Figure 166. — A Case for Books.

With cover and straps for carrying.   In the case
are seven rolls, volumina, corresponding with the
number of the Commentaries on the Gallic War.
A writing tablet leans against the case.

CAESAR'S COMMENTARIES

The Complete Gallic War

With an Introduction, Latin text, Companion, Grammar
Exercises & Vocabularies all based on Francis W. Kelsey

Revised Edition

Edited by
Giles Laurén

*Ave Caesar, morituri
Te salutant*

SOPHRON IMPRIMIT
2012

Revised Edition

copyright 2011 Giles Laurén

ISBN 13: 978-0985081119
ISBN 10: 0985081112

Design by Sophron

PREFACE

The publication of this edition of *Caesar's Gallic War* is due to the inspiration and enthusiam of Dr. Rex Stem, University of California, Davis, who has kindly reviewed and edited the text and notes, made invaluable suggestions and expended countless hours insuring its Latin accuracy. After using the text in his classroom during the Autumn semester of 2011 a number of suggestions for improvement were made and incorporated into this present **revised edition**.

The purpose of yet another edition of Caesar is to bring the best possible text to the student at the lowest possible price in the hope of encouraging classical studies. It is an edition for educators rather than crammers, but will yet be found useful in preparing for the the the Cambridge PreU, the International Baccalaureate, the American Advanced Placement Exam and university programmes that include the study of Caesar.

Frances Kelsey [1858-1927] was a dedicated classical scholar during the golden age of classical scholarship. He was active in the Ancients versus Moderns controversy and it was he who in 1905 determined that the original title of the present work was *C. Iuli Caesaris commentarii rerum gestarum*. His Caesar went into print in 1886 and remained a standard text until after 1918 when the last edition was issued; it has never been surpassed for completeness or accuracy. This present edition is a compilation of the 1897 and the 1918 editions with additions from Hering, emendations and revision as needed to make it a Complete Gallic War. A biography of Kelsey by John Griffiths Pedley: *The Life and Work of Francis Willey Kelsey* has recently appeared from the University of Michigan Press.

Due to the onus of proofing such a complicated text, it is possible that the reader may encounter a mistake or incongruity, probably with reference to an illustration eliminated from this edition. Formatting inconsistancies may I beg be excused as an unavoidable consequence of prefering OpenOffice/LibreOffice, an as yet imperfect programme, over the very expensive alternative. It is hoped the reader will report any textual problems to the editor for correction. Despite minor irritants, this edition of Caesar will be found a most usable text: 'A Complete Caesar,' i.e.: an introduction to Caesar, the complete Latin text, fully annotated, illustrated and keyed to a companion and a grammar section; and with three vocabularies and aids to reading and writing Latin. In brief, it is intended to be the most complete Caesar ever published. An ancillary purpose for this edition is to provide an interesting, useful, and inclusive text for anyone wishing to teach themselves Latin. Perfect books do not appear in this world; Kelsey, a far greater scholar than I, was still correcting after eight editions.

Future improvements, (not dependant on software improvement), may include substituting Hering's text for the somewhat dated text used by Kelsey and will otherwise be responsive to suggestions from readers. Thanks are already in order to one such reader, Vincent DiCarlo, for his well founded suggestions.

Any thoughts, criticisms suggestions and especially corrections will be gratefully received by the undersigned at: (liberdux@gmail.com).

Sacramento
Giles Laurén

PLATE XII

STORMING OF A BESIEGED CITY

CONTENTS

Figure 181. — Horn, with crosspiece by
which it was carried.

ILLUSTRATIONS

Plates

Maps

Figures

Figure 152. — A Roman Calendar.

Of marble. Above the name of each month is a sign of the zodiac associated with it: Capricorn with January, Aquarius with February, Pisces with March, Aries with April, Taurus with May, and Gemini with June.

CHRONOLOGY

100	Born on 12 July, the month subsequently called after him. Son of C. Julius Caesar and Aurelia.
86	Elected *flamen dialis* through his uncle, C. Marius.
84	Married (1) L. Cinna's daughter, Cornelia.
80	Won the "civic crown" of oak-leaves for saving a Roman's life at the storming of Mitylene.
78	Prosecuted Cn. Dolabella for extortion.
76	Captured by pirates.
	Elected *tribunus militum*.
74	Raised a company of volunteers at Rhodes, and held Caria against Mithradates.
68	*Quaestor:* sent to Spain to settle the finances of the country.
67	Married (2) Pompeia, Pompey's cousin.
	Helped to carry *Lex Gabinia,* giving Pompey command against the Mediterranean pirates.
66	Supported *Lex Manilla,* giving Pompey command against Mithradates.
65	*Aedile:* gave public games with great splendour.
63	Elected *Pontifex Maximus.* Spoke in the Senate in the debate on the fellow-conspirators *of* Catiline.
62	*Praetor:* suspended by the Senate for opposition, but at once restored with an apology.
61	Governor, as *Propraetor,* of Further Spain: gained victories over the Lusitanians.
60	Formed with Pompey and Crassus " The First Triumvirate."
59	*Consul* (I) with Bibulus. Appointed governor as *Proconsul,* of Gallia Cisalpina, Gallia Narbonensis (*Provincia*), and Illyricum, for five years; *i.e.* 1 March 59 to 28 February 54 B.C. Married (3) Calpurnia, daughter of L. Calpurnius Piso. Caesar's daughter Julia married to Pompey.
58-51	Operations in Gaul, Germany, and Britain.
56	Conference of the Triumvirs at Luca: Caesar's command to be prolonged for five years; *i.e.* to the end of February 49.
55	Pompey and Crassus consuls.
54	Death of Julia.
53	Crassus killed in action against the Parthians at Carrhae.
51-50	Disputes at Rome about Caesar's command and second consulship.
49	Senate decreed that Caesar should disband his army: he crossed the Rubicon, which meant civil war.
49	*Dictator* (I) for eleven days.
48	*Consul* (II). Defeated Pompey at Pharsalus in Thessaly.
	Dictator (II) till end of 46.
47	Murder of Pompey.
	Settlement of Egypt: Caesar nearly killed at Alexandria.
	Settlement of Asia Minor, after Caesar's victory at Zela ("*Veni, vidi, vici "*) against Pharnaces.
46	*Consul* (III).
	War in North Africa: Caesar victorious at Thapsus over Scipio and the Pompeian army. *Dictator* (III) for ten years.
	Reforms in administration, and in the calendar.
45	Sole *Consul* (IV). *Dictator.*
	War in Spain: Caesar victorious at Munda over the sons of Pompey

(Gnaeus and Sextus) and their army.

Caesar's triumphs. Further honours and offices: *Imperator* for life, *Consul* for the next ten years, *Dictator* and *Praefectus Morum* for life: *Pater Patriae.*

44   *Dictator.*

15 February *(Lupercalia)*. Refused the crown.

15 March *(Ides)* assassinated.

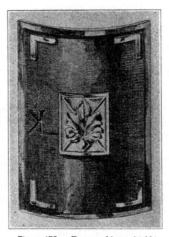

Figure 175. — Roman oblong shield, scutum.

INTRODUCTION
WHY WE STUDY CAESAR

Caesar As A General

Caesar was the greatest general Rome produced. His military genius did not display itself, as did that of Hannibal or Napoleon, in strategic innovation or the introduction of new tactics, but taking the Roman art of war as he found it, he brought it to the highest perfection. The Romans, at all periods of their history, relied for victory not so much on brilliant feats in arms as on the rigid discipline, power of endurance, and persistent courage of their soldiers. In Caesar's ability to make his men do more and endure more for him than they would under any one else lies a chief secret of his success. He had the rare power of binding his army to him with a devotion that nothing could. destroy. In almost every campaign he fought against vastly superior numbers and the most serious disadvantages. For his troops there were long marches, heavy burdens, the constant labour of fortifying, well-grounded fears of the enemy often increased tenfold by exaggeration; yet confidence in their leader inspired them with ever fresh zeal, and his addresses from time to time, reminding them of what he expected of them, fired their courage to the utmost. To this unflagging faithfulness, this unswerving allegiance to him and his cause that he had the faculty of calling forth, fully as much as to skilful handling of forces on the field of battle, his victories were due.

The longer men served under Caesar the more confidence he placed in them; and he did not hesitate to tell them how much he relied on them. Instances of special courage on the part of legions, battalions, or individuals, he made note of, and commended. He made his men think that he was personally interested in each one, just as Napoleon used to go among the common soldiers and inquire into their welfare. He knew his centurions by name, and once at least when the battle was hottest he rushed into the ranks and called out to them individually, urging greater effort; at the battle of the Sambre he seized a shield from a common soldier, and fought in the front rank.

In campaigns Caesar was most careful of the lives of his men, never exposing them to unnecessary risks. Slight delinquencies of conduct he often overlooked; but his general system of discipline was most strict. Active warfare was confined almost entirely to the summer months. During the winter the troops were placed in stationary quarters, where they were kept from idleness by constant drilling. These winter camps, though often distributed about the enemy's country, were nevertheless located away from cities, that the soldiers might not lose their discipline by being brought under corrupting influences, or form attachments with those in whose region they were placed. In this way Caesar avoided one of the fat mistakes of Hannibal, who in the winter allowed his army to revel in the luxuries of South Italy. No matter how well trained a force may be, in a campaign of hard fighting it becomes demoralized, partly by reason of the gaps in the ranks caused by losses, partly on account of irregularity of movement and constant effort toward adaptation to new circumstances. Caesar made his winter encampments a source of fresh strength. From them his soldiers went forth with recruited powers, confident from the experience of past campaigns, and hardened by training. Thus Caesar "made his army, as it were a body, of which he was the soul."

The military movements of Caesar, as of Napoleon, were characterized by an unexpected swiftness. He often appeared in the vicinity of the enemy, or gained possession of important points, before the news had spread that he was on the march. Thus he not infrequently caught his adversaries unprepared, found them with scattered forces, and gained a victory before they could come together. As a consequence, in many cases a panic was excited that paralysed the efforts of the foe and resulted in greater advantage to Caesar than the winning of several battles. When he felt himself too weak in numbers to assume the offensive with the force at hand, he would gain time by parleying, declaring that he must have opportunity for deliberation, while in reality he was awaiting reinforcements, or completing preparations for active measures. He had the power of keeping to himself his designs; his most trusted officers rarely knew his plans till called upon to execute them. He seems to have thought that the best way to assure the secrecy of a project was to carry it out as soon as formed. So his movements often appeared rash; but in the end results revealed his superior judgement and foresight.

No matter how rapidly Caesar advanced, he was always careful to keep up connection with his base of supplies. For these he relied in the Gallic War partly on "the Province," partly on friendly tribes, and partly on the hostile region through which he was marching. That there might be no failure in the regular transportation of supplies to the front he took every precaution. He left no points in possession of the foe behind him; he so secured the route by garrisons at strategic points that in case of defeat he could retreat in safety. Thus, instead of crossing the Rhine by boats, as he could easily have done, he built bridges each time, and left them strongly guarded while he went over into Germany. Once sufficiently near the enemy, his usual practise was to choose immediately a favourable location and fortify a camp. Then by sallies with cavalry he tried to cut off the supplies of the enemy and force them to attack him on his own ground. In this respect his tactics were defensive rather than offensive, and uniformly successful. Sometimes by a feigned retreat, or by marching to one side of the direct route, he drew the enemy away from a point he wished to take, then by a reverse movement fell on it suddenly before they could come to the rescue. He never stopped to besiege a town if he could well avoid it, knowing that a crushing defeat in the field opens the gates of cities. Yet no one was more skilled in the conducting of operations against fortified places than he. The siege of Alesia was one of the most remarkable recorded in history.

None understood better than Caesar how to follow up a victory and turn it to the best advantage. In pursuit of the fleeing he sent detachments of cavalry, and on all sides struck heavy blows before the enemy could gather again or get new courage. Occasionally he authorized indiscriminate slaughter, or the general sale of captives into slavery; but he was not cruel by nature, and in making slaves of those spared by the sword, he acted in accordance with the universal custom of antiquity.[1] In the Civil War he was more compassionate toward the vanquished than any of his contemporaries. In the Gallic War, on conquering a state he usually took under his protection one of the parties in it, placing it in charge of the government, thus binding it to himself by strong ties. His organizing power displayed itself in bringing order out of chaos; while his firmness and moderation

---

1 The number of Gauls and Germans who perished by the sword in the nine years of the Gallic War was perhaps between 1,000,000 and 1,500.000. But in the fifteen years between 1801 and 1816, in wars between Christian nations, the French sacrificed more than 3,000,000 soldiers, and killed at least an equal number of the enemy.

won the respect, if not the esteem, of those whom he had made subject. When he left Gaul and engaged in the war with Pompey, the country was not only once for all subdued, but even contained a strong party devoted to his interests.

The military successes of Caesar have sometimes been attributed to the lack of generalship on the part of his adversaries. This is not just. To say nothing of the fact that in the civil strife the best warriors of Rome were pitted against him, two at least of his northern foes, Ariovistus and Vercingetorix, were men of great natural powers of organization and leadership, consummate masters of the tactics with which they were familiar. The numbers of the barbarian armies were almost beyond compute, their courage well-nigh invincible. From traditions of Gallic invasions the Gauls had become the terror of the Roman soldiery. They were by no means the undisciplined savages that they are sometimes thought to have been; in civilization they were far in advance of the early Britons and Germans. In the earlier campaigns they showed lack of military organization; but toward the end of the Gallic War their troops were organized, armed, and drilled after the Roman fashion, and proved almost a match for the invaders. Sometimes Caesar diminished the awe of his soldiers by trial skirmishes, that the mettle of the enemy might be tested, and the confidence of his army strengthened before the general engagement.

No, the reasons for Caesar's pre-eminence as a general must be sought, not in the weakness of his enemies, but in himself, in his singular power of controlling and organizing men, in his quick and comprehensive grasp of circumstances and ready adaptation to them, in his knowledge of human nature as shown specially in his selection of officers, in his ability to make skilful use of the Roman tactics. But behind all these qualities there was another that defies analysis, that enabled him always to turn things to his own advantage: therein lay his genius. Many generals have studied Caesar's Memoirs very carefully as a military manual; Wellington carried a copy with him on his memorable campaign in India. As the greatest general among the Romans, Caesar takes rank among the most famous military leaders of the world. He will not suffer by comparison with Alexander the Great, with Hannibal, Scipio Africanus and Napoleon.

Caesar as a Politician

The political character of Caesar has long been a subject of controversy. According to some he was a monster of crime, with hardly a redeeming quality, deliberately sacrificing the liberties of his country to an unbounded ambition. Others portray him as a broad-minded statesman, who saw that, in the anarchy arising from the strife of parties, Rome's great need was a single controlling will; who, to give peace and order to his distracted land, made himself its master. Both these views are extreme and unjust. The one emphasizes the destructive side of Caesar's character, while the constructive side is ignored; the other attributes to him that profound knowledge of the tendencies of the Roman state which students of history have been two millennia in acquiring. His character presents, indeed, many apparently conflicting elements. But upon careful study it is evident that in the main he acted in accordance with the spirit of his age; that though his motives may not always have been patriotic, he was in reality a benefactor of his country; and the true significance of his career becomes apparent only when it is considered as the final outworking of a principle which in times past had been asserting itself more and more in Roman politics: the principle of Imperialism.

In entering the arena of political life Caesar no doubt both followed his own inclinations and chose the course reckoned most proper for a Roman youth of fortune and high position. At that time, owing to the proscriptions of Sulla, there was in the popular party a dearth of leaders, a condition which gave ample room for the exercise of his powers. The methods which he employed to make himself the people's favourite were in the highest degree objectionable, if judged by modern standards. Still, they were the usual methods of his time; while in restoring the trophies of Marius to the Capitol he showed a deep insight into the real feelings of the masses as well as a knowledge of the ways of reaching the popular heart. Few of his contemporaries had so great regard for the formalities of the law as he; he avoided unlawful means. At the trial of the Catilinarian conspirators he argued on legal grounds that the accused should not be put to death. The formation of the First Triumvirate was a shrewd move, fraught with momentous consequences. It reveals rare sagacity and foresight; but it had no more and no less significance than the forming of political rings to secure the rewards of office in our day. It proposed not to subvert but to direct the government, and at the same time to turn to private advantage the influence and emoluments of official positions.

The means by which Caesar was enabled finally to obtain the supreme power was the conquest of Gaul. From early times the Gauls, pressed by the tribes beyond, had occasionally made incursions into Italy; and now Roman colonists in "the Province" were not infrequently threatened. To protect these the rest of Transalpine Gaul must be subdued. It has been said that Caesar undertook the task of bringing Gaul into subjection in order to acquire a military power with which to overthrow the home government, but how could he expect, in the subduing of a rough northern country, to develop a force able to cope with a government that had behind it Pompey, conqueror of rich provinces in the East? More likely he planned the Gallic campaigns as an important service to the State. If he should be successful in carrying them out, he would gain a still higher place in the affections of the people, and would add one more laurel to his political honours. Because his remarkable ability as a general rapidly won for him extraordinary successes, which he afterwards employed to further his own ends, we are not warranted in assuming that his aim from the beginning was to obtain the supreme power, and that the conquest of Gaul was the means he took to accomplish it.

The death of Crassus left Pompey and Caesar without rivals in political power. The latter, as master of Gaul, found himself much more nearly on a level with the "great man of Rome" than ever before. A mutual jealousy soon provoked a collision. Pompey undoubtedly had the advantage; for while he was administering a powerful command in Spain through his lieutenants, he was in person at Rome, at the centre of affairs, acting as sole consul by the desire of the people, while Caesar was outside the limits of Italy. As a matter of fact, Rome was under Pompey's control. So it was at Pompey's bidding that the Senate ordered Caesar to disband his legions and resign his command. Caesar was placed in a difficult position. In obeying this decree he would give up everything to his opponent and make himself a political cipher, with but small prospect of ever regaining his former influence. His enemies had woven a net around him. In refusing to obey he would give to the Senate a chance to declare him a traitor, and to his adversary an opportunity of attacking him in the name of the State. Yet simple justice required that all which might be demanded of the one should be demanded of the other also. So at least Caesar thought; and he acted accordingly. If he had previously fought for fame and influence, he must now fight for self-preservation. An appeal to arms was his only means of defence. Delay was dangerous; and he decided on immediate action. If an appeal to arms against the existing authority is ever justifiable in the case of an individual, the crossing of the Rubicon, the first aggressive step of the movement which resulted in Caesar's elevation to supreme power, was attended at least by palliating circumstances.

But in this contest there was a deeper significance than the elevation or, overthrow of an individual. Whoever conquered would be king. There were certain tendencies in the Roman state that rendered a monarchy inevitable. Rome was at first a municipality; her government, a group of institutions developed by and adapted to a city population. When she extended her boundaries she conquered cities, and her government thus had to deal with a collection of municipal organizations similar to her own. The consequence was a constant tendency toward disintegration, toward the separation of this combination of units into its original elements. Opposed to this localizing tendency there was necessarily developed a contrary drift toward centralization. It was found that a body composed of many inharmonious members needed a single will. In times of extreme danger the state was obliged to put almost absolute power into the hands of a **dictator.** The people thus became familiar with the prerogatives of royalty under a different name. Meanwhile the influx of wealth after the period of conquest, the development of large landed estates which absorbed the small farms of the peasant class, and the excessive employment of slave labour which was reducing the free classes within ever narrower limits, gave prominence to individual aspirants to power who made the state a republic only in name. Gaius Gracchus for a time held virtual sovereignty. Marius was supreme for five years. Sulla was as really a king as if he had worn the purple. Matters had at length come to such straits that the very existence of the state demanded a king. There was needed a strong, centralized government, capable of repressing anarchy at home and of enforcing respect abroad.

The murder of Pompey left Caesar without a rival, and under the forms of the old constitution he became in truth monarch of Rome. Thus had he, who at first cherished no more ambitious aim than to become a political leader, risen by the force of circumstances to the absolute mastery of the Roman world. His short administration revealed in him statesmanship of the highest order. Under him the state enjoyed a larger measure of prosperity than before for many decades; and his untimely end only renewed the political disturbances that he had sought to repress. Endowed with so deep insight into men and things, Caesar must have foreseen, faintly at first perhaps, but more and more distinctly as time passed on, what would be the end of the course he was pursuing, as the traveller sees through the breaking mist the summit toward which the upward path is leading. We claim for him, however, that he did not definitely contemplate the subversion of the liberties of the Commonwealth; and that, guided by an overruling Providence, he accomplished an important work for the Roman state and for humanity. Certainly few men have left so strong an impress upon the history of the race as he. The calendar, as reformed by him, is still in use in Greece and Russia. His name became a designation of imperial authority in the Empire which he founded, and remains to-day in the words Kaiser and Czar. Political writers, too, use the word *Caesarism.* What a life, able not simply to make for itself a place in the records of history, but even to hand down a name as synonymous with the highest power!

Caesar as a Man of Letters

Caesar had a natural taste for literature. He enjoyed the best educational advantages of his time in rhetoric and elocution; but the freshness, directness, and vigour of his style indicate not so much careful training as an inborn power over language. As an orator he was considered second only to Cicero. It is to be regretted that none of his orations have come down to us; from the fragments that survive, we know that his manner of speaking was terse, logical, earnest, and convincing. Even during the busiest periods of his life he kept up literary pursuits. He composed a treatise on Latin grammar (*De Analogia*) in two books, in the course of a journey from Cisalpine Gaul across the Alps to the army. About the time of the battle of Munda he wrote a tract "Against Cato," in two books (*Anticatones*); this was in answer to a panegyric by Cicero, and held the hero of Utica up to ridicule. An extensive treatise on astronomy passed under his name, and is several times cited by the elder Pliny. With the exception of a few fragments, all these works, as well as his poems and letters, have perished.

Caesar's most important writings, which still survive, are the 'Commentaries on the Gallic War,' in seven books, describing the conquest of Gaul; and 'Commentaries on the Civil War,' in three books, giving an account of the struggle with Pompey. These works, as the name indicates (*Commentarii*, that is, notes or comments, *Memoirs*), were not intended to be formal historical treatises, but were written in great haste, and given to the world rather as condensed first draughts, as sketches in outline, than as complete and finished productions, The 'Gallic War' was probably written after the fall of Alesia, and published in 51 B.C., before the break with Pompey (Cf. Book VI., chap. i.; VII., chap, vi.); an eighth book was afterwards added to it by Aulus Hirtius. The 'Civil War' was left unfinished, and probably not published till after Caesar's death; it, too, was extended by others, who added narratives of his military operations in Egypt, Africa, and Spain.

The style of the *Memoirs* has always been much admired. Cicero, although a political enemy of the author, did not hesitate to say of them (*Brut.* lxxv. 262): "They are worthy of all praise. They are unadorned, straightforward, and elegant, every embellishment being stripped off as a garment. Caesar desired, indeed, to furnish others who might wish to write history with material upon which they might draw; and perhaps men without good taste, who like to deck out facts in tawdry graces of expression, may think that he has rendered a service in this regard, but he has deterred men of sound sense from trying to improve on them in writing. For in history a pure and brilliant conciseness of style is the highest attainable beauty." The manner of expression, although so condensed, is most clear, and often vivid. It stands as a warning to those who think that a simple, direct, and forcible statement of facts can be made more effective by the use of many words and high-sounding phrases.

Although Caesar is everywhere, as a matter of course, the principal figure in the *Memoirs*, he throws himself into the background, making prominent the deed rather than the doer. He speaks of himself usually in the third person, a mode of expression as rare in personal narrative in his time as to-day, which made possible the belief, current in the Middle Ages, that the *Memoirs* were written by Suetonius. More surprising still is the fact that one finds no bitter aspersions upon his enemies, no extravagant commendations of friends, no professedly special pleas to justify his course. The reasons for important movements are always stated, but in such a way that they seem to have grown out of the attendant circumstances, and to have forced on action; so that no man of discretion could have done other than he had done. In all this there is the highest skill. While keeping himself free from all expressions alike of malice and of self-glorification, he draws the reader along with him, arouses sympathy, and wins to his own view; thus he justifies his course more effectively than if he were to excite the reader's opposition or suspicion by violent statements, or had adopted a more direct way of pleading his cause. There can be little doubt that behind both the 'Gallic' and the 'Civil War' lay a political purpose, to set a favourable explanation of his career before the eyes of his fellow-countrymen and of posterity, and so to offset the malicious rumours about his acts persistently circulated by his enemies. But does this affect the truthfulness of his statements?

In writing his *Memoirs* Caesar had to deal with several classes of facts. First, especially in the 'Gallic War,' there was a fund of interesting information about the strange peoples with which he came in contact. Many of these were previously unknown to the Romans. Caesar was a close and careful observer. He made minute inquiries not only into the numbers and military prowess of his foes, but also into their manner of life, their customs, and religious beliefs. In him, with the circumspection and foresight of the general, was united the eager desire for knowledge of the man of science. His nature was averse to the marvellous. The pages of few ancient writers who present accounts of new peoples are so free from the improbable. Whenever possible he got his information directly, at first hand. In a few instances he seems to have become possessed of erroneous views; but as a whole his statements about lands and peoples are trustworthy. Then, there were the accounts of his military operations in the broad sense, of the general conduct of his campaigns. The accuracy of these has hardly been called in question; while the surveys and excavations carried on under the direction of the Emperor Napoleon III. have furnished in many cases a remarkable confirmation. Finally, there remain the more particular descriptions of battles, sieges, and the like; of successes and reverses. These affect reputation; here if anywhere we should look for untruthfulness. Did Caesar, as some have thought, magnify his victories and obscure his defeats? There is no evidence that he did. The tone throughout his works is candid and fair, besides, with these things most of his readers were to some extent familiar by means of reports brought from the field. Falsifying under such circumstances would have invited all manner of derision and defeated the writer's purposes. Probably Caesar now and then purposely omitted something : his reliability in general we have not the slightest reason to doubt. His statements of his motives of action in certain cases, bearing in mind the circumstances, we are at liberty to accept or reject as we choose; his veracity in regard to facts should not be impugned without good reason. From whatever point of view considered, his works are of great interest and value. The *De Bella Gallico* in particular deserves to be carefully studied, as a masterpiece of concise and spirited writing, as casting light upon the beginnings of the history of Northern Europe, and as revealing the modes of thought and action of one of the world's greatest men.

The Civilization Of The Gauls

Excavations and discoveries in France in recent decades have thrown new light upon the civilization of the Gauls in Caesar's time. To give an account of these within narrow limits is impossible. It may suffice to say that remains of city walls have been found on the site of Bibraete and other Gallic cities, so constructed as completely to verify Caesar's description of a Gallic wall in Book VII (chap. 23); that burial places and unearthed town sites in France, western Switzerland, Belgium, and England have yielded an incalculable number of objects of common life, now available for study in museums; and that with the help of such objects it is permitted to picture to ourselves the varied and picturesque life of ancient Gaul and Britain in a way unknown to previous centuries.

Disregarding the highest estimates, we may reckon the population of Transalpine Gaul in Caesar's time as twelve or thirteen millions; there were perhaps a fourth as many inhabitants as are found in the same area to-day. There were in Gaul not a few cities, some of which, as Avaricum with its 40,000 souls, would be reckoned as important towns in modern times.

The growth of towns implies advancement in both commerce and industry. In Caesar's time there was already developed in Gaul a system of roads, with bridges across the rivers: and there is reason to believe that in many cases the line of a Gallic road was followed later by a Roman road, which in turn is now represented by a highway or railway.

Raw materials for industry and commerce were furnished by farming, by stock raising, and by mining (III. 21, and VII. 22). The Gauls were particularly fond of horses (IV. 2), the quality of which improved under their care. It was therefore no accident which led the Romans to import Gallic horses, and which gave to the Gauls such a lead in the invention of vehicles that the Romans borrowed from them the names of two kinds of cart, **carrus** (I. 3) and **carpentum**. From the Celtic, through the Latin and French, come our words "car" and "chariot" and the Anglo-Saxon, "cart."

The horse is a constantly reoccurs on Gallic coins. The fine quality of the horses still raised on Gallic soil is indicated by the fact that in 1910 there were imported into the United States from France and Belgium more than 4500 horses, nearly four times as many as were imported in that year from all other European countries.

The implications of Caesar's language about importations into Gaul, in Book I (chap. 1), Book II (chap. 15), and Book VI (chap. 24) are borne out by other evidence. The most convincing proof of the influence of both Greek and Italian traders, and of the commercial progress of the country, is to be found in the extensive and varied coinage of the Gallic states[2] in Caesar's time. The Gauls minted their own metal, though they had not the skill to produce coins of so fine workmanship as those of the Greeks and Romans. Their coinage was still in the imitative stage, reproducing, often crudely, designs of foreign coins which circulated among them.

Not a few Gallic coins were copied from a variety of widely current Macedonian coins known as *staters*. An example is thought to have been struck by the Ambarri. The head and the two-horse chariot are unmistakable copies of the obverse and reverse designs of a stater; and the unintelligible letters on the reverse, underneath the chariot, are the work of a Gallic coin-maker who did not know Greek, and imitated, without understanding them, the letters of the Greek name φιλιππου, "of

---

2 In the United States the word **civitas** in passages relating to Gaul should not he translated " tribe," for the reason that the word" tribe" is so closely associated with the American aborigines that it suggests a condition of savagery.

Philip," which is found on the Macedonian coin.

Just as clearly of Roman origin is the type of the two-headed Janus, found on a coin of the Mediomatrici. On the reverse the Gallic designer has made a fanciful use of the chariot design, which appears on Roman coins as well as Greek; the charioteer has been resolved into the graceful curves which we see above the horse, while the chariot seems to be represented by a rosette underneath the horse, symbolizing a chariot wheel. The Gallic craftsman wished to make the horse prominent.

It is not surprising that in Caesar's time the Greek alphabet was in common use in Gaul (VI. 14), employed, for example, in making up the census lists of the Helvetians (I. 29); for Massilia, established originally as a Greek colony and trading post, was already an old city, having commercial relations with many Gallic states.

Nevertheless we occasionally find Roman letters on Gallic coins, as in a coin struck a short time before the downfall of Gallic power, in 52 B.C. The face on the obverse is intended to be a portrait of the Gallic leader Vercingetorix, but is highly conventional. Much more true to life is a later portrait of Vercingetorix on a Roman coin whose designer must have seen him when a captive in Rome. In military matters Vercingetorix confessedly imitated the Romans (VII. 29).

Various objects of metal, pottery, and other permanent materials, strengthen the conviction that while the northern parts of Gaul were more backward, the higher classes in the central and southern portions of the country in Caesar's time had adopted a more refined mode of life (I. 1); thus the terrified women of Gergovia threw down silverware to the Roman soldiers scaling the wall (VII. 47). The common people were housed in round thatched huts, but people of means had houses of stone.

Notwithstanding their use of writing for ordinary purposes, including "documents public and private" (VI. 14) the Gauls did not develop a literature. This may be due in part to the insistence of the Druids that their body of doctrine, poetic and mystical though it was, should be transmitted only by memory (VI. 14). As the Druids were the intellectual leaders of the people, their practise in this respect must have discouraged literary effort. This all-powerful priesthood, regarding which Caesar in Book VI gives the earliest authentic information, in their teachings united a theory of the universe with the doctrine of transmigration of souls. The power of the Druids in temporal affairs came from this fact, that while acting as arbiters and judges in disputes of every kind, they were enabled to enforce their decisions through the terrible penalty of excommunication (VI. 13). Outside the limited field of coins and minor objects the Gauls made almost no progress in art before the Roman Conquest. That they were ready for development in the fuller appreciation of art, if not also in expression, is evident from monuments of Gallic origin dating from the earlier years of the Roman occupation, in which an awakening of the artistic impulse is manifest. An example is a relief showing a Gallic oval shield with metal covering and a war-trumpet with the head of a monster. Wind instruments with heads of animals or monsters, not of Gallic origin, may be seen in collections of musical instruments today.

Gallic and British coins struck after the Conquest indicate to us the adoption of Roman fashions within a few decades after Caesar's death, not only in Gaul but even in Britain. On a coin we find a prominent man of the Treyerans (or of the Leuci), designated in the Roman style as "Germanus, freedman of Indutillus."

Inscribed with Roman letters also are gold coins of the British Virica, as well as gold and silver coins of Tasciovanus. Tasciovanus was a contemporary of the Emperor Augustus. and the father of Cunobelinus, the hero of Shakespeare's drama Cymbeline, as a bronze coin of Cunobelinus shows.

Complete Romanization of at least a part of central Gaul is indicated by a coin struck soon after 31 B.C. at Lugdunum, modern Lyons, which was one of the first Roman colonies established in Gaul outside the Province.

Further Reading

The historians have written more about Julius Caesar than about any other Roman. There are, nevertheless, wide differences of opinion in regard to his motives and character.

In the eyes of some Caesar was a monster of wickedness, a despot guilty of subverting the liberties of his country. Others have viewed him as a statesman and patriot of exalted aims. To others still his career has seemed to mark the culmination of the inevitable trend of the Roman state toward absolutism, and they have interpreted it as the opportune appearance of a will and personality powerful enough to dominate, and fuse into lasting union the inharmonious elements of a political life rapidly drifting into anarchy. Men's views of Caesar have generally been coloured by their attitude toward the type of government which he established.

To the student new to Caesar several fictional works may best serve as an introduction. The two volume autobiography of Caesar by Rex Warner: *The Young Caesar* and *Imperial Caesar* and Olivia Coolidge's Caesar's Gallic War. Any of John Maddox Roberts' *SPQR* series provide entertaining background.

The extant Greek and Latin writings in which Caesar has a prominent place are now accessible in excellent translations; nearly all are included in the *Loeb Classical Library*.[3] Accessible in English also, with few exceptions, are the most important modern works in foreign languages dealing with Caesar and his times.

The earliest characterisation of Caesar which we have, in Sallust's *Catiline* (chaps. 53, 54), forms part of a comparison between him and Cato. A biography of Caesar in Greek, together with biographies of Pompey, Crassus, Brutus, Cato, and Cicero, was included by Plutarch in his *Lives*, published near the end of the first century A.D. (translation by B. Perrin, 10 vols., *Loeb Classical Library*). Plutarch records also a number of Caesar's sayings, with the incidents which called them forth, in his *Moralia*, (translation by Frank C. Babbitt *et al.* 15 vols., *Loeb Classical Library*. In 120 A.D. Suetonius published a biography of Julius Caesar as the first of his *Lives of the Caesars* (*Loeb Classical Library*).

The closing period of the Roman Republic was treated with much detail by two late Greek historians, whose works in great part still survive. About the middle of the second century A.D. Appian wrote the *Civil Wars* (*Loeb Classical Library*); and in the earlier part of the third century Dio Cassius composed his *Roman History* (*Loeb Classical Library*). The ancient literary sources are well summarized and evaluated in the *Annals of Caesar, A Critical Biography with a Survey of the Sources*, by E. G.

---

3 The volumes of the *Loeb Classical Library*, established by James Loeb of New York, have the original text and the English translation on opposite pages (publishers, William Heinemann & Harvard University).

Sihler, which follows the life of Caesar year by year (New York, 1911).

To the ancient material relating to Caesar belong the coins struck by his order, and a number of portraits. The most important coins are interpreted by H. A. Grueber in *Coins of the Roman Republic in the British Museum* (with 123 plates; 3 vols., London, 1910). The portraits of Caesar are discussed at length, but without adequate critical preparation, in *Portraitures of Julius Caesar,* by E. J. Scott (New York, 1903), The bust of Pompey in Copenhagen, three portraits of Cicero, and three of Caesar, are presented in *Greek and Roman Portraits,* by A. Hekler (New York, 1912; plates 155-161). Several gems with the portrait of Caesar are published by A. Furtwaengler, *Die Antiken Gemmen* (3 vols., Berlin, 1899, plates 45, 46).

Among the biographies the first place must be given to *Julius Caesar and the Foundation of the Roman Imperial System,* by W. Warde Fowler. Theodore Dodge's *Cæsar: A History of the Art of War among the Romans down to the End of the Roman Empire, with a detailed account of the Campaigns of Caius Julius Cæsar* has long been in print. There are two very readable modern works: *Julius Caesar: The Pursuit of Power* by Ernle Bradford and *Julius Caesar* by Michael Grant. Christian Meier's *Caesar* is the most complete modern work.

Interesting sidelights on Caesar's career are found in *Cicero and his Friends, A Study of Roman Society in the Time of Caesar,* by G. Boissier; *The Life of Cicero,* by Anthony Trollope; *Cicero and the Fall of the Roman Republic, by J. L. Strachan-Davidson; and Social Life in Rome in the Age of Cicero,* by W. Warde Fowler.

Still of interest for the student of Caesar, though in most respects superseded by later works, are *Lectures on the History of Rome,* by B. G. Niebuhr *History of the Later Roman Commonwealth,* by Thomas Arnold; and *The, Decline of the Roman Republic,* by George Long.

Of special importance are the interpretations of Caesar's career in the fifth volume of *The History of Rome,* by Theodor Mommsen; in the first portion of *The Romans under the Empire,* by C. Merivale; *The Roman Triumvirates,* by C. Merivale, a volume of the series *Epochs of Ancient History;* the third volume of the richly illustrated *History of Rome,* by V. Duruy; the second volume of G. Ferrero's highly imaginative but suggestive *Greatness and Decline of Rome;* and the third volume of *The Roman Republic,* by W. E. Heitland.

It would be interesting if to the diverse modern estimates of Caesar's character and life-work we could add a statement by himself regarding his aims and achievements. In default of the written word, however, we have not a few suggestions in the imagery of the coins issued by his authority, the types of which were suggested, or at least approved, by him. Thus we ire warranted in believing that he wished men to recall the story of his lineage and the origin of the name Caesar as well as his victories in Gaul, Spain, the East, and Africa.

A suggestion of Caesar's attitude toward his task, or at least the attitude he assumed, may be conveyed by a gold coin struck in 49 B.C., after Pompey had fled across the Adriatic. Here we find, on the reverse, a design symbolizing his victories in Gaul; the design of the obverse shows the head of Pietas, the deified personification of loyalty to duty, particularly duty to the gods. Pietas in this connection has no relation to the office of Supreme Pontiff. It suggests that Caesar, like the Trojan Aeneas in the Virgilian epic (*Aen.* I. 378), was the instrument of heaven in the accomplishment of a mission. Illuminating studies relative to Caesar and the transformation of the Roman Republic into the Roman Empire, are *Roman Imperialism,* by J. R. Seeley, in his *Roman Imperialism and Other Lectures and Essays*

(Boston, 1889); *Seven Roman Statesmen of the Later Republic,* by C. Oman, with four studies devoted to Crassus, Cato, Pompey, and Caesar; *Caesar and Alexander,* in *Lectures on Modern History,* to which are added two essays dealing with ancient history, by Friedrich Schlegel; by suggestion rather than by direct bearing, the essay entitled *The Roman Empire and the British Empire in India,* by James Bryce, in his *Studies in History and Jurisprudence.*

Indispensable for the study of Caesar's Commentaries on the historical side are *Caesar's Conquest of Gaul* by T. Rice Holmes, and his *Ancient Britain and the Invasions of Julius Caesar* Very useful are the *History of Julius Caesar,* by Napoleon III, with the Atlas, on which have been founded most of the maps illustrating Caesar's campaigns in Gaul (2 vols., New York, 1866); two works by C. Stoffel, *Guerre de César et d'Arioviste et premieres operations de César en l'an 702* (Paris, 1890), and *Histoire de Jules César, Guerre civile* (2 vols., with Atlas, Paris, 1887); and *Histoire de la Gaule,* by C. Jullian (4 vols., Paris, 1908-13).

Both the historical and the literary significance of Caesar's Commentaries is estimated in *Caesar as a Man of Letters* by F. E. Adcock (Cambridge 1956). *The Commentaries of Caesar* by Anthony Trollope; in the *History of Roman Literature* by C. L. Cruttwell, *History of Latin Literature* by C. A. Simcox (2 vols., New York, 1883), and *Literary History of Rome* 3 by J. W. Duff (London, 1914). The title of the Commentaries is treated by F. W. Kelsey in *The title of Caesar's work on the Gallic and Civil Wars (Transactions of the American Philological Association,* vol. 36, 1905, pp. 211-238).

Caesar In Literature And Myth

Of deep human interest, and touching Caesar at many points, are the *Inciters* of Marcus Cicero; among them are included a few letters written by Caesar and others intimately associated with him (edition, with full notes, by E. Y. Tyrrell and L. C. Purser, 7 vols., in part 3rd. edit., Dublin and London, 1901; translation of the *Letters to Atticus* in the *Loeb Classical Library.*

About a century after Caesar's death Lucan, reacting against the absolutism of Nero, composed the *Pharsalia,* an epic poem in ten books having for its subject the struggle between Caesar and Pompey, commencing with the crossing of the Rubicon. The poet's sympathies were with Pompey and Cato; but, even so, from the very force of his personality Caesar is the dominating character.

In modern times the singular power of Shakespeare's *Julius Caesar* has apparently deterred other dramatists from attempting the theme. The scene of the tragedy, *The False One,* by Beaumont and Fletcher (first published in 1647), is laid at Alexandria after the battle of Pharsalus; the young King Ptolemy, Achillas, and Septimius (C. III. 104), who is "the False One," all appear, as well as Cleopatra, Labienus, and Caesar, who declaims over the head of Pompey, presented to him by Achillas.

John Masefield, in *The Tragedy of Pompey the Great,* has skilfully developed an interpretation of Pompey's actions altogether different from the view that will present itself to most readers of Caesar's *Civil War.* Bernard Shaw's *Caesar and Cleopatra* is an amusing caricature.

Fewer historical novels concern themselves with the closing days of the Roman Republic than with the first century of the Empire. The best of them all is *A Friend of Caesar,* by W. S. Davis. The hero of *The Wonderful Adventures of Phra the*

Phoenician, by E. L. Arnold, son of Edwin Arnold, in the first of his several eventful lives weds the daughter of a British ruler and joins with the natives in trying to prevent the landing of Caesar's forces.

To the domain of the essay, containing much suggestive generalization and psychological analysis, belong the sections and passages relating to Julius Caesar in *The Tragedy of the Caesars, A Study of the Characters of the Caesars of the Julian and Claudian Houses,* by S. Baring-Gould; *Roman Days,* by V. Rydberg (2d edit., New York, 1887); *Imperial Purple,* by Edgar Saltus (Chicago, 1892); *Ave Roma Immortalis,* by F. M. Crawford; as well as the older works, *Causes of the Grandeur and Decadence of the Romans,* by Montesquieu; and *The Caesars,* by Thomas de Quincey.

Wonderful portents accompanying the death of Caesar are described by Virgil in the first book of the *Georgics,* while the transformation of his soul into a comet is set forth by Ovid at the end of the *Metamorphoses;* thus within approximately a half century after his death the miraculous had gathered about his memory and had found literary expression.

Other marvellous stories about Caesar were current in the Roman Empire, and were reflected in later writings. The *Gesta Romanorum,* a collection of edifying tales made about the end of the thirteenth century, tells us how, as Caesar started to cross the Rubicon, a huge ghost stood in his way, and how Caesar met the challenge.

The most persistent tale related to the safe-guarding of Caesar's ashes. In the earlier part of the first century A.D. a massive granite obelisk was brought to Rome from Egypt and erected in a circus near where St. Peter's church was afterwards built; on the top a large ball, or sphere, of bronze was placed (Fig. 26). The obelisk remained standing to until 1586, when the ball was taken down and found to be solid, many believed that it contained the ashes of Julius Caesar, placed there in order that, in the quaint language of a medieval guide-book, "as in his lifetime the-wole world lay subdued before him, even so in his death the-same may lie beneath him forever" *(Mirabilia Urbis Romae.* Latin text, H. Jordan, *Topographie der Stadt Rom,* vol. 2, p. 62; translation by F. M. Nichols, London, 1889, pp. 71-72). One version of the Swan Legend, most commonly associated with Lohengrin, tells us how a sister of Julius Caesar eloped with a Belgian prince, and in her northern home had a beautiful white swan. Her husband joined forces with Ariovistus and fell at the battle of Vesontio. Now in Caesar's army was a hero, Salvius Brabon, who was descended from the Trojan Hector. Hunting near the Rhine he saw a snow-white swan, "playfully pulling at the rope which bound a small skiff to the shore. Salvius leaped into the boat and cast it loose from its mooring. Then the bird swam before him as a guide, and he rowed after it." The swan conducted him to the sister of Caesar, who made herself known to him; he brought Caesar to her castle, and the conqueror embraced his sister with joy. Salvius asked Caesar for the widowed sister's hand; Caesar consented, and Salvius Brabon became the first Luke of Brabant (S. Baring-Gould, *Curious Myths of the Middle Ages,* second series.

MAP I

CAMPAIGNS OF 58 AND 57 B.C.

Book I, 2–54 ; II, 1–33 ; III, 1–6   To face page I

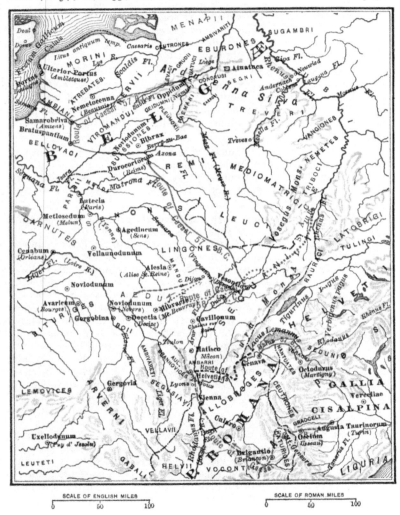

SCALE OF ENGLISH MILES

SCALE OF ROMAN MILES

EXPLANATION

The route of the Helvetians to the Arar is indicated by a broken black
line ; thence their line of march and Caesar's coincide, to Toulon.

COMMENTARIUS PRIMUS

GEOGRAPHY OF GAUL

Divisions and peoples.

1.1 Gallia[2] est omnis divisa in partes tres, quarum unam incolunt[3] Belgae, aliam Aquitani, tertiam, qui ipsorum lingua Celtae,[4] nostra Galli appellantur. **2.** Hi omnes lingua, institutis, legibus inter se[5] differunt. Gallos ab Aquitanis Garumna[6] flumen, a Belgis Matrona et Sequana dividit. **3.** Horum[7] omnium fortissimi sunt Belgae, propterea quod a cultu[8] atque humanitate provinciae longissime absunt, minimeque[9] ad eos mercatores saepe commeant, atque ea, quae ad effeminandos[10] animos pertinent, important; proximique sunt[11] Germanis, qui trans Rhenum incolunt, quibuscum continenter[12] bellum gerunt. **4.** Qua de causa[13] Helvetii quoque reliquos Gallos virtute praecedunt,[14] quod fere cotidianis proeliis cum Germanis contendunt,[15] cum aut suis finibus eos prohibent, aut ipsi in eorum[16] finibus bellum gerunt. **5.** [Eorum una pars, quam Gallos obtinere dictum est, initium capit a flumine Rhodano; continetur Garumna flumine, Oceano, finibus Belgarum; attingit etiam ab Sequanis et Helvetiis flumen Rhenum; vergit ad septentriones. **6.** Belgae ab extremis Galliae finibus oriuntur; pertinent ad inferiorem partem fluminis Rheni; spectant in septentrionem et orientem solem. **7.** Aquitania a Garumna flumine ad Pyrenaeos montes et eam partem Oceani, quae est ad Hispaniam, pertinet; spectat inter occasum solis et septentriones.[17]]

[1] REFERENCES IN ITALIC TYPE ARE TO INTODUCTORY MATTER AND 'POINTS TO BE NOTED IN WRITING LATIN' *p.401*. IN THIS BOOK. AG, B., REFER TO THE LATIN GRAMMARS BY ALLEN AND GREENOUGH, BENNETT. FOR OTHER ABBREVIATIONS CONSULT THE LIST PRECEDING THE VOCABULARY.

[2] **Gallia:** *2a; 286*. **Gallia omnis:** 'Gaul as a whole', contrasted with Gaul in the narrower sense, or Celtic Gaul; Celtic Gaul also is often called *Gallia; 287B* **omnis:** *25a; 80B* **divisa:** 'divided', the perfect passive participle of *divido* used as a predicate adjective; *148c* (AG 495, B 337.2). **in:** 'into'; *124a*. **partes:** 'parts'; *17B* **tres:** *37b; 353c*. **quarum:** 'of which'; *47*. Why genitive? *97a* (AG 346a1, B 201.1). **unam:** sc. *partem*, 'one (part)'; *23a*. Look up the three 'parts' of Gaul ; see GALLIA on the back cover of this book.

[3] **incolunt:** 'inhabit'; *55*. **Belgae:** *19e; 287*. **aliam** [partem]: 'another (part)', less precise than *alteram* (*partem*), 'a second (part)', which might have been used; *23a*. **Aquitani:** sc. *incolunt; 89a*. **tertiam, qui:** = *tertiam partem ei incolunt, qui*, 'a third part is inhabited by those who', lit. 'those inhabit who'; *164a*. **ipsorum:** 'their own'; lit. 'of themselves'; *46*. **ipsorum lingua:** 'in their own language'; *131a* (AG 409, B 218).

[4] **Celtae:** sc. *appellantur; 88; 287B* **nostra:** *nostra lingua* = Latin; *157c*. **appellantur:** 'are called'; *53*. **lingua, institutis, legibus:** 'in respect to language, institutions, and laws'; *142a; 234a* (AG 418, B 226).

[5] **inter se:** 'from one another'; *159* (AG 301f, B 245). **differunt:** 'differ'; *69b*.

[6] **Garumna:** sc. *dividit*, 'separates'. **flumen:** *12e; 91a*. Derivation? *74d*. **Matrona:** *292*. **dividit:** singular number; why? *173a* (AG 317b, B 255.3).

[7] **Horum:** *42b; 97a* (AG 346a2, B 201.1). **fortissimi:** 'the bravest'; *27a*. **propterea:** adverb meaning 'on this account'; closely connected with *quod*, the two words together being translated 'because'. Three reasons are given for the bravery of the Belgians: what are they?

[8] **cultu:** 'mode of life', referring to the outward appearances of civilization; *20*. **atque:** *233a*. **humanitate:** 'refinement' in intellectual interests and in feeling; *10f*. **provinciae:** 'of the Province'; *94a; 290*. **longissime absunt:** 'are furthest removed'; *34a; 66a; 183a*.

[9] **mimime – saepe:** 'very rarely'; lit. 'least often'; *35.* **eos:** *44; 160B* **mercatores:** 'traders' from the Province, especially from Massilia, followed the course of the Rhone, the Saône, and the Loire, so that naturally they did not often go so far north as the Belgian country. **commeant:** 'make their way to'; lit. 'go and come'; *53.* **ea:** 'those things', object of *important; 160c.* Caesar seems to have had in mind particularly the importation of wine (Bk.II, 15; Bk.IV, 2).
[10] **ad effeminandos animos:** 'to weaken the courage'; *230.3* (AG 503, 506; B 339.2). **animos:** *6a; 92a.* **pertinent:** 'tend'; *54.* **important:** 'import'; *53; 175a.*
[11] **proximique sunt:** 'and they are nearest'; *33; 233B* **Germanis:** why dat.? *108a* (AG 384, B 192.1). **trans:** here 'on the other side of'; *122a.* **quibuscum:** *125c.*
[12] **continenter:** 'continually'. **bellum gerunt:** 'they wage war'; *6a; 55.*
[13] **Qua de causa:** 'For this reason'; *167* (AG 308f, B 251.6). **quoque:** 'also'. **reliquos:** 'the rest of the'; *171a.* **Gallos:** only the inhabitants of Celtic Gaul are meant; no comparison with the Belgians and the Aquitanians is implied; *113a.* **virtute:** 'in valour'; *142a* (AG 418, B 226).
[14] **praecedunt:** 'excel'; *113B* **fere:** 'almost'. **cotidianis:** 'every day'; lit. 'daily'; *22B* **proeliis:** 'in battle'; lit. 'by means of battles'; *131a.* **cum:** the preposition *cum* is distinguished from the conjunction *cum* only by the sense and the connection.
[15] **contendunt:** 'contend'; *55.* **cum:** *185a.* **aut . . . aut:** 'either . . . or'; *235B* **suis:** 'their own', referring to the Helvetians; *158a.* **finibus:** 'country'; lit. 'boundaries'; *14b; 127a* (AG 400, B 214.2). **eos:** translate as if *Germanos*, 'the Germans', in order to avoid using 'them' and 'they' with reference to two different peoples in the same sentence. **prohibent:** 'are keeping (the Germans) out'. **ipsi:** 'themselves'; *162a.* There is no detailed record of these border raids.
[16] **eorum:** translate as if *Germanorum.* **finibus:** *124a.*
[17] **Eorum . . . septentriones:** there is reason to believe that this passage was not written by Caesar and was added after his time by someone who thought it useful to describe with greater detail the boundaries of the three divisions of Gaul mentioned by Caesar at the beginning of the chapter; the style is forced and difficult. If it is omitted, the transition from the statement about the Helvetians in Bk.I, 1.4 to the activities of the Helvetian leader, Orgetorix, at Bk.I, 2.1 becomes easy and natural. Translation: 'One part of Gaul taken as a whole (lit. 'of them'), which it has been said the Celts occupy, begins at the river Rhone; it is bounded by the Garonne river, the Ocean, and the country of the Belgians; on the side where the Sequanians and Helvetians are it extends also to the river Rhine; it lies to the north. The country of the Belgians commences at the most distant borders of Celtic Gaul and extends to the lower part of the river Rhine; it faces north and east. Aquitania extends from the Garonne river to the Pyrenees mountains and that part of the Ocean which is off Spain; it faces northwest'.

THE CAMPAIGN AGAINST THE HELVETIANS. 2-2

Orgetorix, a Helvetian, persuades his countrymen to migrate.

2.1. Apud[1] Helvetios longe nobilissimus fuit et ditissimus Orgetorix.[2] Is, M. Messala, M. Pisone consulibus, regni cupiditate[3] inductus, coniurationem nobilitatis fecit, et civitati persuasit,[4] ut de finibus suis cum omnibus copiis exirent; **2.** perfacile[5] esse, cum virtute omnibus praestarent, totius Galliae[6] imperio potiri. **3.** Id[7] hoc facilius eis persuasit, quod undique loci natura Helvetii continentur:[8] una ex parte flumine Rheno, latissimo atque altissimo,[9] qui agrum Helvetium a Germanis dividit; altera[10] ex parte monte Iura altissimo, qui est inter Sequanos et Helvetios; tertia,[11] lacu Lemanno et flumine Rhodano,[12] qui provinciam nostram ab Helvetiis dividit. **4.** His rebus[13] fiebat, ut et minus late vagarentur et minus facile finitimis[14] bellum inferre possent; qua ex parte, homines bellandi[15] cupidi, magno dolore afficiebantur. **5.** Pro multitudine autem[16] hominum et pro gloria belli atque fortitudinis angustos se fines[17] habere arbitrabantur, qui in longitudinem milia passuum[18] CCXL, in latitudinem CLXXX patebant.

[1] **Apud:** *122a.* **longe:** *153B* **nobilissimus:** 'highest in rank'; *27a; 353a.* **ditissimus:** *31.*

[2] **Orgetorix:** *10c.* **M.:** = *Marco; 19a.* **M. ... consulibus:** = 61 B.C.; *144b1; 240a* (AG 419a, B 227.1). **regni:** 'of kingly power', objective genitive; *6a; 102.*

[3] **cupiditate:** 'by a desire'; *10f; 135a* (AG 404b, B 219). **inductus:** 'led on'; *226b; 148B* **coniurationem:** 'conspiracy'; *12c.* **nobilitatis:** here used as a collective noun, lit. 'of the nobility'; trans. 'among the nobles'; *10f; 92B* **fecit:** *57B* **civitati:** *10f; 105* (AG 367, B 187.IIa).

[4] **persuasit:** 'persuaded'; *79B* **ut . . . exirent:** 'to go out', 'to migrate'. What kind of clause? *199a* (AG 563, B 295.1). **cum omnibus copiis:** 'with all (their) effects'; *137a.* **exirent:** plural because *civitati,* '(his) state', to which the unexpressed subject refers, is thought of as if it were *civibus,* 'the people of (his) state'; *68b; 173b; 238h* (B 254.4a).

[5] **perfacile . . . potiri:** indirect discourse, dependent on the idea of saying in *persuasit; 212a; 212c5; 213b* (AG 579, 580; B 314.2). **perfacile esse:** '(saying) that it was exceedingly easy.' The subject of *esse* is *potiri,* 'to obtain possession of'; *222B* Why is *perfacile* neuter? *148d.* **virtute:** *142a* (AG 418, B 226). **omnibus:** *107a* (AG 370, B 187.III.1). **praestarent:** 'they excelled'; *53; 184a* (AG 549, B 286.2). **totius:** *23a.*

[6] **totius Galliae:** 'of the whole (of) Gaul'; *102.* **imperio:** 'sovereignty'. Why ablative? *131c* (AG 410, B 218.1). **potiri:** *60; 61a4.*

[7] **Id:** acc.; 'that (course)'; *117a; 160c* (AG 369, B 176.2). **hoc:** 'on this account', referring to what follows; *135a; 161a* (AG 404, B 219). **facilius:** 'the more easily'; *34a.* **eis:** *44; 105.* **undique:** 'on all sides'. **loci natura:** 'by natural features'; *131a.* How lit.?

[8] **continentur:** 'are hemmed in'; why indicative? *183a.* **una ex parte:** 'on one side', the north side; *126c.* **flumine:** *131a.* **latissimo:** 'very wide'; *153a.*

[9] **altissimo:** here 'very deep', but in the next line 'very high'. **qui:** the antecedent is *Rheno; 163a.* **agrum:** here 'territory'. **a Germanis:** 'from (the territory of) the Germans'; *282; 127c.*

[10] **altera:** for *secunda,* 'second', as often. **monte Iura:** 'by the Jura range'; *mons* sometimes refers to a single mountain, sometimes to a group or chain of mountains, or to a moderate elevation.

[11] **tertia:** sc. *ex parte.* **lacu:** *20b.*

[12] **Rhodano:** the part of the Rhone just below Geneva; see Map 1. **provinciam:** *290.* **nostram:** i.e. *Romanam; 157c.* **Helvetiis:** *282.* Caesar does not deem it necessary to give the boundary on the fourth or east side in the Alps.

[13] **His rebus:** 'Because of these conditions', lit. 'these things'; *135a.* **fiebat:** 'it came about'; *70a.* **ut . . . possent:** subject of *fiebat; 203.1* (AG 569.1, B 297.2). **et . . . et:** *233a.* **minus late vagarentur:** 'they were more restricted in their movements', lit. 'wandered less widely', than they wished; *177a.* **minus:** *35.*

[14] **finitimis:** '(their) neighbours'; *107b; 154a* (AG 370, B 187.III.2). **inferre:** 'wage'; *69B* **possent:** *66B* **qua ex parte:** 'and on that account'; *167.* **homines:** in apposition to the subject of *afficiebantur,* '(being) men'; *12b; 91b.*

[15] **bellandi:** 'of waging war'; *53; 230.1* (AG 349a, B 204.1). **cupidi:** 'fond (of)'; *22B* **magno dolore afficiebantur:** 'they were sorely' (lit. 'with great vexation') 'troubled'; *57B* **dolore:** *11d; 136B* **Pro:** 'Considering'; *125a.* **multitudine hominum:** '(their) population'; how lit.? The number was 263,000 (I.29). The Helvetian territory in 1918 supported a population of about 2,250,000.

[16] **autem:** *236B* **gloria belli atque fortitudinis:** '(their) reputation for war' (lit. 'of war') 'and for bravery'; *102.*

[17] **angustos fines:** 'too small' (lit. 'narrow') 'territories'; *113a.* **se habere:** 'that they had'; *178; 213a.* **arbitrabantur:** 'they thought', lit. 'were thinking'; *175a.* **qui:** i.e. *fines.* **in longitudinem:** 'in length'; *76.*

[18] **milia passuum:** 'miles'. Length of the Roman 'pace' and Roman 'mile'? *243B* **milia:** *38a; 118a* (AG 425, B 181). **passuum:** *20b; 97a.* **CCXL:** *36, 38B* **latitudinem:** 'breadth'; *81.* **CLXXX:** *centum octoginta,* sc. *milia passuum; 38B* As the actual distance across the Helvetian territory was about 80 Roman miles, it has been suggested that Caesar wrote LXXX, *octoginta,* which was changed to CLXXX by an error in copying. **patebant:** 'extended'; *54.* The territory occupied by the Helvetians comprised a large portion, or the whole, of the modern Swiss cantons of Vaud, Neuchâtel, Basel, Freiburg, Bern, Solothurn, and Aargau. At an earlier period the Helvetians had lived north of the Rhine, but they had been forced to the south side by the Germans.

They make preparations; Orgetorix forms a conspiracy.

3.1. His rebus adducti[1], et auctoritate Orgetorigis permoti, constituerunt[2] ea, quae ad proficiscendum pertinerent, comparare, iumentorum[3] et carrorum quam maximum numerum cöemere[4], sementes quam maximas facere, ut in itinere[5] copia frumenti suppeteret, cum proximis civitatibus pacem et amicitiam[6] confirmare. **2.** Ad eas res conficiendas biennium[7] sibi satis esse duxerunt; in tertium annum profectionem lege confirmant.[8] **3.** Ad[9] eas res conficiendas Orgetorix deligitur. Is sibi legationem[10] ad civitates suscepit. **4.** In eo itinere persuadet Castico,[11] Catamantaloedis filio, Sequano, cuius pater regnum in Sequanis multos annos[12] obtinuerat et a senatu populi Romani amicus[13] appellatus erat, ut regnum in civitate sua[14] occuparet, quod pater ante habuerat; **5.** itemque Dumnorigi[15] Aeduo, fratri Diviciaci, qui eo tempore principatum in civitate[16] obtinebat ac maxime plebi acceptus erat, ut idem conaretur,[17] persuadet, eique filiam suam in matrimonium dat.[18] **6.** Perfacile[19] factu esse illis probat conata perficere, propterea quod ipse suae[20] civitatis imperium obtenturus esset; non esse dubium,[21] quin totius Galliae plurimum Helvetii possent; se suis copiis[22] suoque exercitu illis regna conciliaturum confirmat.[23] **7.** Hac oratione adducti,[24] inter se fidem et ius iurandum dant; et, regno occupato[25] per tres potentissimos ac firmissimos populos,[26] totius Galliae sese potiri posse sperant.

---

[1] **His rebus adducti:** 'Prompted by these considerations'. **adducti:** agrees with the unexpressed subject of *constiterunt*. **auctoritate:** ' by the influence'. *135a*. **permoti:** 'stirred to action''.

[2] **constituerunt:** 'they (i.e. *Helvetii*) determined'; followed by **comparare,** 'to make ready'; *221a* (AG 457, B 328.1). **ea:** 'those things'; after *comparare*; *113a*; *160c*. **ad proficiscendum:** 'for emigration', lit. 'for setting out'; *230.3* (AG 506, B 338.3). **pertinerent:** subjunctive as giving the thought of the Helvetians: 'were (as they thought) necessary', lit. 'pertained (to)'; *212d* (AG 592, B 323).

[3] **iumentorum:** 'draft-animals'; horses, mules, and oxen; *97a*. **carrorum:** two-wheeled 'carts', drawn largely by oxen. A Helvetian ox yoke, which was strapped to the horns of the oxen. The hardy Alpine cattle of Switzerland are descended from these Helvetian cattle. **quam maximum:** 'the largest possible'; *153c* (B 240.3). **numerum:** 'number'; *113a*.

[4] **cöemere:** 'to buy up'. **cöemere, facere, confirmare:** after *constituerunt*; *221a*. **sementes quam maximas:** 'as large sowings as possible'; *14b*; *153c*.

[5] **in itinere:** 'on the way'; *18c*. **copia frumenti suppeteret:** 'there might be an adequate supply of grain', lit. 'a supply of grain might be at hand'; *90b*. **suppeteret:** *196a* (AG 531, B 282). **proximis:** 'neighbouring', lit. 'nearest'; *33*.

[6] **pacem et amicitiam:** '(relations of) peace and friendship'. **confirmare:** '(and) to establish'; *234a*. **Ad . . . conficiendas:** gerundive construction, 'to complete these preparations', lit. 'for those things to be completed'; *230.3* (AG 503, B 339.2).

[7] **biennium satis esse:** 'that two years would be sufficient'; *212d*; *214a*. **biennium:** *79b*. **sibi:** 'for them'; *40b*; *158a*. **duxerunt:** here a verb of thought; 'they reckoned'; *213a*. **in:** 'for'. **profectionem:** '(their) departure'; *157a*.

[8] **confirmant:** historical present; trans. by a past tense, 'they fixed'; *175b*. Other historical presents in this chapter which should be translated by a past tense are *deligitur, persuadet, dat, probat, confirmat, dant, sperant.*

[9] **Ad . . . conficiendas:** 'to carry out these arrangements'. **deligitur:** 'was chosen'. **sibi —suscepit:** 'took upon himself'; *104a* (AG 362, B 187.1).

[10] **legationem,** etc.: 'the office of envoy to the states'; *150d*.

[11] **Castico:** *105*. **Catamantaloedis:** *99*. **filio, Sequano:** *91a* (AG 282, B 169.2). **pater:** *11b*. **regnum:** 'the chief authority'; at this time there was no hereditary or fixed monarchy among

the Gauls; *1*; *289a*.

[12] **annos:** *118a* (AG 423, B 181.1). **obtinuerat:** 'had held'; *79b*. **senatu populi Romani:** 'the senate of the Roman people', instead of *senatu populoque*, 'the senate and the Roman people', because the Roman senate had the right to confer honourary titles on foreign rulers without a popular vote.

[13] **amicus:** 'friend'; *88* (AG 284, B 168.2b). Such titles were conferred to recompense services rendered, or as a means of gaining favour.

[14] **sua:** *157b*. **ut . . . occuparet:** 'to seize'; *199a*; *177b*. **quod:** *not* 'because'. **item:** 'also'.

[15] **Dumnorigi:** *10c*; *105*. **fratri:** *11e*. **Diviciaci:** *19d*. **eo tempore:** 'at that time'; *147a*. **principatum:** 'the foremost place'; whether the dominant position of Dumnorix among the Aeduans was due wholly to his influence, or whether in 61 B.C. he had also a magistracy, is not indicated.

[16] **civitate:** '(his) state', i.e. the Aeduan state. **obtinebat:** force of the imperfect? *175a*. **maxime acceptus:** 'most acceptable'; *30*. **plebi:** *108a*. The English expression corresponding with *plebi acceptus* is "popular with the masses".

[17] **ut idem conaretur:** 'to attempt the same thing'; the construction is similar to that of *ut . . . occuparet* above; *61a1*. **idem:** *45*; *117a*. **ei:** *104a*. **in matrimonium:** 'in marriage'.

[18] **dat:** *67a*; *175b*.

[19] **Perfacile . . . possent:** indirect discourse depending on *probat*; *213a*. **Perfacile:** in predicate after *esse* (see Bk.I, 2. 2); *212c5*. **factu:** 'of accomplishment', lit. 'in respect to the doing'; *232* (AG 510.n2, B 340.2). **esse:** *214a*. **illis probat:** 'he (Orgetorix) showed them'; *104a*. **conata:** '(their) undertakings'; *157a*. **perficere:** 'to carry through'; subject of *esse*, *57b*; *79b*; *222b*.

[20] **suae:** 'his own', emphatic; *157b*. **imperium:** 'the sovereign power'; *74b*. **obtenturus esset:** 'he was going to seize'; *63*. Why subjunctive? *214a*. **non esse dubium:** 'that there was no doubt'.

[21] **dubium:** in predicate; neuter because the subject of *esse* is a clause. **quin . . . possent:** 'that the Helvetians were the most powerful (people) in all Gaul', lit. 'were most the able in the whole (of) Gaul'; *201b* (AG 558a, B 298). **Galliae:** *97b* (AG 346a2, B 201.1). **plurimum:** neuter accusative used substantively; *32*; *118b* (AG 214d, B 176.3a).

[22] **se suis copiis:** 'that he with his own means'; *157a*; *131a*. **exercitu:** *not* 'army' but 'armed retinue', like that with which Orgetorix afterwards overawed the judges, as related in the next chapter. **illis:** *104a*. **illis regna conciliaturum** [esse]: 'that he would get kingships for them'; *89c*.

[23] **confirmat:** 'he (Orgetorix) assured (them)'.

[24] **Hac oratione adducti:** 'Won over by this presentation'. **inter se:** *159*. **fidem et ius iurandum:** trans. 'an oath-bound pledge of good faith', lit. 'good faith and oath'; hendiadys, *238d*.

[25] **regno occupato:** 'having seized the supreme power'; *144a* (AG 420.1, B 227.2). **per:** 'with the help of'; *123a*. **potentissimos ac firmissimos:** 'very powerful and very firmly established'; *153a*.

[26] **populos:** the Helvetians, the Sequanians, and the Aeduans. **Galliae:** after *potiri*; *131d* (AG 410a, B 212.2). **sese posse sperant:** 'they hoped that they would be able'; *213a*. **potiri:** after *posse*; *221a*.

The conspiracy is revealed; Orgetorix dies.

4.1. Ea res[1] est Helvetiis per indicium enuntiata. Moribus suis Orgetorigem ex vinculis[2] causam dicere coegerunt; damnatum[3] poenam sequi oportebat, ut igni cremaretur. **2.** Die constituta[4] causae dictionis Orgetorix ad iudicium omnem suam familiam,[5] ad hominum milia decem, undique coegit, et omnes clientes[6] obaeratosque suos, quorum magnum numerum habebat, eodem[7] conduxit; per eos, ne causam diceret,[8] se eripuit. **3.** Cum civitas, ob eam rem incitata,[9] armis ius suum exsequi conaretur,[10] multitudinemque hominum ex agris magistratus cogerent, Orgetorix mortuus[11] est; **4.** neque abest suspicio, ut[12] Helvetii arbitrantur, quin ipse sibi mortem consciverit.

[1] **Ea res:** 'The matter', i.e. Orgetorix's scheme; lit. 'that thing'; *160d*. **Helvetiis:** why dat.? **per**

indicium: 'through (the agency of) informers,' lit. 'through information'; *92b*; *123a*. est enuntiata: 'was reported'; *172a*. Moribus suis: 'In accordance with their customs', as distinguished from the Roman procedure; *136c* (AG 418a, B 220.3).

[2] ex vinculis: 'in chains'; *126c*. causam dicere: 'to plead his case'; *221a*. coegerunt: 'they compelled'; *79b*.

[3] damnatum: agrees with *eum* understood as object of *sequi,* 'if condemned'; *209* (AG 496, B 337.2b). poenam: subject of *sequi,* 'the penalty', defined by the following *ut*-clause. oportebat: *73a,b*. poenam sequi oportebat: 'the penalty would inevitably follow', lit. 'it was necessary that the penalty follow'. igni: *14b*; *131a*. ut igni cremaretur: 'of being burned by fire', lit. 'that he should be burned by fire'; *203.4* (AG 561a, 570; B 297.3). The Gauls punished some offenses by burning alive, and sometimes offered human sacrifices (Bk.VI, 16,19; Bk.VII, 4).

[4] Die constituta: 'On the day appointed'; *21a*; *147a* (AG 423, B 230). dictionis: dependent on *Die,* 'for the pleading'; *102*. iudicium: 'the (place of) judgment', 'the trial'.

[5] familiam: 'slaves'; lit. 'body of slaves', taken collectively. ad: adv. modifying *decem,* 'about'; Caesar often gives a round number where it is impossible to be exact. hominum: *12b*; *97a*. milia: appositive of *familiam*; *38a*; *91a*.

[6] clientes: 'retainers'; *17c*. obaeratos: 'debtors'. In Gaul debtors who were unable to pay might be forced into bondage (Bk.VI, 13).

[7] eodem: 'to the same place,' the place of judgment. conduxit: 'brought', lit. 'led together'. per eos: 'with their help', lit. 'by means of them'; *123a*.

[8] diceret: *196a* (AG 530, 531; B 282). ne . . . eripuit: 'he evaded the pleading of his case', lit. 'he rescued himself that he might not plead his case'; Orgetorix overawed the judges so that they did not dare proceed with the trial.

[9] incitata: 'aroused'; *148b*. ius suum: 'its right' to call traitors to account. exsequi: 'enforce'; *200b*.

[10] conaretur, cogerent: *185c* (AG 546, B 288.1b). Force of the imperfect tense? hominum: *98a*. agris: 'the country'; *7a*; *130a*. magistratus: 'the public officials'; here evidently the local officers are meant; *82b*.

[11] mortuus est: 'died'; *57c*; *176a*. neque abest suspicio: 'and there is ground for suspecting', lit. 'nor is there lacking (ground for) suspecting'; *12c*; *233a*.

[12] ut: meanings of *ut?* See Vocab. quin . . . consciverit: 'that he committed suicide,' lit. 'that he himself inflicted death upon himself'; *201b* (AG 558, B 298). mortem: *17c*.

The Helvetians complete their preparations to migrate.

5.1. Post[1] eius mortem nihilo minus Helvetii id, quod constituerant, facere conantur,[2] ut e finibus suis exeant. **2.** Ubi iam[3] se ad eam rem paratos esse arbitrati sunt, oppida sua omnia, numero[4] ad duodecim, vicos ad quadringentos, reliqua[5] privata aedificia incendunt; **3.** frumentum omne, praeter quod[6] secum portaturi erant, comburunt, ut, domum reditionis[7] spe sublata, paratiores ad omnia pericula subeunda essent;[8] trium mensium molita cibaria sibi quemque domo[9] efferre iubent. **4.** Persuadent Rauracis[10] et Tulingis et Latobrigis, finitimis, uti,[11] eodem usi consilio, oppidis suis vicisque exustis, una cum eis[12] proficiscantur; Boiosque, qui trans Rhenum incoluerant et in agrum[13] Noricum transierant Noreiamque oppugnarant,[14] receptos ad se socios sibi asciscunt.

[1] Post: *122a*. eius: i.e. *Orgetorigis*. nihilo minus: 'nevertheless', lit. 'by nothing less'; *140* (AG 414, B 223). id quod: *160c*.

[2] conantur: *175b*. ut . . . exeant: explains *id*; *203.4*. From the fact that, notwithstanding the treason and death of Orgetorix, the Helvetians carried out the plan of migrating, it is evident that behind the movement there was a general cause stronger than the influence of any individual. It seems probable that this cause was the pressure of the Germans, with whom, as stated in chapter 1, the Helvetians were constantly at war.

[3] Ubi iam: 'As soon as', lit. 'When now'. rem: 'undertaking'. paratos: 'ready'; *148c*. oppida: 'fortified towns'; *6a*.

[4] numero: *142a*; *85* (AG 418, B 226). ad: adverb, (as in Bk.I, 4.2). vicos: 'villages', unfortified.

quadringentos: 'four hundred'; *36.*

[5] **reliqua:** *171a.* **privata aedificia:** 'buildings belonging to individuals', not in the walled towns or villages. **incendunt:** 'they set fire to'.

[6] **praeter quod:** i.e. *praeter id (frumentum) quod.* **secum:** 'with them'; *125c.* **portaturi erant:** 'they were going to take'; *63.* **comburunt:** 'they burned'; *175b.* **domum:** 'home'; *119b* (AG 427.2, B 182.1b).

[7] **reditionis:** 'of returning'; *12c; 102.* **spe:** how declined? *21b,c.* **spe sublata:** 'as a result of taking away the hope', lit. 'the hope having been taken away'; *144b3.* **pericula:** 'dangers'; *6a.* **subeunda:** 'meet', lit. 'to be met'; *68b; 230.3* (AG 503, B 339.2).

[8] **essent:** *196a* (AG 531.1, B 282). **trium:** *37b.* **trium mensium:** 'for (lit. 'of') three months'; *100a.* **molita cibaria:** 'ground rations'. The grain was to be ground to coarse flour before starting, in contrast with the Roman custom of carrying unground grain on campaigns (*317*); the difficulty of carrying the stone mills, in addition to their other effects, probably occasioned the order. **quemque:** *49a; 170b.* **sibi quemque efferre:** 'that each one for himself should carry away'; *178.*

[9] **domo:** *20c; 130b* (AG 427.1, B 229.1b). **efferre:** *69b* (AG 563a, B 331.II). **iubent:** '(and) they gave orders'; *200b; 234a.* On an allowance of three quarters of a pound of coarse flour per day for each person, more than 12,000 tons would be needed to feed 368,000 people (chap. 29) for 90 days. If each cart carried a ton, more than 12,000 carts would have been required to transport the supplies and perhaps half as many more for other purposes; but it is hardly probable that the Helvetians and their allies took so great a quantity of supplies as the order contemplated. If we reckon 20 feet to a cart, 18,000 carts in single file would form a line 68 miles long.

[10] **Rauracis:** why dat.? The Rauraci, Tulingi, and Latobrigi were apparently north of the Helvetians (Map 1), and particularly exposed to the attacks and inroads of the Germans; hence their readiness to join the Helvetians in migrating. **et . . . et:** *234a.* **finitimis:** '(their) neighbours'; *91a; 157a.*

[11] **uti . . . proficiscantur:** trans. by an infinitive, as *ut . . . exirent* in I. 2. 1; *199a; 61a3.* **usi:** 'adopting' or 'to adopt'; lit. 'having used'; *61a3; 228a.* **consilio:** 'plan'; *131c* (AG 410, B 218.1). **oppidis suis vicisque exustis:** 'having burned' (or 'to burn') 'their towns and villages', lit. 'their towns and villages having been burned'; *144b2* (AG 419, B 227). **una:** adverb.

[12] **eis:** *Helvetiis; 160b; 137a.*

[13] **agrum Noricum:** 'the territory of the Norici', corresponding, in general, with the western part of Austria south of the Danube, between Bavaria and Hungary. **transierant:** 'had passed over'; *68b.*

[14] **oppugnarant:** 'had taken' by storming. *340.* Full form? *64a1.* (AG 181, B 116), **recepto socios sibi asciscunt:** 'they received and associated with themselves' (lit. 'to themselves') 'as allies'. *228a* (AG 496, N2, B 337.5). **socios:** *115a.* Cf. IV, 3.2, note 3.

Of two possible routes they choose that through the Province.

6.1. Erant[1] omnino itinera duo, quibus itineribus domo exire possent:[2] unum per Sequanos, angustum et difficile, inter[3] montem Iuram et flumen Rhodanum, vix qua singuli carri ducerentur;[4] mons autem altissimus impendebat, ut facile perpauci[5] prohibere possent; **2.** alterum per provinciam nostram, multo[6] facilius atque expeditius, propterea quod inter fines Helvetiorum et Allobrogum,[7] qui nuper pacati erant, Rhodanus fluit,[8] isque non nullis locis vado transitur. **3.** Extremum[9] oppidum Allobrogum est, proximumque Helvetiorum finibus,[10] Genava. Ex eo oppido pons ad Helvetios pertinet.[11] Allobrogibus sese vel persuasuros, quod nondum bono animo[12] in populum Romanum viderentur, existimabant, vel vi[13] coacturos, ut per suos fines eos ire paterentur. **4.** Omnibus[14] rebus ad profectionem comparatis, diem dicunt, qua die[15] ad ripam Rhodani omnes conveniant. Is dies erat a. d. v. Kal.[16] Apr., L. Pisone, A. Gabinio consulibus.

[1] **Erant:** 'There were'; *90a.* **omnino:** 'only'. **duo:** *37b.* **itineribus:** omit in translation; *165a* (AG 307a, B 251.3). **domo:** (see chap. I. 5. 3).

[2] **possent:** subj. of characteristic; *194a* (AG 535, B 283). **unum . . . alterum:** sc. *iter; 91c* (AG 282a, B 169.5). **per Sequanos:** *282.* **difficile:** 'difficult'; *29.*

[3] **inter . . . Rhodanum:** on the right bank of the Rhone. There was no route across the Jura range practicable for so large a force, while the passage down the left bank of the Rhine, and westward between the Jura and the Vosges Mountains (Map 1), was left out of consideration, not only (we may assume) because it was less direct, but also because it was exposed to the attacks of Ariovistus. **vix:** 'hardly'. **qua:** 'where'; translate as if the order were *qua vix.* **singuli:** 'one at a time'.

[4] **ducerentur:** 'could' (lit. 'would') 'be drawn along'; subj. of characteristic, the relative adverb *qua* having the force of a relative pronoun. The narrowest point of the route is at the "Mill-race Gorge", or Pas de l'Écluse, 19 Roman miles (about 17.5 English miles; *243b*), below Geneva (see Map 2). **mons altissimus:** Mt. Credo, now pierced by a tunnel, 2.5 miles long, through which passes the railroad from Geneva to Lyons. **autem:** 'moreover'; *236a,b.* **impendebat:** 'overhung'; *54.*

[5] **perpauci:** 'very few' men, posted on the heights above the road. Force of *per? 79b* and Vocab. **prohibere:** sc. *eos.* **possent:** *197a* (AG 537.1, B 284.1). **provinciam nostram:** *157c; 290.*

[6] **multo:** 'much', lit. 'by much'; *140.* **facilius:** *29.* **expeditius:** 'more convenient'.

[7] **Allobrogum:** *19e.* **nuper:** 'recently', in 61 B.C., after a revolt; the Allobroges were first conquered by Q. Fabius Maximus, in 121 B.C. (I,45). **pacati erant:** 'had been subdued'; *53; 192.*

[8] **fluit:** 'flows'. **is:** 'it'; *160b.* **non nullis:** 'some'; *23a.* **locis:** *6c; 145c.* **vado transitur:** 'is fordable', lit. 'is crossed by a ford'; *134a; 68c.*

[9] **Extremum:** 'The most remote', lit. 'utmost', from the Roman point of view; *33.*

[10] **finibus:** *108a* (AG 384, B. 192.1). **pons:** *17c.* **Helvetios:** *282.*

[11] **pertinet:** 'reaches across'. **Allobrogibus:** *105.* **vel . . . vel:** *235b.* **persuasuros:** sc. *esse; 89c; 213a, 214a.* **nondum . . . viderentur:** 'did not yet seem' to the Helvetians; why is *viderentur* subjunctive? *183a.*

[12] **bono animo:** 'kindly disposed', lit. 'of kindly feeling'; in predicate after *viderentur; 143b* (AG 415, B 224.1). **in:** here 'toward'. **existimabant:** 'they believed'.

[13] **vi:** 'by force'; *18a.* **coacturos:** i.e. *sese* (the Helvetians) *eos* (the Allobroges) *coacturos esse.* **ut . . . paterentur:** 'to permit', substantive clause after *persuasuros (esse), coacturos (esse); 199a.* **eos:** trans. as if *Helvetios;* (see 1.4, note 15). **ire:** *68a.*

[14] **Omnibus . . . comparatis:** 'when all preparations had been completed'; *144b2.* How lit.? **dicunt:** 'they appointed'.

[15] **qua die:** 'on which'; *147a; 165a* (AG 423, B 230). **ad ripam:** 'on the bank' across from the Province; the north bank of the Rhone. **conveniant:** 'they should assemble'; subjunctive of purpose, as if *qua* were *ut ea,* 'that on that day'; *193* (AG 531.2, B 282.2). **dies:** gender? *21a.*

[16] **a. d. v. Kal. Apr.:** *ante diem quintum Kalendas Apriles,* 'the fifth day before the Calends of April', March 28 by our calendar; *241a,b* (AG 631, B 371.5). **L. . . . . consulibus:** 58 B.C.; *240a; 144b1.*

Caesar hastens to Geneva, and parleys with the Helvetians.

7.1. Caesari[1] cum id nuntiatum esset, eos per provinciam nostram iter facere conari, maturat[2] ab urbe proficisci et, quam maximis potest itineribus,[3] in Galliam ulteriorem contendit et ad[4] Genavam pervenit. **2.** Provinciae toti quam maximum potest militum[5] numerum imperat (erat omnino in Gallia ulteriore legio[6] una); pontem, qui erat ad Genavam, iubet rescindi. **3.** Ubi de eius adventu[7] Helvetii certiores facti sunt, legatos ad eum mittunt[8] nobilissimos civitatis, cuius legationis Nammeius et Verucloetius principem[9] locum obtinebant, qui dicerent, *Sibi*[10] *esse in animo sine ullo maleficio iter per provinciam facere,*[11] *propterea quod aliud iter haberent nullum; rogare, ut eius voluntate*[12] *id sibi facere liceat.* **4.** Caesar, quod memoria[13] tenebat, L. Cassium consulem occisum[14] exercitumque eius ab Helvetiis pulsum et sub iugum missum, concedendum non putabat;[15]

neque homines inimico animo,[16] data facultate per provinciam itineris faciundi, temperaturos[17] ab iniuria et maleficio existimabat. **5.** Tamen,[18] ut spatium intercedere posset, dum milites, quos imperaverat, convenirent,[19] legatis respondit, *Diem*[20] *se ad deliberandum sumpturum; si quid vellent, ad Id. April.*[21] *reverterentur.*

[1] **Caesari:** *19c; 353e.* **nuntiatum esset:** 'had been reported'; *185c* (AG 546, B 288.1b). **eos . . . conari:** infinitive clause in apposition with *id;* the gist of the report, in the direct form, was *Helvetii per provinciam nostram iter facere conantur; 214a.*

[2] **maturat:** 'he hastened'; *255, 256.* **urbe:** Rome, which by way of distinction was *the* city; *17b.*

[3] **quam maximis potest itineribus:** stronger than *quam maximis itineribus;* 'with the utmost possible speed'; *153c.* How lit.? **Galliam ulteriorem:** here including the Province, Caesar's immediate destination; *286; 290.*

[4] **ad:** 'to the vicinity of'; *120a.* **pervenit:** 'came', lit. 'comes through'. If, as Plutarch says, Caesar arrived at the Rhone on the eighth day after leaving Rome, he must have travelled at the rate of about 100 Roman miles (about 92 English miles; *243b*) per day. **Provinciae . . . imperat:** 'he levied upon the Province'; *106a* (AG 369, B 187.1).

[5] **militum:** *10b.* Legionary soldiers are meant.

[6] **legio:** this 'legion' was the tenth, afterwards famous; *307e.* **una:** *23a.* **ad:** 'near'. **pontem . . . rescindi:** 'that the bridge be broken down'; *200b.*

[7] **adventu:** 'approach'; *20b.* **certiores facti sunt:** 'were informed', lit. 'were made more certain', *115c.* **legatos:** 'as envoys'; predicate accusative; *6a; 115a.*

[8] **mittunt:** 'sent'; *175b.* **nobilissimos:** 'the most distinguished men'; *154a.* **cuius legationis:** 'and in this delegation', lit. 'of which delegation'; *167.*

[9] **principem:** 'foremost'; *26b; 10a.* **qui dicerent:** 'in order to say'; *193a* (AG 531.2, B 282.2).

[10] **Sibi . . . liceat:** *212, a,b,* and *c4.* **Sibi esse in animo:** 'that it was their intention'; less freely, 'that they had it in mind'; *Sibi* is a dative of possession; *111; 214a; 178.* **sine:** 'without'; *125a.* **ullo:** *23a.* **maleficio:** 'wrong-doing'; we should say 'without doing any harm'.

[11] **facere:** subject of *esse; 222b.* **haberent:** *214a.* **nullum:** emphatic position; *353d.* **rogare:** sc. *se,* '(and) that they requested'; *215; 234a.*

[12] **eius voluntate:** 'with his consent'; *138.* **ut . . . liceat:** 'that permission might be granted'; subjunctive also in direct discourse. How lit.? *73b; 199a.* **facere:** *222a.*

[13] **memoria:** *131a* (AG 409, B 218). **memoria tenebat:** 'he remembered'; *183a.* **L.:** *Lucium; 19a.*

[14] **occisum:** sc. *esse,* 'had been killed'; *89c; 213a.* **exercitum:** 'army'; *20a,b; 74b.* **pulsum** [esse]: 'had been routed'; *178.* **sub iugum:** 'under the yoke', made by setting two spears upright and placing a third on them horizontally, as a cross-piece; under this captured soldiers were made to pass, bending over, as a token of complete submission and humiliation. The defeat of Cassius by the Helvetians took place in 107 B.C.; *124a.*

[15] **concedendum non putabat:** 'did not think that the request ought to be granted'; less freely, 'that the concession ought to be made'; *63; 73e.* **neque:** trans. as if *et non.*

[16] **inimico animo:** 'of hostile temper'; *143a* (AG 415, B 224). **data facultate:** = *si facultas data esset,* 'if opportunity should have been granted'; *144b4.* **itineris faciundi:** 'of marching'; *64b; 230.1.* How lit?

[17] **temperaturos** [esse]: 'would refrain'; *63.* **iniuria:** 'violence'.

[18] **Tamen:** 'Nevertheless'; *236a.* **spatium:** trans. as if *tempus,* 'time'. **intercedere:** 'intervene'; *221a.* **dum:** 'until'.

[19] **convenirent:** 'should assemble'; *190b* (AG 553, B 293.III.2). **respondit:** 'he made answer'.

[20] **Diem:** 'time'. .... **se:** *158a.* **deliberandum:** 'for consideration'; *230.3.* **sumpturum** [esse]: 'would take'; *63; 214a.* **quid:** 'anything'; *168.* **vellent, reverterentur:** 'they wanted', 'they should return'; in the direct form *si vultis, revertimini; 206.2; 218.1a; 216* (AG 588, B 316).

[21] **Id. April.:** *Idus Apriles,* April 13; *241a,b.*

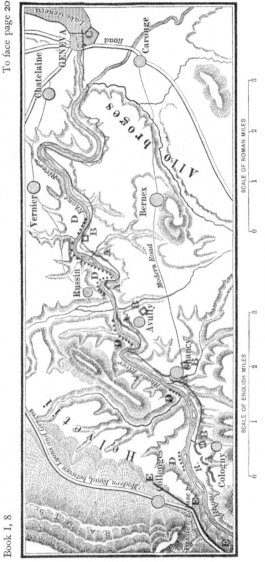

MAP 2

CAESAR'S LINE OF WORKS ALONG THE RHONE FROM GENEVA TO MILL-RACE GORGE (PAS DE L'ÉCLUSE)

Book I, 8   To face page 20

EXPLANATION

A, A. Places where strong fortifications were needed, such as are shown in Figure 34. The lighter red line between these places indicates where less extensive fortifying was required.

B, B. Redoubts, *castella* (chap. 8, l. 6).

C. Site of ancient Geneva, on the south side of the Rhone. The modern city spreads out on both sides of the river.

D, D. Places where the Helvetians probably gathered, in their attempts to force the crossing of the Rhone (chap. 8, ll. 12–16).

E, E. Route of the Helvetian host entering Mill-race Gorge.

Caesar prevents the Helvetians from entering the Province.

8.1. Interea[1] ea legione, quam secum habebat, militibusque, qui ex provincia convenerant, a lacu Lemanno, qui[2] in flumen Rhodanum influit, ad montem Iuram, qui fines Sequanorum ab Helvetiis[3] dividit, milia passuum XVIIII murum[4] in altitudinem pedum sedecim fossamque perducit. **2.** Eo opere perfecto,[5] praesidia disponit, castella communit, quo facilius, si, se invito,[6] transire conarentur, prohibere possit. **3.** Ubi ea dies,[7] quam constituerat cum legatis, venit, et legati ad eum reverterunt,[8] negat, se more et exemplo populi Romani posse iter[9] ulli per provinciam dare; et, si vim facere conentur,[10] prohibiturum ostendit. **4.** Helvetii, ea spe deiecti,[11] navibus iunctis ratibusque compluribus factis, alii[12] vadis Rhodani, qua minima altitudo fluminis erat, non numquam[13] interdiu, saepius noctu, si perrumpere possent,[14] conati, operis munitione et militum concursu[15] et telis repulsi, hoc conatu destiterunt.

[1] **Interea:** 'Meanwhile', while the more distant troops levied on the Province were gathering at the Rhone, and the Helvetians were waiting for Caesar's answer. **legione, militibus:** looked upon as instrument rather than as agent; *131b.* **secum:** *125c.*

[2] **qui . . . influit:** while Caesar's statement is not incorrect, modern geographers consider Lake Geneva as an enlargement of the Rhone, applying the name 'Rhone' also to the principal feeder entering the lake at the upper end.

[3] **Helvetiis:** *282.* **milia:** *118a; 243b; 38a.* **XVIIII:** *undeviginti; 36, 38b.*

[4] **murum:** 'a rampart'; *1.* **in altitudinem pedum sedecim:** 'sixteen feet high'; how lit.? **pedum:** *10b; 100a* (AG 345b, B 203.2). **fossam:** 'trench'. **perducit:** 'he constructed'; *175b.* For much of the distance between Lake Geneva and Mill-race Gorge (17.5 English miles, see I, 6.1, note 4), the left bank of the Rhone is steep enough to make extensive fortifying unnecessary. Caesar apparently made the slopes hard to surmount by cutting the face down from the top for sixteen feet and throwing the dirt out toward the river in such a way as to produce the effect of a rampart and trench; palisades were probably driven in along the edge of the bluff. See Map 2.

[5] **Eo opere perfecto:** 'When this work had been finished'; *13e; 144b2.* **praesidia:** 'detachments' of troops. **disponit:** 'he stationed at intervals'; *79d.* **castella:** 'redoubts'; their probable location is shown on Map 2. **communit:** 'he strongly fortified'. **quo:** why used in place of *ut*? *193b* (B 282.1a).

[6] **se invito:** 'without his permission', lit. 'he (being) unwilling'; *144a.* **conarentur:** *177b; 220* (AG 593, B 324.1). **prohibere:** sc. *eos.*

[7] **ea dies:** April 13; (see I, 7.5).

[8] **reverterunt:** 'returned'; *79d.* **more et exemplo:** 'consistently with the settled usage', lit. 'custom and precedent'; *136c* (B 220.3).

[9] **iter:** 'right of way'. **ulli:** here used as a noun, 'to any one'. **vim facere:** 'use force'; *18a.*

[10] **conentur, [se eos] prohibiturum [esse]:** in the direct form, *si conabimini, prohibebo; 215; 218.1a* (AG 580, B 314.1).

[11] **ea spe deiecti:** 'disappointed in their expectations', lit. 'cast down from that hope'; *57b.* **spe:** *127a.* **navibus . . . factis:** 'joined boats together', attempting to make a floating bridge, 'and made a number of rafts' for poling across; how lit.? *144b2.*

[12] **alii:** 'others', relatively few, compared with the number who tried to cross in the ways just mentioned. **vadis:** *134a.* **minima:** *32.*

[13] **non numquam:** 'sometimes'. **interdiu:** 'by day'. **saepius:** *35.* **noctu:** 'at night'.

[14] **si perrumpere possent:** '(to see) whether they could break through'; after *conati; 204.4* (AG 576a, B 300.3). **conati:** participle, but trans. 'tried'; *61a1; 228a.* **operis munitione:** 'by the strength of the fortifications', i.e. *murus, fossa, castella*; how lit.?

[15] **concursu:** 'by the rapid massing' at points attacked; *1; 20b.* **telis:** 'by (their) missiles'. **repulsi:** 'forced back'. **conatu:** 'they gave up' (lit. 'desisted from') 'the attempt'; *127a* (AG 402, B 214).

The Helvetians get leave to go through the country of the Sequanians.

9.1. Relinquebatur[1] una per Sequanos via, qua, Sequanis invitis, propter angustias[2] ire non poterant. **2.** His cum sua sponte persuadere non possent,[3] legatos ad Dumnorigem Aeduum mittunt, ut, eo deprecatore,[4] a Sequanis impetrarent. **3.** Dumnorix gratia et largitione[5] apud Sequanos plurimum poterat, et Helvetiis[6] erat amicus, quod ex ea civitate Orgetorigis[7] filiam in matrimonium duxerat, et cupiditate regni adductus novis rebus studebat,[8] et quam plurimas civitates suo beneficio habere obstrictas[9] volebat. **4.** Itaque rem[10] suscipit, et a Sequanis impetrat, ut per fines suos Helvetios ire patiantur,[11] obsidesque uti inter sese dent, perficit: Sequani, ne itinere Helvetios[12] prohibeant; Helvetii, ut sine maleficio et iniuria transeant.

[1] **Relinquebatur:** 'There was left'; *90a.* **una via:** 'only the way', described in chap. 6. **qua:** *134a.* **Sequanos:** *282.* **Sequanis invitis:** *144b4.*
[2] **angustias:** 'the narrowness' of the road through the Mill-race Gorge. **His:** *105.* **sua sponte:** 'by their own influence'; *17d; 157b.*
[3] **possent:** *184a; 66b.*
[4] **eo deprecatore:** 'through his intercession'; *144b6.* **impetrarent:** 'they might gain their request'; *177b; 196a* (AG 485e, B 268.3).
[5] **gratia et largitione:** 'on account of his popularity and lavish giving'; *135a.* **plurimum poterat:** 'had very great influence', lit. 'was able to a very great degree'; *118b.* A fuller account of Dumnorix is given in chapter 18, where we learn that he had practical control of the revenues of the Aeduans and was bitterly opposed to Caesar.
[6] **Helvetiis:** *108a* (AG 384, B 192.1).
[7] **Orgetorigis . . . duxerat:** (see I, 3.5, with notes).
[8] **novis rebus studebat:** 'was eager for a revolution'; *105* (AG 368.3, B 187.IIa). **quam plurimas:** 'as many ... as possible'; *153c.*
[9] **suo beneficio obstrictas:** 'placed under obligation to himself', lit. 'bound by his own favour'. **volebat:** *71.* **Itaque:** 'Accordingly'.
[10] **rem:** 'the negotiation'. **impetrat:** 'obtained a promise'; how lit?
[11] **patiantur:** *199a8.* **obsides . . . perficit:** 'and brought about an exchange of hostages' (lit. 'that they should give') 'between them'. Hostages were exchanged as a pledge of good faith; if the agreement were violated, they were liable to be put to death with torture. **uti . . . dent:** after *perficit; 203.3* (AG 568, B 297.1).
[12] **Sequani, Helvetii:** in partitive apposition with the subject of *dent;* freely, 'the Sequanians (giving hostages)'; *91c.* **itinere:** *127a* (AG 400, B 214.2). **ne . . . prohibeant, ut . . . transeant:** substantive clauses with the subjunctive of purpose, expressing the terms of the agreement for the ratification of which the exchange of hostages was arranged.

Caesar, learning of their plan, brings five legions from Italy.

10.1. Caesari renuntiatur,[1] Helvetiis esse in animo per agrum Sequanorum et Aeduorum iter in Santonum fines facere, qui non longe[2] a Tolosatium finibus absunt, quae civitas est in provincia. **2.** Id[3] si fieret, intellegebat magno cum[4] periculo provinciae futurum, ut homines bellicosos, populi Romani inimicos,[5] locis patentibus maximeque frumentariis finitimos haberet. **3.** Ob eas causas ei munitioni,[6] quam fecerat, T. Labienum legatum[7] praefecit; ipse in Italiam magnis itineribus contendit, duasque ibi legiones conscribit,[8] et tres, quae circum Aquileiam[9] hiemabant, ex hibernis educit; et, qua proximum iter in ulteriorem Galliam[10] per Alpes erat, cum his quinque legionibus ire contendit. **4.** Ibi[11] Ceutrones et Graioceli et Caturiges, locis superioribus occupatis, itinere[12] exercitum prohibere conantur. **5.** Compluribus his proeliis[13] pulsis, ab Ocelo, quod est oppidum citerioris provinciae[14] extremum, in fines Vocontiorum ulterioris provinciae[15] die septimo pervenit; inde in Allobrogum fines, ab Allobrogibus in Segusiavos exercitum[16] ducit. Hi sunt extra provinciam trans Rhodanum[17] primi.

[1] **renuntiatur**: 'Word was brought (back) to Caesar', *re*-implying that men had been sent out by him and now returned with the information; *79d*. **esse**: subject of *renuntiatur;* cf. chap. 7, notes 12-14.

[2] **non longe . . . absunt:** the territories of the Santones were on the west coast, more than 100 miles from the nearest point of the Province; see Map back cover GALLIA. If the Helvetians should reach their destination, they would be further from the Province than when they started; yet even at that distance they might become dangerous neighbours because they would no longer be kept on the defensive by the Germans. **quae civitas:** 'a state which', the state of the Tolosates; *165b*.

[3] **Id:** the migration to the territory of the Santones, *iter . . . facere.* **fieret . . . futurum** [esse]: in the direct form, *fiet . . . erit; 70a; 218.1a*.

[4] **cum:** *136a*. **provinciae:** 'to' (lit. 'of') 'the Province'; *102*. **ut . . . haberet:** 'to have'; how lit.? *203.1* (AG 569.2, B 297.2). **bellicosos:** 'warlike'; *75f*.

[5] **inimicos:** *91a*. **locis . . . finitimos:** *108a; 115b* (AG 384, B 192.1). Caesar had no reason to interfere with the passage of the Helvetians through the country of the Sequanians unless it was clear that Roman interests would be unfavourably affected. **patentibus:** 'open' to attack, not protected by natural barriers. **frumentariis:** 'productive' of grain; *30*.

[6] **munitioni:** *107b; 74b*. **T.:** *Titum; 19a*.

[7] **legatum:** 'lieutenant-general' or 'lieutenant'; *313a*. **praefecit:** 'placed in charge (of)'; *57b*. **Italiam:** Cisalpine Gaul is here meant; *283b*.

[8] **duas legiones:** the 11th and 12th. **conscribit:** 'raised' by conscription. **tres:** sc. *legiones,* the 7th, 8th, and 9th legions. **circum:** 'in the neighbourhood of', lit. 'around'; the winter-quarters were not in the town; *122a*.

[9] **Aquileiam:** a flourishing Roman colony near the head of the Adriatic Sea. **hiemabant:** 'were wintering'. **hibernis:** '(their) winter quarters'; *127c; 335a,b*.

[10] **ulteriorem Galliam:** *286*. **Alpes:** *291*. **cum:** *137b*.

[11] **Ibi:** i.e. in the Alps; Caesar's route lay over the pass of Mt. Genèvre, which is one of the best in the Alps. The roads over all the Alpine passes are of the same general character (see Map 1. **locis superioribus occupatis:** 'seized commanding heights and'; how lit.? *144b2*.

[12] **itinere:** *127a* (AG 400, B 214.2). **Compluribus proeliis:** 'in a number of engagements'; *131a*.

[13] **his pulsis:** 'driving them off'; how lit.? *144b2; 160b*. **ab:** here 'from'.

[14] **citerioris provinciae:** 'nearer' as seen from Rome; *284*. **extremum:** i.e. most westerly.

[15] **ulterioris provinciae:** *290*. **pervenit:** 'passed through' *175b*. **inde:** trace on Map 1 Caesar's route from Ocelum.

[16] **exercitum:** three trained legions from near Aquileia, and two legions of recruits just levied in Cisalpine Gaul (the 11th and 12th), with which was joined the tenth legion, released from guarding the fortification below Geneva; for the campaign against the Helvetians Caesar had thus 6 legions, aggregating about 22,000 men, besides cavalry. Light-armed troops, used in the campaign of 57 and afterwards, are not mentioned in Book I; *307e*.

[17] **trans Rhodanum:** Caesar probably crossed the Rhone by a pontoon bridge a short distance above the junction with the Arar. The Segusiavi were clients of the Aeduans, hence on good terms with the Romans. Most of their territory was on the west side of the Rhone, but they seem to have occupied also the narrow corner between the Rhone and the Arar.

The Aeduans, Ambarri and Allobroges entreat Caesar's aid against the Helvetians, who are ravaging their country.

11.1. Helvetii iam per angustias[1] et fines Sequanorum suas copias traduxerant,[2] et in Aeduorum fines pervenerant eorumque agros populabantur.[3] **2.** Aedui, cum se suaque ab eis defendere non possent,[4] legatos ad Caesarem mittunt rogatum[5] auxilium: **3.** [6]*Ita se[7] omni tempore de* *populo Romano meritos esse, ut, paene[8] in conspectu exercitus nostri, agri vastari, liberi eorum in servitutem[9] abduci, oppida expugnari non debuerint.* **4.** Eodem tempore, quo[10] Aedui, Ambarri, necessarii et consanguinei[11] Aeduorum, Caesarem certiorem faciunt, *sese, depopulatis agris,[12] non facile ab oppidis vim hostium prohibere.* **5.** Item Allobroges, qui trans Rhodanum[13] vicos possessionesque habebant, fuga[14] se ad Caesarem recipiunt, et demonstrant,[15] *sibi praeter agri solum nihil esse reliqui.* **6.** Quibus[16] rebus adductus Caesar non exspectandum sibi statuit, dum,[17] omnibus fortunis sociorum consumptis, in Santonos[18] Helvetii pervenirent.

[1] **angustias**: see 9.1; note 2, and 6.1, notes 2-5. It must have taken Caesar 7 or 8 weeks to go to Cisalpine Gaul, gather his forces there, and bring them across the Province to the north side of the Rhone. Meanwhile the Helvetians with their throng of women, children and loaded carts had slowly threaded the narrow Mill-race Gorge, and had advanced only about 100 miles.

[2] **traduxerant**: 'had led (across)'. **Aeduorum fines**: on the west side of the Arar, which the van of the Helvetian host already had crossed. See Map 1.

[3] **populabantur**: 'were laying waste'; *61.a1; 175a.* **sua**: 'their possessions'; *154a.*

[4] **possent**: *184a* (AG 549, B 286.2).

[5] **rogatum**: 'to ask for'; *231a.* **auxilium**: 'help'; *231b.*

[6] **Direct form**: Ita (*nos*) omni tempore de populo Romano *meriti sumus*, ut, paene in conspectu exercitus *tui*, agri vastari, liberi *nostri* in servitutem abduci, oppida expugnari non *debuerint*.

[7] **Ita se . . . meritos esse**: '(saying) that they had so (well) deserved'; *213b.* **omni tempore**: 'at all times'; "every time" has a different force. More than 40 years before, in 121 B.C., the Aeduans had by treaty been recognized as *socii populi Romani*, 'allies of the Roman people'. The Romans were first led to intervene in the affairs of Transalpine Gaul, however, not in the interest of the Aeduans, but in response to a request of Massilia for protection against the incursions of Ligurian tribes east of the Rhone; this was in 155 B.C. **de**: we should say 'of'.

[8] **paene**: 'almost'. **nostri**: *157c.* **vastari**: 'to be laid waste'; *221a.* **liberi eorum**: 'their children'.

[9] **servitutem**: 'slavery', the penalty of capture; *10f.* **abduci**: '(to be) led away'. **expugnari**: '(to be) taken by assault'. **non debuerint**: 'ought not'; *197b.* Why *debeant* in the direct form? *177b; 357b.*

[10] **quo**: *147a.* **Aedui**: sc. *legatos mittunt.* **necessarii**: 'relatives', including connections by marriage; *154a; 91a.*

[11] **consanguinei**: 'kinsmen', comprising only blood relations. Notwithstanding their close relationship with the Aeduans, the Ambarri had a separate coinage.

[12] **depopulatis agris**: '(their) lands had been ravaged and'; how lit.? *59b; 144b2* (AG 190b, B 112b). **prohibere**: *214a; 213a.*

[13] **trans Rhodanum**: i.e. on the north side of the Rhone, probably west of the Mill-race Gorge.

[14] **fuga**: *136b.* **se recipiunt**: 'made their escape'.

[15] **demonstrant**: 'stated'; *175b.* **sibi . . . nihil esse reliqui**: 'that they had nothing left'; *213a.* **sibi**: *111* (AG 373, B 190). **agri solum**: 'the bare ground'; how lit.? **reliqui**: used as a noun, dependent on *nihil; 97a* (B 201).

[16] **Quibus**: *167.* **non exspectandum** [esse] **sibi**: 'that he ought not to wait'; *73e; 89c.* How lit.? **sibi**: *110.*

[17] **dum . . . consumptis**: 'until everything that the allies had should have been destroyed, and'; how lit.? *144b2.*

[18] **Santonos**: 'the (country of) the Santoni'; previously (chap. 10.1) spelled 'Santones'. Caesar was inconsistent in the spelling of this name, which appears in Roman letters on a coin; see Vocab. under *Santones*. The name survives in that of the city Saintes; *19e; 282.* **pervenirent**: *190b* (AG 553, B 293.III.2).

Caesar cuts to pieces one division of the Helvetians at the Arar.

12.1. Flumen est Arar,[1] quod per fines Aeduorum et Sequanorum in Rhodanum influit, incredibili lenitate,[2] ita ut oculis,[3] in utram partem fluat, iudicari non possit. Id Helvetii ratibus ac lintribus[4] iunctis transibant. **2.** Ubi per exploratores[5] Caesar certior factus est, tres iam partes copiarum Helvetios id flumen traduxisse, quartam fere partem citra[6] flumen Ararim reliquam esse, de tertia vigilia cum legionibus tribus[7] e castris profectus ad eam partem pervenit, quae nondum flumen transierat. **3.** Eos[8] impeditos[9] et inopinantes aggressus, magnam partem eorum concidit;[10] reliqui sese fugae mandarunt atque in proximas silvas abdiderunt. **4.** Is pagus[11] appellabatur Tigurinus; nam omnis civitas[12] Helvetia in quattuor pagos divisa est. **5.** Hic pagus unus, cum domo[13] exisset, patrum nostrorum memoria[14] L. Cassium consulem interfecerat et eius exercitum sub iugum miserat. **6.** Ita sive[15] casu sive consilio deorum immortalium, quae pars[16] civitatis Helvetiae insignem calamitatem populo[17] Romano intulerat, ea princeps poenas persolvit. **7.** Qua[18] in re Caesar non solum publicas, sed etiam privatas iniurias ultus est,[19] quod eius soceri L. Pisonis avum, L. Pisonem legatum, Tigurini eodem proelio,[20] quo Cassium, interfecerant.

---

[1] **Flumen est Arar:** 'There is a river, the Arar'; *90a.* **Arar:** now Saône (pronounced sōn); *18e.* **quod:** antecedent? **per fines:** for a part of its course the Arar formed the boundary between the Aeduans and the Sequanians, who engaged in violent strife over the right, claimed by both, to levy tolls on river traffic. The country along the Arar furnished the best quality of bacon and exported it to Rome.

[2] **incredibili lenitate:** 'of incredible sluggishness'; *143a* (AG 415, B 224). **incredibili:** *74f.*

[3] **oculis:** 'with the eye'; *92a; 131a.* **in utram partem:** 'in' (lit. 'into') 'which direction'; *23a.* **fluat:** *204.3* (AG 574, B 300.1). **iudicari:** '(to) be determined'; *221a.* **possit:** the subject is the indirect question *in . . .fluat,* but trans. 'it can not', etc. Near Trévoux, 14 miles north of Lyons, the current of the Saône is today for a short distance as sluggish as in Caesar's time; and here the Helvetians probably crossed the river.

[4] **lintribus iunctis:** 'by (means of) small boats fastened together'; the floats thus constructed, as well as the rafts, could be easily poled across in the still water; *15a; 131a.*

[5] **exploratores:** 'scouting parties'; *327.* **tres ... traduxisse:** trans. as if *Helvetios iam tres partes* ('three quarters') *copiarum trans id flumen duxisse; 114a* (AG 395, B 179.1).

[6] **citra:** 'on this side of', i.e. the east side; *122a.* **Ararim:** *18e.* **de tertia vigilia:** *242d.*

[7] **legionibus tribus:** about 11,000 men; *137b.* **castris:** probably not far from Sathonay, east of the Saône, above its junction with the Rhone. See Map 1. **profectus:** *61a3.*

[8] **Eos:** *160b.*

[9] **impeditos et inopinantes:** 'hampered and off their guard'. The fighting men, scattered throughout the encampment, were completely surprised and had no chance to form a line of battle; the Roman soldiers plied their savage short swords rapidly and effectively; *322e.* **aggressus:** 'attacking'; *57c; 226c.*

[10] **concidit:** how different from *concidit?* **reliqui:** *154a; 171a.* **mandarunt:** = *mandaverunt;* lit. 'committed themselves to flight', i.e. 'took to flight'; *64a1.* **in:** trans. 'in' (lit. 'into') on account of the idea of motion in *abdiderunt,* as if, i.e., they (went) 'into the neighbouring woods' (and) 'concealed themselves'.

[11] **pagus:** 'canton', properly a territorial division, here used of the inhabitants. **Tigurinus:** *148a.*

[12] **civitas:** *288a.* **divisa:** *148c.*

[13] **domo:** *130b* (AG 427.1, B 229.1b). **exisset:** *68b; 185c.*

[14] **memoria:** 'within the memory'; *147b* (AG 423, B 231). **L. Cassium . . . miserat:** see 7.4, notes 13-15.

[15] **sive . . . sive:** *235b.* **casu:** 'by chance' *20a; 135a.* **deorum:** *8d.*

[16] **quae pars:** trans. as if *ea pars civitatis Helvetiae, quae; 165c.* **insignem:** 'notable'; *25a.* **calamitatem:** 'disaster'.

[17] **populo:** *104a.* **princeps persolvit:** 'was the first to pay'; *152b.* **poenas:** *92a.*

[18] **Qua:** *167.* **non solum ... sed etiam:** *236d.*

[19] **ultus est:** *61a3; 176a.* **quod . . . interfecerant:** i.e. *quod Tigurini, eodem proelio quo Cassium (interfecerant), interfecerant Lucium Pisonem legatum, avum Lucii Pisonis, eius* (Caesar's) *soceri.* Lucius Calpurnius Piso, consul in 58 B.C., was the father of Caesar's fourth wife, Calpurnia, whom he had married in the previous year; *253.* **soceri:** *7b.*
[20] **proelio:** *147b* (AG 424d, B 230.2).

Caesar, bridging the Arar, crosses. The Helvetians send envoys.

13.1. Hoc proelio facto,[1] reliquas copias Helvetiorum ut consequi[2] posset, pontem in Arari faciendum curat atque ita exercitum traducit. **2.** Helvetii, repentino[3] eius adventu commoti, cum id, quod ipsi diebus XX[4] aegerrime confecerant, ut flumen transirent, illum uno die fecisse intellegerent, legatos ad eum mittunt; cuius legationis[5] Divico princeps fuit, qui bello Cassiano dux Helvetiorum fuerat. **3.** Is ita cum Caesare egit:[6] *Si pacem[7] populus Romanus cum Helvetiis faceret,[8] in eam partem ituros atque ibi futuros Helvetios, ubi[9] eos Caesar constituisset[10] atque esse voluisset;* **4.** *sin bello persequi perseveraret, reminisceretur[11] et veteris incommodi populi Romani et pristinae[12] virtutis Helvetiorum.* **5.** *Quod[13] improviso[14] unum pagum adortus esset, cum ei, qui flumen transissent, suis[15] auxilium ferre non possent, ne ob eam rem[16] aut suae magnopere virtuti tribueret aut ipsos despiceret;* **6.** *se ita[17] a patribus maioribusque suis didicisse, ut magis[18] virtute contenderent, quam dolo aut insidiis niterentur.* **7.** *Quare[19] ne committeret, ut is locus, ubi constitissent, ex calamitate populi Romani et internecione[20] exercitus nomen caperet[21] aut memoriam proderet.*

[1] **Hoc proelio facto:** trans. as if *post hoc proelium; 144b2.*
[2] **consequi:** 'to pursue'; *61a3.* **posset:** *196a.* **pontem faciendum curat:** 'he (Caesar) had a bridge built', i.e. by the mechanics, *fabri*, of whom there were a number enrolled in the legions; it was doubtless a pontoon bridge; *229b; 310b* (AG 500.4, B 337.8b2). **in:** 'over'.
[3] **repentino:** 'unexpected'. **commoti:** 'alarmed'. **cum,** etc.: trans. as if *cum intellegerent illum* (Caesar) *uno die fecisse* ('had accomplished') *id quod,* etc.; *178; 185c.*
[4] **XX:** *viginti; 38b.* **ut flumen transirent:** a substantive clause explaining *id*; trans. 'the crossing of the river'; *203.4.*
[5] **cuius legationis:** 'and of this delegation'; *167.* **princeps:** *10b.* **bello Cassiano:** 'in the war with Cassius'; *147b.* As the defeat of Cassius took place in 107 B.C., at the time of which Caesar was writing, 58 B.C., Divico must have been between 70 and 80 years old. The Helvetians preferred to avoid a conflict with Caesar, but the tone of Divico's language made a mutual understanding impossible.
[6] **cum Caesare egit:** 'treated with Caesar'; *137c.*
[7] **Direct form:** Si pacem populus Romanus cum Helvetiis *faciet,* in eam partem *ibunt* atque ibi *erunt* Helvetii, ubi eos (*tu*) *constitueris* atque esse *volueris;* sin bello persequi *perseverabis, reminiscere* et veteris incommodi populi Romani et pristinae virtutis Helvetiorum.
[8] **faceret, ituros** [esse], **futuros** [esse]: *89c; 218.1a* (AG 589, B 314.1).
[9] **ubi:** = *in qua.*
[10] **constituisset, voluisset:** in the direct form, future perfect indicative; the tense is influenced by the tense of *egit; 177a* (B 319, Ba). **bello:** *131a.* **persequi:** sc. *eos,* 'to assail (them)'; *61a3; 221a.* **perseveraret:** '(Caesar) should continue'.
[11] **reminisceretur:** 'he should remember'; *216* (AG 588, B 316). **veteris:** *26a.* **incommodi:** the defeat of Cassius. Why genitive? *103a* (AG 350c, B 206.2).
[12] **pristinae:** 'old-time'. **virtutis:** *75c; 81.*
[13] **Direct form:** Quod improviso unum pagum adortus *es,* cum ei, qui flumen *transierant,* suis auxilium ferre non possent, *noli* ob eam rem aut *tuae* magnopere virtuti *tribuere,* aut *nos despicere; (nos)* ita a patribus maioribusque *nostris didicimus,* ut magis virtute *contendamus* quam dolo aut insidiis *nitamur.* Quare *noli committere* ut is locus, ubi *constiterimus* (future perfect), ex calamitate populi Romani et internecione exercitus nomen *capiat* aut memoriam *prodat.*

[14] **Quod:** *198b.* **improviso:** 'suddenly'. **pagum:** what canton? see chap. 12. **adortus esset, transissent:** *214a.*

[15] **suis:** 'to their (countrymen)'; *154a.* **possent:** subjunctive also in the direct form; *185c.*

[16] **rem:** the 'fact' expressed by the clause *Quod . . . adortus esset.* **magnopere:** adverb, takes the place of a direct object; 'that he should not presume overmuch'. **virtuti:** *104b.* **tribueret:** *216* (AG 588.n2, B 316). **aut . . . aut:** *235a, b.* **ipsos:** 'them', i.e. *Helvetios; 162b.*

[17] **ita ... ut:** *197b.* **maioribus:** 'forefathers'; *154a.* **didicisse:** 'had learned'; *178.* **ut . . . contenderent:** 'to fight'; *197a* (AG 537.1, B 284.1).

[18] **magis:** 'rather'; *35.* **quam** [ut] **niterentur:** 'than to rely upon'. **dolo aut insidiis:** 'deceit or ambuscades'; *131c* (AG 431, B 218.3).

[19] **Quare:** *237a.* **ne committeret, ut is locus . . . caperet:** 'he should not allow that place to take'; how lit.? **committeret:** cf. *Tribueret*; note 16. **ubi constitissent:** 'where they should have taken their stand', in order to fight the Romans.

[20] **internecione:** 'annihilation'. **exercitus:** 'of an army', i.e. Caesar's army.

[21] **caperet:** *56; 203.3* (AG 568.n1, B 297.1). **memoriam proderet:** i.e. *memoriam calamitatis posteris proderet* ('transmit').

Caesar lays down conditions: the Helvetians scornfully reject them.

14.1. His[1] Caesar ita respondit: [2]*Eo*[3] *sibi minus dubitationis dari, quod eas res, quas legati Helvetii commemorassent,*[4] *memoria teneret, atque eo gravius ferre, quo minus merito populi Romani*[5] *accidissent;* **2.** *qui si alicuius*[6] *iniuriae sibi conscius fuisset, non fuisse difficile cavere;*[7] *sed eo deceptum, quod neque commissum a se intellegeret, quare timeret,*[8] *neque sine causa timendum putaret.*[9] **3.** *Quod*[10] *si veteris contumeliae oblivisci vellet, num etiam recentium iniuriarum,*[11] *quod, eo invito, iter per provinciam per vim temptassent,*[12] *quod Aeduos, quod Ambarros, quod Allobrogas*[13] *vexassent, memoriam deponere posse?* **4.** [14]*Quod*[15] *sua victoria tam insolenter gloriarentur, quodque tam*[16] *diu se impune iniurias tulisse admirarentur, eodem pertinere.* **5.** *Consuesse*[17] *enim deos immortales, quo gravius homines ex commutatione*[18] *rerum doleant, quos pro scelere eorum ulcisci*[19] *velint, his secundiores interdum res et diuturniorem impunitatem*[20] *concedere.*[21] **6.** *Cum*[22] *ea ita sint, tamen, si obsides ab eis sibi dentur, uti ea,*[23] *quae polliceantur, facturos intellegat, et si Aeduis de iniuriis, quas ipsis*[24] *sociisque eorum intulerint, item si Allobrogibus satisfaciant,*[25] *sese cum eis pacem esse facturum.* **7.** Divico respondit: [26]*Ita*[27] *Helvetios a maioribus suis institutos esse, uti obsides accipere, non dare, consuerint; eius rei populum Romanum esse testem.*[28] Hoc responso[29] dato, discessit.

---

[1] **His:** *legatis Helvetiorum; 104b.*

[2] **Direct form:** Eo *mihi* minus dubitationis *datur,* quod eas res, quas *commemoravistis,* memoria *teneo,* atque eo gravius *fero,* quo minus merito populi Romani *acciderunt;* qui si alicuius iniuriae sibi conscius fuisset, non *fuit* difficile cavere; sed eo *deceptus est,* quod neque commissum [esse] a se *intellegebat,* quare timeret, neque sine causa timendum [esse] *putabat.*

[3] **Eo:** 'for this reason', explained by the following *quod*-clause; *135a; 160c.* **sibi . . . dari:** 'that he had less hesitation', lit. 'that less of hesitation is given to him'; *97b* (AG 346a3, B 201.2). **sibi:** *158a; 104a.*

[4] **commemorassent:** *64a1.* **memoria teneret:** 'he remembered'; *131a.* **eo gravius ferre, quo minus:** sc. *se,* 'that he felt all the more indignant', (lit. 'that he bears them by that the more heavily') 'the less'; *140* (AG 414a, B 223).

[5] **merito populi Romani:** 'in accordance with what was due to' (lit. 'the desert of') 'the Roman people'; *136c* (B 220.3). **accidissent:** 'they had happened'; *214a.* **qui:** =*populus Romanus,* 'it' or 'they'; *167.*

[6] **alicuius:** from *aliqui; 49a.* **iniuriae:** *102* (AG 349.a, B 204.1). **sibi:** *109a.* **fuisse:** why *fuit* in the direct form? *208b* (AG 437a, B 304.3a).

[7] **cavere:** 'to take precautions' (lit. 'to be on guard') against reprisals, which the Roman people would have expected if they had in any way wronged the Helvetians. **eo:** as in note 3. **deceptum:** *eum* (i.e. *populum Romanum) deceptum esse,* 'that they had been deceived'.
neque ... putaret: 'on the one hand they understood that nothing had been done by them which should cause them to fear, and on the other they thought that they ought not to be afraid without cause'. How lit.? **commissum** [esse]: impersonal, but trans. with *neque* as if *et nihil commissum esse.*

[8] **timeret:** subjunctive also in the direct form; trans. *quare* as if *propter quod; 194a* (AG 535a, B 283.1). **timendum** [esse]: impersonal; lit. 'it ought not to be feared'; *73e.*

[9] **Direct form:** Quod si veteris contumeliae oblivisci *volo,* num etiam recentium iniuriarum, quod, *me* invito, iter per provinciam per vim *temptavistis,* quod Aeduos, quod Ambarros, quod Allobrogas *vexavistis,* memoriam deponere *possum?*

[10] **Quod:** lit. 'as to which', referring to the thought of the preceding sentence; trans. 'Even'; *118d.* **veteris:** *28b.* **contumeliae:** 'indignity', the destruction of Cassius's army in 107 B.C.; *103a* (AG 350b, B 206.2). **vellet:** *218.1a.* **num ... posse:** *179b1.*

[11] **recentium iniuriarum:** dependent on *memoriam* near the end of the sentence; 'of fresh outrages', specified in the following appositional clauses introduced by *quod,* 'that'; *198b; 214a* (AG 572, B 299.1a). **eo:** = *Caesare;* 'in despite of him', lit. 'he (being) unwilling'; *144b5* (AG 419a, B 227.1).

[12] **temptassent:** *64a1.* **quod, quod:** sc. *vexassent; 239a; 89a.*

[13] **Allobrogas:** *19f.* **deponere:** 'put aside'; *221a.*

[14] **Direct form:** Quod *vestra* victoria tam insolenter *gloriamini,* quodque tam diu *vos* impune iniurias tulisse *admiramini, eodem* pertinet. Consuerunt enim *di immortales,* quo gravius homines ex commutatione rerum doleant, quos pro scelere eorum ulcisci *volunt,* his secundiores interdum res et diuturniorem impunitatem concedere.

[15] **Quod:** 'The fact that'; two clauses introduced by *quod* stand as subject of *pertinere; 198b; 214a.* **sua victoria:** 'of their victory' over the Romans under Cassius, 107 B.C.; *135a; 81.* **Insolenter:** 'arrogantly'; *34a.* **gloriarentur:** 'they were boasting'; *214a.*

[16] **tam ... tulisse:** 'that they so long had kept on perpetrating wrongs without punishment'; how lit.? **admirarentur:** 'they marvelled'; *61a1.* **eodem pertinere:** 'pointed in the same direction', toward impending retribution for the wrongs committed by the Helvetians.

[17] **Consuesse:** 'are wont'; *64a2; 176b; 214a.* **deos:** *8d.* **quo:** *193b* (AG 531.2a, B 282.1a). **gravius:** 'more bitterly'; *34a.*

[18] **ex commutatione rerum:** 'in consequence of reverses'; how lit.? **doleant:** 'may suffer'. **scelere:** 'wickedness'; *13e.*

[19] **ulcisci:** *223b.* **his:** 'to those', antecedent of *quos* six words prior. **secundiores res:** 'a more prosperous estate'. **diuturniorem:** 'more prolonged'; *76b.*

[20] **impunitatem:** 'escape from punishment'; *106a.* **concedere:** after *Consuesse* in the previous sentence; *221a; 113b.*

[21] **Direct form:** Cum *haec* ita sint, tamen, si obsides *a vobis mihi dabuntur,* uti ea, quae *pollicemini, vos* facturos [esse] *intellegam,* et si Aeduis de iniuriis, quas ipsis sociisque eorum *intulistis,* item Allobrogibus *satisfacietis, vobiscum* pacem *faciam.*

[22] **Cum:** 'Although'; *187* (AG 549, B 309). **ea:** *haec* in the direct form; *160a.* **tamen:** *236a.*

[23] **ea:** object of *facturos* [esse], with which supply *eos* as subject. **polliceantur:** 'they promised'; *61a2.* **Aeduis:** dat. after *satisfaciant; 105.* **de:** 'for'.

[24] **ipsis:** the Aeduans. **sociis:** the Ambarri.

[25] **satisfaciant:** 'they should make restitution'; *79b.*

[26] **Direct form:** Ita *Helvetii* a maioribus suis *instituti sunt,* uti obsides accipere, non dare, *consuerint; huius* rei *populus Romanus est testis.*

[27] **Ita institutos esse:** 'had inherited such traditions'; how lit.? **uti ... consuerint:** 'that they were accustomed'; *64a2; 197b.*

[28] **esse testem:** 'was a witness', i.e. 'could furnish testimony'.

[29] **Hoc responso dato:** 'after making this reply'; *144b2.* **discessit:** 'he (Divico) withdrew'.

The. Helvetians resume their march, defeating Caesar's cavalry; Caesar follows.

15.1. Postero[1] die castra ex eo loco movent. Idem facit Caesar equitatumque[2] omnem, ad numerum quattuor milium, quem ex omni provincia et Aeduis atque eorum sociis coactum habebat,[3] praemittit, qui videant, quas in partes hostes iter faciant.[4] **2.** Qui, cupidius novissimum agmen insecuti,[5] alieno loco cum equitatu Helvetiorum proelium committunt; et pauci de nostris[6] cadunt. **3.** Quo proelio sublati[7] Helvetii, quod quingentis equitibus tantam multitudinem equitum propulerant,[8] audacius subsistere non numquam et novissimo agmine[9] proelio nostros lacessere[10] coeperunt. **4.** Caesar suos a proelio continebat, ac satis habebat[11] in praesentia hostem rapinis, pabulationibus populationibusque prohibere. **5.** Ita[12] dies circiter quindecim iter fecerunt, uti inter novissimum hostium agmen et nostrum primum[13] non amplius quinis[14] aut senis milibus passuum interesset.

[1] **Postero:** 'the following'; *33.* **movent:** sc. *Helvetii; 175b.* **Idem:** neuter accusative; *45.*
[2] **equitatum:** 'his cavalry'; *157a; 309b.*
[3] **coactum habebat:** *229a* (AG 497b, B 337.7). **qui videant:** 'to see'; how lit.? *193a* (AG 531.2, B 282.2). **videant:** plural because the subject *qui* is plural, on account of the idea of *equites* in the antecedent *equitatum; 164d; 238h.* **quas in partes:** 'in what direction'; how lit.? *48a.*
[4] **faciant:** *204.2* (AG 574, B 300.1). **Qui:** *167.* **cupidius:** 'too eagerly'; *153a.* **novissimum agmen:** the 'rear' of the Helvetians; *27b; 12e.*
[5] **insecuti:** *61a3.* **alieno loco:** 'on unfavourable ground', probably too hilly to admit of free movement; *145c, 6c.*
[6] **de nostris:** trans. as if *nostrorum; 97d.* From *pauci . . . cadunt* we infer that the rest made good their escape through flight. The kind of weapons used by the Helvetians may be inferred from their spear and dart heads.
[7] **sublati:** 'elated'; see *tollo* in the Vocab. **quingentis:** *36.* **equitibus:** *131b.*
[8] **propulerant:** 'had routed'; but the 4000 cavalry of Caesar were Gauls, only the officers being Romans. **audacius:** 'with greater boldness'; *34a.* **subsistere:** 'to halt'; as they were marching.
[9] **novissimo agmine:** 'with (their) rear', attacking the Romans who were following them; *131b; 152a.* **proelio:** *131a.* **nostros:** 'our men'; *154a.*
[10] **lacessere:** 'to harass'. **coeperunt:** *72b.* **suos:** 'his soldiers'; *154a.*
[11] **satis habebat:** 'considered (it) sufficient'; the object of *habebat* is *prohibere*, and *satis* is used as a predicate accusative; *115a.* **in praesentia:** 'for the present'. **rapinis, pabulationibus populationibusque:** 'from pillaging, foraging, and laying waste' the country; *92a; 127a* (AG 401, B 214.2).
[12] **Ita:** *197b.* **dies:** *118a* (AG 423, B 181).
[13] **primum** [agmen]: 'van'; *328.* **amplius:** 'more', subject of *interesset; 154a.*
[14] **quinis, senis:** distributive, 'five or six miles' each day; *36.* **milibus:** *129a; 243b; 38a* (AG 406, B 217). **interesset:** 'intervened'; *66a.*

The Aeduans do not bring grain which they have promised; Liscus discloses treachery.

16.1. Interim[1] cotidie Caesar Aeduos frumentum, quod essent publice[2] polliciti, flagitare. **2.** Nam propter frigora, non modo frumenta[3] in agris matura non erant, sed ne pabuli quidem satis magna copia suppetebat, **3.** eo autem frumento,[4] quod flumine Arari navibus subvexerat,[5] propterea minus uti poterat, quod iter ab Arari Helvetii averterant,[6] a quibus discedere nolebat. **4.** Diem ex die ducere[7] Aedui; conferri, comportari, adesse dicere. **5.** Ubi se diutius[8] dici intellexit et diem instare, quo die frumentum[9] militibus metiri oporteret, convocatis eorum principibus, quorum magnam copiam in castris habebat, in his Diviciaco et Lisco,[10] qui summo magistratui praeerat, quem 'vergobretum'[11] appellant Aedui, qui creatur annuus et vitae necisque¹² in suos habet potestatem, graviter eos accusat, **6.** quod, cum neque emi neque ex agris sumi posset,¹³ tam necessario tempore,¹⁴ tam propinquis hostibus, ab eis non sublevetur,¹⁵ praesertim cum, magna ex parte eorum precibus adductus, bellum¹⁶ susceperit; multo etiam gravius, quod sit destitutus,¹⁷ queritur.

¹ **Interim:** 'Meanwhile'. **Aeduos, frumentum:** *116a* (AG 396, B 178.1a). **quod essent polliciti:** 'which (he said) they had promised'; Caesar the writer presents the statement of Caesar the commander as if it were quoted from someone else; *214b* (AG 592.3, B 323).

² **publice:** 'in the name of the state'. **flagitare:** 'kept demanding'; *182* (AG 463, B 335). **frigora:** 'cold seasons', the spring being later than in Italy; *92c*.

³ **frumenta:** the plural is used by Caesar of standing grain; 'crops of grain'. **matura:** 'ripe'; *81*. **ne . . . quidem:** 'not even'; *237c*. **pabuli:** 'of fodder', required for the baggage animals and the horses of the cavalry.

⁴ **autem:** *236a*. **frumento:** after *uti*; *131c* (AG 410, B 218.1).

⁵ **flumine:** *134a* (AG 429a, B 218.9). **Arari:** *18e*. **subvexerat:** 'he had brought up'.

⁶ **averterant:** the Helvetians had at first followed the valley of the Arar (*Saône*) northward, but now 'had turned away from the Arar' and passed westward into the valley of the Liger (*Loire*), avoiding the mountainous country opposite the place where they had crossed the Arar; see Map 1.

⁷ **Diem ex die ducere:** sc. *eum*, 'were putting him off from day to day'. **Diem:** *118a*. **ducere, dicere:** historical infinitives; *182*. **conferri, comportari, adesse:** sc. *frumentum*, 'that (the grain) was being collected' from individuals, 'that it was being brought' to Caesar's headquarters, 'that it was just at hand'; climax, with asyndeton; *238a; 239d*.

⁸ **diutius:** 'too long'; *153a*. **instare:** 'was near'; *178; 213a*. **die:** not translated; *165a*.

⁹ **frumentum:** object of *metiri*. **metiri:** 'to measure out'; *61a4; 222a* (AG 454, B 327.1). How often did the soldiers receive grain? *317*. **oporteret:** *73a,b; 214a*. **convocatis:** 'having called together'; how lit.? *144b2*.

¹⁰ **Diviciaco et Lisco:** sc. *convocatis*. **summo:** *33*. **magistratui:** *107a; 82B* **praeerat:** 'held'; *66a*.

¹¹ **vergobretum:** 'vergobret'; *115a; 289a*. Meaning? See Vocab. **qui:** 'who'; the antecedent is *vergobretum*. **creatur:** 'is elected'. The seat of government was at Bibracte, which was securely situated on the top of a mountain. **annuus:** 'annually'; *151*.

¹² **vitae necisque:** 'of life and death'; *102*. **in suos:** 'over his countrymen'; *154a*. **eos accusat:** 'he took them to task'; *175b*.

¹³ **emi:** 'be purchased'; *55*. **neque . . . neque:** *233a*. **posset:** sc. *frumentum; 220*.

¹⁴ **necessario tempore:** 'at so critical a time'; *147a*. **hostibus:** *144b2*.

¹⁵ **non sublevetur:** with *quod*, 'because (as he said) he received no help from them', lit. 'was not helped by them'; *214B*. See 16.1, note 1, *quod essent polliciti*. **praesertim cum:** 'especially since'; *184a,b* **magna ex parte:** 'in great measure'. **eorum precibus:** 'by their entreaties'; *135a*.

¹⁶ **bellum:** 'campaign' against the Helvetians. **multo:** *140* (AG 414, B 223).

¹⁷ **sit destitutus:** translate as if pluperfect, 'he had been abandoned'; the time is past relatively to that of **queritur**, which is a historical present, 'he complained'; *177b; 214b*.

17.1. Tum demum Liscus, oratione Caesaris adductus, quod¹ antea tacuerat, proponit: *²Esse non nullos,³ quorum auctoritas apud plebem plurimum valeat, qui privatim⁴ plus possint quam ipsi magistratus.* **2.** *Hos seditiosa atque improba oratione⁵ multitudinem deterrere,⁶ ne frumentum conferant, quod debeant.* **3.** *praestare, si iam⁷ principatum Galliae obtinere non possint, Gallorum quam Romanorum imperia⁸ perferre;* **4.** *neque dubitare debere, quin, si Helvetios superaverint⁹ Romani, una cum reliqua Gallia Aeduis¹⁰ libertatem sint erepturi.* **5** *¹¹Ab eisdem nostra¹² consilia, quaeque in castris gerantur, hostibus enuntiari; hos a se coerceri¹³ non posse.* **6.** *Quin etiam, quod¹⁴ necessariam rem coactus Caesari enuntiarit, intellegere sese, quanto id¹⁵ cum periculo fecerit, et ob eam causam, quam diu potuerit, tacuisse.¹⁶*

¹ **quod:** as antecedent supply *id* with *proponit; 160c*. **antea:** 'previously'. **tacuerat:** 'had kept to

himself'; how lit.? **proponit:** 'brought forward (saying)', i.e. 'declared'; *213a*.

[2] **Direct form.** *Non nulli sunt,* quorum auctoritas apud plebem plurimum *valet,* qui privatim plus *possunt* quam ipsi magistratus. *Hi* seditiosa atque improba oratione multitudinem *deterrent,* ne frumentum conferant, quod (*conferre*) *debent;* (*dicunt*) praestare . . . sint erepturi.

[3] **Esse non nullos:** *that there were some men; 90a; 212b, c; 23a; 154a.* **plurimum valeat:** 'carried very great weight'; *32; 118b.*

[4] **privatim:** 'as private individuals'; *77.* **plus possint:** 'had more power'. The state of affairs here depicted arose from the feudal organization of society, which rendered it possible for the great landholders to control multitudes of personal adherents. Cf. I, 4.2, and VI, 15; *288, 289.*

[5] **seditiosa atque improba oratione:** 'by seditious and shameless propaganda'. Among the Aeduans there was a strong party opposed to the Romans.

[6] **deterrere:** 'were holding back' by inspiring fear. **ne . . . conferant:** 'from furnishing'; *201a* (AG 558b, B 295.3). **conferant:** plural because of the idea of plurality in *multitudinem; 173B* **debeant:** 'they were under obligation to furnish'; lit. 'owed'. **praestare . . . erepturi:** parenthetical indirect discourse, summarizing the line of argument (*oratione,* 17.2) by which the anti-Roman leaders influenced the Aeduan populace; '(saying) that it was better', etc.; *213a.*

[7] **si iam . . . non possint:** 'if they (the Aeduans) could no longer'; *218.1a.* Formerly, for a considerable period, the Aeduans had been the leading people in Gaul (VI, 13). **Gallorum:** 'of Gauls', i.e. of Helvetians.

[8] **imperia:** plural as referring to the acts of a sovereign power, trans 'the rule'. **perferre:** 'to endure'; subject of *praestare.* **neque dubitare debere:** sc. *se,* 'and they ought not to doubt that'.

[9] **superaverint:** 'should have vanquished'; *218.1b; 219.* **una:** adverb.

[10] **Aeduis:** dative; *109b* (AG 381, B 188.2d). **sint erepturi:** 'they were going to take away'; subjunctive also in direct discourse; *201c; 63.*

[11] **Direct form:** Ab eisdem *tua* consilia, quaeque in castris *geruntur,* hostibus *enuntiantur;* hi a me *coerceri* non *possunt.* Quin etiam, quod necessariam rem coactus *tibi enuntiavi, intellego,* quanta id cum periculo *fecerim,* et ob eam causam, quam diu *potui, tacui.*

[12] **nostra:** from the Roman point of view. **quaeque . . . gerantur:** 'and whatever is done', lit. 'and what things are done'.

[13] **se:** Liscus. **coerceri:** 'be restrained'; Liscus's 'power of life and death', which he had as vergobret, was here of no avail. **Quin etiam:** 'moreover'.

[14] **quod . . . enuntiarit:** *64a1; 198c.* **coactus:** 'under compulsion', by reason of the vehemence of Caesar's complaints (I, 16.6) and his position as the highest Aeduan official.

[15] **id:** refers to the clause *quod . . . enuntiarit; 160c.* **periculo:** 'danger' *137c; 84.* **fecerit:** trans. as if pluperfect; *204.3.* **quam diu:** 'as long as'.

[16] **tacuisse:** intransitive, sc. *se* as subject; 'he had kept silent'.

Privately Caesar learns that Dumnorix is the arch-traitor.

18.1. Caesar hac oratione Lisci Dumnorigem,[1] Diviciaci fratrem, designari[2] sentiebat; sed, quod pluribus praesentibus eas res[3] iactari nolebat, celeriter concilium dimittit, Liscum retinet.[4] **2.** Quaerit ex solo ea, quae in conventu dixerat; dicit[5] liberius atque audacius. Eadem secreto[6] ab aliis quaerit, reperit esse vera: **3.** [7]*Ipsum*[8] *esse Dumnorigem, summa audacia, magna apud plebem propter liberalitatem*[9] *gratia, cupidum rerum novarum. Complures annos portoria*[10] *reliquaque omnia Aeduorum vectigalia*[11] *parvo pretio redempta habere, propterea quod, illo licente,*[12] *contra liceri audeat nemo.* **4.** [13]*His rebus et*[14] *suam rem familiarem auxisse et facultates ad largiendum*[15] *magnas comparasse;* **5.** *magnum numerum equitatus suo sumptu*[16] *semper alere et circum se habere,* **6.** *neque solum*[17] *domi, sed etiam apud finitimas civitates largiter posse, atque huius potentiae causa*[18] *matrem in Biturigibus homini illic*[19] *nobilissimo ac potentissimo collocasse;* **7.** *ipsum ex Helvetiis uxorem*[20] *habere, sororem ex matre et propinquas* *suas nuptum in*[21] *alias civitates collocasse.* **8.** [22]*Favere et cupere*[23] *Helvetiis propter eam affinitatem, odisse etiam suo nomine*[24] *Caesarem et Romanos, quod eorum adventu potentia eius deminuta*[25] *et Diviciacus frater in antiquum locum gratiae atque honouris sit restitutus.*[26] **9.** *Si quid accidat*[27] *Romanis, summam in spem per Helvetios regni obtinendi venire; imperio*[28] *populi Romani non modo de regno, sed etiam de ea, quam habeat, gratia desperare.* **10.** Reperiebat etiam in quaerendo[29] Caesar, quod proelium equestre adversum paucis ante diebus[30] esset factum,[31] initium eius fugae factum a Dumnorige atque eius equitibus (nam equitatui,[32] quem auxilio Caesari Aedui miserant, Dumnorix praeerat), eorum fuga reliquum esse equitatum[33] perterritum.

[1] **Dumnorigem:** *10c.* **Diviciaci:** *19d; 289c.*
[2] **designari:** 'was meant'; *213a.* **sentiebat:** 'perceived'. **pluribus praesentibus:** 'with many persons present'; *144b2.*
[3] **res:** 'matters', i.e. the real reasons why the state of the Aeduans had not made good its promises. **iactari:** 'should be discussed'; *223a.* **celeriter:** 'quickly'. so as to shut off discussion; *34a.* **concilium:** 'the assembly' of leading Aeduans (*principibus*, chap. 16.5). **dimittit:** 'dismissed'.
[4] **retinet:** '(but) detained'; *238a.* **Quaerit ex [eo] solo ea, quae:** '(Caesar) asked him alone about what', lit. 'those things which'; *116c.* **conventu:** 'the conference'; *1.*
[5] **dicit:** sc. *Liscus.* **liberius:** 'more freely'; *34a.*
[6] **secreto:** 'privately'; *34B* **reperit:** 'he found'. **esse vera:** sc. *ea,* 'that they (Liscus's statements) were true'; *148c.*
[7] **Direct form:** *Ipse est Dumnorix,* summa audacia, magna apud plebem propter liberalitatem gratia, *cupidus* rerum novarum. Complures annos portoria reliquaque omnia Aeduorum vectigalia parvo pretio redempta *habet,* propterea quod, illo licente, contra liceri *audet* nemo.
[8] **Ipsum:** in predicate, but trans. 'that in fact it was Dumnorix', as Caesar had surmised (note 2); how lit.? *162a.* For the indirect discourse see *212a-c.* **summa audacia:** '(a man) of the utmost audacity'; *143a* (AG 415, B 224).
[9] **liberalitatem:** 'lavish giving'.
[10] **annos:** *118a.* **portoria:** 'tolls', levied chiefly, we may assume, upon goods passing through the country along the roads and rivers. **reliqua:** *171a.*
[11] **vectigalia:** 'revenues' in general; *vectigal* (derived from *vectus,* participle of *veho*) means that which is 'brought in' to the public treasury; *16d.* **pretio:** 'price'; *141.* **redempta habere:** trans. as if *redemisse* '(he) had farmed'; *229a.* The Aeduan revenues were "farmed out" as among the Romans; that is, the privilege of collecting taxes was sold at auction to the highest bidder who guaranteed to the state a certain sum, did the collecting through his agents, and kept for himself all that he could make above the amount paid into the public treasury and bore the costs of collection. The "publicans" of the New Testament were collectors of taxes under this system, which afforded large opportunity for corruption and extortion.
[12] **illo licente:** 'when he made a bid'; *61a2; 144a.* **contra:** here an adverb. **nemo:** *12d.* Since no one dared to bid against Dumnorix, he could obtain the right to collect the taxes on terms most favourable to himself.
[13] **Direct form:** His rebus et suam rem familiarem *auxit* et facultates ad largiendum magnas *comparavit.* Magnum numerum equitatus suo sumptu semper *alit* et circum se *habet;* neque solum domi, sed etiam apud finitimas civitates largiter *potest,* atque huius potentiae causa matrem in Biturigibus homini illic nobilissimo ac potentissimo *collocavit; ipse* ex Helvetiis uxorem *habet,* sororem . . . *collocavit.*
[14] **et . . . et:** *233a.* **rem familiarem:** 'private fortune'. **auxisse:** '(he) had increased'.
[15] **ad largiendum:** 'for bribery'; *61a4; 230.3.* **comparasse:** *64a1.*
[16] **suo sumptu:** 'at his own expense'. **alere:** 'maintained'. **neque:** trans. as if *et non; 233a.*
[17] **solum:** 'only'; *236d.* **domi:** *20c; 146.* **largiter posse:** 'had great influence'; how lit.?
[18] **huius potentiae causa:** 'to increase this influence'; how lit.? *135B* **matrem:** *11e.* **Biturigibus:** *10c.*
[19] **illic:** 'of that country'; how lit.? **collocasse:** '(he) had given in marriage'. **ipsum:** '(he) himself', Dumnorix.
[20] **uxorem:** 'wife', a daughter of Orgetorix (3.5, note 17); *13d.* **sororem ex matre:** 'half-sister,

on his mother's side'. **propinquas:** 'his female relatives'.

[21] **nuptum in . . . collocasse:** 'had settled in marriage among...'; how lit.? *231a* (AG 509, B 340.1b).

[22] **Direct form:** *Favet* et *cupit* Helvetiis propter eam affinitatem, *odit* etiam suo nomine Caesarem et Romanos, quod adventu potentia eius *deminuta* [*est*] et Diviciacus frater in antiquum locum gratiae atque honouris *est* restitutus. Si quid accidat Romanis, summam in spem per Helvetios regni obtinendi *veniat*; imperio populi Romani non modo de regno, sed etiam de ea, quam *habet,* gratia *desperat.*

[23] **Favere et cupere:** '(he) favoured and wished (success)'. **affinitatem:** 'relationship'. **odisse:** '(he) hated'; *72a,b.*

[24] **suo nomine:** 'personally'; how lit.? *135a.*

[25] **deminuta [sit]:** 'had been lessened'. **in antiquum locum:** 'to his former position', which the rise of Dumnorix had obscured. Diviciacus was a man of some culture; five years previously, in 63 B.C., he had visited Rome.

[26] **sit restitutus:** 'had been restored'. **Si . . . venire:** *218.2.* **quid:** *49a; 168.*

[27] **accidat:** here used of something unfavourable; the expression "if anything should happen to him" has a similar underlying suggestion. **per:** 'with the help of'; *123a.* **regni obtinendi:** *230.1.*

[28] **imperio:** 'under the supremacy'; *138.* **non modo . . . sed etiam:** *236d.* **de regno:** 'of the kingship'.

[29] **quaerendo:** *230.4.* **quod,** etc.: 'that (in) the disastrous cavalry engagement which had taken place'; *proelium* is attracted into the relative clause, while its proper place in the antecedent clause is taken by *fugae.*

[30] **diebus:** *140.* **initium:** 'the beginning'.

[31] **factum:** sc. *esse.* The implication is that Dumnorix treacherously started with the Aeduan contingent to flee, and that this precipitated a general rout.

[32] **equitatui:** *107a.* **auxilio Caesari:** 'as an aid to Caesar'; *112b* (AG 382.1, B 191.2b).

[33] **esse perterritum:** 'had been thrown into panic'.

Though convinced of the treachery of Dumnorix, Caesar consults his brother
Diviciacus before taking action.

19.1. Quibus rebus cognitis,[1] cum ad has suspiciones certissimae res[2] accederent, quod per fines Sequanorum Helvetios traduxisset, quod obsides inter eos dandos curasset,[3] quod ea omnia, non modo iniussu suo et civitatis,[4] sed etiam inscientibus ipsis,[5] fecisset, quod a magistratu Aeduorum accusaretur, satis esse causae[6] arbitrabatur, quare in eum aut ipse animadverteret,[7] aut civitatem animadvertere iuberet. **2.** His omnibus rebus[8] unum repugnabat, quod Diviciaci fratris[9] summum in populum Romanum studium, summam in se voluntatem, egregiam[10] fidem, iustitiam, temperantiam cognoverat;[11] nam, ne eius supplicio Diviciaci animum offenderet,[12] verebatur. **3.** Itaque prius quam quicquam conaretur,[13] Diviciacum ad se vocari iubet et, cotidianis interpretibus[14] remotis, per C. Valerium Troucillum, principem Galliae provinciae,[15] familiarem suum, cui[16] summam omnium rerum fidem habebat, cum eo[17] colloquitur; **4.** simul commonefacit, quae, ipso praesente, in concilio Gallorum de Dumnorige sint dicta, et ostendit, quae separatim[18] quisque de eo apud se dixerit. **5.** Petit atque hortatur,[19] ut sine eius offensione animi vel ipse de eo, causa cognita, statuat, vel civitatem statuere iubeat.

[1] **Quibus rebus cognitis:** 'Having found out these things'; how lit.? **suspiciones:** 'grounds for suspicion'.

[2] **res:** 'facts', specified in the following *quod*-clauses. **accederent:** trans. as if *adderentur,* 'were added'. **quod . . . accusaretur:** *198b, 220* (AG 593, B 324.1).

[3] **obsides dandos curasset:** 'had effected an exchange of hostages'; *229B* **inter eos:** between

the two peoples, the Sequanians and the Helvetians.
[4] **iniussu suo et civitatis:** 'without his own (Caesar's) authorisation and that of the state' of the Aeduans; *135b*.
[5] **inscientibus ipsis:** 'without their knowledge'; *ipsis = Caesare et Aeduis; 144b2*. **magistratu Aeduorum:** Liscus, the vergobret (chap. 16).
[6] **satis . . . causae:** *97b* (AG 346a4, B 201.2). **esse:** 'that there was'; *90a*. **in eum ipse animadverteret:** 'he himself should punish him', lit. 'should give attention to him'.
[7] **animadverteret:** subjunctive also in direct discourse; *quare = propter quam; 194a*. **aut ... aut:** *235a,b*.
[8] **rebus:** *105*. **unum:** 'one consideration'; *154a*. **repugnabat:** 'weighed against', lit. 'contended against'.
[9] **fratris:** *11e*. **studium:** 'devotion'; *81*.
[10] **egregiam:** 'remarkable'. **temperantiam:** 'self-control'; *238a; 81*.
[11] **cognoverat:** 'was familiar with'; *176B* **eius:** trans. as if *Dumnorigis*. **supplicio:** 'by the punishment'.
[12] **offenderet:** with *ne*, 'that he might offend'; *202*. **verebatur:** 'he was afraid'; *61a2*.
[13] **conaretur:** *189B* **Diviciacum vocari:** 'that Diviciacus be summoned'; *223a*.
[14] **cotidianis interpretibus:** 'the ordinary interpreters'. Diviciacus, notwithstanding his visit to Rome, had evidently not learned to speak Latin, and Caesar did not understand Celtic; *10e*. **per:** *123a*.
[15] **Galliae provinciae:** *290*. **familiarem:** 'intimate friend'.
[16] **cui . . . habebat:** 'in' (lit. 'to') 'whom he had the utmost confidence in' (lit. 'of') 'all matters'.
[17] **eo:** Diviciacus. **colloquitur:** 'he conversed'. **commonefacit:** 'he called to mind'. **quae:** *48a; 204.2*. **ipso:** Diviciacus.
[18] **separatim:** 'separately'; *77*. **quisque:** *49a*. **apud se:** 'in his (Caesar's) presence'; *158a*.
[19] **Petit atque hortatur:** 'He besought and urged (Diviciacus)'; *60*. **ut . . . statuat, iubeat:** *199a*. **eius:** dependent on *animi*; trans., with *sine offensione*, 'without suffering his (Diviciacus's) feelings to be hurt'; how lit.? **vel . . . vel:** *235a,B* **ipse . . . statuat:** lit., 'that he (Caesar) himself pass judgement'; the connection with the preceding *hortatur* shows that the underlying thought is: 'to permit him (Caesar), having heard the case, to pronounce judgement on Dumnorix (*de eo*), or direct the state (of the Aeduans) to pronounce judgement'.

Moved by the pleading of Diviciacus, Caesar pardons Dumnorix, but warns him.

20.1. Diviciacus, multis cum lacrimis[1] Caesarem complexus, obsecrare[2] coepit, ne quid gravius in fratrem statueret: **2.** *Scire se,*[3] *illa esse vera, nec quemquam ex eo plus quam se doloris capere, propterea quod, cum ipse*[4] *gratia plurimum domi*[5] *atque in reliqua Gallia, ille minimum propter adulescentiam posset, per se crevisset;*[6] **3.** *quibus opibus ac nervis non solum ad minuendam gratiam,*[7] *sed paene ad perniciem suam uteretur. Sese tamen et amore fraterno*[8] *et existimatione vulgi commoveri.* **4.** *Quod*[9] *si quid ei a Caesare gravius accidisset, cum*[10] *ipse eum locum amicitiae apud eum teneret, neminem existimaturum, non sua voluntate factum;*[11] *qua ex re futurum, uti totius Galliae animi a se averterentur.* **5.** Haec cum[12] pluribus verbis flens a Caesare peteret, Caesar eius dextram[13] prendit; consolatus rogat, finem orandi[14] faciat; tanti eius apud se gratiam esse ostendit, uti et rei publicae iniuriam et[15] suum dolorem eius voluntati ac precibus condonet.[16] **6.** Dumnorigem ad se vocat, fratrem adhibet;[17] quae in eo reprehendat,[18] ostendit; quae ipse intellegat, quae civitas queratur, proponit; monet,[19] ut in reliquum tempus omnes suspiciones vitet;[20] praeterita se Diviciaco fratri condonare dicit. Dumnorigi custodes[21] ponit, ut, quae agat, quibuscum loquatur, scire possit.

---

[1] **lacrimis:** *136a*. **complexus:** 'embracing'; *61a3; 226c*.
[2] **obsecrare:** 'to entreat (him)'. **ne quid gravius statueret:** 'not to take too harsh measures';

how lit.? **quid:** substantive form; *49a; 117a; 168.* **gravius:** *153a.* **statueret:** *199a.*
[3] **Scire se:** '(saying) that he knew'; *213b; 178.* **nec quemquam:** 'and that no one'; *49a; 168.* **ex eo:** 'on account of that fact'; *160c.* **plus doloris:** *25b; 97b* (AG 346a3, B 201.1).
[4] **ipse:** Diviciacus. **gratia:** *135a.* **plurimum:** sc. *posset; 118b.*
[5] **domi:** i.e. *in Aeduis; 20c; 146.* **ille:** Dumnorix. **minimum:** *32; 118B* **adulescentiam:** 'his youth'. Dumnorix apparently was considerably younger than Diviciacus.
[6] **per se crevisset:** '(Dumnorix) had increased (in resources and strength) through his help'; *123a.* **quibus:** 'and these'; *167.* **opibus:** 'resources'; why ablative? *131c.*
[7] **ad minuendam gratiam:** 'to lessen his (Diviciacus's) popularity'; *230.3.* **perniciem:** 'destruction'.
[8] **fraterno:** i.e. *fratris;* 'by affection for his brother', we would say. **existimatione vulgi:** 'by public opinion'; how lit.? *6b.*
[9] **Quod:** *118d.* **ei:** = *Dumnorigi.* **a Caesare:** 'at the hands of Caesar'. **accidisset:** *218.1b.*
[10] **cum:** 'while'. **eum . . . eum:** 'such a relation of friendship with Caesar'; how lit.?
[11] **non factum** [esse]: 'that it was not done', after *existimaturum* [esse]; *213a.* **sua voluntate:** *136c* (B 220.3). **futurum** [esse]: 'it would come about'; the subject is *uti . . . averterentur; 203.1.*
[12] **cum . . . peteret:** *185c.* **pluribus verbis:** 'with very many words'; i.e., 'at great length'; *138.* **flens:** *226a; 227b.*
[13] **dextram:** 'right hand'. **prendit:** 'grasped'. **consolatus rogat:** 'reassuring (Diviciacus) he asked (him)'; *61a1; 226c.*
[14] **orandi:** 'of his pleading'; *230.1.* **faciat:** 'to make'; *200a* (AG 565a, B 295.8). **tanti . . . esse:** 'that his (Diviciacus's) influence with himself (*se* refers to Caesar) was so great', lit. 'of so great account'; *101* (AG 417, B 203.3).
[15] **et . . . et:** *233a.* **rei publicae:** *102.* **eius voluntati:** 'in response to his wishes'; dative of indirect object on account of the meaning 'give' or 'present' in *con-donet; 104a.*
[16] **condonet:** 'he would disregard'; *177b.*
[17] **fratrem adhibet:** 'he had the brother (Diviciacus) present'; *238a.* **quae:** *48a.*
[18] **reprehendat:** 'he objected to'; *204.2.* **intellegat:** = *sciat.* **civitas:** i.e. of the Aeduans, whose agreement to furnish grain had been broken.
[19] **monet:** 'he warned (Dumnorix)'; *in reliquum tempus:* 'for the future'.
[20] **vitet:** 'he should avoid'; *199a.* **praeterita:** neuter plural, 'the past'; *154a.* **Diviciaco fratri:** dative, but trans. 'for the sake of Diviciacus, his brother'; *104a.*
[21] **custodes:** 'watches', corresponding with the guards of our day; for Dumnorix was not imprisoned. **agat:** *204.2.* **quibuscum:** *125c.*

Caesar plans to crush the Helvetians by a double surprise.

21.1. Eodem die[1] ab exploratoribus certior factus, hostes sub monte[2] consedisse milia passuum ab ipsius castris octo, qualis esset[3] natura montis et qualis in circuitu ascensus, qui cognoscerent,[4] misit. **2.** Renuntiatum est, facilem esse. De tertia vigilia[5] Titum Labienum, legatum pro praetore, cum duabus legionibus et eis ducibus,[6] qui iter cognoverant, summum iugum montis[7] ascendere iubet; quid sui consilii sit, ostendit. **3.** Ipse de quarta vigilia[8] eodem itinere, quo hostes ierant, ad eos contendit equitatumque[9] omnem ante se mittit. **4.** P. Considius, qui rei militaris[10] peritissimus habebatur, et in exercitu L. Sullae,[11] et postea in M. Crassi, fuerat, cum exploratoribus praemittitur.

[1] **Eodem die:** 'on the same day', that he had summoned the council of Gallic leaders in camp (16.5, note 9), and had had the interviews with Diviciacus and Dumnorix. **exploratoribus:** *327.* **hostes. . . octo:** *213a.* The Helvetians were now in the valley of the Liger (*Loire*), southeast of Bibracte; see Map 1.
[2] **sub monte:** 'at the foot of an elevation'; *124a.* **consedisse:** 'had encamped'. **milia passuum:** *118a; 243a,b.*
[3] **qualis esset:** *204.3.* **in circuitu ascensus:** 'the ascent from the opposite side', lit. 'in the going around'. Caesar planned a flank movement, with a surprise attack upon the Helvetians from two sides at once; a Roman force, following a circuitous route, would from the rear secretly

ascend the height at the foot of which the Helvetians were encamped, and charge down upon them from above, while Caesar with the rest of the army attacked them in front.

[4] **cognoscerent:** *193a.* **misit:** sc. *exploratores* as antecedent of *qui.* **esse:** sc. *eum* (= *ascensum*).

[5] **de tertia vigilia:** *242c,d.* **pro praetore:** when a lieutenant was given a special responsibility to act outside the presence of the commander, he was called 'lieutenant in place of the general', or as we say 'second in command'; *313.*

[6] **eis ducibus:** 'with those as guides', referring to the patrols previously sent out.

[7] **summum iugum montis:** 'the highest ridge of the elevation', which was apparently long and uneven. **ascendere:** 'to ascend'; *81; 200b.* **quid sui consilii sit:** 'what his plan was', lit. 'what is of his plan'; *94d* (AG 343b, B 198.3).

[8] **de quarta vigilia:** *242c, d.* **itinere, quo:** *134a* (AG 429a, B 218.9).

[9] **equitatum:** the cavalry were to feel out the enemy; *328.*

[10] **rei militaris:** 'in the art of war'; *21b; 102* (AG 349a, B 204.1). **peritissimus:** *153a; 148c.* This favourable characterization of Considius is presented as a reason for having sent so unreliable an officer on so important a reconnoiter.

[11] **L. Sullae, M. Crassi:** both of high repute as generals, Sulla for his services first in the war with Jugurtha in Africa, then in the Social War, and in the East; Crassus, for his decisive defeat of Spartacus (40.5; note 17); *19a.* **M. Crassi:** sc. *exercitu.*

Through false information the plan miscarries.

22.1. Prima luce,[1] cum summus mons a Labieno teneretur, ipse ab hostium castris non longius mille et quingentis passibus[2] abesset, neque, ut postea ex captivis comperit, aut ipsius adventus aut Labieni cognitus esset, **2.** Considius equo admisso[3] ad eum accurrit, dicit *montem, quem a Labieno occupari* [4] *voluerit, ab hostibus teneri; id se a Gallicis armis atque insignibus*[5] *cognovisse.* **3.** Caesar suas copias in proximum collem[6] subducit, aciem instruit. Labienus, ut erat ei praeceptum[7] a Caesare, ne proelium committeret, nisi[8] ipsius copiae prope hostium castra visae essent, ut undique uno tempore in hostes impetus[9] fieret, monte occupato, nostros[10] exspectabat proelioque abstinebat. **4.** Multo denique die[11] per exploratores Caesar cognovit, et montem a suis teneri et Helvetios castra movisse et Considium, timore[12] perterritum, quod non vidisset, pro viso sibi renuntiavisse. **5.** Eo die, quo consuerat intervallo,[13] hostes sequitur, et milia passuum tria ab eorum castris castra ponit.

[1] **Prima luce:** 'At daybreak'; *152a* (AG 293, B 241.1). As it was now not far from July 1, daybreak was about four o'clock. **summus:** *152a.*

[2] **passibus:** *129a.* **abesset, cognitus esset:** *185c.* **neque:** *233a.* **captivis:** 'prisoners'. **comperit:** 'he ascertained'.

[3] **equo admisso:** *144b7.* **accurrit:** 'hastened'; how lit.?

[4] **occupari:** *occupo,* meaning 'seize', 'take possession of', is generally much stronger than its English derivative 'occupy'; *81.* **voluerit:** *214a.* **Gallicis armis:** *349.*

[5] **insignibus:** 'decorations', used especially of the crests of helmets. Two Gallic helmets are shown in Fig. 46.

[6] **collem:** 'hill'; *14b.* **subducit:** 'led up'. **aciem instruit:** 'drew up a line of battle'; *337a.*

[7] **erat ei praeceptum:** 'he had been ordered', lit. 'it had been ordered to him'; the subject is *ne proelium committeret; 73d; 199b* (AG 566, B 295.1).

[8] **nisi . . . visae essent:** *218.1b.* **prope:** 'near'; *122a.*

[9] **impetus:** 'an attack' *20a, b.* **fieret:** subjunctive of purpose.

[10] **nostros:** the troops with Caesar; *154a.* **proelio:** *127a* (AG 401, B 214.2).

[11] **Multo die:** 'Late in the day'; ablative of time. **per:** *123a.*

[12] **timore:** 'fear', used especially of a cowardly fear; *11d.* **perterritum:** 'thoroughly frightened'; *79b.* **quod:** as antecedent supply *id,* object of *renuntiavisse; 160c.* **pro viso:** 'as seen'; *154a.*

[13] **quo consuerat intervallo:** = *eo intervallo, quo sequi consuerat (consueverat),* but trans. 'at the usual interval'; this was five or six miles (15.5, notes 13-14); *138; 165c.* **milia passuum:** *118a;*

243a.

Caesar turns to go to Bibracte for supplies; the Helvetians attack his marching column on the rear.

23.1. Postridie eius[1] diei, quod omnino biduum supererat, cum[2] exercitui frumentum metiri oporteret, et quod a Bibracte,[3] oppido Aeduorum longe maximo et copiosissimo, non amplius milibus[4] passuum XVIII aberat, rei frumentariae prospiciendum[5] existimavit; iter ab Helvetiis avertit ac Bibracte[6] ire contendit. **2.** Ea res per fugitivos[7] L. Aemilii, decurionis equitum Gallorum, hostibus nuntiatur. **3.** Helvetii, seu quod timore perterritos Romanos discedere a se existimarent,[8] eo magis quod pridie,[9] superioribus locis occupatis, proelium non commisissent, sive eo, quod re[10] frumentaria intercludi posse confiderent,[11] commutato consilio atque itinere converso, nostros a[12] novissimo agmine insequi ac lacessere coeperunt.

[1] **Postridie eius diei:** 'the next day'; *94c.* **biduum supererat:** 'two days remained'; *79b.*
[2] **cum:** trans. freely, 'before'; *185c.* **metiri:** *61a4.* **oporteret:** *73a, b.*
[3] **Bibracte:** *16c,* and Vocab. **oppido:** *91a; 293b.* **longe:** *153b.* **copiosissimo:** 'wealthiest'; *75f.*
[4] **milibus:** *129a; 243b.* How many English miles? **rei frumentariae:** 'the supply of grain', or, more generally, 'supplies'; *105.*
[5] **prospiciendum** [esse]: 'that he ought to provide for'; how lit.? *73e.*
[6] **Bibracte:** here accusative; *119a.* (AG 427.2, B 182.1a).
[7] **fugitivos:** 'runaway slaves'; deserters from an army were called *perfugae* (28.2, note 4); *74g.* **L.:** *19a.* Lucius Aemilius was a Roman officer in charge of a squad of Gallic horsemen. **decurionis:** 'decurion'; *309c.*
[8] **existimarent:** *183a* (AG 592.3, B 286.1). **eo magis:** 'all the more on this account', *eo* being explained by the following *quod*-clause; *135a* (AG 404, B 219).
[9] **pridie:** 'on the day before'. **superioribus locis occupatis:** 'having seized a higher position'. referring to the exploit of Labienus with two legions (chap. 21; notes 5-8). How lit.? *144b5.*
[10] **re:** *127a.* **intercludi:** 'be cut off from'. **posse:** sc. *Romanos.*
[11] **confiderent:** 'were confident.' **commutato, converso:** trans. 'having changed', 'having reversed'; or, 'changing', 'reversing'; how lit.? *144a; 239c.*
[12] **a:** *126c.* **agmine:** derivation? *74d* and Vocab.

Romans and Helvetians prepare for battle,
the Romans on sloping ground. The Helvetians advance.

24.1. Postquam[1] id animum advertit, copias suas Caesar in proximum collem[2] subducit equitatumque, qui sustineret hostium impetum, misit. **2.** Ipse interim[3] in colle medio triplicem aciem instruxit legionum[4] quattuor veteranarum; **3.** atque supra se in summo iugo duas legiones,[5] quas in Gallia citeriore proxime conscripserat, et omnia auxilia[6] collocari ac totum montem hominibus[7] compleri, et interea sarcinas in unum locum conferri et eum ab eis,[8] qui in superiore acie constiterant, muniri[9] iussit. **4.** Helvetii, cum omnibus suis carris secuti,[10] impedimenta in unum locum contulerunt; ipsi,[11] confertissima acie reiecto nostro equitatu, phalange facta[12] sub primam nostram aciem successerunt.

[1] **Postquam:** 'After'; *188.* **id:** why accusative? *113c.*
[2] **collem:** the hill of Armecy, about 16 English miles southeast of Mt. Beuvray, the site of ancient Bibracte, and not far from the village of Montmort. See Map 3, **A. sustineret:** *193a; 328* (AG 531.2, B 282.2).
[3] **interim:** 'meanwhile', while the cavalry were holding back the enemy; it must have taken

Caesar at least two hours to change over his marching column, which was five or six miles long, into battle lines. **in colle medio:** *152a* (AG 293, B. 241.1). **triplicem aciem:** the four legions stood side by side, with the cohorts of each legion arranged in three lines (*337a*). The triple line was not straight, but followed the contour of the hillside, and was about an English mile in length; see Map 3, **B-B.**

[4] **legionum:** *98a.* **veteranarum:** 'veteran'. What four legions are meant? *307e.* **supra se:** Caesar was near the front. **summo:** *152a.*

[5] **legiones . . . conscripserat:** the 11th and 12th legions; see chap. 10; notes 8-9; *284.* **proxime:** *35.*

[6] **auxilia:** *308.* **ac:** 'and (thus)'. **totum montem:** 'the entire upper part' of the hill; see chap. 2; note 10, *monte Iura.*

[7] **hominibus:** *131b.* **compleri:** 'be completely filled'. By occupying the gently rounding crest of the hill, Caesar strengthened his position in case his battle lines, posted halfway up the slope, should be forced back. **interea:** 'in the meantime', while the troops were taking their positions. **sarcinas:** 'packs'; *330.*

[8] **eis:** the two raw legions mentioned in note 5.

[9] **muniri:** 'be fortified', by a trench and a rampart formed from the earth thrown out of the trench. The trench, which for a part of the distance was double, has been traced by excavations; the earthen rampart has disappeared. The line of defence thus hastily made on the highest part of the hill was semicircular in shape (Map 3, **A**).

[10] **secuti:** *226c.* **impedimenta:** 'baggage'. After the Helvetian fighting men turned back in order to attack Caesar, the long line of carts turned and came back also and formed a great corral, or laager, probably at the spot marked "Helvetian Corral" on Map 3; *74d.*

[11] **ipsi:** the fighting men, as distinguished from the old men, women, and children with the baggage. **confertissima acie:** 'by (their) very close formation'; *131a.* **reiecto:** 'hurled back and'; how lit? *144b2.*

[12] **phalange facta:** the Gauls, forming in 'a compact mass', probably fifteen to twenty men deep, moved forward slowly but with almost irresistible momentum; those in the front rank held their large shields so that these would overlap, presenting a firm barrier to the enemy, *18f.* **sub:** the Helvetians advanced uphill, and so 'up against' the first line; *124a.*

The Romans charge, forcing the Helvetians back.

25.1. Caesar, primum suo,[1] deinde omnium ex conspectu remotis equis, ut, aequato[2] omnium periculo, spem fugae tolleret,[3] cohortatus suos proelium commisit. **2.** Milites, e loco superiore pilis missis,[4] facile hostium phalangem perfregerunt.[5] Ea disiecta, gladiis destrictis in eos impetum fecerunt.[6] **3.** Gallis[7] magno ad pugnam erat impedimento, quod, pluribus eorum scutis[8] uno ictu pilorum transfixis et colligatis, cum ferrum[9] se inflexisset, neque evellere neque, sinistra impedita, satis commode[10] pugnare poterant, **4.** multi ut, diu iactato bracchio, praeoptarent[11] scutum manu emittere, et nudo corpore pugnare. **5.** Tandem vulneribus[12] defessi, et pedem referre et, quod mons suberat[13] circiter mille passuum spatio, eo se recipere coeperunt. **6.** Capto[14] monte et succedentibus nostris, Boii et Tulingi, qui hominum[15] milibus circiter XV agmen hostium claudebant et novissimis[16] praesidio erant, ex itinere nostras ab latere aperto aggressi circumvenire;[17] et, id conspicati, Helvetii, qui in montem sese receperant, rursus[18] instare et proelium redintegrare[19] coeperunt. **7.** Romani conversa[20] signa bipertito intulerunt; prima et secunda acies, ut victis ac summotis[21] resisteret, tertia, ut venientes sustineret

---

[1] **suo:** sc. *equo remoto*; *144b2.* **deinde:** *237b.* **omnium equis:** 'the horses of all' the mounted officers and Caesar's staff, not of the cavalry. According to Plutarch Caesar said that after he had won the victory he should need the horse for the pursuit of the enemy.

[2] **aequato:** 'by equalizing'; *144b6.*

[3] **tolleret:** *196a.* **cohortatus:** 'having harangued', or 'harangued and'. It was customary for

Roman commanders to address their soldiers just before going into action; *228a.*

[4] **pilis missis:** 'hurling their pikes', with precision and terrible effect, 'from their higher position' on the slope; *322d, 144b6.*

[5] **perfregerunt:** 'broke up'. **Ea ... destrictis:** 'Having thrown this (formation) into disorder they drew their swords and'; how lit.? *322e.*

[6] **impetum fecerunt:** 'charged'. The first-line soldiers probably allowed the Helvetians to approach within 60 feet before hurling their pikes and charging.

[7] **Gallis ... impedimento:** 'a great hindrance' (lit. 'for a great hindrance') 'to the Gauls'; *112b* (AG 382.1, B 191.2.a). **ad pugnam:** 'in fighting'. **erat:** the subject is the following *quod*-clause; *198b.*

[8] **scutis:** 'shields' (Fig. 48). **uno ictu pilorum:** 'by the blow of a single pike', we should say; *92a.* **transfixis et colligatis:** 'pierced and pinned together'; *144b2.*

[9] **ferrum:** the 'iron' of the pike (*322d*) was long enough to pierce two or more overlapping shields, and was of soft metal, so that it would bend easily; the hard barbed point also hindered withdrawal. **se inflexisset:** 'had become bent'; *185c.* **evellere:** 'to pull (it) out'. **sinistra impedita:** 'since the left hand', which carried the shield, 'was hampered'; *144b3.*

[10] **satis commode:** 'to advantage'; how lit.? **multi:** emphatic position; subject of *praeoptarent*; *353d.* **ut:** 'so that'. **iactato bracchio:** 'having jerked their arms back and forth' in the effort to pull the bent pike iron out of their shields; how lit.? *144b2.*

[11] **praeoptarent:** 'preferred'. **manu:** *127a.* **emittere:** 'to drop'. **nudo:** 'unprotected' by a shield. **corpore:** *13f; 144b7.*

[12] **vulneribus:** *13e; 135a.* **defessi:** 'exhausted'. **pedem referre:** 'to fall back'; *69b; 79d.*

[13] **mons suberat:** 'there was a height near by', southwest of the hill of Armecy; see Map 3; *66a.* **mille:** *38a.* **spatio:** 'at a distance'; *147c.* **eo:** adverb. **se recipere:** 'to retreat'.

[14] **Capto:** 'reached', i.e. by the Helvetians; Map 3, F-F; *144b2.* **Boii et Tulingi:** see chap. 5.4,5.

[15] **hominum:** *97a.* **milibus:** *131a.* **agmen hostium claudebant:** 'were at the end of the enemy's marching column'.

[16] **novissimis** (= *novissimo agmini*), **praesidio:** *112b* (AG 382.1, B 191.2a). **ex itinere:** 'directly after marching', changing from marching order to fighting order as they came up. In the morning as the long column of emigrants started out, the 15,000 Boians and Tulingians formed the vanguard. When the order passed along the column to halt and turn back (chap. 23.3), they became the rearguard, and were several miles away when the battle commenced. As the host of non-combatants were forming a corral with the carts, they marched by it and reached the field of battle just as the Romans were following the retreating Helvetians. **ab latere aperto:** 'on the exposed flank'; *126c.* Since the shield was carried on the left arm, 'the exposed side' of the soldier was the right side, whence the expression was carried over to a body of soldiers in action. In the present instance, the three Roman lines, still retaining, in the confusion of battle, their distinct formation, were following the stubbornly resisting Helvetians toward the southwest from their original position, when the Boians and Tulingians came against them from the west, thus 'attacking' the Romans on the right flank. See Map 3, **H.**

[17] **circumvenire:** 'to move around them', so as to fall upon the Romans in the rear; *sc. coeperunt.* **conspicati:** 'perceiving'; *226c.*

[18] **rursus:** 'again'; derivation? See Vocab.

[19] **redintegrare:** 'to renew', again assuming the offensive. Map 3, **G-G.**

[20] **conversa . . . intulerunt:** 'changed front and advanced in two divisions', one division facing straight ahead (*prima et secunda acies*), the other (*tertia acies*) facing the Boians and Tulingians. Strictly speaking, only the third line changed front (Map 3, **D**); the first and second lines were already in position to meet the new attack of the Helvetians (Map 3, **C-C**); *228a; 325.*

[21] **victis ac summotis:** 'those who had been beaten and driven back'; *154a; 227a4.* **tertia:** sc. *acies; 91c.*

MAP 3

THE BATTLE WITH THE HELVETIANS

Book I, 24–26   To face page 60

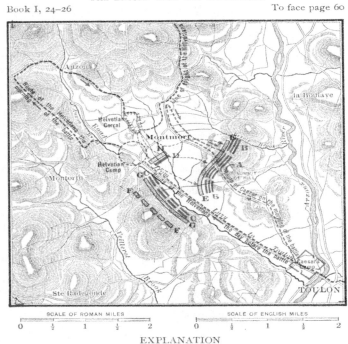

SCALE OF ROMAN MILES   SCALE OF ENGLISH MILES

0   ½   1   ½   2   0   ½   1   ½   2

EXPLANATION

On the day before the battle the Helvetians probably crossed the Arroux at Toulon and encamped near Montmort; a part of the site of the camp is now covered by a pond. Caesar, following, encamped near the Arroux.

A. Semicircular trench hastily dug by the XIth and XIIth legions on the hill (chap. 24, ll. 5–10).

B–B. The four veteran legions in battle order, three lines, first position.

C–C. First and second Roman lines, second position (chap. 25, ll. 21–23).

D. Third Roman line, second position, facing the Boians and Tulingians.

E–E. First position of the Helvetians (chap. 24, ll. 12–14).

F–F. Second position of the Helvetians, on a height (chap. 25, ll. 12–15).

G–G. Third position of the Helvetians, resuming the attack (chap. 25, ll. 18–20).

H. Boians and Tulingians (chap. 25, ll. 15–18).

The Helvetians are totally defeated. Caesar pursues the fleeing.

26.1. Ita ancipiti proelio[1] diu atque acriter pugnatum est. Diutius cum sustinere nostrorum impetus non possent,[2] alteri se, ut coeperant, in montem receperunt, alteri[3] ad impedimenta et carros[4] suos se contulerunt. **2.** Nam hoc toto proelio,[5] cum ab hora septima ad vesperum pugnatum sit, aversum[6] hostem videre nemo potuit. **3.** Ad multam[7] noctem etiam ad impedimenta pugnatum est, propterea quod pro vallo carros obiecerant[8] et e loco superiore in nostros venientes tela coniciebant,[9] et non nulli inter carros rotasque[10] mataras ac tragulas subiciebant nostrosque vulnerabant.[11] **4.** Diu cum esset pugnatum, impedimentis castrisque[12] nostri potiti sunt. Ibi Orgetorigis filia atque unus e filiis[13] captus est. **5.** Ex eo proelio circiter hominum milia CXXX[14] superfuerunt eaque tota nocte[15] continenter ierunt; nullam partem noctis itinere intermisso,[16] in fines Lingonum die quarto pervenerunt, cum[17] et propter vulnera militum et propter sepulturam occisorum[18] nostri, triduum morati, eos sequi non potuissent. **6.** Caesar ad Lingonas[19] litteras nuntiosque misit, ne eos frumento neve alia re iuvarent;[20] qui si iuvissent, se eodem loco, quo Helvetios, habiturum. Ipse, triduo intermisso, cum omnibus copiis eos sequi coepit.

[1] **ancipiti proelio:** 'in two battles', we should say; how lit.? *131a*. **ancipiti:** *26b*. **diu:** *35*. **acriter:** *34a*. **pugnatum est:** *73d*.

[2] **possent:** sc. *hostes*; *185c* (AG 546, B 288.1b).

[3] **alteri, alteri:** 'the combatants on one side' (i.e. *Helvetii*), 'those on the other' (*Boii et Tulingi*); how lit.? *91c*; *154a*.

[4] **carros:** arranged for defence around the corral (Map 3). Cf. 3.1, note 3. **se contulerunt:** 'retired', still fighting; there was no disorderly rout. **Nam:** *237a*.

[5] **proelio:** *147b*. **cum:** 'although'; *187*. **hora:** *242a*. **vesperum:** 'evening'; *7b*.

[6] **aversum:** 'turned to flight'. Caesar speaks with evident admiration of the bravery of the enemy. **nemo:** *12d*.

[7] **Ad multam noctem:** 'Until late at night'; *17b*; *152a*. **ad:** here 'at' or 'by'.

[8] **pro vallo carros obiecerant:** 'had made a rampart of the carts'; how lit.? **loco superiore:** the top of the carts.

[9] **coniciebant:** 'kept hurling'; *175a*.

[10] **rotas:** 'wheels'. These in many cases were doubtless solid disks of wood, which Roman weapons would not pierce. **mataras ac tragulas:** 'spears and darts'; *349*. **subiciebant:** notice the force of *sub-*, 'kept throwing from below' as the Roman soldiers attacked the rampart of carts.

[11] **vulnerabant:** 'were wounding'. There must have been moonlight, or at least clear starlight, else the Gauls could not have aimed their weapons so well.

[12] **castris:** 'encampment', i.e. the corral; *131c* (AG 410, B 218.1). Here were the old men, the women, and the children, of whom a large number were immediately slaughtered.

[13] **e filiis:** trans. as if *filiorum*; *97d*. **captus est:** *172b*.

[14] **CXXX:** *centum triginta*; *36, 38b*.

[15] **nocte:** *147c*. **ierunt:** *68a*. **partem:** *118a*.

[16] **intermisso:** 'breaking'; how lit.? As the survivors seemingly traveled at night only during the first night, the thought in *nullam . . . intermisso* is substantially the same as that in *ea . . . ierunt*; such repetitions are characteristic of dictated matter; *275*. **fines Lingonum:** more than fifty miles north of the battlefield.

[17] **cum:** *184a*. **vulnera militum:** the victory must have cost the Romans dearly. **sepulturam:** burial.

[18] **occisorum:** 'the slain', chiefly Gauls; *154a*. The number of Gauls that perished in this battle has been estimated by some as high as 100,000, or even higher. Prompt burial was necessary for the health of the friendly Aeduans, in whose country Caesar was. **triduum:** 'three days'; *118a*.

[19] **Lingonas:** *19f*. **litteras:** 'letters'. **nuntios:** 'messages', to be delivered orally. **ne:** '(saying) that they should not'; *213b*; *212a*. **eos:** trans. as if *Helvetios*.

[20] **iuvarent:** 'supply', lit. 'aid', *216* (AG 588, B 316). **qui:** *167*. **iuvissent:** sc. *eos = Helvetios*; *218.1b*. **se . . . habiturum:** in full, *se eos (= Lingonas) eodem loco, quo Helvetios haberet, habiturum esse*, but trans. 'he would consider them in the same light as the Helvetians'; *145c*.

The Helvetians beg for terms; one division tries to escape.

27.1. Helvetii, omnium rerum inopia[1] adducti, legatos de deditione[2] ad eum miserunt. **2.** Qui cum eum in itinere convenissent seque ad pedes proiecissent[3] suppliciterque locuti flentes[4] pacem petissent, atque eos in eo loco, quo tum essent,[5] suum adventum exspectare iussisset, paruerunt. **3.** Eo postquam[6] Caesar pervenit, obsides, arma, servos, qui ad eos perfugissent, poposcit.[7] **4.** Dum ea conquiruntur et conferuntur,[8] circiter hominum milia VI eius pagi, qui Verbigenus appellatur, sive timore perterriti,[9] ne, armis traditis, supplicio afficerentur, sive spe salutis[10] inducti, quod in tanta multitudine[11] dediticiorum suam fugam aut occultari aut omnino ignorari[12] posse existimarent, prima nocte e castris Helvetiorum egressi ad Rhenum finesque Germanorum contenderunt.

[1] **inopia:** 'lack'; why ablative? **legatos:** 'envoys'.
[2] **deditione:** 'surrender'. **Qui:** *167.* **convenissent:** *113b.*
[3] **se proiecissent:** 'had prostrated themselves'. **suppliciter:** 'in suppliant fashion'.
[4] **flentes:** *227b.* **eos:** = *Helvetios,* not *legatos.*
[5] **essent:** See chap. 28; note 2 on *vellent.* **iussisset:** *185c; 200b.* **paruerunt:** 'they obeyed'.
[6] **postquam:** *188a.* **servos:** 'slaves'. **qui perfugissent:** 'who (as he said) had fled'; *214b.*
[7] **poposcit:** 'he demanded'. **ea:** comprising *obsides, arma, (fugitivos) servos;* neuter plural under the same rule of agreement as predicate adjectives; *150b.* **conquiruntur:** 'were being sought for'; why present? *190a.*
[8] **conferuntur:** *69b.* **VI:** = *sex; 36.*
[9] **perterriti:** with *milia; 150c; 238h.* **ne:** 'that'; *202.* **armis traditis:** 'after giving up their arms'; *144b2.*
[10] **salutis:** 'of safety'; *10f.*
[11] **in tanta multitudine:** i.e. *cum* ('since') *tanta multitudo dediticiorum esset.* **dediticiorum:** 'of those who had surrendered'. **occultari:** 'be kept hidden'.
[12] **ignorari:** 'remain unnoticed'; how lit.? **existimarent:** *183b.* **prima:** *152a.*

Caesar deals with the fugitive Verbigens, and sends the rest (excepting the Boians) back to the country whence they migrated.

28.1. Quod[1] ubi Caesar resciit, quorum per fines ierant, his, uti conquirerent et reducerent,[2] si sibi purgati esse vellent, imperavit; reductos[3] in hostium numero habuit; **2.** reliquos omnes, obsidibus, armis, perfugis[4] traditis, in deditionem accepit. **3.** Helvetios, Tulingos, Latobrigos in fines suos, unde[5] erant profecti, reverti iussit; et, quod, omnibus frugibus amissis,[6] domi[7] nihil erat, quo famem tolerarent, Allobrogibus imperavit, ut eis frumenti copiam facerent;[8] ipsos oppida vicosque, quos[9] incenderant, restituere iussit. **4.** Id ea maxime ratione fecit,[10] quod noluit, eum locum, unde Helvetii discesserant, vacare,[11] ne propter bonitatem agrorum Germani, qui trans Rhenum incolunt, e suis finibus in Helvetiorum fines transirent[12] et finitimi Galliae provinciae Allobrogibusque essent. **5.** Boios,[13] petentibus Aeduis, quod egregia virtute erant cogniti, ut in finibus suis collocarent,[14] concessit; quibus illi agros dederunt, quosque[15] postea in parem iuris libertatisque condicionem, atque ipsi erant, receperunt.

[1] **Quod . . . resciit:** 'Now when Caesar found this out', referring to the flight of the Verbigens; *167.* **ubi:** *188a.* **quorum:** precedes its antecedent *his,* which is in the dative after *imperavit; 105.*
[2] **reducerent:** 'bring (them) back'; *199a.* **sibi:** 'in his sight'; *109a* (AG 376, B 188.1n). **purgati:** 'free from guilt'; how lit.? *221b* (B 328.2). **vellent:** in indirect discourse as a part of the order; in the direct form, *si vultis; 71.*
[3] **reductos:** sc. *eos,* 'after they had been brought back'; how lit.? *227a4.* **in hostium numero:** 'as enemies'. The 6000 Verbigens were probably massacred, as a terrible warning, but they

may have been sold into slavery. **reliquos:** *171a.*

[4] **perfugis:** 'deserters'. **accepit:** *57a.*

[5] **suos:** *157b.* **unde:** = *e quibus.* **erant profecti:** *61a3.*

[6] **frugibus amissis:** 'since all the produce of the fields was gone'; no crops had been planted this season. How lit.? *144b3.*

[7] **domi:** i.e. in their own country; *146.* **erat:** sc. *eis.* **famem:** 'hunger'; *15b.* **tolerarent:** 'satisfy'; *194a.*

[8] **facerent:** 'furnish'; why subjunctive? **oppida, vicos:** how many? See chap. 5; notes 3-4.

[9] **quos:** *163c.* **incenderant:** when? See chap. 5.

[10] **ea maxime ratione:** 'especially for this reason'; *161a.* **noluit:** *71; 223a.* **unde:** = *e quo.*

[11] **vacare:** 'remain unoccupied.' **bonitatem:** 'good quality'; *76a.*

[12] **transirent:** *196a.* As the Helvetians were now reduced to about one third of their former number, much of their land must have been left unoccupied, and was probably soon seized upon by German immigrants. **provinciae:** *290.* The northernmost part of the Province was held by the Allobroges; see Map 1.

[13] **Boios:** emphatic position; *Aeduis* (dative after *concessit*), *petentibus ut Boios in finibus suis collocarent, quod (Boii) egregia virtute cogniti erant, (Caesar) concessit.* The Aeduans, hard pressed in their strife with the Sequanians, desired an accession of strength; *353d.* **virtute:** *143a.*

[14] **collocarent:** *199a.* **concessit:** 'he granted' the request. **quibus:** trans. as if *et eis; 167.*

[15] **quosque:** = *et eos.* **postea:** after the great uprising in Gaul, narrated in Book VII. **parem** . . . **atque:** 'the same as'; *233c* (AG 324c, B 341.1c).

The number of the Helevetians and their allies

29.1. In castris[1] Helvetiorum tabulae repertae sunt, litteris Graecis confectae, et ad Caesarem relatae,[2] quibus in tabulis nominatim[3] ratio confecta erat, qui numerus domo exisset eorum, qui arma ferre possent,[4] et item separatim pueri, senes[5] mulieresque. **2.** Quarum omnium rerum summa erat capitum Helvetiorum[6] milia CCLXIII, Tulingorum milia XXXVI, Latobrigorum XIIII, Rauracorum XXIII, Boiorum XXXII; ex his, qui[7] arma ferre possent, ad milia nonaginta duo. Summa omnium fuerunt[8] ad milia CCCLXVIII. **3.** Eorum, qui domum redierunt,[9] censu habito, ut Caesar imperaverat, repertus est numerus milium C et X.

[1] **castris:** the corral, indicated on Map 3. **tabulae:** 'tablets', such as those generally used for business documents (p. 370). These were of light-colored wood, and made with a rim like that of a slate. The surface inside the rim was coated with a thin layer of wax, on which writing was done with a pointed stilus. The writing appeared on the wood, which showed through wherever the stilus penetrated the wax. **litteris Graecis confectae:** 'written in Greek characters,', which were used also by the Druids (VI, 14). On account of the antiquity of Massilia (*293a*), the Greek alphabet must have become familiar to the inhabitants of southern Gaul at an early date.

[2] **relatae:** sc. *sunt; 69b.* **tabulis:** *165a.*

[3] **nominatim:** 'by name'; *77.* **ratio:** 'statement'. **qui:** *48b.* **domo:** *130b.* **exisset:** *68b; 204.2.*

[4] **possent:** *194a.* **pueri:** 'children'; *7a.*

[5] **senes:** *18b.* **mulieres:** *11c.* **Quarum:** *167.* **rerum:** 'items', here used of persons; Caesar was thinking of the numbers rather than the personality. **summa:** 'the aggregate..

[6] **capitum Helvetiorum:** trans. as if *Helvetiorum;* we say "so many head" of stock, not of human beings. **CCLXIII:** *ducenta sexaginta tria; 37b, d; 38b.* **XXXVI,** etc.: read in the Latin; *36, 37b.*

[7] **qui,** etc.: i.e. *ei, qui arma ferre possent* (*194a*), *erant,* etc. **ad:** adverb, 'approximately'.

[8] **fuerunt:** plural on account of the influence of the predicate noun *milia; 173b.* **ad:** adverb modifying CCCLXVIII (*trecenta duodeseptuaginta*).

[9] **domum:** *119b.* **redierunt:** 'returned'; *68b.* **censu:** 'a census'; *80b.* How many of the Helvetian host failed to return?

The Campaign against Ariovistus. 30-54

The Gallic leaders congratulate Caesar, request a conference.

30.1. Bello Helvetiorum confecto, totius fere Galliae[1] legati, principes[2] civitatum, ad Caesarem gratulatum convenerunt: **2.** *[3]Intellegere sese, tametsi[4] pro veteribus Helvetiorum iniuriis populi Romani ab his poenas[5] bello repetisset, tamen eam rem non minus ex usu terrae[6] Galliae quam populi Romani accidisse,* **3.** *propterea quod eo consilio,[7] florentissimis rebus, domos suas Helvetii reliquissent, uti[8] toti Galliae bellum inferrent imperioque[9] potirentur, locumque domicilio ex magna copia deligerent, quem ex omni Gallia opportunissimum[10] ac fructuosissimum iudicassent,[11] reliquasque civitates stipendiarias haberent.* **4.** Petierunt, uti sibi[12] concilium totius Galliae in diem certam indicere[13] idque Caesaris voluntate facere liceret; *sese habere quasdam res, quas ex communi consensu[14] ab eo petere vellent.* **5.** Ea re permissa,[15] diem concilio constituerunt et iure iurando, ne quis[16] enuntiaret, nisi quibus communi consilio mandatum esset, inter se sanxerunt.

[1] **Galliae:** Celtic Gaul; *287b.*
[2] **principes:** *10b.* **civitatum:** *10f; 288a, b.* **gratulatum:** *231a.*
[3] **Direct form:** *Intellegimus,* tametsi pro veteribus Helvetiorum iniuriis populi Romani ab his poenas bello *repetieris,* tamen eam rem non minus ex usu terrae Galliae quam populi Romani accidisse, propterea quod eo consilio, florentissimis rebus, domos suas Helvetii *reliquerunt,* uti toti Galliae bellum inferrent, etc.
[4] **Intellegere sese, tametsi:** '(Saying) that they understood that, although'; *212a, b, c1; 213b.* **iniuriis:** with two genitives, *Helvetiorum (95)* and *populi (102);* trans. 'wrongs done to the Roman people by the Helvetians'.
[5] **poenas:** 'punishment'; *92a.* **repetisset:** = *repetivisset* 'had exacted'; *64a3; 214a.* **rem:** 'achievement'.
[6] **ex usu terrae:** 'to the advantage of the country'; how lit.? **accidisse:** 'had turned out'.
[7] **eo consilio:** 'with this design', explained by the following *uti-*clause; *138.* **florentissimis rebus:** 'though their circumstances were exceedingly prosperous'; *144b5; 153a.* **domos:** *20c.*
[8] **uti . . . haberent:** *196a* (AG 531, B 282.1).
[9] **imperio:** *74b; 131c.* **domicilio:** 'for habitation'; *112a* (AG 382, B 191.1). **copia:** sc. *locorum.*
[10] **opportunissimum:** 'the most suitable'. **fructuosissimum:** 'the most productive'; *75f.*
[11] **iudicassent:** *64a1.* **stipendiarias:** predicative: 'tributary (to them)'; *115b.*
[12] **Petierunt, uti sibi . . . liceret:** 'they asked permission'; how lit.? **sibi:** plural; after *liceret; 105.* **in:** 'for'.
[13] **indicere:** 'to appoint'; *222a.* **id:** *160c.* **voluntate:** *138.* **liceret:** *73b.* **sese habere:** *213b.*
[14] **ex communi consensu:** 'in accordance with a general understanding'. **ab eo:** *116b.*
[15] **permissa:** 'granted'. **iure iurando:** *13h.*
[16] **ne quis:** 'that no one'; how lit.? *49a; 168.* **enuntiaret:** 'should make known (its proceedings)'. **nisi quibus:** i.e. *nisi ut ei enuntiarent, quibus . . . mandatum esset* (impersonal), 'except those to whom the task should have been assigned'; *73d.*

In secret session they beseech Caesar to defend Gaul against Ariovistus, Diviciacus stating their ease.

31.1. Eo concilio[1] dimisso, idem principes civitatum, qui ante fuerant,[2] ad Caesarem reverterunt petieruntque, ut sibi secreto,[3] in occulto, de sua omniumque salute cum eo agere liceret. **2.** Ea re impetrata, sese omnes flentes[4] Caesari ad pedes proiecerunt: *[5]Non[6] minus se id contendere et laborare, ne ea, quae dixissent, enuntiarentur,[7] quam uti ea, quae vellent, impetrarent, propterea quod, si enuntiatum esset, summum in cruciatum[8] se* *venturos viderent.* **3.** Locutus est pro his Diviciacus Aeduus: *⁹Galliae¹⁰ totius factiones esse duas; harum alterius principatum tenere Aeduos, alterius Arvernos.¹¹* **4.** *Hi cum tantopere de potentatu¹² inter se multos annos contenderent, factum esse,¹³ uti ab Arvernis Sequanisque Germani mercede¹⁴ arcesserentur.* **5.** *Horum primo circiter milia XV Rhenum transisse;¹⁵ postea quam agros et cultum et copias Gallorum homines feri ac barbari¹⁶ adamassent, traductos plures;¹⁷ nunc esse in Gallia ad centum et XX milium numerum.* **6.** *¹⁸Cum his Aeduos eorumque clientes¹⁹ semel atque iterum armi contendisse; magnam calamitatem pulsos accepisse, omnem nobilitatem,²⁰ omnem senatum, omnem equitatum amisisse.* **7.** *Quibus proeliis calamitatibusque fractos,²¹ qui et sua virtute et populi Romani hospitio²² atque amicitia plurimum ante in Gallia potuissent, coactos esse Sequanis obsides²³ dare nobilissimos²⁴ civitatis et iure iurando civitatem obstringere, sese neque obsides repetituros,²⁵ neque auxilium a populo Romano imploraturos,²⁶ neque recusaturos, quo minus perpetuo sub illorum²⁷ dicione atque imperio essent.* **8.** *²⁸Unum se esse²⁹ ex omni civitate Aeduorum, qui adduci non potuerit, ut iuraret aut liberos suos obsides daret.* **9.** *Ob eam rem se ex civitate profugisse³⁰ et Romam ad senatum venisse auxilium postulatum,³¹ quod solus neque iure iurando neque obsidibus teneretur.* **10.** *³²Sed peius³³ victoribus Sequanis quam Aeduis victis accidisse, propterea quod Ariovistus, rex Germanorum,³⁴ in eorum finibus consedisset tertiamque partem agri Sequani, qui esset optimus totius Galliae, occupavisset,³⁵ et nunc de altera parte tertia Sequanos decedere³⁶ iuberet, propterea quod, paucis mensibus³⁷ ante, Harudum milia hominum XXIIII ad eum venissent, quibus locus ac sedes³⁸ pararentur.* **11.** *Futurum esse paucis annis,³⁹ uti omnes ex Galliae finibus pellerentur atque omnes Germani Rhenum transirent; neque enim conferendum esse⁴⁰ Gallicum cum Germanorum agro, neque hanc consuetudinem victus⁴¹ cum illa comparandam.* **12.** *⁴²Ariovistum autem, ut semel Gallorum⁴³ copias proelio vicerit, quod proelium⁴⁴ factum sit Admagetobrigae, superbe et crudeliter imperare, obsides nobilissimi cuiusque⁴⁵ liberos poscere, et in⁴⁶ eos omnia exempla cruciatusque edere, si qua res non ad nutum⁴⁷ aut ad voluntatem eius facta sit.* **13.** *Hominem esse barbarum, iracundum,⁴⁸ temerarium; non posse eius imperia diutius sustineri.* **14.** *Nisi quid⁴⁹ in Caesare populoque Romano sit auxilii, omnibus Gallis idem esse faciendum, quod Helvetii fecerint, ut domo⁵⁰ emigrent, aliud domicilium, alias sedes, remotas a Germanis, petant, fortunamque, quaecumque⁵¹ accidat, experiantur.* **15.** *⁵²Haec⁵³ si enuntiata Ariovisto sint, non dubitare, quin de omnibus obsidibus, qui apud eum sint, gravissimum supplicium sumat.* **16.** *Caesarem, vel auctoritate sua atque exercitus,⁵⁴ vel recenti victoria, vel nomine populi Romani, deterrere⁵⁵ posse, ne maior multitudo Germanorum Rhenum⁵⁶ traducatur, Galliamque⁵⁷ omnem ab Ariovisti iniuria posse defendere.*

---

¹ **concilio:** where the council of the leading men of Celtic Gaul was held we are not informed; perhaps at Bibracte. **idem:** = *eidem*; 45.

² **fuerant:** i.e. with Caesar. **petierunt . . . liceret:** as in chap. 30.4, note 12.

³ **secreto:** 'privately', as a protection against betrayal. **in occulto:** 'in a secret place', as a precaution against spies. **cum eo:** 137c. **agere:** 'to confer'.

⁴ **flentes:** 227b. **Caesari:** trans. as if *Caesaris*; 109a (AG 377, B 188.1n).

⁵ **Direct form:** Non minus id *contendimus* et *laboramus*, ne ea, quae *dixerimus*, enuntientur, quam uti ea, quae *velimus* (220), *impetremus*, propterea quod, si enuntiatum *erit*, summum in

cruciatum *nos venturos (esse) videmus.*

[6] **Non . . . viderent:** *213b.* **se id contendere et laborare:** 'that they strove and toiled (for) this', explained by the following *ne*-clause; *117a.*

[7] **enuntiatum esset:** impersonal: 'if disclosure should have been made'.

[8] **cruciatum:** 'torture'. **venturos:** *89c.*

[9] **Direct form:** Galliae totius factiones *sunt duae;* harum alterius principatum *tenent Aedui,* alterius, *Arverni.* Hi cum tantopere de potentatu inter se multos annos contenderent (*185c*), factum *est,* uti ab Arvernis Sequanisque Germani mercede arcesserentur. Horum primo circiter milia XV Rhenum *transierunt;* postea quam agros et cultum et copias Gallorum homines feri ac barbari *adamarunt* (= *adamaverunt*), *traducti sunt* plures; nunc *sunt* in Gallia ad centum et XX milium numerum.

[10] **Galliae:** Celtic Gaul; *287b.* For the indirect discourse, see *212a, c1; 214a.* **factiones:** here 'leagues' rather than 'parties', because made up of states. **alterius . . . alterius:** *23a, b; 171b.* **principatum:** 'headship'; *75b.*

[11] **Arvernos:** a powerful state, southwest of the country of the Aeduans. See GALLIA.

[12] **de potentatu:** 'for supremacy'. **annos:** *118a.*

[13] **factum esse:** the subject is *uti . . . arcesserentur;* trans. 'it had come about'; *203.1.* **Sequanis:** these entered into alliance with the Arvernians because of their hatred of the Aeduans. The strife between the Sequanians and the Aeduans arose from the fact that the Arar for a part of its course formed the boundary between the two states, and each claimed the exclusive right to levy tolls on passing vessels. Among the exports was bacon, which was highly esteemed in Rome.

[14] **mercede:** 'for pay'; *141.* **arcesserentur:** 'were brought over'. Finding themselves worsted by the Aeduans, the Sequanians hired Germans to fight for them.

[15] **transisse:** *113b.* **postea quam:** *188a; 214a.*

[16] **feri ac barbari:** 'savage and uncouth'. **adamassent:** 'had formed an eager desire for'; *64a1.* How lit.? **traductos:** *89c.*

[17] **plures:** sc. *Germanos.* **esse:** sc. *Germanos.*

[18] **Direct form:** Cum his *Aedui* eorumque clientes semel atque iterum armis *contenderunt;* magnam calamitatem *pulsi acceperunt,* omnem nobilitatem, omnem senatum, omnem equitatum *amiserunt.* Quibus proeliis calamitatibusque *fracti,* qui et sua virtute et populi Romani hospitio atque amicitia plurimum ante in Gallia *potuerant, coacti sunt* Sequanis obsides dare nobilissimos civitatis et iure iurando civitatem obstringere, etc.

[19] **clientes:** 'dependents', here referring to dependent states. **semel atque iterum:** in our idiom, 'time and again'; how lit.?

[20] **omnem nobilitatem,** etc.: the activity of Aeduan men of rank recorded in Book VII shows that this statement, if accurately reported, was greatly exaggerated. **senatum:** *289b.* **equitatum:** collective, 'knights', mentioned last as the broadest term in the enumeration; apparently the 'nobles' were a subdivision of the 'knights', pre-eminent on account of aristocratic birth as well as the possession of large resources; *288b.*

[21] **fractos:** 'crushed', in agreement with *eos* understood as subject of *coactos esse* and antecedent of *qui.*

[22] **hospitio:** 'relation of hospitality', less close than the relation implied in *amicitia.* Both relations were established by treaties between states; when *hospitium* was established between two states, each was bound to entertain the other's representatives at public expense. **atque:** force? *233a.* **plurimum,** etc.: 'had previously possessed the greatest power'; *118b.* See chap. 11.3, note 7.

[23] **obsides:** accusative, 'as hostages'; *115a.*

[24] **nobilissimos:** as in chap. 7.3. **iure iurando:** *13h.*

[25] **sese neque repetituros** [esse], etc.: 'that they would neither try to get back', etc., the content of the oath; *sese . . . essent* would be in indirect discourse even if the context were in the direct form; *213b.*

[26] **imploraturos** [esse]: 'solicit'. **recusaturos** [esse] 'refuse'. **quo minus – essent:** 'to be'; how lit.? *201a.* **perpetuo:** 'forever'; *34b.*

[27] **illorum:** trans. as if *Sequanorum.* **dicione:** 'sway'.

[28] **Direct form:** *Unus ego sum,* ex omni civitate Aeduorum, qui adduci non *potuerim* (*194a*), ut *iurarem* ('to take the oath'; *199a*) aut liberos *meos* obsides (*115a*) *darem.* Ob eam rem ex civitate *profugi,* et Romam ad senatum *veni* auxilium postulatum, quod solus neque iure iurando

neque obsidibus *tenebar.*

[29] **Unum se esse:** 'That he (Diviciacus) was the only one'.

[30] **profugisse:** 'had fled'. **Romam:** *119a.* At Rome Diviciacus met Cicero, who was much interested in him and in what he had to say about nature, for Diviciacus was a Druid, and the Druids professed knowledge of the Universe (VI, 14).

[31] **postulatum:** 'to demand'; a strong word, justified by the urgency of the cause and the friendly relations between the Aeduan state and Rome; *231a, b.*

[32] **Direct form:** Sed peius victoribus Sequanis quam Aeduis victis *accidit,* propterea quod Ariovistus, rex Germanorum, in eorum finibus *consedit* (*183a*), tertiamque partem agri Sequani, qui *est* optimus totius Galliae, *occupavit;* et nunc de altera parte tertia Sequanos decedere *iubet,* propterea quod, paucis mensibus ante, Ilarudum milia hominum XXIIII ad eum *venerunt,* quibus locus ac sedes *parentur.* Paucis annis omnes ex Galliae finibus *pellentur,* atque omnes Germani Rhenum *transibunt;* neque enim *conferendus est Gallicus* (*ager*) cum Germanorum agro, neque *haec consuetudo* victus cum illa *comparanda* (*est*).

[33] **peius:** 'a worse fate'; *154a; 32.* **victoribus:** here an adjective, 'victorious'. **victoribus . . . victis:** *239c.*

[34] **rex:** *91a.* **Germanorum:** apparently Swabians (37.3, note 5). Ariovistus probably crossed the Rhine as early as 72 or 71 B.C.

[35] **occupavisset:** 'had seized', in the rich level country west of the Rhine, in modern Alsace. **altera parte tertia:** 'a second third-part'.

[36] **decedere:** 'to withdraw'; *200b.*

[37] **mensibus:** *140* (B 223). **Harudum:** *19e.*

[38] **locus ac sedes:** 'places of habitation'; how lit.? *15b.* **pararentur:** 'were to be provided'; *193a.* **Futurum esse:** 'it would come about'; the subject is the following *uti*-clause; *203.1.*

[39] **annis:** *147a.* **omnes:** sc. *Galli.*

[40] **conferendum esse:** *229c.* **Gallicum:** sc. *agrum.* Caesar means that the land in Gaul is incomparably better than that in Germany; we usually state such comparisons in the opposite way.

[41] **consuetudinem victus:** 'standard of living'. **illa:** 'that (of the Germans)'. The civilization of the Gauls was at this time far superior. **comparandam:** *89c.*

[42] **Direct form:** *Ariovistus* autem, ut semel Gallorum copias proelio *vicit,* quod proelium factum *est* Admagetobrigae, superbe et crudeliter *imperat,* obsides nobilissimi cuiusque liberos *poscit,* et in eos omnia exempla cruciatusque *edit,* si qua res non ad nutum aut ad voluntatem eius facta *est. Homo est barbarus, iracundus, temerarius;* non *possunt* eius imperia diutius sustineri. Nisi quid in *te* populoque Romano *erit* auxilii, omnibus Gallis idem *est* faciendum, quod Helvetii *fecerunt,* ut domo emigrent, aliud domicilium, alias sedes, remotas a Germanis, petant, fortunamque, quaecumque accidat, experiantur.

[43] **Gallorum:** the Aeduans and their allies. **vicerit, imperaret,** etc.: representing perfects and presents in the direct form, used for vividness; the pluperfect and perfect or imperfect in the direct form might have been expected, and in translation past tenses should be used.

[44] **quod proelium:** 'a battle which'; *165a.* **Admagetobrigae:** according to the probable meaning of the Gallic name, 'at the stronghold of Admagetos'; where the place was we do not know. The battle was perhaps fought in 61 or 60 B.C., *146.* **superbe et crudeliter:** 'with arrogance and cruelty'.

[45] **nobilissimi cuiusque:** 'of every man of rank'; *170a* (AG 313b, B 252.5c).

[46] **in:** 'upon'. **exempla:** 'kinds of punishment', as warning examples to others. **cruciatus:** 'tortures', as indicating one kind of punishment resorted to by Ariovistus. **edere:** 'inflicted'. **qua:** *49a; 168.*

[47] **ad nutum:** 'at his nod', at the slightest intimation of his desires.

[48] **iracundum:** 'quick-tempered'. **temerarium:** 'reckless'.

[49] **quid — auxilii:** 'some help'; *97b.* **Gallis,** etc.: 'all the Celts would have to do the same thing'; *110; 229c* (AG 374, B 189.1). **idem:** subject of *faciendum esse,* explained by the appositive clause *ut . . . experiantur; 203.4.*

[50] **domo:** *130b.* **emigrent:** 'migrate'.

[51] **quaecumque:** indefinite relative; trans. 'endure whatever fortune might befall them'; *50a.*

[52] **Direct form:** Haec si enuntiata Ariovisto *erunt,* non *dubito,* quin de omnibus obsidibus, qui apud eum *sint,* gravissimum supplicium sumat. *Tu,* vel auctoritate *tua* atque exercitus, vel recenti victoria, vel nomine populi Romani, deterrere *potes,* ne maior multitudo

Germanorum Rhenum traducatur, Galliamque omnem ab Ariovisti iniuria *potes* defendere.
[53] **Haec:** the utterances at the conference, and appeal to Caesar. **non dubitare:** sc. *se*, 'he (Diviciacus) had no doubt'. **quin . . . sumat:** 'that he (Ariovistus) would inflict'; *201c* (AG 558a, B 298). **de:** 'upon'.
[54] **exercitus:** '(that) of his army'; *157d*.
[55] **deterrere ne,** etc.: 'prevent a larger host of Germans from being brought across the Rhine'; how lit.? *201a*.
[56] **Rhenum:** why accusative? *114b* (AG 395n2, B 179.3).
[57] **Galliam:** as in note 10 above. **Ariovisti:** *95*.

The lot of the Sequanians, showing what might happen to all.

32.1. Hac oratione ab Diviciaco habita, omnes, qui aderant, magno fletu[1] auxilium a Caesare petere coeperunt. **2.** Animadvertit Caesar, unos[2] ex omnibus Sequanos nihil earum rerum facere, quas ceteri facerent,[3] sed tristes, capite demisso, terram intueri.[4] Eius rei quae causa esset, miratus, ex ipsis quaesiit.[5] **3.** Nihil Sequani respondere, sed in eadem tristitia[6] taciti permanere. Cum ab his saepius[7] quaereret, neque ullam omnino vocem exprimere[8] posset, idem Diviciacus Aeduus respondit: **4.** *[9]Hoc[10] esse miseriorem et graviorem fortunam Sequanorum quam reliquorum, quod soli ne[11] in occulto quidem queri neque auxilium implorare auderent,[12] absentisque Ariovisti crudelitatem, velut[13] si coram adesset, horrerent,* **5.** *propterea quod reliquis[14] tamen fugae facultas daretur, Sequanis vero, qui intra fines suos Ariovistum recepissent, quorum oppida omnia[15] in potestate eius essent, omnes[16] cruciatus essent perferendi.*

[1] **fletu:** 'weeping'. Shedding of tears by men was much more common among the Gauls and Romans than among us.
[2] **unos:** 'alone'; *23a*. **nihil:** 'none'; how lit.?
[3] **ceteri:** *171a*. **facerent:** *214a; 213a*. **tristes:** 'disconsolately'; *151*. **capite demisso:** 'with bowed heads'; how lit.? *144b7*.
[4] **intueri:** 'looked upon'. **quae:** *48b*. **esset:** *204.2*. **miratus:** *226c*.
[5] **quaesiit:** *116c*. **respondere, permanere:** 'answered', 'remained'; *182*.
[6] **tristitia:** 'state of dejection'. **taciti:** 'silent'; *148c*.
[7] **saepius:** 'again and again'; how lit.? *153a*. **quaereret:** *185c; 116c*. **neque:** = *et non*; *233a*. **vocem:** 'utterance'; *10c*.
[8] **exprimere:** 'to force out'. **Aeduus:** an Aeduan is now speaking for the Sequanians, who were formerly bitter enemies of the Aeduans.
[9] **Direct form:** Hoc *est miserior* et *gravior fortuna* Sequanorum quam reliquorum, quod soli ne in occulto quidem queri neque auxilium implorare *audent*, absentisque Ariovisti crudelitatem, velut si coram *adsit, horrent*, propterea quod reliquis tamen fugae facultas *datur*, Sequanis vero, qui intra fines suos Ariovistum *receperunt*, quorum oppida omnia in potestate eius *sunt*, omnes cruciatus *sunt* perferendi.
[10] **Hoc:** 'On this account', explained by the following *quod*-clause; *135a*. **miseriorem:** 'more wretched'; *22d*.
[11] **ne . . . quidem:** *237c* (B 347).
[12] **auderent:** *62*. **absentis:** 'in his absence'; how lit.? **crudelitatem:** 'cruelty'.
[13] **velut:** 'just as'. **coram:** 'in person'. **adesset:** subjunctive also in the direct form; *210* (AG 524, B 307.1). **horrerent:** 'they shuddered at'.
[14] **reliquis:** 'to the rest' of the Celts; *171a*. **tamen:** 'at any rate', as a last resource. **Sequanis . . . essent perferendi:** 'the Sequanians . . . had to endure'; how lit.? *229c; 110* (AG 374, B 189.1).
[15] **oppida omnia:** exaggeration, for the Sequanians still held Vesontio *(Besançon)*, which was their strongest fortified place (chap. 38).
[16] **omnes:** as we say, 'all possible'.

Caesar, for reasons of state, promises his help against Ariovistus.

33.1. His rebus cognitis, Caesar Gallorum animos verbis confirmavit pollicitusque est, sibi[1] eam rem curae futuram; *magnam se habere spem, et beneficio suo[2] et auctoritate adductum Ariovistum finem iniuriis facturum.[3]* **2.** Hac oratione habita, concilium dimisit. Et secundum[4] ea multae res eum hortabantur, quare sibi eam rem cogitandam[5] et suscipiendam putaret; in primis, quod[6] Aeduos, fratres consanguineosque saepe numero a senatu appellatos, in servitute atque dicione videbat Germanorum teneri, eorumque obsides esse apud Ariovistum ac Sequanos intellegebat; quod[7] in tanto imperio populi Romani turpissimum[8] sibi et rei publicae esse arbitrabatur. **3.** Paulatim[9] autem Germanos consuescere Rhenum transire, et in Galliam magnam eorum multitudinem venire, populo Romano periculosum[10] videbat; **4.** neque sibi homines feros ac barbaros temperaturos existimabat, quin,[11] cum omnem Galliam occupavissent, ut[12] ante Cimbri Teutonique fecissent, in provinciam exirent atque inde in Italiam[13] contenderent, praesertim cum Sequanos[14] a provincia nostra Rhodanus divideret; quibus rebus[15] quam maturrime occurrendum putabat. **5.** Ipse autem Ariovistus tantos sibi spiritus,[16] tantam arrogantiam[17] sumpserat, ut ferendus non videretur.

[1] **sibi . . . futuram** [esse]: 'that this matter should have his attention'; how lit.? *112b.*

[2] **magnam,** etc.: *213b.* **beneficio suo:** Caesar's kindness, when he was consul (59 B.C.), in helping secure a recognition of Ariovistus by the Roman senate (*255*); Caesar reminds Ariovistus of this later (35.2; 43.4).

[3] **iniuriis:** *104a.* **facturum** [esse]: after *habere spem,* used in place of *sperare; 213a.*

[4] **secundum:** preposition; 'besides those considerations'; *122a; 160c.* **quare:** trans. as if *propter quas.* **sibi:** *110.*

[5] **cogitandam** [esse]: 'ought to be taken into consideration'. **putaret:** *194a.* **in primis:** 'first of all'; how lit.?

[6] **quod . . . videbat:** *198b.* **fratres:** predicate accusative after *appellatos; 88b.* **consanguineos:** 'kin', implying blood-relationship, while *fratres,* like our "brethren" might be used as a title implying intimacy of relations without kinship. The use of the title here may imply that the Aeduans claimed descent from the Trojans, as did the Romans, and Caesar himself; *244;.* **numero:** with *saepe,* 'repeatedly'; *142a; 85.*

[7] **quod:** '(a state of affairs) which'; the antecedent of *quod* is the thought expressed by the infinitive clauses depending on *videbat* and *intellegebat.* **in . . . Romani:** 'in view of the greatness of the power of the Roman people'; how lit.?

[8] **turpissimum:** 'exceedingly disgraceful'; *148c; 153a.* **sibi:** *108a.*

[9] **Paulatim,** etc.: 'for the Germans gradually to become accustomed'; *Germanos consuescere* and *multitudinem venire* are the subject of *esse,* 'was', understood after *videbat; 213a.* **autem:** 'moreover'; *236a.*

[10] **periculosum:** 'full of danger'; *148d; 75f; 84.* **sibi . . . temperaturos** [esse]: 'would hold back', lit. 'restrain themselves'; *105.*

[11] **quin . . . exirent:** 'from passing over'; *201a.*

[12] **ut:** 'as'; *188b; 214a.* **ut . . . fecissent:** related in thought with *exirent* and *contenderent.* **Cimbri Teutonique:** the terrible hordes of the Cimbrians and Teutons in the closing years of the second century B.C. swept over Celtic Gaul and passed into the Province, whence the Cimbrians made their way into Cisalpine Gaul. Finally the Teutons were annihilated in a fierce battle at Aquae Sextiae (now Aix), about 20 miles north of Massilia, by Gaius Marius in 102 B.C.; and a year later the Cimbrians met a similar fate at Vercellae, in Cisalpine Gaul, northeast of Turin. See GALLIA, back cover.

[13] **Italiam:** here including Cisalpine Gaul; *283b.* **praesertim cum:** *184b.*

[14] **Sequanos:** *282.* **Rhodanus:** '(only) the Rhone', a slight protection against an invading host.

[15] **quibus rebus:** 'and these conditions'; *107a.* **quam maturrime:** 'at the earliest possible

moment'; *34a; 153c.* **occurrendum** [esse]: sc. *sibi,* 'that he ought to meet'; how lit.?
[16] **tantos spiritus:** 'such insolent airs'; *20b.*
[17] **arrogantiam:** 'arrogance'. **ferendus non:** 'unbearable'; how lit.?

Caesar invites Ariovistus to a conference; he is rebuffed.

34.1. Quam ob rem placuit ei,[1] ut ad Ariovistum legatos mitteret, qui ab eo postularent,[2] uti aliquem locum, medium utriusque, colloquio[3] deligeret: *Velle sese de re publica et summis utriusque[4] rebus cum eo agere.* **2.** Ei legationi Ariovistus respondit: *[5]Si [6] quid ipsi a Caesare opus esset, sese ad eum venturum fuisse; si quid[7] ille se velit, illum ad se venire oportere.* **3.** *Praeterea,[8] se neque sine exercitu in eas partes Galliae venire audere, quas Caesar possideret,[9] neque exercitum sine magno commeatu[10] atque molimento in unum locum contrahere posse.* **4.** *Sibi autem mirum[11] videri, quid in sua Gallia, quam bello vicisset, aut[12] Caesari aut omnino populo Romano negotii esset.*

[1] **placuit ei:** 'he (Caesar) resolved'; how lit.? **ut . . . mitteret:** with *placuit;* 'to send'; *199a7.*
[2] **postularent:** *193a.* **aliquem:** *49a.* **medium utriusque:** 'midway between them'; how lit.? *51; 102.*
[3] **colloquio:** 'for a conference'; *112a.* **Velle sese:** '(stating) that he wished'; *213b.*
[4] **summis utriusque rebus:** 'affairs of the utmost importance to both'; how lit.?
[5] **Direct form:** Si quid *mihi* a Caesare opus esset, ad eum *venissem;* si quid ille *me vult,* ilium ad *me* venire *oportet.* Praeterea, neque sine exercitu in eas partes Galliae, quas Caesar *possidet,* venire *audeo,* neque exercitum sine magno commeatu atque molimento in unum locum contrahere *possum. Mihi* autem mirum *videtur,* quid in *mea* Gallia, quam bello *vici,* aut Caesari aut omnino populo Romano negotii *sit.*
[6] **Si . . . fuisse:** *208c.* **quid,** etc.: 'he himself had wanted anything'; how lit.? *132b.* **ipsi:** *46.*
[7] **quid se:** 'anything of himself', Ariovistus; *116d.*
[8] **Praeterea:** 'furthermore'. Ariovistus was seemingly over near the Rhine, a long distance from Caesar, who was probably in the vicinity of Bibracte.
[9] **possideret:** 'was occupying'.
[10] **commeatu:** 'store of supplies'. **molimento:** 'trouble' in accumulating supplies as well as in mobilizing his forces; for the army of Ariovistus, so long as it was scattered in small detachments, could live off the country. **contrahere:** 'bring together'.
[11] **mirum:** 'a cause for wonder'; *148d.* **bello:** *131a.* **quid . . . esset:** subject of *videri;* 'what business either Caesar or' etc.; *204.2.*
[12] **aut . . . aut:** *235a.* **Caesari, populo:** *111.* **negotii:** *97b.*

Caesar through envoys makes demands of Ariovistus, and threatens.

35.1. His responsis ad Caesarem relatis, iterum ad eum Caesar legatos cum his mandatis[1] mittit: **2.** *[2]Quoniam,[3] tanto suo populique Romani beneficio affectus, cum in consulatu suo[4] rex atque amicus a senatu appellatus esset, hanc sibi populoque Romano gratiam referret,[5] ut, in colloquium venire invitatus,[6] gravaretur, neque de communi re dicendum[7] sibi et cognoscendum putaret, haec esse, quae ab eo postularet:* **3.** *[8]Primum,[9] ne quam multitudinem hominum amplius trans Rhenum in Galliam traduceret;[10] Deinde, obsides, quos haberet ab Aeduis, redderet,[11] Sequanisque permitteret, ut,[12] quos illi haberent, voluntate eius reddere illis liceret; neve Aeduos iniuria lacesseret, neve his sociisque eorum bellum inferret.* **4.** *[13]Si id ita fecisset,[14] sibi populoque Romano perpetuam gratiam atque amicitiam cum eo futuram; si non impetraret, sese, quoniam, M. Messala, M. Pisone consulibus,[15] senatus censuisset,[16] uti, quicumque Galliam provinciam obtineret, quod[17] commodo rei publicae facere posset, Aeduos ceterosque amicos populi Romani defenderet, se[18] Aeduorum iniurias non neglecturum.*

[1] **his mandatis:** 'this message', lit. 'these instructions' to the envoys, which were to be presented orally, and are here summarized; *212c4*.

[2] **Direct form**: Quoniam, tanto *meo* populique Romani beneficio affectus, cum in consulatu *meo* rex atque amicus a senatu appellatus *est,* (Ariovistus) hanc *mihi* populoque Romano gratiam *refert,* ut, in colloquium venire invitatus, *gravetur,* neque de communi re dicendum sibi et cognoscendum *putet,* haec *sunt,* quae ab eo *postulo.*

[3] **Quoniam:** 'Since'. **tanto,** etc.: 'although treated with so great kindness by himself and the Roman people'; how lit.? *157d.*

[4] **consulatu suo:** in the previous year; see chap. 33; note **2. rex . . . senatu:** cf. 3.4, notes 12-13. The truth seems to be that in the strife between the Aeduans and Ariovistus the Roman Senate thought it the best policy to stand in well with both sides. The Senate therefore continued to profess friendship for the Aeduans, but after they sustained a crushing defeat at Admagetos's stronghold (chap. 31.6,7,12) it courted Ariovistus. To what extent Caesar was responsible for the conferring of the titles on Ariovistus in 59 B.C. we do not know.

[5] **referret:** *183a; 214a.* **ut . . . gravaretur:** 'that he . . . raised objections'; explaining *gratiam; 203.4.* **in:** 'to'.

[6] **invitatus:** 'when he had been invited'; *227a.* **neque . . . putaret:** 'and did not consider himself under obligation to discuss, and take under advisement, a matter of mutual interest'; how lit.?

[7] **dicendum** [esse] **sibi:** *73e; 110.* **haec:** *161a; 160c.*

[8] **Direct form**: Primum, *(postulo)* ne *(Ariovistus)* quam multitudinem hominum amplius trans Rhenum in Galliam *traducat;* Deinde, obsides, quos *habet* ab Aeduis, *reddat,* Sequanisque *permittat,* ut (obsides), quos hi habent, voluntate eius reddere illis *liceat;* neve Aeduos iniuria *lacessat,* neve his sociisque eorum bellum *inferat.*

[9] **Primum:** *237b.* **quam:** *49a; 168.* **hominum:** *98a.* **amplius:** 'in addition'; how lit.?

[10] **traduceret . . . lacesseret. . . inferret:** *199a.*

[11] **redderet, permitteret:** sc. *ut; 200a.*

[12] **ut . . . liceret:** 'to have his (Ariovistus's) approval in returning (to the Aeduans the hostages) which' etc.; how lit.? *199a; 73a, b.* **voluntate:** *138.* **reddere:** *67c; 222a.*

[13] **Direct form**: Si id ita *fecerit* (future perfect), *mihi* (111) populoque Romano *perpetua gratia* atque *amicitia* cum eo *erit;* si non *impetrabo,* quoniam, M. Messala, M. Pisone consulibus, senatus *censuit,* uti, quicumque Galliam provinciam obtineret, quod commodo rei publicae facere posset, Aeduos ceterosque amicos populi Romani defenderet, Aeduorum iniurias non *neglegam.*

[14] **fecisset, futuram** [esse]: *218.1b.* **perpetuam:** 'lasting'.

[15] **M. . . . consulibus:** 61 B.C.; *240a; 238a.*

[16] **censuisset:** 'decreed'; *183a; 214a.* **uti . . . defenderet:** *199a; 177b.* **quicumque:** *50a.* **provinciam:** 'as a province'; *115a.*

[17] **quod:** 'so far as'; *194f* (AG 535d, B 283.5). **commodo rei publicae:** 'consistently with the public interest'; *138; 102.* **Aeduos.**

[18] **se:** repeated from *sese* above.

Ariovistus replies, claiming prior rights in Gaul and defying Caesar.

36.1. Ad haec Ariovistus respondit: [1]*Ius esse belli, ut[,] qui[2] vicissent, eis, quos vicissent, quem ad modum vellent, imperarent; item populum Romanum victis non ad alterius praescriptum,[3] sed ad suum arbitrium, imperare consuesse.* **2.** *Si ipse populo Romano non praescriberet,[4] quem ad modum[5] suo[6] iure uteretur, non oportere se a populo Romano in suo iure impediri.* **3.** [7]*Aeduos sibi, quoniam belli fortunam temptassent et armis congressi[8] ac superati essent, stipendiarios esse factos.* **4.** *Magnam Caesarem iniuriam facere, qui[9] suo adventu vectigalia sibi[10] deteriora faceret.* **5.** *Aeduis se obsides redditurum non esse; neque his neque eorum sociis iniuria[11] bellum illaturum, si in[12] eo manerent, quod convenisset, stipendiumque quotannis penderent;[13] si id non fecissent, longe eis fraternum nomen populi Romani afuturum.* **6.** [14]*Quod[15] sibi Caesar denuntiaret, se Aeduorum iniurias non neglecturum, neminem secum sine sua[16] pernicie* *contendisse.* **7.** *Cum vellet, congrederetur;*[17] *intellecturum, quid invicti Germani, exercitatissimi*[18] *in armis, qui inter annos XIIII tectum non subissent,*[19] *virtute possent.*

[1] Direct form: Ius *est* belli, ut, qui *vicerint* (220), eis, quos *vicerint* (220), quem ad modum *velint, imperent* (203.4); item *populus Romanus* victis non ad alterius praescriptum, sed ad suum arbitrium, imperare *consuevit.* Si *ego* populo Romano non *praescribo,* quem ad modum suo iure *utatur* (204.3), non *oportet* (73a) *me* a populo Romano in *meo* iure impediri.

[2] **qui:** the antecedent is the implied subject of *imperarent;* 'that those who had conquered should rule over' etc. **eis:** after *imperarent; 105.* **quem ad modum:** 'in whatever way', lit. 'according to which manner': in full, *ad (eum) modum ad quem.*

[3] **victis:** *227a4.* **ad alterius praescriptum:** 'according to the dictates of another'; how lit.? *23b.* **arbitrium:** 'judgment'.

[4] **non praescriberet:** 'should not dictate'.

[5] **quem ad modum:** 'in what way'; *quem* is here interrogative; *48b.* **suo:** 'its own'. **uteretur:** 'should exercise'.

[6] **suo:** 'his own'.

[7] **Direct form:** *Aedui mihi,* quoniam belli fortunam *temptaverunt* et armis congressi ac superati sunt, stipendiarii facti sunt. Magnam *Caesar* iniuriam *facit,* qui suo adventu vectigalia *mihi* deteriora *faciat.* Aeduis obsides non *reddam;* neque his neque eorum sociis iniuria bellum *inferam,* si in eo *manebunt,* quod *convenit,* stipendiumque quotannis *pendent;* si id non *fecerint* (future perfect), longe eis fraternum nomen populi Romani *aberit.*

[8] **congressi** [essent]: 'had contended'; *57c.* **stipendiarios:** 'subject to the payment of tribute'; *148c.* **Magnam:** emphatic position; *353d.*

[9] **qui:** 'since he'; *194c.* **suo:** refers to Caesar. **vectigalia:** see chap. 18.3, note 11.

[10] **sibi:** refers to Ariovistus. **deteriora:** 'less profitable'; with Caesar's backing, the Aeduans would refuse to pay tribute to Ariovistus.

[11] **iniuria:** 'wrongfully'; *136b* (AG 412b, B 220.2).

[12] **in . . . convenisset:** 'they should abide by' (lit. 'in') 'that which had been agreed upon'. **stipendium:** 'tribute'. **quotannis:** *79b.*

[13] **penderent:** 'should pay'; originally 'weigh out', a meaning appropriate to the early time when payments were made in uncoined metal. There is a similar development of meaning in the English "pound sterling". **longe eis . . . afuturum** [esse]: 'would be far from benefiting them'. **eis:** dative; *109b.* **fraternum . . . Romani:** 'the title of "Brethren of the Roman people"'.

[14] **Direct form:** Quod *mihi* Caesar *denuntiat,* se Aeduorum iniurias non neglecturum, *nemo mecum* sine sua pernicie *contendit.* Cum *volet, congrediatur! Intelleget,* quid invicti Germani, exercitatissimi in armis, qui inter annos XIIII tectum non *subierunt,* virtute *possint.*

[15] **Quod . . . denuntiaret:** 'As for Caesar's warning to him', i.e. to Ariovistus; how lit.? *198c.* **se:** Caesar.

[16] **sua:** 'his own', referring to *neminem.*

[17] **sibi:** 'let him come on!'; *216* (AG 588, B 316). **intellecturum:** *eum* (= *Caesarem*) *intellecturum esse; 215.* **quid Germani – virtute possent:** 'what valour the Germans had'; how lit.? *118b.* **invicti:** 'unconquered'.

[18] **exercitatissimi:** 'most thoroughly trained'. **inter:** 'during'; with *annos,* stronger than the simple accusative of time. **XIIII:** *36, 38b.* **tectum:** 'roof'.

[19] **subissent:** *113b.* **virtute:** *142a.*

Caesar hears further complaints, marches toward Ariovistus.

37.1. Haec eodem tempore Caesari mandata referebantur, et legati ab Aeduis et a Treveris veniebant: **2.** Aedui[1] questum, quod Harudes,[2] qui nuper in Galliam transportati essent, fines eorum popularentur,[3] sese, ne obsidibus quidem datis, pacem Ariovisti redimere potuisse; **3.** Treveri[4] autem, pagos centum Sueborum[5] ad ripas Rheni consedisse, qui Rhenum transire conarentur; his[6] praeesse Nasuam et Cimberium fratres. **4.** Quibus rebus Caesar vehementer[7] commotus maturandum sibi existimavit, ne,[8] si nova manus Sueborum cum veteribus copiis Ariovisti sese coniunxisset,[9] minus facile resisti posset. **5.** Itaque re frumentaria, quam celerrime[10] potuit, comparata, magnis itineribus[11] ad Ariovistum contendit.

[1] **Aedui:** sc. *veniebant.* **questum:** *231a; 61a3.*

[2] **Harudes:** chap. 31.10, notes 37,38. **transportati essent:** 'had been brought over' by Ariovistus.

[3] **popularentur:** 'were (as they said) laying waste'; *214b.* **sese:** '(reporting) that they'; *213b.* **ne obsidibus quidem datis:** 'not even by the giving of hostages'; *144b6.*

[4] **Treveri:** i.e. *Treveri dicebant.*

[5] **Sueborum:** an account of the ancient Swabians is given in IV, 1.

[6] **his:** *107a.* **praeesse:** *66a.* **Nasuam:** *19d.*

[7] **vehementer commotus:** 'greatly disturbed', a strong expression. Caesar does not often give us an insight into his feelings, but the situation now was critical. Why? **maturandum** [esse] **sibi:** 'that he ought to make haste'; *73e.*

[8] **ne,** etc.: 'that it might not be more difficult to cope with him'; how lit.? *73c; 196a.*

[9] **sese coniunxisset:** 'should have united'; *218.1b.*

[10] **quam celerrime potuit:** 'as quickly as possible'; *153c.* **comparata:** *144b2.*

[11] **magnis itineribus:** 'by forced marches'; *329; 18c.* Where Caesar was when the negotiations with Ariovistus were begun, and from where he went to meet Ariovistus, cannot be determined. It seems probable that he overtook the survivors of the Helvetians near the site of Dijon (Map 1); that from there he came back to Bibracte for the Gallic Council; and that from some point near Bibracte 'the forced marches' eastward began, as indicated on Map **1**.

Hearing that Ariovistus has designs on Vesontio, Caesar hastens thither.

38.1. Cum tridui[1] viam processisset, nuntiatum est ei, Ariovistum cum suis omnibus copiis ad occupandum[2] Vesontionem, quod[3] est oppidum maximum Sequanorum, contendere, triduique viam a suis finibus[4] processisse. **2.** Id ne accideret, magnopere sibi praecavendum[5] Caesar existimabat. **3.** Namque omnium rerum, quae ad[6] bellum usui erant, summa erat in eo oppido facultas,[7] **4.** idque natura loci sic muniebatur, ut magnam ad ducendum bellum[8] daret facultatem, propterea quod flumen Dubis, ut circino circumductum,[9] paene[10] totum oppidum cingit; **5.** reliquum spatium, quod est non amplius pedum sescentorum,[11] qua flumen intermittit, mons[12] continet magna altitudine, ita, ut radices montis ex utraque parte ripae fluminis contingant.[13] **6.** Hunc murus circumdatus arcem efficit[14] et cum oppido coniungit. **7.** Huc Caesar magnis nocturnis diurnisque[15] itineribus contendit, occupatoque oppido ibi praesidium collocat.

[1] **tridui:** trans. as if *trium dierum* (see *100a*). **viam:** *118a.*

[2] **occupandum:** gerundive; the gerund in the accusative would not have a direct object; *230.3.*

[3] **quod:** why not *qui,* to agree in gender with *Vesontionem*? *164c* (AG 306, B 250.3).

[4] **suis finibus:** in the country taken from the Sequanians, in Upper Alsace. But the report was unfounded; for if Ariovistus had marched as the report indicated he must have reached Vesontio before Caesar. **Id:** the seizure of Vesontio by Ariovistus.

[5] **sibi praecavendum** [esse]: 'that he ought to take every precaution'; *110; 73e.*

[6] **ad:** 'for'. **usui:** 'useful'; how lit.? *112a.*

[7] **facultas:** 'abundance'. **id:** *oppidum.* **natura loci:** cf. Chap. 2.3, note 7.

[8] **ad ducendum bellum:** 'for prolonging the war', at any rate until Ariovistus could bring the new Swabian hordes (chap. 37.3) to his assistance.

[9] **ut circino circumductum:** 'as though drawn around by a pair of compasses'.

[10] **paene cingit:** 'almost encircles'. The Dubis (modern *Doubs*, 'Black River') here bends into the form of a loop, leaving only one side of the town (*reliquum spatium*) not surrounded by it; and this space is taken up by a high hill, the top of which forms an irregular plateau.

[11] **pedum sescentorum:** 'than six hundred feet' in breadth; a genitive of measure is here used instead of a comparative ablative, *quam* being omitted after *amplius; 100a; 129b.* **sexcentorum:**

the distance across the neck of the loop from the river to the river again is about 1600 Roman feet; but the distance which needed to be fortified, measured across the top of the plateau, was only 600 feet. **intermittit:** 'leaves a neck' of land; how lit.?
[12] **mons:** see chap. 2; note 10. **altitudine:** about 400 feet above the river; *143a* (AG 415, B 224). **ita, ut:** *197b.* **radices:** object of *contingant;* we should say 'base'.
[13] **contingant:** 'touch'. **Hunc:** *i.e. hunc montem;* object of *efficit.* **circumdatus:** 'extended around (it)', at the edge of the small plateau. **murus.**
[14] **arcem efficit:** 'converts (into) a citadel'; *115a.* Vesontio was an important city in Roman times, and afterwards; and Besançon is now a fortress of the first class.
[15] **nocturnis diurnisque:** 'by night and by day'; *76b.* Caesar probably arrived at Vesontio soon after the middle of August.

Panic seizes Caesar's army on account of fear of the Germans.

39.1. Dum paucos dies ad[1] Vesontionem rei frumentariae commeatusque causa moratur,[2] ex percontatione nostrorum vocibusque[3] Gallorum ac mercatorum, qui ingenti magnitudine corporum[4] Germanos, incredibili virtute atque exercitatione in armis esse praedicabant[5] (saepe numero sese cum his congressos ne vultum[6] quidem atque aciem oculorum dicebant ferre potuisse), tantus[7] subito timor omnem exercitum occupavit, ut non mediocriter[8] omnium mentes animosque perturbaret.[9] **2.** Hic primum ortus est a[10] tribunis militum, praefectis, reliquisque, qui, ex urbe amicitiae causa[11] Caesarem secuti, non magnum[12] in re militari usum habebant; **3.** quorum alius alia causa[13] illata, quam sibi ad proficiscendum necessariam esse diceret, petebat, ut[14] eius voluntate discedere liceret; non nulli pudore[15] adducti, ut timoris suspicionem vitarent, remanebant.[16] **4.** Hi neque vultum fingere neque interdum lacrimas tenere poterant; abditi[17] in tabernaculis, aut suum fatum querebantur[18] aut cum familiaribus suis commune periculum miserabantur.[19] **5.** Vulgo totis castris testamenta obsignabantur.[20] Horum vocibus ac timore paulatim etiam ei, qui magnum in castris[21] usum habebant, milites centurionesque, quique equitatui praeerant, perturbabantur. **6.** Qui se ex his[22] minus timidos[23] existimari volebant, non se hostem vereri, sed angustias[24] itineris et magnitudinem silvarum, quae intercederent inter ipsos atque Ariovistum, aut rem[25] frumentariam, ut[26] satis commode supportari posset, timere dicebant. **7.** Non nulli etiam Caesari nuntiabant, cum castra moveri ac signa ferri[27] iussisset, non fore dicto audientes milites neque propter timorem signa laturos.

[1] **ad:** *120a.* Only a 'garrison' (*praesidium*) was stationed in the citadel; the rest of the army were encamped 'near' the town. **rei . . . causa:** 'in order to secure grain and (other) supplies'; how lit.? *135b.*
[2] **moratur:** '(Caesar) was delaying'; *190a.* **ex percontatione:** 'in consequence of the questioning'.
[3] **vocibus:** here 'stories'; *10c.* **mercatorum:** many traders accompanied the army, to trade with friendly natives as well as to purchase loot from the soldiers and supply them with extras not provided in the army rations. **ingenti magnitudine:** 'of huge size'; *143b* (AG 415, B 224.1).
[4] **corporum:** *92a; 13f.* Caesar elsewhere (IV, 1) speaks of the 'huge size' of the Germans, who, by contrast in stature, seemed larger to the Romans than they would have seemed to us. **exercitatione:** 'practiced skill'.
[5] **praedicabant:** 'were declaring'; *84.* **numero:** *142a.* **cum his congressos:** 'meeting Germans'; *57c.* How lit.?
[6] **vultum – ferre:** 'to endure the sight of their faces'; how lit.? Our corresponding phrase is

"to look them in the face". **aciem:** 'fierce look'.

[7] **tantus . . . ut:** *197b.* **subito:** 'suddenly'. **timor:** 'panic'; used of a groundless, cowardly fear.

[8] **non mediocriter:** 'in no slight degree'; litotes; *239g.* **mentes animosque:** as we say, 'hearts and minds'.

[9] **perturbaret:** 'disturbed'.

[10] **ortus est a:** 'started with'; *61b.* **tribunis militum:** 'military tribunes'; *314.* **praefectis:** not the 'cavalry prefects' (*309c*), but 'subsidiary officials' in various positions of slight responsibility, chiefly, we may assume, in connection with the light-armed troops. Caesar's financial and political relations (*251*) made it expedient for him to furnish military appointments for a number of aristocratic young men, who had had no military experience, but wanted a taste of it because that was considered the proper thing. These were in a different class from Publius Crassus, for example, and other young Romans of high social position with Caesar, who attacked their work seriously and became excellent officers.

[11] **urbe:** Rome; *17b.* **amicitiae causa:** *135b.* Caesar is politic as well as polite in ascribing to personal attachment to himself the presence of these ineffectuals in his army.

[12] **non magnum:** *239g.* **re militari:** 'warfare'. **alius alia causa, illata:** '(each) one offering a different excuse'; *171c.*

[13] **causa:** *144b2.* **quam . . . diceret:** 'which, as he said, made it imperative for him to leave'; how lit.? *214b.*

[14] **petebat, ut ... liceret:** 'begged permission'; *199a.* **voluntate:** *138.*

[15] **pudore:** 'by a sense of shame'.

[16] **remanebant:** 'remained' in camp, after the exodus of the others. **vultum fingere:** 'to look unconcerned'; how lit.?

[17] **abditi:** 'shutting themselves up'; *174, 67c.* **tabernaculis:** 'their tents'; *355a.*

[18] **fatum querebantur:** 'they were bewailing their fate'. **familiaribus:** 'intimate friends'.

[19] **miserabantur:** 'were despairingly discussing'. **Vulgo:** adverb, 'generally'. **totis castris:** 'throughout the camp'; *145c.* **testamenta:** 'wills'.

[20] **obsignabantur:** 'were being made', as we say; lit. 'were being sealed', referring to the process by which wax tablets (p. 370), on which wills were ordinarily written, were sealed up.

[21] **in castris:** 'in the army' is our corresponding phrase. **centuriones:** 'the centurions'; *315a.* **quique:** *et (ei) qui;* cavalry prefects and decurions are meant; *309c.*

[22] **Qui ex his:** (*ei*) *ex his, qui; 97d.* **se . . . existimari:** *223a.*

[23] **timidos:** 'cowardly.' **non se vereri:** 'that they were not afraid of'.

[24] **angustias:** the gorges in the valley of the Dubis (*Doubs*), through which the most direct route led northeast to the region where Ariovistus was. **silvarum:** there are still extensive forests on both sides of the upper Doubs.

[25] **rem:** object of *timere,* where a nominative, subject of *posset,* might have been expected; prolepsis; *238g* (B 374.5).

[26] **ut:** 'that not' *202.* **supportari:** 'be brought up'.

[27] **signa ferri:** 'go forward'; how lit.? *324, 325.* **iussisset:** 'should give the order'; future perfect indicative in the direct form; *214a.* **non fore dicto audientes:** 'would not obey the command'; like the Scriptural, "Ye will not hearken unto me"; how lit.? **dicto:** *105.*

Caesar deals with the situation in a persuasive address.

40.1. Haec cum animadvertisset, convocato consilio, omniumque ordinum[1] ad id consilium adhibitis centurionibus, vehementer eos incusavit;[2] primum, quod, aut quam in partem, aut quo consilio[3] ducerentur, sibi quaerendum aut cogitandum putarent: **2.** [4]*Ariovistum,*[5] *se consule, cupidissime populi Romani amicitiam appetisse;*[6] *cur hunc tam temere quisquam ab officio discessurum iudicaret?* **3.** *Sibi quidem persuaderi,*[7] *cognitis suis postulatis*[8] *atque aequitate condicionum perspecta, eum neque suam*[9] *neque populi Romani gratiam repudiaturum.* **4.** [10]*Quod*[11] *si, furore atque amentia impulsus, bellum intulisset, quid tandem*[12] *vererentur? aut cur de sua virtute aut de ipsius diligentia*[13] *desperarent?* **5.** *Factum eius hostis periculum patrum* *nostrorum memoria,[14] cum, Cimbris et Teutonis a Gaio Mario pulsis, non minorem laudem[15] exercitus, quam ipse imperator, meritus[16] videbatur; factum etiam nuper in Italia, servili tumultu,[17] quos tamen aliquid usus ac disciplina, quae[18] a nobis accepissent, sublevarent.* **6.** *Ex quo iudicari posse, quantum[19] haberet in se boni constantia, propterea quod, quos aliquamdiu[20] inermos sine causa timuissent, hos postea armatos[21] ac victores superassent.* **7.** *[22]Denique[23] hos esse eosdem Germanos, quibuscum saepe numero Helvetii congressi,[24] non solum in suis, sed etiam in illorum[25] finibus, plerumque superarint; qui tamen pares esse nostro exercitui non potuerint.* **8.** *[26]Si quos adversum proelium[27] et fuga Gallorum commoveret, hos, si quaererent, reperire posse, diuturnitate[28] belli defatigatis Gallis, Ariovistum, cum multos menses castris se ac paludibus[29] tenuisset neque sui potestatem fecisset, desperantes iam de pugna et dispersos subito adortum, magis ratione et consilio quam virtute vicisse.* **9.** *Cui rationi[30] contra homines barbaros atque imperitos[31] locus fuisset, hac ne ipsum quidem sperare nostros exercitus capi[32] posse.* **10.** *[33]Qui[34] suum timorem in rei frumentariae simulationem angustiasque itineris conferrent, facere arroganter,[35] cum aut de officio imperatoris desperare aut praescribere viderentur.* **11.** *Haec sibi esse curae;[36] frumentum Sequanos, Leucos, Lingones sumministrare,[37] iamque esse in agris frumenta matura; de itinere ipsos brevi tempore iudicaturos.* **12.** *[38]Quod[39] non fore dicto audientes neque signa laturi dicantur, nihil[40] se ea re commoveri; scire enim, quibuscumque exercitus dicto audiens non fuerit, aut, male re gesta,[41] fortunam defuisse, aut, aliquo[42] facinore comperto, avaritiam esse convictam;[43] suam innocentiam perpetua vita, felicitatem Helvetiorum bello[44] esse perspectam.* **13.** *[45]Itaque se, quod in longiorem[46] diem collaturus fuisset, repraesentaturum[47] et proxima nocte de quarta vigilia castra moturum, ut quam primum[48] intellegere posset, utrum apud eos pudor atque officium, an timor, plus valeret.[49]* **14.** *Quod si praeterea nemo sequatur, tamen se cum sola decima legione iturum, de qua non dubitaret,[50] sibique eam praetoriam cohortem futuram.* **15.** Huic legioni[51] Caesar et indulserat praecipue et propter virtutem confidebat maxime.[52]

---

[1] **ordinum:** 'companies'; *12d.* How many in the six legions which Caesar now had? *307c.*
centurionibus: ordinarily only the centurions of first rank, the six centurions of the first cohort of each legion, were invited to a war-council. On this occasion all the centurions of the six legions (360 in number) were brought together doubtless with the lieutenants and other higher officers, not for deliberation, but for an address by the commander in chief.
[2] **vehementer eos incusavit:** 'he severely reprimanded them'. **quod . . . putarent:** 'because (as he told them) they thought'; *214b.* **quam, quo:** *204.2; 48b.*
[3] **consilio:** 'plan'. **quaerendum** [esse] **aut cogitandum** [esse]: the subject is the preceding indirect question; 'that it was their business to inquire or consider'; how lit.? *73e.*
[4] **Direct form:** *Ariovistus, me consule, cupidissime populi Romani amicitiam appetiit; cur hunc tam temere quisquam ab officio discessurum* (esse) *iudicet? Mihi quidem persuadetur, cognitis meis* aequitate atque aequitate condicionum perspecta, eum neque *meam* neque populi Romani gratiam repudiaturum (esse).
[5] **Ariovistum,** etc.: *280.* **se consule:** only a year previously; *255; 144b2.*
[6] **appetisse:** 'strove to secure'; a rhetorical exaggeration. See *33.1*, note 2, and *35.2*, note 4.
temere: 'recklessly'. **quisquam:** *168; 49a.* **ab officio:** 'from his obligation' of allegiance.
[7] **iudicaret:** *179b2.* **Sibi quidem persuaderi:** 'he at least was persuaded'; how lit.? *106b.*
cognitis . . . perspecta: trans. by a clause introduced by 'after'; *239c.* Why ablative?
[8] **postulatis:** 'demands'. **aequitate:** 'fairness'. **perspecta:** 'should have been clearly understood'; how lit.? **eum:** trans. as if *Ariovistum.*
[9] **suam:** *157d.* **repudiaturum** [esse]: 'would reject'.

[10] **Direct form**: Quod si (*Ariovistus*), furore atque amentia impulsus, bellum *intulerit*, quid tandem *vereamini* (*179b2*)? aut cur de *vestra* virtute aut de *mea* diligentia *desperetis* (*179b2*)? Factum (*est*) eius hostis periculum patrum nostrorum memoria, cum, Cimbris et Teutonis a Gaio Mario pulsis, non minorem laudem exercitus, quam ipse imperator, meritus videbatur; factum (*est periculum*) etiam nuper in Italia, servili tumultu, quos tamen aliquid usus ac disciplina, quae a nobis *acceperant, sublevabant*. Ex quo iudicari *potest*, quantum *habeat* (*204.3*) in se boni constantia, propterea quod, quos aliquamdiu inermos sine causa *timuistis*, hos postea armatos ac victores *superavistis*.

[11] **Quod**: 'But'; *118d*. **furore ... impulsus**: 'carried away by rage and madness'.

[12] **quid tandem**: 'what, pray'. **vererentur**: *61a2*.

[13] **diligentia**: 'careful leadership'. **Factum** [esse] . . . **periculum**: 'trial had been made of that enemy', i.e. of the Germans.

[14] **memoria**: *147b*. **Cimbris, Teutonis**: see chap. 33; note 12.

[15] **laudem**: 'praise'; *17c*.

[16] **meritus**: for *meritus esse*; with *videbatur*, 'clearly earned'; how lit.? *148e*. **videbatur**: indicative retained from the direct form; *185b*. **nuper**: fourteen years previously; among the centurions present there were probably a number who had served as soldiers in the war with Spartacus, the term of military service being twenty years; *307a*.

[17] **servili tumultu**: = *tumultu servorum*, 'at the time of the uprising of the slaves', 73-71 B.C.; referring to the insurrection led by Spartacus, the gladiator, who had a succession of victories for two years, but in 71 B.C. was completely crushed. Caesar implies that among the gladiators and other slaves serving under Spartacus there were many of Germanic origin. **tumultu**: used for *bellum* in case of a sudden war in Italy. Why ablative? *147b*. **quos**: *164b* (AG 306b, B 251.2). **quos tamen**, etc.: 'notwithstanding the fact that the experience and training, which they had gained from us, to some extent aided them' (lit. 'whom nevertheless', etc). **aliquid**: *118b*.

[18] **quae**: neuter; *163c* (AG 305a, B 250.2).

[19] **quantum**, etc.: 'how great an advantage there is in steadfastness', lit. 'how much of good steadfastness has in itself'. **boni**: *97b*.

[20] **aliquamdiu**: 'for a long time'. **inermos**: 'without arms', referring to the slaves in the earlier stages of the insurrection, before they were able to supply themselves with weapons. **hos**: antecedent of *quos*.

[21] **armatos**: 'equipped with arms'.

[22] **Direct form**: Denique *hi sunt idem Germani*, quibuscum saepe numero Helvetii congressi, non solum in suis, sed etiam in illorum finibus, plerumque *superaverunt*; qui tamen pares esse nostro exercitui non *potuerunt*.

[23] **Denique**: 'Finally', closing the argument about the Germans. **quibuscum**, etc.: cf. Chap. 1.4; *125c*.

[24] **congressi**: *228a*.

[25] **illorum**: trans. as if *Germanorum*. **plerumque superarint**: *superaverint*; 'generally defeated (them)'. **qui tamen**: 'and they (the Helvetians) nevertheless'; *236a*.

[26] **Direct form**: Si quos adversum proelium et fuga Gallorum *commovet*, hi, si quaerent (*206*), reperire *poterunt*, diuturnitate belli defatigatis Gallis, Ariovistum, cum multos menses (*118a*) castris (*131a*) se ac paludibus tenuisset neque sui potestatem fecisset, (*eos,* = *Gallos*) desperantes iam de pugna et dispersos subito adortum (*226c*), magis ratione et consilio quam virtute vicisse. Cui rationi contra homines barbaros atque imperitos locus *fuit*, hac ne *ipse* quidem *sperat* nostros exercitus capi posse.

[27] **quos**: *168*; *49a*. **adversum proelium**: 'defeat' at Admagetos's stronghold; see 31.12, notes 43-44. **commoveret**: *172b*.

[28] **diuturnitate**, etc.: 'when the Gauls had become exhausted by the length of the war'; *144b2*.

[29] **paludibus**: 'marshes', added to explain how the encampments were shut off from approach; *131a*. **se tenuisset**: 'had kept himself secluded'. **neque sui**, etc.: 'and had given (them) no chance to attack him', lit. 'no power of himself'. **sui**: *102*. **desperantes . . . vicisse**: i.e. *Ariovistum . . . subito adortum* (*eos* = *Gallos*) *desperantes iam de pugna* ('giving up hope of battle') *et dispersos* ('scattered'), *vicisse* (*eos*) *ratione et consilio* ('by cunning and strategy') *magis quam virtute*.

[30] **Cui rationi – hac**: i.e. *hac ratione, cui*, 'by such cunning' – 'for which'; *165c*.

[31] **imperitos**: 'unskilled'. **ipsum**: Ariovistus.

[32] **capi:** 'be caught'; *56*.

[33] **Direct form:** Qui suum timorem in rei frumentariae simulationem angustiasque itineris *conferunt, faciunt* arroganter, cum aut de officio imperatoris desperare aut praescribere *videantur* (*184a*). Haec *mihi* sunt curae; frumentum *Sequani, Leuci, Lingones sumministrant,* iamque *sunt* in agris frumenta matura; de itinere *ipsi* brevi tempore *iudicabitis.*

[34] **Qui:** i.e. *ei, qui;* see chap. 39.6, note 22. **suum,** etc.: 'assigned their fear to a pretended anxiety about supplies'; how lit.?

[35] **arroganter:** 'presumptuously'.

[36] **sibi curae:** *112b* (AG 382.1, B 191.2a). **Leucos.**

[37] **sumministrare:** 'were supplying'. **frumenta:** how different from *frumentum*? Cf. Chap. 16.2, note 3.

[38] **Direct form:** Quod (milites) non fore dicto audientes neque signa laturi dicantur, nihil ea re *commoveor; scio* enim, quibuscumque exercitus dicto audiens non fuerit, aut, male re gesta, fortunam defuisse, aut, aliquo facinore comperto, avaritiam esse convictam: *mea innocentia* perpetua vita, *felicitas* Helvetiorum bello *est perspecta.*

[39] **Quod . . . dicantur:** sc. *milites;* cf. chap. 39, note 29; *198c* (B 299.2). **signa:** *325*. **laturi** [esse] **dicantur:** trans. 'it was said that the soldiers would', etc.; *148e; 172d; 224a*.

[40] **nihil:** 'not at all'; *118c*. **scire:** sc. *se, 215*. **quibuscumque:** after *dicto audiens;* these two words express a single concept, 'obedient', and are followed by the dative; *50a; 108a*. For an antecedent supply *eis* after *defuisse;* trans. 'that in the case of any (commanders) whatever who had found their armies mutinous, either their luck had failed them in consequence of the bad handling of some enterprise, or' etc. How lit.?

[41] **re gesta:** *144b3*. **fortunam:** the Romans were superstitious in avoiding anything that seemed unlucky.

[42] **defuisse:** *66a*. **aliquo:** from *aliqui; 49a*. **facinore:** 'crime'; *13f; 144b3*. **avaritiam:** 'greed', the underlying cause of the crimes committed by generals, according to Caesar.

[43] **esse convictam:** 'had been clearly proved' against them. **suam:** emphatic position; *157b*. **innocentiam:** 'integrity', freedom from the corruption implied in *avaritiam.* **perpetua vita:** 'during his entire life'; *147c* (AG 424b, B 231.1). **felicitatem:** 'good fortune'.

[44] **Helvetiorum bello:** we say 'war with the Helvetians' or 'Helvetian campaign'; *147b*.

[45] **Direct form:** Itaque, quod in longiorem diem collaturus *fui, repraesentabo;* et *hac* nocte de quarta vigilia castra *movebo,* ut quam primum intellegere *possim* (*196a*), utrum apud *milites* pudor atque officium, an timor, plus *valeat* (*204*). Quod si praeterea nem *sequetur* (*218.1a*) tamen *ego* cum sola decima legione *ibo,* de qua non *dubito, mihique ea praetoria cohors erit.*

[46] **longiorem:** 'more distant'. **collaturus fuisset:** 'he had intended to put off'; *63; 69b*.

[47] **repraesentaturum** [esse]: sc. *id,* antecedent of *quod;* 'he would at once do (that)'. **de quarta vigilia:** *242d*.

[48] **quam primum:** *153c*. **utrum ... an:** *204.1* (AG 335, B 300.4).

[49] **plus valeret:** 'should have the stronger influence' with them; *118b*. **Quod:** *118d*.

[50] **non dubitaret:** 'he entertained no doubts'. **praetoriam cohortem:** 'bodyguard', to which a general (originally called *praetor,* see Vocab.) was entitled.

[51] **legioni:** *105; 307e*. **indulserat:** 'had favoured'. **praecipue:** 'especially'; emphatic position; *352a*.

[52] **confidebat maxime:** 'had the fullest confidence'.

Fear and mutiny give place to enthusiasm. Caesar advances.

41.1. Hac oratione habita,[1] mirum in modum conversae sunt omnium[2] mentes, summaque alacritas et cupiditas belli gerendi innata est;[3] **2.** princepsque decima legio per tribunos militum ei gratias egit,[4] quod de se optimum iudicium fecisset, seque esse ad bellum gerendum paratissimam confirmavit. **3.** Deinde reliquae legiones cum tribunis militum et primorum ordinum centurionibus[5] egerunt, uti Caesari satisfacerent; *Se*[6] *neque umquam dubitasse neque timuisse, neque*[7] *de summa belli suum iudicium, sed imperatoris esse existimavisse.* **4.** Eorum satisfactione[8] accepta, et itinere exquisito per Diviciacum, quod ex Gallis ei[9] maximam fidem habebat, ut milium[10] amplius quinquaginta circuitu locis apertis exercitum duceret, de quarta vigilia, ut dixerat, profectus est. **5.** Septimo die,[11] cum iter non intermitteret, ab exploratoribus certior factus est, Ariovisti copias a nostris milibus[12] passuum quattuor et XX[13] abesse.

[1] **Hac oratione habita:** 'After this address'; how lit.? *144b2.* **mirum in modum:** 'in a wonderful way.'

[2] **omnium:** including not only the officers but also the soldiers, to whom the speech was promptly reported by the centurions. **summa alacritas:** 'the utmost enthusiasm.'

[3] **innata est:** 'arose.' **princeps:** adj., 'taking the lead'; how lit.? *152b.* **per:** *123a.* **tribunos militum:** *314.*

[4] **ei gratias egit:** 'conveyed thanks to him'. **fecisset:** 'had passed'. Why subjunctive? *183a.*

[5] **primorum ordinum centurionibus:** 'the centurions of first rank', apparently the six centurions of the first cohort in each legion. **egerunt:** 'arranged'. **uti – satisfacerent:** 'to apologize'; *199a.*

[6] **Se:** '(declaring) that they'; *213b.* **dubitasse:** *64a1.*

[7] **neque:** trans. as if *et non.* **de summa belli iudicium:** 'the determination of the general plan of campaign'; how lit.? **suum, imperatoris:** in predicate after *esse;* 'was not their (business), but the commander's; *94d; 157d.*

[8] **satisfactione:** 'apology'. **exquisito:** 'sought out'. **per:** 'with the help of'.

[9] **ei:** 'in him'; *109a.* **maximam fidem:** 'the fullest confidence'. **ut . . . duceret:** 'so that he could lead'; explains *itinere; 203.4.*

[10] **milium . . . circuitu:** 'although with a detour of more than fifty miles', in order to avoid the dangerous defiles of the Doubs valley; see 39.6, notes 23-26. **milium quinquaginta:** sc. *passuum.* Why genitive? *100a; 129b.* **locis apertis:** 'through open country', marching first north, and then northeast, between the Jura and the Vosegus mountains; see Map 1; *145c.*

[11] **Septimo die:** Caesar had probably covered about 120 miles since leaving Vesontio. He was now in the valley of the Rhine, never previously entered by a Roman general with an army. **exploratoribus:** *327.*

[12] **nostris:** sc. *copiis.* **milibus:** *147c.*

[13] **XX:** read as *viginti; 36, 38b.*

Ariovistus suggests a conference, which is arranged.

42.1. Cognito Caesaris adventu, Ariovistus legatos ad eum mittit: *Quod[1] antea de colloquio postulasset, id per se fieri licere, quoniam propius accessisset, seque id sine periculo facere posse existimare.* **2.** Non respuit[2] condicionem Caesar, iamque eum ad sanitatem reverti arbitrabatur, cum id, quod antea petenti[3] denegasset, ultro[4] polliceretur; **3.** magnamque in spem veniebat, pro[5] suis tantis populique Romani in eum beneficiis, cognitis suis postulatis, fore,[6] uti pertinacia desisteret. Dies colloquio dictus est ex eo die quintus. **4.** Interim saepe cum legati ultro citroque[7] inter eos mitterentur, Ariovistus postulavit, ne quem peditem[8] ad colloquium Caesar adduceret: *Vereri se,[9] ne per insidias ab eo circumveniretur; uterque cum equitatu veniret;[10] alia ratione sese non esse venturum.* **5.** Caesar, quod neque colloquium[11] interposita causa tolli volebat, neque salutem suam Gallorum equitatui[12] committere audebat, commodissimum esse[13] statuit, omnibus equis Gallis equitibus detractis,[14] eo legionarios milites legionis decimae, cui[15] quam maxime confidebat, imponere, ut praesidium quam amicissimum, si[16] quid opus facto esset, haberet. **6.** Quod cum fieret,[17] non irridicule quidam ex militibus decimae legionis dixit: Plus,[18] quam pollicitus esset, Caesarem facere; pollicitum,[19] se in cohortis praetoriae loco decimam legionem habiturum, ad equum rescribere.

[1] **Quod:** the antecedent is *id; 212e.* **postulasset** (= *postulavisset*), **accessisset:** in translating

supply 'Caesar' in order to avoid using 'he' with reference to two persons. **per se:** 'so far as he was concerned'.

[2] **non respuit:** 'did not reject'. **ad sanitatem:** 'to his senses'; *157a*.

[3] **petenti:** sc. *sibi.* **denegasset:** 'he (Ariovistus) had refused'.

[4] **ultro:** 'of his own initiative'. **magnam . . . veniebat:** 'he was coming to have great hopes', we should say.

[5] **pro:** 'in return for'. **suis populique:** *157d.* Cf. chap. 35.2, notes 3-4.

[6] **fore:** after *spem,* as if Caesar had written *sperabat;* the subject is *uti . . . desistere; 225; 203.1.* **pertinacia:** 'obstinate course'; *127a.* **colloquio:** *112a.*

[7] **ultro citroque:** 'back and forth' between the headquarters of the two commanders. **mitterentur:** *185c.*

[8] **quem peditem:** 'any foot soldier'; *49a; 10d.*

[9] **Vereri se:** '(saying) that he was afraid'; *213b.* **ne:** 'that'; *202.*

[10] **veniret:** 'should come'; *veniat* in the direct form; *216.* **alia ratione:** 'on any other condition'; *136c.*

[11] **colloquium . . . tolli:** *223a.* **interposita causa:** 'by putting forward a pretext'; *144b6.*

[12] **Gallorum equitatui:** see chap. 15.1, note 2.

[13] **esse:** the subject is *imponere,* with *commodissimum,* 'the most expedient (thing)', in predicate; *222b; 148d.* **Gallis equitibus:** 'from the Gallic horsemen'; *109b.*

[14] **detractis:** *144b2.* **eo:** = *in eos,* 'on them'.

[15] **cui:** 'in which'; *105.* **quam:** *153c.* **imponere:** 'to mount'.

[16] **si . . . esset:** 'if there should be any need of action'. **quid:** *118b.* **facto:** *132a* (AG 411a, B 218.2).

[17] **Quod cum fieret:** 'While this was being done'; *185c.* **non irridicule:** 'not without wit'; *239g.* **quidam:** *168.*

[18] **Plus:** object of *facere;* 'was doing more' for the legion.

[19] **pollicitum:** 'having promised'; sc. *eum,* referring to Caesar, subject of *rescribere.* **in,** etc.: 'that he would consider ... as a body guard'.

Caesar and Ariovistus meet. Caesar justifies his demands.

43.1. Planities[1] erat magna et in ea tumulus terrenus satis grandis. Hic locus aequo fere spatio a castris Ariovisti et Caesaris aberat.[2] **2.** Eo, ut erat dictum,[3] ad colloquium venerunt. Legionem Caesar, quam equis devexerat,[4] passibus ducentis[5] ab eo tumulo constituit. Item equites Ariovisti pari intervallo[6] constiterunt. **3.** Ariovistus, ex equis ut colloquerentur et praeter se denos[7] ut ad colloquium adducerent, postulavit. **4.** Ubi eo ventum est,[8] Caesar initio orationis sua senatusque in eum beneficia[9] commemoravit, quod rex appellatus esset a senatu, quod amicus,[10] quod munera amplissime missa; quam rem[11] et paucis contigisse et pro magnis hominum officiis consuesse tribui docebat:[12] **5.** *illum, cum neque aditum[13] neque causam postulandi iustam haberet, beneficio ac liberalitate sua[14] ac senatus ea praemia consecutum.* **6.** Docebat etiam, quam veteres[15] quamque iustae causae necessitudinis ipsis[16] cum Aeduis intercederent, **7.** quae senatus consulta,[17] quotiens quamque honorifica, in eos facta essent, ut[18] omni tempore totius Galliae principatum Aedui tenuissent, prius etiam quam[19] nostram amicitiam appetissent: **8.** *Populi Romani hanc[20] esse consuetudinem, ut socios atque amicos non modo[21] sui nihil deperdere, sed gratia, dignitate, honore auctiores[22] velit esse; quod vero ad amicitiam populi Romani attulissent,[23] id eis eripi quis pati posset?* **9.** Postulavit[24] deinde eadem, quae legatis in mandatis dederat: *ne[25] aut Aeduis aut eorum sociis bellum inferret; obsides redderet; si nullam partem Germanorum domum remittere[26] posset, at ne quos amplius Rhenum transire pateretur.*

[1] **Planities:** 'plain' of Alsace, between the Vosges (*Vosegus*) mountains and the Rhine; *21a*. **erat:** *90a*. **tumulus terrenus:** 'an earthy mound', whose sides, free from rocks and ledges, furnished an easy ascent for horsemen. This is identified by Colonel Stoffel with the hill of Plettig, an elevation of oval shape about 24 miles southwest of Strasburg, between the villages of Epfig and Dambach; it rises in isolation more than 160 feet above the surrounding plain.

[2] **aequo fere spatio aberat:** 'was about equally distant'; how lit.? *147c*.

[3] **ut erat dictum:** 'as agreed'; how lit.?

[4] **equis devexerat:** 'had brought on horseback,' lit. 'by means of horses'; *131a*. **passibus:** *147c*.

[5] **ducentis:** *36, 37d*. How many feet in 200 paces? *243b*.

[6] **intervallo:** *138*. **ex equis:** 'on horseback'; *126c*.

[7] **denos:** 'ten men each'; *36; 85*. **adducerent:** *199a*.

[8] **Ubi eo ventum est:** 'when they (had) come to that place'; *73d*. **initio:** *147b*. **sua senatusque:** *157d*.

[9] **beneficia:** explained by the appositional *quod*-clauses following; see chap. 35.2, notes 3-5. **rex:** *88a*.

[10] **amicus:** *89a*. **munera:** what these 'presents' were, we do not know. Gifts considered suitable for a 'king' were a golden crown, an ivory scepter, a chair of state, and embroidered robes. **amplissime:** 'in richest measure'; *34a*.

[11] **missa** [essent]: *214b*. **quam rem:** 'and that this recognition'; *167*. **et . . . et:** *233a*. **paucis:** *105; 154a*. **pro magnis officiis:** 'in return for great services'.

[12] **docebat:** 'he stated'. **illum ... consecutum** [esse]: *213b*.

[13] **aditum:** '(way of) approach' to the Senate.

[14] **sua:** *157b*. **praemia:** 'distinctions'. No special reason is known why Ariovistus, as implied by Caesar, should have sought the recognition of Rome.

[15] **veteres:** *26a*. **necessitudinis:** 'of close relationship'; *12d*.

[16] **ipsis:** i.e. *Romanis*; we should say 'existed between the Romans and the Aeduans'. **intercederent:** *204.3*. **quae:** *48b*.

[17] **consulta:** 'decrees'. **quamque:** = *et quam*. **honourifica:** 'complimentary'; *31*. **in eos facta essent:** 'had been passed in their behalf'; *204.2*.

[18] **ut:** 'how'; *204.3*. **omni tempore:** see chap. 11.3, note 7.

[19] **prius etiam quam:** 'even before'; *189a; 220*. **nostram:** *157c*.

[20] **hanc:** for *hoc; 164c*. **ut . . . velit:** 'to desire'; explaining *hanc; 203.4*.

[21] **non modo – sed:** *236d*. **sui nihil deperdere:** 'should lose nothing of what they had', lit. 'of their own'; *97a; 154a*. **dignitate:** 'in prestige'; *142a*.

[22] **auctiores:** 'the more abounding'. **quod . . . posset:** i.e. *quis posset pati id, quod . . . attulissent, eis eripi?* The reference is to the power and independence of the Aeduans in former times.

[23] **attulissent:** 'had brought'; *69b*. **eis:** dative, 'from them'; *109b* (AG 381, B 188.2d). **posset:** *possit* in the direct form; *179b2*.

[24] **Postulavit eadem:** 'he made the same demands'; *117a*. **dederat:** 'he had entrusted'; see chap. 35; *67a*.

[25] **Ne . . . inferret, redderet, pateretur:** explaining *eadem;* 216 (AG 588, B 316).

[26] **remittere:** 'send back'. **posset:** *218.1a*. **at:** 'at any rate'; *236a*. **quos:** *168*.

The attitude of Ariovistus is uncompromising and defiant.

44.1. Ariovistus ad postulata[1] Caesaris pauca respondit, de suis[2] virtutibus multa praedicavit: **2.** [3]*Transisse Rhenum sese non sua sponte, sed rogatum et arcessitum[4] a Gallis; non sine[5] magna spe magnisque praemiis domum propinquosque reliquisse; sedes habere in Gallia ab ipsis[6] concessas, obsides ipsorum voluntate datos; stipendium capere iure[7] belli, quod victores victis imponere consuerint.* **3.** [8]*Non sese Gallis,[9] sed Gallos sibi bellum intulisse; omnes Galliae civitates ad se oppugnandum venisse ac contra se castra habuisse;[10] eas omnes copias a se uno proelio pulsas ac superatas esse.* **4.** *Si iterum experiri velint, se iterum paratum[11] esse decertare; si pace uti[12] velint, iniquum esse de stipendio recusare, quod sua[13] voluntate ad id tempus pependerint.* **5.**

[14]Amicitiam populi Romani sibi ornamento[15] et praesidio, non detrimento, esse oportere,[16] atque se hac spe petisse. Si per[17] populum Romanum stipendium remittatur et dediticii subtrahantur,[18] non minus libenter sese recusaturum populi Romani amicitiam, quam appetierit. **6.** *[19]Quod[20] multitudinem Germanorum in Galliam traducat, id se sui muniendi,[21] non Galliae impugnandae causa, facere; eius rei testimonium[22] esse, quod nisi rogatus non venerit, et quod bellum non intulerit, sed defenderit.[23]* **7.** *[24]Se prius in Galliam[25] venisse quam populum Romanum. Numquam ante hoc tempus exercitum populi Romani Galliae provinciae finibus[26] egressum.* **8.** *Quid sibi vellet? Cur in suas possessiones veniret? Provinciam suam hanc[27] esse Galliam, sicut illam nostram. Ut[28] ipsi concedi non oporteret, si in nostros fines impetum faceret, sic item nos esse iniquos, quod in suo iure se interpellaremus.[29]* **9.** *[30]Quod[31] fratres a senatu Aeduos appellatos diceret, non se tam barbarum neque tam imperitum[32] esse rerum, ut non sciret, neque bello[33] Allobrogum proximo Aeduos Romanis auxilium tulisse, neque ipsos[34] in his contentionibus, quas Aedui secum et cum Sequanis habuissent, auxilio populi Romani usos esse.* **10.** *[35]Debere se suspicari,[36] simulata Caesarem amicitia, quod exercitum in Gallia habeat, sui opprimendi causa[37] habere.* **11.** *Qui[38] nisi decedat, atque exercitum deducat ex his regionibus, sese illum non pro amico, sed pro hoste, habiturum.[39]* **12.** *Quod si eum interfecerit, multis sese nobilibus principibusque populi Romani gratum[40] esse facturum (id se ab ipsis, per eorum nuntios,[41] compertum habere), quorum omnium gratiam atque amicitiam eius[42] morte redimere posset.* **13.** *Quod si decessisset et liberam[43] possessionem Galliae sibi tradidisset, magno se illum[44] praemio remuneraturum et, quaecumque bella geri vellet, sine ullo eius[45] labore et periculo confecturum.*

---

[1] **postulata:** 'demands'. **pauca:** object of *respondit; 154a.*

[2] **suis:** emphatic; *157b.* **virtutibus:** 'merits'. **multa praedicavit:** 'had much to say'; *84.* How lit.?

[3] **Direct form:** *Transii* Rhenum non *mea* sponte, sed *rogatus* et *arcessitus* a Gallis; non sine magna spe magnisque praemiis domum propinquosque *reliqui*; sedes *habeo* in Gallia ab ipsis concessas, obsides ipsorum voluntate datos; stipendium *capio* iure belli, quod victores victis imponere *consuerunt.*

[4] **rogatum et arcessitum:** 'because he had been asked' etc.; *227a1* (AG 496, B 337.2f).

[5] **non sine:** *239g.*

[6] **ipsis:** the Gauls. **concessas:** 'which had been ceded'; *227a4.* **obsides:** i.e. *se habere sedes et obsides; 238a.* **voluntate:** *138.*

[7] **iure:** 'in accordance with the rights' (lit. 'right') 'of war'; *13g; 136c.* **quod:** the antecedent is *stipendium.* **victis:** 'the vanquished'; *227a4.*

[8] **Direct form:** Non *ego* Gallis, sed *Galli mihi* bellum *intulerunt*; omnes Galliae civitates ad *me* oppugnandum *venerunt* ac contra *me* castra *habuerunt*; eae omnes *copiae* a *me* uno proelio *pulsae* ac *superatae sunt.* Si (Galli) iterum experiri *volunt*, iterum *paratus sum* decertare; si pace uti *volunt*, iniquum *est* de stipendio recusare, quod sua voluntate adhuc *pependerunt.*

[9] **sese Gallis . . . Gallos sibi:** *239b.*

[10] **castra habuisse:** 'had fought'; how lit.? **uno proelio:** see chap. 31.12, note 44.

[11] **paratum decertare:** 'ready to fight it out'; *148c; 221c.*

[12] **uti:** 'to enjoy'; followed by what case? *131c.* **iniquum:** 'unfair'. Why neuter? *148d.* **de stipendio recusare:** 'to refuse to pay the tribute'; how lit.?

[13] **sua:** i.e. of the Gauls; they, however, told a different story, as we learn from chap. 31.10.

[14] **Direct form:** Amicitiam populi Romani *mihi* ornamento et praesidio, non detrimento, esse *oportet*, atque (eam) hac spe *petii.* Si per populum Romanum stipendium *remittetur* et dediticii *subtrahentur*, non minus libenter *recusabo* (206) populi Romani amicitiam, quam *appetii.*

[15] **sibi ornamento:** *112b* (AG 382.1, B 191.2a). **ornamento**, etc.: 'ought to be a source of

prestige and a protection, not a loss'.

[16] **oportere:** the subject is *amicitiam . . . esse.*

[17] **per:** *123a.*

[18] **subtrahantur:** 'should be taken from under' his control. The *dediticii* were 'prisoners of war', held as hostages to force the payment of tribute.

[19] **Direct form:** Quod multitudinem Germanorum in Galliam *traduco,* id *mei* (39) muniendi (*causa*), non Galliae impugnandae causa, *facio;* eius rei testimonium *est,* quod nisi rogatus non *veni,* et quod bellum non *intuli,* sed *defendi.*

[20] **Quod,** etc.: 'In regard to his bringing over', etc.; *198c.* **multitudinem:** 120,000, according to chap. 31, note 17.

[21] **sui muniendi** [causa]: 'in order to protect himself'; *230.1.*

[22] **testimonium:** 'proof'; in predicate with *esse,* to which the *quod*-clauses stand as subject. **quod:** 'the fact that'; *198b.* **nisi rogatus:** 'without being asked.'

[23] **defenderit:** 'had acted on the defensive', lit. 'warded off (war)'.

[24] **Direct form:** Ego prius in Galliam *veni* quam *populus Romanus.* Numquam ante hoc tempus *exercitus* populi Romani Galliae provinciae finibus *egressus est.* Quid *tibi vis?* Cur in *meas* possessiones *venis? Provincia mea est haec* Gallia, sicut *illa* (Gallia) *vestra* (provincia est). Ut *mihi* concedi non *oporteat,* si in *vestros* fines impetum *faciam* (207.1), sic item *vos estis iniqui,* quod *me* in *meo* iure *interpellatis.*

[25] **Galliam:** Celtic Gaul (287b), as in 44.8, note 28; the Province, mentioned in 44.7, note 26, as stated elsewhere, had been under Roman control since 121 B.C.; *290.*

[26] **finibus:** *127a.* **Quid sibi vellet:** 'what did Caesar mean?' How lit.? *217a.*

[27] **hanc Galliam:** 'this (part of) Gaul', toward the Rhine.

[28] **Ut:** 'As.' **ipsi:** *Ariovisto.* **concedi non oporteret:** 'no concession ought to be made'; how lit.?

[29] **se interpellaremus:** 'we were interfering with him'.

[30] **Direct form:** Quod fratres a senatu Aeduos appellatos (*esse*) *dicis,* non tam *barbarus* neque tam *imperitus* rerum *sum,* ut non *sciam,* neque bello Allobrogum proximo Aeduos Romanis auxilium tulisse, neque ipsos in his contentionibus, quas Aedui *mecum* et cum Sequanis *habuerunt,* auxilio populi Romani usos esse.

[31] **Quod – diceret:** 'with reference to his saying'. **fratres:** *88a.* Cf. chap. 33.2, note 6.

[32] **imperitum rerum:** 'unversed in affairs'; *102* (AG 349a, B 204.1). **ut:** *197b.*

[33] **bello:** only three years before, in 61 B.C.; *147b.*

[34] **ipsos, Aedui:** trans. as if *Aeduos, ei.* **contentionibus:** 'struggles'.

[35] **Direct form:** Debeo suspicari, simulata *te* amicitia, quod exercitum in Gallia *habes, mei* opprimendi habere. Nisi *decedes,* atque exercitum *deduces* ex his regionibus, *te* non pro amico, sed pro hoste, *habebo.* Quod si *te interfecero,* multis nobilibus principibusque populi Romani gratum *faciam* (id ab ipsis, per eorum nuntios, compertum *habeo*), quorum omnium gratiam atque amicitiam *tua* morte redimere *possum.* Quod si *decesseris* et liberam possessionem Galliae *mihi tradideris,* magno *te* praemio *remunerabor* et, quaecumque bella geri *voles,* sine ullo *tuo* labore et periculo *conficiam.*

[36] **Debere se suspicari:** 'that he had good reason to suspect'; how lit.? **simulata amicitia:** 'under the guise of friendship'; *144b5.*

[37] **sui opprimendi causa:** 'in order to crush him'; *230.1.* **habere:** sc. *eum,* 'was keeping (it there)'.

[38] **Qui:** Caesar 167. **deducat:** 'withdraw'. **regionibus:** 'regions'; *81.*

[39] **habiturum:** sc. *esse.* **Quod:** 'Moreover'; *118d.*

[40] **gratum:** 'a kindness'. **id:** 'that fact'; *160c.*

[41] **nuntios:** 'agents' rather than 'messengers'. **compertum habere:** trans. as if *comperisse; 229a* (AG 497b, B 337.7). **quorum omnium:** 'of all of whom'; *97c.*

[42] **eius:** Caesar's. It is not impossible that Ariovistus had been in communication with Caesar's enemies; but whether he spoke the truth or not, he was evidently familiar with the party strifes and jealousies at this time in Roman politics. **Quod:** 'On the other hand'; *118d.*

[43] **liberam:** i.e. 'without interference'. **Galliae:** Celtic Gaul, as above.

[44] **illum:** trans. as if *Caesarem.* **remuneraturum** [esse]: 'he would compensate'; *61a1.* **quaecumque:** *50a.*

[45] **eius:** 'on the part of Caesar'; how lit.? **confecturum** [esse]: if Caesar will withdraw, Ariovistus will fight his battles for him. The attitude of Ariovistus seems somewhat less defiant than in his former reply, sent by messengers and summarised in chap. 36.

Caesar declines to make any concessions.

45.1. Multa a Caesare in eam sententiam[1] dicta sunt, quare negotio[2] desistere non posset: *[3]Neque[4] suam neque populi Romani consuetudinem pati, uti [5] optime meritos socios desereret, neque se iudicare, Galliam potius esse Ariovisti[6] quam populi Romani.* **2.** *Bello superatos esse Arvernos et Rutenos[7] a Quinto Fabio Maximo, quibus[8] populus Romanus ignovisset neque in provinciam redegisset neque stipendium imposuisset.* **3.** *[9]Quod si antiquissimum quodque tempus[10] spectari oporteret, populi Romani iustissimum esse in Gallia imperium; si iudicium senatus observari[11] oporteret, liberam debere esse Galliam, quam, bello victam,[12] suis legibus uti voluisset.*

[1] **in eam sententiam:** lit. 'to this purport'; we should say 'to show'.

[2] **negotio:** *127a.* **posset:** *204.3* (AG 574, B 300.1).

[3] **Direct form:** Neque *mea* neque populi Romani *consuetudo patitur,* uti optime meritos socios *deseram,* neque *iudico,* Galliam potius esse *tuam* quam populi Romani. Bello *superati sunt* Arverni et *Ruteni* a Quinto Fabio Maximo, quibus populus Romanus *ignovit,* neque (*eos*) in provinciam *redegit,* neque (*eis*) stipendium *imposuit.*

[4] **Neque,** etc.: *213b.* **suam, populi:** *157d.*

[5] **uti . . . desereret:** after *pati; 199a6.* **neque:** 'and not'.

[6] **esse Ariovisti:** 'belonged to Ariovistus'; *94d* (AG 343b, B 198.3). **Bello:** *131a.*

[7] **Arvernos, Rutenos:** conquered in 121 B.C., but not included in the Province excepting a small division of the Ruteni, called *Ruteni provinciales* (VII, 7); see Map GALLIA.

[8] **quibus:** *105.* **ignovisset:** the Romans with good reason had 'pardoned' them – their country, lying beyond the Cévennes mountains, could have been held only with the greatest difficulty. **neque . . . redegisset:** 'and (whom) it had not reduced'.

[9] **Direct Form:** Quod si antiquissimum quodque tempus spectari *oportet,* populi Romani iustissimum *est* in Gallia imperium; si iudicium senatus observari *oportet, libera debet* esse *Gallia,* quam, bello victam, suis legibus uti *voluit.*

[10] **antiquissimum quodque tempus:** 'priority of time,' lit. 'each earliest time'; *170a; 49a* (AG 313b, B 252.5c).

[11] **observari:** 'to be regarded'; *357b.*

[12] **victam:** 'although it had been conquered'; *227a3.* **suis:** 'its own', referring to the subject of *uti.* **voluisset:** i.e. *senatus voluisset.*

The conference is abruptly ended by an attack of German cavalry.

46.1. Dum haec in colloquio geruntur,[1] Caesari nuntiatum est, equites Ariovisti propius tumulum[2] accedere et ad nostros adequitare,[3] lapides telaque in nostras conicere. **2.** Caesar loquendi finem facit seque ad suos recepit suisque imperavit, ne quod omnino telum[4] in hostes reicerent. **3.** Nam etsi sine ullo periculo legionis delectae[5] cum equitatu proelium fore videbat, tamen committendum[6] non putabat, ut, pulsis hostibus,[7] dici posset, eos ab se per fidem in colloquio circumventos. **4.** Postea quam[8] in vulgus militum elatum est, qua arrogantia in colloquio Ariovistus usus omni Gallia Romanis[9] interdixisset, impetumque ut[10] in nostros eius equites fecissent, eaque res colloquium ut diremisset, multo maior alacritas studiumque pugnandi[11] maius exercitui iniectum est.

[1] **geruntur:** trans. by a past tense; *190a.*

[2] **tumulum:** referred to in chap. 43.1, note 1; *123b* (AG 432a, B 141.3). The German cavalry were about a thousand Roman feet from the hill (chap. 43.2, note 5), the tenth legion at an equal distance.

[3] **adequitare:** 'were riding up (to)'.

[4] **ne quod omnino telum:** 'any missile at all'; *168.*

[5] **legionis delectae**: mounted on horseback (chap. 42.5); 'to the legion', we should say; *102*.
[6] **committendum** [esse] . . . **eos**: 'he thought that he ought not to allow it to be said that, if the enemy were routed, they'; how lit.?
[7] **hostibus**: *144b6*. **per fidem**: 'through a pledge of good faith', used to entrap them.
[8] **Postea quam**: *188a*. **vulgus**: 'rank and file'; *6b*. **elatum est**: *69b*. **qua arrogantia usus**: 'with what arrogance'; how lit.? *131c*.
[9] **Gallia**: *127a*. **Romanis**: why dative? *109c*. **interdixisset,** etc.: 'had denied to the Romans all right to be in Gaul' (lit. 'from all Gaul'); *204.2*.
[10] **ut**: 'how'. **fecissent, diremisset**: *204.3*.
[11] **pugnandi**: 'for fighting', we should say; *230.1*. **exercitui**: *107a*. **iniectum est**: 'were' (lit. 'was') 'infused'; *172b*.

Ariovistus reopens negotiations, but throws Caesar's envoys into chains.

47.1. Biduo[1] post Ariovistus ad Caesarem legatos mittit: *²Velle³ se de his rebus, quae inter eos agi coeptae neque perfectae essent, agere cum eo; uti⁴ aut iterum colloquio diem constitueret aut, si id minus⁵ vellet, e suis legatis aliquem ad se mitteret.* **2.** Colloquendi Caesari causa visa non est,[6] et eo magis, quod pridie eius diei[7] Germani retineri non potuerant, quin in nostros tela conicerent. **3.** Legatum e suis[8] sese magno cum periculo ad eum missurum et hominibus feris obiecturum existimabat. **4.** Commodissimum visum est[9] Gaium Valerium Procillum, C.[10] Valerii Caburi filium, summa virtute et humanitate[11] adulescentem, cuius pater a C. Valerio Flacco civitate[12] donatus erat, et propter fidem et propter linguae Gallicae scientiam, qua multa[13] iam Ariovistus longinqua consuetudine[14] utebatur, et quod in eo peccandi Germanis causa non esset,[15] ad eum mittere, et una M. Metium, qui hospitio Ariovisti utebatur.[16] **5.** His mandavit, ut, quae diceret Ariovistus, cognoscerent et ad se referrent. **6.** Quos cum apud se in castris Ariovistus conspexisset, exercitu suo praesente conclamavit:[17] Quid ad se venirent? an speculandi causa?[18] Conantes dicere prohibuit et in catenas[19] coniecit.

[1] **Biduo**: *140*. **post**: here an adverb.
[2] **Direct form**: *Volo de his rebus, quae inter nos agi coeptae neque perfectae sunt, tecum agere;* (*rogo*) *uti aut iterum colloquio diem constituas, aut, si id minus velis, e tuis legatis aliquem ad me mittas.*
[3] **Velle,** etc.: *212c4; 213b*. **coeptae** [essent]: *72b,c*.
[4] **uti,** etc.: i.e. *se rogare, uti (Caesar)* . . . *constitueret*; the idea of asking is implied in *Velle*, etc.; *199a*.
[5] **minus**: trans. as if *non*. **e legatis**: *97d*. **suis**: *Caesaris*. **aliquem**: *49a*. Ariovistus wanted Caesar to send not a messenger but one of his highest officers, probably in order to hold him as a hostage.
[6] **causa visa non est**: 'there did not seem (to be any) reason'; *90b*. **et eo magis**: 'especially,' lit. 'and on this account the more'; *eo* being explained by the following *quod*-clause; *135a*.
[7] **diei**: *94c* (AG 359b2, B 201.3a). **quin . . . conicerent**: 'from hurling'; *201a* (AG 558, B 295.3).
[8] **Legatum e suis**: 'an envoy from his staff'; one of his officers. **sese . . . missurum** [esse]: 'that it would be exceedingly hazardous for him to send to Ariovistus'; how lit.? **magno cum periculo**: *136a*.
[9] **visum est,** etc.: *visum est mittere Gaium Valerium Procillum,* etc.; *222a*.
[10] **C.** = *Gai; 19a*. **Valerii**: *8a*. **virtute**: *143a*.
[11] **humanitate**: 'refinement'. **adulescentem**: 'a young man'. **C. Valerio Flacco**: governor of the Province of Gaul in 83 B.C.
[12] **civitate**: Roman 'citizenship' was often conferred upon foreigners who had rendered some service. In this case the Gaul *Caburus* took the First Name and Clan Name of *C. Valerius Flaccus,* to whom he was indebted for the distinction, and was known as *C. Valerius Caburus; 19a, b*. **donatus erat**: 'had been presented'.

[13] **qua multa Ariovistus utebatur:** 'which Ariovistus spoke fluently'; how lit.?
[14] **consuetudine:** 'practice'; *135a*. **in eo:** 'in his case.' **peccandi causa:** '(any) reason for offering violence', lit. 'of doing wrong'; for Procillus was a Gaul.
[15] **non esset:** 'because (as he thought) there was not'; *183a*.
[16] **utebatur:** 'enjoyed'. Metius may have been received and entertained by Ariovistus in the course of the negotiations which in 59 B.C. culminated in the recognition of the German ruler by the Roman Senate (chap. 35.2).
[17] **conclamavit:** 'he called out loudly'. **Quid:** 'why'; *118e*. **venirent:** *217a*.
[18] **an speculandi causa:** '(was it) in order to act as spies'; *179a2*. How lit.? **Conantes** [eos], etc.: 'when they tried to speak he stopped them', preventing explanation because he wished his army to believe that they were spies; *227a5*.
[19] **catenas:** 'chains'.

Ariovistus moves camp so as to cut off Caesar's supplies.

48.1. Eodem die castra promovit[1] et milibus passuum sex a Caesaris castris[2] sub monte consedit. **2.** Postridie eius diei praeter[3] castra Caesaris suas copias traduxit et milibus passuum duobus ultra eum castra[4] fecit eo consilio, uti frumento commeatuque, qui[5] ex Sequanis et Aeduis supportaretur, Caesarem intercluderet. **3.** Ex eo die dies continuos quinque Caesar pro castris suas copias produxit et aciem instructam[6] habuit, ut, si vellet Ariovistus proelio contendere, ei potestas non deesset.[7] **4.** Ariovistus his omnibus diebus[8] exercitum castris continuit, equestri proelio[9] cotidie contendit. **5.** Genus[10] hoc erat pugnae, quo se Germani exercuerant. Equitum milia erant[11] sex, totidem numero pedites velocissimi ac fortissimi, quos[12] ex omni copia singuli singulos suae salutis causa delegerant; cum his in proeliis versabantur.[13] **6.** Ad eos[14] se equites recipiebant; hi, si quid erat durius, concurrebant, si qui,[15] graviore vulnere accepto, equo deciderat, circumsistebant;[16] **7.** si quo erat longius prodeundum aut celerius recipiendum, tanta erat horum exercitatione celeritas,[17] ut iubis[18] equorum sublevati cursum adaequarent.

[1] **promovit:** '(Ariovistus) moved forward'. **milibus:** *147c*. How far by our measurement? *243a,b*.
[2] **Caesaris castris:** Caesar's camp is located by Colonel Stoffel between Gemar and Ostheim, about 35 miles southwest of Strassburg. See Map 4, LARGE CAMP. **diei:** *94c*.
[3] **praeter . . . traduxit:** Ariovistus's line of march, as suggested on Map 4, probably skirted or traversed the foothills of the Vosges in such a way that Caesar could not attack him while executing this movement.
[4] **castra:** the camp of Ariovistus, probably at the place so marked on Map 4, was favourably located for defence. **uti . . . intercluderet:** explains *consilio*; *196a*. **frumento:** *127a* (AG 401, B 214.2). Ariovistus thought that by cutting off Caesar's supplies he could force Caesar to retire, or else to fight on ground of his own choosing.
[5] **qui:** *163c*. **supportaretur:** subjunctive by attraction; *220* (AG 593, B 324.1).
[6] **aciem instructam:** 'his army drawn up' in triple line, as indicated on Map 4, CAESAR'S FIRST POSITION; *337a*. **ut:** 'so that'. **vellet:** *220*.
[7] **ei . . . deesset:** 'he did not lack opportunity'; how lit.? *197a*; *239g*.
[8] **diebus:** *147c*. **exercitum:** the German infantry, as we see from the next line. **castris:** 'within the camp'; *131a* (AG 409, B 218).
[9] **equestri proelio:** 'with cavalry skirmishing'. **contendit:** *238a*.
[10] **Genus pugnae:** 'The method of fighting'. **hoc:** *161a*.
[11] **erant:** *90a*. **numero:** *142a*; *85*. **pedites:** sc. *erant*; *10d*. **velocissimi:** 'the fastest'.
[12] **quos,** etc.: 'whom they' (the horsemen) 'had chosen from the entire force, each one (selecting) a foot-soldier'; how lit.? **singulos:** agrees with *quos*; *36*.
[13] **versabantur:** '(the horsemen) associated themselves'.
[14] **eos, hi:** the foot-soldiers. **si . . . erat, concurrebant:** general condition of fact; *205.2*. **quid**

durius: 'unusually serious difficulty'; *153a*. How lit.? **concurrebant**: 'they would rush to the rescue'.

[15] **qui**: 'any one'; *49a, b*. **vulnere**: *13e*. **equo**: *127a*. **deciderat**: 'had fallen'; *205.4*.

[16] **circumsistebant**: 'they would gather round him'. **si quo**, etc.: 'if it was necessary to advance in any direction unusually far, or to retreat with special swiftness'; *73e; 153a*.

[17] **celeritas**: 'swiftness'.

[18] **iubis**: 'by the manes.' **sublevati**: 'supporting themselves'; *174*. **cursum**: 'they kept up with the running' of the horses. Caesar afterwards employed German horsemen as mercenaries, and they rendered him very effective service, as at the siege of Alesia (VII, 80).

Caesar fortifies a camp beyond Ariovistus, reopening the road.

49.1. Ubi eum[1] castris se tenere Caesar intellexit, ne diutius commeatu prohiberetur, ultra eum locum,[2] quo in loco Germani consederant, circiter passus sexcentos ab his, castris[3] idoneum locum delegit acieque triplici instructa ad eum locum venit. **2.** Primam et secundam aciem in armis esse, tertiam castra[4] munire iussit. **3.** Hic locus ab hoste circiter passus sexcentos, uti dictum est, aberat. Eo circiter hominum[5] numero sedecim milia expedita cum omni equitatu Ariovistus misit, quae copiae[6] nostros terrerent et munitione prohiberent. **4.** Nihilo setius[7] Caesar, ut ante constituerat, duas acies hostem propulsare, tertiam opus perficere iussit. **5.** Munitis castris, duas[8] ibi legiones reliquit et partem auxiliorum; quattuor reliquas[9] in castra maiora reduxit.

[1] **eum**: Ariovistus. **se**: object of *tenere*. **ne . . . prohiberetur**: see chap. 48.2, notes 4, 5; *196a*.

[2] **eum locum**: Map 4, CAMP OF ARIOVISTUS. **loco**: *165a*.

[3] **castris**: *108a*. **idoneum**: 'suitable'. **acie triplici**: *337a*.

[4] **castra**: *332*. This camp on Map 4 is called the 'Small Camp', *castra minora*, in order to distinguish it from the 'Large Camp', *castra maiora*. The two camps were not far from two miles apart; both were on somewhat higher ground. Caesar's object in establishing the smaller camp, which was a little more than half a mile from the Germans, was to keep open the road to Vesontio, and so maintain communication with his base of supplies. **munire**: 'fortify'; *333*.

[5] **hominum . . . expedita**: trans. as if *sedecim milia hominum expeditorum*. **expedita**: 'light-armed'.

[6] **quae copiae**: 'in order that these forces'; *193a*.

[7] **Nihilo setius**: 'Nevertheless', lit. 'by nothing the less'; *140*.

[8] **duas**: i.e. *primam et secundam*. **propulsare**: 'to ward off'.

[9] **reliquas**: sc. *legiones*. How many men, probably, in the six legions? *307b, e*.

The Germans, Caesar hears, dare not fight before the new moon.

50.1. Proximo die, instituto suo,[1] Caesar e castris utrisque copias suas eduxit, paulumque a maioribus castris progressus aciem[2] instruxit, hostibus pugnandi potestatem fecit. **2.** Ubi ne[3] tum quidem eos prodire intellexit, circiter meridiem exercitum in castra reduxit. Tum demum Ariovistus partem suarum copiarum, quae[4] castra minora oppugnaret, misit. **3.** Acriter[5] utrimque usque ad vesperum pugnatum est. Solis occasu[6] suas copias Ariovistus, multis et illatis et acceptis vulneribus, in castra reduxit. **4.** Cum ex[7] captivis quaereret Caesar, quam ob rem Ariovistus proelio non decertaret,[8] hanc reperiebat causam, quod apud Germanos ea consuetudo esset,[9] ut matres, familiae eorum sortibus[10] et vaticinationibus declararent, utrum proelium committi ex usu,[11] esset necne; *eas ita dicere,* **5.** *Non*[12] *esse fas Germanos superare, si ante novam lunam proelio contendissent.*

[1] **instituto suo:** 'in accordance with his usual practice' (chap. 48.3); *136c.* **utrisque:** *51.*

[2] **aciem:** Map 4, CAESAR'S SECOND POSITION. **potestatem fecit:** 'gave an opportunity'.

[3] **ne ... quidem:** *237c.* **prodire:** *68b.* **meridiem:** 'midday'.

[4] **quae:** trans. as if *ut ea; 193a.*

[5] **Acriter – pugnatum est:** 'Fiercely the battle raged'; *73d.* **utrimque:** 'on both sides'.

[6] **Solis occasu:** 'At sunset'; *147a.*

[7] **ex:** *116c.* **quam ob rem:** 'for what reason'; *204.2.* How lit.?

[8] **proelio non decertaret:** 'would not fight a decisive battle'; *131a.* How lit.? Ariovistus had used only a part of his forces. **causam:** explained by the following appositional *quod*-clause; *198b.*

[9] **esset:** *214b.* **matres familiae:** 'matrons', married women who were believed to have prophetic powers.

[10] **sortibus:** 'by means of lots', consisting of bits of wood from a branch of a fruit-bearing tree, which were scattered at random over a white cloth and then picked up; *17c.* **vaticinationibus:** 'prophetic utterances,' inspired by "eddies of rivers and whirlings and noises of currents". **declararent:** *203.2.* **utrum . . . necne:** 'whether . . . or not'; *204.1* (AG 335n, B 300.4a).

[11] **ex usu:** 'expedient'; how lit.? **eas,** etc.: *213b.*

[12] **Non,** etc.: indirect discourse, depending on *dicere.* **fas:** 'predestined'. **superare:** 'should be victorious'. **novam lunam:** 'the new moon' of September 18, 58 B.C., according to modern computations. The ancient German superstition about the influence of the moon still lingers in many places, particularly in respect to commencing certain farming operations "in the old of the moon".

MAP 4

The Battle with Ariovistus

Book I, 49–53 To face page 120

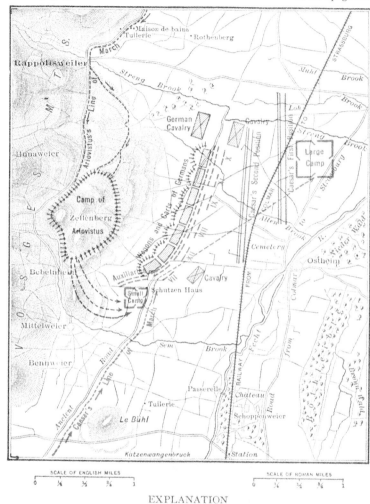

SCALE OF ENGLISH MILES

0   ¼   ½   ¾   1

SCALE OF ROMAN MILES

0   ¼   ½   ¾   1

EXPLANATION

Caesar, marching from the south, encamped north of Modern Ostheim (chap. 48, l. 2). Ariovistus, marching from the north, encamped on Zellenberg.

Taking advantage of their superstition, Caesar forces an engagement.

51.1. Postridie eius diei[1] Caesar praesidio utrisque castris, quod[2] satis esse visum est, reliquit; omnes alarios in conspectu hostium pro castris minoribus constituit, quod minus multitudine[3] militum legionariorum pro hostium numero valebat, ut ad speciem[4] alariis uteretur; ipse, triplici[5] instructa acie, usque ad castra hostium accessit. **2.** Tum demum necessario[6] Germani suas copias castris eduxerunt generatimque[7] constituerunt paribus intervallis, Harudes, Marcomanos, Tribocos, Vangiones, Nemetes, Sedusios, Suebos, omnemque aciem suam raedis[8] et carris circumdederunt,[9] ne qua spes in fuga relinqueretur. **3.** Eo mulieres[10] imposuerunt, quae in proelium proficiscentes passis manibus[11] flentes implorabant, ne se in servitutem Romanis traderent.

[1] **diei:** *94c.* The date was about September 14. **praesidio utrisque castris:** a dative of purpose and a dative of indirect object: 'as a garrison for each camp'; how lit.? *112a; 104a.*
[2] **quod:** as antecedent sc. *id,* object of *reliquit.* **alarios:** 'auxiliaries'; the light-armed troops, called *alarii* because usually stationed on the wings (*alae*) of an army; *308.*
[3] **minus multitudine valebat:** 'was weaker in respect to his force'; how lit.? **pro:** 'in comparison with'.
[4] **ad speciem:** 'for show' in order to hide from the enemy his weakness in heavy infantry; Ariovistus would take the *alarios* for *legionarios.*
[5] **triplici acie:** the front formed by the legions must have been at least a mile long. The probable arrangement of the legions in order of battle is indicated in Map 4; in the rear line only two cohorts to each legion are shown, for the reason that one cohort was probably drawn off for the guard duty indicated at the beginning of this chapter (*praesidio*); *337a.*
[6] **necessario:** 'of necessity'. **castris:** *127a.*
[7] **generatim:** 'by tribes', the soldiers of each tribe being formed into a body by themselves. **intervallis:** *138.*
[8] **raedis:** 'with wagons', probably covered.
[9] **circumdederunt:** 'surrounded', on the rear and wings, as indicated in Map 4. **qua:** *168.* **Eo:** 'thereon', upon the wagons and carts.
[10] **mulieres:** *11c.* **proficiscentes:** sc. *eos; 227a4.*
[11] **passis manibus:** 'with outstretched hands'; *144b2.* **flentes:** *227b.*

Desperate fighting, hand-to-hand; the Roman left, wavering, is reinforced.

52.1. Caesar singulis[1] legionibus singulos legatos et quaestorem praefecit, uti eos testes[2] suae quisque virtutis haberet; **2.** ipse a dextro cornu,[3] quod eam partem minime firmam hostium esse animadverterat, proelium commisit. **3.** Ita[4] nostri acriter in hostes, signo dato, impetum fecerunt, itaque[5] hostes repente celeriterque procurrerunt, ut spatium pila[6] in hostes coniciendi non daretur. **4.** Reiectis pilis, comminus gladiis[7] pugnatum est. At Germani, celeriter ex consuetudine sua phalange[8] facta, impetus gladiorum exceperunt.[9] **5.** Reperti sunt complures nostri, qui in phalanga[10] insilirent et scuta manibus revellerent et desuper vulnerarent. **6.** Cum hostium acies a sinistro cornu[11] pulsa atque in fugam conversa esset,[12] a dextro cornu vehementer multitudine suorum nostram aciem premebant. **7.** Id cum animadvertisset P. Crassus[13] adulescens, qui equitatui praeerat, quod expeditior erat quam ei,[14] qui inter aciem versabantur, tertiam aciem laborantibus[15] nostris subsidio misit.

[1] **singulis,** etc.: Caesar had six legions (*307e*). Over each of five legions he put a lieutenant,

and over the sixth he placed the quaestor. What were the quaestor's ordinary duties? *313b, 251b.*

[2] **testes**: 'as witnesses'; *115a.* **quisque**: *170b.*

[3] **a dextro cornu**: 'on the right wing'; *126c.* **eam partem hostium**: the German left wing, opposite the Roman right. **minime firmam**: 'the weakest'.

[4] **Ita**: modifies *acriter*; *34a.* **signo**: given on the trumpet; *326a1.*

[5] **itaque**: = *et ita.* **repente**: 'suddenly'. **procurrerunt**: 'ran forward'. **spatium**: trans. as if *tempus.*

[6] **pila**: object of *coniciendi*; *322d; 230.1.* **Reiectis pilis – pugnatum est**: 'they threw aside their pikes and fought'; how lit.? *144b2; 73d.* **comminus**: 'at close quarters'.

[7] **gladiis**: *322e.* **ex**: 'in accordance with'.

[8] **phalange**: 'a compact mass', like the formation adopted by the Helvetians; see chap. 24.4, note 12.

[9] **exceperunt**: the Germans apparently did not hurl their javelins (*351*) but relied upon their shields and swords; the German sword was longer than the Roman, and single-edged. **complures nostri**: 'many men on our side'; how lit.? *97c* (AG 346e, B 201.1b).

[10] **phalanga**: *18f.* **insilirent**: 'leaped (upon)'; *194a.* **revellerent**: 'pulled back'. **desuper**: 'from above'. In hand-to-hand fighting the Roman soldier, parrying blows with his own shield, generally tried to strike with his sword under or around the shield of the enemy. In this case the shields of the Germans were interlocked in the close formation, and Caesar's men in their eagerness, as they rushed on the foe, sprang up, pulled back the enemy's shields from the top, and stabbed with their short swords from above.

[11] **a sinistro cornu**: 'on their left wing', facing the Roman right, where Caesar was; *126c.*

[12] **conversa esset**: why subjunctive? **a dextro cornu**: opposite the Roman left.

[13] **P. Crassus**: See Vocab. under *Crassus* (2). **adulescens**: 'young', so called to distinguish him from his father and from his older brother, who was afterwards with Caesar in Gaul; see Vocab. under *Crassus* (3). **equitatui**: *107.* **expeditior**: 'more disengaged', so that he had an opportunity to look about and see where help was most needed; the cavalry, which Crassus commanded, was not fighting.

[14] **ei,** etc.: the officers of the legions. **inter aciem**: 'in action'; how lit.? **tertiam aciem**: the 'third line' was usually kept as a reserve force till needed; *337b.*

[15] **laborantibus**: 'who were hard pressed'; *227a4.* **nostris, subsidio**: *112b.*

Caesar is victorious. The captive envoys are rescued.

53.1. Ita proelium restitutum est,[1] atque omnes hostes terga verterunt neque prius[2] fugere destiterunt, quam ad flumen Rhenum, milia passuum ex eo loco circiter quinquaginta, pervenerunt. **2.** Ibi perpauci aut, viribus[3] confisi, tranare[4] contenderunt aut, lintribus inventis, sibi salutem reppererunt. **3.** In his fuit Ariovistus, qui, naviculam[5] deligatam ad ripam nactus,[6] ea profugit; reliquos omnes consecuti equites[7] nostri interfecerunt. **4.** Duae[8] fuerunt Ariovisti uxores, una Sueba natione, quam domo secum eduxerat, altera Norica, regis Voccionis soror, quam in Gallia duxerat,[9] a fratre missam; utraeque in ea fuga perierunt. Duae filiae;[10] harum altera occisa, altera capta est. **5.** C. Valerius Procillus,[11] cum a custodibus in fuga, trinis catenis vinctus,[12] traheretur, in ipsum Caesarem hostes equitatu insequentem incidit. **6.** Quae[13] quidem res Caesari non minorem quam ipsa victoria voluptatem[14] attulit, quod hominem honestissimum[15] provinciae Galliae, suum familiarem et hospitem,[16] ereptum e manibus hostium, sibi restitutum videbat, neque eius calamitate[17] de tanta voluptate et gratulatione quicquam[18] fortuna deminuerat. **7.** Is, se praesente, de se ter[19] sortibus consultum dicebat, utrum igni statim necaretur an in aliud tempus reservaretur:[20] *sortium beneficio se esse incolumem.* **8.** Item M. Metius[21] repertus et ad eum reductus

est.
¹ **restitutum est**: the language implies that the Roman left wing was ceasing to fight when the reserves were sent to its aid.
² **prius quam**: *189a.* **ad flumen Rhenum**: possibly the fleeing Germans followed the valley of the river Ill and came to the Rhine about '50 miles' northeast of the scene of battle. On the other hand a flight and pursuit of 50 miles seem improbable, and it has been suggested that Caesar wrote *quindecim*, 'fifteen', instead of *quinquaginta*; for the Rhine is about 15 miles east of the supposed battlefield.
³ **viribus**: *135a* (AG 431, B 219.1). **confisi**: *62.*
⁴ **tranare**: 'to swim across'. **lintribus**: *15a.*
⁵ **naviculam**: 'a small boat'. **deligatam**: 'tied'.
⁶ **nactus**: 'coming upon'; *61a3; 226c.* **ea**: 'in it'; *131a.* Ariovistus seems to have died not long afterwards (V, 29).
⁷ **equites**: what were the uses of the cavalry? *339.* **interfecerunt**: the slain numbered 80,000, according to Plutarch.
⁸ **Duae uxores**: the Germans ordinarily had but one wife. **una** [uxor], **altera**: *91c.* **natione**: 'by birth'; how lit.? *142a.*
⁹ **duxerat**: i.e. *in matrimonium duxerat,* 'had married'. **utraeque**: *51.*
¹⁰ **filiae**: sc. *fuerunt; 89a.* **altera, altera**: *171b.* **occisa**: sc. *est; 89b.*
¹¹ **Procillus**: see chap. 47.4-6, notes 9-19. **trinis**: distributive; 'with three chains'; *37e.*
¹² **vinctus**: 'bound.' Principal parts of *vincio, vinco,* and *vivo?* **traheretur**: 'was being dragged along'. **in . . . incidit**: 'fell in the way of'. **hostes**: object of *insequentem.*
¹³ **Quae res**: 'And this circumstance'; *167.*
¹⁴ **voluptatem**: 'pleasure'. **attulit**: *69b.*
¹⁵ **honestissimum**: 'very honourable'; *honestus,* from *honour,* is never our "honest".
¹⁶ **hospitem**: 'guest-friend'; *10d.* **ereptum** [esse], **restitutum** [esse]: *213a.*
¹⁷ **neque**: = *et non.* **eius calamitate**: 'by his' (Procillus's) 'destruction'. **gratulatione**: '(reason for) thankfulness'.
¹⁸ **quicquam deminuerat**: with the negative in *neque,* 'had not detracted', lit. 'had not lessened anything at all'; *168; 117a.* **se praesente**: 'in his presence'; how lit.?
¹⁹ **ter**: considered by some a sacred number. **sortibus consultum** [esse]: 'the lots were consulted'; see chap. 50.4, note 10. How lit.? *73d; 131a.* **utrum . . . an**: *204.1.* **igni**: *14b.* **statim**: *77.* **necaretur**: 'should be killed'.
²⁰ **reservaretur**: 'should be saved up.' **se**, etc.: 'that he was unharmed'.
²¹ **M. Metius**: chap. 47.4, note 15. **eum**: *Caesarem.*

His army in winter quarters, Caesar goes to North Italy.

54.1. Hoc proelio trans Rhenum nuntiato, Suebi,¹ qui ad ripas Rheni venerant, domum reverti coeperunt; quos² ubi, qui proximi Rhenum³ incolunt, perterritos senserunt, insecuti⁴ magnum ex his numerum occiderunt. **2.** Caesar, una aestate⁵ duobus maximis bellis confectis, maturius⁶ paulo, quam tempus anni postulabat, in hiberna in Sequanos⁷ exercitum deduxit; **3.** hibernis Labienum praeposuit; ipse in citeriorem Galliam⁸ ad conventus agendos profectus est.

¹ **Suebi . . . venerant**: see chap. 37.3.
² **quos . . . senserunt**: trans. as if *et ubi ei, qui proximi Rhenum incolunt, eos* (i.e. *Suebos*) *perterritos (esse) senserunt.*
³ **Rhenum**: *123b* (AG 432a, B 141.3).
⁴ **insecuti**: *226c.* **ex his**: *97d.*
⁵ **aestate**: 'summer'; *147a.* The defeat of the Helvetians took place near the end of June, that of Ariovistus the second week in September. With not more than 35,000 soldiers, including cavalry and light-armed troops, Caesar in two campaigns completed in a single season, had practically annihilated fighting forces several times as large as his own, and had destroyed, or rendered docile, two hostile populations aggregating several hundred thousand persons. History affords no more striking instance of a victory of military organization, discipline,

and generalship over numbers, courage, and brute force.

[6] **maturius:** *34a.* **hiberna:** 'winter quarters'; *335a, b.*

[7] **Sequanos:** *282.* The region in which the battle was fought had probably formed a part of the Sequanian territory but had been ceded to Ariovistus. **hibernis:** probably at Vesontio, which possessed great advantages as a military base, as explained in chap. 38. **praeposuit:** 'put in charge of'; *107b.*

[8] **citeriorem Galliam:** *284.* **ad conventus agendos:** 'to hold court'; how lit.? The governor of a province from time to time visited the principal cities in order to preside over provincial courts for the administration of justice. In Cisalpine Gaul, moreover, Caesar would be nearer Rome and so enabled to keep in touch with political conditions there.

FIRST LINE.

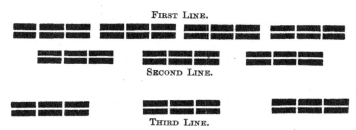

SECOND LINE.

THIRD LINE.

Figure 186. — Acies triplex.

One legion in triple line formation, showing the arrangement of the ten cohorts, and of the three maniples and six centuries in each cohort.

Four cohorts are shown in the first line, three in the second, and three in the third.

In each cohort the three maniples stand side by side. Each maniple is represented as divided into two centuries, one century being behind the other.

The men in each maniple probably stood 8 ranks deep, each century being formed in 4 ranks.

Figure 73. — Slinger, supplied with pebbles.

COMMENTARIUS SECUNDUS

Campaign against the Belgians. 1-28

The Belgians form a league against Caesar.

1.1. Cum esset[1] Caesar in citeriore Gallia, ita uti supra demonstravimus,[2] crebri ad eum rumores afferebantur, litterisque item Labieni certior fiebat,[3] omnes Belgas, quam tertiam esse Galliae[4] partem dixeramus, contra populum Romanum coniurare[5] obsidesque inter se dare: **2.** *[6]Coniurandi[7] has esse causas: primum, quod vererentur, ne,[8] omni pacata Gallia, ad eos exercitus noster adduceretur;* **3.** *deinde, quod ab non nullis Gallis sollicitarentur[9],* partim qui, ut[10] Germanos diutius in Gallia versari noluerant, ita populi Romani exitum hiemare atque inveterascere[11] in Gallia moleste ferebant,[12] partim qui mobilitate et levitate animi novis imperiis[13] studebant; **4.** ab non nullis etiam, quod in Gallia a potentioribus[14] atque eis, qui ad conducendos homines facultates habebant, vulgo regna occupabantur,[15] qui minus facile eam rem[16] imperio nostro consequi poterant.

[1] **esset:** *185c* (AG 546, B 288.1b). **citeriore Gallia:** *124a; 284.* **ita uti:** 'just as'. **supra:** 'above', in the last chapter of Book I. We use the word "above" similarly to refer to the preceding part of a work.

[2] **demonstravimus:** *156* (AG 143a, B 242.3). Caesar the *writer* sometimes speaks in the first person, but always presents Caesar the *doer* in the third. **crebri:** 'frequently'; agrees with *rumores,* 'reports', but has the force of an adverb; *151* (AG 290, B 239). **afferebantur:** force of the imperfect? *175a* (AG 470, B 260.2). **litteris:** *131a* (B 218).

[3] **certior fiebat:** 'he was informed'; how lit.? **dare:** *213a; 214a.* **Belgas:** *19e; 287a.* **quam:** subject accusative with *esse, = quos,* 'who'; attracted to the feminine singular to agree with *partem* in the predicate; *164c; 282.*

[4] **Galliae:** here Transalpine Gaul, as in I, 1.1, referred to in *dixeramus.* **dixeramus:** *214c.*

[5] **coniurare:** 'were conspiring', from the Roman point of view. **inter se dare:** 'were exchanging'; *159.*

[6] **Direct form:** Coniurandi *hae sunt causae*: primum, quod *verentur,* ne, omni pacata Gallia, ad eos exercitus noster *adducatur*; deinde, quod ab non nullis Gallis *sollicitantur.*

[7] **Coniurandi,** etc.: summary of the statement made in the dispatch from Labienus; *212c3; 214a.* **has:** 'as follows'; *161a.* **Coniurandi causas:** explained by the appositional *quod*-clauses following; *230.1; 198b.* **primum, deinde:** *237b.*

[8] **ne:** 'that'; *202.* **omni pacata Gallia:** = *si Gallia omnis pacata esset*; *144b4.* **Gallia:** Celtic Gaul, bordering the Belgian country on the south; the Romans remained in possession of a considerable portion of Celtic Gaul after the defeat of the Helvetians and Ariovistus; *287b.* **ad eos,** etc.: the fear of a Roman invasion was justified, as the event proved. The "conspiracy" of the Belgians was the natural effort of a spirited people to defend their liberties against anticipated encroachment; *158b.* **noster:** *157c.*

[9] **sollicitarentur:** 'were being stirred up'. **partim qui:** 'partly (by those) who'. Caesar here passes to the direct form of statement, presenting as facts on his own authority, details reported by Labienus.

[10] **ut:** 'as'; *188b.* **diutius:** *153a.* **Germanos versari:** *223a.*

[11] **inveterascere:** 'should become established'.

[12] **moleste ferebant:** 'were seriously objecting'. **mobilitate et levitate animi:** 'by reason of temperamental instability and fickleness'; how lit.?

[13] **novis imperiis:** 'a change of rulers'; *105.* How lit.? **non nullis:** i.e. powerful nobles; sc. *sollicitabantur.*

[14] **a potentioribus:** 'by the more powerful'; *154a.* **ad conducendos homines:** 'for hiring men', i.e. mercenary soldiers; *230.3.*

[15] **regna occupabantur:** 'the supreme power was seized'; *92a; 289c.* **qui:** 'and they'.

[16] **eam rem:** 'that object', the obtaining of supreme power. **imperio nostro:** 'under our sovereignty'; *138* (AG 412, B 221). **poterant:** 'would be able'.

He raises two new legions, marches to their territory.

2.1. His nuntiis litterisque[1] commotus, Caesar duas legiones in citeriore Gallia novas conscripsit et inita aestate,[2] in ulteriorem Galliam[3] qui deduceret, Q. Pedium legatum misit. **2.** Ipse, cum primum pabuli copia[4] esse inciperet, ad exercitum[5] venit. **3.** Dat negotium Senonibus reliquisque Gallis, qui finitimi Belgis[6] erant, uti ea, quae apud eos gerantur,[7] cognoscant seque de his rebus certiorem faciant. **4.** Hi constanter[8] omnes nuntiaverunt, manus cogi, exercitum in unum locum[9] conduci. Tum vero dubitandum non existimavit, quin ad[10] eos proficisceretur. **5.** Re frumentaria comparata, castra movet[11] diebusque circiter quindecim ad fines Belgarum pervenit.

[1] **nuntiis litterisque:** cf. I, 26.6, note 19. **duas legiones:** the thirteenth and fourteenth. Caesar now had eight legions, numbered VII to XIV; *307a, e, f.*
[2] **inita aestate:** 'at the beginning of the warm season', probably the latter part of May; how lit.? *68b; 144b1.*
[3] **ulteriorem Galliam:** *286.* **qui** [eas] **deduceret:** 'to lead them', probably over the Great Saint Bernard pass; *193a* (AG 531.2, B 282.2). **legatum:** *313a.* Pedius was a son of Caesar's sister Julia; see Vocab.
[4] **pabuli copia:** forage was needed for the numerous draft animals used to transport the military stores and for the horses of the cavalry and officers. **inciperet:** *185c.*
[5] **exercitum:** probably stationed at or near Vesontio; see Map 1. **Dat negotium:** 'He directed'; *175b.* **reliquis:** *171a.*
[6] **Belgis:** *108a.* **uti . . . faciant:** *199a.*
[7] **gerantur:** 220 (AG 593, B 324). **se:** *158a.*
[8] **constanter:** 'uniformly', with perfect agreement between the reports. **manus:** 'bodies of troops' among the Belgians.
[9] **locum:** why not ablative? *124a.* **dubitandum non** [esse]: sc. *sibi,* 'that he ought not to hesitate'; *73e.*
[10] **ad:** 'against'. **eos:** *Belgas.* **proficisceretur:** *201c.* **Re frumentaria comparata:** 'Having provided for a supply of grain'; *144b2.* How lit.?
[11] **castra movet:** 'he broke camp'; *175b.* **diebus:** *147a.* **circiter:** adverb with *quindecim.* **ad fines pervenit:** 'he reached the territories'. The probable route is indicated on Map 1.

The Remi submit, and give information about the other Belgians.

3.1. Eo[1] cum de improviso celeriusque omni opinione venisset,[2] Remi, qui proximi Galliae ex Belgis sunt, ad eum legatos[3] Iccium et Andecumborium, primos civitatis, miserunt, **2.** qui dicerent:[4] [5]Se[6] suaque omnia in fidem atque potestatem populi Romani permittere,[7] neque se cum reliquis Belgis consensisse, neque contra populum Romanum coniurasse,[8] **3.** paratosque esse et[9] obsides dare et imperata facere et oppidis recipere et frumento ceterisque rebus iuvare. **4.** [10]Reliquos omnes Belgas in armis esse, Germanosque, qui cis Rhenum[11] incolant, sese cum his coniunxisse, **5.** tantumque esse eorum omnium[12] furorem, ut ne Suessiones quidem, fratres consanguineosque suos,[13] qui eodem iure et isdem legibus utantur, unum imperium unumque magistratum cum ipsis habeant, deterrere potuerint,[14] quin cum his consentirent.

[1] **Eo:** = *ad fines Belgarum.* **improviso:** ablative singular neuter of the adjective used as a noun, forming with **de** an adverbial phrase like the English colloquial phrase "of a sudden", "all of a sudden", i.e. 'unexpectedly'. **celerius omni opinione:** 'more quickly than any one had

expected', lit., 'than every expectation'; *129a* (AG 406, B 217.4).

[2] **venisset:** *185c.* **Remi:** the name survives in Reims, modern name of the city occupying the site of the ancient capital of the Remi, Durocortorum. **Galliae:** Celtic Gaul; *287b.* Why dative? *108a.* **ex Belgis:** trans. as if *inter Belgas.*

[3] **legatos:** 'as envoys'; *115a.* **primos:** 'the leading men'; *154a.* **civitatis:** of the Remi.

[4] **qui dicerent**: 'to say'; *193a* (AG 531.2, B 282.2).

[5] **Direct form:** *Nos nostraque omnia in fidem atque potestatem populi Romani permittimus; neque cum reliquis Belgis consensimus, neque contra populum Romanum coniuravimus, parati*que *sumus et obsides dare et imperata facere et (te) oppidis recipere et (te) frumento ceterisque rebus iuvare.*

[6] **Se,** etc.: *212c3.* **Se suaque omnia:** 'themselves and all that they had'; how lit.? **in fidem:** 'to the protection'.

[7] **permittere:** sc. *se* as subject; *214a.* **neque:** 'and not'.

[8] **coniurasse:** = *coniuravisse; 64a1.* **paratos:** adjective, in predicate.

[9] **et, et:** *234a.* **dare, facere,** [eum] **recipere,** [eum] **iuvare:** after *paratos; 221c* (AG 460b, B 328.1). **imperata facere:** 'to obey (his) orders'; *157a.* **oppidis:** 'in (their) towns'; how lit.? *131a.* **frumento:** *131a.*

[10] **Direct form**: *Reliqui omnes Belgae in armis sunt, Germanique, qui cis Rhenum incolunt, sese cum his coniunxerunt; tantus*que *est eorum omnium furor, ut ne Suessiones quidem, fratres consanguineosque nostros, qui eodem iure et isdem legibus utuntur, unum imperium unumque magistratum nobiscum habent, deterrere potuerimus, quin cum his consentirent.*

[11] **cis Rhenum**: on the west side of the Rhine; Caesar writes from the point of view of the Province.

[12] **eorum omnium:** *Belgarum et Germanorum.* **Ne – quidem:** *237c.* **Suessiones:** object of *deterrere.* The name survives in Soissons.

[13] **suos:** 'their own', referring to the Remi. **iure:** '(body of) rights'; *13g; 131c.* **isdem:** *45.*

[14] **potuerint:** *197a,b* (AG 485c, B 268.6). **quin consentirent:** 'from uniting'; *201a* (AG 558, B 295.3a).

Report of the Remi on the history and forces of the Belgians.

4.1. Cum ab eis[1] quaereret, quae civitates quantaeque in armis essent[2] et quid in bello possent, sic reperiebat: [3]*Plerosque Belgas*[4] *esse ortos a Germanis, Rhenumque antiquitus*[5] *traductos, propter loci fertilitatem, ibi consedisse,* **2.** *Gallosque, qui ea loca incolerent, expulisse, solosque*[6] *esse, qui patrum nostrorum memoria,*[7] *omni Gallia vexata, Teutonos Cimbrosque intra suos fines ingredi*[8] *prohibuerint;* **3.** *qua ex re fieri, uti*[9] *earum rerum memoria magnam sibi auctoritatem magnosque spiritus in re militari*[10] *sumerent.* **4.** De numero eorum[11] omnia se habere explorata Remi dicebant, propterea quod,[12] propinquitatibus affinitatibusque coniuncti, quantam quisque[13] multitudinem in communi Belgarum concilio ad id bellum pollicitus sit,[14] cognoverint: **5.** [15]*Plurimum*[16] *inter eos Bellovacos et virtute et auctoritate et hominum numero valere; hos posse conficere*[17] *armata milia centum, pollicitos*[18] *ex eo numero electa sexaginta, totiusque belli imperium sibi postulare.* **6.** [19]*Suessiones suos esse finitimos;*[20] *fines latissimos feracissimosque agros possidere.*[21] **7.** *Apud eos fuisse regem nostra etiam memoria Diviciacum,*[22] *totius Galliae potentissimum, qui cum*[23] *magnae partis harum regionum, tum etiam Britanniae, imperium obtinuerit; nunc esse*[24] *regem Galbam; ad hunc propter iustitiam prudentiamque*[25] *summam totius belli omnium voluntate*[26] *deferri;* **8.** *oppida habere numero XII, polliceri milia armata*[27] *L; totidem Nervios, qui maxime feri inter ipsos*[28] *habeantur longissimeque absint;* **9.** *XV milia Atrebates, Ambianos*[29] *X milia, Morinos XXV milia, Menapios VII milia, Caletos X milia, Veliocasses et Viromanduos totidem, Atuatucos XVIIII*[30] *milia;* **10.** *Condrusos,*

Eburones, Caerosos, Paemanos, qui[31] uno nomine Germani appellantur, *arbitrari se*[32] *posse armare ad XL milia.*

---

[1] **ab eis:** *116c.* **quaereret:** why subjunctive? **quae:** *48b.*

[2] **essent:** *204.2* (AG 574, B 300). **quid – possent:** 'what strength they had', lit. 'to what degree they were able'; *118b* (AG 390c, B 176.3). **sic:** 'as follows'.

[3] **Direct form:** *Plerique Belgae sunt orti* a Germanis, Rhenumque antiquitus *traducti,* propter loci fertilitatem, *hic consederunt,* Gallosque, qui *haec* loca *incolebant, expulerunt; solique sunt,* qui patrum nostrorum memoria, omni Gallia vexata, Teutonos Cimbrosque intra suos fines ingredi prohibuerint (*194a*); qua ex re *fit,* uti earum rerum memoria magnam sibi auctoritatem magnosque spiritus in re militari *sumant.*

[4] **Plerosque Belgas:** 'That most of the Belgians'; *97c.* **a Germanis:** *128b.* The Belgians were of Celtic stock, but had formerly lived on the east side of the Rhine; hence probably arose the belief that they were of Germanic origin. **Rhenum:** accusative after *tra(ns)* in *traductos; 114a.*

[5] **antiquitus:** 'in ancient times'. **fertilitatem:** 'productiveness'. **ibi:** in Gaul.

[6] **solos:** in predicate; 'were the only (people of Gaul) who'.

[7] **memoria:** *147b.* **omni Gallia vexata:** 'when Gaul as a whole was ravaged' by the Cimbrians and Teutons: see I.33; note 12; *144b2; 286.*

[8] **ingredi:** 'from entering'; Caesar uses the infinitive with subject-accusative after *prohibeo; 223a3.* **qua ex re:** 'and in consequence of this achievement'; *167.*

[9] **fieri, uti . . . sumerent:** *203.1.* **memoria:** *135a.*

[10] **in re militari:** 'in respect to the art of war'. **sumerent:** why imperfect? *177a.*

[11] **eorum:** *Belgarum.* **omnia se habere explorata:** 'that they possessed complete information'; how lit.? *229a* (AG 497b, B 337.7).

[12] **propterea quod:** see I, 1.3, note 7. **propinquitatibus affinitatibusque:** 'by blood relationships and intermarriages'; *76a.*

[13] **quisque:** 'each' representative, speaking for his state or tribe. **multitudinem:** 'host'.

[14] **pollicitus sit:** *204.3.* **cognoverint:** *214a.*

[15] **Direct form:** Plurimum inter eos *Bellovaci* et virtute et auctoritate et hominum numero *valent; hi possunt* conficere armata milia centum; *polliciti* (*sunt*) ex eo numero electa sexaginta, totiusque belli imperium sibi *postulant.*

[16] **Plurimum,** etc.: *212c3.* **Plurimum Bellovacos valere:** 'that the Bellovaci were the most powerful'; *118b.* **virtute:** *135a.*

[17] **conficere:** 'muster'; *57b.* **armata milia:** trans. as if *milia hominum armatorum.*

[18] **pollicitos:** *89b.* **electa sexaginta:** sc. *milia,* 'sixty (thousand) picked men'. **totius:** *23a.*

[19] **Direct form:** Suessiones *nostri sunt finitimi;* fines latissimos feracissimosque agros *possident.* Apud eos *fuit rex* nostra etiam memoria *Diviciacus,* totius Galliae *potentissimus,* qui cum magnae partis harum regionum, tum etiam Britanniae, imperium *obtinuit;* nunc est *rex Galba ;* ad hunc propter iustitiam prudentiamque *summa* totius belli omnium voluntate defertur; oppida *habent* numero XII, *pollicentur* milia armata L; totidem *Nervii,* qui maxime feri inter ipsos *habentur* longissimeque *absunt;* XV milia Atrebates, *Ambiani* X milia, *Morini* XXV milia, *Menapii* VII milia, *Caleti* X milia, Veliocasses et *Viromandui* totidem, Atuatuci XVIIII milia; Condrusos, Eburones, Caerosos, Paemanos, qui uno nomine Germani appellantur, *arbitramur* posse armare ad XL milia.

[20] **suos finitimos:** 'their neighbours', neighbours of the Remi. **feracissimos:** 'very productive'; *27a; 153a.*

[21] **possidere:** as subject-accusative supply *eos,* i.e. *Suessiones.* **fuisse:** 'that there had been'; *90a.*

[22] **Diviciacum:** not to be confused with Diviciacus the Aeduan druid, who is mentioned in the next chapter.

[23] **cum . . . tum:** 'not only . . . but also'; *186b.* **regionum:** dependent on *partis,* which limits *imperium.* **Britanniae:** not the whole of Britain – probably only a portion of the island the southeast coast; *294.*

[24] **esse,** etc.: trans. as if *Galbam esse regem; 19d.* **ad hunc – deferri:** 'that upon him – was conferred'; *69b.*

[25] **prudentiam:** 'good judgment'. **summam:** 'the supreme command'.

[26] **voluntate:** *138.* **habere, polliceri:** sc. *eos* (*Suessiones*). **numero:** *142a, 85.* **XII, L,** etc.: *38b, 36.*

[27] **milia armata:** see note 17 above. **totidem:** sc. *milia armata polliceri.* **Nervios:** locate the Nervians, and the other peoples named, upon Map 1. **maxime feri:** in predicate; *30.*

[28] **ipsos:** the Belgians in general, not the Nervians. **habeantur, absint:** vivid use of the present tense where the imperfect (since *cognoverint* above introduces the indirect speech) might have been expected. **absint:** from the country of the Remi. **Atrebates:** *sc. polliceri.*
[29] **Ambianos:** in the region of modern *Amiens.*
[30] **XVIIII:** *undeviginti; 36.*
[31] **qui . . . appellantur:** *214c.* **Germani:** perhaps so called because, although of Celtic stock, they had been the last of the Belgians to remove from the east side of the Rhine to the Belgian country. **uno:** 'a common'.
[32] **se:** *158a.* **ad:** adverb, 'about'.

Caesar, taking hostages from the Remi, crosses the Aisne, and encamps.

5.1. Caesar, Remos[1] cohortatus liberaliterque oratione prosecutus, omnem senatum[2] ad se convenire principumque liberos obsides[3] ad se adduci iussit. Quae omnia ab his diligenter[4] ad diem facta sunt. **2.** Ipse, Diviciacum[5] Aeduum magnopere cohortatus, docet, quanto opere[6] rei publicae communisque salutis intersit, manus[7] hostium distineri, ne cum tanta multitudine uno tempore confligendum sit: **3.** *Id[8] fieri posse, si suas copias Aedui in[9] fines Bellovacorum introduxerint et eorum agros populari coeperint.* His mandatis eum ab se dimittit. **4.** Postquam omnes Belgarum copias in unum locum coactas[10] ad se venire vidit,[11] neque iam longe abesse, ab eis, quos miserat, exploratoribus[12] et ab Remis cognovit, flumen Axonam, quod[13] est in extremis Remorum finibus, exercitum traducere maturavit atque ibi castra posuit.[14] **5.** Quae res et latus unum castrorum ripis[15] fluminis muniebat et, post eum quae[16] erant, tuta ab hostibus reddebat et, commeatus ab Remis reliquisque civitatibus ut sine periculo ad eum portari possent, efficiebat. **6.** In[17] eo flumine pons erat. Ibi praesidium ponit et in altera parte fluminis Q. Titurium Sabinum legatum cum sex cohortibus[18] relinquit; castra in altitudinem pedum duodecim vallo[19] fossaque duodeviginti pedum munire iubet.

[1] **Remos . . . prosecutus:** 'encouraging the Remi and addressing (them) in gracious words'; how lit.? *226c.*
[2] **senatum:** *289b; 75b.* **principum:** *10b.*
[3] **obsides:** 'as hostages'; *88a.* **iussit:** 'gave orders (that)'. **Quae . . . facta sunt:** 'these instructions . . . were carried out'.
[4] **diligenter:** 'carefully'; *34a.* **ad diem:** 'promptly'.
[5] **Diviciacum:** see 4.7, note 22 and I, 18, 20, 31, etc.
[6] **quanto opere,** etc.: 'how important it was for the State and for their mutual welfare'; how lit.? *103e* (AG 355, B 211.1). **rei publicae:** *Romanorum.* **communis:** of Romans and Aeduans. **intersit:** *204.3.*
[7] **manus distineri:** subject of *intersit;* 'that the enemy's forces be kept apart'; *222c; 79d.* **ne . . . confligendum sit:** 'that it might not be necessary to fight'; *73e.*
[8] **Id:** refers to *manus distineri,* 'that (object)'; *213b; 160c.*
[9] **in – introduxerint:** 'should have led – into'; future perfect indicative in the direct form; *218.1b.*
[10] **coactas . . . venire:** 'had been brought together and were coming'; *228a.*
[11] **vidit:** more vivid than *intellexit;* thus do we use the word "see" of things understood but not perceived with the eyes; *188a.* **neque:** trans. as if *et non.* **abesse:** sc. *eas* (= *copias*); dependent on *cognovit.* **eis:** with *exploratoribus.*
[12] **exploratoribus:** *327.* **flumen, exercitum:** *114a* (AG 395, B 179.1). **Axonam:** now *Aisne.* See Map 1.
[13] **quod:** the antecedent is *flumen.* **extremis finibus:** 'the most remote part of the country'; *152a.*

[14] **ibi castra posuit**: Caesar 'encamped' on the north side of the Axona, about a mile and a half northeast of the present village of Berry-au-Bac. See Map 5. **Quae res**: 'Now this movement'; *167*. **et . . . et**: *233d*.

[15] **ripis**: *131a*. **post . . . reddebat**: 'made the rear secure against the enemy'; *331b*. How lit.?

[16] **quae**: i.e. *ea* (*loca*) *quae*. **tuta**: *115b*. **commeatus . . . efficiebat**: 'made it possible for supplies to be brought', etc.; *203.3* (AG 568, B 297.1). **commeatus**: plural because the supplies were furnished by more than one state.

[17] **In**: 'across'. **pons**: *17c*. **erat**: *90a*. **praesidium**: at D on Map 5. **in altera parte**: on the south side of the Aisne, opposite Berry-au-Bac; see Map 5, **C**. Caesar now had both ends of the bridge well guarded. In consequence he was able to get provisions from his allies across the river; to set a watch on the Remi, the sincerity of whose professions of loyalty was not beyond question; and, finally, to keep open an avenue of retreat in case of disaster.

[18] **sex cohortibus**: about how many men? *307c*. **castra**: Map 5, **A**. **pedum**: *100a*. The measurement of twelve feet included both the height of the bank formed by the earth thrown out of the trench and that of the row of palisades along the outer edge; *333*.

[19] **vallo**: why ablative? **duodeviginti pedum**: eighteen Roman feet broad, measured across the top; the trench, with sloping sides, was probably about ten feet deep. Excavations, made in 1862, brought to light traces of this rampart and trench.

The Belgians attack Bibrax, a town of the Remi.

6.1. Ab his castris oppidum Remorum, nomine[1] Bibrax, aberat milia passuum[2] VIII. Id ex itinere magno impetu Belgae oppugnare coeperunt. Aegre eo die sustentatum est.[3] **2.** Gallorum eadem atque Belgarum[4] oppugnatio est haec. Ubi,[5] circumiecta multitudine hominum totis moenibus, undique in murum lapides iaci[6] coepti sunt, murusque defensoribus nudatus est,[7] testudine facta portas succendunt murumque subruunt.[8] Quod tum facile fiebat. **3.** Nam cum tanta multitudo lapides ac tela conicerent,[9] in muro consistendi potestas erat nulli.[10] **4.** Cum finem[11] oppugnandi nox fecisset, Iccius Remus, summa nobilitate[12] et gratia inter suos, qui tum oppido praefuerat, unus ex eis,[13] qui legati de pace ad Caesarem venerant, nuntium[14] ad eum mittit, *nisi subsidium sibi summittatur, sese diutius sustinere[15] non posse.*

[1] **nomine**: 'called'; how lit.? *142a* (AG 418, B 226). **Bibrax**: the name in Celtic meant 'Beavertown'.

[2] **milia passuum VIII**: *118a*; *100a*; *243b*. **ex itinere**: 'from the line of march', attacking the town as soon as they reached it; see Vocab. under **iter**.

[3] **Aegre sustentatum est**: 'With difficulty the defense was maintained'.

[4] **eadem atque Belgarum**: 'the same as (that) of the Belgians'; *233c*. **oppugnatio**: 'the (method of) storming (fortified places)'. **haec**: *161a*.

[5] **Ubi**, etc.: 'When a host of men has encircled the fortifications and'. How lit.? *144b2*. **moenibus**: *104a*.

[6] **iaci**: *57b*. **coepti sunt**: *72c*. **defensoribus**: 'of its defenders'; *127a*; *74a*.

[7] **nudatus est**: 'has been cleared'. **testudine facta**: 'having made a tortoise roof', in the Roman fashion; *345*. **testudine**: *12d*; *144b2*. **succendunt**: 'they', the attacking host, 'set on fire'; *175c*.

[8] **subruunt**: 'undermine'. **Quod tum**: 'Now this, in the present instance', referring to the burning of the gates, and undermining of the walls, of Bibrax.

[9] **conicerent**: *173b*; *184a* (AG 317d, B 254.4). **consistendi**: *230.1*.

[10] **nulli**: trans. as if *nemini* (*12d*; *111*), 'no one was able to stand'; how lit.?

[11] **finem oppugnandi fecisset**: 'had checked the assault'; *185c*. How lit.? **Iccius**: see II.3.1.

[12] **summa nobilitate**: *143a*. **inter suos**: 'among his countrymen'; *154a*. **oppido**: *107a*. **tum praefuerat**: i.e. *praepositus erat et tum praeerat*.

[13] **ex eis**: *97d*. **legati**: in predicate after *venerant*; 'as envoys'.

[14] **nuntium**: here 'a message'. **nisi**: '(saying) that unless', etc.; *213b*. **sibi**: 'to them', the

beleaguered inhabitants of Bibrax. **summittatur:** 'should be sent to their relief'; *218.1a.*
[15] **sustinere:** intransitive, 'hold out'.

MAP 5

THE BATTLE AT THE AISNE (AXONA)

Book II, 7–10

To face page 144

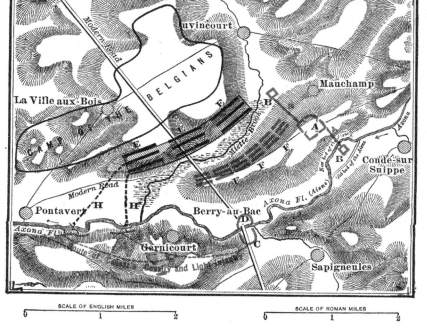

EXPLANATION

Caesar, marching from the South, encamped on the north or right bank of the
Aisne, on a long hill. As the camp was well protected by the streams and the
low ground on the west, in order to secure the east side, he ran intrenchments
from the corners to both the Aisne and the Miette. The widely extended Belgian camp was on the opposite side of the Miette (chap. 7, ll. 11–12).

A. Caesar's camp (chap. 5, l. 15 ; chap. 7, l. 9 ; chap. 8, l. 7).

a, b. Trenches, *fossae* (chap. 8, ll. 11–13).

B, B. Redoubts, *castella* (chap. 8, l. 13).

C. Redoubt at the south end of the bridge, *castellum*, held by Q. Titurius
Sabinus (chap. 5, ll. 20–22 ; chap. 9, l. 11).

D. Guard at the north end of the bridge, *praesidium* (chap. 5, l. 20).

E–E. The Belgians in battle order (chap. 8, l. 20).

F–F. The six legions in battle order (chap. 8, l. 19).

H–H. Probable routes taken by the Belgians to the fords at the Aisne, where
they were met by Caesar's light-armed troops and cavalry (chap. 9, ll. 8–15).

Caesar relieves the town; the Belgians march toward his camp.

7.1. Eo[1] de media, nocte Caesar, isdem ducibus usus, qui nuntii[2] ab Iccio venerant, Numidas et Cretas sagittarios et funditores[3] Baleares subsidio oppidanis mittit; **2.** quorum adventu et[4] Remis cum spe defensionis studium propugnandi accessit, et hostibus,[5] eadem de causa, spes potiundi oppidi discessit. **3.** Itaque paulisper[6] apud oppidum morati agrosque Remorum depopulati, omnibus vicis aedificiisque,[7] quo adire potuerant, incensis, ad castra Caesaris omnibus copiis[8] contenderunt et a[9] milibus passuum minus duobus castra posuerunt; quae castra,[10] ut fumo atque ignibus significabatur, amplius milibus[11] passuum VIII in latitudinem patebant.

[1] **Eo:** toward Bibrax. **de:** *242d.* **isdem:** 'the same men'; *45; 131c.* **ducibus:** 'as guides', predicative; *131f.* **usus:** *226c.*
[2] **nuntii:** construed as *legati* at the end of the previous chapter. **Numidas,** etc.: *308.* **Cretas:** *19f.* **sagittarios:** 'bowmen'.
[3] **funditores:** 'slingers'; *74a;* Fig. 73. **subsidio, oppidanis:** *112b* (AG 382.1, B 191.2). **oppidanis:** 'the inhabitants of the town'. **mittit:** *175b.*
[4] **et . . . et:** *233a.* **spe defensionis:** 'hope of repelling the assault'; how lit.? *74b.* **studium propugnandi:** 'eager desire to take the offensive'; how lit.?
[5] **hostibus:** dative, but trans. 'from the enemy'; *109b.* **potiundi oppidi:** *64b; 230.1.*
[6] **paulisper:** 'for a short time'. **morati,** etc.: sc. *hostes* as subject of *contenderunt; 61a1.*
[7] **vicis, aedificiis:** cf. I, 5.2, notes 4-5; *144b2.* **quo:** adverb; trans. as if *ad quae.*
[8] **omnibus copiis:** *136b* (AG 412, B 220.1).
[9] **a ... duobus:** 'less than two miles away', i.e 'at' (lit. 'from') 'a distance of thousands of paces less than two (thousands)'. The Romans described distances differently than we do.
[10] **quae castra:** 'and this camp', marked CAMP OF THE BELGIANS on Map 5, while Caesar's camp is at **A**; *167.* **fumo:** 'by the smoke'. **significabatur:** 'was indicated'; *73d.*
[11] **milibus:** why ablative? *129a* (AG 407e, B 217.1). **VIII:** *38b, 36.*

Caesar adds to the fortifications of his camp, awaits attack.

8.1. Caesar primo et propter multitudinem hostium et propter eximiam opinionem virtutis[1] proelio supersedere statuit; cotidie tamen equestribus proeliis,[2] quid hostis virtute posset et quid nostri auderent, periclitabatur.[3] **2.** Ubi nostros non esse inferiores intellexit, loco[4] pro castris ad[5] aciem instruendam natura opportuno atque idoneo, quod[6] is collis, ubi castra posita erant, paululum ex planitie editus, tantum[7] adversus in latitudinem patebat, quantum loci[8] acies instructa occupare poterat, atque ex utraque parte lateris deiectus[9] habebat, et in frontem leniter fastigatus paulatim ad planitiem[10] redibat, **3.** ab utroque latere eius collis transversam fossam obduxit[11] circiter passuum quadringentorum **4.** et ad extremas fossas[12] castella constituit ibique tormenta[13] collocavit, ne, cum aciem instruxisset, hostes, quod tantum[14] multitudine poterant, ab lateribus pugnantes, suos circumvenire possent. **5.** Hoc facto, duabus legionibus,[15] quas proxime conscripserat, in castris relictis,[16] ut, si quo opus esset, subsidio duci possent, reliquas VI legiones pro castris in acie[17] constituit. Hostes item suas copias ex castris eductas instruxerant.[18]

[1] **eximiam opinionem virtutis:** 'their extraordinary reputation for bravery'; *102.* **proelio supersedere:** 'to refrain from battle'; *127a.*
[2] **equestribus proeliis:** 'cavalry skirmishes', as distinguished from a general engagement,

with infantry. **quid . . . posset:** 'what mettle the enemy had'; how lit.? *118b.* **virtute:** *142a.*
[3] **periclitabatur:** 'kept trying to find out'; *175d* (AG 470, B 260.2).
[4] **loco . . . idoneo:** trans. as if *cum locus* ('since the space') . . . *opportunus atque idoneus esset; 144b3.*
[5] **ad,** etc.: *230.3.* **natura:** 'naturally'; how lit.? **atque:** *233a.*
[6] **quod . . . redibat:** explains why the ground in front of the camp was well adapted for forming a line of battle. **ubi:** 'on which'. **castra:** Map 5, **A. paululum editus:** 'gradually rising'; how lit.?
[7] **tantum,** etc.: 'on the side toward the enemy extended in width (far enough to provide) just the amount of space that a line of battle would require'; how lit.? **tantum:** *118a.* **adversus:** adjective, agreeing with *collis.* **quantum:** correlative with *tantum,* and object of *occupare,* having *loci* dependent on it.
[8] **loci:** trans. as if dependent on *tantum; 97a.* The long, gently sloping hillside, broad enough to afford room for a Roman triple line, is shown on Map 5, between the Miette brook and the narrowing crest of the hill southwest of Caesar's camp; six legions are there shown in order of battle. **ex utraque parte:** = 'on either side', the side of the camp toward the river, and the opposite side.
[9] **lateris deiectus:** 'steep slopes'; how lit.? *13e.* **in frontem:** 'in' (lit. 'into') 'front' of the camp, on the southwest side. **leniter fastigatus:** 'with gentle slope'; how lit.?
[10] **planitiem:** the level ground between the hill and the river above and below Berry-au-Bac. **redibat:** here 'descended'.
[11] **transversam fossam obduxit:** 'he extended a trench crosswise', that is, at right angles with the length of the hill. Starting from opposite corners of the camp, Caesar prolonged two lines of intrenchments at right angles to the sides, each about a third of a mile in length. One ran down the south slope of the hill, toward the Aisne, the bed of which in Caesar's time is indicated on the plan by the broken line. The other ran down the north slope, toward the Miette brook; both are indicated on Map 5 by lines (**a,b**). At the ends of these intrenchments he constructed 'redoubts' (**B B**), where he stationed troops, with military engines. His purpose was to guard against a flank movement on the part of the enemy, by which they might reach the rear of the camp, and attack from behind while his forces were engaged in front. **passuum quadringentorum:** 'four hundred paces' in length; how lit.? *100a.* How far by our measurement? *243b.*
[12] **ad extremas fossas:** 'at the ends of the trenches'; *152a* (AG 293, B 241.1). **castella:** Map 5, **B B.**
[13] **tormenta:** 'torsioners', such as were used in siege operations; *343.* **instruxisset:** *220.* **quod . . . poterant:** 'because they were so strong in numbers'; why indicative?
[14] **tantum:** *118b.* **ab lateribus:** 'on the flanks'; *126c.* **pugnantes:** with *hostes.* **suos:** 'his men'; *154a.* A glance at the Map shows how well designed the trenches were to protect against an attack upon the right end of the battle line and block access to the rear, which was otherwise protected by the river.
[15] **duabus legionibus:** the thirteenth and fourteenth, enrolled a few months before ; see 2.1. Generally, as in this instance, Caesar exposed his veterans to the brunt of the battle, leaving recruits, whose powers had not been tested, in reserve; *307d, f.*
[16] **relictis:** *144b2.* **quo:** 'at any point'. **esset:** *220.* **subsidio:** 'as a reserve force'; *112a.*
[17] **acie:** undoubtedly a triple line; *337.*
[18] **eductas instruxerant:** 'had led forth and drawn up'; *228a* (AG 496, N.2, B 337.5). For the relative position of the two armies, see Map 5.

The Belgians attempt to cross the Aisne and attack Titurius.

9.1. Palus[1] erat non magna inter nostrum atque hostium exercitum. Hanc[2] si nostri transirent, hostes exspectabant; nostri[3] autem, si ab illis initium transeundi fieret, ut impeditos aggrederentur,[4] parati in armis erant. **2.** Interim proelio equestri inter duas acies contendebatur. Ubi neutri[5] transeundi initium faciunt, secundiore[6] equitum proelio nostris, Caesar suos in castra reduxit. **3.** Hostes protinus[7] ex eo loco ad flumen Axonam contenderunt, quod esse post nostra castra demonstratum est.[8] **4.** Ibi, vadis[9] repertis, partem suarum copiarum traducere conati sunt, eo consilio,[10] ut, si possent, castellum, cui praeerat Q. Titurius legatus, expugnarent pontemque interscinderent; **5.** si minus[11] potuissent, agros Remorum popularentur, qui magno nobis usui[12] ad bellum gerendum erant, commeatuque nostros prohiberent.

[1] **Palus:** the marshy ground along the Miette brook, indicated on Map 5. In the dry weather of 1914 the German army ran first-line and communicating trenches through this marsh, but later these were flooded by the Miette brook. **erat:** *90a.* **nostrum,** etc.: 'our army and that of the enemy'; *157d.*

[2] **Hanc:** *paludem.* **si:** '(to see) whether'; *204.4* (AG 576a,b 300.3).

[3] **nostri . . . erant:** *nostri autem parati in armis erant, ut, si ab illis (hostibus) initium transeundi (paludem) fieret, (eos,* the enemy engaged in crossing over, hence at a disadvantage) *impeditos aggrederentur.* **fieret:** *220* (AG 593, B 324.1).

[4] **aggrederentur:** *57c.* Why subjunctive? **proelio,** etc.: 'a cavalry engagement continued'; how lit.? *73d.*

[5] **neutri:** 'neither side'; each side was waiting for the other to assume the offensive; *23a.*

[6] **secundiore proelio:** *144b5* (AG 420.3, B 227.2c). **nostris:** *108a.*

[7] **protinus:** 'at once'. **eo loco:** on the opposite side of the marsh from the Romans.

[8] **demonstratum est:** 'it has been shown'; see 5.4.

[9] **vadis:** shallow places, suitable for fording, are still found in the Aisne, between the mouth of the Miette brook and the village of Pontavert; for the route of the attacking forces see Map 5, H H.

[10] **eo consilio:** 'with this design', explained by the appositive *ut*-clauses following; *135a; 203.4.* **possent:** *220.* **castellum:** on the south bank of the Aisne; Map 5, **C**, and II.5.6. The Belgians planned to storm the redoubt from the rear. The attempt was justified, from the military point of view; for the destruction of the bridge would have made Caesar's position extremely difficult.

[11] **minus:** trans. as if *non.* **potuissent:** change of tense from *possent,* 'if they could', to *potuissent* 'if (having made the attempt) they should have been unsuccessful'. **popularentur, prohiberent:** sc. *ut,* the clauses being in apposition with *consilio.*

[12] **nobis, usui:** *112b.* **commeatu:** *127a.*

Caesar prevents their crossing; they decide to disperse.

10.1. Caesar, certior factus[1] ab Titurio, omnem equitatum et levis armaturae[2] Numidas, funditores sagittariosque pontem traducit atque ad eos[3] contendit. **2.** Acriter in eo loco pugnatum est.[4] Hostes impeditos nostri in flumine aggressi magnum eorum numerum occiderunt; **3.** per[5] eorum corpora reliquos audacissime transire conantes[6] multitudine telorum reppulerunt; primos, qui transierant, equitatu[7] circumventos interfecerunt. **4.** Hostes,[8] ubi et de expugnando oppido et de flumine transeundo spem se fefellisse[9] intellexerunt neque nostros in locum iniquiorem[10] progredi pugnandi causa viderunt, atque ipsos[11] res frumentaria deficere coepit, consilio convocato constituerunt, optimum esse,[12] domum suam quemque reverti, et, quorum in fines primum Romani exercitum introduxissent,[13] ad eos[14] defendendos undique convenirent, ut potius in suis quam in alienis[15] finibus decertarent et domesticis copiis rei frumentariae uterentur. **5.** Ad eam sententiam cum reliquis causis haec quoque ratio[16] eos deduxit, quod Diviciacum atque Aeduos finibus Bellovacorum appropinquare[17] cognoverant. His persuaderi, ut[18] diutius morarentur neque suis auxilium ferrent, non poterat.

[1] **certior factus:** 'on being informed' of the attempted movement. **equitatum, pontem:** *114a* (AG 395, B 179.1). As Caesar's camp was south of the Miette and east of the bridge over the Aisne, he could send his cavalry across the bridge without danger of interference, and from the south side of the Aisne could attack the enemy in the act of crossing.

[2] **levis armaturae:** 'of light equipment'; trans. 'light-armed'; *308; 100a.* **funditores:** probably provided with leaden shot, though such are not mentioned by Caesar; slingshots of lead were in use both before and after the Gallic Wars.

[3] **eos:** *hostes.* **eo loco:** where the enemy started to cross the river; marked on Map 5 by crossed swords.

[4] **pugnatum est:** *73d.* **aggressi:** *226c.*

[5] **per:** 'over'. The bravery of these Belgians, recorded by Caesar with evident admiration, justifies his characterisation at the beginning of Book I, 1.3.

[6] **conantes:** with *reliquos.* In 1914 this part of the Aisne again became the scene of slaughter. Near Berry-au-Bac French and British troops constructed pontoon bridges in the face of artillery fire accurately directed from the high ground on the north side of the river; and again the Aisne was choked with corpses.

[7] **equitatu:** *131b.* **circumventos interfecerunt:** 'surrounded and killed'; *228a.*

[8] **Hostes:** the main body of the enemy, which remained inactive while a detachment (*partem suarum copiarum*, II, 9.4) tried to cross the river. **oppido:** Bibrax; see II, 6-7; *230.4.*

[9] **spem se fefellisse:** 'that they had been disappointed in their expectations', lit. 'that their expectation had cheated them'. **neque:** trans. as if *et . . . non.* **nostros:** the six legions that had been formed in order of battle and then led back to camp (II, 8.5, and 9.2).

[10] **locum iniquiorem:** 'a less favourable position'; how lit.? **pugnandi causa:** *230.1; 94b.*

[11] **ipsos:** *hostes.* **deficere:** 'to fail'; *57b.* As the Gauls for the most part engaged only in short campaigns, their arrangements for supplies were very defective. It is a maxim of modern warfare that: "the way to victory lies through the soldier's stomach". Caesar, as all great generals, paid the most careful attention to the provisioning of his army; *317.* **consilio:** 'a conference' of the leaders.

[12] **optimum esse:** 'that it was best'. The subject of *esse* is the infinitive clause *quemque reverti,* and *optimum* is in predicate; *148d.* **domum suam:** 'to his own home'; *119b.*

[13] **introduxissent:** *220* (AG 593, B 324).

[14] **eos:** antecedent of *quorum;* 'to defend that people'; *230.3.* **convenirent:** sc. *ut,* 'that they should rally'; *199a; 200a.*

[15] **alienis:** = *aliorum*, 'of others', as opposed to **domesticis,** 'their own'. **decertarent:** *196a.* **copiis:** 'supplies'; *131c.*

[16] **ratio:** 'consideration', explained by the appositive clause *quod* ('that') . . . *cognoverant; 198b.* **Diviciacum,** etc.: cf. II, 5.2-3. **finibus:** *105.*

[17] **appropinquare:** 'were approaching'. **cognoverant:** 'they knew'; *176b.* **His:** the Bellovaci, whose actual fighting force probably did not reach the large estimate of 100,000 given by the Remi (II.4.5); *105.* **His persuaderi:** 'These could not be persuaded'; how lit.? *106b.*

[18] **ut morarentur:** 'to stay' with the united Belgian host. Caesar's plan of dividing the forces of the Belgians, suggested in chap. 5, was thus successful. **neque:** 'and not'.

The Belgians retreat in disorder; Caesar pursues them with great slaughter.

11.1. Ea re[1] constituta, secunda vigilia magno cum strepitu ac tumultu castris[2] egressi, nullo certo ordine neque imperio, cum sibi quisque[3] primum itineris locum peteret et domum pervenire properaret, fecerunt,[4] ut consimilis fugae profectio videretur. **2.** Hac re statim Caesar per[5] speculatores cognita, insidias veritus,[6] quod, qua de causa discederent, nondum perspexerat, exercitum equitatumque castris[7] continuit. **3.** Prima luce, confirmata re[8] ab exploratoribus, omnem equitatum, qui novissimum agmen[9] moraretur, praemisit. His Q. Pedium et L. Aurunculeium Cottam legatos praefecit; T. Labienum legatum[10] cum legionibus tribus subsequi iussit. **4.** Hi,[11] novissimos adorti et multa milia passuum prosecuti, magnam multitudinem eorum fugientium[12] conciderunt, cum ab extremo agmine, ad quos ventum erat, consisterent fortiterque impetum nostrorum militum sustinerent, **5.** priores,[13] quod abesse a periculo viderentur,[14] neque ulla necessitate neque imperio continerentur, exaudito clamore[15] perturbatis ordinibus[16] omnes in fuga sibi praesidium ponerent.[17] **6.** Ita sine ullo periculo tantam eorum multitudinem nostri interfecerunt, quantum[18] fuit diei spatium; sub occasum solis destiterunt seque in castra, ut erat imperatum,[19] receperunt.

[1] **re:** 'conclusion', i.e. to disperse. **secunda vigilia:** *242c; 147a.* **Strepitu:** 'uproar'; *136a.*

[2] **castris:** shown on Map 5; *127a.* **nullo . . . imperio:** ablative of attendant circumstance, explaining *magno . . . tumultu,* and in turn explained by the causal clause *cum . . . properaret;* 'without a fixed order and without discipline'; *138.*

[3] **sibi quisque:** *170b.* **primum:** 'the foremost'. **peteret:** *184a* (AG 549, B 286.2).

[4] **fecerunt . . . videretur:** 'they made their departure look like a rout'; how lit.? *203.3.* **fugae:** *108a.*

[5] **per:** *123a.* **speculatores:** 'spies'; *327.*

[6] **veritus:** *226c.* **discederent:** *204.2.*

[7] **castris:** *131a;* trans. 'in camp'. **Prima luce:** 'at daybreak'; *152a.*

[8] **re:** 'the fact' that the Belgian host had actually dispersed. **exploratoribus:** *327.*

[9] **novissimum agmen:** 'the rear guard' of the retreating Belgians; *27b.* **moraretur:** *193a* (AG 531.2, B 282.2). **His:** plural from the idea of *equites* in *equitatum; 107b.* **Pedium:** see II, 2.1, note 3.

[10] **legatum:** *313a.* **subsequi:** 'to follow closely'.

[11] **Hi:** 'These men', the legionaries under Labienus; the cavalry had gone ahead to retard the Belgian rear till the Roman infantry could catch up with it. **milia:** *118a.*

[12] **eorum fugientium:** 'of them as they fled'. **cum,** etc.: sc. *ei;* 'since those (Belgians) at the rear, whom the Romans had reached, were making a stand'; how lit.? **cum:** *184a.* **15. extremo:** *152a.* **agmine:** here used not of an orderly marching column, but of a mass of soldiers in flight. **ventum erat:** *73d.*

[13] **priores:** 'those in advance', the bulk of the retreating host; *154a; 33.*

[14] **viderentur:** 220 (AG 593, B 324). **neque:** 'and . . . not'. **necessitate:** 'compulsion'.

[15] **exaudito clamore:** 'when they heard the shouting' behind them.

[16] **ordinibus:** 'ranks'. **sibi:** *109a.* **praesidium ponerent:** 'sought safety'; how lit.?

[17] **ponerent:** with *cum,* as *consisterent, sustinerent, continerentur.*

[18] **quantum,** etc.: 'as daylight permitted'; how lit.? **sub:** 'toward'.

[19] **ut erat imperatum:** 'in accordance with their orders'; *73d.*

Noviodunum, besieged by Caesar, surrenders.

12.1. Postridie eius diei[1] Caesar, prius quam se hostes ex terrore ac fuga reciperent in fines Suessionum,[2] qui proximi Remis[3] erant, exercitum duxit et magno itinere ad oppidum Noviodunum[4] contendit. **2.** Id ex itinere oppugnare conatus, quod vacuum ab[5] defensoribus esse audiebat, propter latitudinem fossae murique altitudinem, paucis defendentibus,[6] expugnare non potuit. **3.** Castris[7] munitis, vineas agere, quaeque[8] ad oppugnandum usui erant, comparare coepit. **4.** Interim omnis ex fuga Suessionum multitudo in oppidum proxima nocte[9] convenit. **5.** Celeriter vineis ad oppidum actis, aggere iacto[10] turribusque constitutis, magnitudine operum, quae neque viderant ante Galli neque audierant, et celeritate Romanorum permoti, legatos ad Caesarem de deditione mittunt et, petentibus Remis,[11] ut conservarentur, impetrant.

[1] **diei:** *94c.* **se reciperent:** 'could rally'; why subjunctive? *189b.*

[2] **in fines Suessionum:** see Map 1. Having scattered the great host of united Belgians, Caesar proceeds to the reduction of the different states one by one.

[3] **Remis:** *108a.* **magno itinere:** 'by a forced march'; *329.*
[4] **Noviodunum:** = "Newtown"; thought to have been on the hill of Pommiers, near the modern city of Soissons. **ex itinere:** see Vocab. under *iter.* **oppugnare:** *340.*
[5] **vacuum ab:** 'destitute of'. **esse:** i.e. *id (oppidum) esse vacuum.* **latitudinem fossae:** the wider the 'moat', the more difficult the filling of it so as to gain access to the wall. **latitudinem fossae murique altitudinem:** *239c.*
[6] **paucis defendentibus:** 'though there were but few defending it'; *144b5.*
[7] **Castris:** probably on high ground east of Pommiers, where traces of a Roman camp, thought to date from Caesar's time, have been discovered. **vineas agere:** 'to move forward the arbour sheds'; *342a.*
[8] **quae:** as antecedent supply *ea*, object of *comparare.* **usui:** 'of use.' Why dative? *112a.*
[9] **proxima nocte:** the night following the day on which Caesar reached Noviodunum, encamped, and commenced preparations for besieging the town. **vineis,** etc.: 'arbour sheds', open at the ends, were rapidly constructed, and placed in parallel rows which began outside the range of the enemy's weapons and were extended to the edge of the moat; *144b2.*
[10] **aggere iacto:** 'filling', carried under the lines of arbour sheds, was 'cast' into the moat so as to level it up and make it possible to roll the towers close to the city wall. **turribus:** 'towers'; *342b.* **magnitudine, celeritate:** *135a.* **operum:** 'siege-works'.
[11] **petentibus Remis:** 'at the urgent request of the Remi'; how lit.? **ut conservarentur:** after *petentibus*, 'that they should be spared'; *199a.*

The Suessiones submit; Caesar marches against the Bellovaci, gathered in Bratuspantium.

13.1. Caesar, obsidibus[1] acceptis primis civitatis atque ipsius Galbae[2] regis duobus filiis, armisque omnibus ex oppido traditis, in deditionem Suessiones accipit exercitumque in Bellovacos[3] ducit. **2.** Qui cum[4] se suaque omnia in oppidum Bratuspantium contulissent, atque ab eo oppido Caesar cum exercitu circiter milia passuum V abesset, omnes maiores natu,[5] ex oppido egressi,[6] manus ad Caesarem tendere et voce significare coeperunt, sese in eius fidem[7] ac potestatem venire neque[8] contra populum Romanum armis contendere. **3.** Item, cum ad oppidum accessisset[9] castraque ibi poneret, pueri mulieresque ex muro passis manibus[10] suo more pacem ab Romanis petierunt.

[1] **obsidibus:** 'as hostages'; predicative, after *acceptis; 88b.* **primis:** 'the foremost men'; *154a; 144b2.*
[2] **Galbae:** see II, 4.7.
[3] **Bellovacos:** trans. as if *in fines Bellovacorum; 282.*
[4] **Qui cum:** 'when they'; *167.* **suaque omnia:** 'with everything they had'; how lit.? *154a.* **oppidum:** 'stronghold'; not a city but a fortified place of refuge, occupied only in time of danger.
[5] **maiores natu:** 'the old men'; how lit.? *142a* (AG 418, B 226.1).
[6] **egressi:** 'came out and'; *228a.* **tendere:** 'to stretch out'.
[7] **in eius fidem:** 'under his protection'; *124a.* **venire:** *213b.*
[8] **neque:** trans. as if *et . . . non.* **contendere:** 'struggle' any longer.
[9] **accessisset:** *185c.* **pueri:** 'children', not only 'boys'.
[10] **passis manibus:** 'with hands outstretched'; *144b2.* Principal parts of *pando* and *patior*? **more:** with *passis; 136c.*

Diviciacus presents the case of the Bellovaci.

14.1. Pro his[1] Diviciacus (nam post discessum Belgarum, dimissis Aeduorum copiis,[2] ad eum reverterat) facit verba: **2.** *[3]Bellovacos[4] omni tempore in fide atque amicitia civitatis Aeduae fuisse; impulsos ab suis principibus, qui dicerent,[5] Aeduos, a Caesare in[6] servitutem redactos, omnes* *indignitates; contumeliasque perferre, et* [7]*ab Aeduis defecisse et populo Romano bellum intulisse.* **3.** *Qui*[8] *eius consilii principes fuissent, quod intellegerent, quantam calamitatem civitati intulissent, in Britanniam profugisse.* **4.** [9]*Petere*[10] *non solum Bellovacos, sed etiam pro his Aeduos, ut sua*[11] *clementia ac mansuetudine in eos utatur.* **5.** *Quod si fecerit, Aeduorum auctoritatem apud omnes Belgas amplificaturum, quorum auxiliis atque opibus, si*[12] *qua bella inciderint, sustentare consuerint.*

[1] **his:** *Bellovacis.* **discessum:** 'retreat'; see II, 11.1.
[2] **Aeduorum copiis:** see II, 5.2-3 and II, 10.5. **eum:** Caesar. **facit verba:** 'made a plea'; how lit.?
[3] **Direct form:** *Bellovaci* omni tempore in fide atque amicitia civitatis Aeduae *fuerunt; impulsi* ab suis principibus, qui *dicebant,* Aeduos, a *te* in servitutem redactos, omnes indignitates contumeliasque perferre, et ab Aeduis *defecerunt* et populo Romano bellum *intulerunt.* Qui eius consilii principes *fuerant,* quod *intellegebant,* quantam calamitatem civitati intulissent (204.3), in Britanniam *profugerunt.*
[4] **Bellovacos,** etc.: *213b; 212c1.* **omni tempore:** see I, 11.3, note 7.
[5] **dicerent:** 'kept saying'; *175a.*
[6] **in:** 'to'. **servitutem:** *10f.* **omnes,** etc.: 'every kind of ill-treatment and insult'; *92c.*
[7] **et . . . et:** *234a.* **defecisse:** 'had revolted'; *57b.*
[8] **Qui:** as antecedent supply *eos* with *profugisse.* **principes:** here = *auctores,* 'advisers'.
[9] **Direct form:** *Petunt* non solum *Bellovaci,* sed etiam pro his *Aedui,* ut *tua* clementia ac mansuetudine in eos *utaris.* Quod si *feceris* (future perfect), Aeduorum auctoritatem apud omnes Belgas *amplificabis;* quorum auxiliis atque opibus, si qua bella *inciderunt,* sustentare *consuerunt (176b).*
[10] **petere, utatur:** vivid use of present tenses where past tenses might have been expected.
[11] **sua:** 'his well-known'; *157e.* **clementia:** 'mercifulness', the quality which leads a man to treat with kindness those against whom he has grounds of offense. Near the close of his life a temple was ordered built to 'Caesar's Mercifulness'; *268.* **mansuetudine:** 'compassionateness', the quality that makes one able to realize the sufferings of others. **in:** 'toward'. **Quod:** *118d.* **si,** etc.: *218.1b.*
[12] **si . . . sustentare:** 'to carry through any wars that had arisen'; how lit.? *168; 49a.*

Caesar makes terms with the Bellovaci and Ambiani, learns about the Nervians.

15.1. Caesar, honoris[1] Diviciaci atque Aeduorum causa, sese eos in fidem[2] recepturum et conservaturum dixit; et quod erat civitas[3] magna inter Belgas auctoritate atque hominum multitudine[4] praestabat, DC obsides poposcit. **2.** His traditis omnibusque armis ex oppido collatis,[5] ab eo loco in fines Ambianorum pervenit; qui se suaque omnia sine mora[6] dediderunt. **3.** Eorum[7] fines Nervii attingebant; quorum de natura moribusque Caesar cum quaereret, sic reperiebat: **4.** [8]*Nullum*[9] *aditum esse ad eos mercatoribus; nihil pati vini reliquarumque rerum ad luxuriam pertinentium*[10] *inferri, quod his rebus*[11] *relanguescere animos eorum et remitti virtutem existimarent;*[12] *esse homines feros magnaeque virtutis;* **5.** *increpitare atque incusare*[13] *reliquos Belgas, qui se populo Romano dedidissent patriamque virtutem proiecissent; confirmare, sese*[14] *neque legatos missuros neque ullam condicionem pacis accepturos.*

[1] **honoris:** dependent on *causa;* 'out of regard for Diviciacus'. etc.; *94b.* **Diviciaci:** dependent on *honoris; 102.*
[2] **in fidem:** as in II, 13.2, note 7.
[3] **civitas:** *Bellovacorum.* **auctoritate:** 'prestige'; *143a.*
[4] **multitudine:** *142a* (AG 418, B 226). **DC:** *sescentos; 36.* The fact that for the sake of his Aeduan supporters Caesar had spared the Bellovaci did not prevent him from exacting a large number of hostages to bind them in their pledge of submission.

[5] **collatis:** *69b.* **eo loco:** Bratuspantium. For Caesar's route, see Map 1.
[6] **mora:** 'delay.' **dediderunt:** 'surrendered'.
[7] **Eorum:** the Ambiani. **Nervii attingebant:** 'the country of the Nervians adjoined'; *282.* **de natura:** *116c.*
[8] **Direct form:** *Nullus aditus est* ad eos mercatoribus; nihil *patiuntur* vini reliquarumque rerum ad luxuriam pertinentium inferri, quod his rebus relanguescere animos eorum et remitti virtutem *existimant. Sunt* homines *feri* magnaeque virtutis; *increpitant* atque *incusant* reliquos Belgas, qui se populo Romano *dediderint* patriamque virtutem *proiecerint; confirmant,* sese neque legatos missuros [esse] neque ullam condicionem pacis accepturos [esse].
[9] **Nullum,** etc.: *212c3.* **mercatoribus:** *111.* **nihil vini:** 'no wine'; *97a.* The Nervii were water drinkers. **pati:** sc. *eos* as subject; *60.*
[10] **ad luxuriam pertinentium:** 'which contribute to luxurious living'; how lit.?
[11] **rebus:** *135a.* **relanguescere:** 'becomes weak'. **animos:** *92a.* **virtutem:** 'valour', the manifestation of courage in brave deeds.
[12] **existimarent:** *177a.* **magnae virtutis:** genitive of quality taking the place of an adjective, hence connected by *-que* with *feros; 100a.*
[13] **increpitare atque incusare:** sc. *eos,* 'that they upbraided and condemned'. **reliquos:** *171a.* **qui:** 'because they'; *194c.*
[14] **sese,** etc.: indirect discourse after *confirmare.* **sese:** refers to *eos* understood as subject of *confirmare.*

The Nervians, Atrebatians, and Viromanduans await Caesar at the Sambre.

16.1. Cum per eorum[1] fines triduum iter fecisset, inveniebat ex captivis: *Sabim*[2] *flumen a castris suis non amplius milia passuum X abesse;* **2.** *trans id flumen*[3] *omnes Nervios consedisse adventumque ibi Romanorum exspectare una cum Atrebatibus et Viromanduis, finitimis suis* (nam his utrisque[4] persuaserant, uti eandem belli fortunam experirentur); **3.** *exspectari etiam ab his Atuatucorum copias, atque esse in itinere;*[5] **4.** *mulieres, quique*[6] *per aetatem ad pugnam inutiles viderentur, in eum locum coniecisse, quo*[7] *propter paludes exercitui aditus non esset.*

[1] **eorum:** *Nerviorum.* **triduum:** = *tres dies; 118a.* **iter fecisset:** 'had advanced'; for the route see Map 1. **inveniebat:** = *quaerendo cognoscebat.*
[2] **Sabim,** etc.: *212c3.* **Sabim:** accusative like *turrim; 14c.* **milia:** why not ablative? *129b; 118a.*
[3] **trans id flumen:** they crossed over to the south side of the Sambre, which flows in an easterly direction into the Meuse; *292.*
[4] **his utrisque:** 'both these peoples'; *51; 23a.* The combined forces of the Nervians, Atrebatians, and Viromanduans were estimated at 75,000 (II, 4.7-9). **nam,** etc.: *214c.*
[5] **in itinere:** 'on the way'. **mulieres:** object of *coniecisse.*
[6] **quique:** i.e. *et eos, qui.* **per aetatem:** 'by reason of age'. **inutiles:** predicative, 'useless'. **eum locum:** 'a place', perhaps in the vicinity of the modern city of Mons; *160d.*
[7] **quo:** adverb, = *ad quem.* **esset:** subjunctive also in the direct form; *194a* (AG 535, B 283).

They plan to surprise him on the march.

17.1. His rebus cognitis, exploratores centurionesque praemittit, qui[1] locum idoneum castris deligant. **2.** Cum ex dediticiis Belgis reliquisque Gallis complures, Caesarem secuti, una iter facerent,[2] quidam ex his, ut postea ex captivis cognitum est, eorum[3] dierum consuetudine itineris nostri exercitus perspecta, nocte ad Nervios pervenerunt atque his demonstrarunt,[4] *Inter singulas legiones impedimentorum magnum numerum*[5] *intercedere, neque esse quicquam negotii,*[6] *cum prima legio in castra venisset reliquaeque legiones magnum spatium*[7] *abessent, hanc sub sarcinis adoriri;* **3.** *qua*[8] *pulsa impedimentisque direptis, futurum, ut reliquae*[9] *contra consistere non auderent.* **4.** Adiuvabat[10] etiam eorum consilium, qui rem deferebant, quod

Nervii antiquitus,[11] cum equitatu nihil possent (neque enim ad hoc tempus ei rei[12] student, sed, quicquid possunt, pedestribus valent copiis[13]), quo facilius finitimorum equitatum, si praedandi causa[14] ad eos venissent, impedirent, teneris[15] arbouribus incisis atque inflexis, crebrisque in latitudinem ramis enatis,[16] et rubis sentibusque interiectis, effecerant, ut instar muri[17] hae saepes munimentum praeberent, quo non modo non intrari, sed ne perspici[18] quidem posset. **5.** His rebus cum iter agminis nostri impediretur, non omittendum[19] sibi consilium Nervii existimaverunt.

[1] **qui ... deligant:** 'in order to choose'; *193a; 331a,b.* **ex . . . Gallis:** after *complures; 97d* (AG 346c, B 201.1a). **dediticiis:** the Suessiones (13.1), the Bellovaci (15.1), and the Ambiani (15.2).

[2] **facerent:** *185c.* **quidam:** *168.* **ut:** *188b.*

[3] **eorum . . . exercitus:** 'the marching order of our army in those days', the three days when Caesar was advancing into the country of the Nervians (16.1); how lit.?

[4] **demonstrarunt:** *64a1.* **impedimentorum,** etc.: *311; 74d.*

[5] **numerum:** 'quantity'. **esse:** the subject is *adoriri;* 'and that there was no difficulty — in attacking'; how lit.? *222b.* **quicquam:** *168; 49a.*

[6] **negotii:** *97b.* **castra:** the place selected for a camp ; the camp would not be constructedand fortified until the legions arrived; *332, 333.* **venisset, abessent:** indicative future perfect, and future, in direct discourse.

[7] **spatium:** *118a.* **sarcinis:** 'packs'. The plan was to attack the first legion to come up, just as it reached the place chosen for encampment, before the soldiers could deposit their packs and put themselves into fighting order; *330.*

[8] **qua:** 'when this' legion. **direptis:** 'had been plundered'; how lit.? **futurum** [esse]: the subject is *ut . . . auderent;* 'it would come about that'; *203.1.*

[9] **reliquae:** sc. *legiones.* **contra:** adverb. **contra consistere:** 'to withstand the attack'.

[10] **Adiuvabat:** the subject is *quod . . . effecerant;* 'the plan of those who furnished the information was favoured by the fact that the Nervii', etc. How lit.? *198b.*

[11] **antiquitus:** 'long ago'. **cum . . . possent:** 'not being strong in cavalry'; how lit.? *184a.* **nihil:** *118c.* **neque enim:** 'and in fact . . . not'.

[12] **ei rei student:** 'they give attention to that arm' of the service; *105.* **quicquid . . . copiis:** 'all the strength they have is in infantry'. How lit.? **quicquid:** *118b.*

[13] **copiis:** *142a.* **quo. . . impedirent:** *193b* (AG 531a,b 282.1a).

[14] **praedandi causa:** 'in order to plunder'; *230.1.* **venissent:** *220.*

[15] **teneris . . . inflexis:** 'cutting into young trees and bending them over'; how lit.? *144b2.* **in latitudinem:** 'at the sides', we should say.

[16] **ramis enatis:** with *crebris,* 'letting the branches grow thickly'; *151; 61a3.* How lit.? **rubis,** etc.: 'planting briars and thorn-bushes in the intervening spaces'; how lit.? **effecerant, ut. . . praeberent:** *203.3.* By cutting into young trees near the root they were able to bend them to a horizontal position without killing them. The stem of the tree would then increase in size very slowly, but along the trunk branches would grow out, above and on the sides (*in latitudinem*). In the spaces along the line of defense not filled by trees thus trained, briars and thornbushes were planted. The whole formed a living and impenetrable hedge. Similar hedges are still found in this region.

[17] **instar muri:** 'like a wall', lit. 'the likeness of a wall'; *instar,* indeclinable, is in apposition to *munimentum; 94b.* **saepes:** 'hedges'; *15b.* **munimentum:** 'line of defense'; *74d.* **praeberent:** 'made'. **quo:** adverb = *in quod (munimentum);* but trans. with the impersonal *intrari,* etc., 'which could not only not be penetrated but not even seen through'. How lit.? *73d; 237c.*

[18] **perspici:** *79b.* **posset:** *220.*

[19] **omittendum:** *89c, 73e.* **sibi:** *110.* **consilium:** 'the plan' of attack proposed above in 17.2-3.

The Romans make camp on a height sloping to the river.

18.1. Loci natura erat haec,[1] quem locum nostri castris delegerant. Collis[2] ab summo aequaliter declivis ad flumen Sabim, quod supra[3] nominavimus, vergebat. **2.** Ab eo flumine pari acclivitate collis nascebatur[4] adversus huic et contrarius, passus[5] circiter CC infimus apertus, ab superiore parte silvestris, ut[6] non facile introrsus perspici posset. **3.** Intra eas silvas hostes in occulto sese continebant; in aperto loco[7] secundum flumen paucae stationes equitum videbantur.[8] Fluminis erat altitudo pedum circiter trium.

[1] **haec:** 'as follows'; *161a*. **locum:** *165a*. **castris:** *112a*. The site has been identified, on the left or north bank of the Sambre (*Sabis*), in France, near the Belgian frontier, opposite the city of Hautmont. Map 6, **A.**

[2] **Collis:** on which the camp was laid out. **ab,** etc.: 'sloping evenly from the top, descended'; how lit.?

[3] **supra:** *16.1*. **nominavimus:** 'we have mentioned by name'; *156*. **Ab eo:** 'From the'; *160d*. **pari acclivitate:** 'with similar upward slope'; *143a*.

[4] **nascebatur:** 'arose'. **adversus huic et contrarius:** 'facing this (hill) and opposite (to it)', on the south side of the Sambre; the highest part of the second hill is at **B** on Map 6. **huic:** *108a*.

[5] **passus:** *118a*. **CC:** *ducentos*; *36*. How far? *243b*. **infimus:** 'at the lower edge' of the hill, along the river. **apertus:** free from woods. **ab,** etc.: 'wooded along the upper portion'; *126c*.

[6] **ut:** 'so that'. **introrsus:** 'within'.

[7] **aperto loco:** indicated on Map 6, between the river and the broken line marking the northern limit of the woods. **secundum:** preposition, 'along'. **stationes:** 'pickets.'

[8] **videbantur:** trans. as passive. **pedum:** *100b*. **trium:** *37b*.

A furious attack is made on the Romans while fortifying the camp.

19.1. Caesar, equitatu praemisso,[1] subsequebatur omnibus copiis; sed ratio ordoque[2] agminis aliter se habebat, ac Belgae ad Nervios detulerant. **2.** Nam quod hostibus appropinquabat, consuetudine sua[3] Caesar VI legiones expeditas ducebat; post eas totius exercitus impedimenta[4] collocarat; **3.** inde duae legiones,[5] quae proxime conscriptae erant, totum agmen claudebant praesidioque impedimentis[6] erant. **4.** Equites nostri, cum funditoribus sagittariisque flumen transgressi,[7] cum hostium equitatu proelium commiserunt. **5.** Cum se illi identidem[8] in silvas ad suos reciperent ac rursus ex silva in nostros impetum facerent neque[9] nostri longius, quam quem ad finem[10] porrecta loca aperta pertinebant, cedentes[11] insequi auderent, interim legiones VI, quae primae venerant, opere[12] dimenso castra munire coeperunt. **6.** Ubi prima impedimenta[13] nostri exercitus ab eis, qui in silvis abditi latebant, visa sunt,[14] quod tempus inter eos committendi proelii[15] convenerat, ut intra silvas aciem ordinesque constituerant atque ipsi sese confirmaverant,[16] subito omnibus copiis[17] provolaverunt impetumque in nostros equites fecerunt. **7.** His facile pulsis ac proturbatis,[18] incredibili celeritate ad flumen decucurrerunt,[19] ut paene uno tempore et ad silvas[20] et in flumine et iam in manibus nostris hostes viderentur. **8.** Eadem autem celeritate adverso colle[21] ad nostra castra atque eos, qui in opere occupati[22] erant, contenderunt.

[1] **equitatu praemisso:** *328*. **omnibus copiis:** *137b*.

[2] **ratio ordoque:** 'principle of arrangement', lit. 'principle and arrangement'. **aliter,** etc.: 'were different from what the Belgians'; how lit.? **habebat:** *173a* (AG 317b, B 255.3). **ac:** *233c*.

[3] **consuetudine sua:** 'in accordance with his usual practice', when in the enemy's country; *136c*. **VI:** *38b*. The legions were those numbered 7-12. **expeditas:** predicative, 'in light order'; without the packs (*sarcinae*), which in such cases were doubtless carried with the heavy

baggage; *115b*.
[4] **impedimenta:** *311*. **collocarat:** full form? *64a1*.
[5] **duae legiones:** numbered 13 and 14 (see 2.1). **proxime:** *35*.
[6] **praesidio, impedimentis:** *112b*; *328* (AG 382.1, B 191.2a).
[7] **transgressi:** to the south side of the Sambre. **cum:** *137c*. **equitatu:** the cavalry (18.3) must have been furnished by the Atrebatians and Viromanduans, not by the Nervians (17.4).
[8] **identidem:** 'repeatedly'. **suos:** the enemy's infantry, concealed in the woods (18.3). **reciperent:** *175d*.
[9] **neque:** trans. as if *et* . . *non*. **longius:** 'further'.
[10] **quem ad finem:** = *ad eum finem ad quem*, 'to the limit to which'. **porrecta,** etc.: 'the stretch of open ground extended'; how lit.?
[11] **cedentes:** sc. *eos* (*hostes*), object of *insequi*; 'as they retreated'. **primae venerant:** 'had been the first to come up'; *152b*.
[12] **opere:** 'the trench-work', the first work on the fortifications of the camp; *333*. **dimenso:** 'having measured off'; how lit.? *144b2*; *59b*.
[13] **prima impedimenta:** 'the first part of the baggage train'; Map 6; *152a*.
[14] **visa sunt:** passive in meaning. **quod tempus:** *i.e. tempus* (in thought an appositive of the clause *Ubi . . . visa sunt*, but attracted into the relative clause) . . . *quod convenerat*, 'which had been agreed to'; *165b*.
[15] **committendi proelii:** dependent on *tempus*, 'for beginning the battle'; how lit.? *230.1*. **ut:** 'just as'.
[16] **ipsi sese confirmaverant:** 'had encouraged one another'.
[17] **copiis:** *136b*. **provolaverunt:** 'they rushed forward'. **nostros equites:** who had crossed the river (19.4).
[18] **proturbatis:** 'scattered in a panic'. **incredibili:** *74f*.
[19] **decucurrerunt:** 'they ran down' the sloping ground between the edge of the forest and the river. **ut:** 'so that'. **tempore:** 'instant'.
[20] **ad silvas:** 'near the woods', whence they had just emerged. **in manibus nostris:** in our idiom, 'upon us'; how lit.?
[21] **adverso colle . . . contenderunt:** 'dashed up the hill' on the north side of the Sambre. The Belgians may have covered the distance between the woods on the south side of the Sambre and the site of the Roman camp in ten minutes; the distance is about two-thirds of an English mile.
[22] **occupati:** 'engaged'; *148c*.

Discipline and training enable the soldiers to meet the emergency.

20. Caesari[1] omnia uno tempore erant agenda: vexillum proponendum,[2] quod erat insigne, cum ad arma concurri oporteret; signum tuba[3] dandum ; ab opere revocandi milites; qui[4] paulo longius aggeris petendi causa processerant, arcessendi;[5] acies instruenda, milites cohortandi, signum dandum.[6] **2.** Quarum rerum magnam partem temporis brevitas[7] et incursus hostium impediebat. **3.** His[8] difficultatibus duae res erant subsidio, scientia atque usus militum, quod superioribus proeliis exercitati, quid fieri oporteret,[9] non minus commode ipsi sibi praescribere, quam ab aliis doceri poterant, et quod[10] ab opere singulisque legionibus singulos legatos Caesar discedere,[11] nisi munitis castris, vetuerat. **4.** Hi propter propinquitatem et celeritatem hostium nihil[12] iam Caesaris imperium exspectabant, sed per se,[13] quae videbantur, administrabant.

[1] **Caesari:** emphatic, hence placed at the beginning; *110*; *229c*. **vexillum:** 'the flag'; *324b3*; Fig. 149.
[2] **proponendum, dandum, revocandi,** etc.: sc. *erat, erant*; *229c*. **ad arma concurri:** 'to arm'; how lit.? *73d*.
[3] **tuba:** 'with the trumpet'; the signal was to "form-up"; *326a1*; **opere:** as in 19.5, note 12. **revocandi** [erant]: 'had to be recalled'.

[4] **qui**: as antecedent sc. *ei* (*milites*), subject of *arcessendi* [*erant*]. **paulo longius**: 'a little further' than usual; *140*. **aggeris**: 'material' for the rampart, in this case probably wood; *230.1*.

[5] **arcessendi** [erant]: 'had to be sent for'. **cohortandi** [erant]: see I, 25.1; note 3.

[6] **signum dandum** [erat]: 'the signal' for battle 'had to be given'; *326c*. **Quarum**: *167*.

[7] **brevitas**: 'the shortness'. **incursus**: 'the onrush'. **impediebat**: *173a*.

[8] **His . . . subsidio**: 'Two things served to offset these disadvantages', explained by *scientia . . . poterant* and *quod ab opere . . . vetuerat*; how lit.? *112b*.

[9] **oporteret**: *204.2*. **non minus**, etc.: 'they (themselves) were able to determine for themselves . . . just as fitly as others could instruct them'; How lit.? **ipsi**: agrees with the subject of *poterant*, but need not be translated.

[10] **quod**, etc: 'the fact that Caesar had forbidden the several lieutenants to leave the work and their respective legions'; how lit.? *198b*.

[11] **discedere**: *200b*. **nisi munitis castris**: 'only after the fortifying of the camp had been completed'.

[12] **nihil**: adverbial accusative; *118c*.

[13] **per se**: 'on their own responsibility'. **quae videbantur**: i.e. *quae videbantur administranda*, 'were taking (the measures) which the situation seemed to require'; how lit.? These veterans knew what to do, when they saw the enemy coming, and did not lose their heads.

They form hurriedly; under Caesar's encouragement they fight desperately, against great odds.

21. Caesar, necessariis rebus imperatis,[1] ad cohortandos milites, quam in partem[2] fors obtulit, decucurrit et ad legionem decimam devenit. **2.** Milites non longiore oratione cohortatus, quam uti[3] suae pristinae virtutis memoriam retinerent neu perturbarentur[4] animo, hostiumque impetum fortiter sustinerent, **3.** quod[5] non longius hostes aberant, quam quo telum adigi[6] posset, proelii committendi signum dedit. **4.** Atque in alteram partem[7] item cohortandi causa profectus pugnantibus occurrit.[8] **5.** Temporis[9] tanta fuit exiguitas hostiumque tam paratus ad dimicandum animus, ut non modo ad insignia accommodanda,[10] sed etiam ad galeas induendas[11] scutisque tegimenta detrahenda tempus defuerit. **6.** Quam[12] quisque ab opere in partem casu devenit quaeque[13] prima signa conspexit, ad haec constitit, ne in quaerendis suis[14] pugnandi tempus dimitteret.

[1] **necessariis rebus imperatis**: 'having given (only) the indispensable orders'.

[2] **quam in partem**: = *in eam partem, in quam*; with *fors obtulit*, 'where chance led', a statement introduced to explain why Caesar came first to the tenth legion, which, as the most experienced, had least need of the general's presence; *69b*. **decucurrit**: Caesar was perhaps near the northeast corner of the camp (Map 6, **A**) when he started to rush down the slope to where the troops were forming.

[3] **uti . . . sustinerent**: substantive clauses giving the gist of the words of exhortation; *199a*.

[4] **neu perturbarentur animo**: we might say 'and keep cool'; how lit.? *142a*; *199d*.

[5] **quod . . . aberant**: gives the reason for *signum dedit*. **quam quo**: 'than (the distance) to which'; *194b* (AG 571a,b 283.2a).

[6] **adigi**: 'be thrown'. **signum**: see 20.1, note 6.

[7] **alteram partem**: 'another part' of the hastily formed line; apparently Caesar went across to the right wing, where the seventh and twelfth legions were. See Map 6.

[8] **pugnantibus occurrit**: 'he found (the men already) fighting'; *107a*; *175b*.

[9] **Temporis . . . exiguitas**: 'So short was the time'. How lit.? **hostium**: dependent on *animus*; *233b*; *353d*.

[10] **ad insignia accommodanda**: 'for fitting on their decorations', particularly the crests, which were taken off the helmets on the march. In battle it was important that these crests be in place; by their different forms and colours different legions and cohorts could be distinguished.

[11] **ad galeas induendas**: 'for putting on their helmets' (Fig. 174); *322a*. **scutis**, etc.: 'for

drawing the coverings off the shields', which were protected against moisture; *127a* (AG 401, B 214).

[12] **Quam.** etc.: 'Whatever part (of the line) each (soldier) chanced (to reach as) he came down from the trench-work, (in that part he stayed) and'; how lit.?

[13] **quaeque:** = *et quae*; trans. as if *ad* ('by') *haec signa, quae prima conspexit, constitit* ('he took his stand'). Under ordinary circumstances it was a serious offense for a soldier to be found in a maniple in which he did not belong; *324b2*.

[14] **in quaerendis suis:** sc. *signis*.

MAP 6

THE BATTLE AT THE SAMBRE (SABIS): FIRST PHASE

Book II, 18–22   To face page 164

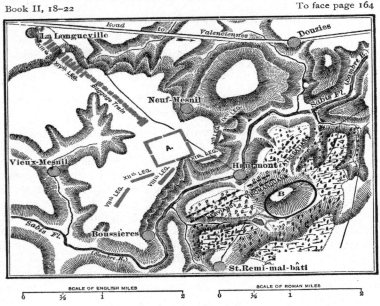

EXPLANATION

Caesar's army, approaching the Sambre from the north, started to make a camp on a hill overlooking the river. The Belgian forces, comprising Nervians, Viromanduans, and Atrebatians, were lying in wait on the south side.

Supposing that each legion would be followed by its baggage train, the Belgians had planned to attack the first legion and destroy it before the others could come to the rescue, and in like manner to destroy the others one by one. Caesar, however, had placed six legions in light marching order first, then all the baggage, and two legions last, the XIIIth and XIVth; he sent cavalry, bowmen, and slingers in advance of the main column.

When the baggage train came into view, the Belgians hurled back the cavalry, bowmen, and slingers, rushed across the river and charged up the hill.

A. The Roman camp (chap. 18, ll. 1–7), with six legions forming in front.
B. The camp of the Belgians (chap. 26, ll. 10–12)

22.1. Instructo exercitu, magis ut loci[1] natura deiectusque collis et necessitas temporis, quam ut rei[2] militaris ratio atque ordo postulabat, cum diversae[3] legiones aliae alia in parte hostibus resisterent, saepibusque densissimis,[4] ut ante demonstravimus, interiectis prospectus[5] impediretur, neque certa subsidia collocari[6] neque, quid in quaque parte opus esset, provideri,[7] neque ab uno omnia imperia administrari poterant. **2.** Itaque in tanta rerum iniquitate[8] fortunae quoque eventus varii[9] sequebantur.

[1] **ut:** 'as'. **loci:** 'of the ground'.

[2] **rei . . . ordo:** 'the arrangement approved by military science'; how lit.?

[3] **diversae:** 'separated'. **aliae alia in parte:** fuller expression of the thought in *diversae;* 'one at one point, another at another'; *171c.*

[4] **densissimis:** 'very thick'; *153a.* **ante:** see 17.4.

[5] **prospectus:** 'the view' over the field of battle.

[6] **certa subsidia collocari** [poterant]: 'could reserves be posted at fixed points'; the movements of the enemy were so obscured by the thickets that Caesar could not tell where reserve forces could be posted to advantage. **certa:** *151* (AG 290, B 239). **quaque:** from *quisque.* **opus esset:** *132b.*

[7] **provideri:** sc. *poterat.* **uno:** 'one person'. **omnia imperia . . . administrari:** 'all orders . . . be given'.

[8] **in tanta rerum iniquitate:** 'under so disadvantageous conditions'; how lit.? **fortunae:** dependent on *eventus.*

[9] **eventus varii:** 'various outcomes'.

Two legions drive the Atrebatians across the river, two force back the Viromanduans, but two are outflanked by the Nervians.

23.1. Legionis VIIII et X[1] milites, ut in sinistra parte aciei constiterant, pilis emissis[2] cursu ac lassitudine exanimatos vulneribusque confectos[3] Atrebates (nam his ea pars obvenerat) celeriter ex loco superiore[4] in flumen compulerunt et, transire conantes[5] insecuti, gladiis magnam partem eorum impeditam[6] interfecerunt. **2.** Ipsi transire flumen non dubitaverunt et, in locum iniquum[7] progressi, rursus resistentes hostes,[8] redintegrato proelio, in fugam coniecerunt. **3.** Item alia in parte[9] diversae duae legiones, XI et VIII, profligatis Viromanduis,[10] quibuscum erant congressae, ex loco superiore, in ipsis fluminis ripis proeliabantur.[11] **4.** At totis fere castris a fronte et a[12] sinistra parte nudatis, cum[13] in dextro cornu legio XII et, non magno ab ea intervallo, VII[14] constitisset, omnes Nervii confertissimo agmine duce Boduognato,[15] qui summam imperii tenebat, ad eum locum contenderunt; **5.** quorum pars ab aperto latere[16] legiones circumvenire, pars summum castrorum locum[17] petere coepit.

[1] **VIIII, X:** *nonae, decimae; 38b.* **aciei:** *21b.* For the position of the legions see Map 6.

[2] **pilis emissis:** 'having hurled their pikes'; *322d.* **lassitudine:** 'fatigue', resulting from the three-quarter mile dash downhill to the river, crossing the river, and uphill to the Roman line. **exanimatos:** 'who were out of breath'; *227a1.*

[3] **vulneribus confectos:** 'disabled by wounds', referring to those struck by the pikes. **ea pars:** the Roman left wing, of which Labienus was in command. **obvenerat:** 'had encountered'.

[4] **loco superiore:** the Romans, being nearer the top of the hill, were on higher ground. **compulerunt:** 'forced'.

[5] **conantes:** sc. *eos* (*Atrebates*), object of *insecuti.*

[6] **impeditam:** by the crossing of the river. **Ipsi:** the soldiers of the ninth and tenth legions. **transire:** *201b.*

[7] **locum iniquum:** the 'ground' south of the Sambre, sloping back from the river and in part covered with woods; Map 7.

[8] **hostes:** object of *coniecerunt.* **redintegrato proelio:** 'they (the Romans) renewed the battle and'; *144b2.*

[9] **alia in parte:** the Roman center, in front of the camp. See Map 7. **diversae:** 'in different

places'; not, as ordinarily, forming a continuous line.
[10] **profligatis Viromanduis:** 'having driven the Viromanduans'. **quibuscum:** *125c.* **erant congressae:** *57c.*
[11] **proeliabantur:** 'were continuing the battle'; *175a.*
[12] **a:** *126b.* **nudatis:** not only the 8th and 11th legions in front, but the 9th and 10th legions on the left of the camp, had abandoned their positions to pursue the enemy, leaving the camp 'unprotected' except on the right, where the 12th and 7th legions stood.
[13] **cum:** 'since'. *184a.* **XII:** *duodecima.* **non:** with *magno; 239g.* **intervallo:** *138.*
[14] **VII:** *(legio) septima.* **constitisset:** why singular? **omnes Nervii:** their fighting force was estimated by the Remi at 50,000 (II, 4.8), but was later reported as 60,000 (II, 28.2). **confertissimo agmine:** a mass formation, like that of the Helvetians (I, 24.4); called 'column', *agmen,* rather than 'battle-line', *acies,* because it was still advancing, not yet having divided in order to deliver the attack at two points.
[15] **duce Boduognato:** 'led by Boduognatus'; how lit.? *144b2.* **summam imperii:** 'the supreme command'.
[16] **ab aperto latere:** 'on the exposed flank', the right flank. **legiones:** the 7th and 12th.
[17] **summum castrorum locum:** 'the height on which the camp was'; how lit.?

The Roman camp is taken; seemingly all is lost.

24.1. Eodem tempore equites nostri levisque armaturae pedites,[1] qui cum eis una[2] fuerant, quos primo hostium impetu pulsos dixeram,[3] cum se in castra reciperent, adversis hostibus occurrebant ac rursus aliam in partem fugam petebant; **2.** et calones,[4] qui ab decumana porta ac summo iugo collis nostros[5] victores flumen transisse conspexerant, praedandi causa egressi, cum respexissent et hostes[6] in nostris castris versari vidissent, praecipites[7] fugae sese mandabant. **3.** Simul eorum, qui[8] cum impedimentis veniebant, clamor fremitusque[9] oriebatur, aliique aliam in partem perterriti ferebantur.[10] **4.** Quibus omnibus rebus permoti, equites Treveri, quorum inter Gallos virtutis opinio[11] est singularis, qui auxilii causa a civitate[12] ad Caesarem missi venerant, cum multitudine hostium castra nostra compleri, legiones[13] premi et paene circumventas teneri, calones, equites, funditores, Numidas diversos dissipatosque[14] in omnes partes fugere vidissent, desperatis nostris rebus, domum contenderunt; **5.** Romanos pulsos superatosque,[15] castris impedimentisque eorum hostes potitos, civitati renuntiaverunt.

[1] **levis armaturae pedites:** slingers and bowmen (II, 19.4).
[2] **cum eis una:** 'along with them', the cavalry.
[3] **dixeram:** II, 19.6-7. **reciperent, respexissent:** force of *re-?* *79d.* **adversis,** etc.: 'were meeting the enemy face to face'; *107a.* The Nervians came up so rapidly that they were already entering the Roman camp at the time when Caesar's cavalry and light-armed troops, which had been routed on the other side of the Sambre, were just coming back to it again. The descriptive force of the imperfects in this chapter adds to the vividness of the picture.
[4] **calones:** 'camp-servants', chiefly, we may assume, servants of officers. **ab decumana porta:** 'at the rear gate' of the camp, which, since the hill sloped toward the river, was on the highest part of the hill. Map 7, **C, C;** *334a.*
[5] **nostros:** the 9th and 10th legions. **praedandi,** etc.: they were leaving the camp by the rear gate to hunt for plunder.
[6] **hostes . . . versari:** 'that the enemy were moving about'.
[7] **praecipites:** 'precipitately'; *151;* (AG 290, B 239).
[8] **eorum, qui:** the drivers of the baggage-train, just coming up; behind it were the 13th and 14th legions bringing up the rear. See Map 7. **clamor:** 'shouting'.
[9] **fremitus:** 'hubbub'. **oriebatur:** *61b; 173a.* **aliique,** etc.: 'some in one direction, others in another'; *171c.*

[10] **ferebantur:** 'were rushing'; *174 (B 256.1)*.

[11] **virtutis opinio:** 'reputation for courage'; meant of the Treveri as a whole, not merely of the cavalry. **singularis:** 'extraordinary'. The implication is that the Treveran horsemen went away not by reason of cowardice but because they thought the day hopelessly lost. **auxilii, etc.:** Caesar must have made an agreement with the Treveri before starting on this campaign.

[12] **civitate:** personified, hence with *a*; *126a*. **cum . . . vidissent:** *185c*.

[13] **legiones:** the 7th and 12th; see Map 7.

[14] **diversos dissipatosque:** 'separated', one body of troops from another, 'and scattered'. **desperatis,** etc.: 'despairing of our victory'; *144b3*.

[15] **pulsos, superatos:** sc. *esse*. **castris, impedimentis:** after *potitos* [*esse*]; *131c*.

Caesar rushes into the fight, calls centurions by name, directs the formation of a double front.

25.1. Caesar[1] ab[2] X legionis cohortatione ad dextrum cornu profectus, ubi suos urgeri[3] signisque in unum locum collatis XII[4] legionis confertos milites sibi ipsos ad pugnam esse impedimento vidit, quartae cohortis[5] omnibus centurionibus occisis signiferoque[6] interfecto, signo amisso, reliquarum cohortium omnibus fere centurionibus aut vulneratis aut occisis, in his primipilo[7] P. Sextio Baculo, fortissimo viro, multis gravibusque[8] vulneribus confecto, ut iam se sustinere non posset, reliquos esse tardiores[9] et non nullos ab novissimis, deserto loco,[10] proelio excedere ac tela vitare, hostes neque[11] a fronte ex inferiore loco subeuntes intermittere et ab utroque latere instare et rem[12] esse in angusto vidit, neque ullum esse subsidium,[13] quod summitti posset; **2.** scuto ab novissimis uni[14] militi detracto, quod ipse eo sine scuto venerat, in primam aciem processit centurionibusque nominatim[15] appellatis, reliquos cohortatus, milites signa inferre et manipulos laxare[16] iussit, quo facilius gladiis uti possent. **3.** Cuius[17] adventu spe illata militibus ac redintegrato animo, cum pro se quisque[18] in conspectu imperatoris etiam in extremis suis rebus operam navare[19] cuperet, paulum hostium impetus tardatus est.[20]

[1] **Caesar:** the beginning of a complex sentence which extends to *possent* at the end of 25.2. The principal clause has for its subject *Caesar*, with which the participles *profectus* and *cohortatus* agree; for its predicate it has the verbs *processit* and *iussit*. The leading subordinate clause is *ubi . . . vidit*, which is so expanded by the introduction of details that *vidit* is repeated for clearness. These details are expressed in part by infinitives with subject-accusatives dependent on *vidit*, in part by ablatives absolute, and in part by the minor clauses *ut . . . posset* and *quod . . . posset*. In translating, the sentence may be broken up into three or four English sentences; most of the ablatives absolute are best rendered by clauses.

[2] **ab . , . cohortatione:** = *ab decima legione, quam cohortatus erat*. Caesar's account of his personal part in this battle, which was interrupted by his description of the progress of the fighting (II, 22-24) is here resumed from 21.1-4. X: *38b, 36*.

[3] **suos urgeri:** 'that his men were hard pressed'. **signis:** 'the standards' of the maniples; *324b2*.

[4] **XII:** *duodecimae*. The crowding together of the soldiers of the 12th legion, which exposed them all the more to the missiles of the enemy, and their consequent losses, were no doubt in part due to their lack of experience in fighting; for this legion, raised in 58 B.C. (I, 10.3, note 8), had been in service only a year. During the battle with the Helvetians it guarded the baggage, having no part in the fray. **sibi . . . impedimento:** 'were hindering one another in fighting'; how lit.? *178; 112b*.

[5] **quartae cohortis:** at the front, perhaps at the end of the first line; *337a*; Fig. 186.

[6] **signifero:** 'the standard-bearer'. Each cohort had three standards, of which there were thirty in the legion. Here the reference probably is to the standard-bearer who carried the standard of the first maniple of the cohort, which was looked upon as the standard of the

cohort; *324b2*.

⁷ **primipilo:** 'the first centurion' of the first cohort, hence regarded as the first centurion of the legion; *315b*.

⁸ **multis gravibusque:** 'many severe wounds'; *152c*. **confecto:** 'exhausted'; with *primipilo*. Baculus did not die, but lived to establish the reputation of being one of the bravest, if not the most brave, among Caesar's men. **ut:** 'so that'.

⁹ **tardiores:** 'less active', having lost their initiative. **ab novissimis:** 'in the rear ranks'; *126c*.

¹⁰ **deserto loco . . . excedere:** 'had abandoned their position and were withdrawing'; how lit.? **proelio:** *127a*. **hostes,** etc.: 'that both in front the enemy did not cease coming up – and on both flanks', etc.; see Map 7. The Nervians outnumbered the men of the 12th and 7th legions five or six to one.

¹¹ **neque . . . et:** *233d*. **ex inferiore loco:** 'from the lower ground' along the river.

¹² **rem,** etc.: 'that matters had reached a crisis'; how lit.? *154a*.

¹³ **subsidium:** 'reserve force': the 13th and 14th legions were not yet available, because too far off. **posset:** *194a* (AG 535a, B 283.2). **scuto,** etc.: 'snatching a shield from a soldier in the rear rank'; how lit.? *144b2*.

¹⁴ **uni:** here 'a', weaker than 'one'; in English "an" and "one" were originally the same word; *23a*. **militi:** *109b* (AG 381, B 188.2d). **eo:** adverb. **sine scuto:** in battle even commanders may have carried shields, for protection in an emergency.

¹⁵ **nominatim:** Caesar's personal knowledge of his men was always an important factor in his success. **signa inferre:** 'to advance'; *325*.

¹⁶ **manipulos laxare:** 'to open up the ranks', we say; lit. 'to spread out the companies'. **quo:** *193b*.

¹⁷ **Cuius:** *167*. **illata:** *69b*. **militibus:** why dative?

¹⁸ **pro se quisque:** *170b*. **in extremis suis rebus:** 'under conditions of the utmost peril to himself'; how lit.?

¹⁹ **operam navare:** 'to do his best'.

²⁰ **tardatus est:** 'was checked'.

26.1. Caesar, cum VII legionem, quae iuxta¹ constiterat, item urgeri ab hoste vidisset,² tribunos militum monuit, ut paulatim sese legiones coniungerent et conversa signa³ in hostes inferrent. **2.** Quo facto, cum aliis alii subsidium ferrent,⁴ neque timerent, ne aversi ab hoste circumvenirentur, audacius resistere ac fortius pugnare coeperunt. **3.** Interim milites legionum duarum,⁵ quae in novissimo agmine praesidio impedimentis fuerant, proelio nuntiato, cursu incitato⁶ in summo colle ab hostibus conspiciebantur, **4.** et T. Labienus castris⁷ hostium potitus et ex loco superiore, quae⁸ res in nostris castris gererentur, conspicatus, X legionem subsidio⁹ nostris misit. **5.** Qui cum ex equitum et calonum fuga, quo in loco res esset,¹⁰ quantoque in periculo et castra et legiones et imperator versaretur,¹¹ cognovissent, nihil¹² ad celeritatem sibi reliqui fecerunt.

¹ **iuxta:** the 7th legion was 'near by' the 12th, on the right wing; see Map 6.

² **vidisset . . . ut . . . inferrent:** *185c*. **ut . . . inferrent:** 'that the (two) legions gradually draw together, face about, and advance against the enemy'. One legion probably simply took up a position behind the other, facing in the opposite direction, so that the rear of both was secure; *199a*.

³ **conversa signa:** *325*; *228a* (AG 496n2, B 337.2).

⁴ **ferrent:** *184a*. **neque:** trans. as if *et . . non*. **ne:** *202*. **aversi:** 'in the rear'; the new formation is shown on Map 7.

⁵ **legionum duarum:** the 13th and 14th; see Map 7.

⁶ **cursu incitato:** 'having quickened their pace'; relation of this ablative absolute to the preceding? **summo colle:** 'the top of the hill' behind the Roman camp; *152a*.

⁷ **castris:** *131c*. **loco superiore:** the height on which the Belgian camp was located; Map 7, **B**. To this height Labienus with the 9th and 10th legions had pursued the Atrebates (23.1-2). The

probable lines of flight and pursuit are indicated on Map 7.

[8] **quae:** *48b.* **gererentur:** *204.2.* **conspicatus:** as spy-glasses were not yet invented, Labienus estimated by eye the distance from camp to camp at over a mile. **X:** *decimam.*

[9] **subsidio, nostris:** *112b.* **Qui cum:** 'And when they'; *167.* **Qui:** plural from the idea of *milites* in *legionem.*

[10] **quo in loco res esset:** 'how matters stood'; how lit.? *204.2* (AG 574, B 300.1).

[11] **versaretur:** agrees with the nearest subject; trans. 'were'; *172b; 204.3.*

[12] **nihil . . . fecerunt:** 'they made the utmost possible speed', more lit. 'left nothing undone in regard to speed'. **sibi:** *109a.* **reliqui:** predicate genitive.

27.1. Horum adventu tanta rerum commutatio est facta, ut nostri, etiam qui[1] vulneribus confecti procubuissent, scutis[2] innixi proelium redintegrarent, calones, perterritos hostes conspicati, etiam inermes[3] armatis occurrerent, **2.** equites vero,[4] ut turpitudinem fugae virtute delerent, omnibus in locis pugnando[5] se legionariis militibus praeferrent. **3.** At hostes etiam[6] in extrema spe salutis tantam virtutem praestiterunt, ut, cum primi eorum[7] cecidissent, proximi iacentibus insisterent[8] atque ex eorum corporibus pugnarent; **4.** his deiectis et coacervatis cadaveribus,[9] qui superessent, ut ex tumulo,[10] tela in nostros conicerent et pila intercepta remitterent; **5.** ut[11] non nequiquam tantae virtutis homines iudicari deberet ausos esse[12] transire latissimum flumen, ascendere altissimas[13] ripas, subire iniquissimum locum, quae[14] facilia ex difficillimis animi magnitudo redegerat.

[1] **qui:** (*ei*) *qui.* **procubuissent:** 'had sunk down'; *220* (AG 593, B 324.1).

[2] **scutis:** *131c.* **innixi:** 'supporting themselves'. **redintegrarent:** *197b.* **perterritos:** predicative.

[3] **inermes:** with *calones;* placed, for the sake of contrast, next to *armatis;* 'unarmed, rushed against armed (men)'.

[4] **vero:** *236a.* **turpitudinem:** 'disgrace'. **delerent:** 'they might wipe out'. **omnibus,** etc.: 'strove to outdo the legionaries at all points in fighting'. Cavalry was considered by the Romans as secondary and auxiliary to the legion; *309.*

[5] **pugnando:** *230.4.* **militibus:** *107b.*

[6] **etiam,** etc.: 'even in utter despair of safety'.

[7] **primi eorum:** 'their foremost ranks'; how lit.? *154a.*

[8] **iacentibus insisterent:** 'mounted upon the fallen'; *227a4.* **ex:** *126c.*

[9] **coacervatis cadaveribus:** 'when their bodies had been heaped' on those of the Nervians that had first fallen. **qui:** as antecedent supply *ei,* subject of *conicerent.* **superessent:** *220.*

[10] **ut ex tumulo:** 'as from a mound'. **conicerent:** 'continued to hurl'. **pila intercepta remitterent:** 'picked up and threw back the pikes', though these could be of little value as weapons; cf. I, 25.3, note 9. **conicerent, remitterent:** in the same construction as *insisterent, pugnarent; 197b.*

[11] **ut,** etc.: a result clause, presenting Caesar's conclusion; 'so that it ought not to be thought that men of so great valour in vain dared', etc.; they fought in a manner worthy of their heroic advance.

[12] **ausos esse:** *62.* **latissimum:** *153a.*

[13] **altissimas:** the banks are steep where the Nervians crossed.

[14] **quae:** 'things (referring to the actions expressed in the preceding infinitives) which, in themselves most difficult, their heroic courage had made easy'; how lit.? **facilia:** *115b.*

MAP 7

THE BATTLE AT THE SAMBRE (SABIS): SECOND PHASE

Book II, 23-27   To face page 172

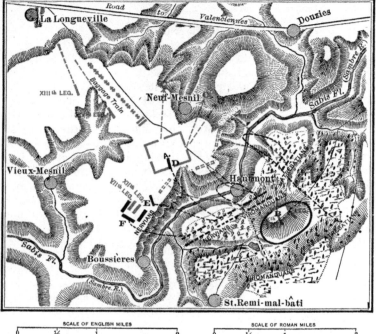

SCALE OF ENGLISH MILES   SCALE OF ROMAN MILES

EXPLANATION

The Atrebatians, having crossed the river, were thrown back by the IXth and X[th] legions, and fled through the woods east of the Belgian camp. The IXth and X[th] legions entered the Belgian camp (**B**), which was on a hill.

In like manner the XIth and VIIIth legions routed the Viromanduans and crossed to the south side of the river in pursuit.

Of the Nervians, one division (**D**) made for the Roman camp (**A**) and entered it; the cavalry, bowmen, and slingers that had taken refuge there fled precipitately (**C**). Other divisions (**E, F**) started to surround the VIIth and XIIth legions, which by Caesar's order took up a position rear to rear.

Hearing the noise of battle the baggage train halted, and the XIIIth and XIVth legions hastened to the scene.

Caesar rushed into the front rank, and saved the day.

Caesar spares the remnant of the Nervians.

28.1. Hoc proelio facto,[1] et prope ad internecionem gente ac nomine Nerviorum redacto, maiores natu, quos una cum pueris mulieribusque in aestuaria[2] ac paludes coniectos dixeramus,[3] hac pugna nuntiata, cum victoribus nihil impeditum, victis[4] nihil tutum arbitrarentur, **2.** omnium, qui supererant, consensu legatos ad Caesarem miserunt seque ei dediderunt; et in commemoranda civitatis calamitate, ex DC[5] ad tres senatores, ex hominum milibus LX vix ad D, qui arma ferre possent, sese redactos esse dixerunt. **3.** Quos Caesar, ut in[6] miseros ac supplices usus misericordia videretur, diligentissime conservavit suisque finibus atque oppidis uti iussit et finitimis imperavit, ut[7] ab iniuria et maleficio se suosque prohiberent.

[1] **Hoc proelio facto:** 'Now that this battle was over'; how lit.? **internecionem:** 'utter destruction'. Six years later, however, the Nervians were expected to send a force of 6000 warriors to Alesia (VII, 75.3). **gente:** 'stock'.
[2] **aestuaria:** here 'tidal marshes', surrounded by salt water at high tide. **paludes:** 'swamps'. **coniectos:** *89c.*
[3] **dixeramus:** 16.4. **cum:** *184a.* **nihil impeditum:** 'that there was nothing to oppose'; how lit.?
[4] **victis:** *227a4.* **nihil tutum:** 'no safety', we should say. **omnium:** masculine, dependent on *consensu.*
[5] **DC:** *sescentis (senatoribus).* Reckoning the Nervian army at 60,000 (10,000 more than the Remi reported; 4.8), 600 *senatores* would average one to every 100 men. It is possible, therefore, that the Latin word *senator* is here applied to a leader of a hundred; and this suggestion seems to be confirmed by the losses of the *senatores* in battle. **D:** *quingentos,* modified by *vix,* 'barely'. Exaggeration on the part of the suppliants was to be expected. **qui . . . possent:** subjunctive in the direct form; *194a.*
[6] **in:** 'toward'. **usus:** sc. *esse;* *221b* (AG 582, B 328.2). **misericordia:** 'compassion'; cf. 14.4; *131c.*
[7] **ut,** etc.: *199a.* **iniuria et maleficio:** 'wrong-doing and ill-treatment' of the weak remnant of the Nervians.

CAPTURE OF THE STRONGHOLD OF THE ATUATUCI. 29-33

The Atuatuci gather in one stronghold.

29.1. Atuatuci, de quibus supra[1] scripsimus, cum omnibus copiis auxilio Nerviis[2] venirent, hac pugna nuntiata, ex itinere domum reverterunt; **2.** cunctis oppidis castellisque[3] desertis, sua omnia in unum oppidum,[4] egregie natura munitum, contulerunt. **3.** Quod cum[5] ex omnibus in circuitu partibus altissimas rupes[6] deiectusque haberet, una ex parte leniter acclivis aditus in latitudinem non amplius ducentorum pedum[7] relinquebatur; quem locum duplici altissimo muro munierant; tum magni ponderis[8] saxa et praeacutas trabes in[9] muro collocabant. **4.** Ipsi erant ex Cimbris Teutonisque[10] prognati, qui, cum iter in provinciam[11] nostram atque Italiam facerent, eis impedimentis, quae secum agere ac portare non poterant, citra[12] flumen Rhenum depositis, custodiam ex suis ac praesidium VI milia hominum una reliquerunt. **5.** Hi[13] post eorum obitum[14] multos annos a finitimis exagitati, cum alias bellum inferrent, alias illatum[15] defenderent, consensu eorum omnium pace facta, hunc sibi domicilio[16] locum delegerunt.

¹ **supra:** see II.16.3. **cum:** *185c.* **omnibus copiis:** 19,000 men, if they reached the estimate of the Remi (II, 4.10); *136b* (AG 412, B 220.1).

² **auxilio Nerviis:** *112b.* **ex itinere:** see Vocab., under *iter.*

³ **castellis:** 'fortresses'; small fortified places, perhaps occupied only in time of danger.

⁴ **oppidum:** 'stronghold', like that of the Bellovaci; see II, 13.2, note 4. Some locate this stronghold on the hill where now the citadel of Namur is, at the junction of the Meuse and the Sambre and across the Sambre from the city of Namur; see Map 8. Others, considering the hill at Namur too small, prefer, as the site of the stronghold, the hill of Falhize, which lies on the north bank of the Meuse, opposite the town of Huy, 19 miles below Namur. **egregie:** 'admirably'.

⁵ **Quod cum:** 'And although this'; *187*; *167.* **ex,** etc.: 'on all sides round about'; how lit.?

⁶ **rupes:** 'cliffs'; *15b.***leniter acclivis:** 'gently rising'. If the stronghold was on the hill across from Namur, this narrow 'approach' was on the southwest side.

⁷ **pedum:** the case is not influenced by *amplius;* *100a*; *129b.* **duplici:** 'double'; *26a.*

⁸ **ponderis:** *100a.* **praeacutas trabes:** 'beams sharpened at the ends'; *17c.*

⁹ **in:** 'on'. **collocabant:** 'they were placing', at the time (*tum*) when Caesar came up; the change of tense from the pluperfect (*munierant*) is to be noted.

¹⁰ **Cimbris Teutonisque,** etc.: see I, 33.4, note 12. **prognati:** 'descended'; *128b.*

¹¹ **provinciam:** *290.***impedimentis:** 'cattle and goods'; the use of *agere*, 'drive', with *portare,* shows that cattle as well as portable possessions are here included.

¹² **citra:** on the west side. **depositis:** with *impedimentis.* **custodiam:** 'as a guard' of the *impedimenta;* *115a.* **ex suis:** i.e. *sex milia hominum ex suis; 97d.* **praesidium:** 'as a garrison'.

¹³ **Hi:** the 6000 Atuatuci. **eorum:** the great host of the Cambrians and Teutons.

¹⁴ **obitum:** 'destruction', at Aquae Sextiae in 102 B.C. and at Vercellae in 101 B.C. **exagitati:** 'harassed'. **alias . . . alias:** 'sometimes . . . sometimes'.

¹⁵ **illatum:** sc. *bellum;* 'were repelling attack'. **eorum omnium:** 'of them all', including the Atuatuci and their neighbours.

¹⁶ **domicilio:** *112a.* **locum:** 'district'.

Caesar besieges it; the Atuatuci ridicule the siege-works.

30.1. Ac primo adventu¹ exercitus nostri crebras ex oppido excursiones² faciebant parvulisque proeliis cum nostris contendebant; **2.** postea vallo³ pedum XII, in circuitu XV milium crebrisque castellis circummuniti⁴ oppido sese continebant. **3.** Ubi, vineis actis,⁵ aggere exstructo, turrim procul constitui viderunt, primum irridere⁶ ex muro atque increpitare vocibus, quod⁷ tanta machinatio a tanto spatio institueretur: **4.** *Quibusnam⁸ manibus aut quibus viribus, praesertim homines tantulae staturae* (nam⁹ plerumque omnibus Gallis prae magnitudine corporum suorum brevitas nostra contemptui est) *tanti oneris¹⁰ turrim in muro sese collocare posse confiderent?*

¹ **primo adventu:** i.e. *primo post adventum tempore,* 'Immediately after the arrival'; *147b.*

² **excursiones:** 'sallies'. **parvulis proeliis:** 'skirmishes'; how lit.? *76c.*

³ **vallo, castellis:** these formed the line of contravallation; see Map 8. It has been thought strange that, if the site of the stronghold was opposite Namur, or at Falhize, no mention in this description is made of the Sambre or the Meuse. The brow of the hill on which the stronghold stood was so steep and high that perhaps the rivers hardly entered into Caesar's calculations in planning the contravallation. **pedum XII:** in height; *38b*; *100a.* **XV milium:** sc. *pedum,* though Caesar in such cases elsewhere has *passuum.* A circuit of three Roman miles seems to satisfy the conditions; *243b.*

⁴ **circummuniti:** 'closed in'; how lit.? **oppido:** *131a.*

⁵ **vineis actis:** *342a.* **aggere exstructo:** '(and) after an embankment had been built up'; *341.* **turrim:** *14b*; *342b.*

⁶ **irridere:** 'they (the Atuatuci) scoffed'; *182.* **increpitare vocibus:** 'made taunting remarks'; how lit.? *182*;*131a.*

⁷ **quod,** etc.: 'because (as they said) so big an engine', etc.; *214b* (AG 592.3, B 286.1). **a tanto**

spatio: 'so far off'; i.e., 'at' (lit. 'from') 'so great a distance'; cf. II, 7.3, note 9.

[8] **Quibusnam . . . confiderent:** *213b; 212c6.* **Quibusnam:** *48c.* **viribus:** *18a.* **homines,** etc.: contemptuous, '(being) men of so small size', 'such little chaps'; *91b; 100a.*

[9] **nam . . . est:** *214c.* **Gallis, contemptui:** both datives, but trans. 'held in contempt by the Gauls'; how lit.?

[10] **oneris:** 'weight'; *13e.* The Atuatuci seem to have thought that the Romans would have to pick up the tower in order to move it. **confiderent:** *217a* (AG 586, B 315.1).

> *Frightened by the approach of the moveable tower, they sue for peace; they*
> *secretly keep back arms.*

31.1. Ubi vero moveri[1] et appropinquare moenibus viderunt, nova atque inusitata[2] specie commoti, legatos ad Caesarem de pace miserunt, qui,[3] ad hunc modum locuti, **2.** *Non se existimare, Romanos sine ope[4] deorum bellum gerere, qui[5] tantae altitudinis machinationes tanta celeritate promovere possent, se suaque omnia[6] eorum potestati permittere* dixerunt; **3.** *Unum[7] petere ac deprecari: si forte pro sua clementia ac mansuetudine, quam ipsi ab aliis audirent,[8] statuisset, Atuatucos esse conservandos, ne se armis[9] despoliaret.* **4.** *Sibi omnes fere finitimos esse inimicos ac suae virtuti[10] invidere; a quibus se defendere, traditis armis,[11] non possent.* **5.** *Sibi praestare,[12] si in eum casum deducerentur, quamvis fortunam a[13] populo Romano pati, quam ab his per cruciatum interfici, inter quos dominari[14] consuessent.*

[1] **moveri,** etc.: sc.*turrim.* **moenibus:** *105.* **viderunt:** *Atuatuci.*

[2] **inusitata:** 'unwonted'. **specie:** 'sight'; *21b.*

[3] **qui:** subject of *dixerunt,* the last word of II, 31.2. **hunc:** 'the following'; *161a.*

[4] **ope:** 'help'. **deorum:** *8d.*

[5] **qui:** 'since they'; *194c* (AG 535e, B 283.3a).

[6] **se suaque omnia:** 'themselves and all they had'; how lit.? **eorum:** of the Romans.

[7] **Unum:** 'one thing (only)', explained by *ne . . . despoliaret.* **deprecari:** 'begged to escape'. **clementia,** etc.: cf. II, 14.4, note 11.

[8] **audirent:** 'they kept hearing about'; *audivissent,* implying a single instance, would have been less complimentary. **statuisset,** etc.: in the direct form, *si statueris* (future perfect) . . . *noli nos armis despoliare; 218.1b; 216.*

[9] **armis:** *127a.* **Sibi:** after *inimicos.*

[10] **virtuti:** *105.* **invidere:** 'envied'. **a:** we say 'against'.

[11] **traditis armis:** i.e. *si arma tradita essent; 144b4* (AG 420.4, B 227.2b).

[12] **praestare:** 'it was better'. **eum casum:** 'such a condition', involving a choice between the mercy of the Romans and the treatment of their neighbours. **quamvis fortunam:** 'any lot whatever'; *49a.*

[13] **a:** 'at the hands of'. **pati:** subject of *praestare; 222b.*

[14] **dominari:** 'to exercise dominion'; *61a1.* **consuessent:** *64a2.*

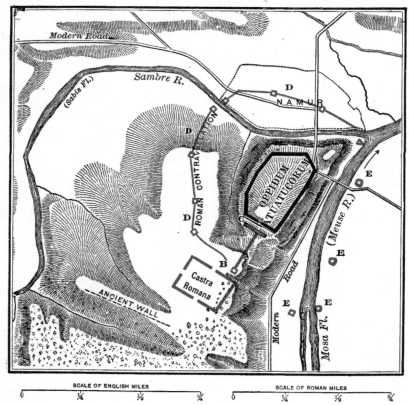

EXPLANATION

The Atuatuci abandoned their towns and gathered in a stronghold protected by steep cliffs except on one side, where there was an easy approach not more than 200 Roman feet wide.

Caesar blockaded the stronghold with a rampart and redoubts. Afterwards he ran an embankment up the inclined approach, and made ready to attack.

A. Incline along which Caesar-constructed his siege embankment, *agger*.

B. General's gate, *porta praetōria*, of Caesar's camp.

C. Upper end of the inclined approach, fortified with a double wall (chap. 29, ll. 8–10) and moat (chap. 32, ll. 9, 10).

D–D. Rampart, *vallum* (chap. 30, l. 3).

E–E. Redoubts, *castella* (chap. 30, l. 4).

32.1. Ad haec Caesar respondit: *Se magis consuetudine sua[1] quam merito eorum civitatem conservaturum, si,[2] prius quam murum aries attigisset, se dedidissent; sed deditionis nullam esse condicionem nisi armis traditis.[3]* **2.** *Se id, quod in Nerviis fecisset, facturum finitimisque imperaturum, ne[4] quam dediticiis populi Romani iniuriam inferrent.* **3.** Re nuntiata ad suos, illi se, quae imperarentur,[5] facere dixerunt. **4.** Armorum magna multitudine[6] de muro in fossam, quae erat ante oppidum, iacta, sic ut[7] prope summam muri aggerisque altitudinem acervi[8] armorum adaequarent, et tamen circiter parte tertia, ut postea perspectum est, celata[9] atque in oppido retenta, portis patefactis,[10] eo die pace sunt usi.

[1] **consuetudine sua:** 'in accordance with his practice' of mercifully treating a prostrate foe; *136c*. **merito:** *135a*.

[2] **si, etc.:** in the direct form, *civitatem conservabo, si, prius quam . . . attigerit* (future perfect), *vos dedideritis* (future perfect). **aries:** 'battering-ram'. It was a rule of war that besieged cities which did not capitulate before the battering-ram touched the walls, should when captured be given over to destruction; *10e; 342c*.

[3] **armis traditis:** *144b2*. **id, quod:** *160c*. **in:** 'in the case of'. **facturum:** *89c*.

[4] **ne, etc.:** *199a*. **quam:** *168; 49a*. **dediticiis:** *107b*.

[5] **imperarentur:** *214a*. **se facere:** 'that they carried out'; vivid use of the present tense where the future might have been expected.

[6] **multitudine:** 'quantity'; with *iacta*. **fossam:** Map 8, **C**.

[7] **sic ut, etc.:** *197b*. **summam . . . altitudinem:** 'the full height'; *152a*. The 'embankment' had been prolonged to the edge of the moat; the deep space between the end of the 'embankment' and the 'wall', from the bottom of the moat up, was nearly filled with weapons.

[8] **acervi:** 'heaps'.

[9] **celata:** 'concealed.'

[10] **patefactis:** 'thrown open'. **pace sunt usi:** 'they kept quiet'; lit. 'they enjoyed peace'.

They make a treacherous attack; are defeated, and sold into slavery.

33. Sub[1] vesperum Caesar portas claudi militesque ex oppido exire iussit, ne[2] quam noctu oppidani a militibus iniuriam acciperent. **2.** Illi, ante inito,[3] ut intellectum est, consilio, quod, deditione facta, nostros praesidia deducturos[4] aut denique[5] indiligentius servaturos crediderant, partim cum[6] eis, quae retinuerant et celaverant, armis, partim scutis ex cortice[7] factis aut viminibus intextis, quae subito, ut temporis exiguitas postulabat, pellibus[8] induxerant, tertia vigilia,[9] qua minime arduus ad nostras munitiones ascensus[10] videbatur, omnibus copiis repente ex oppido eruptionem[11] fecerunt. **3.** Celeriter, ut ante Caesar imperaverat, ignibus[12] significatione facta, ex proximis castellis eo[13] concursum est, **4.** pugnatumque ab hostibus ita acriter est, ut[14] a viris fortibus in extrema spe salutis iniquo loco,[15] contra eos, qui ex vallo turribusque[16] tela iacerent, pugnari debuit, cum in una virtute omnis spes salutis consisteret. **5.** Occisis ad[17] hominum milibus IIII, reliqui in oppidum reiecti sunt. **6.** Postridie eius diei[18] refractis portis, cum iam defenderet nemo, atque intromissis[19] militibus nostris, sectionem eius oppidi universam Caesar vendidit.[20] **7.** Ab eis, qui emerant, capitum[21] numerus ad eum relatus est milium LIII.

[1] **Sub:** 'Towards'. **vesperum:** *7b*.

² **ne**, etc.: *196a*. **quam**: *168; 49a* (as in II.32.2; note 4). **a**: as in II.31.4; note 10.
³ **ante inito – consilio**: 'having previously formed a plot'; how lit.?
⁴ **praesidia deducturos** [esse]: 'would withdraw the outposts' from the redoubts and the line of circumvallation, where the Roman sentries kept watch.
⁵ **denique**: 'at any rate'. **indiligentius**: 'less carefully'; *153a*. **servaturos** [esse]: 'would maintain (them)' the outposts.
⁶ **cum**: with *armis*, and understood with *scutis*.
⁷ **cortice**: 'bark'; *98b*. **viminibus intextis**: '(of) wicker-work', lit. 'withes interwoven'.
⁸ **pellibus**: 'with skins'. The Atuatuci had driven cattle into the enclosure.
⁹ **tertia vigilia**: *242c*. **arduus**: 'steep'; *30*.
¹⁰ **ascensus**, etc.: implies that the Roman line of contravallation, at the point it was attacked, was on ground somewhat above the level of the plain, so that the enemy, after rushing down from the town, must advance up a height in order to storm the Roman fortifications. **copiis**: *137b*.
¹¹ **eruptionem**: 'sortie'.
¹² **ignibus**: 'by fire-signals'. See Plate IV, 2. **significatione**: 'warning'.
¹³ **eo**: to the point attacked. **concursum est**: 'the soldiers rushed'; *73d*.
¹⁴ **ut**, etc.: 'as brave men were bound to fight'. **in . . . salutis**: cf. II, 27.3, note 5.
¹⁵ **iniquo loco**: *145c*. **vallo**: the Roman line of contravallation.
¹⁶ **turribus**: stationed at intervals along the line of contravallation, as on the rampart around a camp; cf. Plate IX, 6. **iacerent**: *194a* (AG 535, B 283.2). **una**: 'alone'.
¹⁷ **ad**: adverb, 'about', modifying *quattuor* (IIII).
¹⁸ **diei**: *94c*. **refractis**: 'had been burst in'; how lit.? **cum**: *184a*. **iam**: 'any longer'.
¹⁹ **intromissis**: 'had been sent in', lit. 'into', the stronghold. **sectionem universam**: 'the booty in one sale', at auction; in such cases the buyers who joined in the bid afterwards divided up the purchase among themselves for resale in smaller lots. Such wholesale buyers accompanied Roman armies. In this instance the booty included not only everything that the captured Atuatuci had, but the people themselves, who were sold into slavery.
²⁰ **vendidit**: 'sold.'
²¹ **capitum**: 'of persons'; cf. I, 29.2, note 6. **LIII**: *quinquaginta trium; 38b, 36*. Some of the Atuatuci, however, were still left in the country; cf. V, 38.1 and 39.3.

SUCCESSFUL CLOSING OF THE YEAR. 34, 35

Maritime states in northwestern Gaul submit to Publius Crassus.

34.1. Eodem tempore a P.¹ Crasso, quem cum legione una miserat ad Venetos,² Venellos, Osismos, Coriosolitas, Esuvios, Aulercos, Redones, quae³ sunt maritimae civitates Oceanumque⁴ attingunt, certior factus est, omnes eas civitates in dicionem potestatemque populi Romani esse redactas.

¹ **P.**: *19a*. **Crasso**: see Vocab. under *Crassus*, (2). **legione una**: the 7th, which must have started for western Gaul soon after the battle of the Sambre.
² **Venetos**: see III, 8.1, note 3. **Venellos**: for the location of the Venelli and other peoples mentioned, see GALLIA, back cover of this volume. **Coriosolitas**: *19f*.
³ **quae**: *164c*. **maritimae**: 'maritime'.
⁴ **Oceanum**: the Atlantic; see Vocab.

German tribes offer submission; the army goes into winter quarters; a thanksgiving is decreed at Rome.

35.1. His rebus gestis, omni Gallia pacata, tanta huius belli ad barbaros opinio perlata est, uti ab eis nationibus, quae trans Rhenum incolerent,¹ legati ad Caesarem mitterentur, qui se² obsides daturas, imperata facturas pollicerentur.³ **2.** Quas legationes Caesar, quod in Italiam Illyricumque⁴ properabat, inita proxima aestate ad se reverti iussit. **3.** Ipse, in Carnutes,⁵

Andes, Turonos, quaeque civitates propinquae his locis erant, ubi bellum gesserat, legionibus in hiberna[6] deductis, in Italiam profectus est. **4.** Ob easque res ex[7] litteris Caesaris dierum XV supplicatio decreta est, quod[8] ante id tempus accidit nulli.

[1] **incolerent:** *220* (AG 593, B 324.1).

[2] **se:** feminine, taking the gender of *nationibus*; hence *daturas* and *facturas* (sc. *esse*) are feminine.

[3] **pollicerentur:** *193a.* **Quas:** *167.* **Italiam:** here including Cisalpine Gaul; *283b.*

[4] **Illyricum:** *298.*

[5] **Carnutes,** etc.: *282.* See Map I. **quaeque civitates:** *et in eas civitates quae*; *165c.*

[6] **hiberna:** *335b.* **easque:** *233b.*

[7] **ex:** 'after receipt of'. **litteris:** 'dispatches' to the Roman Senate, reporting his victories. **supplicatio:** 'solemn thanksgiving', services of prayer to avert misfortune as well as giving of thanks to the gods for victory. Usually such services lasted only three or four days; the longest previous 'thanksgiving' was of twelve days, decreed after Pompey had brought to a close the war with Mithridates.

[8] **quod:** sc. *id*, referring to the fact stated in the preceding clause. **nulli:** = *nemini*; *12d.*

PLATE II   OFFICERS, STANDARD-BEARERS, AND MUSICIANS

1. Commander, *imperator*.   2. Lieutenant-general, *legatus*.
3. Centurion, *centurio*.   4. *Lictor*.   5. Standard-bearers, *signiferi*.
6. Eagle-bearer, *aquilifer*. 7. Trumpeter, *tubicen*. 8. Hornblower, *cornicen*
9. Eagle, *aquila*.   10. Banner, *vexillum*.

COMMENTARIUS TERTIUS

Caesar stations Galba with a small force in the Alps; Galba locates his winter quarters in Octodurus.

1.1. Cum in Italiam proficisceretur[1] Caesar, Ser. Galbam, cum legione XII[2] et parte equitatus, in Nantuates, Veragros Sedunosque misit, qui a finibus Allobrogum et lacu Lemanno et flumine Rhodano ad summas Alpes[3] pertinent. **2.** Causa mittendi[4] fuit, quod iter per Alpes, quo magno cum periculo[5] magnisque cum portoriis mercatores ire consuerant, patefieri[6] volebat. **3.** Huic permisit, si opus esse arbitraretur, uti in his locis legionem[7] hiemandi causa, collocaret. **4.** Galba, secundis aliquot proeliis[8] factis castellisque compluribus eorum expugnatis, missis ad eum undique legatis obsidibusque datis et pace facta, constituit cohortes duas[9] in Nantuatibus collocare et ipse, cum reliquis[10] eius legionis cohortibus, in vico[11] Veragrorum, qui appellatur Octodurus, hiemare; **5.** qui[12] vicus, positus in valle, non magna adiecta planitie, altissimis montibus undique continetur. **6.** Cum hic in duas partes flumine[13] divideretur, alteram partem eius vici Gallis concessit, alteram, vacuam[14] ab his relictam, cohortibus ad hiemandum attribuit. Eum locum vallo fossaque munivit.

[1] **proficisceretur:** Caesar 'was starting' on the trip referred to in II, 35.3; *185c.* The events of Book III, as a whole, belong to the year 56 B.C., but the uprising of the Alpine tribes, narrated in chapters 1-6, took place in the latter part of the autumn and early winter of B.C. 57. **Italiam:** Cisalpine Gaul; *283b.* **Ser.** = *Servium*; *19a.* **Galbam:** see Vocab. under Galba, (1).

[2] **XII:** *duodecimo*; *38b.* Caesar had eight legions, numbered 7 to 14 inclusive. **Nantuates:** *282.* Locate the states mentioned on Map 1.

[3] **summas Alpes:** 'the highest part of the Alps'; *152a.*

[4] **mittendi:** *230.1.* **iter:** 'route' to Italy, over the pass now known as the Great St. Bernard, where the famous hospice is. Napoleon used this route in 1800 with an army of 36,000.

[5] **periculo:** the danger arose not so much from the precipitous way over the mountains as from the hostility of the natives. These lived in part by plundering and by levying tolls on the goods of traders going over the pass. **portoriis:** see I, 18.3, note 11.

[6] **patefieri:** 'be kept open'; the subject is *iter*; *70c; 223a.* **Huic:** Galba. **opus esse:** 'that it was necessary'. **arbitraretur:** *arbitraberis* in the unattracted form; *220.*

[7] **legionem,** etc.: the 12th legion had suffered so severely in the battle of the Sambre (II, 25) that Caesar would hardly have stationed it at so difficult a post if he had anticipated serious opposition. **collocaret:** *199a.*

[8] **proeliis,** etc.: the ablatives absolute indicate successive events, and should be rendered by clauses. First come the engagements, then the taking of strongholds: later, the sending of envoys, then the giving of hostages; finally, the ratification of peace.

[9] **cohortes duas:** how many men? *307c.* **in Nantuatibus:** perhaps where St. Maurice is on the upper Rhone; *282.*

[10] **reliquis cohortibus:** doubtless the two strongest cohorts were detailed for the separate post; how many men were in the remaining eight is difficult to estimate.

[11] **vico:** how different from *oppidum*? **Octodurus:** near Martigny; see Map 1.

[12] **qui:** *167.* **valle:** 'valley'. **non magna:** *239g.* **adiecta:** 'adjoining'; how lit.?

[13] **flumine:** the Dranse, which flows into the Rhone, from the south, at the point where the Rhone turns northwest toward Lake Geneva. **alteram . . . alteram:** *171b.*

[14] **vacuam:** predicative, after *relictam*; Galba expelled the inhabitants from the part of Octodurus which was on the west bank of the Dranse, and turned the dwellings into winter quarters; *88b.*

There is a sudden uprising of the mountaineers.

2.1. Cum dies hibernorum[1] complures transissent, frumentumque eo[2] comportari iussisset, subito per exploratores certior factus est, ex ea parte vici, quam Gallis concesserat,[3] omnes noctu discessisse, montesque, qui impenderent,[4] a maxima multitudine Sedunorum et Veragrorum teneri.
2. Id[5] aliquot de causis acciderat, ut subito Galli belli renovandi legionisque opprimendae consilium caperent: **3.** primum, quod legionem, neque eam plenissimam,[6] detractis cohortibus duabus et compluribus[7] singillatim, qui commeatus petendi causa missi erant, absentibus, propter paucitatem despiciebant; **4.** tum etiam,[8] quod propter iniquitatem loci, cum ipsi[9] ex montibus in vallem decurrerent et tela conicerent, ne primum quidem impetum suum posse sustineri existimabant. **5.** Accedebat, quod[10] suos ab se liberos abstractos obsidum nomine[11] dolebant, et Romanos non solum itinerum causa, sed etiam perpetuae possessionis culmina[12] Alpium occupare conari et ea loca finitimae provinciae[13] adiungere sibi persuasum habebant.

[1] **hibernorum:** 'of the (life in) winter quarters'. **transissent:** *68b; 185c.*
[2] **eo:** to the part of the town used for winter quarters. **iussisset:** sc. *Galba.* **exploratores:** *327.*
[3] **concesserat:** *214c.* The Gauls occupied the part of the town on the east bank.
[4] **impenderent:** *214a.* **a:** with the ablative of agent because of the idea of *homines* in *multitudo; 126b.*
[5] **Id:** explained by the clause *ut . . . caperent; 203.4.* **renovandi:** 'of renewing'. *230.1.*
[6] **neque eam plenissimam:** 'and that lacking its full strength'; the reason is explained by the following ablatives absolute. How lit.? *161e.*
[7] **compluribus:** sc. *militibus.* **singillatim:** 'as individuals', not sent out as cohorts or maniples. **commeatus,** etc.: *230.1.*
[8] **tum etiam:** *deinde* is more common as correlative with *primum; 237b.*
[9] **ipsi:** *Galli.* **decurrerent:** 'should rush down'.
[10] **quod . . . dolebant:** subject of *Accedebat;* 'There was the further consideration that', etc.; *198b* (AG 572, B 299.1). **abstractos:** 'had been taken away'; *89c; 223a2.*
[11] **nomine:** 'under the name'; *136b.* **itinerum causa:** cf. III.1.2.
[12] **culmina:** 'summits', commanding the passes; *12e.*
[13] **provinciae:** *107b; 290.* **adiungere:** 'annex'. **sibi persuasum habebant,** etc.: 'were convinced that the Romans were trying', lit. 'had persuaded themselves', etc.; *229a* (AG 497b, B 337.7). **persuasum:** predicative, in agreement with the infinitive clause *Romanos . . . conari,* object of *habebant; 148d.*

Galba, calling a council, decides not to retreat.

3.1. His nuntiis acceptis, Galba, cum neque[1] opus hibernorum munitionesque plene[2] essent perfectae, neque de frumento reliquoque commeatu satis esset provisum,[3] quod, deditione facta obsidibusque acceptis, nihil[4] de bello timendum existimaverat, consilio[5] celeriter convocato, sententias exquirere coepit. **2.** Quo[6] in consilio, cum tantum repentini periculi praeter opinionem accidisset ac iam omnia fere superiora loca multitudine armatorum completa[7] conspicerentur, neque subsidio veniri neque commeatus supportari, interclusis itineribus,[8] possent, prope iam desperata salute non nullae eius modi[9] sententiae dicebantur, ut, impedimentis relictis eruptione facta, isdem[10] itineribus, quibus eo pervenissent, ad salutem[11] contenderent. **3.** Maiori tamen parti placuit, hoc reservato ad extremum[12] consilio, interim rei eventum experiri et castra defendere.

[1] **neque. . .neque**: 'not. . . and not'. **opus hibernorum, munitiones**: 'the work on the winter quarters', in general, including most importantly, 'the fortifications' (III, 1.6).

[2] **plene**: 'quite'. **perfectae**: agreement? *172b*. **de**: 'for'.

[3] **satis esset provisum**: 'sufficient provision had been made'.

[4] **nihil . . . timendum** [esse]: 'that he had no occasion to fear hostilities'; how lit.? *73e*.

[5] **consilio**: doubtless of the centurions; cf. I, 40.1. **sententias exquirere**: 'to ask for opinions' regarding the best course to pursue.

[6] **Quo**: *167*. **tantum repentini periculi**: 'so great danger suddenly', lit. 'so much of sudden danger'; *97b*. **praeter opinionem**: 'contrary to expectation'.

[7] **completa** [esse]: participle here used as a predicate adjective; *221b*. **neque subsidio veniri**: sc. *posset* 'and help could not come'; how lit.? *73d; 112a*.

[8] **interclusis itineribus**: *144b3*.

[9] **eius modi**: 'of the following purport'; *100a*. **ut**, etc.: *203.4*.

[10] **isdem**: *45*. **itineribus**: *134a*. **pervenissent**: *220*.

[11] **ad salutem**: 'to (a place of) safety'. **Maiori parti placuit**: 'the majority decided'; *73c*.

[12] **ad extremum**: 'to the last'; *154a*. **eventum experiri**: 'to await the outcome'.

The mountaineers, superior in numbers, make a furious attack.

4.1. Brevi spatio interiecto,[1] vix ut eis rebus, quas constituissent, collocandis atque administrandis tempus daretur, hostes ex omnibus partibus, signo dato, decurrere,[2] lapides gaesaque[3] in vallum conicere. **2.** Nostri primo integris[4] viribus fortiter repugnare neque ullum frustra[5] telum ex loco superiore mittere, et quaecumque pars castrorum nudata defensoribus[6] premi videbatur, eo[7] occurrere et auxilium ferre; **3.** sed hoc superari, quod diuturnitate pugnae hostes defessi[8] proelio excedebant, alii integris viribus[9] succedebant. **4.** Quarum rerum a nostris propter paucitatem fieri nihil poterat, ac non modo[10] defesso ex pugna excedendi,[11] sed ne saucio quidem eius loci, ubi constiterat, relinquendi ac sui recipiendi[12] facultas dabatur.

[1] **Brevi spatio interiecto**: 'After a brief interval'; how lit.? **ut**: 'so that'. **rebus — collocandis**: *230.2*. **constituissent**: *220*.

[2] **decurrere, conicere**: *182* (AG 463, B 335).

[3] **gaesa**: Gallic 'javelins'; *349*; Fig. 40.

[4] **integris**: 'unimpaired'; *22f; 80b; 135a*. **neque ullum telum**: 'and no missile'.

[5] **frustra**: 'in vain'. **ex loco superiore**: the rampart of the camp; see III, 1.6. **quaecumque**: *50a; 192*.

[6] **defensoribus**: *127a; 74a*.

[7] **eo** = *in eam partem*; 'to that part they rushed'. **ferre**: *182*. **hoc superari**: 'on this account they were at a disadvantage'; how lit.? *135a*.

[8] **defessi**: '(when) exhausted'. **proelio**: *127a*. **alii**: '(and) others'; *238a*.

[9] **viribus**: *143a*. **succedebant**: 'were taking their places'. **rerum**: dependent on *nihil*; *97a*.

[10] **non modo**: trans. as if *non modo non*; 'not only not to one (who was) exhausted', i.e. one on the Roman side; *236d; 154a* (AG 288, B 343.2a).

[11] **excedendi**: dependent on *facultas*. **saucio**: 'to one (who was) wounded'; *154a; 237c*. **loci — relinquendi**: *230.1*.

[12] **sui recipiendi**: 'of looking after himself'.

The Romans, forced to extremities, resolve upon a sally.

5.1. Cum iam[1] amplius horis sex continenter pugnaretur ac non solum vires, sed etiam tela nostras deficerent, atque hostes acrius[2] instarent languidioribusque nostris vallum scindere et fossas[3] complere coepissent, resque esset iam ad extremum[4] perducta casum, **2.** P. Sextius Baculus, primi pili centurio, quem Nervico proelio[5] compluribus confectum vulneribus diximus, et item C. Volusenus,[6] tribunus militum, vir et consilii magni[7] et virtutis, ad Galbam accurrunt atque unam[8] esse spem salutis docent, si, eruptione facta, extremum auxilium experirentur. **3.** Itaque, convocatis centurionibus,[9] celeriter milites certiores facit, paulisper intermitterent proelium[10] ac tantum modo tela missa exciperent seque ex labore reficerent; post, dato signo, ex castris erumperent[11] atque omnem spem salutis in virtute ponerent.

[1] **Cum iam – pugnaretur:** 'When fighting had been going on'; *175f; 73d.* **horis:** *129a.*
[2] **acrius:** *34a.* **languidioribus nostris:** 'as our men became weaker'; how lit.? *144b3.* **vallum scindere:** 'to destroy the rampart' by pulling up the palisades along the outer edge.
[3] **fossas:** plural because the parts of the moat on the four sides are thought of as separate trenches.
[4] **ad extremum casum:** 'to the last crisis'. **P. Sextius Baculus, primi pili centurio:** see II.25.1; note 8; *315b.*
[5] **proelio:** *147b.* **Nervico:** 'with the Nervians', we should say. The battle had taken place not long before this time; see II, 19-28.
[6] **Volusenus:** the suggestion was evidently made first by Baculus to his ranking officer, Volusenus, who hurried with him to Galba. **tribunus:** *314*
[7] **consilii magni:** 'of excellent judgment'; *100a.*
[8] **unam spem:** 'that the only hope'. **facta:** 'by making', etc.; *144b6.* **extremum auxilium:** 'the last resource'.
[9] **centurionibus:** how many ordinarily in 8 cohorts? *315b.* **milites certiores facit:** 'he directed the soldiers', through the centurions.
[10] **intermitterent proelium:** 'to stop fighting'; *216* (AG 588, B 316). **tantum modo.** etc.: 'only to parry', with their shields, 'the missiles hurled' by the enemy, in order to save their strength for the sortie.
[11] **erumperent:** 'to burst forth', suddenly assuming the offensive; *216.*

The Romans win; but Galba withdraws to the Province.

6.1. Quod[1] iussi sunt, faciunt, ac subito, omnibus portis eruptione facta, neque cognoscendi, quid fieret, neque sui colligendi[2] hostibus facultatem relinquunt. **2.** Ita, commutata fortuna, eos,[3] qui in spem potiundorum castrorum venerant, undique circumventos intercipiunt; et ex[4] hominum milibus amplius[5] XXX, quem numerum barbarorum ad castra venisse constabat, plus tertia parte interfecta,[6] reliquos perterritos in fugam coniciunt ac ne in locis[7] quidem superioribus consistere patiuntur. **3.** Sic, omnibus hostium copiis fusis[8] armisque exutis, se in castra munitionesque suas recipiunt. **4.** Quo proelio[9] facto, quod saepius fortunam temptare Galba nolebat, atque alio[10] se in hiberna consilio venisse meminerat, aliis occurrisse[11] rebus viderat, maxime frumenti commeatusque inopia permotus, postero die, omnibus eius vici[12] aedificiis incensis, in provinciam reverti contendit, **5.** ac, nullo hoste prohibente aut iter demorante,[13] incolumem legionem in Nantuates, inde in Allobroges, perduxit, ibique hiemavit.

[1] **Quod,** etc.: *id, quod facere iussi sunt, faciunt; 160c.* **portis:** *134a; 334a* (AG 429a, B 218.9).
[2] **sui colligendi:** 'of collecting their forces', scattered on all sides of the camp, in order to resist the four mass attacks launched from the four gates; *154b* (AG 504c, B 339.5).
[3] **eos – circumventos intercipiunt:** 'they surrounded and slew those'; *228a.* **potiundorum:** *64b.*

[4] **ex,** etc.; i.e. *plus tertia parte, ex amplius triginta hominum milibus, numero barbarorum* ('of natives') *quem ad castra venisse constabat, interfecta.* **ex:** *97d.*

[5] **amplius, plus:** *129b.* **numerum:** *165b.* It seems hardly credible that a force of more than 30,000 men, attacking under conditions very favorable to themselves, could have been beaten off even by a Roman force less than one tenth as large; perhaps the estimate of the number of the enemy was exaggerated.

[6] **plus tertia parte interfecta:** on this basis the Roman soldiers on the average accounted for three to five Gauls apiece.

[7] **locis superioribus:** the heights round about; see III, 1.5.

[8] **fusis:** 'routed'. **armisque exutis:** 'and bereft of their arms', which they cast away in their flight. **armis:** *127a.*

[9] **Quo proelio facto:** 'After this battle'; how lit.? **saepius:** 'too often'; *153a.*

[10] **alio – consilio:** 'with one design', stated in III, 1.2,3; *138; 171c.*

[11] **aliis occurrisse rebus:** '(but) that he had found conditions different', implying the impossibility of carrying out the original design with the force at his disposal.

[12] **eius vici:** Octodurus, of which the part assigned to the natives, as well as that occupied by the Romans (III, 1.6), was now burned.

[13] **iter demorante:** 'delaying his march'; *61a1.* **incolumem:** predicative, 'in safety'.

Crassus, wintering near the Ocean, sends to the nearest states for grain.

7.1. His rebus gestis, cum[1] omnibus de causis Caesar pacatam[2] Galliam existimaret, superatis Belgis, expulsis Germanis, victis in Alpibus Sedunis,[3] atque ita inita hieme in Illyricum[4] profectus esset, quod eas quoque nationes adire et regiones cognoscere volebat, subitum bellum in Gallia coortum est.[5] **2.** Eius belli haec[6] fuit causa. P. Crassus adulescens cum legione VII[7] proximus mare Oceanum in Andibus hiemabat. **3.** Is, quod in his locis inopia frumenti erat, praefectos[8] tribunosque militum complures in finitimas civitates frumenti commeatusque petendi causa dimisit; **4.** quo in numero est T. Terrasidius missus in Esuvios, M. Trebius Gallus in Coriosolitas,[9] Q. Velanius cum T. Silio in Venetos.

[1] **cum:** 'although'; *187.* **omnibus de causis:** with *existimaret,* 'had every reason to think'; how lit.?

[2] **pacatam:** sc. *esse.* **Galliam:** *287b.* **superatis Belgis:** see II.1-33. **expulsis Germanis:** see I, 30-54.

[3] **Sedunis:** of the Alpine tribes the Seduni, as the most important, are alone mentioned. **inita hieme:** 'at the beginning of winter'; how lit.? *68b; 144b1.*

[4] **Illyricum:** *298; 255.* See II, 35.2.

[5] **coortum est:** ' broke out'; how lit.? *61b.*

[6] **haec:** 'as follows'; *161a.* **adulescens:** cf. I, 52.7, note 13 and Vocab. under *Crassus,* (2).

[7] **VII:** *septima; 38b.* **proximus,** etc.: 'very near the Ocean'; lit. 'very near the sea', designated 'the Ocean' to distinguish it from the Mediterranean sea; *123b.*

[8] **praefectos:** 'subsidiary officers'; cf. I, 39.2, note 10. **tribunos militum:** *314.* **complures:** with *civitates.*

[9] **Coriosolitas:** *19f; 282.* Locate, on Map 9, the peoples mentioned.

MAP 9.

OPERATIONS OF THE YEAR 56 B.C.

Book III, 7–27   To face page 198

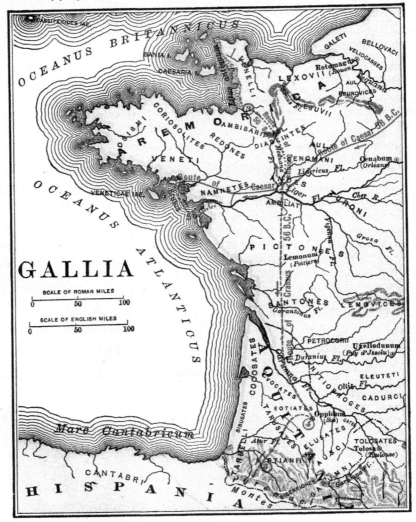

EXPLANATION

1. Base whence Caesar sent Sabinus north and Crassus south.   2. Sea-fight
with the Venetans (chap. 13–15).   3. Battle of Sabinus (17–19).   4. Battle
of Crassus with the Sotiates (20–22).   5. Final victory of Crassus (23–26).

The Venetans detain his representatives and lead a revolt.

8.1. Huius[1] est civitatis longe amplissima auctoritas omnis orae maritimae regionum earum, quod et[2] naves habent Veneti plurimas, quibus in[3] Britanniam navigare consuerunt, et scientia[4] atque usu rerum nauticarum reliquos antecedunt, et in[5] magno impetu maris atque aperto, paucis portibus interiectis, quos tenent ipsi, omnes[6] fere, qui eo mari uti consuerunt, habent vectigales.[7] **2.** Ab his fit initium retinendi Silii atque Velanii, quod per eos[8] suos se obsides, quos Crasso dedissent,[9] recuperaturos existimabant. **3.** Horum auctoritate[10] finitimi adducti, ut sunt Gallorum subita et repentina consilia, eadem de causa Trebium Terrasidiumque retinent; et celeriter, missis legatis, per suos principes inter se[11] coniurant, nihil, nisi communi consilio, acturos eundemque[12] omnes fortunae exitum esse laturos: **4.** reliquasque[13] civitates sollicitant, ut in ea libertate, quam a maioribus acceperint,[14] permanere, quam Romanorum servitutem perferre malint. **5.** Omni ora maritima celeriter ad suam sententiam perducta, communem legationem ad P. Crassum mittunt: si[15] velit suos recuperare, obsides sibi remittat.

[1] **Huius civitatis:** of the Venetans. **omnis orae,** etc.: trans. as if *omnium civitatum orae maritimae earum regionum.*
[2] **et . . . et . . . et:** *233d.*
[3] **in – navigare:** 'to make the voyage to'. The Venetans had developed an extensive carrying business between Gaul and Britain; Britain was less advanced than Gaul in most respects but was regarded as the center of Druidism (VI, 13.11). **Britanniam:** *294.* **consuerunt:** *64a2; 176b.*
[4] **scientia:** *142a.* **rerum nauticarum:** 'nautical matters'. **antecedunt:** 'excel'.
[5] **in,** etc.: 'since the violence of the open sea is great, with harbours few and far between'; how lit.?
[6] **omnes:** object of *habent.* **eo mari:** the modern Bay of Biscay. *16b; 131c.*
[7] **vectigales:** 'subject to tribute'; predicative; *115a, b.* On account of the violence of the sea and the scarcity of harbours, navigators were obliged to take refuge in the harbours of the Venetans who mulcted them in tolls. **Ab his,** etc.: 'These took the first step by detaining', etc.; how lit.?
[8] **per eos:** as an exchange; *123a.* **suos,** etc.: *se recuperaturos [esse] suos obsides.*
[9] **dedissent:** *214a.* **recuperaturos** [esse]: 'would get back'.
[10] **Horum auctoritate:** 'by their example'. **ut,** etc.: 'consistently with the practice of the Gauls, to form plans suddenly and without reflection'; how lit.? The fickleness of the Gauls is more than once alluded to by Caesar; see III, 19.6, note 14.
[11] **inter se:** *159.* **nihil,** etc.: *se nihil acturos esse . . . laturos esse; 213b.*
[12] **eundem:** *45.* **exitum:** 'issue'.
[13] **reliquas:** *171a.* **ut . . .malint:** *199a; 71.*
[14] **acceperint:** *220.* **quam:** '(rather) than'.
[15] **si,** etc.: in the direct form: *si vis tuos recuperare, obsides nobis remitte; 218.1a; 216.*

Caesar orders ships built; the coast states prepare for war.

9.1. Quibus de rebus Caesar a Crasso certior factus, quod ipse aberat longius,[1] naves interim longas aedificari in flumine Ligeri,[2] quod influit in Oceanum, remiges ex provincia institui, nautas[3] gubernatoresque comparari iubet. **2.** His rebus celeriter administratis, ipse, cum[4] primum per anni tempus potuit, ad exercitum contendit. **3.** Veneti reliquaeque item civitates, cognito Caesaris adventu, simul quod, quantum in se[5] facinus admisissent, intellegebant, legatos[6], quod nomen ad omnes nationes sanctum inviolatumque[7] semper fuisset, retentos ab se et in vincula coniectos, pro magnitudine periculi bellum parare et maxime ea, quae ad usum navium pertinent, providere instituunt,[8] hoc maiore spe, quod multum natura loci confidebant. **4.** Pedestria[9] esse itinera concisa aestuariis, navigationem impeditam propter inscientiam locorum[10] paucitatemque portuum sciebant, **5.** neque[11] nostras exercitus propter inopiam frumenti diutius apud se morari posse confidebant; **6.** *ac[12] iam ut[13] omnia contra opinionem acciderent, tamen se plurimum navibus posse, Romanos neque ullam facultatem habere navium, neque eorum locorum, ubi[14] bellum gesturi essent, vada, portus, insulas[15] novisse;* **7.** ac longe aliam esse navigationem in concluso mari[16] atque in vastissimo atque apertissimo Oceano perspiciebant. **8.** His initis consiliis, oppida muniunt, frumenta[17] ex agris in oppida comportant, naves in Venetiam, ubi Caesarem primum esse bellum gesturum constabat, quam plurimas possunt, cogunt. **9.** Socios[18] sibi ad id bellum Osismos, Lexovios, Namnetes, Ambiliatos, Morinos, Diablintes, Menapios asciscunt; auxilia[19] ex Britannia, quae contra eas regiones posita est, arcessunt.

[1] **longius:** 'too far away'. Caesar was probably in Cisalpine Gaul; for the revolt of the Venetans came to a head in the early spring, and in April of 56 B.C. Caesar met Pompey and Crassus at Luca; *256; 153a.* **naves longas:** 'galleys'; *346a.* **interim:** 'meanwhile', pending his return to the army. **aedificari:** 'be built'.

[2] **Ligeri:** *18e.* See Maps 9 and 10. **quod,** etc.: explains why, although the Venetans were strong on the ocean, the ships were ordered built on the Loire. **remiges:** 'rowers'.

[3] **nautas:** 'sailors'. **gubernatores:** 'steersmen', who managed the rudders; *346b; 84.* The fighting on these ships was to be done by legionaries (III, 14.3).

[4] **cum,** etc.: 'as soon as the season of the year permitted'; how lit.? *185b.* Caesar probably rejoined the army in May.

[5] **in se . . . admisissent:** 'they had committed'; *se* refers to the subject of *admisissent.* How lit.? *204.3.*

[6] **legatos . . . coniectos** [esse]: explains *quantum . . . admisissent:* 'in that envoys had been', etc. **quod nomen:** 'a title which', the title of envoy or ambassador; *165b.* **ad:** 'among'.

[7] **sanctum inviolatumque:** 'sacred and inviolable'.

[8] **instituunt:** *175b.* **hoc:** 'on this account'. **spe:** *138.* **multum confidebant:** 'had much confidence'; *118b.* **natura:** *135a.*

[9] **Pedestria,** etc.: 'that the land routes were cut by inlets of the sea', making progress of an army difficult; see Map 10. **navigationem:** 'navigation', by the Romans; sc. *esse; 81.*

[10] **inscientiam locorum:** 'lack of knowledge of the country'.

[11] **neque:** trans. as if *et . . . non.*

[12] **ac . . . novisse:** a brief summary in indirect discourse; 'and (they believed) that', etc.; *212c6.*

[13] **ut:** with *iam,* 'even granting that'. **acciderent:** subjunctive also in direct discourse; *191b* (AG 527a, B 308). **plurimum posse:** cf. I, 3.6, note 21.

[14] **ubi:** = *in quibus.* **gesturi essent:** *63.*

[15] **insulas:** 'islands'. **longe aliam . . . atque:** 'far different . . . from what it was'; *233c.*

[16] **in concluso mari:** 'on a land-locked sea', referring to the Mediterranean. **vastissimo, apertissimo:** 'illimitable, unconfined'; how lit.?

[17] **frumenta:** unthreshed 'grain', just ripening in the fields, hurriedly cut and transported into the towns; see I, 16.2, note 3. The time was near the beginning of July.

[18] **Socios:** 'as allies'; *115a.* **Osismos,** etc.: locate these states on the Map on the back cover.

[19] **auxilia,** etc.: help furnished to his enemies by the Britons gave Caesar a pretext later for invading the island (IV, 20).

Caesar considers it equally important to check this uprising and to distribute his forces so as to prevent revolts elsewhere.

10.1. Erant[1] hae difficultates belli gerendi, quas supra ostendimus, sed multa tamen Caesarem ad id bellum incitabant: **2.** iniuria[2] retentorum equitum Romanorum, rebellio facta post deditionem, defectio[3] datis obsidibus, tot civitatum coniuratio, in primis ne,[4] hac parte neglecta, reliquae nationes sibi idem[5] licere arbitrarentur. **3.** Itaque cum[6] intellegeret, omnes fere Gallos novis rebus studere et ad bellum mobiliter[7] celeriterque excitari, omnes autem homines natura libertati studere[8] et condicionem servitutis odisse,[9] prius quam plures civitates conspirarent, partiendum[10] sibi ac latius distribuendum exercitum putavit.

[1] **Erant:** *90a.* **supra:** III, 9, the previous chapter.
[2] **iniuria,** etc.: 'the wrong done by the detention of Roman knights', referring to the envoys (III.8.2-3), who, as the other tribunes in Caesar's army, had the rank of *equites*; *228b* (AG 497, B 337.6). **equitum:** *96.* **rebellio:** 'renewal of war'.
[3] **defectio:** 'revolting'. **datis obsidibus:** *144b5.*
[4] **ne . . . arbitrarentur:** the clause is in the same construction as *iniuria, rebellio,* etc., in apposition with *multa;* '(the fear) that', etc.; *202.* **hac parte neglecta:** 'if this part (of Gaul)', etc.; *144b4.*
[5] **idem:** subject accusative with *licere;* 'the same course'. **licere:** *73b.*
[6] **cum:** *184a.* **novis rebus studere:** 'were eager for a change of rule'; *105.*
[7] **mobiliter:** 'easily'. **excitari:** 'were stirred'.
[8] **natura libertati studere:** 'have a natural desire for liberty'; how lit.?
[9] **odisse:** *72b; 176b.* **prius quam:** with the subjunctive also in direct discourse; *189b.* **conspirarent:** 'should league together'.
[10] **partiendum** [esse], etc.: 'that he ought to divide up his army and distribute (it) more widely', in order to hold all parts of the country in check; *73e.*

11.1. Itaque T. Labienum legatum in Treveros,[1] qui proximi flumini Rheno sunt, cum equitatu mittit. **2.** Huic mandat, Remos reliquosque Belgas adeat[2] atque in officio contineat, Germanosque, qui auxilio[3] a Belgis arcessiti dicebantur, si per vim navibus flumen transire conentur,[4] prohibeat. **3.** P. Crassum, cum cohortibus legionariis XII[5] et magno numero equitatus, in Aquitaniam[6] proficisci iubet, ne ex his nationibus auxilia in Galliam[7] mittantur ac tantae nationes coniungantur. **4.** Q. Titurium Sabinum legatum cum legionibus tribus in Venellos, Coriosolitas Lexoviosque mittit, qui[8] eam manum distinendam[9] curet. **5.** D.[10] Brutum adulescentem classi Gallicisque navibus, quas ex Pictonibus et Santonis reliquisque pacatis regionibus convenire iusserat, praeficit et, cum primum possit,[11] in Venetos proficisci iubet. Ipse eo[12] pedestribus copiis contendit.

[1] **Treveros:** see Map on the back cover; *282.* **proximi:** here followed by the dative; *108a.*
[2] **adeat:** *sc.ut; 200a; 199a.* **in officio:** 'in allegiance'.
[3] **auxilio:** *112a.* **arcessiti** [esse]: *148e.*
[4] **conentur:** *220* (AG 593, B 324).
[5] **XII:** *duodecim;* Crassus had a legion and two cohorts of infantry.
[6] **Aquitaniam:** *287c.*
[7] **Galliam:** Celtic Gaul; *287b.* As the Aquitanians were of different stock, their relations with their Celtic neighbors seem ordinarily not to have been intimate.
[8] **qui . . . curet:** 'in order to keep their forces at a distance'; how lit.? *193a.*

⁹ **distinendam:** *79d; 229b* (B 337.8b2).
¹⁰ **D.:** *19a.* **classi:** 'fleet', built on the Loire (III, 9.1-2). **Gallicis navibus:** used as supply ships.
¹¹ **possit:** indicative in the direct form.
¹² **eo:** *in Venetos.* **copiis:** *137b.*

The capture of strongholds of the Venetans proves fruitless.

12.1. Erant eius modi[1] fere situs oppidorum, ut, posita in extremis[2] lingulis promunturiisque, neque pedibus aditum haberent, cum[3] ex alto se aestus incitavisset (quod bis accidit[4] semper horarum XII spatio), neque navibus, quod, rursus minuente aestu, naves in vadis afflictarentur.[5] **2.** Ita utraque[6] re oppidorum oppugnatio impediebatur; ac si quando,[7] magnitudine operis forte superati, extruso mari aggere ac molibus[8] atque his oppidi moenibus adaequatis, suis fortunis[9] desperare coeperant, magno numero navium appulso,[10] cuius rei summam facultatem habebant, omnia sua deportabant[11] seque in proxima oppida recipiebant; ibi se rursus isdem[12] opportunitatibus loci defendebant. **3.** Haec eo facilius magnam partem aestatis faciebant, quod nostrae naves tempestatibus detinebantur,[13] summaque erat vasto[14] atque aperto mari, magnis aestibus, raris ac prope nullis portibus, difficultas navigandi.

[1] **eius modi . . . ut:** 'of such a character that'; *100b; 197b.* **situs:** 'locations'.
[2] **extremis,** etc.: 'at the ends of tongues of land,', relatively low, 'and promontories', high points of land, projecting into the sea. *152a.* **pedibus:** 'by land'; how lit.? *131a.* **aditum:** i.e. for an attacking army.
[3] **cum,** etc.: 'when the tide had rushed in from the deep'; how lit.? **quod:** 'which', referring to the preceding clause; hence neuter. **bis,** etc.: On July 1 the sun rises in Quiberon Bay at 4:12 and sets at 7:48 and the tide reaches high-water at 5 a.m. and 5:25 p.m.: there are thus two tides in one day. The interval between the forenoon and afternoon tides, in general, is less than the length of the summer days when Caesar was in this region (see the *American Journal of Philology,* 1916, p. 297).
[4] **accidit:** 'happened'. **horarum:** the long 'hours', of the summer days; *242a.* **spatio:** 'within the period'; *147c.* **rursus minuente aestu:** 'at ebb tide'; how lit.?
[5] **afflictarentur:** 'would be stranded', in case they should be over the shallow places when the tide went out.
[6] **utraque re:** 'by both conditions', both the rising and the ebbing of the tide. How lit.?
[7] **quando:** 'at any time'. **operis:** = *munitionum,* explained by what follows. **superati:** agrees with *oppidani,* understood as subject of *coeperant.* **extruso mari:** 'when the sea had been shut out'. *144b2.* Starting from the nearest point of land which remained dry at high tide, the Romans prolonged toward the town two massive parallel embankments, or dikes, working whenever the tide would allow, since at high tide the enclosed space would be under water. Having prolonged their dikes almost to the city, quickly, when the tide was low, they filled in the last stretch and shut out the water from both sides, thus giving a dry avenue of approach between the dikes from the adjacent country to the town. But by the time they were ready to attack, using each embankment as an *agger* (341), the townspeople had already taken ship and departed. See Map 10, **A.**
[8] **aggere ac molibus:** 'by massive dikes'; hendiadys; how lit.? *238d* (AG 640, B 374.4). **his,** etc.: 'when these had been built up to a level with the walls'. **moenibus:** *107a.*
[9] **fortunis:** dative; *109a.*
[10] **appulso:** 'having brought up' to the threatened town; how lit.? **cuius rei:** instead of *quarum;* we should say, 'of which they had the greatest abundance'; how lit.?
[11] **deportabant:** repeated action, 'they would carry off'; *175d.*
[12] **isdem:** 45. **opportunitatibus:** 'advantages'. **defendebant:** *175d.*
[13] **tempestatibus detinebantur:** 'were held back' in the Loire (III, 9.1), 'by storms'. **summa . . . difficultas:** *353d.*
[14] **vasto,** etc.: *144b3.* There is an implied contrast with the more sheltered and almost tideless

waters of the Mediterranean. **raris ac prope nullis:** 'infrequent, in fact, almost entirely lacking'; how lit.?

MAP 10

SEA-FIGHT WITH THE VENETANS

Book III, 7–16

To face page 208

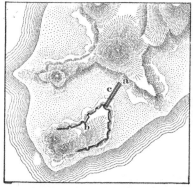

SCALE OF ENGLISH MILES

0 5 10 15 20

SCALE OF ROMAN MILES

0 5 10 15 20

EXPLANATION

Caesar's fleet was built on the Loire (Liger, chap. 9, ll. 2–4), and placed in command of Brutus. From the mouth of the Loire it followed a northerly course till it met the Venetan fleet (chap. 14).

MAP 10, **A**

OPERATIONS AGAINST A VENETAN TOWN
(III, 12)

a. Mainland.

b. Stronghold, *oppidum*, surrounded by water at high tide.

c. Parallel dikes over land submerged except at low tide. The dikes, or embankments, were high enough to keep out the water at high tide.

SCALE OF MILES

0 ¼ ½ ¾ 1 1¼ 1½

MAP 10, **A**

Advantages of the sea-going Venetan ships over Roman galleys.

13.1. Namque ipsorum[1] naves ad hunc modum factae armataeque[2] erant: carinae aliquanto planiores quam nostrarum navium, quo[3] facilius vada ac decessum aestus excipere possent; **2.** prorae[4] admodum erectae, atque item   puppes,   ad   magnitudinem   fluctuum[5]   tempestatumque accommodatae; **3.** naves totae[6] factae ex robore ad quamvis vim et contumeliam perferendam; transtra,[7] ex pedalibus in altitudinem trabibus, confixa clavis ferreis digiti pollicis crassitudine;[8] ancorae pro[9] funibus ferreis catenis revinctae; **4.** pelles pro velis alutaeque tenuiter confectae,[10] sive propter lini inopiam atque eius[11] usus inscientiam, sive eo, quod est magis veri simile, quod tantas tempestates Oceani tantosque impetus[12] ventorum sustineri ac tanta onera navium[13] regi velis non satis commode posse arbitrabantur. **5.** Cum his navibus nostrae classi[14] eius modi congressus erat,[15] ut una celeritate et pulsu remorum praestaret; reliqua pro   loci   natura,   pro[16]   vi   tempestatum   illis   essent   aptiora   et accommodatiora. **6.** Neque enim his[17] nostrae rostro nocere poterant (tanta in eis erat firmitudo[18]), neque propter altitudinem facile telum adigebatur,[19] et eadem de causa, minus commode copulis continebantur.[20] **7.** Accedebat, ut,[21] cum saevire ventus coepisset et se vento dedissent, et tempestatem ferrent[22] facilius et in vadis consisterent tutius[23] et, ab aestu relictae, nihil saxa et cautes timerent; quarum rerum omnium nostris navibus[24] casus erat extimescendus.

---

[1] **Namque ipsorum:** closely connected with the preceding; 'And (the Venetans have not the same difficulty in navigating these waters) for their'. **hunc:** 'the following'.

[2] **armatae:** 'equipped'. **carinae:** 'keels'; sc. *erant*. **aliquanto planiores:** 'considerably flatter', so that the ships were more flat-bottomed than the Roman galleys. **quam:** 'than (those)'.

[3] **quo:** *193b.* **decessum:** 'the ebbing'.

[4] **prorae,** etc.: 'the prows were very high'; sc. *erant* in this and the following clauses. **puppes:** 'sterns'.

[5] **fluctuum:** 'of sea-waves'. **accommodatae:** 'adapted'.

[6] **totae:**'wholly'; *151.* **robore:** 'oak'; *13f.* **quamvis:** 'no matter how great', lit. 'any you please'; *49a.* **vim et contumeliam:** 'violence and buffeting'; *230.3.*

[7] **transtra,** etc.: 'the cross-timbers, (made) of beams a foot thick' (lit. 'in height'), were 'fastened (to the sides) with iron bolts of the thickness of a thumb'. **trabibus:** *17c.*

[8] **crassitudine:** *143a.* **ancorae:** 'anchors', like those in use to-day.

[9] **pro:** 'instead of'. **funibus:** 'ropes'. As the Romans used only cables of rope, the chain cables of the Venetans seemed noteworthy. **revinctae:** were 'held'. **pelles:** 'hides'. **velis:** 'sails' of canvas.

[10] **alutae tenuiter confectae:** 'leather dressed thin'. **sive . . . sive:** *235a, b.* **lini:** 'flax'.

[11] **eius:** *lini.* **eo:** 'on this account,' explained by *quod . . . arbitrabantur; 135a.* **quod:** relative, refers to the thought of the following *quod*-clause. **veri:** *108b.*

[12] **impetus:** 'gusts.'

[13] **tanta onera navium:** trans. 'so heavy vessels'; how lit? **onera:** *13e.* **regi:** 'be managed'. **velis:** 'with (canvas) sails'.

[14] **nostrae classi congressus:** 'the encounter of our fleet'; how lit.? *111.* **eius modi:** 'such'; how lit.? *100b.*

[15] **erat:** 'would be'. **una:** 'only'. **pulsu remorum:** 'propulsion by oars', which gave to the galley a rapidity and freedom of movement comparable with that of a modern steamship. **reliqua:** 'other conditions'; *154a.*

[16] **pro:** 'in regard to'. **illis:** the Venetan ships. **aptiora:** 'better suited'.

[17] **his:** *105.* **nostrae:** sc. *naves.* **rostro:** 'by ramming', lit. 'with the beak'; *346c; 347.* **nocere:** 'do injury'.

[18] **firmitudo:** 'solidity'.

[19] **telum adigebatur:** 'could a missile be thrown up' on to them. The galleys were built relatively low, and light.

[20] **copulis continebantur:** 'could they be held with grappling hooks', thrown out from a galley to catch and hold a hostile ship so that the Romans could board it; *347*.

[21] **Accedebat, ut:** 'There was the further advantage, that'; *203.1*. **saevire:** 'to blow a gale'; how lit.? **se vento dedissent:** 'they ran before the wind'; *220*. How lit.?

[22] **ferrent:** 'they would weather'. **consisterent:** 'would ride'.

[23] **tutius:** *34b*. **aestu:** personified, hence with *ab*; *126b*. **relictae:** the Venetan ships, being flat-bottomed, when left by the tide settled easily and safely on the ground. **nihil:** = emphatic *non*; *118c* (AG 390d and n.2, B 176.2b).

[24] **navibus:** *110*; *239h* (AG 374, B 189.1). **casus,** etc.: 'the occurrence was greatly to be feared'; *229c*.

Caesar's fleet, commanded by Brutus, arrives; desperate sea-fight.

14.1. Compluribus expugnatis oppidis, Caesar, ubi intellexit, frustra tantum laborem sumi, neque hostium fugam, captis[1] oppidis, reprimi neque eis noceri posse, statuit exspectandam classem. **2.** Quae[2] ubi convenit ac primum ab hostibus visa est, circiter CCXX[3] naves eorum, paratissimae atque omni genere armorum[4] ornatissimae, profectae ex portu nostris adversae constiterunt; **3.** neque[5] satis Bruto, qui classi praeerat, vel tribunis[6] militum centurionibusque, quibus singulae naves erant attributae, constabat, quid agerent[7] aut quam rationem pugnae insisterent. **4.** Rostro[8] enim noceri non posse cognoverant; turribus[9] autem excitatis, tamen has altitudo puppium ex[10] barbaris navibus superabat, ut neque ex inferiore loco satis commode tela adigi possent[11] et missa a Gallis gravius[12] acciderent. **5.** Una erat magno usui[13] res praeparata a nostris, falces praeacutae insertae affixaeque longuriis, non[14] absimili forma muralium falcium.[15] **6.** His cum funes, qui antemnas ad malos destinabant,[16] comprehensi adductique erant, navigio remis incitato, praerumpebantur.[17] **7.** Quibus abscisis, antemnae necessario concidebant;[18] ut, cum omnis Gallicis navibus spes in velis armamentisque[19] consisteret, his ereptis, omnis usus navium uno[20] tempore eriperetur. **8.** Reliquum[21] erat certamen positum in virtute, qua nostri milites facile superabant, atque eo magis, quod in conspectu Caesaris atque omnis exercitus res[22] gerebatur, ut nullum paulo fortius[23] factum latere posset; **9.** omnes enim colles ac loca superiora, unde erat propinquus despectus in mare,[24] ab exercitu tenebantur.

[1] **captis,** etc.: 'could be checked by taking the towns'; *144b6*. **eis noceri posse:** 'harm could be done them'; *106b*; *105*. **exspectandam:** in full, *sibi exspectandam esse*.

[2] **Quae:** *167*. **convenit:** 'arrived'.

[3] **CCXX:** *ducentae et viginti*; *38b*; *36*. **paratissimae:** 'fully ready'; *153a*. **genere:** *133*.

[4] **armorum:** 'of equipment', including everything needed to make a ship ready for action. **ornatissimae:** 'completely rigged'. **ex portu,** etc.: the sea-fight probably took place in the bay of Quiberon, Caesar's army being drawn up in sight on the heights of St. Gildas. The courses of the fleets may be traced on Map 10.

[5] **neque . . . constabat:** 'and it was not quite clear to Brutus', etc. After the Gallic war Brutus, as an official of the Roman mint, struck a coin commemorating Gallic victories; *73c*.

[6] **tribunis,** etc.: the legionaries on the Roman galleys were under their regular officers. We do not know how many galleys participated in the battle.

[7] **quid agerent:** 'what they were to do'; *217b* (AG 587, B 315.3).

[8] **Rostro:** as in III, 13.6. **noceri:** sc. *eis*, the enemy's ships.
[9] **turribus excitatis:** 'even though the towers had been erected' on the Roman ships; *144b5*; *346d.*
[10] **ex:** 'on'; *126c.* **inferiore loco:** the decks and towers of the Roman vessels.
[11] **adigi possent:** cf. III, 13.6, note 19. **missa:** sc. *tela.*
[12] **gravius:** 'with greater force', because thrown from a considerable height down upon the decks of the galleys.
[13] **magno usui:** 'very useful'; how lit.? *112a.* **praeparata:** 'made ready beforehand'. **falces,** etc.: 'hooks sharpened at the ends, let into (the ends of) long poles and fastened to (them)'. **falces:** *17c; 91a.*
[14] **non,** etc.: = *forma non absimili formae muralium falcium,* 'of a shape not unlike that of wall hooks'; *143a; 238b.*
[15] **muralium falcium:** used on long poles to pull stones out of walls; *342c.* **His:** *131a.* **cum:** 'whenever'; *186a* (B. 288b3). **antemnas:** 'sail-yards'. **malos:** 'masts'.
[16] **destinabant:** 'fastened'. **adducti erant:** 'had been pulled taut'. **navigio incitato:** 'when the ship', that had caught its hook in the enemy's rigging, 'was driven forward', etc.; *144b2.*
[17] **praerumpebantur:** 'they were severed'. **abscisis:** 'cutoff'.
[18] **concidebant:** 'fell down'. **cum:** *184a.* **Gallicis navibus:** 'in the case of the Gallic ships'; dative; *109a* (AG 376, B 188.1n).
[19] **armamentis:** 'rigging'; they had no oars. **usus:** 'control'.
[20] **uno:** trans. as if *eodem.*
[21] **Reliquum:** emphatic position; *353d.* **certamen:** 'contest'. **erat positum in:** 'depended on'; how lit.?
[22] **res:** 'the struggle'. **gerebatur:** force of the imperfect?
[23] **paulo fortius:** 'unusually brave', lit. 'a little braver (than usual)'. **factum:** 'deed'. **latere:** 'be unobserved'. **colles,** etc.: heights of St. Gildas; see Map 10.
[24] **despectus in mare:** 'view over the sea', *de* implying a view from an elevation.

Roman courage, ingenuity, and good luck win the day.

15.1. Deiectis, ut diximus, antemnis, cum[1] singulas binae ac ternae naves circumsteterant, milites summa vi transcendere[2] in hostium naves contendebant. **2.** Quod postquam barbari fieri animadverterunt, expugnatis compluribus navibus, cum ei[3] rei nullum reperiretur auxilium, fuga salutem petere contenderunt. **3.** Ac iam conversis in eam partem navibus, quo[4] ventus ferebat, tanta subito malacia[5] ac tranquillitas exstitit, ut se ex loco movere non possent.[6] **4.** Quae quidem res ad negotium conficiendum maxime fuit opportuna; nam singulas[7] nostri consectati[8] expugnaverunt, ut perpaucae ex omni numero noctis interventu[9] ad terram pervenerint, cum ab hora fere IIII usque ad solis occasum pugnaretur.

[1] **cum:** *186a.* **singulas,** etc.: 'two or' (lit. 'and') 'three galleys had surrounded a single ship' of the enemy. We are not to suppose that Caesar's fleet outnumbered that of the Venetans; the Romans simply concentrated their forces on one vessel at a time, instead of engaging the whole line of the enemy at once. **singulas:** sc. *naves.* **binae:** *36.*
[2] **transcendere in:** 'to board', in the nautical sense. **contendebant:** 'would hasten'. *175d* (AG 470, B 260.2). **Quod:** trans. as if *et hoc.*
[3] **ei auxilium:** 'no remedy', i.e. counter-tactic, 'was discovered against this', the boarding of their vessels by the legionaries. "Thus was this naval battle", says Mommsen (*History of Rome,* Vol. V, p. 57) – "so far as historical knowledge reaches, the earliest fought on the Atlantic Ocean – just like the engagement at Mylae two hundred years before, and despite the most unfavourable circumstances, was decided in favour of the Romans by a lucky invention suggested by necessity."
[4] **quo:** trans. as if *in quam.* **ventus ferebat:** 'the wind was blowing'.
[5] **malacia ac tranquillitas:** 'calm and stillness'. **exstitit:** 'ensued'; in the latter part of summer a morning wind in these regions is usually followed by a calm in the afternoon; *176a; 173a.*

[6] **non possent**: relying entirely on sails, the Venetans were helpless when the wind failed them. **res**: 'circumstance'.

[7] **singulas**: 'one by one'; sc. *naves*.

[8] **consectati**: 'pursuing'; *226c*. **numero**: *97d*.

[9] **interventu**: 'because of the coming'; *135a*. **cum**: 'although'; *187*. **hora quarta**: a little before ten o'clock by our reckoning; the battle took place toward the end of summer, before the autumnal equinox; *242a, b*.

The captive Venetans are sold into slavery as a warning.

16.1. Quo proelio bellum Venetorum totiusque orae maritimae confectum est. **2.** Nam cum[1] omnis iuventus, omnes etiam gravioris[2] aetatis, in quibus aliquid consilii aut dignitatis fuit,[3] eo convenerant, tum, navium quod ubique fuerat, in unum locum coegerant; **3.** quibus[4] amissis, reliqui neque quo se reciperent,[5] neque quem ad modum oppida defenderent, habebant. Itaque se suaque omnia[6] Caesari dediderunt. **4.** In quos eo[7] gravius Caesar vindicandum statuit, quo diligentius in reliquum tempus[8] a barbaris ius legatorum conservaretur. Itaque, omni[9] senatu necato, reliquos sub corona vendidit.

[1] **cum . . . tum**: *186b* (B. 290.2).

[2] **gravioris**: 'more advanced'. **aliquid . . . dignitatis**: 'any weight of judgement or influence'; *97b*.

[3] **fuit**: *90a*. **eo**: to the country of the Venetans. **navium quod**: i.e. *id navium, quod eis ubique fuerat*, 'all the ships that they had had anywhere'; *97b*.

[4] **quibus**: including men as well as ships. **reliqui**: 'those who survived'; how lit.? **neque,** etc.: 'had (in mind) neither a place to which they might make their escape, nor any means by which they might defend', etc.; how lit.?

[5] **reciperent,** etc.: indirect question; it would have the subjunctive also as a direct question; *217b*.

[6] **suaque omnia**: 'and all they had'; how lit.?

[7] **eo . . . quo**: 'on this account ... in order that'; *193b*. **gravius vindicandum** [esse]: 'that a severer punishment ought to be inflicted'; how lit.?

[8] **in reliquum tempus**: 'for the future'. **ius legatorum**: 'the rights of ambassadors', whose persons, from the beginning of civilized life, have been considered inviolable.

[9] **omni,** etc.: 'killed all the senate and'; how lit.? *144b2; 289b*. **sub corona**: 'into slavery'; lit. 'under the wreath', referring to the wreath placed on the heads of captives sold at auction. We can hardly suppose that the entire population was sold into slavery; yet these maritime states were so reduced in strength that they afterwards gave Caesar no trouble.

Expedition of Sabinus against the Venellans. 17-19

Sabinus encamps in the country of the Venelli and pretends fear.

17.1. Dum haec in Venetis[1] geruntur, Q. Titurius Sabinus cum eis[2] copiis, quas a Caesare acceperat, in fines Venellorum pervenit. **2.** His praeerat Viridovix[3] ac summam imperii tenebat earum omnium civitatum, quae defecerant, ex quibus exercitum[4] magnasque copias coegerat; **3.** atque his paucis diebus[5] Aulerci Eburovices[6] Lexoviique, senatu suo interfecto, quod auctores[7] belli esse nolebant, portas clauserunt seque cum Viridovice coniunxerunt; **4.** magnaque praeterea multitudo undique ex Gallia perditorum[8] hominum latronumque convenerat, quos spes praedandi studiumque bellandi ab agri cultura[9] et cotidiano labore sevocabat. **5.** Sabinus idoneo omnibus rebus[10] loco castris sese tenebat, cum[11] Viridovix contra eum duorum milium spatio consedisset cotidieque, productis copiis, pugnandi potestatem faceret, ut[12] iam non solum hostibus in contemptionem Sabinus veniret, sed etiam nostrorum militum vocibus non nihil[13] carperetur;[14] **6.** tantamque opinionem timoris praebuit, ut iam ad vallum castrorum hostes accedere auderent. **7.** Id[15] ea de causa faciebat, quod cum tanta multitudine hostium, praesertim eo absente, qui[16] summam imperii teneret, nisi aequo loco aut opportunitate aliqua data, legato dimicandum[17] non existimabat.

[1] **Venetis:** *282.* **geruntur:** trans. by a past tense; *190a.*

[2] **eis copiis:** three legions, as related in III, 11.4. **in fines Venellorum:** the probable route of Sabinus is shown on Map 9.

[3] **Viridovix:** *19d.* **summam imperii:** 'the chief command'; how lit.? Viridovix not only commanded the forces of the Venellans, but was commander in chief of all the forces raised by the revolting states.

[4] **exercitum:** 'an army', trained and equipped, as distinguished from **copias,** 'forces' hastily levied and organized.

[5] **his paucls diebus:** 'within the few days' after the arrival of Sabinus; *147a; 160d.*

[6] **Aulerci Eburovlces:** one name; see Map 9.

[7] **auctores:** 'favourers'; why nominative? *221b.* **nolebant:** plural because *senatu* is thought of as *senatoribus; 173b.* **portas clauserunt:** the shutting of city gates on the approach of an army was taken as a declaration of war.

[8] **perditorum:** 'desperate'. **latronum:** 'bandits.'

[9] **agri cultura:** 'farming'. **sevocabat:** 'lured away'; how lit.? *79d.*

[10] **omnibus rebus:** 'in all respects'; *142a.* **loco:** *145c.* **castris:** *131a.* The camp of Sabinus was probably near the small river Sée, in the southern part of the Venellan territory (Map 9).

[11] **cum:** *187.* **duorum,** etc.: '(only) two miles away'. **spatio:** *147c.*

[12] **ut:** 'so that'. **hostibus:** 'in the eyes of the enemy'; *109a* (AG 377, B 188.1n). **contemptionem:** 'contempt'.

[13] **non nihil:** 'rather sharply'; how lit.? *118c.*

[14] **carperetur:** 'was criticised'. **opinionem:** 'impression'; *81.* **praebuit:** 'produced'.

[15] **Id:** the holding of the Roman soldiers in camp.

[16] **eo absente, qui:** 'in the absence of him (Caesar) who'; *144b3.* **teneret:** *214a.* **nisi:** i.e. *nisi dimicaret.* **aequo loco:** 'advantageous position'; sc. *dato; 144b2.*

[17] **dimicandum** [esse], etc.: 'a lieutenant ought not', etc.; *110.*

By a ruse he leads the enemy to attack him.

18.1. Hac confirmata opinione timoris, idoneum quendam hominem et callidum[1] delegit, Gallum, ex eis, quos auxilii causa secum habebat. **2.** Huic magnis praemiis pollicitationibusque persuadet, uti ad hostes transeat, et, quid fieri velit,[2] edocet. **3.** Qui[3] ubi pro perfuga ad eos venit, timorem Romanorum proponit; quibus angustiis ipse Caesar a Venetis prematur, docet, **4.** neque[4] longius abesse, quin proxima nocte Sabinus clam ex castris exercitum educat et ad Caesarem auxilii ferendi causa proficiscatur. **5.** Quod ubi auditum est, conclamant omnes, occasionem[5] negotii bene gerendi amittendam non esse; ad castra iri[6] oportere. **6.** Multae res ad hoc consilium Gallos hortabantur: superiorum[7] dierum Sabini cunctatio, perfugae confirmatio, inopia cibariorum, cui rei parum diligenter ab eis erat provisum, spes Venetici belli, et quod fere libenter homines id, quod[8] volunt, credunt. **7.** His rebus adducti, non prius[9] Viridovicem reliquosque duces ex concilio dimittunt, quam ab his sit concessum, arma uti capiant et ad castra contendant. **8.** Qua re concessa, laeti,[10] ut explorata victoria, sarmentis virgultisque collectis, quibus[11] fossas Romanorum compleant, ad castra pergunt.

[1] **callidum:** 'tactful'. **ex eis:** *97d.*

[2] **velit, prematur:** *204.2.* **edocet:** 'explained'; *175b.*

[3] **Qui, Quod:** *167.* **pro perfuga:** 'as if a deserter'. **venit:** *188a.*

[4] **neque,** etc.: *neque longius abesse proxima nocte, quin . . . proficiscatur,* 'and that no later than the following night Sabinus would stealthily lead', etc.; *201b* (AG 558, B 298).

[5] **occasionem,** etc.: 'the chance to score a notable success'; how lit.?

[6] **iri,** etc.: 'that they ought to attack the camp'; how lit.? *68d; 73d* (AG 208d, B 138.iv).

[7] **superiorum:** 'preceding'. **cunctatio:** 'inaction'; *91a; 74b.* **confirmatio:** 'the assurance'.

[8] **quod . . . credunt:** appositive of *res; 198b; 175c.* **fere:** 'as a rule'. Caesar's keen insight into human nature was an important factor in his success.

[9] **prius – quam – sit concessum:** 'until permission had been granted'; *189b* (B 292).

[10] **laeti:** 'joyfully'; *151.* **ut explorata victoria:** 'as if victory were (already) assured'. **sarmentis:** 'brushwood', cut from trees. **virgultis:** 'fascines', bundles of shoots and bushes tied together for convenience in handling. **collectis:** 'they gathered and'; how lit.?

[11] **quibus . . . compleant:** trans. as if *ut eis . . . compleant; 193a; 131a.*

He surprises them, and wins a decisive victory.

19.1. Locus[1] erat castrorum editus et paulatim ab imo acclivis circiter passus[2] mille. Huc magno cursu contenderunt, ut quam minimum spatii[3] ad se colligendos armandosque Romanis daretur, exanimatique pervenerunt. **2.** Sabinus, suos hortatus,[4] cupientibus signum dat. Impeditis hostibus propter ea, quae ferebant, onera, subito duabus portis[5] eruptionem fieri iubet. **3.** Factum est opportunitate loci, hostium inscientia[6] ac defatigatione, virtute militum et superiorum pugnarum exercitatione, ut ne unum quidem nostrorum impetum ferrent[7] ac statim terga verterent. **4.** Quos impeditos integris viribus[8] milites nostri consecuti, magnum numerum eorum occiderunt; reliquos[9] equites[10] consectati, paucos, qui ex fuga evaserant, reliquerunt. **5.** Sic, uno tempore, et de navali pugna Sabinus et de Sabini victoria Caesar certior factus est, civitatesque omnes se statim Titurio[11] dediderunt. **6.** Nam ut ad bella suscipienda Gallorum alacer[12] ac promptus est animus, sic mollis[13] ac minime resistens ad calamitates perferendas mens[14] eorum est.

[1] **Locus:** 'site'. **ab imo:** 'from the bottom' of the hill; *154a.*

[2] **passus:** *118a.* **Huc:** up the slope to the camp. **magno cursu:** 'at full speed'.

[3] **quam minimum spatii:** 'as little time as possible'; *97b; 153c.*

[4] **hortatus:** see I, 25.1, note 3; *226c.* **cupientibus:** sc. *eis.*

[5] **duabus portis:** sc. *castrorum:* probably the gates on the right and left sides of the camp; *334a; 134a.* **Factum est:** 'the result was'; how lit.? **opportunitate:** *135a.*

[6] **inscientia:** 'lack of skill'. **defatigatione:** 'exhaustion'.

[7] **ferrent:** sc. *hostes; 203.1.* **ac:** 'but'; *234b.*

[8] **viribus:** *135a; 18a.* **consecuti:** *226c.*

[9] **reliquos:** 'the rest' of the Gauls not slain by the legionaries.

[10] **equites:** = *equites nostri.* **paucos:** '(only) a few'; *154a.*

[11] **Titurio:** for the full name see III, 11.4; *19b.* **ut:** 'just as'. The subjugation of these states was now complete; the submission reported the previous year (II, 34) had been only nominal.

[12] **alacer:** 'impetuous'; *24.* **promptus:** 'ready'. **animus:** 'temperament'.

[13] **mollis:** 'yielding'. **resistens:** adjective; with *minime,* 'not at all capable of resistance'. Caesar again comments on the fickleness of the Gauls (cf. III, 8.3 and 10.3; IV, 5.2-3).

[14] **mens:** 'character'.

Crassus, entering Aquitania, meets a force of the Sotiates.

20.1. Eodem fere tempore P. Crassus,[1] cum in Aquitaniam pervenisset, quae, ut ante dictum est, tertia pars Galliae est, cum[2] intellegeret, in eis locis sibi bellum gerendum, ubi paucis ante annis[3] L. Valerius Praeconinus legatus, exercitu pulso, interfectus esset, atque unde[4] L. Manlius proconsul, impedimentis amissis, profugisset, non mediocrem[5] sibi diligentiam adhibendam intellegebat. **2.** Itaque re frumentaria provisa, auxiliis equitatuque comparato, multis praeterea viris fortibus[6] Tolosa et Carcasone et Narbone, quae sunt civitates Galliae provinciae finitimae his regionibus, nominatim[7] evocatis, in Sotiatium fines exercitum introduxit. **3.** Cuius adventu cognito Sotiates, magnis copiis coactis, equitatuque,[8] quo plurimum valebant, in itinere agmen nostrum adorti, primum equestre proelium commiserunt; **4.** deinde, equitatu[9] suo pulso atque insequentibus nostris, subito pedestres copias, quas in convalle in insidiis collocaverant, ostenderunt. Hi,[10] nostros disiectos adorti, proelium renovarunt.

[1] **P. Crassus:** with twelve cohorts and a large body of cavalry (III, 11.3). The cavalry would have been of no use to Caesar in the campaign against the Venetans, but could be employed by Crassus to advantage in the mountainous regions of Aquitania.
[2] **cum:** *184a.* **gerendum:** sc. *esse.* **ubi:** = *in quibus.*
[3] **paucis ante annis:** twenty-two years before (*140*), in 78 B.C. In that year Praeconinus, mentioned only here, and Lucius Manlius, proconsul of the Province, were routed by Hirtuleius, the quaestor of Sertorius. Cf. III, 23.5, note 7.
[4] **unde:** = *e quibus.* **L.:** *19a.*
[5] **non mediocrem:** 'no ordinary'; *239g.* **sibi:** *110.*
[6] **viris fortibus:** soldiers who, having served their time (20 years), were living in the Province; *307a.* **Tolosa:** *127a; 293a.*
[7] **nominatim:** requests to re-enter the service were sent to the veterans individually. **evocatis:** 'called out'. **Sotiatium:** see Map 9; *19e.*
[8] **equitatu:** with *adorti; 131a.* **quo:** *142a.* **plurimum:** *118b.*
[9] **equitatu**, etc: apparently the flight of the cavalry was a ruse, to draw the pursuing Romans into the valley (*convalle*) where the infantry of the Sotiates was in ambush.
[10] **Hi:** referring to *pedestres copias.* Why masculine?

In a fierce fight he defeats them and captures their city.

21.1. Pugnatum est diu atque acriter, cum Sotiates, superioribus victoriis[1] freti, in sua virtute totius Aquitaniae salutem positam putarent,[2] nostri autem, quid sine imperatore et sine reliquis legionibus, adulescentulo duce,[3] efficere possent, perspici cuperent; tandem confecti vulneribus hostes terga verterunt. **2.** Quorum magno numero interfecto, Crassus ex itinere[4] oppidum Sotiatum oppugnare coepit. Quibus[5] fortiter resistentibus, vineas turresque egit. **3.** Illi, alias[6] eruptione temptata, alias cuniculis ad aggerem vineasque actis (cuius rei[7] sunt longe peritissimi Aquitani, propterea quod multis locis[8] apud eos aerariae secturaeque sunt[9]), ubi diligentia nostrorum nihil his rebus profici posse intellexerunt, legatos ad Crassum mittunt, seque in deditionem ut recipiat, petunt. Qua re impetrata, arma tradere iussi faciunt.

[1] **victoriis:** *131e* (AG 431a, B 218.3). **freti:** 'relying on'.
[2] **putarent:** *184a.* **quid . . . possent:** subject of *perspici; 204.2.*
[3] **adulescentulo duce:** 'with a youth as leader', referring to Crassus; *144b2.*
[4] **ex itinere:** Vocab. under *iter.* **oppidum:** identified with Sos, the name of which is derived from *Sotiates.* **oppugnare:** Crassus tried to take the town by sudden storming; *340.*
[5] **Quibus:** *167.* **vineas, turres:** appliances for besieging; *342a,b.*
[6] **alias . . . alias:** 'at one time ... at another'. **cuniculis:** 'tunnels', underground passageways from which the Roman works could be undermined, so that they would fall in, or could be set on fire.
[7] **cuius rei:** 'an operation', the driving of tunnels, 'in which'; *102; 165b.*
[8] **locis:** *145c.* **aerariae:** 'copper mines'. **securae:** 'excavations', probably open cuts from which iron ore was taken, as distinguished from the more elaborate tunnels of the copper mines. Remains of ancient copper and iron mines have been found in the region of the Sotiates, and mining operations are still carried on there.
[9] **sunt:** *90a.* **diligentia:** *135a.* **his rebus:** 'by these devices'; *131a.*

Adiatunnus with a devoted band makes a sortie, is captured.

22.1. Atque in[1] ea re omnium nostrorum intentis animis, alia ex parte oppidi Adiatunnus,[2] qui summam imperii tenebat, cum DC[3] devotis, quos illi 'soldurios' appellant. **2.** quorum haec est condicio, uti[4] omnibus in vita commodis una cum eis fruantur, quorum se amicitiae[5] dediderint; si quid his per vim[6] accidat, aut eundem casum una ferant aut sibi mortem consciscant **3.** (neque adhuc[7] hominum memoria repertus est quisquam, qui, eo interfecto, cuius se amicitiae devovisset, mortem recusaret[8]). **4.** cum his Adiatunnus eruptionem facere conatus, clamore ab ea parte munitionis sublato, cum ad arma milites concurrissent vehementerque ibi pugnatum esset, repulsus in oppidum tamen, uti[9] eadem deditionis condicione uteretur, a Crasso impetravit.

[1] **in:** 'upon'. **intentis animis:** 'while the attention was fixed'; how lit.? *144b2.*
[2] **Adiatunnus:** a coin has been found bearing his name in Roman letters; the spelling of the name is not the same as that given by Caesar. **summam imperii:** see III, 17.2, note 3.
[3] **DC:** *sescentis; 38b.* **devotis:** 'faithful followers'. **soldurios:** 'the vow-beholden'. **quorum,** etc.: 'the terms of whose association are these'; how lit.?
[4] **uti . . . fruantur:** *203.4.* **commodis:** *131c* (AG 410, B 218.1).
[5] **amicitiae:** dative. **dediderint:** *220.* **si quid,** etc.: cf. I, 18.9, note 27.
[6] **vim:** 'violence'. **eundem casum una:** 'the same fate at the same time'. **ferant:** sc. *ut.* **sibi,** etc.: cf. I, 4.4, note 12.
[7] **adhuc:** 'up to this time'. **memoria:** *147b.*
[8] **recusaret:** *194a* (AG 535a, B 283.2). **his:** = *devotis* in III, 22.1, resuming the narrative interrupted by the long explanation.
[9] **uti,** etc.: *199a.* **eadem:** 'the same' as the rest.

Proceeding further, Crassus finds a formidable army.

23.1. Armis obsidibusque acceptis, Crassus in fines Vocatium et Tarusatium profectus est. **2.** Tum vero barbari, commoti, quod oppidum[1] et natura loci et manu munitum paucis diebus, quibus[2] eo ventum erat, expugnatum cognoverant, legatos quoque versus[3] dimittere, coniurare, obsides inter se dare, copias parare coeperunt. **3.** Mittuntur etiam ad eas civitates legati, quae sunt citerioris Hispaniae[4] finitimae Aquitaniae; inde auxilia ducesque arcessuntur. **4.** Quorum adventu[5] magna cum auctoritate et magna hominum[6] multitudine bellum gerere conantur. **5.** Duces vero ei deliguntur, qui una cum Q. Sertorio[7] omnes annos fuerant summamque scientiam rei militaris habere existimabantur. **6.** Hi consuetudine populi Romani loca capere,[8] castra munire, commeatibus nostros intercludere instituunt. **7.** Quod[9] ubi Crassus animadvertit, suas copias propter exiguitatem non facile diduci,[10] hostem et vagari et vias obsidere et[11] castris satis praesidii relinquere, ob eam causam minus commode frumentum commeatumque sibi supportari, in dies[12] hostium numerum augeri, non cunctandum existimavit, quin[13] pugna decertaret. **8.** Hac re ad consilium delata, ubi omnes idem sentire[14] intellexit, posterum diem pugnae constituit.

[1] **oppidum:** *oppidum Sotiatium,* III, 21.2. **manu:** the natural defences of the town had been strengthened by fortifications.

[2] **quibus:** 'after', lit. 'within which'; *147a.* **ventum erat:** *73d.* **expugnatum:** sc. *esse.*

[3] **quoque versus:** 'in all directions'.

[4] **citerioris Hispaniae:** *94d; 296.* **finitimae:** agrees with *quae.*

[5] **adventu:** *147b.* **magna,** etc.: to be taken closely with *adventu.* **auctoritate:** 'prestige'.

[6] **hominum:** *98a.* **Duces:** in predicate; *88a.*

[7] **Q. Sertorio:** a military leader of the popular party in the first Civil War at Rome, the war between Marius and Sulla. After the death of Marius, and Sulla's return to Rome, Sertorius organized an army in Spain, and held his own against the government for ten years, until at length he was treacherously assassinated in 72 B.C. **omnes annos:** 'during all (those) years', 82-72 B.C., when Sertorius had an army in the field.

[8] **loca capere:** 'to choose locations' for encampment. The Aquitanians were in this respect in advance of the Gauls, who did not begin to fortify their camps until four years later (VII, 29.7).

[9] **Quod:** 'Now – this (fact)', explained by the following infinitive clauses.

[10] **diduci:** 'spread out', so as to cope at all points with the numerically superior enemy. **hostem,** etc.: '(but) that the enemy both roamed' at will 'and'.

[11] **et:** 'and (still)'.=. **castris:** of the enemy. **praesidii:** *97b.*

[12] **in dies:** 'day by day'. **non cunctandum** [esse]: sc. *sibi,* 'that he ought not to delay'.

[13] **quin,** etc.: 'to fight a decisive battle'; how lit.? *201b.*

[14] **omnes idem sentire:** 'that all held the same opinion'; *117a.*

Forming battle order, he waits, then attacks the enemy's camp.

24.1. Prima luce productis omnibus copiis, duplici acie[1] instituta, auxiliis[2] in mediam aciem coniectis, quid hostes consilii caperent,[3] exspectabat. **2.** Illi, etsi propter multitudinem et veterem belli gloriam paucitatemque[4] nostrorum se tuto[5] dimicaturos existimabant, tamen tutius esse arbitrabantur, obsessis viis,[6] commeatu intercluso, sine ullo vulnere victoria potiri, **3.** et, si propter inopiam rei frumentariae Romani sese recipere[7] coepissent, impeditos in agmine et sub sarcinis[8] infirmiores animo adoriri cogitabant. **4.** Hoc consilio probato ab ducibus, productis Romanorum copiis, sese castris tenebant. **5.** Hac re perspecta Crassus, cum sua cunctatione atque opinione[9] timoris hostes nostros milites alacriores ad pugnandum effecissent, atque omnium[10] voces audirentur, *exspectari[11] diutius non oportere, quin ad castra iretur,* cohortatus suos, omnibus cupientibus,[12] ad hostium castra contendit.

[1] **duplici acie:** not so strong as the customary triple line, but necessary here because the Roman force was so greatly outnumbered by the enemy; *337.* **duplici:** *26a.*

[2] **auxiliis:** the auxiliary troops were usually stationed upon the wings; in this instance they were placed at the middle of the line because Crassus did not have confidence in them (III, 25.1). **quid consilii:** 'what plan'; *97b.*

[3] **caperent:** 'would adopt'; *204.2.* **exspectabat:** 'was waiting (to see)'. **multitudinem:** estimated at 50,000 (III, 26.6).

[4] **paucitatem:** the whole force under the command of Crassus (see III, 11.3 and 20.2) can hardly have amounted to 10,000 men.

[5] **tuto:** *34b.* **tutius:** predicative with *esse,* of which the subject is *potiri; 222b; 148d.*

[6] **obsessis viis:** 'having blocked the roads (and)'; how lit.? *238a.*

[7] **sese recipere:** 'to retreat'. **impeditos:** sc. *eos* [*Romanos*].

[8] **sarcinis:** *330.* **infirmiores animo:** 'less courageous'; how lit.? *142a.* **cogitabant:** 'they were proposing'.

[9] **opinione:** 'impression'. **hostes:** nominative.

[10] **omnium:** i.e. *omnium militum.* **voces:** 'remarks'.

[11] **exspectari,** etc.: '(to the effect) that they ought not to delay further to attack the camp'; how lit.? *213b.* **iretur:** *68d; 73d; 201b.*

[12] **omnibus cupientibus:** *144b3.* **ad hostium castra:** this is the only attack of the Romans on a fortified camp recorded in the Gallic War.

He learns that the enemy's rear gate is not well guarded.

25.1. Ibi cum alii[1] fossas complerent, alii, multis telis coniectis, defensores vallo[2] munitionibusque depellerent, auxiliaresque,[3] quibus ad pugnam non multum Crassus confidebat, lapidibus[4] telisque sumministrandis et ad aggerem caespitibus[5] comportandis speciem atque opinionem pugnantium praeberent; cum item ab hostibus constanter ac non timide pugnaretur telaque ex loco superiore[6] missa non frustra acciderent, **2.** equites, circumitis hostium castris,[7] Crasso renuntiaverunt, non eadem esse diligentia ab decumana porta[8] castra munita facilemque aditum habere.

[1] **alii . . . alii:** *milites Romani; 171b.* **fossas:** see III, 5.1.

[2] **vallo:** constructed in the Roman fashion (III, 23.6); *127a; 333.*

[3] **auxiliares:** see III, 24.1, note 2. **quibus:** dative; *105.*

[4] **lapidibus . . . comportandis:** 'by bringing', etc., ablatives of means; *230.4.* **ad aggerem:** sc. *faciundum.* The rampart of the enemy's camp was so high that the Romans began to make a sloping mound up to it, like the *agger* used in besieging a town.

[5] **caespitibus:** 'sods'; *10d.* **speciem . . . pugnantium:** 'the appearance and impression of combatants'.

[6] **loco superiore:** the top of the rampart of the camp; the camp lay in a plain (III, 26.6).

[7] **circumitis hostium castris:** 'having ridden about the enemy's camp'; *334a.*

[8] **ab decumana porta:** 'on the side of the rear gate'; *126c.*

Surprising the enemy by a rear attack, he routs them.

26.1. Crassus, equitum praefectos[1] cohortatus, ut magnis praemiis pollicitationibusque suos[2] excitarent, quid fieri velit, ostendit. **2.** Illi,[3] ut erat imperatum, eductis eis cohortibus, quae, praesidio castris relictae, intritae[4] ab labore erant, et longiore itinere circumductis, ne ex hostium castris conspici possent, omnium[5] oculis mentibusque ad pugnam intentis, celeriter ad eas,[6] quas diximus, munitiones pervenerunt, **3.** atque, his prorutis,[7] prius in hostium castris constiterunt, quam plane ab his videri[8] aut, quid rei gereretur, cognosci posset. **4.** Tum vero, clamore[9] ab ea parte audito, nostri, redintegratis viribus, quod[10] plerumque in spe victoriae accidere consuevit, acrius impugnare coeperunt. **5.** Hostes undique circumventi, desperatis[11] omnibus rebus, se per munitiones deicere et fuga salutem petere contenderunt. **6.** Quos equitatus apertissimis[12] campis consectatus, ex milium L numero, quae[13] ex

Aquitania Cantabrisque convenisse constabat, vix quarta parte relicta, multa nocte[14] se in castra recepit.

[1] **equitum praefectos:** *309c.* **ut,** etc.: *199a.*
[2] **suos:** the cavalrymen, on whom the success of the surprise depended.
[3] **Illi:** the cavalry prefects who guided cohorts of infantry to the rear of the enemy's camp. It is possible that the cavalrymen took the legionaries with them on their horses in order to transport them quickly by a roundabout way. **praesidio castris:** *112b.*
[4] **intritae:** 'unfatigued'. **longiore:** *153a.*
[5] **omnium:** *hostium.* **oculis,** etc.: *144b2.*
[6] **eas – munitiones:** at the rear of the enemy's camp (III, 25.2).
[7] **prorutis:** 'demolished'. **prius – quam:** *189b.* **plane:** 'clearly'.
[8] **videri:** sc. *possent*, 'they could be seen'. **quid,** etc.: 'what was going on'; how lit.?
[9] **clamore,** etc.: from the shouting at the rear of the camp the Romans fighting in front knew that the attack there was in progress, and were inspired to greater efforts.
[10] **quod:** relative, refers to the thought in *redintegratis viribus;* trans., with *plerumque,* 'as generally'.
[11] **desperatis omnibus rebus:** 'in utter despair'; how lit.? **per:** 'over'.
[12] **apertissimis:** 'wide and open'. Cf. *153a.* **campis:** *145c.* **consectatus:** *226c.*
[13] **quae:** subject accusative of *convenisse;* the antecedent is *milium.*
[14] **multa nocte:** 'late at night'; *152a.*

Crassus receives the submission of other Aquitanian states.

27.1. Hac audita pugna, maxima pars Aquitaniae sese Crasso dedidit obsidesque ultro misit; quo in numero[1] fuerunt Tarbelli,[2] Bigerriones, Ptianii, Vocates, Tarusates, Elusates, Gates, Ausci, Garumni, Sibusates, Cocosates; **2.** paucae ultimae nationes,[3] anni tempore confisae, quod hiems suberat, hoc facere neglexerunt.

[1] **quo in numero:** we should say 'in the number of whom', 'among whom'.
[2] **Tarbelli,** etc.: see Map 9. The Tarbelli have left a trace of their name in modern Tarbes; the Bigerriones, in Bagnères de Bigorre, a wateringplace in the Pyrenees; the Elusates, in Eauze; the Ausci, in Auch; the Sibusates, in Saubusse.
[3] **paucae ultimae nationes:** i.e. *paucae nationes, quae ultimae erant;* 'a few remote peoples'. **tempore:** *135a* (AG 431, B 219.1).

EXPEDITION OF CAESAR AGAINST THE MORINI AND THE MENAPII. 28, 29

Caesar proceeds against the Morini and the Menapii.

28.1. Eodem[1] fere tempore Caesar, etsi prope exacta iam aestas erat, tamen, quod, omni Gallia,[2] pacata, Morini Menapiique supererant,[3] qui in armis essent neque ad eum umquam legatos de pace misissent, arbitratus[4] id bellum celeriter confici posse, eo exercitum duxit;[5] qui longe alia ratione ac reliqui Galli bellum gerere coeperunt. **2.** Nam quod intellegebant, maximas nationes, quae proelio contendissent, pulsas superatasque esse, continentesque[6] silvas ac paludes habebant,[7] eo se suaque omnia contulerunt. **3.** Ad quarum initium silvarum cum Caesar pervenisset castraque munire instituisset, neque hostis interim visus esset, dispersis in opere nostris, subito ex omnibus partibus silvae evolaverunt[8] et in nostros impetum fecerunt. **4.** Nostri celeriter arma ceperunt eosque in silvas reppulerunt et, compluribus interfectis, longius[9] impeditioribus locis secuti, paucos ex suis deperdiderunt.

[1] **Eodem fere tempore:** 'About the same time' that Crassus completed the reduction of

Aquitania, perhaps in the latter part of August. The narrative of Caesar's own military operations, interrupted chap. 16, is here resumed. **prope exacta:** 'almost over'.
[2] **omni Gallia:** 'Gaul as a whole'.
[3] **supererant,** etc.: 'were the only remaining (peoples) that were'. The Morini and Menapii were more backward than most of the Gauls, but were good fighters. **essent:** *194a.* **neque:** trans. as if *et non.*
[4] **arbitratus:** *226c.*
[5] **exercitum duxit:** the distance traversed in the march from the sea-coast of the country of the Venetans could hardly have been less than 400 English miles. **qui:** 'but they'; *167.* **longe,** etc.: 'in a way far different from that of the rest of the Gauls'; how lit.? *233c.*
[6] **continentes:** 'continuous'.
[7] **habebant:** coordinate with *intellegebant;* sc. *quod,* **eo:** *in eas* [*silvas ac paludes*].
[8] **evolaverunt:** 'rushed forth'; how lit.?
[9] **longius:** 'too far'; *153a.* **impeditioribus locis:** 'in places (that were) much obstructed' by trees and marshes.

Hiding in forests, favoured by rains, they elude him.

29.1. Reliquis deinceps[1] diebus Caesar silvas caedere instituit et, ne quis[2] inermibus imprudentibusque militibus ab latere impetus fieri posset, omnem eam materiam,[3] quae erat caesa, conversam[4] ad hostem collocabat et pro vallo ad utrumque latus exstruebat. **2.** Incredibili celeritate magno spatio paucis diebus confecto,[5] cum iam pecus atque extrema impedimenta a nostris tenerentur, ipsi[6] densiores silvas peterent, eius modi sunt tempestates consecutae, uti opus necessario intermitteretur et continuatione[7] imbrium diutius sub pellibus[8] milites contineri non possent. **3.** Itaque vastatis omnibus eorum agris, vicis aedificiisque incensis, Caesar exercitum reduxit et in Aulercis[9] Lexoviisque, reliquis[10] item civitatibus, quae proxime bellum fecerant, in hibernis collocavit.

[1] **deinceps:** 'without interruption'. **caedere:** 'to cut down'.
[2] **quis:** *49a.* **imprudentibus:** 'off their guard'. *144b2.*
[3] **materiam:** 'timber', here used of untrimmed trees.
[4] **conversam,** etc.: 'turned toward the enemy and laid in order and built up as a rampart'; how lit.? As the Romans advanced they felled trees, and placed them, with the tops outwards, at either side of the space which they cleared, thus forming an effective defense against the enemy.
[5] **confecto:** 'cleared'. **iam . . . tenerentur:** 'were already in our hands'. **pecus:** 'cattle'; *13f.* **extrema impedimenta:** 'the rear of their baggage-train'; *152a.*
[6] **ipsi:** the people themselves, as distinguished from their possessions; as Caesar cut his way through the woods, they retreated further and further into the forest; *238a.*
[7] **continuatione:** 'continuation'; *135a; 81.* **imbrium:** 'rainstorms'; *15c.*
[8] **sub pellibus:** 'in tents'; how lit.? *335a.*
[9] **Aulercis,** etc.: see Map 9. **Lexoviis:** see III, 11.4.
[10] **reliquis civitatibus:** Venetans (chapters 12-16), Venellans (17-19), and Sotiates (20-27).

PLATE III   ROMAN SOLDIERS, INFANTRY AND CAVALRY

1. Slinger, *funditor*.   2-3. Legionaries, with different types of equipment.
4. Pack, *sarcinae*.   5. Cavalry.

COMMENTARIUS QUARTUS

Pressed by the Suebi, the Usipetes and Tencteri enter Gaul; Customs, hardihood, and prowess of the Suebi.

1.1. Ea, quae secuta est, hieme,[1] qui fuit annus Cn. Pompeio, M. Crasso consulibus,[2] Usipetes Germani et item Tencteri magna cum multitudine hominum flumen Rhenum transierunt, non longe a mari, quo[3] Rhenus influit. **2.** Causa transeundi[4] fuit, quod, ab Suebis complures annos exagitati, bello premebantur[5] et agri cultura prohibebantur. **3.** Sueborum gens est longe maxima et bellicosissima Germanorum omnium. **4.** Hi centum pagos habere dicuntur, ex quibus quotannis singula milia[6] armatorum bellandi causa ex finibus educunt.[7] Reliqui, qui domi manserunt, se atque illos[8] alunt; **5.** hi rursus in vicem anno post in armis sunt, illi domi remanent. **6.** Sic neque agri cultura nec ratio[9] atque usus belli intermittitur.[10] **7.** Sed privati ac separati agri apud eos nihil est, neque longius anno[11] remanere uno in loco colendi causa[12] licet. **8.** Neque multum frumento,[13] sed maximam partem lacte atque pecore[14] vivunt, multumque sunt in venationibus; **9.** quae res,[15] et cibi genere et cotidiana exercitatione et libertate vitae, quod, a pueris[16] nullo officio aut disciplina assuefacti, nihil omnino contra voluntatem faciunt, et[17] vires alit et immani[18] corporum magnitudine homines efficit. **10.** Atque in[19] eam se consuetudinem adduxerunt, ut, locis frigidissimis, neque vestitus[20] praeter pelles habeant quicquam, quarum propter exiguitatem magna est corporis pars aperta, et laventur[21] in fluminibus.

[1] **hieme:** *12a; 147a.* **qui:** in agreement not with the antecedent *hieme,* but with the predicate noun *annus; 164c* (AG 306, B 250.3). **annus:** 55 B.C.; Pompey and Crassus entered upon their consulship January 1 of that year. The winter of 56-55 B.C., according to the calendar in use, fell wholly in 55 B.C.; for the old Roman calendar, which was still used, had fallen so far behind that January 1 of the official year came on November 30 of the solar year. A corrected calendar was introduced in 46 B.C. by Julius Caesar.

[2] **consulibus:** *240a.* **Germani:** appositive of both *Usipetes* and *Tencteri.*

[3] **quo:** = *in quod.* The horde of Usipetes and Tencteri is thought to have crossed the Rhine near Xanten or Emmerich, below Cologne, in the region where the Rhine receives the Lippe as tributary. (Map 11)

[4] **transeundi:** *68b.* **Suebis:** ancestors of the modern Swabians ; see GALLIA. **annos:** *118a.*

[5] **premebantur:** force of Imperfect? *175a.* **cultura:** *127a.*

[6] **singula milia:** 'a thousand each'; if each clan furnished a thousand warriors, the armed force of the Swabians must have reached a total of 100,000 men. **bellandi:** *230.1.*

[7] **ex finibus educunt:** invasion of neighbouring territory is implied. **qui domi manserunt:** 'who (each year) have remained at home'.

[8] **illos:** 'the others'; those in the field. **hi, illi:** 'the latter', 'the former'; *161b.* **in vicem:** 'in turn'. **anno:** *140.*

[9] **ratio . . . belli:** 'the pursuit of war in theory and practice'; how lit.?

[10] **intermittitur:** *173a.* **privati ac separati:** 'assigned to an individual and marked off' by boundaries; the land was held in common. **agri nihil:** 'no land'; *97a.*

[11] **anno:** *129a.* **remanere:** *222a.*

[12] **colendi causa:** 'in order to till the soil'; how lit.? Changes of location were doubtless made each year in order to obtain the best results from the primitive farming.

[13] **frumento:** ablative of means; trans. with *vivunt,* 'they live on grain'; how lit.? **partem:** *118c.* **lacte:** 'milk'; *10g.*

[14] **pecore:** *13f.* **multum sunt in:** 'devote much time to'; how lit.? **venationibus:** 'hunting', we should say; *92a.*

[15] **quae res:** 'this circumstance', their devotion to hunting; *167.* **et cibi genere:** 'both by reason of the kind of food' obtained by hunting; *135a.*

[16] **a pueris:** 'from childhood'; how lit.? **officio:** ablative; 'habituated to no obligation or training'; how lit.? *139.*

[17] **et . . . et:** *233a.* **vires:** *18a.*

[18] **immani:** 'huge'. **homines:** predicate accusative, with *eos* understood as object of *efficit.* Cf. I, 39.1, note 4.

[19] **in,** etc.: 'they have trained themselves to'; how lit.? **locis frigidissimis:** '(even) in the coldest places'; *145c.*

[20] **neque vestitus – quicquam:** 'no clothing'; how lit.? **neque . . . et:** *233d.* **habeant:** *203.4.* **quicquam:** *49a.*

[21] **laventur:** 'to bathe'; how lit.? *174.*

2.1. Mercatoribus[1] est aditus magis eo, ut, quae bello ceperint,[2] quibus vendant, habeant, quam quo ullam rem ad se importari desiderent.[3] **2.** Quin etiam iumentis, quibus maxime[4] Galli delectantur quaeque impenso parant pretio, Germani importatis non utuntur, sed quae sunt apud eos nata, parva atque deformia,[5] haec cotidiana exercitatione, summi[6] ut sint laboris, efficiunt. **3.** Equestribus proeliis saepe ex equis desiliunt[7] ac pedibus proeliantur, equosque eodem[8] remanere vestigio assuefecerunt, ad quos se celeriter, cum usus est,[9] recipiunt; **4.** neque eorum moribus[10] turpius quicquam aut inertius habetur, quam ephippiis[11] uti. **5.** Itaque ad quemvis numerum ephippiatorum equitum quamvis pauci[12] adire audent. **6.** Vinum[13] omnino ad se importari non patiuntur, quod ea re ad laborem ferendum remollescere[14] homines atque effeminari arbitrantur.

[1] **Mercatoribus,** etc.: *Mercatoribus est aditus (ad Suebos) magis eo* ('on this account'), *ut (eos) habeant quibus vendant (ea), quae bello ceperint, quam,* etc.

[2] **ceperint:** *220.* [eos] **quibus vendant:** 'those to whom they may sell'; purchasers for their booty are meant; *194a.* **quam quo:** = *quam eo quod,* 'than for the reason that'; *183c.*

[3] **desiderent:** 'desire'. **iumentis:** with *utuntur* (*131c*); emphatic by position. Horses alone are meant; *353d.*

[4] **maxime delectantur:** 'have very great pleasure'; how lit.? **impenso pretio:** 'at an extravagant price'; *141.* **parant:** 'obtain'. So great was the interest of the Gauls in horses that they developed choice breeds, and Gallic horses were in demand in Rome. The horse figures prominently on Gallic coins.

[5] **deformia:** 'unsightly'.

[6] **summi laboris:** '(capable) of the greatest endurance'; *100b* (AG 345, B 203.5). **sint:** *203.3.*

[7] **desiliunt:** 'leap down'. **pedibus:** 'on foot'. Why ablative?

[8] **eodem vestigio:** 'on the same spot' where they have been left; *145c.*

[9] **cum usus est:** 'when it is necessary'; *186a.* **neque – quicquam:** *168.*

[10] **eorum moribus:** 'according to their view'; how lit.? *136c.* **inertius:** 'more unmanly'. **habetur:** 'is regarded'.

[11] **ephippiis:** 'saddle-cloths', padded, spread over the horse's back, and taking the place of our saddles. **quemvis:** *49a.* **ephippiatorum:** 'riding with saddle-cloths'.

[12] **quamvis pauci:** 'however few' in number.

[13] **Vinum,** etc.: cf. II, 15.4. **re:** *135a.*

[14] **remollescere:** 'lose their vigor'.

MAP II

OPERATIONS OF 55 AND 54 B.C.

Books IV, V.   To face page 232

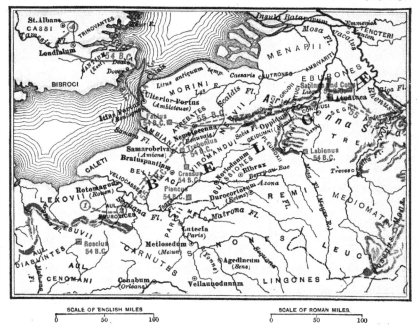

SCALE OF ENGLISH MILES   SCALE OF ROMAN MILES.
0   50   100   0   50   100

EXPLANATION

MAP II

1, 2. Winter quarters, 56–55 B.C.(III.29).
3. Expedition into Germany, 55 B.C. (IV. 19).
4. March into Britain, 54 B.C. (V. 21).

MAP II, A

Heavy broken red line, route of main fleet in 55 B.C. (IV. 23).

Light broken red lines, route of transports with cavalry, part driven back, part driven down the channel (IV. 28).

Unbroken red line, route of fleet in 54 B.C. (V. 8).

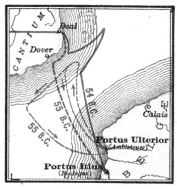

MAP II, A

Detail of Caesar's crossings to Britain.

3.1. Publice[1] maximam putant esse laudem, quam latissime a suis finibus vacare agros;[2] hac re significari, magnum numerum civitatum suam vim sustinere non posse. **2.** Itaque una ex parte[3] a Suebis circiter milia passuum C agri vacare dicuntur. **3.** Ad alteram partem[4] succedunt Ubii, quorum fuit civitas ampla atque florens, ut est captus Germanorum;[5] ei paulo sunt eiusdem generis ceteris[6] humaniores, propterea quod Rhenum attingunt, multumque[7] ad eos mercatores ventitant, et ipsi propter propinquitatem Gallicis sunt[8] moribus assuefacti. **4.** Hos cum Suebi, multis saepe bellis experti,[9] propter amplitudinem gravitatemque[10] civitatis finibus expellere non potuissent, tamen vectigales[11] sibi fecerunt ac multo humiliores infirmioresque redegerunt.

[1] **Publice:** 'for a people'; how lit.? **laudem:** *88a.* **quam:** *153c.*
[2] **vacare agros:** subject of *esse*. **significari:** the subject is the infinitive clause following.
[3] **una ex parte:** 'on one side'. The east side is meant, and the country left vacant was probably Bohemia, from which the Boii had withdrawn; cf. I, 5.4. The name *Boii* survives in 'Bohemia'. **Suebis:** *282.* **milia:** *118a.* **C:** *36. 38b,* **agri:** nominative plural; *172d.*
[4] **Ad alteram partem:** 'On the opposite side', toward the Rhine; how lit.? **fuit:** the past tense implies that the condition described no longer exists.
[5] **ut est captus Germanorum:** 'according to the German standard'; how lit.?
[6] **eiusdem generis ceteris:** i.e. than the rest of the Germans; *129a.* **humaniores:** 'more civilized'.
[7] **multum ventitant:** 'freely come and go'; *78a.*
[8] **sunt,** etc.: 'have become familiar with', etc. Caesar gives an interesting comparison between Gallic and German customs later (VI, 11-24); *139.*
[9] **experti:** 'although they had tried'; how lit.? *227a3.*
[10] **gravitatem:** here 'power of resistance'. **civitatis:** of the Ubii. **finibus:** *127a.*
[11] **vectigales:** predicate accusative; 'made (them) tributary'; *115b.* **multo,** etc.: 'caused them to become much less prominent and powerful'; how lit.?

By strategy the Usipetes and Tencteri overcome the Menapii.

4.1. In eadem causa[1] fuerunt Usipetes et Tencteri, quos supra[2] diximus, qui complures annos Sueborum vim sustinuerunt; ad extremum[3] tamen, agris expulsi et multis locis Germaniae triennium[4] vagati, ad Rhenum pervenerunt, **2.** quas regiones Menapii incolebant. Hi ad utramque ripam fluminis agros, aedificia vicosque[5] habebant; **3.** sed, tantae multitudinis aditu perterriti, ex eis aedificiis, quae trans flumen[6] habuerant, demigraverunt[7] et cis Rhenum, dispositis praesidiis, Germanis transire[8] prohibebant. **4.** Illi,[9] omnia experti, cum neque vi contendere propter inopiam navium neque clam transire propter custodias Menapiorum possent, reverti se in suas sedes regionesque simulaverunt et, tridui[10] viam progressi, rursus reverterunt **5.** atque, omni hoc itinere[11] una nocte equitatu confecto, inscios inopinantesque Menapios oppresserunt, **6.** qui, de Germanorum discessu per exploratores certiores facti, sine metu trans[12] Rhenum in suos vicos remigraverant. **7.** His interfectis navibusque eorum occupatis, prius quam ea pars Menapiorum, quae citra Rhenum erat, certior fieret,[13] flumen transierunt atque, omnibus eorum aedificiis occupatis, reliquam partem[14] hiemis se eorum copiis aluerunt.

[1] **eadem causa:** 'the same condition' of subjection to the Swabians.
[2] **supra:** chap. IV, 1.1-2. **annos:** *118a.*
[3] **ad extremum:** 'finally'. **multis locis:** 'over many parts'; *145c.*

[4] **triennium:** used instead of *tres annos.* **quas regiones:** '(to) the districts which': in full, *ad eas regiones quas; 165c.*

[5] **aedificia, vicos:** cf. I, 5.2, notes 4-5. **tantae multitudinis:** reported as 430,000 (IV, 15.3.

[6] **trans flumen:** on the east side of the Rhine; Caesar writes from the point of view of one in Gaul.

[7] **demigraverunt:** 'they moved away'.

[8] **Germanos transire:** 'the Germans from crossing'; *223a3.*

[9] **Illi:** *Germani.* **omnia experti:** 'having tried every expedient'; how lit.? **vi contendere:** 'to force a passage'.

[10] **tridui:** trans. as if *trium dierum; 100a.* **viam:** *117b.*

[11] **omni hoc itinere confecto:** 'covered the entire distance – and'; how lit.? *144b2.* **equitatu:** *131a.* **inscios:** 'being in ignorance' of what the Germans were doing.

[12] **trans:** to the east side. **remigraverant:** 'had moved back'.

[13] **fieret:** *189b* (AG 551b, B 292.1b).

[14] **partem:** *118a.* **eorum:** the Menapii on the west side of the Rhine. **eorum copiis:** 'with their supplies'.

Caesar fears the effect of this victory upon the fickle Gauls.

5.1. His de rebus Caesar certior factus et infirmitatem[1] Gallorum veritus, quod sunt in consiliis capiendis mobiles et novis plerumque rebus student, nihil his committendum[2] existimavit. **2.** Est[3] enim hoc Gallicae consuetudinis, uti et viatores, etiam invitos,[4] consistere cogant et, quid quisque eorum de quaque[5] re audierit aut cognoverit, quaerant, et mercatores in oppidis vulgus[6] circumsistat, quibusque ex regionibus veniant quasque[7] ibi res cognoverint, pronuntiare cogat. **3.** His rebus atque auditionibus[8] permoti, de summis saepe rebus consilia ineunt, quorum[9] eos in vestigio paenitere necesse est, cum incertis[10] rumoribus serviant et plerique ad voluntatem eorum ficta respondeant.

[1] **infirmitatem:** 'fickleness'. Cf. III, 19.6, notes 11-14.

[2] **nihil his committendum** [esse]: 'that no reliance whatever ought to be placed on them'; *73e.* **nihil:** = emphatic *non; 118c* (AG 390d2, B 176.2b).

[3] **Est . . . cogant:** 'For it is a custom of the Gauls to compel', etc.; how lit.? **consuetudinis:** *100b.* **uti cogant, quaerant, circumsistat, cogat:** explain *hoc; 203.4.* **viatores:** 'travellers', on country roads.

[4] **invitos:** *151.* **cogant:** the subject is supplied in thought from *Gallicae,* as if it were *Gallorum.* **quid:** *204.2.* **eorum:** *97a.*

[5] **quaque:** *49a.* **audierit:** *64a3.*

[6] **vulgus:** *6b.* **quibusque:** = *quibus* (*48b*) + *-que.*

[7] **quasque:** = *quas* + *-que; 204.2.* **pronuntiare:** '(them) to declare'.

[8] **His rebus atque auditionibus:** 'reports and mere hearsay'; how lit.? **summis:** 'of the utmost importance'.

[9] **quorum:** 'of which they must immediately repent'; how lit.? *103c* (AG 354b, B 209.1). **paenitere:** subject of *est; 73a.*

[10] **incertis:** 'indefinite.' **serviant:** 'they subject themselves'; *184a.* **plerique:** 'most men', when questioned. **ad,** etc.: 'make up answers to gratify them'; how lit.?

He resolves to fight the Usipetes and Tencteri.

6.1. Qua consuetudine cognita, Caesar, ne graviori[1] bello occurreret, maturius,[2] quam consuerat, ad exercitum proficiscitur. **2.** Eo[3] cum venisset, ea, quae fore suspicatus erat, facta[4] cognovit; **3.** missas legationes ab non nullis civitatibus ad Germanos invitatosque eos, uti[5] ab Rheno discederent; *omniaque,[6] quae postulassent, ab se fore parata.* **4.** Qua spe adducti, Germani latius iam vagabantur et in fines Eburonum[7] et

Condrusorum, qui sunt Treverorum clientes, pervenerant. **5.** Principibus
Galliae evocatis, Caesar ea, quae cognoverat, dissimulanda[8] sibi
existimavit eorumque animis permulsis et confirmatis, equitatuque
imperato, bellum cum Germanis gerere constituit.[9]

[1] **graviori:** 'quite serious', in case the fickle Gauls and the Germans should unite against him;
153a. **bello:** *107a.*
[2] **maturius:** 'earlier' in the spring, perhaps in the first part of April; *34a.* **exercitum:** divided
up for winter quarters, among the Lexovii and other states, in the autumn of 56 B.C. (III, 29.3);
now probably brought together again, near the lower Seine, in advance of Caesar's arrival.
[3] **Eo:** *ad exercitum.* **fore:** 'would take place'.
[4] **facta, missas, invitatos:** sc. *esse.*
[5] **uti,** etc.: i.e. to proceed toward the interior of Gaul in order to help drive the Romans out.
[6] **omniaque:** 'and (with the promise) that everything'; *213b.* **postulassent:** future perfect
indicative in the direct form; *64a1.* **fore parata:** a substitute for the future infinitive passive.
Qua spe: 'by this prospect'; *167.*
[7] **Eburonum, Condrusorum.** etc.: see GALLIA.
[8] **dissimulanda** [esse]: 'ought to be kept secret'. **permulsis:** 'having soothed'; how lit.?
[9] **constituit:** here not 'determined', but 'announced his intention'; he had previously made
up his mind.

He marches near; the Germans parley, assert their rights in Gaul, and request lands.

7.1. Re frumentaria comparata equitibusque delectis, iter[1] in ea loco facere
coepit, quibus in locis esse Germanos audiebat. **2.** A quibus[2] cum
paucorum dierum iter abesset, legati ab his venerunt, **3.** quorum[3] haec fuit
oratio: *Germanos[4] neque priores populo Romano bellum inferre, neque tamen
recusare, si lacessantur,[5] quin armis contendant, quod Germanorum consuetudo
sit a maioribus tradita, quicumque[6] bellum inferant, resistere neque deprecari.
[7]Haec tamen dicere,[8] venisse invitos, eiectos domo;* **4.** *si suam gratiam Romani
velint, posse eis utiles esse amicos; vel sibi agros attribuant vel patiantur eos
tenere, quos armis possederint:[9]* **5.** *sese unis Suebis concedere, quibus ne di
quidem immortales pares esse possent; reliquum[10] quidem in terris esse neminem,
quem non superare possint.*

[1] **iter facere:** 'to march'. **locis:** *165a.*
[2] **quibus:** 'these (places)'; *167.* **dierum:** *100a.* **iter:** *118a; 243c.*
[3] **quorum,** etc.: 'whose plea was as follows'; *161a.*
[4] **Germanos,** etc.: 'that the Germans did not take the lead in making war . . . and that,
nevertheless, they would not refuse to fight'; how lit.? **priores:** *152b.*
[5] **lacessantur:** present, used for greater vividness, where a past tense might have been
expected; *218.1a.* **contendant:** subjunctive also in the direct form; *201a.*
[6] **quicumque:** *50a.* **resistere:** sc. *eis* (105), as antecedent of *quicumque; 79d.* **neque deprecari:**
'and not to beg for mercy'.
[7] **Direct form:** Haec tamen *dicimus,* (nos) venisse invitos, eiectos domo; si (vos Romani)
nostram gratiam *vultis, possumus vobis* utiles esse amicos; vel *nobis* agros *attribuite* (216) vel
patimini (nos) eos (agros) tenere, quos armis *possedimus;* unis Suebis *concedimus,* quibus ne di
quidem immortales pares esse *possint* (194a); *reliquus* quidem in terris est *nemo,* quem non
superare *possimus.*
[8] **dicere, venisse, posse, tenere:** sc *se; 215.* **eiectos:** 'because they had been driven forth';
227a1. **domo:** *127a.*
[9] **possederint:** from *possido.* **unis:** 'alone'; *23a.* **di:** *8d; 237c.* **concedere:** 'admitted inferiority'.
[10] **reliquum neminem:** 'no one else'; *12d.* **in terris:** 'on earth'; why is *terris* plural?

Caesar insists that they go back to Germany; the parley continues.

8.1. Ad haec Caesar, quae visum est,[1] respondit; sed exitus fuit orationis: *Sibi*[2] *nullam cum his amicitiam esse posse, si in Gallia remanerent;* **2.** *neque verum*[3] *esse, qui suos fines tueri non potuerint, alienos*[4] *occupare; neque ullos in Gallia vacare agros, qui dari, tantae praesertim multitudini, sine iniuria possint;*[5] **3.** *sed licere, si velint, in Ubiorum finibus considere, quorum sint legati apud se*[6] *et de Sueborum iniuriis querantur et a se auxilium petant; hoc se*[7] *Ubiis imperaturum.*

[1] **visum est:** sc. *respondere.* Caesar does not give the whole of his answer, which perhaps followed the same line of argument as his statement to Ariovistus (I, 45).
[2] **Sibi,** etc.: in the direct form, *Mihi nulla cum vobis amicitia esse potest,* 'I can have no friendly relations with you'; *111, 212c1.*
[3] **verum:** consistent with what is true, 'a fair thing'. **qui:** for antecedent supply *eos* as subject-accusative with *occupare.*
[4] **alienos:** sc. *fines;* 'of others'.
[5] **possint,** etc.: the present tense is used for the sake of vividness. **licere:** sc. *eis; 73a, b.*
[6] **apud se:** 'with him'. **Sueborum iniuriis:** IV, 3.3-4.
[7] **hoc,** etc.: 'that he would order the Ubii (to allow them to do) this'; lit. 'he would command this to the Ubii'. Caesar could 'order' the Ubii because he held hostages from that people (IV, 16.5).

9.1. Legati haec se ad suos relaturos dixerunt et, re deliberata, post diem tertium[1] ad Caesarem reversuros; interea ne propius se[2] castra moveret, petierunt. **2.** Ne id quidem Caesar ab[3] se impetrari posse dixit. **3.** Cognoverat enim, magnam partem equitatus ab eis, aliquot diebus[4] ante, praedandi frumentandique causa[5] ad Ambivaritos trans Mosam missam; hos exspectari[6] equites atque eius rei causa moram interponi arbitratur.

[1] **post diem tertium:** 'in three days', i.e. 'the next day but one'; in such expressions the Romans included the days with which a period began and ended.
[2] **propius se:** *123b.* **moveret:** *199a.*
[3] **ab:** 'from'.
[4] **diebus:** 140 (AG 424f, B 223).
[5] **frumentandi causa:** 'to forage'; how lit.? **trans:** 'across' to the west side of the Meuse; the main body, and Caesar, were on the east side, between the Meuse and the Rhine.
[6] **hos exspectari,** etc.: in order that an attack with all their forces might be made upon the Romans. **rei:** the return of the cavalry.

Description of the Rhine region.

[**10.1.** Mosa profluit ex monte Vosego, qui est in finibus Lingonum, et parte quadam ex Rheno recepta, quae appellatur Vacalus, insulam efficit Batavorum, **2.** neque longius ab eo milibus passuum LXXX in Oceanum influit. **3.** Rhenus autem oritur ex Lepontiis, qui Alpes incolunt, et longo spatio per fines Nantuatium, Helvetiorum, Sequanorum, Mediomatricorum, Tribocorum, Treverorum citatus fertur **4.** et, ubi Oceano appropinquavit, in plures diffluit partes, multis ingentibusque insulis effectis, quarum pars magna a feris barbarisque nationibus incolitur **5.** (ex quibus sunt, qui piscibus atque ovis avium vivere existimantur), multisque capitibus in Oceanum influit.][1]

[1] On account of certain difficulties and inconsistencies in this chapter many think that it was not written by Caesar, but added later by someone who wished to supply a geographical background for this part of the narrative; the Meuse, for example, does not rise in the Vosges

mountains, and the Rhine could hardly have flowed through the country of the Nantuates. Nevertheless the rapid current of the Rhine is referred to, which is particularly noticeable in the upper part of its course, as at Schaffhausen; and we cannot assume that Caesar had accurate knowledge of regions so far from those which he himself had visited.

If the chapter is omitted, there is an easy transition from chap. 9 to chap. 11. Translation: 'The Meuse rises in the Vosges mountains, which are in the country of the Lingones; receiving from the Rhine an affluent, which is called the Waal, it forms (with this) the island of the Batavians, and not further from this than eighty miles it flows into the Ocean.

'The Rhine, moreover, rises in the country of the Lepontii, who dwell in the Alps, and in a long course flows rapidly through the territories of the Nantuates, the Helvetians, the Sequanians, the Mediomatrici, the Triboci, and the Treverans; where it approaches the Ocean it divides up into several branches, forming many large islands. Of these (islands) a considerable portion are inhabited by wild and savage tribes, some of whom are believed to live on fish and birds' eggs. (The Rhine) flows into the Ocean through many mouths.'

The parley, Caesar concludes, is being continued merely to gain lime.

11.1. Caesar cum ab hoste[1] non amplius passuum XII milibus abesset, ut erat constitutum,[2] ad eum legati revertuntur; qui in itinere congressi[3] magnopere, ne longius progrederetur, orabant. **2.** Cum id non impetrassent, petebant, uti ad eos equites, qui agmen antecessissent,[4] praemitteret eosque pugna[5] prohiberet, sibique ut potestatem faceret in Ubios legatos mittendi; **3.** *quorum si principes ac senatus sibi iure iurando[6] fidem fecisset, ea condicione, quae a Caesare ferretur, se usuros* ostendebant; *ad has res conficiendas sibi tridui spatium daret.[7]* **4.** Haec omnia Caesar eodem illo pertinere[8] arbitrabatur, ut, tridui mora interposita, equites eorum, qui abessent,[9] reverterentur; tamen *sese non longius milibus passuum IIII, aquationis causa,[10] processurum eo die* dixit; **5.** *huc postero die quam frequentissimi[11] convenirent, ut de eorum postulatis cognosceret.* **6.** Interim ad praefectos,[12] qui cum omni equitatu antecesserant, mittit, qui nuntiarent,[13] ne hostes proelio lacesserent et, si ipsi lacesserentur, sustinerent,[14] quoad ipse cum exercitu propius accessisset.[15]

[1] **cum ab hoste**, etc.: after denying the request of the Germans (IV, 9.1), Caesar evidently had marched toward them. **XII:** *38b, 36.* **milibus:** *129a*

[2] **ut erat constitutum:** the agreement was that the envoys should return in three days (IV, 9.1); *73d.*

[3] **congressi:** sc. *cum eo*, 'meeting him'; *57c; 226c.* **progrederetur:** *199a.*

[4] **antecessissent:** *220; 328.* **praemitteret:** here without an object; with *ad eos equites*, 'that he send forward to', etc.

[5] **pugna:** *127a.* **sibi,** etc.: 'that he would give them permission to send'; how lit. ?

[6] **iure iurando fidem fecisset:** 'should have bound themselves by an oath'; *13h.* How lit.? **fecisset:** agrees with the nearer subject; *172b.* **ea,** etc.: 'that they would accept the terms proposed by Caesar'; *131c.* How lit.?

[7] **daret:** *da* in the direct form; *216.*

[8] **eodem illo pertinere:** 'had the same end in view'; how lit.? **ut,** etc.: explaining *eodem illo; 199a.*

[9] **abessent:** *220.* Cf. IV, 9.3.

[10] **aquationis causa:** 'in order to get water'; *94b.* **huc:** to the place where he was at the time of the conference.

[11] **quam frequentissimi:** 'in as great numbers as possible'; *153c.* **convenirent:** *convenite* in the direct form; *216.*

[12] **praefectos:** *309c.* **equitatu:** *137a.*

[13] **qui nuntiarent:** '(men) to convey the order'; *193a.*

[14] **sustinerent:** sc. *ut; 200a.* The Roman cavalry were ordered to act on the defensive.

[15] **accessisset:** subjunctive also in the direct form; *190c* (AG 553, B 293.3.2).

The German cavalry surprises and routs the cavalry of Caesar; bravery of Piso the Aquitanian in the skirmish.

12.1. At hostes, ubi primum[1] nostros equites conspexerunt, quorum erat V milium[2] numerus, cum ipsi non amplius DCCC equites[3] haberent, quod ei, qui frumentandi causa erant trans Mosam profecti, nondum redierant, nihil timentibus nostris, quod legati eorum paulo ante a Caesare discesserant atque is dies indutiis[4] erat ab his petitus, impetu facto celeriter nostros perturbaverunt; **2.** rursus his[5] resistentibus, consuetudine[6] sua ad pedes desiluerunt, subfossisque equis compluribusque nostris deiectis, reliquos[7] in fugam coniecerunt atque ita perterritos egerunt, ut non prius fuga desisterent, quam in conspectum agminis[8] nostri venissent. **3.** In eo proelio ex equitibus[9] nostris interficiuntur IIII et LXX, **4.** in his vir fortissimus, Piso[10] Aquitanus, amplissimo genere natus, cuius avus in civitate sua regnum obtinuerat, amicus[11] a senatu nostro appellatus. **5.** Hic cum fratri, intercluso ab hostibus, auxilium ferret, illum ex periculo eripuit, ipse, equo vulnerato, deiectus,[12] quoad potuit, fortissime restitit; **6.** cum circumventus, multis vulneribus acceptis, cecidisset, atque id[13] frater, qui iam proelio excesserat, procul animadvertisset, incitato equo[14] se hostibus obtulit atque interfectus est.

[1] **ubi primum:** *188c.* **nostros equites:** the Roman cavalry had apparently advanced in the direction of the German camp.

[2] **V milium:** *309b; 100a.* **cum:** *187.* **DCCC:** *octingentos; 38b, 36.*

[3] **equites:** *129b.* **ei . . . profecti:** IV, 9.3.

[4] **indutiis:** 'for a truce'; *112a.* Caesar explains why his cavalry were caught off their guard. **impetu facto:** 'charged and'; how lit.? *144b2.*

[5] **his:** the Roman cavalry.

[6] **consuetudine:** *136c.* **sua:** *157b.* **ad pedes:** 'to the ground', we should say; *10b.* **desiluerunt:** from their horses. **subfossis . . . deiectis:** 'stabbed the horses (of our cavalry) underneath and dismounted quite a number of our men and'; how lit.?

[7] **reliquos:** sc. *nostros.* **fugam:** the flight of the Gallic cavalry, as in a previous instance (I, 18.10), may have been stimulated by treachery among the native leaders.

[8] **agminis:** the main force. **venissent:** subjunctive by attraction; *189a; 220.*

[9] **ex equitibus:** *97d.* **IIII et LXX:** *quattuor et septuaginta; 38b.* The result of the skirmish showed the superiority of the German over the Gallic cavalry. Caesar afterwards hired German horsemen, and made much use of them (VII, 80.6, note 14).

[10] **Piso:** a Roman name, probably conferred on some Aquitanian with Roman citizenship; cf. I.47, note 13. **genere:** *128a* (AG 403.2a, B 215).

[11] **amicus:** cf. I, 3.4, note 13; *88a.*

[12] **deiectus:** 'although thrown' from his horse, he continued to fight on foot; *227a3.* **potuit:** *190c.*

[13] **id:** 'that (mishap)'. **proelio:** *127a.*

[14] **incitato equo:** 'urging his horse forward'; how lit.? **se hostibus obtulit:** 'he hurled himself upon the enemy'. Many instances of individual bravery and devotion are recorded by Caesar.

The German leaders come to offer apology; Caesar detains them.

13.1. Hoc facto proelio[1] Caesar neque iam sibi legatos audiendos[2] neque condiciones accipiendas arbitrabatur ab eis, qui per dolum atque insidias,[3] petita pace, ultro bellum intulissent; **2.** exspectare[4] vero, dum hostium copiae augerentur equitatusque reverteretur, summae dementiae esse[5] iudicabat; **3.** et, cognita Gallorum infirmitate,[6] quantum iam apud eos hostes uno proelio auctoritatis essent consecuti, sentiebat; quibus[7] ad consilia capienda nihil spatii dandum existimabat. **4.** His constitutis rebus et consilio[8] cum legatis et quaestore communicato, ne quem diem pugnae praetermitteret, opportunissima res accidit, quod postridie eius diei[9] mane, eadem[10] et simulatione et perfidia usi, Germani frequentes, omnibus principibus maioribusque natu adhibitis, ad eum in castra venerunt, simul,[11] ut dicebatur, sui purgandi causa, **5.** quod[12] contra, atque esset dictum et ipsi petissent, proelium pridie commisissent,[13] simul ut, si quid possent, de indutiis fallendo[14] impetrarent. **6.** Quos sibi Caesar oblatos gavisus, illos retineri iussit; ipse omnes copias castris eduxit equitatumque, quod recenti proelio perterritum esse existimabat, agmen subsequi[15] iussit.

[1] **Hoc facto proelio:** 'After this battle'; how lit.?

[2] **audiendos:** *89c.* **ab:** 'from'; Caesar had arranged to take up their proposals (IV, 11.5) on the following day.

[3] **per dolum atque insidias:** 'craftily and treacherously'; how lit.? **ultro:** 'without provocation'; how lit.? **bellum intulissent:** 'had made an attack'.

[4] **exspectare:** subject of *esse; 222b.* **dum:** 'until', with the subjunctive also in the direct form; *190b* (AG 553, B 293.3.2).

[5] **summae dementiae esse:** 'that it was the height of folly'; how lit.? *100b.*

[6] **infirmitate:** cf. IV, 5.1. **quantum – auctoritatis:** 'how great prestige'; *97b; 204.3.*

[7] **quibus:** trans. as if *et eis.* **ad,** etc: *230.3.* **nihil spatii:** 'no time'; *97a.*

[8] **consilio:** 'determination', explained by the appositive clause *ne . . . praetermittet,* 'not to let slip any chance to fight'; lit. 'any day of battle'. **cum – communicato:** 'after he had imparted to'; how lit.? *137c.* **quaestore:** *313b.*

[9] **diei:** *94c.* **mane:** 'early in the morning'.

[10] **eadem:** 'the same' as before. **perfidia:** 'treachery'. To justify his own course Caesar accuses the Germans of bad faith. But if they did not mean what they said, why did so many of them trust themselves in Caesar's power? The collision on the previous day may have been precipitated by hotheads, without the approval of the leaders of the German host.

[11] **simul – simul:** 'both – and'. **sui purgandi causa:** 'in order to clear themselves'; *154b; 230.1* (AG 504c, B 339.5).

[12] **quod,** etc.: 'because, contrary to what had been said'. **contra:** adverb. **atque:** *233c.*

[13] **commisissent:** '(as they admitted) they had started the battle'; *183a.* **si quid possent:** 'if in any degree possible'; how lit.? *118b.* **de:** 'in the matter of'.

[14] **fallendo:** 'by playing false'. **Quos:** *167.* **oblatos** [esse]: *69b.* **gavisus:** 'rejoicing'; *62; 226e.*

[15] **agmen subsequi:** 'to follow the main force', i.e. to bring up the rear, instead of leading the van, as the cavalry usually did; *328.*

Surprising the leaderless German host, he utterly destroys it.

14.1. Acie triplici[1] instituta et celeriter VIII milium itinere confecto, prius[2] ad hostium castra pervenit, quam, quid ageretur, Germani sentire possent. **2.** Qui omnibus rebus subito perterriti, et[3] celeritate adventus nostri et discessu suorum,[4] neque consilii habendi neque arma capiendi spatio dato, perturbantur,[5] copiasne adversus hostem ducere, an castra defendere, an fuga salutem petere praestaret. **3.** Quorum[6] timor cum fremitu et concursu significaretur, milites nostri, pristini diei[7] perfidia incitati, in castra irruperunt. **4.** Quo loco,[8] qui celeriter arma capere potuerunt, paulisper nostris restiterunt[9] atque inter carros impedimentaque proelium commiserunt; **5.** at[10] reliqua multitudo puerorum mulierumque (nam cum[11] omnibus suis domo excesserant

Rhenumque transierant) passim fugere coepit; ad quos[12] consectandos Caesar equitatum misit.

[1] **Acie triplici:** *337a.* **VIII:** *38b.* **itinere:** the army probably marched in three parallel columns, which deployed as they neared the camp of the enemy. The country must have been open and fairly level to admit of the rapid execution of the movement.

[2] **prius ... quam ... possent:** *189b* (AG 551b, B 292.1b). **hostium castra:** a corral protected by carts, like that of the Helvetians (I, 26.3).

[3] **et – et:** 'both – and'; *233a.*

[4] **suorum:** the German leaders who had gone to Caesar and were held by him under guard. **consilii ... capiendi:** gerundive and gerund in coordinate construction; trans. 'for,' etc.; *230.1.* **spatio:** *tempore.*

[5] **perturbantur:** 'were (too) confused (to decide)'. **ne ... an ...an:** 'whether ... or ... or'; *204.1.* **ducere:** *222a.*

[6] **Quorum:** *167.* **cum:** *185c.*

[7] **pristini diei:** 'of the previous day'. **irruperunt:** 'burst into'.

[8] **Quo loco:** *castris Germanorum.*

[9] **restiterunt:** sc. *ei,* antecedent of *qui.* **inter carros,** etc.: cf. I, 26.3.

[10] **at:** *236a.* **reliqua,** etc.:'the rest of the host (consisting) of women and children'; *98a.*

[11] **cum:** cf. I, 1.4, note 14. **excesserant:** i.e. *Usipetes et Tencteri.*

[12] **quos:** the antecedent is *multitudo; 164d.* Caesar's conduct in detaining the German leaders, who had come to him under a flag of truce, and then attacking and pursuing the leaderless host without mercy, seems treacherous and unlike his ordinary procedure. When afterwards his friends proposed, in the Roman senate, a thanksgiving for the victory, Cato urged that Caesar be delivered up to those whom he had treacherously entrapped, as an atonement for the wrong. Not much weight should be attached to this as a judgement on Caesar's course, however, for debates in the Roman senate, as in our own, were coloured by political and personal antagonisms.

15.1. Germani,[1] post tergum clamore audito, cum suos interfici viderent, armis abiectis signisque militaribus relictis, se ex castris eiecerunt, **2.** et cum ad confluentem[2] Mosae et Rheni pervenissent, reliqua[3] fuga desperata, magno numero interfecto, reliqui se in flumen[4] praecipitaverunt atque ibi timore, lassitudine,[5] vi fluminis oppressi perierunt. **3.** Nostri ad unum[6] omnes incolumes, perpaucis vulneratis, ex tanti belli timore, cum hostium numerus capitum[7] CCCCXXX milium fuisset, se in castra receperunt. **4.** Caesar eis, quos in castris retinuerat, discedendi potestatem fecit. **5.** Illi, supplicia cruciatusque Gallorum veriti,[8] quorum agros vexaverant, remanere se apud eum velle dixerunt. His Caesar libertatem[9] concessit.

[1] **Germani:** the warriors who armed for defence when the camp was attacked (IV, 14.4). **clamore:** 'the shrieking' of the women and children, part of whom were cut down by the legionaries entering the camp, part by the cavalry after they had fled from the camp.

[2] **confluentem:** 'confluence'. **Mosae:** probably the Moselle is here meant, not the Meuse; *Mosellae* may have been written and changed to *Mosae* in copying. It seems probable that the German camp was south of the Moselle and that the fleeing warriors came to the region of Coblenz, which lies in the angle formed by the Moselle as it enters the Rhine.

[3] **reliqua,** etc.: 'abandoning hope of further flight'; how lit.? *144b2.*

[4] **flumen:** the Rhine, at Coblenz.

[5] **lassitudine:** in consequence of the fighting and running.

[6] **ad unum:** 'to a man'. **incolumes:** 'in safety'. **ex ... cum:** 'notwithstanding (their) apprehension of a hard campaign, since'; *184a.* How lit.?

[7] **capitum ... fuisset:** 'had amounted to 430,000'; cf. I, 29.2, note 6; *100b.* **CCCCXXX:** = *quadringentorum triginta; 38b, 36.* If, as among the Helvetians, one fourth were fighting-men, the Usipetes and Tencteri mustered an army of more than 130,000. The number seems greatly

exaggerated.
[8] **veriti:** *61a2; 226c.*
[9] **libertatem:** 'leave' to stay. They probably entered his service as mercenaries.

FIRST EXPEDITION INTO GERMANY. 16-19

Caesar resolves to cross the Rhine and enter Germany.

16.1. Germanico bello confecto, multis de causis Caesar statuit sibi Rhenum esse transeundum; quarum[1] illa fuit iustissima,[2] quod, cum videret Germanos tam facile impelli, ut[3] in Galliam venirent, suis quoque rebus eos timere voluit, cum[4] intellegerent, et posse et audere populi Romani exercitum Rhenum transire. **2.** Accessit etiam, quod[5] illa pars equitatus Usipetum et Tencterorum, quam supra[6] commemoravi praedandi frumentandique causa Mosam transisse neque proelio interfuisse, post fugam suorum se trans Rhenum in fines Sugambrorum receperat seque cum eis coniunxerat. **3.** Ad quos[7] cum Caesar nuntios misisset, qui postularent, eos, qui sibi Galliaeque bellum intulissent, sibi dederent,[8] responderunt: **4.** *Populi Romani imperium Rhenum finire;[9] si, se invito, Germanos in Galliam transire non aequum[10] existimaret, cur sui[11] quicquam esse imperii aut potestatis trans Rhenum postularet?[12]* **5.** Ubii autem, qui uni[13] ex Transrhenanis ad Caesarem legatos miserant,[14] amicitiam fecerant, obsides dederant, magnopere orabant, ut sibi auxilium ferret, quod[15] graviter ab Suebis premerentur: **6.** *Vel,[16] si id facere occupationibus rei publicae prohiberetur, exercitum[17] modo Rhenum transportaret; id sibi ad auxilium spemque reliqui temporis satis futurum.* **7.** *Tantum esse nomen atque opinionem[18] eius exercitus, Ariovisto pulso et hoc novissimo proelio facto, etiam ad ultimas Germanorum nationes, uti opinione et amicitia populi Romani tuti esse possint.* **8.** Navium magnam copiam ad transportandum exercitum pollicebantur.

---

[1] **quarum:** *97a.* **illa:** *161a.*
[2] **iustissima:** 'the most weighty'. **quod ... voluit:** explains *illa [causa].*
[3] **ut ... venirent:** 'to come'; *199a.* **suis quoque rebus:** 'for their own interests also'.
[4] **cum:** *cum* temporal has here a conditional force also: 'in case'.
[5] **Accessit etiam quod:** 'There was the further reason that'; *198a,b.*
[6] **supra:** IV, 9.3. **commemoravi:** cf. *demonstravimus,* II, 1.1, note 2.
[7] **quos:** *Sugambros.* **postularent:** *193a.*
[8] **dederent:** *200a* (AG 565a, B 295.8).
[9] **imperium Rhenum finire:** *i.e. Rhenum* (subject accusative) *esse finem* ('limit') *imperii.* **se invito:** cf. I, 8.2, note 6.
[10] **aequum:** 'right'; in predicate, neuter, accusative, in agreement with the infinitive clause *Germanos transire,* which stands as object of *existimaret.*
[11] **sui,** etc.: 'that anything beyond the Rhine was under his authority or power'; *94d.*
[12] **postularet:** with *cur,* 'why should he claim'; *217a.*
[13] **uni:** 'alone'; *23a.* **ex Transrhenanis:** 'of the peoples across the Rhine'; *97d.*
[14] **miserant, fecerant, dederant:** *234a; 238a.*
[15] **quod ... premerentur:** *183a.*
[16] **Vel:** *213b; 235a.* **id facere:** 'from doing that'; *223a3.* **occupationibus rei publicae:** 'by the requirements of public business'.
[17] **exercitum, Rhenum:** *114a.* **transportaret:** *216.* **id:** 'that (movement)'. **ad ... temporis:** 'for (present) help and (for) hope in respect to the future'; how lit.?
[18] **opinionem:** 'reputation'. **eius:** 'his,' i.e. *Caesaris.* **Ariovisto pulso:** 'in consequence of the

defeat of Ariovistus' (related in Book I); how lit.? *144b3.*
He builds a bridge across the Rhine.

17.1. Caesar his de causis, quas commemoravi, Rhenum transire[1] decreverat; sed navibus transire neque satis tutum esse arbitrabatur, neque suae[2] neque populi Romani dignitatis[3] esse statuebat. **2.** Itaque, etsi summa difficultas faciendi pontis proponebatur propter latitudinem,[4] rapiditatem altitudinemque fluminis, tamen id[5] sibi contendendum, aut[6] aliter non traducendum exercitum, existimabat. Rationem[7] pontis hanc instituit: **3.** tigna bina[8] sesquipedalia, paulum ab imo praeacuta, dimensa[9] ad altitudinem fluminis, intervallo pedum duorum inter se[10] iungebat. **4.** Haec cum, machinationibus immissa in flumen, defixerat[11] fistucisque adegerat, non sublicae modo derecte[12] ad perpendiculum, sed prone ac fastigate, ut secundum naturam fluminis[13] procumberent, **5.** his item contraria duo[14] ad eundem modum iuncta, intervallo pedum quadragenum ab inferiore parte,[15] contra vim atque impetum fluminis conversa, statuebat. **6.** Haec utraque,[16] insuper bipedalibus trabibus immissis, quantum[17] eorum tignorum iunctura distabat, binis utrimque fibulis ab extrema parte distinebantur; **7.** quibus[18] disclusis atque in contrariam partem revinctis, tanta erat operis firmitudo atque ea rerum natura,[19] ut, quo maior vis aquae se incitavisset, hoc[20] artius illigata tenerentur. **8.** Haec[21] derecta materia iniecta contexebantur ac longuriis cratibusque[22] consternebantur; **9.** ac nihilo setius sublicae et ad[23] inferiorem partem fluminis oblique agebantur, quae, pro ariete subiectae[24] et cum omni opere coniunctae, vim fluminis exciperent; **10.** et aliae[25] item supra pontem mediocri spatio, ut, si arborum trunci[26] sive naves deiciendi operis causa essent a barbaris missae, his defensoribus[27] earum rerum vis minueretur, neu[28] ponti nocerent.

[1] **transire:** *222b.* **tutum:** predicative; *148d.* Caesar was always careful to have the country in the rear of his army well secured, not only for the transportation of supplies but also to make a retreat safe in case of necessity.

[2] **suae, populi:** *157d.*

[3] **dignitatis,** etc.: 'would be inconsistent with the prestige'; *94d.* How lit.? **etsi:** *191a.*

[4] **latitudinem:** between 1300 and 1600 feet in the region where Caesar built the bridge, that is, near Neuwied, between Coblenz and Andernach (Map 11). **rapiditatem:** 'swiftness'; *76a.*

[5] **id,** etc.: sc. *esse,* 'that he ought to make every effort (to accomplish) this'.

[6] **aut:** *235a.*

[7] **Rationem,** etc.: 'the plan of the bridge (which) he devised (was) as follows'. *161a.* How lit.?

[8] **Tigna bina:** 'a pair of logs', to be driven into the river bed and used as posts to support the bridge; see Plate VI, **a a**; *36.* **sesquipedalia:** 'a foot and a half thick'; *79b.* **ab imo:** 'at the lower end'; *154a, 126c.*

[9] **dimensa:** passive; with *ad,* etc., 'measured off to correspond with the depth of the river', the longer piles for use near the middle, the shorter for driving nearer the banks. How lit.? *59b.* **intervallo,** etc.: 'two feet apart'; how lit.? *138.*

[10] **inter se:** 'together'; *159.* **iungebat:** sc. *Caesar;* the object is *Tigna.* The two logs of each pair were apparently fastened together on the bank, before they were driven into the river bed. **machinationibus immissa:** 'had let down by mechanical appliances', rafts equipped with suitable tackle. How lit.? *228a.*

[11] **defixerat,** etc.: 'had planted these firmly and driven [them] home with pile-drivers', in the case of each pair; the pluperfect with *cum* implies repeated action; *186a* (B 288.3). **non sublicae modo:** 'not like an (ordinary) pile', because ordinarily piles are driven in perpendicularly, while these pairs were driven with a slant. How lit.?

[12] **derecte:** 'straight up and down'. **ad perpendiculum:** 'according to a plumb-line'. **prone ac fastigate:** 'leaning forward with a decided slant'; how lit.? **secundum:** 'in conformity with'; *122a.*

[13] **naturam fluminis:** 'the direction of the current'; *74d.* **his contraria:** 'opposite these'; *108a.* Plate VI, **a´ a´.**

[14] **duo:** sc. *tigna; bina* might have been used. **ad eundem modum:** 'in the same manner'; *45.* **quadragenum:** 'forty' Roman feet in each case; *22c.* The distance must have been measured on the surface of the water.

[15] **ab inferiore parte:** 'on the lower side', i.e. downstream from the first pair. **contra,** etc.: 'against the violent rushing of the current'; how lit.? As the first pair of posts slanted downstream, so the second pair slanted upstream.

[16] **Haec utraque . . . distinebantur:** 'the two pairs' of posts 'were held apart'; *51.* **insuper:** 'above'. **bipedalibus,** etc.: 'after a beam having the thickness of two feet, corresponding with the space between the posts' (of each pair) 'had been let in'; how lit.? The heavy crossbeam, or sill, is marked **b b** on Plate VI.

[17] **quantum:** representing the idea of measure in *bipedalibus;* accusative: *118a.* **binis . . . parte:** 'by a pair of braces on each side' (i.e. with each pair of posts) 'at the very end' of the sill. What these 'pairs of braces' were it is not easy to understand. If of wood, they may have been like those represented in the Plate VI, **c c** ; for with such braces the greater the pressure the more closely the structure would have been bound together. If the braces were of iron – a less probable supposition because of the amount of iron required – the arrangement must have been altogether different.

[18] **quibus . . . revinctis:** i.e. *tignis;* 'now that these' (the two pairs of posts, one pair above and one below) 'were kept' (at the proper distance) 'apart, and were braced in opposite directions', the lower posts slanting upstream, the upper posts slanting downstream. How lit.? *144b3.*

[19] **ea rerum natura:** 'such the character of the structure' as a whole; how lit.? **quo,** etc.: 'the greater the force of the water rushing against it'; *220.* How lit.? **quo . . . hoc:** *140* (AG 414a, B 223).

[20] **hoc,** etc.: 'the more closely they' (the opposite pairs of posts, *tigna*) 'were tied and held together'. **illigata:** *228a.*

[21] **Haec:** 'These piers', each pier formed by fastening the sill, two feet thick, securely to the pair of posts at either end. **derecta:** 'in the direction of the bridge'; how lit.? **materia iniecta:** 'by laying timber', i.e. girders, **d** on the Plates; these were, of course, at right angles with the direction of the current; *92b; 144b6.* **contexebantur:** 'were joined'. As the bridge was designed to carry a moving load of cavalry and draft animals as well as infantry, and was obviously built hastily of rough timbers, with a wide margin of safety, we may suppose that the length of the girders between the sills was not more than 25 English feet, possibly not more than 20 feet; the number of piers was probably between sixty and seventy. **longuriis:** 'joists', laid on the girders, in the direction of the current; marked **h** on the Plates.

[22] **cratibus:** 'wickerwork', woven of supple branches, laid over the joists and taking the place of the planks on a modern bridge; marked **i** on the Plates. **consternebantur:** 'were covered.. nihilo setius:** 'nevertheless', in order still further to assure the safety of the bridge; *140.* **et:** 'also'.

[23] **ad,** etc.: 'on the down-stream side'; how lit.? **oblique agebantur:** 'were driven with a slant'; these piles, slanting upstream, braced the piers against the force of the current; marked **e** on the Plates. **quae:** 'in order that they'; *193a.*

[24] **pro ariete subiectae:** 'set below as props'; *10e.* How lit.?

[25] **aliae:** *aliae sublicae agebantur,* marked **f f** on the Plates. These vertical piles protected the bridge against floating logs or other objects in the current liable to damage it. **mediocri spatio:** 'a short distance'; *140.*

[26] **trunci:** 'tree-trunks'; *81.* **navos:** barges loaded with stones or earth are probably meant. **operis:** 'the structure'; *230.1.* **essent missae:** *220.*

[27] **his defensoribus:** ablative absolute, = *his defendentibus, his* being personified; trans. 'by these defences'. **earum rerum:** tree-trunks and weighted barges.

[28] **neu:** 'and not'; lit. 'or not'; *196b.*

PLATE VI

CAESAR'S BRIDGE ACROSS THE RHINE

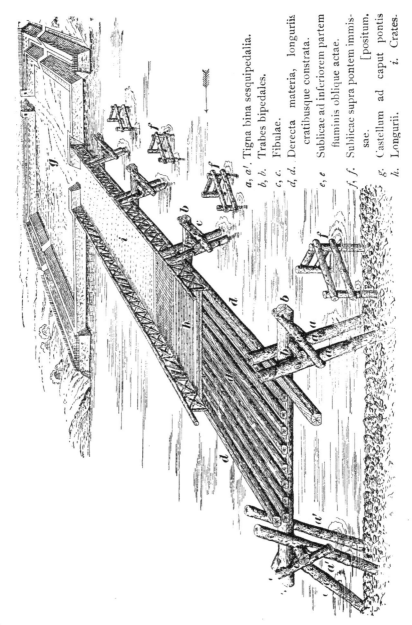

a, a'. Tigna bina sesquipedalia.
b, b. Trabes bipedales.
c, c. Fibulae.
d, d. Derecta materia, longuriis cratibusque constrata.
e, e Sublicae ad inferiorem partem fluminis oblique actae.
f, f. Sublicae supra pontem immissae. [positum.
g. Castellum ad caput pontis
h. Longurii.　*i.* Crates.

Entering Germany, he finds some tribes submissive; but the Sugambrians flee.

18.1. Diebus X, quibus[1] materia coepta erat comportari, omni opere effecto, exercitus traducitur. **2.** Caesar, ad utramque partem[2] pontis firmo praesidio relicto, in fines Sugambrorum contendit. **3.** Interim a compluribus civitatibus ad eum legati veniunt; quibus,[3] pacem atque amicitiam petentibus, liberaliter respondit obsidesque ad se adduci iubet. **4.** At[4] Sugambri ex eo[5] tempore, quo pons institui coeptus est, fuga comparata, hortantibus eis,[6] quos ex Tencteris atque Usipetibus apud se habebant, finibus suis excesserant suaque omnia exportaverant[7] seque in solitudinem ac silvas abdiderant.

[1] **Diebus X, quibus:** 'Within ten days after'; *147a.* **comportari:** *72c.* The rapidity and skill with which the bridge was built bear witness to Caesar's genius in practical affairs as well as to the efficiency of his engineers and mechanics; *310b.*
[2] **partem:** we should say 'end'. **praesidio relicto:** 'having left', etc.; *144b2.* Plate VI, **g.**
Sugambrorum: the German end of the bridge led into the country of the Ubians; north of the Ubians were the Sugambrians. See GALLIA.
[3] **quibus:** dative. **liberaliter respondit:** 'be returned a gracious answer'; how lit.? *175b.*
[4] **At:** *236a.* **ex:** 'immediately after'.
[5] **eo:** 'the'; *160d.* **fuga comparata:** 'taking to flight'; how lit.?
[6] **hortantibus eis:** 'at the instigation of those'. From IV, 15.1-2, it might be inferred that few of the Tencteri and the Usipetes escaped besides cavalry (IV, 16.2).
[7] **exportaverant:** 'had carried away'. **in:** cf. I, 12.3, note 10; 'into the recesses of the forests'.

He ravages the country of the Sugambrians, encourages the Ubians, and returns to Gaul.

19.1. Caesar, paucos dies in eorum[1] finibus moratus, omnibus vicis[2] aedificiisque incensis frumentisque succisis, se in fines Ubiorum recepit; atque his auxilium suum pollicitus, si[3] ab Suebis premerentur, haec ab eis cognovit: **2.** *Suebos, postea quam[4] per exploratores pontem fieri comperissent, more[5] suo concilio habito, nuntios in omnes partes dimisisse, uti[6] de oppidis demigrarent, liberos, uxores suaque omnia in silvis deponerent, atque omnes, qui arma ferre possent, unum in locum convenirent;* **3.** *hunc[7] esse delectum medium fere[8] regionum earum, quas Suebi obtinerent; hic Romanorum adventum exspectare[9] atque ibi decertare constituisse.* **4.** Quod[10] ubi Caesar comperit, omnibus eis rebus confectis, quarum rerum[11] causa traducere exercitum constituerat, ut Germanis metum iniceret, ut Sugambros ulcisceretur, ut Ubios obsidione[12] liberaret, diebus omnino XVIII trans Rhenum consumptis, satis et ad laudem et ad utilitatem profectum[13] arbitratus, se in Galliam recepit pontemque rescidit.

[1] **eorum:** *Sugambrorum.* **moratus:** *226c.*
[2] **vicis,** etc.: cf. I, 5.2, notes 4-5. **frumentis succisis:** 'cut down the standing grain and'; how lit.? *144b2.*
[3] **si . . . premerentur:** indirect, from the idea of 'saying' in *pollicitus;* future indicative in the direct form; *213b.*
[4] **postea quam:** with the indicative in the direct form; *188a.*
[5] **more:** *136c.* **nuntios:** 'messengers'.
[6] **uti,** etc.: '(directing the people) to move away from the strongholds', etc.; the substantive clauses give the gist of the instructions conveyed by the messengers; *199a.*
[7] **hunc:** predicative after *delectum esse,* with which *locum* is to be supplied as subject; 'that there had been chosen, as this (mustering point), a place'.
[8] **medium fere:** 'nearly (at) the center'. **regionum:** *102.*

[9] **exspectare:** sc. *eos* (*Suebos*). **ibi:** 'at that point'.
[10] **Quod:** 'this fact'; *167.* **eis rebus confectis:** 'having accomplished the objects', explained by the appositive *ut*-clauses following; *144b3.* In reality Caesar accomplished very little by the march into Germany. The formal enumeration which follows seems intended to justify an expedition barren of tangible results.
[11] **rerum:** *165a.* **ut,** etc.: *199a.*
[12] **obsidione:** 'from oppression'; the Ubii had been forced to pay tribute to the Swabians (IV, 3.4); *127a.* **ut . . . liberaret:** 'to free'. **XVIII:** *38b, 36.*
[13] **profectum** [esse]: the subject is *satis; 57b.*

FIRST EXPEDITION TO BRITAIN. 20-38

Caesar resolves to invade Britain; he lacks information.

20.1. Exigua[1] parte aestatis reliqua, Caesar, etsi in his locis, quod omnis Gallia[2] ad septentriones vergit, maturae sunt hiemes, tamen in Britanniam[3] proficisci contendit, quod, omnibus fere Gallicis bellis,[4] hostibus nostris inde sumministrata auxilia intellegebat **2.** et, si tempus anni ad bellum gerendum deficeret,[5] tamen magno sibi usui fore arbitrabatur, si modo insulam adisset,[6] genus hominum perspexisset, loca, portus, aditus[7] cognovisset; quae omnia fere Gallis erant incognita.[8] **3.** Neque enim temere, praeter mercatores, illo adit quisquam, neque[9] eis ipsis quicquam praeter oram maritimam atque eas regiones, quae sunt contra Gallias,[10] notum est. **4.** Itaque vocatis ad se undique mercatoribus, neque quanta esset insulae magnitudo, neque quae aut quantae nationes incolerent,[11] neque quem usum belli haberent aut quibus institutis uterentur, neque qui essent ad[12] maiorem navium multitudinem idonei portus, reperire poterat.

[1] **Exigua . . . reliqua:** ablative absolute; 'As a small part', etc.; it was now near the end of July.
[2] **omnis Gallia:** cf. I, 1.1, note 2. **ad . . . vergit:** 'lies toward the north', in relation to the latitude of Italy; cf. Map 12.
[3] **Britanniam:** *294.* **quod . . . intellegebat:** the aid given by the Britains to the Venetans (III, 9.9) and to the other Gauls, as for example to refugees from the Bellovaci (II, 14.2-3), seems to have been of slight account; it furnished, however, a plausible pretext for the invasion of Britain.
[4] **bellis:** *147b.* **inde:** *e Britannia.* **sumministrata:** sc. *esse.*
[5] **deficeret:** 'was insufficient'. **sibi usui fore:** *112b.* **arbitrabatur:** *183a.*
[6] **adisset:** *adiret* might have been expected; Caesar conceives of the expedition as an accomplished fact; *218.1b.*
[7] **aditus:** 'approaches'; points, outside the regular harbours, where a landing could be made. **quae omnia fere:** 'for nearly all of these things'; *167; 97c.*
[8] **incognita:** the Venetans at least must have been informed about Britain (III, 8.1), but they had been well-nigh exterminated, and it was not to be expected that Gauls having the knowledge desired by Caesar would be free in imparting it to him; **Neque enim –
quisquam:** 'for no one'; *168.* **temere:** 'without good reason'; only traders and students of Druidic theology (VI, 13.11) had occasion to go to Britain. **illo:** adverb.
[9] **neque . . . quicquam:** 'and nothing'. **eis:** *108a.*
[10] **Gallias:** plural because referring to the different divisions; we should say, 'the (several) parts of Gaul'.
[11] **incolerent:** sc. *eam; 204.2, 3.* **quem:** *48b.* **usum belli:** 'methods of warfare'; how lit.?
[12] **ad . . . multitudinem:** i.e. for a fleet, whose requirements were very different from those of trading vessels coming to port singly or in small numbers.

He sends Volusenus to Britain and makes preparations; he receives British envoys, and sends Commius also to Britain.

21.1. Ad haec cognoscenda, prius[1] quam periculum faceret, idoneum[2] esse arbitratus C. Volusenum cum navi longa praemittit.[3] **2.** Huic mandat, ut, exploratis omnibus rebus, ad se quam primum[4] revertatur. **3.** Ipse cum omnibus copiis in Morinos proficiscitur, quod inde[5] erat brevissimus in Britanniam traiectus. **4.** Huc naves undique ex finitimis regionibus et, quam[6] superiore aestate ad Veneticum[7] bellum effecerat classem, iubet convenire. **5.** Interim, consilio eius cognito et per mercatores perlato ad Britannos, a compluribus insulae civitatibus ad eum legati veniunt, qui polliceantur[8] obsides dare atque imperio populi Romani obtemperare. **6.** Quibus auditis, liberaliter pollicitus hortatusque, ut in ea sententia permanerent, **7.** eos domum remittit; et cum eis una Commium, quem ipse, Atrebatibus[9] superatis, regem ibi constituerat, cuius et virtutem et consilium probabat[10] et quem sibi fidelem esse arbitrabatur, cuiusque auctoritas in his regionibus magni habebatur,[11] mittit. **8.** Huic imperat, quas possit,[12] adeat civitates horteturque, ut populi[13] Romani fidem sequantur, seque celeriter eo venturum nuntiet. **9.** Volusenus, perspectis regionibus omnibus, quantum[14] ei facultatis dari potuit, qui[15] navi egredi ac se barbaris committere non auderet, quinto die ad Caesarem revertitur, quaeque ibi perspexisset, renuntiat.

[1] **prius . . . faceret:** 'before making the attempt'; *189b.*
[2] **idoneum:** adj. in predicate; trans. 'a suitable person'. **navi longa:** *346a.*
[3] **praemittit:** sc. *eum.* **ut,** etc.: *199a.*
[4] **quam primum:** *153c.*
[5] **inde:** 'from their country'; how lit.? See Map 11. **in Britanniam:** after *traiectus; 150d.*
traiectus: 'passage'. **Huc:** to the vicinity of modern Boulogne.
[6] **quam — classem:** = *eam classem, quam; 165c* (AG 307b, B 251.4a).
[7] **ad Veneticum bellum:** III, 11.5, notes and III. chaps. 14, 15.
[8] **polliceantur:** *193a.* **dare:** i.e. *se daturos esse; 178.* **imperio obtemperare:** 'submit to the authority'; *105.*
[9] **Atrebatibus:** conquered in the battle at the Sambre, two years previously (II, 23.1,2). **regem:** *115a.* **ibi:** among the Atrebatians. **virtutem et consilium:** 'energy and discretion'.
[10] **probabat:** 'he appreciated'. **fidelem:** 'loyal'. Afterwards Commius was disloyal to Caesar; cf. VII, 75.5.
[11] **magni habebatur:** 'was considered great', lit. 'of great (value)'; *101* (AG 417, B 203.3).
[12] **possit:** *sc.adire.* Why subjunctive? *220.* **adeat:** *200a* (AG 565a, B 295.8).
[13] **populi . . . sequantur:** 'fix their confidence in the Roman people'; how lit.? *199a.* **se:** Caesar.
[14] **quantum facultatis:** 'so far as opportunity'; *97b.*
[15] **qui:** 'since he'; *194c.* **navi:** *14b; 127a.*

Opportunely he receives the submission of the Morini. He assembles a fleet.

22.1. Dum in his locis[1] Caesar navium parandarum causa moratur,[2] ex magna parte Morinorum ad eum legati venerunt, qui se[3] de superioris temporis consilio excusarent, quod,[4] homines barbari et nostrae consuetudinis imperiti, bellum populo Romano fecissent, seque ea, quae imperasset,[5] facturos pollicerentur. **2.** Hoc sibi Caesar satis opportune accidisse arbitratus, quod neque post tergum hostem relinquere volebat neque belli gerendi propter anni tempus[6] facultatem habebat neque has[7] tantularum rerum occupationes Britanniae anteponendas iudicabat, magnum eis numerum obsidum imperat. Quibus adductis, eos in fidem recepit. **3.** Navibus[8] circiter LXXX onerariis coactis contractisque, quot[9] satis esse ad duas transportandas legiones existimabat, quod[10] praeterea navium longarum habebat, quaestori, legatis praefectisque[11] distribuit. **4.** Huc accedebant XVIII onerariae naves, quae ex eo loco[12] a milibus passuum VIII vento tenebantur, quo minus[13] in eundem portum venire possent; has equitibus[14] distribuit. **5.** Reliquum exercitum[15] Q. Titurio Sabino et L. Aurunculeio Cottae legatis in Menapios atque in[16] eos pagos Morinorum, a quibus ad eum legati non venerant, ducendum dedit; **6.** P. Sulpicium Rufum legatum cum eo praesidio,[17] quod satis esse arbitrabatur, portum tenere iussit.

[1] **his locis:** in the country of the Morini, probably in the vicinity of modern Boulogne.

[2] **moratur:** *190a* (AG 556, B 293.1).

[3] **qui se . . . excusarent, pollicerentur:** 'to offer excuse', lit. 'excuse themselves', etc.; *193a.* **de . . . consilio:** 'for their conduct the previous season', 56 B.C. (III.28).

[4] **quod . . . fecissent:** 'because (as they said) they had made'; *183a.* **homines barbari:** '(being) uncivilized people'; *91b.* **consuetudinis:** sing., but trans. 'usages'; the reference is particularly to the Roman practice of treating with consideration peoples that submitted to Roman rule; *102.*

[5] **imperasset:** *64a1; 214a.*

[6] **anni tempus:** it was already August, too late in the season to enter upon an extended campaign. **neque,** etc.: 'and he judged that the exactions of such trivial affairs ought not to have precedence over (the invasion of) Britain'; how lit.?

[7] **has:** *160d.* **tantularum:** *76c.* **Britanniae:** *107a.*

[8] **Navibus onerariis:** 'transports'; these were sailing vessels, while the galleys were propelled by oars; *346a.* **LXXX:** *octaginta; 38b.* **coactis contractisque:** 'pressed into service and brought together' in a single harbour.

[9] **quot:** 'as many as'. **duas legiones:** the 7th and the 10th. The smallness of the force is consistent with Caesar's statement that the purpose of the expedition was not conquest but the obtaining of information. If the two legions, after three years of hard fighting, contained each about 3600 men (*307b*) fit for service, the total of 7200 men divided up among the 80 transports would have averaged 90 men to a ship. The vessels were not large; and the supplies, not merely provisions but tents and other equipment, must have taken up considerable space.

[10] **quod navium longarum:** 'the galleys which'; lit. 'what of long ships'; *97b.* **quaestori:** *313b.*

[11] **praefectis:** 'subsidiary officers'. The galleys seem also to have carried slingers, bowmen, and artillery (chap. 25). **Huc accedebant:** 'In addition to this number there were'; how lit.? *90b.*

[12] **eo loco:** portus Itius, now Boulogne; see Map 11. **a:** 'off.' The small harbour eight Roman miles up the coast, where the 18 transports were detained, is now called Ambleteuse. Map 11 A.

[13] **quo minus:** 'so that ... not'; *201a.* **eundem portum:** portus Itius.

[14] **equitibus:** the cavalry contingents of the two legions, 500 or 600 horsemen in all; *309a.* **equitibus distribuit:** the horsemen could more easily go across the country to the smaller harbour (IV, 23.1).

[15] **Reliquum exercitum:** five legions, if we assume that one legion was assigned to duty at the harbour; for Caesar had eight legions in all, and only two were required for the expedition.

[16] **in – ducendum:** 'for operations against'; how lit.? *229b.*

[17] **eo praesidio, quod:** = *tanto praesidio, quantum.*

Caesar sails to Britain, and makes preparation to land.

23.1. His constitutis rebus, nactus[1] idoneam ad navigandum tempestatem,[2] tertia fere vigilia solvit equitesque in ulteriorem portum[3] progredi et naves conscendere et se sequi iussit. **2.** A quibus[4] cum paulo tardius esset administratum, ipse hora[5] diei circiter quarta cum primis navibus Britanniam attigit,[6] atque ibi in omnibus collibus expositas hostium copias armatas conspexit. **3.** Cuius loci haec[7] erat natura, atque ita montibus angustis mare continebatur, uti ex locis superioribus[8] in litus telum adigi posset. **4.** Hunc ad egrediendum nequaquam idoneum locum arbitratus, dum reliquae naves eo convenirent,[9] ad horam nonam[10] in ancoris exspectavit. **5.** Interim legatis tribunisque militum[11] convocatis, et quae ex Voluseno cognovisset, et quae fieri vellet, ostendit, monuitque, ut[12] rei militaris ratio, maxime ut maritimae res postularent, ut,[13] cum celerem atque instabilem motum haberent, ad nutum[14] et ad tempus omnes res ab eis administrarentur. **6.** His dimissis, et ventum et aestum uno tempore nactus secundum,[15] dato signo et sublatis ancoris, circiter milia passuum VII ab eo loco[16] progressus, aperto ac plano litore naves constituit.[17]

[1] **nactus:** *61a3; 226c.*

[2] **tempestatem:** 'weather.' As might be inferred from its derivation from *tempus*, 'time', *tempestas* may imply good or bad weather according to the connection. We use 'time' similarly: one can have a good time or a bad one. **tertia fere vigilia:** 'about the third watch'; indefinite because the embarkation must have taken two or three hours; *242c.* **solvit:** sc. *naves,* 'got under way, from Boulogne. The date was probably August 26.

[3] **ulteriorem portum:** Ambleteuse, northeast of Boulogne (IV, 22.4). **progredi:** i.e. by land. **naves conscendere:** 'to embark'.

[4] **quibus:** 'them', the cavalry; *167.* **paulo tardius:** 'with a little too much delay', probably due to the difficulty of getting the horses aboard; *153a.* **esset administratum:** 'the orders were carried out'; how lit.? *73d.*

[5] **hora quarta:** the beginning of 'the fourth hour' on August 26 in the latitude of Dover by Roman reckoning was about 8:30 a.m. by our time; *242b.*

[6] **Britanniam attigit:** 'reached Britain', near Dover; see Map 11. **expositas:** 'arrayed'.

[7] **haec:** 'such'. **ita,** etc.: 'the sea was so closely bordered by abrupt cliffs'; *angustis,* lit. 'narrow', implies sharp outlines, as seen from the sea, and an abrupt descent. The chalk cliffs near Dover run almost straight up from the water's edge.

[8] **locis superioribus:** the top of the cliffs. **litus:** 'shore'; *13f.*

[9] **convenirent:** *190b* (AG 553, B 293.3.2).

[10] **horam nonam:** the beginning of the ninth hour was about 2:20 p.m. by our time; *242b.* **in ancoris:** 'at anchor'. The ancient anchors were like those of today.

[11] **tribunis mllitum:** *314.* **et . . . et:** *233a.* **quae:** *204.2.* The information derived from Volusenus was probably to the effect that there was a good landing place further up the coast.

[12] **ut . . . postularent:** 'as military practice, above all, as marine service required'; *220.* How lit.?

[13] **ut . . . omnes,** etc.: after *monuit;* 'that all orders be executed'; *199a.* **cum,** etc.: 'since (these conditions) involved quick and unsteady movement'.

[14] **ad nutum:** 'on the instant'; how lit.? **ad tempus:** 'at the (right) time'.

[15] **secundum:** 'favorable', both wind and tide bearing toward the northeast.

[16] **eo loco:** Dover. **progressus:** *226c.* **aperto ac plano litore:** between Walmer and Deal, about seven miles northeast of Dover; *145c.*

[17] **naves constituit:** 'he ran the ships aground'; how lit.?

The legionaries attempt to land; the Britons resist fiercely.

24.1. At barbari, consilio Romanorum cognito, praemisso equitatu et essedariis,[1] quo plerumque genere in proeliis uti consuerunt, reliquis copiis subsecuti, nostros navibus egredi[2] prohibebant. **2.** Erat[3] ob has causas summa difficultas, quod naves propter magnitudinem, nisi in alto,[4] constitui non poterant; militibus autem, ignotis locis,[5] impeditis manibus, magno et gravi onere armorum oppressis,[6] simul et de navibus desiliendum et in fluctibus consistendum et cum hostibus erat pugnandum, **3.** cum[7] illi, aut ex arido aut paulum in aquam progressi, omnibus membris expeditis, notissimis locis,[8] audacter tela conicerent et equos insuefactos[9] incitarent. **4.** Quibus rebus nostri perterriti, atque huius omnino generis[10] pugnae imperiti, non eadem[11] alacritate ac studio, quo in pedestribus uti proeliis consuerant, utebantur.[12]

[1] **essedariis:** 'chariot-fighters', described in chap. 33. **quo genere:** 'a type (of warrior) which'; *165b.*

[2] **copiis:** the Britons followed by land, as near the shore as possible; *137b.* **navibus egredi:** 'from disembarking'; *223a; 127a.*

[3] **Erat:** *90a.* **has:** refers to what follows; *161a.*

[4] **in alto:** 'in deep (water)'; *154a.* **constitui:** 'be grounded', so as to remain firm. **militibus ... desiliendum** [erat]: 'the soldiers . . . had to jump down'; how lit.? *73e; 110.*

[5] **ignotis locis:** '(being) on unfamiliar ground'; how lit.? *145c.*

[6] **oppressis:** agrees with *militibus;* 'weighed down'. **et . . . et . . . et:** *238f.*

[7] **cum:** 'while'; *187.* **illi:** *Britanni.* **ex arido:** 'from dry land'.

[8] **notissimis locis:** 'thoroughly acquainted with the ground'; how lit.? *153a; 144b2.* **audacter, etc.:** the British were provided with weapons much like those of the Gauls.

[9] **insuefactos:** 'trained' to go into the water.

[10] **generis:** with *imperiti; 102* (AG 349a, B 204.1).

[11] **eadem:** *150a.* **quo:** *163c.* **pedestribus:** i.e. *terrestribus,* 'on land'.

[12] **utebantur:** 'were displaying'.

The standard-bearer of the Tenth leaps overboard, bidding the others follow.

25.1. Quod[1] ubi Caesar animadvertit, naves longas, quarum et species[2] erat barbaris inusitatior et motus ad usum expeditior, paulum removeri ab onerariis navibus et remis incitari et ad latus apertum[3] hostium constitui, atque inde fundis,[4] sagittis, tormentis hostes propelli ac summoveri iussit; quae res[5] magno usui nostris fuit. **2.** Nam, et navium figura[6] et remorum motu et inusitato genere tormentorum permoti, barbari constiterunt ac paulum modo[7] pedem rettulerunt. **3.** Atque nostris militibus cunctantibus, maxime propter altitudinem[8] maris, qui[9] decimae legionis aquilam ferebat, obtestatus deos, ut ea res legioni feliciter eveniret, 'Desilite', inquit, 'commilitones,[10] nisi vultis aquilam hostibus prodere; ego[11] certe meum rei publicae atque imperatori officium praestitero'.[12] **4.** Hoc cum[13] voce magna dixisset, se ex navi proiecit atque in hostes aquilam ferre coepit. **5.** Tum nostri, cohortati[14] inter se, ne tantum dedecus[15] admitteretur, universi ex navi desiluerunt. **6.** Hos item ex proximis primi navibus cum conspexissent, subsecuti[16] hostibus appropinquarunt.

[1] **Quod:** 'Now . . . this'; *167.* **animadvertit:** *188a.*

[2] **species:** 'appearance'; *80b.* **inusitatior:** 'less familiar.. Oar-driven galleys were not so well adapted to withstand the buffeting of northern waters as solidly built sailing vessels, such as those of the Venetans (III, 13-14). **ad usum:** i.e. *ad navigandum;* 'the movement was more

easily controlled'; how lit.? The galleys could be driven faster, and in any direction.
³ **ad latus apertum:** 'over against the exposed flank', the right flank of the enemy. The galleys were to be placed parallel with the shore. **inde:** = *e navibus longis.*
⁴ **fundis:** 'with slings', which hurled slingshots of lead when material was available; such slingshots were sometimes inscribed (cf. II, 10.1, note 2). **sagittis:** 'arrows'; *308.* **tormentis:** 'artillery'; our word 'artillery' was applied to engines of war, whose propelling force was derived from tension, before it came to be restricted to cannon, which derive their propelling force from explosives. The *'torsioners'* used on the galleys were probably small catapults, which Caesar elsewhere calls 'scorpions' (*343a*).
⁵ **quae res:** 'and this manoeuvre'. **usui:** *112b.*
⁶ **figura:** the galleys were relatively long, narrow, and low.
⁷ **paulum modo:** 'just a little', from the water's edge.
⁸ **altitudinem:** the sailing vessels which had been run aground on the sandy bottom formed a line, irregular because of the variation in depth, at least two thirds of a mile long; the water where the bows were driven into the sand was probably up to the soldiers' necks.
⁹ **qui:** as antecedent sc. *is,* subject of *inquit.* **aquilam:** 'eagle'; *324b1.* **obtestatus,** etc.: 'praying the gods that his effort might turn out fortunately for the legion'; *199a.*
¹⁰ **commilitones:** 'fellow-soldiers'; *93.* **vultis:** *71.*
¹¹ **ego:** *87b.* **certe:** 'at any rate'.
¹² **praestitero:** *176c.*
¹³ **cum:** *185c.* **voce:** *136b.* **magna:** 'loud'.
¹⁴ **cohortati inter se:** *159; 226c.*
¹⁵ **dedecus:** ' disgrace', the loss of the eagle of the legion; *13f.* **universi:** 'all together'.
¹⁶ **subsecuti:** 'they followed and'; how lit.? *228a.* **appropinquarunt:** *64a1.*

Finally the Romans force the enemy back, and land.

26.1. Pugnatum¹ est ab utrisque acriter. Nostri tamen, quod neque ordines servare² neque firmiter insistere neque signa³ subsequi poterant, atque alius alia ex navi, quibuscumque signis occurrerat, se aggregabat, magnopere perturbabantur; **2.** hostes vero, notis omnibus vadis, ubi ex litore aliquos singulares⁴ ex navi egredientes conspexerant, **3.** incitatis equis⁵ impeditos adoriebantur, plures paucos circumsistebant, alii ab latere aperto⁶ in universos tela coniciebant. **4.** Quod cum animadvertisset Caesar, scaphas⁷ longarum navium, item speculatoria navigia,⁸ militibus compleri iussit et, quos laborantes conspexerat, his subsidia summittebat. **5.** Nostri, simul in arido⁹ constiterunt, suis omnibus consecutis, in hostes impetum fecerunt atque eos in fugam dederunt; neque¹⁰ longius prosequi potuerunt, quod equites cursum tenere atque insulam capere¹¹ non potuerant. Hoc unum ad pristinam fortunam Caesari defuit.

¹ **Pugnatum,** etc.: 'sharp fighting was kept up by both sides'; how lit.? **utrisque:** *51.*
² **ordines servare:** 'to keep the ranks'. **firmiter insistere:** 'to get a firm footing'.
³ **signa:** *324b2.* **alius,** etc.: 'one from this ship, another from that'; *171c.* **quibuscumque . . . aggregabat:** 'they were joining any standards that they had fallen in with'; how lit.? *50a.*
⁴ **singulares:** 'one by one'. **conspexerant:** *188,d.*
⁵ **incitatis equis:** 'urging their horses forward'; *144b2.* **adoriebantur:** 'they would attack'; *175d.* **plures paucos:** *plures hostes paucos Romanos.*
⁶ **ab latere aperto:** 'on the exposed flank', the right side, unprotected by a shield. **universos:** 'groups of soldiers', contrasted with the individuals referred to in I. 6.
⁷ **scaphas:** 'small boats', carried on the galleys.
⁸ **speculatoria navigia:** 'scouting vessels', smaller and lighter than the galleys, without a beak, and designed for rapid movement.
⁹ **in arido:** 'on dry ground'; *154a.* **constiterunt:** *188a.*
¹⁰ **neque:** 'but . . . not'. **equites:** still at Ambleteuse (IV, 23.2).
¹¹ **insulam capere:** 'to make the island'. **Hoc,** etc.: 'in this respect only was Caesar's usual good fortune incomplete'; how lit.?

The Britons offer to submit, and return Commius to Caesar.

27.1. Hostes proelio superati, simul atque se ex fuga receperunt,[1] statim ad Caesarem legatos de pace miserunt; obsides sese daturos,[2] quaeque imperasset, facturos polliciti sunt. **2.** Una cum his legatis Commius Atrebas venit, quem supra[3] demonstraveram a Caesare in Britanniam praemissum. **3.** Hunc illi e navi egressum, cum ad eos oratoris modo[4] Caesaris mandata deferret, comprehenderant atque in vincula coniecerant; tum, proelio facto,[5] remiserunt.[6] **4.** In petenda pace eius rei culpam in multitudinem contulerunt et, propter imprudentiam[7] ut ignosceretur, petiverunt. **5.** Caesar questus,[8] quod, cum ultro, in continentem legatis missis, pacem ab se petissent,[9] bellum sine causa intulissent, ignoscere[10] se imprudentiae dixit obsidesque imperavit; **6.** quorum illi partem statim dederunt, partem, ex longinquioribus locis arcessitam,[11] paucis diebus sese daturos dixerunt. **7.** Interea suos[12] remigrare in agros iusserunt, principesque undique convenire[13] et se civitatesque suas Caesari commendare coeperunt.

[1] **receperunt:** *188a.* **statim:** *77.* **legatos:** 'envoys'.

[2] **daturos:** *89c.* **quaeque,** etc.: i.e. *et ea, quae imperavisset, facturos esse; 214a.*

[3] **supra:** IV, 21.7-8. **demonstraveram:** cf. II, 1.1, note 2.

[4] **oratoris modo:** 'in the character of an envoy,' lit. 'of a pleader'; *80b.*

[5] **proelio facto:** i.e. *post hoc proelium; 144b2.*

[6] **remiserunt:** sc. *eum.* **eius rei:** i.e. *quod Commius, orator Caesaris, comprehensus atque in vincula coniectus erat.*

[7] **imprudentiam:** 'lack of knowledge'. **ignosceretur:** sc. *sibi,* 'that pardon be granted them'; *199a; 106b.*

[8] **questus:** *226c.* **quod . . . intulissent:** 'because (as he said) they had', etc.; *183a* (AG 540, B 286.1). **continentem:** 'the continent', Gaul.

[9] **petissent:** *187.* **sine causa:** from the Roman point of view; but the Romans would have considered the defence of the shores of Italy against an armed force a most noble action. Thus do conditions alter opinions.

[10] **ignoscere se:** 'that he would pardon'. **imprudentiae:** *105.*

[11] **arcessitam:** i.e. *cum ea (pars) arcessita esset; 227a1.*

[12] **suos:** 'their people'; the demobilization of the British host was ordered. **iusserunt:** sc. *ei,* the British envoys.

[13] **convenire:** *ad Caesarem.* **Caesari commendare:** 'to put under Caesar's protection'.

The ships with the cavalry are prevented from landing by a storm.

28.1. His rebus[1] pace confirmata, post diem quartum, quam est[2] in Britanniam ventum, naves XVIII, de quibus supra[3] demonstratum est, quae equites sustulerant, ex superiore portu[4] leni vento solverunt. **2.** Quae cum appropinquarent Britanniae et ex castris[5] viderentur, tanta tempestas[6] subito coorta est, ut nulla earum cursum tenere posset, sed aliae[7] eodem, unde erant profectae, referrentur,[8] aliae ad inferiorem partem insulae, quae est propius[9] solis occasum, magno suo cum periculo deicerentur; **3.** quae,[10] tamen ancoris iactis, cum fluctibus complerentur, necessario adversa nocte[11] in altum provectae continentem petierunt.

[1] **His rebus:** the giving of hostages, the demobilization of the British host, and the presence of British leaders in Caesar's camp. **post – quam:** = *quarto die postquam,* 'three days after' by our reckoning; cf. IV, 9.1, note 1.

[2] **est ventum:** *73d.*

[3] **supra:** IV, 22.4. **sustulerant:** 'had taken on board'.

[4] **superiore portu:** Ambleteuse. **leni vento:** 'with a light breeze', blowing north or northeast; *138*. **solverunt:** 'sailed'.
[5] **ex castris:** Caesar's camp was on rising ground, not far from the shore, so that it commanded a wide view of the sea. **viderentur:** trans. as passive.
[6] **tempestas:** 'storm', a northeaster. Cf. IV, 23.1, note 2.
[7] **aliae . . . aliae:** *171b*. **eodem,** etc.: Ambleteuse.
[8] **referrentur:** sc. *ut*. **ad . . . occasum:** southwest from Caesar's landing place. See Map 11, **A.**
[9] **propius:** *123b* (AG 432a, B 141.3). **suo:** 'to themselves'; how lit.? **deicerentur:** ' were driven'. *57b*.
[10] **quae . . . cum:** 'nevertheless they anchored and when they'; how lit.? *167; 144b2.*
[11] **adversa nocte:** 'in the face of the night', a metaphorical form of expression transferred from physical space (as *adverso colle, 134a*) to time. **in altum provectae:** 'they put out to sea and'; how lit.? *226c; 228a.*

The fleet on the British shore is wrecked by a high tide.

29.1. Eadem nocte[1] accidit, ut esset luna plena, qui dies maritimos aestus[2] maximos in Oceano efficere consuevit, nostrisque id erat incognitum. **2.** Ita uno tempore et longas naves, quibus Caesar exercitum[3] transportandum curaverat, quasque in aridum subduxerat, aestus complebat, et onerarias, quae ad ancoras erant deligatae, tempestas afflictabat, neque ulla nostris facultas aut administrandi[4] aut auxiliandi[5] dabatur. **3.** Compluribus navibus fractis, reliquae cum essent, funibus,[6] ancoris reliquisque armamentis amissis, ad navigandum inutiles, magna,[7] id quod necesse erat accidere, totius exercitus perturbatio[8] facta est. **4.** Neque enim naves erant aliae, quibus reportari[9] possent, et omnia deerant, quae ad reficiendas naves erant usui,[10] et quod omnibus constabat, hiemari in Gallia oportere, frumentum in his locis[11] in hiemem provisum non erat.

[1] **eadem nocte:** the night of August 30, as determined by astronomical calculations. **accidit . . . plena:** 'it happened to be full moon'; how lit.? **qui dies:** 'and this date'.
[2] **aestus . . . incognitum:** the rise and fall of the tide in the Mediterranean is hardly perceptible. Caesar's men had learned of the existence of tides in the Ocean the previous year (III, 12); what they had failed to notice was the coincidence of the highest tides with the time of the full moon. At Dover the highest tide rises about 19 feet; at Boulogne, 25 feet.
[3] **exercitum,** etc.: 'had had the army brought over'; *229b.*
[4] **administrandi:** 'of managing' the vessels, the crews being on shore.
[5] **auxiliandi:** by getting men on to the ships.
[6] **funibus . . . amissis:** 'on account of the loss of', etc. *144b3.*
[7] **magna** with *perturbatio; 353d.* **id,** etc.: 'as was bound to happen'; how lit.? *160c.*
[8] **perturbatio:** 'commotion'. **Neque,** etc.: 'for there were no other ships'; *90a.* How lit.?
[9] **reportari:** 'be carried back'. **possent:** *194a.*
[10] **usui:** trans. as if *utilia; 112a.* **constabat,** etc.: 'it was clear that they would have to winter'; how lit.?
[11] **his locis:** in Britain. **in hiemem:** 'for the winter'; *12a.* Rations had been taken for only a limited stay in Britain.

The Britons, learning of the disaster, secretly plan a revolt.

30.1. Quibus rebus cognitis, principes Britanniae, qui post proelium ad Caesarem convenerant, inter se collocuti,[1] cum equites et naves et frumentum Romanis deesse intellegerent, et paucitatem militum ex castrorum exiguitate cognoscerent, quae[2] hoc erant etiam angustiora, quod sine impedimentis Caesar legiones transportaverat, **2.** optimum factu esse[3] duxerunt,[4] rebellione facta, frumento commeatuque nostros prohibere et rem[5] in hiemem producere; quod, his superatis aut reditu[6] interclusis, neminem postea belli inferendi causa in Britanniam transiturum confidebant. **3.** Itaque, rursus coniuratione facta, paulatim[7] ex castris discedere ac suos clam ex agris deducere coeperunt.

[1] **inter se collocuti:** *159* (AG 301f, B 245.1).

[2] **quae erant:** 'which was'. **hoc etiam angustiora:** 'even smaller (than usual for two legions) for this reason', explained by the; *quod*-clause. **impedimentis:** left in Gaul; *311*.

[3] **optimum factu esse:** 'that the best thing to do was'; how lit.? **optimum:** in predicate, after *esse*; *148d*. **factu:** *232*.

[4] **duxerunt:** 'decided'; the subject is *principes* in the first line of the chapter. **rebellione facta:** 'renewing hostilities'; how lit.? *144b2*. **frumento:** *127a*.

[5] **rem:** 'their operations'. **his,** etc.: 'if these (invaders) should be', etc.; *144b4*.

[6] **reditu:** 'return'; *127a*. **postea:** 'in future'.

[7] **paulatim:** one or two at a time. That the British leaders were assembled in the Roman camp is clear from the beginning of this chapter.

Caesar, anticipating trouble, gathers supplies and hastens repairs on the ships.

31.1. At Caesar, etsi nondum eorum consilia cognoverat,[1] tamen et ex[2] eventu navium suarum, et ex eo, quod obsides dare intermiserant, fore id, quod accidit, suspicabatur. **2.** Itaque ad[3] omnes casus subsidia comparabat. Nam et frumentum[4] ex agris cotidie in castra conferebat et, quae gravissime afflictae erant naves, earum materia atque aere ad reliquas reficiendas utebatur et, quae[5] ad eas res erant usui, ex continenti comportari iubebat. **3.** Itaque, cum summo studio[6] a militibus administraretur, XII navibus amissis, reliquis[7] ut navigari commode posset, effecit.

[1] **cognoverat:** 'was familiar with'; *176b*.

[2] **ex . . . suarum:** 'from what had happened to his ships'; how lit.? **ex eo, quod:** 'from the fact that'; *198b*.

[3] **ad . . . comparabat:** 'he was providing for every emergency'.

[4] **frumentum:** from the new harvest. Later a head of wheat on British coins became an appropriate symbol of the island's staple crop. **quae . . . naves, earum:** = *earum navium, quae*; *165c*.

[5] **quae:** as antecedent sc. *ea,* subject-accusative with *comportari*. **ad eas res:** 'for that purpose'.

[6] **summo studio:** 'with the utmost enthusiasm'. **administraretur:** 'the work was carried on'; *184a*.

[7] **reliquis,** etc.: sc. *navibus* (*131a*); 'he made it possible to utilize the others fairly well for navigation'; how lit.? *203.3*.

The Britons make a treacherous attack, using war-chariots.

32.1. Dum ea geruntur,[1] legione ex consuetudine una frumentatum[2] missa, quae appellabatur VII, neque ulla ad id tempus belli suspicione interposita, cum pars hominum[3] in agris remaneret, pars etiam in castra ventitaret,[4] ei, qui pro portis castrorum[5] in statione erant, Caesari nuntiaverunt, pulverem[6] maiorem, quam consuetudo ferret, in ea parte videri, quam in partem[7] legio iter fecisset. **2.** Caesar id, quod erat, suspicatus,[8] aliquid novi a barbaris initum consilii, cohortes,[9] quae in stationibus erant, secum in eam partem proficisci, ex reliquis duas in stationem cohortes succedere, reliquas[10] armari[11] et confestim sese subsequi iussit. **3.** Cum paulo longius[12] a castris processisset, suos ab hostibus premi atque aegre sustinere[13] et, conferta legione, ex omnibus partibus tela conici[14] animadvertit. **4.** Nam quod, omni ex reliquis partibus demesso[15] frumento, pars una erat reliqua, suspicati hostes, huc nostros esse venturos, noctu in silvis delituerant;[16] **5.** tum dispersos, depositis armis, in metendo[17] occupatos subito adorti, paucis interfectis reliquos, incertis ordinibus,[18] perturbaverant, simul equitatu atque essedis[19] circumdederant.

[1] **geruntur:** *190a.* **legione:** with *missa.*
[2] **frumentatum:** 'to get grain', from the fields; *231a.* **VII:** *septima; 38a, 36.* **neque,** etc.: 'without any suspicion of hostilities up to that time'; how lit.?
[3] **hominum:** *Britannorum; 98a.*
[4] **ventitaret:** 'came frequently', a frequentative from *venio; 78a.* **ei:** *milites.*
[5] **portis castrorum:** *334a.* **in statione:** 'on guard'; *81.*
[6] **pulverem:** '(a cloud of) dust'; *13g.* **quam,** etc.: 'than usual'; *197c.* **parte:** 'direction'.
[7] **quam in partem:** 'in which'; *165a.* **quod erat:** 'which was actually the case'.
[8] **suspicatus:** *226c.* **aliquid,** etc.: 'some new scheme had been worked up'; how lit.? **aliquid:** *168; 49a.* **initum:** sc. *esse; 68b, c.* **consilii:** *97b.*
[9] **cohortes:** probably four in number, one at each of the four gates of the camp. How many men? *307c.* **in stationibus:** 'on guard'; plural because each gate was thought of as a separate post.
[10] **reliquis:** six cohorts, of the 10th legion. The four cohorts on guard went with Caesar; two stood guard in their place, and the last four cohorts of the legion were ordered to arm and follow Caesar as soon as they could; *307c.* **in stationem succedere:** 'to relieve guard'.
[11] **armari:** 'to arm', lit. 'to arm themselves'; *174.* **confestim:** 'with all haste'.
[12] **paulo longius:** 'some little distance'; *153a.* **suos:** the men of the 7th legion.
[13] **aegre sustinere:** 'were holding their own with difficulty'. **conferta legione:** 'since the legion was crowded together'; *144b3.* The more closely the men stood the more effective were the missiles of the enemy surrounding them.
[14] **conici:** sc. *in eam; 57b.*
[15] **demesso:** 'cut'; *144b3.* **una:** 'only one'.
[16] **delituerant:** 'had hidden'. **dispersos, occupatos:** sc. *eos* (= *nostros* just above), object of *adorti.* **depositis armis:** 'having laid aside their weapons'.
[17] **in metendo:** 'in reaping'; *230.4.* **adorti:** *226c.*
[18] **incertis ordinibus:** 'since their ranks were in disorder', a proper formation being impossible under the circumstances.
[19] **essedis:** 'with war chariots'. Scythed war chariots, with a long sharp blade projecting from each end of the axle, were in use in Oriental countries, but the British chariots to which Caesar refers were apparently without scythes. Remains of chariot wheels have been found in the graves of warriors.

The way the Britons use war-chariots in battle.

33.1. Genus hoc est ex essedis[1] pugnae: Primo per[2] omnes partes perequitant et tela coniciunt, atque ipso terrore equorum[3] et strepitu rotarum ordines plerumque perturbant; et cum se[4] inter equitum turmas insinuaverunt, ex essedis desiliunt et pedibus[5] proeliantur. **2.** Aurigae[6] interim paulatim ex proelio excedunt, atque ita currus collocant, ut, si illi[7] a multitudine hostium premantur, expeditum ad suos[8] receptum habeant. **3.** Ita mobilitatem equitum, stabilitatem[9] peditum in proeliis praestant;[10] ac tantum usu cotidiano et exercitatione efficiunt, uti in declivi ac praecipiti loco incitatos equos sustinere[11] et brevi[12] moderari ac flectere, et per temonem percurrere et in iugo[13] insistere, et se inde in currus citissime recipere consuerint.

[1] **ex essedis:** with *pugnae; 150d* (B. 353.5).

[2] **per . . . perequitant:** sc. *essedarii;* 'they' (the chariot-fighters) 'ride everywhere'. Each chariot carried a driver and one fighter. As the drivers dashed against the enemy, the men in the chariots sprang out and fought on foot. The chariots meanwhile withdrew a little from the thick of the fight, so that the drivers could see how the battle was going. If they saw their warriors defeated in any part of the line they swiftly drove to that part, took on board those hard pressed, and quickly passed beyond the reach of danger.

[3] **terrore equorum:** 'fright caused by the horses'; subjective genitive; *95*. **ordines:** 'the ranks' of the enemy.

[4] **se . . . insinuaverunt:** 'they have penetrated'; the British cavalry were so deployed as to leave spaces through which the chariots could be driven against the enemy.

[5] **pedibus:** 'on foot'; *131a*.

[6] **Aurigae:** 'the drivers'. **ita . . . ut:** *197b*.

[7] **illi:** the chariot-fighters. **premantur:** *220*.

[8] **ad suos:** 'to their own lines', we should say. **receptum:** 'a retreat'.

[9] **stabilitatem:** 'steadiness'. **peditum:** *10d*.

[10] **praestant:** 'exhibit'; sc. *essedarii*. **tantum . . . efficiunt:** 'they become so expert'; how lit.?

[11] **incitatos equos sustinere:** 'to keep control of their horses at full gallop'; how lit.?

[12] **brevi:** for *brevi tempore,* 'in an instant.' **moderari:** 'to check'. **flectere:** 'to turn'. **per,** etc.: 'to run along the pole'.

[13] **iugo:** yokes were used with horses as well as cattle. **citissime:** 'with the utmost quickness'; *34b*.

Caesar brings aid; the Britons prepare to attack the camp.

34.1. Quibus rebus[1] perturbatis nostris, novitate pugnae, tempore opportunissimo Caesar auxilium tulit; namque eius adventu hostes constiterunt, nostri se ex timore receperunt. **2.** Quo facto,[2] ad lacessendum hostem et ad committendum proelium alienum[3] esse tempus arbitratus, suo se loco continuit et, brevi tempore intermisso, in castra legiones reduxit. **3.** Dum haec geruntur, nostris[4] omnibus occupatis, qui erant in agris reliqui, discesserunt. **4.** Secutae sunt continuos complures dies tempestates, quae[5] et nostros in castris continerent et hostem a pugna prohiberent. **5.** Interim barbari nuntios in omnes partes dimiserunt paucitatemque nostrorum militum suis praedicaverunt et, quanta praedae faciendae[6] atque in perpetuum sui liberandi facultas daretur,[7] si Romanos castris expulissent, demonstraverunt. **6.** His rebus[8] celeriter magna multitudine peditatus equitatusque coacta, ad castra venerunt.

[1] **rebus:** ablative of means. **nostris:** dative after *tulit; 154a*. **novitate:** 'strangeness'; *135a*.

[2] **Quo facto:** 'Though this had been accomplished', referring to the effects of Caesar's arrival; *144b5*.

[3] **alienum:** 'unfavourable'. **suo:** 'favourable', to himself; how lit.?

[4] **nostris,** etc.: while the Romans were busy repairing ships and strengthening their defences, the Britons 'withdrew' from the open country, gathering for attack. **qui:** as antecedent, sc. *ei* as subject of *discesserunt*.

[5] **quae . . . continerent:** *194a* (B 283).

[6] **praedae faciendae:** 'of securing booty'. **in perpetuum:** 'forever'. **sui:** *154b* (AG 504c, B 339.5).

[7] **daretur:** *204.3*. **expulissent:** *218.1b*.

[8] **His rebus:** 'by means of these statements'; how lit.? **equitatus:** apparently including also the *essedarii*, the close connection of whom with the cavalry has already been noted.

Caesar repels the attack on the camp and pursues the Britons.

35.1. Caesar, etsi idem,[1] quod superioribus diebus acciderat, fore videbat, ut, si essent hostes pulsi, celeritate periculum effugerent,[2] tamen nactus equites circiter XXX, quos Commius Atrebas, de quo ante[3] dictum est, secum transportaverat, legiones in acie pro castris constituit. **2.** Commisso proelio diutius[4] nostrorum militum impetum hostes ferre non potuerunt ac[5] terga verterunt. **3.** Quos tanto spatio secuti, quantum cursu et viribus efficere potuerunt, complures[6] ex eis occiderunt; deinde, omnibus longe lateque aedificiis incensis, se in castra receperunt.

[1] **idem:** subject of *fore*, explained by the appositive clause *ut . . . effugerent*; *203.4.*
[2] **effugerent:** 'they would escape from'. **nactus:** *61a3*; *226c.* **XXX:** a squad (*turma*); *38b*; *309c.*
[3] **ante:** see IV, 21.7. The 30 horsemen were too few to be of service except in scouting or in following up a fleeing enemy.
[4] **diutius:** 'very long'; *153a.*
[5] **ac:** 'but'; *234b.* **tanto spatio,** etc.: 'so far as their speed and strength allowed'; how lit.? *147c.* **secuti,** etc.: sc. *nostri.*
[6] **complures:** accusative. **ex eis:** *97d.*

The Britons sue for peace. Caesar sails back to Gaul.

36.1. Eodem die legati, ab hostibus missi, ad Caesarem de pace venerunt. **2.** His[1] Caesar numerum obsidum, quem ante imperaverat, duplicavit,[2] eosque in continentem adduci iussit, quod, propinqua die aequinoctii,[3] infirmis navibus hiemi[4] navigationem subiciendam non existimabat. **3.** Ipse, idoneam tempestatem nactus, paulo post mediam noctem naves solvit; quae omnes incolumes ad continentem pervenerunt, **4.** sed ex eis onerariae duae eosdem portus,[5] quos reliquae,[6] capere non potuerunt, et paulo infra delatae sunt.

[1] **His:** with *duplicavit*; kind of dative? *109a.* **quem,** etc.: see IV, 27.5-7.
[2] **duplicavit:** 'doubled'.
[3] **propinqua die aequinoctii:** 'since the season of the equinox was near at hand', a period when storms are unusually prevalent; *144b3.* The equinox fell on September 26, and Caesar probably left Britain at least a week before that date. He had been on the island about three weeks, and had hardly been able to go out of sight of the seashore.
[4] **hiemi,** etc.: 'that the voyage ought to run the risk of stormy weather'; how lit.?
[5] **eosdem portus:** probably Boulogne and Ambleteuse.
[6] **reliquae:** 'as the rest'; sc. *naves ceperunt.* **capere:** 'make'. **paulo infra:** i.e. southwest. Whether the two transports made some harbor, or were stranded on the beach, Caesar does not say.

Legionaries from two transports are attacked by the Morini.

37.1. Quibus[1] ex navibus cum essent expositi milites circiter CCC[2] atque in castra contenderent, Morini, quos Caesar, in Britanniam proficiscens, pacatos reliquerat, spe praedae adducti primo non ita magno[3] suorum numero circumsteterunt ac, si[4] sese interfici nollent, arma ponere iusserunt. **2.** Cum illi, orbe facto,[5] sese defenderent, celeriter ad clamorem hominum[6] circiter milia VI convenerunt. Qua re nuntiata, Caesar omnem[7] ex castris equitatum suis auxilio misit. **3.**Interim nostri milites impetum hostium sustinuerunt atque amplius horis quattuor fortissime pugnaverunt; et, paucis vulneribus acceptis, complures ex his occiderunt. **4.** Postea[8] vero quam equitatus noster in conspectum venit, hostes, abiectis armis, terga verterunt magnusque eorum numerus est occisus.

[1] **Quibus navibus:** 'these vessels', the two transports mentioned near the end of the preceding chapter. **essent expositi:** 'had been landed'.
[2] **CCC:** *trecenti,* averaging about 150 men to a ship. **castra:** probably constructed by Publius

Sulpicius Rufus for the protection of the harbor at *portius Itius*, Boulogne; cf. IV, 22.6. **Morini,** etc.: belonging to the part of the Morini who had given hostages to Caesar just before he sailed for Britain ; cf. IV, 22.1,2.

[3] **non ita magno:** 'not very large'. **circumsteterunt:** sc. *eos*, 'the three hundred'.

[4] **si . . . nollent, ponere:** in the direct form, *si . . . non vultis, ponite.* **ponere:** here = *deponere*, 'lay down'.

[5] **orbe facto:** 'formed a circle and'; how lit.? *144b2.* The 'circle' formed by soldiers for defence was hollow and corresponded with our 'hollow square'; *338.* **ad clamorem:** 'on (hearing) the shouting' of the attacking Morini. In Gaul news was transmitted quickly by shouting across the country (VII, 3.2).

[6] **hominum:** i.e. *Morinorum;* dependent on *milia; 98a.* **VI:** *sex.* The number is probably exaggerated; in any case it evidences a much denser population in this region than is implied for the regions penetrated in the expedition against the Morini and Menapii the previous year; cf. III, 28-29.

[7] **omnem equitatum:** including probably the cavalry that had embarked in the 18 transports but had failed to reach Britain (IV, 22.4), as well as the contingent left with Sulpicius (IV, 22.6); the rest must have gone with Titurius Sabinus and Cotta (IV, 22.5).

[8] **Postea quam:** *188a.* **vero:** *236a.*

Caesar inflicts punishment upon the Morini and Menapii; winter quarters in Belgium; thanksgiving decreed at Rome.

38.1. Caesar postero die T. Labienum[1] legatum cum eis legionibus, quas ex Britannia reduxerat, in Morinos, qui rebellionem fecerant, misit. **2.** Qui cum[2] propter siccitates paludum, quo[3] se reciperent, non haberent (quo perfugio superiore anno[4] fuerant usi), omnes fere in potestatem Labieni pervenerunt. **3.** At Q. Titurius et L. Cotta legati, qui in Menapiorum[5] fines legiones duxerant, omnibus eorum agris vastatis, frumentis succisis, aedificiis incensis, quod Menapii se omnes in[6] densissimas silvas abdiderant, se ad Caesarem receperunt. **4.** Caesar in Belgis omnium legionum hiberna constituit. Eo duae omnino civitates ex Britannia obsides miserunt, reliquae neglexerunt.[7] **5.** His rebus gestis, ex litteris Caesaris dierum XX supplicatio[8] a senatu decreta est.

[1] **T. Labienum:** he had probably accompanied Caesar to Britain.

[2] **Qui cum:** ' And since they'; *184a.* **siccitates:** plural because there was dryness in a number of marshes; trans. 'dryness'; *92c.*

[3] **quo,** etc.: '(a place) to which they might escape'; *194a.* **quo perfugio:** i.e. *perfugium, quo:* 'the refuge which'; *165b.*

[4] **superiore anno:** 56 B.C. ; cf. III.28-29.

[5] **Menapiorum:** cf. III, 28.1, note 3.

[6] **in,** etc.: cf. I, 12.3, note 10.

[7] **reliquae neglexerunt:** *obsides mittere.* The expedition to Britain, as that into Germany, was followed by no tangible results; but great fame was thereby won by the daring general for having opened up to his countrymen new and extensive regions. Hence the thanksgiving decreed at Rome, obtained by his friends for Caesar in the face of all the opposition that his enemies could stir up (see note 12 to IV, 14.5).

[8] **supplicatio:** cf. II, 35.4. This 'thanksgiving' was to be 5 days longer than the one decreed at the end of 57 B.C., though that was the longest known up to that time.

PLATE IV   WEAPONS, STANDARDS, AND ROMAN CAMP

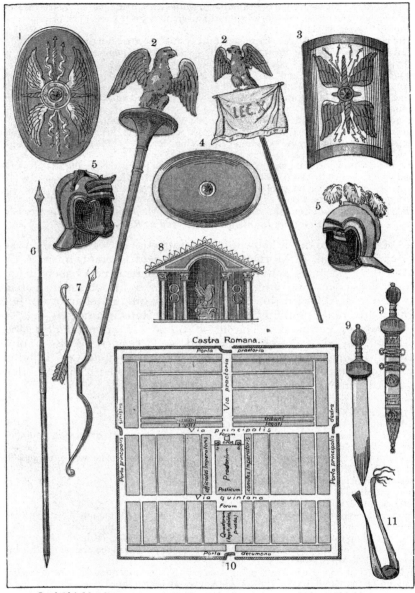

1. Oval Shield, *clipeus*.   2, 2. Eagle of the Legion.   3. Oblong Shield, *scutum*.
4. Light Shield, *parma*.   5, 5. Cavalry Helmet, *cassis*.   6. Pike, *pilum*.
7. Bow, *arcus;* Arrow, *sagitta*.   8. Shrine for the Eagle, *sacellum*.
9, 9. Sword, *gladius;* Scabbard, *vagina*.   10. Roman Camp.
11. Sling, *funda*.

COMMENTARIUS QUINTUS

SECOND EXPEDITION TO BRITAIN. 1-23

Caesar orders ships built, and quiets disturbances in Illyricum.

1.1. L. Domitio,[1] Ap. Claudio consulibus, discedens ab hibernis[2] Caesar in Italiam, ut quotannis facere consuerat, legatis imperat, quos legionibus praefecerat, uti, quam plurimas possent, hieme naves aedificandas veteresque reficiendas curarent. Earum modum formamque demonstrat. **2.** Ad celeritatem onerandi[3] subductionesque paulo facit humiliores, quam quibus in nostro mari uti consuevimus, atque id eo magis, quod propter crebras commutationes aestuum[4] minus magnos ibi fluctus fieri cognoverat; ad onera ac multitudinem iumentorum transportandam paulo latiores,[5] quam quibus in reliquis utimur maribus. **3.** Has omnes actuarias[6] imperat fieri, quam ad rem humilitas[7] multum adiuvat. **4.** Ea, quae sunt usui ad armandas naves, ex Hispania[8] apportari iubet. **5.** Ipse, conventibus Galliae citerioris peractis,[9] in Illyricum proficiscitur, quod a Pirustis finitimam partem provinciae incursionibus[10] vastari audiebat. **6.** Eo cum venisset, civitatibus milites imperat certumque in locum convenire iubet. **7.** Qua re nuntiata, Pirustae legatos ad eum mittunt, qui doceant, nihil earum rerum publico factum consilio, seseque paratos esse demonstrant omnibus rationibus de iniuriis satisfacere. **8.** Percepta oratione eorum, Caesar obsides imperat eosque ad certam diem adduci iubet; nisi ita fecerint, sese bello civitatem persecuturum demonstrat. **9.** Eis ad diem adductis, ut imperaverat, arbitros[11] inter civitates dat, qui litem[12] aestiment poenamque constituant.

[1] **L. Domitio, Ap. Claudio consulibus:** 54 B.C.; *240a; 234a.*
[2] **hibernis:** in Belgium (IV, 38). **Italiam:** *283b.*
[3] **onerandi:** 'of loading'. **subductiones:** 'beaching'; *92a.* **humiliores:** 'shallower'. **quam quibus:** i.e. *quam eae* [*naves*] *sunt, quibus.*
[4] **commutationes aestuum:** cf. IV, 29.1, note 2.
[5] **latiores:** predicative; sc. *eas facit.*
[6] **actuarias:** predicative, 'for rapid movement', with the use of oars as well as sails.
[7] **humilitas:** 'lowness' of the deck above the water.
[8] **Hispania:** *296.* **apportari:** 'be brought'.
[9] **peractis:** 'finished'. **Illyricum:** *298.*
[10] **incursionibus:** 'raids'.
[11] **arbitros:** ' referees'; *7c; 80b.*
[12] **litem:** 'the (matter of) damages'.

Proceeding to Gaul he finds ships ready, visits the Treverans.

2.1. His confectis rebus conventibusque peractis, in citeriorem Galliam revertitur atque inde ad exercitum proficiscitur. **2.** Eo cum venisset, circumitis omnibus hibernis, singulari militum studio in summa omnium rerum inopia circiter DC[1] eius generis, cuius supra demonstravimus, naves, et longas[2] XXVIII, invenit instructas, neque multum abesse ab eo, quin paucis diebus deduci possint. **3.** Collaudatis[3] militibus atque eis, qui negotio praefuerant, quid fieri velit, ostendit, atque omnes ad portum Itium convenire iubet, quo ex portu commodissimum in Britanniam traiectum esse cognoverat, circiter milium passuum XXX a continenti; huic rei,[4] quod satis esse visum est militum, reliquit. **4.** Ipse cum legionibus expeditis IIII et equitibus DCCC in fines Treverorum proficiscitur, quod hi neque ad concilia veniebant neque imperio parebant, Germanosque Transrhenanos sollicitare dicebantur.

[1] **DC:** *sescentas.* **cuius:** *cuius generis naves;* trans. *cuius* as if *quod.* **supra:** in chap. 1.
[2] **longas:** i.e. *naves duodetriginta; 346a.* **neque,** etc.: 'and that in a few days they would be about ready to launch'; how lit.?
[3] **Collaudatis:** 'warmly commending'; how lit.?
[4] **huic rei:** 'for this purpose.' **quod militum:** 'so many soldiers as'; *97, b.*

By means of hostages he binds Indutiomarus to keep the peace.

3.1. Haec civitas longe plurimum totius Galliae equitatu valet magnasque habet copias peditum, Rhenumque, ut supra[1] demonstravimus, tangit. **2.** In ea civitate duo de principatu inter se contendebant, Indutiomarus et Cingetorix; **3.** e quibus alter, simul atque de Caesaris legionumque adventu cognitum est, ad eum venit, se suosque omnes in officio futuros neque ab amicitia populi Romani defecturos confirmavit, quaeque in Treveris gererentur, ostendit. **4.** At Indutiomarus equitatum peditatumque cogere, eisque, qui per aetatem[2] in armis esse non poterant, in silvam Arduennam abditis, quae, ingenti magnitudine, per medios fines Treverorum a flumine Rheno ad initium Remorum pertinet, bellum parare instituit. **5.** Sed postea quam non nulli principes ex ea civitate, et familiaritate Cingetorigis adducti et adventu nostri exercitus perterriti, ad Caesarem venerunt et de suis privatim rebus ab eo petere coeperunt, quoniam civitati consulere non possent, veritus, ne ab omnibus desereretur, Indutiomarus legatos ad Caesarem mittit: **6.** *Sese[3] idcirco ab suis discedere atque ad eum venire noluisse, quo facilius civitatem in officio contineret, ne omnis nobilitatis discessu plebs propter imprudentiam[4] laberetur;* **7.** *itaque civitatem in sua potestate esse, seque, si Caesar permitteret, ad eum in castra venturum, et suas civitatisque fortunas eius fidei permissurum.*

[1] **supra:** see III, 11.1. **tangit:** 'extends to', lit. 'touches'.
[2] **per aetatem:** 'by reason of age'. **in armis esse:** i.e. **arma ferre.**
[3] **Sese,** etc.: '(saying) that he.' **idcirco:** 'on this account'.
[4] **imprudentiam:** 'lack of foresight'. **laberetur:** 'fall away', becoming disloyal.

4.1. Caesar, etsi intellegebat, qua de causa ea dicerentur, quaeque eum res ab instituto consilio[1] deterreret, tamen, ne aestatem in Treveris consumere cogeretur, omnibus ad Britannicum bellum rebus comparatis, Indutiomarum ad se cum CC obsidibus venire iussit. **2.** His adductis, in eis filio propinquisque eius omnibus, quos nominatim evocaverat,[2] consolatus Indutiomarum hortatusque est, uti in officio maneret; **3.** nihilo tamen setius, principibus Treverorum ad se convocatis, hos singillatim Cingetorigi conciliavit; quod cum[3] merito eius[4] ab se fieri intellegebat, tum magni interesse arbitrabatur, eius auctoritatem inter suos quam plurimum valere, cuius tam egregiam in se voluntatem perspexisset. **4.** Id factum graviter tulit Indutiomarus, suam gratiam inter suos minui, et, qui[5] iam ante inimico in nos animo fuisset, multo gravius[6] hoc dolore exarsit.

[1] **ab instituto consilio:** 'from (carrying out) the plan (which he had) formed'.
[2] **evocaverat:** sc. *Caesar.*
[3] **quod cum,** etc.: 'and not only did he understand that he was doing this in accordance with what Cingetorix deserved'; how lit.? *186b.*
[4] **eius:** *Cingetorigis; 19d.* **magni:** *103d.*
[5] **qui:** 'although he'; *187* (B 283.3b).
[6] **gravius ... exarsit:** 'on account of this grievance he became much more indignant'; how lit.?

Caesar gathers his forces at portus Itius.

5.1. His rebus constitutis, Caesar ad portum Itium cum legionibus pervenit. **2.** Ibi cognoscit, LX naves,[1] quae in Meldis factae erant, tempestate reiectas cursum tenere non potuisse atque eodem, unde erant profectae, revertisse; reliquas paratas ad navigandum atque omnibus rebus instructas invenit. **3.** Eodem equitatus totius Galliae convenit, numero[2] milium quattuor, principesque ex omnibus civitatibus; **4.** ex quibus perpaucos, quorum in se fidem perspexerat, relinquere in Gallia, reliquos obsidum loco secum ducere decreverat, quod, cum ipse abesset,[3] motum Galliae verebatur.

[1] **naves,** etc.: these vessels had to be taken down the Marne and the Seine to the Channel, then north to Boulogne (portus Itius); see Map 11.
[2] **numero:** *142a; 85.* **milium:** dependent on *equitatus; 100a; 309b.*
[3] **abesset:** *185c.*

Dumnorix attempts to elude Caesar's vigilance, and is slain.

6.1. Erat una cum ceteris Dumnorix Aeduus, de quo ante[1] a nobis dictum est. Hunc secum habere in primis constituerat, quod eum[2] cupidum rerum novarum, cupidum imperii, magni animi, magnae inter Gallos auctoritatis cognoverat. **2.** Accedebat huc, quod in concilio Aeduorum Dumnorix dixerat, sibi[3] a Caesare regnum civitatis deferri; quod dictum Aedui graviter ferebant, neque recusandi aut deprecandi causa legatos ad Caesarem mittere audebant. **3.** Id factum ex suis hospitibus Caesar cognoverat. Ille omnibus primo precibus petere contendit, ut in Gallia relinqueretur, partim quod, insuetus navigandi,[4] mare timeret, partim quod religionibus[5] impediri sese diceret. **4.** Postea quam id obstinate[6] sibi negari vidit, omni spe impetrandi adempta, principes Galliae sollicitare, sevocare[7] singulos hortarique coepit, uti in continenti remanerent; metu territare:[8] *Non sine causa fieri, ut Gallia omni nobilitate spoliaretur;*[9] **5.** *id esse consilium Caesaris, ut, quos in conspectu Galliae interficere vereretur, hos omnes in Britanniam traductos necaret;* **6.** fidem reliquis interponere, ius iurandum poscere, ut, quod esse ex usu Galliae intellexissent, communi consilio administrarent. **7.** Haec a compluribus ad Caesarem deferebantur.

[1] **ante:** see I, 16-20. Dumnorix had always opposed Caesar.
[2] **eum:** sc. *esse; 289c.*
[3] **sibi . . . deferri:** contrary to the constitution of the Aeduans, who elected a Vergobret annually; see I, 16.5.
[4] **insuetus navigandi:** 'unused to sailing'; *230.1.*
[5] **religionibus:** 'by religious scruples'. **diceret:** *183b.*
[6] **obstinate:** 'persistently'.
[7] **sevocare:** 'to call aside', for secret conference; *19d.*
[8] **territare:** sc. *eos;* 'he worked upon their fears, (saying)'; *182; 213b.* How lit.?
[9] **spoliaretur:** 'was being stripped', by taking the leading men to Britain.

7.1. Qua re cognita Caesar, quod tantum civitati Aeduae dignitatis tribuebat, coercendum atque deterrendum, quibuscumque rebus posset, Dumnorigem statuebat; **2.** quod longius eius amentiam progredi videbat, prospiciendum,[1] ne quid sibi ac rei publicae nocere posset. **3.** Itaque dies circiter XXV in eo loco[2] commoratus, quod Corus ventus navigationem impediebat, qui magnam partem omnis temporis in his locis flare consuevit, dabat operam,[3] ut in officio Dumnorigem contineret, nihilo tamen setius omnia eius consilia cognosceret; **4.** tandem idoneam nactus tempestatem[4] milites equitesque conscendere naves iubet. **5.** At, omnium impeditis animis, Dumnorix cum equitibus Aeduorum a castris, insciente Caesare, domum discedere coepit. **6.** Qua re nuntiata, Caesar, intermissa profectione atque omnibus rebus postpositis, magnam partem equitatus ad eum insequendum mittit retrahique[5] imperat; **7.** si vim faciat neque pareat, interfici iubet, nihil hunc, se absente, pro sano[6] facturum arbitratus, qui praesentis imperium neglexisset. **8.** Ille autem revocatus resistere ac se manu defendere suorumque fidem implorare coepit, saepe clamitans,[7] liberum se liberaeque esse civitatis. **9.** Illi, ut erat imperatum, circumsistunt hominem atque interficiunt; at equites Aedui ad Caesarem omnes revertuntur.

[1] **prospiciendum:** sc. *esse statuebat.*
[2] **eo loco:** portus Itius, Boulogne. **commoratus:** 'while waiting'. **Corus:** 'from the northwest'.
[3] **dabat operam:** 'was taking pains'.
[4] **tempestatem:** cf. IV, 23.1, note 2.
[5] **retrahi:** sc. *eum,* 'that he be brought back'.
[6] **pro sano:** 'like a man in his senses'; how lit.? **praesentis:** sc. *sui,* i.e. *Caesaris.*
[7] **clamitans:** 'crying out'; *78a.*

Caesar sails to Britain, lands, and captures a stronghold.

8.1. His rebus gestis, Labieno in continenti cum III legionibus et equitum milibus duobus relicto, ut portus tueretur et rem frumentariam provideret, quaeque in Gallia gererentur, cognosceret, consiliumque pro[1] tempore et pro re caperet, **2.** ipse cum V legionibus et pari[2] numero equitum, quem in continenti reliquerat, ad solis occasum naves solvit. Et leni Africo[3] provectus, media circiter nocte vento intermisso, cursum non tenuit et, longius delatus aestu, orta luce sub sinistra Britanniam relictam conspexit. **3.** Tum, rursus aestus[4] commutationem secutus, remis contendit, ut eam partem insulae caperet,[5] qua optimum esse egressum superiore aestate cognoverat. **4.** Qua in re admodum fuit militum virtus laudanda,[6] qui vectoriis[7] gravibusque navigiis, non intermisso remigandi[8] labore, longarum navium cursum adaequarunt. **5.** Accessum est ad Britanniam omnibus navibus meridiano[9] fere tempore, neque in eo loco hostis est visus; **6.** sed, ut postea Caesar ex captivis cognovit, cum magnae manus eo convenissent, multitudine navium perterritae, quae cum annotinis[10] privatisque, quas sui quisque commodi causa fecerat, amplius DCCC[11] uno erant visae tempore, a litore discesserant ac se in superiora loca abdiderant.

[1] **pro ... re:** 'as conditions at the time might require'; how lit.?
[2] **pari:** trans. as if *eodem.*

[3] **Africo:** 'southwest wind'. Caesar probably sailed about July 6.
[4] **aestus,** etc.: the change of course is shown on Map 11, **A.**
[5] **caperet:** 'reach'.
[6] **laudanda:** 'praiseworthy'.
[7] **vectoriis,** etc.: 'heavy transports'.
[8] **remigandi:** 'of rowing'; the transports were provided with oars, in addition to the usual sails (in Vocab.).
[9] **meridiano tempore:** 'midday'.
[10] **annotinis:** sc. *navibus,* 'ships of the previous year'.
[11] **DCCC:** *octingentae;* with *quae,* 'of which more than 800'; *97c; 129b.*

9.1. Caesar, exposito exercitu et loco castris idoneo capto, ubi ex captivis cognovit, quo in loco hostium copiae consedissent, cohortibus X ad mare relictis et equitibus CCC, qui[1] praesidio navibus essent, de tertia vigilia ad hostes contendit, eo minus veritus navibus,[2] quod in litore molli atque aperto deligatas ad ancoras relinquebat; ei praesidio navibusque Q. Atrium praefecit. **2.** Ipse, noctu progressus milia passuum circiter XII, hostium copias conspicatus est. **3.** Illi, equitatu atque essedis[3] ad flumen progressi, ex loco superiore nostros prohibere et proelium committere coeperunt. **4.** Repulsi ab equitatu se in silvas abdiderunt, locum nacti egregie et natura et opere munitum, quem domestici belli, ut videbatur, causa iam ante praeparaverant; nam crebris arboribus succisis omnes[4] introitus erant praeclusi. **5.** Ipsi ex silvis rari propugnabant,[5] nostrosque intra munitiones ingredi prohibebant.[6] **6.** At milites legionis septimae, testudine[7] facta et aggere ad munitiones adiecto, locum ceperunt eosque ex silvis expulerunt, paucis vulneribus acceptis. **7.** Sed eos fugientes longius Caesar prosequi vetuit, et quod loci naturam ignorabat, et quod, magna parte diei consumpta, munitioni castrorum tempus relinqui volebat.

[1] **qui . . . essent:** 'to guard the ships'; how lit.? *193a; 112b.*
[2] **navibus:** dative. **molli:** affording good anchorage.
[3] **essedis:** see IV, 33 and notes. **flumen:** the Great Stour; see Map 11.
[4] **omnes,** etc.: 'all the entrances were obstructed'.
[5] **rari propugnabant:** 'in small bodies were hurling missiles'; how lit.? The British stronghold was perhaps near Canterbury.
[6] **prohibebant:** 'were trying to prevent'; *175e; 223a.*
[7] **testudine:** *345.* **aggere:** probably made of tree trunks; *341.*

A storm shatters the fleet; Caesar orders repairs, returns inland.

10.1. Postridie eius diei mane tripertito[1] milites equitesque in expeditionem[2] misit, ut eos, qui fugerant, persequerentur. **2.** His aliquantum itineris[3] progressis, cum iam extremi essent in prospectu, equites a Q. Atrio ad Caesarem venerunt, qui nuntiarent, superiore nocte maxima coorta tempestate, prope omnes naves afflictas atque in litus eiectas esse, quod neque ancorae funesque subsisterent, neque nautae gubernatoresque vim tempestatis pati possent; **3.** itaque ex eo concursu navium magnum esse incommodum acceptum.

[1] **tripertito:** 'in three columns'.
[2] **in expeditionem:** 'for a rapid march', with light equipment.
[3] **aliquantum itineris:** 'some distance'; how lit.? **extremi:** 'the rear' of the Roman force was just visible to those in camp.

11.1. His rebus cognitis, Caesar legiones equitatumque revocari atque in itinere resistere[1] iubet, ipse ad naves revertitur; **2.** eadem fere, quae ex nuntiis[2] litterisque cognoverat, coram perspicit, sic ut, amissis circiter XL navibus, reliquae tamen refici posse magno negotio[3] viderentur. **3.** Itaque ex legionibus fabros[4] deligit et ex continenti alios arcessi iubet; **4.** Labieno scribit, ut, quam plurimas posset, eis legionibus,[5] quae sint apud eum, naves instituat. **5.** Ipse, etsi res[6] erat multae operae ac laboris, tamen commodissimum esse statuit, omnes naves subduci[7] et cum castris una munitione coniungi. **6.** In his rebus circiter dies X consumit, ne nocturnis quidem temporibus ad laborem militum intermissis. **7.** Subductis navibus castrisque egregie munitis, easdem copias, quas ante, praesidio navibus relinquit, ipse eodem,[8] unde redierat, proficiscitur. **8.** Eo cum venisset, maiores iam undique in eum locum copiae Britannorum convenerant, summa imperii bellique administrandi communi consilio permissa Cassivellauno; cuius fines a maritimis civitatibus flumen dividit, quod appellatur Tamesis,[9] a mari circiter milia passuum LXXX. **9.** Huic superiore tempore cum reliquis civitatibus continentia bella intercesserant; sed, nostro adventu permoti, Britanni hunc toti bello imperioque praefecerant.

[1] **in itinere resistere:** to beat off the enemy, without halting for a pitched battle.
[2] **nuntiis:** 'messengers', mounted (V, 10.2). **litteris:** 'dispatch', from Quintus Atrius.
[3] **negotio:** 'trouble'.
[4] **fabros:** 'mechanics'; 7c; 310b.
[5] **eis legionibus:** 'with (the help of) the legions', at portus Itius; 160d.
[6] **res,** etc.: 'it was a wearisome and laborious undertaking'; how lit.? 100b.
[7] **subduci:** the ships were built so that they could be beached; V, 1.1-2.
[8] **eodem,** etc.: the British stronghold, near modern Canterbury (V, 9.4-6).
[9] **Tamesis:** only the upper Thames formed the boundary of the territories ruled by Cassivellaunus; 14c. **mari:** at the point where Caesar landed, near Deal.

The Britons and their island.

12.1. Britanniae pars interior ab eis incolitur, quos[1] natos in insula ipsa memoria proditum dicunt;[2] **2.** maritima pars ab eis, qui praedae ac belli inferendi causa ex Belgio transierunt (qui[3] omnes fere eis nominibus civitatum appellantur, quibus orti ex civitatibus eo pervenerunt), et, bello illato, ibi permanserunt atque agros colere coeperunt. **3.** Hominum[4] est infinita multitudo creberrimaque aedificia[5] fere Gallicis consimilia, pecorum magnus numerus. **4.** Utuntur aut aere[6] aut nummo aureo,[7] aut taleis ferreis ad certum pondus examinatis, pro nummo. Nascitur[8] ibi plumbum album in mediterraneis regionibus, in maritimis ferrum,[9] sed eius exigua est copia; aere utuntur importato. **5.** Materia cuiusque generis, ut in Gallia, est, praeter fagum[10] atque abietem. **6.** Leporem[11] et gallinam et anserem gustare fas non putant; haec[12] tamen alunt animi voluptatisque causa. **7.** Loca sunt temperatiora quam in Gallia, remissioribus[13] frigoribus.

[1] **quos,** etc.: quos natos [esse] is subject of proditum [esse]; 'who, they say, according to tradition, originated in the island itself'; how lit.? 294.
[2] **dicunt:** 172c. Several ancient peoples considered themselves "autochthones", sprung from the soil in the region in which they dwelt.
[3] **qui,** etc.: there was, for example, a British tribe called Atrebates.

[4] **Hominum,** etc.: 'The population is beyond number'; how lit.?

[5] **aedificia:** sc. *sunt.* **Gallicis** [aedificiis]: large round huts of timbers and wickerwork, with conical thatched roofs.

[6] **aere:** 'bronze': bronze coins. The earliest British bronze coins yet discovered date from a few years after Caesar's time.

[7] **nummo aureo:** 'gold coins', we should say. Gold coins began to be struck in Britain at least a hundred years before Caesar's invasions. **taleis ferreis:** 'iron bars'. **ad,** etc.: 'weighed to a certain standard', lit. 'weight'. The iron currency bars that have been found represent several different weights, the heaviest being twice as heavy as the second, and so on.

[8] **Nascitur:** 'is found'. **plumbum album:** 'tin', which began to be exported from Cornwall as early as the ninth century B.C. **mediterraneis:** 'inland'. The Cornish tin mines were in reality near the sea, but they were a long distance from Caesar's landing-place.

[9] **ferrum:** iron mines were worked in Sussex from the prehistoric period to the nineteenth century. **aere:** some bronze seems to have been imported into Britain, but most of the bronze objects found in Britain were made there, from native mixtures of the component metals.

[10] **fagum:** 'beech'; *5b.* Caesar seems to have been mistaken in saying that the beech was not found in Britain; but his opportunities for direct observation were limited. **abietem:** 'fir'; *10e.*

[11] **Leporem,** etc.: 'hare, chicken, and goose'. The origin of the superstition is difficult to understand; *13g; 234a.* **anserem:** *11c.* **gustare:** 'to taste'.

[12] **haec alunt:** 'they raise these'. **animi,** etc.: 'for pastime and amusement'. **Loca:** 'the region'; *6c.* **sunt temperatiora:** 'has a milder climate'; how lit.?

[13] **remissioribus frigoribus:** 'the cold being less severe'; how lit.? *92c; 13f.*

MAP 12

MAP OF BRITAIN AS CONCEIVED BY CAESAR

Book V, 13   To face page 300

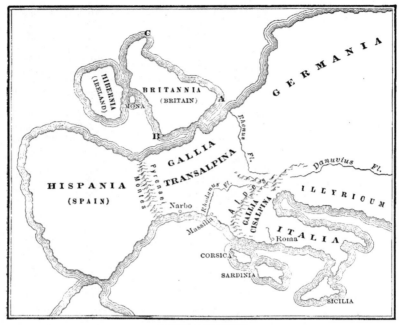

EXPLANATION

In view of the meagerness of Caesar's information, his statement about the geography of Britain is surprisingly near the truth in essential particulars. In this respect it compares favorably with the statements of modern travelers and explorers in regard to regions of which they have seen only a small part.

He knew that the Island was triangular in shape, and in his two expeditions he had himself seen a portion of the coast facing Gaul (chap. 13, l. 1). He could easily believe that one corner (**A**) faced east, another (**B**) toward the south. His language implies that he had a vague idea of a projection eastward (**C**) at the northern extremity (l. 18). He knew the location, and approximately the size, of Ireland (l. 7).

Caesar, as other ancients, found it more difficult to estimate distances north and south than east and west. He fell easily into the error of supposing that the northern end of Spain extended so far that it lay west of the southern part of Britain (l. 6); and his conception of the relative positions of the two Gauls, Italy and Illyricum, was probably very nearly as represented.

The strait between Italy and Sicily, now Strait of Messina, is called by Caesar *Fretum* (C. II, l. 3).

13.1. Insula natura[1] triquetra, cuius unum latus est contra Galliam. Huius lateris alter angulus,[2] qui est ad Cantium, quo[3] fere omnes ex Gallia naves appelluntur, ad orientem solem, inferior[4] ad meridiem spectat. Hoc latus pertinet circiter milia passuum D.[5] **2.** Alterum[6] vergit ad Hispaniam atque occidentem solem; qua ex parte[7] est Hibernia, dimidio minor, ut existimatur, quam Britannia,[8] sed pari spatio transmissus, atque ex Gallia est in Britanniam. **3.** In[9] hoc medio cursu est insula, quae appellatur Mona;[10] complures praeterea minores subiectae insulae[11] existimantur; de quibus insulis non nulli scripserunt, dies continuos XXX sub bruma[12] esse noctem. **4.** Nos[13] nihil de eo percontationibus reperiebamus, nisi certis ex aqua[14] mensuris breviores esse quam in continenti noctes videbamus. **5.** Huius est longitudo lateris, ut[15] fert illorum opinio, DCC[16] milium. **6.** Tertium[17] est contra septentriones; cui parti nulla est obiecta terra, sed eius angulus lateris maxime ad Germaniam spectat. Hoc[18] milia passuum DCCC in longitudinem esse existimatur. **7.** Ita omnis insula est in circuitu vicies centum[19] milium passuum.

[1] **natura**: 'in shape'; lit. 'by nature'. **triquetra**: 'triangular'. **contra**: 'opposite'.
[2] **alter angulus**: 'one corner'. **ad Cantium**: 'by Kent' (Map 12, **A**); the boundaries of Kent in Caesar's time are not known with exactness.
[3] **quo**: refers to *angulus*. **appelluntur**: 'come to land'; how lit.? **ad orientem solem**: 'toward the east'. How lit.?
[4] **inferior** [angulus]: see Map 12, **B**. **ad meridiem**: 'toward the south'.
[5] **D**: *quingentorum;* how many English miles in 500 Roman miles? *243a,b.*
[6] **Alterum** [latus], etc.: 'The second side has a westerly trend, toward Spain'. How lit.? Caesar's erroneous belief that Spain extended north nearly to Britain was shared by his contemporaries, and even by some writers after his time. See Map 12.
[7] **qua ex parte**: 'and on this side'. **dimidio minor**: 'a half smaller'; how lit.? *140.*
[8] **Britannia**: sc. *est.* **pari**, etc.: '(reached by) a passage just as long as that from Gaul to Britain'; how lit.? **pari spatio**: descriptive ablative, taking the place of an adjective, and coordinated with *minor* by *sed*. **transmissus**: genitive, depending on *spatio*. **atque**: *233c.*
[9] **In . . . cursu**: 'half way across', between Britain and Ireland; how lit.? *152a.*
[10] **Mona**: see Map 12. **subiectae** [esse], etc.: 'are thought to lie off (the coast on this side)'.
[11] **insulae**: probably the Hebrides are referred to. **non nulli scripserunt**: perhaps Greek writers, whose works have perished, are meant.
[12] **sub bruma**: 'about the winter solstice'. The statement regarding a period of thirty days without the sun is not true of the Hebrides or of the other islands near Scotland.
[13] **Nos**: *156.* **percontationibus**: 'through inquiries'. **certis**, etc.: 'by exact measurements (made) with a water-clock'; how lit.? A water-clock, *clepsydra*, was used in a Roman camp, especially to mark the watches; *242e.*
[14] **ex aqua**: with *mensuris; 150d.* **breviores**: Caesar's observations were made in summer; in winter the nights would of course be longer.
[15] **ut**, etc.: 'according to their idea', i.e. of the Britons; how lit.?
[16] **DCC**: *septingentorum.* **milium**: *100b.*
[17] **Tertium** [latus]: cf. *unum* and *alterum* in the two previous paragraphs.
[18] **Hoc**: *hoc latus.* **DCCC**: *octingenta.*
[19] **vicies centum**: 'two thousand'; how lit.? Caesar's estimate is nearer the truth than might have been expected; no Roman is known to have sailed around the island until more than a century after Caesar's time, in 84 A.D.

14.1. Ex his omnibus[1] longe sunt humanissimi, qui Cantium incolunt, quae regio est maritima omnis[2], neque multum a Gallica differunt consuetudine. **2.** Interiores plerique[3] frumenta non serunt,[4] sed lacte et carne vivunt pellibusque sunt vestiti.[5] **3.** Omnes vero se[6] Britanni vitro inficiunt, quod caeruleum efficit colorem, atque hoc[7] horridiores sunt in pugna aspectu; capilloque[8] sunt promisso atque omni parte corporis rasa praeter caput et labrum superius. **4.** Uxores habent deni duodenique inter se communes, et maxime fratres cum fratribus parentesque cum liberis; **5.** sed, qui sunt ex eis nati, eorum habentur liberi, quo primum virgo quaeque deducta est.

[1] **his omnibus:** the Britons; *97d.* **humanissimi:** 'most civilized'.
[2] **omnis:** 'wholly'; *151.* **neque:** 'and . . . not'.
[3] **Interiores plerique:** 'Those living in the interior, for the most part'.
[4] **serunt:** 'sow'. **lacte:** cf. IV, 1.8; *131a.* **carne:** 'meat'; *18a.*
[5] **sunt vestiti:** 'clothe themselves'; *174.* Caesar was misinformed about the life of the inland tribes of Britain. It has been proved by discoveries that, long before his time, at least the more progressive raised crops and had woollen and linen clothes.
[6] **se vitro inficiunt:** 'stain themselves with woad', a plant from the leaves of which is made a dye resembling indigo in color. **caeruleum colorem:** 'a bluish colour'; *80b.*
[7] **hoc:** 'on this account'. **horridiores aspectu:** 'rather wild-looking'; how lit.? *142a.*
[8] **capillo**, etc.: 'they let their hair grow long'; how lit.?

The Britons fight fiercely, but Caesar defeats them.

15.1. Equites[1] hostium essedariique acriter proelio cum equitatu nostro in itinere conflixerunt, ita tamen, ut nostri omnibus partibus superiores fuerint atque eos in silvas collesque compulerint; **2.** sed, compluribus interfectis, cupidius insecuti non nullos ex suis amiserunt. **3.** At illi, intermisso spatio, imprudentibus nostris atque[2] occupatis in munitione castrorum, subito se ex silvis eiecerunt, impetuque in eos facto, qui erant in statione pro castris collocati, acriter pugnaverunt; **4.** duabusque missis subsidio cohortibus a Caesare, atque his primis legionum duarum, cum hae perexiguo[3] intermisso loci spatio inter se constitissent, novo[4] genere pugnae perterritis nostris, per medios audacissime perruperunt seque inde incolumes receperunt. **5.** Eo die Q. Laberius Durus, tribunus militum, interficitur. Illi, pluribus summissis cohortibus, repelluntur.

[1] **Equites**, etc.: cf. IV, 33 and notes. The narrative, interrupted by the description of Britain, is here resumed from chap. 11.
[2] **atque**, etc.: 'and those the first'; *161c.*
[3] **perexiguo:** 'very small'; *79b.* **inter se:** 'apart'.
[4] **novo**, etc.: the two cohorts had evidently not been on the first expedition. **per medios:** between the cohorts.

16.1. Toto hoc in genere[1] pugnae, cum sub oculis omnium ac pro castris dimicaretur, intellectum est,[2] nostros propter gravitatem armorum, quod neque insequi cedentes possent neque ab signis discedere auderent, minus aptos esse ad huius generis hostem; **2.** equites autem magno cum periculo proelio dimicare, propterea quod illi[3] etiam consulto plerumque cederent et, cum paulum ab legionibus nostros removissent, ex essedis desilirent et pedibus dispari proelio[4] contenderent. **3.** Equestris autem proelii ratio et cedentibus et insequentibus par atque idem periculum inferebat. **4.** Accedebat[5] huc, ut numquam conferti, sed rari[6] magnisque intervallis proeliarentur stationesque dispositas haberent, atque alios[7] alii deinceps exciperent, integrique et recentes defatigatis[8] succederent.

[1] **genere**, etc.: 'throughout the engagement, with fighting of this sort'; how lit.? **sub oculis**

omnium: i.e. *in conspectu omnium.*
[2] **intellectum est:** 'it was evident'; how lit.?
[3] **illi,** etc.: 'they', the Britons, 'would fall back purposely'.
[4] **dispari proelio:** 'in battle with the advantage on their side', because Caesar's Gallic cavalry were no match for warriors fighting on foot. How lit.?
[5] **Accedebat huc:** 'There was the further fact that'. **conferti:** 'in close formation'.
[6] **rari:** 'in small bodies'. **stationes:** here 'reserves'.
[7] **alios,** etc.: 'were relieving one another in turn'; *171b.*
[8] **defatigatis:** *227a4.*

17.1. Postero die procul a castris hostes in collibus constiterunt, rarique se ostendere et lenius, quam pridie, nostros equites proelio lacessere coeperunt. **2.** Sed meridie, cum Caesar, pabulandi causa,[1] III legiones atque omnem equitatum cum C. Trebonio legato misisset, repente ex omnibus partibus ad pabulatores[2] advolaverunt sic, uti ab signis legionibusque non absisterent. **3.** Nostri, acriter in eos impetu facto, reppulerunt neque finem sequendi fecerunt, quoad,[3] subsidio confisi, equites, cum[4] post se legiones viderent, praecipites hostes egerunt; **4.** magnoque eorum numero interfecto, neque sui colligendi[5] neque consistendi, aut ex essedis desiliendi, facultatem dederunt. **5.** Ex[6] hac fuga protinus, quae undique convenerant, auxilia discesserunt, neque post id tempus umquam summis nobiscum copiis hostes contenderunt.

[1] **pabulandi causa:** 'to forage.' Three legions and the cavalry made a foraging party of extraordinary size.
[2] **pabulatores:** 'foragers'. **advolaverunt:** 'rushed upon'; how lit.? **ab . . . absisterent:** 'they did not hold back from the standards of the legions', lit. 'and the legions'; the Britons even charged upon the legionaries, formed in order of battle; *238d; 324b2.*
[3] **quoad:** *190c.* **subsidio:** 'on the support (of the legions)'; *135a.*
[4] **cum:** *184a.* **praecipites:** accusative, 'head over heels'; *151.*
[5] **sui colligendi:** *154b* (AG 504c, B 339.5).
[6] **Ex:** 'after'. **auxilia:** *auxilia Britannorum.*

With great dash Caesar's men force the passage of the Thames.

18.1. Caesar, cognito consilio[1] eorum, ad flumen Tamesim in fines Cassivellauni exercitum duxit; quod flumen uno omnino loco[2] pedibus, atque hoc aegre, transiri potest. **2.** Eo cum venisset, animadvertit, ad alteram fluminis ripam magnas esse copias hostium instructas. **3.** Ripa autem erat acutis sudibus[3] praefixis munita, eiusdemque generis sub aqua defixae sudes flumine tegebantur. **4.** His rebus cognitis a captivis perfugisque, Caesar, praemisso equitatu, confestim legiones subsequi iussit. **5.** Sed ea celeritate atque eo impetu milites ierunt, cum[4] capite solo ex aqua exstarent, ut hostes impetum legionum atque equitum sustinere non possent ripasque dimitterent ac se fugae mandarent.

[1] **consilio:** the 'plan' of the Britons, revealed in chap. 19.
[2] **loco:** *145c.* **hoc:** sc. *loco.*
[3] **acutis sudibus:** 'with sharp stakes'. **praefixis:** 'driven in front', at the water's edge.
[4] **cum,** etc.: 'though they were in water up to the chin'; how lit.? Caesar crossed the Thames from the south to the north side; precisely where he crossed is not known. See Map 11.

Cassivellaunus harasses Caesar's army on the march.

19.1. Cassivellaunus, ut supra demonstravimus, omni deposita spe contentionis,[1] dimissis amplioribus copiis, milibus circiter IIII[2] essedariorum relictis, itinera nostra servabat; paulumque ex via excedebat locisque impeditis ac silvestribus sese occultabat, atque eis regionibus, quibus nos iter facturos cognoverat, pecora atque homines ex agris in silvas compellebat; 2. et, cum equitatus noster, liberius praedandi vastandique causa, se[3] in agros effuderat, omnibus viis semitisque essedarios ex silvis emittebat, et magno cum periculo nostrorum equitum[4] cum eis confligebat atque hoc metu latius vagari[5] prohibebat. 3. Relinquebatur, ut neque longius ab agmine legionum discedi[6] Caesar pateretur, et tantum in agris vastandis incendiisque faciendis hostibus noceretur, quantum labore atque itinere[7] legionarii milites efficere poterant.

[1] **contentionis:** 'of a general engagement'. **amplioribus copiis:** 'the greater part of his forces'.
[2] **IIII:** *quattuor*. It is not possible to determine whether Caesar means that Cassivellaunus kept in the field 4000 chariot-drivers, each having a chariot and accompanied by a warrior (see IV, 33.1, note 2), making a force of 8000 men, or whether in *essedariorum* both drivers and warriors are included; in the latter case there would be 2000 chariots, each with two men, making a total of 4000 men.
[3] **se effuderat:** 'had dashed forth' **omnibus,** etc.: 'by all the roads and passage-ways', well known to the Britons; *134a*.
[4] **equitum:** *102*. **hoc metu:** 'from fear of this' danger.
[5] **vagari,** sc. *nostros*.
[6] **discedi:** i.e. *equitibus*, 'that (the cavalry) should leave', etc. **tantum – noceretur:** 'that so great harm be done'; how lit.?
[7] **labore atque itinere:** 'by toilsome marching'; *238d*.

The Trinovantes and other peoples submit. Caesar takes Cassivellaunus' stronghold.

20.1. Interim Trinovantes, prope firmissima earum regionum civitas, ex qua Mandubracius adulescens, Caesaris fidem secutus,[1] ad eum in continentem venerat (cuius pater in ea civitate regnum obtinuerat interfectusque erat a Cassivellauno, ipse fuga mortem vitaverat), legatos ad Caesarem mittunt pollicenturque, sese ei dedituros atque imperata facturos; **2.** petunt, ut Mandubracium ab iniuria Cassivellauni[2] defendat, atque in civitatem mittat, qui praesit imperiumque obtineat. **3.** His Caesar imperat obsides XL frumentumque exercitui Mandubraciumque ad eos mittit. **4.** Illi imperata celeriter fecerunt, obsides ad numerum frumentumque miserunt.

[1] **Caesaris fidem secutus:** 'attaching himself to Caesar'; how lit.?
[2] **Cassivellauni:** 'at the hands of Cassivellaunus'; *95*. **qui:** *193a*.

21.1. Trinovantibus defensis atque ab omni militum iniuria prohibitis, Cenimagni,[1] Segontiaci, Ancalites, Bibroci, Cassi, legationibus missis, sese Caesari dedunt. **2.** Ab his cognoscit, non longe ex eo loco[2] oppidum Cassivellauni abesse, silvis paludibusque munitum, quo satis magnus hominum pecorisque numerus convenerit. **3.** Oppidum[3] autem Britanni vocant, cum silvas impeditas vallo atque fossa munierunt, quo, incursionis hostium vitandae causa, convenire consuerunt. **4.** Eo proficiscitur cum legionibus. Locum reperit egregie natura atque opere munitum; tamen hunc duabus ex partibus oppugnare contendit. **5.** Hostes, paulisper morati, militum nostrorum impetum non tulerunt seseque alia ex parte oppidi eiecerunt. **6.** Magnus ibi numerus pecoris repertus, multique in fuga sunt comprehensi atque interfecti.

[1] **Cenimagni,** etc.: some of these small states are located on GALLIA.

[2] **eo loco**: where Caesar met the envoys. **oppidum:** 'the stronghold of Cassivellaunus' is thought to have been in the vicinity of St. Albans.

[3] **Oppidum vocant**: 'call (it) a stronghold'. Several fortified enclosures of extreme antiquity, intended not for permanent habitation but only for refuge and defence in time of danger, have been found in England.

An attack on the naval camp is repulsed. Cassivellaunus yields.

22.1. Dum haec in his locis[1] geruntur, Cassivellaunus ad Cantium, quod esse ad mare supra[2] demonstravimus, quibus regionibus IIII reges praeerant, Cingetorix, Carvilius, Taximagulus, Segovax, nuntios mittit atque his imperat, uti, coactis omnibus copiis, castra navalia[3] de improviso adoriantur atque oppugnent. **2.** Hi cum ad castra venissent, nostri, eruptione facta, multis eorum interfectis, capto etiam nobili duce Lugotorige,[4] suos incolumes reduxerunt. **3.** Cassivellaunus, hoc proelio nuntiato, tot detrimentis acceptis, vastatis finibus, maxime etiam permotus defectione civitatum, legatos per Atrebatem Commium de deditione ad Caesarem mittit. **4.** Caesar, cum constituisset hiemare in continenti propter repentinos Galliae motus, neque multum aestatis superesset, atque id[5] facile extrahi posse intellegeret, obsides imperat et, quid[6] in annos singulos vectigalis populo Romano Britannia penderet, constituit; **5.** interdicit[7] atque imperat Cassivellauno, ne Mandubracio neu Trinovantibus noceat.

[1] **in his locis:** in the region of St. Albans.

[2] **supra**: at the opening of chap. 14.

[3] **castra navalia**: see V, 11.5-6.

[4] **Lugotorige**: *10c.* **incolumes**: predicative.

[5] **id**, etc.: 'and that this could easily be wasted', lit. 'drawn out', in profitless negotiations.

[6] **quid – vectigalis**: *97b.* **in annos singulos**: 'each year'.

[7] **interdicit**, etc.: 'laid the strictest injunctions on Cassivellaunus'; how lit.? *175b.*

Caesar returns to the coast, finds ships ready, sails to Gaul.

23.1. Obsidibus acceptis, exercitum reducit ad mare, naves invenit refectas.[1] **2.** His deductis, quod et captivorum magnum numerum habebat et non nullae tempestate deperierant naves, duobus commeatibus[2] exercitum reportare instituit. **3.** Ac sic accidit, uti ex tanto navium numero tot navigationibus neque hoc neque superiore anno ulla omnino navis, quae milites portaret, desideraretur, **4.** at ex eis, quae inanes ex continenti ad eum remitterentur, et[3] prioris commeatus, expositis militibus, et quas postea Labienus faciendas curaverat, numero LX, perpaucae locum caperent,[4] reliquae fere omnes reicerentur. **5.** Quas[5] cum aliquamdiu Caesar frustra exspectasset, ne anni tempore a navigatione excluderetur, quod aequinoctium[6] suberat, necessario angustius[7] milites collocavit ac, summa tranquillitate consecuta, **6.** secunda inita cum solvisset vigilia, prima luce terram attigit omnesque incolumes naves perduxit.

[1] **refectas:** 'repaired'; cf. chapters 10 and 11. **deductis:** 'launched', lit. 'drawn down' to the water, from the fortified enclosure (*castra navalia*, V, 22.1) in which they had been guarded and repaired.
[2] **duobus commeatibus:** 'in two trips'; *136b.*
[3] **et,** etc.: 'both (the ships used) in the first trip, (sent back) after the soldiers had been landed, and (other ships) which'.
[4] **locum caperent:** 'reached their destination', Britain.
[5] **Quas:** 'these' ships, sent from the continent; *167.*
[6] **aequinoctium:** Caesar must have left Britain shortly after the middle of September, having been two months or more on the island.
[7] **necessario angustius:** 'of necessity rather closely'; *153a.*

DIVISION OF THE ARMY FOR THE WINTER. 24, 25

Grain being scarce, Caesar for the winter divides his army.

24.1. Subductis[1] navibus concilioque Gallorum Samarobrivae peracto, quod eo anno frumentum in Gallia, propter siccitates,[2] angustius provenerat, coactus est aliter ac superioribus annis exercitum in hibernis collocare legionesque in plures civitates distribuere. **2.** Ex quibus unam, in Morinos ducendam,[3] C. Fabio legato dedit, alteram in Nervios Q. Ciceroni, tertiam in Esuvios L. Roscio; quartam in Remis cum T. Labieno in confinio Treverorum[4] hiemare iussit; **3.** tres in Bellovacis collocavit: his M. Crassum[5] et L. Munatium Plancum et C. Trebonium legatos praefecit. **4.** Unam legionem, quam proxime trans Padum[6] conscripserat, et cohortes V in Eburones, quorum pars maxima est inter Mosam ac Rhenum, qui sub imperio Ambiorigis et Catuvolci erant, misit. **5.** His militibus Q. Titurium Sabinum et L. Aurunculeium Cottam legatos praeesse iussit. **6.** Ad hunc modum distributis legionibus, facillime inopiae[7] rei frumentariae sese mederi posse existimavit. **7.** Atque harum tamen omnium legionum hiberna praeter eam, quam L. Roscio in pacatissimam et quietissimam partem ducendam dederat, milibus passuum C[8] continebantur. **8.** Ipse interea, quoad legiones collocatas munitaque hiberna cognovisset, in Gallia morari constituit.

[1] **Subductis:** cf. V, 1.6-7. **Samarobrivae:** *4a.*
[2] **siccitates:** cf. IV, 38.2, note 2. **aliter ac:** *233c.*
[3] **ducendam,** etc.: 'to be led into the country of the Morini'; *229b.*
[4] **in confinio Treverorum:** 'on the Treveran frontier'. The site of Labienus's camp is indicated on Map 11.
[5] **M. Crassum:** quaestor; see Vocab. under *Crassus,* (3).
[6] **trans Padum:** north of the Po. in Cisalpine Gaul; Caesar writes from the point of view of one in Rome.
[7] **Inopiae – mederi:** 'to remedy the shortage'; *106b.*
[8] **C:** *centum.* Caesar perhaps means that no two camps were more than 100 Roman miles apart; if so, his estimate is somewhat under the truth; *81.*

Tasgetius murdered, Caesar transfers Plancus to the country of the Carnutes.

25.1. Erat in Carnutibus, summo loco natus,[1] Tasgetius, cuius maiores in sua civitate regnum obtinuerant. **2.** Huic Caesar pro eius virtute[2] atque in se benevolentia, quod in omnibus bellis singulari eius opera fuerat usus, maiorum locum restituerat. **3.** Tertium iam hunc annum regnantem, inimici palam, multis ex civitate auctoribus, interfecerunt. **4.** Defertur ea res ad Caesarem. Ille veritus, quod[3] ad plures pertinebat, ne civitas eorum impulsu deficeret, L. Plancum cum legione ex Belgio celeriter in Carnutes proficisci iubet ibique hiemare, quorumque opera cognoverat Tasgetium interfectum, hos comprehensos[4] ad se mittere. **5.** Interim ab omnibus legatis quaestoreque, quibus legiones tradiderat, certior factus est, in hiberna perventum locumque esse munitum.

[1] **summo loco natus:** 'of the highest rank by birth'; *128a.*
[2] **virtute:** 'efficiency'. **in se benevolentia:** 'loyalty to himself'; *150d.*
[3] **quod,** etc.: 'because a large number were implicated'; how lit.?
[4] **comprehensos,** etc.: 'to take into custody and send to him'; *228a.*

ATTACKS OF THE GAULS UPON CAESAR'S WINTER CAMPS

1. DESTRUCTION OF THE FORCE UNDER SABINUS AND COTTA BY AMBIORIX, 26-37

Ambiorix attacks the camp of Sabinus and Cotta, parleys.

26.1. Diebus[1] circiter XV, quibus in hiberna ventum est, initium repentini tumultus ac defectionis ortum est ab Ambiorige[2] et Catuvolco; **2.** qui cum ad fines regni sui Sabino Cottaeque praesto fuissent frumentumque in hiberna comportavissent, Indutiomari Treveri[3] nuntiis impulsi, suos concitaverunt, subitoque oppressis lignatoribus,[4] magna manu ad castra oppugnatum venerunt. **3.** Cum celeriter nostri arma cepissent vallumque[5] ascendissent, atque una ex parte, Hispanis equitibus emissis, equestri proelio superiores fuissent, desperata re, hostes suos ab oppugnatione reduxerunt. **4.** Tum suo more conclamaverunt, uti aliqui[6] ex nostris ad colloquium prodiret: *Habere sese, quae de re communi dicere vellent, quibus rebus controversias[7] minui posse sperarent.*

[1] **Diebus ... quibus:** ' About fifteen days after.'
[2] **Ambiorige et Catuvolco:** V. 24.4; *19d; 10c.* **Sabino,** etc.: 'had met Sabinus and Cotta', whom they came to meet at the Eburonian frontier (*ad fines regni sui*); how lit.?
[3] **Treveri:** genitive. **suos:** the Eburones.
[4] **lignatoribus:** 'wood foragers', soldiers detailed to get wood. **manu:** *137b.*
[5] **vallum:** the camp of Sabinus and Cotta was perhaps on the site of modern Limburg; see Map 11.
[6] **aliqui:** *49a.*
[7] **controversias:** 'the questions at issue'.

27.1. Mittitur ad eos colloquendi causa C. Arpineius, eques Romanus, familiaris Q. Titurii,[1] et Q. Iunius ex Hispania quidam, qui iam ante, missu Caesaris,[2] ad Ambiorigem ventitare consuerat; apud quos Ambiorix ad hunc modum locutus est: **2.** *Sese[3] pro Caesaris in se beneficiis plurimum ei confiteri debere, quod, eius opera, stipendio liberatus esset, quod Atuatucis, finitimis suis, pendere consuesset, quodque ei[4] et filius et fratris filius a Caesare remissi essent, quos Atuatuci, obsidum numero missos, apud se in servitute et catenis tenuissent;* **3.** *neque id, quod fecerit de oppugnatione castrorum, aut iudicio[5] aut voluntate sua fecisse, sed coactu civitatis, suaque esse eius modi imperia, ut non minus haberet iuris in se multitudo, quam ipse in multitudinem.* **4.** *Civitati porro hanc fuisse belli causam, quod repentinae Gallorum coniurationi resistere non potuerit. Id se facile ex humilitate sua probare posse, quod non adeo sit imperitus rerum, ut suis copiis populum Romanum superari posse confidat.* **5.**

Sed esse Galliae commune consilium; omnibus hibernis Caesaris oppugnandis hunc esse dictum diem, ne qua legio alteri legioni subsidio venire posset. **6.** *Non facile Gallos Gallis negare potuisse, praesertim cum de recuperanda communi libertate consilium initum[6] videretur.* **7.** *Quibus[7] quoniam pro pietate satisfecerit, habere nunc se rationem officii pro beneficiis Caesaris; monere, orare Titurium pro hospitio, ut suae ac militum saluti consulat.* **8.** *Magnam manum Germanorum conductam[8] Rhenum transisse; hanc affore biduo.* **9.** *Ipsorum[9] esse consilium, velintne prius quam finitimi sentiant, eductos ex hibernis milites aut ad Ciceronem, aut ad Labienum, deducere, quorum alter milia passuum circiter L, alter paulo amplius ab eis absit.* **10.** *Illud se polliceri et iure iurando confirmare, tutum se iter per suos fines daturum.* **11.** *Quod cum faciat,[10] et civitati sese consulere, quod hibernis levetur,[11] et Caesari pro eius meritis gratiam referre.* Hac oratione habita, discedit Ambiorix.

¹ **Q. Titurii:** Q. Titurius Sabinus, called *Sabinus* in V, 24.5, *a-c.*
² **missu Caesaris:** 'sent by Caesar'; how lit.?
³ **Sese,** etc.: *Sese confiteri, pro Caesaris beneficiis in se, (se) ei plurimum debere*; *213b.*
⁴ **ei:** for *sibi*, referring to Ambiorix.
⁵ **iudicio:** *138.* **coactu civitatis:** 'forced by his state'; how lit.? **suaque,** etc.: 'and that the conditions of his authority were such'.
⁶ **initum:** sc. *esse.*
⁷ **Quibus,** etc.: 'Since he had done his duty by them and by his country', in attacking the Roman camp. Duty to one's country is here expressed by *pietate.* How lit.? **habere,** etc.: 'he recognized (his) obligation'; how lit.?
⁸ **conductam:** i.e. *conductam mercede;* 'mercenaries'.
⁹ **Ipsorum esse consilium:** 'They (the Roman officers) were to decide'; how lit.? *94d.* **velintne:** *204.1.*
¹⁰ **Quod cum faciat:** 'in doing this'. **civitati:** *105.*
¹¹ **hibernis levetur:** 'it would be relieved of the winter encampment'; *127a; 335b.* **gratiam referre:** 'and would show his gratitude'. This wily and lying speech lured the Roman force to its destruction.

Cotta refuses to receive advice from Ambiorix, an enemy; Sabinus trusts him.

28.1. Arpineius et Iunius, quae audierunt, ad legatos deferunt. Illi, repentina re perturbati, etsi[1] ab hoste ea dicebantur, tamen non neglegenda existimabant, maximeque hac re permovebantur, quod civitatem ignobilem[2] atque humilem Eburonum sua sponte populo Romano bellum facere ausam[3] vix erat credendum. **2.** Itaque ad consilium rem deferunt, magnaque inter eos exsistit controversia. **3.** L. Aurunculeius compluresque tribuni militum et primorum ordinum centuriones[4] nihil temere agendum, neque ex hibernis iniussu Caesaris discedendum existimabant; **4.** quantasvis[5] Gallorum, magnas etiam copias Germanorum sustineri posse, munitis hibernis, docebant: **5.** *Rem esse testimonio, quod primum hostium impetum, multis ultro vulneribus illatis, fortissime sustinuerint; re[6] frumentaria non premi;* **6.** *interea et ex proximis hibernis et a Caesare conventura subsidia;* **7.** *postremo, quid esse[7] levius aut turpius, quam, auctore hoste,[8] de summis rebus capere consilium?*

¹ **etsi ... dicebantur:** implies Caesar's disapproval of the consideration afforded to Ambiorix's statement.
² **ignobilem:** 'obscure'.
³ **ausam [esse]:** *62.* **vix erat credendum:** 'was hardly credible'; how lit.?
⁴ **primorum ordinum centuriones:** cf. I, 41.3, note 5.

[5] **quantasvis:** *copias;* 'any force of Gauls', no matter how great.
[6] **re,** etc.: 'that there was no difficulty about supplies'; how lit.?
[7] **quid esse:** *217c.*
[8] **auctore hoste:** 'on the advice of an enemy'; *144b2.*

29.1. Contra ea Titurius *sero[1] facturos* clamitabat, *cum maiores manus hostium, adiunctis Germanis, convenissent, aut cum aliquid calamitatis in proximis hibernis esset acceptum.***2.** *Brevem consulendi esse occasionem. Caesarem, se arbitrari, profectum in Italiam;[2] neque aliter Carnutes interficiendi Tasgetii consilium fuisse capturos, neque Eburones, si[3] ille adesset, tanta contemptione nostri[4] ad castra venturos esse.* **3.** *Sese[5] non hostem auctorem, sed rem spectare: subesse Rhenum; magno esse Germanis dolori[6] Ariovisti mortem et superiores nostras victorias;[7]* **4.** *ardere Galliam, tot contumeliis acceptis, sub populi Romani imperium redactam, superiore gloria rei militaris exstincta.[8]* **5.** *Postremo, quis hoc sibi persuaderet, sine certa spe Ambiorigem ad[9] eius modi consilium descendisse ?* **6.** *Suam sententiam in utramque partem[10] esse tutam: si nihil esset durius, nullo cum periculo ad proximam legionem perventuros; si Gallia omnis cum Germanis consentiret, unam[11] esse in celeritate positam salutem.* **7.** *Cottae quidem atque eorum, qui dissentirent,[12] consilium quem habere exitum? in quo si non praesens periculum, at certe longinqua obsidione fames esset timenda.*

[1] **sero:** 'too late'. **facturos:** *se facturos esse.* **clamitabat:** 'kept protesting loudly'; *78a.*
[2] **Italiam:** *283b.* **interficiendi,** etc.: chap. 25.
[3] **si adesset . . . venturos esse:** *218.3.*
[4] **nostri:** *155.* **ad,** etc.: i.e. *castra oppugnaturos esse.*
[5] **Sese,** etc.: 'that he had regard not for the enemy as adviser, but for (the facts of) the situation'.
[6] **Germanis, dolori:** *112b.* **Ariovisti mortem:** nothing is known about the death of Ariovistus, who was last mentioned in Book I. chap 53.
[7] **victorias:** over Ariovistus (I, 30-54), the Usipetes and Tencteri (IV, 1-15), and the expedition into Germany in the previous year (IV, 16-19). **ardere:** 'was ablaze'.
[8] **exstincta:** 'obscured'. **quis,** etc.: *217a.*
[9] **ad . . . descendisse:** 'had resorted to'.
[10] **in utramque partem:** 'for either alternative.' **si . . . durius:** 'if nothing serious should happen'; how lit.?
[11] **unam — salutem:** 'their only safety'; *353 d.*
[12] **dissentirent:** 'disagreed with him'. **habere:** *217c.*

After heated argument Sabinus persuades Cotta to accept Ambiorix's guarantees of safety and leave the camp.

30.1. Hac in utramque partem[1] disputatione habita, cum a Cotta primisque ordinibus[2] acriter resisteretur, 'Vincite,'[3] inquit, 'si ita vultis,' Sabinus, et id clariore voce, ut magna pars militum exaudiret; **2.** 'neque is sum,' inquit, 'qui gravissime ex vobis[4] mortis periculo terrear. Hi sapient;[5] si gravius quid acciderit, abs te rationem reposcent; **3.** qui, si[6] per te liceat, perendino die, cum proximis hibernis coniuncti, communem cum reliquis belli casum sustineant, non, reiecti et relegati[7] longe a ceteris, aut ferro aut fame intereant.'

[1] **in utramque partem:** 'on both sides' **disputatione:** 'discussion'.
[2] **ordinibus:** = *centurionibus.* **acriter resisteretur:** ' vigorous opposition was still offered'.
[3] **Vincite:** 'Have your own way'. **et id:** *161c.* **clariore voce:** 'raising his voice'; how lit.?

⁴ **ex vobis:** *97d.* **terrear:** *194a.*
⁵ **Hi sapient:** 'These', the soldiers, spoken with a gesture, 'will understand'. **si,** etc.: *206.4.*
⁶ **si . . . liceat:** 'if you would consent'. **perendino die:** 'day after tomorrow.'
⁷ **relegati:** 'treated as outlaws'.

31.1. Consurgitur[1] ex consilio; comprehendunt utrumque et orant, ne sua dissensione[2] et pertinacia rem in summum periculum deducant; **2.** *facilem esse rem, seu maneant, seu proficiscantur, si modo unum omnes sentiant ac probent; contra in dissensione nullam se salutem perspicere.* **3.** Res disputatione ad mediam noctem perducitur. Tandem dat[3] Cotta, permotus, manus; superat sententia Sabini. **4.** Pronuntiatur, prima luce ituros. Consumitur vigiliis reliqua pars noctis, cum sua quisque miles circumspiceret, quid[4] secum portare posset, quid ex instrumento[5] hibernorum relinquere cogeretur. **5.** Omnia excogitantur, quare nec sine periculo maneatur et languore militum et vigiliis periculum augeatur. **6.** Prima luce sic ex castris proficiscuntur, ut[6] quibus esset persuasum, non ab hoste, sed ab homine amicissimo consilium datum, longissimo[7] agmine maximisque impedimentis.

¹ **Consurgitur:** 'all stood up'; how lit.? **comprehendunt:** by the hand. **utrumque:** Sabinus and Cotta.
² **dissensione:** 'disagreement'.
³ **dat – manus:** 'yielded'; Sabinus was the senior officer.
⁴ **quid:** '(to see) what'.
⁵ **instrumento:** 'outfit'. **Omnia,** etc.: 'Every reason was thought of (to prove to themselves) both why they could not remain without danger and (why) the danger would be increased by the exhaustion of the soldiers resulting from (unrelieved) watches'. How lit.?
⁶ **ut . . . persuasum:** 'like men convinced', i.e. *ut* ('as') *ei, quibus persuasum esset* (subjunctive of characteristic).
⁷ **longissimo,** etc.: with disregard of every precaution.

The Roman force, enticed into a defile, is treacherously attacked.

32.1. At hostes, postea quam ex nocturno fremitu vigiliisque de profectione eorum senserunt, collocatis insidiis bipertito[1] in silvis opportuno atque occulto loco a milibus passuum circiter duobus, Romanorum adventum exspectabant; **2.** et cum se[2] maior pars agminis in magnam convallem demisisset, ex utraque parte eius vallis subito se ostenderunt novissimosque[3] premere et primos prohibere ascensu atque, iniquissimo nostris loco, proelium committere coeperunt.

¹ **bipertito:** 'at two points', on opposite sides of a depression through which the road ran. **a:** 'off'; see II, 8.2, note 19.
² **se . . . demisisset:** 'had passed down'. **convallem:** 'defile'.
³ **novissimos,** etc.: the enemy crowded toward those in the rear and checked the advance of those in front.

33.1. Tum demum Titurius, qui[1] nihil ante providisset, trepidare[2] et concursare cohortesque disponere, haec tamen ipsa timide atque ut[3] eum omnia deficere viderentur; quod plerumque eis accidere consuevit, qui in ipso negotio[4] consilium capere coguntur. **2.** At Cotta, qui cogitasset, haec posse in itinere accidere, atque ob eam causam profectionis auctor[5] non fuisset, nulla in re communi saluti deerat; et in appellandis cohortandisque militibus imperatoris, et in pugna militis, officia praestabat. **3.** Cum propter longitudinem agminis non facile per se omnia obire[6] et, quid quoque loco faciendum esset, providere possent, iusserunt pronuntiari,[7] ut impedimenta relinquerent[8] atque in orbem consisterent. **4.** Quod consilium, etsi in eius modi casu reprehendendum non est,[9] tamen incommode accidit;[10] **5.** nam et nostris militibus spem minuit et hostes ad pugnam alacriores effecit, quod non sine[11] summo timore et desperatione id factum videbatur. **6.** Praeterea accidit, quod fieri necesse erat, ut vulgo milites ab signis discederent, quaeque quisque eorum carissima[12] haberet, ab impedimentis petere atque arripere properaret, clamore et fletu omnia complerentur.

[1] **qui**: 'since he'; *194c* (AG 535e, B 283.3a).

[2] **trepidare**: 'was greatly agitated'. *182*. **concursare**: 'rushed from place to place'.

[3] **ut**, etc.: '(in such a way) that all (his resources) seemed to fail him'. **quod**: *id, quod.*

[4] **in ipso negotio**: 'in the emergency'.

[5] **auctor**: 'in favour of'; how lit.?

[6] **omnia obire**: 'to look after everything'.

[7] **iusserunt pronuntiari**: 'they', Cotta and Sabinus, 'gave orders that the word be passed'.

[8] **relinquerent**: 'that (the men) should abandon.' **orbem**: 'circle', corresponding with our hollow square; *338*.

[9] **reprehendendum non est**: 'it is not to be criticized'.

[10] **incommode accidit**: 'turned out unfortunately'. **militibus**: *109a*.

[11] **non sine**: *239g*. **desperatione**: 'despair'.

[12] **carissima**: 'most dear', predicative; *petere ab impedimentis (ea) quae quisque carissima haberet.* **haberet**: *220*. **arripere**: 'carry off', before the enemy should loot the abandoned baggage.

34.1. At barbaris consilium[1] non defuit. Nam duces eorum tota acie pronuntiari iusserunt, ne quis ab loco discederet: *illorum esse praedam atque illis reservari, quaecumque Romani reliquissent; proinde omnia in victoria posita existimarent.* **2.** Erant et virtute et studio pugnandi pares nostri; tametsi ab duce et a fortuna deserebantur, tamen omnem spem salutis in virtute ponebant, et quotiens quaeque cohors procurrerat, ab ea parte magnus numerus hostium cadebat. **3.** Qua re animadversa Ambiorix pronuntiari iubet, ut procul tela coniciant[2] neu propius accedant et, quam in partem Romani impetum fecerint, cedant **4.** (levitate armorum et cotidiana exercitatione nihil[3] eis noceri posse), rursus se[4] ad signa recipientes insequantur.

[1] **consilium**: 'presence of mind', contrasted with the confusion and panic on the Roman side.

[2] **coniciant**: 'that (his men) hurl'.

[3] **nihil**, etc.: '(saying that) no harm could be done to them'.

[4] **se**: object of *recipientes*; '(the Romans) returning to their standards', to the place in the circle from which they had made a charge.

35.1. Quo praecepto[1] ab eis diligentissime observato, cum quaepiam[2] cohors ex orbe excesserat atque impetum fecerat, hostes velocissime refugiebant.[3] **2.** Interim eam partem nudari necesse erat et ab latere aperto[4] tela recipere. **3.** Rursus, cum in eum locum,[5] unde erant egressi, reverti coeperant, et ab eis, qui cesserant, et ab eis, qui proximi steterant, circumveniebantur; **4.** sin autem locum tenere[6] vellent, nec virtuti locus relinquebatur, neque ab tanta multitudine coniecta tela conferti vitare poterant. Tamen, tot incommodis conflictati,[7] multis vulneribus acceptis, resistebant, **5.** et magna parte diei consumpta, cum a prima luce ad horam octavam[8] pugnaretur, nihil, quod ipsis esset indignum, committebant. **6.** Tum T. Balventio,[9] qui superiore[10] anno primum pilum duxerat, viro forti et magnae auctoritatis,[11] utrumque femur tragula traicitur; **7.** Q. Lucanius, eiusdem ordinis,[12] fortissime pugnans, dum circumvento filio subvenit,[13] interficitur; **8.** L. Cotta legatus, omnes cohortes ordinesque[14] adhortans, in adversum os funda vulneratur.

[1] **praecepto:** 'order'. **eis:** *barbaris.*
[2] **quaepiam:** 'any'; *49a.*
[3] **refugiebant:** 'would rush back in flight'; *175d.* **eam partem:** the charging cohort.
[4] **ab latere aperto:** 'on the exposed side', the right side, unprotected by a shield; *126c.*
[5] **eum locum:** in the circle. **egressi,** etc.: sc. *milites.*
[6] **locum tenere:** in the circle, without charging.
[7] **conflictati:** 'although harassed'.
[8] **horam octavam:** *242a.* **pugnaretur:** *184a.* **ipsis indignum:** 'unworthy of them'; *142b.*
[9] **T. Balventio:** *109a.*
[10] **superiore,** etc.: Balventius had been the first centurion of the legion the year before; he was now serving probably as a veteran volunteer (*evocatus*); *316.*
[11] **auctoritatis:** 'influence'; *100a.* **femur:** 'thigh'; *18d.*
[12] **eiusdem ordinis:** 'of the same rank', a first centurion. **circumvento:** 'who had been surrounded'; *227a4.*
[13] **filio subvenit:** 'came to the rescue of his son'; *175b.*
[14] **ordines:** here 'centuries'. **in adversum os:** 'full in the face'. **funda:** by a sling-shot.

Sabinus and others surrender to Ambiorix, and are cut down.

36.1. His rebus permotus, Q. Titurius, cum procul Ambiorigem suos cohortantem[1] conspexisset, interpretem suum, Cn. Pompeium, ad eum mittit rogatum, ut sibi militibusque parcat.[2] **2.** Ille appellatus respondit: *Si velit secum colloqui, licere; sperare, a multitudine impetrari[3] posse, quod[4] ad militum salutem pertineat; ipsi vero nihil nocitum iri,[5] inque eam rem se suam fidem interponere.* **3.** Ille[6] cum Cotta saucio communicat, si videatur pugna ut excedant et cum Ambiorige una colloquantur; *sperare, ab eo de[7] sua ac militum salute impetrari posse.* Cotta se ad armatum hostem iturum negat, atque in eo perseverat.

[1] **cohortantem:** *228c.* **interpretem:** *10e.*
[2] **parcat:** 'to spare'; *199a.*
[3] **impetrari,** etc.: 'that the request might be granted, so far as the safety of the soldiers was concerned'.
[4] **quod:** the antecedent is implied in *impetrari; 194f.* **ipsi:** Titurius Sabinus. **vero:** *236a.*
[5] **nocitum iri:** future infinitive passive; 'that no harm should be done'; *54; 73d.*
[6] **Ille:** Titurius Sabinus. **videatur:** *204.4.*
[7] **de,** etc.: 'for their own safety and that of the soldiers'; *157d.*

Cotta dies heroically fighting. The soldiers spared by the day's slaughter end their own lives that night.

37.1. Sabinus, quos[1] in praesentia tribunos militum circum se habebat, et primorum ordinum centuriones, se sequi iubet et, cum propius Ambiorigem[2] accessisset, iussus arma abicere, imperatum facit suisque, ut idem faciant, imperat. **2.** Interim, dum de condicionibus inter se agunt longiorque consulto ab Ambiorige instituitur sermo,[3] paulatim circumventus interficitur. **3.** Tum vero suo more[4] 'Victoriam' conclamant atque ululatum tollunt impetuque in nostros facto ordines perturbant. **4.** Ibi L. Cotta pugnans interficitur cum maxima parte militum. Reliqui se in castra recipiunt, unde erant egressi. **5.** Ex quibus L. Petrosidius aquilifer,[5] cum magna multitudine hostium premeretur, aquilam intra vallum proiecit; **6.** ipse pro castris fortissime pugnans occiditur. Illi aegre ad[6] noctem oppugnationem sustinent; noctu ad unum omnes, desperata salute, se ipsi[7] interficiunt. **7.** Pauci, ex proelio elapsi, incertis itineribus per silvas ad T. Labienum legatum in hiberna perveniunt atque eum de rebus gestis certiorem faciunt.

[1] **quos tribunos:** *eos tribunos, quos.* **in praesentia:** 'at the time'
[2] **Ambiorigem:** *123b.*
[3] **sermo:** 'talk'; *12b.*
[4] **more:** *136c.* **ululatum:** 'yell', a kind of war whoop.
[5] **aquilifer:** 'eagle bearer'; *324b1.* **cum:** 'although.'
[6] **ad unum:** 'to a man'. They probably killed one another.
[7] **se ipsi:** *162c.* The number of Roman soldiers that perished was probably above 5000. We are told that when Caesar heard of this disaster he vowed that he would cut neither hair nor beard till he had wreaked vengeance on Ambiorix and the Eburones. Ambiorix is now regarded by some as **a** national hero, as a defender of his people's liberties against Roman aggression; a statue has been erected in his honour at Tongres.

2. HEROIC DEFENCE OF CICERO'S CAMP AGAINST THE NERVIANS. 38-45

A fierce attack, inspired by Ambiorix, is made on Cicero's camp.

38.1. Hac victoria sublatus, Ambiorix statim cum equitatu in Atuatucos, qui erant eius regno finitimi, proficiscitur; neque noctem neque diem intermittit, peditatumque sese subsequi iubet. **2.** Re[1] demonstrata Atuatucisque concitatis, postero die in Nervios pervenit hortaturque, ne[2] sui in perpetuum liberandi atque ulciscendi Romanos pro eis, quas acceperint, iniuriis occasionem dimittant; **3.** *interfectos esse legatos[3] duos magnamque partem exercitus interisse* demonstrat; **4.** *nihil[4] esse negotii, subito oppressam legionem, quae cum Cicerone hiemet, interfici;* se[5] ad eam rem profitetur adiutorem. Facile hac oratione Nerviis persuadet.

[1] **Re:** 'what had been done'. **concitatis:** 'stirred up'; *144b2.*
[2] **ne,** etc.: 'not to lose the chance'. **sui:** *154b.*
[3] **legatos duos:** Sabinus and Cotta. **magnam partem:** in reality about one fifth of Caesar's legionaries.
[4] **nihil,** etc.: 'that it would be no trouble suddenly to crush the legion . . . and destroy it'; how lit.? *97a; 228a.*
[5] **se,** etc.: 'he promised his cooperation'; how lit.? *115a.*

39.1. Itaque confestim dimissis nuntiis ad Ceutrones,[1] Grudios, Levacos, Pleumoxios, Geidumnos, qui omnes sub eorum[2] imperio sunt, quam maximas possunt manus, cogunt, et de improviso ad Ciceronis hiberna advolant, nondum ad eum fama de Titurii morte perlata. **2.** Huic[3] quoque accidit, quod fuit necesse, ut non nulli milites, qui lignationis[4] munitionisque causa in silvas discessissent, repentino equitum adventu interciperentur. **3.** His circumventis, magna manu Eburones, Nervii, Atuatuci atque horum omnium socii et clientes legionem oppugnare incipiunt. Nostri celeriter ad arma concurrunt, vallum conscendunt.[5] **4.** Aegre is dies sustentatur, quod omnem spem hostes in celeritate ponebant atque, hanc adepti victoriam,[6] in perpetuum se fore victores confidebant.

[1] **Ceutrones**, etc.: small Belgic peoples, clients of the Nervii.
[2] **eorum:** *Nerviorum.* **quam maximas:** *153c.*
[3] **Huic:** Cicero; the probable location of his camp is indicated on Map 11. **quod:** for *id, quod.*
[4] **lignationis,** etc.: 'to get timber for the fortification' of the camp; how lit.? **discessissent**: *220.*
[5] **vallum conscendunt:** they stood on the rampart, behind the palisades (*valli*); *333.*
[6] **hanc adepti victoriam:** = *si hanc victoriam adepti essent; 227a2.*

40.1. Mittuntur[1] ad Caesarem confestim a Cicerone litterae, magnis propositis praemiis, si pertulissent;[2] obsessis omnibus viis, missi[3] intercipiuntur. **2.** Noctu ex ea materia, quam munitionis causa comportaverant, turres[4] admodum CXX excitantur;[5] incredibili celeritate, quae deesse operi videbantur, perficiuntur. **3.** Hostes postero die, multo maioribus coactis copiis, castra oppugnant, fossam complent. Eadem ratione, qua pridie, a nostris resistitur. **4.** Hoc idem reliquis deinceps fit diebus. **5.** Nulla pars nocturni temporis ad laborem intermittitur; non aegris, non vulneratis[6] facultas quietis datur. **6.** Quaecumque ad proximi diei oppugnationem opus sunt, noctu comparantur; multae praeustae sudes,[7] magnus muralium pilorum numerus instituitur; turres contabulantur,[8] pinnae loricaeque ex cratibus attexuntur.[9] **7.** Ipse Cicero, cum[10] tenuissima valetudine esset, ne nocturnum quidem sibi tempus ad quietem relinquebat, ut ultro militum concursu ac vocibus sibi parcere cogeretur.

[1] **Mittuntur:** emphatic position; *353a.* **ad Caesarem:** at Samarobriva.
[2] **si pertulissent:** *si nuntii eas litteras pertulissent.*
[3] **missi:** 'those who had been sent'; *227a4.*
[4] **turres:** *333.* **admodum:** 'fully'. **CXX:** *centum viginti.* Unless the camp were larger than would seem to have been required for a single legion, the 120 towers must have been about 40 feet apart; if so, men on the towers could defend the short spaces between with any kind of missile. Ordinarily such towers were about 80 feet apart.
[5] **excitantur:** 'were erected'.
[6] **vulneratis:** *227a4.* **facultas quietis:** 'chance to rest'; how lit.? *10e.* **Quaecumque:** *50a.*
[7] **praeustae sudes:** 'stakes hardened at the ends by burning'; the stock of ordinary weapons had given out. **muralium pilorum:** 'of wall-pikes'; heavy pikes, to be hurled from the towers.
[8] **contabulantur:** 'were provided with floors'. **pinnae:** 'battlements'. **loricae ex cratibus:** 'breastworks of wattle', made by interweaving branches, and put up as screens to protect the soldiers in the towers; *98b; 150d.*
[9] **attexuntur:** 'were attached' (lit. 'woven') 'to the towers'.
[10] **cum:** *187.* **tenuissima valetudine:** 'in very delicate health'; *143a.*

The crafty parleying, which was Sabinus's undoing, has no effect on Cicero.

41.1. Tunc duces principesque Nerviorum, qui aliquem sermonis aditum[1] causamque amicitiae cum Cicerone habebant, colloqui sese velle dicunt. **2.** Facta potestate, eadem, quae Ambiorix cum Titurio egerat, commemorant: **3.** *Omnem Galliam esse in armis; Germanos Rhenum transisse; Caesaris reliquorumque hiberna oppugnari.* **4.** Addunt etiam de Sabini morte; Ambiorigem ostentant[2] fidei faciundae[3] causa. **5.** *Errare eos dicunt, si quicquam ab his[4] praesidii sperent, qui suis rebus diffidant; Sese tamen hoc esse[5]* *in Ciceronem populumque Romanum animo, ut nihil nisi hiberna recusent, atque hanc inveterascere consuetudinem[6] nolint;* **6.** *licere illis per se incolumibus ex hibernis discedere et, quascumque in partes velint, sine metu proficisci.* **7.** Cicero ad haec unum modo respondit: *Non esse consuetudinem populi Romani, accipere ab hoste armato[7] condicionem;* **8.** *si ab armis discedere velint, se adiutore utantur legatosque ad Caesarem mittant; sperare,[8] pro eius iustitia, quae petierint, impetraturos.*

[1] **sermonis aditum:** 'pretext for an interview'.

[2] **ostentant,** etc.: 'they pointed to Ambiorix in order to inspire credence'.

[3] **faciundae:** *64b.* **Errare:** 'were deluding themselves'. **eos:** Cicero and his men. **quicquam praesidii:** 'any help at all'; *49a.*

[4] **his:** the Romans in the other camps. **qui,** etc.: 'who were in desperate straits'; how lit.? *62; 135a.*

[5] **hoc esse – animo:** 'had this feeling'; how lit.? *143b.*

[6] **consuetudinem:** 'custom' of imposing winter camps upon them. **per se:** 'so far as they', the Nervii, 'were concerned'.

[7] **armato:** 'in arms'. **ab armis discedere:** in our idiom, 'to lay down their arms'. **se,** etc.: 'they might utilize him as mediator'; *131f.*

[8] **sperare:** sc. *se,* Cicero.

The Nervians besiege the camp. Fire rages among the huts.

42.1. Ab hac spe[1] repulsi, Nervii vallo pedum X et fossa pedum[2] XV hiberna cingunt. **2.** Haec et superiorum annorum consuetudine a nobis cognoverant et, quosdam de exercitu nacti captivos, ab his docebantur; **3.** sed nulla[3] ferramentorum copia, quae esset[4] ad hunc usum idonea, gladiis caespites circumcidere,[5] manibus sagulisque terram exhaurire cogebantur. **4.** Qua quidem ex re hominum multitudo cognosci potuit; nam minus horis tribus milium passuum III in circuitu munitionem perfecerunt. **5.** Reliquis diebus turres[6] ad altitudinem valli, falces[7] testudinesque, quas idem captivi docuerant, parare ac facere coeperunt.

[1] **spe:** 'hope' of deceitfully coaxing Cicero. **pedem X:** in height.

[2] **pedum XV:** in width, at the top; *100a.*

[3] **nulla,** etc.: 'having no stock of iron tools'; *144b3.*

[4] **esset:** *194a.* **caespites:** *10d.*

[5] **circumcidere:** 'cut'; lit. 'cut around'. **sagulis:** 'in their cloaks'; *348; 131a.* **exhaurire:** 'to take out'.

[6] **turres:** movable 'towers'. **ad:** 'proportioned to'.

[7] **falces:** large 'hooks' for pulling down the palisade. **testudines:** 'turtle-shell sheds', probably less solid than those built by the Romans; *342a.*

43.1. Septimo oppugnationis die, maximo coorto vento, ferventes[1] fusili ex argilla glandes fundis et fervefacta iacula in casas,[2] quae more Gallico stramentis erant tectae, iacere coeperunt. **2.** Hae celeriter ignem comprehenderunt et venti magnitudine[3] in omnem locum castrorum distulerunt. **3.** Hostes maximo clamore, sicuti[4] parta iam atque explorata victoria, turres testudinesque agere[5] et scalis vallum ascendere coeperunt. **4.** At[6] tanta militum virtus atque ea praesentia animi fuit ut, cum[7] undique flamma torrerentur maximaque telorum multitudine premerentur, suaque omnia impedimenta atque omnes fortunas conflagrare[8] intellegerent, non modo demigrandi causa[9] de vallo decederet nemo, sed paene ne respiceret quidem quisquam, ac tum[10] omnes acerrime fortissimeque pugnarent. **5.** Hic dies nostris longe gravissimus fuit; sed tamen hunc habuit eventum, ut eo die maximus numerus hostium vulneraretur atque interficeretur, ut[11] se sub ipso vallo constipaverant recessumque[12] primis ultimi non dabant. **6.** Paulum quidem intermissa flamma,[13] et quodam loco turri adacta. et contingente vallum, tertiae cohortis centuriones ex eo, quo stabant, loco recesserunt[14] suosque omnes removerunt, nutu vocibusque hostes, si[15] introire vellent, vocare coeperunt; quorum progredi ausus est nemo. **7.** Tum ex omni parte lapidibus[16] coniectis deturbati, turrisque succensa est.

[1] **ferventes**, etc.: 'red-hot balls of kneaded clay', which would not crack to pieces when heated. Experiments have shown that red-hot balls of clay the size of one's fist when thrown will retain their heat long enough to ignite straw; 98b. **fervefacta iacula**: 'burning javelins'.
[2] **casas**: 'huts'; 335b. **stramentis**: 'with thatch'.
[3] **venti magnitudine**: 'by reason of the force of the wind'. **distulerunt**: *hae casae ignem distulerunt*, the huts being looked upon as agents. Probably the high wind carried bits of burning thatch all over the camp; 239h.
[4] **sicuti**: 'just as if'.
[5] **agere**: 'to move up'. The Gauls were using Roman methods of attack; 342a, b. **scalis**: 'with scaling-ladders'; 342d.
[6] **At**: 236a. **ea praesentia animi**: 'such their presence of mind'.
[7] **cum**: 187. **flamma torrerentur**: 'they were being scorched by the flames'; 92b.
[8] **conflagrare**: 'were on fire'.
[9] **demigrandi causa**: 'in order to withdraw' temporarily to rescue his valuables or get a brief respite. **paene**, etc.: 'but hardly any one even looked around'.
[10] **tum**: emphatic, 'then', above all other times.
[11] **ut**: 'since'. **sub**, etc.: 'had crowded together close up to the rampart'.
[12] **recessum . . . dabant**: 'those behind would not give those in front a chance to draw back'.
[13] **intermissa flamma**: the Gauls dared not risk moving forward the wooden towers while the flames were at their height. **loco**: 145c.
[14] **recesserunt**: 'drew back'.
[15] **si**: 204.4. **introire**: 'to come inside'.
[16] **lapidibus**: the supply of ordinary weapons had given out. Practice in hurling the pike enabled Roman soldiers to throw stones effectively. Both pike-hurling and stone-throwing find a parallel in the throwing of hand grenades in modern wars. **deturbati**: sc. *sunt*; 'they were forced back in disorder'.

Brave deeds of two rival centurions, Pullo and Vorenus.

44.1. Erant[1] in ea legione fortissimi viri, centuriones, qui primis ordinibus appropinquarent, T. Pullo et L. Vorenus. **2.** Hi perpetuas inter se controversias habebant, uter alteri anteferretur,[2] omnibusque annis de loco summis simultatibus contendebant. **3.** Ex his Pullo, cum acerrime[3] ad munitiones pugnaretur, 'Quid[4] dubitas,' inquit, 'Vorene? aut quem locum tuae probandae virtutis exspectas? hic dies de nostris controversiis iudicabit.' **4.** Haec cum dixisset, procedit extra munitiones, quaeque pars hostium confertissima est visa, in eam[5] irrumpit. **5.** Ne Vorenus quidem sese tum vallo continet, sed, omnium veritus existimationem, subsequitur. **6.** Mediocri spatio relicto,[6] Pullo pilum in hostes immittit atque unum ex multitudine procurrentem traicit; quo[7] percusso et exanimato, hunc scutis protegunt[8] hostes, in illum universi tela coniciunt neque dant progrediendi facultatem. **7.** Transfigitur scutum Pulloni[9] et verutum in balteo defigitur. **8.** Avertit hic casus vaginam[10] et gladium educere conanti dextram moratur manum, impeditumque[11] hostes circumsistunt. **9.** Succurrit[12] inimicus illi Vorenus et laboranti subvenit. **10.** Ad hunc se confestim a Pullone omnis multitudo convertit; **11.** illum veruto transfixum arbitrantur. Vorenus gladio rem comminus gerit[13] atque, uno interfecto, reliquos paulum propellit; dum cupidius instat, in[14] locum deiectus inferiorem concidit. **12.** Huic rursus circumvento subsidium fert Pullo, atque ambo[15] incolumes, compluribus interfectis, summa cum laude sese intra munitiones recipiunt. **13.** Sic fortuna in contentione et certamine[16] utrumque versavit, ut alter alteri[17] inimicus auxilio salutique esset, neque diiudicari[18] posset, uter utri virtute anteferendus videretur.

[1] **Erant:** *90a.* **qui,** etc.: 'who were nearing the first rank', the position of centurion of first rank; *194a; 315a.*

[2] **anteferretur,** etc.: 'should have the preference over the other', as the better man; *69b; 204.3.* **omnibus annis:** 'year in year out'. **de loco:** 'for advancement.' **summis simultatibus:** 'with the utmost bitterness'.

[3] **acerrime – pugnaretur:** 'the fighting was the very hottest'.

[4] **Quid:** 'Why'; *118e.* **locum:** 'opportunity'.

[5] **eam:** *eam partem; 165c.* **irrumpit:** 'he rushed'.

[6] **Mediocri spatio relicto:** 'At a moderate distance', perhaps four or five rods from the enemy.

[7] **quo:** refers to the wounded Gaul, who, as *protegunt* implies, was not killed; trans. as if *et hoc,* 'and since he was made breathless by the blow'; how lit.?

[8] **protegunt:** 'protected'. **illum:** Pullo.

[9] **Pulloni:** *109a.* **verutum:** the same 'dart' that pierced Pullo's shield. **balteo:** 'sword-belt'; *322e.*

[10] **vaginam:** 'scabbard'. **conanti:** sc. *ei,* 'as he' (lit. 'to him') 'was attempting'.

[11] **impeditum:** sc. *eum.*

[12] **Succurrit illi:** 'ran to his rescue'; how lit.? **inimicus:** 'adversary'.

[13] **rem comminus gerit:** 'engaged in close fighting'; *175b.*

[14] **in,** etc.: 'stumbling' (lit. 'thrown down') 'into a hollow'.

[15] **ambo:** 'both'; *37c.*

[16] **contentione et certamine:** 'in contest and combat'. **utrumque versavit:** 'shifted (the positions of) both'.

[17] **alter alteri:** *171b.* **alteri, auxilio:** *112b.*

[18] **diiudicari:** 'be determined'. **utri:** 'to the other'; *23a; 107a.* **virtute,** etc.: 'should seem worthy to be considered superior in point of valour'; *142a.*

Word of Cicero's desperate plight finally reaches Caesar.

45.1. Quanto[1] erat in dies gravior atque asperior oppugnatio, et maxime quod,[2] magna parte militum confecta vulneribus, res ad paucitatem defensorum pervenerat, tanto crebriores litterae nuntiique ad Caesarem mittebantur; quorum pars, deprehensa,[3] in conspectu nostrorum militum cum cruciatu necabatur. **2.** Erat unus[4] intus Nervius, nomine Vertico, loco natus honesto, qui a prima obsidione[5] ad Ciceronem perfugerat suamque ei fidem praestiterat. **3.** Hic servo spe libertatis magnisque persuadet praemiis, ut litteras ad Caesarem deferat. **4.** Has ille in iaculo illigatas[6] effert et, Gallus inter Gallos sine ulla suspicione versatus, ad Caesarem pervenit. **5.** Ab eo[7] de periculis Ciceronis legionisque cognoscitur.

[1] **Quanto,** etc.: 'The harder and more violent – the more frequently dispatches'; how lit.? *140* (AG 414a, B 223). **in dies:** 'day by day'.

[2] **maxime quod:** 'chiefly because'. **confecta:** 'enfeebled'.

[3] **deprehensa:** 'caught'.

[4] **unus:** 'one', the only Nervian. **intus:** in the camp. **loco,** etc.: 'of good family'; *128a.*

[5] **a prima obsidione:** 'soon after the beginning of the siege'; *152a.*
[6] **in iaculo illigatas:** 'tied in a javelin'. The javelin may have been split; the dispatch, written on papyrus, may have been put between the parts, the javelin then being tied with cords as if accidentally split and repaired. **inter Gallos versatus:** 'mingling with Gauls'.
[7] **Ab eo – cognoscitur:** *Caesar ab eo cognoscit.*

3. CRUSHING DEFEAT OF THE BESIEGING GAULS BY CAESAR. 46-52

Caesar makes hurried preparations, and proceeds by forced marches to relieve Cicero.

46.1. Caesar,[1] acceptis litteris hora circiter undecima diei, statim nuntium in Bellovacos ad M. Crassum quaestorem mittit, cuius hiberna aberant ab eo milia passuum XXV; **2.** iubet media nocte legionem proficisci celeriterque ad se venire. **3.** Exit cum nuntio Crassus. Alterum[2] ad C. Fabium legatum mittit, ut[3] in Atrebatium fines legionem adducat, qua sibi iter faciendum sciebat. **4.** Scribit Labieno, si rei publicae commodo[4] facere posset, cum legione ad fines Nerviorum veniat.[5] **5.** Reliquam partem exercitus, quod paulo aberat longius, non putat exspectandam; equites circiter CCCC ex proximis hibernis cogit.

[1] **Caesar:** at Samarobriva. **hora undecima:** about 5 p.m.; it was now early autumn; *242a,b.*
[2] **Alterum:** sc. *nuntium.* **C. Fabium:** V, 24.2.
[3] **ut:** '(directing him) to'; *199a.* Caesar would have to march through the country of the Atrebatians in order to reach Cicero's camp, in the country of the Nervians. See Map 11.
[4] **rei publicae commodo:** 'consistently with the public interest'; *138.*
[5] **veniat:** *216.* **Reliquam partem exercitus:** V, 24.2-3.

47.1. Hora circiter tertia ab antecursoribus[1] de Crassi adventu certior factus, eo die milia passuum XX procedit. **2.** Crassum[2] Samarobrivae praeficit legionemque ei attribuit, quod ibi impedimenta[3] exercitus, obsides civitatum, litteras publicas frumentumque omne, quod eo, tolerandae hiemis causa, devexerat, relinquebat. **3.** Fabius, ut imperatum erat, non ita[4] multum moratus, in itinere cum legione occurrit. **4.** Labienus, interitu Sabini et caede cohortium cognita, cum omnes ad eum Treverorum copiae venissent, veritus ne, si ex hibernis fugae similem profectionem fecisset, hostium impetum sustinere non posset, **5.** praesertim quos[5] recenti victoria efferri sciret, litteras Caesari remittit, quanto[6] cum periculo legionem ex hibernis educturus esset; rem gestam[7] in Eburonibus perscribit; docet, omnes equitatus peditatusque copias Treverorum III milia passuum longe ab suis castris consedisse.

[1] **antecursoribus:** 'advance guard' of Crassus.
[2] **Crassum,** etc.: Caesar left Samarobriva before Crassus arrived.
[3] **impedimenta:** *311.* **litteras publicas:** 'state documents', such as dispatches and accounts.
[4] **non ita,** etc.: 'with very little delay'; how lit.? **occurrit:** sc. *Caesari.*
[5] **praesertim quos,** etc: 'especially since he knew that they'; *184b.*
[6] **quanto,** etc.: '(explaining) how dangerous it would be for him to withdraw the legion'; how lit.? *204.3.*
[7] **rem gestam:** 'what had taken place', referring to the destruction of the force under Sabinus and Cotta.

48.1. Caesar, consilio eius probato, etsi opinione[1] trium legionum deiectus ad duas redierat, tamen unum communis salutis auxilium in celeritate ponebat. **2.** Venit magnis itineribus[2] in Nerviorum fines. Ibi ex captivis cognoscit, quae apud Ciceronem gerantur, quantoque in periculo res sit. **3.** Tum cuidam ex equitibus Gallis magnis praemiis persuadet, uti ad Ciceronem epistulam[3] deferat. **4.** Hanc Graecis[4] conscriptam litteris mittit, ne, intercepta epistula, nostra ab hostibus consilia cognoscantur. **5.** Si adire[5] non possit, monet, ut tragulam cum epistula ad ammentum deligata intra munitionem castrorum abiciat. **6.** In litteris scribit, se cum legionibus profectum celeriter affore; hortatur, ut pristinam virtutem retineat. **7.** Gallus, periculum veritus, ut erat praeceptum, tragulam mittit. **8.** Haec casu ad turrim[6] adhaesit, neque a nostris biduo animadversa, tertio die a quodam milite conspicitur, dempta[7] ad Ciceronem defertur. **9.** Ille perlectam[8] in conventu militum recitat maximaque omnes laetitia afficit.[9] **10.** Tum fumi incendiorum procul videbantur; quae res omnem dubitationem adventus legionum expulit.

[1] **opinione,** etc.: 'disappointed in his expectation of (having) three legions he had been reduced to two', the legion which he had had at Samarobriva, and the one under Fabius that had joined him.
[2] **magnis itineribus:** *329.*
[3] **epistulam:** 'letter'.
[4] **Graecis litteris:** in Greek characters, not Greek words; some of the Nervians apparently could read Latin.
[5] **adire:** 'to reach' the camp. **ammentum:** 'thong' attached to a javelin and used in throwing.
[6] **turrim:** *14b.* **adhaesit. neque:** 'and not'.
[7] **dempta:** 'was taken down and'; *228a.*
[8] **perlectam – recitat:** sc. *eam;* 'after he had read it through he read it aloud'; *227a.*
[9] **afficit:** 'filled'. **fumi incendiorum:** of burning villages, set on fire as Caesar's relieving force passed through; the plural implies more than one fire.

Caesar approaching, the Gauls turn from Cicero's camp to attack him.

49.1. Galli, re[1] cognita per exploratores, obsidionem relinquunt, ad Caesarem omnibus copiis contendunt. Haec erant armata circiter milia LX. **2.** Cicero, data facultate, Gallum[2] ab eodem Verticone, quem supra[3] demonstravimus, repetit, qui litteras ad Caesarem deferat; hunc[4] admonet, iter caute diligenterque faciat; **3.** perscribit in litteris, hostes ab se discessisse omnemque ad eum multitudinem convertisse. **4.** Quibus litteris circiter media nocte Caesar allatis suos facit certiores eosque ad dimicandum animo confirmat. **5.** Postero die, luce prima, movet castra; et circiter milia passuum IIII progressus, trans vallem magnam et rivum[5] multitudinem hostium conspicatur. **6.** Erat[6] magni periculi res, tantulis copiis iniquo loco dimicare; tum, quoniam obsidione liberatum Ciceronem sciebat, aequo[7] animo remittendum de celeritate existimabat. **7.** Consedit et, quam aequissimo potest loco, castra communit, atque haec,[8] etsi erant exigua per se, vix[9] hominum milium VII, praesertim nullis cum impedimentis, tamen angustiis[10] viarum, quam maxime potest, contrahit, eo consilio,[11] ut in summam contemptionem hostibus veniat. **8.** Interim, speculatoribus in omnes partes dimissis, explorat, quo commodissime itinere vallem transire possit.

[1] **re:** 'the fact' of Caesar's approach. **per:** *123a.*
[2] **Gallum,** etc.: 'asked the same Vertico . . . for another Gaul'; *116b.*

³ **supra:** V, 45.2. **qui,** etc.: *193a.*
⁴ **hunc,** etc.: 'warned him' (Caesar) 'to proceed with caution'; *200a.*
⁵ **rivum:** 'brook', flowing in a 'wide valley'.
⁶ **Erat,** etc.: 'It was extremely hazardous'; how lit.?
⁷ **aequo,** etc.: 'that without anxiety he could slacken his pace'; how lit.?
⁸ **haec:** object of *contrahit*; 'this' camp, 'although it was', etc.
⁹ **vix,** etc.: '(containing) barely 7000 men'; the two legions with Caesar averaged hardly 3500
men each; *100b; 307b.*
¹⁰ **angustiis,** etc.: 'by making the passages as narrow as possible'; *334b.*
¹¹ **consilio:** *138.* **hostibus:** trans. as if *hostium; 109a.*

Caesar, encamped, pretends fear, lures the Gauls on, routs them.

50.1. Eo die, parvulis equestribus proeliis ad aquam¹ factis, utrique sese
suo loco continent: **2.** Galli, quod ampliores copias, quae nondum
convenerant, exspectabant; **3.** Caesar,² si forte timoris simulatione hostes
in suum locum³ elicere posset, ut citra vallem pro castris proelio
contenderet; si id efficere non posset, ut, exploratis itineribus, minore cum
periculo vallem rivumque transiret. **4.** Prima luce hostium equitatus ad
castra accedit proeliumque cum nostris equitibus committit. **5.** Caesar
consulto equites cedere seque in castra recipere iubet; simul ex omnibus
partibus castra altiore vallo muniri portasque obstrui⁴ atque in his
administrandis rebus quam maxime concursari⁵ et cum simulatione agi
timoris iubet.

¹ **ad aquam:** 'by the water', the brook mentioned in V, 49.5.
² **Caesar,** etc.: *Caesar [se continet suo loco] ut, si . . . posset, citra vallem . . . contenderet.*
³ **suum locum:** 'a position favourable to himself'; *157e.* **elicere:** 'to entice'.
⁴ **obstrui:** 'be blocked up'.
⁵ **concursari:** 'that the men rush about'; *73d.* **agi:** 'go through their motions'; how lit.?

51.1. Quibus omnibus rebus hostes invitati copias traducunt¹ aciemque
iniquo loco constituunt; nostris vero etiam de vallo deductis, propius
accedunt et tela intra munitionem ex omnibus partibus coniciunt **2.**
praeconibusque² circummissis pronuntiari iubent: *Seu quis, Gallus seu
Romanus, velit ante horam tertiam ad se transire, sine periculo licere; post id
tempus non fore potestatem.***3.** Ac sic nostros contempserunt, ut, obstructis in
speciem³ portis singulis ordinibus caespitum, quod ea⁴ non posse
introrumpere videbantur, alii vallum manu scindere, alii fossas complere
inciperent.**4.** Tum Caesar, omnibus portis eruptione facta equitatuque
emisso, celeriter hostes in fugam dat, sic uti omnino⁵ pugnandi causa
resisteret nemo, magnumque ex eis numerum occidit atque omnes armis
exuit.

¹ **copias traducunt:** *copias rivum traducunt; 114a.*
² **praeconibus,** etc.: 'they sent criers around' the camp, 'directing that the announcement be
made'; how lit.?
³ **in speciem:** 'for show'. The barriers in the gates, of turf and only the breadth of a sod in
thickness, seemed solid but were easily pushed over from the inside.
⁴ **ea — introrumpere:** 'to break in that way', through the gates.
⁵ **omnino – nemo:** 'no one at all'.

Caesar, joining Cicero, praises him and his men.

52.1. Longius prosequi veritus, quod silvae paludesque intercedebant neque[1] etiam parvulo detrimento illorum locum relinqui videbat, omnibus suis incolumibus eodem die ad Ciceronem pervenit. **2.** Institutas turres,[2] testudines munitionesque hostium admiratur; producta[3] legione, cognoscit, non decimum quemque esse reliquum militem sine vulnere; **3.** ex his omnibus iudicat rebus, quanto cum periculo et quanta cum virtute res[4] sint administratae. **4.** Ciceronem pro eius merito legionemque collaudat; centuriones singillatim tribunosque militum appellat,[5] quorum egregiam fuisse virtutem testimonio Ciceronis cognoverat. De casu Sabini et Cottae certius[6] ex captivis cognoscit. **5.** Postero die, contione[7] habita, rem gestam proponit, milites consolatur et confirmat; **6.** quod detrimentum[8] culpa et temeritate legati sit acceptum, hoc[9] aequiore animo ferundum docet, quod, beneficio deorum immortalium et virtute eorum expiato[10] incommodo, neque hostibus diutina laetitia neque ipsis longior dolor relinquatur.

[1] **neque ... relinqui**: 'and that no opportunity was left for (inflicting) even a trifling loss upon them'; how lit.?
[2] **turres,** etc.: V, 42.5, notes 6-7.
[3] **producta**: 'drawn up' for review. **non,** etc.: 'that not one soldier in ten had escaped unwounded'; how lit.? *170a.*
[4] **res,** etc.: 'the operations' for defence 'were handled'. **eius merito:** Cicero's heroic defence is famous in military annals.
[5] **appellat**: 'he addressed' in complimentary terms.
[6] **certius**: an earlier report had come from Labienus (chap. 37).
[7] **contione**: 'an assembly'. **rem,** etc.: 'set forth what had happened'.
[8] **quod detrimentum:** *id detrimentum, quod.* **culpa et temeritate:** 'through the culpable rashness'; *238d.*
[9] **hoc**: 'on this account'. **aequiore animo:** 'with the greater tranquillity'.
[10] **expiato:** 'atoned for'.

4. Labienus defends his camp from, then routs, Indutiomarus and the Treverans. 53-58

A proposed attack on Labienus is abandoned; but almost all Gaul is stirred up.

53.1. Interim ad Labienum per Remos[1] incredibili celeritate de victoria Caesaris fama perfertur, ut, cum ab hibernis Ciceronis milia passuum abesset[2] circiter LX, eoque post horam nonam diei Caesar pervenisset, ante mediam noctem[3] ad portas castrorum clamor oreretur, quo clamore significatio victoriae gratulatioque ab Remis Labieno fieret. **2.** Hac fama ad Treveros perlata, Indutiomarus,[4] qui postero die castra Labieni oppugnare decreverat, noctu profugit copiasque omnes in Treveros reducit.[5] **3.** Caesar Fabium[6] cum sua legione remittit in hiberna, ipse cum tribus legionibus[7] circum Samarobrivam trinis hibernis hiemare constituit et, quod tanti motus Galliae exstiterant, totam hiemem ipse ad exercitum manere decrevit. **4.** Nam, illo incommodo de Sabini morte perlato, omnes fere Galliae civitates de bello consultabant, nuntios legationesque in omnes partes dimittebant et, quid[8] reliqui consili caperent atque unde initium belli fieret, explorabant[9] nocturnaque in locis desertis concilia habebant. **5.** Neque ullum fere totius hiemis tempus sine sollicitudine Caesaris intercessit, quin[10] aliquem de consiliis ac motu Gallorum nuntium acciperet. **6.** In his[11] ab L. Roscio, quem legioni tertiae decimae praefecerat, certior factus est, magnas Gallorum copias earum civitatum, quae Aremoricae appellantur, oppugnandi sui[12] causa convenisse **7.** neque longius milia passuum octo ab hibernis suis afuisse, sed nuntio allato de victoria Caesaris discessisse, adeo ut fugae similis discessus videretur.

[1] **per Remos:** 'through the (country of the) Remi', on the border of which the camp of Labienus was situated.

[2] **abesset:** sc. *Labienus* (AG 326, B 309.3). **eo:** to Cicero's camp.

[3] **ante mediam noctem:** from the ninth hour (about 2.00 P.M., for it was now autumn) to midnight would be about ten hours. The way that messages were transmitted so rapidly is explained in VII, 3.2-3.

[4] **Indutiomarus:** he had prompted the attack on Titurius Sabinus and Cotta; see V, 26.2.

[5] **reducit, remittit:** force of *re-*?

[6] **Fabium:** he had left his winter-quarters among the Morini (V, 24.2), to go with Caesar to the relief of Cicero (V, 47.3).

[7] **tribus legionibus:** Caesar now had the legion of Cicero with him, in addition to the two legions mentioned in V, 48.1. **trinis:** why is the distributive numeral used instead of the cardinal? (AG 137b, B. 81.4b).

[8] **reliqui:** sc. *Galli*; nominative.

[9] **explorabant:** 'were trying to find out'.

[10] **quin – acciperet:** 'without his receiving'.

[11] **In his** [nuntiis]: we should say 'among others'. **L. Roscio:** see V, 24.7 and Map.

[12] **sui:** refers not to the subject, but to the agent, *L. Roscio*. **milia:** (AG 407c, B 217.3).

54.1. At Caesar, principibus cuiusque civitatis ad se evocatis, alias territando, cum se scire, quae fierent, denuntiaret, alias[1] cohortando magnam partem Galliae in officio[2] tenuit. **2.** Tamen Senones, quae est civitas in primis firma et magnae inter Gallos auctoritatis, Cavarinum, quem Caesar apud eos regem constituerat, cuius frater Moritasgus[3] adventu[4] in Galliam Caesaris, cuiusque maiores regnum obtinuerant, interficere publico consilio[5] conati, cum ille praesensisset ac profugisset, usque ad fines insecuti regno domoque expulerunt **3.** et, missis ad Caesarem satis faciendi causa legatis, cum is omnem[6] ad se senatum venire iussisset, dicto audientes[7] non fuerunt. **4.** Tantum[8] apud homines barbaros valuit, esse aliquos repertos principes[9] belli inferendi, tantamque omnibus voluntatum commutationem attulit, ut praeter Aeduos et Remos, quos praecipuo semper honoure Caesar habuit, alteros[10] pro vetere ac perpetua erga populum Romanum fide, alteros pro recentibus Gallici belli[11] officiis, nulla fere civitas fuerit non suspecta nobis.[12] **5.** Idque adeo haud scio mirandumne sit, cum compluribus aliis de causis, tum maxime, quod ei, qui virtute belli omnibus gentibus praeferebantur, tantum se eius opinionis[13] deperdidisse, ut a populo Romans imperia perferrent, gravissime dolebant.

[1] **alias – alias:** see Vocab. **cum . . . denuntiaret:** causal, 'giving them to understand'; *denuntio* is used of an important, solemn, or threatening announcement.

[2] **in officio:** 'in allegiance'.

[3] **frater Moritasgus:** sc. *regnum obtinebat*.

[4] **adventu:** abl. of time. **in Galliam:** why not *in Gallia*?

[5] **publico consilio:** through the decision of some tribunal that tried those guilty of crimes against the state.

[6] **omnem:** 'as a body'. **senatum:** a council consisting of the chief men of the state, to whom Caesar applies the name of the corresponding body at Rome.

[7] **dicto audientes:** see I, 39.7, note 27.

[8] **Tantum – valuit:** 'so great influence had the fact', etc. The subject of *valuit* is the following infinitive clause.

[9] **principes,** etc.: 'the leaders in making war', thus setting an example for the rest.

[10] **alteros – alteros:** 'the one people – the other'.

[11] **Gallici belli:** 'in the Gallic war'.

[12] **non suspecta nobis:** 'beyond suspicion in our view' (AG 375, B 189.2). **Idque . . . cum:** 'and this (the fact last stated) I am inclined to think is so far remarkable, not only', etc. The indirect question is the object of *scio*, a construction which, with *haud* preceding *scio*, generally implies an affirmative point of view (B 300.5).

[13] **tantum eius opinionis:** 'so much of that reputation'.

55.1. Treveri vero atque Indutiomarus totius hiemis nullum tempus intermiserunt, quin trans Rhenum legatos mitterent, civitates sollicitarent, pecunias pollicerentur, magna parte exercitus nostri interfecta multo minorem superesse dicerent partem. **2.** Neque tamen ulli civitati Germanorum persuaderi[1] potuit, ut Rhenum transiret, cum se bis expertos dicerent, Ariovisti bello[2] et Tencterorum transitu; non esse amplius fortunam temptaturos. **3.** Hac spe lapsus[3] Indutiomarus nihilo minus copias cogere, exercere, a finitimis equos parare, exsules damnatosque tota Gallia[4] magnis praemiis ad se allicere coepit. **4.** Ac tantam sibi iam his rebus in Gallia auctoritatem comparaverat, ut undique ad eum legationes concurrerent, gratiam atque amicitiam publice privatimque[5] peterent.

[1] **persuaderi:** 'but no state could be persuaded' (B 187.2b). **cum . . . dicerent:** 'since, as they (the Germans) said, they had tried it twice' (AG 549, B 286.2).

[2] **Ariovisti bello:** see Book I, chaps. 30-54. **Tencterorum transitu:** see Book IV., chaps., 1-15.

[3] **lapsus:** 'disappointed'.

[4] **tota Gallia:** 'throughout Gaul'.

[5] **publice, privatim:** see IV, 3, note 1.

Indutiomarus attacks the camp of Labienus, and is killed.

56.1. Ubi intellexit,[1] ultro ad se veniri, altera ex parte Senones Carnutesque conscientia facinoris[2] instigari, altera Nervios Aduatucosque bellum Romanis parare, neque sibi voluntariorum copias defore, si ex finibus suis progredi coepisset, armatum concilium indicit. **2.** Hoc[3] more Gallorum est initium belli; quo[4] lege communi omnes puberes armati convenire consuerunt; qui ex eis novissimus venit, in conspectu multitudinis omnibus cruciatibus[5] affectus necatur. **3.** In eo concilio Cingetorigem, alterius principem factionis, generum suum, quem supra[6] demonstravimus Caesaris secutum fidem[7] ab eo non discessisse, hostem iudicat bonaque eius publicat. **4.** His rebus confectis in concilio pronuntiat, arcessitum se a Senonibus et Carnutibus aliisque compluribus Galliae civitatibus; **5.** huc[8] iturum per fines Remorum eorumque agros populaturum ac, prius quam id faciat, castra Labieni oppugnaturum. Quae fieri velit, praecipit.

[1] **intellexit:** sc. *Indutiomarus.* **ultro:** 'of their own accord'. **veniri:** 'that (they) were coming'.

[2] **facinoris:** the uprising of a conquered people to recover their former liberties Caesar regards as a crime. Cf. IV, 27.5, note 8.

[3] **Hoc:** i.e. *armatum concilium indicere.*

[4] **quo:** = *ad quod,* 'to this'.

[5] **cruciatibus:** cf. VI, 16.4, note 7.

[6] **supra:** see V, 3.1-3.
[7] **ab eo non discessisse:** = *in eius fide mansisse.*
[8] **huc:** = *ad eas civitates.* On the way to the Senones he would need to pass through the territory of the Remi. See Map p. 250.

57.1. Labienus, cum et loci natura et manu munitissimis castris sese teneret, de suo ac legionis periculo nihil timebat,[1] ne quam occasionem[2] rei bene gerendae dimitteret, cogitabat. **2.** Itaque a Cingetorige atque eius propinquis oratione Indutiomari cognita, quam in concilio habuerat, nuntios mittit ad finitimas civitates equitesque undique evocat; his certam diem conveniendi dicit. **3.** Interim prope cotidie cum omni equitatu Indutiomarus sub castris eius vagabatur, alias ut situm castrorum cognosceret, alias colloquendi aut territandi causa; equites plerumque omnes tela intra vallum coniciebant. **4.** Labienus suos intra munitionem continebat timorisque opinionem,[3] quibuscumque poterat rebus, augebat.
[1] **nihil timebat:** 'was feeling no anxiety'.
[2] **occasionem . . . rei gerendae:** 'the change of fighting of successful battle'.
[3] **timoris opinionem:** 'the impression of fear'. Labienus was trying the same tactic that Caesar had lately made use of with so great success (see V, 50.4-5), and Sabinus two years before (see III, 17.5-6).

58.1. Cum maiore in dies[1] contemptione Indutiomarus ad castra accederet, nocte una intromissis[2] equitibus omnium finitimarum civitatum, quos[3] arcessendos curaverat, tanta diligentia omnes suos custodiis[4] intra castra continuit, ut nulla ratione ea res enuntiari aut ad Treveros perferri posset. **2.** Interim ex consuetudine cotidiana Indutiomarus ad castra accedit atque ibi magnam partem diei consumit; equites tela coniciunt et magna cum contumelia verborum nostros ad pugnam evocant. **3.** Nullo ab nostris dato responso, ubi visum est,[5] sub vesperum dispersi ac dissipati discedunt. **4.** Subito Labienus duabus portis omnem equitatum emittit; praecipit[6] atque interdicit, proterritis hostibus atque in fugam coniectis (quod fore, sicut accidit, videbat) unum omnes peterent Indutiomarum, neu quis quem prius vulneret, quam illum interfectum viderit, quod mora[7] reliquorum spatium nactum illum effugere nolebat; **5.** magna proponit eis, qui occiderint,[8] praemia; summittit cohortes equitibus subsidio. **6.** Comprobat[9] hominis consilium fortuna, et cum unum[10] omnes peterent, in ipso fluminis vado deprehensus Indutiomarus interficitur caputque eius refertur in castra; redeuntes equites, quos possunt,[11] consectantur atque occidunt. **7.** Hac re cognita, omnes Eburonum et Nerviorum, quae convenerant, copiae discedunt, pauloque[12] habuit post id factum Caesar quietiorem Galliam.
[1] **in dies:** 'day by every', 'every day.'
[2] **intromissis:** 'introduced' into the camp. Labienus had no cavalry of his own with which to carry out his design against the Treveri.
[3] **quos . . . curaverat:** 'that he had caused to be collected'. **tanta diligentia:** 'with so great carefulness'.
[4] **custodiis:** 'by keeping guard'. Once having conveyed the cavalry into his camp, Labienus took care that the fact should not become known to the enemy.
[5] **visum est:** 'they thought best'; sc. *discedere.* **dispersi, dissipati, discedunt:** alliteration. (AG 641, B 375.3).

[6] **praecipit:** followed by *unum . . . peterent;* **interdicit** applies to *neu . . . vulneret.*
[7] **mora . . . nactum:** gaining time in the delay caused by the cavalry following up the others.
[8] **occiderint:** sc. *eum* (AG 535, B 283.2).
[9] **Comprobat:** 'justifies'.
[10] **unum** [ilium]: 'him alone'. **fluminis:** perhaps the Ourthe.
[11] **possunt:** sc. *consectari et occidere.*
[12] **pauloque . . . Galliam:** notice the brevity and force of this closing sentence. **habuit:** 'found'.

Figure 148. — Legionary's cuirass.

Pompey's soldiers had the same armor and weapons as Caesar's ; there was no such disparity in equipment as there had been between Caesar's soldiers and the Gauls.

Figure 174.—Legion-
ary's helmet, galea,
without the crest.

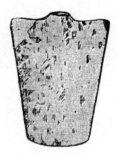

Figure 184. —
Roman spade.

Of iron ; such,
with wooden
handles, were
used by Caesar's
soldiers.

COMMENTARIUS SEXTUS

Caesar, increasing his forces, proceeds against several rebellious states.

1.1. Multis de causis¹ Caesar, maiorem Galliae motum exspectans, per M. Silanum, C. Antistium Reginum, T. Sextium legatos dilectum habere instituit; **2.** simul ab Cn. Pompeio² proconsule petit, quoniam ipse ad urbem³ cum imperio rei publicae causa⁴ remaneret, quos⁵ ex Cisalpina Gallia consul sacramento rogavisset, ad signa convenire et ad se proficisci iuberet,⁶ **3.** magni interesse etiam in reliquum tempus ad opinionem⁷ Galliae existimans, tantas videri Italiae facultates, ut, si quid⁸ esset in bello detrimenti acceptum, non modo id brevi tempore sarciri, sed etiam maioribus augeri copiis posset. **4.** Quod cum Pompeius et rei publicae⁹ et amicitiae tribuisset, celeriter confecto per suos dilectu tribus¹⁰ ante exactam hiemem et constitutis et adductis legionibus duplicatoque earum cohortium numero, quas cum Q. Titurio amiserat, et celeritate et copiis docuit, quid¹¹ populi Romani disciplina atque opes possent.

¹ **causis**: well stated by Moberly: "the death of Dumnorix, the comparative failure in Britain, the loss of the entire division of Cotta and Sabinus, the hostility stirred up among the Treveri by Indutiomarus, and, above all, the general longing for freedom felt throughout Gaul".
² **Cn. Pompeio:** Pompey had been consul in 70 B.C. and a second time in 55. As proconsul of Spain, he had at this time six legions under his command; instead of administering the affairs of his province himself, however, he remained near Rome, watching the course of events, and left the governing of Spain to his lieutenants.. He was still on good terms with Caesar.
³ **ad urbem:** 'near the city', see I, 7.1, note 2. A general having a military command (*imperium*) was by law prohibited from entering Rome.
⁴ **rei publicae causa**: 'in public service'. Pompey was nominally superintending the supply of grain to Rome, but in reality giving his attention to politics, and making every effort to win for himself a position of undisputed supremacy as a political leader. **remaneret:** 'since (as Caesar said) he (Pompey) was staying' (AG 592.3, B 286.1).
⁵ **quos consul . . . rogavisset:** 'which he as consul had enlisted in Cisalpine Gaul', in 55 B.C. **sacramento:** ablative. The soldiers took an oath that they would meet at the order of the consuls and not leave the standards without their command. **rogavisset:** subjunctive by attraction.
⁶ **iuberet:** why subjunctive, and why imperfect tense? **magni:** (AG 417, B. 203.3).
⁷ **opinionem:** the opinion of the Roman power entertained by Gaul.
⁸ **quid detrimenti:** 'any loss'.
⁹ **rei publicae:** 'for the public good'. **amicitiae:** between Pompey and Caesar.
¹⁰ **tribus**, etc.: as the three new legions contained cohorts, the number of the 15 cohorts lost under Cotta and Sabinus was doubled. One of the legions took the place of the Fourteenth that had perished; the other two were numbered I and XV. Caesar had now ten legions; cf. II, 2.1 note 1. **ante exactam hiemem:** 'before the end of winter'.
¹¹ **quid – possent:** see II, 4.1, note 2.

2.1. Interfecto Indutiomaro, ut docuimus,¹ ad eius propinquos a Treveris imperium defertur. Illi finitimos Germanos sollicitare² et pecuniam polliceri non desistunt. **2.** Cum a proximis impetrare non possent, ulteriores³ temptant. Inventis non nullis civitatibus iure iurando inter se confirmant⁴ obsidibusque⁵ de pecunia cavent; Ambiorigem sibi societate et foedere adiungunt. **3.** Quibus rebus cognitis Caesar, cum undique bellum parari videret, Nervios, Aduatucos, Menapios, adiunctis Cisrhenanis⁶ omnibus Germanis, esse in armis, Senones⁷ ad imperatum non venire et cum Carnutibus finitimisque civitatibus consilia communicare, a Treveris Germanos crebris legationibus sollicitari, maturius[8] sibi de bello cogitandum putavit.

[1] **docuimus:** cf. V, 58.4 et seq. **ad eius propinquos:** when Caesar was starting on the second expedition to Britain he held as hostages the son and all the other relatives of Indutiomarus (V, 4.1-2). On his return he probably set these at liberty; otherwise Indutiomarus would hardly have dared to become leader of a revolt.

[2] **Germanos sollicitare:** cf. I, 31.4 and V, 27.8.

[3] **ulteriores:** 'those further off'.

[4] **inter se confirmant:** 'strengthen the compact with one another'.

[5] **obsidibus:** ablative; 'exchange hostages as a guarantee (for the payment) of money'.

[6] **Cisrhenanis:** in Gaul; cf. I, 31.5 and IV, 1.1, note 3.

[7] **Senones:** see V, 54.2-3.

[8] **maturius:** 'earlier (than usual)'; see IV, 6, note 2. Caesar does not speak of coming to Transalpine Gaul, as in the corresponding passages (I, 7.1; II, 1.1-2; IV, 6.1; V, 2.1), for the reason that he had spent the entire winter of 54-53 with the army, giving up his usual circuit of Cisalpine Gaul and Illyricum Cf V, 53.3.

3.1. Itaque nondum hieme confecta, proximis[1] quattuor coactis legionibus **2.** de improviso[2] in fines Nerviorum contendit et, prius quam illi aut convenire aut profugere possent,[3] magno pecoris atque hominum numero capto atque ea[4] praeda militibus concessa vastatisque agris, in deditionem venire atque obsides sibi dare coegit. **3.** Eo celeriter confecto negotio rursus in hiberna[5] legiones reduxit. **4.** Concilio Galliae primo vere,[6] ut instituerat, indicto, cum reliqui praeter Senones, Carnutes Treverosque venissent,[7] initium[8] belli ac defectionis hoc esse arbitratus, ut omnia postponere videretur, concilium Lutetiam Parisiorum[9] transfert. **5.** Confines erant hi Senonibus civitatemque[10] patrum memoria coniunxerant, sed ab hoc consilio[11] afuisse existimabantur. **6.** Hac[12] re pro suggestu pronuntiata, eodem die cum legionibus in Senones proficiscitur magnisque itineribus eo pervenit.

[1] **proximis . . . legionibus:** probably the three legions that had been placed in winter-quarters about Samarobriva, and that under Fabius among the Morini (V, 53.3, V, 24.2).

[2] **de improviso:** see II, 3.1, note 1.

[3] **possent:** why not indicative?

[4] **ea . . . concessa:** = *eis loco praedae* ('as booty') *militibus concessis.*

[5] **hiberna:** at Samarobriva (Amiens).

[6] **primo vere:** 'at the beginning of spring', probably the earlier part of March. **ut instituerat:** = *ut facere consuerat,* 'according to his practice..

[7] **venissent:** to the council.

[8] **initium:** in predicate, emphatic position. **omnia postponere:** 'to make everything (else) second'.

[9] **Lutetiam Parisiorum:** the first mention of Paris in history. Lutetia occupied only the island in the Seine, which forms but a small part of the modern city. Paris did not become an important town until the sixth century.

[10] **civitatem coniunxerant:** i.e. making one state out of two.

[11] **consilio:** = *consilio belli.* The political union between the Senones and the Parisii could not have been very close or binding.

[12] **Hac re:** the defection of the Senones, Carnutes, and Treveri. **pronuntiata:** at the council held at Lutetia.

MAP 13
OPERATIONS OF 53 AND 52 B.C.

Books VI, VII.

To face page 338

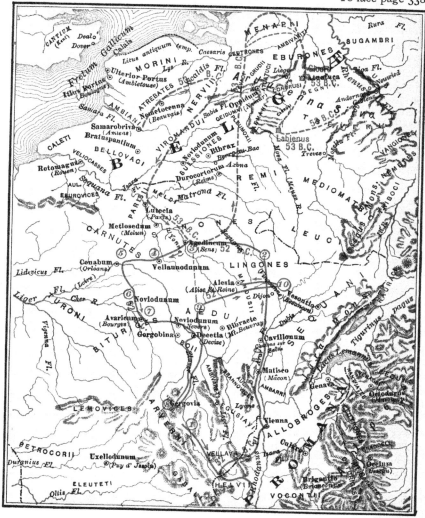

EXPLANATION

1. March into the Arvernian country, 52 B.C. (VII. 8). 2. Winter quarters (VII. 9). 3. Base, 52 B.C. (VII. 10). 4. Vellaunodunum captured (VII. 11). 5. Cenabum destroyed (VII. 11). 6. Noviodunum captured (VII. 12). 7. Avaricum destroyed (VII. 14–28). 8. Gergovia blockaded (VII. 36 ff.). 9. Junction with Labienus (VII. 62). 10. Defeat of Vercingetorix (VII. 67).

4.1. Cognito eius adventu Acco, qui princeps eius consili[1] fuerat, iubet in oppida multitudinem convenire. Conantibus,[2] prius quam id effici posset, adesse Romanos nuntiatur. **2.** Necessario sententia[3] desistunt legatosque deprecandi causa ad Caesarem mittunt; adeunt per Aeduos,[4] quorum antiquitus erat in fide[5] civitas. **3.** Libenter Caesar petentibus Aeduis dat veniam excusationemque accipit, quod aestivum tempus instantis belli, non quaestionis esse arbitratur. **4.** Obsidibus imperatis C, hos Aeduis[6] custodiendos[7] tradit. **5.** Eodem[8] Carnutes legatos obsidesque mittunt, usi deprecatoribus Remis,[9] quorum erant in clientela; eadem ferunt responsa. **6.** Peragit concilium Caesar equitesque imperat civitatibus.

[1] **princeps eius consili**: 'the leader in that scheme'.
[2] **Conantibus** [eis]: dative.
[3] **sententia desistunt**: 'give up the notion'.
[4] **per Aeduos**: 'with the support of the Aedui'.
[5] **fide**: 'protection'.
[6] **Aeduis**: why ablative? Cf. I, 28.5 and II, 12.5, note 11. The Aedui were eager in every way to extend their sway and regain the headship among the states of Gaul which they had once possessed; for which see I, 31.3 et seq. **aestivum . . . belli**: 'the summer ought to be devoted to the impending war'.
[7] **custodiendos**: why is *esse* not to be supplied? (AG 500.4, B 337.7b2).
[8] **Eodem**: probably Agedincum.
[9] **Remis**: the Remi had been on friendly terms with Caesar since *57*; see II, 3.1-2; II, 5.1; V, 54.4-5.

5.1. Hac parte Galliae pacata, totus[1] et mente et animo in bellum Treverorum et Ambiorigis insistit. **2.** Cavarinum cum equitatu Senonum secum proficisci iubet, ne quis aut ex huius[2] iracundia aut ex eo, quod meruerat, odio civitatis motus exsistat. **3.** His rebus constitutis, quod pro explorato[3] habebat, Ambiorigem proelio non esse concertaturum, reliqua eius consilia[4] animo circumspiciebat. **4.** Erant Menapii propinqui Eburonum finibus, perpetuis[5] paludibus silvisque muniti, qui uni[6] ex Gallia de pace ad Caesarem legatos numquam miserant. Cum his esse hospitium[7] Ambiorigi sciebat; item per Treveros venisse Germanis[8] in amicitiam cognoverat. **5.** Haec prius illi detrahenda auxilia existimabat, quam ipsum bello lacesseret, ne, desperata salute, aut se in Menapios abderet aut cum Transrhenanis congredi[9] cogeretur. **6.** Hoc inito consilio, totius exercitus impedimenta ad Labienum in Treveros mittit[10] duasque legiones ad eum proficisci iubet; ipse cum legionibus expeditis quinque in Menapios proficiscitur. **7.** Illi, nulla coacta manu, loci praesidio freti, in silvas paludesque confugiunt suaque eodem conferunt.

[1] **totus . . . animo**: 'heart and soul', 'with his entire attention'.
[2] **huius**: objective genitive, 'at him'. **ex . . . odio**: these petty tyrants among the Gauls seem generally to have been capricious and cruel. **civitatis**: dependent on *motus*.
[3] **pro explorato**: 'as certain'.
[4] **reliqua eius consilia**: 'what other plans he might have on foot'.
[5] **perpetuis**: 'continuous'; see III, 28.2.
[6] **uni**: difference in meaning between singular and plural of this word?
[7] **hospitium**: see I, 53., note 16. **venisse**: sc. *eum*.
[8] **Germanis**: (AG 377, B 188.1n).
[9] **congredi**: = *se coniungere*. **cogeretur**: = *necessitate coactus conaretur*; sc. *Ambiorix*.
[10] **mittit**: sc. *Caesar*.

6.1. Caesar, partitis[1] copiis cum C. Fabio legato et M. Crasso quaestore celeriterque effectis pontibus,[2] adit tripertito, aedificia vicosque[3] incendit, magno pecoris atque hominum numero potitur. **2.** Quibus rebus coacti Menapii legatos ad eum pacis petendae causa mittunt. **3.** Ille obsidibus acceptis hostium[4] se habiturum numero confirmat, si aut Ambiorigem aut eius legatos finibus suis recepissent. **4.** His confirmatis rebus Commium[5] Atrebatem cum equitatu custodis loco in Menapiis relinquit; ipse in Treveros proficiscitur.

---

[1] **partitis:** passive.
[2] **pontibus:** bridges across the streams, and causeways over the marshes.
[3] **aedificia vicosque:** see I, 5.2, note 3.
[4] **hostium numero:** 'as enemies.'
[5] **Commium:** one of Caesar's puppet-kings; see IV, 21.7; cf. V, 6.2, note 3. **custodis loco:** 'as a guard'.

Meanwhile Labienus conquers the Treveri.

7.1. Dum haec a Caesare geruntur,[1] Treveri magnis coactis peditatus equitatusque copiis Labienum cum una legione, quae in eorum finibus[2] hiemaverat, adoriri parabant, **2.** iamque ab eo non longius bidui via[3] aberant, cum duas venisse legiones missu Caesaris[4] cognoscunt. **3.** Positis castris a[5] milibus passuum XV, auxilia Germanorum exspectare constituunt. **4.** Labienus, hostium cognito consilio, sperans, temeritate eorum fore aliquam dimicandi facultatem, praesidio quinque cohortium impedimentis relicto, cum viginti quinque cohortibus magnoque equitatu[6] contra hostem proficiscitur et mille[7] passuum intermisso spatio castra communit. **5.** Erat[8] inter Labienum atque hostem difficili transitu flumen[9] ripisque praeruptis. Hoc neque ipse transire habebat in animo neque hostes transituros[10] existimabat. **6.** Augebatur auxiliorum cotidie spes. Loquitur in consilio[11] palam, quoniam Germani appropinquare dicantur, sese suas exercitusque fortunas in dubium[12] non devocaturum, et postero die prima luce castra moturum. **7.** Celeriter haec ad hostes deferuntur, ut ex magno Gallorum equitum[13] numero non nullos Gallicis rebus favere natura cogebat. **8.** Labienus, noctu tribunis militum primisque ordinibus[14] convocatis, quid[15] sui sit consili, proponit et, quo facilius hostibus timoris det suspicionem,[16] maiore strepitu et tumultu, quam[17] populi Romani fert consuetudo, castra moveri iubet. His rebus fugae similem profectionem effecit. **9.** Haec quoque per exploratores ante lucem in[18] tanta propinquitate castrorum ad hostes deferuntur.

---

[1] **geruntur:** (AG 576, e, B 293.1).
[2] **in eorum finibus:** see V, 24.2-3, and Map. **hiemaverat:** pluperfect, because it was now summer (VI, 4.3).
[3] **via:** why ablative?
[4] **missu Caesaris:** 'being sent by Caesar'.
[5] **a:** 'off'; construction of **milibus**?
[6] **equitatu:** 'body of cavalry'.
[7] **mille:** here a noun, indeclinable (AG 134dN, B 80.5a).
[8] **Erat:** see I, 7.1, note 1.
[9] **flumen:** perhaps the Ourthe. **habebat in animo:** 'was intending'.
[10] **neque hostes traasituros:** i.e. unless he could in some way induce them to make the

crossing. **Augebatur**: sc. *enim hostibus*.
[11] **in consilio**: 'as a part of his plan'. Labienus prepares a ruse for the enemy.
[12] **in dubium devocaturum**: = *in discrimen vocalurum* [*esse*].
[13] **equitum**: the cavalry of Caesar's army was mainly composed of Gauls. **non nullos**, etc.: 'from force of nature some were favouring the Gallic cause'; *natura* is nominative.
[14] **ordinibus**: = *centurionibus*.
[15] **quid . . . consili**: 'what his plan was'.
[16] **suspicionem**: 'impression'.
[17] **quam . . . consuetudo**: 'than is customary for Romans'.
[18] **in . . . castrorum**: causal, 'because the camps were so near each other'.

8.1. Vix agmen novissimum extra munitiones processerat, cum Galli, cohortati[1] inter se, ne speratam praedam ex manibus dimitterent — longum esse,[2] perterritis Romanis, Germanorum auxilium exspectare, neque suam pati dignitatem, ut tantis copiis tam exiguam manum, praesertim fugientem atque impeditam, adoriri non audeant — flumen transire et iniquo loco committere proelium non dubitant. **2.** Quae fore suspicatus Labienus, ut omnes citra flumen eliceret, eadem usus simulatione itineris[3] placide progrediebatur. **3.** Tum praemissis paulum impedimentis atque in tumulo quodam collocatis, **4.** 'Habetis,' inquit, 'milites, quam petistis, facultatem: hostem impedito atque iniquo loco tenetis; praestate eandem nobis ducibus[4] virtutem, quam saepe numero imperatori[5] praestitistis, atque illum adesse et haec coram cernere existimate.' **5.** Simul signa[6] ad hostem converti aciemque derigi iubet et, paucis turmis praesidio ad impedimenta dimissis, reliquos equites ad latera disponit. **6.** Celeriter nostri, clamore sublato, pila in hostes immittunt. Illi, ubi praeter spem, quos fugere credebant, infestis signis ad se ire viderunt, impetum modo[7] ferre non potuerunt ac primo concursu in fugam coniecti proximas silvas petierunt. **7.** Quos Labienus equitatu consectatus, magno numero interfecto, compluribus captis, paucis post diebus civitatem[8] recepit. Nam Germani, qui auxilio veniebant, percepta Treverorum fuga sese domum receperunt. **8.** Cum his propinqui Indutiomari, qui defectionis auctores fuerant, comitati eos[9] ex civitate excesserunt. Cingetorigi, quem ab initio permansisse in officio demonstravimus,[10] principatus atque imperium est traditum.

[1] **cohortati inter se**: 'having urged one another on'.
[2] **longum esse**: '(saying) that it would be wearisome'.
[3] **simulatione itineris**: = *simulato itinere*, 'feigned march'.
[4] **nobis ducibus**: dative, the editorial 'we' (AG 143a, B 242.3).
[5] **imperatori**: Caesar. Labienus used a similar exhortation with good effect also on another occasion (VII, 62.2). How soldiers fought when under the eye of Caesar may be inferred from II, 25.2-3 and III, 14.8.
[6] **signa . . . converti**: 'face about towards the enemy'.
[7] **impetum modo**: 'the bare onset'.
[8] **civitatem recepit**: 'recovered the state' of the Treveri from its condition of insurrection.
[9] **comitati eos**: not a repetition of the thought in *cum his*; they not only went off at the same time as the Germans, but accompanied these into Germany. Cf. VI, 2.1, notes 1-2.
[10] **demonstravimus**: see V, 3.3 and V, 56.3.

Caesar bridges the Rhine, crosses, makes terms with the Ubii.

9.1. Caesar, postquam ex Menapiis in Treveros venit, duabus de causis

Rhenum transire constituit; **2.** quarum una erat, quod Germani auxilia contra se Treveris miserant, altera, ne ad eos Ambiorix[1] receptum haberet. **3.** His constitutis rebus, paulum supra eum locum, quo ante[2] exercitum traduxerat, facere pontem instituit. **4.** Nota[3] atque instituta ratione, magno militum studio, paucis diebus opus efficitur. **5.** Firmo in Treveris ad pontem praesidio relicto, ne quis ab his subito motus oreretur,[4] reliquas copias equitatumque traducit. **6.** Ubii, qui ante obsides dederant atque in deditionem venerant, purgandi sui[5] causa ad eum legatos mittunt, qui doceant, neque auxilia ex sua civitate in Treveros missa neque ab se fidem laesam;[6] **7.** petunt atque orant, ut sibi parcat, ne communi odio[7] Germanorum innocentes pro nocentibus poenas pendant; si amplius obsidum[8] velit dari, pollicentur. **8.** Cognita Caesar causa reperit, ab Suebis auxilia missa esse; Ubiorum satisfactionem accipit, aditus viasque in Suebos[9] perquirit.

[1] **Ambiorix:** see V, 37.6, note 7.

[2] **ante:** in 55 B.C.; see IV, 17-19, and notes..

[3] **Nota . . . studio:** 'Since the plan (of such a bridge) was familiar and had been tried, (and) the soldiers worked with much enthusiasm'; how lit.?

[4] **oreretur:** *61b.*

[5] **sui:** *154b; 230.1.* **qui doceant:** *193a.*

[6] **fidem laesam** [esse]: '(their) pledge had been violated'.

[7] **communi odio:** 'indiscriminate hatred.. **innocentes,** etc.: 'the innocent for the guilty'; *81.*

[8] **amplius obsidum:** 'more hostages'; *97b* (AG 346a3, B 201.2).

[9] **Suebos:** *282.* **perquirit:** 'made careful inquiry about'.

10.1. Interim paucis post diebus fit ab Ubiis certior, Suebos omnes in unum locum[1] copias cogere atque eis nationibus, quae sub eorum sint imperio, denuntiare, ut auxilia peditatus equitatusque mittant. **2.** His cognitis rebus, rem frumentariam providet, castris idoneum locum deligit; Ubiis imperat, ut pecora deducant suaque omnia ex agris in oppida conferant, sperans, barbaros atque imperitos homines, inopia cibariorum adductos, ad iniquam pugnandi condicionem posse deduci; **3.** mandat, ut crebros[2] exploratores in Suebos mittant, quaeque apud eos gerantur, cognoscant. **4.** Illi imperata faciunt et, paucis diebus intermissis, referunt: *Suebos omnes, postea quam certiores nuntii de exercitu Romanorum venerint, cum omnibus suis sociorumque copiis, quas coegissent, penitus ad extremos fines[3] se recepisse;* **5.** *silvam esse ibi infinita magnitudine, quae appellatur Bacenis; hanc longe introrsus pertinere et, pro nativo muro[4] obiectam, Cheruscos ab Suebis Suebosque ab[5] Cheruscis iniuriis[6] incursionibusque prohibere; ad eius silvae initium Suebos adventum Romanorum exspectare constituisse.*

[1] **in unum locum,** etc.: cf. IV, 19.2.

[2] **crebros:** 'a great many'. The scouts were of course Ubians; cf. VI, 29.1.

[3] **extremos fines:** 'the most remote part of their country'; *152a.*

[4] **pro nativo muro:** 'as a natural barrier'.

[5] **ab:** 'on the part of'.

[6] **iniuriis,** etc.: 'protected . . . from destructive raids'; *238d; 127a.*

The customs of the Gauls and Germans contrasted. 11-28.

Political conditions in Gaul; motives for leadership.

11.1. Quoniam [1] ad hunc locum perventum est, non alienum esse videtur, de[2] Galliae Germaniaeque moribus et, quo differant hae nationes inter sese, proponere. **2.** In Gallia non solum in omnibus civitatibus atque in omnibus pagis partibusque,[3] sed paene etiam in singulis domibus[4] factiones sunt, **3.** earumque factionum principes sunt, qui summam auctoritatem eorum[5] iudicio habere existimantur, quorum[6] ad arbitrium iudiciumque summa omnium rerum consiliorumque redeat. **4.** Idque[7] eius rei causa antiquitus institutum videtur, ne quis ex plebe contra potentiorem auxilii[8] egeret; suos enim quisque[9] opprimi et circumveniri non patitur, neque, aliter si faciat, ullam inter suos habet auctoritatem. **5.** Haec eadem ratio[10] est in summa totius Galliae; namque omnes civitates divisae[11] sunt in duas partes.

---

[1] **Quoniam**, etc.: 'Since we have reached this point' in the narrative; *73d*. **alienum:** 'out of place'. The digression which follows was introduced to gratify Roman readers, who were eager to have information about the new countries; it is regarded by historians as a source of information of prime importance regarding political institutions and conditions of life in Northern Europe in antiquity.

[2] **de – proponere:** 'to give an account of'. **quo:** 'in what respect', introduces an indirect question.

[3] **partibus:** 'districts'; *289c*.

[4] **domibus:** *20c.* **factiones:** 'party divisions'.

[5] **eorum:** *Gallorum.* **iudicio:** *138.*

[6] **quorum:** refers to (*ei*) *qui . . . existimantur*; 'so that the final decision in respect to all affairs and projects is referred to their authority and judgement'; how lit.? *194a*.

[7] **Id – institutum** [esse] **videtur:** 'that practice seems to have become established'. **eius rei causa:** 'with this object in view', referring to the clause *ne . . . egeret*; how lit.? *161a*.

[8] **auxilii:** *127d.* **egeret:** 'lack'.

[9] **quisque:** 'each (leader)'. **neque . . . faciat, habet:** *207.2*.

[10] **ratio**, etc.: 'This same condition holds true of the whole of Gaul'; how lit.?

[11] **divisae:** *148c.* **partes:** 'groups', explained in chap. 12.

12.1. Cum[1] Caesar in Galliam venit, alterius factionis principes erant Aedui, alterius Sequani. **2.** Hi[2] cum per se minus valerent, quod summa auctoritas antiquitus erat in Aeduis magnaeque eorum erant clientelae,[3] Germanos atque Ariovistum sibi adiunxerant eosque ad se[4] magnis iacturis pollicitationibusque perduxerant. **3.** Proeliis vero compluribus factis secundis, atque omni nobilitate[5] Aeduorum interfecta, **4.** tantum[6] potentia antecesserant, ut magnam partem clientium[7] ab Aeduis ad se traducerent obsidesque ab eis principum filios acciperent, et publice[8] iurare cogerent, nihil se contra Sequanos consilii inituros, et partem finitimi agri per vim occupatam possiderent[9] Galliaeque totius principatum obtinerent. **5.** Qua necessitate adductus, Diviciacus,[10] auxilii petendi causa, Romam ad senatum profectus, infecta[11] re redierat. **6.** Adventu[12] Caesaris facta commutatione rerum, obsidibus Aeduis[13] redditis, veteribus clientelis restitutis, novis per Caesarem comparatis,[14] quod ei, qui se ad eorum amicitiam aggregaverant, meliore condicione atque aequiore imperio se uti[15] videbant, reliquis rebus eorum gratia dignitateque amplificata, Sequani principatum dimiserant. **7.** In eorum locum Remi successerant; quos[16] quod adaequare apud Caesarem gratia intellegebatur, ei, qui propter veteres inimicitias[17] nullo modo cum Aeduis coniungi poterant, se Remis[18] in clientelam dicabant. **8.** Hos illi diligenter tuebantur; ita et novam et repente collectam[19] auctoritatem tenebant. **9.** Eo tum statu res erat, ut longe principes haberentur Aedui, secundum locum dignitatis Remi obtinerent.

---

[1] **Cum:** '(At the time) when'; *185b.* **alterius:** *23b; 171b.*

[2] **Hi:** 'The latter'. Previously the Arvernians had held a position of leadership; see I, 31.3-7.

[3] **clientelae:** 'dependencies', states acknowledging the sovereignty of the Aeduans.

[4] **eos ad se . . . perduxerant:** 'had won them over'. **iacturis:** 'pecuniary sacrifices'.

[5] **omni nobilitate:** see I, 31.6, note 20.

[6] **tantum – antecesserant:** 'they had so far outstripped (the Aeduans)'.

[7] **clientium:** dependent states are here meant.

[8] **publice:** 'for the state'. **iurare:** as subject sc. *eos*, i.e. *Aeduorum principes.* **nihil – consilii:** 'no scheme'; *97a.*

[9] **occupatam possiderent:** 'seized . . . and retained in their possession'; *228a.*

[10] **Diviciacus,** etc.: the statement of Diviciacus himself on this point is summarized by Caesar at I, 31.8-9.

[11] **infecta re:** 'without accomplishing his purpose'; how lit.?

[12] **Adventu:** *147b.* **facta,** etc.: the ablatives absolute are best translated by clauses. 144b2, 3. **commutatione rerum:** 'a complete change of relations'.

[13] **Aeduis:** dative. **novis:** sc. *clientelis.*

[14] **comparatis:** for the Aeduans. **se,** etc.: 'had joined themselves to them as allies'; how lit.?

[15] **se uti:** 'that they enjoyed'. **reliquis rebus:** 'in all other respects' also.

[16] **quos . . . intellegebatur:** 'and since it was understood that they (the Remi) stood equally high in Caesar's favour'; how lit.?

[17] **inimicitias:** 'enmities'. **coniungi:** *174.*

[18] **Remis,** etc.: 'attached themselves as dependants to the Remi'; how lit.?

[19] **repente collectam:** 'suddenly acquired', in the brief period since the defeat of Ariovistus, five years before.

The two ruling classes, and the common people, in Gaul. The Druids: their power as priests and judges, their organization, their teachings about the soul.

13.1. In omni Gallia eorum hominum, qui aliquo[1] sunt numero atque honoure, genera sunt duo; nam plebes paene servorum[2] habetur loco, quae nihil audet per se, nulli adhibetur consilio. **2.** Plerique, cum aut aere alieno[3] aut magnitudine tributorum[4] aut iniuria potentiorum premuntur, sese in servitutem dicant nobilibus; quibus[5] in hos eadem omnia sunt iura, quae[6] dominis in servos. **3.** Sed de his duobus generibus alterum[7] est druidum, alterum equitum. **4.** Illi[8] rebus divinis intersunt, sacrificia publica ac privata procurant, religiones interpretantur;[9] ad hos magnus adulescentium numerus disciplinae causa[10] concurrit, magnoque hi[11] sunt apud eos honoure. **5.** Nam fere de omnibus controversiis publicis privatisque constituunt et, si quod[12] est facinus admissum, si caedes facta,[13] si de hereditate, de finibus[14] controversia est, idem decernunt, praemia poenasque constituunt; **6.** si qui,[15] aut privatus aut populus, eorum decreto[16] non stetit, sacrificiis interdicunt. Haec poena apud eos est gravissima. **7.** Quibus[17] ita est interdictum, hi numero[18] impiorum ac sceleratorum habentur, his[19] omnes decedunt, aditum eorum sermonemque defugiunt, ne quid ex contagione[20] incommodi accipiant, neque his petentibus[21] ius redditur neque honos ullus communicatur. **8.** His autem omnibus druidibus praeest unus, qui summam inter eos habet auctoritatem. **9.** Hoc mortuo[22] aut, si qui ex reliquis excellit[23] dignitate, succedit, aut, si sunt plures pares,[24] suffragio druidum, non numquam etiam armis, de principatu contendunt. **10.** Hi certo anni tempore in finibus Carnutum, quae regio[25] totius Galliae media habetur, considunt[26] in loco consecrato. Huc omnes undique, qui controversias habent, conveniunt eorumque decretis iudiciisque parent. **11.** Disciplina[27] in Britannia reperta atque inde in Galliam translata esse existimatur, et nunc, qui diligentius[28] eam rem cognoscere volunt, plerumque illo discendi causa proficiscuntur.

[1] **aliquo**, etc.: 'are of any account and (receive) recognition'; how lit.? *143b.*
[2] **servorum loco:** 'as slaves'; *288b.* **nulli consilio:** 'to no consultation'; *23a.*
[3] **aere alieno:** 'by debt'; how lit.?
[4] **tributorum:** 'of the taxes'. **sese,** etc.: 'attach themselves as bondsmen'; how lit.?
[5] **quibus,** etc.: 'and these have over them'; *167; 111.*
[6] **quae,** etc.: sc. *sunt;* 'as masters (have) over slaves'.
[7] **alterum** [genus]: *171b.* **druidum:** '(that of) the Druids', a priesthood possessing great power in Gaul and Britain. Very little is known of the Druids in Caesar's time beyond what he tells us in this book.
[8] **Illi,** etc.: 'the former have charge of the services of worship'. **sacrificia – procurant:** 'regulate the sacrifices'.
[9] **religiones interpretantur:** 'settle religious questions'; *238a.*
[10] **disciplinae causa:** 'in order to receive instruction'; how lit.? *81.*
[11] **hi:** the Druids. **eos:** *Gallos.*
[12] **quod:** adjective form; *49a; 168.*
[13] **facta:** sc. *est.* **hereditate:** 'an inheritance'.
[14] **finibus:** here 'boundaries'. **idem decernunt:** 'they likewise render judgement'.
[15] **qui:** substantive form; 'any (party)' to a controversy, 'whether . . . or', etc.; *49a.*
[16] **decreto:** 'decision'; *138.* **sacrificiis interdicunt:** 'they exclude (the offender) from the sacrifices'; *127a.*
[17] **Quibus:** dative; 'on whom such an interdict has been laid'.
[18] **numero,** etc.: 'as wicked and crime-polluted men'; how lit.?
[19] **his:** dative; 'these all men avoid'; *109b.* **defugiunt:** 'shun'.
[20] **contagione:** 'contact' with the excommunicated.
[21] **petentibus:** 'though they may seek (justice)'. **honos:** *13a,b.*
[22] **Hoc mortuo:** 'When he' (the arch-Druid) 'dies'; *160b.*
[23] **excellit:** 'is preeminent'; *205.1.* **dignitate:** 'in standing'; *142a.*
[24] **pares:** i.e., *pares dignitate.* **suffragio:** 'by vote'.
[25] **quae regio:** 'a region which'; *165b.* **Carnutum.**
[26] **considunt:** 'hold a meeting'. **loco consecrato:** the 'hallowed spot' was probably a sacred grove; *145a.*
[27] **Disciplina:** 'The system' of the Druids. **reperta, translata:** *221b.* It is not now possible to determine the truth of the tradition, as recorded by Caesar, that Druidism originated in Britain.
[28] **diligentius:** 'with special thoroughness'. **eam rem:** 'the system'; *160d.*

14.1. Druides a bello abesse consuerunt neque tributa una[1] cum reliquis pendunt, militiae vacationem omniumque rerum habent immunitatem. **2.** Tantis excitati praemiis, et sua sponte multi in disciplinam[2] conveniunt et a parentibus propinquisque mittuntur.[3] **3.** Magnum ibi numerum versuum[4] ediscere dicuntur. Itaque annos non nulli vicenos[5] in disciplina permanent. Neque fas esse existimant ea[6] litteris mandare cum in reliquis fere rebus, publicis privatisque rationibus,[7] Graecis litteris utantur. **4.** Id mihi duabus de causis instituisse videntur, quod[8] neque in vulgus disciplinam efferri velint, neque eos, qui discunt,[9] litteris confisos, minus memoriae studere; quod[10] fere plerisque accidit, ut praesidio litterarum diligentiam in perdiscendo[11] ac memoriam remittant. **5.** In primis hoc volunt persuadere, non interire animas,[12] sed ab aliis[13] post mortem transire ad alios; atque hoc maxime ad virtutem excitari[14] putant, metu mortis neglecto. **6.** Multa[15] praeterea de sideribus atque eorum motu, de mundi ac terrarum[16] magnitudine, de rerum natura, de deorum immortalium vi ac potestate disputant et iuventuti tradunt.

[1] **una cum reliquis:** 'at the same rate as the rest'; the Druids paid taxes at a lower rate than ordinary citizens, or were not legally bound to pay taxes at all. **pendunt:** see I, 36.5, note 13. **militiae:** *80b.* **vacationem,** etc.: 'exemption from' (lit. 'of') 'military service and freedom from all (public) burdens'; *81.*

[2] **in disciplinam:** 'to receive instruction', from the Druids; how lit.? **parentibus:** *81.*

[3] **mittuntur:** sc. *multi*; so to-day many "are sent" to school.

[4] **versuum:** 'lines'; the metrical form was probably adopted to facilitate memorizing. **ediscere:** 'to learn by heart'.

[5] **vicenos:** *36.* **in disciplina:** 'under instruction'.

[6] **ea:** the teachings set forth in verse. **litteris:** 'to writing', we should say. **cum:** 'although'; *187.*

[7] **rationibus:** 'accounts', included under *rebus* but added as a concrete example; trans. 'as in', etc. **Graecis litteris:** 'Greek characters,' used in writing the Gallic languages (cf. I, 29.1). Gallic coins occasionally had inscriptions in the Latin alphabet, in imitation of Roman coins.

[8] **quod . . . velint:** 'because (as it has been suggested) they do not wish to have their body of teachings spread abroad among the common people', who would remain in subjection to the druidical priesthood only so long as they should be kept in ignorance; *183a.*

[9] **discunt:** vivid use of the indicative; cf. *220.* **litteris:** *135a.* **minus – studere:** 'pay too little heed'.

[10] **quod:** 'and this'; *167.* **praesidio litterarum:** 'through reliance upon written records'; how lit.?

[11] **perdiscendo:** 'learning by heart'; *230.4.* The truth of this statement is unquestioned.

[12] **animas:** 'the soul', as life-principle; this is the doctrine of transmigration of souls, or metempsychosis; *92a.*

[13] **aliis, alios:** *171b; 154a.* **hoc:** 'by this (belief)'.

[14] **excitari:** impersonal; 'men are spurred on'. **metu,** etc.: *144b3.*

[15] **Multa – disputant:** 'They treat many subjects'. **sideribus:** 'heavenly bodies'. **mundi:** 'the universe'.

[16] **terrarum:** for *orbis terrarum*, 'the earth'.

The knights: their warlike occupation, and their retainers.

15.1. Alterum[1] genus est equitum. Hi, cum est usus atque aliquod[2] bellum incidit (quod fere ante Caesaris adventum quotannis accidere solebat, uti aut ipsi iniurias inferrent aut illatas propulsarent), omnes in bello versantur, **2.** atque eorum[3] ut quisque est genere copiisque amplissimus, ita plurimos circum se ambactos clientesque habet. Hanc[4] unam gratiam potentiamque noverunt.

[1] **Alterum:** cf. VI, 13.3. **cum:** 'whenever', *186a.*

[2] **aliquod:** *49a.* **incidit:** 'breaks out'. **quod:** 'and this'.

[3] **eorum,** etc.: 'each knight has about him the greatest number of vassals and retainers that his social position and resources will warrant'; how lit.? A notable example is Orgetorix (I,

4.2).

[4] **Hanc**, etc.: 'This (numerousness of retinue) is the only sign of influence and power that they recognize'; how lit.? *170b*.

Superstitions of the Gauls; their human sacrifices.

16.1. Natio est omnis[1] Gallorum admodum dedita religionibus, **2.** atque ob eam causam, qui sunt affecti gravioribus morbis[2] quique in proeliis periculisque versantur, aut pro victimis homines immolant[3] aut se immolaturos vovent, administrisque ad ea sacrificia druidibus utuntur, **3.** quod, pro vita hominis nisi hominis vita reddatur, non posse deorum immortalium numen[4] placari arbitrantur; publiceque eiusdem generis habent instituta[5] sacrificia. **4.** Alii immani magnitudine simulacra[6] habent, quorum contexta viminibus membra vivis[7] hominibus complent; quibus succensis, circumventi flamma exanimantur homines. **5.** Supplicia[8] eorum, qui in furto aut latrocinio aut aliqua noxia[9] sint comprehensi, gratiora dis immortalibus esse arbitrantur; sed cum eius generis copia defecit, etiam ad innocentium supplicia descendunt.[10]

[1] **omnis:** 'as a whole'. **dedita:** 'devoted'; *148c*. **religionibus:** 'religious observances'.
[2] **morbis:** 'diseases'. **pro victimis:** 'as victims.'
[3] **immolant:** 'offer up'. **se immolaturos:** i.e. *se immolaturos esse homines pro victimis*. **vovent:** 'vow'. **administris:** 'as officiating priests'; *7c; 131f*.
[4] **numen:** 'majesty'; lit. 'nod'. **placari:** 'be appeased'.
[5] **habent instituta:** *229a* (AG 497b, B 337.7). **sacrificia:** human sacrifices were offered at times in Eastern lands (cf., for example, 2 Kings, 3.27), and in ancient Mexico; and even at Rome an instance of human sacrifice is reported as late as 216 B.C.
[6] **simulacra:** 'images' of wickerwork, having some resemblance to the human form.
[7] **vivis:** 'living'. **quibus:** *et eis* (*simulacris*).
[8] **Supplicia:** *92a*. **furto:** 'theft'. **latrocinio:** 'highway robbery'.
[9] **noxia:** 'crime'. **gratiora:** 'more acceptable'.
[10] **descendunt:** 'resort'.

The gods worshipped by the Gauls.

17.1. Deorum[1] maxime Mercurium colunt. Huius sunt plurima simulacra;[2] hunc omnium inventorem artium ferunt, hunc viarum[3] atque itinerum ducem, hunc ad quaestus pecuniae mercaturasque[4] habere vim maximam arbitrantur; **2.** post hunc, Apollinem[5] et Martem et Iovem et Minervam. De his eandem fere, quam reliquae gentes, habent opinionem: Apollinem morbos depellere, Minervam operum atque artificiorum initia tradere, Iovem imperium caelestium[6] tenere, Martem bella regere. **3.** Huic, cum proelio dimicare constituerunt, ea, quae bello ceperint,[7] plerumque devovent; cum superaverunt, animalia capta immolant reliquasque res in unum locum conferunt. **4.** Multis in civitatibus harum rerum exstructos tumulos[8] locis consecratis conspicari licet; **5.** neque saepe accidit, ut neglecta quispiam[9] religione aut capta apud se occultare aut posita tollere[10] auderet, gravissimumque ei rei supplicium cum cruciatu constitutum est.

[1] **Deorum:** dependent on *maxime*; *97e*. **Mercurium:** in the case of Mercury and the other gods mentioned, Caesar gives the name of the Roman divinity whose attributes and functions seemed to him to correspond most nearly with those of the Gallic divinity; the Gallic names were of course not known to Roman readers.
[2] **simulacra:** since the Gauls began making statues only after the Roman conquest, it has been

suggested that the 'images' of Mercury referred to here were the huge upright stones (menhirs) of which several groups must have been seen by Caesar in Gaul and that these were associated in some way with the worship of the Gallic divinity identified by him with this god. Pillars of a certain type were sacred to Hermes, the Greek god corresponding with Mercury. **inventorem:** *80b.* **artium:** 'arts'; *81.* **ferunt:** *172c.*

[3] **viarum:** Mercury is 'guide for roads' in that he points out the road, and 'for journeys' because he accompanies the traveler on the way. **quaestus:** 'acquisition'; *92a.*

[4] **mercaturas:** 'commercial transactions'.

[5] **Apollinem,** etc.: the infinitive clauses are appositional; *12d.* **operum,** etc.: 'imparts the elements of the trades and crafts'.

[6] **caelestium:** 'the gods' as dwellers in the sky (*caelum*).

[7] **ceperint:** subjunctive in implied indirect discourse, for the future perfect indicative. **cum superaverunt:** *post victoriam.* **animalia:** *16b; 80b.*

[8] **tumulos:** such piles of booty would after a time rot down and be covered with vegetation, presenting the appearance of a mound.

[9] **quispiam:** *49a.* **capta:** neuter plural, accusative; *227a4.* **apud se:** 'in his possession'.

[10] **posita tollere:** 'to take away what had been deposited' as an offering to the gods.

Strange customs of the Gauls.

18.1. Galli se omnes ab Dite patre[1] prognatos praedicant idque ab druidibus proditum dicunt. **2.** Ob eam[2] causam spatia omnis temporis non numero dierum, sed noctium finiunt;[3] dies natales et mensium et annorum initia sic observant, ut[4] noctem dies subsequatur. **3.** In reliquis vitae institutis hoc[5] fere ab reliquis differunt, quod suos liberos, nisi cum adoleverunt,[6] ut munus militiae sustinere possint, palam ad se[7] adire non patiuntur, filiumque puerili aetate[8] in publico in conspectu patris assistere turpe[9] ducunt.

[1] **Dite patre:** Caesar identifies the Gallic divinity with a Roman god of the Underworld known in earlier times as 'Father Dis' (*Dis pater*), later generally called Pluto; *128b.*

[2] **Ob eam causam:** because sprung from the god of the Underworld, the realm of darkness and night.

[3] **finiunt:** 'measure'. The ancient Germans also reckoned time by the number of nights; a trace of this reckoning remains in our word "fortnight" (= fourteen nights). **dies natales:** 'birthdays'.

[4] **ut,** etc.: instead of saying "the first day of the month", as we do, the Gauls said 'the first night of the month', 'the first night of the year', 'birthright', etc. It is more difficult to keep track of time by days than by nights because it is easier to note the changes of the moon than of the sun.

[5] **hoc:** *142a.* **ab reliquis:** 'from all other people'; *171a.*

[6] **adoleverunt:** 'have grown up'. **munus militiae:** 'military service'.

[7] **se:** only the fathers are referred to, as shown by what follows.

[8] **puerili aetate:** 'while in the age of childhood'; how lit.? *143a.*

[9] **turpe:** predicative, 'consider it disgraceful for a son ... to appear'. On public occasions the Gauls would appear armed; it was thought in bad form for an armed man to have with him, in a public place, a son who was not also armed.

19.1. Viri,[1] quantas pecunias ab uxoribus dotis nomine acceperunt, tantas ex suis bonis,[2] aestimatione facta, cum dotibus communicant.[3] **2.** Huius omnis pecuniae coniunctim ratio habetur fructusque[4] servantur; uter eorum vita superavit, ad eum pars utriusque[5] cum fructibus superiorum temporum pervenit. **3.** Viri in[6] uxores, sicuti in liberos, vitae necisque habent potestatem; et cum pater familiae,[7] illustriore loco natus, decessit, eius propinqui conveniunt et, de[8] morte si res in suspicionem venit, de uxoribus[9] in servilem modum quaestionem habent et, si compertum est,[10] igni atque omnibus tormentis excruciatas interficiunt. **4.** Funera[11] sunt pro cultu Gallorum magnifica et sumptuosa; omniaque, quae vivis cordi fuisse[12] arbitrantur, in ignem inferunt, etiam animalia, **5.** ac paulo supra, hanc[13] memoriam servi et clientes, quos ab eis dilectos esse[14] constabat, iustis funebribus confectis, una[15] cremabantur.

[1] **Viri:** 'husbands'; German *Mann* is similarly used. **pecunias:** 'property' in general; trans. as if *tantas pecunias, quantas.* **dotis nomine:** 'as dowry'; *17c.*

[2] **bonis:** 'possessions'. **aestimatione facta:** 'making an estimate of value'; *144b2.*

[3] **communicant:** 'set aside'. From his own property the husband set aside an amount equal to the dower received with the wife. The income from this common fund, or estate, was saved up and added to the principal; when the husband or wife died the whole went to the survivor. **coniunctim,** etc.: 'a joint account is kept'; how lit.?

[4] **fructus:** 'income'; *92a.* **uter:** 'whichever', husband or wife. **vita:** *142a.*

[5] **utriusque:** 'of both'; *51.* The custom could have prevailed only among the higher classes, on account of the abject poverty of the common folk (VI, 13.1).

[6] **in:** 'over'. **vitae,** etc.: among the early Romans also the father had 'the power of life and death' over his household.

[7] **pater familiae:** 'the head of a family'. **illustriore loco natus:** 'of higher rank'; *128a.*

[8] **de,** etc.: 'if suspicion has arisen regarding (the cause of) death'; how lit.?

[9] **uxoribus:** the plural implies the existence of polygamy among the higher classes in Gaul. **in,** etc.: 'an examination like that of slaves', under torture; how lit.? Roman law and custom sanctioned the torture of slaves on the death of a master under suspicious circumstances.

[10] **compertum est:** impersonal, '(their guilt) has been proved'. **igni,** etc.: 'agonize and kill them with fire and every instrument of torture'; *228a; 205.3.*

[11] **Funera:** 'funerals'; *13e.* **pro cultu:** 'considering the civilization'. **magnifica:** 'splendid'; *31.* **sumptuosa:** 'costly'; *75f.*

[12] **cordi fuisse:** 'were dear'; how lit.? *10g; 112b.* **ignem:** of the funeral pyre. The ashes were sometimes buried in wooden buckets adorned with bronze ornaments.

[13] **supra hanc memoriam:** 'before our time'; how lit.?

[14] **dilectos esse:** 'were loved'. **iustis,** etc.: 'on the completion of the regular funeral rites'.

[15] **una:** 'at the same time', with the body of the master. The burning of favourite dependants on their master's funeral pyre was probably intended to continue their service for him in the other world. Interment without burning was also in vogue in Gaul.

Their precautions in dealing with rumors affecting public safety.

20.1. Quae civitates[1] commodius suam rem publicam administrare existimantur, habent[2] legibus sanctum, si quis quid de re publica[3] a finitimis rumore aut fama acceperit, uti ad magistratum deferat neve[4] cum quo alio communicet, **2.** quod saepe homines temerarios atque imperitos falsis[5] rumoribus terreri et ad facinus impelli et de summis rebus consilium capere cognitum est. **3.** Magistratus, quae visa sunt,[6] occultant, quaeque esse ex usu iudicaverunt, multitudini produnt. De re publica nisi per concilium[7] loqui non conceditur.

[1] **Quae civitates:** i.e. *eae civitates, quae.* **rem publicam:** 'public affairs'.

[2] **habent,** etc.: 'have it ordained by law that if anybody has heard anything'; *49a.*

[3] **de re publica:** 'touching the public interest'; how lit.?

[4] **neve:** 'and not'. **quo:** *49a.*

[5] **falsis:** 'baseless'; *83a.* Cf. IV, 5.2-3.

[6] **visa sunt:** i.e. *visa sunt occultanda,* 'which they have thought best to conceal'. **quaeque:** *et (ea) quae.*

[7] **per concilium:** 'at an assembly' duly convoked, lit. 'through (the medium of) an assembly'. Very few states could have enforced this regulation for any length of time.

Altogether different are the beliefs and customs of the Germans.

21.1. Germani[1] multum ab hac consuetudine differunt. Nam neque druides[2] habent, qui rebus divinis praesint, neque sacrificiis student. **2.** Deorum[3] numero eos solos ducunt, quos cernunt et quorum aperte opibus iuvantur, Solem et Vulcanum[4] et Lunam; reliquos ne fama quidem acceperunt. **3.** Vita omnis in venationibus[5] atque in studiis rei militaris consistit; a parvis[6] labori ac duritiae student. **4.** Qui diutissime impuberes permanserunt, maximam inter suos ferunt laudem; hoc alii staturam, alii vires nervosque confirmari putant. **5.** Intra annum vero vicesimum feminae notitiam habuisse in turpissimis habent rebus; cuius rei nulla est occultatio, quod et promiscue in fluminibus perluuntur et pellibus aut parvis renonum tegimentis utuntur, magna corporis parte nuda.

[1] **Germani**, etc.: 'The German mode of life and government differs greatly from that described'; how lit.? *238b*.
[2] **druides**: there were priests among the Germans, but they did not form a dominant class, as the Druids did in Gaul. **rebus divinis**: see VI, 13.4, note 8. **praesint**: *193a* (AG 531.2, B 282.2).
[3] **Deorum**, etc.: the religion of the Germans in Caesar's time was a primitive nature-worship.
[4] **Vulcanum**: god of fire. **Lunam**: the host of Ariovistus dared not fight before the new moon (I, 50.4). **reliquos**: sc. *deos.*
[5] **venationibus**: 'hunting'; *92a.* **in**, etc.: 'in warlike pursuits'.
[6] **a parvis**: 'from childhood'. **duritiae**: 'hardship'.

The Germans do not take to farming, and have no private land.

22.1. Agri culturae non student, maiorque pars eorum victus in lacte,[1] caseo, carne consistit. **2.** Neque quisquam agri modum certum aut fines[2] habet proprios; sed magistratus ac principes in annos singulos[3] gentibus cognationibusque hominum, quique[4] una coierunt, quantum et quo loco visum est[5] agri, attribuunt, atque anno post alio transire cogunt. **3.** Eius rei[6] multas afferunt causas: ne, assidua consuetudine capti, studium belli gerendi agri cultura[7] commutent; ne latos fines parare studeant, potentioresque humiliores possessionibus expellant; ne accuratius[8] ad frigora atque aestus vitandos aedificent; ne qua oriatur pecuniae cupiditas, qua ex re factiones dissensionesque[9] nascuntur; **4.** ut animi aequitate[10] plebem contineant, cum suas quisque opes cum potentissimis[11] aequari videat.

[1] **lacte**: *10g.* **caseo**: 'cheese'. **carne**: *18a.*
[2] **fines proprios**: 'lands of his own'; there was no private ownership of land Cf. IV, 1.7.
[3] **in annos singulos**: 'each year'. **gentibus**: 'clans'. **cognationibus**: 'those connected by blood', groups of families.
[4] **quique**, etc.: 'and (to those) who have joined together', associating themselves for the purpose. **quantum – agri**, etc.: 'as much land as they deem proper, and in whatever place (they think best)'.
[5] **visum est**: sc. *eis* (*magistratibus ac principibus*). **anno**: *140.* Cf. IV, I.4-6. **alio**: adverb, 'to another place'.
[6] **Eius rei causas**: 'explanations of this practice', defined by the *ne*-clauses and *ut*-clause following. **assidua**, etc.: 'captivated by the attractiveness of permanent residence'; how lit.?
[7] **cultura**: *139* (AG 417b).
[8] **accuratius**: 'with too great pains'. **frigora**: *92c.*
[9] **dissensiones**: 'dissensions'; *81.* **nascuntur**: indicative as expressing the view of the writer: cf. 220.
[10] **animi aequitate**: 'in a state of contentment'; how lit.? **cum**, etc.: 'each one seeing'.

[11] **cum potentissimis:** *cum opibus potentissimorum; 238b.*

Their ambitions are military; but they protect a guest.

23.1. Civitatibus maxima laus[1] est, quam latissime circum se, vastatis finibus, solitudines habere. **2.** Hoc proprium virtutis[2] existimant, expulsos agris finitimos cedere, neque quemquam[3] prope audere consistere; **3.** simul hoc se fore tutiores arbitrantur, repentinae incursionis[4] timore sublato. **4.** Cum bellum[5] civitas aut illatum defendit aut infert, magistratus, qui ei bello praesint[6] et vitae necisque habeant potestatem, deliguntur. **5.** In pace nullus est communis[7] magistratus, sed principes[8] regionum atque pagorum inter suos ius dicunt[9] controversiasque minuunt. **6.** Latrocinia[10] nullam habent infamiam, quae extra fines cuiusque civitatis fiunt, atque ea iuventutis exercendae ac desidiae[11] minuendae causa fieri praedicant. **7.** Atque ubi quis ex principibus in concilio dixit, *se ducem[12] fore, qui sequi velint, profiteantur,*[13] consurgunt ei, qui et causam et hominem probant, suumque auxilium pollicentur atque a multitudine collaudantur; **8.** qui ex his[14] secuti non sunt, in desertorum[15] ac proditorum numero ducuntur, omniumque his[16] rerum postea fides derogatur. **9.** Hospitem violare[17] fas non putant; qui quacumque de causa ad eos venerunt, ab iniuria prohibent, sanctos habent, hisque omnium domus patent victusque communicatur.

[1] **maxima laus:** 'the highest distinction'. **quam:** *153c.*
[2] **proprium virtutis:** 'a proof of valour'; how lit.? *102.* Cf. IV, 3.1-2.
[3] **neque quemquam:** 'and that no one'; *168; 49a.*
[4] **incursionis:** 'raid'. **timore:** *144b3.*
[5] **bellum illatum defendit:** 'repels an attack that has been made'.
[6] **praesint:** *193a* (AG 531.2, B 282.2).
[7] **communis:** 'common' to a whole people or tribe.
[8] **principes**, etc.: the head men of divisions and districts. Nothing is known about the details of the German civil administration in Caesar's time; these probably varied somewhat among the different peoples.
[9] **ius dicunt:** 'administer justice'.
[10] **Latrocinia:** 'marauding expeditions' outside their own borders. **habent infamiam:** 'disgrace'.
[11] **desidiae:** 'indolence'. **praedicant:** 'they (the Germans) declare.' **quis:** *49a.*
[12] **ducem:** 'leader' of an expedition or raid. **qui:** as antecedent supply *ei*, subject of *profiteantur.*
[13] **profiteantur:** 'that they . . . are to volunteer'; *216.*
[14] **ex his:** 'of those' who have offered to follow. In this voluntary relation between the chieftain as leader and his followers lies the origin of the peculiar relation between lord and vassal in the Middle Ages.
[15] **desertorum**, etc.: 'as deserters and traitors'; *81.* **omnium rerum fides:** 'confidence in all matters', not merely in respect to warlike prowess.
[16] **his:** dative; *109b.* **derogatur:** 'is withdrawn'.
[17] **Hospitem violare:** 'to maltreat a guest'. **qui:** as antecedent supply *eos*, object of *prohibent.* **quacumque:** *50a.*

References. The statements in chapters 22 and 23 about the institutions of the early Germans are of particular interest; they reveal the application of principles of government, whose fuller employment in the feudal system and in the English Constitution have had much to do with shaping the political history of Europe and its siblings. References: Stubbs, *Constitutional History of England*, vol. I., chaps. I and 2; Taylor, *Origin and Growth of the English Constitution*, book I., chaps. 1, 2;

Adams, *Civilization during the Middle Ages*, chap. 5; Hallam, *View of the State of Europe during the Middle Ages*, chap. 2.

The Gauls, once superior to the Germans, are now inferior.

24.1. Ac fuit antea tempus, cum Germanos Galli virtute superarent, ultro bella inferrent,[1] propter hominum multitudinem agrique inopiam trans Rhenum[2] colonias mitterent. **2.** Itaque ea, quae fertilissima[3] Germaniae sunt, loca, circum Hercyniam silvam,[4] quam Eratostheni et quibusdam Graecis fama notam esse video,[5] quam illi Orcyniam appellant, Volcae Tectosages[6] occupaverunt atque ibi consederunt; **3.** quae[7] gens ad hoc tempus his sedibus sese continet summamque habet iustitiae et bellicae[8] laudis opinionem. **4.** Nunc, quod in eadem inopia, egestate, patientia, qua ante, Germani permanent, **5.** eodem victu et cultu corporis utuntur, Gallis autem provinciarum[9] propinquitas et transmarinarum rerum notitia multa[10] ad copiam atque usus largitur, **6.** paulatim assuefacti superari multisque victi proeliis, ne se quidem ipsi[11] cum illis virtute comparant.

[1] **inferrent, mitterent:** *238a.*
[2] **trans Rhenum:** the Gauls in earlier times had not only held extensive regions east of the Rhine, but had pressed far down into Italy, giving to Cisalpine Gaul its name. **colonias:** *81.*
[3] **fertilissima:** 'most productive'; *81.* **loca:** accusative.
[4] **Hercyniam silvam:** see Vocab. Eratostheni: see Vocab. **quibusdam:** *168.*
[5] **video:** Caesar evidently had before him the works of the unnamed Greek writers referred to. He probably kept at his headquarters copies of writings that he thought might be in any way useful in his campaigns.
[6] **Volcae Tectosages:** see Vocab. under *Tectosages.*
[7] **quae gens:** 'and that people'. **ad . . . continet:** 'to this day continues to maintain itself'; a Gallic outpost, as it were, on German soil. **summam:** *353d.*
[8] **bellicae,** etc.: 'reputation for . . . prowess in war'. **in,** etc.: 'in the (same condition of) poverty, privation, (and) endurance as before'; *234a.*
[9] **provinciarum:** the two provinces, Cisalpine Gaul and "the Province" in Transalpine Gaul. **transmarinarum,** etc.: 'familiarity with products brought across the sea', which entered Gaul chiefly through the port of Massilia; how lit.? *293a.*
[10] **multa:** 'many articles', not contributing to the "simple life". **ad . . . largitur:** 'supply in abundance for common use'; how lit.?
[11] **ipsi:** *Galli.* **illis:** trans. as if *Germanis.*

The Hercynian forest, and the wonderful animals found in it.

25.1. Huius Hercyniae silvae, quae supra[1] demonstrata est, latitudo[2] VIIII dierum iter expedito patet; non enim aliter finiri potest, neque[3] mensuras itinerum noverunt. **2.** Oritur ab Helvetiorum et Nemetum et Rauracorum finibus,[4] rectaque fluminis Danuvii regione[5] pertinet ad fines Dacorum et Anartium; **3.** hinc se flectit sinistrorsus,[6] diversis a flumine regionibus, multarumque gentium fines propter magnitudinem attingit; **4.** neque quisquam est huius Germaniae,[7] qui se aut adisse ad initium[8] eius silvae dicat, cum dierum iter LX processerit, aut, quo ex loco oriatur, acceperit; **5.** multaque in ea genera ferarum[9] nasci constat, quae reliquis in locis visa non sint; ex quibus quae[10] maxime differant a ceteris et memoriae[11] prodenda videantur, haec sunt.

[1] **supra:** VI, 24.2.
[2] **latitudo:** 'breadth', from north to south. **VIII,** etc.: *243c.* **expedito:** 'for an unencumbered (traveler)', who might average 20 miles a day; if so, the 'nine days' journey' would be a

rough equivalent of 180 miles.

[3] **neque, etc.:** 'and (the people) have no system of measuring distances', by paces and miles (*243a*) such as the Romans had. How lit.? **Oritur:** sc. *ea* (*Hercynia silva*).

[4] **finibus:** 'frontiers'. **recta, etc.:** 'following the line of the Danube it extends'; how lit.?

[5] **regione:** *136b.*

[6] **sinistrorsus:** 'to the left' of the Danube, spreading out northward, toward the Carpathian Mountains. **diversis, etc.:** 'in a direction away from the river'; *92a.*

[7] **huius Germaniae:** 'of this (part of) Germany', the western part.

[8] **initium:** the eastern limit. **dicat:** *194a.* **cum:** *187.*

[9] **ferarum:** 'wild animals'. **quae:** 'such as'; *194a.* **reliquis locis:** 'any other places'.

[10] **ex quibus quae:** *et ex eis* (*ea*) *quae.*

[11] **memoriae:** dative; 'seem worthy of mention'; how lit.? **haec:** *161a.*

26.1. Est[1] bos cervi figura, cuius a media fronte inter aures unum cornu[2] exsistit, excelsius magisque derectum his, quae nobis nota sunt, cornibus; ab eius summo[3] sicut palmae ramique late diffunduntur. **2.** Eadem est feminae[4] marisque natura, eadem[5] forma magnitudoque cornuum.

[1] **Est:** *90a.* **bos, etc.:** 'an ox having the form of a stag'. Caesar is describing the reindeer, with which the American caribou is closely related. As a descriptive term *bos* was applied also to the elephant, one name of which was *Luca bos*, 'Lucanian cow'; *18a.* **figura:** *143a.* **media:** *152a.* **aures:** 'ears'; *82c.*

[2] **unum cornu:** reindeer and caribou shed their antlers each year, and Caesar's informant may have seen a reindeer which had lost one antler, but had not yet shed the other. In the Provincial Museum at Victoria, British Columbia, there is a degenerate caribou which, when shot, had only one antler. **excelsius, etc.:** 'higher and straighter'; *30; 129a.*

[3] **ab eius summo:** 'at the end of the antler'; how lit.? **sicut, etc.:** 'hands' (i.e. with fingers extended) 'and branches, as it were, are widely spread out'. The aptness of the description, and the comparison with the deer-horns familiar to the Romans (*nobis nota sunt*), suggest that Caesar had probably obtained an antler of a reindeer. The error of placing a single antler at the middle of the forehead of the reindeer may be due to an interpreter's misunderstanding; if so, the error is certainly no more remarkable than that mistranslation of Exodus (chapter 34, verse 29), which led Michelangelo to put horns on his famous statue of Moses.

[4] **feminae, etc.:** 'the natural characteristics of the male and the female'. **maris:** *13g.*

[5] **eadem, etc.:** here again Caesar was misinformed; the antlers of the female reindeer are somewhat smaller than those of the male.

27.1. Sunt item, quae appellantur alces.[1] Harum est consimilis capris[2] figura et varietas pellium, sed magnitudine paulo antecedunt[3] mutilaeque sunt cornibus et crura sine nodis articulisque[4] habent, **2.** neque quietis causa procumbunt, neque, si quo afflictae[5] casu conciderunt, erigere sese aut sublevare possunt. **3.** His sunt[6] arbores pro cubilibus; ad eas se applicant, atque ita, paulum modo reclinatae,[7] quietem capiunt. **4.** Quarum ex vestigiis cum[8] est animadversum a venatoribus, quo se recipere consuerint, omnes[9] eo loco aut ab radicibus subruunt aut accidunt[10] arbores, tantum, ut summa species earum stantium relinquatur. **5.** Huc[11] cum se consuetudine reclinaverunt, infirmas arbores pondere affligunt atque una ipsae concidunt.

[1] **alces:** 'moose'. The American moose closely resembles the European elk, to which Caesar refers; the American elk belongs to a different genus.

[2] **capris:** i.e. *figurae* (dative) *caprarum*, '(like) that of goats'; brachylogy. *238b.* **varietas:** 'mottled appearance'.

[3] **antecedunt:** 'they surpass (the reindeer)'. **mutilae, etc.:** 'their horns present a broken

appearance'; how lit.? **cornibus:** *142a.* **crura:** 'legs'; *13g.*

[4] **nodis articulisque:** 'nodes and joints'. In this statement Caesar reflects the condition of scientific knowledge in his time. The even more marvellous unicorn found a place in a textbook of Natural History as late as the fourteenth century. In England down to the nineteenth century the belief was still current that elephants have no joints in their legs. **quietis:** *10e.*

[5] **afflictae:** 'thrown down'. **erigere,** etc.: 'to assume a standing position, or raise themselves up'.

[6] **sunt pro cubilibus:** 'serve as resting-places'. **ad,** etc.: 'they lean up against these'.

[7] **reclinatae:** 'leaning to one side'; lit. 'leaned back'.

[8] **cum:** *185b.* **venatoribus:** 'hunters'; *74a.*

[9] **omnes:** with *arbores; 353d.* **ab:** 'at'; *126c.*

[10] **accidunt:** 'cut into'. **tantum,** etc.: '(only) so much that the trees retain perfectly the appearance of standing firmly'; how lit.?

[11] **Huc:** *in has arbores.* **consuetudine:** *136c.* This wonderful story may have originated in a distorted account of a kind of pitfall, made by covering a deep hole with timber so weakened by notches that a heavy animal passing above would break through.

28.1. Tertium est genus eorum, qui uri[1] appellantur. Hi sunt magnitudine paulo infra elephantos,[2] specie et colore et figura tauri.[3] **2.** Magna vis eorum est et magna velocitas, neque homini neque ferae, quam conspexerunt, parcunt.[4] **3.** Hos studiose[5] foveis captos interficiunt. Hoc se labore durant adulescentes atque hoc genere venationis exercent, et qui plurimos ex his interfecerunt, relatis[6] in publicum cornibus, quae sint[7] testimonio, magnam ferunt laudem. **4.** Sed assuescere[8] ad homines et mansuefieri ne parvuli quidem excepti possunt. **5.** Amplitudo cornuum et figura et species multum a nostrorum boum cornibus differt. **6.** Haec studiose conquisita[9] ab labris argento circumcludunt atque in amplissimis[10] epulis pro poculis utuntur.[11]

[1] **uri:** 'wild cattle', now extinct; sometimes confused with the aurochs, or European buffalo, of which a few herds still exist in game preserves. The 'wild cattle' had spreading horns, like those of Texas cattle, and it is thought that they represented the primitive stock from which our domestic cattle are descended. The last specimen died in 1627.

[2] **elephantos:** 'the elephant'; *92a.* **specie:** *143a.* **colore:** *80b.*

[3] **tauri:** i.e. of a domestic 'bull'.

[4] **parcunt:** 'spare'; they attack indiscriminately; *105.*

[5] **studiose:** 'diligently'. **foveis:** 'by means of pitfalls'. **captos:** *228a.* **se durant:** 'they develop hardihood'; how lit.?

[6] **relatis,** etc.: 'publicly exhibiting the horns as a trophy'.

[7] **sint:** *193a.* **testimonio:** *112a.*

[8] **assuescere,** etc.: 'become domesticated'. **mansuefieri:** 'be tamed'. **ne,** etc.: 'not even if very young when caught'.

[9] **conquisita:** 'collect and'; *228a.* **ab labris,** etc.: 'mount them with silver at the rim'; how lit.?

[10] **in amplissimis epulis:** 'at their more elaborate feasts'. The principal beverage was beer.

[11] **utuntur:** sc. *his;* 'use them as drinking cups'. Such drinking horns continued in use in the Middle Ages; in later times horns of cattle were made into "powder-horns", the use of which in America continued until after the Revolutionary War. Drinking horns were used also by the early Greeks.

Caesar returns to Gaul, cuts down the farther end of the bridge.

29.1. Caesar,[1] postquam per Ubios exploratores comperit, Suebos sese in silvas recepisse, inopiam frumenti veritus, quod, ut supra[2] demonstravimus, minime omnes Germani agri culturae student, constituit non progredi longius; **2.** sed, ne omnino metum reditus sui barbaris[3] tolleret atque ut eorum auxilia[4] tardaret, reducto exercitu, partem ultimam pontis, quae ripas Ubiorum contingebat, in longitudinem pedum CC rescindit, **3.** atque in extremo ponte[5] turrim tabulatorum IV constituit praesidiumque cohortium XII, pontis tuendi causa, ponit magnisque eum locum munitionibus[6] firmat. **4.** Ei loco praesidioque C. Volcacium Tullum adulescentem praefecit. Ipse, cum maturescere frumenta[7] inciperent, ad bellum Ambiorigis profectus, per Arduennam silvam, quae est totius Galliae maxima atque ab ripis Rheni finibusque Treverorum ad Nervios pertinet milibusque[8] amplius quingentis in longitudinem patet, L. Minucium Basilum cum omni equitatu praemittit, si[9] quid celeritate itineris atque opportunitate temporis proficere posset; **5.** monet, ut ignes in castris fieri prohibeat, ne qua eius adventus procul significatio fiat; sese confestim subsequi[10] dicit.

[1] **Caesar,** etc.: the narrative, broken off at chapter 10, is here resumed.
[2] **supra:** VI, 22.1; cf. IV, 1.7. **demonstravimus:** see II, 1.1, note 2.
[3] **barbaris: B.** 214; **A.** 243
[4] **auxilia:** forces that the Germans might send to help the rebellious Gauls. Cf. VI, 10.1.
[5] **in extremo ponte:** 'on the end of the bridge', in the river, 200 Roman feet from the east bank. The bridge probably crossed a small island, which furnished a secure foundation for the tower. **tabulatorum IV:** 'four stories high'; how lit.? *100a.*
[6] **munitionibus:** of a fortified enclosure at the end of the bridge, on the west bank.
[7] **frumenta:** why pl.? It was now the latter part of July, or early in August.
[8] **milibus:** sc. *passuum.* The distance is seemingly exaggerated.
[9] **si:** '(to see) whether' (AG 576a, B 300.3).
[10] **subsequi:** for the tense cf. II, 32.3, note 5.

30.1. Basilus, ut imperatum est, facit. Celeriter contraque omnium opinionem confecto itinere, multos in agris inopinantes deprehendit; eorum indicio ad ipsum Ambiorigem contendit, quo in loco[1] cum paucis equitibus esse dicebatur. **2.** Multum[2] cum in omnibus rebus, tum in re militari potest fortuna. Nam ut magno accidit casu, ut in ipsum incautum etiam atque imparatum incideret,[3] priusque eius adventus ab omnibus videretur, quam fama ac nuntius afferretur, sic magnae fuit fortunae,[4] omni militari instrumento, quod circum se habebat, erepto, raedis equisque comprehensis, ipsum effugere mortem. **3.** Sed hoc factum est, quod aedificio circumdato silva, ut sunt fere domicilia Gallorum,[5] qui vitandi aestus causa plerumque silvarum atque fluminum petunt propinquitates, comites familiaresque eius angusto in loco paulisper equitum nostrorum vim sustinuerunt. **4.** His pugnantibus illum in equum quidam ex suis intulit; fugientem silvae texerunt. Sic et ad subeundum periculum et ad vitandum multum fortuna valuit.

[1] **quo in loco:** = *ad eum locum, in quo.*
[2] **Multum – potest:** 'has great influence'; cf. I, 3.6, note 21 (*plurimum*).
[3] **incideret:** sc. *Basilus.* **prius, quam:** use of moods after *prius quam?*
[4] **magnae fuit fortunae:** 'it was a case of rare good luck'. The clause corresponds to *ut . . . casu* above; the power of fortune was manifested both by the way that Ambiorix fell into danger, and by the way that he got out of it.
[5] **domicilia Gallorum:** see V, 12.3, note 5.

31.1. Ambiorix copias suas iudicione[1] non conduxerit, quod proelio dimicandum non existimaret, an tempore exclusus[2] et repentino equitum adventu prohibitus, cum[3] reliquum exercitum subsequi crederet, dubium est; **2.** sed certe dimissis per agros nuntiis sibi quemque consulere iussit. Quorum pars in Arduennam silvam, pars in continentes[4] paludes profugit; **3.** qui proximi Oceano fuerunt, hi insulis[5] sese occultaverunt, quas aestus efficere consuerunt; **4.** multi ex suis finibus egressi se suaque omnia alienissimis crediderunt. **5.** Catuvolcus, rex dimidiae partis Eburonum, qui una cum Ambiorige consilium inierat, aetate iam confectus, cum laborem belli aut fugae ferre non posset, omnibus[6] precibus detestatus Ambiorigem, qui[7] eius consili auctor fuisset, taxo,[8] cuius magna in Gallia Germaniaque copia est, se exanimavit.

[1] **iudicio:** ablative of cause, 'purposely' (AG 335, B 162.4).
[2] **tempore exclusus:** 'prevented (from gathering his forces) by (the shortness of) time'.
[3] **cum:** 'since'.
[4] **continentes:** 'continuous'.
[5] **insulis:** low tracts of land that became islands when the tide ran in.
[6] **omnibus ... Ambiorigem:** 'calling down on Ambiorix all manner of curses'. More likely he cursed Caesar.
[7] **qui:** 'since he' (AG 535e, B 283.3a).
[8] **taxo:** the juice of yew-leaves is poisonous; the fruit is not, excepting the seeds, which are very poisonous.

32.1. Segni Condrusique,[1] ex gente et numero Germanorum, qui sunt inter Eburones Treverosque, legatos ad Caesarem miserunt oratum, ne se in hostium numero duceret neve omnium Germanorum, qui essent citra Rhenum, unam[2] esse causam iudicaret; nihil se de bello cogitasse, nulla Ambiorigi auxilia misisse. **2.** Caesar, explorata re quaestione captivorum, si[3] qui ad eos Eburones ex fuga convenissent, ad se ut reducerentur, imperavit; si ita fecissent, fines eorum se violaturum negavit. **3.** Tum copiis in tres partes distributis impedimenta omnium legionum Aduatucam contulit. **4.** Id castelli nomen est. Hoc fere est in mediis Eburonum finibus, ubi Titurius atque Aurunculeius hiemandi causa consederant. **5.** Hunc cum reliquis rebus locum probabat, tum quod superioris anni munitiones[4] integrae manebant, ut militum laborem sublevaret.[5] **6.** Praesidio impedimentis legionem quartam decimam reliquit, unam ex his tribus,[6] quas proxime conscriptas ex Italia traduxerat. **7.** Ei legioni castrisque Q. Tullium Ciceronem praeficit ducentosque equites ei attribuit.

[1] **Segni, Condrusi:** west of the Rhine; see Map.
[2] **unam:** 'one and the same'.
[3] **si ... violaturum:** in direct discourse, *si ita feceritis, ... non violabo* (AG 589; B 319A, Ba).
[4] **munitiones:** the fortifications of the camp abandoned by Cotta and Sabinus. See V, 26-37; VI, 37.7.
[5] **sublevaret:** sc. *Caesar.* The soldiers could occupy the old camp and be spared the labour of fortifying.
[6] **tribus:** see VI.1.4, notes 9-11.

33.1. Partito exercitu T. Labienum cum legionibus tribus[1] ad Oceanum versus in eas partes, quae Menapios attingunt, proficisci iubet; **2.** C.

Trebonium cum pari legionum numero ad eam regionem, quae ad
Aduatucos adiacet, depopulandam mittit; **3.** ipse cum reliquis tribus[2] ad
flumen Scaldim,[3] quod influit in Mosam, extremasque Arduennae partes
ire constituit, quo cum paucis equitibus profectum Ambiorigem audiebat.
4. Discedens post diem septimum[4] sese reversurum confirmat; quam[5] ad
diem ei legioni, quae in praesidio[6] relinquebatur, frumentum deberi
sciebat. **5.** Labienum Treboniumque hortatur, si rei publicae commodo[7]
facere possint, ad eum diem revertantur, ut, rursus communicato consilio
exploratisque hostium rationibus, aliud initium belli capere possent.

[1] **Partito:** passive.
[2] **tribus:** as one legion was left at Aduatuca (Tongres) under Cicero, and as Labienus,
Trebonius, and Caesar each had three, the ten legions were all disposed of. We must
suppose, therefore, that Caesar had now withdrawn the twelve cohorts left to guard the
bridge over the Rhine (VI, 29.3), which is highly improbable (cf. VI, 35.6), or that these were
cohorts of auxiliaries outside the regular legions.
[3] **Scaldim:** in point of fact the Schelde does not flow into the Meuse; and its distance from
Tongres seems too great to be twice traversed, as Caesar travelled, in seven days. It has been
suggested that *Scaldim* is a mistake in the manuscripts for *Sabim;* the Sambre meets all the
conditions of Caesar's statement.
[4] **post diem septimum:** 'on (lit. 'during') the seventh day after'.
[5] **quam diem:** notice the change of gender from the preceding line, because '(limit of) time' or
'date' rather than 'day' is meant (AG 97a, B. 53).
[6] **in praesidio:** at Aduatuca.
[7] **rei publicae commodo:** 'consistently with the public interest', 'to the advantage of the
commonwealth'.

34.1. Erat,[1] ut supra demonstravimus, manus certa nulla, non oppidum,
non praesidium, quod se armis defenderet,[2] sed in omnes partes dispersa
multitudo. **2.** Ubi cuique aut valles abdita[3] aut locus silvestris aut palus
impedita spem praesidi aut salutis aliquam offerebat, consederat. **3.** Haec
loca vicinitatibus[4] erant nota, magnamque res diligentiam requirebat, non
in[5] summa exercitus tuenda (nullum enim poterat universis a perterritis
ac dispersis periculum accidere), sed in singulis militibus conservandis;
quae tamen ex parte res[6] ad salutem exercitus pertinebat. **4.** Nam et
praedae cupiditas multos longius evocabat, et silvae incertis occultisque
itineribus confertos[7] adire prohibebant. **5.** Si negotium confici stirpemque
hominum sceleratorum[8] interfici vellet, dimittendae plures manus
diducendique erant milites; **6.** si continere ad signa manipulos vellet, ut
instituta ratio et consuetudo exercitus Romani postulabat, locus ipse erat
praesidio barbaris, neque ex occulto insidiandi et dispersos
circumveniendi singulis deerat audacia. **7.** Ut[9] in eius modi difficultatibus,
quantum diligentia provideri poterat, providebatur, ut[10] potius in nocendo
aliquid praetermitteretur, etsi omnium animi ad ulciscendum ardebant,
quam cum aliquo militum detrimento noceretur. **8.** Dimittit ad finitimas
civitates nuntios Caesar; omnes evocat spe praedae ad diripiendos
Eburones, ut potius in silvis Gallorum vita quam legionarius miles
periclitetur, simul ut magna multitudine circumfusa pro tali facinore
stirps ac nomen civitatis tollatur. **9.** Magnus undique numerus celeriter
convenit.

[1] **Erat:** see I, 6.1, note 1. **supra:** VI, 31.1-2. **certa:** 'definite', i.e. among the Gauls.

[2] **defenderet:** 'was able to defend'; subjunctive of characteristic.

[3] **abdita:** 'secluded'.

[4] **vicinitatibus:** abstract for concrete; 'neighbours'.

[5] **in . . . tuenda:** 'in protecting the army as a whole'.

[6] **quae tamen ex parte res:** 'a circumstance which, nevertheless, in a degree'.

[7] **confertos:** in masses, or divisions, for mutual protection.

[8] **sceleratorum:** referring to the Eburones, for whom on account of their having destroyed the fifteen cohorts under Cotta and Sabinus, Caesar felt the most bitter hatred; cf. V.37, note 10. Their "wickedness" in Caesar's view lay in the fact that they had fought bravely for their freedom, and had inflicted a telling blow upon him.

[9] **Ut . . . difficultatibus:** 'Considering the nature of the difficulties'.

[10] **ut,** etc.: that he might rather do less damage to the foe than cause any hurt to his soldiers. Caesar let loose upon the Eburones their savage neighbours.

The Sugambri storm Cicero's camp, and are repulsed.

35.1. Haec in omnibus Eburonum partibus gerebantur, diesque appetebat septimus, quem ad diem[1] Caesar ad impedimenta legionemque[2] reverti constituerat. **2.** Hic, quantum in bello fortuna[3] possit et quantos afferat casus, cognosci potuit. **3.** Dissipatis ac perterritis hostibus, ut demonstravimus, manus erat nulla, quae parvam modo causam timoris afferret. **4.** Trans Rhenum ad Germanos pervenit fama, diripi Eburones atque ultro omnes ad praedam evocari. **5.** Cogunt equitum duo milia Sugambri, qui sunt proximi Rheno, a quibus receptos ex fuga Tencteros atque Usipetes supra docuimus.[4] **6.** Transeunt Rhenum navibus ratibusque triginta milibus passuum infra eum locum, ubi pons[5] erat perfectus praesidiumque a Caesare relictum; primos Eburonum fines adeunt; multos ex fuga[6] dispersos excipiunt, magno pecoris numero,[7] cuius sunt cupidissimi barbari, potiuntur. Invitati praeda longius procedunt. **7.** Non hos palus in bello latrociniisque natos,[8] non silvae morantur. Quibus in locis sit Caesar, ex captivis quaerunt; profectum longius reperiunt omnemque exercitum discessisse cognoscunt. **8.** Atque unus ex captivis, 'Quid vos,' inquit, 'hanc miseram ac tenuem[9] sectamini praedam, quibus licet iam esse fortunatissimos? **9.** Tribus horis Aduatucam venire potestis; huc omnes suas fortunas exercitus Romanorum contulit; praesidi tantum[10] est, ut ne murus quidem cingi possit, neque quisquam[11] egredi extra munitiones audeat.' **10.** Oblata spe Germani, quam[12] nacti erant praedam, in occulto relinquunt; ipsi Aduatucam contendunt usi eodem duce,[13] cuius haec indicio cognoverant.

[1] **diem:** see VI, 33.4. (AG 307a, B 251.3).

[2] **legionem:** the XIVth, under Cicero, with the military stores at Aduatuca; see VI, 32.3-6.

[3] **fortuna,** etc.: cf. VI, 30.4.

[4] **supra docuimus:** see IV, 16.2-4.

[5] **pons, praesidium:** see VI, 9.3; and VI, 29.3, note 5.

[6] **ex fuga:** 'in flight'.

[7] **numero:** what other case is sometimes found after *potior*?

[8] **latrociniis natos:** see VI, 23.6, note 10.

[9] **tenuem:** 'trifling'.

[10] **praesidi tantum:** 'so small a garrison'. **ut . . . possit:** 'that not even the rampart in its entire extent can be manned'.

[11] **neque quisquam:** 'and no one'.

[12] **quam praedam:** trans. as if *eam praedam, quam.*

[13] **duce:** 'as guide'; why abl.?

36.1. Cicero,[1] qui omnes superiores dies praeceptis Caesaris cum summa diligentia milites in castris continuisset ac ne calonem quidem quemquam extra munitionem egredi passus esset, septimo die, diffidens de numero dierum Caesarem fidem servaturum, quod longius progressum[2] audiebat neque ulla de reditu eius fama afferebatur, **2.** simul eorum permotus vocibus, qui illius[3] patientiam paene obsessionem appellabant, si quidem ex castris egredi non liceret, nullum eius modi casum exspectans, quo,[4] novem oppositis legionibus maximoque equitatu, dispersis ac paene deletis hostibus, in milibus passuum tribus offendi posset, quinque cohortes frumentatum in proximas segetes mittit, quas inter et castra unus[5] omnino collis intererat. **3.** Complures erant in castris ex legionibus[6] aegri relicti; ex quibus qui hoc spatio[7] dierum convaluerant, circiter CCC, sub vexillo una mittuntur; **4.** magna praeterea multitudo calonum, magna vis iumentorum, quae in castris subsederant, facta potestate[8] sequitur.

[1] **Cicero:** the year before (autumn of B.C. 54) Cicero had bravely withstood a most violent attack on his camp among the Nervii; see V, 38-52. **qui:** = 'although he', hence followed by the subjunctive (B 283.3b). **praeceptis:** 'according to the instructions'.

[2] **progressum:** sc. *eum esse.*

[3] **illius:** Cicero.

[4] **quo . . . posset:** 'by which hurt could be received in (a march of only) three miles'.

[5] **unus:** 'only a.'

[6] **legionibus:** the nine legions off on expeditions.

[7] **hoc spatio,** etc.: they had recovered in the few days that Caesar had been gone. **sub vexillo:** being of different legions and maniples, they went off by themselves under a flag, instead of with a regular standard.

[8] **facta potestate:** 'having obtained permission'.

37.1. Hoc[1] ipso tempore et casu Germani equites interveniunt protinusque eodem illo,[2] quo venerant, cursu ab[3] decumana porta in castra irrumpere conantur, **2.** nec prius sunt visi, obiectis[4] ab ea parte silvis, quam castris appropinquarent, usque eo ut, qui sub vallo tenderent[5] mercatores, recipiendi sui[6] facultatem non haberent. **3.** Inopinantes nostri re nova perturbantur, ac vix primum impetum cohors in statione sustinet. **4.** Circumfunduntur[7] hostes ex reliquis partibus,[8] si quem aditum reperire possent. **5.** Aegre portas nostri tuentur; reliquos aditus locus[9] ipse per se munitioque defendit. **6.** Totis[10] trepidatur castris, atque alius ex alio causam tumultus quaerit; neque quo signa ferantur,[11] neque quam in partem quisque conveniat, provident. **7.** Alius castra iam capta pronuntiat, alius deleto exercitu atque imperatore victores barbaros venisse contendit; **8.** plerique novas sibi ex[12] loco religiones fingunt Cottaeque et Tituri calamitatem,[13] qui in eodem occiderint castello, ante oculos ponunt. **9.** Tali timore omnibus perterritis, confirmatur opinio barbaris,[14] ut ex captivo audierant, nullum esse intus praesidium. **10.** Perrumpere nituntur seque ipsi adhortantur, ne tantam fortunam ex manibus dimittant.

[1] **Hoc . . . casu:** 'Just at this critical moment'.

[2] **eodem illo cursu:** 'with that same gallop'.

[3] **ab:** 'on the side of'.

[4] **obiectis silvis**: causal ablative absolute. **appropinquarent**: (AG 551b, B 292).
[5] **tenderent**: 'had their tents' (AG 593, B 324.1). The tents of the traders were in this case just outside the rear gate.
[6] **recipiendi sui**: (AG 504c, B 339.5).
[7] **Circumfunduntur**: 'pour around', 'swarm around' (AG 156aN, B 256.1).
[8] **ex reliquis partibus**: 'on the other sides'. **si**: '(to see) whether' (AG 576a, B 300.3).
[9] **locus**: the camp was no doubt situated on a hill.
[10] **Totis . . . castris**: 'there is a panic throughout the camp'.
[11] **signa ferantur**: 'an advance should be made'. **quam . . . conveniat**: 'where the men should fall in'.
[12] **ex . . . fingunt**: 'draw superstitions from the locality'.
[13] **calamitatem**: described in V, 26-37. **occiderint**: subjunctive because Caesar is giving the thought of the soldiers.
[14] **barbaris**: trans. as if *barbarorum* (AG 377, B 188.1n).

38.1. Erat aeger in praesidio relictus P. Sextius Baculus, qui primum pilum[1] apud Caesarem duxerat, cuius mentionem superioribus proeliis[2] fecimus, ac diem iam quintum cibo caruerat. **2.** Hic, diffisus suae atque omnium saluti, inermis ex tabernaculo prodit; videt, imminere hostes atque in summo rem esse discrimine; capit arma a proximis atque in porta consistit. **3.** Consequuntur hunc centuriones eius cohortis, quae in statione[3] erat; paulisper una proelium sustinent. **4.** Relinquit animus Sextium,[4] gravibus acceptis vulneribus; aegre per manus tractus [5]servatur. Hoc spatio interposito, reliqui sese confirmant tantum, ut in munitionibus consistere audeant speciemque defensorum praebeant.

[1] **primum pilum duxerat**: Baculus had been first centurion, *primipilus*. **apud Caesarem**: 'under Caesar', in Caesar's army.
[2] **superioribus proeliis**: 'in (the narrative of) previous battles', viz., that with the Nervii (see II, 25.1), and that in the Alps (see III, 5.2).
[3] **in statione**: 'on guard'.
[4] **Relinquit animus Sextium**: 'Sextius faints'.
[5] **per manus tractus**: 'dragged from hand to hand'.

39.1. Interim, confecta frumentatione, milites nostri clamorem exaudiunt; praecurrunt equites; quanto res sit in periculo, cognoscunt. **2.** Hic[1] vero nulla munitio est, quae perterritos recipiat;[2] modo conscripti atque usus militaris imperiti ad tribunum militum centurionesque ora convertunt; quid ab his praecipiatur, exspectant.[3] **3.** Nemo est tam fortis, quin[4] rei novitate perturbetur. **4.** Barbari signa procul conspicati oppugnatione desistunt; redisse primo legiones credunt, quas longius discessisse ex captivis cognoverant; postea, despecta paucitate, ex omnibus partibus impetum faciunt.

[1] **Hic nulla munitio**: the foragers were apparently three miles from camp (see VI, 36.2).
[2] **recipiat**: force of the subjunctive? **modo conscripti**: the XIVth legion had been recently enrolled. See VI, 32.6; VI, 1.4, note 10.
[3] **exspectant**: 'they wait (to see) what order will be given'.
[4] **quin**: = *qui non*; 'as not to be upset'.

40.1. Calones in proximum tumulum procurrunt. Hinc celeriter deiecti se in[1] signa manipulosque coniciunt; eo magis timidos perterrent milites. **2.** Alii,[2] cuneo facto ut celeriter perrumpant, censent, quoniam[3] tam propinqua sint castra, et si pars aliqua circumventa ceciderit, at[4] reliquos servari posse confidunt; **3.** alii,[5] ut in iugo consistant atque eundem omnes ferant casum. **4.** Hoc veteres non probant milites, quos sub vexillo una profectos docuimus.[6] Itaque inter se cohortati duce C. Trebonio, equite Romano, qui eis erat praepositus, per medios hostes perrumpunt incolumesque ad unum omnes in castra perveniunt. **5.** Hos subsecuti calones equitesque eodem impetu militum virtute servantur. **6.** At ei, qui in iugo constiterant, nullo etiam nunc usu rei militaris percepto, neque in eo, quod probaverant, consilio permanere, ut se loco superiore defenderent, neque eam,[7] quam prodesse aliis vim celeritatemque viderant, imitari potuerunt, sed se in castra recipere conati iniquum in locum demiserunt. **7.** Centuriones, quorum non nulli ex inferioribus ordinibus reliquarum legionum virtutis causa,[8] in superiores erant ordines huius legionis traducti, ne ante partam rei militaris laudem amitterent, fortissime pugnantes conciderunt. **8.** Militum pars,[9] horum virtute summotis hostibus, praeter spem incolumis in castra pervenit, pars a barbaris circumventa periit.

[1] **in . . . manipulos:** the drivers try to force their way in among the soldiers of the companies.
[2] **Alii censent:** 'some (of the soldiers) propose'.
[3] **quoniam – sint:** 'since (they say) the camp is'; reason for subjunctive?
[4] **at:** 'at least'.
[5] **alii:** sc. *censent*.
[6] **docuimus:** see VI, 36.3. **inter se cohortati:** (AG 145c, B 245.1).
[7] **eam:** *vim celeritatemque.*
[8] **virtutis causa:** 'on account of bravery'. Caesar had promoted into higher positions in the new XIVth legion some centurions of lower rank from the other legions, both as a reward of merit and as an example of courage to the recruits.
[9] **pars:** two cohorts perished, more than 700 men; see VI, 44.1.

41.1. Germani, desperata expugnatione castrorum, quod nostros iam constitisse in munitionibus videbant, cum ea praeda, quam in silvis deposuerant, trans Rhenum sese receperunt. **2.** Ac tantus fuit etiam post discessum hostium terror, ut ea nocte, cum C. Volusenus missus cum equitatu in castra venisset, fidem non faceret,[1] adesse cum incolumi Caesarem exercitu. **3.** Sic omnium animos timor[2] occupaverat, ut paene alienata mente,[3] deletis omnibus copiis, equitatum se ex fuga recepisse dicerent, neque[4] incolumi exercitu Germanos castra oppugnaturos fuisse contenderent. **4.** Quem timorem Caesaris adventus sustulit.

[1] **fidem non faceret:** 'he could not convince (Cicero and the soldiers)'.
[2] **timor:** see I, 39.1, note 7.
[3] **alienata mente:** ablative absolute, 'bereft of reason'.
[4] **neque . . . contenderent:** 'and they were maintaining that, had the Roman army been unharmed, the Germans would not have attacked the camp'. **incolumi exercitu:** ablative absolute (AG 521a, B 305.1)

42.1. Reversus ille, eventus[1] belli non ignorans, unum, quod cohortes ex statione et praesidio essent emissae,[2] questus (ne minimo quidem casui[3] locum relinqui debuisse) multum[4] fortunam in repentino hostium adventu potuisse iudicavit,[5] **2.** multo etiam amplius, quod paene ab ipso vallo portisque castrorum barbaros avertisset. **3.** Quarum omnium rerum maxime admirandum[6] videbatur, quod Germani, qui eo consilio Rhenum transierant, ut Ambiorigis fines depopularentur, ad castra Romanorum delati optatissimum Ambiorigi beneficium obtulerunt.

[1] **eventus:** accusative, 'issues', 'chances'. **unum:** after *questus* '(only) one thing'.
[2] **essent emissae:** when is *quod* causal found with the subjunctive?
[3] **casui:** '(saying) that . . . for not even the least chance'.
[4] **multum – potuisse:** see VI, 30.2, note 2.
[5] **iudicavit:** 'concluded'. **amplius:** sc. *fortunam potuisse.*
[6] **admirandum:** sc. *hoc* (= *haec res*).

Caesar lays waste the country of the Eburones; holds a council; places his army in winter quarters, and goes to Italy.

43.1. Caesar rursus ad vexandos hostes profectus, magno coacto equitum numero[1] ex finitimis civitatibus, in omnes partes dimittit.[2] **2.** Omnes vici atque omnia aedificia, quae quisque conspexerat, incendebantur; **3.** praeda[3] ex omnibus locis agebatur; frumenta[4] non solum a tanta multitudine iumentorum atque hominum consumebantur, sed etiam anni tempore[5] atque imbribus procubuerant, ut, si qui etiam in praesentia[6] se occultassent, tamen his, deducto exercitu, rerum[7] omnium inopia pereundum videretur. **4.** Ac saepe in eum locum ventum est, tanto in omnes partes diviso[8] equitatu, ut[9] modo visum ab se Ambiorigem in fuga circumspicerent captivi, nec plane etiam abisse ex conspectu contenderent, **5.** ut, spe consequendi illata atque infinito labore suscepto, qui se summam a Caesare gratiam inituros putarent, paene[10] naturam studio vincerent, semperque paulum ad summam felicitatem defuisse videretur, **6.** atque ille[11] latebris aut saltibus se eriperet et noctu occultatus alias regiones partesque peteret non maiore equitum praesidio quam IV, quibus solis vitam suam committere audebat.

[1] **numero, etc.:** cf. VI, 34.7, note 10.
[2] **dimittit:** sc. *eos.*
[3] **praeda:** cattle, and perhaps other animals, as shown by *agebatur;* cf. also VI, 35.6.
[4] **frumenta:** force of the plural?
[5] **anni tempore:** autumn; the autumn rains had begun.
[6] **in praesentia:** 'for a time'. **deducto exercitu:** 'after the army should have been led away'.
[7] **rerum omnium inopia pereundum:** 'they would have to perish from want of all things'. **in eum locum:** 'to such a pass'.
[8] **in omnes partes diviso:** 'sent apart in all directions'.
[9] **ut, etc.:** 'that those captured were looking about for Ambiorix, just seen by them in flight, and were maintaining', etc.
[10] **paene . . . vincerent:** 'in their eagerness (of pursuit) were almost surpassing their natural powers'.
[11] **ille, etc.:** Ambiorix seemed to be living a charmed life. In 51 B.C. we find him still eluding Caesar's grasp (B. G. VIII, 24).

44.1. Tali modo vastatis regionibus exercitum Caesar duarum cohortium damno[1] Durocortorum Remorum reducit, concilioque in eum locum Galliae indicto de coniuratione Senonum et Carnutum quaestionem habere instituit; **2.** et de Accone, qui princeps eius consili fuerat, graviore sententia pronuntiata, more[2] maiorum supplicium sumpsit. **3.** Non nulli iudicium veriti profugerunt. Quibus cum aqua[3] atque igni interdixisset, duas legiones ad fines Treverorum, duas in Lingonibus, VI reliquas in

Senonum finibus Agedinci in hibernis collocavit; frumentoque exercitui proviso, ut instituerat, in Italiam[4] ad conventus agendos profectus est.

[1] **duarum cohortium damno:** see VI, 40.8, note 9.

[2] **more . . . sumpsit:** 'punished after the ancient fashion'. The ancient Roman custom referred to was that of putting traitors to death.

[3] **aqua . . . interdixisset:** 'forbid the use of fire and water'. This was the usual Roman formula of exile, by which every one within certain limits was forbidden to furnish the outcast with fire and water, these representing the necessaries of life.

[4] **Italiam:** see I, 10.3, note 7. **ad conventus agendos:** see I, 54.3, note 8.

PLATE IX   APPLIANCES FOR SIEGE AND DEFENSE

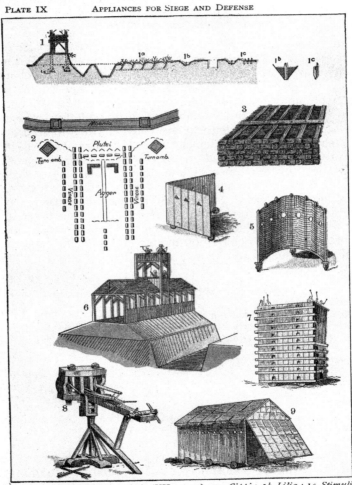

1. Caesar's Works before Alesia (VII. 72, 73): 1a, *Cippi*; 1b, *Lilia*; 1c, *Stimuli*.
2. *Agger*, etc. (VII. 24).   3. Gallic City Wall (VII. 23).
4, 5. Movable Breastworks, *plutei*.
6. Rampart of Camp, with Passageway and Towers.
7. Movable Tower, *turris ambulatoria*.   8. Catapult, *catapulta*.
9. Sapper's Hut, *vinea*.

COMMENTARIUS SEPTIMUS

<small>BEGINNING OF A GENERAL UPRISING; FIRST MOVEMENTS. 1-10</small>

The Gauls secretly plan a general uprising.

1.1. [1]Quieta Gallia,[2] Caesar, ut constituerat, in Italiam ad conventus agendos proficiscitur. Ibi cognoscit de P. Clodii[3] caede; de senatusque consulto certior factus, ut omnes iuniores[4] Italiae coniurarent, dilectum tota provincia habere instituit. **2.** Eae res in Galliam Transalpinam celeriter perferuntur. Addunt ipsi et affingunt[5] rumoribus Galli, quod res poscere videbatur, retineri urbano motu[6] Caesarem neque in tantis dissensionibus[7] ad exercitum venire posse. **3.** Hac impulsi occasione, qui[8] iam ante se populi Romani imperio subiectos dolerent, liberius atque audacius de bello consilia inire incipiunt. **4.** Indictis inter se principes Galliae conciliis silvestribus ac remotis locis queruntur de Acconis[9] morte; hunc casum ad ipsos recidere[10] posse demonstrant; **5.** miserantur communem Galliae fortunam; omnibus pollicitationibus[11] ac praemiis deposcunt, qui belli initium faciant et sui[12] capitis periculo Galliam in libertatem vindicent. **6.** In primis rationem esse habendam[13] dicunt, prius quam eorum clandestina consilia efferantur, ut Caesar ab exercitu intercludatur. **7.** *Id esse facile, quod neque legiones audeant, absente imperatore, ex hibernis[14] egredi, neque imperator sine praesidio ad legiones pervenire possit;* **8.** *postremo in acie praestare interfici, quam non veterem belli gloriam libertatemque, quam a maioribus acceperint, recuperare.*

---

[1] **The Circumstances.** During the sixth year of the Gallic War (53 B.C.) the restlessness of the conquered states became increasingly manifest, but all attempts to revolt were sternly repressed by Caesar. After his return from the second expedition into Germany (VI, 29), Caesar devoted himself particularly to the chastisement of the Eburones, but narrowly escaped the loss of a legion, which was stationed at Atuatuca ,under the command of Quintus Cicero, and attacked by a force of marauding Sugambrians (VI, 30-44). Before the close of the winter 53-52 B.C. the Gauls began to organize a general rebellion. The earlier part of the Seventh Book, which is devoted to the events of 52 B.C., deals with the first movements of the Gauls and with Caesar's counter-movements, which were characterized by amazing quickness of decision, energy, and despatch.

[2] **Quieta Gallia:** the "calm before the storm"; *144b3*. **Italiam:** Cisalpine Gaul; *283b*. **ad,** etc.: see I, 54.3, note 8.

[3] **P. Clodii:** killed in January, 52 B.C., in an encounter with his personal enemy, T. Annius Milo. Riots ensued at Rome, and the Senate called up all men throughout Italy capable of bearing arms.

[4] **iuniores:** men between the ages of 17 and 46. **coniurarent:** 'should together take the oath' that they would obey the consuls. **dilectum:** 'levy'; *307a*. **Provincia:** = *citeriore provincia; 284.*

[5] **Addunt et affingunt:** 'added to (the facts) and embellished (them) with rumors'; *175b*. **quod:** = *id quod*, explained by *retineri . . . posse;* "the wish" was "father to the thought". **res:** 'the condition of affairs'.

[6] **urbano motu:** 'the disturbances in the city', in Rome.

[7] **dissensionibus:** 'strifes'.

[8] **qui:** 'since they'; *194c.* **ante:** adverb.

[9] **Acconis:** a leader in uprisings the previous year (VI, 4.1).

[10] **ad ipsos recidere:** 'might fall upon themselves'.

[11] **omnibus pollicitationibus:** 'by every sort of promise'.

[12] **sui,** etc.: 'at the risk of their lives would assert the freedom of Gaul'. How lit.?

[13] **rationem esse habendam:** 'that a plan should be devised'.

[14] **hibernis**: 6 legions at Agedincum (3, Map 13), 2 among the Lingones (2, Map 13), and 2 near the Treveran frontier.

The Carnutes lead in revolt, massacre the Romans in Cenabum.

2.1. His rebus agitatis, profitentur[1] Carnutes, se nullum periculum communis salutis causa, recusare, principesque[2] ex omnibus bellum facturos pollicentur **2.** et, quoniam[3] in praesentia obsidibus cavere inter se non possint, ne res efferatur, at iure iurando ac fide[4] sanciatur, petunt, collatis militaribus signis, quo more eorum[5] gravissima caerimonia continetur, ne, facto initio belli, ab reliquis deserantur. **3.** Tum, collaudatis Carnutibus, dato iure iurando ab omnibus, qui aderant, tempore eius rei[6] constituto, a concilio disceditur.[7]

[1] **profitentur**: at a meeting of representatives of Gallic states.
[2] **principes**, etc.: 'that they will be the first of all to make war'.
[3] **quoniam**, etc.: 'since at the time they could not bind one another for mutual protection by an exchange of hostages'.
[4] **fide**: 'a pledge of honour'. **sanciatur**: sc. *ut*; 'that (the compact) be ratified'; *199a.* **collatis signis**: 'by placing their standards close together'. signifying inviolable alliance for war.
[5] **more eorum**: 'in accordance with their custom'; *136c.* **gravissima**: 'most solemn'.
[6] **eius rei**: the commencing of hostilities.
[7] **disceditur**: 'they went away'; *73d; 176b.*

3.1. Ubi ea dies[1] venit, Carnutes, Cotuato et Conconnetodumno ducibus, desperatis[2] hominibus, Cenabum signo dato concurrunt civesque Romanos, qui negotiandi[3] causa ibi constiterant, in his C. Fufium Citam, honestum equitem Romanum, qui rei frumentariae iussu Caesaris praeerat, interficiunt[4] bonaque eorum diripiunt. **2.** Celeriter ad omnes Galliae civitates fama perfertur. Nam ubi quae[5] maior atque illustrior incidit res, clamore per agros[6] regionesque significant; hunc alii deinceps excipiunt et proximis tradunt, ut tum accidit. **3.** Nam quae Cenabi[7] oriente sole gesta essent, ante primam confectam vigiliam in finibus Arvernorum audita sunt, quod spatium[8] est milium passuum circiter CLX.

[1] **dies**: the 'day' appointed for commencing hostilities; *21a.*
[2] **desperatis**: here an adjective. **Cenabum**: Map 13; *119a.*
[3] **negotiandi**: the Roman citizens engaged in business in Gallic cities were chiefly money-lenders who furnished capital for various enterprises, and dealers in supplies, particularly of grain.
[4] **interficiunt**: the massacre of the Roman citizens, well organized in advance, took place at daybreak.
[5] **quae**: 'any'; *168.* **clamore**: 'by shouting'.
[6] **per agros regionesque**: 'across the country'; how lit.? **hunc** [clamorem], etc.: 'others in turn take up the shouting'.
[7] **Cenabi**: *146.* **gesta essent**: adversative, 'although these things had been done'; *194d.* **ante . . . vigiliam**: *228b, 242c.*
[8] **quod spatium**: 'a distance which'. Perhaps men had been posted in advance along the roads leading from Cenabum, in readiness to transmit the news: otherwise the population must have been so dense over the country that neighbors were within hailing distance; *165b.*

The Arverni revolt, under the leadership of Vercingetorix.

4.1. Simili ratione ibi[1] Vercingetorix, Celtilli filius, Arvernus, summae potentiae adulescens, cuius pater principatum totius Galliae[2] obtinuerat et ob eam[3] causam, quod regnum appetebat, a civitate erat interfectus, convocatis suis clientibus[4] facile incendit. **2.** Cognito eius consilio, ad arma concurritur.[5] Prohibetur a Gobannitione, patruo suo, reliquisque principibus, qui hanc[6] temptandam fortunam non existimabant; expellitur ex oppido Gergovia; **3.** non destitit tamen, atque in agris habet dilectum egentium ac perditorum. Hac coacta manu, quoscumque[7] adit ex civitate, ad suam sententiam perducit; **4.** hortatur, ut communis libertatis causa arma capiant, magnisque coactis copiis adversarios[8] suos, a quibus paulo ante erat eiectus, expellit ex civitate. **5.** Rex ab suis appellatur. Dimittit quoque versus legationes; obtestatur,[9] ut in fide maneant.

Vercingetorix wins over many states, including the Bituriges.

6. Celeriter sibi Senones, Parisios, Pictones, Cadurcos, Turonos, Aulercos, Lemovices, Andos reliquosque omnes, qui Oceanum attingunt, adiungit; omnium consensu ad eum defertur imperium. **7.** Qua oblata potestate, omnibus his civitatibus obsides imperat, certum numerum militum ad se celeriter adduci iubet, **8.** armorum quantum[10] quaeque civitas domi[11] quodque ante tempus efficiat, constituit; in primis equitatui studet. **9.** Summae diligentiae summam imperii severitatem addit; magnitudine supplicii dubitantes[12] cogit. **10.** Nam, maiore commisso delicto,[13] igni atque omnibus tormentis necat, leviore de causa[14] auribus desectis, aut singulis effossis oculis, domum remittit, ut sint reliquis documento[15] et magnitudine poenae perterreant alios.

[1] **ibi:** in the country of the Arvernians; Map 13.
[2] **principatum totius Galliae:** 'a position of leadership throughout the Celtic country', on account of his influence; *287b.*
[3] **eam:** *161a.* **causam:** explained by the *quod*-clause.
[4] **clientibus:** a feudal following, like that of Orgetorix (I, 4).
[5] **ad arma concurritur:** 'they rushed to arms'; how lit.? *73d.* **patruo:** 'uncle' on his father's side.
[6] **hanc,** etc.: 'that fortune ought not to be tempted in this way'. How lit.?
[7] **quoscumque,** etc.: 'all the men of his state whom he approached'; *50a.*
[8] **adversarios:** 'opponents', such as Gobannitio.
[9] **obtestatur:** 'he adjured (his allies)'. through his envoys.
[10] **armorum quantum,** etc.: 'how great a supply of arms each state should furnish'; *97b.*
[11] **domi:** 'of its own manufacture', lit. 'at home'; *146.* **quod,** etc.: 'and before what time'; Vercingetorix fixed the date for delivery.
[12] **dubitantes:** 'those who hesitated' to join him; *227a4.*
[13] **delicto:** 'offense'. **necat:** sc. *eum qui id commiserat.*
[14] **leviore de causa:** i.e. *si qui levius peccaverunt.* **auribus,** etc.: 'he cut off their ears, or gouged out one eye, and'; *144b2.*
[15] **documento:** 'a warning'; *112b.*

5.1. His suppliciis celeriter coacto exercitu, Lucterium Cadurcum, summae hominem audaciae, cum parte copiarum in Rutenos[1] mittit; ipse in Bituriges proficiscitur. **2.** Eius adventu Bituriges ad Aeduos, quorum[2] erant in fide, legatos mittunt subsidium rogatum,[3] quo facilius hostium copias sustinere possint. **3.** Aedui de consilio legatorum,[4] quos Caesar ad exercitum reliquerat, copias equitatus peditatusque subsidio Biturigibus[5] mittunt. **4.** Qui cum ad flumen Ligerim venissent, quod Bituriges ab Aeduis dividit, paucos dies ibi morati neque flumen transire ausi,[6] domum revertuntur **5.** legatisque nostris renuntiant, *se Biturigum perfidiam veritos[7] revertisse, quibus id consilii fuisse cognoverint, ut, si flumen transissent,* *una ex parte ipsi, altera Arverni se circumsisterent.* **6.** Id eane[8] de causa, quam legatis pronuntiarunt, an perfidia adducti fecerint,[9] quod nihil nobis constat, non videtur pro certo esse ponendum. **7.** Bituriges eorum discessu statim se cum Arvernis coniungunt.

[1] **Rutenos,** etc.: Vercingetorix proceeds with great energy against the states friendly to Caesar.
[2] **quorum,** etc.: 'in whose allegiance they were'. The Aeduans were at the head of one league of Gallic states, the Arvernians of the other (I, 31.3-7).
[3] **rogatum:** *281a.* **hostium:** the Arvernian army.
[4] **legatorum:** these had been left 'with the army' when it was placed in winter quarters at the end of 53 B.C.; *313a.*
[5] **Biturigibus:** *19e, 112b.* **Qui:** *167.* **Ligerim:** *18e.*
[6] **ausi:** *62.* **domum:** *20c, 119b.*
[7] **veritos:** *61a2; 227a1.* **quibus,** etc.: 'having found out that the Bituriges had the design'; *97b; 214a.*
[8] **-ne . . .an:** *204.1* (AG 335, B 162.4).
[9] **fecerint:** the object is *Id.* **nihil:** adverbial accusative; *118c.* **nobis:** *156.* **pro certo:** 'ascertain'; *154a.*

Caesar leaves Cisalpine Gaul, proceeds to Narbo, in the Province.

6.1. His rebus in Italiam[1] Caesari nuntiatis, cum iam ille urbanas[2] res virtute Cn. Pompei commodiorem in statum pervenisse intellegeret, in Transalpinam Galliam profectus est. **2.** Eo cum venisset, magna[3] difficultate afficiebatur, qua ratione ad exercitum pervenire posset.[4] **3.** Nam si legiones in provinciam arcesseret, se absente in itinere proelio dimicaturas intellegebat; **4.** si ipse[5] ad exercitum contenderet, ne eis quidem eo tempore,[6] qui quieti viderentur, suam salutem recte committi videbat.

[1] **Italiam:** Caesar was in Cisalpine Gaul; *283b; 256.*
[2] **urbanas res:** 'affairs in the city', Rome: see VII, 1.1-2, and notes 3-7. **virtute:** ' through the energetic action'. The break between Caesar and Pompey did not come till two years later; *258.*
[3] **magna,** etc.: 'he experienced great difficulty in devising a plan for reaching his army'; how lit.?
[4] **Posset:** *204.2.* **legiones:** see VII, 1.7, note 14.
[5] **ipse:** alone, or with only a small military escort.
[6] **eo tempore:** 'at so critical a time'; how lit.?

7.1. Interim Lucterius Cadurcus in Rutenos[1] missus eam civitatem Arvernis conciliat. **2.** Progressus in Nitiobroges[2] et Gabalos, ab utrisque obsides accipit et, magna coacta manu, in provinciam Narbonem versus[3] irruptionem facere contendit. **3.** Qua re nuntiata, Caesar omnibus consiliis antevertendum existimavit, ut Narbonem proficisceretur. **4.** Eo cum venisset, timentes confirmat, praesidia in Rutenis provincialibus,[4] Volcis Arecomicis, Tolosatibus circumque Narbonem, quae loca[5] hostibus erant finitima, constituit, **5.** partem copiarum ex provincia supplementumque,[6] quod ex Italia adduxerat, in Helvios, qui fines Arvernorum contingunt, convenire iubet.

[1] **Rutenos:** *282.* **missus:** see VII, 5.1.1.
[2] **Nitiobroges, Gabalos:** west, and east, of the Ruteni; see Map GALLIA.
[3] **versus:** 'in the direction of''; *123c.* **irruptionem:** ' raid'. **omnibus,** etc.: 'that setting out for

Narbo should precede all (forming of) plans'; how lit.?
[4] **provincialibus**: a part of the Ruteni were in the Province.
[5] **quae loca**: (in) locis quae; 165c.
[6] **supplementum**: 'raw contingent'; cf. VII, 1.1.

Caesar crosses the Cévennes through deep snow, surprising the Arverni.

8.1. His[1] rebus comparatis, represso iam Lucterio et remoto, quod intrare intra praesidia[2] periculosum putabat, in Helvios proficiscitur.[3] **2.** Etsi mons Cebenna, qui Arvernos ab Helviis discludit, durissimo tempore[4] anni altissima nive iter impediebat, tamen, discussa nive[5] in altitudinem pedum sex atque ita viis patefactis summo[6] militum sudore, ad fines Arvernorum pervenit. **3.** Quibus oppressis inopinantibus, quod se Cebenna ut muro munitos existimabant, ac ne[7] singulari quidem umquam homini eo tempore anni semitae[8] patuerant, equitibus imperat, ut, quam latissime possint, vagentur et quam maximum hostibus terrorem inferant. **4.** Celeriter haec fama[9] ac nuntiis ad Vercingetorigem perferuntur; quem perterriti omnes Arverni circumsistunt atque obsecrant, ut suis[10] fortunis consulat neu se ab hostibus diripi patiatur, praesertim cum[11] videat omne ad se bellum translatum. **5.** Quorum ille precibus permotus, castra ex Biturigibus movet in[12] Arvernos versus.

[1] **His**, etc.: 'Having completed these preparations'.
[2] **intra praesidia**: 'within the (chain of) garrisons' by which Caesar had secured the western frontier of the Province. **periculosum**: 75f; 84; 148d. **putabat**: sc. *Lucterius*.
[3] **proficiscitur**: sc. *Caesar*.
[4] **durissimo tempore**: 'the most inclement season'.
[5] **discussa nive**: 'the snow was cleared away' in the pass by which he crossed the Cevennes. Cf. Map 13, (1); 144b2.
[6] **summo sudore**: 'with the utmost effort'; 136b. How lit.?
[7] **ne**, etc.: 'not even for one man alone', not to speak of an army.
[8] **semitae**: mountain 'trails'. **patuerant**: 'were passable'.
[9] **fama**: 'by report'; less definite than **nuntiis**, 'by messages'.
[10] **suis**: 'their own'. **neu**: 199d.
[11] **cum**: 184b. **omne**: 353d.
[12] **in...versus**: 123c. **Arvernos**: 282.

9.1. At Caesar, biduum in his locis moratus, quod haec de Vercingetorige[1] usu ventura[2] opinione praeceperat, per causam[3] supplementi equitatusque cogendi ab exercitu discedit, **2.** Brutum adulescentem his copiis praeficit; hunc monet, ut in omnes partes equites quam latissime pervagentur: *Daturum[4] se operam, ne longius triduo a castris absit.* **3.** His constitutis rebus, suis inopinantibus, quam maximis potest itineribus, Viennam pervenit. **4.** Ibi nactus[5] recentem equitatum, quem multis ante diebus eo praemiserat, neque diurno neque nocturno itinere intermisso, per fines Aeduorum in Lingones contendit, ubi duae legiones[6] hiemabant, ut, si quid[7] etiam de sua salute ab Aeduis iniretur consilii, celeritate[8] praecurreret. **5.** Eo cum pervenisset, ad reliquas legiones mittit priusque omnes in unum locum cogit, quam de eius adventu Arvernis nuntiari posset.[9] **6.** Hac re cognita, Vercingetorix rursus in Bituriges exercitum reducit, atque inde profectus Gorgobinam, Boiorum[10] oppidum, quos ibi, Helvetico proelio victos, Caesar collocaverat Aeduisque attribuerat, oppugnare instituit.

[1] **haec de Vercingetorige:** 'these movements on the part of Vercingetorix'.
[2] **usu ventura** [esse]: 'would take place', lit., 'would come in experience'; *142a.* **opinione praeceperat:** 'had conjectured'.
[3] **per causam,** etc.: 'making a pretext of bringing together his new force', etc. How lit.?
[4] **Daturum** [esse] . . . **absit:** said as a blind, to prevent information regarding his plans from reaching the enemy.
[5] **nactus,** etc.: 'finding his cavalry refreshed'.
[6] **duae legiones:** see (2) on Map 13.
[7] **quid,** etc.: 'any design involving his personal safety'; *97b; 353d.*
[8] **celeritate:** 'by quickness of movement'. **praecurreret:** that he might forestall (it)'.
[9] **nuntiari posset:** 'any report could reach'; *73d; 189b.*
[10] **Boiorum,** etc.: cf. I, 28.5; and VI, 24.1, note 2.

10.1. Magnam haec res[1] Caesari difficultatem ad consilium capiendum afferebat: si reliquam partem hiemis uno loco legiones contineret, ne,[2] stipendiariis Aeduorum expugnatis, cuncta Gallia[3] deficeret, quod nullum amicis in eo praesidium videret positum esse; si maturius ex hibernis educeret,[4] ne ab re frumentaria duris subvectionibus laboraret. **2.** Praestare visum est tamen omnes difficultates perpeti, quam, tanta contumelia accepta,[5] omnium suorum voluntates alienare. **3.** Itaque cohortatus Aeduos de supportando commeatu, praemittit ad Boios, qui[6] de suo adventu doceant, hortenturque, ut in fide maneant atque hostium impetum magno animo sustineant. **4.** Duabus Agedinci legionibus atque impedimentis totius exercitus[7] relictis, ad Boios proficiscitur.

[1] **haec res:** 'This movement' of Vercingetorix.
[2] **ne,** etc.: if Caesar failed to protect the Gauls pledged to his interest, he would soon find them enemies.
[3] **cuncta Gallia:** 'the whole of Gaul'. **amicis:** 'for those (who were) friendly (to him)'. **eo:** Caesar.
[4] **educeret:** sc. *legiones.* **ab:** 'in respect to'. **duris subvectionibus:** 'on account of difficulties of transportation', caused by the bad state of the roads toward the end of winter.
[5] **tanta contumelia accepta:** 'by acquiescing in so great an indignity' as the capture of Gorgobina by Vercingetorix would be. **suorum:** 'who were loyal to him'. **voluntatis:** 'the good will'.
[6] **qui,** etc.: '(messengers) to explain'; *193a.*
[7] **totius exercitus:** ten legions, besides auxiliary troops; *308.*

Caesar takes Vellaunodunum, Cenabum, Noviodunum; marches toward
Avaricum. The Bituriges burn all their towns except Avaricum.

11.1. Altero[1] die cum ad oppidum Senonum, Vellaunodunum, venisset, ne quem post se hostem relinqueret, quo[2] expeditiore re frumentaria uteretur, oppugnare instituit idque biduo circumvallavit; **2.** tertio die missis ex oppido legatis de deditione, arma conferri, iumenta produci, sexcentos obsides dari iubet. Ea qui conficeret, C. Trebonium legatum relinquit, **3.** ipse ut quam primum[3] iter faceret. Cenabum Carnutum proficiscitur; **4.** qui, tum primum allato nuntio de oppugnatione Vellaunoduni, cum longius eam rem ductum iri[4] existimarent, praesidium[5] Cenabi tuendi causa, quod eo mitterent, comparabant. **5.** Huc biduo pervenit.[6] Castris ante oppidum positis, diei tempore[7] exclusus in posterum oppugnationem differt, quaeque[8] ad eam rem usui sint, militibus imperat **6.** et, quod oppidum Cenabum pons fluminis Ligeris contingebat, veritus, ne noctu ex oppido profugerent,[9] duas legiones in armis excubare iubet. **7.** Cenabenses paulo ante mediam noctem silentio ex oppido egressi flumen transire coeperunt. **8.** Qua re per exploratores nuntiata, Caesar legiones, quas expeditas esse iusserat, portis incensis intromittit atque oppido potitur, perpaucis ex hostium numero desideratis, quin cuncti caperentur, quod pontis atque itinerum angustiae multitudini fugam intercluserant. **9.** Oppidum diripit atque incendit, praedam[10] militibus donat, exercitum Ligerim traducit atque in Biturigum fines pervenit.

[1] **Altero:** = *postero.*

[2] **quo:** why instead of *ut?* Caesar's base of operations was now Agedincum. The transportation of supplies to the front as he kept marching south would be endangered if he left towns behind him in possession of the enemy.

[3] **quam primum:** see Idioms. **iter faceret:** to Gorgobina, which Vercingetorix was besieging.

[4] **ductum iri:** 'that it (the siege) would be prolonged'; fut. pass, infin.

[5] **praesidium,** etc.: *praesidium, quod Cenabum mitterent* (subj. of purpose), *eius tuendi causa, comparabant.*

[6] **pervenit:** sc. *Caesar.*

[7] **diei tempore:** i.e. by the lateness of the hour; Caesar reached Cenabum late in the afternoon. **posterum:** sc. *diem.*

[8] **quaeque ... imperat:** = *et ea, quae ad eam rem usui sint, exponit et fieri imperat.* **sint:** why not *sunt?*

[9] **profugerent:** sc. *Cenabenses.*

[10] **praedam:** including probably the inhabitants of the town as well as their possessions. Caesar thus rewarded his men for the pluck and endurance they had shown during the few weeks preceding.

12.1. Vercingetorix, ubi de Caesaris adventu cognovit, oppugnatione[1] desistit atque obviam Caesari proficiscitur. **2.** Ille[2] oppidum Biturigum positum in via, Noviodunum, oppugnare instituerat. **3.** Quo ex oppido cum legati ad eum venissent oratum, ut[3] sibi ignosceret suaeque vitae consuleret, ut celeritate reliquas res conficeret, qua pleraque erat consecutus, arma conferri, equos produci, obsides dari iubet. **4.** Parte iam obsidum tradita, cum reliqua administrarentur, centurionibus et paucis militibus intromissis, qui arma iumentaque conquirerent, equitatus hostium procul visus est, qui agmen Vercingetorigis antecesserat. **5.** Quem[4] simul atque oppidani conspexerunt atque in spem[5] auxili venerunt, clamore sublato arma capere, portas claudere, murum complere[6] coeperunt. **6.** Centuriones in oppido, cum ex significatione[7] Gallorum novi aliquid ab eis iniri consili intellexissent, gladiis destrictis portas occupaverunt suosque omnes incolumes[8] receperunt.

[1] **oppugnatione:** cf. VII, 9.6.

[2] **Ille:** Caesar. **in via:** 'on the way' to Gorgobina.

[3] **ut ... consuleret:** object of *oratum;* while **ut ... conficeret** explains the purpose of Caesar's action.

[4] **Quem:** 'Now – this', the cavalry.

[5] **in spem venerunt:** see Idioms, under *spem.*

[6] **murum complere:** 'to man the wall'. **in oppido:** = *qui erant in oppido.*

[7] **significatione:** 'demeanor', 'behavior'. **novi aliquid – consili:** 'some new scheme'.

[8] **omnes incolumes:** acc.

13.1. Caesar ex castris equitatum educi iubet, proelium equestre committit; laborantibus iam suis Germanos equites circiter CCCC summittit, quos ab initio[1] secum habere instituerat. **2.** Eorum impetum Galli sustinere non potuerunt atque in fugam coniecti, multis amissis, se ad agmen receperunt. Quibus profligatis rursus oppidani perterriti comprehensos eos, quorum opera plebem concitatam existimabant, ad Caesarem perduxerunt seseque ei dediderunt. **3.** Quibus rebus confectis, Caesar ad oppidum Avaricum, quod erat maximum munitissimumque in finibus Biturigum atque agri fertilissima regione,[2] profectus est, quod eo oppido recepto civitatem Biturigum se in potestatem redacturum confidebat.

[1] **ab initio:** 'from the beginning' of the Gallic war. German horsemen are prominent in the operations narrated in Book VII.
[2] **regione:** dep. on *in* before *finibus*.

14.1. Vercingetorix, tot continuis incommodis Vellaunoduni,[1] Cenabi, Novioduni acceptis, suos ad concilium convocat. **2.** Docet, longe alia[2] ratione esse bellum gerendum, atque antea gestum sit. Omnibus modis huic rei studendum, ut pabulatione et commeatu Romani prohibeantur. **3.** Id esse facile, quod equitatu ipsi abundent et quod anni tempore[3] subleventur. **4.** Pabulum secari non posse; necessario dispersos hostes[4] ex aedificiis petere; hos omnes cotidie ab equitibus deleri posse. **5.** Praeterea, salutis causa rei familiaris commoda[5] neglegenda; vicos atque aedificia incendi oportere hoc spatio[6] ab via quoque versus, quo pabulandi causa adire posse videantur. **6.** Harum ipsis rerum copiam suppetere, quod, quorum in finibus bellum geratur, eorum opibus subleventur; **7.** Romanos aut inopiam non laturos aut magno periculo longius a castris processuros; **8.** neque interesse, ipsosne[7] interficiant impedimentisne exuant, quibus[8] amissis bellum geri non possit. **9.** Praeterea, oppida incendi oportere, quae non munitione et loci natura ab omni sint[9] periculo tuta, ne suis sint ad detrectandam militiam receptacula neu Romanis proposita[10] ad copiam commeatus praedamque tollendam. **10.** Haec[11] si gravia aut acerba videantur, multo illa gravius aestimari debere, liberos, coniuges in servitutem abstrahi, ipsos interfici; quae sit necesse accidere victis.[12]

[1] **Vellaunoduni,** etc.: AG 427.3, B 232.1.
[2] **alia – atque:** 'different from what'.
[3] **anni tempore:** probably March by the Calendar.
[4] **hostes:** the Romans. **aedificiis:** the granaries and barns where grain and fodder were stored.
[5] **rei familiaris commoda:** 'private interests'. Such an appeal to the sentiment of patriotism, in the face of invaders, might well bring response.
[6] **hoc spatio . . . quo:** 'for so great a distance from their (the Romans') track in every direction, as'.
[7] **-ne – ne** = *utrum – an.*
[8] **quibus amissis**: 'without which'.
[9] **sint:** subj. also in dir. disc; characteristic. **ne neu:** = *ne aut – aut.*
[10] **proposita:** 'handy'.
[11] **Haec:** refers to what precedes, **illa** to what follows. This policy of avoiding a decisive battle, cutting off the enemy's supplies and harassing him at every turn, was the very best that, under the circumstances, the Gauls could pursue. The proposal of it reveals in

Vercingetorix generalship of a high order. Similar tactics have been successfully employed by many generals, among others, Fabius Maximus, who wore out Hannibal.
[12] **victis**: i.e. to the Gauls, if conquered.

15.1. Omnium consensu hac sententia probata, uno die amplius XX urbes[1] Biturigum incenduntur. **2.** Hoc idem fit in reliquis civitatibus. In omnibus partibus incendia conspiciuntur; quae etsi magno cum dolore omnes ferebant, tamen hoc sibi solaci proponebant, quod se, prope explorata victoria, celeriter amissa[2] recuperaturos confidebant. **3.** Deliberatur[3] de Avarico in communi concilio, incendi placeret an defendi. **4.** Procumbunt[4] omnibus Gallis ad pedes Bituriges, ne pulcherrimam[5] prope totius Galliae urbem, quae praesidio et ornamento sit civitati, suis manibus succendere cogerentur; **5.** facile se loci natura defensuros dicunt, quod, prope ex omnibus partibus flumine[6] et palude circumdata, unum habeat et[7] perangustum aditum. **6.** Datur petentibus venia, dissuadente primo Vercingetorige, post concedente et precibus ipsorum[8] et misericordia vulgi. Defensores oppido idonei deliguntur.

[1] **urbes**: AG 407c, B 217.3. This voluntary burning of cities, especially at such a season, evinces a heroic spirit.
[2] **amissa**: neut. pl. of part. used as noun.
[3] **Deliberatur**: see Vocabulary.
[4] **Procumbunt**: the falling is emphasized by the position of the word. **Gallis**: AG 377, B 188.1n.
[5] **pulcherrimam**: Avaricum occupied a beautiful site, and had many fine open squares.
[6] **flumine**, etc.: see Plan X.
[7] **et**: omit in trans.
[8] **ipsorum**: the delegates of the Bituriges. **vulgi**: 'of the general body' of delegates from the other states. The exemption of Avaricum from the general destruction of cities was the first great mistake of the Gauls in this campaign, the outcome of which was to be for them so disastrous.

Caesar, though harassed by Vercingetorix, besieges Avaricum. Vercingetorix, being accused of treachery, clears himself.

16.1. Vercingetorix minoribus[1] Caesarem itineribus subsequitur et locum castris deligit paludibus silvisque munitum, ab Avarico longe milia passuum XVI. **2.** Ibi per certos exploratores in[2] singula diei tempora, quae ad Avaricum agerentur, cognoscebat et, quid fieri vellet, imperabat. **3.** Omnes nostras pabulationes frumentationesque observabat dispersosque,[3] cum longius necessario procederent, adoriebatur magnoque incommodo afficiebat, etsi,[4] quantum ratione provideri poterat, ab nostris occurrebatur, ut incertis temporibus diversisque itineribus iretur.

[1] **minoribus**: 'shorter', 'easy'.
[2] **in . . . tempora**: i.e. hourly.
[3] **dispersos . . . adoriebatur:** The Britons had tried the same tactics in the year 55.
[4] **etsi**, etc.: 'although, so far as provision could be made by calculating in advance, our men met the emergency by going out at uncertain times and in different directions'.

17.1. Castris ad eam partem oppidi positis Caesar, quae intermissa flumine et palude aditum, ut supra[1] diximus, angustum habebat, aggerem apparare, vineas agere, turres duas constituere coepit; nam circumvallare loci natura prohibebat. **2.** De re frumentaria Boios atque Aeduos adhortari non destitit; quorum alteri,[2] quod nullo studio agebant, non multum adiuvabant, alteri non magnis facultatibus, quod[3] civitas erat exigua et infirma, celeriter, quod habuerunt, consumpserunt. **3.** Summa difficultate rei frumentariae affecto exercitu[4] tenuitate Boiorum, indiligentia Aeduorum, incendiis aedificiorum, usque eo, ut complures dies frumento milites caruerint[5] et pecore ex longinquioribus vicis adacto extremam famem sustentarent, nulla[6] tamen vox est ab eis audita populi Romani maiestate et superioribus victoriis indigna. **4** Quin etiam Caesar cum in opere[7] singulas legiones appellaret et, si acerbius inopiam ferrent, se dimissurum oppugnationem diceret, universi ab eo, ne id facerent, petebant: **5.** Sic se complures annos illo imperante[8] meruisse, ut nullam ignominiam acciperent,[9] nusquam infecta re discederent; **6.** hoc se ignominiae[10] laturos loco, si inceptam oppugnationem reliquissent; **7.** praestare omnes perferre acerbitates, quam non civibus Romanis, qui Cenabi perfidia Gallorum interissent, parentarent.[11] **8.** Haec eadem centurionibus tribunisque militum mandabant, ut per eos ad Caesarem deferrentur.

[1] **supra:** see VII, 17.3, cf. Plan X.
[2] **alteri:** the Aedui. **nullo studio:** 'without enthusiasm', The Aedui had doubtless found the Roman yoke galling, and would gladly have thrown it off if they had dared. Once before they had given Caesar serious trouble by not bringing promised supplies; see I, 16.
[3] **quod:** as antecedent supply *frumentum* with *consumpserunt*.
[4] **affecto exercitu:** 'although the army was involved'; modified by the ablatives of cause, *tenuitate, indiligentia, incendiis.*
[5] Notice the change of tense from **caruerint,** stating a historical fact, to **sustentarent** ('were bearing up against'), giving the resulting condition and implying that the hunger continued so long as the grain was scarce.
[6] **nulla . . . indigna:** the dignity of expression well suits the noble courage exhibited.
[7] **in opere:** engaged 'in the work' of building the *agger,* etc.
[8] **illo imperante:** 'under him as commander'.
[9] **ignominiam acciperent:** 'suffer defeat'.
[10] **ignominiae loco:** 'in the light of a disgrace', 'as a disgrace'.
[11] **parentarent:** subj. also in dir. disc. (AG 571a, B 284.4).

18.1. Cum iam muro turres appropinquassent, ex captivis Caesar cognovit, Vercingetorigem, consumpto pabulo, castra movisse propius Avaricum[1] atque ipsum cum equitatu expeditisque,[2] qui inter equites proeliari consuessent, insidiandi causa eo profectum, quo nostros postero die pabulatum venturos arbitraretur. **2.** Quibus rebus cognitis media nocte silentio profectus ad hostium castra mane pervenit.[3] **3.** Illi, celeriter per exploratores adventu Caesaris cognito, carros impedimentaque sua in artiores silvas abdiderunt, copias omnes in loco edito atque aperto instruxerunt. **4.** Qua re nuntiata Caesar celeriter sarcinas conferri, arma expediri iussit.

[1] **Avaricum:** AG 432a, B 141.3.
[2] **expeditis,** etc.: light-armed foot-soldiers fought among the cavalry. Vercingetorix had adopted the German tactics, the superiority of which over their own the Gauls had learned to their cost.

19. Collis¹ erat leniter ab infimo acclivis. Hunc ex omnibus fere partibus palus difficilis atque impedita cingebat, non latior² pedibus quinquaginta. **2.** Hoc se colle interruptis pontibus Galli fiducia loci continebant generatimque distributi omnia vada ac saltus³ eius paludis obtinebant, sic animo parati, ut, si eam paludem Romani perrumpere conarentur, haesitantes premerent ex loco superiore; **3.** ut, qui⁴ propinquitatem loci videret, paratos prope aequo Marte⁵ ad dimicandum existimaret, qui iniquitatem condicionis perspiceret, inani simulatione⁶ sese ostentare cognosceret. **4.** Indignantes milites Caesar, quod conspectum suum⁷ hostes perferre possent tantulo spatio interiecto, et signum proeli exposcentes edocet, quanto detrimento et quot virorum fortium morte necesse sit constare victoriam; **5.** quos cum⁸ sic animo paratos videat, ut nullum pro sua laude periculum recusent, summae se iniquitatis⁹ condemnari debere, nisi eorum vitam sua salute¹⁰ habeat cariorem. **6.** Sic milites consolatus eodem die reducit in castra reliquaque, quae ad oppugnationem oppidi pertinebant, administrare instituit.

¹ **Collis:** on which the Gauls had taken up their position; = *locus editus atque apertus* at the end of the previous chapter.
² **non latior:** concessive, 'although not wider'.
³ **saltus:** places in the bog grown over with bushes and underbrush, by which the Romans might attempt to cross. **sic – ut:** ' firmly resolved – to'.
⁴ **qui – videret:** 'if one should look at'.
⁵ **aequo Marte:** see Vocabulary.
⁶ **inani simulatione:** 'with mere parade', spoken contemptuously. Caesar intimates, rather ungraciously, that the Gauls knew that they were safe from all attack where they were, and that they were simply showing themselves off.
⁷ **conspectum suum:** 'the sight of them', the Roman soldiers.
⁸ **cum:** AG 549, B 309.3. **sua:** = *Caesaris*.
⁹ **iniquitatis:** AG 352, B 208.2.
¹⁰ **salute:** 'reputation', rather than 'safety'.

20.1. Vercingetorix, cum ad suos redisset, proditionis¹ insimulatus, quod² castra propius Romanos movisset, quod cum omni equitatu discessisset, quod sine imperio³ tantas copias reliquisset, quod eius discessu Romani tanta opportunitate et celeritate venissent; **2.** non haec omnia fortuito aut sine consilio accidere potuisse; regnum illum Galliae malle Caesaris concessu quam ipsorum habere beneficio: **3.** tali modo accusatus ad haec respondit: Quod castra movisset,⁴ factum inopia pabuli etiam ipsis hortantibus; quod propius Romanos accessisset, persuasum⁵ loci opportunitate, qui se ipse sine munitione defenderet; **4.** equitum vero operam neque in loco palustri desiderari debuisse et illic fuisse utilem, quo sint profecti. **5.** Summam imperi se consulto nulli discedentem tradidisse, ne is⁶ multitudinis studio ad dimicandum impelleretur; cui rei⁷ propter animi mollitiem studere omnes videret, quod diutius laborem ferre non possent. **6.** Romani si casu intervenerint, fortunae, si alicuius indicio vocati, huic habendam gratiam, quod et paucitatem eorum ex loco superiore cognoscere et virtutem despicere potuerint, qui⁸ dimicare non ausi turpiter se in castra receperint. **7.** Imperium se a Caesare per proditionem nullum desiderare, quod habere victoria posset, quae iam esset sibi atque omnibus Gallis explorata; quin etiam ipsis remittere,[9] si sibi magis honorem tribuere quam ab se salutem accipere videantur. **8.** 'Haec ut intellegatis', inquit, 'a me sincere pronuntiari, audite Romanos milites', **9.** Producit servos, quos in pabulatione paucis ante diebus exceperat et fame vinculisque excruciaverat. **10.** Hi iam ante edocti, quae interrogati pronuntiarent, milites se esse legionarios dicunt; fame et inopia adductos clam ex castris exisse, si[10] quid frumenti aut pecoris in agris reperire possent; **11.** simili omnem exercitum inopia premi, nec iam vires sufficere cuiusquam nec ferre operis laborem posse; itaque statuisse imperatorem,[11] si nihil in oppugnatione oppidi profecissent, triduo exercitum deducere. **12.** 'Haec,' inquit, 'a me', Vercingetorix, 'beneficia habetis, quem proditionis insimulatis; cuius opera sine vestro sanguine tantum exercitum victorem fame paene consumptum videtis; quem turpiter se ex fuga recipientem ne qua civitas suis finibus recipiat, a me provisum est'.

_____

[1] **proditionis:** AG 352, B 208.1.

[2] **quod,** etc.: 'because (as they said) he had', etc.

[3] **sine imperio:** i.e. _sine imperatore;_ Vercingetorix had left his army temporarily without placing any one in command.

[4] **Quod castra movisset:** 'In regard to having moved the camp' (AG 572a, B 299.2).

[5] **persuasum:** sc. _ei esse._

[6] **is:** the one appointed commander-in-chief temporarily.

[7] **cui rei:** i.e. immediate battle with the Romans. Even the Romans at times lost faith in Fabius Maximus as he was slowly breaking the strength of Hannibal.

[8] **qui:** 'since they'.

[9] **ipsis remittere** [imperium]: 'resign (his generalship) to them, if they thought they were', etc.

[10] **si:** '(to see) whether' (AG 576a, B 300.3).

[11] **imperatorem:** Caesar.

21.1. Conclamat omnis multitudo et suo more armis concrepat,[1] quod facere in eo[2] consuerunt, cuius orationem approbant; summum[3] esse Vercingetorigem ducem, nec de eius fide dubitandum, nec maiore ratione[4] bellum administrari posse. **2.** Statuunt, ut X milia hominum delecta ex omnibus copiis in oppidum summittantur, **3.** nec solis Biturigibus communem[5] salutem committendam censent, quod paene in eo,[6] si id oppidum retinuissent, summam victoriae constare intellegebant.

[1] **armis concrepat:** the early Germans also at their war-councils expressed approval by beating with their spears upon their shields; see Tac. _Germ._ 11.

[2] **in eo:** 'in (the case of him)'.

[3] **summum,** etc.: the ingenious ruse of Vercingetorix had turned the fickle Gauls at once; they were now as much in favour of him as a few hours previous they had been against him.

[4] **maiore ratione:** 'on a more reasonable method'.

[5] **communem:** to the Gauls. If the Bituriges single-handed should succeed in resisting Caesar, they would have all the credit of the victory.

[6] **in eo:** = _in ea re._ **oppidum:** Avaricum.

22.1. Singulari militum nostrorum virtuti consilia cuiusque modi Gallorum occurrebant, ut est summae[1] genus sollertiae atque ad omnia imitanda et efficienda, quae a quoque[2] traduntur, aptissimum. **2.** Nam et laqueis falces avertebant, quas, cum destinaverant, tormentis introrsus reducebant, et aggerem cuniculis subtrahebant,[3] eo scientius, quod apud eos magnae sunt ferrariae[4] atque omne genus cuniculorum notum atque usitatum est. **3.** Totum autem murum ex omni parte turribus contabulaverant[5] atque has coriis[6] intexerant. **4.** Tum crebris diurnis nocturnisque eruptionibus aut aggeri ignem inferebant aut milites occupatos in opere adoriebantur et nostrarum turrium altitudinem, quantum has cotidianus[7] agger expresserat, commissis[8] suarum turrium malis adaequabant, **5.** et apertos cuniculos[9] praeusta et praeacuta materia et pice fervefacta et maximi ponderis saxis morabantur moenibusque appropinquare prohibebant.

[1] **summae sollertiae**, etc.: versatility is a striking characteristic of the French.

[2] **quoque**: from *quisque*; trans. 'any one'. **falces**: = *falces murales*, strong poles, to one end of which was fastened a heavy point for prying, with a hook for pulling stones out of the enemy's wall; whether they were usually worked by hand or by machinery is not known. In this case the Gauls caught hold of the *falces* with nooses, turned them aside, and having gotten a firm grip on them, drew them over inside the walls by means of windlasses (*tormentis*).

[3] **subtrahebant**: 'drew away' the *agger* by running mines under it.

[4] **ferrariae**: iron is still mined in the region about Bourges (Avaricum).

[5] **turribus contabulaverant**: = *turribus contabulatis instruxerant,* or *compleverant.* The towers were built of wood, and two or more stories in height above the wall. See Plan X.

[6] **coriis**: the hides were put on to protect the towers against the firebrands of the besiegers.

[7] **cotidianus agger expresserat**: 'the daily (addition to the) *agger* had raised'. On the *agger* the Romans had wooden towers, which were raised gradually as the height of the *agger* was increased. See Plan X., 4, a.

[8] **commissis . . . malis**: 'by building up between the corner-posts of their towers'. When the Gauls erected a tower on the walls they left the upright posts at the corners of full length, projecting above the stories at first built; the height could readily be increased, as circumstances might demand, by laying crosspieces above, between these corner-posts already in position.

[9] **apertos cuniculos**: 'the exposed (ends of the) gangways' in the *agger*, through which timber and other material were carried to the front; as the *agger* was prolonged nearly to the wall, the enemy hurled sharp darts and other things into the ends of these passage-ways and so 'were hindering' the progress of the work.

The Siege and Destruction of Avaricum. 23-31

The ingenious construction of Gallic city walls.

23.1. Muri autem omnes Gallici hac fere forma sunt. Trabes[1] derectae, perpetuae in longitudinem paribus intervallis, distantes inter se binos pedes, in solo collocantur. **2.** Hae revinciuntur introrsus[2] et multo aggere vestiuntur;[3] ea autem, quae diximus, intervalla grandibus in fronte[4] saxis efferciuntur.[5] **3.** His collocatis et coagmentatis, alius insuper ordo additur, ut idem illud intervallum[6] servetur neque inter se contingant trabes, sed, paribus intermissis spatiis, singulae[7] singulis saxis interiectis arte contineantur. **4.** Sic deinceps omne opus contexitur, dum iusta[8] muro altitudo expleatur.[9] **5.** Hoc cum in speciem varietatemque[10] opus deforme non est alternis trabibus ac saxis, quae rectis lineis suos ordines servant, tum ad utilitatem et defensionem urbium summam habet opportunitatem, quod et ab incendio lapis et ab ariete materia defendit, quae perpetuis[11] trabibus pedes quadragenos plerumque introrsus revincta neque perrumpi[12] neque distrahi[13] potest.

[1] **Trabes,** etc.: beams at right angles to the course of the wall were laid in a row two feet apart along the entire length of the wall.

[2] **revinciuntur introrsus:** 'are made fast inside' the wall, probably by means of crossbeams parallel with the line of the wall, as indicated in Plate IX, 3.

[3] **vestiuntur:** 'are covered'.

[4] **fronte:** the outside of the wall; the large stones tightly fitted the spaces between the ends of the beams.

[5] **efferciuntur:** 'are closely packed'. **coagmentatis:** 'fastened together'.

[6] **idem illud intervallum:** two feet. **inter,** etc.: 'touch one another'; *159*.

[7] **singulae,** etc.: 'the individual (beams) are held in position by tightly fitting a stone between' each two; how lit.?

[8] **iusta:** 'proper'. **expleatur:** 'is reached'; *100b*.

[9] **expleatur:** why not indic?

[10] **in speciem varietatemque:** 'in point of diversified appearance'.

[11] **perpetuis:** by a 'continuous' line of tie pieces each 40 feet long and fastened to each other.

[12] **perrumpi:** 'broken to pieces' by the battering-ram and heavy missiles.

[13] **distrahi:** 'wrenched asunder' by the *falces murales*.

The Gauls set the agger on fire and make a fierce attack.

24.1. His tot rebus impedita oppugnatione,[1] milites, cum toto tempore[2] frigore et assiduis imbribus tardarentur, tamen continenti labore omnia haec superaverunt et diebus XXV aggerem latum pedes CCCXXX,[3] altum pedes LXXX exstruxerunt. **2.** Cum is murum hostium paene contingeret, et Caesar ad opus consuetudine excubaret[4] militesque hortaretur, ne quod omnino tempus ab opere intermitteretur, paulo ante tertiam vigiliam est animadversum, fumare aggerem,[5] quem cuniculo[6] hostes succenderant, **3.** eodemque tempore, toto muro clamore sublato, duabus portis[7] ab utroque latere turrium eruptio fiebat; **4.** alii faces[8] atque aridam materiem de muro in aggerem eminus iaciebant, picem reliquasque res, quibus ignis excitari potest, fundebant, ut,[9] quo primum occurreretur aut cui rei ferretur auxilium, vix ratio iniri posset. **5.** Tamen, quod instituto[10] Caesaris duae semper legiones pro castris excubabant pluresque, partitis temporibus, erant in opere, celeriter factum est, ut alii eruptionibus resisterent, alii turres[11] reducerent aggeremque interscinderent, omnis vero ex castris multitudo ad restinguendum[12] concurreret.

[1] **oppugnatione:** *340*. **cum:** 'although'.

[2] **tempore:** *147c.* **frigore:** it was still winter, probably in March. **assiduis:** 'continual'; *81*.

[3] **CCCXXX:** *trecentos et triginta,* measured where the siege bank faced the wall (Map 14). **LXXX:** *octoginta.* The unusual height is explained by the existence of a gully in front of the wall.

[4] **excubaret:** 'was watching'.

[5] **fumare aggerem:** 'that the siege embankment was smoking'.

[6] **cunicuio:** 'by means of a countermine', run out underneath.

[7] **portis:** *134a.* **ab utroque latere:** 'on both sides' of the siege embankment, designated by the movable towers now at the corners (Plate IX, 2).

[8] **faces:** 'firebrands'; *17c.* **aridam:** *81*.

[9] **ut,** etc.: 'so that it was hardly possible to decide at what point a counter-attack should first be made, or to what part reinforcements should be sent'; how lit.?

[10] **Instituto,** etc.: *136c.* The legionaries on duty worked in shifts.

[11] **turres,** etc.: they first drew back the towers, so as to remove these beyond the reach of the flames, then cut the siege embankment in two in order to confine the fire to the part already

burning.

[12] **ad restinguendum:** 'to put out (the fire)'; *230.3.*

MAP 14

The Siege of Avaricum

Book VII, 15–28

To face page 374

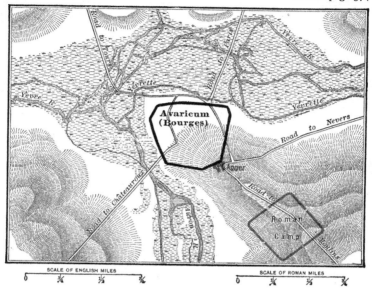

EXPLANATION

The city of Avaricum, on the site of modern Bourges, was situated at the confluence of two streams, now called Yèvre and Auron, and was protected by marshes on three sides. It was surrounded by a strong wall (outlined in blue), and was reckoned by its inhabitants the most beautiful city in Gaul.

Caesar encamped on the higher ground on the side of the city free from marshes. Selecting a favorable point of approach he commenced the construction of a huge embankment, agger, consisting of two parallel dikes, or viaducts, terminating in a long embankment near the wall and parallel with it.

The siege embankment, composed largely of timber, was in part destroyed by fire, and the city was finally taken by assault.

An instance of extraordinary bravery.

25.1. Cum in omnibus locis, consumpta iam reliqua parte noctis, pugnaretur semperque hostibus[1] spes victoriae redintegraretur, eo magis, quod deustos[2] pluteos turrium videbant nec[3] facile adire apertos ad auxiliandum animadvertebant, semperque ipsi[4] recentes defessis succederent omnemque Galliae salutem in illo vestigio temporis positam arbitrarentur, accidit,[5] inspectantibus nobis, quod, dignum[6] memoria visum, praetereundum non existimavimus. **2.** Quidam ante portam oppidi Gallus per[7] manus sebi ac picis traditas glebas in ignem e regione turris[8] proiciebat; scorpione[9] ab latere dextro traiectus exanimatusque, concidit. **3.** Hunc[10] ex proximis unus iacentem transgressus, eodem illo munere fungebatur; eadem ratione, ictu scorpionis, exanimato altero, successit tertius,[11] et tertio quartus, **4.** nec prius ille est a propugnatoribus[12] vacuus relictus locus, quam, is restincto aggere atque omni ex parte summotis hostibus, finis est pugnandi factus.

[1] **hostibus:** *109a* (AG 377, B 188.1n).
[2] **deustos,** etc.: sc. *esse,* 'that the breastworks of the towers were burned'; these were wooden screens, probably protected by hides, on the front of the towers.
[3] **nec,** etc.: sc. *milites;* 'and that it was not easy for the men exposed' to the enemy's missiles 'to come forward to help' in putting out the fire. The artillery was placed in the towers, which were therefore special objects of attack; the towers were finally saved, perhaps by throwing earth against the parts that caught fire.
[4] **ipsi:** 'on their side'. **recentes, defessis:** *227a4.*
[5] **accidit:** sc. *id;* 'there happened, under my own observation, (something) which'; how lit.? *156.*
[6] **dignum:** predicative, after *visum; 142b.*
[7] **per,** etc.: 'lumps of tallow and pitch passed from hand to hand', till they reached the Gaul who threw them. The siege embankment, built of green timber and earth and stones, did not burn readily.
[8] **e regione turris:** 'directly in a line with one of the towers' on the siege embankment, hence within range. How lit.?
[9] **scorpione,** etc.: 'his right side pierced with a (bolt from a) scorpion'; how lit.? *343a.*
[10] **Hunc,** etc.: 'stepping over him as he lay'.
[11] **tertio:** *ictu scorpionis exanimato tertio (Gallo), successit quartus (Gallus).* **prius .... quam:** *189a.*
[12] **propugnatoribus:** 'defenders'. **vacuus:** predicative.

The defenders, despairing, plan to flee, but are thwarted.

26.1. Omnia experti Galli, quod res nulla successerat, postero die consilium ceperunt ex oppido profugere, hortante et iubente Vercingetorige. **2.** Id silentio noctis conati, non magna[1] iactura suorum sese effecturos sperabant, propterea quod neque longe ab oppido castra Vercingetorigis aberant, et[2] palus perpetua, quae intercedebat, Romanos ad insequendum tardabat.[3] **3.** Iamque hoc facere noctu apparabant,[4] cum matres familiae repente in publicum procurrerunt flentesque proiectae[5] ad pedes suorum omnibus precibus petierunt, ne se et communes liberos hostibus ad supplicium dederent, quos ad capiendam fugam naturae et virium infirmitas impediret. **4.** Ubi eos in sententia perstare viderunt, quod plerumque in summo periculo timor misericordiam non[6] recipit, conclamare et significare de fuga Romanis coeperunt. **5.** Quo[7] timore perterriti Galli, ne ab equitatu Romanorum viae praeoccuparentur,[8] consilio destiterunt.

[1] **non magna:** 'no great'; *239g.*
[2] **et:** correlative with *neque; 233a.*
[3] **tardabat:** 'would delay'.
[4] **apparabant:** 'they were preparing'.
[5] **proiectae:** 'casting themselves'. **suorum:** 'of their (husbands)'.
[6] **non,** etc.: 'knows no pity'; *177c; 175c.*

[7] **Quo,** etc.: 'frightened by this' (giving of notice to the Romans) 'and fearing that'; how lit.?
[8] **praeoccuparentur:** 'be seized in advance'; 202.

In a final assault the Romans capture Avaricum, sparing none.

27.1. Postero die Caesar, promota turri perfectisque operibus, quae facere instituerat, magno coorto imbri,[1] non inutilem hanc ad capiendum consilium tempestatem arbitratus, quod paulo incautius[2] custodias in muro dispositas videbat, suos quoque languidius[3] in opere versari iussit et, quid fieri vellet, ostendit. **2.** Legiones intra vineas in occulto expeditas cohortatus, ut aliquando pro tantis laboribus fructum victoriae perciperent, eis, qui primi murum ascendissent, praemia[4] proposuit militibusque signum dedit. **3.** Illi subito ex omnibus partibus evolaverunt murumque celeriter compleverunt.

[1] **imbri:** 15c. **non inutilem:** 239g.
[2] **incautius:** 'rather carelessly'; 153a.
[3] **languidius:** 'quite lazily' according to appearances, in order to deceive the enemy.
[4] **praemia:** 318. **signum:** 326b.

28.1. Hostes, re nova perterriti, muro turribusque[1] deiecti, in foro ac locis patentioribus cuneatim[2] constiterunt, hoc animo, ut, si[3] qua ex parte obviam veniretur, acie instructa depugnarent.[4] **2.** Ubi neminem in aequum locum sese demittere, sed toto undique muro circumfundi[5] viderunt, veriti, ne omnino spes fugae tolleretur, abiectis armis ultimas oppidi partes continenti impetu petiverunt, **3.** parsque ibi, cum angusto exitu portarum se ipsi premerent, a militibus,[6] pars iam egressa portis ab equitibus est interfecta. Nec fuit quisquam,[7] qui praedae studeret. **4.** Sic, et Cenabi caede et labore operis incitati, non[8] aetate confectis, non mulieribus, non infantibus pepercerunt. **5.** Denique ex omni numero, qui fuit circiter milium XL, vix DCCC, qui, primo clamore audito, se ex oppido eiecerant, incolumes ad Vercingetorigem pervenerunt. **6.** Quos ille multa iam nocte silentio ex fuga excepit, et veritus, ne qua in castris ex eorum concursu et misericordia vulgi seditio[9] oreretur,[10] procul in via dispositis familiaribus suis principibusque civitatum, disparandos[11] deducendosque ad suos curavit, quae cuique civitati pars castrorum ab initio obvenerat.

[1] **turribus:** on the walls of Avaricum (VII, 22.3); 127a.
[2] **cuneatim:** 'in wedge-shaped masses'; 77.
[3] **si,** etc.: 'if an attack should be made from any quarter'; how lit.?
[4] **depugnarent:** 'they would fight it out'.
[5] **circumfundi:** impersonal, 'that they' (the Romans) 'distributed themselves thickly'; how lit.? 174.
[6] **a militibus:** sc. *interfecta est.*
[7] **quisquam:** 168. **studeret:** 194a. **Cenabi:** 146.
[8] **non,** etc.: 239a. **aetate confectis:** 'the aged'; how lit.?
[9] **seditio:** 'mutiny'.
[10] **oreretur:** 61b. **procul,** etc.: 'he stationed personal representatives and leading men of the (different) states along the road at a distance' from the camp, in order to intercept the fugitives, '(and)'.
[11] **disparandos,** etc.: 'he had them' (the fugitives) 'divided up and conducted in each case to the men of their own state, (who were) in the part of the camp that had from the first been assigned to that state'. How lit.? The 10,000 defenders of Avaricum had been drawn from

different states (VII, 21.2); *229b.* "It is probable," says Desjardins, "that if the orders of the Gallic chief had been obeyed, and Avaricum had been burned, as he wished to have it, Caesar and his army would have had the lot of Napoleon after the burning of Moscow."

Vercingetorix continues the war with great courage. Caesar settles a feud among the Aedui.

29.1. Postero die, concilio convocato, consolatus[1] cohortatusque est, ne[2] se admodum animo demitterent, neve perturbarentur incommodo: **2.** Non virtute neque in acie vicisse Romanos, sed artificio quodam[3] et scientia oppugnationis, cuius rei fuerint ipsi imperiti. **3.** Errare, si qui[4] in bello omnes secundos rerum proventus exspectent. **4.** Sibi numquam placuisse Avaricum defendi, cuius rei testes ipsos haberet; sed factum[5] imprudentia Biturigum et nimia obsequentia reliquorum, uti hoc incommodum acciperetur. **5.** Id tamen se celeriter maioribus commodis sanaturum. **6.** Nam quae ab reliquis Gallis civitates dissentirent, has sua diligentia adiuncturum atque unum consilium totius Galliae effecturum, cuius consensui ne orbis quidem terrarum possit obsistere; idque se prope iam effectum habere.[6] **7.** Interea aequum esse ab eis communis salutis causa impetrari, ut castra munire instituerent, quo facilius repentinos hostium impetus sustinerent.

[1] **consolatus,** etc.: sc. *Vercingetorix.*
[2] **ne ... demitterent:** 'not to lose heart altogether'.
[3] **artificio quodam:** 'by a kind of cunning'; spoken with contempt.
[4] **si qui:** 'whoever'.
[5] **factum** [esse]: 'it had come about'; the subject is *uti ... acciperetur.*
[6] **effectum habere:** trans. as if *effecisse.* (AG 497b, B 337.6).

30.1. Fuit haec oratio non ingrata Gallis, et maxime, quod ipse[1] animo non defecerat, tanto accepto incommodo, neque se in occultum abdiderat et conspectum multitudinis fugerat; **2.** plusque animo providere et praesentire existimabatur, quod re integra[2] primo incendendum Avaricum, post deserendum, censuerat. **3.** Itaque ut reliquorum imperatorum res adversae auctoritatem minuunt, sic huius ex contrario dignitas incommodo accepto in dies augebatur. **4.** Simul in spem veniebant[3] eius affirmatione de reliquis adiungendis civitatibus, primumque eo tempore Galli castra munire[4] instituerunt; et sic sunt animo consternati homines insueti laboris,[5] ut omnia, quae imperarentur, sibi patienda existimarent.

[1] **ipse non ... fugerat:** the implication is that as a rule Gallic leaders who had made a failure gave up at once and went into hiding.
[2] **re integra:** 'at the outset'.
[3] **in spem veniebant:** see Idioms under *spem.*
[4] **castra munire:** Vercingetorix wisely adopted the Roman method of encampment, as he had previously adopted the cavalry tactics of the Germans.
[5] **insueti laboris:** 'though unused to labour'.

31.1. Nec minus, quam est pollicitus, Vercingetorix animo laborabat, ut reliquas civitates adiungeret, atque earum principes donis pollicitationibusque alliciebat. **2.** Huic rei idoneos homines deligebat, quorum quisque aut oratione subdola aut amicitia facillime capere posset.[1] **3.** Qui Avarico expugnato refugerant, armandos vestiendosque curat; **4.** simul, ut deminutae copiae redintegrarentur, imperat certum numerum militum civitatibus, quem et quam[2] ante diem in castra adduci velit, sagittariosque[3] omnes, quorum erat permagnus numerus in Gallia, conquiri et ad se mitti iubet. His rebus celeriter id, quod Avarici deperierat, expletur. **5.** Interim Teutomatus, Olloviconis filius, rex Nitiobrogum, cuius pater ab senatu nostra amicus erat appellatus, cum magno equitum suorum numero et quos ex Aquitania conduxerat[4] ad eum pervenit.

[1] **capere posset**: 'could win over' the Gauls yet remaining out of the league. **posset:** AG 535f, B 282.3.
[2] **quem,** etc.: '(stating) what number and before what time'.
[3] **sagittarios**: these were to match Caesar's light-armed troops.
[4] **conduxerat**: sc. *mercede,* 'had hired'. The Aquitanians did not join the general movement against Caesar on patriotic grounds.

32.1. Caesar Avarici complures dies commoratus summamque ibi copiam frumenti et reliqui commeatus nactus exercitum ex labore atque inopia reficit. **2.** Iam prope hieme confecta, cum[1] ipso anni tempore ad gerendum bellum vocaretur et ad hostem proficisci constituisset, sive eum ex paludibus silvisque elicere sive obsidione premere posset, legati[2] ad eum principes Aeduorum veniunt oratum, ut maxime necessario tempore[3] civitati subveniat: **3.** Summo esse in periculo rem,[4] quod, cum singuli magistratus antiquitus creari atque regiam potestatem annum obtinere consuessent, duo magistratum gerant et se uterque eorum legibus creatum esse dicat. **4.** Horum esse alterum Convictolitavem, florentem et illustrem adulescentem, alterum Cotum, antiquissima familia natum atque ipsum hominem summae potentiae et magnae cognationis, cuius frater Valetiacus proximo anno eundem magistratum gesserit. **5.** Civitatem esse omnem in armis; divisum senatum, divisum populum, suas[5] cuiusque eorum clientelas. **6.** Quod si diutius alatur controversia, fore, uti pars cum parte civitatis confligat; id ne accidat, positum[6] in eius diligentia atque auctoritate.

[1] **cum**: 'although'.
[2] **legati**: 'as envoys'.
[3] **maxime uecessario tempore**: 'at a most urgent crisis'.
[4] **rem**: the public weal.
[5] **suas . . . clientelas**: 'that each of them had his own backers'.
[6] **positum in**: 'depended on'.

33.1. Caesar, etsi a bello atque hoste discedere detrimentosum esse existimabat, tamen non ignorans, quanta ex dissensionibus incommoda oriri consuessent, ne tanta et tam coniuncta populo Romano civitas, quam ipse semper aluisset[1] omnibusque rebus ornasset, ad vim atque arma descenderet, atque ea[2] pars, quae minus sibi confideret, auxilia a Vercingetorige arcesseret, huic rei praevertendum existimavit **2.** et, quod[3] legibus Aeduorum eis, qui summum magistratum obtinerent, excedere ex finibus non liceret, ne quid de iure aut de legibus eorum deminuisse videretur, ipse in Aeduos proficisci statuit senatumque omnem et, quos inter[4] controversia esset, ad se Decetiam evocavit. **3.** Cum prope omnis civitas eo convenisset, docereturque, paucis clam convocatis alio[5] loco, alio tempore, atque oportuerit, fratrem[6] a fratre renuntiatum, cum leges duo ex una familia vivo utroque non solum magistratus creari vetarent, sed etiam in senatu esse prohiberent, Cotum imperium deponere coegit, Convictolitavem, qui per sacerdotes more civitatis intermissis magistratibus[7] esset creatus, potestatem obtinere iussit.

[1] **aluisset, ornasset:** subj. by attraction. **ad . . . descenderet:** i.e. go so far as to resort to.
[2] **ea . . . confideret:** 'that party which had least confidence' in its power, = 'the weaker party'.
[3] **quod,** etc.: as the chiefs, according to the laws of the Aedui, could not leave the state to come to Caesar, he must go to them.
[4] **quos inter:** = *(eos), inter quos* (AG 435, B 144.3).
[5] **alio . . . oportuerit:** 'at a time and place other than was proper'.
[6] **fratrem:** Cotus. **fratre:** Valetiacus. **renuntiatum:** 'declared elected'; sc. *esse.* **duo . . . prohiberent:** the excellence of this regulation throws light upon the political advancement of the Aedui.
[7] **intermissis magistratibus:** 'in case of vacancies in the magistracy'; properly the interval between the going out of one magistrate and the inauguration of his successor. As a rule, the retiring Vergobret appointed his successor; since Valetiacus had unlawfully chosen his brother to the office, the Druids, by virtue of the right they had to fill the magistracy in case of vacancy, proceeded to nominate and install Convictolitavis, treating the appointment of Cotus as null and void. Possibly Caesar has not told the whole truth in regard to the matter. It seems probable that the division of parties among the Aedui was on the question of loyalty to himself; at any rate, a number of the Aedui soon joined the rebellion against him.

Caesar sends four legions north under Labienus, encamps with the rest before Gergovia; he checks a defection of Aeduan troops.

34.1. Hoc decreto interposito, cohortatus Aeduos, ut controversiarum[1] ac dissensionis obliviscerentur atque, omnibus omissis rebus,[2] huic bello servirent eaque, quae meruissent, praemia ab se, devicta Gallia,[3] exspectarent equitatumque omnem et peditum milia decem sibi celeriter mitterent, quae in praesidiis rei frumentariae causa disponeret, exercitum in duas partes divisit; **2.** quattuor legiones in Senones Parisiosque Labieno ducendas dedit, sex ipse in Arvernos ad oppidum Gergoviam secundum flumen Elaver duxit; equitatus partem illi attribuit, partem sibi reliquit. **3.** Qua re cognita Vercingetorix, omnibus interruptis eius fluminis pontibus, ab altera[4] fluminis parte iter facere coepit.

[1] **controversiarum:** AG 350, B 206.2.
[2] **omnibus omissis rebus:** 'laying everything (else) aside'.
[3] **devicta Gallia:** = *cum Gallia devicta esset.*
[4] **ab altera parte:** Vercingetorix was on the west side of the Allier (Elaver). Caesar, leaving Decize (Decetia) marched along the east bank in the direction of Gergovia, which he could not reach without crossing the stream. See Map.

35.1. Cum uterque[1] utrique esset exercitus in conspectu fereque e regione[2] castris castra poneret, dispositis exploratoribus, necubi effecto ponte Romani copias traducerent, **2.** erat in magnis Caesari difficultatibus res, ne maiorem aestatis partem flumine[3] impediretur, quod non fere ante autumnum Elaver vado[4] transiri solet. **3.** Itaque, ne id accideret, silvestri loco castris positis e regione unius eorum pontium, quos Vercingetorix rescindendos curaverat, postero die cum duabus legionibus in occulto restitit **4.** reliquas copias cum omnibus impedimentis, ut consueverat, misit, distractis quibusdam cohortibus, uti numerus legionum constare[5] videretur. **5.** His, quam longissime possent, progredi iussis, cum iam ex diei tempore coniecturam caperet, in castra perventum,[6] isdem sublicis, quarum pars inferior[7] integra remanebat, pontem reficere coepit. **6.** Celeriter effecto opere legionibusque traductis et loco castris idoneo delecto reliquas copias revocavit. **7.** Vercingetorix re cognita, ne contra suam voluntatem dimicare cogeretur, magnis itineribus antecessit.

[1] **uterque . . . conspectu**: 'each army was in sight of the other'.

[2] **e regione**: 'directly opposite' each other. **dispositis**: by Vercingetorix.

[3] **flumine**: swollen by the melting of the snow upon the mountains.

[4] **vado**: the Allier is now almost everywhere fordable in summer, apparently on account of the filling up of the river-bed.

[5] **constare**: 'to be full'. From the 6 legions with him Caesar seems to have chosen out 20 cohorts (= 2 legions); he then arranged the remaining 40 cohorts so that on the march they presented the appearance of 6 full legions, and sent them on in the direction that he had been following.

[6] **perventum** [esse]: i.e. that the legions had gone about the usual distance of a day's march, and had halted to encamp. Vercingetorix, following along on the other side of the river, would naturally encamp too, leaving the coast clear for Caesar and the two legions that had stayed back to build the bridge. Thus Caesar's ruse succeeded perfectly. Vercingetorix had not yet learned to keep scouts in the rear.

[7] **pars inferior**: the piles had not been destroyed below the water line.

THE SIEGE OF GERGOVIA. 36-51

Caesar arrives at Gergovia and fortifies two camps.

36.1. Caesar ex eo loco[1] quintis castris Gergoviam pervenit equestrique[2] eo die proelio levi facto, perspecto urbis situ, quae, posita in altissimo monte,[3] omnes aditus difficiles habebat, de oppugnatione[4] desperavit, de obsessione non prius agendum constituit, quam rem frumentariam expedisset.[5] **2.** At Vercingetorix, castris[6] prope oppidum positis, mediocribus circum se intervallis separatim[7] singularum civitatum copias collocaverat, atque omnibus eius iugi collibus[8] occupatis, qua[9] despici poterat, horribilem speciem praebebat: **3.** principesque earum civitatum, quos sibi ad consilium capiendum delegerat, prima luce cotidie ad se convenire iubebat, seu quid communicandum, seu quid administrandum videretur; **4.** neque[10] ullum fere diem intermittebat, quin equestri proelio, interiectis sagittariis,[11] quid in quoque esset animi ac virtutis suorum, periclitaretur. **5.** Erat e regione oppidi[12] collis sub ipsis radicibus montis, egregie munitus[13] atque ex omni parte circumcisus; quem si tenerent nostri, et aquae[14] magna parte et pabulatione libera prohibituri hostes[15] videbantur. **6.** Sed is locus praesidio ab his non nimis firmo tenebatur. **7.** Tamen silentio noctis Caesar, ex castris[16] egressus, prius quam subsidio ex oppido veniri posset, deiecto praesidio, potitus loco,[17] duas ibi legiones collocavit fossamque[18] duplicem duodenum pedum a maioribus castris ad minora[19] perduxit, ut tuto ab repentino hostium incursu etiam singuli commeare possent.

[1] **eo loco**: the place where Caesar encamped after crossing the Elaver (Allier). **quintis castris:**

'in five marches', encampments being counted as marches because at the close of each day's march a camp was fortified; *147c, 331a*. **Gergoviam:** *110a*.

[2] **equestri,** etc.: Vercingetorix had reached Gergovia first.

[3] **monte,** etc.: Gergovia lay on a high, narrow plateau, accessible only from the south and southeast. See Map 15.

[4] **oppugnatione, obsessione:** *340*.

[5] **expedisset:** 'had arranged for'; *189b*.

[6] **castris . . . positis:** on an elevated terrace, adjoining the town on the south; marked Gallic Encampment on Map 15.

[7] **separatim:** the soldiers of each state had a separate camp.

[8] **eius iugi collibus:** 'the minor elevations of the height', the points of vantage on the mountain, about and below the town; *160d*.

[9] **qua,** etc.: 'where a view over the plain could be had'; how lit.? *73d*. **horribilem:** 'formidable'; *81*.

[10] **neque,** etc.: 'and he allowed hardly a day to pass without trying'; *201a*.

[11] **interiectis sagittariis:** 'placing archers among (the cavalry)'; how lit.? **quid,** etc.: i.e. *quid animi ac virtutis (97b) in quoque suorum (97a) esset (204.2)*.

[12] **e regione oppidi:** 'directly opposite the town', on the south. **collis:** White Rock *(La Roche Blanche)*, near the village of the same name (Map 15).

[13] **munitus:** principally by nature. **circumcisus:** 'precipitous'.

[14] **aquae,** etc.: the Gauls probably obtained water from the Auzon.

[15] **hostes:** accusative. **ab his:** *ab hostibus*.

[16] **castris:** marked Large Camp on Map 15. **subsidio,** etc.: 'before relief could come'; how lit.? *73d, 112a*.

[17] **loco:** *131c*. **ibi:** on White Rock.

[18] **fossam,** etc.: 'two (parallel) trenches, each 12 feet wide'; how lit.? According to the excavations, which have brought to light many traces of Caesar's works near Gergovia, the hastily dug trenches were hardly more than six feet wide. **duodenum:** *22c*.

[19] **minora** [castra]: on White Rock, marked Small Camp on Map 15. As this contained two legions, in the large camp there must have been stationed four legions besides the cavalry and auxiliaries.

37.1. Dum haec ad Gergoviam geruntur, Convictolitavis Aeduus, cui magistratum adiudicatum a Caesare demonstravimus,[1] sollicitatus ab Arvernis pecunia cum quibusdam adulescentibus colloquitur; quorum erat princeps Litaviccus atque eius fratres, amplissima familia nati adulescentes. **2.** Cum his praemium[2] communicat hortaturque, ut se liberos et imperio[3] natos meminerint: **3.** Unam[4] esse Aeduorum civitatem, quae certissimam Galliae victoriam distineat;[5] eius auctoritate reliquas contineri; qua traducta locum consistendi Romanis in Gallia non fore. **4.** Esse non nullo se Caesaris beneficio affectum, sic[6] tamen, ut iustissimam apud eum causam obtinuerit; sed plus communi libertati tribuere. **5.** Cur enim potius Aedui de suo iure et de legibus ad Caesarem disceptatorem, quam Romani ad Aeduos veniant?[7] **6.** Celeriter adulescentibus et oratione magistratus et praemio deductis, cum se vel principes eius consili fore profiterentur, ratio perficiendi[8] quaerebatur, quod civitatem temere ad suscipiendum bellum adduci posse non confidebant. **7.** Placuit,[9] ut Litaviccus decem illis milibus, quae Caesari ad bellum mitterentur,[10] praeficeretur atque ea ducenda curaret, fratresque[11] eius ad Caesarem praecurrerent. Reliqua, qua ratione agi placeat, constituunt.

[1] **demonstravimus:** in VII, 32-33.

[2] **praemium:** received from the Arverni.

[3] **imperio:** dat. of purpose.

[4] **Unam**: 'the only one'.

[5] **distineat**: subj. also in dir. disc. (AG 535b, B 283.2).

[6] **sic**, etc.: 'yet only so far as this, that he had been sustained in a perfectly just claim'.

[7] **veniant**: AG 444, B 277.

[8] **ratio perficiendi**: 'a way of carrying out (their plan)'.

[9] **Placuit** [eis]: 'They resolved'.

[10] **mitterentur**: 'were on the point of being sent', having been raised in response to Caesar's request.

[11] **fratres**: these were to try to win over to the scheme of revolt the Aeduan contingent already serving under Caesar.

38.1. Litaviccus, accepto exercitu,[1] cum milia passuum circiter XXX a Gergovia abesset, convocatis subito militibus lacrimans, **2.** 'Quo proficiscimur,' inquit, 'milites? Omnis noster equitatus, omnis nobilitas interiit; principes civitatis, Eporedorix et Viridomarus,[2] insimulati proditionis, ab Romanis indicta[3] causa interfecti sunt. **3.** Haec ab his cognoscite, qui ex ipsa caede fugerunt; nam ego, fratribus atque omnibus meis propinquis interfectis, dolore prohibeor, quae gesta sunt, pronuntiare.[4] **4.** Producuntur hi, quos ille edocuerat, quae dici vellet, atque eadem, quae Litaviccus pronuntiaverat, multitudini exponunt: **5.** equites Aeduorum interfectos, quod collocuti[5] cum Arvernis dicerentur; ipsos se inter multitudinem militum occultasse atque ex media caede fugisse. **6.** Conclamant Aedui et Litaviccum obsecrant, ut sibi consulat. **7.** 'Quasi vero,' inquit ille, 'consili sit res,[6] ac non necesse sit nobis Gergoviam contendere et cum Arvernis nosmet coniungere. **8.** An[7] dubitamus, quin nefario facinore admisso Romani iam ad nos interficiendos concurrant? Proinde, si quid in nobis animi est, persequamur[8] eorum mortem, qui indignissime interierunt, atque hos latrones interficiamus.' **9.** Ostendit cives Romanos,[9] qui eius praesidi fiducia una erant; continuo magnum numerum frumenti commeatusque diripit, ipsos crudeliter excruciatos interficit. **10.** Nuntios tota civitate Aeduorum dimittit, eodem mendacio de caede equitum et principum permovet;[10] hortatur, ut simili ratione, atque[11] ipse fecerit, suas iniurias persequantur.

[1] **exercitu**: the 10,000 soldiers intended for Caesar.

[2] **Eporedorix, Viridomarus**: both favourites of Caesar, though afterwards traitors to his cause; Litaviccus was lying. **proditionis**: AG 352, B 208.1.

[3] **indicta**: see Vocabulary.

[4] **pronuntiare**: 'from uttering'.

[5] **collocuti** [esse]: AG 582, B 328.2.

[6] **consili sit res**: 'it were a matter of choice' (AG 524, B 307.1, 2).

[7] **An**: AG 335b, B 162.4a.

[8] **persequamur**: 'let us avenge'.

[9] **cives Romanos**: these, relying on the protection of the Aedui, were probably conveying to Caesar the supplies mentioned in the next line.

[10] **permovet**: sc. *totam civitatem*.

[11] **atque**: AG 384n2, B 341.1c. **suas iniurias** = *iniurias sibi illatas*.

MAP 15

THE SIEGE OF GERGOVIA

Book VII, 36–51

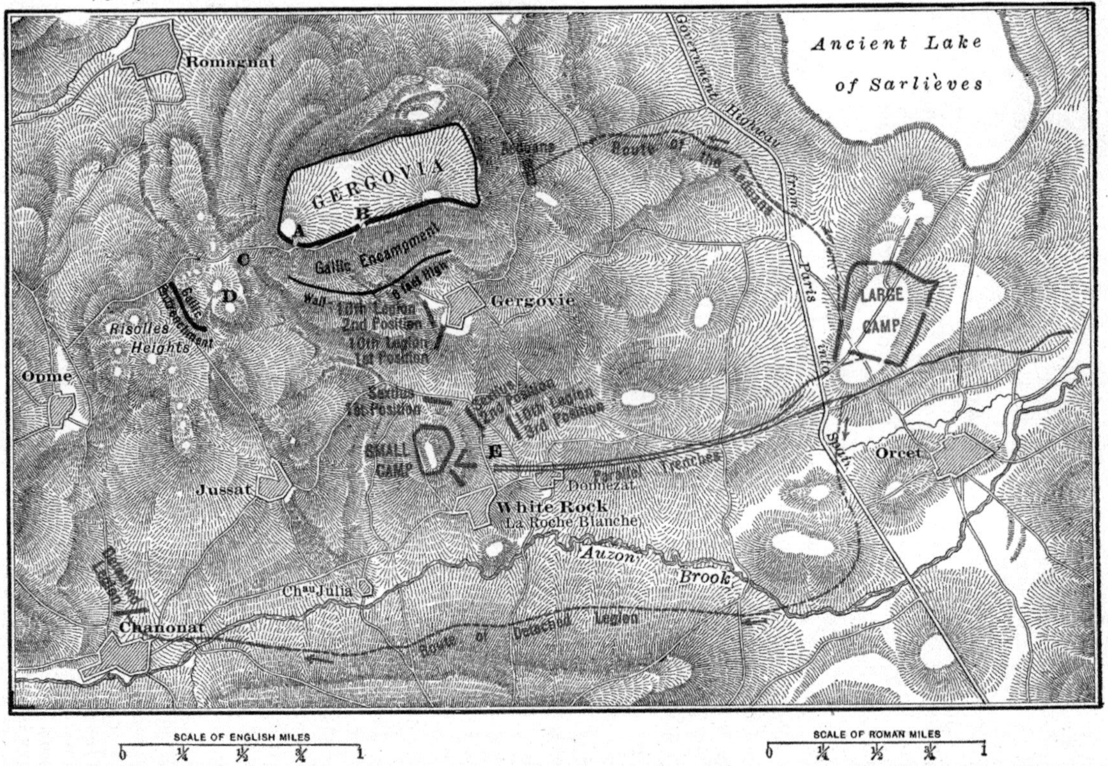

39.1. Eporedorix Aeduus, summo loco natus adulescens et summae domi potentiae, et una Viridomarus, pari aetate et gratia, sed genere dispari, quem Caesar ab Diviciaco sibi traditum[1] ex humili loco ad summam dignitatem perduxerat, in equitum numero convenerant nominatim[2] ab eo evocati. **2.** His erat inter se de principatu contentio, et in illa[3] magistratuum controversia alter pro Convictolitavi, alter pro Coto summis opibus[4] pugnaverant. **3.** Ex his Eporedorix, cognito Litavicci consilio, media fere nocte rem ad Caesarem defert; orat, ne patiatur civitatem pravis adulescentium consiliis ab amicitia populi Romani deficere; quod[5] futurum provideat, si se tot hominum milia cum hostibus coniunxerint, quorum salutem neque propinqui neglegere neque civitas levi momento[6] aestimare posset.

[1] **traditum:** 'introduced'.
[2] **nominatim evocati:** 'specially summoned'.
[3] **illa:** 'that' already spoken of in VII, 33.
[4] **summis opibus:** 'with all their might'.
[5] **[id] quod . . . provideat:** considered a subordinate clause; hence the subj.
[6] **levi momento:** 'of small account'; abl. of price.

40.1. Magna affectus sollicitudine hoc nuntio Caesar, quod semper Aeduorum civitati praecipue indulserat, nulla interposita dubitatione legiones expeditas quattuor equitatumque omnem ex castris educit, **2.** nec fuit spatium tali tempore ad contrahenda castra,[1] quod res posita in celeritate videbatur; **3.** C. Fabium legatum cum legionibus duabus castris praesidio relinquit. Fratres Litavicci cum comprehendi iussisset, paulo ante reperit ad hostes profugisse. **4.** Adhortatus milites, ne necessario tempore[2] itineris labore permoveantur, cupidissimis omnibus progressus milia passuum XXV, agmen Aeduorum conspicatur; immisso equitatu iter eorum moratur atque impedit interdicitque omnibus,[3] ne quemquam[4] interficiant. **5.** Eporedorigem et Viridomarum, quos illi[5] interfectos existimabant, inter equites versari suosque appellare iubet. **6.** His[6] cognitis et Litavicci fraude perspecta, Aedui manus tendere, deditionem significare et proiectis armis mortem deprecari[7] incipiunt. **7.** Litaviccus cum suis clientibus, quibus more Gallorum nefas est etiam in extrema fortuna deserere patronos, Gergoviam profugit.

[1] **ad contrahenda castra:** to reduce the size of the camp so that it could be defended by the two legions left behind; for Caesar had but six legions at Gergovia, four having been sent with Labienus to the north. **posita [esse] in:** 'to depend on'.
[2] **necessario tempore:** 'in the emergency'.
[3] **omnibus:** Caesar's soldiers.
[4] **quemquam:** 'a single person'; more emphatic than *quem*.
[5] **illi:** the soldiers of the Aedui deceived by Litaviccus.
[6] **His:** masc.
[7] **mortem deprecari:** 'to plead for life'.

A fierce attack is made upon the Roman camp before Gergovia. The Aedui revolt.

41.1. Caesar, nuntiis ad civitatem Aeduorum missis, qui suo beneficio conservatos[1] docerent, quos iure belli interficere potuisset, tribusque horis exercitui ad quietem datis, castra[2] ad Gergoviam movit. **2.** Medio fere itinere equites a Fabio missi, quanto[3] res in periculo fuerit, exponunt. Summis copiis castra[4] oppugnata demonstrant, cum crebro integri defessis succederent[5] nostrosque assiduo labore defatigarent, quibus propter magnitudinem castrorum perpetuo esset isdem in vallo[6] permanendum. 3. Multitudine sagittarum atque omni genere telorum multos vulneratos; ad haec sustinenda magno usui fuisse tormenta. 4. Fabium discessu eorum[7] duabus relictis portis obstruere[8] ceteras pluteosque vallo addere et se in posterum diem similemque casum apparare. His rebus cognitis, Caesar summo studio militum ante[9] ortum solis in castra pervenit. _____

[1] **conservatos:** sc. *esse eos.*

[2] **castra – movit:** Caesar had encamped after having received the submission of the Aedui.

[3] **quanto . . . fuerit:** 'how critical the condition of affairs had been'.

[4] **castra:** the camps before Gergovia.

[5] **succederent:** 'were relieving'.

[6] **in vallo:** on the 'rampart'.

[7] **discessu eorum:** 'on the departure of the enemy'.

[8] **obstruere, addere, apparare:** the present tense implies that the messengers left Fabius engaged in the work.

[9] **ante . . . pervenit:** Caesar had learned of the defection stirred up by Litaviccus about midnight; he started with his troops immediately, and marched 25 miles; after three hours' rest he brought his force back again, reaching Gergovia before sunrise. His men had marched 50 Roman miles in less than 28 hours.

42.1. Dum haec ad Gergoviam geruntur, Aedui primis nuntiis ab Litavicco acceptis nullum sibi ad cognoscendum spatium relinquunt. **2.** Impellit alios avaritia, alios iracundia et temeritas, quae maxime illi hominum generi est innata, ut levem auditionem habeant pro re comperta.[1] **3.** Bona civium Romanorum diripiunt, caedes faciunt, in servitutem abstrahunt. **4.** Adiuvat rem proclinatam[2] Convictolitavis plebemque ad furorem impellit, ut facinore admisso ad sanitatem reverti pudeat. **5.** M. Aristium, tribunum militum, iter ad legionem[3] facientem fide data ex oppido Cabillono educunt; idem facere[4] cogunt eos, qui negotiandi causa ibi constiterant. **6.** Hos continuo in itinere adorti omnibus impedimentis exuunt; repugnantes diem noctemque obsident; multis utrimque interfectis maiorem multitudinem armatorum concitant.

[1] **pro re comperta:** 'as an assured fact'.

[2] **Adiuvat rem proclinatam:** 'helps to precipitate matters'.

[3] **ad legionem:** probably going to join his legion at Gergovia. Aristius seems to have been accompanied by a detachment of soldiers, and probably the traders put themselves under his protection.

[4] **idem facere:** i.e. to leave Cabillonum at once. The number of traders at Chalon must have been considerable.

43.1. Interim nuntio allato, omnes eorum milites in potestate Caesaris teneri, concurrunt ad Aristium, **2.** nihil publico factum consilio demonstrant; quaestionem de bonis direptis decernunt, Litavicci fratrumque bona publicant, legatos ad Caesarem sui purgandi[1] gratia mittunt. **3.** Haec faciunt recuperandorum suorum causa; sed contaminati facinore et capti compendio ex direptis bonis, quod ea res[2] ad multos pertinebat, et timore poenae exterriti consilia clam de bello inire incipiunt civitatesque reliquas legationibus sollicitant. **4.** Quae tametsi Caesar intellegebat, tamen, quam mitissime potest, legatos appellat: Nihil[3] se propter inscientiam levitatemque vulgi gravius de civitate iudicare neque de sua in Aeduos benevolentia deminuere. **5.** Ipse maiorem Galliae motum exspectans, ne ab omnibus civitatibus circumsisteretur, consilia inibat, quem ad modum a Gergovia discederet ac rursus omnem exercitum contraheret,[4] ne profectio nata ab timore defectionis similisque fugae videretur.

[1] **sui purgandi:** AG 504c, B 339.5. **gratia:** = *causa.*
[2] **ea res:** the profit accruing from the booty.
[3] **Nihil – gravius iudicare:** 'that he would pass no very severe judgement'.
[4] **exercitum contraheret:** i.e. unite his forces with the four legions under Labienus.

Caesar orders an engagement at Gergovia; there is brave fighting, but without success.

44.1. Haec[1] cogitanti accidere visa est facultas bene gerendae rei. Nam cum in minora castra[2] operis perspiciendi causa venisset, animadvertit collem,[3] qui ab hostibus tenebatur, nudatum hominibus, qui superioribus diebus vix prae multitudine cerni poterat. **2.** Admiratus quaerit ex perfugis causam, quorum magnus ad eum cotidie numerus confluebat. **3.** Constabat inter omnes,[4] quod iam ipse Caesar per exploratores cognoverat, dorsum esse eius iugi[5] prope aequum, sed silvestre et angustum, qua esset aditus ad alteram partem[6] oppidi; **4.** vehementer huic illos loco timere, nec iam aliter sentire, uno colle ab Romanis occupato, si alteram amisissent, quin paene circumvallati atque omni exitu et pabulatione interclusi viderentur. Ad hunc muniendum locum omnes a Vercingetorige evocatos.

[1] **Haec:** i.e. how to get away from Gergovia without giving the impression of flight. **cogitanti:** sc. *Caesari* (AG 490, B 336.2).
[2] **minora castra:** on la Roche-Blanche.
[3] **collem:** a part of the Risolle Heights, marked Collis Nudatus on the Plan.
[4] **Constabat inter omnes:** 'All agreed'. **quod:** = *id, quod.*
[5] **eius iugi:** the northwestern slope of the Risolle Heights, along which there was a narrow approach to the town grown up with brush.
[6] **alteram partem:** the west side, from the point of view of the main camp. **illos:** the Gauls. Now that one hill (la Roche-Blanche, VII, 36) had been lost, if Caesar should get possession of another he might extend his line of works along the whole south side of the city, thus shutting the Gauls off from their main water supply and from foraging in the plain.

45.1. Hac re cognita Caesar mittit[1] complures equitum turmas eo de media nocte; imperat, ut paulo tumultuosius omnibus locis vagarentur. **2.** Prima luce magnum numerum impedimentorum[2] ex castris mulorumque produci deque his stramenta[3] detrahi mulionesque cum cassidibus equitum specie ac simulatione collibus circumvehi iubet. **3.** His paucos addit equites, qui latius ostentationis causa vagarentur. Longo circuitu easdem[4] omnes iubet petere regiones. **4.** Haec procul ex oppido videbantur, ut erat a Gergovia despectus in castra, neque[5] tanto spatio, certi quid esset, explorari poterat. **5.** Legionem[6] unam eodem iugo mittit et paulum progressam inferiore constituit loco silvisque occultat. **6.** Augetur Gallis suspicio, atque omnes illo[7] ad munitionem copiae traducuntur. **7.** Vacua castra hostium Caesar conspicatus, tectis insignibus[8] suorum occultatisque signis militaribus, raros[9] milites, ne ex oppido animadverterentur, ex maioribus castris in minora traducit **8.** legatisque, quos singulis legionibus praefecerat, quid fieri velit, ostendit; in primis monet, ut contineant milites, ne studio pugnandi aut spe praedae longius progrediantur; **9.** quid iniquitas loci habeat incommodi,[10] proponit; hoc una celeritate posse vitari; occasionis[11] esse rem, non proeli. **10.** His rebus expositis signum dat et ab dextra parte alio ascensu[12] eodem tempore Aeduos mittit.

[1] **mittit:** towards the point which the Gauls were engaged in fortifying. By seeming to concentrate his forces against this position, Caesar drew the attention of the enemy altogether from his real design, the seizing of their camp.

[2] **impedimentorum:** here 'beasts of burden'.

[3] **stramenta:** 'pack-saddles', used only for the conveyance of burdens and not adapted **for** riding. In southern countries frequently these are left on the animals for weeks at a time without being removed.

[4] **easdem regiones:** the lower ground southwest of the smaller camp, toward Chanonat; as they proceeded in this direction the purpose of the manoeuvre would seem to the Gauls to be, to skirt the base of the Risolle Heights on the south, and make a dash from the west against the point which they were fortifying.

[5] **neque:** 'and (yet) not'. **spatio:** 'distance'. The invention of the spy-glass has had an important influence in determining the methods of modern warfare.

[6] **Legionem:** marked Detached Legion on Map 15.

[7] **illo:** adv. **ad munitionem:** 'for (the work of) fortifying'.

[8] **insignibus:** The crests and standards could be seen by the enemy from the plateau of Gergovia, above the embankment thrown up inside the trenches connecting the two camps.

[9] **raros:** 'in scattered parties'.

[10] **incommodi:** dep. on *quid.*

[11] **occasionis . . . proeli:** 'that they were attempting a surprise, not a battle'. Caesar's purpose was not to hold the Gallic encampment but simply to raid it, thinking that after a successful dash of this sort he could withdraw from the siege with his credit good.

[12] **alio ascensu:** i.e. to the plateau of Gergovia, on the east; see Map 15.

46.1. Murus oppidi a planitie[1] atque initio ascensus recta regione, si[2] nullus anfractus intercederet, MCC passus aberat; **2.** quicquid[3] huc circuitus ad molliendum clivum accesserat, id spatium itineris augebat. **3.** A[4] medio fere colle in[5] longitudinem, ut natura montis ferebat, ex grandibus saxis VI pedum murum,[6] qui nostrorum impetum tardaret, praeduxerant Galli atque, inferiore[7] omni spatio vacuo relicto, superiorem partem collis,[8] usque ad murum oppidi, densissimis castris[9] compleverant. **4.** Milites, dato signo, celeriter ad munitionem perveniunt eamque transgressi trinis castris[10] potiuntur; **5.** ac tanta fuit in castris capiendis celeritas, ut Teutomatus, rex Nitiobrogum, subito in tabernaculo oppressus, ut meridie conquieverat,[11] superiore corporis parte nuda, vulnerato equo, vix se ex manibus praedantium militum eriperet.

[1] **planitie,** etc.: the lower ground at the right of the Small Camp and just above the Parallel Trenches; E on Map 15. **recta regione:** 'in a straight line'.

[2] **si,** etc.:'if there should be no deviation'; how lit.? **anfractus:** *79d.* **MCC:** *mille ducentos,* somewhat more than an English mile; *38a, b; 243b.*

[3] **quicquid . . . augebat:** 'the distance to be traversed was increased by every detour (made)

in order to render (the ascent of) the slope easy'. How lit.? The wall of Gergovia lay almost 1000 feet above the point where the legions started.

[4] **A**, etc.: 'about halfway up the height'; *126c, 152a.*

[5] **in**, etc.: 'following the long side of the mountain as the contour permitted'; how lit.?

[6] **murum:** marked Wall 6 feet high on Map 15. **tardaret:** *193a.*

[7] **inferiore spatio:** the sloping mountain side below the wall. **vacuo:** predicative. *148c.*

[8] **superiorem partem collis:** Gallic Encampment on Map 15.

[9] **densissimis castris:** 'with camps (standing) close together': each camp contained the troops of a single state, in accordance with the arrangement described in VII, 36.2; *153a.*

[10] **trims castris:** 'three camps'; *37e, 131c.*

[11] **conquieverat:** 'he was having a nap'; lit.' had taken complete rest'.

Flushed with victory, the soldiers do not retreat as ordered.

47.1. Consecutus id,[1] quod animo proposuerat, Caesar receptui[2] cani iussit, legionisque X, quacum erat, continuo signa constituit.[3] **2.** At reliquarum legionum milites, non exaudito sono tubae,[4] quod satis magna valles intercedebat, tamen a tribunis militum legatisque, ut erat a Caesare praeceptum, retinebantur;[5] **3.** sed, elati spe celeris victoriae et hostium fuga et superiorum temporum secundis proeliis, nihil adeo arduum sibi esse existimaverunt, quod non virtute consequi possent, neque finem prius sequendi fecerunt quam muro oppidi portisque[6] appropinquarunt. **4.** Tum vero, ex omnibus urbis partibus orto clamore, qui longius[7] aberant, repentino tumultu perterriti, cum hostem intra portas esse existimarent, sese ex oppido eiecerunt. **5.** Matres familiae de muro vestem[8] argentumque iactabant et, pectore[9] nudo prominentes, passis manibus obtestabantur Romanos, ut sibi parcerent neu,[10] sicut Avarici fecissent, ne a mulieribus quidem atque infantibus abstinerent; **6.** non nullae de muro per manus demissae[11] sese militibus tradebant. **7.** L. Fabius, centurio legionis VIII, quem inter suos eo die dixisse constabat, excitari se Avaricensibus praemiis[12] neque commissurum, ut prius quisquam murum ascenderet, tres suos[13] nactus manipulares atque ab eis sublevatus, murum ascendit; hos[14] ipse rursus singulos exceptans in murum extulit.

[1] **id**, etc.: 'what he had in mind', that is, to give the enemy a good scare by a bold dash, so as to be able to retire from Gergovia without discredit.

[2] **receptui**, etc.: 'gave orders that the recall be sounded'; *326c.* How lit.? *112a, 73d.*

[3] **signa constituit:** 'brought to a halt the standards'; *324b2.* **non exaudito:** 'though they did not hear'; how lit.? *144B5.*

[4] **tubae:** *326a1.* **valles:** a depression in the slope, just west of the village of Gergovie; Caesar with the tenth legion was east of this depression (Map 15, 10th Legion, 1st Position).

[5] **retinebantur:** 'an attempt was being made ... to hold the soldiers . . . back'; how lit.? *175e.*

[6] **portis:** probably at the points marked A and B on Map 15.

[7] **longius**, etc.: the Gauls who were some distance inside the wall. **hostem:** the Romans.

[8] **vestem:** 'clothing', **argentum:** 'silver'.

[9] **pectore:** 'breast'. **prominentes:** 'leaning forward'.

[10] **neu**, etc.: 'and not refuse to spare even women'; how lit.? *199d.* **Avarici:** *146.* **fecissent:** *220.*

[11] **demissae:** 'being let down' outside the wall.

[12] **Avaricensibus praemils:** 'the prizes (offered) at Avaricum' see VII, 27.2. **neque,** etc.: 'and that he was not going to let any one scale the wall ahead of him'. How lit.?

[13] **suos manipulares:** 'men of his maniple'.

[14] **hos singulos exceptans:** 'taking hold of them, one at a time'.

The Gauls rally and attack the Romans.

48.1. Interim ei,[1] qui ad alteram partem oppidi, ut supra demonstravimus, munitionis causa convenerant, primo exaudito clamore, inde etiam crebris nuntiis incitati, oppidum a Romanis teneri, praemissis equitibus magno cursu eo contenderunt. **2.** Eorum[2] ut quisque primus venerat, sub muro consistebat suorumque pugnantium numerum augebat. **3.** Quorum cum magna multitudo convenisset, matres familiae, quae paulo ante Romanis de muro manus tendebant, suos obtestari et more Gallico passum capillum[3] ostentare liberosque in conspectum proferre[4] coeperunt. **4.** Erat Romanis nec loco nec numero aequa contentio; simul et cursu et spatio[5] pugnae defatigati, non facile recentes atque integros sustinebant.

[1] **ei:** *Galli.* **alteram partem:** see VII, 44. **supra:** VII, 44; and VII, 45.
[2] **Eorum,** etc.: 'In succession as each came up'. **sub muro;** 'at the foot of the wall', on the outside.
[3] **passum capillum:** 'their hair disheveled'.
[4] **proferre:** 'to bring out'; *69b.*
[5] **spatio:** 'duration'. **non,** etc.: 'they could not easily hold out against'.

49.1. Caesar cum iniquo loco pugnari hostiumque copias augeri videret, praemetuens suis,[1] ad T. Sextium legatum, quem minoribus castris praesidio reliquerat, misit, ut cohortes ex castris celeriter educeret et sub infimo colle[2] ab dextro latere hostium constitueret, ut, si nostros loco depulsos[3] vidisset, quo[4] minus libere hostes insequerentur, terreret. **2.** Ipse, paulum ex eo loco cum legione progressus,[5] ubi constiterat, eventum pugnae exspectabat.

[1] **praemetuens suis:** 'becoming anxious about his men'.
[2] **sub infimo colle:** 'at the foot of the hill' on which the small camp was; see Map 15, Sextius, 1st Position.
[3] **loco depulsos:** 'forced from their position'.
[4] **quo,** etc.: 'deter the enemy from pursuing them further'; how lit.? *201a.*
[5] **progressus,** etc.: see Map 15, 10th Legion, 2d Position.

The Romans fight stubbornly, though against overwhelming odds.

50.1. Cum acerrime comminus pugnaretur, hostes[1] loco et numero, nostri virtute confiderent, subito sunt Aedui[2] visi ab latere nostris aperto, quos Caesar ab dextra parte alio ascensu, manus[3] distinendae causa, miserat. **2.** Hi similitudine armorum[4] vehementer nostros perterruerunt, ac tametsi dextris[5] umeris exsertis animadvertebantur, quod[6] insigne pacatorum esse consuerat, tamen id ipsum sui[7] fallendi causa milites ab hostibus factum existimabant. **3.** Eodem tempore L. Fabius centurio, quique una murum ascenderant, circumventi atque interfecti, muro praecipitabantur.

The heroic self-sacrifice of Marcus Petronius.

4. M. Petronius, eiusdem legionis[8] centurio, cum portas excidere conatus esset, a multitudine oppressus ac sibi desperans, multis iam vulneribus acceptis, manipularibus[9] suis, qui illum secuti erant, 'Quoniam,'[10] inquit, 'me una vobiscum servare non possum, vestrae[11] quidem certe vitae prospiciam, quos, cupiditate gloriae adductus, in periculum deduxi. Vos, data facultate, vobis consulite.' **5.** Simul in medios hostes irrupit duobusque interfectis reliquos a porta paulum summovit. **6.** Conantibus auxiliari suis, 'Frustra,' inquit, 'meae vitae[12] subvenire conamini, quem iam sanguis viresque deficiunt. Proinde abite, dum est facultas, vosque[13] ad legionem recipite.' Ita pugnans, post paulum concidit ac[14] suis saluti fuit.

[1] **hostes:** sc. *confiderent.* **loco:** *135a.*
[2] **Aedui,** etc.: see VII, 45; Map 15, Aeduans.
[3] **manus,** etc.: 'to separate the (enemy's) forces' by a diversion.
[4] **similitudine armorum:** 'from the likeness of their arms' to those of the hostile Gauls.
[5] **dextris,** etc.: 'it was noticed that they had their right shoulders bare'; how lit.? *172d, 191a.*
[6] **quod,** etc.: 'the customary sign indicating those at peace'; how lit.?
[7] **sui:** *154b* (AG 504c, B 339.5).
[8] **eiusdem legionis:** the 8th; see VII, 47.7. **excidere:** 'to hew down'.
[9] **manipularibus:** dative after *inquit.*
[10] **Quoniam,** etc.: *211b2.* **me:** *158b.* **vobiscum:** *125c.*
[11] **vestrae vitae, quos:** 'for the lives of you, whom'; how lit.? *92b, 164b.*
[12] **meae vitae, quem**: i. e. *vitae mei* (genitive), *quem.*
[13] **vos:** object of *recipite; 158b.*
[14] **ac,** etc.: 'and saved his men'; how lit.? *112b.*

The Romans retire, with severe losses.

51.1. Nostri, cum undique premerentur, XLVI[1] centurionibus amissis, deiecti sunt loco.[2] Sed intolerantius Gallos insequentes legio X tardavit, quae pro subsidio paulo aequiore loco[3] constiterat. **2.** Hanc rursus XIII legionis cohortes exceperunt, quae, ex castris minoribus eductae, cum T. Sextio legato ceperant locum superiorem.[4] **3.** Legiones, ubi primum planitiem attigerunt, infestis[5] contra hostes signis constiterunt. **4.** Vercingetorix ab radicibus collis suos intra munitiones reduxit. Eo die milites sunt paulo minus DCC[6] desiderati.

[1] **XLVI:** *quadraginta sex.* As the centurions led their men, the percentage of casualties was proportionally much higher than among the common soldiers.
[2] **deiecti sunt loco**: 'were forced down from their position'. **intolerantius**: 'with considerable violence'.
[3] **paulo aequiore loco:** see Map 15, 10th Legion, 3d Position.
[4] **locum superiorem:** see Map 15, Sextius, 2d Position.
[5] **infestis,** etc.: 'they halted and faced the enemy'; how lit.? *325, 144b2.* That the soldiers, swept down the slope by an overwhelming force, rallied even when supported by the 10th and 13th legions, is all the more remarkable in view of the severe losses among their officers.
[6] **DCC:** *septingenti; 129b.* If the losses among the common soldiers had been in proportion to those among the centurions, the number would have been considerably above two thousand.

Caesar addresses the army, raises the siege, and marches against the rebellious Aedui.

52.1. Postero die Caesar, contione advocata, temeritatem cupiditatemque[1] militum reprehendit, quod sibi ipsi iudicavissent, quo procedendum aut quid agendum videretur, neque signo recipiendi dato constitissent neque a tribunis militum legatisque retineri potuissent. **2.** Exposuit, quid[2] iniquitas loci posset, quod ipse ad Avaricum sensisset, cum sine duce et sine equitatu deprehensis hostibus exploratam victoriam[3] dimisisset, ne parvum modo detrimentum in contentione propter iniquitatem loci accideret. **3.** Quanto opere[4] eorum animi magnitudinem admiraretur, quos non castrorum munitiones, non altitudo montis, non murus oppidi tardare potuisset, tanto opere licentiam arrogantiamque reprehendere, quod plus se quam imperatorem de victoria atque exitu rerum sentire existimarent; **4.** nec minus se a milite modestiam et continentiam quam virtutem atque animi magnitudinem desiderare.

[1] **cupiditatem:** 'eager desire' for victory, not for booty. **sibi:** 'for themselves'.
[2] **quid . . . posset:** 'what the effect of a disadvantageous position is'. **posset:** trans. as if pres. (AG 485d, B 268.1).
[3] **exploratam victoriam:** Caesar was not so sure about the victory at the time; cf. VII, 19, and note 6.
[4] **Quanto opere – tanto opere:** see Vocab. under *Quantus*.

53.1. Hac habita contione et ad extremam orationem[1] confirmatis militibus, ne ob hanc causam animo permoverentur neu, quod iniquitas loci attulisset, id virtuti hostium tribuerent, eadem de profectione cogitans, quae ante senserat, legiones ex castris eduxit aciemque idoneo loco[2] constituit. **2.** Cum Vercingetorix nihilo magis in aequum locum descenderet, levi facto equestri proelio atque eo secundo, in castra exercitum reduxit. **3.** Cum hoc idem postero die fecisset, satis[3] ad Gallicam ostentationem minuendam militumque animos confirmandos factum existimans in Aeduos movit castra. **4.** Ne tum quidem insecutis hostibus, tertio die ad flumen Elaver venit; pontem refecit eoque[4] exercitum traducit.

[1] **ad extremam orationem:** 'at the close of his address'.
[2] **idoneo loco:** Caesar wished to entice the Gauls into a general engagement, in which they would be at a great disadvantage. Vercingetorix, however, was wise enough to avoid a regular battle.
[3] **satis . . . factum:** these words hardly conceal the fact that the siege of Gergovia resulted in a serious reverse.
[4] **eo:** AG 429a, B 218.9.

54.1. Ibi[1] a Viridomaro atque Eporedorige Aeduis appellatus discit, cum omni equitatu Litaviccum ad sollicitandos Aeduos profectum; opus esse[2] ipsos antecedere ad confirmandam civitatem. **2.** Etsi multis iam rebus perfidiam Aeduorum perspectam habebat[3] atque horum discessu maturari defectionem civitatis existimabat, tamen eos retinendos non constituit, ne aut inferre iniuriam videretur aut daret timoris aliquam suspicionem. **3.** Discedentibus his[4] breviter sua in Aeduos merita exposuit; quos et quam humiles[5] accepisset, compulsos in oppida, multatos agris, omnibus ereptis copiis, imposito stipendio, obsidibus summa cum contumelia extortis, **4.** et quam in fortunam quamque in amplitudinem deduxisset, ut non solum in pristinum statum redissent, sed omnium temporum[6] dignitatem et gratiam antecessisse viderentur. His datis mandatis[7] eos ab se dimisit.

[1] **Ibi:** on the east side of the Elaver (Allier), in the territory of the Aedui.

² **opus esse**: see Idioms. Viridomarus and Eporedorix were going to turn traitors to Caesar, and wished for an excuse to get away from him.
³ **perspectam habebat**: trans. as if *perspexerat* (AG 497b, B 337.6).
⁴ **his**: Viridomarus and Eporedorix.
⁵ **quam humiles**: cf. VI, 12 and I, 31.
⁶ **omnium temporum:** 'of all (previous) periods'.
⁷ **mandatis**: 'instructions', points which Caesar gave Viridomarus and Eporedorix to understand they were to use with their fellow-countrymen.

55.1. Noviodunum¹ erat oppidum Aeduorum ad ripas Ligeris, opportuno loco positum. **2.** Huc Caesar omnes obsides Galliae, frumentum, pecuniam publicam,² suorum atque exercitus impedimentorum magnam partem contulerat; **3.** huc magnum numerum equorum huius belli causa, in Italia atque Hispania coemptum miserat. **4.** Eo cum Eporedorix Viridomarusque venissent et de statu civitatis cognovissent, Litaviccum Bibracte ab Aeduis receptum, quod est oppidum apud eos maximae auctoritatis, Convictolitavim magistratum magnamque partem senatus ad eum convenisse, legatos ad Vercingetorigem de pace et amicitia concilianda publice missos, non praetermittendum tantum commodum existimaverunt. **5.** Itaque interfectis Novioduni custodibus, quique eo negotiandi causa convenerant, pecuniam atque equos inter se partiti sunt, **6.** obsides civitatum³ Bibracte ad magistratum deducendos curaverunt; **7.** oppidum, quod a se teneri non posse iudicabant, ne cui esset usui Romanis, incenderunt; **8.** frumenti quod⁴ subito potuerunt, navibus avexerunt, reliquum flumine atque incendio corruperunt. **9.** Ipsi ex finitimis regionibus copias cogere, praesidia custodiasque ad ripas Ligeris disponere equitatumque omnibus locis iniciendi timoris causa ostentare coeperunt, si⁵ ab re frumentaria Romanos excludere aut adductos inopia in provinciam expellere possent. **10.** Quam ad spem multum eos adiuvabat, quod Liger ex nivibus⁶ creverat, ut omnino vado non posse transiri videretur.

¹ **Noviodunum**: now *Nevers;* this town Caesar had made his permanent base of supplies.
² **pecuniam publicam:** the military chest.
³ **obsides civitatum:** held by Caesar as pledges of loyalty. The capture of these by the Aedui had much to do with hastening the spread of the rebellion.
⁴ **frumenti quod:** 'whatever grain'; sc. *avehere.*
⁵ **si:** '(to see) whether' (AG 576a, B 300.3).
⁶ **ex nivibus:** the melting of the snow on the mountains. It was now harvest-time (July).

56.1. Quibus rebus cognitis Caesar maturandum sibi censuit, si¹ esset in perficiendis pontibus periclitandum, ut prius, quam essent maiores eo coactae copiae, dimicaret. **2.** Nam ne, commutato consilio, iter in provinciam converteret, ut non nemo tum quidem necessario faciundum existimabat, cum infamia atque indignitas rei et oppositus mons Cebenna viarumque difficultas impediebat, tum maxime quod, abiuncto Labieno² atque eis legionibus, quas una miserat, vehementer timebat. **3.** Itaque admodum magnis diurnis nocturnisque itineribus confectis, contra omnium opinionem ad Ligerim venit, **4.** vadoque³ per equites invento pro rei necessitate opportuno, ut bracchia modo atque umeri ad sustinenda arma liberi ab aqua esse possent, disposito equitatu,[4] qui vim fluminis refringeret, atque hostibus primo aspectu perturbatis, incolumem exercitum traduxit, **5.** frumentumque in agris et pecoris copiam nactus, repleto his rebus exercitu iter in Senones facere instituit.[5]

[1] **si ... periclitandum**: haste was necessary in order to get across to the north side of the Ligcr before the enemy should have gathered greater forces to prevent his crossing. Retreat to the Province was out of the question; he must push to the north, and effect a junction with Labienus at all hazards.

[2] **Labieno**: dat.

[3] **vado**: probably at Bourbon-Lancy, where there has always been a ford. **pro ... opportuno**: 'good enough considering the emergency', though under ordinary circumstances dangerous and impracticable.

[4] **disposito equitatu**: by stationing the cavalry in a compact line across the stream, the force of the current was broken, so that the infantry could keep their footing in the deep water while marching over.

[5] **instituit**: = *coepit*. Caesar's objective point was Agedincum.

<small>E<small>XPEDITION</small> OF L<small>ABIENUS</small> AGAINST THE P<small>ARISII</small>, LVII-LXII.</small>

Meanwhile the expedition of Labienus against the Parisii is successful. He joins Caesar.

57.1. Dum haec apud Caesarem geruntur, Labienus eo supplemento, quod nuper ex Italia venerat, relicto Agedinci,[1] ut esset impedimentis praesidio, cum quattuor legionibus Lutetiam proficiscitur. Id est oppidum Parisiorum, quod positum est in insula fluminis Sequanae. **2.** Cuius adventu ab hostibus cognito, magnae ex finitimis civitatibus copiae convenerunt. **3.** Summa imperi[2] traditur Camulogeno Aulerco, qui prope confectus aetate tamen propter singularem scientiam rei militaris ad eum est honorem evocatus. **4.** Is cum animadvertisset, perpetuam[3] esse paludem, quae influeret in Sequanam atque illum omnem locum magnopere impediret, hic consedit nostrosque transitu prohibere instituit.

[1] **Agedinci**: AG 427.3, B 232.1.

[2] **Summa imperi**: see Idioms.

[3] **perpetuam paludem**: this 'continuous marsh' probably lay-along the little stream Essonne, extending back from its junction with the Seine. On the north side of it the Gauls were securely posted. See Map p. 250.

58.1. Labienus primo vineas agere,[1] cratibus atque aggere paludem explere atque iter munire[2] conabatur. **2.** Postquam id difficilius confieri[3] animadvertit, silentio e castris tertia vigilia egressus eodem,[4] quo venerat, itinere Metiosedum pervenit. **3.** Id est oppidum Senonum, in insula Sequanae positum, ut paulo ante de Lutetia diximus. **4.** Deprehensis navibus circiter quinquaginta celeriterque coniunctis atque eo[5] militibus iniectis et rei novitate perterritis oppidanis, quorum magna pars erat ad bellum evocata, sine contentione oppido potitur. **5.** Refecto ponte,[6] quem superioribus diebus hostes resciderant, exercitum traducit et secundo flumine[7] ad Lutetiam iter facere coepit. **6.** Hostes re cognita ab eis, qui Metiosedo fugerant, Lutetiam incendi pontesque eius oppidi rescindi iubent; ipsi profecti a palude ad ripas Sequanae e regione Lutetiae[8] contra Labieni castra considunt.

[1] **vineas agere,** etc.: Labienus proposed, under cover of *vineae,* to build a causeway over the marsh in the face of the enemy, throwing in fascines and earth as if filling up the moat of a besieged city.

[2] **iter munire:** 'to construct a road'.

[3] **id difiicilius confieri:** the implication is that the difficulty arose less from the attacks of the enemy than from the yielding nature of the marsh.

[4] **eodem . . . pervenit:** Labienus had come from Agedincum along the left bank of the Seine as far as the Essonne. Not being able to cross this, he marched back the way he came as far as Melun, there passed over to the east side of the Seine, and followed the course of the river down to Paris unhindered. See Map p. 250.

[5] **eo:** 'thereon'.

[6] **ponte:** across the Seine at Melun.

[7] **secundo flumine:** see Idioms.

[8] **e regione Lutetiae:** 'directly opposite Paris'. For the positions of the camps of Labienus and the Gauls, see Map p. 250.

59.1. Iam Caesar[1] a Gergovia discessisse audiebatur, iam de Aeduorum defectione et secundo Galliae motu rumores afferebantur, Gallique in colloquiis interclusum itinere et Ligeri[2] Caesarem, inopia frumenti coactum, in provinciam contendisse confirmabant. **2.** Bellovaci autem, defectione Aeduorum cognita, qui iam ante erant per se infideles, manus cogere atque aperte bellum parare coeperunt. **3.** Tum Labienus tanta rerum[3] commutatione longe aliud sibi capiendum consilium, atque antea senserat, intellegebat, **4.** neque iam, ut[4] aliquid acquireret proelioque hostes lacesseret, sed ut incolumem exercitum Agedincum reduceret, cogitabat. **5.** Namque altera ex parte[5] Bellovaci, quae civitas in Gallia maximam habet opinionem virtutis, instabant, alteram Camulogenus parato atque instructo exercitu tenebat; tum legiones a praesidio atque impedimentis interclusas maximum flumen[6] distinebat. **6.** Tantis subito difficultatibus obiectis ab animi virtute[7] auxilium petendum videbat.

[1] **Caesar – audiebatur:** 'men were hearing that Caesar', etc.

[2] **itinere et Ligeri:** 'from marching, and from (crossing) the Loire'.

[3] **rerum:** 'circumstances'. **aliud - atque:** 'different from what'.

[4] **ut:** introducing a subj. of purpose. Labienus had now to plan not merely about inflicting damage upon the enemy, but even about making sure his retreat and getting back in safety to Agedincum.

[5] **altera ex parte:** on the north; see Map p. 250. **quae civitas:** 'a state which'.

[6] **flumen:** the Seine; Labienus was on the east side, while Agedincum lay to the southwest of the river.

[7] **virtute:** 'determination.'

60.1. Itaque sub vesperum consilio convocato, cohortatus, ut ea, quae imperasset, diligenter industrieque administrarent, naves, quas Metiosedo deduxerat, singulas equitibus Romanis[1] attribuit et, prima confecta vigilia, quattuor milia passuum secundo flumine silentio progredi ibique[2] se exspectare iubet. **2.** Quinque cohortes, quas minime firmas ad dimicandum esse existimabat, castris praesidio relinquit; **3.** quinque eiusdem legionis reliquas de media nocte cum omnibus impedimentis adverso flumine[3] magno tumultu proficisci imperat. **4.** Conquirit etiam lintres; has magno sonitu remorum incitatas in eandem partem mittit. Ipse post paulo silentio egressus cum tribus legionibus eum locum[4] petit, quo naves appelli iusserat.

[1] **singulas equitibus Romanis:** 'each to a Roman knight'. These knights were officers waiting for an appointment in the army.

[2] **ibi:** four miles below Paris, near the site of the village of Point-du-Jour.

[3] **adverso flumine:** see Idioms. The skill shown in this stratagem reveals good generalship in Labienus; but see Vocabulary.

[4] **eum locum:** see note to *ibi* above.

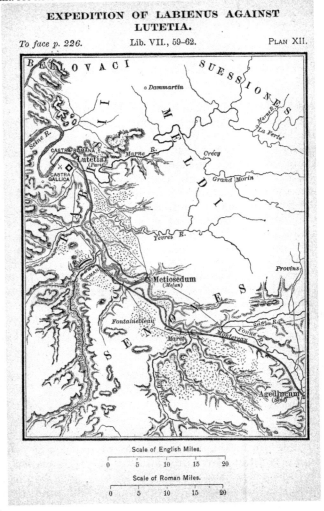

EXPEDITION OF LABIENUS AGAINST LUTETIA.

To face p. 226.   Lib. VII., 59–62.   PLAN XII.

61.1. Eo cum esset ventum, exploratores hostium, ut omni fluminis parte erant dispositi, inopinantes, quod magna subito erat coorta tempestas, a nostris opprimuntur; **2.** exercitus equitatusque, equitibus Romanis administrantibus, quos ei negotio praefecerat, celeriter transmittitur.[1] **3.** Uno fere tempore sub lucem hostibus nuntiatur, in castris Romanorum praeter consuetudinem tumultuari,[2] et magnum ire agmen adverso flumine sonitumque remorum in eadem parte exaudiri, et paulo infra milites navibus transportari. **4.** Quibus rebus auditis, quod existimabant, tribus locis[3] transire legiones atque omnes perturbatos defectione Aeduorum fugam parare, suas quoque copias in tres partes distribuerunt. **5.** Nam praesidio e regione castrorum[4] relicto et parva manu Metiosedum versus missa, quae tantum progrederetur,[5] quantum naves[6] processissent, reliquas copias contra Labienum duxerunt.

[1] **transmittitur:** across the Seine, not far below the Gallic camp.
[2] **tumultuari:** pass, used impers.
[3] **tribus locis:** the Gauls heard the uproar in the Roman Camp, learned that a detachment was going up the river, and were informed by scouts of the approach of Labienus from below. Accordingly they separated their forces into three divisions, one of which went upstream, another mounted guard on the bank of the Seine opposite the Roman camp, and a third went to meet Labienus. Thus the ruse of Labienus was successful in scattering the forces of the enemy, though not in taking them on the rear by surprise as he had perhaps intended.
[4] **e regione castrorum:** on the bank of the Seine, 'directly opposite', 'in a line with', 'the camp'.
[5] **progrederetur:** 'which was to advance (only) so far'.
[6] **naves:** the *lintres*, which were being rowed upstream with great noise.

62.1. Prima luce et nostri[1] omnes erant transportati et hostium acies[2] cernebatur. **2.** Labienus milites cohortatus, ut suae pristinae virtutis et secundissimorum proeliorum retinerent memoriam atque ipsum Caesarem, cuius ductu saepe numero hostes superassent, praesentem adesse existimarent, dat signum proeli. **3.** Primo concursu ab dextro cornu, ubi septima legio constiterat, hostes pelluntur atque in fugam coniciuntur; **4.** ab sinistro, quem locum[3] duodecima legio tenebat, cum primi ordines hostium transfixi pilis concidissent, tamen acerrime reliqui resistebant, nec dabat suspicionem[4] fugae quisquam.[5] **5.** Ipse dux hostium Camulogenus suis aderat atque eos cohortabatur. **6.** At incerto etiam nunc exitu victoriae, cum septimae legionis[6] tribunis esset nuntiatum, quae in sinistro cornu gererentur, post tergum hostium legionem ostenderunt signaque intulerunt. **7.** Ne eo quidem tempore quisquam loco cessit, sed circumventi omnes interfectique sunt. Eandem fortunam tulit Camulogenus. **8.** At ei, qui in praesidio contra castra Labieni erant relicti, cum proelium commissum audissent, subsidio suis ierunt collemque ceperunt,[7] neque nostrorum militum victorum impetum sustinere potuerunt. **9.** Sic cum suis fugientibus permixti, quos[8] non silvae montesque texerunt, ab equitatu sunt interfecti. **10.** Hoc negotio confecto Labienus revertitur Agedincum, ubi impedimenta totius exercitus relicta erant; inde cum omnibus copiis ad Caesarem[9] pervenit.

[1] **nostri:** Labienus with three legions and the cavalry; five cohorts had remained at the camp, and the remaining five of the same legion had gone up-stream.

[2] **hostium acies:** the division of the enemy that had marched down-stream from their camp. The probable scene of the battle is indicated on the Plan by crossed swords.

[3] **quem locum:** 'the position, which'. **cum:** 'although'.

[4] **suspicionem:** 'indication'.

[5] **quisquam:** emphatic by position. **suis aderat:** he was not simply present, but took part in the fighting.

[6] **septimae legionis:** the VIIth legion made a flank movement and turned the enemy's rear.

[7] **collem ceperunt:** 'reached an elevation' on which they could make a stand. **neque:** = *et tamen non.*

[8] **quos:** sc. *ei.*

[9] **Caesarem:** Caesar had been marching to the north of the Loire, and met Labienus probably near Joigny, on the Yonne. See Map.

GENERAL UPRISING, WITH VERCINGETORIX IN COMMAND. 63-68

The Aeduans lead; Vercingetorix assumes command.

63.1. Defectione Aeduorum[1] cognita, bellum augetur. Legationes in omnes partes circummittuntur;[2] **2.** quantum gratia, auctoritate, pecunia valent, ad sollicitandas civitates nituntur; **3.** nacti obsides, quos Caesar apud eos deposuerat, horum supplicio dubitantes territant.[3] **4.** Petunt a Vercingetorige Aedui, ut ad se veniat rationesque[4] belli gerendi communicet. **5.** Re impetrata contendunt, ut ipsis summa imperii tradatur, et, re in controversiam deducta, totius Galliae concilium Bibracte[5] indicitur. **6.** Eodem conveniunt undique frequentes. Multitudinis suffragiis res permittitur; ad unum[6] omnes Vercingetorigem probant imperatorem. **7.** Ab hoc concilio Remi, Lingones, Treveri afuerunt: illi,[7] quod amicitiam Romanorum sequebantur; Treveri, quod aberant longius et a Germanis premebantur, quae fuit causa, quare toto[8] abessent bello et neutris auxilia mitterent. **8.** Magno dolore Aedui ferunt se deiectos principatu,[9] queruntur fortunae commutationem et Caesaris in se indulgentiam[10] requirunt, neque tamen, suscepto bello, suum consilium ab reliquis separare audent. **9.** Inviti[11] summae spei adulescentes, Eporedorix et Viridomarus, Vercingetorigi parent.

[1] **Defectione Aeduorum:** the Aeduans, after much dissension, had finally cast in their lot with Vercingetorix.

[2] **circummittuntur:** 'were sent in all directions' by the Aeduans. **quantum,** etc.: 'to the limit of their influence'.

[3] **dubitantes territant:** cf. VII, 4.9, and note 12.

[4] **rationes,** etc.: 'work out the plan of campaign with (them)'.

[5] **Bibracte;** *145b, 16c.*

[6] **ad unum:** 'to a man'; the vote was unanimous.

[7] **illi:** 'the former', including both the Remi and the Lingones.

[8] **toto bello:** *147c.* **abessent:** 'they held aloof'.

[9] **se deiectos** [esse] **principatu:** 'that they had been forced out of their position of leadership'; cf. VI, 12.9.

[10] **indulgentiam:** 'favour'. **requirunt:** 'they greatly missed'.

[11] **Inviti:** 'Unwillingly'; *151.* **summae spei:** 'of the greatest promise'; *100a.*

64.1. Ille[1] imperat reliquis civitatibus obsides itemque ei rei constituit diem; omnes equites, XV milia numero, celeriter convenire iubet. **2.** Peditatu,[2] quem antea habuerit, se fore contentum dicit, neque[3] fortunam temptaturum aut in acie dimicaturum; *Sed, quoniam abundet equitatu,* *perfacile esse factu frumentationibus[4] pabulationibusque Romanos prohibere;* **3.** *aequo modo animo sua ipsi frumenta corrumpant aedificiaque incendant, qua[5] rei familiaris iactura perpetuum imperium libertatemque se consequi videant.* **4.** His constitutis rebus, Aeduis Segusiavisque, qui sunt finitimi provinciae,[6] X milia peditum imperat; huc addit equites DCCC. **5.** His praeficit fratrem Eporedorigis bellumque inferri Allobrogibus iubet. **6.** Altera ex parte Gabalos proximosque pagos Arvernorum in Helvios,[7] item Rutenos Cadurcosque ad fines Volcarum Arecomicorurn depopulandos mittit. **7.** Nihilo minus clandestinis nuntiis legationibusque Allobrogas sollicitat, quorum mentes nondum ab superiore bello[8] resedisse sperabat. **8.** Horum principibus pecunias, civitati autem imperium totius provinciae pollicetur.

[1] **Ille:** Vercingetorix. **ei rei:** the delivery of the hostages to him.
[2] **Peditatu:** *135a* (B. 219.1).
[3] **neque . . . videant:** the policy infantry.
[4] **frumentationibus:** 'from getting grain'.
[5] **qua . . . iactura:** 'since by this sacrifice of property'.
[6] **provinciae:** *290.* **huc:** for *his*, 'to these'.
[7] **Helvios:** west of the Rhone; see Map GALLIA.
[8] **superiore bello:** the uprising of the Allobroges in 61 B.C.

Caesar takes account of his forces, sends for German cavalry.

65.1. Ad hos omnes casus[1] provisa erant praesidia cohortium duarum et viginti, quae, ex ipsa coacta provincia ab[2] L. Caesare legato, ad omnes partes opponebantur. **2.** Helvii sua sponte cum finitimis proelio congressi pelluntur et, C. Valerio Donnotauro, Caburi filio,[3] principe civitatis, compluribusque aliis interfectis, intra[4] oppida murosque compelluntur. **3.** Allobroges, crebris ad Rhodanum dispositis praesidiis, magna cura et diligentia suos fines tuentur. **4.** Caesar, quod hostes equitatu superiores esse intellegebat et, interclusis[5] omnibus itineribus, nulla re ex provincia atque Italia sublevari poterat, trans Rhenum in Germaniam mittit ad eas civitates,[6] quas superioribus annis pacaverat, equitesque ab his arcessit et levis armaturae pedites, qui[7] inter eos proeliari consuerant. **5.** Eorum adventu, quod minus idoneis equis[8] utebantur, a tribunis militum reliquisque equitibus Romanis atque evocatis equos sumit Germanisque distribuit.

[1] **Ad hos omnes casus:** 'To meet all these conditions'.
[2] **ad opponebantur:** 'were posted to secure every point'.
[3] **Caburi filio:** see I, 47.4. **principe:** 'first magistrate'.
[4] **intra,** etc.: 'into their fortified towns and behind walls'.
[5] **interclusis,** etc: 'since all the roads were blocked'.
[6] **eas civitates:** the Ubil were friendly to Caesar (IV, 16.5); what other German states are here referred to we do not know. **superioribus annis:** 55 and 53 B.C. (IV, 16-19 and VI, 9-28).
[7] **qui . . consuerant:** in the manner previously described (I, 48.5-7). Caesar had previously had a division of German cavalry.
[8] **minus idoneis equis:** cf. IV, 2.2.

MAP 16

VICTORY OF CAESAR OVER VERCINGETORIX

Book VII, 66–68

To face page 392

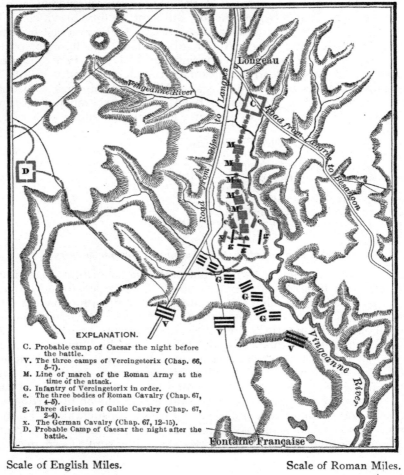

EXPLANATION.

C. Probable camp of Caesar the night before the battle.
V. The three camps of Vercingetorix (Chap. 66, 5–7).
M. Line of march of the Roman Army at the time of the attack.
G. Infantry of Vercingetorix in order.
e. The three bodies of Roman Cavalry (Chap. 67, 4–5).
g. Three divisions of Gallic Cavalry (Chap. 67, 2–4).
x. The German Cavalry (Chap. 67, 12–15).
D. Probable Camp of Caesar the night after the battle.

Scale of English Miles.

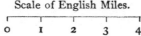

0   1   2   3   4

Scale of Roman Miles.

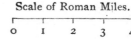

0   1   2   3   4

EXPLANATION

Vercingetorix drew up his infantry in front of his three camps, on the bank of a river, and ordered his cavalry to attack Caesar's army, which was marching toward the river on the opposite side.

Caesar's legionaries, though surprised, held their own until finally the German cavalry in Caesar's employ hurled back the Gallic cavalry, which suffered complete defeat.

Vercingetorix encamps near Caesar, addresses his troops.

66.1. Interea, dum[1] haec geruntur, hostium copiae ex Arvernis equitesque, qui toti Galliae erant imperati, conveniunt. **2.** Magno horum coacto numero, cum Caesar in Sequanos per extremos Lingonum fines[2] iter faceret, quo facilius subsidium provinciae ferri posset, circiter milia passuum X ab Romanis trinis castris[3] Vercingetorix consedit, **3.** convocatisque ad concilium praefectis equitum, venisse tempus victoriae demonstrat: *Fugere[4] in provinciam Romanos Galliaque excedere.* **4.** *Id sibi ad praesentem obtinendam libertatem satis esse; ad reliqui temporis pacem atque otium parum profici; maioribus enim coactis copiis reversuros[5] neque finem bellandi facturos.* **5.** *Proinde in agmine impeditos[6] adoriantur. Si pedites suis auxilium ferant atque in eo morentur, iter facere non posse; si, id quod magis futurum confidat, relictis impedimentis suae saluti consulant, et usu rerum necessariarum et dignitate spoliatum iri.[7]* **6.** *Nam de equitibus hostium, quin nemo eorum progredi modo extra agmen audeat, ne ipsos quidem debere dubitare. Id[8] quo maiore faciant animo, copias se omnes pro castris habiturum et terrori hostibus futurum.* **7.** Conclamant equites, sanctissimo iure iurando[9] confirmari oportere, ne tecto recipiatur,[10] ne ad liberos, ne ad parentes, ne ad uxorem aditum habeat, qui non bis per agmen hostium perequitarit.

[1] **dum**, etc.: while Caesar was collecting forces from the Province and from Germany; *190a.*
[2] **extremos Lingonum fines:** 'the most distant (part of the) country of the Lingones'; i.e. the southeastern part, 'most distant' from Agedincum, chief city of the Senones, which was Caesar's principal base for the operations of 52 B.C. See Map 13.
[3] **trinis castris:** marked V, V, V, on Map 16, which represents the location as fixed by Napoleon, about 40 miles northeast of Dijon. The battle was probably fought north of Dijon, and much nearer; but Napoleon's plan indicates the relative positions clearly. **trinis:** *37e.*
[4] **Fugere**, etc.: *213b.* **Id:** the retreat to the Province.
[5] **reversuros** [esse]: sc. *Romanos.*
[6] **impeditos:** sc. *eos (= Romanos)*. If the legionaries, thus caught at a disadvantage, should attempt to defend the baggage-train, their retreat would be stopped; if they should abandon the baggage-train and try to defend only themselves, they would be cut off from their supplies.
[7] **dignitate spoliatum iri:** 'would be despoiled of their prestige.. **hostium:** the Romans.
[8] **Id faciant:** 'That they might make the attack'; how lit.?
[9] **iure iurando:** explained by the *ne*-clauses following.; *13h.*
[10] **recipiatur:** '(the man) who'.

The cavalry of Vercingetorix is defeated by Caesar's cavalry.

67.1. Probata re atque omnibus iure iurando[1] adactis, postero die, in tres partes distributo equitatu, duae[2] se acies ab duobus lateribus[3] ostendunt, una a primo agmine iter impedire coepit. Qua re nuntiata, Caesar suum quoque equitatum, tripertito divisum,[4] contra hostem ire iubet. **2.** Pugnatur una omnibus in partibus. **3.** Consistit agmen; impedimenta[5] intra legiones recipiuntur. **4.** Si qua in parte nostri laborare aut gravius premi videbantur, eo signa inferri Caesar aciemque constitui iubebat; quae res et hostes ad insequendum tardabat et nostros spe auxilii confirmabat. **5.** Tandem Germani[6] ab dextro latere summum iugum nacti hostes loco depellunt; fugientes usque ad flumen, ubi Vercingetorix cum pedestribus copiis[7] consederat, persequuntur compluresque interficiunt. 6. Qua re animadversa, reliqui, ne circumirentur, veriti, se fugae mandant. 7. Omnibus locis fit caedes. Tres nobilissimi Aedui capti ad Caesarem perducuntur: Cotus, praefectus equitum, qui controversiam cum Convictolitavi proximis comitiis habuerat, et Cavarillus, qui post defectionem Litavicci pedestribus copiis praefuerat, et Eporedorix, quo duce ante adventum Caesaris Aedui cum Sequanis bello contenderant.

[1] **iure iurando:** the oath given above.
[2] **duae acies, una** [acies]: the three divisions of Gallic cavalry, marked g, g, g, on Map 16.
[3] **lateribus, primo agmine:** 'flanks', 'van', of the Romans.
[4] **equitatum, tripertito divisum:** marked e, e, e, on Map 16.
[5] **impedimenta,** etc.: each legion formed a hollow square (*orbis, 338*) about its baggage (*328*). Caesar was surprised.
[6] **Germani:** from the favourable position which they had reached on the height (x on Map 16) the German cavalry charged the Gallic cavalry with irresistible momentum. Cf. VII, 70, 2-4; and 80, 6.
[7] **pedestribus copiis:** Map 16, G, G, G.

Vercingetorix and his army take refuge at Alesia.

68.1. Fugato omni equitatu, Vercingetorix copias suas, ut pro castris collocaverat, reduxit protinusque Alesiam, quod est oppidum Mandubiorum, iter facere coepit celeriterque impedimenta ex castris educi et se subsequi iussit. **2.** Caesar, impedimentis in proximum collem deductis, duabus legionibus[1] praesidio relictis, secutus hostes, quantum diei tempus est passum, circiter III milibus ex novissimo agmine interfectis, altero die[2] ad Alesiam castra fecit. **3.** Perspecto urbis situ perterritisque hostibus, quod equitatu, qua maxime parte exercitus confidebant, erant pulsi, adhortatus ad laborem milites circumvallare instituit.

[1] **legionibus:** abl. abs. with *relictis*. **praesidio:** *112a*.
[2] **altero die:** = *postero die*, 'the next day'. Cf. Map 13.

THE SIEGE AND FALL OF ALESIA. 69-90

Caesar commences to surround Alesia with a line of works.

69.1. Ipsum erat oppidum Alesia[1] in colle summo, admodum edito loco, ut nisi obsidione[2] expugnari non posse videretur. **2.** Cuius collis radices duo duabus ex partibus flumina[3] subluebant. **3.** Ante oppidum planities[4] circiter milia passuum III in longitudinem patebat; **4.** reliquis ex omnibus partibus colles, mediocri interiecto spatio,[5] pari altitudinis fastigio oppidum cingebant. **5.** Sub muro,[6] quae pars collis ad orientem solem spectabat, hunc omnem locum[7] copiae Gallorum compleverant fossamque et maceriam[8] in altitudinem VI pedum praeduxerant. **6.** Eius munitionis,[9] quae ab Romanis instituebatur, circuitus XI milia passuum tenebat.[10] **7.** Castra opportunis locis erant posita ibique castella XXIII facta; quibus in castellis interdiu stationes[11] ponebantur, ne qua subito eruptio fieret; haec eadem noctu excubitoribus ac firmis praesidiis[12] tenebantur.

[1] **Alesia,** etc.: Alesia was situated on the top of an oval hill now called *Mont Auxois*, a part of which is occupied by the village of *Alise-Ste-Reine* (see Map 17). The highest point is more

than 500 feet above the beds of the small streams on either side. The accuracy of Caesar's description has been attested by discoveries made in the course of excavations in 1862-65, and since 1900.

[2] **obsidione:** *340*.

[3] **flumina:** the *Ose* and the *Oserain*. **subluebant:** 'washed'.

[4] **planities:** 'the plain' of *Les Laumes*.

[5] **spatio:** the average distance between the height of Alesia and the tops of the surrounding hills is about a mile. **pari,** etc.: 'having a like elevation'; how lit.?

[6] **Sub muro,** etc.: 'Below the wall', on the side facing the east.

[7] **hunc omnem locum:** 'all the space'; *160d*.

[8] **maceriam:** 'wall of loose stones', without mortar; Map 17.

[9] **Eius munitionis:** 'of the line of investment', a series of fortified camps, between which at intervals were the 'redoubts', *castella*.

[10] **tenebat:** 'extended'. **Castra:** plural. The infantry camps are those marked **A, B, C, D** on Map 17; the camps marked **G, H, I, K** were probably occupied by cavalry.

[11] **stationes:** 'outposts'.

[12] **excubitoribus ac firmis praesidiis:** 'by strong garrisons of men in bivouac', sleeping under arms in the open; the redoubts were fortified enclosures without tents; *238d*.

The Gauls attempt to stop the work, and are driven back.

70.1. Opere instituto fit equestre proelium in ea planitie, quam, intermissam collibus,[1] tria milia passuum in longitudinem patere supra[2] demonstravimus. Summa vi ab utrisque contenditur. **2.** Laborantibus[3] nostris Caesar Germanos summittit legionesque pro castris[4] constituit, ne qua subito irruptio ab hostium peditatu fiat. **3.** Praesidio[5] legionum addito, nostris animus augetur; hostes, in fugam coniecti, se ipsi multitudine impediunt atque angustioribus portis[6] relictis coartantur. **4.** Germani acrius usque ad munitiones persequuntur. Fit magna caedes; **5.** non nulli, relictis equis, fossam transire et maceriam transcendere conantur. Paulum legiones Caesar, quas pro vallo[7] constituerat, promoveri iubet. **6.** Non minus, qui intra munitiones erant, Galli perturbantur; veniri[8] ad se confestim existimantes, ad arma conclamant; non nulli, perterriti, in oppidum irrumpunt. **7.** Vercingetorix iubet portas[9] claudi, ne castra nudentur. Multis interfectis, compluribus equis captis, Germani sese recipiunt.

[1] **intermissam collibus:** 'free from hills,' lit. 'left off by hills'.

[2] **supra:** VII.69. **Summa,** etc.: 'Both sides fought with their utmost strength'; how lit.?

[3] **Laborantibus:** 'hard pressed'; how lit.? **Germanos:** mercenaries, consisting of cavalry, and light-armed troops, trained to fight with them, brought from Germany to offset the superiority of Vercingetorix in cavalry (VII, 65, 4-5).

[4] **castris:** plural. **irruptio:** 'attack'.

[5] **Praesidio:** 'support.' **nostris:** *109a*.

[6] **portis,** etc.: 'gate-openings' in the wall of loose stones (see VII, 69.5; **a, b, c**, on Map 17), '(which had been) left rather narrow'; it is not probable that gates had been placed in the openings. **coartantur:** 'were jammed together'; *352a*.

[7] **pro vallo:** probably the rampart of the infantry camps alone (**A, B, C, D**, on Map 17) is meant.

[8] **veniri:** trans, 'that the Romans were coming'. *73, d*.

[9] **portas:** here 'gates' of the town, through which panic-stricken Gauls rushed, in the effort to escape from their threatened camp into the city. **castra:** on the east side of Alesia, between the city wall and the wall of loose stones.

MAP 17

THE SIEGE OF ALESIA

Book VII, 69–90

To face page 400

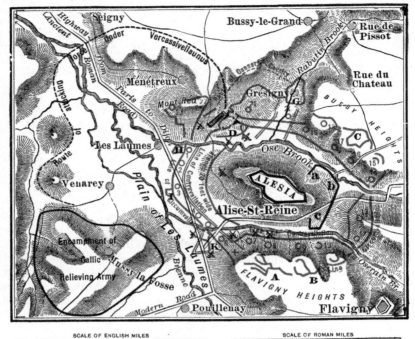

SCALE OF ENGLISH MILES

SCALE OF ROMAN MILES

EXPLANATION

Caesar's lines of works about Alesia encompassed a circuit of 11 Roman miles on the inside, 14 miles on the outside.

In the plain west of the city, and at other points where required, there were two systems of defenses, one to protect Caesar's men against the attacks of Vercingetorix in the city, the other as a defense against the relieving army.

Camps of infantry were probably located at **A, B, C, D**; of cavalry, at **G, H, I, K.** The redoubts, castella (chap. 69), are numbered 1 to 23.

On the west, along the edge of the plain, a trench, or moat, 20 feet wide, with vertical sides, was constructed (chap. 72, ll. 3–5). Further west, in this order, 'goads,' stimulī ; 'wolf-holes,' līlia ; 'boundary posts,' cippī ; two V-shaped 'trenches,' fossae; 'rampart,' agger, and 'palisade,' vallus, with a 'breastwork,' lōrīca, and 'battlements,' pinnae ; also 'towers,' turrēs, at intervals of 80 feet. These defenses formed the LINE OF CONTRAVALLATION (chap. 72–73).

The same defenses, in a reverse series, the 'goads' being furthest outside, the rampart inside, formed the LINE OF CIRCUMVALLATION (chap. 74).

Vercingetorix summons all Gaul to the rescue, and apportions the available provisions.

71.1. Vercingetorix, prius quam munitiones ab Romanis perficiantur,[1] consilium capit, omnem ab se equitatum noctu dimittere. **2.** Discedentibus[2] mandat, ut suam quisque eorum civitatem adeat omnesque,[3] qui per aetatem arma ferre possint, ad bellum cogant. **3.** Sua in illos merita proponit obtestaturque, ut suae salutis rationem habeant, neu se, optime de communi libertate meritum,[4] hostibus in cruciatum dedant. Quod[5] si indiligentiores fuerint, milia hominum delecta LXXX una secum interitura demonstrat; **4.** *ratione inita,[6] se exigue dierum XXX[7] habere frumentum, sed paulo etiam longius tolerari posse parcendo[8].* **5.** His datis mandatis, qua erat[9] nostrum opus intermissum, secunda vigilia[10] silentio equitatum dimittit. **6.** Frumentum omne ad se referri iubet; capitis poenam[11] eis, qui non paruerint, constituit; **7.** pecus, cuius magna erat copia a Mandubiis compulsa, viritim distribuit; **8.** frumentum parce et paulatim metiri instituit. Copias omnes, quas pro oppido[12] collocaverat, in oppidum recipit. **9.** His rationibus auxilia Galliae exspectare et bellum administrare parat.

[1] **perficiantur:** *189b* (AG 551b.n2, B 292).
[2] **Discedentibus:** sc. *eis (equitibus),* implied in the preceding *equitatum.*
[3] **omnes:** object of *cogant.* **per aetatem:** 'by reason of age'.
[4] **meritum:** participle; 'who had rendered most excellent service in behalf of their common liberty'; how lit.?
[5] **Quod:** *118d.* **indiligentiores:** 'too remiss'.
[6] **ratione inita:** '(he said that), having made calculation'; *213b.*
[7] **dierum XXX:** '(to last) 30 days'; how lit.? *100a.*
[8] **parcendo:** 'by reducing the rations'; how lit.? *230.4.*
[9] **erat,** etc.: 'there was a break in our line of works', the contravallation, which there had not been time to complete.
[10] **secunda vigilia:** *242c.* **Frumentum omne:** in the city; Vercingetorix put the inhabitants under martial law.
[11] **capitis poenam:** 'the penalty of death'. **paruerint:** subjunctive in implied indirect discourse, as part of the notice given to the Alesians.
[12] **pro oppido:** in the encampment on the east side.

Description of the inner line of Caesar's siege works.

72.1. Quibus rebus cognitis ex perfugis et captivis, Caesar haec[1] genera munitionis instituit. Fossam[2] pedum XX derectis lateribus duxit, ut eius fossae solum[3] tantundem pateret, quantum summae fossae labra distarent. **2.** Reliquas omnes munitiones ab ea fossa pedes CCCC[4] reduxit, hoc consilio, quoniam tantum esset necessario spatium complexus, nec[5] facile totum opus corona militum cingeretur, ne de improviso aut noctu ad munitiones multitudo hostium advolaret, aut interdiu tela in nostros, operi destinatos, conicere possent. **3.** Hoc intermisso spatio,[6] duas fossas XV pedes latas, eadem altitudine, perduxit; quarum interiorem[7] campestribus ac demissis[8] locis aqua, ex flumine derivata, complevit. **4.** Post eas[9] aggerem ac vallum XII pedum exstruxit. Huic loricam[10] pinnasque adiecit, grandibus cervis eminentibus ad commissuras[11] pluteorum atque aggeris, qui ascensum hostium tardarent,[12] et turres toto opere circumdedit, quae pedes[13] LXXX inter se distarent.

[1] **haec**: 'the following'; *161a*. **munitionis**: 'works', together forming the contravallation, the purpose of which was to hem in Vercingetorix and protect Caesar's forces against attack from within (Map 17, Contravallation). *92b*.

[2] **Fossam**, etc.: 'a trench twenty feet (in width), with vertical sides', much harder for an enemy to fill and cross than the ordinary triangular trench *(333)*; it ran across the plain west of the town, between the Ose and the Oserain (Map 17, Trench 20 Feet Wide).

[3] **solum,** etc.: 'the bottom was as broad as the distance between the edges at the top'; how lit.?

[4] **CCCC**: *quadringentos*. The distance, as shown by excavation, averages so much more than 400 Roman feet, that it has been suggested that Caesar intended to write *passus* or *passibus*. **hoc,** etc.: i.e. *hoc consilio, ne, quoniam . . . cingeretur, de improviso . . . possent.* **esset — complexus, cingeretur:** *220*.

[5] **nec,** etc.: 'and the whole line of works could not easily be manned with a continuous cordon of soldiers'; how lit.?

[6] **spatio:** refers to *pedes CCCC* above. **duas fossas:** Map 17, where it will be observed that the outer trench ran only to the edges of the plain, while the inner trench was continued around the town, forming a part of the contravallation. **eadem altitudine:** of the same depth, 8 or 9 feet; these trenches were V-shaped.

[7] **interiorem:** sc. *fossam*. **campestribus:** 'in the plain'.

[8] **demissis:** 'low'. **flumine:** the Oserain. **derivata:** 'drawn'. Silt, evidencing the action of running water, was found in the inner trench.

[9] **Post eas:** 'Behind these', on the side away from the town. **aggerem:** 'bank', made of the earth thrown out of the nearer trench. **vallum:** masculine, 'palisade', like the palisade of a camp *(333)*. **XII pedum:** measured from the surface of the ground beside the 'bank' to the top of the 'palisade'. **Huic:** singular because the 'bank' and the 'palisade' are thought of as forming one fortification; 'to this rampart'.

[10] **loricam:** a 'breastwork', made by weaving supple branches closely together on the exposed side of the palisade. **pinnas:** 'battlements', covered with wickerwork and projecting above the palisade, behind which the soldiers could find shelter after hurling their weapons over the palisade. **cervis:** 'stags', large limbs of trees and tops of young trees, from which the foliage and twigs had been removed, the branches being stripped of their bark and sharpened; these were planted along the bank at the foot of the palisade, projecting outwards over the trench and towards the town (Plate IX.1, the projecting branches at the foot of the tower). **eminentibus:** 'projecting'.

[11] **ad commissuras**, etc.: 'along the line where the wood construction was fitted to the *bank'*, *pluteorum* here including the 'palisade' *(vallus)*, the 'breastwork' *(lorica)*, and the 'battlements' *(pinnas)*. How lit.?

[12] **tardarent:** *193a*. **opere:** 'the line of works'. **quae,** etc.: *194a*.

[13] **pedes LXXX:** artillery was mounted in the towers (VII, 81.5; and 82.1); the spaces between the towers could be covered also by hand-thrown missiles, in case the enemy should burst through the palisade.

73.1. Erat[1] eodem tempore et materiari et frumentari et tantas munitiones fieri necesse, deminutis[2] nostris copiis, quae longius[3] a castris progrediebantur; ac non numquam opera nostra Galli temptare atque eruptionem ex oppido pluribus portis summa vi facere conabantur. **2.** Quare ad haec rursus opera addendum[4] Caesar putavit, quo minore numero militum munitiones defendi possent. Itaque, truncis arborum aut admodum firmis ramis[5] abscisis, atque horum[6] delibratis ac praeacutis cacuminibus, perpetuae[7] fossae quinos pedes altae ducebantur. **3.** Huc[8] illi stipites demissi, et ab infimo revincti,[9] ne revelli possent, ab[10] ramis eminebant. **4.** Quini erant ordines, coniuncti inter se atque implicati;[11] quo qui intraverant, se ipsi acutissimis vallis[12] induebant. Hos cippos appellabant. **5.** Ante[13] hos, obliquis ordinibus in quincuncem dispositis, scrobes[14] in altitudinem trium pedum fodiebantur, paulatim angustiore[15] ad infimum fastigio. **6.** Huc teretes stipites feminis crassitudine, ab[16] summo praeacuti et praeusti, demittebantur ita, ut non amplius[17] digitis IIII ex terra eminerent; **7.** simul, confirmandi et stabiliendi[18] causa, singuli ab infimo solo pedes terra exculcabantur; reliqua pars scrobis ad occultandas insidias[19] viminibus ac virgultis integebatur. **8.** Huius generis octoni ordines[20] ducti ternos inter se pedes distabant. Id, ex similitudine floris,[21] lilium appellabant. **9.** Ante haec taleae,[22] pedem longae, ferreis hamis infixis, totae in terram infodiebantur,[23] mediocribusque intermissis spatiis, omnibus locis disserebantur,[24] quos stimulos nominabant.

[1] **Erat – necesse:** as subject *materiari* and *frumentari* are coordinated with *munitiones fieri*; 'it was necessary both to get timber and to secure grain and to carry on the construction of these extensive fortifications'; how lit.?

[2] **deminutis,** etc.: 'with (consequent) weakening of our forces'; how lit.?

[3] **longius:** the supplies of timber and grain near the camp were soon exhausted.

[4] **addendum** [esse]: 'that an addition ought to be made'; *73e*.

[5] **admodum firmis ramis:** 'very large limbs', probably not less than four or five inches in diameter.

[6] **horum,** etc.: 'the ends (of their branches) barked and sharpened to a point'.

[7] **perpetuae:** 'continuous', running parallel with the rampart, at the points where needed, on the side toward the town. **quinos:** distributive; 'each five feet deep'.

[8] **Huc:** 'Into these', the parallel trenches. **illi stipites:** 'the stocks' of trees, prepared as described; *160d*.

[9] **revincti:** 'fastened down'; how the stocks were fastened at the bottom we do not know. **ab infimo**: *126c, 154a*.

[10] **ab,** etc.: 'had their branches' (these having been barked and sharpened) 'projecting' above the ground; how lit.? *126c*. **Quini ordines:** 'five rows', one in 'each (trench)'; cf. Plate IX.1.

[11] **implicati:** 'interwoven', the parallel trenches being near together. **quo,** etc.: 'and any who tried to enter these' rows of branches, corresponding with the barbed wire entanglements of modern fortifications. How lit.?

[12] **valis:** 'points'. **se induebant:** 'would pierce themselves'. **cippos:** 'boundary posts', jestingly named from their resemblance to the firmly set stocks of trees and posts used by surveyors to mark boundaries, especially in regions where boundary posts of stone were hard to procure. **appellabant:** 'the soldiers called'; *172c*.

[13] **Ante:** 'In front of', on the side toward the town. **obliquis.** etc.: 'in slanting rows having a quincuncial arrangement'; how lit.?

[14] **scrobes:** 'holes'. **fodiebantur:** 'were dug'; *57b*.

[15] **angustiore,** etc.: 'the side gradually narrowing toward the bottom', like a funnel; how lit.? **Huc:** 'Into these'. **teretes:** 'smooth'. **feminis crassitudine:** 'of the thickness of a thigh'; *18d, 143a*.

[16] **ab,** etc.: 'sharpened at the top and hardened (at the point) by burning'.

[17] **amplius,** etc.: 'more than four finger-breadths', about equivalent to three inches; *243a*.

[18] **stabiliendi,** etc.: 'to give them a solid setting'; how lit.? **singuli,** etc.: 'earth was packed about them by treading, to the depth of a foot from the bottom', lit. 'feet in each case from the bottom were trodden with earth'.

[19] **insidias:** 'the pitfall'. **integebatur:** 'was covered up'.

[20] **octoni ordines:** 'eight rows in each case', wherever the wolfholes were used; they were not needed at all points of the contravallation.

[21] **floris:** *13c*. **lilium:** 'lily', the name being suggested by the appearance of the stalk of the lily rising from its funnel-shaped circlet of leaves; now "wolf-pit" or "wolf-hole".

[22] **taleae:** 'blocks'. **ferreis,** etc.: 'with barbed hooks, of iron, set in'.

[23] **infodiebantur,** etc.: 'were buried in the earth'. only the barbed iron projecting; how lit.?

[24] **disserebantur:** 'were planted here and there'. Several of the irons have been found. **stimulos:** 'goads', so called from the likeness of the projecting points to the sharp end of a

goad.

Caesar completes a similar outer line of works.

74.1. His rebus perfectis, regiones[1] secutus quam potuit aequissimas pro loci natura, XIIII milia passuum complexus[2] pares[3] eiusdem generis munitiones, diversas ab his, contra exteriorem hostem[4] perfecit, ut ne magna quidem multitudine, si[5] ita accidat, munitionum praesidia circumfundi possent; **2.** ac ne cum periculo ex castris egredi[6] cogatur, dierum XXX[7] pabulum frumentumque habere omnes convectum iubet.

[1] **regiones,** etc.: 'following a course over the most nearly level stretches that the configuration of the country afforded'; how lit.?
[2] **complexus:** participle; 'he embraced (a circuit of) fourteen miles and'; *228a.*
[3] **pares:** 'corresponding'. **diversas:** 'facing in the opposite direction' from the inner line of works; see Map 17, Circumvallation.
[4] **exteriorem hostem:** a relieving force. **multitudine:** sc. *hostium.*
[5] **si,** etc.: *si magna multitudo veniat.* **circumfundi:** 'be completely surrounded'.
[6] **ex castris egredi:** in order to secure forage and grain.
[7] **XXX:** cf. VII, 71.4, note 7. **omnes:** 'all' his forces. **convectum:** 'collected'; *229a.*

The Gauls gather a great army for the relief of Alesia.

75.1. Dum haec ad[1] Alesiam geruntur, Galli, concilio principum indicto, non omnes, qui arma ferre possent, ut censuit Vercingetorix, convocandos statuunt, sed certum numerum cuique civitati imperandum, ne,[2] tanta multitudine confusa, nec moderari nec discernere suos nec frumentandi[3] rationem habere possent. **2.** Imperant Aeduis atque eorum clientibus,[4] Segusiavis, Ambivaretis, Aulercis Brannovicibus, milia XXXV; parem numerum Arvernis, adiunctis Eleutetis, Cadurcis, Gabalis, Vellaviis, qui sub imperio Arvernorum esse consuerunt; **3.** Sequanis, Senonibus, Biturigibus, Santonis, Rutenis, Carnutibus duodena milia;[5] Bellovacis X; totidem Lemovicibus; octona Pictonibus et Turonis et Parisiis et Helvetiis; sena Andibus, Ambianis, Mediomatricis, Petrocoriis, Nerviis, Morinis, Nitiobrogibus; quinque milia Aulercis Cenomanis; totidem Atrebatibus; IIII Veliocassis; Aulercis Eburovicibus III; Rauracis et Boiis bina: **4.** XXX universis civitatibus, quae Oceanum attingunt quaeque eorum consuetudine Aremoricae appellantur, quo sunt in numero Coriosolites, Redones, Ambibarii, Caletes, Osismi, Veneti, Lexovii, Venelli.[6] **5.** Ex his Bellovaci suum numerum[7] non compleverunt, quod se suo[8] nomine atque arbitrio cum Romanis bellum gesturos dicerent neque cuiusquam imperio obtemperaturos; rogati tamen a Commio, pro eius hospitio[9] duo milia una miserunt.

[1] **ad:** *120a.* **Galli,** etc.: in response to the appeal of Vercingetorix (VII, 71).
[2] **ne,** etc.: '(fearing) that . . . they would not be able either to manage (it) or . . . or'. **tanta,** etc.: 'if so enormous a host should be massed together'; *144b4.*
[3] **frumentandi,** etc.: 'to make systematic provision for supplying grain'.
[4] **clientibus:** 'dependent states'.
[5] **duodena milia:** 'twelve thousand each', or 72,000 for these six states. The total levy, amounting to 287,000 men, shows that after six years of war the population of Gaul must have been considerably larger than is ordinarily supposed. The population, in Caesar's time, of the territory west of the Rhine has been estimated as high as 20 to 30 million.
[6] **Venelli:** in the list of revolting states we do not find the Remi and the Lingones, who remained friendly, nor the Treverans, who were pressed by the Germans (VII, 63.7), nor the

Aquitanian states.

[7] **numerum:** 'contingent'. **quod . . . dicerent:** *183b.*

[8] **suo,** etc.: 'on their own responsibility and in their own way'; how lit.?

[9] **pro eius hospitio:** 'in consideration of their relations of hospitality with him'. **una:** 'at the same time' with the other states.

Commius, Viridomarus, Eporedorix, and Vercassivellaunus are placed in command of the Gallic army of relief.

76.1. Huius opera Commii,[1] ut antea demonstravimus, fideli atque utili superioribus annis erat usus in Britannia Caesar; quibus[2] ille pro meritis civitatem eius immunem esse iusserat, iura legesque reddiderat atque ipsi[3] Morinos attribuerat. **2.** Tanta[4] tamen universae Galliae consensio fuit libertatis vindicandae, et pristinae belli laudis recuperandae, ut neque beneficiis neque amicitiae memoria moverentur,[5] omnesque[6] et animo et opibus in id bellum incumberent. **3.** Coactis equitum milibus VIII et peditum circiter CCL, haec in Aeduorum finibus recensebantur,[7] numerusque inibatur, praefecti constituebantur; **4.** Commio Atrebati, Viridomaro et Eporedorigi Aeduis, Vercassivellauno Arverno, consobrino[8] Vercingetorigis, summa imperii traditur. His delecti[9] ex civitatibus attribuuntur, quorum consilio bellum administraretur. **5.** Omnes alacres et fiduciae[10] pleni ad Alesiam proficiscuntur; neque erat omnium quisquam, qui aspectum modo tantae multitudinis sustineri posse arbitraretur, praesertim ancipiti proelio,[11] cum ex oppido eruptione pugnaretur, foris[12] tantae copiae equitatus peditatusque cernerentur.

[1] **Commii:** after the final defeat of the Gauls Commius seems to have established himself as a ruler in Britain, and to have left sons who were rulers, who issued coins in imitation of Roman coins struck near the beginning of the Empire. Three sons of Commius are named on coins: Verica or Virica, Tincommius. and Eppillus (294).

[2] **quibus.** etc.: trans. as if *et pro his meritis.* **civitatem:** the Atrebates. **immunem:** 'free from tribute'. Apparently, as implied also by *iura legesque reddiderat.* the Atrebates had become a dependency of king, son of Commius'. some other state.

[3] **ipsi:** to Commius; the Morini had been hard to manage.

[4] **Tanta,** etc.: 'So strong was the common purpose of entire Gaul to recover its liberty'.

[5] **moverentur:** the subject is implied in *Galliae;* 'men were influenced'.

[6] **-que:** 'but'; *234b.* **incumberent:** 'were devoting themselves'.

[7] **recensebantur:** 'were reviewed'; we would say 'mobilized'.

[8] **consobrino:** 'cousin'. **summa imperii:** the commander-in-chief, Vercingetorix, was shut up in Alesia.

[9] **delecti:** 'men chosen'; delegates, forming a kind of general staff. **quorum consilio:** 'in accordance with whose counsel'; *193a.*

[10] **fiduciae:** 'confidence'. **ad:** 'for'; *120a.*

[11] **ancipiti proelio:** 'with fighting on two sides'.

[12] **foris:** 'on the outer side'.

The Gallic force in Alesia faces starvation; Critognatus proposes to sustain life by eating the non-combatants.

77.1. At ei, qui Alesiae[1] obsidebantur, praeterita die, qua auxilia suorum exspectaverant, consumpto omni frumento, inscii, quid in Aeduis gereretur, concilio coacto de exitu suarum fortunarum consultabant. **2.** Ac variis dictis sententiis, quarum pars deditionem, pars, dum vires suppeterent,[2] eruptionem censebat, non praetereunda oratio Critognati videtur[3] propter eius singularem et nefariam crudelitatem. **3.** Hic, summo in Arvernis ortus loco[4] et magnae habitus auctoritatis, 'Nihil,'[5] inquit, 'de eorum sententia dicturus sum, qui turpissimam servitutem deditionis nomine appellant; neque hos habendos civium loco neque ad concilium adhibendos censeo. **4.** Cum[6] his mihi res sit, qui eruptionem probant; quorum in consilio, omnium[7] vestrum consensu, pristinae residere[8] virtutis memoria videtur. **5.** Animi est ista mollitia, non virtus, paulisper inopiam ferre non posse. Qui se ultro morti offerant,[9] facilius reperiuntur, quam qui dolorem patienter ferant. **6.** 'Atque ego[10] hanc sententiam probarem (tantum apud me dignitas potest), si nullam praeterquam vitae nostrae iacturam[11] fieri viderem; **7.** sed in consilio capiendo omnem Galliam respiciamus,[12] quam ad nostrum auxilium concitavimus. **8.** Quid,[13] hominum milibus LXXX uno loco interfectis, propinquis consanguineisque nostris animi fore existimatis, si paene in ipsis cadaveribus proelio decertare cogentur? **9.** Nolite[14] hos vestro auxilio exspoliare, qui vestrae salutis causa suum periculum neglexerunt, nec stultitia[15] ac temeritate vestra aut animi imbecillitate omnem Galliam prosternere et perpetuae servituti subicere. **10.** 'An,[16] quod ad diem non venerunt, de eorum fide constantiaque dubitatis? Quid ergo? Romanos in illis ulterioribus munitionibus animine causa[17] cotidie exerceri putatis? **11.** Si illorum[18] nuntiis confirmari non potestis, omni aditu praesaepto,[19] his utimini testibus, appropinquare eorum adventum; cuius rei timore exterriti, diem noctemque in opere versantur. **12.** Quid[20] ergo mei consilii est? Facere, quod nostri maiores nequaquam pari bello Cimbrorum[21] Teutonumque fecerunt; qui in oppida compulsi ac simili inopia subacti,[22] eorum corporibus, qui aetate ad bellum inutiles videbantur, vitam toleraverunt neque se hostibus tradiderunt. **13.** Cuius[23] rei si exemplum non haberemus, tamen libertatis causa institui[24] et posteris prodi pulcherrimum iudicarem. **14.** Nam quid[25] illi simile bello fuit? Depopulata Gallia, Cimbri, magnaque illata calamitate, finibus quidem nostris aliquando excesserunt atque alias terras petierunt; iura, leges, agros, libertatem nobis reliquerunt. **15.** Romani vero quid petunt aliud aut quid volunt, nisi, invidia[26] adducti, quos fama nobiles potentesque bello[27] cognoverunt, horum in agris civitatibusque considere atque his aeternam iniungere[28] servitutem? Neque enim umquam alia condicione[29] bella gesserunt. **16.** Quod si ea, quae in longinquis nationibus geruntur, ignoratis, respicite finitimam Galliam,[30] quae, in provinciam redacta, iure et legibus commutatis, securibus[31] subiecta, perpetua premitur servitute.'

---

[1] **Alesiae:** *146.* **praeterita die:** the limit of 30 days had passed (VII, 71.4); *21a.*

[2] **suppeterent:** subjunctive in implied indirect discourse; *214b.*

[3] **videtur,** etc.: sc. *mihi;* 'the speech of Critognatus should not, I think, be passed over'. **nefariam:** 'atrocious'.

[4] **loco:** *128a.* **magnae auctoritatis:** *100b.*

[5] **Nihil,** etc.: *211b3; 280.*

[6] **Cum,** etc.: 'Let me deal (only) with those'; *180b.*

[7] **omnium,** etc.: 'according to the common feeling of you all'; *97c; 138.*

[8] **residere – videtur:** 'is seen to linger'. **ista:** for *istud*, addressed to those who would risk all

by an immediate sortie, explained by the appositional infinitive clause *paulisper . . . posse;*
'that is lack of resolution on your part'; *160a, e.*

[9] **offerant:** *194a.* **reperiuntur:** sc. *ei.* **quam:** *quam ei.*

[10] **ego:** *87b.* **hanc sententiam:** in favour of a sortie. **tantum,** etc.: 'so great weight does the
standing (of its advocates) carry with me'.

[11] **iacturam:** 'loss'; *nullam iacturam praeterquam vitae nostrae (iacturam).*

[12] **respiciamus:** *180a.* **concitavimus:** 'we have summoned'.

[13] **Quid – animi:** 'what feelings'. **milibus LXXX:** the number of the army of Vercingetorix. not
counting the inhabitants of Alesia (VII, 71.3).

[14] **Nolite – exspoliare:** 'do not rob'; *181b.* **auxilio:** *127a.* **qui,** etc.: the relieving force.

[15] **stultitia,** etc.: 'by your folly and rashness or weakness of resolution, utterly cast down'.

[16] **An:** *179a2* (AG 335b, B 162.4a). **venerunt:** *176a.*

[17] **animi causa:** 'for the sake of amusement'. **-ne:** *179a1.* **exerceri:** 'are exerting themselves';
174.

[18] **illorum:** the Gallic forces on the way.

[19] **praesaepto:** 'shut off'. **his:** the Romans.

[20] **Quid,** etc.: 'What, then, is my proposal?' **Facere:** i.e. *meum consilium est facere.*

[21] **Cimbrorum:** 'with the Cimbrians' and Teutons.

[22] **subacti:** 'reduced to straits'.

[23] **Cuius,** etc.: 'And if we had no precedent for such a course'; how lit.?

[24] **institui:** sc. *exemplum,* 'that a precedent be established'. **pulcherrimum:** 'a most noble
thing'; *28a.*

[25] **quid,** etc.: 'what resemblance had that war to the present one?' How lit.? **Depopulata:** *59b.*

[26] **invidia:** 'envy'.

[27] **fama nobiles potentesque bello:** *239c.*

[28] **iniungere:** 'to fasten upon', as a yoke is fastened upon oxen.

[29] **alia condicione:** 'on (any) other principle'.

[30] **finitimam Galliam:** 'the neighboring (part of Gaul)'; *152a.*

[31] **securibus:** 'the axes' of the lictors, symbols of authority.

The residents of Alesia with wives and children are driven outside the walls; Caesar refuses to receive them.

78.1. Sententiis dictis, constituunt, ut ei, qui valetudine[1] aut aetate inutiles
sint bello, oppido excedant, atque omnia prius experiantur, quam ad
Critognati sententiam descendant; **2.** *Illo tamen potius utendum consilio, si
res cogat atque auxilia morentur, quam aut deditionis aut pacis subeundam*[2]
condicionem. **3.** Mandubii,[3] qui eos oppido receperant, cum liberis atque
uxoribus exire coguntur. **4.** Hi, cum ad munitiones Romanorum
accessissent, flentes omnibus precibus orabant, ut se[4] in servitutem
receptos cibo iuvarent. **5.** At Caesar, dispositis in vallo custodiis, recipi[5]
prohibebat.

[1] **valetudine:** 'by reason of health'.

[2] **subeundam** [esse] **condicionem:** 'submit to terms'.

[3] **Mandubii:** the inhabitants of Alesia and those who had fled into the city from the
surrounding country.

[4] **se – receptos:** 'receive them – and'; *228a.*

[5] **recipi:** sc. *eos.* Cast out by Vercingetorix and rejected by Caesar, the women and children
and men unfit for war perished miserably in the spaces between the town walls and the
Roman contravallation. Caesar's army at the time was suffering from lack of supplies; *223a.*

The cavalry of the Gallic army of relief attacks fiercely, is repulsed.

79.1. Interea Commius[1] reliquique duces, quibus summa imperii permissa
erat, cum omnibus copiis ad Alesiam perveniunt et, colle exteriore[2]

occupato, non longius mille passibus ab nostris munitionibus considunt.

2. Postero die, equitatu ex castris educto, omnem eam planitiem,[3] quam in longitudinem tria milia passuum patere demonstravimus, complent, pedestresque copias, paulum ab eo loco abditas,[4] in locis superioribus constituunt. 3. Erat ex oppido Alesia despectus in campum. Concurrunt,[5] his auxiliis visis; fit gratulatio inter eos atque omnium animi ad laetitiam excitantur. 4. Itaque, productis copiis, ante oppidum considunt et proximam fossam[6] cratibus atque aggere explent seque ad eruptionem atque omnes casus comparant.

[1] Commius: VII, 76.1, duces: see VII, 76.3.
[2] colle exteriore: southwest of Alesia; see Map 17, Encampment of Gallic Relieving Army.
[3] planitiem, etc.; see VII, 69.3-4.
[4] abditas: 'drew back and'; 228a.
[5] Concurrunt: 'They' (the Gauls in the town) 'rushed together'.
[6] proximam fossam: the trench nearest the city; "Trench 20 feet wide" on Map 17.

80.1. Caesar, omni exercitu ad utramque[1] partem munitionum disposito, ut, si usus veniat, suum quisque locum teneat et noverit, equitatum ex castris[2] educi et proelium committi iubet. 2. Erat ex omnibus castris,[3] quae summum undique iugum tenebant, despectus, atque omnes milites intenti pugnae proventum[4] exspectabant. 3. Galli inter equites raros sagittarios expeditosque levis armaturae interiecerant, qui[5] suis cedentibus auxilio succurrerent et nostrorum equitum impetus sustinerent. Ab his complures,[6] de improviso vulnerati, proelio excedebant. 4. Cum suos pugna superiores esse Galli confiderent et nostros[7] multitudine premi viderent, ex omnibus partibus et ei, qui munitionibus[8] continebantur, et hi, qui ad auxilium convenerant, clamore et ululatu[9] suorum animos confirmabant. 5. Quod in conspectu omnium res gerebatur[10] neque recte[11] aut turpiter factum celari poterat, utrosque et laudis cupiditas et timor ignominiae[12] ad virtutem excitabat. 6. Cum[13] a meridie prope ad solis occasum dubia victoria pugnaretur, Germani[14] una in parte confertis turmis in hostes impetum fecerunt eosque propulerunt; 7. quibus in fugam coniectis, sagittarii[15] circumventi interfectique sunt. 8. Item ex reliquis partibus nostri, cedentes[16] usque ad castra insecuti, sui[17] colligendi facultatem non dederunt. 9. At ei, qui ab Alesia processerant, maesti,[18] prope victoria desperata, se in oppidum receperunt.

[1] utramque, etc.: both the inner and the outer lines of works.
[2] castris: the cavalry camps were probably those marked G, H, I, K on Map 17.
[3] castris, etc.: the infantry camps (A, B, C, D), in which were the milites.
[4] proventum: 'issue'.
[5] qui, etc.: 'in order that these might furnish support'; 193a; 112a.
[6] complures: of Caesar's cavalry.
[7] nostros: equites; the infantry did not go into action.
[8] munitionibus: of the town.
[9] ululatu: cf. V, 37.3, note 4. If upwards of 200,000 men were shouting and shrieking at once, the noise in the Roman lines across the plain, where the sounds from both sides met, must have been terrific; even the noise at one of the great football games would furnish no standard of comparison. The Romans under arms in the camps were probably silent, awaiting a signal for action.
[10] res gerebatur: 'the engagement was going on'.

[11] **recte,** etc.: 'and no brave or cowardly action'; how lit.?

[12] **ignominiae:** 'disgrace'; *81.*

[13] **Cum,** etc.: 'After the battle had been raging . . . with victory in doubt'; how lit.?

[14] **Germani**: the German cavalry rendered effective service on several critical occasions (VII, 67.6; and 70.2-3).

[15] **sagittarii,** etc.: among the cavalry; they had not yet learned to keep up with the horsemen by taking hold of the horses' manes, as the Germans did (I, 48.7).

[16] **cedentes:** 'the enemy in retreat'; how lit.? *227a4.*

[17] **sui:** *154b* (AG 504c, B 339.5).

[18] **maesti:** 'in sadness'; *151.*

A second attack, by night, is equally unsuccessful.

81.1. Uno die intermisso, Galli, atque hoc spatio[1] magno cratium, scalarum,[2] harpagonum numero effecto, media nocte silentio ex castris egressi, ad campestres[3] munitiones accedunt. **2.** Subito clamore sublato, qua significatione,[4] qui in oppido obsidebantur,[5] de suo adventu cognoscere possent, crates proicere, fundis, sagittis, lapidibus nostros de vallo[6] proturbare reliquaque, quae ad oppugnationem pertinent, parant administrare. **3.** Eodem tempore, clamore exaudito, dat tuba signum[7] suis Vercingetorix atque ex oppido educit. **4.** Nostri, ut superioribus diebus suus cuique erat locus attributus, ad munitiones accedunt; fundis librilibus[8] sudibusque, quas in opere disposuerant,[9] ac glandibus Gallos proterrent.[10] **5.** Prospectu tenebris adempto, multa utrimque vulnera accipiuntur. Complura tormentis tela coniciuntur. **6.** At M. Antonius[11] et C. Trebonius legati, quibus hae partes ad defendendum obvenerant, qua ex parte nostros premi intellexerant, his auxilio ex ulterioribus castellis deductos summittebant.

[1] **hoc spatio:** 'during this interval'; *147c.*

[2] **scalarum:** 'ladders'. **harpagonum:** 'grappling-hooks', for pulling down the Roman breastworks and palisades; *12c.*

[3] **campestres:** west of the town, and nearest the Gallic encampment.

[4] **qua significatione:** *ut ea significatione,* 'that by this sign'; *193a.*

[5] **obsidebantur:** vivid use of the indicative. Cf. *220.*

[6] **vallo:** of the circumvallation, running from the Ose to Flavigny Heights. **proturbare:** 'dislodge'.

[7] **dat tuba signum:** Vercingetorix had adopted the Roman system of signals; *326a1;* II.20.1.

[8] **fundis librilibus:** 'pound-weight slings'; whether these were slingshots of stone weighing about a Roman pound, or stones of a pound weight hurled with the help of a cord attached to them, we do not know; Balearic slingers were trained to hurl stones weighing a pound; *85.* **sudibus;** 'stakes,, with pointed ends hardened by fire, for use as javelins *(praeustae sudes);* cf. V, 40.6, note 7).

[9] **disposuerant:** 'had piled at intervals', as reserve ammunition; *79d.* **glandibus:** probably leaden 'bullets' (cf. II, 10.1).

[10] **proterrent:** 'drove back'. **tenebris:** 'by the darkness'; the attack began at midnight. **multa,** etc.: the soldiers could not parry the blows with their shields because they could not see the missiles coming.

[11] **M. Antonius:** the first mention of Mark Antony by Caesar. **hae partes:** 'this portion' of the fortifications, in the plain.

82.1. Dum longius a munitione aberant Galli, plus multitudine telorum proficiebant; postea quam propius successerunt, aut se stimulis[1] inopinantes induebant aut in scrobes[2] delati transfodiebantur aut ex vallo ac turribus traiecti[3] pilis muralibus interibant. **2.** Multis undique vulneribus acceptis, nulla munitione perrupta, cum lux appeteret, veriti, ne ab latere aperto ex superioribus castris[4] eruptione circumvenirentur, se ad suos receperunt. **3.** At interiores,[5] dum ea, quae a Vercingetorige ad eruptionem praeparata erant, proferunt, priores fossas[6] explent, **4.** diutius in his rebus administrandis morati, prius suos discessisse cognoverunt, quam munitionibus appropinquarent. Ita re infecta[7] in oppidum reverterunt.

[1] **stimulis, scrobes.**: cf. VII, 73.9, notes 22-24.
[2] **delati:** 'stumbling'; how lit.? **transfodiebantur:** 'were impaled'; 57*b*.
[3] **traiecti**, etc.: 'transfixed by wall pikes'.
[4] **superioribus castris:** on Map 17, Flavigny Heights; marked **A, B**.
[5] **interiores**: the Gallic army in Alesia.
[6] **priores fossas**: precisely what trenches are meant we do not know; evidently not the same as *proximam fossam* in VII, 79.4.
[7] **re infecta:** 'without accomplishing their purpose'.

The Gauls plan a surprise, and make a last desperate assault.

83.1. Bis[1] magno cum detrimento repulsi, Galli, quid agant, consulunt; locorum[2] peritos adhibent; ex his superiorum castrorum situs munitionesque cognoscunt. **2.** Erat a septentrionibus[3] collis, quem propter magnitudinem circuitus opere circumplecti non potuerant nostri; necessario paene iniquo loco et leniter declivi[4] castra fecerant. **3.** Haec C. Antistius Reginus et C. Caninius Rebilus legati cum duabus legionibus obtinebant. **4.** Cognitis per exploratores regionibus, duces hostium LX milia ex omni numero deligunt earum civitatum, quae maximam virtutis opinionem[5] habebant; **5.** quid quoque pacto agi placeat, occulte inter se constituunt; adeundi[6] tempus definiunt, cum meridies esse videatur. **6.** His copiis Vercassivellaunum Arvernum, unum ex IIII[7] ducibus, propinquum Vercingetorigis, praeficiunt. **7.** Ille ex castris prima vigilia egressus, prope confecto sub lucem[8] itinere,[9] post montem se occultavit, militesque ex nocturno labore sese reficere iussit. **8.** Cum iam meridies appropinquare videretur, ad ea castra,[10] quae supra demonstravimus, contendit; eodemque tempore equitatus ad campestres[11] munitiones accedere et reliquae copiae pro castris sese ostendere coeperunt.

[1] **Bis . . . repulsi:** first in an attack with cavalry (VII, 80), then in an attack with infantry (VII, 81-82).
[2] **locorum,** etc.: 'they brought in men who knew the ground'; how lit.? 102.
[3] **a septentrionibus:** 'on the north'. **collis:** Mont Rea.
[4] **leniter declivi:** 'gently sloping' toward the city; hence offering an advantage to a force attacking from the north. **castra:** D on Map 17.
[5] **virtutis opinionem:** 'reputation for courage'. **quid,** etc.: 'what plan they would deem it best to carry out, and in what way'.
[6] **adeundi,** etc.: 'they fixed as the hour of attack'.
[7] **IIII ducibus:** 'the four commanders' named in VII, 76.4.
[8] **sub lucem:** 'toward daybreak'.
[9] **itinere:** shown on Map 17, Route of Attacking Force under Vercassivellaunus. **post montem:** behind Mont Réa.
[10] **castra:** marked D.
[11] **campestres:** cf. VII, 72.3, note 7.

Vercingetorix attacks the Roman works on the inner side.

84.1. Vercingetorix, ex arce Alesiae suos conspicatus, ex oppido egreditur; crates, longurios,[1] musculos, falces reliquaque, quae eruptionis causa paraverat, profert. **2.** Pugnatur uno tempore omnibus locis, atque omnia temptantur; quae minime visa pars firma est, huc concurritur. **3.** Romanorum manus tantis munitionibus distinetur nec[2] facile pluribus locis occurrit. **4.** Multum ad terrendos nostros valet clamor, qui post tergum pugnantibus[3] exsistit, quod suum periculum in aliena vident virtute constare; **5.** omnia enim plerumque, quae absunt,[4] vehementius hominum mentes perturbant.

[1] **longurios:** 'poles', sharpened at the end, for thrusting; much longer than the ordinary javelin. **musculos:** 'mousies'; Vercingetorix had adopted the Roman siege appliances (*342a*). **falces:** *falces murales*; cf. VII, 22.1, note 2; *342c*.

[2] **nec,** etc.: 'could not easily meet (the enemy) at several points (at the same time)'.

[3] **post tergum pugnantibus:** 'at the rear of the men in action'; the shouting of those fighting on the outer line of works was heard by those defending the inner line, and vice versa; *109a*.

[4] **absunt, perturbant:** *175c*.

Caesar surveys the field, meets crises wherever they arise.

85.1. Caesar idoneum locum[1] nactus, quid quaque in parte geratur, cognoscit; laborantibus subsidium summittit. **2.** Utrisque[2] ad animum occurrit, unum esse illud tempus, quo maxime contendi conveniat: **3.** Galli, nisi perfregerint munitiones, de omni salute desperant; Romani, si[3] rem obtinuerint, finem laborum omnium exspectant. **4.** Maxime ad superiores munitiones laboratur, quo Vercassivellaunum missum demonstravimus.[4] Iniquum loci ad declivitatem fastigium magnum habet momentum. **5.** Alii tela coniciunt, alii, testudine[5] facta, subeunt; defatigatis in vicem integri succedunt. **6.** Agger,[6] ab universis in munitionem coniectus, et ascensum dat Gallis et ea, quae[7] in terra occultaverant Romani, contegit;[8] nec iam arma nostris nec vires suppetunt.

[1] **locum,** etc.: Caesar's post of observation was probably on the Flavigny Heights, at the point marked with a cross on Map 17.

[2] **Utrisque,** etc.: 'To both sides came the conviction, that now was the time for a supreme final effort'; how lit.?

[3] **si,** etc.: 'if they could (only) maintain their position, looked forward to'.

[4] **demonstravimus:** VII, 83.4-8. **Iniquum,** etc.: 'The unfavourable ground' (above the camp marked D), 'sloping downwards' (cf. VII, 83.2), 'proved a serious factor'; how lit.?

[5] **testudine facta:** 'formed a turtle-shell roof (in the Roman fashion) and'. *144b2; 338; 345*.

[6] **Agger:** 'earth'; no regular siege embankment was made.

[7] **ea, quae,** etc.: cf VII, 73.2-9.

[8] **contegit:** 'covered up'.

86.1. His rebus cognitis, Caesar Labienum cum cohortibus VI subsidio laborantibus[1] mittit; **2.** imperat, si sustinere non possit, deductis[2] cohortibus eruptione pugnet; id, nisi necessario, ne faciat. **3.** Ipse[3] adit reliquos; cohortatur, ne labori succumbant; omnium superiorum dimicationum[4] fructum in eo die atque hora docet consistere.

The attack of Vercingetorix is repulsed.

4. Interiores,[5] desperatis campestribus locis propter magnitudinem munitionum, loca[6] praerupta ascensu temptant; huc ea, quae[7] paraverant, conferunt. **5.** Multitudine telorum ex turribus propugnantes[8] deturbant, **6.** aggere et cratibus fossas explent, falcibus[9] vallum ac loricam rescindunt.

[1] **laborantibus:** the troops under Antistius Reginus and Caninius Rebilus, in the fiercely assaulted camp at D.
[2] **deductis.** etc.: 'to draw off the cohorts (from the engagement) and make a sortie'. A similar tactic had saved the day for Galba at Octodurus (III, 5.2-3).
[3] **Ipse:** 'in person'. **reliquos:** the other divisions besides that to which Labienus had been sent.
[4] **dimicationum:** 'combats'.
[5] **Interiores:** as in VII, 82.3.
[6] **loca.** etc.: 'places with a steep ascent' (lit. 'steep in respect to ascent'), along the side of Flavigny Heights, which it had not been thought necessary to provide with defences as elaborate as those in the plain of Les Laumes.
[7] **ea, quae,** etc.: see VII, 84.1.
[8] **propugnantes,** etc.: 'forced back (our) men (who were) fighting from the towers'.
[9] **falcibus:** VII, 84, 1. **vallum, loricam:** VII, 72.4.

87.1. Mittit[1] primo Brutum adulescentem cum cohortibus Caesar, post cum aliis C. Fabium legatum; postremo ipse, cum vehementius pugnaretur, integros subsidio adducit.

A charge and a flank movement on the north rout the enemy.

2. Restituto[2] proelio ac repulsis hostibus, eo, quo Labienum miserat, contendit; cohortes IIII ex proximo castello deducit, equitum partem se sequi, partem circumire[3] exteriores munitiones et a tergo hostes adoriri iubet. **3.** Labienus, postquam neque aggeres[4] neque fossae vim hostium sustinere poterant, coactis una XI cohortibus, quas ex proximis praesidiis[5] deductas fors obtulit, Caesarem per nuntios facit certiorem, quid faciendum existimet. Accelerat[6] Caesar, ut proelio intersit.

[1] **Mittit:** to the point attacked by Vercingetorix. **cohortibus:** the number is not given.
[2] **Restituto,** etc.: re-enforced, the men defending the ramparts attacked by Vercingetorix rallied and beat him off.
[3] **partem circumire:** sc. *equitum.* The division of cavalry ordered to execute the flank movement probably started from the camp at G; Map 17, Route of Caesar's Cavalry.
[4] **aggeres:** here 'ramparts', at camp D.
[5] **praesidiis:** detachments under arms at the redoubts; cf. VII, 69.7, note 12.
[6] **Accelerat:** 'hastened'.

88.1. Eius adventu ex colore[1] vestitus cognito, quo insigni in proeliis uti consuerat, turmisque equitum et cohortibus visis, quas se sequi iusserat, ut de locis superioribus[2] haec declivia et devexa cernebantur, hostes proelium committunt.[3] **2.** Utrimque[4] clamore sublato, excipit rursus ex vallo atque omnibus munitionibus clamor. Nostri, omissis pilis,[5] gladiis rem gerunt. **3.** Repente post tergum[6] equitatus cernitur; cohortes aliae appropinquant. Hostes terga vertunt; fugientibus equites occurrunt. Fit magna caedes. **4.** Sedulius, dux et princeps Lemovicum, occiditur; Vercassivellaunus Arvernus vivus in fuga comprehenditur; signa militaria

LXXIIII ad Caesarem referuntur; pauci ex tanto numero[7] se incolumes in castra recipiunt. **5.** Conspicati ex oppido[8] caedem et fugam suorum, desperata salute, copias a munitionibus reducunt. **6.** Fit protinus, hac re audita, ex castris Gallorum fuga. Quod[9] nisi crebris subsidiis ac totius diei labore milites essent defessi, omnes hostium copiae deleri potuissent. **7.** De media nocte[10] missus equitatus novissimum agmen consequitur; magnus numerus capitur atque interficitur, reliqui ex fuga in civitates discedunt.

[1] **colore:** scarlet. **vestitus:** cloak (*paludamentum); 321.* **cognito:** by the enemy. **insigni:** 'as a distinguishing mark'.

[2] **locis superioribus:** Mont Réa. **haec declivia et devexa:** 'these descending slopes', on the northwest side of Flavigny Heights, down which Caesar passed, on horseback, in full view of the enemy.

[3] **committunt:** with the division under Labienus just coming into action.

[4] **Utrimque,** etc.: the extraordinary vividness of the following description is due in part to the brevity of the sentences, some of which a writer of less restraint would have expanded into paragraphs; to the omission of connectives *(238a),* and to the sparing use of adjectives. **excipit – clamor:** 'the cheering was taken up' by those not in the action; how lit.? *353a.*

[5] **omissis pilis:** the legionaries were charging up hill, so that pikes could not be hurled to advantage.

[6] **tergum:** sc. *hostium.* **equitatus:** from camp G. **cohortes aliae:** the fresh cohorts with Caesar.

[7] **numero:** 60,000 (VII, 83.4).

[8] **Conspicati ex oppido:** brief for *ei, qui in oppido sunt, conspicati,* etc.

[9] **Quod:** *118d.* **nisi,** etc.: *208a2.* **crebris subsidiis:** 'with frequent (service in) supporting forces'.

[10] **De media nocte:** *242d.*

Vercingetorix surrenders.

89.1. Postero die Vercingetorix, concilio convocato, id bellum se suscepisse non suarum necessitatum, sed communis libertatis causa demonstrat, **2.** et quoniam sit fortunae cedendum, ad utramque rem[1] se illis offerre, seu morte sua Romanis satisfacere seu vivum tradere velint. **3.** Mittuntur de his rebus ad Caesarem legati. **4.** Iubet arma tradi, principes produci. Ipse[2] in munitione pro castris consedit; eo duces producuntur. Vercingetorix[3] deditur, arma proiciuntur. **5.** Reservatis[4] Aeduis atque Arvernis, si per eos civitates recuperare posset, ex reliquis captivis toti exercitui capita singula[5] praedae nomine distribuit.[6]

[1] **ad utramque rem:** 'for either alternative'.

[2] **Ipse:** Caesar.

[3] **Vercingetorix,** etc.: Vercingetorix, as we learn from Plutarch, having arrayed himself in splendid armour, mounted a horse adorned with trappings, passed slowly out from Alesia, and rode around Caesar sitting to receive the prisoners; then, halting before Caesar, he sprang from his horse, laid off his armour, and without a word seated himself at the feet of his conqueror, "every inch a king!" For six years after this Vercingetorix was confined in a Roman prison (doubtless the Mamertine Prison). At length, in 46 B.C., he was led along the streets of Rome to grace Caesar's great triumph; then, in accordance with Roman custom, "while his conqueror was offering solemn thanks to the gods on the summit of the Capitol, Vercingetorix was beheaded at its foot as guilty of high treason against the Roman nation". Thus ended the career of the greatest of the Gauls, the first national hero of France.

[4] **Reservatis,** etc.: afterwards 20,000 prisoners were returned to the Aeduans and Arvernians (VII., 90.3). **si:** '(to see) whether'; *204.4* (AG 576a, B 300.3).

[5] **capita singula,** etc.: each soldier in Caesar's army received a prisoner as his share of the booty *(318);* the number was probably not far from 50,000.

[6] **Historical Significance of the Siege of Alesia.** Caesar's devices for rendering impassable his lines of defence at Alesia, in ingenuity and adaptation to the purpose for which they were intended, have never been excelled in the annals of military engineering. Caesar's success, again, well illustrates the superiority of generalship, discipline, persistence, and hard work over vastly greater numbers, even in the face of every disadvantage of position and surroundings. For the Gauls the fall of Alesia was the crowning disaster of a hopeless struggle. They staked all on the relief of the city, and lost. But if Caesar had here suffered complete defeat, probably Gaul would long have remained unconquered, and the course of European history would have been changed. The siege of Alesia may well rank among the decisive military operations of the world.

All Gaul submits to Caesar. He places his army in winter quarters. A thanksgiving is decreed at Rome.

90.1. His rebus confectis in Aeduos proficiscitur; civitatem recipit.[1] **2.** Eo legati ab Arvernis missi, quae imperaret, se facturos pollicentur. Imperat magnum numerum obsidum. Legiones in hiberna[2] mittit. **3.** Captivorum circiter XX milia Aeduis Arvernisque reddit. **4.** T. Labienum duabus cum legionibus et equitatu in Sequanos proficisci iubet; huic M. Sempronium Rutilum attribuit. **5.** C. Fabium legatum et Lucium Minucium Basilum cum legionibus duabus in Remis collocat, ne quam a finitimis Bellovacis[3] calamitatem accipiant. **6.** C. Antistium Reginum in Ambivaretos, T. Sextium in Bituriges, C. Caninium Rebilum in Rutenos cum singulis legionibus mittit. **7.** Q. Tullium Ciceronem et P. Sulpicium Cabilloni et Matiscone in Aeduis ad Ararim rei frumentariae causa collocat. **8.** Ipse Bibracte hiemare constituit. His rebus ex[4] Caesaris litteris cognitis, Romae dierum viginti supplicatio redditur.

[1] **civitatem recipit**: 'he recovered the state' from its condition of rebellion.

[2] **in hiberna**: the legions were distributed so as to be a support to one another in case of need, and at the same time so as to command the whole country. The strength of Gaul had been so far broken that little danger was to be apprehended from rebellion.

[3] **Bellovacis**: they were subdued the following year; see VIII.6-23.

[4] **ex litteris**: 'from despatches'.

COMMENTARIUS OCTAVUS

[Praefatio] **1.** Coactus adsiduis tuis vocibus, Balbe, cum cotidiana mea recusatio non difficultatis excusationem, sed inertiae videretur deprecationem habere, difficillimam rem suscepi. **2.** Caesaris nostri commentarios rerum gestarum Galliae, non comparantibus superioribus atque insequentibus eius scriptis, contexui novissimumque inperfectum ab rebus gestis Alexandriae confeci usque ad exitum non quidem civilis dissensionis, cuius finem nullum videmus, sed vitae Caesaris. **3.** Quos utinam qui legent scire possint, quam invitus susceperim scribendos, quo facilius caream stultitiae atque arrogantiae crimine, qui me mediis interposuerim Caesaris scriptis. **4.** Constat enim inter omnes nihil tam operose ab aliis esse perfectum, quod non horum elegantia commentariorum superetur. **5.** qui sunt editi, ne scientia tantarum rerum scriptoribus deesset, adeoque probantur omnium iudicio, ut praerepta, non praebita facultas scriptoribus videatur. **6.** Cuius tamen rei maior nostra quam reliquorum est admiratio. ceteri enim, quam bene atque emendate, nos etiam, quam facile atque celeriter eos perfecerit, scimus. **7.** Erat autem in Caesare cum facultas atque elegantia summa scribendi, tum verissima scientia suorum consiliorum explicandorum. **8.** Mihi ne illud quidem accidit, ut Alexandrino atque Africano bello interessem. quae bella quamquam ex parte nobis Caesaris sermone sunt nota, tamen aliter audimus ea, quae rerum novitate aut admiratione nos capiunt, aliter quae pro testimonio sumus dicturi. **9.** Sed ego nimirum dum omnes excusationis causas colligo, ne cum Caesare conferar, hoc ipso crimen adrogantiae subeo, quod me iudicio cuiusquam existimem posse cum Caesare comparari. Vale.

1. 1. Omni Gallia devicta Caesar cum a superiore aestate nullum bellandi tempus intermisisset militesque hibernorum quiete reficere a tantis laboribus vellet, complures eodem tempore civitates renovare belli consilia nuntiabantur coniurationesque facere. **2.** cuius rei verisimilis causa adferebatur, quod Gallis omnibus cognitum esset neque ulla multitudine in unum locum coacta resisti posse [a] Romanis nec, si diversa bella complures eodem tempore intulissent civitates, satis auxilii aut spatii aut copiarum habiturum exercitum populi Romani ad omnia persequenda. **3.** non esse autem alicui civitati sortem incommodi recusandam, si tali mora reliquae possent se vindicare in libertatem.

2. 1. Quae ne opinio Gallorum confirmaretur, Caesar Marcum Antonium quaestorem suis praefecit hibernis. ipse cum equitum praesidio pridie Kalendas Ianuarias ab oppido Bibracte proficiscitur ad legionem XIII, quam non longe a finibus Haeduorum conlocaverat in finibus Biturigum, eique adiungit legionem undecimam, quae proxima fuerat. **2.** binis cohortibus ad impedimenta tuenda relictis reliquum exercitum in copiosissimos agros Biturigum inducit, qui cum latos fines et complura oppida haberent, unius legionis hibernis non potuerant contineri quin bellum pararent coniurationesque facerent.

3.1. Repentino adventu Caesaris accidit, quod inparatis disiectisque accidere fuit necesse, ut sine timore ullo rura colentes prius ab equitatu opprimerentur, quam confugere in oppida possent. **2.** namque etiam illud vulgare incursionis hostium signum, quod incendiis aedificiorum intellegi consuevit, Caesaris id erat interdicto sublatum, ne aut copia pabuli frumentique, si longius progredi vellet, deficeretur aut hostes incendiis terrerentur. **3.** multis hominum milibus captis perterriti Bituriges, qui primum adventum potuerant effugere Romanorum, in finitimas civitates aut privatis hospitiis confisi aut societate consiliorum confugerant. **4.** frustra: nam Caesar magnis itineribus omnibus locis occurrit nec dat ulli civitati spatium de aliena potius quam de domestica salute cogitandi. qua celeritate et fideles amicos retinebat et dubitantes terrore ad condiciones pacis adducebat. **5.** tali condicione proposita Bituriges cum sibi viderent clementia Caesaris reditum patere in eius amicitiam finitimasque civitates sine ulla poena dedisse obsides atque in fidem receptas esse, idem fecerunt.

4.1. Caesar milititbus pro tanto labore ac patientia, qui brumalibus diebus, itineribus difficillimis, frigoribus intolerandis studiosissime permanserant in labore, ducenos sestertios, centurionibus tot milia nummum praedae nomine condonata pollicetur legionibusque in hiberna remissis ipse se recipit die XXXX Bibracte. **2.** ibi cum ius diceret, Bituriges ad eum legatos mittunt auxilium petitum contra Carnutes, quos intulisse bellum sibi querebantur. **3.** qua re cognita, cum dies non amplius X et VIII in hibernis esset moratus, legiones XIIII et sextam ex hibernis ab Arari ducit, quas ibi conlocatas explicandae rei frumentariae causa superiore commentario demonstratum est. ita cum duabus legionibus ad persequendos: Carnutes proficiscitur.

5.1. Cum fama exercitus ad hostes esset perlata, calamitate ceterorum ducti Carnutes desertis vicis oppidisque, quae tolerandae hiemis causa constitutis repente exiguis ad necessitatem aedificiis incolebant, nuper enim devicti complura oppida dimiserant, dispersi profugiunt. **2.** Caesar erumpentes eo maxime tempore acerrimas tempestates cum subire milites nollet, in oppido Carnutum Cenabo castra ponit atque in tecta partim Gallorum, partim qu<a>e conlatis celeriter stramentis tentoriorum integendorum gratia erant inaedificata, milites conpegit. **3.** equites tamen et auxiliarios pedites in omnes partes mittit, quascumque petisse dicebantur hostes. nec frustra: nam plerumque magna praeda potiti nostri revertuntur. **4.** oppressi Carnutes hiemis difficultate, terrore periculi, cum tectis expulsi nullo loco diutius consistere auderent nec silvarum praesidio tempestatibus durissimis tegi possent, dispersi magna parte amissa suorum dissipantur in finitimas civitates.

6.1. Caesar tempore anni difficillimo, cum satis haberet convenientes manus dissipare, ne quod initium belli nasceretur, quantumque in ratione esset, exploratum haberet sub tempus aestivorum nullum summum bellum posse conflari, Gaium Trebonium cum duabus legionibus, quas secum habebat, in hibernis Cenabi conlocavit. **2.** ipse cum crebris legationibus Remorum certior fieret Bellovacos, qui belli gloria Gallos omnes Belgasque praestabant, finitimasque his civitates duce Correo Bellovaco et Commio Atrebate exercitus comparare atque in unum locum cogere, ut omni multitudine in fines Suess<i>onum, qui Remis erant attributi, facerent inpressionem, pertinere autem non tantum ad dignitatem, sed etiam ad salutem suam iudicaret nullam calamitatem socios optime de re publica meritos accipere, **3.** legionem ex hibernis evocat rursus undecimam, litteras autem ad Gaium Fabium mittit, ut in fines Suessionum legiones duas, quas habebat, adduceret, alteramque ex duabus a Tito Labieno arcessit. **4.** ita quantum hibernorum opportunitas bellique ratio postulabat, perpetuo suo labore invicem legionibus expeditionum onus iniungebat.

7.1. His copiis coactis ad Bellovacos proficiscitur castrisque in eorum finibus positis equitum turmas dimittit in omnes partes ad aliquos excipiendos, ex quibus hostium consilia cognosceret. **2.** equites officio functi renuntiant paucos in aedificiis esse inventos atque hos non qui agrorum colendorum causa remansissent, namque esse undique diligenter demigratum, sed qui speculandi causa essent remissi. **3.** a quibus cum quaereret Caesar, quo loco multitudo esset Bellovacorum quodve esset consilium eorum, **4.** inveniebat Bellovacos omnes, qui arma ferre possent, in unum locum convenisse itemque Ambianos, Aulercos, Caletes, Veliocasses, Atrebates. locum castris excelsum in silva circumdata palude delegisse, impedimenta omnia in ulteriores silvas contulisse. conplures esse principes belli auctores, sed multitudinem maxime Correo obtemperare, quod ei summo esse odio nomen p. R. Intellexissent. **5.** paucis ante diebus ex his castris Atrebatem Commium discessisse ad auxilia Germanorum adducenda, quorum et vicinitas propinqua et multitudo esset infinita. **6.** constituisse autem Bellovacos omnium principum consensu, summa plebei cupiditate, si, ut diceretur, Caesar cum tribus legionibus veniret, sese offerre ad dimicandum, ne miseriore ac duriore postea condicione cum toto exercitu decertare cogerentur. **7.** si maiores copias adduceret, in eo loco permanere, quem delegissent, pabulatione autem, quae propter anni tempus cum exigua tum disiecta esset, et frumentatione et reliquo commeatu ex insidiis prohibere Romanos.

8.1. Quae Caesar consentientibus pluribus eum cognosset atque ea, quae proponerentur, consilia plena prudentiae longeque a temeritate barbarorum remota esse iudicaret, omnibus rebus inserviendum statuit, quo celerius hostes contempta suorum paucitate prodirent in aciem. **2.** singularis enim virtutis veterrimas legiones VII, VIII, VIIII habebat, summae spei delectaeque iuventutis XI, quae octavo iam stipendio tamen in conlatione reliquarum nondum eandem vetustatis ac virtutis ceperat opinionem. **3.** itaque consilio advocato rebus iis, quae ad se essent delatae, omnibus expositis animos multitudinis confirmat. si forte hostes trium legionum numero posset elicere ad dimicandum, agminis ordinem ita constituit, ut legio VII, VIII, VIIII ante omnia irent impedimenta, deinde omnium impedimentorum agmen, quod tamen erat mediocre, ut in expeditionibus esse consuevit, cogeret XI, ne maioris multitudinis species accidere hostibus posset, quam ipsi depoposcissent. **4.** hac ratione paene quadrato agmine instructo in conspectum hostium celerius opinione eorum exercitum adducit.

9.1. Quas legiones repente instructas velut in acie certo gradu accedere Galli cum viderent, quorum erant ad Caesarem plena fiduciae consilia perlata, sive certaminis periculo sive subito adventu sive ex<s>pectatione nostri consilii copias instruunt pro castris nec loco superiore decedunt. **2.** Caesar etsi dimicare optaverat, tamen admiratus tantam multitudinem hostium valle intermissa magis in altitudinem depressa quam late patente castra castris hostium confert. **3.** haec imperat vallo pedum duodecim muniri, loriculam pro [hac] ratione eius altitudinis inaedificari, fossam duplicem pedum denum quinum lateribus deprimi derectis, turres excitari crebras in altitudinem trium tabulatorum, pontibus traiectis constratisque coniungi, quorum frontes viminea loricula munirentur, **4.** ut ab hostibus duplici fossa, duplici propugnatorum ordine defenderentur, quorum alter ex pontibus, quo tutior altitudine esset, hoc audacius longiusque permitteret tela, alter qui propior hostem in ipso vallo conlocatus esset, ponte ab incidentibus telis tegeretur. portis fores altioresque turres inposuit.

10.1. Huius munitionis duplex erat consilium. namque et operum magnitudinem et timorem suum sperabat fiduciam barbaris allaturum, et cum pabulatum frumentatumque longius esset proficiscendum, parvis copiis castra munitione ipsa videbat posse defendi. **2.** interim crebro paucis utrimque procurrentibus inter bina castra palude interiecta contendebatur. quam tamen paludem nonnumquam aut nostra auxilia [aut] Gallorum Germanorumque transibant acriusque hostes insequebantur, aut vicissim hostes ea<n>dem transgressi nostros longius summovebant. **3.** accidebat autem cotidianis pabulationibus, id quod accidere erat necesse, cum raris disiectisque ex aedificiis pabulum conquireretur, ut impeditis a locis dispersi pabulatores circumvenirentur. **4.** quae res etsi mediocre detrimentum iumentorum ac servorum nostris adferebat, tamen stultas cogitationes incitabat barbarorum, atque eo magis, quod Commius, quem profectum ad auxilia Germanorum arcessenda docui, cum equitibus venerat. qui tametsi numero non amplius erant quingenti, tamen Germanorum adventu barbari inflabantur.

11.1. Caesar cum animadverteret hostem complures dies castris palude et loci natura munitis se tenere neque oppugnari castra eorum sine dimicatione perniciosa nec locum munitionibus claudi nisi a maiore exercitu posse, litteras ad Trebonium mittit, ut, quam celerrime posset, legionem XIIII, quae cum T. Sextio legato in Biturigibus hiemabat, arcesseret atque ita cum tribus legionibus magnis itineribus ad se veniret. **2.** ipse equites invicem Remorum ac Lingonum reliquarumque civitatum, quorum magnum numerum evocaverat, praesidio pabulationibus mittit, qui subitas hostium incursiones sustinerent.

12.1. Quod cum cotidie fieret ac iam consuetudine diligentia minueretur, quod plerumque accidit diuturnitate, Bellovaci delecta manu peditum cognitis stationibus cotidianis equitum nostrorum silvestribus locis insidias disponunt eodemque equites postero die mittunt, **2.** qui primum elicerent nostros <in> insidias, deinde circumventos adgrederentur. **3.** cuius mali sors incidit Remis, quibus ille dies fungendi muneris obvenerat. namque hi, cum repente hostium equites animadvertissent ac numero superiores paucitatem contempsissent, cupidius insecuti a peditibus undique sunt circumdati. **4.** quo facto perturbati celerius, quam consuetudo fert equestris proelii, se receperunt amisso Vertisco principe civitatis praefecto equitum. **5.** qui cum vix equo propter aetatem posset uti, tamen consuetudine Gallorum neque aetatis excusatione in suscipienda praefectura usus erat neque dimicari sine se voluerat. **6.** inflammantur atque incitantur hostium animi secundo proelio, principe et praefecto Remorum interfecto, **7.** nostrique detrimento admonentur diligentius exploratis locis stationes disponere ac moderatius cedentem insequi hostem.

13.1. Non intermittunt interim cotidiana proelia in conspectu utrorumque castrorum, quae ad vada transitusque fiebant paludis. **2.** qua contentione Germani, quos propterea Caesar tra[ns]duxerat Rhenum, ut equitibus interpositi proeliarentur, cum constantius universi paludem transissent paucisque resistentibus interfectis pertinacius reliquam multitudinem essent insecuti, perterriti non solum ii, qui aut comminus opprimebantur aut eminus vulnerabantur, sed etiam qui longius subsidiari consueverant, **3.** turpiter refugerunt nec prius finem fugae fecerunt saepe amissis superioribus locis, quam se aut in castra suorum reciperent aut nonnulli pudore coacti longius profugerent. **4.** quorum periculo sic omnes copiae sunt perturbatae, ut vix iudicari posset, utrum secundis parvulis rebus insolentiores an adverso mediocri casu timidiores essent.

14.1. Compluribus diebus isdem <in> castris consumptis, cum propius accessisse legiones et Gaium Trebonium legatum cognossent, duces Bellovacorum veriti similem obsessionem Alesiae noctu dimittunt eos, quos aut aetate aut viribus inferiores aut inermes habebant, unaque reliqua impedimenta. **2.** quorum perturbatum et confusum dum explicant agmen, magna enim multitudo carrorum etiam expeditos sequi Gallos consuevit, oppressi luce copias armatorum pro suis instruunt castris, ne prius Romani persequi se inciperent, quam longius agmen impedimentorum suorum processisset. **3.** at Caesar neque resistentes adgrediundos tanto collis ascensu iudicabat neque non usque eo legiones admovendas, ut discedere ex eo loco sine periculo barbari militibus instantibus non possent. **4.** ita, cum palude inpedita a castris castra dividi videret, quae transeundi difficultas celeritatem insequendi tardare posset, atque id iugum, quod trans paludem paene ad hostium castra pertineret, mediocri valle a castris eorum intercisum animadverteret, pontibus palude constrata legiones traducit celeriterque in summam planitiem iugi pervenit, quae declivi fastigio duobus ab lateribus muniebatur. **5.** ibi legionibus instructis ad ultimum iugum pervenit aciemque eo loco constituit, unde tormento missa tela in hostium cuneos conici possent.

15.1. Barbari confisi loci natura, cum dimicare non recusarent, si forte Romani subire collem conarentur, paulatimque copias distributas dimittere non auderent, ne dispersi perturbarentur, in acie permanserunt. **2.** quorum pertinacia cognita Caesar XX cohortibus instructis castrisque eo loco metatis muniri iubet castra. **3.** absolutis operibus pro vallo legiones instructas collocat, equites frenatis equis in stationibus disponit. **4.** Bellovaci cum Romanos ad insequendum paratos viderent neque pernoctare aut diutius permanere sine periculo eodem loco possent, tale consilium sui recipiendi ceperunt. **5.** fasces ubi consederant, namque in acie sedere Gallos consuesse superioribus commentariis declaratum est, per manus stramentorum ac virgultorum, quorum summa erat in castris copia, inter se traditos ante aciem conlocarunt extremoque tempore diei signo pronuntiato uno tempore incenderunt. **6.** ita continens flamma copias omnes repente a conspectu texit Romanorum. quod ubi accidit, barbari vehementissimo cursu refugerunt.

16.1. Caesar etsi discessum hostium animadvertere non poterat incendiis oppositis, tamen id consilium cum fugae causa initum suspicaretur, legiones promovet, turmas mittit ad insequendum. ipse veritus insidias, ne forte in eodem loco subsistere hostis atque elicere nostros in locum conaretur iniquum, tardius procedit. **2.** equites cum intrare fumum et flammam densissimam timerent ac, si qui cupidius intraverant, vix suorum ipsi priores partes animadverterent equorum, insidias veriti liberam facultatem sui recipiendi Bellovacis dederunt. **3.** ita fuga timoris simul calliditatisque plena sine ullo detrimento milia non amplius decem progressi hostes loco munitissimo castra posuerunt. **4.** inde cum saepe in insidiis equites peditesque disponerent, magna detrimenta Romanis in pabulationibus inferebant.

17.1. Quod cum crebrius accideret, ex captivo quodam comperit Caesar Correum Bellovacorum ducem fortissimorum milia sex peditum delegisse equitesque ex omni numero mille, quos in insidiis eo loco conlocaret, quem in locum propter copiam frumenti ac pabuli Romanos pabulatum missuros suspicaretur. **2.** quo cognito consilio Caesar legiones plures, quam solebat, educit equitatumque, qua consuetudine pabulatoribus mittere praesidio consuerat, praemittit. **3.** huic interponit auxilia levis armaturae. ipse cum legionibus, quam potest maxime, adpropinquat.

18.1. Hostes in insidiis dispositi, cum sibi delegissent campum ad rem gerendam non amplius patentem in omnes partes passibus mille, silvis undique inpeditissimis aut flumine altissimo munitum, velut indagine hunc insidiis circumdederunt. **2.** explorato hostium consilio nostri ad proeliandum animo atque armis parati, cum subsequentibus legionibus nullam dimicationem recusarent, turmatim in eum locum devenerunt. **3.** quorum adventu cum sibi Correus oblatam occasionem rei gerendae existimaret, primum cum paucis se ostendit atque in proximas turmas impetum fecit. **4.** nostri constanter incursum sustinent insidiatorum neque plures in unum locum conveniunt, quod plerumque equestribus proeliis cum propter aliquem timorem accidit, tum multitudine ipsorum detrimentum accipitur.

19.1. Cum dispositis turmis invicem rari proeliarentur neque ab lateribus circumveniri suos paterentur, erumpunt ceteri Correo proeliante ex silvis. fit magna contentione diversum proelium. **2.** quod cum diutius pari Marte iniretur, paulatim ex silvis instructa multitudo procedit peditum, quae nostros cogit cedere equites. quibus celeriter subveniunt levis armaturae pedites, quos ante legiones missos esse docui, turmisque nostrorum interpositi constanter proeliantur. **3.** pugnatur aliquamdiu pari contentione. deinde, ut ratio postulabat proelii, qui sustinuerant primos impetus insidiarum, hoc ipso fiunt superiores, quod nullum ab insidiantibus inprudentes acceperant detrimentum. **4.** accedunt propius interim legiones crebrique eodem tempore et nostris et hostibus nuntii adferuntur imperatorem instructis copiis adesse. **5.** qua re cognita praesidio cohortium confisi nostri acerrime proeliantur, ne, si tardius rem gessissent, victoriae gloriam communicasse cum legionibus viderentur. **6.** hostes concidunt animis atque itineribus diversis fugam quaerunt. nequiquam: nam quibus difficultatibus locorum Romanos claudere voluerant. his ipsi tenebantur. **7.** victi tamen perculsique, maiore parte amissa, quo fors tulerat, consternati profugiunt partim silvis petitis, partim flumine. **8.** qui tamen in fuga a nostris acriter insequentibus conficiuntur, cum interim nulla calamitate victus Correus excedere proelio silvasque petere aut invitantibus nostris ad deditionem potuit adduci, quin fortissime proeliando compluresque vulnerando cogeret elatos iracundia victores in se tela conicere.

20.1. Tali modo re gesta recentibus proelii vestigiis ingressus Caesar. cum victos tanta calamitate existimaret hostes nuntio accepto locum castrorum relicturos, quae non longius ab ea caede abesse plus minus VIII milibus dicebantur, tametsi flumine impeditum transitum videbat, tamen exercitu traducto progreditur. **2.** at Bellovaci reliquaeque civitates repente ex fuga paucis atque his vulneratis receptis, qui silvarum beneficio casum evitaverant, omnibus adversis, cognita calamitate, interfecto Correo, amisso equitatu et fortissimis peditibus, cum adventare Romanos existimarent, concilio repente cantu tubarum convocato conclamant. legati obsidesque ad Caesarem mittantur.

21.1. Hoc omnibus probato consilio Commius Atrebas ad eos confugit Germanos, a quibus ad id bellum auxilia mutuatus erat. **2.** ceteri e vestigio mittunt ad Caesarem legatos petuntque, ut ea poena sit contentus hostium, quam si sine dimicatione inferre integris posset, pro sua clementia atque humanitate numquam profecto esset inlaturus. **3.** adflictas opes equestri proelio Bellovacorum esse; delectorum peditum multa milia interisse, vix refugisse nuntios caedis. **4.** tamen magnum, ut in tanta calamitate, Bellovacos eo proelio commodum esse consecutos, quod Correus, auctor belli, concitator multitudinis, esset interfectus; numquam enim senatum tantum in civitate illo vivo quantum inperitam plebem potuisse.

22.1. Haec orantibus legatis commemorat Caesar: eodem tempore superiore anno Bellovacos ceterasque Galliae civitates suscepisse bellum; pertinacissime hos ex omnibus in sententia permansisse neque ad sanitatem reliquorum deditione esse perductos; **2.** scire atque intellegere se causam peccati facillime mortuis delegari. neminem vero tantum pollere, ut invitis principibus, resistente senatu, omnibus bonis repugnantibus infirma manu plebis bellum concitare et gerere posset; sed tamen se contentum fore ea poena, quam sibi ipsi contraxissent.

23.1. Nocte insequenti legati responsa ad suos referunt. obsides conficiunt. concurrunt reliquarum civitatum legati, quae Bellovacorum speculabantur eventum. **2.** obsides dant, imperata faciunt, excepto Commio, quem timor prohibebat cuiusquam fidei suam committere salutem. **3.** nam superiore anno Titus Labienus Caesare in Gallia citeriore ius dicente, cum Commium comperisset sollicitare civitates et coniurationem contra Caesarem facere, infidelitatem eius sine ulla perfidia iudicavit comprimi posse. **4.** quem quia non arbitrabatur vocatum in castra venturum, ne temptando cautiorem faceret, Gaium Volusenum Quadratum misit, qui eum per simulationem conloquii curaret interficiendum. ad eam rem delectos idoneos ei tradidit centuriones. **5.** cum in conloquium ventum esset et, ut convenerat, manum Commii Volusenus arripuisset, centurio vel[ut] insueta re permotus vel celeriter a familiaribus prohibitus Commii conficere hominem non potuit. **6.** graviter tamen primo ictu gladio caput percussit. cum utrimque gladii destricti essent, non tam pugnandi quam diffugiendi fuit utrorumque consilium: nostrorum, quod mortifero vulnere Commium credebant adfectum, Gallorum, quod insidiis cognitis plura, quam videbant, extimescebant. quo facto statuisse Commius dicebatur numquam in conspectum cuiusquam Romani venire.

24.1. Bellicosissimis gentibus devictis Caesar cum videret nullam iam esse civitatem, quae bellum pararet, quo sibi resisteret, sed nonnullos ex oppidis demigrare, ex agris diffugere ad praesens imperium evitandum, plures in partes exercitum dimittere constituit. **2.** M. Antonium quaestorem cum legione duodecima sibi coniungit. C. Fabium legatum cum cohortibus XXV mittit in diversissimam partem Galliae, quod ibi quasdam civitates in armis esse audiebat neque C. Caninium Rebilum legatum, qui in illis regionibus erat, satis firmas duas legiones habere existimabat. **3.** Titum Labienum ad se evocat. legionem autem duodecimam, quae eum eo fuerat in hibernis, in togatam Galliam mittit ad colonias civium Romanorum tuendas, ne quod simile incommodum accideret decursione barbarorum ac superiore aestate Tergestinis acciderat, qui repentino latrocinio atque impetu illorum erant oppressi. **4.** ipse ad vastandos depopulandosque fines Ambiorigis proficiscitur. quem perterritum ac fugientem cum redigi posse in suam potestatem desperasset, proximum suae dignitatis esse ducebat adeo fines eius vastare civibus aedificiis pecore, ut odio suorum Ambiorix, si quos

Fortuna reliquos fecisset, nullum reditum propter tantas calamitates haberet in civitatem.

25.1. Cum in omnes partes finium Ambiorigis aut legiones aut auxilia dimisisset atque omnia caedibus, incendiis, rapinis vastasset, magno numero hominum interfecto aut capto Labienum cum duabus legionibus in Treveros mittit, **2.** quorum civitas propter Germaniae vicinitatem cotidianis exercitata bellis cultu et feritate non multum a Germanis differebat neque imperata umquam nisi exercitu coacta faciebat.

26.1. Interim C. Caninius Rebilus legatus cum magnam multitudinem convenisse hostium in fines Pictonum litteris nuntiisque Durati cognosceret, qui perpetuo in amicitia Romanorum permanserat, cum pars quaedam civitatis eius defecisset, ad oppidum Lemonum contendit. **2.** quo cum adventaret atque ex captivis certius cognosceret multis hominum milibus a Dumnaco, duce Andium, Duratium clausum Lemoni oppugnari neque infirmas legiones hostibus committere auderet, castra posuit loco munito. **3.** Dumnacus cum adpropinquare Caninium cognosset, copiis omnibus ad legiones conversis castra Romanorum oppugnare instituit. **4.** cum complures dies in oppugnatione consumpsisset et magno suorum detrimento nullam partem munitionum convellere potuisset, rursus ad obsidendum Lemonum redit.

27.1. Eodem tempore C. Fabius legatus complures civitates in fidem recipit, obsidibus firmat litterisque Gai Canini Rebili fit certior. quae in Pictonibus gerantur. quibus rebus cognitis proficiscitur ad auxilium Duratio ferendum. **2.** at Dumnacus adventu Fabii cognito desperata salute, si eodem tempore coactus esset [et Romanum] et externum sustinere hostem et respicere ac timere oppidanos, repente ex eo loco eum copiis recedit nec se satis tutum fore arbitratur, nisi flumen Ligerim. quod erat ponte propter magnitudinem transeundum, copias traduxisset. **3.** Fabius etsi nondum in conspectum hostium venerat neque se cum Caninio coniunxerat, tamen doctus ab iis, qui locorum noverant naturam, potissimum credidit hostes perterritos eum locum, quem petebant, petituros. **4.** itaque cum copiis ad eundem pontem contendit equitatumque tantum praecedere ante agmen imperat legionum, quantum, cum processisset, sine defatigatione equorum in eadem se reciperet castra. **5.** consequuntur equites nostri, ut erat praeceptum, invaduntque Dumnaci agmen et fugientes perterritosque sub sarcinis in itinere adgressi magna praeda multis interfectis potiuntur. ita re bene gesta se recipiunt in castra.

28.1. Insequenti nocte Fabius equites praemittit sic paratos, ut confligerent atque omne agmen morarentur, dum consequeretur ipse. **2.** cuius praeceptis ut res gereretur, Quintus [Tit]Atius Varus praefectus equitum, singularis et animi et prudentiae vir, suos hortatur agmenque hostium consecutus turmas partim idoneis locis disponit, partim equitum proelium committit. **3.** confligit audacius equitatus hostium succedentibus sibi peditibus, qui toto agmine subsistentes equitibus suis contra nostros ferunt auxilium. fit proelium acri certamine. **4.** namque nostri contemptis pridie superatis [que] hostibus, cum subsequi legiones meminissent, et pudore cedendi et cupiditate per se conficiendi proelii fortissime contra pedites proeliantur, **5.** hostesque nihil amplius copiarum accessurum credentes, ut pridie cognoverant, delendi equitatus nostri nacti occasionem videbantur.

29.1. Cum aliquamdiu summa contentione dimicaretur, Dumnacus instruit aciem, quae suis esset equitibus invicem praesidio, cum repente confertae legiones in conspectum hostium veniunt. **2.** quibus visis perculsae barbarorum turmae ac perterrita acies hostium, perturbato impedimentorum agmine, magno clamore discursuque passim fugae se mandant. **3.** at nostri equites, qui paulo ante cum resistentibus fortissime conflixerant, laetitia victoriae elati. magno undique clamore sublato cedentibus circumfusi, quantum equorum vires ad persequendum dextraeque ad caedendum valent, tantum eo proelio interficiunt. **4.** itaque amplius milibus passuum duodecim aut armatorum aut eorum, qui timore arma proiecerant, interfectis omnis multitudo capitur impedimentorum.

30.1. Qua ex fuga cum constaret Drappetem Senonem, qui, ut primum defecerat Gallia, collectis undique perditis hominibus, servis ad libertatem vocatis, exulibus omnium civitatum adscitis, receptis latronibus impedimenta et commeatus Romanorum interceperat, non amplius hominum duobus milibus ex fuga collectis provinciam petere unaque consilium cum eo Lucterium Cadurcum cepisse, quem superiore commentario prima defectione Galliae facere in provinciam voluisse impetum cognitum est, **2.** Caninius legatus cum legionibus duabus ad eos persequendos contendit, ne detrimento aut timore provinciae magna infamia perditorum hominum latrociniis caperetur.

31.1. Gaius Fabius cum reliquo exercitu in Carnutes ceterasque proficiscitur civitates, quarum eo proelio, quod cum Dumnaco fecerat, copias esse accisas sciebat. **2.** non enim dubitabat, quin recenti calamitate summissiores essent futurae, dato vero spatio ac tempore eodem instigante Dumnaco possent concitari. **3.** qua in re summa felicitas celeritasque in recipiendis civitatibus Fabium consequitur. **4.** nam Carnutes, qui saepe vexati numquam pacis fecerant mentionem, datis obsidibus veniunt in deditionem, ceteraeque civitates positae in ultimis Galliae finibus Oceanoque coniunctae, quae Aremoricae appellantur, auctoritate adductae Carnutum adventu Fabii legionumque imperata sine mora faciunt. **5.** Dumnacus suis finibus expulsus errans latitansque solus extremas Galliae regiones petere est coactus.

32.1. At Drappes unaque Lucterius, cum legiones Caniniumque adesse cognoscerent nec se sine certa pernicie persequente exercitu putarent provinciae fines intrare posse nec iam libere vagandi latrociniorumque faciendorum facultatem haberent, in finibus consistunt Cadurcorum. **2.** ibi cum Lucterius apud suos cives quondam integris rebus multum potuisset semperque auctor novorum consiliorum magnam apud barbaros auctoritatem haberet, oppidum Uxellodunum, quod in clientela fuerat eius, egregie natura loci munitum occupat suis et Drappetis copiis oppidanosque sibi coniungit.

33.1. Quo cum confestim Gaius Caninius venisset animadverteretque omnes oppidi partes praeruptissimis saxis esse munitas, quo defendente nullo tamen armatis ascendere esset difficile, magna autem impedimenta oppidanorum videret, quae si clandestina fuga subtrahere conarentur, effugere non modo equitatum, sed ne legiones quidem possent, tripertito cohortibus divisis trina excelsissimo loco castra fecit, **2.** a quibus paulatim, quantum copiae patiebantur, vallum in oppidi circuitum ducere instituit.

34.1. Quod cum animadverterent oppidani miserrimaque Alesiae memoria solliciti similem casum obsessionis vererentur maximeque ex omnibus Lucterius, qui fortunae illius periculum fecerat, moneret frumenti rationem esse habendam, constituunt omnium consensu parte ibi relicta copiarum ipsi cum expeditis ad importandum frumentum proficisci. **2.** eo consilio probato proxima nocte duobus milibus armatorum relictis reliquos ex oppido Drappes et Lucterius educunt. **3.** hi paucos dies morati ex finibus Cadurcorum, qui partim re frumentaria sublevare eos cupiebant, partim prohibere, quominus sumerent, non poterant, magnum numerum frumenti conparant, nonnumquam autem expeditionibus nocturnis castella nostrorum adoriuntur. **4.** quam ob causam Gaius Caninius toto oppido munitiones circumdare moratur, ne aut opus effectum tueri non possit aut plurimis in locis infirma disponat praesidia.

35.1. Magna copia frumenti conparata considunt Drappes et Lucterius non longius ab oppido decem milibus, unde paulatim frumentum in oppidum subportarent. **2.** ipsi inter se provincias partiuntur. Drappes castris praesidio cum parte copiarum resistit, Lucterius agmen iumentorum ad oppidum ducit. **3.** dispositis ibi praesidiis hora noctis circiter decima silvestribus angustisque itineribus frumentum inportare in oppidum instituit. **4.** quorum strepitum vigiles castrorum cum sensissent exploratoresque missi, quae gererentur, renuntiassent, Caninius celeriter cum cohortibus armatis ex proximis castellis in frumentarios sub ipsam lucem impetum facit. hi repentino malo perterriti diffugiunt ad sua praesidia. **5.** quae nostri ut viderunt, acrius contra armatos incitati neminem ex eo numero vivum capi patiuntur. profugit inde cum paucis Lucterius nec se recipit in castra.

36.1. Re bene gesta Caninius ex captivis comperit partem copiarum cum Drappete esse in castris a milibus non amplius XII qua re ex compluribus cognita, cum intellegeret fugato duce altero perterritos reliquos facile opprimi posse, magnae felicitatis esse arbitrabatur neminem ex caede refugisse in castra, qui de accepta calamitate nuntium Drappeti perferret. **2.** sed in experiundo cum periculum nullum videret, equitatum omnem Germanosque pedites, summae velocitatis homines, ad castra hostium praemittit. ipse legionem unam in trina castra distribuit, alteram secum expeditam ducit. **3.** cum propius hostes accessisset, ab exploratoribus, quos praemiserat, cognoscit castra eorum, ut barbarorum fere consuetudo est, relictis locis superioribus ad ripas esse fluminis demissa, at Germanos equitesque inprudentibus omnibus de inproviso advolasse proeliumque commisisse. **4.** qua re cognita legionem armatam instructamque adducit. ita repente omnibus ex partibus signo dato loca superiora capiuntur. quod ubi accidit, Germani equitesque signis legionis visis vehementissime proeliantur. **5.** confestim cohortes undique impetum faciunt omnibusque aut interfectis aut captis magna praeda potiuntur. capitur ipse eo proelio Drappes.

37.1. Caninius felicissime re gesta sine ullo paene militis vulnere ad obsidendos oppidanos revertitur externoque hoste deleto, **2.** cuius timore antea dividere praesidia et munitione oppidanos circumdare prohibitus erat, opera undique imperat administrari. venit eodem cum suis copiis postero die Gaius Fabius partemque oppidi sumit ad obsidendum.

38.1. Caesar interim M. Antonium quaestorem cum cohortibus XV in Bellovacis relinquit, ne qua rursus novorum consiliorum capiendorum Belgis facultas daretur. **2.** ipse reliquas civitates adit, obsides plures imperat, timentes omnium animos consolatione sanat. **3.** cum in Carnutes venisset, quorum in civitate superiore commentario Caesar exposuit initium belli esse ortum, quod praecipue eos propter conscientiam facti timere animadvertebat, quo celerius civitatem timore liberaret, principem sceleris illius et concitatorem belli Gutuatrum ad supplicium deposcit. **4.** qui etsi ne civibus quidem suis se committebat, tamen celeriter omnium cura quaesitus in castra perducitur. **5.** cogitur in eius supplicium contra naturam suam Caesar maximo militum concursu, qui ei omnia pericula et detrimenta belli a Gutuatro accepta referebant, adeo ut verberibus exanima-tum corpus securi feriretur.

39.1. Ibi crebris litteris Caninii fit certior, quae de Drappete et Lucterio gesta essent quoque in consilio permanerent oppidani. **2.** quorum etsi paucitatem contemnebat, tamen pertinaciam magna poena esse adficiendam iudicabat, ne universa Gallia non sibi vires defuisse ad resistendum Romanis, sed constantiam putaret, neve hoc exemplo ceterae civitates locorum opportunitate fretae vindicarent se in libertatem, **3.** cum omnibus Gallis notum esse sciret reliquam esse unam aestatem suae provinciae, quam si sustinere potuissent, nullum ultra periculum vererentur. **4.** itaque Q. Calenum legatum cum legionibus duabus reliquit, qui iustis itineribus se subsequeretur. ipse cum omni equitatu, quam potest celerrime, ad Caninium contendit.

40.1. Caesar cum contra ex<s>pectationem omnium Uxellodunum venisset oppidumque operibus clausum animadverteret neque ab oppugnatione recedi videret ulla condicione posse, magna autem copia frumenti abundare oppidanos ex perfugis cognosset, aqua prohibere hostem temptare coepit. **2.** flumen infimam vallem dividebat, quae totum paene montem cingebat, in quo positum erat praeruptum undique oppidum Uxellodunum. **3.** hoc avertere loci natura prohibebat. sic enim imis radicibus montis ferebatur, **4.** ut nullam in partem depressis fossis derivari posset. erat autem oppidanis difficilis et praeruptus eo descensus, ut prohibentibus nostris sine vulneribus ac periculo vitae neque adire flumen neque arduo se recipere possent ascensu. **5.** qua difficultate eorum cognita Caesar sagittariis funditoribusque dispositis, tormentis etiam quibusdam locis contra facillimos descensus conlocatis, aqua fluminis prohibebat oppidanos.

41.1. Quorum omnis postea multitudo aquatorum unum in locum conveniebat. sub ipsum enim oppidi murum magnus fons aquae prorumpebat ab ea parte, quae fere pedum trecentorum intervallo a fluminis circuitu vacabat. **2.** hoc fonte prohiberi posse oppidanos cum optarent reliqui, Caesar unus videret, e regione eius vineas agere adversus montem et aggerem instruere coepit magno cum labore et continua dimicatione. **3.** oppidani enim loco superiore decurrunt et eminus sine periculo proeliantur multosque pertinaciter succedentes vulnerant. non deterrentur tamen milites nostri vineas proferre et labore atque operibus locorum vincere difficultates. **4.** eodem tempore cuniculos tectos ad vineas agunt et caput fontis, quod genus operis sine ullo periculo et sine suspicione hostium facere licebat. **5.** ex<s>truitur agger in altitudinem pedum sexaginta. conlocatur in eo turris decem tabulatorum, non quidem quae moenibus adaequaret, id enim nullis operibus effici poterat, sed quae superare fontis fastigium posset. **6.** ex ea cum tela tormentis iacerentur ad fontis aditum nec sine periculo possent aquari oppidani, non tantum pecora atque iumenta, sed etiam magna hominum multitudo siti consumebatur.

42.1. Quo malo perterriti oppidani cupas sebo, pice, scandulis complent. eas ardentes in opera provolvunt eodemque tempore acerrime proeliantur, ut ab incendio restinguendo dimicationis periculo deterreant Romanos. magna repente in ipsis operibus flamma existit. **2.** quaecumque enim per locum praecipitem missa erant, ea vineis et aggere suppressa comprehendebant id ipsum, quod morabatur. **3.** milites contra nostri quamquam periculoso genere proelii locoque iniquo premebantur, tamen omnia fortissimo sustinebant animo. **4.** res enim gerebatur et excelso loco et in conspectu exercitus nostri magnusque utrimque clamor oriebatur. ita quam quisque poterat maxime insignis, quo notior testatiorque virtus esset eius, telis hostium flammaeque se offerebat.

43.1. Caesar cum conplures suos vulnerari videret, ex omnibus oppidi partibus cohortes montem ascendere et simulatione moenium occupandorum clamorem undique iubet tollere. **2.** quo facto perterriti oppidani, cum quid ageretur in locis reliquis essent suspensi, revocant ab inpugnandis operibus armatos murisque disponunt. **3.** ita nostri fine proelii facto celeriter opera flamma comprehensa partim resting<u>unt, partim interscindunt. **4.** cum pertinaciter resisterent oppidani, magna etiam parte amissa siti suorum in sententia permanerent, ad postremum cuniculis venae fontis intercisae sunt atque aversae. **5.** quo facto repente perennis exaruit fons tantamque attulit oppidanis salutis desperationem, ut id non hominum consilio, sed deorum voluntate factum putarent. itaque se necessitate coacti tradiderunt.

44.1. Caesar cum suam lenitatem cognitam omnibus sciret neque vereretur, ne quid crudelitate naturae videretur asperius fecisse, neque exitum consiliorum suorum animadverteret, si tali ratione diversis in locis plures consilia inissent, exemplo supplicii deterrendos reliquos existimavit. itaque omnibus, qui arma tulerant, manus praecidit vitamque concessit, quo testatior esset poena improborum. **2.** Drappes, quem captum esse a Caninio docui, sive indignitate et dolore vinculorum sive timore gravioris supplicii paucis diebus cibo se abstinuit atque ita interiit. **3.** eodem tempore Lucterius, quem profugisse ex proelio scripsi, cum in potestatem venisset Epasnacti Arverni, crebro enim mutandis locis multorum fidei se committebat, quod nusquam diutius sine periculo commoraturus videbatur, cum sibi conscius esset quam inimicum deberet Caesarem habere, hunc Epasnactus Arvernus amicissimus p. R. sine dubitatione ulla vinctum ad Caesarem deduxit.

45.1. Labienus interim in Treveris equestre proelium facit secundum compluribusque Treveris interfectis et Germanis, qui nullis adversus Romanos auxilia denegabant, principes eorum vivos redigit in suam potestatem atque in his Surum Haeduum, **2.** qui et virtutis et generis summam nobilitatem habebat solusque ex Haeduis ad id tempus permanserat in armis.

46.1. Ea re cognita Caesar cum in omnibus partibus Galliae bene res geri videret iudicaretque superioribus aestivis Galliam devictam subactamque esse, Aquitaniam numquam ipse adisset, sed per Publium Crassum quadam ex parte devicisset, cum duabus legionibus in eam partem Galliae est profectus, ut ibi extremum tempus consumeret aestivorum. **2.** quam rem sicuti cetera celeriter feliciterque confecit. namque omnes Aquitaniae civitates legatos ad Caesarem miserunt obsidesque ei dederunt. **3.** quibus rebus gestis ipse cum praesidio equitum Narbonem profectus est; exercitum per legatos in hiberna deduxit: **4.** quattuor legiones in Belgio conlocavit cum M. Antonio et C. Trebonio et P. Vatinio legatis, duas legiones in Haeduos deduxit, quorum in omni Gallia summam esse auctoritatem sciebat, duas in Turonis ad fines Carnutum posuit, quae omnem illam regionum coniunctam Oceano continerent, duas reliquas in Lemovicum finibus non longe ab Arvernis, ne qua pars Galliae vacua ab exercitu esset. **5.** paucos dies ipse in provincia moratus, cum celeriter omnes conventus percucurrisset, publicas controversias cognosset, bene meritis praemia tribuisset. **6.** cognoscendi enim maximam facultatem habebat quali quisque fuisset animo totius Galliae defectione, quam sustinuerat fidelitate atque auxiliis provinciae illius, his confectis rebus ad legiones in Belgium se recepit hibernavitque Nemetocennae.

47.1. Ibi cognoscit Commium Atrebatem proelio cum equitatu suo contendisse. **2.** nam cum Antonius in hiberna venisset civitasque Atrebatium in officio maneret, Commius, qui post illam vulnerationem, quam supra commemoravi, semper ad omnes motus paratus suis civibus esse consuesset, ne consilia belli quaerentibus auctor armorum duxque deesset parente Romanis civitate, cum suis equitibus latrociniis se suosque alebat infestisque itineribus commeatus complures, in hiberna Romanorum qui comportabantur, intercipiebat.

48.1. Erat attributus Antonio praefectus equitum, qui cum eo hibernaret, C. Volusenus Quadratus. hunc Antonius ad persequendum hostium equitatum mittit. **2.** Volusenus ad eam virtutem, quae singularis erat in eo, magnum odium Commii adiungebat, quo libentius id faceret, quod imperabatur. itaque dispositis insidiis saepius equites eius adgressus secunda proelia faciebat. **3.** novissime cum vehementius contenderetur ac Volusenus ipsius intercipiendi Commii cupiditate pertinacius eum cum paucis insecutus esset, ille autem fuga vehementi Volusenum produxisset longius, inimicus homini repente omnium suorum invocat fidem atque auxilium, ne sua vulnera perfidia interposita paterentur inpunita, conversoque equo se a ceteris incautius permittit in praefectum. **4.** faciunt hoc idem omnes eius equites paucosque nostros convertunt atque insequuntur. **5.** Commius incensum calcaribus equum coniungit equo Quadrati lanceaque infesta ac magnis viribus medium femur traicit Voluseni. **6.** praefecto vulnerato non dubitant nostri resistere et conversis equis hostem pellere. **7.** quod ubi accidit, complures hostium magno nostrorum impetu perculsi vulnerantur ac partim in fuga proteruntur, partim intercipiuntur. quod [ubi] malum dux equi velocitate evitavit, ac si<c> proelio secundo graviter ab eo vulneratus praefectus, ut vitae periculum aditurus videretur, refertur in castra. **8.** Commius autem sive expiato suo dolore sive magna parte amissa suorum legatos ad Antonium mittit seque et ibi futurum, ubi praescripserit, et ea facturum, quae imperarit, obsidibus datis firmat. **9.** unum illud orat, ut timori suo concedatur, ne in conspectum veniat cuiusquam Romani. cuius postulationem Antonius cum iudicaret ab iusto nasci timore, veniam petenti dedit, obsides accepit. **10.** Scio Caesarem singulorum annorum singulos commentarios confecisse. quod ego non existimavi mihi esse faciendum, propterea quod insequens annus L. Paulo C. Marcello consulibus nullas res Galliae habet magno opere gestas. **11.** ne quis tamen ignoraret, quibus in locis Caesar exercitusque eo tempore fuissent, pauca esse scribenda coniungendaque huic commentario statui.

49.1. Caesar in Belgio cum hiemaret, unum illud propositum habebat continere in amicitia civitates, nulli spem aut causam dare armorum. **2.** nihil enim minus volebat quam sub decessum suum necessitatem sibi aliquam inponi belli gerendi, ne, cum exercitum deducturus esset, bellum aliquod relinqueretur, quod omnis Gallia libenter sine praesenti periculo susciperet. **3.** itaque honorifice civitates appellando, principes maximis praemiis adficiendo, nulla onera nova iniungendo defessam tot adversis proeliis Galliam condicione parendi meliore facile in pace continuit.

50.1. Ipse hibernis peractis contra consuetudinem in Italiam quam maximis itineribus est profectus, ut municipia et colonias appellaret, quibus M. Antonii, quaestoris sui, commendaverat sacerdotii petitionem. **2.** contendebat enim gratia cum libenter pro homine sibi coniunctissimo, quem paulo ante praemiserat ad petitionem, tum acriter contra factionem et potentiam paucorum, qui M. Antonii repulsa Caesaris decedentis gratiam convellere cupiebant. **3.** hunc etsi augurem prius factum, quam Italiam attingeret, in itinere audierat, tamen non minus iustam sibi causam municipia et colonias adeundi existimavit, ut iis gratias ageret, quod frequentiam atque officium suum Antonio praestitissent, **4.** simulque se et honorem suum insequentis anni commendaret petitione, propterea quod insolenter adversarii sui gloriarentur L. Lentulum et C. Marcellum consules creatos, qui omnem honorem et dignitatem Caesaris spoliarent, ereptum Ser. Galbae consulatum, cum is multo plus gratia suffragii valuisset, quod sibi coniunctus et familiaritate et consuetudine legationis esset.

51.1. Exceptus est Caesaris adventus ab omnibus municipiis et coloniis incredibili honore atque amore. tum primum enim veniebat ab illo universae Galliae bello. **2.** nihil relinquebatur, quod ad ornatum portarum, itinerum, locorum omnium, qua Caesar iturus erat, excogitari poterat. **3.** cum liberis omnis multitudo obviam procedebat, hostiae omnibus locis immolabantur, tricliniis stratis fora templaque occupabantur, ut vel exspectatissimi triumphi laetitia praecipi posset. tanta erat magnificentia apud opulentiores, cupiditas apud humiliores.

52.1. Cum omnes regiones Galliae togatae Caesar percucurrisset, summa celeritate ad exercitum Nemetocennam rediit legionibusque ex omnibus hibernis ad fines Treverorum evocatis eo profectus est ibique exercitum lustravit. **2.** T. Labienum Galliae praefecit togatae, quo maiore commendatione conciliaretur ad consulatus petitionem. ipse tantum itinerum faciebat, quantum satis esse ad mutationem locorum propter salubritatem existimabat. **3.** ibi quamquam crebro audiebat Labienum ab inimicis suis sollicitari certiorque fiebat id agi paucorum consiliis, ut interposita senatus auctoritate aliqua parte exercitus spoliaretur, tamen neque de Labieno credidit quicquam neque contra senatus auctoritatem ut aliquid faceret adduci potuit. iudicabat enim liberis sententiis patrum conscriptorum causam suam facile obtineri. **4.** nam C. Curio tr. pl., cum Caesaris causam dignitatemque defendendam suscepisset, saepe erat senatui pollicitus, si quem timor armorum Caesaris laederet et quoniam Pompei dominatio atque arma non minimum terrorem foro inferrent, discederet uterque ab armis exercitusque dimitteret. fore eo facto liberam et sui iuris civitatem. **5.** neque hoc tantum pollicitus est, sed etiam s. c. per discessionem facere coepit. quod ne fieret, consules amicique Pompei evicerunt atque ita rem mo[de]rando discesserunt.

53.1. Magnum hoc testimonium senatus erat universi conveniensque superiori facto. nam Marcellus proximo anno cum inpugnaret Caesaris dignitatem, contra legem Pompei et Crassi rettulerat ante tempus ad senatum de Caesaris provinciis, sententiisque dictis discessionem faciente Marcello, qui sibi omnem dignitatem ex Caesaris invidia quaerebat, senatus frequens in alia omnia transiit. **2.** quibus non frangebantur animi inimicorum Caesaris, sed admonebantur, quo maiores pararent necessitates, quibus cogi posset senatus id probare, quod ipsi constituissent.

54.1. Fit deinde senatus consultum, ut ad bellum Parthicum legio una a Cn. Pompeio, altera a C. Caesare mitteretur. neque obscure duae legiones uni detrahuntur. **2.** nam Cn. Pompeius legionem primam, quam ad Caesarem miserat, confectam ex dilectu provinciae Caesaris, eam tamquam ex suo numero dedit. **3.** Caesar tamen, cum de voluntate minime dubium esset adversariorum suorum, Cn. Pompeio legionem remisit et suo nomine quintam decimam, quam in Gallia citeriore habuerat, ex s. c. iubet tradi. in eius locum tertiam decimam legionem in Italiam mittit, quae praesidia tueretur, ex quibus praesidiis quinta decima deducebatur. **4.** ipse exercitui distribuit hiberna: C. Trebonium cum legionibus IIII in Belgio conlocat, C. Fabium cum totidem in Haeduos deducit. **5.** sic enim existimabat tutissimam fore Galliam, si Belgae, quorum maxima virtus, et Haedui, quorum auctoritas summa esset, exercitibus continerentur. ipse in Italiam profectus est.

55.1. Quo cum venisset, cognoscit per C. Marcellum consulem legiones duas ab se missas, quae ex s. c. deberent ad Parthicum bellum duci, Cn. Pompeio traditas atque in Italia retentas esse. **2.** hoc facto quamquam nulli erat dubium, quidnam contra Caesarem pararetur, tamen Caesar omnia patienda esse statuit, quoad sibi spes aliqua relinqueretur iure potius disceptandi quam belligerandi. contendit . . .

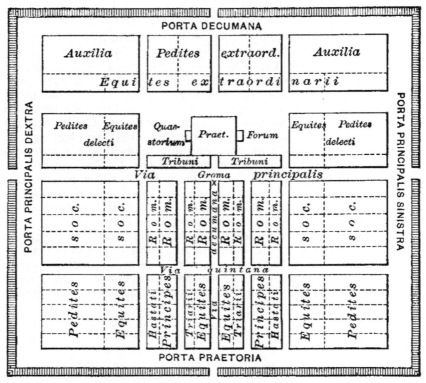

FIG. 119. — CASTRA ROMANA.

SELECTIONS FOR SIGHT READING

1. The Pig's Last Will and Testament

Testāmentum Porcellī.

Incipit[1] testāmentum porcellī.

M. Grunnius Corocotta,[2] porcellus, testāmentum fēcit. Quoniam manū meā scrībere nōn potuī, scrībendum[3] dictāvī.

Magīrus,[4] cocus, dīxit:

'Venī hūc, ēversor[5] domī, solivertiātor, fugitīve porcelle, et hodiē[6] tibi dirimō vītam.'

Corocotta, porcellus, dīxit:

'Sī qua fēcī, sī qua[7] peccāvī, sī qua vāscella pedibus meīs cōnfrēgī,[8] rogō, domine coce, vītam petō, concēde rogantī.' Magīrus, cocus, dīxit:

'Trānsī, puer,[9] affer mihi dē cocīnā cultrum, ut hunc porcellum faciam cruentum.'[10]

Porcellus comprehenditur ā famulīs,[11] ductus, sub diē XVI kal. lucernīnās,[12] ubi abundant cymae, Clībanātō et Piperātō cōnsulibus. Et ut vīdit, sē moritūrum esse, hōrae spatium petiit, et cocum rogāvit, ut testāmentum facere posset.

Clāmāvit[13] ad sē suōs parentēs, ut dē cibāriīs suīs aliquid dīmitteret eīs.[14] Quī ait:

'Patrī meō, Verrīnō Lārdīnō,[15] dō, lēgō darī glandis modiōs XXX; et mātrī meae, Veturīnae Scrōfae,[16] dō, lēgō darī Lacōnicae[17] silīginis modiōs XL; et sorōrī meae Quirīnae, in cuius vōtum[18] interesse nōn potuī, dō, lēgō darī hordeī modiōs XXX.

'Et dē meīs vīsceribus[19] dabō, dōnābō, sūtōribus saetās, rīxōribus[20] capitīnās, surdīs auriculās, causidicīs et verbōsīs linguam, isiciāriīs[21] femora, cursōribus et vēnātōribus tālōs, latrōnibus ungulās.[22]

'Et nec nōminandō[23] cocō lēgātō dīmittō popiam et pīstillum, quae mēcum attuleram, dē[24] Tebeste ūsque ad Tergeste; liget[25] sibi collum dē reste.

'Et volō mihi fierī monumentum,[26] aureīs litterīs scrīptum,

M • GRUNNIUS • COROCOTTA • PORCELLUS
VĪXIT • ANNĪS • DCCCC XC VIIII • ET • S[27]
QUOD[28] • SĪ • SĒMISSEM • VĪXISSET
MĪLLE • ANNŌS • IMPLĒSSET[29]

'Optimī amātōrēs[30] meī, vel cōnsulēs vītae, rogō vōs, ut cum corpore meō bene faciātis, bene condiātis[31] dē bonīs condīmentīs[32] nucleī, piperis et mellis, ut nōmen meum in sempiternum[33] nōminētur.

'Meī dominī[34] vel cōnsobrīnī meī, quī in mediō testāmentō interfuistis, iubēte signārī.'[35]

[36]Lārdiō signāvit.
Ofellicus signāvit.
Cymīnātus signāvit.
Lūcānicus signāvit.

Tergillus signāvit.
Celsīnus signāvit.
Nūptiālicus signāvit.
Explicit³⁷ testāmentum porcellī, sub diē XVI kal. lucernīnās, Clībanātō et
Piperātō cōnsulibus, fēlīciter.³⁸

---

1 **Incipit**: '(Here) begins.' **testāmentum:** in our legal phrase, 'the last will and testament.' The
Pig's Will, the author of which is unknown, afforded amusement to many generations of
Roman schoolboys. **porcellus, -ī,** m., 'pig.' *75a.*
2 **M. Grunnius Corocotta,** gen. **Mārcī Grunniī Corocottae,** m., 'Marcus Grunter Bristleback.'
All the names of the Will are made up, and their meaning, although obvious to a Roman, can
be only approximated in translation.
3 **scrībendum:** gerundive, 'for writing'; sc. *testāmentum.* **dictō, -āre, -āvī, -ātus,** [frequentative
of **dīcō,** *78a*], 1, ' dictate.'
4 **Magīrus, -ī,** [ΜΑΓΕΙΡΟΣ], m., 'Chef;' Greek word meaning 'cook,' here used as a name.
cocus, -ī, m., 'cook.'
5 **ēversor, -ōris,** [**ēvertō**], m., 'overturner.' **solivertiātor, -ōris,** [**solum,** 'ground,' **vertō**], m., a
made-up word, 'rooter.'
6 **hodiē:** adv., 'to-day.' **dirimō:** colloquial present instead of the future.
7 **qua:** 'anything,' lit. 'anythings.' **peccō, -āre, -āvī, -ātus,** 1, 'transgress,' 'do mischief.' **qua
peccāvī:** 'have done any mischief.' **qua:** 'any.' **vāscellum, -ī,** n., 'dish.'
8 **cōnfringō, -ere, cōnfrēgī, -frāctus,** 3, 'smash,' 'break to pieces.' **dominus, -ī,** m., 'master.'
rogantī: sc. *mihi.*
9 **puer:** the cook's helper. **cocīna, -ae,** f., 'kitchen.' **culter, -trī** *(7c),* m., 'butcher-knife.'
10 **cruentus, -a, -um,** adj., 'bloody'; here, 'all bloody.'
11 **famulus, -ī,** m., 'servant.'
12 **lucernīnus, -a, -um,** adj., a made-up word, 'of candle-light;' the expression 'the kalends of
candle-light' humorously suggests the beginning of the long winter nights — the season
when spring pigs (and turkeys) are in demand. **cyma, -ae,** f., 'young cabbage.' **Clībanātus, -ī,**
[**clībanus,** 'baking-pan'], m., 'Roastingpan.' **Piperātus, -ī** [**piper,** ' pepper'], m. 'Blackpepper.'
13 **clāmō, -āre, -āvī, -ātus,** I, 'call.'
14 **dīmitteret eīs** : 'bestow upon them.' **Quī ait:** 'And he said.'
15 **Verrīnus Lārdīnus, -ī -ī,** [**verrēs,** 'boar,' **lārdum,** 'bacon'], m., 'Boar Bacon.' **lēgō, -āre, -āvī,
-ātus,** I, 'appoint.' **lēgō darī:** 'I bequeath,' lit. 'I appoint to be given'; legal formality and
redundancy of expression. **glandis:** singular where we use the plural; 'of acorns.'
modius, -ī, m., 'peck.'
16 **Veturīna Scrōfa, -ae -ae,** 'Dame Hogg.'
17 **Lacōnicus, -a, -um,** adj. 'Lacedaemonian.' **silīgō, -inis,** f., 'white wheat.' **Quirīna, -ae,** f.,
'Squealy.' **in** : 'at.'
18 **vōtum:** 'wedding.' **hordeum, -ī,** n., 'barley.'
19 **vīscus, -eris,** *(13e),* n., 'flesh.' **sūtor, -ōris,** m., 'shoemaker.' **saeta, -ae,** f., 'bristle,' used by
cobblers in the waxed end of their threads.
20 **rīxor, -ōris,** m., 'quarreler.' **capitīna, -ae,** [**caput**], f., 'head-meat,' suggesting our word
"headcheese." **surdus, -a, -um,** adj., 'deaf.' **auricula, -ae,** [diminutive of **auris**], f., 'ear'; the
hearing of pigs is very keen. **causidicus, -ī,** [**causa, dīcō**], m., 'pleader.' **verbōsus, -ī,**
[**verbum**], m., 'talkative person.'
21 **isiciārius, -ī,** m., 'sausage-maker.' **cursor, -ōris,** [**currō**], m., 'runner.' **tālus, -ī,** m.,
'knucklebone.'
22 **ungula, -ae,** f., 'hoof.'
23 **nec nōminandō:** 'unspeakable.' **lēgātum, -ī,** n., 'legacy;' here dative of purpose. **popia,-ae,**
f., 'soup-ladle.' **pīstillum, -ī,** n., 'pestle' of a mortar.
24 **dē,** etc.: like "from Dan to Beersheba." **Tebeste, -is,** n., 'Tebeste,' a city in Numidia, now
Tébessa. **Tergeste, -is,** n., now Trieste.
25 **ligō, -āre, -āvī, -ātus,** I, 'bind.' **collum, -ī,** n., 'neck.' **dē:** we should say 'with.' **restis, -is,** f.,
'rope;' the cook is exhorted to hang himself.
26 **monumentum, -ī,** [**moneō;** *74d*], n., 'monument.'

27 **S**: for **sēmisse**, abl. **sēmis, sēmissis**, m., 'half.'

28 **quod**: 'but.' **sēmissem**: 'half' of a year.

29 **impleō, -ēre, implēvī, -ētus**, 2, ' fill out;' satirical in respect to the veracity of inscriptions on tombstones.

30 **amātor, -ōris**, [**amō**], m., 'lover.' **meī**: 'of me.' **cōnsulēs** : translate as if *cōnsulentēs; double* meaning, 'ye who have regard for (my) life,' 'ye who are fond of good living.'

31 **condiō, -īre, -īvī, -ītus**, 4, word of double meaning: 'embalm' from the pig's point of view, ' season' from the point of view of the lovers' of roast pig. **condiātis**: sc. *id.* **dē**: 'with.'

32 **condīmentum, -ī**, [**condiō**], n., 'seasoning.' **nucleus, -ī**, m., 'nut-meat.' **piper, -eris**, n., 'pepper.' **meī, mellis**, n., 'honey.'

33 **sempiternus, -a, -um**, [**semper**], adj., 'everlasting;' neuter as noun, **in sempiternum**, 'forever and ever.'

34 **Meī dominī**: title of respect; 'good sirs.' **cōnsobrīnus, -ī**, m., 'cousin.' **in mediō testāmentō**: i.e. 'at the making of my will.'

35 **signō, -āre, -āvī, -ātus**, [**signum**], I, 'affix a seal;' **signārī**, 'that the seals be affixed.' Each of the seven witnesses of a will was supposed to stamp his signet in the wax covering the ends of the string with which the tablets were tied together (Fig. 203).

36 **Lārdiō** : 'Fatbacon.' **Ofellicus**: 'Tidbit.' **Cymīnātus**: 'Youngcabbager. **Lūcānicus**: 'Porksausager.' **Tergillus**: 'Porkrind.' **Celsīnus**: 'Porkpie.' **Nūptiālicus**: 'Weddingporker,' suggesting a dish in favor for wedding-feasts.

37 **explicō, -āre, explicuī, explicitus**, [**ex** + **plicō**], I, 'unroll,' as a book written in the form of a scroll. **Explicit**: in full, *explicitum est*, lit. 'is unrolled;' we should say, 'Here ends.' The form of expression, while not suitable for the tablets on which wills were written, is appropriate for the scroll-shaped book in which the Pig's Will is represented as being recorded (Figures 166 and 191).

38 **fēlīciter**: 'happily,' a word of good omen, often added at the end of a writing.

2. WITTICISMS ATTRIBUTED TO CICERO

On Lentulus, his son-in-law.

Cicerō cum Lentulum, generum suum, exiguae statūrae hominem, longō gladiō accīnctum[1] vīdisset,
'Quis,' inquit, 'generum meum ad gladium alligāvit?'[2]

On Piso, a son-in-law, who walked effeminately.

Cicerō, cum Pisō gener eius mollius[3] incēderet, fīlia autem concitātius,[4] ait fīliae: 'Ambulā tamquam vir!'

On a portrait of his brother Quintus, larger than life.

Nec Q. Cicerōnī frātrī circā[5] similem mordācitātem pepercit. Nam cum in eā prōvinciā, quam ille rēxerat,[6] vīdisset clipeātam[7] imāginem eius, ingentibus liniāmentīs, ūsque ad pectus ex mōre[8] pīctam (erat autem Quīntus ipse statūrae parvae), ait:
'Frāter meus[9] dīmidius maior est quam tōtus.'

On a certain foppishness of Caesar's attire.

In Caesarem quoque mordācitās Cicerōnis dentēs suōs strīnxit.[10] Nam prīmum post victōriam[11] Caesaris interrogātus, cūr in ēlectiōne[12] partis errāsset, respondit: 'Praecinctūra mē dēcēpit,' iocātus[13] in Caesarem, quī ita togā praecingēbātur, ut trahendō laciniam[14] velut mollis incēderet.

On Caesar's enlargement of the Senate.

Cicerō aliās facilitātem[15] Caesaris in allēgandō senātū irrīsit palam.
Nam cum ab hospite suō, P. Malliō,[16] rogārētur, ut decuriōnātum[17]
prīvignō eius expedīret, assistente frequentiā,[18] dīxit:
'Rōmae,[19] sī vīs, habēbit; Pompeiīs difficile est.'

A play upon words.

Nē illa[20] quidem (ōrātōribus conveniunt), quae Cicerōnī aliquandō, sed
nōn in agendō,[21] excidērunt, ut dīxit, cum is candidātus,[22] quī cocī fīlius
habēbātur, cōram eō suffrāgium ab aliō peteret:
'Ego, quoque,[23] tibi favēbō.'

To Vatinius, Caesar's friend, anticipating a compliment.

Vatīnius, pedibus aeger,[24] cum vellet vidērī commodiōris[25] valētūdinis
factus et dīceret, sē iam bīna mīlia ambulāre:
'Diēs enim,'[26] inquit Cicerō, 'longiōrēs sunt.'

On the consulship of Vatinius, which lasted a few days.

In cōnsulātū Vatīniī, quem paucīs diēbus gessit, notābilis[27] Cicerōnis
urbānitās[28] circumferēbātur:
'Magnum ostentum,'[29] inquit, 'annō Vatīniī factum est, quod illō
cōnsulātū nec brūma nec vēr nec aestās nec autumnus fuit.'
Querentī deinde Vatīniō, quod gravātus esset,[30] domum ad sē
īnfīrmātum[31] venīre, respondit:
'Voluī in cōnsulātū tuō venīre, sed nox mē comprehendit.'

On the consulship of Caninius Rebilus, formerly a lieutenant of Caesar, which lasted only a few hours, at the end of 45 B.C.

'Hōc cōnsecūtus est Rebilus, ut quaererētur,[32] quibus cōnsulibus cōnsul
fuerit.'
'Vigilantem[33] habēmus cōnsulem Canīnium, quī in cōnsulātū suō
somnum nōn vīdit.'

Retorts for persons who lie about their age.

Redarguimus[34] interim apertē, ut Cicerō Vibium Curium, multum dē
annīs aetātis suae mentientem:[35]
'Tum ergō, cum ūnā dēclāmābāmus,[36] nōn erās nātus!' Interim et
simulātā assēnsiōne,[37] ut īdem, Fabiā Dolābellae dīcente *trīgintā*[38] *sē annōs
habēre,* 'Vērum est,' inquit, 'nam hōc[39] illam iam vīgintī annīs audiō!'

On a man from Africa, who wished to pass as an aristocrat.

Octāvius, quī nātū nōbilis vidēbātur, Cicerōnī recitantī ait: 'Nōn audiō, quae
dīcis.'
Ille respondit: 'Certē solēbās bene forātās[40] habēre aurēs!' Hōc eō dictum,
quia Octāvius Libys[41] oriundus dīcēbātur, quibus[42] mōs est aurem forāre.

1 **accingō, -cingere, -cīnxī, -cīnctus**, [ad + cingō], 3, 'gird on,' 'arm.'

2 **alligō, -āre, -āvī, -ātus**, [ad + ligō], I, 'tie (to).'

3 **molliter**, [mollis], adv., 'lazily.'

4 **concitātē**, [concitātus, participle of concitō], adv., 'energetically.' **ambulō, -āre, -āvī**, I, 'walk.' **tamquam**, [tam + quam], adv., 'just as.' **vir**: '(your) husband (does).'

5 **circā**: 'in the use of;' lit. 'around.' **mordācitās, -ātis**, [mordāx], f., 'sharpness' of speech. **pepercit**: sc. M. Cicerō.

6 **rēxerat**: 'had governed;' Quintus Cicero was governor of the province of Asia (302c) for three years, before he became a lieutenant of Caesar in Gaul.

7 **clipeātus, -a, -um**, [clipeus], adj., 'shield-shaped,' i.e. 'oval,' like the *clipeus*. **imāgō, -inis**, f., 'portrait.' **līniāmentum, -ī**, n., 'feature.' **ūsque**, etc.: the painted portrait resembled a bust.

8 **ex mōre**: 'in the usual fashion.' **pingō, -ere, pīnxī, pīctus**, 3, 'paint.'

9 **Frāter meus dīmidius**: 'the half of my brother.'

10 **dentēs suōs strīnxit**: 'showed its teeth,' we should say.

11 **victōriam**: at Pharsalus; Cicero had joined the party of Pompey.

12 **ēlectiō, -ōnis**, [ēligō], f., 'choice.' **praecinctūra, -ae**, [praecingō], f., manner of dress,' referring to the effeminate way that Caesar draped his toga.

13 **iocor, -ārī, -ātus**, I, dep., 'jest.' **toga, -ae**, f., 'toga,' the principal outer garment worn by Roman men. **praecingō, -cingere, -cīnxī, -cīnctus**, [prae + cingō], 3, 'gird about.' The passive is here used in a middle sense; 'would wrap his toga about him in such a way,' lit. 'would so wrap himself up with his toga.'

14 **lacinia, -ae**, f., 'end' of a toga; 'by letting the end of his toga drag,' instead of carefully tucking it in.

15 **facilitās, -ātis**, [facilis], f., 'ready compliance.' **allēgō, -āre, -āvī, -ātus**, I, 'depute;' 'in appointing (men to) the Senate.'

16 **P. Mallius**. gen. **Publiī Malliī**, m., a friend of Cicero.

17 **decuriōnātus, -ūs**, m., 'membership in a town council,' probably at Pompeii, near which Cicero had a countryseat. **prīvignus, -ī**, m., 'step-son.' **expedīret**: 'help to secure.'

18 **frequentia, -ae**, [frequēns], f., 'crowd.'

19 **Rōmae**: locative. 146. **Pompeiīs**: 'at Pompeii.' 145d.

20 **illa**: 'those (sayings).' **ōrātōribus conveniunt**: 'are proper for an orator.' **Cicerōnī — excidērunt**: 'fell from the lips of Cicero.' 109b.

21 **in agendō**: 'while arguing' in court.

22 **candidātus, -ī**, [candidus, 'white'], m., 'candidate.' **cocī**: gen. of **cocus**, 'cook,' pronounced as if spelled **quoquus**. **cōram**: here a preposition with the ablative; 'in his presence.'

23 **quoque**: either the adverb, or the vocative of *quoquus = cocus*.

24 **pedibus aeger**: Vatinius had the gout

25 **commodiōris valētūdinis; factus [esse]**: 'to have improved in health,' lit. 'to have become of better health.' **bīna mīlia [passuum]**: 'two miles (a day).'

26 **enim**: '(Of course), for.'

27 **notābilis, -e**, [nota], adj., 'remarkable.'

28 **urbānitās, -ātis**, [urbānus], f., 'pleasantry;' trans. 'witticism.' **circumferō, -ferre, -tulī, -lātus**, [circum + ferō], 3, 'carry around;' here 'circulate.'

29 **ostentum, -ī**, [ostendō], n., 'marvel.'

30 **gravātus esset**: 'because (as he said, Cicero) had been unwilling.' **domum ad sē**: 'to his house to (see) him.'

31 **īnfīrmō, -āre, -āvī, -ātus**, [īnfīrmus], I, 'enfeeble.' **īnfīrmātum**: 'when he was laid up.'

32 **ut quaererētur**: 'that the question should be raised.' **quibus cōnsulibus**: 'in whose consulship.'

33 **vigilāns, -antis** [vigilō, 'keep awake'], adj. of double meaning, 'watchful' and 'wakeful.'

34 **redarguō, -ere, -uī**, 3, 'show up;' 'we show up (people).' **interim**: 'sometimes.' **Vibius Curius, -ī -ī**, m., an acquaintance of Cicero's; sc. *redarguit*.

35 **mentior, -īrī, -ītus**, 4, dep., 'lie.'

36 **dēclāmō, -āre**, etc., [dē + clāmō], I, 'practice declamation.'

37 **assēnsiō, -ōnis**, f., 'agreement.' **īdem**: Cicero; subject of *inquit*. **Fabia, -ae**, f., wife of Dolabella. **Dolābella, -ae**, m., P. Cornelius Dolabella, who was born in 70 B.C., and was prominent in Roman politics at the time of the Civil War.

38 **trīgintā**, etc.: 'that she was thirty years old.'
39 **hōc**, etc.: sc. *dīcere;* 'I've been hearing her say that.'
40 **forō, -āre, -āvī, -ātus**, I, 'bore;' of the ear, 'pierce.'
41 **Libys, -yos**, m., 'a Libyan'; 'was said to be a Libyan by birth.'
42 **quibus** : *et eīs*, the Libyans.

3. LEGAL MAXIMS

Fundamental maxims of right conduct.

Iūris praecepta sunt haec: honestē[1] vīvere, alterum nōn laedere, suum cuique[2] tribuere.

Definition of justice.

Iūstitia est cōnstāns[3] et perpetua voluntās iūs suum cuique tribuendī.[4]

The principal is responsible for his agent.

Quī facit per alium, facit per sē.

The plea, "I did not know the law," is not valid.

Ignōrantia[5] lēgis nēminem excūsat.

We cannot confer upon another ampler rights than we ourselves possess.

Nēmō plūs iūris in alium trānsferre potest quam ipse habet.

A single-crime, a single punishment.

Nēmō dēbet bis pūnīrī[6] prō ūnō dēlīctō.

In heated argument men lose sight of the truth.

Nimium altercandō[7] vēritās āmittitur.

1 **honestē**, [**honōs**]: adv., 'honorably.'
2 **suum cuique**: 'to each what belongs to him.'
3 **cōnstāns, -tis**, adj., 'unvarying.' **voluntās**: 'determination.' **iūs suum cuique**: 'to each his due.'
4 **tribuendī**: translate as if an infinitive.
5 **ignōrantia, -ae**, f., 'ignorance.'
6 **pūniō, -īre, -īvī, -ītus**, 4, 'punish.'
7 **altercor, -ārī, -ātus**, [**alter**], I, dep., 'dispute.' **vēritās, -ātis**, [**vērus**], f., 'truth.'

4. FABLES

In union lies safety; in discord, weakness.

In eōdem prātō[1] pāscēbantur trēs bovēs in maximā concordiā, et sīc ab omnī ferārum incursiōne tūtī erant. Sed discidiō[2] inter illōs ortō, singulī ā ferīs petītī et laniātī sunt.
Fābula[3] docet, quantum bonī sit in concordiā.

1 **prātum, -ī**, n., 'meadow.' **pāscor, -ī, pāstus**, 3, dep., 'feed.' **concordia, -ae**, f., 'harmony.'
2 **discidium, -ī**, n., 'discord.' **laniō, -āre**, etc., I, 'tear to pieces.'
3 **fābula, -ae**, f., 'fable.'

Circumstances may make cowards brave.

Haedus,[4] stāns in tēctō domūs, lupō praetereuntī male dīxit. Cui lupus, 'Nōn tū,' inquit, 'sed tēctum mihi maledīcit.'
Saepe locus et tempus hominēs timidōs audācēs reddit.

The dog in the manger.

Canis[5] iacēbat in praesēpī bovēsque lātrandō ā pābulō arcēbat.[6] Cui ūnus boum, 'Quanta ista,' inquit, 'invidia est, quod nōn pateris, ut eō cibō vescāmur,[7] quem tū ipse capere nec possīs!
Haec fābula invidiae indolem[8] dēclārat.

"Who will put the bell on the cat?"

Mūres[9] aliquandō habuērunt cōnsilium, quō modō sibi ā fēle[10] cavērent. Multīs aliīs prōpositīs, omnibus placuit, ut eī tintinnābulum[11] annecterētur; sīc enim ipsōs sonitū admonitōs eam fugere posse. Sed cum iam inter mūrēs quaererētur, quī fēlī tintinnābulum annecteret, nēmō repertus est.
Fābula docet, in suādendō[12] plūrimōs esse audācēs, sed in ipsō perīculō timidōs.

He who urges others on, shares the responsibility.

Tubicen[13] ab hostibus captus, 'Nē mē,' inquit, 'interficite; nam inermis sum, neque quicquam habeō praeter hanc tubam.'
At hostēs, 'Propter hōc ipsum,' inquiunt,[14] 'tē interimēmus, quod, cum ipse pugnandī sīs imperītus, aliōs ad pugnam incitāre solēs.'
Fābula docet, nōn sōlum maleficōs[15] esse pūniendōs, sed etiam eōs, quī aliōs ad male faciendum irritent.[16]

5. THE FIRST PSALM

Beātus[1] vir, quī nōn abiit in cōnsiliō impiōrum,
   et in viā peccātōrum[2] nōn stetit,
   et in cathedrā[3] pestilentiae nōn sēdit;
sed in lēge Dominī[4] voluntās eius,

---

4 **haedus, -ī,** m., 'kid.' **lupus, -ī,** m.,' wolf.' **maledīcō, -dīcere, -dīxī, -dictus,** 3, 'rail at.'
5 **canis, -is,** m., 'dog.' **praesēpe, -is,** n., 'manger.' **lātrō, -āre, -āvī,** I, 'bark.'
6 **arceō, -ēre, -uī,** 2, 'keep (from).' **invidia, -ae,** f., 'meanness.'
7 **vescor, -ī,** 3, dep., 'eat.'
8 **indolēs, -is,** f., 'true nature.'
9 **mūs, mūris,** m., 'mouse.'
10 **fēlis, -is,** f., 'cat.'
11 **tintinnābulum, -ī,** n., 'bell.' **annectō, -nectere, -nexuī, -nexus,** 3, 'tie (to).' **sonitus, -ūs,** m., 'sound.'
12 **suādeō, -ēre, -sī,** 2, 'advise.'
13 **tubicen, -inis,** m., 'trumpeter.'
14 **inquiunt:** from *inquam;* 'say.' **interimō, -imere, -ēmī, -ēmptus,** 3, 'kill.'
15 **maleficus, -ī,** m., 'evildoer.'
16 **irritō, -āre, -āvī, -ātus,** I, 'stir up.'

et in lēge eius meditābitur[5] diē ac nocte.

Et erit tamquam lignum,[6] quod plantātum est secus dēcursūs aquārum,

  quod fructum suum dabit in tempore suō,

et folium[7] eius nōn dēfluet,

  et omnia, quaecumque faciet, prosperābuntur.[8]

Nōn sīc impiī,[9] nōn sīc;

  sed tamquam pulvis, quem prōicit ventus ā faciē[10] terrae.

Ideō nōn resurgent[11] impiī in iūdiciō,

  neque peccātōrēs in conciliō iūstōrum;

quoniam nōvit Dominus viam iūstōrum,[12]

  et iter impiōrum perībit.

---

1 **Beātus, -a, -um**, adj., 'happy,' 'blessed.' **impius, -a, -um**, [in- + pius], adj., 'wicked,' 'ungodly;' as a noun, **impius, -ī**, m., 'wicked man.'
2 **peccātor, -ōris**, [peccō], m., 'sinner.'
3 **cathedra, -ae**, [ΚΑΘΕΔΡΑ], f., 'chair,' 'seat.' **pestilentia, -ae**, [pestilēns, 'unwholesome'], f.,'plague;' here 'they that are a plague,' 'the scornful.' **sedeō, -ēre, sēdī**, sup. **sessum**, 2, 'sit.'
4 **Dominus, -ī**, m., 'Lord.' **voluntās**: sc. *est.*
5 **meditor, -ārī, -ātus**, I, dep., 'reflect,' 'meditate.'
6 **lignum, -ī**, n., 'wood,' 'tree.' **plantō, -āre, -āvī, -ātus**, [planta, 'a plant'], I, 'plant.' **secus**, prep., 'along,' 'beside.' **dēcursus, -ūs**, [dēcurrō], m., 'course' of a brook or stream, 'river.'
7 **folium, -ī**, n.,'leaf.' **dēfluō, -fluere, -flūxī**, [dē + fluō], 3, 'flow away;' of a leaf, 'fade,' 'wither.'
8 **prosperō, -āre, -āvī, -ātus**, [prosper, 'favorable'], I, 'succeed,' 'prosper.'
9 **impiī**: sc. *sunt.*
10 **faciēs, -eī**, f., 'face.'
11 **resurgō, -ere, resurrēxī, resurrēctus**, [re- + surgō], 3, 'rise again,' 'stand.'
12 **iūstus, -ī**, [iūstus, -a, -um], m., 'just man,' 'righteous man.'

6. The Twenty-third Psalm

Dominus regit mē, et nihil mihi deerit.

  In locō pāscuae[1] ibi mē collocāvit;

super aquam refectiōnis[2] ēducāvit mē,

  animam meam convertit.

Dēdūxit mē super sēmitās iūstitiae[3] propter nōmen suum.

Nam, et[4] sī ambulāverō in mediō umbrae mortis,

  nōn timēbō mala, quoniam tū mēcum es:

virga[5] tua et baculus tuus, ipsa mē cōnsōlāta sunt.

Parāstī in cōnspectū meō mēnsam,[6] adversus eōs quī trībulant mē:

  impinguāstī[7] in oleō caput meum,

---

1 **pascua,-ae**, f., ' pasturage,"pasture.'
2 **refectio, -orris**, [reficio], f., 'refreshing.' **educo, -are, -avi, -Stus**, [e + duco, from dux], 1, 'rear'; 'support,' 'nourish.'
3 **iustitiae**: 'righteousness.'
4 **et**: 'even.' **ambulo, -are, -avi**, 1, 'walk.' **umbra, -ae**, f., •shadow.'
5 **virga,-ae**, f., a slender branch,'rod.' **baculus,-1**, m.,'staff.' **ipsa** : neuter plural as referring to both *virga* and *baculus* (cf. *163, c*) ; emphatic ' they.'
6 **mensa,-ae**, f.,'table.'**tribulo,-are, I**, 'thresh'; 'afflict,' 'torment.'
7 **impinguo, -are, -avi, -atus**, [in + pinguis], i, -make fat'; 'anoint.' **in**: 'with.' **oleum, -I**, n., 'oil' of the olive.

et calix[8] meus inēbriāns quam praeclārus est!
Et misericordia tua subsequētur mē omnibus diēbus vītae meae,
  et ut inhabitem[9] in domō Dominī in longitūdinem diērum.

8 **calix, -icis, m.,** 'cup.' **inebrio, -are,** I, 'fill full'; 'over flow.' **praeclarus, -a, -um, [prae + clarus],** adj.,
-glorious,' 'splendid.'
9 **inhabito, -are, -avi, [in + habito], 1,** 'dwell in,' 'dwell.' **in longitudinem dierum:**   'forever.'

PLATE VII   MILITARY DEVICES

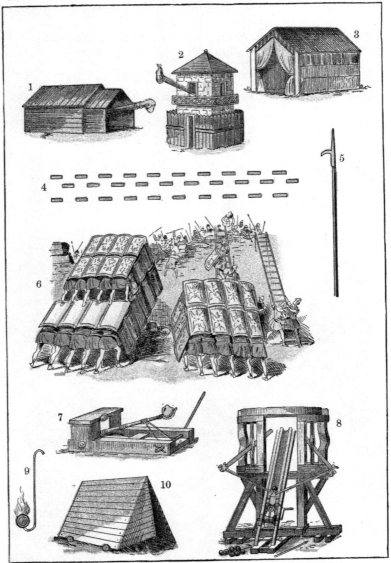

1. Timbered Shed, *testudo*, with Battering Ram.   2. Fire-signal Tower.
3. Tent, *tabernaculum*.   4. Order of Battle.   5. Wall Hook, *falx muralis*.
6. Turtle-shell roof, *testudo*.   7. *Onager*.   8. *Ballista*.
9. *Glans fusili ex argilla* (V. 43).   10. Turtle-shell shed, *testudo*.

GRAMMAR FOR THE STUDY OF CAESAR

INFLECTIONS

NOUNS

1. The Latin language has no article. In translating into English, the definite article *the*, or the indefinite article *a*, should be supplied with nouns in the different cases as the sense may require.

FIRST DECLENSION

2. *a*. The Nominative Singular of nouns of the First Declension ends in **-ă**.

b. Nouns of the First Declension are nearly all of the Feminine Gender; a few nouns referring to males are masculine, as **nauta**, sailor (III. 9); **Cotta**, a man's name (C. I. 6).

3. An example of the First Declension is: **via** (stem **viā-**), F., way (1.9):

SINGULAR

Case		Meaning	Termination
Nom.	*via*	*a way, the way*	-ă
Gen.	*viae*	*of a way, of the way*	-ae
Dat.	*viae*	*to or for a way, or the way*	-ae
Acc.	*viam*	*a way, the way*	-am
Abl.	*viā*	*from, by, in a way or the way*	-ā
Voc.	*via*	*O way!*	-ă

PLURAL

Nom.	*viae*	*ways, the ways*	-ae
Gen.	*viārum*	*of ways, of the ways*	-ārum
Dat.	*viīs*	*to or for ways, or the ways*	-īs
Acc.	*viās*	*ways, the ways*	-as
Abl.	*viīs*	*from, by, in ways, or the ways*	-īs
Voc.	*viae*	*O ways !*	-ae

4. *a*. Besides the six cases of the First Declension there is a rare Locative Case, of which the Singular is exactly like the Genitive, as **Samarobrīvae**, *at Samarobriva* (V. 24).

b. The Greek Name **Achillās** (C. III. 104) is of the First Declension, and declined as follows: *Nom.* **Achillās**, *Gen.* **Achillae**, *Dat.* **Achillae**, *Acc.* **Achillam**, *Abl.* **Achillā**, *Voc.* **Achillā** or **Achilla**.

SECOND DECLENSION

5. *a*. The Nominative Singular of the Second Declension ends in **-um** for Neuter Nouns and **-us, -er, -ir** for all others.

b. Nouns of the Second Declension in **-us, -er**, and **-ir** are generally Masculine. Feminine are most names of Trees and Plants, as **fāgus**, *beech* (V. 12), and most names of Countries, Islands, and Cities, as **Aegyptus**, *Egypt* (C. III. 104).

6. *a*. Examples of Nouns of the Second Declension in **-us** and **-um** are **lēgātus** (I. 7) and **bellum** (I. 1):

lēgātus (stem **lēgāto-**), M., *envoy, lieutenant*   **bellum** (stem **bello-**), N., *war*

SINGULAR

Case		Termination	Case	Termination
Nom.	*lēgātus*	-us	*bellum*	-um
Gen.	*lēgātī*	-ī	*bellī*	-ī

Dat.	lēgātō	-ō	bellō	-ō
Acc.	lēgātum	-um	bellum	-um
Abl.	lēgātō	-ō	bellō	-ō
Voc.	lēgāte	-e	bellum	-um

PLURAL

Nom.	lēgātī	-ī	bella	-a
Gen.	lēgātōrum	-ōrum	bellōrum	-ōrum
Dat.	lēgātīs	-īs	bellīs	-īs
Acc.	lēgātōs	-ōs	bella	-a
Abl.	lēgātīs	-īs	bellīs	-īs
Voc.	lēgātī	-ī	bella	-a

b. Caesar uses the Neuter **vulgus** in the Nominative (IV. 5), Genitive **vulgī** (I. 20), and the Accusative **vulgus** (I. 46).

c. Caesar uses **locus, -ī,** M., *place,* with a Neuter Plural declined thus: *Nom.* **loca,** *Gen.* **locōrum,** *Dat.* **locīs,** *Acc.* **loca,** *Abl.* **locīs.**

d. The Second Declension has a rare Locative Case, of which the Singular is like the Genitive; as **Cavillōnī,** *at Cavillonum* (VII. 90).

7. *a.* Examples of Nouns of the Second Declension in **-er** and **-ir** are **puer,** *boy* (I. 29), **ager,** *field* (I. 4), and **vir,** *man* (II. 25):

puer (stem **puero-**), M., *boy*   **ager** (stem **agro-**), M., *field*   **vir** (stem **viro-**), M., *man*

SINGULAR

Nom.	puer	ager	vir	
Gen.	puerī	agrī	virī	-ī
Dat.	puerō	agrō	virō	-ō
Acc.	puerum	agrum	virum	-um
Abl.	puerō	agrō	virō	-ō
Voc.	puer	ager	vir	

PLURAL

Nom.	puerī	agrī	virī	-ī
Gen.	puerōrum	agrōrum	virōrum	-ōrum
Dat.	puerīs	agrīs	virīs	-īs
Acc.	puerōs	agrōs	virōs	-ōs
Abl.	puerīs	agrīs	virīs	-īs
Voc.	puerī	agrī	virī	-ī

b. Declined like **puer** are **socer,** M., *father-in-law* (I. 12), **gener,** M., *son-in-law* (V. 56), **vesper,** M., *evening* (I. 26), **līberī,** M., plural only, *children* (I. 11), and compounds of **-fer** and **-ger,** as **signifer,** *standard-bearer* (II. 25).

c. Like **ager** is **arbiter, -trī,** M., *referee* (V. 1); also **faber, -brī,** M., *mechanic,* Gen. Plural generally **fabrum** (V. 11), **administer, -trī,** M., *helper* (VI. 16), **culter, -trī,** M., *butcher-knife.*

8. *a.* In Caesar's time nouns of the Second Declension in **-ius** and **-ium** formed the Genitive Singular in **-ī** (not **-iī**), retaining the accent on the penult of words of more than two syllables even when this was short; thus, **fīlī, Vale'rī, negō'tī, impe'rī.** Afterwards Common Nouns in **-ius,** and many Proper Names in **-ius,** were written with the Genitive in **-iī,** and for the sake of consistency such Genitives are frequently printed with **-iī** today, as **cōnsiliī** (I. 21), **Valeriī** (I. 47).

b. The Genitive of **Pompeius** is written with **-ī, Pompe'ī** (VII. 6, C. III. 84), as are also the Genitives of some other Proper Names in **-ius.**

c. The Vocative of **fīlius** and of Proper Names in **-ius** ends in **-ī** (not **-ie**), the accent remaining on the penult of vocatives containing more than two syllables; thus: **Pompe'ī** (C. III. 87).

d. The declension of **deus,** M., *god* (I. 12), is irregular:

	SINGULAR	PLURAL
Nom.	deus	dī, deī. diī
Gen.	deī	deōrum, deum
Dat.	deō	dīs, deīs, diīs
Acc.	deum	deōs
Abl.	deō	dīs, deīs. diīs
Voc.	deus	dī, deī, diī

THIRD DECLENSION

9. In the Third Declension are comprised nouns with stems ending in a consonant (mute stems, liquid stems, nasal stems, and **-s** stems), nouns with stems ending in **-i**, nouns with mixed stems, and nouns of irregular declension. The stem rarely appears unchanged in the Nominative, but may usually be recognized in the Genitive.

10. *a.* Mute Stems may end in a Labial, **p, b**; in a Guttural, **c, g**; or in a Dental, **t, d**. In Guttural Stems the **-s** of the case ending in the Nominative unites with the **c** or **g** of the stem, producing **x**; thus **dux** for **duc-s**, in which the stem is **duc-**, the termination **-s**; and **rēx** for **rēg-s**.

b. Examples of nouns with mute stems are **prīnceps** (I. 13), **rēx** (I. 31), **pēs** (I. 8), **mīles** (I. 7), **virtūs** (I. 1) and **caput** (I. 29):

prīnceps, (stem in oblique cases **prīncip-**), M., *leader, leading man*

rēx (stem **rēg-**), M., *king*

pēs (stem in oblique cases **ped-**), M., *foot*

SINGULAR

	prīnceps	rēx	pēs	
Nom.	prīnceps	rēx	pēs	-s
Gen.	prīncipis	rēgis	pedis	-is
Dat.	prīncipī	rēgī	pedī	-ī
Acc.	prīncipem	rēgem	pedem	-em
Abl.	prīncipe	rēge	pede	-e
Voc.	prīnceps	rēx	pēs	-s

PLURAL

	prīncipēs	rēgēs	pedēs	
Nom.	prīncipēs	rēgēs	pedēs	-ēs
Gen.	prīncipum	rēgum	pedum	-um
Dat.	prīncipibus	rēgibus	pedibus	-ibus
Acc.	prīncipēs	rēgēs	pedēs	-ēs
Abl.	prīncipibus	rēgibus	pedibus	-ibus
Voc.	prīncipēs	rēgēs	pedēs	-ēs

mīles (stem in oblique cases **mīlit-**), M., *soldier*

virtūs (stem in oblique cases **virtūt-**), F., *valour, virtue*

caput (stem in oblique cases **capit-**), N., *head*

SINGULAR

	mīles	virtūs	caput
Nom.	mīles	virtūs	caput
Gen.	mīlitis	virtūtis	capitis
Dat.	mīlitī	virtūtī	capitī
Acc.	mīlitem	virtūtem	caput
Abl.	mīlite	virtūte	capite
Voc.	mīles	virtūs	caput

PLURAL

	mīlitēs	virtūtēs	capita
Nom.	mīlitēs	virtūtēs	capita
Gen.	mīlitum	virtūtum	capitum
Dat.	mīlitibus	virtūtibus	capitibus
Acc.	mīlitēs	virtūtēs	capita
Abl.	mīlitibus	virtūtibus	capitibus
Voc.	mīlitēs	virtūtēs	capita

c. Like **rēx** are declined Gallic Proper Names in **-rīx**, as, in Singular only, **Orgetorīx**, *Gen.* **Orgetorīgis** (I. 2), and **Dumnorīx, -rīgis** (I. 3), and, in Plural only, **Biturīgēs, Biturīgum** (I. 18); also **dux, ducis**, M., *leader* (I. 13), **pāx, pācis**, F., *peace* (I. 3), **pix, picis**, F., *pitch* (VII. 22), and **vōx, vōcis**, F., *voice, utterance* (I. 32).

d. Like **mīles** in Declension are **eques, equitis**, M., *horseman* (I. 15), **pedes, peditis**, M., *foot-soldier* (I. 42); and **caespes**, M., *sod* (III. 25), **comes**, M. *companion* (VI. 30), **hospes**, M., *guest-friend* (I. 53), **stīpes**, M., *tree-trunk* (VII. 73).

e. **Quiēs**, F., *repose* (V. 40). is declined **quiēs, quiētis, quiētī**, etc.; but **ariēs**, M., *battering-ram* (II. 32), **abiēs**, F., *fir-tree* (V. 12), **interpres**, M., *interpreter* (I. 19), **seges**, F., *grainfield* (VI. 36) have **-ĕtis** in the Genitive and are declined **ariēs, arietis, arietī, arietem**, etc.

f. Like **virtūs** are **salūs, salūtis**, F., in Singular only, *safety* (I. 27), **servitūs, servitūtis**, F., *slavery* (I. 11); here also belong the Feminine Nouns whose Nominative ends in **-tās**, as **cīvitās, cīvitātis**, *state* (I. 2), **aestās, aestātis**, *summer* (I. 54).

g. Lacking the Dental in the Nominative are the Neuters **cor, cordis**, *heart* (VI. 19), and **lac, lactis**, *milk* (IV. 1).

11. *a.* Liquid stems end in **-l** or **-r.**

b. Examples of nouns with liquid stems are **cōnsul** (I. 2), **victor** (I. 31) and **pater** (I. 3):

cōnsul (stem cōnsul-) M., *consul*	victor (stem victōr-) M., *victor*	pater (stem patr-) M., *father*

SINGULAR

Nom.	*cōnsul*	*victor*	*pater*
Gen.	*cōnsulis*	*victōris*	*patris*
Dat.	*cōnsulī*	*victōrī*	*patrī*
Acc.	*cōnsulem*	*victōrem*	*patrem*
Abl.	*cōnsule*	*victōre*	*patre*
Voc.	*cōnsul*	*victor*	*pater*

PLURAL

Nom.	*cōnsulēs*	*victōrēs*	*patrēs*
Gen.	*cōnsulum*	*victōrum*	*patrum*
Dat.	*cōnsulibus*	*victōribus*	*patribus*
Acc.	*cōnsulēs*	*victōrēs*	*patrēs*
Abl.	*cōnsulibus*	*victōribus*	*patribus*
Voc.	*cōnsulēs*	*victōrēs*	*patrēs*

c. Like **cōnsul** are **sōl, sōlis**, M., *sun* (I. 1), **exsul, exsulis**, M., *exile* (V. 55), **sāl, salis**, M., *salt* (C. II. 37); also some **-r** stems, as **Caesar, Caesaris**, M., *Caesar (19c)*; **agger, aggeris**, M., *mound* (II. 20), **ānser, -eris**, M., *goose* (V. 12), **mulier, mulieris**, F., *woman* (I. 29), **arbor, arboris**, F., *tree* (II. 17).

d. Like **victor** are declined Masculine nouns of Agency in **-tor**, as **mercātor, -ōris**, *trader* (I. 1), **dēprecātor, -ōris**, *intercessor* (I. 9); and Abstract nouns in **-or**, as **timor, -ōris**, M., *fear* (I. 22).

e. Like **pater** are declined **frāter, frātris**, M., *brother* (I. 3), and **māter, mātris**, F., *mother* (I. 18).

12. *a.* Nasal Stems end in **-n**, excepting in **hiems, hiemis**, F., *winter* (IV. 1), of which the stem ends in **-m.**

b. Examples are **sermō** (V. 37), **homō** (I. 2) and **nōmen** (I. 13):

sermō (stem sermōn-) M., *conversation*	homō (stem homin-) M., *man*	nōmen (stem nōmin-) N., *name*

SINGULAR

Nom.	*sermō*	*homō*	*nōmen*
Gen.	*sermōnis*	*hominis*	*nōminis*
Dat.	*sermōnī*	*hominī*	*nōminī*
Acc.	*sermōnem*	*hominem*	*nōmen*

Abl.	*sermōne*	*homine*	*nōmine*
Voc.	*sermō*	*homō*	*nōmen*

PLURAL

Nom.	*sermōnēs*	*hominēs*	*nōmina*
Gen.	*sermōnum*	*hominum*	*nōminum*
Dat.	*sermōnibus*	*hominibus*	*nōminibus*
Acc.	*sermōnēs*	*hominēs*	*nōmina*
Abl.	*sermōnibus*	*hominibus*	*nōminibus*
Voc.	*sermōnēs*	*hominēs*	*nōmina*

c. Like **sermō** are declined **harpagō, harpagōnis**, M., *grappling-hook* (VII. 81); **latrō, latrōnis**, M., *bandit* (III. 17); **Dīvicō, Dīviconis**, M., (I. 13; in Singular only); and nouns in **-iō**, as **suspīciō, suspīciōnis**, F., *suspicion* (I. 4), **coniūrātiō, -ōnis**, F., *league* (I. 2), **Cūriō, Cūriōnis**, M., (C. II. 3; in Singular only).

d. Like **homō** are declined **ōrdō, ōrdinis**, M., *rank* (I. 40); **necessitūdō, -inis**, F., *close connection* (I. 43); **testūdō, testūdinis**, F., *testudo* (II. 6); **nēmō**, *Dat.* **nēminī**, *Acc.* **nēminem** (the place of the *Gen.* and *Abl.*, and sometimes the *Dat.*, being supplied by *Gen.* **nūllīus**, *Abl.* **nūllō**, *Dat.* **nūllī**, from **nūllus**), M., *no one*; **Apollo, Apollinis**, M., (VI. 17, in Singular only); **sōlitūdo, sōlitūdinis**, F., *wilderness* (IV. 18); and **virgō, -inis**, F., *maiden* (C. II. 4).

e. Like **nōmen** are declined other Neuters in **-men**, as **flūmen, flūminis**, *river* (I. 1), **agmen, agminis**, *column* (I. 15), and **certāmen, -inis**, *contest* (III. 14).

13. *a.* The **-s-** of **-s** Stems becomes **r** between vowels in the oblique cases. In **honōs, -r** generally appears also in the Nominative; **-r** is always found in the Nominative of **rūmor** and many other nouns of this class.

b. Examples of nouns with **-s** stems are **mōs** (I. 4), **honōs** (VI. 13), or **honour**, and **genus** (I. 48):

mōs (oblique stem **mōr-**) M., *custom*	**honōs, honor** (oblique stem **honōr-**) M., *honour*	**genus** (oblique stem **gener-**) N., *race*

SINGULAR

Nom.	*mōs*	*honōs or honor*	*genus*
Gen.	*mōris*	*honōris*	*generis*
Dat.	*mōrī*	*honōrī*	*generī*
Acc.	*mōrem*	*honōrem*	*genus*
Abl.	*mōre*	*honōre*	*genere*
Voc.	*mōs*	*honor*	*genus*

PLURAL

Nom.	*mōrēs*	*honōrēs*	*genera*
Gen.	*mōrum*	*honōrum*	*generum*
Dat.	*mōribus*	*honōribus*	*generibus*
Acc.	*mōrēs*	*honōrēs*	*genera*
Abl.	*mōribus*	*honōribus*	*generibus*
Voc.	*mōrēs*	*honōrēs*	*genera*

c. Like **mōs** is declined **flōs**, M., *flower* (VII. 73).

d. Like **honour** are **soror, sorōris**, F., *sister* (I. 18), **uxor, uxōris**, F., *wife* (I. 18).

e. Like **genus** are declined the Neuters **fūnus, fūneris**, *funeral* (VI. 19); **latus, lateris**, *side* (I. 25); **mūnus, mūneris**, *gift* (I. 43); **onus, oneris**, *burden, load* (II. 30); **opus, operis**, *work* (I. 8); **scelus, sceleris**, *crime* (I. 14); **vulnus, vulneris**, *wound* (I. 25), etc.

f. Similar in declension to **genus**, but having a different vowel before the Endings of the Oblique Cases, are the Neuters **corpus, corporis**, *body* (I. 25); **dēdecus, -oris**, *disgrace* (IV. 25); **facinus, -oris**, *evil deed* (I. 40); **frīgus, frīgoris**, *cold* (I. 10); **lītus, lītoris**, *shore* (IV. 23); **pectus, pectoris**, *breast* (VII. 47); **pecus, pecoris**, *cattle* (III. 29); **tempus, temporis**, *time* (I. 16); and **rōbur, rōboris**, *oak* (III. 13).

g. Among other Nouns of the Third Declension with Nominative in **-s** and Genitive in **-ris** are the Masculine **pulvis, pulveris**, *dust* (*Acc.* **pulverem**, IV. 32), **lepus, leporis**, *hare* (*Acc.* **leporem**, V. 12), **mās, maris**, *male* (Gen. VI. 26); and the Neuters **iūs, iūris** (I. 4; *Nom.* Plural *iūra*, VI. 13), **aes, aeris**, *copper* (IV. 31), **crūs, crūris**, *leg* (VI. 27), and **ōs, ōris**, *mouth, face* (V. 35; *Acc.* Plural **ōra**, VI. 39).

h. **iūs iūrandum**, N., *oath* (I. 3), is thus declined, in the Singular:
Nom. **iūs iūrandum**, *Gen.* **iūris iūrandī**, *Dat.* **iūrī iūrandō**, *Acc.* **iūs iūrandum**, *Abl.* **iūre iūrandō**.

14. *a.* The Nominative Singular of Masculine and Feminine nouns with **-i** Stems ends ordinarily in **-is**, the Genitive Plural always in **-ium**.

b. Examples of Masculine and Feminine **-i** Stems with Nominative Singular in **-is** are **turris** (II. 30), **īgnis** (I. 4) and **hostis** (I. 21):

	turris (stem **turri-**),	**īgnis** (stem **īgni-**)	**hostis** (stem **hosti-**)	
	F., *tower*	M., *fire*	M. & F., *enemy*	

SINGULAR

Nom.	*turris*	*īgnis*	*hostis*	-is
Gen.	*turris*	*īgnis*	*hostis*	-is
Dat.	*turrī*	*īgnī*	*hostī*	-ī
Acc.	*turrim* or *-em*	*īgnem*	*hostem*	-im, -em
Abl.	*turrī* or *-e*	*īgnī* or *-e*	*hoste*	-e, -ī
Voc.	*turris*	*īgnis*	*hostis*	-is

PLURAL

Nom.	*turrēs*	*īgnēs*	*hostēs*	-ēs
Gen.	*turrium*	*īgnium*	*hostium*	-ium
Dat.	*turribus*	*īgnibus*	*hostibus*	-ibus
Acc.	*turrīs* or *-ēs*	*īgnīs* or *-ēs*	*hostīs* or *-ēs*	-īs, -ēs
Abl.	*turribus*	*īgnibus*	*hostibus*	-ibus
Voc.	*turrēs*	*īgnēs*	*hostēs*	-ēs

c. Like **turris**, but in the Singular only, is **Sabis, -is**, *Acc.* **-im**, M., *the Sambre* (II. 16); also **Tamesis, -is**, *Acc.* **-im**, M., *the Thames* (V. 11, 18).

15. *a.* The Nominative Singular of some nouns with **-i** Stems ends in **-ēs**, of a few others in **-er**. Examples are **caedēs** (V. 47) and **linter** (I. 12):

     caedēs (stem **caedi-**), F., *slaughter*   **linter** (stem **lintri-**), F., *skiff*

	Singular	Plural	Singular	Plural
Nom.	*caedēs*	*caedēs*	*linter*	*lintrēs*
Gen.	*caedis*	*caedium*	*lintris*	*lintrium*
Dat.	*caedī*	*caedibus*	*lintrī*	*lintribus*
Acc.	*caedem*	*caedēs* or *-īs*	*lintrem*	*lintrēs, -īs*
Abl.	*caede*	*caedibus*	*lintrī* or *-ē*	*lintribus*
Voc.	*caedēs*	*caedēs*	*linter*	*lintrēs*

b. Like **caedēs** are declined the Feminine Nouns **cautēs, cautis**, *jagged rock* (III. 13), **mōlēs, mōlis**, *dike* (III. 12), **rūpēs, -is**, *cliff* (II. 29), **sēdēs, -is**, *abode* (I. 31), **saepēs, -is**, *hedge* (II. 17), **alcēs, -is**, *moose* (VI. 27); also **famēs, -is**, *hunger* (I. 28), which, however, has **famē** in the Ablative Singular (VII. 20).

c. Like **linter** is **imber, imbris**, M., *rainstorm* (III. 29).

16. *a.* The Nominative Singular of Neuter nouns with **-i** Stems ends in **-e, -al**, and **-ar**; the Ablative Singular ends in **-ī**, the Genitive Plural in **-ium**.

b. Examples of neuter nouns with **-i** Stems are **mare** (III. 7) and **animal** (VI. 17):

mare (stem mari-), N., *sea*   animal (stem animāli-), N., *animal*

	SINGULAR	PLURAL	SINGULAR	PLURAL	TERMINATIONS	
					SINGULAR	PLURAL
Nom.	mare	maria	animal	animālia	-e or wanting	-ia
Gen.	maris	marium	animālis	animālium	-ī	-ium
Dat.	marī	maribus	animālī	animālibus	-ī	-ibus
Acc.	mare	maria	animal	animālia	-e or wanting	-ia
Abl.	marī	maribus	animālī	animālibus	-ī	-ibus
Voc.	mare	maria	animal	animālia	-e or wanting	-ia

c. **Bibracte**, N., is declined thus: *Nom.* **Bibracte**, *Gen.* **Bibractis**, *Dat.* **Bibractī**, *Acc.* **Bibracte**, *Abl.* **Bibracte**; no Plural.

d. Like **animal** is **vectīgal, -ālis** (I. 18).

17. *a.* The declension of nouns with Mixed Stems in the Singular conforms to that of Mute Stems, in the Plural to that of **-i** Stems.

b. Examples of nouns with Mixed Stems are **mōns** (I. 1), **pars** (I. 1), **nox** (I. 26) and **urbs** (I. 39):

	mōns (stem **mont-**) M., *height*	**pars** (stem **part-**) F., *part*	**nox** (stem **noct-**) F., *night*	**urbs** (stem **urb-**) F., *city*
		SINGULAR		
Nom.	mōns	pars	nox	urbs
Gen.	montis	partis	noctis	urbis
Dat.	montī	partī	noctī	urbī
Acc.	montem	partem	noctem	urbem
Abl.	monte	parte	nocte	urbe
Voc.	mōns	pars	nox	urbs
		PLURAL		
Nom.	montēs	partēs	noctēs	urbēs
Gen.	montium	partium	noctium	urbium
Dat.	montibus	partibus	noctibus	urbibus
Acc.	montēs, -īs	partēs, -īs	noctēs, -īs	urbēs, -īs
Abl.	montibus	partibus	noctibus	urbibus
Voc.	montēs	partēs	noctēs	urbēs

c. Among Nouns with Mixed Stems used by Caesar are **pōns, pontis**, M., *bridge* (I. 6); **cliēns, clientis**, M., *retainer* (I. 4); **parēns, -entis**, M. and F., *parent* (V. 14); **falx, falcis**, F., *sickle, hook* (III. 14); **fax, facis**, F., *torch* (VII. 24); **glāns, glandis**, F., *acorn, slingshot* (V. 43); **dōs, dōtis**, F., *dowry* (VI. 19); **fraus, fraudis**, F., *deception* (VII. 40); **frōns, frontis**, F., *front* (II. 8); **laus, laudis**, F., *praise* (I. 40); **līs, lītis**, F., *damages* (V. 1); **mors, mortis**, F., *death* (I. 5); **nix, nivis**, F., *snow* (VII. 8); **plēbs, plēbis**, F., *people* (I. 3); **trabs, trabis**, F., *beam* (II. 29); **sors, sortis**, F., *lot* (I. 50); **stirps, stirpis**, F., *stock* (VI. 34).

d. Defective is the noun with the stem **spont-**, which has only a Genitive, **spontis**, and Ablative, **sponte** (I. 9).

18. *a.* The declension of the nouns **vīs** (I. 6), **bōs** (VI. 26), **carō** (V. 14), and **Iuppiter** (VI. 17), is exceptional, not conforming to any of the types which have been given:

	vīs (stems **vi-, vīr-**) F., *force*	**bōs** (stem **bov-**) M. & F., *ox, cow*	**carō** (stem **carn-**) F., *flesh*	**Iuppiter** (stem **iov-**, + **pater** in the Nom.) M., *Jupiter*
		SINGULAR		
Nom.	vīs	bōs	carō	Iuppiter

Gen.	—	*bovis*	*carnis*	*Iovis*
Dat.	—	*bovī*	*carnī*	*Iovī*
Acc.	*vim*	*bovem*	*carnem*	*Iovem*
Abl.	*vī*	*bove*	*carne*	*Iove*
Voc.	*vis*	*bōs*	*carō*	*Iuppiter*

PLURAL

Nom.	*vīrēs*	*bovēs*	*carnēs*
Gen.	*vīrium*	*boum* or *bovum*	*carnium*
Dat.	*vīribus*	*bōbus* or *būbus*	*carnibus*
Acc.	*vīrēs*	*bovēs*	*carnēs*
Abl.	*vīribus*	*bōbus* or *būbus*	*carnibus*
Voc.	*vīrēs*	*bovēs*	*carnēs*

b. **Senex**, M., *old man* (I. 29), stem **seni-** in oblique cases, is declined thus: **senex, senis, senī, senem, sene, senex; senēs, senum, senibus, senēs, senibus, senēs.**

c. **Iter**, N., *journey, route* (I. 3), has a stem **itiner-** in the oblique cases: **iter, itineris, itinerī, iter, itinere iter; itinera, itinerum, itineribus, itinera, itineribus, itinera.**

d. **Femur**, N., *thigh*, in the oblique cases has two stems, **femor-** and **femin-**, thus: *Nom.* **femur**, *Gen.* **femoris** or **feminis** (VII. 73), etc.

e. **Arar**, M., *the Arar* (I. 12, 13, 16), is declined thus: **Arar, Araris, Ararī, Ararim, Ararī, Arar;** similar is **Liger, Ligeris**, M., *the Liger* (III. 9).

f. **Phalanx**, F., *mass formation, mass*, is declined thus: *Nom.* **phalanx**, *Gen.* **phalangis**, *Dat.* **phalangī**, *Acc.* **phalangem** or **phalanga**, *Abl.* **phalange**.

g. **Taurois**, F., *Taurois*, is thus declined: **Taurois**, *Gen.* **Tauroëntis**, *Acc.* **Tauroënta** (C. II. 4).

NAMES OF THE FIRST, SECOND, AND THIRD DECLENSIONS

19. *a.* Of the Second Declension are all Roman First Names (**praenōmina**) used by Caesar, and in reading the text the name should be supplied, in the proper case form, from the abbreviation. The First Names are **Aulus**, *Gen.* **Aulī** (abbreviation A.), **Appius** (Ap.), **Gāius** (abbreviation C, an old form of G.), **Decimus** (D.), **Gnaeus** (Cn.), **Lūcius** (L.), **Mārcus** (M.), **Pūblius** (P.), **Quīntus** (Q.), **Servius** (Ser.), and **Titus** (T.).

b. The Clan Names (**nōmina**), ending in **-ius** (as **Iūlius, Tullius**), are of the Second Declension.

c. The Family Names or Surnames (**cognōmina**) are partly of the First Declension, as **Galba** (**Servius Sulpicius Galba**); of the Second, as **Baculus** (**Pūblius Sextius Baculus**); and of the Third, as **Caesar** (*11c*), the full name being declined thus: *Nom.* **Gāius Iūlius Caesar**, *Gen.* **Gāī Iūlī Caesaris** or **Gāiī Iūliī Caesaris** (*8a*), *Dat.* **Gāiō Iūliō Caesarī**, *Acc.* **Gāium Iūlium Caesarem**, *Abl.* **Gāiō Iūliō Caesare**, *Voc.* **Gāī Iūlī Caesar** (*8c*).

d. The names of Gauls or Germans are generally of the Second Declension, as **Dīviciācus, -ī**, or of the Third, as **Dumnorīx**, *Gen.* **Dumnorīgis**; of the First Declension are **Galba** (II. 4, 13) and **Nasua** (I. 37), as well as the Numidian names **Juba, Saburra** (C.II. 38).

e. The names of Foreign Peoples are ordinarily declined in the Plural only. A few are of the First Declension, as **Belgae, -ārum** (I. 1); the rest are of the Second Declension, as **Helvetiī, -ōrum** (I. 1), or of the Third, as **Allobrogēs, -um** (I. 6).

f. In the Accusative Plural of names of foreign peoples Caesar sometimes has the Greek ending **-as** instead of **-ēs**; as **Allobrogas** (I. 14), **Crētas** (II. 7), **Coriosolitas** (II. 34).

FOURTH DECLENSION

20. *a.* Nouns of the Fourth Declension ending in **-us** are generally Masculine, nouns ending in **-ū** are Neuter; **domus, manus**, and **Īdūs** (Plural) are Feminine.

b. Examples of nouns of the Fourth Declension are **frūctus** (VI. 19) and **cornū** (I. 52):

frūctus (stem **frūctu-**) M., *fruit*   **cornū** (stem **cornu-**), N., *horn*

	SINGULAR	PLURAL	SINGULAR	PLURAL
Nom.	frūctus	frūctūs	cornū	cornua
Gen.	frūctūs	frūctuum	cornūs	cornuum
Dat.	frūctuī	frūctibus	cornū	cornibus
Acc.	frūctum	frūctūs	cornū	cornua
Abl.	frūctū	frūctibus	cornū	cornibus
Voc.	frūctus	frūctūs	cornū	cornua

c. **Domus** (stem **domu-**), F., *house*, has also a stem **domo-** of the Second Declension, from which are formed a Locative Singular, **domī**, *at home* (I. 18, 20, etc.), an Ablative Singular, **domō**, *from home*, (I. 5, 6, etc.), an Accusative Plural, **domōs** (I. 30), and some forms not used by Caesar.

d. Many nouns of the Fourth Declension are defective, being used only in the Ablative Singular, as **iniussū** (I. 19), **iussū** (VII. 3), **nātū** (II. 13).

FIFTH DECLENSION

21. *a.* Nouns of the Fifth Declension end in **-ēs**, and are Feminine except **diēs**, *day*, and **merīdiēs**, *midday* (I. 50), which are Masculine; but **diēs** is usually Feminine when referring to a certain day (as I. 4, 8, 30), or to time in general.

b. Examples of nouns of the Fifth Declension are:

diēs (stem **diē-**), **rēs** (stem **rē-**), M., *day* F., *thing*

	SINGULAR	PLURAL	SINGULAR	PLURAL
Nom.	diēs	diēs	rēs	rēs
Gen.	diēī	diērum	reī	rērum
Dat.	diēī	diēbus	reī	rēbus
Acc.	diem	diēs	rem	rēs
Abl.	diē	diēbus	rē	rēbus
Voc.	diēs	diēs	rēs	rēs

c. In the Genitive and Dative Singular **-ēī** becomes **-eī** when a consonant precedes, as in **reī** (I. 21); so **speī** (VII. 63, C. II. 5).

ADJECTIVES

22. *a.* In Adjectives of the First and Second Declensions the Masculine is declined like **lēgātus** (6a), **puer** (7a), or **ager** (7a), the Feminine like **via** (3), and the Neuter like **bellum** (6a).

b. Declined like **lēgātus**, **via**, **bellum**, are many Adjectives, as **bonus, bona, bonum**, *good*:

	SINGULAR			PLURAL		
	MASCULINE	FEMININE	NEUTER	MASCULINE	FEMININE	NEUTER
Nom.	bonus	bona	bonum	bonī	bonae	bona
Gen.	bonī	bonae	bonī	bonōrum	bonārum	bonōrum
Dat.	bonō	bonae	bonō	bonīs	bonīs	bonīs
Acc.	bonum	bonam	bonum	bonōs	bonās	bona
Abl.	bonō	bonā	bonō	bonīs	bonīs	bonīs
Voc.	bone	bona	bonum	bonī	bonae	bona

c. Distributive adjectives are declined like **bonus** except that in the Genitive Plural they have **-um** instead of **-ōrum**, as **quadrāgēnum** (IV. 17).

d. A few Adjectives are declined like **puer, via, bellum**, as **miser, misera, miserum**, *wretched* (I. 32):

	Singular			Plural		
	Masculine	Feminine	Neuter	Masculine	Feminine	Neuter
Nom.	miser	misera	miserum	miserī	miserae	misera
Gen.	miserī	miserae	miserī	miserōrum	miserārum	miserōrum
Dat.	miserō	miserae	miserō	miserīs	miserīs	miserīs
Acc.	miserum	miseram	miserum	miserōs	miserās	misera
Abl.	miserō	miserā	miserō	miserīs	miserīs	miserīs
Voc.	miser	misera	miserum	miserī	miserae	misera

e. Like **miser** are declined **asper** (V. 45), **līber** (I. 44), and **tener** (II.17).

f. Declined like **ager, via, bellum,** are most adjectives in **-er**, as **aeger, aegra, aegrum,** *sick* (V. 40), **integer** (III. 4), etc.:

	Singular			Plural		
	Masculine	Feminine	Neuter	Masculine	Feminine	Neuter
Nom.	aeger	aegra	aegrum	aegrī	aegrae	aegra
Gen.	aegrī	aegrae	aegrī	aegrōrum	aegrārum	aegrōrum
Dat.	aegrō	aegrae	aegrō	aegrīs	aegrīs	aegrīs
Acc.	aegrum	aegram	aegrum	aegrōs	aegrās	aegra
Abl.	aegrō	aegrā	aegrō	aegrīs	aegrīs	aegrīs
Voc.	aeger	aegra	aegrum	aegrī	aegrae	aegra

23. *a.* Six Adjectives in **-us** (**ūnus**, *one*; **sōlus**, *alone*; **tōtus**, *whole*; **alius**, *other*; **ūllus**, *any*; **nūllus**, *none*) and three in **-er** (**alter**, *the other*; **ūter**, *which (of two)?* and **neuter**, *neither*), have **-īus** (or **-ius**) in the Genitive and **-ī** in the Dative Singular of all genders, and lack the Vocative; the Plural is regular. They are thus declined in the Singular:

	Singular			Plural		
	Masculine	Feminine	Neuter	Masculine	Feminine	Neuter
Nom.	alius	alia	aliud	alter	altera	alterum
Gen.	[alīus	alīus	alīus]	alterius	alterius	alterius
Dat.	aliī	aliī	aliī	alterī	alterī	alterī
Acc.	alium	aliam	aliud	alterum	alteram	alterum
Abl.	aliō	aliā	aliō	alterō	alterā	alterō
Nom.	tōtus	tōta	tōtum	uter	utra	utrum
Gen.	tōtius	tōtīus	tōtīus	utrīus	utrīus	utrīus
Dat.	tōtī	tōtī	tōtī	utrī	utrī	utrī
Acc.	tōtum	tōtam	tōtum	utrum	utram	utrum
Abl.	tōtō	tōtā	tōtō	utrō	utrā	utrō

b. The Genitive Singular of **alter** is generally **alterius**, instead of **alterīus**; and **alterius** is ordinarily used in place of the Genitive **alīus**.

24. Some Adjectives of the Third Declension have three endings in the Nominative Singular, others two, and others only one. Adjectives with three endings are declined like **ācer, ācris, ācre,** *sharp* (C. III. 72):

	Singular			Plural		
	Masculine	Feminine	Neuter	Masculine	Feminine	Neuter
Nom.	ācer	ācris	ācre	ācrēs	ācrēs	ācria
Gen.	ācris	ācris	ācris	ācrium	ācrium	ācrium
Dat.	ācrī	ācrī	ācrī	ācribus	ācribus	ācribus
Acc.	ācrem	ācrem	ācre	ācrēs, -īs	ācrēs, -īs	ācria
Abl.	ācrī	ācrī	ācrī	ācribus	ācribus	ācribus
Voc.	ācer	ācris	ācre	ācrēs	ācrēs	ācria

25. *a.* Adjectives of the Third Declension with two endings are in part formed on **-i** Stems, like nouns, and in the Positive Degree, as **fortis, forte,** *strong* (II. 33); in part they are Comparatives formed on **-s** Stems (*13a*), as **fortior, fortius,** *stronger* (III. 14), **melior, melius,**

better (VI. 12):

	SINGULAR		PLURAL	
	MASCULINE AND FEM.	NEUTER	MASCULINE AND FEM.	NEUTER
Nom.	*fortis*	*forte*	*fortēs*	*fortia*
Gen.	*fortis*	*fortis*	*fortium*	*fortium*
Dat.	*fortī*	*fortī*	*fortibus*	*fortibus*
Acc.	*fortem*	*forte*	*fortēs or -īs*	*fortia*
Abl.	*fortī*	*fortī*	*fortibus*	*fortibus*
Voc.	*fortis*	*forte*	*fortēs*	*fortia*

	SINGULAR		PLURAL	
	MASCULINE AND FEM.	NEUTER	MASCULINE AND FEM.	NEUTER
Nom.	*melior*	*melius*	*meliōrēs*	*meliōra*
Gen.	*meliōris*	*meliōris*	*meliōrum*	*meliōrum*
Dat.	*meliōrī*	*meliōrī*	*meliōribus*	*meliōribus*
Acc.	*meliōrem*	*melius*	*meliōrēs or -īs*	*meliōra*
Abl.	*meliōre*	*meliōre*	*meliōribus*	*meliōribus*
Voc.	*melior*	*melius*	*meliōrēs*	*meliōra*

b. **Plūs**, *more*, is defective, in the Singular having only the neuter forms, *Nom.* **plūs**, *Gen.* **plūris**, *Acc.* **plūs**, *Abl.* **plūre**; the Plural is declined *Nom.* **plūrēs, plūra**, *Gen.* **plūrium**, *Dat.* **plūribus, plūribus**. *Acc.* **plūrēs** or **plūrīs, plūra**, *Abl.* **plūribus, plūribus**.

26. *a.* With Adjectives of the Third Declension having one ending in the Nominative Singular are included also present participles. Examples are **duplex**, *double* (II. 29), **regēns**, *ruling*, and **vetus**, *old* (I. 13):

	SINGULAR		PLURAL	
	MASCULINE AND FEM.	NEUTER	MASCULINE AND FEM.	NEUTER
Nom.	*duplex*	*duplex*	*duplicēs*	*duplicia*
Gen.	*duplicis*	*duplicis*	*duplicium*	*duplicium*
Dat.	*duplicī*	*duplicī*	*duplicibus*	*duplicibus*
Acc.	*duplicem*	*duplex*	*duplicēs or -īs*	*duplicia*
Abl.	*duplicī*	*duplicī*	*duplicibus*	*duplicibus*
Voc.	*duplex*	*duplex*	*duplicēs*	*duplicia*

	SINGULAR		PLURAL	
	MASCULINE AND FEM.	NEUTER	MASCULINE AND FEM.	NEUTER
Nom.	*regēns*	*regēns*	*regentēs*	*regentia*
Gen.	*regentis*	*regentis*	*regentium*	*regentium*
Dat.	*regentī*	*regentī*	*regentibus*	*regentibus*
Acc.	*regentem*	*regēns*	*regentēs or -īs*	*regentia*
Abl.	*regente (participle)*	*regente (participle)*	*regentibus*	*regentibus*
	regentī (adjective)	*regentī (adjective)*		
Voc.	*regēns*	*regēns*	*regentēs*	*regentia*

	SINGULAR		PLURAL	
	MASCULINE AND FEM.	NEUTER	MASCULINE AND FEM.	NEUTER
Nom.	*vetus*	*vetus*	*veterēs*	*vetera*
Gen.	*veteris*	*veteris*	*veterum*	*veterum*
Dat.	*veterī*	*veterī*	*veteribus*	*veteribus*
Acc.	*veterem*	*vetus*	*veterēs*	*vetera*
Abl.	*vetere*	*vetere*	*veteribus*	*veteribus*
Voc.	*vetus*	*vetus*	*veterēs*	*vetera*

b. The Adjective **prīnceps, -cipis** (I. 7) is declined like the Noun (*10b*); the Adjectives **anceps, ancipitis** (I. 26), **particeps, cipis**, (C. III. 60), and **praeceps, -cipitis** (II. 24), also have additional syllables in the oblique cases.

COMPARISON OF ADJECTIVES

27. *a.* Examples of the Regular Comparison of Adjectives, and of participles used as Adjectives, are:

Positive	Comparative	Superlative
altus, -a, -um, high	*altior, altius, higher*	*altissima, -a, -um, very high, highest*
antīquus, -a, -um, ancient	*antīquior, -ius*	*antīquissimus*
fortis, -e, brave	*fortior, fortius*	*fortissimus*
nōbilis, -e, noble	*nōbilior, nobilius*	*nōbilissimus*
ferāx, fertile	*ferācior, feracius*	*ferācissimus*
potēns, able	*potentior, potentius*	*potentissimus*
apertus, open, exposed	*apertior, apertius*	*apertissimus*

b. **Novus,** *new,* lacks the Comparative, but has a Superlative, **novissimus,** *last* (I. 15).

28. *a.* Examples of Adjectives in **-er,** with Comparative in **-ior** and Superlative in **-rimus,** are:

asper, -ra, -rum, rough	*asperior, -ius*	*asperrimus, -a, -um*
celer, -eris, -ere, swift	*celerior, -ius*	*celerrimus*
crēber, -bra, -brum, frequent	*crēbrior, crebrius*	*crēberrimus*
pulcher, -chra, -chrum, beautiful	*pulchrior, -ius*	*pulcherrimus*

b. **Vetus,** *Gen.* **veteris,** *old, Sup.* **viterrimus,** lacks the Comparative.

29. Six Adjectives in **-ilis** have **-limus** in the Superlative: **facilis, difficilis, gracilis, humilis, similis, dissimilis:**

facilis, -e, easy	*facilior, facilius*	*facillimus, -a, -um*
difficilis, -e, difficult	*difficilior, -ius*	*difficillimus*
humilis, -e, low	*humilior, -ius*	*humillimus*
similis, -e, like	*similior, -ius*	*simillimus*

30. Some Adjectives form the Comparative and the Superlative by prefixing **magis,** *more,* and **maximē,** *most,* as **magis dērēctum,** *straighter* (VI. 26), and **maximē acceptus,** *very acceptable* (I. 3), **maximē frūmentāriīs,** *exceedingly fertile* (I. 10), **maximē ferī,** *most barbarous* (II. 4).

31. The Adjectives **dīves** or **dīs,** *rich* (I. 2), **honōrificus,** *complimentary* (I. 43), and **magnificus,** *splendid* (VI. 19) are thus compared:

dīves or dīs	*dīvitior or dītior*	*dīvitissimus or dītissimus*
honōrificus	*honōrificentior*	*honōrificentissimus*
magnificus	*magnificentior*	*magnificentissimus*

32. Several common Adjectives are irregular in Comparison:

bonus, -a, -um, good	*melior, melius, better*	*optimus, -a, -um, best*
malus, bad	*peior, peius, worse*	*pessimus, worst*
parvus, small	*minor, minus, less*	*minimus, least*
magnus, great	*maior, maius, greater*	*maximus, greatest*
multus, much	*plūs, gen. plūris (25b)*	*plūrimus, most*

33. Several Adjectives lack the Positive, though the Stem appears in Prepositions and Adverbs; others have a Positive only in a limited or special use. Examples are:

(citrā, on this side)	*citerior, citerius, on this side, hither*	*citimus, -a, -um, nearest*
(ultrā, beyond)	*ulterior, ulterius, farther*	*ultimus, farthest*
(intrā, within)	*interior, interius, inner*	*intimus, inmost*
(prope, near)	*propior, propius, nearer*	*proximus, nearest*
(dē, down)	*dēterior, dēterius, inferior*	*dēterrimus, worst*
(prae, prō, before)	*prior, prius, former*	*prīmus, first*
posterus, following	*posterior, later*	*postrēmus, latest, last*

(citrā, on this side)	citerior, citerius, on this side, hither	citimus, -a, -um, nearest
īnferus, below	inferior, inferius, lower	īnfimus, lowest
		īmus, lowest
superus, above	superior, superius, higher	suprēmus, last
exterus, foreign (C. III. 43)	exterior, outer	summus, highest
		extrēmus, outermost

ADVERBS

34. *a.* Adverbs regularly formed from Adjectives have the Positive in -ē (-ĕ in **facile**) or -ter, the Comparative in -ius, and the Superlative in -ē:

Positive	Comparative	Superlative
amplē (amplus), fully	amplius, more fully	amplissimē, most fully
aegrē (aeger), ill	aegrius	aegerrimē
mātūrē (mātūrus), early	mātūrius	mātūrrimē
facile (facilis), easily	facilius	facillimē
fortiter (fortis), bravely	fortius	fortissimē
audācter (audāx), boldly	audācius	audācissimē
ācriter (ācer), fiercely	ācrius	ācerrimē

b. Some Adverbs formed from Adjectives end in -ō (-ŏ in **cito**), as **continuō, subitō, prīmō**; such, with Comparative and Superlative, are:

crēbrō (crēber), frequently	crēbrius	crēberrimē
tūtō (tūtus), safely	tūtius	tūtissimē
cito (citus), quickly	citius	citissimē

c. A few Adverbs formed from Adjectives end in -um (Acc. Singular Neuter), as **multum** (**multus**), *much* (III. 9); in -**tim**, as **prīvātim** (**prīvātus**), *privately* (I. 17); and in -**tus**, as **antīquitus** (**antīquus**), *in ancient times* (II. 4).

35. The following Adverbs have irregularities in Formation or in Comparison:

bene, well	melius, better	optimē, best
male, ill	peius, worse	pessimē, worst
magnopere, greatly	magis, more	maximē, most
multum, much	plūs, more	plūrimum, most
nōn multum, little		
parum, little	minus, less	minimē, least
nūper, recently		nūperrimē, most recently, very recently
diū, long	diūtius, longer	diūtissimē, longest
saepe, often	saepius, oftener	saepissimē, most often, oftenest
prope, near	propius, nearer	proximē, nearest, next
	potius, rather	potissimum, especially, above all
satis, enough	satius, better	
	prius, before	prīmum, first

NUMERALS

36. The Roman Notation, and Cardinal, Ordinal, and Distributive Adjectives are presented in the following list:

Roman Notation	Cardinals	Ordinals	Distributives
I.	ūnus, ūna, ūnum	prīmus, first	singulī, one by one
II.	duo, duae, duo	secundus, second	bīnī, two each
III.	trēs, tria, three	tertius, third	ternī, trīnī, three by three, three each

IIII., or IV.	quattuor, *four*	quārtus, *fourth*	quaternī, *four by four, four each*
V.	quīnque, *five*	quintus, *fifth*	quini, *five by five, five each*
VI.	sex, *six*	sextus, *sixth*	sēnī, *six by six, six each*
VII.	septem, *seven*	septimus, *seventh*	septēnī, *by sevens, seven each*
VIII.	octō, *eight*	octāvus, *eighth*	octōnī, *by eights, eight apiece*
IX.	novem, *nine*	nōnus, *ninth*	novēnī, *nine each*
X.	decem, *ten*	decimus, *tenth*	dēnī, *ten each*
XI.	ūndecim, *eleven*	ūndecimus, *eleventh*	ūndēnī, *eleven each*
XII.	duodecim, *twelve*	duodecimus, *twelfth*	duodēnī, *twelve each*
XIII.	tredecim, *thirteen*	tertius decimus, *thirteenth*	ternī dēnī, *thirteen each*
XIIII., or XIV.	quattuordecim, *fourteen*	quārtus decimus, *fourteenth*	quaternī dēnī, *fourteen each*
XV.	quīndecim, *fifteen*	quīntus decimus, *fifteenth*	quīnī dēnī, *fifteen each*
XVI.	sēdecim, *sixteen*	sextus decimus, *sixteenth*	sēnī dēnī, *sixteen each*
XVII.	septendecim, *seventeen*	septimus decimus, *seventeenth*	septēnī dēnī, *seventeen each*
XVIII.	duodēvīgintī, *eighteen*	duodēvīcēsimus, *eighteenth*	duodēvīcēnī, *eighteen each*
XVIIII., or XIX.	ūndēvīgintī, *nineteen.*	ūndēvīcēsimus, *nineteenth*	ūndēvīcēnī, *nineteen each*
XX.	vīgintī, *twenty*	vīcēsimus, *twentieth*	vīcēnī, *twenty each*
XXI.	vīgintī ūnus, ūnus et vīgintī, *twenty-one*	vīcēsimus prīmus, ūnus et vīcēsimus, *twenty-first*	vīcēnī singulī, singulī et vīcēnī, *twenty-one each*
XXII.	vīgintī duo, duo et vīgintī, *twenty-two*	vīcēsimus secundus, alter et vīcēsimus, *twenty-second*	vīcēnī bīnī, bīnī et vīcēnī, *twenty-two each*
XXX.	trīgintā, *thirty*	trīcēsimus, *thirtieth*	trīcēnī, *thirty each*
XXXX. XL.	quadrāgintā, *forty*	quadrāgēsimus, *fortieth*	quadrāgēnī, *forty each*
L.	quīnquāgintā, *fifty*	quīnquāgēsimus, *fiftieth*	quīnquāgēnī, *fifty each*
LX.	sexāgintā, *sixty*	sexāgēsimus, *sixtieth*	sexāgēnī, *sixty each*
LXX.	septuāgintā, *seventy*	septuāgēsimus, *seventieth*	septuāgēnī, *seventy each*
LXXX.	octōgintā, *eighty*	octōgēsimus, *eightieth*	octōgēnī, *eighty each*
LXXXX. XC.	nōnāgintā, *ninety*	nōnāgēsimus, *ninetieth*	nōnāgēnī, *ninety each*
C.	centum, *one hundred*	centēsimus, *one hundredth*	centēnī, *one hundred each*
CI.	centum ūnus, centum et ūnus, *one hundred and one*	centēsimus prīmus, centēsimus et prīmus, *hundred and first*	centēnī singulī, *one hundred and one each*
CC.	ducentī, -ae, -a, *two hundred*	ducentēsimus, *two hundredth*	ducēnī, *two hundred each*
CCC.	trecentī, -ae, -a, *three hundred*	trecentēsimus, *three hundredth*	trecēnī, *three hundred each*
CCCC.	quadringentī, *four hundred*	quadringentēsimus, *four hundredth*	quadringēnī, *four hundred each*
D.	quīngentī, *five hundred*	quīngentēsimus, *five hundredth*	quīngēnī, *five hundred each*
DC.	sescentī, *six hundred*	sescentēsimus, *six hundredth*	sescēnī, *six hundred each*
DCC.	septingentī, *seven hundred*	septingentēsimus, *seven hundredth*	septingēnī, *seven hundred each*
DCCC.	octingentī, *eight hundred*	octingentēsimus, *eight hundredth*	octingēnī, *eight hundred each*
DCCCC.	nōngentī, *nine hundred*	nōngentēsimus, *nine hundredth*	nōngēnī, *nine hundred each*
M.	mīlle, *thousand*	mīllēsimus, *thousandth*	singula mīlia, *a thousand each*
MM.	duo mīlia, *two thousand*	bis mīllēsimus, *a two thousandth*	bīna mīlia, *two thousand each*

37. *a.* **Ūnus** is declined like **tōtus** (23*a*).

b. **Duo** (I. 48) and **trēs** (I. 1) are declined thus:

Nom.	duo	duae	duo	trēs	tria
Gen.	duōrum	duārum	duōrum	trium	trium
Dat.	duōbus	duābus	duōbus	tribus	tribus
Acc.	duōs, duo	duās	duo	trēs, trīs	tria
Abl.	duōbus	duābus	duōbus	tribus	tribus

c. Like **duo** is declined **ambō** (V. 44), excepting **-ō** instead of **-o**.

d. **Ducentī, -ae, -a** (I. 43) and the other words for hundreds to **nōngentī, -ae, -a** (C. III. 71) are declined like the Plural of **bonus**, but the Genitive Plural generally ends in **-um**.

e. When Plural Nouns, which generally have a Singular Meaning, are used with a Plural Meaning, a Numeral in agreement must be Distributive; with such Nouns **trīnī** is always used instead of **ternī**. Thus, **trīnīs catēnīs**, *with three chains* (I. 53).

38. *a.* **Mīlle** (I. 22) in the Singular is used as an Indeclinable Adjective. In the Plural it is used as a Substantive and thus declined: *Nom.* **mīlia**, *Gen.* **mīlium**, *Dat.* **mīlibus**, *Acc.* **mīlia**, *Abl.* **mīlibus**

b. The Roman numerical symbols are frequently used in place of Ordinal as well as Cardinal Adjectives. In reading Latin the proper form of the Adjective should be supplied; thus **ducenta quadrāgintā** should be read for **CCXL** in **mīlia passuum CCXL** (I. 2); **decimā** for **X** in **legiōne X** (C. III. 91).

PRONOUNS

39. *a.* The Personal Pronouns of the First and the Second Person are declined as follows:

	SINGULAR	PLURAL	SINGULAR	PLURAL
Nom.	ego, I	nōs, we	tū, thou	vōs, you
Gen.	meī	nostrum, nostrī	tuī	vestrum, vestrī
Dat.	mihi	nōbīs	tibi	vōbīs
Acc.	mē	nōs	tē	vōs
Voc.	—	—	tū	vōs
Abl.	mē	nōbīs	tē	vōbīs

b. The place of a Personal Pronoun of the Third Person is taken by the demonstratives (*160a* and *b*).

40. *a.* In the oblique cases the Pronouns of the First and Second Person may be used in a Reflexive sense, as **vōs recipite**, lit. *take yourselves back, retreat* (VII. 50); **meī**, may mean *of myself*, **tibi**, *to* or *for thyself, yourself*, etc.

b. The Reflexive Pronoun of the Third Person has no separate forms for the three genders, and is declined in Singular and Plural alike, as follows:

Gen.   **suī**, *of himself, of herself, of itself, of themselves*

Dat.   **sibi**, *to* or *for himself, herself, itself, themselves*

Acc.   **sē** or **sēsē**, *himself, herself, itself, themselves*

Abl.   **sē** or **sēsē**, *with*, or *by, himself, herself, itself, themselves*

41. The Possessive Pronouns are declined like Adjectives. They are: **meus, mea, meum**, *my*; **noster, nostra, nostrum**, *our*; **tuus, tua, tuum**, *thy*; **vester, vestra, vestrum**, *your*; and **suus, sua, suum**, *his, her, its, their*. **Suus** is used only in a Reflexive sense.

42. *a.* The Demonstrative Pronouns are **hīc**, *this, such*; **iste**, *that of yours, that*: **ille**, *that, such*; **is**, *that, he, such*, and **īdem**, *the same*.

b. **Hīc,** *this, such,* is declined thus:

	SINGULAR			PLURAL		
	MASCULINE	FEMININE	NEUTER	MASCULINE	FEMININE	NEUTER
Nom.	hīc	haec	hōc	hī	hae	haec
Gen.	huius	huius	huius	hōrum	hārum	hōrum
Dat.	huic	huic	huic	hīs	hīs	hīs
Acc.	hunc	hanc	hōc	hōs	hās	haec
Abl.	hōc	hāc	hōc	hīs	hīs	hīs

43. *a*. The Demonstrative Pronoun ille, *that, such,* is declined as follows:

	SINGULAR			PLURAL		
	MASCULINE	FEMININE	NEUTER	MASCULINE	FEMININE	NEUTER
Nom.	ille	illa	illud	illī	illae	illa
Gen.	illīus	illius	illīus	illōrum	illārum	illōrum
Dat.	illī	illī	illī	illīs	illīs	illīs
Acc.	illum	illam	illud	illōs	illās	illa
Abl.	illō	illā	illō	illīs	illīs	illīs

b. The Demonstrative Pronoun **iste, ista, istud,** *that of yours, that,* is declined like **ille**.

44. The Demonstrative Pronoun **is**, *that, he, such,* is thus declined:

	SINGULAR			PLURAL		
	MASCULINE	FEMININE	NEUTER	MASCULINE	FEMININE	NEUTER
Nom.	is	ea	id	eī, iī	eae	ea
Gen.	eius	eius	eius	eōrum	eārum	eōrum
Dat.	eī	eī	eī	eīs, iīs	eīs, iīs	eīs, iīs
Acc.	eum	eam	id	eōs	eās	ea
Abl.	eō	eā	eō	eīs, iīs	eīs, iīs	eīs, iīs

45. The Demonstrative Pronoun **īdem,** *the same,* is declined as follows:

	SINGULAR			PLURAL		
	MASCULINE	FEMININE	NEUTER	MASCULINE	FEMININE	NEUTER
Nom.	īdem	eadem	idem	eīdem, iīdem, or īdem	eaedem	eadem
Gen.	eiusdem	eiusdem	eiusdem	eōrundem	eārundem	eōrundem
Dat.	eīdem	eīdem	eīdem	eīsdem, iīsdem, or īsdem	eīsdem, iīsdem, or īsdem	eīsdem, iīsdem, or īsdem
Acc.	eundem	eandem	idem	eōsdem	eāsdem	eadem
Abl.	eōdem	eādem	eōdem	eīsdem, iīsdem, or īsdem	eīsdem, iīsdem, or īsdem	eīsdem, iīsdem, or īsdem

46. The Intensive Pronoun **ipse,** *self,* is thus declined:

	SINGULAR			PLURAL		
	MASCULINE	FEMININE	NEUTER	MASCULINE	FEMININE	NEUTER
Nom.	ipse	ipsa	ipsum	ipsī	ipsae	ipsa
Gen.	ipsīus	ipsīus	ipsīus	ipsōrum	ipsārum	ipsōrum
Dat.	ipsī	ipsī	ipsī	ipsīs	ipsīs	ipsīs
Acc.	ipsum	ipsam	ipsum	ipsōs	ipsās	ipsa
Abl.	ipsō	ipsā	ipsō	ipsīs	ipsīs	ipsīs

47. The Relative Pronoun **quī,** *who, which,* is declined as follows:

	SINGULAR			PLURAL		
	MASCULINE	FEMININE	NEUTER	MASCULINE	FEMININE	NEUTER
Nom.	quī	quae	quod	quī	quae	quae
Gen.	cuius	cuius	cuius	quōrum	quārum	quōrum
Dat.	cui	cui	cui	quibus	quibus	quibus
Acc.	quem	quam	quod	quōs	quās	quae
Abl.	quō	quā	quō	quibus	quibus	quibus

48. *a.* The Substantive Interrogative Pronoun is **quis, quid,** *who? what?* It is declined as follows:

	SINGULAR		PLURAL		
	MASC. & FEM.	NEUTER	MASCULINE	FEMININE	NEUTER
Nom.	quis	quid	quī	quae	quae
Gen.	cuius	cuius	quōrum	quārum	quōrum
Dat.	cui	cui	quibus	quibus	quibus
Acc.	quem	quid	quōs	quās	quae
Abl.	quō	quō	quibus	quibus	quibus

b. The Adjective Interrogative Pronoun is **quī, quae, quod,** *what?* as **quī numerus,** *what number?* (I. 29). It is declined like the Relative Pronoun (47).

c. Interrogative **quis** and **quī** may be strengthened by **-nam,** as **quibusnam manibus,** *by what hands, pray?* (II. 30).

49. *a.* The Indefinite Pronouns follow the Declension of the Relative and Interrogative Pronouns, but only the Pronominal Part of the Compounds is declined. The following Indefinite Pronouns are used by Caesar, in both Substantive and Adjective forms:

Substantive Forms				*Adjective Forms*		
Masc. And Fem.		*Neut.*		*Masc.*	*Fem.*	*Neut.*
quis or quī (Masc.) quid,		any one, anything		quī or quis	quae or qua	quod, any

Nom. and *Acc.* Pl. Neut., quae *or* quā

aliquis aliquī (V. 26)	aliquid	some one, something	aliquī	aliqua	aliquod	any
quispiam	quidpiam	some one, something	quispiam	quaepiam	quodpiam	some
quisquam	quicquam	anyone, any thing at all	quisquam		quicquam	any (rare)

(Plural lacking.) — *(Plural lacking.)*

quisque	quidque		each one, each thing	quisque	quaeque quodque	each
quīvīs Acc. quemvīs	quaevīs quamvīs	quidvīs quidvīs	anyone, any thing you please	quīvīs Acc. quemvīs, quamvīs, quodvīs,	quaevīs quodvīs,	any you please
quīdam Acc. quendam	quaedam quandam	quiddam quiddam	a certain person, or thing	quīdam Acc. quendam quandam quodam	quaedam quoddam	a certain

b. The Indefinite Pronoun **quis, quī,** is used by Caesar only after **sī, nisī, seu, nē, neu,** and **ubi.**

50. *a.* The Indefinite Relative **quīcumque, quaecumque, quodcumque,** *whoever, whatever,* the first part **quī-** being declined like the relative **quī,** is used both as an Adjective and as a Substantive; as **quaecumque bella,** *whatever wars* (I. 44), **quīcumque bellum īnferant,** *whoever,* or *no matter who, should wage war* (IV. 7).

b. The parts of the Indefinite Relative **quisquis, quidquid** or **quicquid,** *whoever, whatever,* are both declined like **quis** (48), but only **quisquis, quicquid** (II. 17), and **quōquō** are in common use.

51. Caesar uses two compounds of **uter** (23a) with the force of Indefinite Pronouns, **uterque, utraque, utrumque (utrīusque,** etc.), *each of two,* Plural *both, the two;* and **alteruter, alterutra, alterutrum,** *one or the other,* as **alterutrō exercitū,** *the one or the other army* (C. III. 90).

52. The verb **sum** is inflected as follows:

Principal parts:

Pres. Indicative	Pres. Infinitive	Perf. Indicative	Fut. Part. (Perf. Part. lacking)
sum	*esse*	*fuī*	*futūrus*

VERBS[1]

INDICATIVE MOOD		SUBJUNCTIVE	
Present Tense		Present Tense	
Singular	Plural	Singular	Plural
sum, I am	*sumus, we are*	*sim*	*sīmus*
es, thou art	*estis, you are*	*sīs*	*sītis*
est, he (she, it) is	*sunt, they are*	*sit*	*sint*

IMPERFECT

eram, I was	*erāmus, we were*	*essem*	*essēmus*
erās, thou wast	*erātis, you were*	*essēs*	*essētis*
erat, he was	*erant, they were*	*esset*	*essent*

FUTURE

erō, I shall be	*erimus, we shall be*
eris, thou will be	*eritis, you will be*
erit, he will be	*erunt, they will be*

PERFECT

fuī, I have been, I was	*fuimus, we have been, we were*	*fuerim*	*fuerīmus*
fuistī, thou hast been, you were	*fuistis, you have been, you were*	*fuerīs*	*fuerītis*
fuit, he has been, he was	*fuērunt, fuēre, they have been, they were*	*fuerit*	*fuerint*

PLUPERFECT

fueram, I had been	*fuerāmus, we had been*	*fuissem*	*fuissēmus*
fuerās, thou hadst, you had been	*fuerātis, you had been*	*fuissēs*	*fuissētis*
fuerat, he had been	*fuerant, they had been*	*fuisset*	*fuissent*

FUTURE PERFECT

fuerō, I shall have been	*fuerimus, we shall have been*
fueris, thou wilt have been	*fueritis, you will have been*
fuerit, he will have been	*fuerint, they will have been*

IMPERATIVE			INFINITIVE	
Pres.	*es, be thou*	*este, be ye*	Pres.	*esse, to be*
Fut.	*estō, thou shalt be*	*estōte, ye shall be*	Perf.	*fuisse, to have been*
	estō, he shall be	*suntō, they shall be*	Fut.	*futūrus esse*, or *fore, to be about to be*

PARTICIPLE

Fut.　*futūrus, about to be*

FIRST CONJUGATION

53. Verbs of the First Conjugation are inflected like **amō**, *I love.*

Principal Parts:

PRES. INDICATIVE	PRES. INFINITIVE	PERF. INDICATIVE	PERF. PASS. PARTICIPLE
Active. amō	amāre	amāvī	amātus
PRES. INDICATIVE	PRES. INFINITIVE	PERF. INDICATIVE	
Passive. amor	amārī	amātus sum	

ACTIVE VOICE	PASSIVE VOICE
INDICATIVE MOOD	INDICATIVE MOOD
Present Tense	Present Tense

[1] Since the Principal Parts of all the Verbs in the Latin Text of this book are given in the Vocabulary, it has not been thought necessary to extend this outline by presenting either a List of Verbs or a discussion of the Stems.

SINGULAR	PLURAL	SINGULAR	PLURAL
		I am loved, etc.	
amō, I love	*amāmus, we love*	*amor*	*amāmur*
amās, you love	*amātis, you love*	*amāris or -re*	*amāminī*
amat, he loves	*amant, they love*	*amātur*	*amantur*

IMPERFECT		IMPERFECT	
		I was loved, etc.	
amābam, I was loving	*amābāmus, we were loving*	*amābar*	*amābāmur*
amābās, you were loving	*amābātis, you were loving*	*amābāris, or -re*	*amābāminī*
amābat, he was loving	*amābant, they were loving*	*amābātur*	*amābantur*

FUTURE		FUTURE	
amābō, I shall love	*amābimus, we shall love*	*amābor*	*amābimur*
amābis, thou wilt, thou will love	*amābitis, you will love*	*amāberis, or -re*	*amābiminī*
amābit, he will love	*amābunt, they will love*	*amābitur*	*amābuntur*

PERFECT		PERFECT	
		I have been loved, I was loved, etc.	
amāvī, I have loved, I loved	*amāvimus, we have loved, we loved*	*amātus (-a, -um) sum*	*amātī (-ae, -a) sumus*
amāvistī, you have loved, you loved	*amāvistis, you have loved, you loved*	*amātus es*	*amātī estis*
amāvit, he has loved, he loved	*amāvērunt, -ēre, they have loved, they loved*	*amātus est*	*amātī sunt*

ACTIVE VOICE   PASSIVE VOICE
INDICATIVE MOOD

PLUPERFECT		PLUPERFECT		
		I had been loved, etc.		
amāveram, I had loved	*amāverāmus, we had loved*	*amātus eram*[1]	*amātī erāmus*	
amāverās, you had loved	*amāverātis, you had loved*	*amātus eras*	*amātī erātis*	
amāverat, he had loved	*amāverant, they had loved*	*amātus erat*	*amātī erant*	

FUTURE PERFECT
I shall have been loved, etc.

amāverō, I shall have loved	*amāverimus, we shall have loved*	*amātus erō*[1]	*amātī erimus*
amāveris, you will have loved	*amāveritis, you will have loved*	*amātus eris*	*amātī eritis*
amāverit, he will have loved	*amāverint, they will have loved*	*amātus erit*	*amātī erunt*

SUBJUNCTIVE

PRESENT   PRESENT
I may love, let us love, etc. *I may be loved,* etc.

SINGULAR	PLURAL		
amem amēmus	*amer*	*amēmur*	
amēs amētis	*amēris, or -re*	*amēminī*	
amet ament	*amētur*	*amentur*	

IMPERFECT

I might love   *I might be loved*

amārem amārēmus	*amārer*	*amārēmur*
amārēs amārētis	*amārēris, or -re*	*amārēminī*
amāret amārent	*amārētur*	*amārentur*

---

[1] In the Perfect Passive **fuī, fuistī, fuit,** *etc.*, are sometimes used for **sum, es, est,** *etc.*, and **fueram, fuerās, fuerō,** *etc.,* for **eram, erō,** *etc.*

PERFECT

I may have loved		I may have been loved	
amāverim	amāverīmus	amātus sim[1]	amatī sīmus
amāverīs	amāverītis	amātus sīs	amātī sītis
amāverit	amāverint	amātus sit	amatī sint

PLUPERFECT

I might have loved		I might have been loved	
amāvissem	amāvissēmus	amātus essem[1]	amātī essēmus
amāvissēs	amāvissētis	amātus essēs	amātī essētis
amāvisset	amāvissent	amātī esset	amātī essent

IMPERATIVE

ACTIVE VOICE

Pres.   amā, love thou   amāte, love ye
Fut.   amātō, thou shalt love   amātōte, ye shall love
     amātō, he shall love   amantō, they shall love

PASSIVE VOICE

Pres.   amāre, be thou loved
Fut.   amātor, thou shalt be loved
     amātor, he shall be loved
Pres.   amāminī, be ye loved
Fut.   amantor, they shall be loved

INFINITIVE

Pres.   amāre, to love   Pres.   amārī, to be loved

Perf.   amāvisse, to have loved   Perf.   amātus esse, to have been loved

Fut.   amātūrus esse, to be about to love   Fut.   amātum īrī, to be about to be loved

PARTICIPLE

Pres.   amāns, loving   Perfect.   amātus, loved, having been loved
     (Gen. amantis)
Fut.   amātūrus, about to love   Gerundive.   amandus, to be loved, worthy to be loved

GERUND   **SUPINE**

Gen.   amandī, of loving
Dat.   amandō, for loving
Acc.   amandum, loving   Acc.   amātum, to love
Abl.   amandō, by loving   Abl.   amātū, to love, to be loved

SECOND CONJUGATION

54. Verbs of the Second Conjugation are conjugated like **moneō,** *I advise.*
PRINCIPAL PARTS:

PRES. INDICATIVE	PRES. INFINITIVE	PERF. INDICATIVE	PERF. PASS. PARTICIPLE
Active. moneō	monēre	monuī	monitus

PERF. INDICATIVE	PRES. INFINITIVE	PERF. INDICATIVE	
Passive. moneor	monērī	monitus sum	

ACTIVE VOICE   PASSIVE VOICE

INDICATIVE MOOD

PRESENT TENSE   PRESENT TENSE

singular	plural	singular	plural
moneō	monēmus	moneor	monēmur

---

[1] Here **fuerim, fuerīs, fuissem,** *etc.*, are sometimes used for **sim, essem,** *etc.*

mon*ēs*	mon*ētis*	mon*ēris* or *-re*	mon*ēminī*
monet	monent	mon*ētur*	monentur

ACTIVE VOICE   PASSIVE VOICE

INDICATIVE MOOD

IMPERFECT
I was advising, or I advised, etc.

IMPERFECT
I was advised, etc.

mon*ēbam*	mon*ēbāmus*	mon*ēbar*	mon*ēbāmur*
mon*ēbās*	mon*ēbātis*	mon*ēbāris, or -re*	mon*ēbāminī*
mon*ēbat*	mon*ēbant*	mon*ēbātur*	mon*ēbantur*

FUTURE

I shall advise   *I shall be advised*

mon*ēbō*	mon*ēbimus*	mon*ēbor*	mon*ēbimur*
mon*ēbis*	mon*ēbitis*	mon*ēberis, or -re*	mon*ēbiminī*
mon*ēbit*	mon*ēbunt*	mon*ēbitur*	mon*ēbuntur*

PERFECT

I have advised, or I advised   *I have been advised, I was advised*

monu*ī*	monu*imus*	monitus **sum**	monitī **sumus**
monu*istī*	monu*istis*	monitus **es**	monitī **estis**
monu*it*	monu*ērunt, or -ēre*	monitus **est**	monitī **sunt**

PLUPERFECT

I had advised   *I had been advised*

monu*eram*	monu*erāmus*	monitus **eram**	monitī **erāmus**
monu*erās*	monu*erātis*	monitus **erās**	monitī **erātis**
monu*erat*	monu*erant*	monitus **erat**	monitī **erant**

FUTURE PERFECT

I shall have advised   *I shall have been advised*

monu*erō*	monu*erimus*	monitus **erō**	monitī **erimus**
monu*eris*	monu*eritis*	monitus **eris**	monitī **eritis**
monu*erit*	monu*erint*	monitus **erit**	monitī **erunt**

SUBJUNCTIVE

PRESENT TENSE

I might advise, you would advise   *I may be advised, etc.*

mone*am*	mone*āmus*	mone*ar*	mone*āmur*
mone*ās*	mone*ātis*	mone*āris, or -re*	mone*āminī*
mone*at*	mone*ant*	mone*ātur*	mone*antur*

IMPERFECT

I may have advised, etc.   *I might be advised*

mon*ērem*	mon*ērēmus*	mon*ērer*	mon*ērēmur*
mon*ērēs*	mon*ērētis*	mon*ēreris, or -re*	mon*ērēminī*
mon*ēret*	mon*ērent*	mon*ērētur*	mon*ērentur*

ACTIVE VOICE   PASSIVE VOICE

SUBJUNCTIVE

PREFECT

I may have advised, etc.   *I may have been advised, etc.*

monu*erim*	monu*erīmus*	monitus **sim**	monitī **sīmus**
monu*erīs*	monu*erītis*	monitus **sīs**	monitī **sītis**
monu*erit*	monu*erint*	monitus **sit**	monitī **sint**

PLUPERFECT

I might have advised, you would   *I might have been advised have advised, etc.*

monuissem	monuissēmus	monitus essem	monitī essēmus
monuissēs	monuissētis	monitus essēs	monitī essētis
monuisset	monuissent	monitus esset	monitī essent

IMPERATIVE

Pres.	monē, advise thou	monēte, advise ye	Pres. monēre, be thou advised	monēminī, be ye advised
Fut.	monētō, thou shalt advise	monētōte, ye shall advise	Fut. monētor, thou shalt be advised	
	monētō, he shall advise	monentō, they shall advise	monētor, he shall be advised	monentor, they shall be advised

INFINITIVE	PARTICIPLE	INFINITIVE	PARTICIPLE
Pres. monēre, to advise	Pres. monēns, advising	Pres. monērī, to be advised	Perf. monitus, advised, having been advised
Perf. monuisse, to have advised	Gen. (monentis)	Perf. monitus esse, to have been advised	Gerundive monendus, to be advised, worthy to be advised
Fut. monitūrus esse, to be about to advise	Fut. monitūrus, about to advise	Fut. monitum īrī, to be about to be advised	

GERUND   SUPINE

Gen.	monendī, of advising		
Dat.	monendō, for advising		
Acc.	monendum, advising	Acc.	monitum, to advise
Abl.	monendō, by advising	Abl.	monitū, to advise, to be advised

THIRD CONJUGATION

55. Verbs of the Third Conjugation are inflected like **regō**, *I rule.*

PRINCIPAL PARTS:

	PRES. INDICATIVE	PRES. INFINITIVE	PERF. INDICATIVE	PERF. PASS. PARTIC.
Active.	reg**ō**	reg**ere**	rēx**ī**	rēctus
	PRES. INDICATIVE	PRES. INFINITIVE	PERF. INDICATIVE	
Passive.	reg**or**	reg**ī**	rēctus **sum**	

ACTIVE VOICE   PASSIVE VOICE
INDICATIVE MOOD
PRESENT TENSE   PRESENT TENSE
I rule, etc.   *I am ruled, etc.*

SINGULAR	PLURAL	SINGULAR	PLURAL
regō	regimus	regor	regimur
regis	regitis	regeris or -re	regiminī
regit	regunt	regitur	reguntur

IMPERFECT   IMPERFECT
I was ruling, or I ruled   *I was ruled*

regēbam	regēbāmus	regēbar	regēbāmur
regēbās	regēbātis	regēbāris, or -re	regēbāminī
regēbat	regēbant	regēbātur	regēbantur

FUTURE   FUTURE
I shall rule   *I shall be ruled*

regam	regēmus	regar	regēmur
regēs	regētis	regēris, or -re	regēminī
reget	regent	regētur	regentur

PERFECT PERFECT
I have ruled, or *I ruled*   *I have been ruled*, or *I was ruled*

rēxī	rēximus	rēctus sum	rēctī sumus
rēxistī	rēxistis	rēctus es	rēctī estis
rēxit	rēxērunt, *or -ēre*	rēctus est	rēctī sunt

PLUPERFECT PLUPERFECT
I had ruled   *I had been ruled*

rēxeram	rēxerāmus	rēctus eram	rēctī erāmus
rēxerās	rēxerātis	rēctus erās	rēctī erātis
rēxerat	rēxerant	rēctus erat	rēctī erant

FUTURE PERFECT FUTURE PERFECT
I shall have ruled   *I shall have been ruled*

rēxerō	rēxerimus	rēctus erō	rēctī erimus
rēxeris	rēxeritis	rēctus eris	rēctī eritis
rēxerit	rēxerint	rēctus erit	rēctī erunt

ACTIVE VOICE PASSIVE VOICE
SUBJUNCTIVE

PRESENT TENSE PRESENT TENSE
I may rule, let us rule, etc.   *I may be ruled, etc.*

Singular	Plural	Singular	Plural
regam	regāmus	regar	regāmur
regās	regātis	regāris, *or -re*	regāminī
regat	regant	regātur	regantur

IMPERFECT IMPERFECT
I might rule, you would rule, etc.   *I might be ruled, you would be ruled*

regerem	regerēmus	regerer	regerēmur
regerēs	regerētis	regerēris, *or -re*	regerēminī
regeret	regerent	regerētur	regerentur

PERFECT PERFECT
I may have ruled   *I may have been ruled*

rēxerim	rēxerīmus	rēctus sim	rēctī sīmus
rēxerīs	rēxerītis	rēctus sīs	rēctī sītis
rēxerit	rēxerint	rēctus sit	rēctī sint

PLUPERFECT PLUPERFECT
I might have ruled, you would have ruled   *I might have been ruled, you would have been ruled*

rēxissem	rēxissēmus	rēctus essem	rēctī essēmus
rēxissēs	rēxissētis	rēctus essēs	rēctī essētis
rēxisset	rēxissent	rēctus esset	rēctī essent

IMPERATIVE

Pres.	rege, *rule thou*	regite, *rule ye*	regere, *be thou ruled*	regiminī, *be ye ruled*
Fut.	regitō, *thou shalt rule*	regitōte, *ye shall rule*	regitor, *thou shalt be ruled*	
	regitō, *he shall rule*	reguntō, *they shall rule*	regitor, *he shall be ruled*	reguntor, *they shall be ruled.*

INFINITIVE	PARTICIPLE	INFINITIVE		PARTICIPLE
Pres. *regere*, to rule	*regēns*, ruling	*regī*, to be ruled	*Pref.*	*rēctus*, ruled, having been ruled
Perf. *rēxisse*, to have ruled	(*Gen.* *regentis*)	*rēctus esse*, to have been ruled	*Ger.*	*regendus*, to be ruled, deserving to be ruled
Fut. *rēctūrus esse*, to be about to rule	*rēctūrus*, about to rule	*rēctum īrī*, to be about to be ruled		

Active Voice

GERUND	SUPINE
Gen. *regendī*, of ruling	
Dat. *regendō*, for ruling	
Acc. *regendum*, ruling	*Acc.* *rēctum*, to rule
Abl. *regendō*, by ruling	*Abl.* *rēctū*, to rule, to be ruled

56. Verbs in **-iō** of the Third Conjugation have in the present system forms in which **-i-** is followed by a vowel; these forms are like the corresponding forms of the Fourth Conjugation. An example is **capiō**, *I take.*
Principal Parts:

	Pres. Indicative	Pres. Infinitive	Perf. Indicative	Perf. Pass. Partic.
Active	*capiō*	*capere*	*cēpī*	*captus*
Passive	*capior*	*capī*	*captus sum*	

ACTIVE VOICE   PASSIVE VOICE
INDICATIVE MOOD

Present Tense		Present Tense	
Singular	Plural	Singular	Plural
capiō	*capimus*	*capior*	*capimur*
capis	*capitis*	*caperis, or -re*	*capiminī*
capit	*capiunt*	*capitur*	*capiuntur*
Imperfect		Imperfect	
capiēbam	*capiēbāmus*	*capiēbar*	*capiēbāmur*
capiēbās	*capiēbātis*	*capiēbāris*	*capiēbāminī*
capiēbat	*capiēbant*	*capiēbātur*	*capiēbantur*
Future		Future	
capiam	*capiēmus*	*capiar*	*capiēmur*
capiēs	*capiētis*	*capiēris*	*capiēminī*
capiet	*capient*	*capiētur*	*capientur*
Perfect		Perfect	
cēpī	*cēpimus*	*captus sum*	*captī sumus*
cēpistī	*cēpistis*	*captus es*	*captī estis*
cēpit	*cēpērunt or -ēre*	*captus est*	*captī sunt*
Pluperfect		Pluperfect	
cēperam	*cēperāmus*	*captus eram*	*captī erāmus*
cēperās	*cēperātis*	*captus erās*	*captī erātis*
cēperat	*cēperant*	*captus erat*	*captī erant*
Future Perfect		Future Perfect	
cēperō	*cēperimus*	*captus erō*	*captī erimus*
cēperis	*cēperitis*	*captus eris*	*captī eritis*
cēperit	*cēperint*	*captus erit*	*captī erunt*

ACTIVE VOICE		PASSIVE VOICE	
		SUBJUNCTIVE	
Present Tense		Present Tense	
Singular	Plural	Singular	Plural
capiam	*capiāmus*	*capiar*	*capiāmur*
capiās	*capiātis*	*capiāris or -re*	*capiāminī*
capiat	*capiant*	*capiātur*	*capiantur*
Imperfect		Imperfect	
caperem	*caperēmus*	*caperer*	*caperēmur*
caperēs	*caperētis*	*caperēris*	*caperēminī*
caperet	*caperent*	*caperētur*	*caperentur*
Perfect		Perfect	
cēperim	*cēperīmus*	*captus sim*	*captī sīmus*
cēperis	*cēperitis*	*captus sīs*	*captī sītis*
cēperit	*cēperint*	*captus sit*	*captī sint*
Pluperfect		Pluperfect	
cēpissem	*cēpissēmus*	*captus essem*	*captī essēmus*
cēpissēs	*cēpissētis*	*captus essēs*	*captī essētis*
cēpisset	*cēpissent*	*captus esset*	*captī essent*

IMPERATIVE

ACTIVE VOICE		PASSIVE VOICE	
Pres. *cape*	*capite*	Pres. *capere*	*capiminī*
Fut. *capitō*	*capitōte*	Fut. *capitor*	
capitō	*capiuntō*	*capitor*	*capiuntor*

INFINITIVE	PARTICIPLE	INFINITIVE	PARTICIPLE
Pres. *capere*	*capiēns*	Pres. *capī*	
Perf. *cēpisse*	(Gen. *capientīs*)	Perf. *captus esse*	Perf. *captus*
Fut. *captūrus esse*	*captūrus*	Fut. *captum īrī*	Gen. *capiendus*

GERUND	SUPINE
Gen. *capiendī*	
Dat. *capiendō*	
Acc. *capiendum*	Acc. *captum*
Abl. *capiendō*	Abl. *captū*

57. *a.* Inflected like **capiō** are its Compounds, **accipiō, concipiō, dēcipiō, excipiō, incipiō, percipiō, praecipiō, recipiō,** and **suscipiō.**

b. The following verbs in **-iō**, inflected like **capiō**, are used by Caesar: **cupiō**, *ardently desire, wish well to* (I. 18, etc.); **faciō**, *do, make,* and its Compounds **afficiō, cōnficiō, dēficiō, efficiō, īnficiō, perficiō, prōficiō, reficiō** and **sufficiō; ēliciō,** *entice* (V. 50), **fodiō,** *dig* (VII. 73) and its Compounds **effodiō** (VII. 4), **īnfodiō** (VII. 73), **subfodiō** (IV. 12), **trānsfodiō** (VII. 82); **fugiō**, *run away,* and its Compounds **cōnfugiō, dēfugiō, effugiō, perfugiō, prōfugiō,** and **refugiō; iaciō,** *throw,* and its Compounds **abiciō, coniciō, dēiciō, disiciō, ēiciō, iniciō, obiciō, prōiciō, reiciō,** and **subiciō; pariō,** *bring forth, gain* (C. III. 82); two Compounds of **quatiō,** *shake,* **discutiō** (VII. 8) and **percutiō** (V. 44); five Compounds of **rapiō,** *seize,* **arripiō** (V. 33), **corripiō, dīripiō, ēripiō** and **praeripiō; sapiō,** *have sense* (V. 30); **alliciō,** *attract* (V. 55, VII. 31); and Compounds of **speciō,** *look,* **cōnspiciō, dēspiciō, perspiciō, prōspiciō,** and **respiciō.**

c. Similar in inflection to the Passive of **capiō** are the following Deponent Verbs in **-ior** used by Caesar: **patior,** *suffer* (inflected below, 60), and its Compound **perpetior** (C. III. 47); **morior,** *die* (1.4, etc.); and the following Compounds of **gradior,** *step:* **aggredior, congredior, dēgredior, dīgredior, ēgredior, ingredior, praegredior, prōgredior,** and **regredior.**

FOURTH CONJUGATION

58. Verbs of the Fourth Conjugation are inflected like **audiō,** *I hear.*

Principal Parts:

	PRES. INDICATIVE	PRES. INFINITIVE	PRES. INDICATIVE	PERF.PASS. PARTIC.
Active	*audiō*	*audīre*	*audīvī*	*audītus*
	PRES. INDICATIVE	PRES. INFINITIVE	PERF. INDICATIVE	
Passive	*audior*	*audīrī*	*audītus sum*	

ACTIVE VOICE		PASSIVE VOICE	
INDICATIVE MOOD			
PRESENT TENSE		PRESENT TENSE	
I hear, etc.		*I am heard, etc.*	
SINGULAR	PLURAL	SINGULAR	PLURAL
audiō	*audīmus*	*audior*	*audīmur*
audīs	*andītis*	*audīris*, or *-re*	*audīminī*
audit	*andiunt*	*audītur*	*audiuntur*

IMPERFECT		IMPERFECT	
I was hearing, or *I heard*		*I was heard*	
audiēbam	*audiēbāmus*	*audiēbar*	*audiēbāmur*
audiēbās	*audiēbātis*	*audiēbāris*, or *-re*	*audiēbāminī*
audiēbat	*audiēbant*	*audiēbātur*	*audiēbantur*

FUTURE		FUTURE	
I shall hear		*I shall be heard*	
audiam	*audiēmus*	*audiar*	*audiēmur*
audiēs	*audiētis*	*audiēris*, or *-re*	*audiēminī*
audiet	*audient*	*audiētur*	*audientur*

Active Voice		Passive Voice	
INDICATIVE MOOD			
PERFECT		PERFECT	
I have heard, or *I heard*		*I have been heard*, or *I was heard*	
audīvī	*audīvimus*	*audītus sum*	*audītī sumus*
audīvistī	*audīvistis*	*audītus es*	*audītī estis*
audīvit	*audīvērunt*, or *-ēre*	*audītus est*	*audītī sunt*

PLUPERFECT		PLUPERFECT	
I had heard		*I had been heard*	
audīveram	*andīverāmus*	*audītus eram*	*audītī erāmus*
audīverās	*audīverātis*	*audītus erās*	*audītī erātis*
audīverat	*audīverant*	*audītus erat*	*audītī erant*

FUTURE PERFECT		FUTURE PERFECT	
I shall have heard		*I shall have been heard*	
audīverō	*audīverimus*	*audītus erō*	*audītī erimus*
audīveris	*andīveritis*	*audītus eris*	*audītī eritis*
audīverit	*audīverint*	*audītus erit*	*audītī erunt*

ACTIVE VOICE		PASSIVE VOICE	
SUBJUNCTIVE			
PRESENT TENSE		PRESENT TENSE	
I may hear, let us hear, etc.		*I my be heard, let us be heard, etc.*	
SINGULAR	PLURAL	SINGULAR	PLURAL
audiam	*audiāmus*	*audiar*	*audiāmur*
audiās	*audiātis*	*audiāris, or -re*	*audiāminī*
audiat	*audiant*	*audiātur*	*audiantur*

IMPERFECT		IMPERFECT	
I might hear, you would hear		*I might be heard, you would be heard*	
audīrem	audīrēmus	audīrer	audīrēmur
audīrēs	audīrētis	audīrēris, or -re	audīrēminī
audīret	audīrent	audīrētur	audīrentur

PERFECT		PERFECT	
I may have heard		*I may have been heard*	
audīverim	audīverīmus	audītus sim	audītī sīmus
audīverīs	audīverītis	audītus sīs	audītī sītis
audīverit	audīverint	audītus sit	audītī sint

PLUPERFECT		PLUPERFECT	
I might have heard, you would have heard		*I might have been heard, you would have been heard*	
audīvissem	audīvissēmus	audītus essem	audītī essēmus
audīvissēs	audīvissētis	audītus essēs	audītī essētis
audīvisset	audīvissent	audītus esset	audītī essent

ACTIVE VOICE   PASSIVE VOICE

IMPERATIVE

Pres. audī, *hear thou*	audīte, *hear ye*	*Pres.* audīre, *be thou heard*	audīminī, *be ye heard*
Fut. audītō, *thou shalt hear*	audītōte, *ye shall hear*	*Fut.* audītor, *thou shalt be heard*	
audītō, *he shall hear*	audiuntō, *they shall hear*	audītor, *he shall be heard*	audiuntor, *they shall be heard*

INFINITIVE	PARTICIPLE	INFINITIVE	PARTICIPLE
Pres. audīre, *to hear*	audiēns, *hearing*	*Pres.* audīrī, *to be heard*	*Perf.* audītus, *heard, having been heard*
Perf. audīvisse, *to have heard*	(Gen. audientis)	*Perf.* audītus esse, *to have been heard*	
Fut. audītūrus esse, *to be about to hear*	audītūrus, *about to hear*	*Fut.* audītum īrī, *to be about to be heard*	Ger. audiendus, *to be heard, worthy to be heard*

GERUND   SUPINE

Gen. audiendī, *of hearing*
Dat. audiendō, *for hearing*
Acc. audiendum, *hearing*   Acc. audītum, *to hear*
Abl. audiendō, *by hearing*   Abl. audītū, *to hear, to be heard*

DEPONENT VERBS

59. *a.* The forms of Deponent Verbs are generally Passive, while the meaning is Active.

b. The Passive meaning is found in the Gerundive of Deponent Verbs, and sometimes in the Perfect Participle; as **dīmēnsō**, *measured off* (II. 19); **dēpopulātīs**, *having been ravaged* (I. 11).

c. Deponent Verbs have in the Active form a Future Infinitive, Present and Future Participles, Gerund, and Supine.

60. Deponent Verbs in the four conjugations are inflected, as **hortor**, *urge* (I. 19); **vereor**, *fear* (I. 19); **sequor**, *follow* (I. 22), and **patior**, *suffer, allow* (I. 6, 9); **largior**, *give freely* (I. 18):

INDICATIVE MOOD

	FIRST CONJUGATION	SECOND CONJUGATION	THIRD CONJUGATION	THIRD CONJ. IN -IOR	FOURTH CONJUGATION
Pres.	hortor	vereor	sequor	patior	largior
	hortāris, -re	verēris, -re	sequeris, -re	pateris, -re	largīris, -re
	hortātur	verētur	sequitur	patitur	largītur
	hortāmur	verēmur	sequimur	patimur	largīmur
	hortāminī	verēminī	sequiminī	patiminī	largīminī
	hortantur	verentur	sequuntur	patiuntur	largiuntur
Imp.	hortābar, etc.	verēbar, etc.	sequēbar, etc.	patiēbar, etc.	largiēbar, etc.
Fut.	hortābor	verēbor	sequar	patiar	largiar
Perf.	hortātus sum	veritus sum	secūtus sum	passus sum	largītus sum
Plup.	hortātus eram	veritus eram	secūtus eram	passus eram	largītus eram
F.P.	hortātus erō	veritus erō	secūtus erō	passus erō	largītus erō

SUBJUNCTIVE

Pres.	horter	verear	sequar	patiar	largiar
Imp.	hortārer	verērer	sequerer	paterer	largīrer
Perf.	hortātus sim	veritus sim	secūtus sim	passus sim	largītus sim
Plup.	hortātus essem	veritus essem	secūtus essem	passus essem	largītus essem

IMPERATIVE

Pres.	hortāre	verēre	sequere	patere	largīre
Imp.	hortātor	verētor	sequitor	patitor	largītor

INFINITIVE

Pres.	hortārī	verērī	sequī	patī	largīrī
Perf.	hortātus esse	veritus esse	secūtus esse	passus esse	largītus esse
Fut.	hortātūrus esse	veritūrus esse	secūtūrus esse	passūrus esse	largītūrus esse

PARTICIPLES

Pres.	hortāns	verēns	sequēns	patiēns	largiēns
Fut.	hortātūrus	veritūrus	secūtūrus	passūrus	largītūrus
Perf.	hortātus	veritus	secūtus	passus	largītus
Ger.	hortandus	verendus	sequendus	patiendus	largiendus

GERUND

Gen.	hortandī	verendī	sequendī	patiendī	largiendī
Dat.	hortandō	verendō	sequendō	patiendō	largiendō
Acc.	hortandum	verendum	sequendum	patiendum	largiendum
Abl.	hortandō	verendō	sequendō	patiendō	largiendō

SUPINE

Acc.	hortātum	veritum	secūtum	passum	largītum
Abl.	hortātū	veritū	secūtū	passū	largītū

61. a. Of the Deponent Verbs used by Caesar, besides those previously mentioned, the most important are:

(1) First Conjugation, **arbitror**, *think* (I. 4), **cohortor**, *urge on* (I. 25), **cōnor**, *attempt* (I. 3), **cōnsector**, *pursue* (III. 19), **cōnsōlor**, *reassure* (I. 20), **cōnspicor**, *catch sight of* (I. 25), **cunctor**, *delay* (III. 23), **dominor**, *hold sway* (II. 31), **frūmentor**, *get supplies* (IV. 9), **glōrior**, *boast* (I. 14), **grātulor**, *congratulate* (I. 30), **interpretor**, *expound* (VI. 13); **mīror**, *wonder* (I. 32) and **admīror** (I. 14); **miseror**, *lament* (I. 39); **moror**, *delay* (I. 39), and **dēmoror** (III. 6); **pābulor**, *get fodder* (V. 17), **populor**, *lay waste* (I. 11), and **dēpopulor**, *completely lay waste* (II. 7); **recordor**, *recall* (C. III. 72), **remūneror**, *compensate* (I. 44), and **speculor**, *spy out* (I. 47).

(2) Second Conjugation, **fateor**, *acknowledge* (C. III. 20), and its Compounds **cōnfiteor** (V. 27) and **profiteor** (VI. 23); **liceor**, *bid* (I. 18), and **polliceor**, *promise* (I. 14); **mereor**, *earn* (I. 40); **tueor**, *protect* (IV. 8), and **intueor**, *look upon* (I. 32); **vereor**, *be afraid* (I. 19).

(3) Third Conjugation, **complector**, *embrace* (I. 20), **dēfetīscor**, *become exhausted* (VII. 88);

fruor, *enjoy* (III. 22); **lābor**, *slip, fall away* (V. 3), and **ēlābor**, *escape* (V. 37); **loquor**, *speak* (I. 20); **nāscor**, *be born, rise* (II. 18), and **ēnāscor**, *grow out*, (II. 17); **nancīscor**, *obtain* (I. 53); **nītor**, *strive, rely on* (I. 13), and **innītor**, *lean upon* (II. 27); **oblīvīscor**, *forget*, (I. 14), **proficīscor**, *set out* (I. 3), **queror**, *complain* (I. 16); the Compounds of **sequor**, **cōnsequor**, **exsequor**, **īnsequor**, **persequor**, **prōsequor**, **subsequor**; **reminīscor**, *remember* (I. 13), **ulcīscor**, *avenge* (I. 12); and **ūtor**, *use, adopt* (I. 5).

(4) Fourth Conjugation, **experior**, *try* (I. 31), **largior**, *give freely, bribe* (I. 18); **mētior**, *measure* (I. 16), and **dīmētior**, *measure off* (II. 19, IV. 17); **partior**, *divide* (III. 10), and **potior**, *become master of* (I. 3).

b. To the Fourth Conjugation belongs the Deponent **orior**, *rise*, with its Compounds **adorior**, *attack* (I. 13) and **coörior**, *arise* (III.7); but Caesar uses certain forms of **orior** which are like those of Deponents in **-ior** of the Third Conjugation, as **oritur** (VI. 25) and **orerētur** (Imperfect Subjunctive; VI. 9, VII. 28).

62. Semi-Deponent Verbs have a Perfect System Passive in form but Active in meaning; they are **audeō** (I. 18), **fīdō** (C. III. 111) with its compounds **cōnfīdō** (I. 23) and **diffīdō** (V. 41); **gaudeō** (IV. 13), and **soleō** (VI. 15):

> *audeō, audēre, ausus sum, dare.*
> *fīdō, fīdere, fīsus sum, trust.*
> *gaudeō, gaudēre, gāvīsus sum, rejoice.*
> *soleō, solēre, solitus sum, be wont.*

PERIPHRASTIC CONJUGATION

63. The Periphrastic Conjugation has an Active and a Passive form, made up by combining the Future Active Participle and the Future Passive Participle, or Gerundive, with the verb **sum**, thus:

ACTIVE PERIPHRASTIC CONJUGATION

INDICATIVE MOOD		SUBJUNCTIVE MOOD	
Pres.	*amātūrus (-a, -um) sum*, I am about to love	Pres.	*amātūrus sim*, I may be about to love
Imp.	*amātūrus eram*, I was about to love	Imp.	*amātūrus essem*, I might be about to love
Fut.	*amātūrus erō*, I shall be about to love	Perf.	*amātūrus fuerim*, I may have been about to love
Perf.	*amātūrus fuī*, I have been, was, about to love	Plup.	*amātūrus fuissem*, I might have been about to love
Plup.	*amātūrus fueram*, I had been about to love		
Fut. P.	*amātūrus fuerō*, I shall have been about to love		

INFINITIVE
Pres. *amātūrus esse*, to be about to love
Perf. *amātūrus fuisse*, to have been about to love

PASSIVE PERIPHRASTIC CONJUGATION

INDICATIVE		SUBJUNCTIVE	
Pres.	*amandus (a, -um) sum*, I am to be loved, I must be loved	Pres.	*amandus sim*, I may have to be loved
Imp.	*amandus eram*, I had to be loved	Imp.	*amandus essem*, I might have to be loved
Fut.	*amandus erō*, I shall have to be loved	Perf.	*amandus fuerim*, I may have had to be loved
Perf.	*amandus fuī*, I have had to be loved, had to be loved	Plup.	*amandus fuissem*, I might have had to be loved

PASSIVE PERIPHRASTIC CONJUGATION

Plup. **amandus fueram**, *I had deserved to be loved*

Fut. P. **amandus fuerō**, *I shall have had to be loved*

INFINITIVE

Pres. **amandus esse**, *to have to be loved*
Perf. **amandus fuisse**, *to have had to be loved*

64. a. Perfects in **-āvī, -ēvī**, and **-īvī**, and other tenses formed from the same stems, are sometimes contracted by the loss of **-vi-** or **-ve-** before **-s-** or **-r-**; Perfects in **-īvī** lose the **-v-** before **-r-** but retain the vowel. Examples are:

(1) **oppugnārant** (I. 5) for **oppugnāverant; adamāssent** (I. 31) for **adamāvissent; commemorāssent** (I. 14) for **commemorāvissent; superārint**, Perfect Subjunctive (I. 40) for **superāverint; superāssent** (I. 40) for **superāvissent.**

(2) **cōnsuērunt** (III. 8, etc.) for **cōnsuēvērunt; cōnsuērint** (I. 44, etc.) for **cōnsuēverint; cōnsuēsse** (I. 14) for **cōnsuēvisse.**

(3) **audiērunt** (V. 28) for **audīvērunt; audierit** (IV. 5) for **audīverit; audierant** (II. 12, VI. 37) for **audīverant; audīssent** (VII. 62) for **audīvissent; audīstis** (C. III. 87) for **audīvistis.**

b. The Future Passive Participle, or Gerundive, sometimes has the ending **-undus** instead of **-endus**, as **faciundī** (I. 7), **potiundī** (II. 7).

IRREGULAR VERBS

65. Of the Irregular Verbs Caesar most frequently uses **sum, dō, eō, ferō, fīō, volō** and certain compounds.

66. a. Of the compounds of **sum** Caesar uses **absum, adsum, dēsum, intersum, possum, praesum, prōsum, subsum,** and **supersum.** These are inflected like **sum** (53), excepting **possum;** but in **prōsum (prōfuisse,** VI. 40) the preposition has the form **prōd-** before vowels, as **prōdest.**

b. **Possum,** *I am able,* is inflected as follows:

Principal Parts:

possum   posse   potuī

	INDICATIVE MOOD			SUBJUNCTIVE MOOD	
	Singular	Plural		Singular	Plural
Pres.	*possum*	*possumus*	*Pres.*	*possim*	*possīmus,*
	potes	*potestis*		*possīs*	*possītis,*
	potest	*possunt*		*possit*	*possint*
Imp.	*poteram, poterās, etc.*	*poterāmus, -erātis, etc.*	*Imp.*	*possem*	*possēmus*
				possēs	*possētis*
Fut.	*poterō, poteris, etc.*	*poterimus*		*posset*	*possent*
			Perf.	*potuerim*	*potuerīmus*
Perf.	*potuī, potuistī, etc.*	*potuimus*		*potuerīs*	*potuerītis*
				potuerit	*potuerint*
Plup.	*potueram, potuerās, etc.*	*potuerāmus*	*Plup.*	*potuissem*	*potuissēmus*
				potuissēs	*potuissētis*
Fut. P.	*potuerō, potueris, etc.*	*potuerimus*		*potuisset*	*potuissent*

	INFINITIVE		PARTICIPLE
Pres.	*posse*		*Pres.* potēns (used as an adjective)
Perf.	*potuisse*		*Gen.* potentis

67. a. Dō, dare, *give,* has **-a-** instead of **-ā-** in the Present System except in the Second Person of the Present Indicative and the Present Imperative. The inflection of the Perfect System (**dedī,** *etc.*), is regular.

Principal Parts:

$$d\bar{o} \quad dare \quad ded\bar{i} \quad datus$$

ACTIVE VOICE

	INDICATIVE MOOD			SUBJUNCTIVE MOOD	
Pres.	*dō*	*damus*	Pres.	*dem*	*dēmus*
	dās	*datis*		*dēs*	*dētis*
	dat	*dant*		*det*	*dent*
Imp.	*dabam, etc.*	*dabāmus*	Imp.	*darem*	*darēmus*
Fut.	*dabō, etc.*	*dabimus*		*darēs*	*darētis*
Perf.	*dedī, etc.*	*dedimus*		*daret*	*darent*
Plup	*dederam, etc.*	*dederāmus*	Perf.	*dederim, etc.*	*dederīmus, etc.*
Fut. P.	*dederō, etc.*	*dederimus*	Plup.	*dedissem, etc.*	*dedissēmus, etc.*

	IMPERATIVE			INFINITIVE	PARTICIPLE
Pres.	*dā*	*date*	Pres.	*dare*	*dāns*
Fut.	*datō*	*datōte*	Perf.	*dedisse*	
	datō	*dantō*	Fut.	*datūrus esse*	*datūrus*

GERUND
dandī, etc.

SUPINE
datum, datū

b. The Passive of **dō** has **-a-** instead of **-ā-**, as **darī, datur, dabar, dabor, darer, datus,** *etc.;* the First Person of the Present Indicative Passive is not in use.

c. The compounds of **dō** are of the Third Conjugation except **circumdō,** which is inflected like **dō.**

68. *a.* **Eō, īre,** *go,* is thus inflected:

Principal Parts:

$$e\bar{o} \quad \bar{i}re \quad i\bar{i}\ (\bar{i}v\bar{i}) \quad itum\ (est)$$

	INDICATIVE MOOD			SUBJUNCTIVE MOOD	
Pres.	*eō*	*īmus*	Pres.	*eam*	*eāmus*
	īs	*ītis*		*eās*	*eātis*
	it	*eunt*		*eat*	*eant*
Imp.	*ībam, etc.*	*ībāmus*	Imp	*īrem*	*īrēmus*
Fut.	*ībō, etc.*	*ībimus*		*īrēs*	*īrētis*
Perf.	*iī*	*iimus*		*īret*	*īrent*
	īstī or iistī	*īstis or iistis*	Perf.	*ierim*	*ierīmus*
	iit	*iērunt or iēre*		*ierīs*	*ierītis*
Plup.	*ieram, etc.*	*ierāmus*		*ierit*	*ierint*
Fut. P.	*ierō, etc.*	*ierimus*	Plup.	*īssem, etc.*	*īssēmus, etc.*

	IMPERATIVE			INFINITIVE		PARTICIPLE	
Pres.	*ī*	*īte*	Pres.	*īre*	Pres.	*iēns*	Gen. *euntis*
Fut.	*ītō*	*ītōte*	Perf.	*īsse*			
	ītō	*euntō*	Fut.	*itūrus esse*	Fut.	*itūrus*	Gerundive *eundum*
			Pass.	*īrī*			

GERUND
eundī, eundō, etc.

SUPINE
itum, itū

b. Caesar uses the Compounds **abeō, adeō, coeō** (VI. 22), **exeō, ineō, obeō, prōdeō, redeō, subeō,** and **trānseō,** inflected like **eō.**

c. Transitive compounds of **eō** are used also in the Passive, as **numerus inībātur,** *the number was cast up* (VII. 76); **initā aestāte,** *at the beginning of summer* (II. 2); **trānsītur,** *is crossed* (I. 6).

d. Impersonal Passive forms of **eō** are **īrī** (III. 18), **īrētur** (III. 24).

69. *a.* **Ferō, ferre,** *bear, carry,* is inflected as follows:

Principal Parts:

Active.	**ferō**	**ferre**	**tulī**	**lātus**
Passive.	**feror**	**ferrī**		**lātus sum**

ACTIVE VOICE   PASSIVE VOICE

INDICATIVE MOOD

	SINGULAR	PLURAL		SINGULAR	PLURAL
Pres.	ferō	ferimus	*Pres.*	feror	ferimur
	fers	fertis		ferris	feriminī
	fert	ferunt		fertur	feruntur
Imp.	ferēbam, *etc.* ferēbāmus		*Imp.*	ferēbar	ferēbāmur
Fut.	feram	ferēmus	*Fut.*	ferar	ferēmur
Perf.	tulī	tulimus	*Perf.*	lātus sum	lātī sumus
Plup.	tuleram	tulerāmus	*Plup.*	lātus eram	lātī erāmus
Fut. P.	tulerō	tulerimus	*Fut. P.*	lātus erō	lātī erimus

SUBJUNCTIVE MOOD

Pres.	feram	ferāmus	*Pres.*	ferar	ferāmur
	ferās	ferātis		ferāris, *or* -re	ferāminī
	ferat	ferant		ferātur	ferantur
Imp.	ferrem	ferrēmus	*Imp.*	ferrer	ferrēmur
	ferrēs	ferrētis		ferrēris	ferrēminī
	ferret	ferrent		ferrētur	ferrentur
Perf.	tulerim	tulerīmus	*Perf.*	lātus sim	lātī sīmus
Plup.	tulissem	tulissēmus	*Plup.*	lātus essem	lātī essēmus

IMPERATIVE

Pres.	fer	ferte	*Pres.*	ferre	feriminī
Fut.	fertō	fertōte	*Fut.*	fertor	
	fertō	feruntō		fertor	feruntor

ACTIVE VOICE   PASSIVE VOICE

INFINITIVE	PARTICIPLE		INFINITIVE	PARTICIPLE
Pres. ferre	*Pres.* ferēns	*Pres.*	ferrī	
Perf. tulisse	(*Gen.* ferentis)	*Perf.*	lātus esse	*Perf.* lātus
Fut. lātūrus esse	*Fut.* lātūrus	*Fut.*	lātum īrī	*Gen.* ferendus *or* ferundus

GERUND   SUPINE

Gen. ferendī	
Dat. ferendō	
Acc. ferendum	*Acc.* lātum
Abl. ferendō	*Abl.* lātū

b. Caesar uses the Compounds, **afferō, anteferō, conferō, dēferō, differō, efferō, īnferō, offerō, perferō, praeferō, prōferō** and **referō**, which are inflected like **ferō**.

70. a. **Fiō**, *become* (with -ī- except in **fit** and before -e-), is used as the Passive of **faciō**, with the meaning *be made, be done*. It is inflected as follows:

Principal Parts:

          fīō   **fierī**   **factus sum**

INDICATIVE MOOD   SUBJUNCTIVE MOOD

	SINGULAR	PLURAL		SINGULAR	PLURAL
Pres.	fīō	fīmus	*Pres.*	fīam	fīāmus
	fīs	fītis		fīās	fīātis
	fit	fīunt		fīat	fīant
Imp.	fīēbam, *etc.*	fīēbāmus	*Imp.*	fierem	fierēmus
Fut.	fīam	fīēmus		fierēs	fierētis
Perf.	factus sum	factī sumus		fieret	fierent
Plup.	factus eram	factī erāmus	*Perf.*	factus sim	factī sīmus
Fut. P.	factus erō	factī erimus	*Plup.*	factus essem	factī essēmus

IMPERATIVE

Pres.	*fī*		*fīte*

	INFINITIVE		PARTICIPLE
Pres.	*fierī*		
Perf.	*factus esse*	*Perf.*	*factus*
Fut.	*factum īrī*	*Ger.*	*faciendus*

b. Of compounds of **fīō** Caesar uses **cōnfierī** (VII. 58) and **collabefierī** (C. II. 6).

c. Compounds of **faciō** with Prepositions have their own Passive forms; so **cōnfecta erat,** *had been made* (I. 29); **patefierī,** *be kept open* (III. 1).

71. Volō, *I wish,* and its compounds **nōlō,** *I am unwilling,* and **mālō,** *I prefer,* are inflected as follows:

Principal Parts:

volō	*velle*	*voluī*
nōlō	*nōlle*	*nōluī*
mālō	*mālle*	*māluī*

INDIC. PRESENT	SUBJ. PRESENT	INDIC. PRESENT	SUBJ. PRESENT	INDIC. PRESENT	SUBJ. PRESENT
volō	*velim*	*nōlō*	*nōlim*	*mālō*	*mālim*
vīs	*velīs*	*nōn vīs*	*nōlīs*	*māvīs*	*mālīs*
vult	*velit*	*nōn vult*	*nōlit*	*māvult*	*mālit*
volumus	*velīmus*	*nōlumus*	*nōlīmus*	*mālumus*	*mālīmus*
vultis	*velītis*	*nōn vultis*	*nōlītis*	*māvultis*	*mālītis*
volunt	*velint*	*nōlunt*	*nōlint*	*mālunt*	*mālint*

IMPERFECT

volēbam, etc.	*vellem*	*nōlēbam*	*nōllem*	*mālēbam*	*mālem*

FUTURE

volam, etc.	*nōlam*	*mālam*

PERFECT

voluī, etc.	*voluerim*	*nōluī*	*nōluerim*	*māluī*	*māluerim*

PLUPERFECT

volueram	*voluissem*	*nōlueram*	*nōluissem*	*mālueram*	*māluissem*

FUTURE PERFECT

voluerō, etc.	*nōluerō*	*māluerō*

IMPERATIVE

Pres.	*nōlī*	*nōlīte*
Fut.	*nōlītō*	*nōlītōte*
	nōlītō	*nōluntō*

INFINITIVE

Pres.	*velle*	*nōlle*	*mālle*
Perf.	*voluisse*	*nōluisse*	*māluisse*

PARTICIPLE

Pres.	*volēns*	*nōlēns*

DEFECTIVE VERBS

72. *a.* Caesar uses one or more forms of each of the following Defective Verbs: **inquam,** *I say,* which he uses only in direct quotations, in the Third Person Singular Indicative Present, **inquit,** *he says, says he;* **coepī,** *I have begun, I began,* which belongs chiefly to the Perfect System; **meminī,** *I remember,* and **ōdī,** *I hate,* which are Perfect in form, but Present in meaning.

b. **Coepī, meminī,** and **ōdī** are inflected as follows:

INDICATIVE MOOD				SUBJUNCTIVE MOOD		
Perf.	*coepī, etc.*	*meminī*	*ōdī*	*coeperim*	*meminerim*	*ōderim*
Plup.	*coeperam*	*memineram*	*ōderam*	*coepissem*	*meminissem*	*ōdissem*
Fut. P.	*coeperō*	*meminerō*	*ōderō*			

IMPERATIVE				INFINITIVE	
Sing.	*mementō*	*Perf.*	*coepisse*	*memini* *sse*	*ōdisse*
		Fut.	*coeptūrus esse*		*ōsūrus esse*
Plur.	*mementōte*				

PARTICIPLE		
Perf.	*coeptus, begun*	*ōsus*
Fut.	*coeptūrus esse*	*ōsūrus*

c. The Passive forms of **coepī** are used with the Passive Infinitive, as **lapidēs iacī coeptī sunt,** *stones began to be thrown* (II. 6).

IMPERSONAL VERBS

73. *a.* Of the Impersonal Verbs Caesar most often uses **licet,** *it is permitted* (I. 7) and **oportet,** *it is necessary, it behooves* (I. 4); he has also **paenitet,** *it makes sorry* (IV. 5) and **pudet,** *it makes ashamed* (VII. 42).

b. The Impersonal **licet** is inflected as follows:

INDICATIVE			SUBJUNCTIVE	
Pres.	licet, *it is permuted*		*Pres.*	liceat, *it may be permitted*
Imp.	licēbat, *it was permitted*		*Imp.*	licēret, *it might be permitted*
Fut.	licēbit, *it will be permitted*			
Perf.	licuit, *it has been permitted* or *it was permitted*		*Perf.*	licuerit, *it may have been permitted*
Plup.	licuerat, *it had been permited*		*Plup.*	licuisset, *it might have been permitted*
Fut. P.	licuerit, *it will have been permitted*			

INFINITIVE
Pres. licēre, *to be permitted*   *Perf.* licuisse, *to have been permitted*

c. Caesar uses Impersonally the Third Person Singular of a number of Verbs, among which are **accēdit,** *it is added, there is the further fact that* (III. 13); **accidit,** *it happens, it turns out* (I. 31); **cōnstat,** *it is certain* (III. 6); **interest,** *it is important* (II. 5); **placet,** *it pleases* (I. 34); and **praestat,** *it is better* (I. 17).

d. Caesar uses Impersonally the Passive of several Intransitive Verbs, making prominent the action rather than the doer; as **pugnātur,** *fighting goes on,* lit. *it is fought* (VII. 67, 84); **pugnātum est,** *fighting went on* (I. 26); **Ubi eō ventum est,** *when (they) had come thither,* lit. *when it was come thither,* the *coming* being made prominent (I. 43).

e. Verbs are often used impersonally in the Passive Periphrastic Conjugation, denoting Obligation or Necessity (229c); as, **reī frūmentāriae prōspiciendum [esse],** *that he should provide for supplies,* lit. *that it ought to be provided for supplies by him* (I. 23).

WORD FORMATION

74. The following classes of words are derived from Verbs:

a. Nouns with the Suffix **-tor** denoting the agent, as **vic-tor,** (I. 31), *victor,* from **vincō; dēfēn-sor** (II. 6; for **dēfend-tor,** as **dēfēn-sus** for **dēfend-tus**), *defender,* from **dēfendō.**

b. Nouns with the Suffixes **-tiō (-siō), -tus, -tūra, -ium,** denoting an action or the result of an action, as **coniūrā-tiō** (I. 2), *a swearing together, league* (**coniūrō**); **mūnī-tiō** (I. 10), *a fortifying, a fortification* conceived as a result of fortifying (**mūniō**); **adven-tus** (I. 22), *arrival* (**adveniō**); **exerci-tus** (I. 13), *army,* conceived as a product of training (**exerceō**); **armā-tūra** (II. 10), *equipment* (**armō**); **imperium** (I. 3), *command, sovereignty* (**imperō**); **iūdic-ium** (I. 4), *judgement, trial* (**iūdicō**).

c. Nouns with the Suffix **-or**, denoting a condition or state, as **tim-or** (I. 22), *fear* (**timeō**).

d. Nouns with the Suffixes **-men** or **-mentum, -ulum, -bulum, -crum**, denoting process, means, or result, as **flū-men** (I. 12), *stream, river,* conceived as a flowing or current (**fluō**); **impedī-mentum** (I. 25), *hindrance* (**impediō**), pl. **impedīmenta** (I. 24), *baggage,* conceived as an aggregation of hindrances; **vinc-ulum** (I. 4), *bond, chain,* conceived as a means of binding (**vinciō**); **pā-bulum** (I. 16), *fodder,* conceived as a means of feeding (**pāscō**): **simulā-crum** (VI. 16), *image,* conceived as something made like something else (**simulō,** *make like*).

e. Adjectives with the Suffix **-āx**, denoting a quality or tendency, as **ferāx** (II. 4), *productive, fertile* (**ferō,** *bear*).

f. Adjectives with the Suffixes **-ilis** and **-bilis**, denoting passive qualities, or capacity, as **fac-ilis** (I. 6), *easy,* i.e. capable of being done or made (**faciō**); **mō-bilis** (IV. 5), *easily moved, changeable* (**moveō**); **incrēdibilis** (I. 12), *incredible* (negative **in-** + **crēdibilis,** *capable of being believed,* from **crēdō**).

g. A few Adjectives in **-tīvus**, as **cap-tīvus** (I. 50), *captive* (**capiō**), **fugi-tīvus** (I. 23), *fugitive* (**fugiō**).

75. The following classes of words are derived from Nouns:

a. Diminutive Nouns, ending in **-lus** (Fem. **-la,** Neut. **-lum**), and in **-ulus, -olus, -culus,** *etc.,* as **arti-culus** (VI. 27), *joint* (**artus**); **tabella** (C. III. 83), *voting tablet* (**tabula**); **porcellus,** *pig,* dim. from **porculus,** *young hog, pig,* which is itself a dim. from **porcus,** *hog.*

b. Nouns with the Suffix **-ātus**, denoting an official position or body, as **cōnsul-ātus** (I. 35), *consulship* (**cōnsul**); **magistrātus** (I. 4), *magistracy, magistrate* (**magister**); **senātus** (I. 3), *senate* (**senex**).

c. A few Abstract Nouns in **-tās** and **-tūs**, as **cīvi-tās** (I. 2), *citizenship, state* (**cīvis**); **vir-tūs** (I. 1), *valour* (**vir**).

d. Adjectives with the Suffix **-eus**, denoting material, as **aureus** (V. 12), *of gold* (**aurum**); **ferreus** (III. 13), *of iron* (**ferrum**).

e. Adjectives with the Suffixes **-ius, -icus, -cus, -ānus, -īnus, -nus, -ālis, -īlis, -ārius, -āris, -īvus,** meaning *connected with, belonging to, from, etc.,* as **patr-ius** (II. 15), *of a father, ancestral* (**pater**); **bell-icus** (VI. 24), *of war* (**bellum**); **Gall-icus** (I. 31), *Gallic;* **Germān-icus** (IV. 16), *Germanic;* **urb-ānus** (VII. 1), *of a city, of the city* (**urbs**); **Rōm-ānus,** *of Rome,* (**Rōma**); **Lat-īnus,** *of Latium, Latin;* **nāv-ālis** (III. 19), *naval* (**nāvis**); **legiōn-ārius** (I. 51), *of a legion, legionary* (**legiō**); **cōnsul-āris** (C. III. 82), *consular;* **aest-īvus** (VI. 4), *of summer.*

f. Adjectives with the suffix **-ōsus**, denoting fullness, as **perīculōsus** (I. 33), *full of danger* (**perīculum**); **bellic-ōsus** (I. 10), *warlike* (**bellic-us, bellum**).

g. Denominative Verbs, of the different conjugations, as **cūrō, -āre** (I. 19), *care for, take care* (**cūra**); **laudō, -āre** (C. III. 87), *praise* (**laus, laudis**); **tribuō, -ere** (I. 13), *assign* (**tribus**); **fīniō, -īre** (IV. 16), *limit* (**fīnis**); **partior, -īrī** (III. 10), *divide* (**pars, partis**).

76. *a.* Derived from Adjectives are Abstract Nouns with the Suffixes **-tia, -ia, -tās,** and **-tūdō**, denoting quality or condition, as **dūri-tia** (VI. 21), *hardness* (**dūrus**); **audāc-ia** (I. 18), *boldness* (**audāx**); **grāt-ia** (I. 9), *favour* (**grātus**); **cupidi-tās** (I. 2), *desire* (**cupidus**); **forti-tūdō** (I. 2), *bravery* (**fortis**).

b. Derived from Adverbs are several Adjectives in **-urnus, -turnus, -tinus**, referring to Time, as **diū-turnus** (I. 14), *long-continued* (**diū**), and **diū-tinus** (V. 52), *protracted* (**diū**); so **Crāstinus** (C. III. 91), like the English name *Morrow,* from **crās-tinus,** *of to-morrow* (**crās**).

c. A fewer Adjectives have a Diminutive in **-ulus**; as **tantulus,** *so small,* from **tantus** (IV. 22).

77. Adverbs[1] are sometimes formed from the Stem of the Perfect Passive Participle with the suffix **-im**, as **stat-im** (I. 53), *immediately,* (**status, stō**); and from nouns, with the ending **-tim** (or **-im**), as **virī-tim** (VII. 71), *man by man* (**vir**), and **part-im** (II. 1), *partly,* which was

---

[1] The formation of Adverbs from Adjectives is treated under Adverbs, *34, 35.*

originally an Accusative of **pars**.

78. Verbs derived from Verbs are:

a. Frequentatives, expressing repeated or intensive action; frequentatives derived from Verbs of the First Conjugation end in **-itō**, as **clāmitō** (V. 7), *cry out loudly, shout* (**clāmō**); others end in **-tō** or **-sō**, as **iactō** (I. 25), *toss about, cast* (**iaciō**), **concursō** (V. 33), *rush hither and yon, rush about* (**concurrō**).

b. Inchoatives, or Inceptives, expressing the beginning of an action or state, a becoming; they end in **-scō**, preceded by **-ā-, -ē-,** or **-ī-,** as **mātūrēscō** (VI. 29), *become ripe* (**mātūrō**).

79. *a.* In the first part of a Compound Word the final vowel of the Stem of a Noun or Adjective is dropped before a vowel, and becomes **-i-** before a consonant, while in the case of consonant Stems **-i-** is often inserted; in the second part vowel changes frequently appear. Thus **signi-fer** (II. 25), *standard-bearer* (for **signo-fer, signum** + **fer-** in **ferō**); **prīn-ceps** (I. 30), *leader,* i.e. *taking foremost place* (for **prīmo-cap-s, prīmus** + **cap-** in **capiō**); **ampli-ficō** (II. 14), *enlarge* (for **amplo-fac-ō, amplus** + **fac-** in **faciō**).

b. The first part of a Compound is often a Preposition or other indeclinable word, as **perficiō** (I. 3), *carry through* (**per** + **faciō**); **in-iussū** (I. 19), *without orders* (negative **in-** + **iussū**); **bi-enn-ium** (I. 3), (*period of*) *two years* (for **bi-anno-ium, bis** + **annus** + suffix **-ium**); **quotannīs** (I. 36), *annually* (**quot** + Ablative of **annus**).

c. Compounds originating in phrases are sometimes declinable, as **prō-cōnsul,** *proconsul,* Abl. **prō-cōnsule** (VI. 1); sometimes indeclinable, as **ob-viam,** *in the way* (VII. 12, 28).

d. The following indeclinable prefixes are found only in Compound Words:

amb-, am-, (an-), *about,* as in **ān-frāctus** (VII. 46), *curve.*

com-, co- (old form of **cum,** *with*), *with, together;* see under **cum** in Vocabulary.

dis-, appearing also as **dir-, dī-,** *apart,* as in **dis-cēdō** (I. 16), *go apart;* **dir-īmō** (I. 46), *take apart, break off;* **dī-mīttō** (I. 18), *send about, send off.*

in-, = **un-,** *not,* as in **incertus** (IV. 5); to be carefully distinguished from the preposition **in** in composition.

por-, *forth, forward,* as in **por-rigō** (II. 19), *extend.*

re-, red-, *back,* as in **re-maneō** (I. 39), *stay behind;* **red-eō** (I. 29), *return.*

sē-, sēd-, *apart,* as in **sē-parō** (VII. 63), *separate,* **sēd-itiō** (VII. 28), *mutiny.*

THE DERIVATION OF ENGLISH WORDS FROM THE LATIN[1]

80. *a.* Very many of the Words in the English Language in common use are derived, indirectly or directly, from the Latin. The percentage of classical Latin words that have been taken over into English directly,[2] however, is exceedingly small; the people whose name survives in the word "English" reached Britain too late for any direct contact with classical Latin. But in the Middle Ages a modified Latin was spoken and written by educated men all over Europe; and classical Latin authors continued to be read, less in the Middle Ages, but extensively after the Revival of Learning. Meanwhile the Latin spoken by the common people in Italy, France, Spain, and other countries conquered by the Romans, had developed into the Romance languages, French, Italian, Spanish and kindred tongues; and after the Norman Conquest, in the eleventh century, French was both spoken and written in England. Thus it happens that words of Latin origin have come down into the English of today in various ways, some through the writings and speech of those who read classical Latin, a great many through mediaeval Latin, but far the greatest number through the Romance languages, particularly French.

---

[1] Classes in Caesar find it a useful exercise to make, on separate slips or cards, a list of Latin words in each lesson having English derivatives, adding the words derived from them. The Latin words from time to time can be classified, in groups corresponding with the numbered paragraphs *80-85,* the words in each group being arranged in alphabetial order.

[2] The editor is indebted to Professor O.F. Emerson, of Western Reserve University, for helpful suggestions.

b. Some Latin words appear in English in their Latin forms, though they may have passed through other forms and may now have a different meaning; as "arbor" (II. 17), "census" (I. 29), "colour" (V. 14), "duplex" (II. 29), "senator" (II. 28), "victor" (I. 31), and "omnibus," meaning originally *for all*, from the Dative Plural Masculine of **omnis** (I. 1).

81. Many Latin Words appear in English with slight change of spelling, as "cent" from **centum** (I. 37), "condition" from **condicio** (I. 28) through a late spelling **conditio**; "difficulty" from **difficultas** (II. 20), "fort" from **fortis** (I. 48), "future" from **futurus** (I. 10), the Future Participle associated with **sum**; "office" from **officium** (I. 40), "senate" from **senatus** (I. 3), and "victory" from **victoria** (I. 53); "false" from **falsus** (VI. 20), and "pedal" from **pedalis** (III. 13), which goes back to **pes**, Gen. **pedis**, *foot* (I. 25); "admire" from **admiror** (I. 14), "ascend" from **ascendo** (I. 21), "accept'" from **accipio** (I. 14) through the Frequentative **accepto**, *accept*, which is formed from **acceptus** (I. 48), Participle of **accipio**.

82. *a.* Some English Words have been formed from Latin Words by Analogy of Latin or French Words already in the language. Examples are "magistracy" and "classical."

b. "Magistracy" goes back to **magistratus** (I. 4). From **magistratus** came "magistrate," to which the suffix "-cy" was added from Analogy to the English nouns of Latin origin ending in "-cy"[1]; this suffix represents the Latin termination **-tia**, as in "clemency," from **clementia** (II. 14). With the addition of the suffix "-cy" the last two letters of "magistrate" disappeared; hence "magistracy."

c. "Classical" comes from the Adjective **classicus**, *first class*, which goes back to **classis**, *a class*, though in Caesar **classis** (III. 14, etc.) has only the meaning *fleet*, as a class or division of military forces. From **classicus** comes "classic"; the suffix "-al" was added from Analogy to the English Words which are derived from the Latin Adjectives ending in **-alis**, as "social" from **socialis** (ultimately from **socius**, *fellow, ally*, I. 5), "hospital" from **hospitalis** (ultimately from **hospes**, Gen. **hospitis**, *guest-friend*, I. 53), and "legal" from **legalis** (ultimately from **lex**, **legis**, *law*, I. 1). Similarly, "aural" is derived from **auris**, *ear* (VI. 26), "continual" from **continuus** (I. 48), and "senatorial" from **senatorius** (C. III. 83), the suffix "-al" replacing the Latin terminations.

83. *a.* Some English Words are formed from Words of ultimate Latin origin by the addition of a suffix of English origin. Thus "falsehood" comes from "false" (Latin **falsus**, VI. 20) with the suffix "-hood" denoting quality; "citizenship" from "citizen," which goes back ultimately to Latin **civis** (VII. 77), with the suffix "-ship" denoting state or office; "instantly" from " instant " (Latin **instans**, Gen. **instantis**, Present Participle of **insto**, I. 16), and "nobly" from "noble" (Latin **nobilis**, I. 2), by addition of the suffix "-ly," which has the same origin as the English word "like."

b. A few English Words are formed from Latin Words by the addition of an English suffix of Greek origin; as "jurist" from **ius**, Gen. **iuris** (I. 4) with the suffix "-ist," which represents a Greek termination denoting the agent; "Caesarism," "nihilism," "terrorism" from **Caesar** (I. 7), **nihil** (I. 11), and **terror** (II. 12) with the suffix "-ism," also of Greek origin, implying doctrine or practise.

84. Many Latin Words, especially those that have come into English through the French, have undergone so great changes that their Latin origin is not at once perceived, though it can always be traced through intermediate forms. Such are "captaincy," from "captain," which is ultimately derived from **caput** (I. 29), *head*, with the suffix "-cy" (*82, b*); "city," from **civitas** (I. 2); "lieutenant," from **locum tenens** (Present Participle of **teneo**, *hold*), one holding another's office or place; "madam," "Madonna," from **mea domina**, Feminine corresponding to the Masculine **meus dominus** (Dative **dominis**, VI. 13); "governor" from **gubernator** (III. 9); "peril" from **periculum** (f. 17), and "perilous" from **periculosus** (I. 33), "preach" from **praedico** (I. 44), and "receive" from **recipio** (I. 5).

85. A few common abbreviations represent Latin Words; as "no." in "no. 9," where "no."

---

[1]This suffix has no connection with a similar suffix of Greek origin found in "democracy" and a few other English words.

stands not for "number" but for **numerō** (I. 5), the Ablative of **numerus**. Also, the symbols for English money, £ s. d., now read as "pounds, shillings, pence," are derived from Latin words: £ = **lībra**, a *pound* in weight, whence **lībrīlis**, *weighing a pound* (VII. 81); s. = **solidus**, a Roman gold coin; and d. = **dēnārius**, a Roman silver coin, translated *penny*, though its value as silver was originally between fifteen and twenty cents in our currency. **Solidus**, the name of the coin, came from the Adjective **solidus**, from which our word "solid" is derived; it survives in our word "soldier" as "one having pay" for military service. **Dēnārius** came from **dēnī**, *ten each* (I. 43) because it originally contained ten of the monetary units called **as**, and **as** survives in our word "ace." Our abbreviation "Mr." is for "Master," but "Master" is of Latin origin, being derived from **magister** (C. III. 43).

86. The value of the contribution which the English language has received from the Latin cannot be measured in percentages of words. The words of English origin which we use are largely concrete, and well fitted to express fundamental ideas; but we are indebted to the Latin for a very large proportion of the words employed in the arts, science, and education, which fit the English language to be the vehicle of expression for a constantly developing civilization.

SYNTAX

SUBJECT AND PREDICATE

87. *a.* A Noun or Pronoun, or an Adjective taking the place of a Noun, when used as the Subject of a Finite Verb is in the Nominative Case; as, **lēgātī revertērunt**, *the envoys returned* (I. 3); **integrī dēfessīs succēderent,** *fresh men were relieving the exhausted* (VII. 41).

b. A Personal Pronoun used as a Subject is expressed only when there is emphasis or contrast; as, **Dēsilīte, commīlitōnēs, nisi vultis aquilam hostibus prōdere; ego certē meum . . . officium praestiterō,** *Leap down, comrades, unless you want to abandon your eagle to the enemy; I at any rate shall have done my duty.* Here **ego** is emphatic, but the subject of the Plural Verbs is not emphatic, and hence is not expressed (IV. 25).

c. Instead of a Noun or other Substantive word an Infinitive or a Clause may be used as the Subject of a Verb; as, **Commodissimum vīsum est Gāium Valerium Procillum . . . mittere,** *It seemed most expedient to send Gaius Valerius Procillus,* where **mittere** is the subject of **vīsum est** (I. 47).

88. *a.* A Predicate Noun, in the same case as the Subject, is used with **sum** and the Passives of Verbs of calling, choosing, making, esteeming, and the like; as, **Dīvicō prīnceps fuit,** *Divico was the leading man* (I. 13); **quī . . . Gallī appellantur,** *who are called Gauls* (I. 1); **ducēs eī dēliguntur,** *those are chosen (as) leaders* (III. 23).

b. A Predicate Noun after Passive Participles is similarly used; as, **obsidibus acceptīs prīmīs cīvitātis,** *having received the foremost men of the state as hostages,* lit. *the foremost men of the state having been received as hostages* (II. 13).

89. *a.* A Verb is sometimes omitted when it can easily be supplied from the context; as, **aciēs** (I. 25), where **intulit** is to be supplied.

b. Forms of **sum** are often omitted in the compound tenses; as, **occīsa** (I. 53) for **occīsa est,** *was killed.*

c. In the Future Active and Perfect Passive Infinitive, and also in the Present Passive Infinitive of the Periphrastic Conjugation, **esse** is frequently omitted; as, **conciliātūrum** (I. 3) for **conciliātūrum esse**; **itūrōs atque futūrōs** (I. 13) for **itūrōs esse atque futūrōs esse**; **lātūrī** for **lātūrī esse** (I. 40); **occīsum . . . pulsum . . . missum** (I. 7) for **occīsum esse . . . pulsum esse . . . missum esse**; **exspectandum** (I. 11) for **exspectandum esse.**

90. *a.* In certain connections **est, erat,** etc., may best be translated *there is, there was,* etc., with the Subject following; as, **Flūmen est Arar,** *There is a river, the Arar* (I. 12); **Erant itinera duo,** *There were two routes* (I. 6).

b. Occasionally *there* may be used in like manner in translating other verbs than **sum**; as, **Relinquēbātur ūna via,** *There remained only the route* (I. 9).

NOUNS

91. *a.* Nouns used as Appositives, whether in the Nominative or in the Oblique cases, agree in case with the Nouns to which they belong; as, **Ariovistus, rēx Germānōrum,** *Ariovistus, king of the Germans* (I. 31); **ā Bibracte, oppidō** (Ablative) **Aeduōrum,** *from Bibracte, a town of the Aeduans* (I. 23).

b. Nouns in Predicate Apposition sometimes agree with an unexpressed Subject, which is implied in the Verb; as, **hominēs . . . (eī) afficiēbantur,** *(being) men . . . they were sorely troubled* (I. 2).

c. A Noun referring to a Part may be in Apposition to a Noun expressing the Whole (Partitive Apposition); as, **itinera duo: ūnum (iter), alteram (iter),** *two routes: the one (route) . . . , the other . . .* (I. 6).

92. *a.* A Plural Noun is often used in Latin where English usage prefers the Singular; as, **ad effēminandōs animōs,** *to weaken the courage* (I. 1).

b. An Abstract Noun is sometimes used in Latin where English usage expects a Concrete Plural Noun; as, **coniūrātiōnem nōbilitātis,** *a conspiracy of the nobles,* lit. *of the nobility* (I. 2).

c. Abstract Nouns are sometimes used in the Plural to denote instances of the Quality; as; **ad frīgora atque aestūs vītandōs,** *to avoid heat and cold* (VI. 22).

THE VOCATIVE CASE

93. The Vocative Case is used only in Direct Address; as, **Quid dubitās, Vorēne?** *Vorenus, why do you hesitate?* (V. 44).

THE GENITIVE CASE

94. *a.* In the Possessive Genitive the idea of Possession or of Close Connection is generally prominent: as, **fīnēs Sēquanōrum,** *the territory of the Sequanians, the Sequanians' country* (I. 8); **ā hūmānitāte prōvinciae,** *from the refinement of the Province* (I. 1).

b. The Possessive Genitive is used idiomatically with **causā, grātiā** and **īnstar**; as, **auxiliī causā,** *as an auxiliary force,* lit. *for the sake of support* (II. 24); **suī pūrgandī grātiā,** *in order to clear themselves* (VII. 43); **īnstar mūrī mūnīmentum,** *a barrier like a wall,* lit. *the image of a wall* (II. 17).

c. A Genitive, perhaps Possessive in Origin, is used with **prīdiē** and **postrīdiē**; as, **prīdiē eius diēī,** *the day before that day, on the previous day* (I. 47); **postrīdiē eius diēī,** *the next day* (II. 12).

d. With **sum** and **fīō** the Possessive Genitive is used Predicatively with the meaning (*the business*) *of belonging to,* etc.; as, **neque sē iūdicāre Galliam potius esse Ariovistī quam populī Rōmānī,** *and he judged that Gaul did not belong to Ariovistus* (lit. *was not Ariovistus's*) *any more than to the Roman people* (1. 45).

95. The Subjective Genitive designates the Person or Agent whose act or feeling is expressed in the Noun on which the Genitive depends; as, **ab Ariovistī iniūriā,** *from the wrongdoing of Ariovistus* (I. 31); **terrōre equōrum,** *the fright caused by the horses,* lit. *of the horses* (IV. 33).

96. The Appositional Genitive defines or explains the Noun on which it depends; as, **iniūria retentōrum equitum,** *the wrong (committed by) detaining the knights,* the detaining of the knights being the wrong expressed in **iniūria** (III. 10).

97. *a.* The Partitive Genitive, or Genitive of the Whole, designates the Whole of which a Part is expressed in the Noun, Pronoun, Adjective, or Numeral on which it depends; as, quārum ūnam (**partem**), *of which* (i.e. *three parts*) *one* (*part*) (I. 1); **mīlia passuum CCXL**, *two hundred and forty miles*, lit. *two hundred and forty thousands of paces* (I. 2); **prīmōs cīvitātis**, *the first* (*men*) *of the state* (II. 3); **nihil reliquī . . . fēcērunt**, *they spared no effort*, lit. *nothing of the rest* (II. 26).

b. The Part on which the Genitive of the Whole depends may be indefinitely expressed by the Singular Neuter of a Pronoun or of an Adjective, used substantively, or by the Adverb **satis** used substantively; as, **quid negōtiī**, *what business*, lit. *what of business* (I. 34); **quid suī cōnsiliī sit**, *what his plan was* (I. 21); **aliquid novī cōnsiliī**, *some new scheme or other* (IV. 32); **quantum bonī**, *how great good* (I. 40); **plūs dolōris**, *more suffering* (I. 20); **tōtīus Galliae plūrimum possent**, *were the most powerful of all Gaul* (I. 3); **satis causae**, *sufficient ground*, lit. *enough of cause* (I. 19).

c. In the English phrase *all of these* there is no Partitive idea, because *these* and *all* refer to the same whole. Such phrases are not expressed in Latin by the Partitive Genitive but by words agreeing in Case; as, **Hī omnēs**, *all these* (I. 1); **complūrēs nostrī**, *a large number of our men* (I. 52); **omnium vestrum**, *of all of you, of you all* (VII. 77).

d. Caesar sometimes uses **dē** or **ex** with the Ablative instead of the Genitive of the Whole; so regularly with **quīdam** and words referring to Number. Thus, **quīdam ex hīs**, *some of these* (II. 17); **paucī dē nostrīs**, *a few of our men* (I. 15).

e. A Genitive of the Whole may be used with an Adverb in the Superlative Degree; as **Deōrum maximē Mercurium colunt**, *of the gods they worship Mercury above all others* (VI. 17).

98. *a.* A variety of the Genitive of the Whole is the Genitive of Material, which is used to designate the Material or Units included in the Noun on which it depends; as, **multitūdinem hominum**, *a force of men*, lit. *a multitude* (*made up*) *of men* (I. 4); **aciem legiōnum quattuor**, *a line* (*consisting*) *of four legions* (I. 24).

b. The Material of which anything is made is expressed by the Ablative with **ex**; as, **scūtīs ex cortice factīs**, *with shields made of bark* (II. 33).

99. The Genitive is used to express Origin; as, **Catamantāloedis fīliō**, *son of Catamantaloedes* (I. 3).

100. *a.* The Genitive of Quality and the Genitive of Measure are modified by Adjectives or Numerals; as, **hominēs magnae virtūtis**, *men of great valour* (II. 15); **mūrum in altitūdinem pedum sēdecim**, *a rampart sixteen feet high*, lit. *to the height of sixteen feet* (I. 8).

b. The Genitive of Quality and Genitive of Measure may be used predicatively; as, **Erant eius modī sitūs oppidōrum**, *The strongholds were so situated*, lit. *the situations of the strongholds were of such a character* (III. 12).

101. The Neuter Genitives **magnī**, **tantī**, and some others are used predicatively, without a Noun, to express Indefinite Value; as, **magnī habēbātur**, *was considered of great weight* (IV. 21); **tantī**, *of so great account* (I. 20).

102. The Objective Genitive is used with Nouns to denote the Object toward which Action or Feeling is directed, and with Adjectives to limit their application: as, **reī pūblicae** (Genitive) **iniūriam**, *the wrong done to the state* (I. 20); **rēgnī cupiditāte inductus**, *led by desire of kingly power* (I. 2); **imperītum rērum**, *unversed in affairs* (I. 44); **alicuius iniūriae cōnscius**, *conscious of any wrong-doing* (I. 14).

a. Caesar uses **reminīscor** and **oblīvīscor** with a Genitive of the thing remembered or forgotten; as, **reminīscerētur incommodī**, *he should recall the disaster* (I. 13); **contumēliae oblīvīscī**, *to be forgetful of an affront* (I. 14).

b. A Genitive of the Charge is used with Verbs of Accusing and Condemning; as, **prōditiōnis īnsimulātus**, *accused of treachery* (VII. 20); **capitis damnārent**, *should condemn* (*to loss*) *of civil rights*, lit. *of head* (C. III. 83).

c. Caesar uses the impersonal **paenitet** with the Accusative of the Person repenting and the Genitive of the Object of Repentance; as, **quōrum eōs paenitēre necesse est,** *of which they of necessity repent*, lit. *of which it is necessary that it repent them* (IV. 5).

d. Caesar uses **interest** with a Genitive Neuter to express the degree of concern; as, **magnī**

interesse arbitrābātur, *he thought that it was of great importance* (V. 4).

e. With **interest** Caesar uses a Genitive of the Interest concerned; as, **reī pūblicae commūnisque salūtis intersit** (Historical Present), *it concerned the State and their mutual welfare* (II. 5).

THE DATIVE CASE

104. *a.* The Dative of the Indirect Object is used with Transitive Verbs which have a Direct Object in the Accusative, or an Infinitive Clause as Object, and also with the Passive of such Verbs; as, **dat** (Historical Present) **negōtium Senonibus**, *He assigned the task to the Senones* (II. 2); **nostrīs — dabātur**, *was given to our men* (IV. 29).

b. With such Verbs the place of the Direct Object may be taken by an Adverb or a Clause; as, **nē suae magnopere virtūtī tribueret**, *that he should not presume over-much upon his valour* (I. 13).

105. The Dative of the Indirect Object is used with many Intransitive Verbs meaning *persuade, trust, distrust; command, obey, serve, resist; pardon, spare; please, displease, favour, indulge; approach; envy, threaten, rebuke,* and some others; as, **persuādet Casticō**, *he persuades Casticus* (I. 3), that is, *he prevails upon Custicus.* The Roman point of view in these verbs is somewhat different from that of the English, which with corresponding verbs generally uses a Direct Object. The following are among the Intransitive Verbs thus used with the Dative by Caesar: **accidit**, *happens to* (I. 18); **appropinquō**, *approach* (II. 10); **cēdō**, *yield to* (VII. 89); **concēdō**, *acknowledge inferiority to* (IV. 7); **cōnfīdō**, *trust* (I. 42); **cōnsulō**, *look out for* (VI. 31); **contingit**, *it falls to the lot of* (I. 43); **crēdō**, *intrust* (VI. 31); **cupiō**, *wish well to* (I. 18). **dēspērō**, *despair of* (III. 12); **diffīdō**, *lose confidence in* (VI. 38); **ēvenit**, *it turns out* (IV. 25); **faveō**, *favour* (VI. 7); **ignōscō**, *pardon* (I. 45); **imperō**, *command* (I. 28); **indulgeō**, *treat with favour* (I. 40); **invideō**, *envy, be jealous of* (II. 31). **licet**, *it is permitted* (I. 30); **medeor**, *remedy* (V. 24); **noceō**, *do injury to* (III. 13); **obtemperō**, *submit to* (IV. 21); **parcō**, *spare* (VI. 28); **pāreō**, *obey* (VI. 13); **persuādeō**, *persuade* (I. 2); **placet**, *it pleases* (I. 34); **prōspiciō**, *arrange for* (I. 23); **prōsum**, *be of benefit to* (VI. 40). **repugnō**, *contend against* (I. 19); **resistō**, *oppose* (I. 25); **satisfaciō**, *make restitution* (I. 14); **serviō**, *be the slave of* (IV. 5), *devote one's self to* (VII. 34); **studeō**, *be eager for* (I. 9), *give attention to* (II. 17); **temperō**, *restrain* (I. 33).

106. *a.* A few Intransitive Verbs are also used Transitively by Caesar, and govern the Accusative: examples are, **impūnitātem concēdere**, *grant escape from punishment* (I. 14); **mīlitēs, quōs imperāverat**, *the soldiers that he had levied* (I. 7).

b. Verbs which take the Dative of the Indirect Object are in the Passive used only Impersonally; as, **Sibi persuādērī**, *That the conviction was forced upon him, that he was persuaded* (I. 40).

107. *a.* The Dative of the Indirect Object is used after many Verbs compounded with the Prepositions **ad, ante, com-** (for **cum**), **in, inter, ob, prae, sub**, and **super**; as, **omnibus praestārent**, *they excelled all* (I. 2).

b. Transitive Verbs compounded with these Prepositions may have both a Direct and an Indirect Object, the Dative depending not on the Preposition but on the Compound; as, **fīnitimīs bellum īnferre**, *to wage war on their neighbours* (I. 2).

108. *a.* The Dative is used after Adjectives meaning *agreeable, friendly, hurtful, hostile, like, unlike, near, subject, obedient, suitable, appropriate,* and many others; as, **plēbī acceptus**, *acceptable to the people* (I. 3); **proximī Germānīs**, *next to the Germans* (I. 1); **locum idōneum castrīs**, *a place suitable for a camp* (II. 17).

b. **Similis** is used with the Genitive when referring to an inner or complete resemblance, as, **vērī simile**, *probable*, lit. *having the likeness of truth* (III. 13); otherwise with the Dative; as, **fugae similis**, *like a rout.* (V. 53).

109. *a.* The Dative of Reference designates the Person or Interest affected by the action or state expressed in a Verb, or in a Clause as a whole; it should be translated with *to, for, of,* *from, in,* or left untranslated, according to the meaning of the clause in which it appears, and the requirements of English idiom. Thus, **iniūriae sibi cōnscius fuisset,** *had been conscious of wrong-doing,* lit. *had been conscious, to itself, of wrong-doing* (I. 14); **sī sibi pūrgātī esse vellent,** *if they wanted to clear themselves in his sight,* lit. *to clear themselves with reference to himself* (I. 28); **sēsē Caesarī ad pedēs prōiēcērunt,** *prostrated themselves at Caesar's feet,* lit. *in relation to Caesar* (I. 31).

b. A Dative of Reference is used with Verbs of *taking away,* especially those compounded with **ab, dē,** and **ex** (sometimes called Dative of Separation); thus, **Aeduīs lībertātem sint ēreptūrī,** *that they were going to take away liberty from the Aeduans,* lit. *that as regards the Aeduans, they are,* etc. (I. 17); **scūtō ūnī mīlitī dētrāctō,** *snatching a shield from a soldier,* lit. *to a soldier,* the Dative expressing the point of view of the soldier (II. 25); **longē eīs āfutūrum,** *would be far from benefiting them,* lit. *would be far away with reference to them* (I. 36).

c. A Dative of Reference is used with **interdīcō,** which may take also the Ablative of the Thing; as, **Galliā Rōmānīs interdīxisset,** *had denied to the Romans any rights in Gaul,* lit. *from Gaul* (I. 46).

110. The Dative is used with the Passive Periphrastic Conjugation to express Agency; as, **omnibus Gallīs idem esse faciendum,** *that all the Celts would have to do the same thing* (I. 31); **Caesarī omnia erant agenda,** *Caesar had to see to everything* (II. 20).

111. The Dative is used with the Verb **sum** to denote Possession; as, **Mercātōribus est aditus,** *Traders have access* (IV. 2); **quid . . . Caesarī . . . negōtiī esset,** *what business Caesar . . . had* (I. 34).

112. *a.* The Dative is used with Verbs to denote the Purpose or Tendency of an action; as, **locum domiciliō dēligerent,** *might select a place for a permanent habitation* (I. 30); **locum castrīs dēligit** (Historical Present), *selected a place for a camp* (VII. 16 and often); **Diēs colloquiō dictus est,** *a day was appointed for a conference* (I. 42).

b. **Sum** and several other Verbs may have two Datives, a Dative of Purpose or Tendency and a Dative of Reference; as, **sibi eam rem cūrae futūram,** *that this matter should have his attention,* lit. *should be to him for a care* (I. 33); **cum auxiliō Nerviīs venīrent,** *when they were coming to the assistance of the Nervians,* lit. *for an aid to the Nervians* (II. 29).

THE ACCUSATIVE CASE

113. *a.* The Direct Object of a Transitive Verb is in the Accusative Case; as, **frūmentum combūrunt** (Historical Present), *they burned the grain* (I. 5).

b. Caesar uses as Transitive Verbs several Intransitives compounded with **ad, ante, circum, com-, in, ob, prae, praeter, sub,** and **trāns;** as, **sī īnsulam adīsset,** *if he should have visited the island* (IV. 20); **reliquōs antecēdunt,** *surpass the rest* (III. 8); **eum convēnissent,** *had met him* (I. 27); **sē grātiam initūrōs [esse],** *that they would gain favour* (VI. 43): **initā hieme,** *at the beginning of winter,* lit. *winter having been begun* (III. 7); **tēctum nōn subīssent,** *had not found shelter under a roof,* lit. *had not passed under a roof* (I. 36); **tantam virtūtem praestitērunt,** *displayed so great valour* (II. 27).

c. Caesar uses both **animadvertō** and **animum advertō** with the Accusative of the Direct Object conceived as the object of the mental action expressed by the Compound; thus, **id animum advertit,** *he noticed that* (I. 24); **haec animadvertisset,** *had noticed this* (I. 40).

114. *a.* Transitive Verbs compounded with **trāns** or **circum** may have two Accusatives, one dependent on the Verb, the other on the Preposition; as, **trēs partēs cōpiārum Helvētiōs id flūmen trādūxisse,** *that the Helvetians had taken three-fourths of their forces across the river* (I. 12), **partēs** being the object of **dūcere,** while **flūmen** is governed by **trāns.**

b. In the Passive the Object of the Verb used with two Accusatives becomes a Subject, while the Accusative governed by the Preposition remains; as, **nē maior multitūdō Rhēnum trādūcātur,** *that no greater host be brought across the Rhine* (I. 31).

115. *a.* Verbs of *making, choosing, regarding, giving, sending, having, calling, showing,* and some others, may have two Accusatives, one a Direct Object, the other a Predicate Accusative; as, **quem rēgem constituerat,** *whom he had made king* (IV. 21); **quem 'vergobretum' appellant Aeduī,** *which the Aeduans call Vergobret* (I. 10).

b. In the construction of Verbs of *making, choosing, calling,* etc., with two Accusatives, the Predicate Accusative may be an Adjective; as, **utī . . . cīvitātēs stīpendiāriās habērent,** *that they might have states tributary to them* (I. 30).

c. In the Passive of Verbs of *making, choosing, calling,* etc., the Direct Object of the Active is made the Subject and the Predicate Accusative becomes a Predicate Nominative; as, **quī Celtae appellantur,** *who are called Celts* (I. 1); **Helvētiī certiōrēs factī sunt,** *the Helvetians were informed,* where **certiōrēs,** an adjective in the comparative degree, is predicative (I. 7).

116. *a.* Verbs of *asking, demanding, teaching* may have two Accusatives, one of the Person, the other of the Thing; as, **Aeduōs frūmentum flāgitāre,** *kept pressing the Aeduans for the grain* (I. 10).

b. With Verbs of *asking* and *demanding,* the Person may be expressed by the Ablative with a Preposition, the Thing asked by an Accusative or by a Clause; as, **abs tē ratiōnem reposcent,** *they will demand an accounting from you* (V. 30); **cum ab eīs quaereret quae cīvitātēs . . . essent,** *making inquiry of them what states were* . . . (II. 4).

c. With **quaerō** the Person may be expressed by the Ablative with **ab** or **ex**; as, **quaerit ex sōlō ea,** *asked,* lit. *asks, (him) alone about those things* (I. 18); the Accusative of the Thing may be replaced by an Ablative with **dē**; as, **quōrum dē nātūrā cum quaereret,** *making inquiry about the character of whom* (II. 15).

d. **Volō** is sometimes used like a Verb of *asking,* with two Accusatives; as, **sī quid** (Accusative) **ille sē** (Accusative) **velit,** *if he (Caesar) wished anything of him* (I. 34).

117. *a.* With both Intransitive and Transitive Verbs Caesar some times uses a Neuter Pronoun as an Accusative of Result produced, to carry forward or qualify the meaning: as, **Id eīs persuāsit,** *he persuaded them (to adopt) that (course),* lit. *he persuaded that to them* (I. 2); **hōc facere,** *to do this* (III. 27).

b. The Accusative of Result may be a Noun of kindred meaning with the Verb (Cognate Accusative); thus, **tūtam vītam vīvere,** *to live a safe life.*

118. *a.* The Accusative is used to express Extent and Duration; as, **mīlia passuum XVIIII** (for **undēvīgintī),** *nineteen miles* (I. 8); **multōs annōs,** *many years* (I. 3); **magnam partem aestātis,** *during a great part of the summer* (III. 12); **trīduī viam prōcessisset,** *had advanced a three days' march* (I. 38).

b. Indefinite Extent or Degree may be expressed with certain Verbs by the Neuter Accusative of Pronouns, or of Adjectives used substantively; as, **quicquid possunt,** *whatever strength they have,* lit. *to whatever degree they are able* (II. 17); **quid Germānī virtūte possent,** *what mettle the Germans had,* lit. *to what degree the Germans were able in respect to bravery* (I. 36); **quōrum auctōritās plūrimum valeat** (Historical Present), *whose influence carried very great weight,* lit. *is strong to the highest degree* (I. 17); **sī quid** (Accusative) **opus esset,** *if there should be any need,* lit. *need to any extent* (I. 42).

c. Extent is expressed by the Accusative of **nihil,** and also by **partem** (Accusative of **pars**) used indefinitely, a construction often called Adverbial Accusative; as, **nihil Caesaris imperium exspectābant,** *were not waiting at all for Caesar's orders,* lit. *to extent of nothing, to no extent* (II. 20); **maximam partem lacte atque pecore vīvunt,** *they live mostly on milk and meat,* where **partem** is used indefinitely, not being limited to a definite idea, as it is when a Genitive is dependent upon it (IV. 1).

d. Caesar uses **quod,** Singular Neuter of the Relative **quī,** as an Adverbial Accusative before **sī, nisi,** and **ubi,** where it may be translated *now, moreover, but, and,* or *even,* lit. *as to which;* as, **Quod sī . . . vellet,** *even if he were willing* (I. 14); **Quod sī quid . . .,** *Now if anything* (I. 20).

e. Caesar uses **quid,** Singular Neuter of the Interrogative **quis,** as an Adverbial Accusative with the meaning *why?* lit. *as to what thing?* Thus, **Quid dubitās,** *Why do you hesitate?* (V. 44).

119. *a.* Names of Towns or Small Islands are put in the Accusative to express the Limit of

Motion; as, **Bibracte īre contendit** (Historical Present), *he made haste to go to Bibracte* (I. 23).

b. In like manner **domum**, the Accusative of **domus**, is used to express Limit of Motion; as, **quī domum rediērunt,** *who returned home* (I. 29).

120. *a.* The Accusative of names of towns is used with **ad** to express *to the vicinity of, in the neighbourhood of*; as, **ad Genavam pervenit,** *he proceeded to the vicinity of Geneva* (I. 7); **Caesar . . . ad Alesiam castra fēcit,** *Caesar encamped in the neighbourhood of Alesia* (VII. 68); but Caesar has **Vercingetorīx . . . Alesiam iter facere coepit,** *Vercingetorix began to march to Alesia,* without **ad**, because Vercingetorix fled to the town itself for refuge, **Alesiam** here expressing the Limit of Motion (VII. 68).

b. In such phrases as **ad oppidum Noviodūnum** (II. 12) the Name of the Town is in the Accusative, not because expressing a Limit of Motion, but as an appositive of **oppidum**.

121. The Subject of the Infinitive is in the Accusative; as, **diem īnstāre,** *that the day was at hand* (I. 16).

122. *a.* Caesar uses the following Prepositions with the Accusative only: **ad**, *to;* **adversus**, *against;* **ante**, *before;* **apud**, *near, with, among;* **circā**, *around* (C only); **circiter**, *about;* **circum**, *around;* **cis**, *on this side of;* **citrā**, *on this side of;* **contrā**, *against;* **ergā**, *towards;* **extrā**, *outside of;* **infrā**, *below;* **inter**, *between;* **intrā**, *within;* **iuxtā**, *near;* **ob**, *on account of;* **penes**, *in the possession of;* **per**, *through;* **post**, *after;* **praeter**, *excepting;* **prope**, *near;* **propter**, *on account of;* **secundum**, *along, after, besides, according to;* **suprā**, *above;* **trāns**, *across, on the other side of;* **ultrā**, *beyond;* **versus**, *toward.*

b. Several of these Prepositions are used by Caesar also as Adverbs; as, **contrā**, *in opposition* (I. 18); **suprā**, *above* (II. 18).

123. *a.* With Nouns referring to Persons Caesar often uses **per** with the Accusative to express the Means through which something is done, as distinguished from Direct Agency, which is expressed by the Ablative with **ab**; as, **per eōs**, *with their help,* lit. *by means of them* (I.4).

b. Caesar uses also **propius**, *nearer*, the Comparative of **prope**, and **proximus**, *next*, the Superlative of **propior**, with the Accusative; as, **propius sē**, *nearer to themselves* (IV. 9); **quī proximī Rhēnum incolunt,** *who dwell next to the Rhine* (I. 54).

c. Versus follows its Noun, and is sometimes used in a separable Compound with **ad** and **in**; as, **Metlosēdum versus,** *towards Metlosedum* (VII. 61); **ad Oceanum versus,** *towards the Ocean* (VI. 33).

124. *a.* The Prepositions **in** and **sub** are used with the Accusative to denote Motion, with the Ablative to denote Rest; as, **in partēs trēs,** *into three parts* (I. 1); **in eōrum fīnibus,** *in their country* (I. 1); **sub iugum missum,** *sent under the yoke* (I. 7); **sub aquā,** *under water* (V. 18).

b. **Super** is used ordinarily with the Accusative, but occasionally with the Ablative.

THE ABLATIVE CASE

125. *a.* Caesar uses the following Prepositions with the Ablative: **ā**, or **ab**, **abs**, *away from, by;* **cum**, *with;* **dē**, *down from, concerning;* **ex** or **ē**, *out from, out of;* **prae**, *before;* **prō**, *in front of, for, considering, as;* **sine**, *without.*

b. The form **abs** appears only in **abs tē** (V. 30). **Ab** and **ex** are regularly used before vowels and **h**; **ā** and **ē**, before consonants, but before consonants **ab** and **ex** are also used.

c. With the Ablative of the Personal, Reflexive, and Relative Pronouns **cum** is ordinarily joined; thus **nōbīscum**, *with us* (V. 17); **sēcum**, *with him* (I. 8), *with himself* (I. 36); **quībuscum**, *with whom* (I. 1).

126. *a.* Direct Agency with the Passive is expressed by **ā**, **ab**, with the Ablative; as, **ab Helvētiīs pulsum,** *routed by the Helvetians* (I. 7).

b. Caesar sometimes uses an Abstract or Collective Noun with **ā**, **ab**, to express Agency; as, **ā multitūdine,** *by a host* (III. 2).

c. Caesar often uses **ā**, **ab**, and sometimes **ex**, to indicate a Local Relation, where we use *on,*

in, or *at*; as, **ā dextrō cornū,** *on the right wing,* lit. *from* (*the point of view of*) *the right wing* (I. 52);
ā novissimō agmine, *on the rear* (I. 23); **ā fronte,** *in front* (II. 23).

127. *a.* An Ablative of Separation without a Preposition is regularly used by Caesar with
many Verbs meaning *keep from, refrain from; withdraw from; strip, deprive of; free from; lack, be
without;* as, **proeliō abstinēbat,** *was refraining from battle* (I. 22); **eā spē dēiectī,** *deprived of this
hope* (I. 8).

The most important of the Verbs thus used by Caesar are: **abstineō,** *refrain from;* **careō,** *be
without* (VI. 38); **dēiciō,** *cast down from;* **dēsistō,** *desist from, leave off* (I. 8); **egeō,** *lack* (C. III. 32);
emittō, *let go from* (I. 25); **excēdō,** *withdraw from, leave* (II. 25); **exuō,** *strip* (III. 6); **interclūdō,**
cut off (I. 23). **levō,** *relieve from* (V. 27); **līberō,** *free from* (IV. L9); **nūdō,** *clear* (II. 6); **prohibeō,**
keep from (I. 1); **spoliō,** *rob of, despoil* (V. 6), and **exspoliō,** *rob* (VII. 77).

b. With several of these Verbs the idea of Separation may be expressed by a Preposition; as,
ab oppidīs vim hostium prohibēre, *to defend the towns against the violence of the enemy,* lit. *to
hold back the violence of the enemy from the towns* (I. 11).

c. With other Verbs the Ablative of Separation is regularly accompanied by a Preposition;
as, **exercitum dēdūcat ex hīs regiōnibus,** *leads his army out of these regions* (I. 44).

d. Caesar uses **egeō** with the Genitive also: **nē quis . . . auxiliī egēret,** *that not any one be
without help* (VI. 11).

128. *a.* A variety of the Ablative of Separation is the Ablative of Source, or Origin, which
Caesar uses with **nātus,** participle of **nāscor,** and **ortus,** participle of **orior;** as, **amplissimō
genere nātus,** *sprung from most illustrious stock* (IV. 12); **summō ortus locō,** *born to the highest
station in life,* lit. *risen from the highest place* (VII. 77).

b. Origin is more broadly stated with Prepositions; as, **quibus ortī ex cīvitātibus,** *tribes from
which they* (*were*) *descended* (V. 12); **ortōs ā Germānīs,** *descendants* (lit. *descended*) *from the
Germans* (II. 4); **ab Dīte patre prōgnātōs,** *descendants from Father Dis* (VI. 18).

129. *a.* The Ablative of Comparison is used by Caesar after Comparative Adjectives and
Adverbs; as, **paulō cēterīs hūmāniōrēs, cēterīs** being used instead of **quam cēterī (sunt),** *a
little more civilized than the rest* (IV. 3); **nōn amplius quīnīs aut sēnīs mīlibus passuum,** *not
more than five or six miles each day* (I. 15); **celerius omnī opīniōne,** *more quickly than any one had
anticipated,* lit. *than every expectation* (II. 3).

b. In a few instances Caesar uses **amplius, longius,** and **minus** as if in place of **amplius
quam, longius quam, minus quam,** without influence upon the construction of the Noun
following; as, **nōn amplius pedum sescentōrum** (Genitive of Measure), *not more than six
hundred feet* (I. 38); **neque longius mīlia** (Accusative of Extent) **passuum VIII,** *and not further
than eight miles* (V. 53); **mīlitēs sunt paulō minus DCC dēsīderātī,** *almost seven hundred men
were lost,* lit. *by a small degree less than 700* (VII. 51).

130. *a.* The Place Whence is regularly expressed by the Ablative with a Preposition,
generally **ex** or **dē;** as, **ex agrīs,** *from the country* (I. 4).

b. **Domō,** Ablative of **domus,** is used in the Ablative of the Place Whence without a
Preposition; as, **domō exīre,** *to go out from home* (I. 6).

131. *a.* The Ablative is used to denote Means or Instrument; as, **gladiīs partem eōrum
interfēcērunt,** *killed a part of them with swords* (II. 23); **proeliīs contendunt,** *they contend in
battle,* lit. *by means of battles* (I. 1); **memoriā tenēbat,** *he remembered,* lit. *held by means of memory*
(I. 7).

b. The Ablative of Means may denote persons as well as things; as, **quīngentīs equitibus,**
with five hundred horsemen (I. 15).

c. Caesar uses the Ablative of Means with **ūtor, abūtor, fruor, fungor, nītor, innītor,** and
ordinarily with **potior;** thus **ephippiīs ūtī,** *to use saddle-cloths,* lit. *to assist themselves by means
of saddle-cloths* (IV. 2); **impedīmentīs potītī sunt,** *obtained possession of the baggage,* that is *made
themselves masters by means of the baggage* (I. 26).

d. Caesar uses **potior** also with the Genitive; as, **tōtīus Galliae potīrī,** *to become masters of
the whole* (*of*) *Gaul* (I. 3).

e. Caesar uses an Ablative of Means with **frētus**, *relying on*, lit. *supported by*; as, **victōriīs frētī**, *relying on their victories* (III. 21).

f. The Ablative with **ūtor** is sometimes accompanied by a Predicate Ablative, the construction resembling that of two Accusatives after verbs of *having* {115a}; thus **īsdem ducibus ūsus**, *employing the same men as guides* (II. 7).

132. *a.* **Opus est**, *there is need*, is used with the Ablative of the Thing needed, which may be expressed by a Perfect Passive Participle; thus, **sī quid opus factō esset**, *if anything should require action*, lit. *if there should be need of (something) done, to any extent* (I. 42).

b. With **opus est** the Thing needed may be expressed by a Neuter Pronoun in the Nominative; as, **sī quid** (Subject) **ipsī ā Caesare opus esset**, *if he himself had wanted anything of Caesar*, lit. *if anything were necessary to himself from Caesar* (I. 34); **quid . . . opus esset**, *what was necessary* (II. 22); **Quaecumque opus sunt**, *Whatever is* (lit. *whatever things are*) *necessary* (V. 40).

133. The Ablative of Means is used with a few Adjectives; as, **nāvēs . . . omnī genere armōrum ōrnātissimae**, *ships completely fitted out with every kind of equipment* (III. 14).

134. *a.* Caesar uses the Ablative of the Way by Which with several words referring to Natural Features and Military Operations; as, **adversō colle**, *up the hill*, lit. *by the hill facing them* (II. 19); **quod flūmine subvexerat**, *which he had brought up the river*, lit. *by means of the river* (I. 16); **duābus portīs ēruptiōnem fierī**, *that a sally be made from* (lit. *by*) *two gates* (III. 19).

The words thus used are:

collis, flūmen; fretum (C. II. 3); **iter**, especially in **magnīs itineribus**, *by forced marches* (I. 37); **iugum** (C. III. 97); **pōns** (C. I. 55); **porta, vadum** (I. 6, 8), and **via** (V. 19).

b. The Ablative of the Way by Which is sometimes used indefinitely with words referring to Distance; as, **tantō spatiō secūtī quantum efficere potuērunt**, *following so great a distance* (lit. *by so great a space*) *as they were able to cover* (IV. 35).

135. *a.* An Ablative denoting Cause is used with many Verbs and Adjectives, particularly those which express *pleasure, pain, trust, distrust, boastfulness*, and the like; as, **annī tempore cōnfīsae**, *trusting in the time of year*, lit. *confident because of the time of year* (III. 27); **Quod sua victōriā glōriārentur**, *the fact that they were boasting of* (lit. *by reason of*) *their victory* (I. 14).

b. In some phrases the force of the Ablative of Cause has become obscured, as in **causā** and **grātiā**, *for the sake of*, with the Genitive, and in **iussū, iniussū**, and the like; as, **auxiliī causā**, *as an auxiliary force*, lit. *for the sake of support* (III. 18; II. 24); **iussū Caesaris**, *by (reason of) Caesar's orders* (VII. 3); **iniussū suō et cīvitātis**, *without his own authorization and (that) of the state*, i.e. because of unauthorization (I. 19).

136. *a.* The Ablative of Manner (answering the question "How?") is used by Caesar with **cum**, especially when the Noun is modified by an Adjective; as, **cum cruciātū necābātur**, *was put to death with torture* (V. 45); **multīs cum lacrimīs**, *with many tears* (I. 20).

b. The Ablative of Manner is often used without a Preposition; as, **et mente et animō**, *with heart and soul* (VI. 5).

c. In certain connections Caesar uses an Ablative with the meaning *in accordance with*; as, **Mōribus suīs**, *in accordance with their customs* (I. 4); **cōnsuētūdine populī Rōmānī**, *in accordance with the practise of the Roman people* (III. 23).

137. *a.* The Ablative is used with **cum** to express Accompaniment; as, **cum suīs omnibus cōpiīs**, *with all his forces* (I. 38).

b. An Ablative of Accompaniment referring to Military Operations, when qualified by an Adjective, may be used without **cum**; but if the modifier is a Numeral, **cum** must be used. Thus, **omnibus cōpiīs contendērunt**, *they hastened with all their forces* (II. 7); **cum duābus legiōnibus**, *with two legions* (I. 21).

c. The use of **cum** with the Ablative of Accompaniment is much broader than the meaning *together with*. Examples are: **cōnstituerat cum lēgātīs**, *had appointed with the envoys* (I. 8); **cōnsiliō cum lēgātīs commūnicātō**, *having imparted his determination to his lieutenants* (IV. 13); **cum Caesare ēgit**, *treated with Caesar* (I. 13); **cum illā (cōnsuētūdine) comparandam**, *to be* *compared with that manner of life* (I. 31).

138. An Ablative of Attendant Circumstance is used by Caesar with an Adjective, Pronominal Adjective, or Genitive as modifying word, and without a Preposition; as, **paribus intervāllīs**, *at equal intervals* (I. 51); **imperiō nostrō**, *under our sovereignty* (II. 1); **commodō reī pūblicae**. *with advantage to* (lit. *of*) *the State* (I. 35); **Caesaris voluntāte**, *with Caesar's approval* (I. 30).

139. The Ablative is used with certain Verbs meaning *exchange, mix,* and *accustom;* thus, **nē studium bellī gerendī agrī cultūrā commūtent**, *that they may not exchange their devotion to aggressive warfare for farming* (VI. 22); **nūllō officiō aut dīsciplīnā assuēfactī**, *habituated to* (lit. *familiarized with) no obligation or training* (IV. 1); **admixtum lacte**, *mixed with milk* (C. III. 48).

140. The Ablative of Degree of Difference is used with Comparatives, and with Adverbs or Phrases implying Comparison; as, **paulō longius**, *a little further,* lit. *further by a little* (II. 20); **paucīs ante diēbus**, *a few days before* (I. 18); **mīlibus passuum duōbus ultrā eum**, *two miles beyond him,* lit. *beyond him by two miles* (I. 48).

141. The Ablative of Price is used by Caesar only in indefinite expressions; thus, **parvō pretiō redēmpta**, *purchased at a low price* (I. 18); **impēnsō pretiō**, *at a high price* (IV. 2); **quantō dētrīmentō**, *at how great a loss* (VII. 19); **levī mōmentō**, *of slight account* (VII. 39).

142. *a.* The Ablative of Specification (answering the question "In respect to what?") is used with Verbs and Adjectives and the Adverb **saepe**; as, **cum virtūte omnibus praestārent**, *since they surpassed all in valour* (I. 2); **Suēba nātiōne**, *a Sueban by birth* (I. 53); **numerō ad duodecim**, *about twelve in number,* lit. *in number about twelve* (I. 5); **saepe numerō**, *frequently,* lit. *often in respect to number* (I. 33).

b. The Ablative of Specification is used with **dignus** and **indignus**; as, **nihil, quod ipsīs esset indignum, committēbant**, *they did nothing that was unworthy of them,* lit. *in respect to themselves* (V. 35).

143. *a.* The Descriptive Ablative, or Ablative of Quality, is modified by an Adjective or, more rarely, by a Noun in the Genitive; as, **hominēs inimīcō animō**, *men of unfriendly* (*attitude of*) *mind* (I. 7).

b. The Descriptive Ablative may be used predicatively; as, **ingentī magnitūdine Germānōs esse**, *that the Germans were of huge size* (I. 39); **sunt speciē . . . taurī**, *they have* (lit. *are of*) *the appearance of a bull* (VI. 28).

144. *a.* The Ablative Absolute consists of a Noun or Pronoun in the Ablative with a Participle, Adjective, or Noun in the same case, and is loosely related with the rest of the sentence; as, **rēgnō occupātō**, *having seized the governing power,* lit. *the governing power having been seized* (I. 3).

b. The Ablative Absolute may express Time, Attendant Circumstance, Cause, Condition, Concession, Means, or Manner, and may often be translated by a clause; thus:

(1) Time: **M. Messālā, M. Pisōne cōnsulibus**, *in the consulship of Marcus Messala and Marcus Piso,* lit. *Marcus Messala, Marcus Piso (being) consuls* (I. 2).

(2) Attendant Circumstance: **convocātīs eōrum prīncipibus**, *having called together their leading men* (I. 16); **captō monte et succēdentibus nostrīs**, *after they had reached the height and our men were coming up* (I. 25).

(3) Cause: **omnibus frūgibus āmissīs**, *since all the produce of the fields was gone,* lit. *all . . . having been lost* (I. 28).

(4) Condition: **data facultate**, *if opportunity should have been granted* (I. 7).

(5) Concession or Opposition: **superiōribus locīs occupātīs**, *though the higher positions had been seized* (I. 23).

(6) Means: **eō dēprecātōre**, *through his intercession,* lit. *he (being) intercessor* (I. 9).

(7) Manner: **equō admissō**, *with (his) horse at top speed,* lit. *his horse having been let go* (I. 22).

145. *a.* The Place Where is regularly expressed by the Ablative with a Preposition; as, **in eōrum fīnibus**, *in their territories* (I. 1).

b. Names of Towns, excepting those in the Singular of the First and Second Declensions, are put in the Ablative of the Place Where, without a Preposition; as, **Bibracte,** *at Bibracte* (VII. 90).

c. The Noun **locus**, Singular and Plural, is often used in the Ablative of the Place Where without a Preposition, as are also several other Nouns when modified by an Adjective, particularly **tōtus**; thus, **aliēnō locō**, *on unfavourable ground*, lit. *in an unfavourable place* (I. 15); **tōtīs castrīs**, *throughout the camp*, lit. *in the whole camp* (I. 39); **eōdem vēstīgiō**, *in the same spot* (IV. 2).

146. With Names of Towns of the First and Second Declensions, Singular, Place Where is expressed by the Locative; as, **Cēnabī**, *at Cenabum* (VII. 14); also **domī**, Locative of **domus**, *at home* (I. 18).

147. *a.* The Time When, and Time Within Which anything happens, may be denoted by the Ablative without a Preposition; as, **diē quārtō**, *on the fourth day* (I. 26); **paucīs annīs**, *within a few years* (I. 31).

b. Words that have only an indirect reference to Time are some times put in the Ablative of Time When or Within Which; as, **patrum nostrōrum memoriā**, *within the memory of our fathers* (I. 12); **initiō ōrātiōnis**, *at the beginning of his statement* (I. 43).

c. Intervals of Space and Duration of Time are sometimes expressed by the Ablative, especially when modified by an Adjective or Genitive; as, **mīlibus passuum sex**, *six miles* (*distant*), lit. *by six thousands of paces* (I. 48); **tōtā nocte iērunt**, *all night long they went on* (I. 26).

ADJECTIVES

148. *a.* Adjectives and Participles, whether Attributive or Predicative, agree in Gender, Number, and Case with the Noun or Pronoun to which they belong.

b. Attributive Adjectives and Participles stand in direct relation with a Noun or Pronoun; as, **fortissimō virō** (Abl.), *a very brave man* (II. 25); **Is, rēgnī cupiditāte inductus,** *He, led on by a desire of kingly power* (I. 2).

c. Predicate Adjectives, and Participles in Predicate used as Adjectives, are connected with a Noun or Pronoun through a Verb or Participle; as, **fortissimī sunt Belgae,** *the Belgians are the bravest* (I. 1); **quī perītissimus habēbātur,** *who was considered highly skilled* (I. 21); **Gallia est dīvīsa,** *Gaul is divided*, the Perfect Passive Participle of **dīvidō** being used as an Adjective; if **est dīvīsa** were here a Perfect Passive tense, it would have to be translated *has been divided* or *was divided* (I. 1).

d. A Predicate Adjective or Participle limiting an Infinitive or Clause is Neuter; as, **perfacile esse . . . potīrī,** *that it was exceedingly easy* (or, *a very easy thing*) *to obtain possession of*, **perfacile** being the Predicate after **esse**, to which **potīrī** stands as subject (I. 2).

e. A Participle forming part of an Infinitive may agree with the Subject of the Principal Verb; as, **meritus [esse] vidēbātur,** *was seen to have earned* (I. 40).

149. Demonstrative and other Pronouns used like Adjectives agree with the word to which they belong; as, **eō tempore**, *at that time* (I. 8); **quā arrogantiā**, *what presumption* (I. 40); **id ipsum**, *that very thing* (VII. 50).

150. *a.* An Attributive Adjective used with two or more Nouns regularly agrees with the Nearest; as, **eādem alacritāte ac studiō**, *the same eagerness and enthusiasm* (IV. 24).

b. A Predicate Adjective used with two or more Nouns is regularly Plural; when the Nouns are of Different Genders, the Adjective is generally Masculine if Persons are referred to, Neuter if only Things or Abstract Qualities are denoted, though even in this case the agreement may be with the nearer substantive; as, **frāter et soror eōrum bonī sunt**, *their brother and sister are good*; **et mūrus et porta alta erant**, *both the wall and the gate were high*; **ut bracchia atque umerī . . . līberī esse possent**, *that their arms and shoulders might be free* (VII. 56).

c. An Adjective or Participle may agree with a Noun in Sense, without regard to Grammatical Gender or Number; as, **hominum mīlia** (Neuter) **VI, perterritī** (Masculine), *six* *thousand (of) men, thoroughly frightened* (I. 27).

d. A Noun, particularly a Noun with Verbal Force, is sometimes modified by a prepositional phrase; as, **lēgātiōnem ad cīvitātēs,** *the office of envoy to the states* (I. 3).

151. Adjectives are sometimes used in Latin where in English an Adverb or a Phrase is required; as, **laetī . . . ad castra pergunt** (Historical Present), *joyfully . . . they advanced against the camp* (III. 13); **viātōrēs etiam invītōs cōnsistere cōgant,** *they oblige travelers, even against their will, to stop* (IV. 5).

152. *a.* Certain Adjectives often designate a part of that to which they refer; as, **in colle mediō,** *halfway up the hill* (I. 24); **prīmā nocte,** *in the first part of the night* (I. 27); **summus mōns,** *the top of the height* (I. 22).

The Adjectives thus used by Caesar are **extrēmus** (as II. 5); **īnfimus** (II. 18); **medius; multus** (I. 22); **novissimus,** in **novissimum agmen** (I. 15 and often), *the rear of a marching column* as the *latest part* of a column to pass a given point; **prīmus** and **summus.**

b. The Adjectives **prīnceps, prior, primus** are sometimes used by Caesar to designate the first to do or experience something; as, **prīnceps poenās persolvit,** *was the first to pay the penalty* (I. 12); **neque priōrēs bellum īnferre,** *did not take the lead in waging war,* where **prior** is used because only two peoples, the Germans and the Romans, are referred to (IV. 7).

c. The Adjective **multus** and another Adjective agreeing with the same Noun are joined by **et** or **-que;** as, **multīs gravibusque vulneribus,** *many severe wounds* (II. 25).

153. *a.* The Comparative and Superlative of both Adjectives and Adverbs sometimes have shades of meaning best expressed in English by *too, rather, very, exceedingly,* or *highly,* and the like, with the Positive; as, **paulō fortius,** *unusually brave,* lit. *a little braver than usual* (III. 14); **lātissimō atque altissimō,** *very wide and very deep* (I. 2).

b. A Superlative is sometimes modified by an Adverb; as, **longē nōbilissimus,** *far the highest in rank* (I. 2).

c. The highest possible degree is expressed by **quam** with the Superlative, as **quam maximum numerum,** *as great a number as possible, the greatest possible number* (I. 3); **quam celerrimē potuit,** *as quickly as possible* (I. 37); **quam prīmum,** *as soon as possible* (I. 40).

154. *a.* Adjectives and Participles are used as Substantives, frequently in the Plural, less often in the Singular; as, **vērī** (Neuter) **simile,** *probable,* lit. *like truth* (III. 13); **nostrī,** *our men* (I. 52); **novissimīs** (Masculine), *for the rear,* lit. *for those last* (I. 25); **sua,** *their possessions* (I. 11); **prō vīsō,** *as seen,* lit. *for (that which was) seen* (I. 22).

b. Caesar uses the Genitive Singular Neuter **suī** with a collective force in the Gerundive Construction, and in such cases it should be translated as if plural; as, **suī colligendī facultātem,** *opportunity of collecting their forces,* lit. *of collecting themselves* (III. 6).

PRONOUNS

155. The Genitives **meī, nostrī, tuī,** and **vestrī** (39a) are regularly Objective, **nostrum** and **vestrum** being used in other relations; as, **tantā contemptiōne nostrī,** *with so great contempt for us* (V. 29); **omnium vestrum,** *of you all* (VII. 77).

156. The Plural is often used for the Singular of the Pronoun of the First Person, just as in our "editorial we"; thus Caesar when referring to himself as writer often uses a Plural Verb, as, **ut ante dēmōnstrāvimus,** *as we have previously shown* (II. 22).

157. *a.* The Possessive Pronouns are expressed only when required for the sake of Clearness, Emphasis, or Contrast; in translating they must be supplied in accordance with English idiom: as, **Cōnsidius, equō admissō,** *Considius with (his) horse at top speed* (I. 22).

b. When expressed for Clearness, and unemphatic, the Possessive Pronoun follows its Noun, as, **in cīvitāte suā,** *in his state* (I. 3); when used for Emphasis or Contrast, the Possessive Pronoun precedes its Noun, as, **meum ofiicium,** *MY duty* (IV. 25).

c. Caesar often uses **noster** to designate that which is Roman; as, **nostram amīcitiam,** *our friendship* (I. 43).

d. A Possessive Pronoun and a Genitive are sometimes coordinated in construction; as, **suō populīque Rōmānī beneficiō**, *with his own kindness and that of the Roman people*, that is, *kindness of himself and of the Roman people* (I. 35).

e. **Suus** may mean *his characteristic, his well-known*; as **suā clēmentiā**, *his well-known clemency* (II. 14).

158. *a.* The Reflexive Pronoun of the Third Person, **sē**, and the corresponding Possessive **suus**, refer to the Subject of the Verb; in a Subordinate Clause they may refer to the Subject of the Principal Clause (Indirect Reflexive). Thus, **sē ēripuit,** *he rescued himself* (I. 4); **legiō . . . eī grātiās ēgit, quod dē sē optimum iūdicium fēcisset,** *the legion . . . conveyed thanks to him because he had passed an extremely favourable opinion on it* (I. 41).

b. In the Pronouns of the First and Second Persons the regular forms are sometimes Reflexive, as, **mē servāre nōn possum,** *I cannot save myself* (VII. 50); so also *is*, as **eōs,** *themselves* (II. 1).

c. In translating into Latin the English Possessives "his," "her," "its," "their," when referring to the subject of the Verb must be rendered by forms of the Reflexive **suus.**

159. The Reciprocal Relation is expressed by **inter sē** (lit. *among themselves*), which must be translated in accordance with the requirements of English idiom; as, **inter sē dant,** *they gave* (lit. *give*) *to one another* (I. 3); **inter sē differunt,** *they differ from one another* (I. 1); **inter sē collocūtī,** *having conferred with one another* (IV. 30); **cohortātī inter sē,** *urging one another on* (IV. 25); **inter sē contenderent,** *they strove together* (I. 31); **inter sē,** *referring to two persons, with each other* (V. 44).

160. *a.* The Demonstrative Pronoun **hīc,** *this,* refers to something near the speaker or the subject of thought; **iste,** *that of yours,* to something near the person addressed; **ille,** *that,* to something more remote; and **is,** *that,* to something thought of in a less definite relation. Thus: **Hīc pāgus,** *This canton* (I. 12); **Animī est ista mollitia,** *That is lack of resolution on your part* (VII. 77); **illī simile bellō,** *like that war* with the Cimbrians and Teutons (VII. 77); **Is diēs,** *That day* just referred to (I. 6).

b. Caesar frequently uses the Demonstrative **is,** less frequently **hīc** and **ille,** where the English has a Personal Pronoun of the Third Person; as, **ad eōs,** *to them* (I. 1); **cur hunc quisquam discessūrum iūdicāret,** *why should any one suppose that he* (Ariovistus) *would withdraw* (I. 40); **illum ūnō diē fēcisse . . .**, *that he* (Caesar) *had in one day accomplished* (I. 13).

c. Caesar frequently uses the Neuter Singular and Neuter Plural of **hīc, ille,** and **is** with the meaning *this* (thing), *that* (thing), *it, these things, those things*; a Noun may sometimes be supplied in translation. Thus, **id quod,** *that which* (I. 5); **Id eīs persuāsit,** *he persuaded them* (to) *that course* (I. 2); **illa esse vēra,** *that those statements were true* (I. 20).

d. A Demonstrative Pronoun is sometimes used in Latin where English usage prefers an Article; thus, **Ea rēs,** *The matter,* lit. *that thing* (I. 4); **eum locum,** *a place* (II. 16).

e. A Demonstrative Pronoun used as Subject is regularly attracted into agreement with a Noun in the Predicate; as **Animī est ista mollitia,** for **istud est animī mollitia,** *that is lack of resolution on your part* (VII. 77).

161. *a.* The Demonstratives **hīc** and **ille** sometimes refer to what follows; as, **hōc facilius . . . quod,** *the more easily on this* (account) *because* (I. 2); **multīs dē causīs . . . quārum illa fuit iūstissima . . . quod,** *for many reasons, of which this was the most weighty, that* (IV. 16).

b. Caesar sometimes uses **hīc** and **ille** in contrast, with the meaning *the latter* (that last mentioned) and *the former* (that previously mentioned); as, **Reliquī . . . sē atque illōs alunt; hī rūrsus annō post in armīs sunt, illī domī remanent,** *The rest support themselves and those in the field; the latter after one year are again in arms, the former remain at home* (IV. I).

c. A Conjunction followed by **is** or **hīc** may express an Emphatic Characterization; as, **legiōnem, neque eam plēnissimam** (sc. **legiōnem**), *the legion, and that lacking its full strength,* lit. *and that not most full* (III. 2).

162. *a.* The Intensive Pronoun **ipse** with Nouns and Pronouns has the meaning *self, very*; as, **ipsī magistrātūs,** *the magistrates themselves* (I. 17); **ipsum esse Dumnorīgem,** *that Dumnorix* *was the very man* (I. 18); **in ipsīs rīpīs,** *on the very banks* (II. 23).

b. In Subordinate Clauses **ipse** may be used as an Indirect Reflexive referring to the Principal Subject, or to avoid ambiguity; as, **Ariovistus respondit, sī quid ipsī ā Caesare opus esset,** *Ariovistus answered that if he himself had wanted anything of Caesar*, lit. *if anything were necessary to himself from Caesar* (I. 34).

c. Contrasted pronouns are often placed in proximity; as, **sē ipsī interficiunt,** *they all killed one another*, lit. *they themselves slay themselves* (V. 37).

163. *a.* A Relative Pronoun agrees with its Antecedent in Gender and Number, but its Case depends upon its construction in the clause to which it belongs; as, **trēs (legiōnēs,** Fem., Acc.), **quae** (Fem., Pl., Nom.) **. . . hiemābant,** *three legions which were wintering* (I. 10).

b. A Relative referring to two or more Antecedents of the same Gender and Number agrees with them in Gender, but in Number may agree with the nearest Antecedent, or be Plural; as, **prō suā clēmentiā ac mānsuētūdine, quam audīrent,** *in accordance with his forbearance and graciousness, of which they were hearing* (II. 31); **fīlius et frātris fīlius, . . . quōs . . . ,** *his son and his brother's son, whom . . .* (V. 27).

c. A Relative referring to two or more Antecedents of different Gender or Number may agree with the nearest Antecedent, or be Masculine Plural in case one Antecedent denotes a man, Feminine Plural in case one Antecedent denotes a woman and the others things, or Neuter Plural in case only things are denoted; thus, **frūmentō** (Neut.) **commeātūque, quī** (M., Sing.), *grain and (other) supplies which . . .* (I. 48); **mātrēs familiae . . . petiērunt, nē sē** (Fem.), **et līberōs dēderent, quōs . . . ,** *the matrons besought not to give up themselves and the children whom* (VII. 26); **ūsus ac disciplīna, quae** (Neuter Plural) **. . . ,** *experience and training, which . . .* (I. 40).

164. *a.* The Antecedent of a Relative Pronoun is sometimes omitted; as, **(eī incolunt) quī,** *those inhabit who* (I. 1).

b. Caesar sometimes uses a Relative referring to an implied Antecedent; as, **servīlī tumultū, quōs . . . ,** as if he had said **tumultū servōrum, quōs . . . ,** *in the uprising of the slaves, whom . . .* (I. 40).

c. A Noun in Predicate attracts a Relative Pronoun standing as subject into agreement with it; as, **Belgās, quam** (for **quōs) tertiam esse Galliae partem dīxerāmus,** *the Belgians who, we had said, form* (lit. *are) a third of Gaul* (II. 1).

d. A Plural Relative may refer for its Antecedent to a Singular Collective Noun which suggests Plurality; as, **equitātum . . . quī videant,** *cavalry . . . to see*, lit. *who should see* (I. 15).

165. *a.* An Antecedent is sometimes repeated in a Relative Clause, and should be translated only once; as, **itinera duo, quibus itineribus,** *two routes by which* (I. 6), not *by which routes*.

b. An Appositional Antecedent is sometimes incorporated in a Relative Clause, and should be translated; as, **quod tempus convēnerat,** *the time which had been agreed on* (II. 19).

c. An Antecedent is often incorporated in a Relative Clause; as, **Cui ratiōnī, . . . hāc,** *By the cunning, . . . for which* (I. 40).

166. Caesar uses the Neuter of a Relative or Demonstrative Pronoun, sometimes both a Demonstrative and a Relative, referring to a Clause or Thought as a whole; as, **supplicātiō dēcrēta est, quod . . . ,** *a thanksgiving was decreed, (a distinction) which . . .* (II. 35); **magna, id quod necesse erat accidere, perturbātiō facta est,** *a great commotion, as was bound to be the case, ensued* (IV. 29).

167. A Relative is often used in Latin at the beginning of a Clause or Sentence where English idiom requires a Demonstrative, with or without a connective; as, **Quā dē causā,** *And for this reason, For this reason* (I. 1); **Quī . . . proelium committunt** (Historical Present), *They (or And they) . . . joined battle* (I. 15).

168. Of the Indefinite Pronouns, Caesar uses **quīdam,** *a certain*, in respect to persons or things distinctly thought of but not described; **aliquis,** *some, any, somebody*, of persons or things referred to in a general way; **quis** and **quī,** *any, some*, still more vaguely, with **sī, nisi, seu, nē,** and **ubi;** and **quisquam,** *any at all*, in Interrogative or Negative Clauses or in a

Clause following a Comparative; as, **quāsdam rēs,** *certain things* (I. 30); **quīdam ex mīlitibus,** *a certain one* (or *one*) *of the soldiers* (I. 42); **alicuius iniūriae,** *of any wrong-doing* (I. 14); **sī quid vellent,** *if they wanted anything* (I. 7); **Cur quisquam iūdicāret,** *Why should any one suppose* (I. 40); **prius quam quicquam cōnārētur,** *before taking any measures,* lit. *before he should attempt anything at all* (I. 19).

169. Caesar uses the Indefinite Distributive Pronoun **uterque,** *each of two,* in the Plural as well as the Singular; as, **utrīsque castrīs,** *for each camp* (I. 51); **ab utrīsque,** *by those on each side* (IV. 26).

170. a. Caesar sometimes uses the Indefinite Distributive Pronoun **quisque,** *each,* with a Superlative to designate a Class, or with a Numeral Ordinal to indicate a Proportion; thus, **nōbilissimī cuiusque līberōs,** *the children of every man of high rank* (I. 31); **decimum quemque mīlitem,** *one soldier in ten,* lit. *each tenth soldier* (V. 52).

b. Caesar uses **quisque,** *each,* in close connection with **sē** and **suus;** as, **cum sibi quisque . . . peteret,** *when each one was seeking for himself* (II. 11); **utī eōs testēs suae quisque virtūtis habēret,** *that each might have them as witnesses of his own valour* (I. 52).

171. a. Of the Pronominal Adjectives, **cēterī** (Plural) means *the other, the rest besides those mentioned;* **reliquī,** *the rest* in the sense *those remaining* after some are taken; as, **Aeduōs cēterōsque amīcōs populī Rōmānī,** *the Aeduans and the other friends of the Roman people* (I. 35); **reliquōs Gallōs,** *the rest of the Gauls,* after the Helvetians have been singled out (I. 1).

b. Caesar repeats **alter** and **alius** in a Correlative Relation; as, **hārum altera occīsa, altera capta est,** *of these* (*daughters*) *one was killed, the other captured* (I. 53); **aliae (nāvēs) . . . aliae . . . ,** *some* (*ships*) *. . . others* (IV. 28); **alterī — alterī,** *the latter — the former* (VII. 17).

c. Caesar repeats **alius** with the sense *one . . . one, another . . . another;* as, **legiōnēs aliae aliā in parte resisterent,** *legions were offering resistance, one at one point, another at another* (II. 22).

VERBS

AGREEMENT, MOODS AND TENSES, QUESTIONS

172. a. A Finite Verb agrees with its Subject in Number and Person; in compound forms of the Verb the Participle must agree with the Subject also in Gender. Thus, **Orgetorīx dēligitur,** *Orgetorix is chosen* (I. 3); **Ea rēs est ēnūntiāta,** *The matter* (lit. *that thing*) *was made known* (I. 4).

b. When a Verb is used with more than one Subject, it may agree with the nearest Subject, or be Plural; as, **fīlia et ūnus ē fīliīs captus est,** *a daughter and one of the sons were taken captive* (I. 26); **Nammeius et Verucloetius . . . obtinēbant,** *Nammeius and Verucloetius held* (I. 7).

c. Verbs are sometimes used in the Third Person Plural with an implied indefinite subject, as, **dīcunt,** *they say* (V. 12).

d. A verb in Latin is sometimes used with a Personal Subject where the English prefers the Impersonal Construction with "it"; as, **Quod nōn fore dictō audientēs . . . dīcantur,** *As to the fact that it was said that they would not be obedient,* lit. *that they are said not to be about to be,* etc. (I. 40).

173. a. When two Subjects express a single idea, the Verb may be Singular; as, **Matrona et Sēquana dīvidit,** *the Marne and the Seine separate . . . ,* the two rivers being thought of as forming one boundary (I. 1).

b. A Plural Verb may be used with a Singular Noun, or with an unexpressed Subject representing a Singular Noun, where the sense suggests Plurality; as, **cum tanta multitūdō lapidēs conicerent,** *when so great a host were hurling stones* (II. 6).

174. Caesar rarely uses a Passive Verb or Participle in a Reflexive Sense; as, **sublevātī,** *supporting themselves* (I. 48); **armārī,** *to arm themselves* (IV. 32).

175. a. The Present, Imperfect, and Future Tenses represent an action as going on in Present, Past, or Future Time; as, **eōrumque agrōs populābantur,** *and were laying waste their country* (I. 11).

b. In vivid narration Caesar often thinks of past events as in progress and uses the Present Indicative (Historical Present). In translating the Historical Present a past tense should generally be used; as, **dīcit līberius**, *he spoke* (lit. *speaks*) *more freely* (I. 18).

c. The Present is used in statements true at all times (Universal Present), and statements about Customs; as, **hominēs id, quod [crēdere] volunt, crēdunt**, *men readily believe what they wish to believe* (III. 18).

d. The Imperfect may be used of Repeated or Customary Action; as, **perīclitābatur**, *he kept trying* (II. 8); **adoriēbantur . . . circumsistēbant . . . coniciēbant**, *would attack . . . would surround . . . would hurl* (IV. 26)

e. The Imperfect is sometimes used of Attempted Action (Conative Imperfect); as, **nostrōs intrā mūnītiōnēs ingredī prohibēbant**, *were trying to prevent our men from getting inside the fortification* (V. 9).

f. The Imperfect with **iam**, used of an action already in progress for a considerable period, should be translated with a Progressive Pluperfect; as, **Cum iam amplius hōrīs sex pugnārētur**, *when fighting had now been going on more than six hours* (III. 5).

176. *a.* Caesar generally uses the Historical Perfect, as **discessit**, *he withdrew* (I. 14); very rarely he uses the Perfect in the sense of the English Present Perfect, as **nōn vēnērunt**, *they have not come* (VII. 77).

b. The Perfect and Pluperfect of **nōscō, cognōscō, cōnsuēscō** express a state resulting from action, and are generally best translated by the Present and Imperfect; as, **nōvērunt**, *they are familiar with*, lit. *have come to know* (VI. 15); **īre cōnsuērant**, *were accustomed (had become accustomed) to go* (III. 1). The Perfect and Pluperfect of **meminī** and **ōdī** also are translated by the Present and Imperfect.

c. The Latin Future Perfect is used with great precision where frequently in English a Future or Present Tense might be employed: as, **meum officium praestiterō**, *I shall have done my duty*, where we should ordinarily say, *I shall do my duty* (IV. 25).

177. *a.* In the Sequence of Tenses a Primary Tense (Present, Future, or Future Perfect[1]) in the Principal Clause is ordinarily followed by a Primary Tense in the Subordinate Clause; and a Secondary Tense (Imperfect, Perfect, or Pluperfect[2]) of the Principal Clause by a past tense in the Subordinate Clause. Thus, **Mercātōribus est aditus ut, quae bellō cēperint, quibus vēndant, habeant**, *Traders have access (to them) . . . that they may have purchasers for the things that they have captured in war*, lit. *that they may have (those) to whom they may sell (those things) which they have taken in war* (IV. 2); **equitātumque, quī sustinēret impetum, mīsit**, *and he sent his cavalry to sustain the attack* (I. 24).

b. A Historical Present in the Principal Clause is sometimes followed by a Primary Tense, sometimes by a Secondary Tense, in the Subordinate Clause; as, **diem dīcunt, quā diē . . . conveniant**, *they set a day on which they were* (lit. *are*) *to come together* (I. 6); **pontem, quī erat ad Genavam, iubet rescindī**, *he gave* (lit. *gives*) *orders that the bridge, which was near Geneva, be cut down* (I. 7).

c. A verb in a Subordinate Clause containing a Statement of Fact or a General Truth may be in the Present Tense even though the verb of the Principal Clause is in a Past Tense; as, **eīs persuāsit, quod Helvetiī . . . continentur**, *he persuaded them, because the Helvetians are hemmed in* (I. 2).

178. The Tenses of the Infinitive in Indirect Discourse express time relative to that of the Verbs on which they depend, the Present Infinitive expressing the same time as the Governing Verb; the Perfect Infinitive, time earlier than that of the Governing Verb; and the Future Infinitive, time later than that of the Governing Verb. Thus, **nōn sē hostem verērī . . . dīcēbant**, *were saying that they did not fear the enemy* (I. 39); **illum fēcisse intellegerent**, *they understood that he had done* (I. 13); **Caesar . . . sēsē eōs . . . cōnservātūrum [esse] dīxit**, *Caesar*

---

[1] The Primary Tenses of the Indicative, referring to Present and Future Time, are the Present, Future, and Future Perfect. The Primary Tenses of the Subjunctive are the Present and Perfect. Cf. *354*

[2] The Secondary Tenses of the Indicative, referring to Past Time, are the Imperfect, Perfect, and Pluperfect. The Secondary Tenses of the Subjunctive are the Imperfect and Pluperfect.

said that he would spare their lives (II. 15).

179. *a.* Direct Questions in Latin are introduced by Question Words and are of two kinds:

(1) Single Questions, introduced by Interrogative Pronouns and Adverbs, or by the Enclitic **-ne** attached to the emphatic word of the question and asking for information, by **nōnne** implying the answer "Yes," or **num** implying the answer "No." Thus: **quem locum . . . exspectās?** *what (kind of a) chance are you waiting for* (V. 44)? **Audīsne?** *Do you hear?* **Nōnne audīs?** *Do you not hear?* **Num audīs?** *You don't hear, do you?*

(2) Double Questions, which ordinarily have utrum or the Enclitic -ne in the First Member, and **an**, *or*, or **annōn**, *or not*, in the second; as, **utrum officium, an timor, plūs valet**, *Is sense of duty, or cowardice, stronger?* The First Member of a Double Question may be omitted, **An** alone introducing the second; as, **An . . . dubitātis?** *Do you have (any) doubt* (VII. 77)?

b. In Indirect Discourse Caesar uses Rhetorical Questions, implying a Negative Answer, Doubt, or Perplexity; these in the Direct Form would have had the Indicative, or the Deliberative Subjunctive. Thus:

(1) Indicative in the Direct Form: **num . . . memoriam dēpōnere posse?** *could he lay aside the recollection?* As a Direct Question: **Num . . . memoriam dēpōnere possum,** *can I put aside the recollection?* implying the answer "No"; as when we say "How can I do that?" meaning, emphatically, "I cannot do that" (I. 14).

(2) Deliberative Subjunctive in the Direct Form: **cūr quisquam . . . iūdicāret,** *why should any one infer?* in the Direct form, **cūr iūdicet?** (I. 40); **neque satīs Brūtō . . . centuriōnibusque . . . cōnstābat, quid agerent,** *and Brutus and the centurions . . . did not quite know what to do,* lit. *and it was not quite clear to Brutus and the centurions . . . what they should do;* as a Direct Question, **Quid agāmus?** *What are we to do?* (III. 14).

180. *a.* Caesar rarely uses the Subjunctive in the First Person to express an Exhortation (Hortatory Subjunctive); as, **hōs latrōnēs interficiāmus,** *let us kill these bandits* (VII. 38); **sīmus parātī,** *let us be ready* (C. III. 85).

b. Caesar rarely uses the Subjunctive in the Third Person to express a Command (Jussive Subjunctive); as, **Cum hīs mihi rēs sit,** *let me deal* (lit. *let the issue be to me) with those* (VII. 77).

c. A Wish Capable of Realization is expressed by the Present Subjunctive, often with **utinam**; as, **utinam redeant,** *may they return!*

d. A Wish Incapable of Realization is expressed in Present Time by utinam with the Imperfect Subjunctive and in Past Time by **utinam** with the Pluperfect Subjunctive; as, **utinam adessent,** *oh that they were here* (but they are not); **utinam redīssent,** *oh that they had come back* (but they did not).

181. *a.* Caesar rarely uses the Imperative, in Direct Quotations, as **Dēsilīte,** *Jump down* (IV. 25).

b. Caesar uses the Imperatives **nōlī, nōlīte** with the Infinitive to express Prohibition; as, **Nōlīte hōs vestrō auxiliō exspoliāre,** *Do not* (lit. *be unwilling to) rob them of your assistance* (VII. 77).

182. Caesar rarely uses an Infinitive in a Principal Clause in the place of an Imperfect or Perfect Indicative (Historical Infinitive), the Subject being in the Nominative; as, **Caesar Aeduōs frūmentum flāgitāre,** *Caesar kept pressing the Aeduans for the grain* (I. 16); **hostēs . . . signō datō dēcurrere,** *the enemy at a given signal rushed down* (III. 4).

CAUSAL AND TEMPORAL CLAUSES, RELATIVE CLAUSES, CLAUSES OF PURPOSE AND RESULT

183. *a.* In Causal Clauses introduced by **quod** and **quoniam** Caesar uses the Indicative when the reason is stated as that of Caesar the Writer, the Subjunctive when the reason is presented as some one else's. Thus, **Dumnorīx . . . Helvētiīs erat amīcus, quod . . . dūxerat,** *Dumnorix was friendly to the Helvetians, because he had taken . . .,* the **quod**-clause containing Caesar's explanation of the reason why Dumnorix favoured the Helvetians (I. 9); **eī grātiās**

ēgit, quod optimum iūdicium fēcisset, *thanked him because* (as the delegation said) *he had passed a most favourable judgement,* the **quod**-clause here having the Subjunctive because it presents the reason given by the delegation for the expression of thanks (I. 41).

b. In Causal Clauses Caesar sometimes uses the Subjunctive of a Verb of Saying or Thinking to introduce a statement of a reason ascribed to some one else; as, **Bellovacī suum numerum nōn complēvērunt, quod sē suō nōmine . . . bellum gestūrōs dīcerent,** *the Bellovaci did not furnish their full contingent because, as they said, they were going to wage war on their own account . . .* (VII. 75).

c. The Subjunctive introduced by **nōn quod,** *not because,* or **quam quō** (= **quam eō quod**), *than because,* may be used to express an alleged or assumed reason; as, **quam quō . . . dēsīderent,** *than because they desire* (IV. 2).

184. *a.* A Causal Clause introduced by **cum,** *since,* has its verb in the Subjunctive; as, **cum . . . persuādēre nōn possent,** *since they were not able to persuade* (I. 9).

b. Caesar sometimes uses the adverb **praesertim,** *especially,* to make prominent the Causal Idea in a Clause introduced by **cum;** as, **praesertim cum eōrum precibus adductus bellum suscēperit,** *especially since, in response to* (lit. *prevailed upon by*) *their entreaties, he had undertaken the campaign* (I. 16).

185. *a.* **Cum** Temporal, *when,* referring to the Present or Future is used with the Indicative; as, **cum . . . premuntur,** *when they are overwhelmed* (VI. 13).

b. With **cum** Temporal, *when,* and **cum prīmum,** *as soon as,* referring to Past Time, Caesar uses the Indicative when the force of **cum** is purely Temporal; as, **cum . . . exercitus . . . meritus (esse) vidēbātur,** *when the army clearly earned,* lit. *was seen to have earned* (1. 40); **cum prīmum potuit,** *as soon as he could* (III. 9).

c. With **cum** Temporal, *when,* and **cum prīmum,** *as soon as,* referring to Past Time, Caesar uses the Subjunctive when an idea of Circumstance, Condition, or Cause is involved; as, **cum ferrum sē īnflexisset,** *when* (i.e. *when and because*) *the iron had become bent,* lit. *had bent itself* (I. 25); **cum prīmum pābulī cōpia esse inciperet,** *as soon as* (*and because*) *there began to be plenty of forage* (II. 2).

186. *a.* Caesar sometimes uses **cum** Temporal or **ubi** with the Indicative to denote recurrent action; as, **cum ūsus est,** *whenever it is necessary* (IV. 2).

b. Caesar sometimes uses **cum** Temporal correlatively with the Adverb **turn** in the sense *not only . . . but also, but, both . . . and;* as, **cum omnia iuventūs . . . convēnerant, tum nāvium quod ubīque fuerat,** *not only* (lit. *when*) *had all the youth . . . assembled but* (lit. *then*) *all the ships they had* (III. 16).

187. Caesar sometimes uses **cum** Adversative, *although, while,* with the Subjunctive; as, **cum ea ita sint,** *although this* (lit. *those things*) *is true* (I. 14).

188. *a.* Caesar uses the Temporal Conjunctions **ubi, ut,** *when,* **postquam,** *after,* **posteā quam** (written as two words) *after that, after,* and **simul atque, simul,** *as soon as,* with the Indicative, usually in the Perfect Tense. Thus, **Quod ubi Caesar resciit,** *When Caesar found this out* (I. 28); **postquam Caesar pervēnit,** *after Caesar arrived* (I. 27); **simul atque sē recēpērunt,** *so soon as they rallied* (IV. 27).

b. The conjunction **ut,** *as,* introducing a comparison, is used with the Indicative; as, **ut . . . nōluerant, ita,** *as they had been unwilling so . . .* (II. 1).

c. **Ubi prīmum,** *as soon as* (lit. *when first*), is used with the Perfect Indicative; as, **ubi prīmum nostrōs equitēs cōnspexērunt,** *as soon as they saw our horsemen* (IV. 12).

d. The Pluperfect Indicative with **ubi** may denote a Repeated Action; as, **ubi . . . cōnspexerant,** *whenever they saw,* lit. *when they had seen* (IV. 26).

189. *a.* Caesar uses **prius quam,** *until, before,* with the Indicative to denote an actual occurrence or a fact; as, **neque prius fugere dēstitērunt quam ad flūmen Rhēnum . . . pervēnērunt,** *and they did not stop their flight until they reached the river Rhine* (I. 53).

b. Caesar uses **prius quam** and **ante quam,** *sooner than, before,* with the Subjunctive, implying Expectancy or Purpose in an action; as, **prius quam sē hostēs reciperent,** *before the* *enemy could rally* (II. 12).

190. *a.* Caesar uses **dum** Temporal in the sense of while with the Indicative Historical Present; in the sense of *so long as, while,* with the Indicative Present, Imperfect, and Perfect. Thus, **Dum ea conquīruntur,** *while those things were* (lit. *are*) *being sought out* (I. 27); **Dum longius aberant Gallī,** *so long as the Gauls were further away* (VII. 82).

b. Caesar uses **dum,** *until,* with the Subjunctive to denote Intention or Expectancy; as, **dum . . . Helvētiī pervenīrent,** *until the Helvetians should reach* (I. 11).

c. Caesar uses **quoad** in the Temporal sense of *so long as, until,* with the Indicative; in the sense of until denoting Intention or Expectancy, with the Subjunctive. Thus, **quoad potuit,** *so long as he could* (IV. 12); **quoad ipse propius . . . accessisset,** *until he himself should have come up nearer* (IV. 11).

191. *a.* Caesar uses.the Adversative Conjunctions **etsī, tametsī,** *although,* with the, Indicative; as, **etsī . . . vidēbat,** *although he saw* (I. 46).

b. Concessive **ut,** meaning granted that, *although,* is followed by the Subjunctive; as, **ut omnia contrā opīniōnem accidant,** *granted that everything turn out contrary to expectation* (in Indirect Form III. 9).

192. Relative Clauses, introduced by a Relative or General Relative Pronoun, have their Verb in the Indicative unless an idea of Purpose, Characteristic, Cause, Result, or Condition is involved; as, **Allobrogum, quī nūper pācātī erant,** *of the Allobroges, who had lately been subdued* (I. 6); **quaecumque pars castrōrum . . . premī vidēbātur,** *whenever any part* (lit. *whatever part*) *of the camp seemed to be hard pressed* (III. 4).

193. *a.* A Relative Clause of Purpose may be introduced by **quī** (= **ut is,** *in order that he*), or by the Relative Adverbs **quō** (= **ut eō**), **quā** (= **ut eā**), and has its Verb in the Subjunctive; as, **lēgātōs mittunt** (Historical Present) **nōbilissimōs cīvitātis . . . quī dīcerent,** *they sent as envoys the citizens of highest rank to say,* lit. *who should say* (I. 7); **quō gravius hominēs . . . doleant,** *in order that men may more bitterly suffer* (I. 14). Cf. 355

b. In Relative Clauses of Purpose **quō** is generally used with a Comparative; as, **quō facilius . . . possit,** *that he might* (lit. *may*) *be able the more easily* (I. 8).

194. *a.* A Relative Clause with the Subjunctive, introduced by a Relative Pronoun or Relative Adverb, may characterize an Indefinite Antecedent (Clause of Characteristic); as, **itinera duo, quibus itineribus . . . exīre possent,** *two routes by which they could go out,* i.e. *two routes of such a character that by them they could go out* (I. 6); **nihil [eīs] erat quō famem tolerārent,** *they had nothing with which they could satisfy hunger* (I. 28).

b. A Clause of Characteristic may be used after a Comparative; as **nōn longius aberant quam quō tēlum adigī posset,** *were already within range,* lit. *not further away than* (the distance) *to which a dart could be thrown* (II. 21).

c. A Relative Clause with the Subjunctive may have a Causal Force; as, **Catuvolcus . . . dētestātus Ambiorīgem, quī eius cōnsiliī auctor fuisset, . . . sē exanimāvit,** *cursing Ambiorix, since he* (lit. *who*) *had been the originator of that scheme, Catuvolcus killed himself* (VI. 31).

d. A Relative Clause with the Subjunctive may have an Adversative Force; as, **Cicerō, quī . . . mīlitēs in castrīs continuisset,** *Cicero, although he had kept the soldiers in camp* (VI. 36).

e. A Relative Clause with the Subjunctive may have a Conditional Force; as **quī . . . vidēret,** *if one should look at* (VII. 19).

f. A Restrictive Clause may be introduced by the Relative **quod** and have the Subjunctive; as, **quod . . . posset,** *so far as he might be able,* (lit. *that*) *which,* etc. (I. 35).

195. A Relative Clause of Result may be introduced by **quī** (= **ut is,** *so that he*), or **quīn** (= **quī nōn, quae nōn, quod nōn**), and has its Verb in the Subjunctive; as, **Nēmō est tam fortis, quīn reī novitāte perturbētur,** *No one* (*of them*) *was so strong that he was not upset by the unexpectedness of the occurrence* (VI. 39).

196. *a.* Clauses of Purpose in Caesar are most often introduced by **ut, utī,** *in order that, that,* or **nē,** *in order that not, lest,* and have their Verb in the Subjunctive; as, **ut spatium intercēdere**

posset, *in order that a period of time might* (lit. *might be able to*) *intervene* (I. 7); **Id nē accideret**, *in order that this might not happen* (I. 38).

b. In Clauses of Purpose Caesar uses **nē . . . nēve (neu)** in the sense of *that not . . . nor*, and **ut (utī) . . . nēve (neu)** in the sense of *that . . . and that not*, with the Subjunctive; as, **ut . . . eārum rērum vīs minuerētur, neu pontī nocērent,** *that the force of these things might be lessened and that they might not damage the bridge* (IV. 17).

197. *a.* Clauses of Result are most often introduced by **ut** or **utī**, *so that, that* (negative **nōn**), and have their Verb in the Subjunctive; as, **ut perpaucī prohibēre possent,** *so that a very few* (*men*) *could stop them* (I. 6); **ut . . . iūdicārī nōn possit,** *that it cannot be determined* (I. 12).

b. Clauses of Result are often preceded by a word of Measure or Quality, **tam, tantus, ita, sīc,** etc.; as, **tanta rērum commūtātiō est facta, ut nostrī . . . proelium redintegrārent,** *so great a change was brought about that our* (*men*) *renewed the fight* (II. 27); **sīc mūniēbātur, ut magnam . . . daret facultātem,** *was so fortified that it afforded a great resource* (I. 38).

c. A Clause of Result with the Subjunctive may be introduced by **quam** after a Comparative, with or without **ut**; as, **pulverem maiōrem, quam cōnsuētūdo ferret,** *a cloud of dust greater than usual* lit. *greater than* (*so that*) *an ordinary condition would bring it* (IV. 32).

SUBSTANTIVE CLAUSES

198. *a.* Substantive Clauses are used as Subject of a Verb, as Object of a Verb, and in other Relations similar to those in which Nouns are used.

b. A Substantive Clause introduced by **quod,** meaning *the fact that, that*, has its Verb in the Indicative, and may stand as Subject, or Predicate, or Object of a Verb, or in Apposition. Thus, **magnō erat impedīmentō, quod . . . neque . . . poterant,** *A great hindrance . . . was the fact that they were able neither to . . .* , the **quod**-clause being the Subject of **erat** (I. 25); **causa mittendī fuit quod . . . volēbat,** *the reason for sending was the fact that he wanted . . .* , the **quod**-clause being in Predicate (III. 1); **multae rēs in prīmīs quod . . . vidēbat,** *many circumstances, first of all the fact that he saw . . .* , the **quod**-clause being in Apposition with **rēs** (I. 33).

c. A Substantive Clause introduced by **quod,** meaning *As to the fact that, As regards the fact that,* may have the force of an Accusative or Ablative of Specification. Thus, **quod . . . ēnūntiārit,** *As to the fact that he had reported*; in the direct form, **quod ēnūntiāvī,** *as to the fact that I have reported* (I. 17).

199. *a.* Substantive Clauses with the Subjunctive introduced by **ut,** or **utī,** *that*, and **nē,** *that not,* are used after Verbs of *Commanding, Urging, Reminding, Asking, Persuading, Conceding* and *Permitting, Deciding, Striving*; the Subjunctive may often best be translated by an Infinitive. Thus, **Allobrogibus imperāvit, ut . . . cōpiam facerent,** *ordered the Allobroges to furnish* (lit. *that they should furnish*) *a supply* (I. 28); **persuādet** (Historical Present) **Casticō . . . ut rēgnum . . . occupāret,** *persuaded Casticus to seize the kingly power* (I. 3).

Such Verbs and Phrases used by Caesar are:

(1) Commanding: **imperō,** *order*; **interdīcō,** *enjoin* (VII. 40); **mandō,** *command* (I. 47); **negōtium dō,** *assign the task* (II. 2); **praecipiō,** *enjoin, direct* (I. 22); **dēnūntiō,** *enjoin,* (C. III. 86); **praedīcō,** *order in advance* (C. III. 92).

(2) Urging: **cohortor,** *encourage* (II. 21); **hortor,** *urge* (I. 19); **sollicitō,** *press* (III. 8).

(3) Reminding: **admoneō,** *admonish* (V. 49); **moneō,** *warn* (I. 20).

(4) Asking: **dēprecor,** *beg to escape* (II. 31); **ōrō,** *beg* (IV. 16); **obsecrō,** *beseech* (I. 20); **obtestor,** *pray* (IV. 25); **petō,** *ask earnestly* (I. 28); **postulō,** *demand* (I. 34); **rogō,** *ask* (I. 7).

(5) Persuading: **addūcō,** *prevail upon* (I. 31); **persuādeō,** *persuade*; **impellō,** *incite* (IV. 16).

(6) Conceding and Permitting: **concēdō,** *grant* (III. 18); **patior,** *suffer, allow* (I. 45); **permittō,** *permit* (I. 35).

(7) Deciding: **cēnseō,** *decree* (I. 35); **cōnstituō,** *determine* (II. 10); **placuit,** *it pleased* (I. 34); **sanciō,** *bind* (I. 30).

(8) Striving: **agō,** *arrange* (I. 41); **contendō,** *strive* (I. 31); **dō operam,** *take pains* (V. 7); **impetrō,** *obtain one's request* (I. 9); **labōrō,** *put forth effort* (I. 31).

b. Such Verbs are sometimes used impersonally in the Passive, the Substantive Clause taking the place of a Subject; as **erat eī praeceptum, nē proelium committeret,** *he had been ordered not to join battle,* lit. *it had been ordered to him that he should not,* etc. (I. 22).

c. With such Verbs the Substantive Clause is sometimes replaced by the Infinitive, with or without a Subject Accusative; as, **loquī concēditur,** *permission is given to speak* (VI. 20); **Hās [nāvēs] āctuāriās imperat** (Historical Present) **fierī,** *he ordered that these (ships) be built for fast movement* (V. 1).

d. As a Negative Connective between Substantive Subjunctive Clauses Caesar uses **nēve** (before vowels and **h**) and **neu** (before consonants), with the meaning *and that . . . not,* or *that . . . not.*

200. *a.* In Substantive Clauses with **ut** after **admoneō, cohortor, cōnstituō, imperō, mandō, nūntiō,** *order,* **postulō,** *demand,* and **rogō,** *ask,* and a few phrases, the **ut** is sometimes omitted; as, **rogat** (Historical Present), **fīnem ōrandī faciat,** *asked him to make an end of his pleading* (I. 20).

b. **Iubeō,** *order, bid,* and **vetō,** *forbid,* are regularly used by Caesar with the Infinitive and Subject Accusative; **cōnor,** *attempt,* with the Infinitive; as, **quemque efferre iubent,** *they gave* (lit. *give) orders that each person carry away* (I. 5); **exsequī cōnārētur,** *attempted to enforce* (I. 4).

201. *a.* Substantive Clauses with the Subjunctive introduced by **nē,** *that not,* **quō minus,** *that not* (lit. *by which the less),* and **quīn,** *that not,* are used after Verbs of *Hindering, Preventing,* and *Refusing;* the Conjunction often may best be rendered by *from* with a Participle. Thus, **hōs . . . dēterrēre nē frūmentum cōnferant,** *these through fear were holding back (the people) from furnishing the grain* (I. 17); **retinērī nōn potuerant quīn . . . tēla conicerent,** *could not be restrained from hurling darts* (I. 47). Such Verbs used by Caesar are: **dēterreō,** *hold back through fear;* **recūsō,** *refuse* (I. 31); **retineō,** *restrain;* **temperō,** *restrain one's self* (I. 33); **teneō,** *hold back* (IV. 22); **terreō,** *frighten* (VII. 49).

b. Substantive Clauses with the Subjunctive introduced by **quīn** are used also after general expressions of Doubt and Negation, **quīn** being translated *that.* Thus, **nōn esse dubium, quīn . . . ,** *that there was no doubt that* (I. 3); **neque abest suspīciō . . . quīn,** *and there is ground for suspecting that,* lit. *and there is not lacking suspicion that* (I. 4).

c. After **dubitō,** meaning *doubt,* Caesar uses a Substantive Clause with **quīn** and the Subjunctive; after **dubitō,** *hesitate,* generally the Infinitive, rarely a clause with **quīn.** Thus, **nōn dubitāre quīn . . . sūmat,** *he did not doubt that he (Ariovistus) would inflict* (I. 31); **trānsīre flūmen nōn dubitāvērunt,** *did not hesitate to cross the river* (II. 23); **dubitandum nōn exīstimāvit quīn . . . proficīscirētur,** *thought that he ought not to hesitate to set out* (II. 2).

202. Substantive Clauses with the Subjunctive introduced by **ut** and **nē** are used after Verbs of Fearing; after such Verbs **ut** is to be translated *that not,* and **nē,** *that,* or *lest.* Thus, **nē . . . offenderet verēbātur,** *was afraid that he might offend* (I. 19); **ut . . . supportārī posset, timēre dīcēbant,** *were saying that they feared that (the supply of grain) could not be brought up* (I. 39).

203. Clauses of Result introduced by **ut** or **utī** and **ut nōn** are used as Substantive Clauses in four ways:

(1) As the Subject of Impersonal Verbs; thus, **fīēbat ut . . . vagārentur,** *it came about that they wandered* (I. 2); **Accēdēbat ut . . . tempestātem ferrent,** *There was the additional fact that they weathered the storm* (III. 13). The more important Impersonal Forms thus used by Caesar are **accēdēbat; accidit,** *it happened* (IV. 29); **fit** (C. II. 4); **fīēbat; factum est** (III. 19); **factum esse** (I. 31), **fierī** (II. 4); **īnstitūtum est,** *the custom became fixed* (C. III. 92); **Relinquēbātur,** *the result was,* lit. *it was left* (V. 19); and the Future Infinitive of **sum** in both forms, **futūrum esse** (I. 10, 20, 31), and **fore** (I. 42).

(2) As Predicate or Appositive with **cōnsuētūdō est** and **iūs est;** thus, **ea cōnsuētūdō esset, ut mātrēs familiae . . . dēclārārent,** *there was the custom that the matrons should declare* (I. 50).

(3) As Object after Verbs of Action and Accomplishment; thus, **committeret ut is locus . . .**

nōmen caperet, lit. *bring it about that the place . . . should assume a name* (I. 13); **commeātūs ut . . . portārī possent, efficiēbat,** *made it possible for supplies to be brought,* lit. *was accomplishing that supplies could be brought* (II. 5). The Verbs thus used by Caesar are **committō, efficiō, perficiō** (I. 9).

(4) As Appositive of a Noun or Neuter Pronoun whose meaning the ut-clause defines; thus, **poenam, ut īgnī cremārētur,** *the penalty of being burned by fire,* lit. *that he should be burned by fire* (I. 4); **id, quod cōnstituerant . . . ut ē fīnibus suīs exeant,** *that which they had resolved upon, a migration from their country,* lit. *that they should go out from their territories* (I. 5).

204. Indirect Questions are used as Substantive Clauses after Expressions of Inquiry, Narration, Deliberation, and Uncertainty, and have the Subjunctive. The following types of Indirect Questions are used by Caesar:

(1) Introduced by the Interrogative Particles **-ne** (V. 27), **num** (I. 14) in Single Questions; in Double Questions, by the Correlative Particles **utrum . . . an,** *whether . . . or* (I. 40); **utrum . . . necne,** *whether . . . or not,* **necne** representing **annōn** of the Direct Form (I. 50); **-ne . . . an,** *whether . . . or* (VI. 31); **-ne . . . an . . . an,** *whether . . . or . . . or* (IV. 14); **-ne . . . -ne,** *whether . . . or* (VII. 14); and **an** alone, **utrum** being omitted, *or* (VII. 15). Thus, **cōnsultum [esse], utrum īgnī statim necārētur an . . . reservārētur,** *that counsel was taken whether he should at once be put to death by burning, or saved up for another occasion* (I. 53).

(2) Introduced by an Interrogative Pronoun; as, **Dumnorīgī cūstōdēs pōnit** (Historical Present), **ut, quae agat, quibuscum loquātur, scīre possit,** *(Caesar) set guards over Dumnorix, in order to be able to know what* (lit. *what things*) *he did, with whom he talked* (I. 20).

(3) Introduced by Pronominal Adjectives, and Adverbs used Interrogatively; as, **in utram partem fluat,** *in which direction it flows* (I. 12). Adjectives and Adverbs thus used by Caesar are **quālis,** *of what sort* (I. 21); **quam** with an Adjective, *how* (I. 43); **quantus,** *how great* (I. 17); **quem ad modum,** *in what way* (I. 36); **uter,** *which;* **cūr,** *why* (I. 40); **quārē,** *wherefore, why* (I. 45); **quō,** *whither* (III. 16); **quot,** *how many* (VII. 19); **quotiēns,** *how often* (I. 43); **unde,** *whence* (V. 53); **ut,** *how* (I. 43).

(4) Introduced by **sī,** *if, whether,* after Verbs of Effort and Expectation; as, **sī perrumpere possent, cōnātī,** *trying (to see) whether they could break through* (I. 8).

CONDITIONAL SENTENCES

205. Caesar has General Conditions of the First Type (Conditions of Fact) introduced by **sī,** *if,* with the Indicative in both Protasis and Apodosis, the Protasis implying Customary or Repeated Action; **sī** is almost equivalent to *whenever.* Thus:

(1) Present Tense in both Protasis and Apodosis: **sī quī ex reliquīs excellit, succēdit,** *if anyone of the rest is preeminent, he becomes the successor* of the arch-druid (VI. 13).

(2) Imperfect Tense in both Protasis and Apodosis: **sī quid erat dūrius, concurrēbant,** *if there was unusually serious difficulty* (lit. *if there was anything rather hard*) *they would rush to the rescue* (I. 48).

(3) Perfect Tense in the Protasis, Present in the Apodosis: **sī compertum est, interficiunt,** *if the fact (of crime) has been established, they kill* (VI. 19).

(4) Pluperfect Tense in the Protasis, Imperfect in the Apodosis: **sī quī . . . equō dēciderat, circumsistēbant,** *if anyone had fallen from his horse, they would gather around him* (I. 48).

206. Caesar has Specific Conditions of the First Type (Conditions of Fact) introduced by **sī,** *if,* or **nisi,** *unless,* with the Indicative in the Protasis, and the Indicative, Imperative, or Hortatory Subjunctive in the Apodosis. Thus:

(1) Present Indicative in both Protasis and Apodosis: **Cuius sī vōs paenitet, vestrum vōbīs beneficium remittō,** *if you regret this, I give you back your favour* (C. II. 32).

(2) Present Indicative in the Protasis, Present Imperative in the Apodosis: **Dēsilīte . . . nisi vultis aquilam hostibus prōdere,** *jump down, unless you wish to abandon your eagle to the enemy* (IV. 25).

(3) Present Indicative in the Protasis, Hortatory Subjunctive in the Apodosis: **Sī quid in nōbīs animī est, persequāmur mortem,** *if we have any vestige of courage in us, let us avenge the death* (VII. 38).

(4) Future Perfect Indicative in the Protasis, Future Indicative or Imperative in the Apodosis: **sī gravius quid acciderit, ratiōnem reposcent,** *if any disaster shall befall them* (lit. *anything rather heavy shall have happened*), *they will demand an accounting* (V. 30); **Tuēminī castra, et dēfendite, sī quid dūrius acciderit,** *guard the camp, and defend it in case of any trouble,* lit. *if anything rather hard shall have happened* (C. III. 94).

207. Caesar has conditions of the Second Type (Conditions of Possible Realization), introduced by **sī,** *if,* **nisi,** *unless,* or **sīn,** *but if,* with the Subjunctive in the Protasis, and the Potential Subjunctive, or the Indicative (emphasizing the situation as an actual one) in the Apodosis; thus:

(1) Present Subjunctive in both Protasis and Apodosis: **quī, sī per tē liceat, . . . cum reliquīs bellī cāsum sustineant,** *if they should have your permission, they would share the fortune of war with the rest* (V. 30).

(2) Present Subjunctive in the Protasis, Present Indicative in the Apodosis: **neque, aliter sī faciat, ūllam habet auctōritātem,** *and if (a leading man) does* (lit. *should do*) *otherwise, he has no influence at all* (VI. 11).

(3) Imperfect Subjunctive in the Protasis, Imperfect Indicative in the Apodosis: **sī continēre ad signa manipulōs vellet, locus ipse erat praesidiō barbarīs,** *if he desired to keep his companies with the standards, the very (character of the) region was a protection to the natives* (VI. 34).

208. *a.* Caesar has Conditions of the Third Type (Conditions Contrary to Fact), introduced by **sī,** *if,* or **nisi,** *unless,* with the Subjunctive in both Protasis and Apodosis, the Imperfect referring to Present Time, the Pluperfect to Past Time. Thus:

(1) Imperfect: **ego hanc sententiam probārem . . . sī nūllam praeterquam vītae nostrae iactūram fierī vidērem,** *I should approve this view if I saw that no (loss) was involved except the loss of our own lives,* implying that the speaker did not approve the view, and that other loss was involved (VII. 77).

(2) Pluperfect: **nisi . . . mīlitēs essent dēfessī, omnēs hostium cōpiae dēlērī potuissent,** *if the soldiers had not been exhausted . . ., the entire forces of the enemy might have been wiped out,* implying that the soldiers were exhausted, and that many of the enemy escaped (VII. 88).

b. The Indicative is used in the Apodosis of Conditions Contrary to Fact when there is present an idea of Necessity, Propriety, or Possibility; as, **sī populus Rōmānus alicuius iniūriae sibi cōnscius fuisset, nōn fuit difficile cavēre,** *if the Roman people had been conscious of any wrongdoing it would not have been* (lit. *was not*) *difficult (for them) to take precautions* (from the Indirect Form in I. 14).

c. The Imperfect Subjunctive, referring to Past Time, may be used in Conditions Contrary to Fact, if a lasting state of affairs is implied; as, **sī quid mihi ā Caesare opus esset, ad eum vēnissem,** *If I had wanted (or now wanted) anything of Caesar, I should have come to him* (from the Indirect Form in I. 34).

209. In the Protasis of a Conditional Sentence an Ablative Absolute, a Participle, or other form of expression implying a Condition, may be used in place of the clause with **sī;** as, **datā facultāte,** taking the place of **sī facultās data esset,** *if an opportunity should have been granted,* in the Direct Form, **sī facultās data erit** (I. 7); **damnātum (eum),** *him, if condemned,* **damnātum** taking the place of **sī damnātus esset** (I. 4).

210. Caesar has Conditional Clauses of Comparison with the Subjunctive introduced by **velut sī, quasi,** and **proinde ac sī.** Thus: **quod . . . absentis Ariovistī crūdēlitātem velut sī cōram adesset, horrērent,** *that is . . .* **velut horrērent, sī cōram adesset, horrērent,** *because they dreaded Ariovistus's cruelty when he was away just as (they would dread it) if he were present* (I. 32); **Quasi vērō cōnsiliī sit rēs,** *As if indeed it were a matter of choice,* i.e. *as it would be, if it should be a matter of choice* (VII. 38); **proinde ac sī . . . vellent,** *just as if they proposed* (C. III. 60).

DIRECT AND INDIRECT QUOTATION AND INDIRECT DISCOURSE
GENERAL STATEMENT

211. *a.* Caesar presents the language of another person in two ways, either in Direct Quotation, or in Indirect Quotation, a form of Indirect Discourse.

b. In Direct Quotation Caesar quotes:

(1) Words spoken directly to him, as the brave words of Crastinus just before going into action at the battle of Pharsalus (C. III. 91).

(2) Words reported to him, presumably by his officers; as the exhortation of the unnamed standard-bearer of the Tenth Legion when landing on the British shore, if this was spoken outside of Caesar's hearing (IV. 25), and the challenge of Pullo to Vorenus (V. 44).

(3) Words or Speeches, sometimes in dialects foreign to Caesar, which he presents in his own language, but throws into the form of Direct Quotation in order to enhance the effect; such are the words of the Eburonian captive to the Sugambrian leaders (VI. 35), and the speech of the cold-blooded Critognatus at the war council in Alesia (VII. 77); also the words of the dying eagle-bearer (C. III. 64), and the remarks of Pompey and Labienus before Pharsalus (C. III. 86, 87).

212. *a.* In Indirect Quotation, or Indirect Discourse in the narrower sense, Caesar in most cases aims to present, not a word-for-word reproduction of what was said or written, but a summary, as brief as possible, of the main points. For example, in order to move to action the other prominent Helvetians, and carry through the negotiations with Casticus and Dumnorix, Orgetorix must have had many conferences, extending over a considerable period of time; yet the gist of the argument by which, according to Caesar, he persuaded the whole Helvetian nation to migrate, is given in ten words of Indirect Discourse (I. 2), while the gist of the argument by which Casticus and Dumnorix were induced to join him in forming a triumvirate of usurpation is summarized in thirty-one words (I. 3).

b. The kind of Summary found in the longer passages of Caesar's Indirect Discourse has a parallel in the condensed reports of addresses in the newspapers. A reporter, sent to prepare a synopsis of a lecture an hour in length, on the Moon, might on his return to the news paper office find his space reduced, by pressure of matter, to sixty words; he might nevertheless summarize the main points thus: "The lecturer said *that the moon is nearly two hundred and thirty-nine thousand miles from the earth; that under the telescope it has the appearance of a dead planet; that most careful observations have failed to detect the presence of air or water; and that, notwithstanding the moon's brightness, due to reflection, its surface must be as cold as ice.*"

c. In a manner somewhat similar, but with marvelous clearness and cogency in view of the degree of condensation, Caesar in Indirect Discourse presents summarizing statements, or outlines, including —

(1) Conferences with Gallic and German leaders, conducted, no doubt haltingly, through interpreters, as with Divico (I. 13, 14), Liscus and other Aeduans (I. 17, 18), the Gallic delegation (I. 30-33), and Ariovistus (I. 43-45).

(2) His own addresses; as the speech with which he quelled an incipient mutiny (I. 40), and his exhortation to his soldiers at Pharsalus (C. III. 90).

(3) Reports made to him; as by Labienus (II. 1) and the envoys of the Remi (II. 3. 4).

(4) Requests and replies, messages and instructions; as the request of the Helvetian envoys, and Caesar's answer (I. 7); the plea of the Aeduans (I. 11), Caesar's message to the Lingones (I. 26), messages to and from Ariovistus (I. 34-36, 47).

(5) Arguments; as the arguments of Orgetorix (I. 2, 3), and of disloyal natives (II. 17).

(6) Brief reports, explanations or speeches, presented in some cases with little or no condensation, as the hurried report of Considius (I. 22), the apology of the soldiers (I. 41), the joke by the soldier of the Tenth Legion (I. 42), and the taunt of the Atuatuci as translated into Latin (II. 30).

d. Indirect Discourse in a broader sense includes all statements in the Indirect Form after words of Thought as well as Speech; as, **biennium satis esse dūxērunt**, *they reckoned that two years would be sufficient* (I. 3).

e. In the Latin text of this book the more important Indirect Quotations and Summaries are printed in Italic Type.

213. *a.* Indirect Discourse is introduced by a Verb or other Expression of *Saying, Perceiving, Ascertaining, Thinking, Knowing,* or *Remembering*; as, **sē . . . condōnāre dīcit** (Historical Present) *he said that he would pardon* (I. 20). Such Verbs and Expressions used by Caesar are: **agō**, *present a case* (I. 13); **animadvertō**, *notice* (I. 32); **arbitror**, *think* (I. 2); **audiō**, *hear* (IV. 7); **cēnseō**, *decide, think* (VII. 21); **certiōrem faciō**, *inform* (I. 11); **certior fit**, *is informed* (I. 12); **clāmitō**, *cry out* (V. 7), **cogitō**, *think* (V. 33); **cognōscō**, *learn* (I. 22); **commemorō**, *relate* (IV. 16); **comperiō**, *ascertain* (IV. 19); **conclāmō**, *shout* (III. 18); **cōnfīdō**, *be confident, trust* (III. 9); **cōnfīrmō**, *assure* (I. 3); **coniectūram capiō**, *infer* (VII. 35); **cōnspiciō**, *see* (II. 24); **cōnstat**, *it is agreed* (II. 6); **cōnstituō**, *resolve* (II. 10); **contendō**, *insist* (VI. 41); **crēdō**, *believe* (II. 33). **dēmōnstrō**, *show, prove* (I. 11); **dēnūntiō**, *threaten* (I. 36); **dīcō**, *say*; **diffīdō**, *lose confidence* (VI. 36); **discō**, *learn* (VII. 54); **doceō**, *explain* (I. 43); **dūcō**, *reckon* (I. 3); **exīstimō**, *reckon, think* (I. 6); **faciō verba**, *make a plea* (II. 14); **intellegō**, *understand* (I. 16); **inveniō**, *find out* (II. 16); **iūdicō**, *judge* (I. 45); **iūrō**, *swear* (VI. 12); **loquor**, *speak, say* (II. 31). **meminī**, *remember* (III. 6); **memoriā teneō**, *hold in memory, remember* (I. 7); **mihi persuāsum habeō**, *am convinced* (III. 2); **moneō**, *explain* (C. III. 89); **negō**, *declare that . . . not* (I. 8); **nūntiō**, *announce* (II. 2); **nūntium mittō**, *send word* (II. 6); **ostendō**, *make plain* (I. 8); **perscrībō**, *write fully* (V. 49); **perspiciō**, *perceive* (III. 9); **polliceor**, *promise* (I. 33); **praedicō**, *declare* (I. 39); **prō explōrātō habeō**, *consider certain* (VI. 5); **probō**, *show, prove* (I. 3); **profiteor**, *declare* (VII. 2); **prōnūntiō**, *announce* (V. 56); **provideō**, *foresee* (VII. 39); **putō**, *think* (IV. 3). **recordor**, *recall* (C. III. 47); **referō**, *report* (VI. 10); **renūntiō**, *bring (back) report* (I. 10); **reperiō**, *find out, ascertain* (I. 18); **respondeō**, *answer* (I. 14); **sciō**, *know* (I. 20); **scrībō**, *write* (V. 13); **sentiō**, *perceive* (I. 18); **spem habeō**, *have hope that* (I. 33); **significō**, *give intimation* (II. 13); **simulō**, *pretend* (IV. 4); **spērō**, *hope* (I. 3); **statuō**, *determine* (I. 42); **suspicor**, *suspect* (I. 44); **testibus ūtor**, *take as witnesses that* (VII. 77); **videō**, *see* (I. 33); **voveō**, *vow* (VI. 16).

b. The Verb of Saying, on which Indirect Discourse depends, is sometimes not expressed, but implied in the Context; as, **Caesarem complexus obsecrāre coepit . . . scīre sē**, *throwing his arms around Caesar began to beseech* (*him, saying*) *that he knew* (I. 20).

RULES FOR INDIRECT DISCOURSE

214. *a.* In Indirect Discourse the Principal Statements, corresponding with the Principal Clauses of Direct Discourse, are expressed by the Subject Accusative and the Infinitive; Subordinate Clauses have the Subjunctive. Thus, **Cōnsuēsse deōs immortālēs . . . quōs prō scelere eōrum ulcīscī velint, hīs secundiōrēs interdum rēs, et diūturniōrem impūnitātem, concēdere,** *The immortal gods are wont to grant a more prosperous estate meanwhile, and longer freedom from punishment, to those whom they desire to punish for their wickedness*; in the Direct Form **cōnsuēsse deōs** would be come **cōnsuērunt dī**, and **velint** in the Subordinate Clause would be **volunt**, the other words remaining unchanged, and the sentence would read **Cōnsuērunt dī immortālēs . . . quōs prō scelere eōrum ulcīscī volunt, hīs secundiōrēs interdum rēs et diūturniōrem impūnitātem concēdere** (I. 14).

b. A Subordinate Clause containing an implied quotation may have the Subjunctive; as, **frūmentum, quod essent pollicitī,** *the grain which* (*as he said*) *they had promised* (I. 16).

c. In Indirect Discourse a Subordinate or Parenthetical Clause, presenting a Statement of Fact which is not necessarily a part of the Indirect Discourse, may have the Indicative; as, **Condrūsōs . . . Paemānōs, quī Germānī appellantur,** *that the Condrusi . . . and the Paemani, who are called Germans* (II. 4).

215. The Subject Accusative in Indirect Discourse is sometimes omitted when it is easily understood from the Context, especially when it refers to the same person as the Subject of the Verb on which the Indirect Discourse depends; as, **scīre**, for **sē scīre**, *that he knew* (I. 40, I. 41); **prohibitūrum ostendit**, for **sē prohibitūrum esse ostendit** (Historical Present), *he showed that he would prevent them* (I. 8).

216. Commands expressed in Direct Quotation by the Imperative, or by the Jussive Subjunctive, in Indirect Discourse have the Subjunctive, the Negative being **nē**. Thus, **reminīscerētur**, *let him remember*, which in the Direct Form would be Imperative, **reminīscere**, *remember* (I. 13); **nē . . . tribueret**, *that he should not presume*, the Direct Form being **nōlī tribuere** (I. 13).

a. Ordinary Questions in Indirect Discourse have the Subjunctive; as, **Cūr in suās possessiōnēs venīret**, *Why did he (Caesar) come into his possessions?* in the Direct Form this would be, **Cūr in meās possessiōnēs venīs?** *Why do you come into my possessions* (I. 44)?

b. Deliberative Questions in Indirect Discourse retain the Subjunctive, but the Tense is governed by that of the Verb on which the Indirect Discourse depends (*177a, b*); thus, **Quid agāmus?** *What are we to do?* after a Past Tense in Indirect Discourse becomes **Quid agerent**; as, **neque satis . . . cōnstābat, quid agerent**, *and it was not quite clear . . . what they should do* (III. 14).

c. Rhetorical Questions in Indirect Discourse have the Infinitive (*179b*); as, **quid esse levius**, *what is more capricious*, implying that nothing could be more capricious (V. 28).

218. An Apodosis of a Conditional Sentence containing a Statement is expressed in Indirect Discourse by the Accusative and Infinitive, containing a Command, by the Subjunctive; the Protasis, containing the Condition, has the Subjunctive, as follows:

(1) *a.* In the First Type (Conditions of Fact), the Tense of the Infinitive in Indirect Discourse corresponds with the Tense of the Apodosis in the Direct Form, while the Tense of the Protasis, introduced by **sī** or **sīn**, is governed by that of the Verb on which the Indirect Discourse depends (*177a, b*). Thus, **Is ita cum Caesare ēgit: sī pācem populus Rōmānus cum Helvētiīs faceret, in eam partem itūrōs [esse] atque ibi futūrōs [esse] Helvētiōs, ubi eōs Caesar cōnstituisset atque esse voluisset**, *He took up (the matter) with Caesar thus: If the Roman people would make peace with the Helvetians, they would go wherever Caesar should have appointed and wished them to be, and would there remain*; in the Direct Form, **Sī pācem populus Rōmānus cum Helvētiīs faciet, in eam partem ībunt atque ibi erunt Helvētiī, ubi eōs tū cōnstitueris** (Future Perfect Indicative) **atque esse volueris** (I. 13).

b. In the Protasis of the First Type a Perfect or Pluperfect Subjunctive in Indirect Discourse may represent a Future Perfect Indicative in the Direct Form; as, **Quod sī fēcerit** (Perfect Subjunctive), **Aeduōrum auctōritātem amplificātūrum [esse]**, *If he should do this, he would increase the prestige of the Aeduans*; in the Direct Form, **Quod sī fēceris** (Future Perfect Indicative) **Aeduōrum auctōritātem amplificābis**, *If you will do* (lit. *shall have done*) *this, you will increase the prestige of the Aeduans* (II. 14).

(2) In the Second Type (Conditions of Possible Realization) the Infinitive in Indirect Discourse represents the Subjunctive of the Direct Form; the Tense of the Present Subjunctive in the Protasis is Present after a Present Tense, but Imperfect in case the Indirect Discourse follows a Past Tense. Thus, after a Present Tense, **Sī quid accidat Rōmānīs, summam in spem . . . venīre**, *if any (disaster) should befall the Romans, he would entertain the highest expectation*, lit. *would come into the highest hope*; in the Direct Form, **sī quid accidat Rōmānīs, summam in spem veniat** (I. 18).

(3) In the Third Type (Conditions Contrary to Fact) in Indirect Discourse the Perfect Infinitive of the Active Periphrastic Conjugation corresponds to the Active Pluperfect Subjunctive in the Apodosis of the Direct Form, while a Passive Pluperfect Subjunctive in the Apodosis is represented by **futūrum fuisse** (Impersonal) **ut . . .** with a Passive Imperfect Subjunctive, the Protasis being in the Subjunctive; as, **neque Eburōnēs, sī ille adesset, (fuisse) ventūrōs**, *nor would the Eburones have come if he (had been and) were at hand* (V. 29; cf. *208c*); **nisi nūntiī essent allātī, exīstimābant plērīque futūrum fuisse, utī (oppidum) amitterētur**, *if news had not been brought, most people were of the opinion that the town would have* *been lost*, in the Direct Form, **nisi nūntiī essent allātī, oppidum amissum esset** (C. III. 101).

219. The Apodosis of a Conditional Sentence is sometimes incorporated in a Substantive Clause introduced by **ut, nē,** or **quīn.** Thus, **ut, sī vellet Ariovistus proeliō contendere, eī potestās non deesset,** *in order that, if Ariovistus wished to contend in battle, opportunity might not be lacking to him*, in the Direct Form, **Sī . . . volet . . . nōn deerit** (I. 48); **neque dubitāre debēre quīn, sī Helvētiōs superāverint** (Perfect Subjunctive) **Rōmānī . . . Aeduīs lībertātem sint ēreptūrī,** *and that they ought not to doubt that, if the Romans should have overpowered the Helvetians, they were going to take away liberty from the Aeduans*, in the Direct Form, **sī Helvētiōs superāverint** (Future Perfect Indicative) **Rōmānī . . . ēreptūrī sunt** (I. 17).

220. The Verb of a clause subordinate to a clause having its Verb in the Subjunctive, or in the Infinitive, is ordinarily put in the Subjunctive (Subjunctive by Attraction); as, **utī frūmentō commeātūque, quī . . . supportārētur, Caesarem interclūderet,** *that he might cut Caesar off from the grain and other supplies which were being brought up* (I. 48).

THE INFINITIVE

221. *a.* Caesar uses the Infinitive after many Verbs to complete the Meaning (Complementary Infinitive); as, **. . . exīre possent,** *they were able to go out*, **exīre** filling out the sense which with **possent** alone would be incomplete (I. 6).

b. A Participle, Adjective, or Noun in Predicate with a Complementary Infinitive is attracted to the case of the Subject of the Verb on which the Infinitive depends; as, **pūrgātī esse vellent,** *they should wish to be guiltless* (I. 28).

c. Caesar has the Infinitive after certain Participles used as Adjectives; as, **parātum** (Accusative) **dēcertāre,** *ready to fight it out* (I. 44).

222. *a.* An Infinitive may be the Subject of an Impersonal Verb, or of other Verbs used Impersonally; as, **Maiōrī partī placuit . . . dēfendere,** *The majority decided* (lit. *to the greater part it was pleasing*) *to defend . . .* (III. 3); **Commodissimum vīsum est . . . mittere,** *It seemed most expedient to send*, **mittere** being the Subject of **vīsum est** (I. 47).

b. An Infinitive is sometimes used as the Subject of an Infinitive, especially in Indirect Discourse; as, **commodissimum esse statuit . . . impōnere,** he *decided that the most expedient (thing) was to place . . . on*, **impōnere** being the Subject of **esse** used impersonally (I. 42).

c. An Infinitive used as Subject may have a Subject Accusative; as, **intersit** (Historical Present) **manūs distinērī,** *it was important that the forces be kept apart* (II. 5).

223. *a.* Caesar uses the Accusative with the Infinitive not only after words of Speech and Thought (Indirect Discourse, *212d*), but also after Words expressing *Will* or *Desire, Feeling, Permission* and *Prevention, Persuasion, Command, Training* and *Compulsion*; as, **eās rēs iactārī nōlēbat,** *he was unwilling that those matters should be discussed* (I. 18); **eōs īre paterentur,** *would allow them to go* (I. 6).

Such Words used by Caesar are:

(1) Expressing Will or Desire: **dēsīderō,** *desire* (IV. 2); **mālō,** *prefer* (C. III. 80); **nōlō,** *be unwilling;* **studeō,** *be eager* (C. I. 4); **vōlō,** *wish* (I. 13).

(2) Expressing Feeling: **admīror,** *be surprised* (I. 14); **doleō,** *grieve* (III. 2); **gaudeō,** *rejoice* (IV. 13); **glōrior,** *boost* (C. I. 4); **queror,** *complain* (C. III. 96; usually followed by a **quod** clause); **magnō dolōre ferō,** *feel deeply chagrined* (VII. 63); **molestē ferō,** *feel irritation* (II. 1).

(3) Expressing Permission or Prevention: **patior,** *suffer, allow* (sometimes followed by an **ut**-clause); **prohibeō,** *prevent . . . from* (II. 4, etc.).

(4) Expressing Command, Training, or Compulsion: **iubeō,** *order* (I. 5); **vetō,** *forbid* (II. 20); **assuēfaciō,** *train* (IV. 2); **cōgō,** *force* (I. 4).

b. **Cupiō, mālō, nōlō, studeō,** and **volō** frequently have the Infinitive without a Subject Accusative (Complementary Infinitive); as, **ulcīscī velint,** *may wish to punish* (I. 14).

224. *a.* When Verbs which, in the Active Voice, have the Accusative and Infinitive, are used in the Passive, a Subject Nominative may take the place of the Accusative, the Infinitive remaining the same; in translating, the English Impersonal construction should often be used. Thus, **nōn fore dictō audientēs . . . dīcantur,** *that it is said they will not be obedient to the command,* lit. *that they are said not to be about to be obedient* (I. 40).

b. The Accusative and the Infinitive may stand as the Subject of an Impersonal Verb, or of other Verbs used Impersonally; as, **poenam sequī oportēbat,** *the penalty would inevitably follow,* lit. *that the penalty follow, was inevitable* (I. 4); **Nōn esse fās Germānōs superāre,** *That it was not right for the Germans to conquer,* **Germānōs superāre** being the Subject of **esse** used Impersonally (I. 50).

225. The place of the Future Infinitive may be taken by **fore** or **futūrum esse** and a clause with **ut** and the Subjunctive; as, **fore, utī pertināciā dēsisteret,** *that he would desist from his obstinate course,* lit. *that it would be that he would desist* (I. 42).

PARTICIPLES

226. a. The Time denoted by a Present Participle is the same as that of the Principal Verb; as, **flēns peteret,** *with tears* (lit. *weeping) he was entreating* (I. 20).

b. The Time denoted by a Perfect Participle is prior to that of the Principal Verb; as, **cupiditāte inductus,** *led on* (lit. *having been led) by a desire* (I. 2).

c. Caesar sometimes uses Perfect Participles of Deponent and Semi-deponent Verbs where English usage prefers a Present Participle; as, **Caesarem complexus,** *embracing Caesar,* lit. *having embraced* (I. 20). Examples are: **arbitrātus,** *thinking* (III. 28); **complexus; commorātus,** *delaying* (V. 7); **cōnfīsus,** *trusting* (I. 53); **cōnsōlātus,** *comforting* (I. 20); **diffīsus,** *distrusting* (VI. 38); **gāvīsus,** *rejoicing* (IV. 13); **mīrātus,** *wondering* (I. 32); **secūtus,** *following* (I. 24); **ūsus,** *using* (II. 7); **veritus,** *fearing* (II. 11).

227. a. A Participle is often used to express concisely an idea which might have been expanded into a Clause, particularly an idea of *Cause, Condition, Opposition, Characterization,* or *Description.* Thus:

(1) Expressing Cause: **sē, Biturīgum perfidiam veritōs, revertisse,** *that they, fearing the treachery of the Bituriges, had come back,* that is, *that they had come back because they feared the treachery of the Bituriges* (VII. 5).

(2) Expressing Condition: **hanc adeptī victōriam, in perpetuum sē fore victōrēs cōnfīdēbant,** *having won this victory, they were confident that they would be victorious for all time,* **adeptī** being equivalent to **sī adeptī essent** (V. 39).

(3) Expressing Opposition: **in colloquium venīre invītātus,** *although invited to come to a conference* (I. 35).

(4) Expressing Characterization or Description: **victīs, venientēs,** *those beaten, those coming up,* meaning *those who had been beaten, those who were coming up* (I. 25).

(5) Expressing Time: **cōnantēs,** *when they were attempting* (I. 47).

b. A Participle may express Manner or Circumstance; as, **flēns peteret,** *with tears* (lit. *weeping) he was entreating* (I. 20); **pugnāns interficitur,** *is killed while fighting* (V. 37).

228. a. Caesar sometimes uses a Perfect Participle in agreement with the Subject or the Object of a Verb where English usage prefers a coordinate clause. Thus, **Persuādent** (Historical Present) **Rauracīs . . . utī, eōdem ūsī cōnsiliō, . . . cum eīs proficīscantur,** *Persuaded the Rauraci . . . to adopt the same plan, and set out with them,* lit. *that, having used the same plan, they should set out* (I. 5); **Boiōs . . . receptōs ad sē sociōs sibi ascīscunt,** *they received and associated with themselves the Boians,* lit. *the Boians, having been received . . . they associated* (I. 5).

b. Caesar sometimes uses a Perfect Passive Participle in agreement with a Noun where the Participle has the main idea and is best translated by a Noun; as, **ante prīmam cōnfectam vigiliam,** *before the end of the first watch,* lit. *before the first watch having been completed* (VII. 3).

c. Caesar sometimes uses a Participle in agreement with the Object of a Verb to depict an Action or a Situation more vividly. Thus, **aliquōs ex nāvī ēgredientēs cōnspexerant,** *had seen* *some (soldiers) disembarking,* is more vivid than **aliquōs . . . ēgredī,** *that some (soldiers) were disembarking* (IV. 26).

229. *a.* **Habeō** with a Perfect Passive Participle in agreement with its Object may have almost the force of a Perfect or Pluperfect tense; as, **quem . . . coāctum habēbat,** *which he had collected,* lit. *which, having been collected, he was having* (I. 15).

b. Caesar uses the Future Passive Participle (Gerundive) in agreement with the Object of Certain Verbs to express Purpose or Accomplishment; as, **pontem faciendum cūrat** (Historical Present), *he had a bridge built, he attended to the building of a bridge,* lit. *cared for a bridge to be built* (I. 13).

The verbs thus used are **cūrō,** *arrange, provide;* **dō,** *give* (IV. 22); and **trādō,** *deliver* (VI. 4).

c. The Future Passive Participle combined with the forms of **sum** in the Passive Periphrastic Conjugation (63) is often used to express *Obligation, Necessity,* or *Propriety;* as, **revocandī [erant] mīlitēs,** *the soldiers had to be called back* (II. 20). Cf. *357a, b*

GERUND AND GERUNDIVE CONSTRUCTION

230. In place of the Gerund, Caesar more often uses the Gerundive Construction, with the Noun in the case in which the Gerund might have been put, and the Gerundive agreeing with it. His use of the Gerund and of the Gerundive Construction is as follows:

(1) Genitive after Nouns and Adjectives, and with **causā** and **grātiā,** expressing Purpose: **bellandī cupidī,** *desirous of waging war* (I. 2); **Galliae impugnandae causā,** *in order to attack Gaul* (I. 44). Cf. *355*

(2) Dative after Verbs (Gerundive Construction only): **vix ut eīs rēbus . . . collocandīs . . . tempus darētur,** *barely time (enough) was given for making those arrangements,* lit. *for those things to be arranged* (III. 4).

(3) Accusative after **ad** to express Purpose: **ad dēlīberandum,** *for consideration* (I. 7); **Ad eās rēs cōnficiendās,** *To complete these preparations,* lit. *for these things to be accomplished* (I. 3). Cf. *355*

(4) Ablative of Means without a Preposition, and Ablative with the Prepositions **in** or **dē**: **fallendō,** *by practising deception* (IV. 13); **in quaerendō,** *on making inquiry* (I. 18); **dē expugnandō oppidō,** *in regard to storming the stronghold* (II. 10).

THE SUPINES

231. *a.* The Supine in **-um** is used, chiefly after Verbs of Motion, to express Purpose; as, **ad Caesarem grātulātum convēnērunt,** *came to Caesar to offer congratulations* (I. 30). Cf. *355*

b. The Supine in **-um** may be followed by a Direct Object, or by a Clause; as, **lēgātōs mittunt** (Historical Present) **rogātum auxilium,** *sent envoys to ask for help* (I. 11); **questum, quod Harūdēs . . . fīnēs eōrum populārentur,** *to make complaint because the Harudes were laying waste their country* (I. 37).

232. Caesar uses the Supine in **-ū** after a few adjectives to denote in What Respect their Meaning is to be taken; as, **Perfacile factū,** *very easy of accomplishment,* lit. *very easy in respect to the doing* (I. 3).

The Adjectives thus used by Caesar are **horridus** (V. 14), **optimus** (IV. 30), and **perfacilis** (I. 3, VII. 64).

CONJUNCTIONS

233. *a.* Of the Copulative Conjunctions Caesar uses **et,** *and,* **et . . . et,** *both . . . and,* on the one hand . . . on the other, to express simple connection; **-que,** *and,* **-que . . . -que,** *both . . . and,* to express a closer connection; **atque** or **ac,** *and also, and indeed, and,* to express a close connection and also make that which follows slightly more prominent; and **neque** or **nec,**

and .. . not, **neque** (or **nec**) . . . **neque** (or **nec**), *neither . . . nor, not . . . and not;* **et . . . neque,**
both . . . and not; **neque** or **nec . . . et,** *and not . . . and,* to express a connection with a negative
idea.

b. The enclitic Conjunction **-que,** *and,* is attached to the word introduced by it, or to the first
word of a Phrase or Clause which it introduces, excepting a Prepositional Phrase; **-que**
introducing a Prepositional Phrase may be attached to the first word after the Preposition.
Thus, **ob eāsque rēs,** *and on account of these things* (II. 35).

c. After words expressing Similarity, or the Opposite, **atque** or **ac** has the force of *than, as;*
as, **in parem . . . condiciōnem atque ipsī erant,** *into the same condition . . . as themselves,* lit. *as
(and) they themselves were* (I. 28).

d. Caesar uses the conjunctions **et, -que, atque, ac,** and **neque** in various combinations,
sometimes joining more than two members; as, **et . . . que** (III. 11), **-que . . . et** (II. 22), **et . . .
atque** (I. 15), **atque . . . et** (II. 8), **atque . . . -que** (VI. 11), **neque . . . atque** (II. 10), **neque . . . et**
(II. 25), **-que . . . -que . . . -que** (I. 30), **ac . . . atque . . . -que** (III. 5), **et . . . atque . . . et . . . et . . .
et** (IV. 33).

234. *a.* When more than two words stand in the same relation, the Copulative Conjunction
may be expressed with all, or omitted with all, or the last two words may be joined by **-que;**
in each case English usage generally prefers "and" between the last two words. Thus,
Rauracīs et Tulingīs et Latobrīgīs, *the Rauraci, Tulingi, and Latobrigi* (I. 5); **linguā, īnstitūtīs,
lēgibus,** *in respect to language, institutions, and laws* (I. 1); **puerī, senēs mulierēsque,** *children,
old men, and women* (I. 29).

b. Sometimes, especially after a negative expression, Caesar uses **et, -que,** and **atque** or **ac,**
where English usage prefers *but;* as, **portūs . . . capere nōn potuērunt, et paulō īnfrā dēlātae
sunt,** *could not make the harbors but were carried a short distance below* (IV. 36).

235. *a.* Of the Disjunctive Conjunctions Caesar uses **aut,** *or,* to connect alternatives that
cannot, in most cases, both be true at the same time; **vel,** *or,* negative **nēve** or **neu,** *or not, and
not,* to connect alternatives between which there might be a choice; and **sīve** or **seu,** *or if,* to
connect alternatives involving a condition. Thus, **quīnīs aut sēnīs mīlibus passuum,** *five or
six miles each day* (1.15); **Brūtō . . . vel tribūnīs,** *to Brutus or the tribunes* (III. 14).

b. The Disjunctive Conjunctions are often used in pairs, as **aut . . . aut,** *either . . . or* (I. 1),
vel . . . vel, *either . . . or* (I. 6), **sīve . . . sīve,** *whether . . . or, either . . . or* (I. 12).

236. *a.* Of the Adversative Conjunctions Caesar uses **at,** *but, at any rate,* to express Contrast
or Restriction; **autem,** *however, on the other hand, moreover,* to express Contrast or Addition;
sed, *but,* to correct or limit a Preceding Statement; **tamen,** *nevertheless, yet,* to emphasize the
importance of something that follows in opposition to a Preceding Statement; and **vērō,** *in
fact, but in truth,* to emphasize a contrast with a Preceding Statement.

b. The Adversative Conjunctions **autem** and **vērō** are regularly placed after the First Word
of a Clause.

c. The Adversative Conjunction **tamen** sometimes stands after the First Word of a Clause.

d. Caesar uses correlatively **nōn sōlum . . . sed etiam,** *not only. . . but also;* **nōn modo . . . sed
etiam,** *not only . . . but also;* **nōn modo . . . sed,** *not only . . . but;* **nōn modo nōn . . . sed nē . . .
quidem,** *not only not . . . but not even.*

e. In **nōn modo . . . nē — quidem** Caesar uses **nōn modo** as equivalent to **nōn modo nōn,**
when a verb appears only in the second member; as **nōn modo defessō . . . sed nē sauciō
quidem,** *not only not to one (who was) exhausted . . . but even to a wounded man* (III. 4).

237. *a.* Of the Conjunctions denoting Logical Relations Caesar uses chiefly **itaque,**
accordingly (lit. *and so*), to introduce a statement of a fact or situation naturally resulting from
what preceded; **proinde,** *hence,* to introduce a Command; **nam** or **enim,** *for,* to introduce an
Explanation of a Preceding Statement; and **quārē,** *wherefore, and therefore,* to introduce a
Logical Consequence, or a Command.

b. In presenting a succession of points Caesar often uses **prīmum,** *first,* and **deinde,** *then, in
the second place;* sometimes, also, **dēnique,** *in fine,* to introduce the conclusion of an argument.

c. In the Adverbial Phrase **nē . . . quidem**, *not even*, the word or phrase emphasized is placed between the two words; as, **nē pabulī quidem**, *not even of fodder* (I. 16).

FIGURES OF SPEECH

238. Caesar uses the following Grammatical Figures:

a. Asyndeton (a-sin'de-ton),[1] the omission of a Conjunction where a Connective might have been used; as, **loca, portūs, aditūs cognōvisset**, *should have become acquainted with the natural features, the harbors, (and) the approaches* (IV. 20); **L. Pīsōne, A. Gabīniō cōnsulibus**, *in the Consulship of Lucius Piso (and) Aulus Gabinius* (I. 6).

b. Brachylogy (bra-kil'ọ-ji), a condensed form of expression; as, **cōnsimilis caprīs figūra**, *shape like (that of) goats*, that is, **figūra cōnsimilis figūrae** (Dative) **caprārum** (VI. 27).

c. Ellipsis (e-lip'sis), the omission of words essential to the meaning; as, **Duae fīliae**, for **Duae fīliae fuērunt**, *There were two daughters* (I. 53).

d. Hendiadys (hen-dī'a-dis), the use of two Nouns with a Connective where a noun with a Modifying Genitive or Adjective might have been expected; as, **fidem et iūs iūrandum**, *a pledge of good faith bound by an oath*, lit. *good faith and oath* (I. 3).

e. Parenthesis (pa-ren'the-sis), the insertion of an Independent Sentence or phrase, interrupting the Construction; as, **quam maximum potest mīlitum numerum imperat** (**erat . . . legiō ūna**), **pontem . . . iubet** (Historical Present), **rescindī**, *he levied as many soldiers as possible (there was only one legion, altogether, in further Gaul) and gave orders that the bridge be cut down* (I. 7).

f. Polysyndeton (pol-i-sin'de-ton), the use of more Conjunctions than the sense requires; as, **Ceutronēs et Graiocelī et Caturīgēs**, *The Ceutrones, the Graioceli, and the Caturiges* (I. 10).

g. Prolepsis (prō-lep'sis), or *Anticipation*, the use of a Noun as Object in a clause preceding that in which it naturally belongs as Subject; as, **rem frūmentāriam, ut supportārī posset, timēre**, *that they feared that the supply of grain could not be brought up*, lit. *they feared the supply of grain, that it . . .* (I. 39).

h. Synesis (sin'ẹ-sis), construction according to the Sense, without regard to the Grammatical Form; as, **cīvitātī persuāsit, ut . . . exīrent**, *persuaded the (people of his) state to go out*, lit. *persuaded his state that they should go out* (I. 2).

239. Caesar uses the following Rhetorical Figures: *a. Anaphora* (an-af'o-ra), the Repetition of the same word at the beginning of Successive Phrases or Clauses; as, **nōn aetāte cōnfectīs, nōn mulieribus, nōn īnfantibus pepercērunt**, *they spared not the aged, not the women, not the children* (VII. 28).

b. Antithesis (an-tith'e-sis), the juxtaposition of contrasted expressions in like order; as, **Nōn sēsē Gallīs, sed Gallōs sibi, bellum intulisse**, *He did not make war on the Gauls, but the Gauls on him* (I. 44).

c. Chiasmus (kī-as'mus), an arrangement of contrasted words in inverse order; as, **fāmā nōbilēs potentēsque bellō**, *in reputation notable, and powerful in war* (VII. 77).

d. Climax (klī'max), an arrangement of words, phrases, or clauses with gradual increase of interest or vigour of expression to the end; as, **cōnferre, comportārī, adesse**, *that it was being collected, was on the way, was at hand* (I. 16).

e. Euphemism (ū'fe-mizm), the use of a mild expression in order to avoid a word of bad omen; as, **sī quid accidat Rōmānīs**, *if anything should happen to the Romans*, meaning *if any disaster should befall the Romans* (I. 18).

f. Hyperbaton (hī-per'ba-ton), the arrangement of words in unusual order, as the separation of words that belong together, such as the insertion of one or more words between the parts of an Ablative Absolute; thus, **simulātā Caesarem amīcitiā**, *that Caesar under the pretense of friendship*, the usual order being **Caesarem, simulātā amīcitiā** (I. 44).

g. Litotes (lit'ọ-tēz), the Affirmation of an idea through the Negation of its Opposite; as,

[1]The key to the Pronunciation is given at the beginning of the Vocabulary.

neque tam imperītum esse rērum ut nōn scīret, *and he was not so unversed in affairs as not to know,* meaning *that he was so worldly wise that he very well knew* (I. 44).

h. Personification (pèr-son'i-fi'kā'shun), the representation of something inanimate or abstract as endowed with Life and Action; as **Cōnspicātae nāvēs trirēmēs duae nāvem D. Brūtī,** *Two triremes, sighting the ship of Decimus Brutus* (C. II. 6).

EXPRESSIONS RELATING TO TIME

240. *a.* The Roman year (**annus**) is usually dated by the consuls in office, their names being given in the Ablative Absolute with **cōnsulibus**; as, **Cn. Pompeiō, M. Crassō cōnsulibus,** *in the consulship of Gnaeus Pompey and Marcus Crassus* (IV. 1), 55 B.C.

b. In Caesar's time the year commenced on January 1, and the months were named (**mēnsis**) **Iānuārius, Februārius, Mārtius** (originally the first month of the year), **Aprīlis, Maius, Iūnius, Quīnctīlis** (from **quīnque;** named the *fifth* month when the year began with March), **Sextīlis** (**sex**), **September, Octōber, November, December** (the *tenth* month, reckoning March as the first). Afterwards **Quīnctīlis** was changed to **Iūlius** (our *July*) in honour of Julius Caesar, and **Sextīlis** to **Augustus** (our *August*) in honour of the Emperor Augustus.

241. *a.* Dates in the month were reckoned backward from three points, the mode of reckoning being similar to that which we use when we say "Four days yet before the New Moon." These points, designated by Plural Feminine Nouns, are *the Calends,* **Kalendae,** the *first* day of the month; *the Nones,* **Nōnae** (ninth before the Ides), the *seventh* day of March, May, July, and October, the *fifth* day of other months; and *the Ides* (**Īdūs**), the *fifteenth* day of March, May, July, and October, the *thirteenth* of other months.

b. In giving dates the days at the beginning and end of a given period were both included, and abbreviations were employed. Thus, **a. d. v. Kal. Apr.** (I. 6), in full would be **ante diem quīntum Kalendās Aprīlēs,** which is translated as if it were (**diēs**) **quīntus ante Kalendās Aprīlēs,** *the fifth* (*day*) *before the Calends of April;* since March had 31 days, we start from April 1 and count back:

Day I	Day II	Day III	Day IV	Day V
'1 April'	'31 March'	'30 March'	'29 March'	'28 March'

and so we find the fifth day, which is March 28 according to our method of writing dates.

c. In 46 B.C. the Calendar was reformed by Julius Caesar by virtue of his authority as Supreme Pontiff (252), and since that year it has undergone slight change. As the dates of the Gallic War and of the Civil War are prior to 46 B.C., they fall in the period of the Unreformed Calendar, when there was much confusion. Thus, the twenty-eighth day of March of the Unreformed Calendar in 58 B.C. (I. 6) is considered by some to be the same as March 24 of our Calendar; by others, the same as March 25; by others still, as April 16 of our Calendar.

242. *a.* The day from sunrise to sunset was divided into twelve hours, **hōrae,** which varied in length according to the season of the year, and were numbered 1-12; thus, **hōrā septimā,** *the seventh hour* (I. 26). Since the sixth hour ended at noon, the seventh hour at the equinoxes would correspond exactly with the hour between twelve and one o'clock according to our reckoning; at other times the seventh hour would end after, or before, one o'clock.

b. The method of reducing the Roman hours to our system of reckoning may be illustrated by the following problem: *Question.* "What, approximately, is our equivalent of the fourth Roman hour in the last week of August in the region of Dover, England?" *Answer.* In the region of Dover in the last week in August the sun rises about 5 o'clock and sets about 7. The length of the day is therefore about 14 hours by our reckoning. Since the Romans divided the full day into 12 equal hours, we divide 14 by 12 and have 1.167, that is, the Roman hour in this problem = 1.167 of our hours. At the beginning of the fourth Roman hour 3 Roman hours have passed; 3 x 1.167 = 3.5, that is, at the beginning of the fourth Roman hour 3.5 of our hours have passed since sunrise. As sunrise is reckoned about 5 o'clock by our time, we add 3.5 to 5, making 8:30; that is, 8:30 a.m., by our reckoning from midnight, will approximately represent the beginning of the fourth hour of the day by Roman reckoning under the conditions of the problem.

c. In military usage the night was divided into four watches of three hours each: **prīma vigilia,** *first watch* (VII. 3), commencing at sunset, 6 to 9 o'clock by Roman reckoning; **secunda vigilia** (II. 11), ending at midnight, 9 to 12 o'clock; **tertia vigilia** (II. 33), commencing at midnight, 12 to 3 o'clock a.m.; **quārta vigilia** (I. 21), ending at sunrise, 3 to 6 o'clock a.m., by Roman reckoning.

d. Caesar uses the Preposition **dē** in certain expressions of time with the meaning *just after, in the course of;* as **dē mediā nocte,** *just after midnight* (II. 7); **dē tertiā vigiliā,** *soon after the beginning of the third watch* (I. 12), which lasted from midnight to 3:00 a. m.

e. When the sun was not visible, recourse might be had to water clocks, **ex aquā mensūrae** (V. 13), for the measurement of time.

EXPRESSIONS RELATING TO LENGTH AND DISTANCE

243. *a.* Of the terms denoting measurement Caesar uses **digitus,** *finger-breadth* (VII. 73); **pēs,** *foot* (I. 8), which measured approximately 0.97 of the English foot; **passus,** *pace* (I. 49); and **mīlle passūs,** *mile,* Plural **mīlia passuum,** *miles* (I. 2). The **passus** contained two ordinary steps (**gradus**), and measured the distance between the points where the same heel is lifted and touches the ground again.

b. The relations of the units of measurement, and their modern equivalents, are as follows:

		English Feet	Meters
	1 digitus	= 0.728 inch	= 0.0185 m
16 digiti	= *1 pes*	= 11.65 inches	= 0.296 m
2.5 pedes	= 1 gradus	= 2 feet 5.125 inches	= 0.74 m
2 gradus	= 1 passus	= 4 feet 10.25 inches	= 1.48 m
1000 passus	= mille passus	= 4854 feet	= 1480 m

Since the Roman foot was approximately 0.97 of the English foot in length, the Roman mile, 4854 English feet in length, was 426 feet shorter than the English mile of 5280 feet; 12 English miles are a little more than the equivalent of 13 Roman miles.

c. Long distances may be loosely expressed by **iter** (Accusative) with the Genitive; as, **novem diērum iter,** *a nine days' journey* (VI. 25).

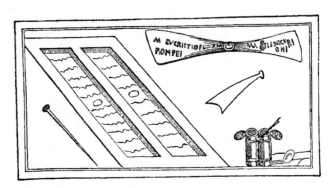

Fig. 27. — Writing Materials.

244. "My aunt Julia," said Julius Caesar in an address in 68 B.C. at the funeral of his aunt, wife of the famous Marius, " My aunt Julia on her mother's side traced her ancestry back to kings, on her father's side to the immortal gods. For those who bear the name Marcius Rex, her mother's family, are descended from Ancus Marcius;[1] from Venus the Julii are sprung, and to that clan our family belongs. In our stock therefore are blended the sacred authority of kings, whose power is greatest among men, and a right to the reverence due to the gods, under whose power kings themselves are.

Whatever the truth may be about the origin of the Julian clan (*gens*), in these proud words the man who was destined to become its most distinguished representative asserted, unmistakably, its aristocratic standing. Twenty years afterwards, when Caesar had the authority to strike coins, he gave a visible expression to the popular belief in the Trojan origin of the Julii, from Venus and Anchises; stamped upon a denarius Aeneas appears, in the flight from burning Troy, carrying his aged father Anchises upon his left shoulder and in his right hand the sacred image, the Palladium, which, men said, had fallen from heaven.

245. Toward the end of the Republic the Caesar family far outstripped the other families of the Julian gens in prominence. In the two centuries immediately preceding the Christian era it furnished a full score of names sufficiently distinguished to find mention in biographical dictionaries two thousand years afterwards. Of the father of Julius Caesar, however, nothing important is of record except his sudden death, at Pisa, when he was putting on his shoes.

246. Gaius Julius Caesar was born on 12 July, in the year 100 B.C.; he was thus six years younger than Pompey and the orator Cicero. It is assumed that his birthplace was Rome. His mother was Aurelia, a Roman matron of the highest type. She not only watched over the education of her son, and Julius was the only son, with great care, but followed his career with solicitude, and on one occasion at least rendered him a notable service. She was not spared, however, to see her son at the head of the State, or to be harrowed by civil war; she died when Caesar was in Gaul. We know nothing about the education of the young Julius, except that he had as private teacher, at his own home, Antonius Gnipho, a distinguished rhetorician, who had studied at Alexandria and was well versed in Greek. We may assume that the youth received the usual training of the time in Greek as well as in declamation, numbers, and music, for Greek was then the foundation of liberal studies.

247. The only career deemed suitable for a young patrician was in the service of the State, either through public office, or through service in the

---

1 The fourth king of Rome, following Tullus Hostilius.

field, as occasion might require. We do not understand how high-born Caesars were first led to espouse the cause of the common people and champion the interests of the masses as opposed to the aristocracy, which believed in the government of the many by the few and had its stronghold in the Senate, but when Julius was old enough to take an active interest in public affairs, his uncle by marriage, Marius, was leader of the popular or democratic party, which was then dominant. Marius died in 86 B.C., and was succeeded by Cornelius Cinna as democratic leader.

248. The daughter of this Cinna, Cornelia, in 83 B.C. became Caesar's wife. To them was born a daughter Julia who, in 59 B.C., in her early twenties, became the fourth wife of Pompey.

249. In 82 B.C. Sulla returned from a series of victories in the East and restored the power of the Senate, taking vengeance upon political enemies. There was a reign of terror. Cinna had been killed, and Sulla ordered Caesar to divorce his wife, Cinna's daughter. This Caesar refused, at the risk of his life. In disguise he made his escape to the mountains. He was tracked by Sulla's emissaries, one of whom found him; he purchased his life with a large bribe. After a time, through influential friends, pardon was obtained from Sulla, who is said to have granted it with the warning that in young Caesar there were many Mariuses.

Advancement in Rome, however, was blocked so long as Sulla lived. Caesar went East and joined the army. At the siege of Mytilene. on the island of Lesbos, in 80 B.C., he was awarded the Civic Crown for conspicuous bravery. This crown, though made of oak leaves, represented a military distinction rarely conferred, and most highly esteemed. It was given only to the soldier who had saved the life of a Roman citizen in battle, had killed his adversary, and held the position where the rescue was made, without retreating. There is a good representation of a Civic Crown on a coin of the Emperor Augustus.

250. Returning to Rome, after Sulla's death (78 B.C.), Caesar brought charges of extortion in provincial management first against Gnaeus Dolabella, who had been proconsul in Macedonia, and afterwards against Gaius Antonius, who had plundered Greece; at that time the bringing of delinquent officials to justice was a common way of introducing one's self to public notice. Though both Dolabella and Antonius seem to have escaped punishment, Caesar showed marked oratorical power, and in prosecuting them attracted favourable attention. Wishing to perfect himself in oratory, in 76 Caesar started for Rhodes, to study under Apollonius Molo, the most eminent teacher of the art. In the Eastern Mediterranean the pirates were still active; near Miletus his ship was captured, and he was held a prisoner on an island for thirty-eight days, until his retinue could return and bring to the pirates a ransom of fifty talents. As a captive he showed himself merry and sociable, and he jokingly told his captors that some day he would come back and crucify them. Being released, he at once manned ships at Miletus, attacked the pirates suddenly, and captured most of them. True to his word, he crucified them, but ordered their throats cut first, Suetonius adds, as an example of Caesar's humaneness, in order to spare needless suffering. The quickness of action, daring, and success of this adventure reveal in Caesar at the age of twenty-four the qualities that characterized his entire career.

251. *a.* During the next sixteen years Caesar followed the usual course of political promotion, neglecting no means by which he might increase his popularity. He bestowed gifts with a free hand, assumed the debts of bankrupt young nobles who had squandered their inheritance, gave largesses to the people. When his own means were exhausted, he borrowed large sums at high rates of interest, with the design of obtaining reimbursement, from the spoils of office. According to Plutarch his indebtedness, before he held a single office, had reached the enormous sum of thirteen hundred talents.

b. In 68 B.C. Caesar was quaestor, and accompanied Antistius Vetus to Spain. Here his duties were chiefly financial; the provincial quaestor had charge of the military stores and supervised the keeping of accounts for the provincial governor. This was doubtless a good business training for Caesar, which he turned to excellent use later in his administration in Gaul.

c. In 65 B.C. Caesar was **curule aedile**, with Bibulus as colleague. The curule aediles had charge of the streets and public buildings, the markets, and the celebration of the public games. In this office, by extravagant expenditures on games and public improvements, he raised the enthusiasm of the populace to the highest pitch. He even dared by night to set up in the Capitol the statue of Marius, and trophies of victories in the Jugurthine and Cimbrian wars, which had been thrown down by Sulla seventeen years before, and the people wept for joy at the revival of old memories. He secured so many gladiators for public shows that the Senate became alarmed, on account of the presence of so great an armed force, and passed a law restricting the number, but he nevertheless exhibited three hundred and twenty pairs, all resplendent in silver armour. Caesar's political methods were not unlike those of his contemporaries, but he excelled them in daring and foresight, and succeeded.

252. It has been believed by many that Caesar was connected with the Catilinarian conspiracy of 65 B.C., if not also with that of 63, but the evidence is meagre Much more important was his election, in 63 B.C., after a bitter contest, to the office of Supreme Pontiff, **Pontifex Maximus.** The tenure of this office was for life. As the head of the college of pontiffs, then fifteen in number, the Supreme Pontiff was virtually the head of the

Roman religious system. He decided questions relating to religious law and usage, and he had charge of the Calendar; the priests of Jupiter and of other divinities, as well as the Vestal Virgins, were under his jurisdiction. The first coin struck by Caesar in Gaul on one side bears the symbols of his sacred office, the ax for striking victims in offering sacrifice, the close-fitting cap, with point of olive wood, worn by certain priests, the brush-shaped sprinkler for holy water, and the ladle for dipping up wine, for use in pouring libations.

253. In 62 B.C., the year of the Bona Dea scandal, Caesar held the office of **praetor,** in the discharge of which, amid scenes of violence, he carried himself with firmness and dignity; the functions of the praetor were judicial, and in stormy times the administration of justice is doubly difficult. In 61 he served as governor of Hispania Ulterior. Returning to Rome in the summer of 60, with abundant means of satisfying his creditors thanks to Crassus, he was decreed a public thanksgiving for his victories, and was soon elected consul for the year 59.

In the year of his consulship, 59, Caesar married Calpurnia, familiar to readers of Shakespeare's "Julius Caesar"; she was the daughter of Calpurnius Piso (I. 12), and was Caesar's fourth wife. For his first wife, Cossutia, was divorced before he married Cornelia, his second wife (248), who had died before his quaestorship and Pompeia, whom Caesar married in 67 B.C., as his third wife, was divorced six years later.

254. For some years Pompey had been the most conspicuous Roman. His successes in the campaign against the pirates and the war with Mithridates, and his conquest of Syria and Palestine, had made him the national hero. But in the qualities needful for a political leader he was quite lacking, so that even from his own party, the aristocratic, he was unable to win either the recognition he desired or the privileges to which he was entitled. More than once the Senate snubbed him outright. Here Caesar saw an opportunity. Relying on his own popularity, he proposed to Pompey that they work in harmony, and by uniting their influence accomplish what either might desire. Pompey agreed, and with these two, Crassus, the wealthiest man of Rome, was joined, making a political coalition really supreme, which is known as the First Triumvirate. It had no official existence; it was simply a political ring, of only three members but of unlimited power. It was to cement this union that Pompey, then a widower for the third time, married Caesar's daughter Julia (248), who was less than half his age.

255. During his consulship in 59, among other measures Caesar caused a law to be passed regarding the division of the public lands, which, though bitterly opposed by the Senate, pleased the people greatly. With his aid, too, Pompey gained favours previously denied. While consul he seems to have used his influence with the Senate to secure a recognition of

Ariovistus, the German ruler, with whom he afterwards fought (I. 33, 35, 40).

At the close of his consulship, as it was the custom to give to ex-consuls the charge of provinces, Caesar easily obtained for five years the government of both Cisalpine Gaul (284) and Illyricum (298), together with the part of Transalpine Gaul previously subdued, which in this book is called the Province (290).

256. Caesar was soon engaged in the conquest of Transalpine Gaul beyond the Province. The first summer (58 B.C.) he drove back to their homes the Helvetians, who had at tempted to migrate from the country now called Switzerland, to the west of Gaul, and he annihilated the army of the German king, Ariovistus. The following year he subdued the Belgic States in the north.

The third campaign (56 B.C.) was against the peoples of northwest Gaul, that had leagued together to resist Caesar. In April of this year at Luca, near the southern border of Cisalpine Gaul, Caesar had renewed his compact with Pompey and Crassus, who agreed to see to it that his command should be extended for five years longer. A part of every winter except one (54-53), he spent in Cisalpine Gaul, so as to be near Rome and retain his influence in home politics; it was contrary to law that a provincial governor having an army should enter Italy while in office.

In 55 B.C. Caesar chastised several German tribes and bridged the Rhine; then he crossed over to Britain. The campaign of the next summer (54) was principally against the Britons, part of whom he reduced to nominal subjection. In the fall a division of his army in Belgium, under the command of Sabinus and Cotta, was cut off by a sudden uprising of the enemy.

In 53 Caesar had to face an extensive rebellion of the Gallic states, which, however, he speedily crushed. But the next year almost all Gaul rose against him, and under the leadership of Vercingetorix taxed his powers to the utmost. He finally prevailed; and after the fall of Alesia (52 B.C.) the strength of the Gauls was forever broken.

In the eighth campaign, summer of 51, the states that had not submitted were one by one reduced to complete subjection. The following spring, in 50 B.C., Caesar left his army and went into Cisalpine Gaul. Here he resolved to remain till the expiration of his command in 49, returning to Transalpine Gaul only for a short time during the summer to review the troops.

257. Caesar's Gallic victories are symbolically portrayed on several coins. On one we see in the middle a trophy, draped; on the top is a Gallic helmet, with a bull's horns. Suspended on one side of the trophy is an oval shield; opposite is a Gallic war trumpet, with the mouth carved to represent the head of a serpent. Nearer the edge of the coin, is a sacrificial ax. The base of the trophy divides the victor's name, Caesar. A trophy appears less distinctly on another coin of Caesar, but at the foot is Vercingetorix, sitting, with his hands tied behind him; his head is turned toward the left as he looks upward.

258. During Caesar's absence in Gaul, in 55 B.C., Crassus undertook a campaign of conquest against the Parthians, in the Far East; he was defeated and killed in 53 B.C. The triumvirate was thus brought to an end, and with it speedily ended the cooperation between Caesar and Pompey.

Pompey began to view Caesar's successes with distrust and alarm. He entered into alliance again with the aristocracy. In 50 B.C. the Senate in Pompey's interest passed a decree that he and Caesar should each give up a legion for service in the East. Since 53 Caesar had had one of Pompey's legions; this was now demanded back. Caesar let it go, and one of his own too, without a complaint, although the intent of the whole action was evidently to weaken his forces. As it was not lawful for him to proceed in person to Rome, he stationed himself in Ravenna, the town of Cisalpine Gaul nearest the boundary of Italy (*283*), on the east side; thence he sent agents and friends to the City to negotiate for him, to try to offset the influence now openly brought to bear against him, but the negotiations were fruitless.

Pompey and the Senate both hated and feared Caesar. A decree was passed that he should disband his army by a certain date, or be considered an outlaw. In the state of public affairs at the time, this was simply to wrest from him the fruits of his hard-won successes, without leaving him even a guaranty of his personal safety. Caesar hesitated. The Senate voted further, that the consuls should "provide that the state receive no hurt," which is like a proclamation of martial law in our day.

259. This action of the Senate was virtually a declaration of war against Caesar, inspired by the jealousy of his opponent. With one legion he at once (in January, 49 B.C.) crossed the Rubicon, the boundary of his province (*283*), and marched south. Soon all Italy was in his power; Pompey, the Senate, and their followers had fled to Macedonia, on the east side of the Adriatic (*299*).

After arranging matters at Rome to suit himself, in April, 49 B.C., Caesar went to Spain, where lieutenants devoted to Pompey, Afranius and Petreius, had a strong army. They were soon crushed, the main force being captured near Ilerda in August of 49. On his return from Spain to Italy, Massilia (*Marseilles*), which had closed its gates to him on the way out, and had been besieged with great energy in his absence by Trebonius, gave itself into his hands; its fleet had been destroyed, in two engagements, by Decimus Brutus (p. 425).

260. Operations in Africa in 49 were not so fortunate, for the force dispatched under Curio to defeat the followers of Pompey in Africa, led by Varus, was utterly destroyed through the aid of the wily Numidian king, Juba.

261. At the end of 49 Caesar had control of all Roman territories west of the Adriatic; the provinces east of the Adriatic, however, were in the hands of Pompey, who was mobilising forces in Macedonia obviously for a descent upon Italy from across the sea. In consequence Caesar also now gathered his forces on the east side of the Adriatic. For some months, in the earlier part of 48, the armies of Pompey and Caesar faced each other near **Dyrrachium** (Durazzo), but Caesar was obliged to withdraw into the interior. The decisive battle was fought 9 August 48 B.C., near the city of **Pharsalus**, in Thessaly. Caesar's forces numbered about twenty-two thousand men, with one thousand cavalry; Pompey had forty-seven thousand infantry, seven thousand cavalry, and some light-armed troops. But superior generalship and the courage of desperation won the day against overwhelming odds. The Senatorial forces were entirely routed. Pompey fled to Egypt, where he was treacherously murdered.

262. Caesar also went with a small force to Egypt, where, in Alexandria, he became involved in the Alexandrine War. For a time this war occasioned him great difficulty because of his inability to secure reinforcements, but finally Mithridates of Pergamum came to his assistance with an army, marching down through Cilicia and Syria to Egypt. By April of 47 B.C. Caesar had the country under complete control, but he himself is said to have fallen a victim to the charms of the young and beautiful Egyptian princess, Cleopatra.

263. Leaving Cleopatra and a younger brother on the Egyptian throne, Caesar in June proceeded through Syria north to Pontus, where at Zela he easily crushed the rebellious King Pharnaces, reporting the quick victory to a friend in the laconic message, veni, vidi, vici. He soon afterwards returned to Rome.

264. Caesar had only three months in Rome before he was obliged to take the field against the Pompeiau forces, now gathered in Africa under the leadership of Scipio and Labienus. In January, 46, he landed with a small army near Hadrumetum, south-east from Carthage, where he maintained his position until sufficient forces could be brought over. At the battle of **Thapsus,** April 6, 46 B.C., he won a complete victory over the Pompeians and Juba, who was still helping them.

265. Caesar was now everywhere master. In accordance with legal forms he promulgated several laws of great benefit to the people. He reformed the calendar also (*241,* c). In August of 46 in Rome Caesar celebrated his great triumph. On four different days triumphal processions wound along the Sacred Way through the Forum and up the Capitoline Hill, displaying to the astonished multitudes the spoils of victories in Gaul, Egypt, and Pontus, and over Juba in Africa. Treasure amounting to 65,000 talents was carried in the procession, and a conspicuous figure was the Gallic commander-in-chief, Vercingetorix, who had been kept in prison six years awaiting this event. In honour of the triumph twenty-two thousand tables were spread for the feasting of the populace, and games and gladiatorial shows were given with a magnificence previously unheard of.

266. In 45 B.C. a large army was collected against Caesar in Spain, commanded by the two sons of Pompey. Caesar marched against it, and at the battle of **Munda** (17 March) totally defeated it. On a coin struck in Spain in 45, and perhaps put into circulation in order to pay his soldiers, Caesar commemorates Spanish as well as Gallic victories. A large trophy supports, in the middle, a coat of mail, above which is a helmet; on either side is a spear (disproportionately short), then a shield, and a war-trumpet. At the foot, on the right, is a seated captive, with his hands tied behind him and face turned backward, looking up, his hair streaming down; this we may safely identify as Vercingetorix. At the left sits a female figure, weeping, a personification of Hispania.

267. On Caesar's return to Rome the Senate, whose members were now mainly of his own choosing, loaded him with honours. By conferring upon him all the important offices, especially the dictatorship in life tenure, it centred the whole authority in his hands. Finally it ordered his portrait struck on coins, from which previously faces of living men had been excluded, and decreed that statues of him should be placed in the temples of the gods in Rome.

268. Caesar's use of absolute power was marked by unexpected clemency towards former opponents; in recognition of this the Senate shortly before his death ordered a temple built and dedicated to 'Caesar's Mercifulness,' personified as a divinity. He contemplated large projects for the public weal; nevertheless his foresight and breadth of view counted for nothing in the bitter hatred of his political enemies. A conspiracy was formed to take his life. On 15 March 44 B.C. as Caesar had just entered the hall where the Senate met, near Pompey's Theatre, he was set upon with daggers, and fell, pierced by twenty-three wounds, at the foot of a statue of his vanquished rival. Though the assassination of Caesar was commemorated by a coin, the plans of the murderers all miscarried. It is said that not one of them died a natural death, and before many years Caesar's nephew and heir, Octavianus, afterwards called Augustus, was Emperor of the Roman world.

269. Caesar was tall and of commanding presence. His features were angular and prominent. He had a fair complexion, with keen black eyes. In later years he was bald; at no time of life did he wear a beard. Suetonius says that among all the honours conferred upon Caesar by the

Senate and the People none was more acceptable to him than the privilege of wearing at all times a, laurel crown, by which his baldness was concealed. Though endowed with a constitution naturally by no means robust, he became inured to hardship, and exhibited astonishing powers of endurance. In matters of dress he was particular to the verge of effeminacy.

270. Of all the Romans Caesar was without doubt the greatest. In him the most varied talents were united with a restless ambition and tireless energy. While deliberate and far-seeing in forming his plans, in carrying them out he often acted with a haste that seemed like recklessness. He could occasion scenes of the most shocking cruelty, yet none could be more forgiving, or more gracious in granting pardon. Apparently believing, with the Epicurean philosophy, that death ends all and life is worth living only for the pleasure to be gotten out of it, he mingled freely with the dissolute society of Rome; yet when it was time for action, he spurned indulgences, gave himself to the severest toil, and endured privations without a murmur.

Caesar's faults were those he shared in common with his age; his genius belongs to all ages.

The Name Caesar

271. Roman surnames, which in many cases became family names, were generally derived from some personal characteristic or association. For the name Caesar scholars in antiquity suggested four derivations, of which one was, that the first of the Julii to bear the name Caesar received it because he was born with a thick head of hair, caesaries; another was, that it came from the colour of the eyes, bluish grey, caesius. There was also a tradition that the first Julius to be called Caesar had killed an elephant and received the name from the word for elephant in the language of the Mauri, in Africa, from whose country elephants came. This derivation seems to have commended itself to Julius Caesar, for on a coin struck by him in Gaul, we see, over his name, an elephant trampling upon a Gallic war trumpet with a serpent's head, symbolising his utter defeat of the Gauls and conquest of the country. To the end of the Empire Roman emperors adopted the name Caesar as a title, and it survives in two imperial titles of modern times, "Kaiser," of Germany and Austria, and "Czar," of Russia. What an impress the life of Julius Caesar made upon the world, not merely to leave a heritage of influence in government and literature, but to transmit his very name across the ages as a designation of the highest authority recognized among men!

The Portraits of Caesar

272. After Caesar attained supremacy innumerable likenesses of him must have been made. Men ordered the erection of statues of him in all cities, and in all the temples of Rome; his features were stamped on coins and cut in gems. Of the many extant busts and statues bearing his name only a few can be considered genuine. Though the two best of these, a colossal bust at Naples and a large statue at Rome, have been somewhat restored, the expression of face has not been materially affected; a bust in the British Museum, representing Caesar at a somewhat later period of life, is singularly well preserved. In the well-known statue with the arms (as restored by a French artist) he appears as commander, making an address to his troops. To judge from the manner of treatment, both this statue and the bust at Naples were made near the end of the first century A.D.

Caesar's Commentaries

273. The Commentaries of Caesar were not designed to be a biographical work, nor yet, strictly speaking, a military history. They were rather, as the title Commentaries of Deeds, **Commentarii Rerum Gestarum**, implies, an informal record of events. For **commentarius** comes from **commentor**, a verb used by speakers with the meaning make preparation for a speech by gathering material and preparing outlines; whence **liber commentarius**, or **commentarius**, commentary, came to designate a collection of materials for future use.

Had Caesar intended that the Commentaries should be a formal history, the matter, in accordance with the universal custom of antiquity, would have been arranged in such a, way that the books would be of about the same length, but he grouped his material by years without regard to the length of the divisions, and we find that the first book, or Commentary, is as long as the second and third combined, while the seventh is almost as long as the second, third, and fourth taken together. Approximate uniformity in the length of the books comprised in a literary work was usual on account of convenience in handling, since each book formed a separate roll; hence the name for the roll or book, **volumen** (from **volvo**, roll up), which survives in our word "volume" (Figure 166).

274. Nevertheless it is evident that the Commentaries were not prepared as a diary, for private use, but written at one time and intended for circulation. We are safe in believing that Caesar intended through them not only to give to the public an authoritative account of the important events treated, but also to supply to historians of the period a collection of authentic material on which they might draw; hence, perhaps, the peculiar restraint under which he refers to himself in the third person, a practise as rare in narratives of the kind in antiquity as it is to-day; hence, also, presumably, the frequent use of indirect discourse near the beginning, while in the later books the style is more often enlivened, as generally in Greek and Latin historical works, by direct quotation (211, b).

275. The Seven Commentaries of the Gallic War were probably composed soon after the fall of Alesia, in the winter of 52-51 B.C.; they were probably taken down from dictation and circulated through the multiplication of copies from the original copy or copies sent from Gaul to Rome in 51.

276. The Civil War was seemingly incomplete at the time of Caesar's death; only two Commentaries, narrating the events of 49 and 48 B.C., were finished. Later the first Commentary, dealing with the events of 49, was divided into two books, the other remaining undivided; consequently in manuscripts and editions the Civil War now appears in three books, the first and second being devoted to the events of 49, the third to those of 48 B.C.

277. A gap of two years was left between the Commentaries of the Gallic War, covering the period 58-52 B.C., and those of the Civil War, covering the years 49 and 48. This was filled by Aulus Hirtius, who added to the Gallic War an eighth book narrating briefly the events of 51 and 50 B.C. in Gaul. Other writers afterwards extended the Civil War also by adding narratives of Caesar's military operations in Egypt, Africa, and Spain.

278. Notwithstanding Caesar's aim in composing the Commentaries as source books rather than finished works, the clearness, conciseness, and vigour of his style, and the importance of the matter, have given them a place in the first rank of historical writings. Of the Commentaries on the Gallic-War Cicero wrote (*Brut.* lxxv. 262): "They are worthy of all praise. They are unadorned, straightforward, and elegant, every embellishment being stripped off as a garment. Caesar desired, indeed, to furnish others, who might wish to write history, with material upon which they might draw, and perhaps men without good taste, who like to deck out facts in tawdry graces of expression, may think that he has rendered a service to historians by providing them with raw material, but he has deterred men of sound sense from trying to improve on the Commentaries in literary expression. For in history a pure and brilliant conciseness of style is the highest attainable beauty."

279. The question has been much discussed whether or not in the Commentaries Caesar warped the truth in self-justification. No one will deny that he had a complete command of the facts, and that, when the Commentaries on the Gallic War were published, there were many officers and men who would instantly have detected untruths and condemned them. Caesar seems to have been too large a man to condescend to misrepresentation even in narrating his own defeats, as at Gergovia and Dyrrachium; while there may have been occasional lapses of memory in respect to details, we have no reason to question the substantial accuracy of the Commentaries as historical documents.

The Commentaries themselves convey no impression of exaggeration. Plutarch, who had at hand other sources of information, no longer extant, thus summarizes the results of the Gallic war: "Caesar was engaged in the Gallic war less than ten years. In that time he captured more than eight hundred towns, brought into submission three hundred peoples, fought against three million foes, killed a million, and took a million prisoners." Caesar took part in thirty battles.

Chateaubriand declares that Caesar was the most complete man of all history, for his genius was transcendent in three directions: in politics, in war, and in literature. Let us try to form some estimate of this threefold life-work by considering him specially as a General, as a Politician, and as a Man of Letters.

Caesar As An Orator

280. As an orator Caesar was rated second only to Cicero. His orations have perished, but apart from other evidence a favourable judgement of Caesar's oratorical style might be formed from the speech which he puts into the mouth of Critognatus (VII. 77), and the outline of the argument by which he quelled an incipient mutiny (I. 40).

THE GEOGRAPHY OF CAESAR'S COMMENTARIES

281. The Geography of the Commentaries on the Gallic War touches Italy, Cisalpine Gaul, Illyricum, and Transalpine Gaul; that of the Civil War touches also Spain, Macedonia, Epirus and Thessaly, Asia Minor, Syria, Egypt, and Africa.

282. Caesar frequently uses the name of a people for that of the country inhabited by them, where English usage expects the word "country" or "land" or an equivalent; as **qui agrum Helvetium a Germanis dividit,** *which separates the Helvetian territory from that of the Germans,* lit. *from the Germans* (I. 2); **unum per Sequanos,** *one (route) through the country of the Sequanians,* lit. *through the Sequanians* (I. 6).

Italy And Cisalpine Gaul

283. Caesar uses Italia, *Italy,* in two senses:

a. Italy in the narrower sense as a political unit (C. I. 6), Italy proper, having as its northern boundary on the east side the small river Rubicon, on the west the lower course of the river Auser, and between the two rivers a line running a short distance south of Luca (modern *Lucca*).

b. Italy in the geographical sense (I. 10), designating the entire peninsula as far as the Alps, and including Cisalpine Gaul in addition to Italy proper.

284. Cisalpine Gaul is designated by Caesar as **Cisalpina Gallia** (VI. 1), **Gallia citerior,** *Hither Gaul* (I. 24), and **citerior provincia,** *the nearer province* (I. 10). It comprised the great drainage area of the **Padus,** *Po* (V. 24), extending from

Italy proper to the Alps. The entire region was brought under Roman domination in the second century B.C., but Cisalpine Gaul was not joined with Italy politically till the reign of Augustus.

285. Of the cities of Cisalpine Gaul Caesar mentions two, **Aquileia** (I. 10), at the head of the Adriatic Sea, chief city of the Cisalpine Veneti, who gave their name to modern "Venice;" and **Ocelum** (I. 10), in the extreme western part.

Transalpine Gaul

286. Transalpine Gaul is designated by Caesar as **Transalpina Gallia** (VII. 6), or **Gallia Transalpina** (VII. 1) *Transalpine Gaul;* **Gallia ulterior** (I. 7), or **ulterior Gallia** (I. 10), *Further Gaul;* or simply **Gallia,** *Gaul* (I. 1). It extended from the Alps and the Rhine to the Atlantic Ocean, comprising the countries now known as France and Belgium, the German possessions west of the Rhine, and the greater part of Switzerland and Holland. In this book where "Gaul" stands alone, *Transalpine Gaul* is meant. (See back cover). After the conquest, **Gallia** as a subject country was personified as a female figure, sometimes with the characteristic Gallic war-trumpet, as on a coin struck in Rome in 48 B.C.; only the head is shown, with long hair, dishevelled, the war-trumpet being behind the head.

287. On account of differences in speech, and other characteristics, Caesar describes Transalpine Gaul as divided into three parts:

a. *The land of the Belgians,* **Belgium,** in the northeast, extending from the rivers **Sequana,** *Seine,* and **Matrona,** *Marne,* to the river **Rhenus,** *Rhine.* The Belgium described by Caesar was much larger than the modern country. The ancient Belgian stock survives in the Walloons. The language was mostly Celtic.

b. *The land of the Galli, the Celtic country, Celtic Gaul,* extending from the *Seine* and *Marne* to the river **Garumna,** *Garonne.* This part is often called Gallia (I. 1, I. 20: I. 30). The numerous dialects of Celtic Gaul belonged to the great Celtic family, which has modern representatives in Armoric, spoken in Brittany, and the Welsh language.

c. *The land of the Aquitanians,* **Aquitania,** extending from the Garonne River to the Pyrenees. The language of the Aquitanians seems to have been related to the Basque.

288. *a.* The three divisions of Gaul were made up of many small *states,* **civitates,** each of which had its own political organization. A number of the states had their own coinage in gold and other metals, but the coins were mostly imitations of those struck by Greek states and at Rome.

b. In Celtic Gaul the governing power was in the hands of two classes, the knights and the Druid priests; the condition of the common people was not much above slavery (VI. 13).

289. *a.* Government in Gaul was administered by *magistrates,* **magistrates,** chosen by the dominant classes, such as the Vergobrets (I. 16); a few of the more backward states had *kings,* **reges,** as Galba, king of the Suessiones (II. 4), and Commius, king of the Atrebates (IV. 21).

b. In some states there was a *council of elders,* **senatus** (II. 5).

c. Politically Gaul in Caesar's time was in a condition of unrest. Usurpations of power and changes of rulers were frequent (II. 1). Not only in the different states but in the subdivisions of states, and even in powerful families, there were party divisions (VI. 11), from which strife of great bitterness arose. A conspicuous example is the irreconcilable antagonism between the brothers Diviciacus and Dumnorix (I. 18), of whom the former did everything possible to advance Caesar's interests (II. 5, 10), while the latter, as leader of an anti-Roman party among the Aeduans, sought in all ways to thwart Caesar, until finally he was killed while resisting capture, by Caesar's cavalry (V. 7).

290. The southeastern part of Gaul, not specified in Caesar's threefold division, had been conquered by the Romans and organized into a province in 121 B.C. This was the only part of Transalpine Gaul that properly came under Caesar's jurisdiction when he went out as governor in 58 B.C. *(255).* It is designated by Caesar as **Gallia provincia** (I. 19) or **provincia Gallia** (I. 53), *Gallic Province;* as **ulterior provincia,** *Further Province* (I. 10); as **provincia nostra,** *Our Province* (I. 2); or simply **provincia,** *Province* (I. 1).

291. Of the mountains of Gaul the most important are: **Alpes,** *the Alps* (I. 10), of which the western and southern portion, the French and the Swiss Alps, were known to Caesar; **mons Cebenna,** *the Cevennes* (VII. 8), in Southern Gaul; **mons Iura,** *the Jura Mountains* (I. 2), extending from the Rhone below Geneva northeast to the Rhine; **mons Vosegus,** *the Vosges* (IV. 10), west of the Rhine and north of the Jura range; **Pyrenaei montes,** *the Pyrenees,* on the border toward Spain (1.1).

292. The more important rivers of Gaul mentioned by Caesar are: **Rhodanus,** *the Rhone* (I. 2), which flows through **lacus Lemannus,** *Lake Geneva* (I. 2), and empties into the Mediterranean; **Arar,** *Saône* (I. 12), a tributary of the Rhone, which it enters from the north; **Sequana,** *the Seine* (I. 1); **Matrona,** *Marne* (I. 1), a tributary of the *Seine,* which it enters from the east; **Axona,** *Aisne* (II, 5), a tributary of the *Oise,* which in turn flows into the *Seine* from the northeast, below the confluence with the Marne; **Rhenus,** *Rhine* (I.1); **Garumna,** *Garonne* (I. 1): **Liger,** *Loire* (III. 9), the largest river of Gaul, flowing into the Bay of Biscay; **Mosa,** *Meuse* (IV. 9), in northeastern Gaul; **Sabis.** *Sambre,* a tributary of the *Meuse,* which it enters from the west (II. 16).

293. The cities of Gaul in Caesar's time were situated on or near a coast, on a river, or on the top of a high mountain. The more noteworthy were:

a. In the Province: **Massilia,** *Marseilles* (C. II. 3), founded by Greeks from Phocaea about 600 B.C., a prosperous city, which retained its Greek character, carried on an extensive commerce, and became an important civilising influence **Narbo,** *Narbonne* (III. 20), on the river Atax not far from the sea, colonised by the Romans in 118 B.C.; **Tolosa.** *Toulouse* (III. 20), on the Garonne river; **Genava,** *Geneva* (I. 6), on **lacus Lemannus,** *Lake Geneva* (I. 2).

b. In Celtic Gaul: **Agedincum,** *Sens* (VI. 14): **Alesia,** *Alise-Sainte-Reine* (VII. 68); **Avaricum,** *Bourges* (VII. 13); **Bibracte,** on *Mt. Beuvray* (I. 23); **Cenabum,** *Orléans* (VII. 3); **Decetia,** *Decize* (VII. 33); **Gergovia** (VII. 36); **Lutecia Parisiorum,** *Paris* (VI. 3); **Vesontio,** *Besancon* (I. 38V

c. In Belgium: **Bibrax** (II. 6) near the *Aisne;* **Durocortorum,** *Reims* (VI. 44); **Noviodunum** of the Suessiones, near *Soissons* (II. 12); **Samarobriva,** *Amiens* (V. 24).

Britain, Germany, And Spain

294. Caesar uses **Britannia,** *Britain* (II. 4), to designate the island of Great Britain, including modern England, Scotland, and Wales. He was the first Roman general to invade the island, whose inhabitants he found similar to those of Celtic Gaul in language and institutions, but not so far advanced in civilization. His two expeditions, in 55 and 54 B.C., had slight apparent effect, but they stimulated commerce and prepared the way for the introduction of Roman wares and customs. The subjugation of Britain by the Romans began in 43 A.D.

295. Caesar uses **Germania,** *Germany* (IV. 4), to designate a country of indefinite extent east of the Rhine and north of the Danube. He came into contact only with the German peoples near the Rhine. His two expeditions across the Rhine, in 55 and 53 B.C., produced slight effect; the Romans never conquered more of Germany than a narrow strip along the Rhine and the Danube.

296. Ancient *Spain,* **Hispania,** included modern Spain and Portugal. After the Roman Conquest, about 200 B.C., it was divided into two provinces, **citerior Hispania.** *Hither Spain* (III. 23), including the northern and eastern part of the peninsula, and **ulterior Hispania,** *Further Spain* (C. I. 38), on the south and west.

297. Caesar sometimes uses **Hispania,** *Spain,* to designate the peninsula as a whole (V. 1): sometimes the plural, **Hispaniae,** *the Spains* (C. III. 73), referring to the two Spanish provinces.

Illyricum, Macedonia, Epirus, And Thessaly

298. Illyricum was a narrow province that bordered Cisalpine Gaul for a short distance at the head of the Adriatic Sea, and extended down the east side of the Adriatic as far as the river **Drilo,** *Drin.* It included parts of modern Albania, Montenegro, Herzegovina, Dalmatia, Croatia, and Istria. It came under Roman control about 167 B.C.

299. Belonging, in Caesar's time, to the province of Macedonia, was a strip of coast between Illyricum and Epirus with the important cities **Apollonia** (C. III. 75), about five miles from the sea, and **Dyrrachium**, *Durazzo* (C. III. 53), on the coast (Map 19).

300. **Epirus** was the northernmost division of Greece on the west side; it occupied a part of modern Albania. It was conquered by the Romans in 168 B.C. (Map 19). Towns of Epirus mentioned by Caesar are **Buthrotum** (C. III. 16) and **Oricum** (C. III. 90), both on the coast (Map 19).

301. **Thessalia.** *Thessaly*, in northeastern Greece, corresponded roughly with the division of modern Greece called by the same name. Towns of Thessaly mentioned by Caesar are **Gomphi** (C. III. 80), **Larisa**, *Larissa* (C. III. 96), and **Metropolis** (C. III. 80). Cf. Map 19.

Asia, Syria, Egypt, And Africa

302. The Romans used **Asia** in three senses, designating:

(*a.*) The continent Asia, as we use the name to-day.

(*b.*) The western projection of the continent, between the Mediterranean and the Black Sea; called **Asia Minor** in order to distinguish it from the mass of the continent as a whole.

(*c.*) The Roman province **Asia**, which was organized in 129 B.C. The Roman province Asia included only the western part of Asia Minor, with the countries Caria, Lydia, Mysia, and Phrygia. Caesar uses Asia (C. III. 53) to designate the Roman province, not Asia Minor or the continent.

303. At the time of the Civil War **Bithynia**, including a part of Pontus (C. III. 3), and **Cilicia** in Asia Minor (C. III. 102) were already organized as separate provinces.

304. **Syria** (C. III. 103), including **Phoenicia** and **Palestine**, was conquered by Pompey and became a Roman province about 64 B.C. At Jerusalem Pompey profaned the Holy of Holies in the Temple by entering it, but be refrained from carrying off the treasure. The treasure, however, a few years later fell a prey to Crassus, who, on his way to attack the Parthians (*258*), delayed in Jerusalem in order to rob the Temple.

305. **Aegyptus**, *Egypt* (C. III. 104), at the time of the Civil War was an independent kingdom. It was not made subject to Rome till 29 B.C. Its principal city, **Alexandria**, *Alexandria* (C. III. 103), was founded by Alexander the Great, who gave to it his name.

306. Caesar uses **Africa** (C. II. 37) to designate, not the continent, but the comparatively small Roman province of *Africa*, which was organized after the destruction of Carthage in 146 B.C. After the battle of Thapsus and the death of Juba *(262)* Caesar made another province out of the Kingdom of Numidia, which adjoined the province Africa on the south and west, and later after his death was added to it.

Africa was personified as a female figure, wearing as a headdress the spoils of an elephant.

THE ROMAN ART OF WAR IN CAESAR'S TIME

Composition Of The Army

307. The legion. *a.* The *legion,* **legio** (I. 7), in Caesar's time was composed exclusively of Roman citizens. Probably Caesar's *legionary soldiers,* **legionarii** (C. III. 63) or simply **milites** (I. 7), were mainly volunteers who were willing to enlist for the regular term of twenty years on account of the certainty of the pay, and of provision for their old age in case they lived beyond the period of service. However, citizens between the ages of seventeen and forty-six were liable to be called out by a *levy,* **dilectus** (C. I. 6), at any time. Romans of the upper classes who wished to serve in the army, or found themselves unable to evade conscription, were employed as officers, or attached to the bodyguard of the commander.

b. The normal strength of a legion at the end of the Republic was 6,000 men, but the average number of men in Caesar's legions probably did not exceed 3,600 in the Gallic War, and 3,000 in the Civil War.

c. The legion was divided into ten *cohorts,* **cohortes** (III. 1), averaging, in Caesar's army, about 360 men each; the cohort was divided into three *maniples,* **manipuli** (II. 25), of 120 men; the maniples into two *centuries* or *companies,* **ordines** (I. 40). In legions having a full complement of men each century would contain 100; in Caesar's army the number could hardly have averaged more than 60.

d. The legions that had seen long service, apparently not less than nine or ten years, were called *veteran,* **legiones veteranae** (I. 24); the rest, *last levied,* or *raw,* **legiones proxime conscriptae** (I. 24), or **legiones tironum** (C. III. 28). The legions were designated by number.

e. In the first year of the Gallic War Caesar had four veteran legions, numbered VII., VIII., IX., these three apparently brought from the vicinity of Aquileia (I. 10), and X.; the tenth legion was in the Province at the time of his arrival in Gaul (I. 7). After Caesar learned that the Helvetians proposed to go through the country of the Sequanians and Aeduans he hastily raised in Cisalpine Gaul two legions (I. 10), which were numbered XI. and XII. With these six legions he gained two of his most brilliant victories, over the Helvetians and over Ariovistus.

f. In the second year of the war Caesar raised two new legions in

Cisalpine Gaul (II. 2), numbered XIII. and XIV., so that he now had four veteran and four raw legions, eight in all.

g. In the fifth year (54 B.C.) the XIVth legion and half of another were annihilated in the ambuscade set by Ambiorix (V. 26-37). At the beginning of the next year Caesar raised two more legions in Cisalpine Gaul, one replacing the lost XIVth (VI. 32), the other numbered XV., and besides obtained a legion from Pompey, which was numbered VI. (VI. 1; VIII. 54). In the last two years of the war he had thus ten legions (VII. 34), numbered VI. to XV. inclusive. It appears probable that the whole force of legionary soldiers engaged in the siege of Alesia fell short of forty thousand.

308. The infantry auxiliaries. In addition to the legions, a Roman army contained bodies of infantry and cavalry drawn from allied and subject peoples, or hired outright from independent nations, called *auxiliaries* or *auxiliary troops,* auxilia (I. 24). These in some eases retained their native dress, equipment, and mode of fighting, in others were armed and trained after the Roman fashion. To the former class belong the *light-armed troops,* levis armaturae pedites (II. 24), including as special classes the slingers (Plate III. 1), and bowmen. In the Gallic War Caesar availed himself of the help of *slingers,* funditores, from the Balearic Islands (II. 7), *bowmen,* sagittarii, from Crete and from Numidia (II. 7), and light-armed German troops (VII. 65). He utilised also contingents from the Gallic States that he subdued (III. 18, VIII. 10). In 52 B.C. he had a force of ten thousand Aeduans (VII. 34). Caesar, as other Roman writers, is generally not careful to state the exact number of the auxiliary troops; they were regarded as relatively unimportant. The officers of the auxiliaries, both infantry and cavalry, were Romans. Auxiliary troops posted on the wing of an army might be called *wing-men,* alarii (I. 51).

309. The cavalry. *a.* A troop of cavalry usually accompanied each legion. While the evidence is not conclusive, it is probable that in the latter part of the Gallic War, if not from the beginning, Caesar had contingents of cavalry in connection with his legions, averaging 200 to 300 men each. These horsemen were foreigners, serving for pay; they were drawn from Spain, *Spanish horsemen,* Hispani equites (V. 26), from Germany, *German horsemen,* Germani equites (VII. 13), and from Gaul.

b. Apart from the legionary contingents, Caesar had a force of cavalry raised from the Gallic States subject or friendly to Rome, which was reckoned as a single body, numbering under ordinary circumstances about 4000 (I. 15; V. 5), or 5000 men (IV. 12).

c. The cavalry was divided into *squads* or *squadrons,* turmae, of about 30 horsemen; such a squad went with Commius to Britain (IV. 35). Probably the squad contained three *declines,* decuriae, of 10 men each, under the command of *decurions,* decuriones (I. 23). The higher officers were called *cavalry prefects,* **praefecti equitum** (III. 26). See Plate III, 5.

310. The non-combatants. *a.* There were two classes of non-combatants, slaves employed for menial services, and free men, or freedmen. In the former class were included the officers' servants and *camp servants,* **calones** (II. 24), as well as the drivers and *muleteers* with the heavy baggage, **muliones** (VII. 45); in the latter class were citizens or others who were allowed to accompany the army but. were obliged to find quarters outside of the camp, as *traders,* **mercatores** (VI. 37).

b. The *mechanics,* **fabri** (V. 11), were not enrolled as a separate corps, but were drawn from the ranks of the legionary soldiers whenever needed.

311. The baggage train. Each legion had a separate baggage train. The heavy *baggage,* **impedimenta** (II. 19), comprised tents, hand-mills for grinding grain, artillery, extra weapons, and other military stores, as well as supplies of food. In the enemy's country for better defence the baggage trains of a number of legions might be formed into a single column (II. 19). From the baggage of the legion, or heavy baggage, the baggage of the soldiers, carried in individual *packs,* **sarcinae,** should be clearly distinguished (Figure 6).

The Officers

312. The general was properly called *leader,* **dux,** until he had won a victory; after the first victory he had a right to the title **imperator,** *commander* or *general* (I. 40). Caesar used the title **Imperator** from the time that he defeated the Helvetians, in 58 B.C., until his death (I. 40, etc.).

313. *a.* Next in rank came the *lieutenant,* or *lieutenant-general,* **legatus** (I. 10), who was frequently placed by Caesar in command of separate legions, or of corps containing more than one legion. When acting in the absence of the general the lieutenant became *lieutenant in the general's place,* **legatus pro praetore** (I. 21), and exercised unusual authority. The title "lieutenant general" would more accurately define the military position of Labienus, for example, than that of "lieutenant."

b. The *quaestor,* **quaestor** (I. 52), was charged with the care of the military chest and the supplies, but was sometimes clothed with purely military authority, and assumed the functions of a lieutenant. The quaestor and the lieutenants belonged to the staff of the general, and had with him the distinction of a *body-guard,* **cohors praetoria** (I. 40), composed of picked soldiers and of young men of rank who wished to acquire military experience.

314. The *military tribunes,* **tribuni militum** (I. 39), numbered six to a legion. In Caesar's army the tribunes appear to have received appointment for personal rather than military reasons and they were entrusted with subordinate services, such as the leading of troops on the march, the command of detachments smaller than a legion (cf. VI. 39), the securing of supplies (III. 7), and the oversight of the watches. Only one military tribune, Gaius Volusenus (III. 5), is mentioned by Caesar in terms of praise.

315. *a.* In marked contrast with the higher officers, who were of good social position, were the captains, or *centurions,* **centuriones, ordines** (V. 30). These were often of the humblest origin; they were promoted from the ranks simply on account of bravery and ability At the drill, on the march, and in battle, they were at the same time the models and the leaders of the soldiers.

b. As each century had a centurion, there were 2 centurions in each **maniple** (distinguished as *first,* **prior,** and *second,* **posterior**), 6 in each cohort, and 60 in the legion. The first in rank was the *first centurion* (of the first **maniple**) *of the first cohort,* **primipilus** (II. 25). The first centurion of the second **maniple** of a cohort was called **princeps prior** (C. III. 64).

316. Below the centurions, but ranking above the common soldiers, were the privileged soldiers, who were relieved from picket duty as well as work on fortifications and other manual labour Such were the *veteran volunteers,* **evocati** (G. III. 53), soldiers who had served their full time but had re-enlisted at the general's request; the musicians, and the *standard-bearers,* **signiferi.**

Provisioning And Pay Of The Soldiers

317. Caesar was careful to have ample supplies always at hand.

The care of the stores was in the hands of the quaestor, with his staff. Not bread or flour, but *grain,* **frumentum** (1.16), usually wheat, was served out to the soldiers for rations. This they themselves ground with *hand-mills,* **molae manuales,** and prepared for food by boiling into a paste or by making it into bread without yeast.

The grain was portioned out every fifteen days, and on the march each soldier carried his share in a sack. The amount furnished does not seem large when we reflect that the men lived almost exclusively on a vegetable diet. The allowance for the fifteen days was two Roman *pecks,* **modii,** about half a bushel by our measure. As the weight of this was not far from thirty pounds, the soldier had about two pounds per day. On difficult or forced marches extra rations were served out.

If the soldier desired to do so he could trade off his grain for bread, or buy other articles of food from the numerous *traders,* **mercatores** (I. 39), who accompanied the army and had a flourishing business. When wheat was scarce, *barley,* **hordeum** (C. III. 47), was substituted, Rations of barley were frequently served out also instead of wheat as a punishment for slight offences. In traversing an enemy's country fresh meat was often secured.

318. The wages of the Roman soldier were very small, hut in successful campaigns the men had a share of the *booty,* **praeda** (G. III. 97), consisting largely of captives, who were sold as slaves (VII. 89). These were bought up on the spot by the traders, and thus readily turned into cash. Sometimes Caesar gave money realized from the sale of booty; thus after the conquest of the Bituriges in 51 B.C. the soldiers received 200 sesterces apiece, the centurions a much larger sum (VIII. 4). As other *rewards,* **praemia** (V. 58), the commander could make special *gifts,* **militaria dona** (G. III. 53), such as disk-shaped *decorations* of metal for the breast, **phalerae** (Figure 62), clothing, and double pay (C. III. 53). When convicted of cowardly or disgraceful conduct the soldier was deprived of his weapons and driven from the camp, or in extreme cases put to death; officers and privileged soldiers might be reduced in rank, as were certain standard-bearers after an engagement before Dyrrachium (C. III. 74).

319. At the close of his period of service, twenty years, or on reaching his fiftieth year, the soldier who had served well was entitled to an *honourable discharge,* **missio honesta,** or **missio** (C. I. 86), together with an allotment of land, or a payment of money.

The Dress And Equipment

320. The legionary soldier wore a thick woollen undergarment, *tunic,* **tunica,** reaching nearly to the knees (cf. C. III. 44). His *cloak,* **sagum** (G. I. 75), which served also as a blanket, was likewise of undyed wool, and fastened by a *clasp,* **fibula,** on the right shoulder, so as not to impede the movement of the right arm. The soldier's *shoes,* **caligae,** were like a sandal, but had heavy soles which were fastened on by straps over the foot and instep.

321. The *cloak* of the commander, **paludamentum,** differed from that of the soldier only in being more ample, of finer quality, and ornamented; it was ordinarily scarlet in colour (VII. 88).

322. The weapons of the legionary were in part offensive, in part defensive. As defensive *weapons,* **arma,** he had:

a. A helmut, **galea,** ornamented with a *crest,* **crista** (Plate III, 3). On the march the helmet was hung on a cord which passed through the ring at the top and around the soldier's neck. The crest was fastened on before going into action.

b. A *cuirass,* or *coat of mail,* **lorica,** of leather, or of leather strengthened with strips of metal, or of metal (Figure 150).

c. A *shield,* ordinarily rectangular, **scutum** (II. 25; Figure 175; Plate IV, 3), but in some cases oval, **clipeus** (Plate IV, 1), made of two layers of boards fastened together, strengthened on the out side by layers of linen or of leather, and at the edges by a rim of metal. At the middle of the out side was an iron knob, **umbo,** used in striking.

On the march the shield was protected from the wet by a leather *covering,* tegimentum, (II. 21). In battle it was held on the left arm.

The offensive weapons of the legionary were:

d. A *pike,* pilum (I. 25), a heavy and formidable javelin. It consisted of a shaft of wood about four feet- long, into the end of which was fitted a small iron shaft, ferrum (I. 25), with a pointed head, which projected two feet beyond the end of the wood (see Plate IV, 6). The weight of the whole was not far from ten or eleven pounds. Pikes could be thrown only about 75 feet, but they were hurled with such skill and force that the first hurling often decided the battle.

e. A *sword,* gladius (I. 25), called *Spanish sword,* gladius Hispanus, because made according to a pattern brought from Spain after the Second Punic War. The Spanish sword was short, broad, two-edged, and pointed, better adapted for stabbing than for slashing, though used for both purposes (Plate IV, 9). It was kept in a *scabbard,* vagina (V. 44), fastened to a *belt,* balteus (V. 44), which was passed over the left shoulder (Plate III, 3); this brought the sword on the right side, so that it was not in the way of the shield.

f. In the time of the Empire, and probably also in Caesar's day, officers carried a *dagger,* pugio, which was attached to a belt running around the waist.

323. The dress and equipment of the light-armed soldiers varied greatly (Plate III, 1; PL IV, 7, 11). They, as well as the cavalry, seem generally to have had a light round or oval *shield,* parma, about three feet in diameter (Plate IV, 4). The cavalry had *helmets* of metal, cassides (VII. 45), light lances for hurling, and a longer sword than that used by the infantry (Plate III, 5).

The Standards

324. *a.* While the ancient battle lacked the noise and smoke of modern death-dealing devices, great clouds of dust were raised and obscured the movements of the combatants; the standards, or ensigns, were consequently more numerous, and had a relatively more important place, than flags have to-day.

b. The ensigns of Caesar's army were: (1) The *eagle* of the legion, aquila (IV. 25), of silver, carried in battle on the end of a pole by the *eagle-bearer,* aquilifer (V. 37). In camp it was kept in a little *shrine,* sacellum (Plate IV, 8). It was the standard of the legion as a whole; the eagle with extended wings borne aloft seemed to signify that the bird sacred to Jupiter, god of victory, was ready to lead the legion to success, and the loss of the eagle was the deepest disgrace that could be incurred (IV. 25; V. 37; C. III. 64). See Plate IV, 2.

The ancient Persians had a golden eagle as the royal standard and today the eagle appears among the emblems of many nations.

(2) The *standards,* signa (II. 21), one to each maniple, carried by *standard-bearers,* signiferi (II. 25). These varied in appearance. One type, known from a coin struck in 49 B.C., had small streamers attached to the end of the pole, underneath which were two crescents (perhaps for good luck), one just above the other; below these were two disks of metal, phalerae, no doubt presented to the maniple for meritorious conduct, and last of all a square plate of metal, indicating by a letter the place of the maniple (H = hastati, P = principes). In some cases figures of animals appeared. There was no separate standard for the cohort. (3) The *banners,* vexilla, rectangular flags of different sizes used for a variety of purposes (Figure 149). A large red flag was the special ensign of the commander (II. 20). Smaller banners were used by special detachments not formed of regular maniples (VI. 36), or attached to the standards of the maniples.

325. On the march the standard was at the front, in battle some distance behind the front, of the maniple. From the immediate association of the manipular standards with military movements arose several idiomatic expressions used by Caesar. Such are: signa ferre, *to go forward* (I. 39). signa inferre, *to advance* (II. 26). signa convertere, *to face about* (I. 25). ad signa convenire, *to assemble* (VI. 1). infestis signis, *in battle formation,* lit. *with hostile standards* (VII. 51; C. III. 93).

The Musical Instruments

326. *a.* The musical instruments were:

(1) The *trumpet,* tuba (II. 20), about three feet long, with a funnel-shaped opening (Plate II, 7); it had a deep tone, and was sounded by the *trumpeters,* tubicines (VII. 47).

(2) The *horn,* cornu, a large curved instrument, with a shriller note (Plate II. 8).

(3) The *shell trumpet,* bucina, perhaps resembling the large shells in use in modem times about Naples as dinner horns; such at least is Triton's bucina described by Ovid (*Met.* I, 333-338).

The shell trumpet was used especially in camp for giving the signals to change the watches (C. 11. 35).

b. As the maniple was the unit of military movement, signals were addressed to the standard-bearers, signiferi.

c. The order "to advance " or "to fall back" was conveyed by the general to the *trumpeters,* tubicines (cf. VII. 47); their signal was taken up by the horn blowers, cornicines, of whom thee was one to each maniple. The notes of the instruments could be heard above the din of battle much more clearly than the spoken words of the officers.

The Army On The March

327. When in an enemy's country Caesar maintained an exceedingly efficient information service. Parties of mounted *patrols,* **exploratores** (I. 21), scoured the country, and their observation was supplemented by single *scouts* or *spies,* **speculatores** (II. 11), who gathered information wherever they could.

328. The army advanced ordinarily in three divisions. At the *front,* **primum agmen** (VII. 67), came the cavalry, with perhaps a division of light-armed troops, sent ahead to feel out the enemy (I. 15), and in case of attack, to hold him at bay until the rest of the army could prepare for action (II. 19). Next came the main force, each legion being accompanied by its baggage train, but when there was danger of attack the legions marched in single column, with the baggage of the whole army united (II. 19). The *rear,* **novissimum agmen,** might in case of danger be formed of part of the legionary force, the baggage being between the rear and the main body (II. 19).

329. The regular *day's march,* **iustum iter,** was from six to seven hours long. The start was usually made at sunrise, but in emergencies the army got under way at midnight, or two or three o'clock in the morning. The distance ordinarily traversed was about 15 or 16 English miles; on *a, forced march,* **iter magnum** (II. 12), a much greater distance might be made, as 25 or 30 English miles (VII. 41). Caesar's forced marches manifested astonishing powers of endurance on the part of his soldiers. Rivers were often crossed by fording; in such operations the ancient army had the advantage over the modern, because it carried no miscellaniea that would be spoiled by submersion in water (V. 18, VII. 56).

330. On the march the soldier carried his rations, his cooking utensils, his arms, blanket, and one or two *rampart stakes,* or *palisades,* **valli;** palisades for defence were carried by dragoons as late as the seventeenth century.

The luggage was done up in tight *bundles* or *packs,* **sarcinae** (Plate III, 4), which were fastened to forked poles, and raised over the shoulder. This arrangement was introduced by Marius, in memory of whom soldiers so equipped were called *Marius's mues,* **muli Mariani.** The helmet was hung by a cord from the neck, the other weapons disposed of in the most convenient way. When it rained, the oblong *shields,* **scuta** (822, c), could be put over the head like a roof.

The Army In Camp

331. *a.* A camp (Figure 119, *p.290*) was fortified at the close of every day's march. When the army was still on the march, men were sent forward to choose a suitable location for a camp and measure it off.

b. Whenever possible, a site for the camp was selected on a slight elevation, with abundance of water, and of wood for fuel, near at hand. The proximity of a dense forest or overhanging mountain was avoided, that a favourable opportunity of attack might not be given to the enemy Sometimes the rear or one side was placed parallel with a river (II. 5).

332. The camp was usually rectangular (see Maps 3, 4, 6, 20); in a few cases there were camps of irregular shapes, adapted to the nature of the ground (Maps 5, 15). The size of the camp varied according to the size of the force.

333. In fortifying a camp, first an embankment was thrown up on all four sides; for digging the soldiers used spades. Outside of this embankment was a trench, usually triangular in section (V-shaped), from which the earth for the embankment was taken (Plate IV, 10). On the outer edge of the embankment a row of strong *rampart stakes* or *palisades,* **valli,** was driven firmly in, forming a *stockade.* The *rampart,* **vallum** (II. 5), thus made, was several feet high and wide enough so that the soldiers could stand on it behind the palisades. The *trench, or moat,* **fossa** (II. 8), was from twelve to eighteen feet wide (II. 5) and from seven to ten feet deep. When the army expected to remain in the same place for a long time, as in *winter quarters,* **hiberna** (I. 54), or a *stationary camp,* **castra stativa** (C. III. 30), sometimes *towers,* **turres** (V. 40), were added at brief intervals, and the intervening spaces further protected by a roof (Plate IX, 6). The labour of fortifying a camp was prodigious.

334. *a.* The camp had four gates (Plate IV, 10). That in the direction of the advance, toward the enemy, was called the *general's gate,* **porta praetoria** (C. III. 94), the one opposite to this, at the rear, *the decuman gate,* **porta decumana** (II, 24); the gates on the right and left side respectively, as one faced the front, *main right gate,* **porta principalis dextra,** and *main left gate,* **porta principalis sinistra.** The last two were connected by the *main street,* **via principalis.** The entrances were made more easily defensible by an approach so laid out that an enemy attempting to enter would expose the right, or unprotected side.

b. Inside the rampart, between it and the tents, a vacant space two hundred feet wide was left on all sides. The remaining room in the enclosure was systematically divided, so that every maniple, decuria, and body of light-armed troops knew its place and could find its quarters at once. The *general's quarters,* **praetorium** (C. III. 94), was near the middle of the camp; near it was an open space where he could address his troops from a *platform,* **suggestus** (VI. 3). Access to all parts of the camp was made by means of *passageways,* **viae** (V. 49).

335. *a.* The *tents,* **tabernacula** (I. 39), were of leather (Plate VII, 3); hence **sub**

pellibus, lit. *under hides,* means *in tents* (III. 29). Each was calculated to hold ten men, but a centurion seems generally to have had more room to himself than the soldiers.

b. The *winter quarters,* **hiberna,** were made more comfortable by the substitution of straw-thatched *huts,* **casae** (V. 43), for tents.

c. In a hostile country a strong guard was kept before the gates of the camp (IV. 32). In the earlier times, and probably in Caesar's army, the password, admitting to the camp, was different each night; it was written on slips of wood, which were given by the commander to the military tribunes, and passed by these to the men on duty.

336. Many Roman camps became the nucleus of permanent settlements, which survive in cities to-day. A marked instance is the city of *Chester,* England, the name of which is derived from **castra;** *Rochester* comes from **Rodolphi castra.**

The Army In Battle Array

337. *a.* When the Roman force was far outnumbered by the enemy, the legionary soldiers might be arranged in a *double line,* **duplex acies** (III. 24), or even in a *single line,* **acies simplex,** as at the battle of Ruspina, near Hadrunietum *(264).* But under ordinary circumstances Caesar drew up his legions in a *triple line,* **triplex acies,** as in the battles with the Helvetians, Ariovistus, and the Usipetes and Tencteri. This arrangement was probably as follows (Figure 186, *p.63*): (1) Four cohorts of each legion stood in the first line; about 160 feet behind them stood three cohorts, and ordinarily the remaining three cohorts of the legion were posted still farther back as a reserve. At the battle of Pharsalus there were only two cohorts in Caesar's third line (as indicated on Map 20), one cohort from each legion having been drawn off to form a fourth line, and there were probably only two cohorts in the third line at the battle with Ariovistus (Map 4), one cohort from each legion being required for guard duty at the camps. (2) In each cohort the three maniples stood side by side, one of the centuries in each maniple being behind the other. The soldiers in each battle line stood about three feet apart each way, and there is some reason for supposing that in Caesar's cohorts the men stood 8 ranks deep. The standard-bearers did not stand in the front rank, but were protected by soldiers selected for their agility and strength, *the men before the standards,* **antesignani** (C. III. 84).

b. As the first line went into action the second followed closely behind; as the men of the first fell or withdrew exhausted, those of the second pressed forward and took their places; in case of need the third line advanced and in like manner relieved the combined first and second. In the battle with the Helvetians the whole third line faced about and repelled an attack on the rear (Map 3).

338. When circumstances required it, soldiers were massed in serried ranks, as in a wedge-shaped column, *wedge*, **cuneus** (VI. 40), or under a *turtle-shell roof*, **testudo** (used by the Gauls, VII. 85). For defence sometimes a force was formed into a *circle*, **orbis**, corresponding with our hollow square (IV. 37).

339. The place of the light-armed troops and cavalry was ordinarily at first in front of the triple line, or on the wings. They opened the engagement by skirmishing, prevented flank movements of the enemy, drew the brunt of the attack if the legions wished to take another position, and were employed in various other ways as occasion demanded. The cavalry were utilized especially to cut down the fleeing.

Operations Against Fortified Places

340. The taking of walled towns was accomplished by *sudden storming* without long preparation, **repentina oppugnatio** (C. III. 80), **oppugnatio** (VII. 36); *siege blockade*, **obsidio** (VII. 69), or **obsessio** (VII. 36), which aimed to repel all attempts of the enemy to escape or secure supplies, and to reduce him by starvation, as at Alesia (VII. 69-90); or by *siege and storming*, **longinqua oppugnatio** (C. III. 80), with the help of machines to break down the enemy's fortifications and gain admission to the city, as at Avaricum (VII. 16-28).

In storming a city the forces rushed forward, tried to batter down the gates, fill up the moat, and mount the walls with ladders.

341. The siege was begun by extending a line of works, in case the nature of the site allowed, entirely around the place to be reduced. Then a *siege embankment*, or *mole*, **agger**, a wide roadway of timber and earth, was begun outside the reach of the enemy's weapons; it was gradually prolonged toward the city wall, and raised until at the front the top was on a level with the wall, or even higher.

342. *a.* The workmen at the front were protected by movable *breastworks*, **plutei** (cf. Plate IX, 4, 5), or by arbour-sheds, or sappers' huts, **vineae** (II, 12; see Plate IX, 9), made of timber or of thick wickerwork, with rawhides stretched over the outside as a protection against fire, Rows of arbour-sheds were placed along the sides of the mole to afford passageways to the front (Plate IX, 2); a long arbour-shed was called a *mousie*, **musculus** (VII. 84; C. II. 10). A sappers' shed with a sloping roof of strong boards specially adapted for use in undermining a wall was called a *turtle-shell shed*, **testudo** (Plate VII, 10).

b. *Movable towers*, **turres ambulatoriae** (II. 12,31), to be filled with soldiers, were built out of range of the enemy's missiles and brought up near the walls, usually on the siege embankment, which sloped gently from the rear up to the wall (Plate IX, 7; Plate XII).

c. In the lowest story of the movable tower, or under a separate roof, was the *battering ram,* aries (II. 32), an enormous beam with a metallic head which was swung against the walls with terrific force (Plate VII, 1). The attacking force tried also to pry stones out of the walls with wall hooks, falces (murales), light poles with a strong iron hook at the end (VII. 22), and clear the walls of defenders by means of *artillery* of the *torsioner* type, tormenta.

d. Walls and ramparts were mounted by means of *scaling ladders,* scalae (V. 43).

343. For throwing heavy missiles the Romans had *torsioners,* tormenta (VII. 81), so named from the method of developing the force required for hurling; tormentum is derived from torqueo, *twist.* This was obtained by twisting with great tension strong ropes of hair, which were suddenly released by means of a trigger; the force was utilized for the shooting of missiles by a mechanism of which there were three principal types:

a. The *catapult,* catapulta (Plate IX, 8), for shooting large arrows or darts. A small catapult is called *scorpion,* scorpio, by Caesar (VII. 25).

b. The *ballista,* ballista (Plate VII, 8), which cast stones; the trough was sharply inclined, while that of the catapult was nearly horizontal. The ballista is not mentioned by Caesar.

c. The *wild ass,* onager (Plate VII, 7), which hurled stones, but was probably not used in Caesar's time.

Where the ground allowed, the walls were undermined and tunnels run under the town.

344. The besieged met mines by counter-mines. With great hooks they tried to catch the head of the battering ram and hold it, or let down masses of wood or wickerwork along the side of the wall to deaden the force of the blow, or drew the wall hooks over into the city with windlasses (VII. 22). By frequent *sallies,* eruptiones (VII. 22), they endeavoured to destroy the works of the besiegers, drove the workmen from their posts, and hurled firebrands into the sheds and towers.

345. Owing to the amount of wood used in siege works the danger from fire was great. Once even the siege embankment was burned (VII. 24). When a breach had been made in the wall, or a gate battered down, an attack was begun wherever it was thought possible to force an entrance. The siege embankment and towers were connected with the top of the wall by means of planks and beams thrown across (Plate XII). Detachments of soldiers, holding their oblong shields close together above their heads, formed a *turtle-shell roof,* testudo, under which they marched up close to the walls and tried to scale them, or entered the breach (Plate VII, 6).

The Roman Battleships

346. *a*. The *battleships* or *galleys*, **naves longae** (III. 9), of Caesar's time were propelled mainly by oars; they had only one mast, and generally one large sail. There were usually three rows or banks of oars, hence the name *trireme*, **navis triremis** (C. II. 6) or **triremis** (C. III. 101), but some times vessels with two banks of oars were used, *bireme*, **biremis** (C. III. 40), and even five banks, *quinquereme*, **quinqueremis** (C. III. 101). The rowers kept time to the sound of a horn or click of a hammer.

***b*.** The *rudders*, **gubernacula**, were not like those of to-day, but consisted of two large paddles thrust down into the sea, one on each side of the stern; they were controlled by the *steersman*, **gubernator** (III. 9). The anchor was like those of our own time.

***c*.** At the prow, near the water line, was the ship's *beak*, **rostrum** (III. 13), consisting of one or more sharp metal-pointed beams projecting in front, for use in ramming a hostile ship. When the galleys were not in use they might be drawn up on the shore (IV. 29).

***d*.** Before the galley went into action the sail was rolled up and the mast taken down; a *tower*, **turris** (III. 14), was raised on the front part of the ship, from which missiles could be hurled over into a vessel near at hand; *grappling-hooks*, **ferreae manus** (lit. *iron hands*; G. II. 6), were provided, by which the opposing ship might be seized, and a movable bridge that could be thrown across in boarding.

***e*.** For the carrying of his troops Caesar used *transports*, **onerariae naves** (IV. 22), which were broader and slower than the galleys and were accompanied by galleys as escort (V. 8). The admiral's ship, or flag-ship, was distinguished by a red *banner*, **vexillum**, resembling that used by the general on land (*824, b, 3*).

347. The naval tactics of the Romans consisted mainly in either propelling a vessel with great force against a rival and crushing the side by ramming, or in catching hold of the hostile craft with grappling-hooks, pulling alongside, springing over on it, and settling the conflict with a hand-to-hand fight (Plate XI). In the seafight with the Venetans, who had only sailing vessels, the Roman sailors crippled the enemy's ships by cutting down the sail yards; the legionaries on the galleys then boarded the Venetan ships and despatched the crews (III. 13-15). Galleys were used on the Mediterranean until the beginning of the nineteenth century.

Dress And Equipment Of The Gauls And Germans

348. The Gauls wore trousers, **bracae**, which the Romans considered barbaric. The Gallic military *cloak*, **sagulum** (V. 42), was apparently smaller than that of the Roman soldiers.

349. The Gallic infantry were protected by large oblong or oval shields, of wood or metal (called by Caesar, scuta, I. 25), and by helmets of metal on which sometimes horns, and even wheels, appeared. (Figure 46).

The offensive weapons of the Gauls were a long sword, and several types of missile for throwing, as *javelins,* gaesa (III. 4), spears, matarae (I. 26), and *darts,* tragulae (I. 26), or veruta (V. 44).

350. The Gallic standard, in many cases at least, was an image of a boar mounted on a pole. Signals in Gallic armies were given on a curved *war-trumpet,* carnyx, which terminated in the head of an animal or serpent.

351. The clothing of the Germans was largely of skins (IV. 1), but the more advanced wore trousers, like the Gauls, and confined their long hair in a kind of knot. The principal weapons of the Germans were a shield and spear, and a long sword with a single edge.

Figure 150. — Symbols of Victory.
Cuirass, two spears, and a banner, suggesting
victory over a civilized nation. From a relief.

EXERCISES IN LATIN COMPOSITION

Forty Exercises reprinted, by permission, from *Latin Composition*, by Bernard M. Allen and John L. Phillips, of Phillips Academy, Andover, Massachusetts.

POINTS TO BE NOTED IN WRITING LATIN

ORDER OF WORDS

352. Normal Order, *a.* When the emphasis is evenly distributed in a Latin sentence, the Subject comes first, the Predicate last, and the Modifiers of the Predicate precede the Verb in this order: Indirect Object, Direct Object, Adverb or Adverbial Phrase; as, **Is sibi legationem ad civitates suscepit,** *he took upon himself the misson of envoy to the states* (I. 3).

b. Genitives, Adjectives, Possessive Pronouns, and Ordinal Numerals when unemphatic follow their Nouns; as **gloria belli,** *reputation for war* (I. 2); **cupiditate regm,** *by desire of kingly power* (I. 9); **locis patentibus maximeque frumentariis,** *open and exceedingly productive country* (I. 10); **filiam suam,** *his daughter* (I. 3); **die quarto,** *on the fourth day* (I. 26).

c. The Demonstrative Pronouns **hie, iste, ille,** is, the Intensive **ipse,** and Adjectives indicating quantity or position when unemphatic precede their Nouns; as, *these conditions* (I. 3); **ipse imperator,** *the general himself* (I. 40); **tres populos,** *three peoples* (I. 3); **magnum numerum,** *a great number* (1. 4); **extremum oppidum,** *the furthest town* (I. 6); **superiore acie,** *the upper line* (I. 24).

353. Order according to Emphasis, *a.* For the sake of emphasis the Normal Order of words in the sentence may be reversed, the Subject being placed last; as, **Apud** Helvetios **longe nobilissimus fuit** et **diitissimus** Orgetorix, *Among the Helvetians Orgetorix was far the highest in rank, and wealthiest* (I. 2).

b. Genitives, Adjectives, Possessive Pronouns, and Ordinal Numerals when emphatic precede their Nouns; as, **regni cupiditate,** *by desire of kingly power* (1.2); **inimico animo,** *of hostile disposition* (I. 7); **decima legio,** *the tenth legion* (I. 41).

c. When emphatic, the Demonstratives hie. **iste, ille,** is, the Intensive **ipse** and Adjectives indicating quantity or position follow their nouns; as, in **insula ipsa,** *in the island itself* (V. 12); **Galliae totius,** *of entire Gaul* (I. 31); **partes tres,** *three parts* (I. 1); **locis superioribus,** *the higher places* (I. 10).

d. For the sake of emphasis words belonging together in construction are often separated; as, **aliud iter haberent nullum,** *they had no other way* (I. 7); **magno ad pugnam erat impedimento,** *was a great hindrance* (I. 25).

e. An important word in a clause may be made emphatic by placing it before the conjunction introducing the clause; as **Diu cum esset pugnatum,** *When the fighting had continued a I on a time* (1.26).

THE SEQUENCE OF TENSES

354. In writing Latin the Sequence of Tenses should be particularly noted when a Subjunctive is required in a Dependent Clause. For convenience of reference the statement of the grammar *(177, a)* is here supplemented by a tabular outline:

PRIMARY SEQUENCE

rogat	**quid faciam**	*He asks, is asking*	*what*
rogabit	*(incomplete*	*He will ask*	*I am*
rogaverit	*action)*	*He will have asked*	*doing*
rogat	**quid fecerim**	*He asks, is asking*	*what I did,*
rogabit	*(completed*	*He will ask*	*or have*
rogaverit	*action)*	*He will have asked*	*done*

SECONDARY SEQUENCE

rogabat	**quid facerem**	*He asked, was asking*	*what I*
rogavit	*(incomplete*	*He asked*	*was*
rogaverat	*action)*	*He had asked*	*doing*
rogabat	**quid fecissem**	*He asked, was asking*	*what I*
rogavit	*(completed*	*He asked*	*had*
rogaverat	*action)*	*He had asked*	*done*

TABLE ILLUSTRATING SEQUENCE OF TENSES

	Main Verb	Followed by Referring to the Same or Later Time	Subjunctive Referring to Previous Time
Primary Tenses	*Present* *Future* *Future Perfect*	*Present*	*Perfect*
Secondary Tenses	*Imperfect* *Perfect* *Pluperfect*	*Imperfect*	*Pluperfect*

WAYS OF EXPRESSING PURPOSE

355. Purpose in Latin may be expressed in live ways:
By the use of **ut** with the Subjunctive *(196, a)*;
By the use of a Relative with the Subjunctive *(193, a)*;
By **ad** with the Accusative of the Gerund or the Gerundive Construction *(230, 3)*;
By **causa** with the Genitive of the Gerund or the Gerundive Construction *(230, 1)*;
By the Supine in **-um** *(231, a* and *h)*.

"MAY," "MIGHT," AND "MUST," "OUGHT" IN LATIN

356. *a.* "May" and "might" often appear in clauses expressing Purpose, which are translated into Latin by **ut** with the Subjunctive; as, "in order that they might be more ready," **ut paratiores essent** (I. 5). *196, a.*

b. "May" and "might" may also express Permission and be best translated by **licet** with the Dative of the Person and the Infinitive; as, " We may discuss with him," **nobis cum eo agere licet**, lit.' it is permitted to us,' etc. *73, b,* and *222, a.*

357. *a.* "Must" implies Necessity, and is translated by the Passive Periphrastic conjugation *(73, e,* and *229, c)*, or by **necesse est** with the Infinitive, or Infinitive with Subject-Accusative, the Infinitive with **necesse est** being the Subject of est; as, 'as was bound to happen,' **quod necesse erat accidere**, lit. 'which was necessary to happen,' **quod accidere** being the subject of erat (IV. 29).

b. " Ought," implying Obligation or Propriety, is translated either by the Passive Periphrastic conjugation *(73, e,* and *229, c)*, by **oportet** and the Present Infinitive with Subject Accusative *(73, a)*, or by **debed** with a Present Infinitive; since "ought" is a defective verb, past time is expressed in English by the Past Infinitive with "ought," while in Latin past time is expressed by the Principal Verb and only the Present Infinitive is used. Thus:

Present Time	
They ought to fight bravely	**fortiter pugnare debent**
	eos fortiter pugnare oportet
	eis fortiter pugnandum est
Past Time	
He ought to have sent hostages	**obsides mittere debuit**
	eum obsides mittere oportuit
	obsides ei mittendi erant

LESSON I - PRONOUNS

Personal. *39, a* and *b*; *87, a* and *b*; *155, 15ii.* B. 242; A. 295; H. 500.
Demonstrative and Intensive. *42-45,46*; *160-162*; B. 24(i-249; A. 296-298; H. 505-507.
Reflexive. *40, a* and *6*; *158, a* and *b*; *150.* B. 244; A. 299, and 300, 1, 2; H. 502-504.

Book I. 1, 2. 1. These often carry on war with them. **2.** That river separates all these from the Belgians. **3.** We call you Gauls. **4.** They call themselves Celts. **5.** The Helvetians carry on war with the Germans, and fight in their territory. **6.** They all differ from one another. **7.** The Belgians inhabit this part of Gaul, and call themselves the bravest of all. **8.** Their boundaries are narrow in proportion to the number of men.

LESSON II - PRONOUNS

Relative. *47*; *163, a* and *6.* B. 250, 251; A. 304-306, and 308, *a*; H. 510.
Possessive. *41*; *157,* ct-c, *158, c.* B. 243; A. 302, *a, c,d,e*; H. 501.

Book I. 3, 4. 1. Casticus had been called our friend. **2.** He will seize the royal power in his own state. **3.** Diviciacus, who held the leadership, was a brother of Dumnorix. **4.** They will establish peace with those states which are nearest. **5.** They were influenced by his speech, and gave a pledge to one another. **6.** His father held the royal power for many years. **7.** He will take all his clients with him to the trial. **8.** Dumnorix, to whom he gave his daughter in marriage, was very powerful. **9.** You attempted the same thing in your state.

LESSON III - PRONOUNS

Interrogative. *48, a* and *b.* B. 90; A. 148, 152; H. 511.
Indefinite. *49, a* and 6; *168.* B. 252; A. 309-314; H. 512-515.
Direct Questions. *179, a.* B. 102; A. 330-333; H. 378.
Ablative of Agent and Means. *126, a; 131, a, b,* and c. B. 210; A. 405; H. 468, and 1.
Book I. 5, 6. 1. Were all the towns and villages burned by the Helvetians? **2.** Certain[1] of the Kauraci adopted the same plan, and started out with them. **3.** If there is any road by which we can[2] go from home, we will burn all our towns and villages. **4.** What did they try to do when[3] they went out from home ? **5.** They cannot persuade their neighbour, can they, to attempt to do this ? **6.** They permitted them to go through their territory.
1. *certain;* quidam and numerals take ex with the Ablative instead of the Partitive Genitive. *97, d.* 2. *can;* note mood in text. *194, a.* 3. *when;* use **ubi**. Note construction in text.

LESSON IV - REVIEW

Book I. 7, 8. Lake Geneva empties into the Rhone, which is a river in Gaul between the (country of the) Sequanians[1] and the (country of the) Allobroges. Caesar built a rampart ten feet high from this lake to the Jura mountains, which separate the (country of the) Helvetians from the (country of the) Sequanians. When this rampart was finished, he fortified redoubts; and after stationing[2] garrisons, he was able very easily to stop those who tried to cross over. The Helvetians were intending to march through the Province because they could not go by any other route; and so[3] they fastened many boats together, and made rafts by which they crossed the Rhone at its shallowest point.
1. *282.* 2. *after stationing;* use *Ablative Absolute. 144, a* and *b.* 3. *and so, itaque. 237, a.*

LESSON V

Indirect Questions. *204.* B. 300; A. 573, 574; H. 649, 11.
Sequence of Tenses. *177, a,* and *354.* B. 267, 268; A. 482-484; H. 543-S45.
Book I. 9, 10. 1. He does not understand why they are sending envoys. **2.** Ho announced what[1] the Helvetians were planning. **3.** They found out why he had enrolled two legions. **4.** Did Caesar know whether Dumnorix was a friend of the Helvetians or not? **5.** Caesar knew what[1] was being done by the Helvetians. **6.** He does not know whether they obtained their request. **7.** Can he find out why they led their legions out from winter quarters ? **8.** I asked him whether Caesar was passing the winter there, or had gone into Gaul.
1 *what,* plural.

LESSON VI

Subjunctive of Purpose. *196, a, b,* and *193, a, b.* B. 282; A. 531; H. 568, 590.
Constructions of Place. *119, a, b,* and *120, a: 130, a* and *b: 145, a, b, c; 146.* B. 182, 228, 229, 232; A. 426, 427; H. 418, and 4, 419, 1, and 461, 462, 483, 484.
Book I. 11, 12. 1. The Aeduans, in order to defend themselves and their possessions, asked help of[1] Caesar. **2.** They sent an army to keep off the attack of the enemy. **3.** They had nothing left at home. **4.** When the Tigurini had gone out from home, they sent Cassius's army under the yoke. **5.** He will cross the river in order to be able to judge in which direction it flows. **6.** Caesar inflicted a great disaster on this state, with the design of avenging[2] his personal wrongs. **7.** He will send envoys to Eome to ask help.
1 *ask of,* peto, with **ab** and Ablative, *lie, b.* 2. *with the design of avenging;* in Latin, *with this design that he might avenge.*

LESSON VII - REVIEW

Book I. 13. Caesar led his army across the Arar, so that he might follow up the forces of the Helvetians. His sudden arrival alarmed them, and they sent envoys to him to make peace, for[1] they could not understand how[2] he had crossed the river so quickly.[3] Divico was the leader of this embassy, and he asked Caesar where he wished the Helvetians to go. He inquired if Caesar remembered the former valour[4] of the Helvetians, and the destruction of the army which had crossed from the Roman Province[5] into their territory.
1 *for,* nam. 2. *how,* quern ad modum 3. *quickly,* celeriter. 4 *valour;* note case after reminiscor in text 5. *province,* provincia.

LESSON VIII

Subjunctive of Result. *197, a* and *b.* B. 284; A. 537; H. 570.
Ablative of Means. *131, a.* B. 218; A. 409; H. 476.
Dative of Possession. *111.* B. 190; A. 373; H. 430.
Book I. 14, 15. 1. They boasted so insolently that Caesar could not put aside the memory of the injuries. **2.** Caesar had less doubt because he remembered what the envoys had mentioned. **3.** They will march in such a way that we cannot attack them. **4.** By this battle he kept the enemy from foraging. **5.** The gods had granted prosperity to them for so long that they were grieved at the change of circumstances. **6.** The number of the enemy is so large that they cannot drive them back. **7.** He stationed men to see in what direction the enemy were marching.

LESSON IX

Indirect Discourse: Simple Declarative Sentences. *212, d; 213, a* and *6; 214, a; 178.* B. 313, 314, 1, 2, and 317; A. 579-582, 584; H. 642, 644.
Partitive Genitive. *97, a, b, c,* and *d.* B. 201, 1, 2; A. 346, *a, c;* H. 440, 5, and 441-443.
Book I. 16, 17. 1. Caesar said that the grain in the fields was not ripe. **2.** He knew that many of their chiefs had been called together to complain about the leadership of the Aeduans. **3.** For this reason he thought Caesar would take away liberty from the Gauls.[1] **4.** Day after day he declared that the Aeduans were not collecting the grain. **5.** They have a large supply of grain, which they can use if Caesar undertakes[2] the war. **6.** He said that he thought we knew with how great danger he had reported our plans.
1 *Gauls;* note case in text. 2 *undertakes;* what time is referred to ?

LESSON X - REVIEW

Book I. 18. Caesar realized that Liscus referred to Dumnorix, and that these matters had been discussed very freely and boldly; but because Dumnorix was in charge of the cavalry and was utterly reckless,[1] he wished him to favour the Romans. After dismissing[2] the council he asked many questions,[3] and discovered that for several years Dumnorix had been enlarging his private property and had very great power both at home and among the Helvetians. Caesar knew that Dumnorix, by means of this power, could restore himself to his former position of influence, and that he had amassed so much[4] wealth that he entertained hopes of getting the royal power. He learned also that Dumnorix and his horsemen had started the flight of the cavalry a few days before.
1 *utterly reckless;* in Latin, *of supreme recklessness.* 2 *after dismissing;* use Ablative Absolute. *144, a* aud *b.* 3 *questions;* omit, and use neuter adjective as a noun. 4 *so much,* tantus.

LESSON XI - INDIRECT DISCOURSE

Complex Sentences. *214, a; 218; 158, a; 354.* B. 314, land 318; A. 580, and 585, *a;* H. 643.
Prepositions. *122, a; 124, a; 125, a.* B. 141, 142, 143; A. 220, *a, b, c;* H. 420, 2 and 3, and 490, 2.
Book I. 19, 20. 1. He knew that everything[1] which was said to him was true. **2.** Caesar hoped not to hurt (that he should not hurt) the feelings of Diviciacus, if he should punish his brother. **3.** We all know that Procillus was a man in whom "- he had great confidence. **4.** Diviciacus thought that Caesar would punish Dumnorix because he had led an army through the territory of the Sequanians. **5.** He will order Diviciacus to be called to him, in order that he may tell him what he knows. **6.** Caesar replied that he would tell what had been said in the council.
1 *everything;* in Latin, *all things.* 2 *in whom;* use the Dative.

LESSON XII - ABLATIVE ABSOLUTE

Ablative Absolute. *144, a* and *b.* B. 227; A. 411), 420; H. 489.
Book I. 21, 22. 1. Caesar, having sent ahead all his cavalry, ordered Labienus to climb to the summit of the mountain. **2.** While our men were seizing this mountain, the Helvetians moved camp. **3.** After seizing the mountain, Labienus did not begin battle, but waited for Caesar. **4.** Caesar led his forces to the nearest hill, but did not make an attack on the enemy. **5.** When they had pitched camp three miles from Caesar's camp, the enemy refrained from battle.

LESSON XIII - REVIEW

Book I. 23, 24. On the following day it was announced to the enemy that Caesar had changed his route and gone to Bibracte, which was the richest city of the Helvetians, to provide for grain. The Helvetians thought that he was withdrawing because he was frightened, and attacked him in the rear; but Caesar, after leading his forces to the nearest hill and drawing up his line of battle, stationed two legions on the top of the ridge, and collected the packs in [1] one place. The Helvetians, following with all their baggage, formed a phalanx close by[2] the line of battle of the Romans.

1 *in*; in Latin, *into. 124, a.* 2 *close by*, sub, with the Ablative.

LESSON XIV

Reminding, B. 294, 295,

Substantive Clauses with Verbs of *Commanding, Urging, Persuading,* and *Permitting. 199, a; 200, b; 223, a,* (1) and (4). 1, 2, and 296, 1; A. 503; H. 564, 565, 568.

Ablative of Accompaniment. *137, a, b,* and c. B. 222; A. 413; H. 473, and 474, 2, N. 1.

Book I. 25, 26. 1. They threw away their shields, and fought with the enemy with swords. **2.** Caesar ordered the soldiers to make an attack on the Helvetians with drawn swords. **3.** Having noticed this, he bade the cavalry surround the enemy and renew the battle. **4.** He urges them to retreat to the mountain with their baggage and carts. **5.** We persuaded them not to help the soldiers with wagons or anything else. **6.** They fought a long time near the baggage, and got possession of the camp and the horses.

LESSON XV

Substantive Clauses with Verbs of *Asking* and *Fearing. 199, a,* and *202.* K. 295, 1, and 296, 2; A. 563, 564; H. 565, 567.

Book I. 27, 28. 1. Caesar demanded that they should await his [1] arrival in that place. **2.** The Helvetians feared that Caesar would ask that they surrender their arms. **3.** They begged Caesar not to regard them as enemies. **4.** He will ask that envoys be sent to him. **5.** He was afraid that the Germans might cross into the territory of the Helvetians. **6.** Caesar asked the Helvetians to return to their own territory, so that the lands [2] might not be unoccupied. **7.** They urge him to accept their surrender.[3] **8.** They fear that they may not be able to conceal their flight.

1 *his*, indirect reflexive. *158, a.* 2 *lands*, agri. 3 *accept their surrender*; note the text.

LESSON XVI - REVIEW

Book I, 29, 30. The soldiers found records in the camp showing[1] the number of Helvetians who could bear arms. These had gone out from home with all the women and children. Caesar ordered his men to make an enumeration of those who had returned home, and the total was about 120,000. The envoys of the Gauls, who had come to Caesar, feared that he would inflict punishment on their states, but nevertheless asked him not to take possession of all Gaul. This war had turned out to the advantage of Gaul, and they begged Caesar that they might be permitted to appoint a council, and to ask of him the things which they wished.[2] This request was granted, and they agreed together not to disclose anything except with Caesar's consent.

1 *showing*; in Latin, *which showed.* 2 *wished*; use Subjunctive, Subordinate Clause in implied Indirect Discourse. *214, b.*

LESSON XVII

Ablative of Separation or Source. *127, a, b,* and c. B. 214, 215; A. 400-402, and 403, 1; H. 401-465, 467.

Ablative of Comparison. *129, a* and 6. B. 217; A. 406 and 407, *a*; H. 471.

Ablative of Degree of Difference. *140.* B. 223; A. 414; H. 479.

Book I. 31 (*first half*). **1.** They asked back their hostages from the Sequanians, and sought aid of the Roman people. **2.** The Germans are much fiercer than the Gauls,[1] and covet their lands. **3.** Diviciacus fled from his state, and came to Rome many years before. **4.** The Aeduans are less powerful in Gaul than the Sequanians, being weakened by great disasters. **5.** We are working to induce [2] Diviciacus to give his children as hostages to the Germans. **6.** About a thousand of the Germans crossed the Rhine, and contended in arms with the Aeduans and their dependants.

1 *than the Gauls*; express in two ways. 2 *to induce*, 196, a.

LESSON XVIII

Substantive Clauses of Result. *203.* B. 297; A. 568, 569; H. 571.

Ablative of Manner. *13(i, a* and 6. B. 220; A. 412; H. 473, 3.

Ablative of Accordance, *136, c.* B. 220, 3; A. 418, *a*; H. 475, 3.

Book I. 31 (*latter half*). **1.** The result was that they could not longer endure his cruelty. **2.** He will cause a place to be prepared for the Ilarudes. **3.** He saw that the best part of entire Gaul would be occupied by Ariovistus. **4.** All these things were done with the greatest injustice. **5.**

He says that they will not be able to drive the Germans from the Gallic territory. **6.** The cruelty of Ariovistus caused them to seek another home. **7.** It happened that a larger number of Germans crossed the Rhine.

LESSON XIX - REVIEW

Book I. 32, 33. The lot of the Sequanians was much more unhappy than (that) of the others, because the cruelty of Ariovistus had caused them to fear him in his absence, and they did not dare to seek aid from Caesar.

Therefore [1] when Caesar asked why they did not do what the others did, it happened that they made no answer,[2] but remained silent. Diviciacus finally told what the reason was. Caesar promised to put an end to the outrages of Ariovistus, and dismissed the council. The Roman Province was separated by the Rhone from the territory of the Sequanians, and Caesar thought it would be dangerous to the Roman people (for) the Germans to cross from their own boundaries into Gaul.

1 *therefore,* itaque. 2 *made no answer;* in Latin, *answered nothing.*

LESSON XX

Verbs of Hindering, Preventing, Doubting. *201, a, b,* and c. B. 295, 3ₛ and 298; A. 558; H. 568, 8, and 595, 1, 2, and 596, 2.

Ablative of Time. *147, a* and *b.* B. 230, 231; A. 423; H. 486, 487. _

Accusative of Extent. *IIS, a.* B. 181; A. 423, 425; H. 417.

Book I. 34, 35. 1. They could not be restrained from sending envoys to Caesar. **2.** In three days he will advance many miles. **3.** There was no doubt that these replies had been brought back to Caesar. **4.** He talked[1] with him a large part of the day about very important matters. **5.** Caesar demanded of him that he prevent a large number from being led across the Rhine. **6.** This river was half a mile (five hundred paces) wide.[2]

1 *talked,* ago. 2 36, and 243, *a* and *b.*

LESSON XXI

Dative with Special Verbs. *105.* B. 187, n; A. 367; H. 426.

Dative with Compounds. *107, a* and *b.* B. 187, m; A. 370; H. 429.

Book I. 36. 1. The Germans rule those whom they conquer, as they wish. **2.** We do not prescribe to you how you shall pay the tax. **3.** I shall not make war on their allies unjustly. **4.** They could not be persuaded to return the hostages. **5.** No one had resisted him without his own destruction. **6.** They put him in command' of the conquered. **7.** He ordered[2] them not to make the revenues less. **8.** He will persuade them to do what he wishes. **9.** They had been ordered[2] to do all these things.

1 *put in command,* praeficio. 2 *ordered;* use impero iu one sentence, and iubeo in the other.

LESSON XXII - REVIEW

Book I. 37, 38. The Harudes, who had lately come into Gaul, could not be kept from laying waste the lands of the Aeduaus. The latter resisted bravely for many days, and did not doubt that Caesar was hurrying by forced marches against the Swabians, commanded by Nasua,[1] in order to prevent them from crossing the Rhine. Caesar thought that he ought to advance as quickly as possible to seize Vesontio, and after getting ready a grain supply, he hastened to that town with all his forces. The town is almost surrounded by a river of great width, which touches the base of a mountain six hundred feet high. Caesar fortified this town with a very high wall, so that a great opportunity was given to prolong the war, and having stationed a garrison there, he advanced a three days' march toward Ariovistus.

1 *commanded by Nasua;* in Latin, *whom Nasua commanded.*

LESSON XXIII

Gerund and Gerundive. *230.* B. 338, 339; A. 501-507; H. 623-631.

Supine. *231,232.* B. 340; A. 509; H. 633.

Active Periphrastic Conjugation. *63.* B. 115; A. 193-195, and a98, *a*; H. 236, 531.

Passive Periphrastic Conjugation. *63, 73, e,* and *229, c.* B. 115, and 337, 8, *b,* 1; A. 193, 194, 196, and 500, 2; H. 237, and 621, 1, 2.

Dative of Agent. *HO.* B. 189,1; A. 374, *a*; H. 431.

Book I. 39. 1. One assigned one reason for departing, another another. **2.** He remained in camp for the sake of avoiding suspicion. **3.** Caesar intended to delay a few days near Vesontio. **4.** Caesar sent some of his men to bring up the grain.[1] **5.** We shall have to break camp in a few days. **6.** He said that he was going to report this to Caesar. **7.** Having sealed their wills, they remained in their tents to lament the common danger. **8.** The Germans, with whom they were going to contend, had[2] incredible valour.

1 *to bring up the grain;* write in five ways. *355.* 2 *had;* in Latin, *were of.*

LESSON XXIV - MAY, MIGHT, MUST, OUGHT

May, Might. *336, a* and *b.* B. 327, 1; A. 565, u. 1, 2; H. 564, 2.
Must, Ought. *357, a* and *6.* B. 115, 270, 2, and 337, 8, *b,* 1; A. 191,196, 486, a, and 500, 2; H. 237, 618, 2, and 621, 1, 2.
Book I. 40 *(first half).* **1.** Caesar ought[1] to summon to the council the centurions of all ranks. **2.** A centurion is not allowed to inquire by what plan he is being led. **3.** Caesar said he did this in order that Ariovistus might not reject his friendship. **4.** This he should not have said (= ought not to have said). **5.** After learning their plans, you may stay in camp if you wish. **6.** The Romans did not need to fear that these unarmed men would conquer them.[2]

1 *ought;* write in three ways. *357, b.* 2. *them, 158, a.*

LESSON XXV - REVIEW

Book I. 40 *(latter half).* Caesar urged the Roman soldiers not to despair in regard to grain, which was then already ripe in the fields. He told them that they ought not to be disturbed by the narrow roads, and that they were not permitted to dictate to the commander concerning his duties. He desired to know as soon as possible whether the soldiers were going to be ' obedient to his command or not, and so he ordered them to move camp on the next night. He had the greatest confidence in the tenth legion, and did not[2] doubt that they would follow[3] him,[4] and do what[5] had to be done.

1 *were going to be,* etc., S3, and 204, (1). 2 *and ... not,* neque. 3 *follow, 201, b.* 4 *him, 158, a.* 5 *what;* in Latin, = *those things which.*

LESSON XXVI

Temporal Clauses with Ubi, Vt, Postquam, Simui alque. *188,a.* B. 287, 1; A. 513; H. «02.
Temporal Clauses with Cum, Cum primum. *185, a, b, c.* B. 288, 1, and 289: A. 545-547; H. 600, 601.
Ablative with Certain Deponents. *131, c.* B. 218,1; A. 410; H. 477.
Book I. 41, 42. 1. When Caesar had delivered this speech, the military tribunes thanked him. **2.** As soon as Ariovistus learned of Caesar's arrival, he promised many things of his own accord. **3.** After getting possession of the horses, he put on them his bravest soldiers. **4.** When he saw that Ariovistus wished a conference, he decided not to use the Gallic horsemen. **5.** As soon as they came, they said that the enemy's forces were twenty miles away.

LESSON XXVII

Temporal Clauses with Priusquam. *189, a* and &. B. 291,292; A. Ml; H. 605.
Temporal Clauses with Dum and Quoad. *190, a, b,* and c. B. 293; A. 0C3-556; H. 603, 604, 1.
Ablative of Specification. *142, a* and *b.* B. 226; A. 418; H. 480.
Ablative of Cause. *135, a* and *6.* B. 219; A. 404; H. 475.
Book I. 43. 1. Caesar stationed the legion two hundred paces from the mound, before he came to the conference. **2.** While he was making war on their allies, a part of the Germans crossed the Rhine. **3.** The Aeduans had held the leadership before Ariovistus came into Gaul. **4.** They had been able to secure these gifts through his kindness. **5.** They did not send back the hostages until[1] he demanded them. **6.** They were his allies, and for this reason he made these demands. **7.** He waited[2] until they should seek our friendship.

1. *until. 190, 6.* 2. *wait,* **exspecto.**

LESSON XXVIII - REVIEW

Book I. 44 *(first half).* After Ariovistus was summoned by the Gauls, he crossed the Rhine, and took possession of the settlements which the Gauls had granted him. When they made war upon him, they were routed in one battle, and after being defeated, paid tribute and enjoyed peace. While this was going on, Caesar was marching to attack Ariovistus, and wished to come into Gaul before he[1] should impose tribute on all the states. As soon as he came there, he pitched camp, and waited[2] until Ariovistus should reply to his demands. The latter[3] was ready to fight if Caesar wished to, but Caesar made objection; about the tribute, which up to this time had been paid willingly by the Gauls.

1 *he,* **ille.** 2 *wait,* **exspectii.** 3 *the, latter,* here **ille.**

LESSON XXIX

Causal Glauses with Quod, Quia, Quoniam. *1S3, a* and *b.* B. 286, 1; A. 540; H. 588.
Causal Clauses with Cum. *184, a* and *b.* B. 280, 2; A. 549; H. 598.
Dative with Adjectives, *108, a* and 6. B. 192; A. 383-385; H. 434.

Book I. 44 (*latter half*). **1.** He withdrew his army into those regions, because they were nearest the province (of) Gaul. **2.** Since the Aeduans had been called brothers by the senate, they ought to have enjoyed the assistance of the Romans. **3.** Ariovistus complained because we had made an attack on his territories. **4.** The friendship of the Roman people was pleasing to the Aeduans, since they did not wish to be overwhelmed. **5.** Since he has withdrawn from Gaul, we shall consider him as a friend, and not as an enemy.

LESSON XXX

Adversative or Concessive Clauses. *187,* and *191, a* and 6. B. 308, and 309, 2, 3; A. 527, 549; H. 585, 586, 598.
Genitive with Adjectives. *102.* B. 204,1; A. 349, *a*; H. 450, 451.

Book I. 45, 46. 1. Although Fabius conquered the Avernians, he did not reduce them to a province. **2.** Since the horsemen were hurling weapons against our men, Caesar stopped speaking.[1] **3.** Although the soldiers were eager for the battle, Caesar ordered them not to make an attack. **4.** Even if Gaul is free, still it cannot use its own laws. **5.** When this had been announced to Caesar, he ordered his men to return to camp. **6.** Although they are ignorant of the custom of the Roman people, he will not pardon them.
1 *stopped speaking;* note the expression in the text.

LESSON XXXI - REVIEW

Book I. 47. Ariovistus sent a messenger to Caesar, to ark that he should a second time appoint a day for a conference. Although the matters which they had begun to discuss the day before had not been finished, Caesar was unwilling to go himself, or to send envoys and expose them to so great danger. However,[1] because he desired to know what Ariovistus would say (was going to say),[2] it seemed best to him to send Valerius Proeillus and Marcus Mettius. When they had come to Ariovistus in[3] camp, and were attempting to speak, he called out that they were spies, and threw them into chains. Caesar ought not to have sent these men to Ariovistus, since there was no reason for a conference, and he knew that the danger to[4] them would be great.
1 *however,* autem, the second word of its clause. *236, a* and *b.* 2 *would say, 63.* 3 *in,* in with accusative. *124, a.* 4 *to;* in Latin, *of.*

LESSON XXXII

Subjunctive of Characteristic. *194, a.* B. 283, 1, 2; A. 535, *a,b*; H. 591,1,2,4,5.
Ablative of Description. *143, a* and *b.* B. 224; A. 415; H. 473, 2.
Genitive of Quality and Measure, *wo, a* and *b.* B. 203; A. 345; H. 440,3.

Book I. 48, 49. 1. A place about six hundred paces long was picked out, suitable for two legions. **2.** The forces of Ariovistus are the only ones which can keep our troops from supplies. **3.** The Germans were very swift and of great courage, and terrified our men. **4.** There is no army in all Gaul that can overcome the forces of the Romans. **5.** They were (men) of so great swiftness that they equalled the speed of the horses. **6.** They were cut off from grain and supplies by a river two hundred feet in width.[1]
1 *Two hundred feet in width;* express in two ways.

LESSON XXXIII

Exhortations, and Jussive Subjunctive. *ISO, a* and 6. B. 273-275; A. 439; H. 559, 1,2.
Commands and Prohibitions. *181, a* and *b.* B. 276, *b*; A. 450; H. 561, 1.
Wishes. *180,* c and *d.* B. 279; A. 441; H. 558.
Dative of Purpose; Two Datives. *112, a* and *b.* B. 191, 1, 2; A. 382; H. 425, 3, and 433.

Book I. 50, 51. 1. Let us lead out the troops from camp, and draw up our line of battle. **2.** Would that we had not given them an opportunity for fighting! **3.** Caesar left the auxiliaries as a protection for the smaller camp. **4.** 0 that they would not deliver us into slavery! **5.** Do not fight before the new moon, if you wish to conquer. **6.** Let him not use the auxiliaries for a show. **7.** Would that it were not ordained that the Germans should conquer !

LESSON XXXIV

CONDITIONS. *205-209.* B. 301-304, 1; A. 515-517; II. 574-579.

Book I. 52. 1. If the enemy should suddenly make an attack on our men, they would not be able to hurl their javelins. **2.** They would have sent the lieutenant to our assistance, if they had noticed this. **3.** If Caesar were in command of the troops, they would not be in difficulty. **4.** I shall not begin battle on the left wing, unless I see that that part of the line is the strongest. **5.** They said that if they leaped upon the enemy from above, they would put them to flight. **6.** Do not throw your javelins against the enemy, unless they make an attack upon you. **7.** Had he not put a lieutenant in charge of our men, they would have been routed.

LESSON XXXV - REVIEW

Book I. 53, 54. When the battle had been renewed, the enemy were put to flight, and lied to the river. A few, who trusted in their strength, swam across. There were some who crossed over in boats which they found, but the rest were put to death by our cavalry. Ariovistus himself would have been killed, if he had not found a skiff fastened to the shore, and sought safety in it.

While he was following the enemy, Caesar fell in with Valerius Procillus, whom the guards were dragging along. Having rescued him, Caesar said: 'I should have little pleasure in this victory, if you were now in the hands of the enemy. Would that the other envoys, whom I sent to Ariovistus, had also been restored to me ! Let us hope that they may be found and brought back."

LESSON XXXVI - REVIEW
CAUSAL AND CONCESSIVE CLAUSES (LESSONS XXIX AND XXX).

Book IV. 27, 28. As soon as the hostages, whom the enemy sent to Caesar, did what he had ordered, he pardoned them, and begged them not to make war on him without good cause. Although he pardoned their ignorance, he complained because they had thrown Commius the Atrebatian into chains, and had not sent him back. Since part of the hostages which they promised were at a distance, he ordered them to be sent to the continent in a few days. The ships in which the cavalry were carried approached Britain, but could not hold their course because a great storm suddenly came up and carried them back to the continent.

LESSON XXXVII - REVIEW
CLAUSES OF RESULT, AND SUBSTANTIVE CLAUSES OF RESULT (LESSONS VIII AND XVIII).

Book IV. 29-31. 1. It happened that the tides were very high on that night because there was a full moon. **2.** He caused those things which were of use to be brought from the continent. **3.** We must keep them from supplies, and prolong the affair until winter. **4.** The tide was so[1] high that it filled the ships which had been drawn up on dry land. **5.** Although they were going to pass the winter in Gaul, they had made no provision for grain. **6.** The ships arc so damaged by the storm that they cannot be repaired. **7.** He brought it about that no one afterwards crossed to Britain to bring on war. **8.** It happened that everything was lacking which was useful for carrying on war.
1 *so,* **tam.**

LESSON XXXVIII - REVIEW
EXHORTATIONS, COMMANDS, PROHIBITIONS AND WISHES (LESSON XXIII).

Book IV. 32, 33. 1. Let part of the legion march in that direction in which the dust was seen. **2.** Would that Caesar had suspected the plans of the barbarians, and attacked them when their arms were laid aside! **3.** It was reported to the general that the cohorts which were on guard had started in the same direction. **4.** If the enemy attack you, throw your weapons quickly; let the cavalry dismount and fight on foot. **5.** Do not be disturbed by the noise of the chariots, for if hard pressed, you will have an easy retreat. **6.** The Britons fight with chariots, and daily practise makes them able to do many things with their horses at full speed.

LESSON XXXIX - REVIEW

Purpose Clauses, and Substantive Clauses after Certain Verbs (Lessons VI, XIV, and XV).

Book IV. 34, 35. 1. Caesar will keep his men in camp that they may not be attacked by the enemy. **2.** The barbarians sent messengers in. all directions to tell what had happened. **3.** Storms followed for so many days[1] that. the enemy were kept from a battle. **4.** Caesar feared that the same thing would happen. **5.** They urged the rest, who were in the fields, to depart. **6.** Disturbed by the strange sort of fighting, they begged Caesar to send aid to them. **7.** They gathered a large number of cavalry and infantry, in order that they might the more easily[2]

drive the Romans from the camp. **8.** He ordered them to burn the buildings far and near, and return to camp. **9.** Having killed many, they prevented the rest from escaping.[3]
1 *days, 118, a.* 2 *easily,* facile. 3. *from escaping, 201, a,* and *223, a,* (3).

LESSON XL - REVIEW
CONDITIONS (LESSON XXXIV).

Book IV. 32, 33. 1. Let part of the legion march in that direction in which the dust was seen. **2.** Would that Caesar had suspected the plans of the barbarians, and attacked them when their arms were laid aside! **3.** It was reported to the general that the cohorts which were on guard had started in the same direction. **4.** If the enemy attack you, throw your weapons quickly; let the cavalry dismount and fight on foot. **5.** Do not be disturbed by the noise of the chariots, for if hard pressed, you will have an easy retreat. **6.** The Britons fight with chariots, and daily practise makes them able to do many things with their horses at full speed.

Book IV. 36-38. If Caesar had not sailed on that night, the hostages which he ordered would have been brought to him, but the equinox was near, and he thought if he hastened he would arrive safely at the continent. After finding a suitable place, he disembarked some three hundred men, who started for the camp, but were surrounded by the Morini, who said, " Lay down your arms if you do not wish to be killed. If Caesar and his cavalry were here, they would defend you, but you cannot withstand our attack and will be all killed unless he comes to your assistance." But after those who said this saw that our cavalry were coming, they quickly turned and fled.

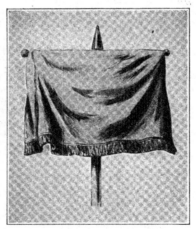

Figure 149. — Banner, vēxillum.

IDIOMS AND PHRASES

For distinctions of meaning and usage in a more general study of Latin Idioms Meissner's Latin Phrasebook (New York, 1895) will be found helpful.

A dextro cornu, *on the right wing.*

a fronte, *in front.*

a milibus paasuum minus duobus, *about two miles off* (V 32).

a milibus passuum minus duobus, *less than two miles off* (II. 7).

a novissimo agmine, *in the rear.*

a pueris, *from childhood.*

a sinistro cornu, *on the left wing.*

a tanto spatio, *so far off* (II. 30).

a tergo, *on the rear.*

ab armis discedere, *to lay down arms.*

urbem ab eis defendere, *to defend the city against them.*

se absente, *in his absence.*

accedit ut, or quod, *there is the additional fact (or circumstance) that, and besides.*

accedit huc ut, accedit quod, *there is, further, the consideration that, or the fact that.*

aciem convertere, *to face about.*

acies media, *the middle of the line.*

acies oculorum, *the keen glance of their eyes* (I. 39).

ad ancoras deligatae naves, *ships lying at anchor.*

ad conducendos homines, *for hiring men* (II. 1).

ad equum rescribere, (1) *to enroll in the cavalry,* (2) *to raise to knighthood* (I. 42).

ad extremum, *at the end, at last, finally.*

ad Genavam pervenit, *he arrived in the vicinity of Geneva* (I. 7).

ad hunc modum, *after this fashion, thus.*

ad milia quindecim, *about fifteen thousand.*

ad salutem contendere, *to hasten to a place of safety* (III. 3).

ad speciem, *for show.*

ad unum, *to a man.*

ad urbem, *near the city.*

vulnera adversa, *wounds in front.*

adversis hostibus occurrere, *to meet the enemy face to face* (II. 24).

in adversum os, *right in the face.*

adverso colle, *up the hill.*

adverso flumine, *up the stream, upstream, against the current.*

aegre ferre, *to take to heart, to be vexed.*

aequo animo, *without anxiety, contentedly.*

aere alieno premi, *to be in debt.*

afficere supplicio, *to punish.*

afflei magno dolore, *to be greatly annoyed.*

agere cum eo, *to confer with him.*

cum tribunis agunt, *they arrange with the tribunes* (I. 41).

agere gratias, *to thank,*

agmen claudere, *to bring up the rear.*

alias — alias, *at one time — at another.*

alienum tempus, *an unfavourable time.*

alienus locus, *an unfavourable place, location.*

alii aliam in partem, *some in one direction, others in another; in different directions.*

aliter atque (or **ac**), *otherwise than, different from what.*

alius alia causa illata, *one presenting one pretext, another another; each one presenting a different excuse* (I. 39).

aliis alii subsidium ferunt, *one part renders aid to the other* (II. 26).

rem esse in angusto, *that matters had reached a crisis* (II. 25).

animum advertere, *to notice.*

ante exactam hiemem, *before the end of winter* (VI. 1).

longe alius atque, or **ac,** *far other than, very different from.*

contra atque erat dictum, *contrary to what had been agreed upon* (IV. 13).

idem atque, *the same as.*

audiens dicto esse, *to be obedient.*

aversi circumveniri, *to be surrounded on the rear* (II. 26).

aversum hostem videre, *to see a foe in flight* (I. 26).

Bellum defendere, *to wage a defensive war, repel invasion,*

bellum ducere, *to prolong a war* (I. 38).

bellum gerere, *to carry on war, wage war.*

bellum inferre, *to make war.*

bono animo esse in (with acc), *to cherish a kindly feeling toward, to be well disposed toward* (I. 6).

Consilium capere, *to form a plan.*

locum capere, *to capture a place* (V. 9), *to reach a destination* (V. 23).

portum, insulam capere, *to make a harbour* (IV. 36), *to reach an island* (IV. 26).

oppidum capere, *to take a town.*

capite solo ex aqua exstare, *lo stand up to the chin in water* (V, 18).

capitis poenam, *capital punishment, the death penalty.*

capitum decem milia, *ten thousand souls.*

castra movere, *to break camp.*

castra ponere, *to pitch camp, encamp.*

causa, with gen., *for the sake of, on account of.*

honoris Diviciaci causa, *out of regard for Diviciacus* (II. 15).

qua de causa (*and*) *for this reason.*

causam dicere, *to plead a case.*

cedentibus et insequentibus, *to the pursued and the pursuing* (V. 16).

celerius opinione, *sooner than was expected* (II. 3).

certiorem Caesarem facere, *to inform Caesar.*

certior fieri, *to be informed.*

civitate donatus, *granted citizenship, made a citizen* (I. 47).

collocare nuptum, *to give in marriage* (I. 18).

proelium committere, *to commence an engagement, join battle.*

commodo (abl.) **rei publicae,** *consistently with the pubic interest, to the advantage of the commonwealth.*

idem conari, *to make the same attempt, attempt the same thing* (I. 3).

bellum conficere, *to finish a war.*

vulneribus confectus, *exhausted with wounds.*

aetate confectus, *weakened by age.*

in fugam conicere, *to put to flight, rout.*

sibi mortem consciscere, *to commit suicide* (I. 4; III. 22).

conspicari licet, *one may. see* (VI. 17)

consulere alicui, *to have regard for any one, look out for the interest of any one.*

sibi quemque consulere, *that each one took out for himself* (VI. 31).

consulere aliquem, *to consult any one, ask advice of any one* (not in Caesar),

consulto cedere, *to retreat purposely, designedly.*

quod tempus convenerat, *the time which had been agreed upon* (II. 19).

sub corona vendere, *to sell into slavery.* (III. 16).

eum primum, *as soon as.*

eum — tum, *not only — but also, both — and.*

cursu incitato, *having quickened their pace.*

Dare manus, *to yield* (V. 31).

dare operam, *to take pains.*

in matrimonium dare, *to give in marriage* (I. 3).

in fugam dare, *to put to flight.*

inter se dare, *to exchange.*

de improviso, *unexpectedly, suddenly.*

hae spe deiecti, *disappointed in this expectation* (I. 8).

se animo demittere, *to lose heart, despair* (VII. 29).

mortem deprecari, *to plead for life* (VII. 40).

diem dicere, *to appoint a day.*

dimidio minor, *smaller by half, a half smaller* (V. 13).

transire flumen non dubitant, *they do not hesitate* (or delay) *to cross the river* (II. 23).

non dubitat, quin, *he does not doubt that.*

non dubium est, quin, *there is no doubt that.*

duce Boduognato, *under the leadership of Boduognatus* (II. 23).

in matrimonium ducere, *to marry* (I. 9).

uxorem ducere, *to marry* (I. 53).

Ex navi egredi, navi egredi, *to disembark.*

eo, before comparatives, *all the;* as **eo magis,** *all the more.*

esse in animo, *to intend.*

ex aqua mensurae, *water-clocks* (V. 13).

ex equis, *on horseback* (I. 43).

ex inferiore loco, *from a tower position ; from a lower level* (III. 14).

ex loco superiore, *from a higher position ; from a higher point of view.*

ex usu Galliae (gen.), *of advantage to Gaul, expedient for Gaul.*

exspectabat si transirent, *he was waiting to see whether they would cross* (II. 9).

legio expedita, *legion unencumbered* with baggage.

extremi, *as part of an army, the rear* (V. 10).

ad extremas fossas, *at the ends of the trenches* (II. 8).

in extremo ponte, *at the end of the bridge* (VI. 29).

in extremis suis rebus, *under circumstances of the greatest danger to himself* (II. 25).

Facinus in se admittere, facinus admittere, *to become guilty of a crime, commit a crime.*

excursiones facere, *to make sallies.*

idem facere, *to convince; to give a pledge* (IV. 11).

imperata facere, *to do what was commanded, to carry out the orders.*

impetum facere, with in and acc., *to make an attack on ; to charge.*

hoc proelio facto, *after this battle.*

proelio facto secundo, *after a successful engagement; since the result of the battle was favourable.*

facultas navium, *supply of skips.*

auxilium, subsidium ferre, *to render aid, to bring aid,*

condicionem ferre, *to propose terms* (IV. 11).

graviter, moleste ferre, *to be annoyed, to be vexed.*

consuetudo fert, *is usually* (VI. 7).

ut fert illorum opinio, *as their opinion goes, according to their idea* (V. 13).

idem habere alicui, *to have confidence in any one.*

idem interponere, *to pledge one's honour.*

idem praestare, *to give proof of one's good faith* (V. 45).

Caesaris fidem sequi, *to attach one's self to Caesar.*

in eius fidem venire, *to put one's self under his protection.*

sibi fingere, *to imagine.*

vultum fingere, *to control the features* (I. 39).

Gratiam habere, *to feel thankful.*

gratiam referre, *to make return, to make*

requital.
gratias agere, *to thank.*
gratum facere, *to do a favour* (I. 44).
graviter ferre, *to take to heart, to be annoyed.*
Habere in animo, *to intend* (VI. 7).
eodem loco habere quo Helvetios, *to regard (them) in the same light as the Helvetians* (I. 26).
hostium numero habere, *to consider as enemies.*
equitatum coactum habere, *to have a body of cavalry collected, to have gathered a body of cavalry together* (I. 15).
id compertum habebat, *he had learned that* (I. 44).
orationem habere, *to make a speech.*
sibi persuasum habere, *to be convinced* (III. 2).
Idem qui, *the same as.* idem sentire, *to have the same feeling.*
equitibus imperat, ut —, *he commands the cavalry to —.*
civitatibus obsides imperat, *he levies hostages upon the states, obliges the states to furnish hostages.*
pons in Arare, *a bridge over the Arar* (I. 13).
in arido, *on dry land.*
in circuitu, *in case one should go around* (I. 21).
in dies, *every day, daily.*
in itinere, *on the march,*
in perpetuum, *forever.*
in praesentia, *for the present.*
in reliquum tempus, *for the future.*
in servilem modum, *as in the case of slaves* (VI. 19).
in statione, *on guard.*
in vicem, *in turn.*
bellum incidit, *a war breaks out.*
in ipsum Caesarem ineidit, *he fell in the way of Caesar himself* (I. 53).
iniuriam inferre, *to inflict an injury.*
collis infimus apertus, *a hill cleared at the base* (II. 18).
consilium inire, *to enter into a project, to form a plan.*
inita aestate, *at the beginning of summer.*
iniussu Caesaris, *without Caesar's bidding.*
inter se cohortati, *urging one another on.*
inter se dare, *to exchange.*
inter se differunt, *they differ from one another,*
inter annos xiiii, *during fourteen years* (I. 36)
aqua atque igni interdicere, *to forbid the use of fire and water, to banish* (VI. 44).
sacrificiis interdicere, *to prohibit from attendance at sacrifices, excommunicate* (VI. 13).
omni Gallia Romanis interdixit, *he forbade the Romans occupying any part of Gaul* (I. 46).
se ipsi interficiunt, *they kilt themselves* (V. 37).
ipsius eastra, *his own camp.*
iter faeere, *to march.*

in itinere, *on the march.*
ex itinere, *from the line of march, leaving the line of march ;* the expression is used of a force which turns from marching order at once, without encamping, to attack an enemy in the field (I. 25), or storm a town (II. 6, 12; III. 21), or retreat (II. 29).
magnum iter, *forced march.*
optimum iudicium facere, *to pass a very favourable opinion* (I. 41).
ius dicere, *to administer justice* (VI. 23).
Largiter posse, *to have great influence.*
maxima laus, *the highest merit.*
legionem conscribere, *to enrol a legion.*
alieno loco, *in an unfavourable place.*
obsidum loco, *as hostages.*
Maior pars, *the greater part, the majority.*
in manibus nostris esse, *to be close to us* (II. 19).
manipulos laxare, *to spread out the maniples, open the ranks.*
manus conducta, *a force serving for pay, a mercenary force* (V. 27).
medio in colle, *half-way up the hill.*
memoria nostra (abl.), *in our own day.*
memoria tenere, *to remember.*
memoriam deponere, *to cease to remember, to forget.*
memoriam prodere, *lo transmit the remembrance.*
missu Caesaris, *sent by Caesar.*
oratoris modo, *as an envoy.*
moleste ferre, *to be annoyed.*
more maiorum supplicium sumere, *to punish after the ancient fashion.*
lingua Galliea multa uti, *to speak the Gallic language fluently* (I. 47).
ad multam noctem, *tilt late at night.*
multo die, *late in the day.*
multum valere, *to be very powerful.*
Natura atque opere (manu), *naturally and artificiality.*
naves conscendere, *to go on board, embark.*
naves armare, *to fit out ships.*
naves deducere, *to launch ships.*
naves in litore eiectae, *ships stranded.*
naves longae, *war-ships, galleys.*
naves onerariae, *freight-ships, transport-ships.*
naves solvere, *to set sail, weigh anchor.*
naves subducere, *to draw skips up on land, beach.*
navi, ex navi egredi, *to disembark.*
ex navibus expositi, *landed, placed on shore.*
nihilo minus, setius, *none the less, no less, just so.*
nisi rogatus, *without being asked* (I. 44).
novis rebus (imperiis) studere, *to desire a revolution.*
non ita magnus numerus, *not a very large*

number, not very many.

Occupationes rei publicae, *business of state, public affairs* (IV. 16).

officium praestare, *to do one's duty.*

operam dare, *to take pains.*

operam navare, *to do one's best.*

opinio timoris, *impression of fear.*

opinio virtutis, *reputation for courage.*

opus est, *there is need, it is necessary.*

opus facto est, *there is need of action.*

in orbem consistere, *to form a circle.*

ordines servare, *to keep the ranks, remain in tine.*

primi ordines, *the centurions of the first rank* (V. 30).

ordinibus perturbatis, *the ranks being broken, out of order.*

ratio ordoque agminis, *system and arrangement, regular order, of the line of march.*

Pedem referre, *to retreat.*

sub pellibus, *in tents* (III. 29).

stipendium pendere, *to pay tribute.*

per manus tractus, *dragged, passed, from hand to hand* (VI. 38).

ad Alpes pertinent, *extend as far as the Alps.*

eodem pertinere, *point to the same thing.*

petere, ut liceat, *to ask permission.*

placuit ei mittere, *he thought best to send.*

plurimum posse, *to have the greatest influence, be very powerful.*

plus posse, *to have greater influence, be more powerful.*

poenas pendere, persolvere, *to pay the penalty.*

poenas repetere, *to inflict punishment.*

castris potiri, *to obtain possession of the camp.*

totius Galliae potiri, *to obtain the mastery over the whole of Gaul* (I. 3).

prae magnitudine sua, *in comparison with his own greatness.*

se praesente, *in his presence.*

virtute omnibus praestare, *to excel all (the rest) with respect to courage.*

fidem praestare, *to give proof of one's good faith.*

officia ducis praestare, *discharge the duties of a commander.*

virtutem praestare, *to show courage.*

praestat pati, quam, *it is better to suffer than.*

Sabino praesto fuit, *he met Sabinus* (V. 26).

milites premi videt, *he sees that the soldiers are hard pressed.*

prima aestate, primo vere, *at the beginning of summer, of spring.*

prima luce, *at early dawn.*

prima nocte, *at the beginning of night, at night-fall.*

primum agmen, *the van.* See Companion,

328. (VII. 67).

principes consili, *the leaders in the scheme.*

pro beneficiis, *in return for favours*

pro his, *on behalf of these.*

pro multitudine, *in proportion to the population.*

pro perfuga, *as a deserter.*

pro vallo, *as a rampart.*

pro sano, *as a sane man, like a man in his senses.*

pro tempore, pro re, *as the time, as the circumstances demanded.*

proeliis parvulis, *in skirmishes.*

publice — privatim, *as a state or in the name of the state- —as individuals.*

Quae cum ita sint, *since this is true, since the case stands thus.*

quaevis fortuna, *any lot whatever* (II. 30).

post diem quartum, quam, *four days after, the fourth day after* (IV. 28).

quam maximus, *as great as possible, the greatest possible.*

quam primum, *as soon as possible.*

quanto — tanto, quo — eo, quo — hoc, *with comparatives, the —; as,*

quanto gravior — tanto crebriores, *the severer — the more frequently.*

decem diebus, quibus, *ten days after* (IV. 18).

quinis aut senis milibus passuum, *five or six miles each day* (I. 15).

nullum tempus intermiserunt, quin legatos mitterent, *they let no time pass without sending envoys* (V. 55).

nobilissimus quisque, *all the nobles.*

antiquissimum quodque tempus, *priority of time* (I. 45).

Rari propugnabant, *they were all in scattered parties, in small bodies* (V. 9).

se recipere, *to withdraw, retreat.*

mortem recusare, *to shrink from death.*

recusare quo minus sub illorum dicione sint, *to refuse to be under their sway* (I. 31).

religiones interpretari, *to settle religious questions* (VI. 13).

religionibus impediri, *to be hindered by religious scruples* (V. 6).

male re gesta, *after an unsuccessful venture* (I. 40).

occasio rei bene gerendae, negoti bene gerendi, *a chance of fighting a successful battle, of gaining an advantage.*

res communis, *a common interest, common interests.*

res gestae, *what has been done, deeds, exploits.*

res secundae, *prosperity.*

Sacramento rogare, *to enlist.*

satis commode, *very conveniently.*

se suaque omnia, *themselves and all their*

possessions.

secundo flumine, *down the stream, downstream, with the current.*

secundum ea, *besides those considerations* (I. 33).

secundum flumen, *next to the stream, along the river.*

secundum naturam fluminis, *according to the current* (i.e. *natural course) of the river* (IV. 17).

sententia desistere, *to give up the notion* (VI. 4).

si quid erat durius, *in case of any difficulty* (I. 48).

ad signa eonvenire, *to muster.*

signa inferre, etc, see Companion, 325. (II. 26).

signa conversa inferre, *to face about and advance.*

oriens sol, *the East.*

solis occasus, *sunset; the West.*

occidens sol, *the West.*

in spem venire, *to begin to have hope.*

sub bruma, *at the time of the winter sotstice, in winter.*

sub monte, *at the foot of the height.*

sub occasum solis, *about sunset.*

sub vesperum, *towards evening.*

diem sumere, *to take time* (I. 7).

supplicium de aliquo sumere, *to inflict punishment on any one, punish anyone.*

in summa, *as a whole.*

summa belli, *the general management of the war* (I. 41).

summa exercitus, *the army as a whole* (VI. 34).

summa imperi, *the supreme power, chief authority.*

summa omnium rerum, *the final decision of everything* (VI. 11).

summa vi, *with might and main.*

summis copiis, *with all their forces, in full force* (V. 17).

ab summo, *from the top.*

equos sustinere, *to check the horses* (IV. 33).

se sustinere non potest, *he can no longer hold himself up, stand* (II. 25).

Una per Sequanos via, *only the way through the country of the Sequani* (I. 9).

in una virtute eonsistere, *to depend on courage atone* (II. 33).

uni Sequani, *the Sequam alone* (I. 32).

Veniam dare, *to pardon.*

vereor ne, *I fear that.*

vereor ut, I fear *that not.*

in castris versari, *to be in the camp* (II. 24).

in periculo versari, *to be in danger.*

in proeliis periculisque versari, *to be in the midst of warfare and danger* (VI. 16).

terga vertere, *to turn to flee, flee.*

eos in vestigio paenitet, *they regret immediately, on the spot* (IV. 5).

IDIOMATIC GENATIVES

i. Genitive of the whole. B. 201; AG. 216.

Aliquid calamitatis, *some disaster.*

novi aliquid consili, *some new scheme (or other).*

aliquid itineris, some *distance.*

amplius obsidum, *more hostages.*

minus dubitationis, *less doubt.*

multum aestatis, *a great part of the summer.*

nihil agri, *no land, no territory.*

nihil negoti, *no trouble.*

nihil reliqui, *nothing left* (I. 11).

nihil vini, *no wine.*

plus doloris, *more grief more pain.*

quam minimum spati, *as little time as possible* (III. 19).

eodem vestigio remanere, *to remain in the same place* (IV. 2).

vim facere, *to use violence.*

in aliquem vindicare, *to punish anyone* (III. 16).

quantum boni, *how much advantage, good.*

neque vestitus quicquam, *no clothing.*

quid negoti ? *what business?*

quid rei est ? *what is the mater?*

quod navium longarum, *what warships, whatever galleys* (IV. 22).

satis causae, *reason enough, sufficient cause.*

satis praesidi, *a sufficient garrison.*

sui nihil deperdere, *to lose none of their standing* (I. 43).

tantum repentini periculi, *so great sudden danger.*

ii Objective Genitive. B. 200; AG. 217.

Helvetiorum iniuriae populi Romani, *wrongs done to the Roman people by the Helvetians.* (I. 30)

magno sui cum perieulo, *with great danger to themselves* (IV. 28).

magno eum periculo nostrorum equitum, *with great danger to our horsemen* (V, 19).

sui potestatem facere, *to give (the enemy} a chance at him* (I. 40).

iii. Genitive of value. B. 203, 3; AG. 252, *a.*

Magni haberi, *to be considered of much account, much thought of.*

rei publicae (gen.) **magni interest,** *it deeply concerns the general interest, it greatly concerns the state.*

iv. Genitive after adjectives. B. 204; AG. 218.

Peritus rerum, belli, skilled *in affairs, in war.*

locus medius utriusque, *a place midway between both* (I. 34).

v. Genitive after adverbs. B. 201, 3, *a;* AG. 214,g.

Postridie eius diei, *on the next day after, the following day*
pridie eius diei, *on the previous day, the day before.*

PASSIVE USED IMPERSONALLY.

Accessum est ad Britanniam, *they reached Britain* (V. 8).
committendum non putabat, *he was thinking that he ought not (so) to act, that occasion ought not to be given* (I. 46).
concedi non oportet, *it ought not to be granted, concession ought not to be made.*
constabat hiemari in Gallia oportere, *it was clear that they must spend the winter in Gaul* (IV. 29).
consurgitur, *they rise in a body, all rise* (V. 31).
proelio equestri contendebatur, *the contest was continued with an engagement of the cavalry* (II. 9).
nobis non cunctandum est, quin pugna decertemus, *we must not delay to fight a decisive battle* (III. 23).
deliberatur, *the question is discussed* (VII. 15).
militibus de navibus desiliendum et in fluctibus consistendum et cum hostibus erat pugnandum, *the soldiers had to jump down from the ships and get their footing in the water and fight with the enemy* (IV. 24).
de eius fide non dubitandum, *his good faith ought not to be questioned* (VII. 21).
dubitandum non existimavit, quin proficisceretur, *he thought that he ought not to delay about setting out* (II. 2).
in vulgus militum elatum est, *it got abroad among the rank and file of the soldiers* (I. 46).
si enuntiatum esset, *if disclosure should have been made* (I. 31).
exspectari non oportet, quin eatur, *ought not to delay to go.*
quibus [sacrificiis] interdictum est, *who have been forbidden participation in sacrifices* (VI. 13).
ut ignosceretur, petiverunt, *they begged that pardon he granted them* (IV. 27).
mandatum est, *a commission was given, the matter was entrusted* (I. 30).
maturandum sibi existimavit, *he thought that he ought to make all haste.*
navibus nocetur, *the ships are damaged.*
quibus rebus occurrendum est, *these circumstances ought to be provided for, this emergency ought to be met* (I. 33).
rerum omnium inopia nobis pereundum est, *we must perish from want of all things.*
mihi persuadetur, *I am convinced.*
praecavendum est, *every precaution should be taken* (I. 38).
ei praeceptum est, *he was instructed, directed.*

ut erat praeceptum, *as (he, they) had been instructed, according to instructions.*
prodeundum erat, *it became necessary to advance* (I. 48).
pronuntiatur, *notice is given, announcement is made* (V. 31).
rei frumentariae prospiciendum est, *arrangement ought to be made for supplies,*
pugnatum est, *fighting went on, the battle raged.*
minus facile resisti potest, *resistance cannot so easily be made* (I. 37).
aegre sustentatum est, *the defense was maintained with difficulty* (II. 6).
totis trepidatur castris, *there is a panic throughout the camp* (VI. 37).
ventum est, *he (they) came,*
in eos vindicandum est, *punishment ought to be inflicted on them* (III. 16).

ESSE IN IDIOMATIC EXPRESSIONS.

i. <u>With predicate genitive.</u> B. 198, 3; AG. 214, c.

Aestivum tempus instantis belli est, *the summer ought to be devoted to the impending war* (VI. 4).
quid consili Caesaris est? *what plan has Caesar in mind? what does Caesar intend to do?*
est hoc Gallicae consuetudinis, *this is a peculiar custom of the Gauls* (IV. 5).
exspectare summae dementiae est, *it is the highest folly to wail* (IV. 13).
suae dignitatis esse, *to be consistent with his dignity* (IV. 17).
magnae fuit fortunae, *it was a case of rare good luck* (VI. 30).
iudicium imperatoris est, *it is for the general to decide* (I. 41).
cur sui quicquam esse imperi postularet, *why should he claim anything as under his sway.*
haec summi ut sint laboris efficiunt, *these (by training) they make capable of the greatest exertion, of the greatest endurance* (IV. 2).
est legati, *it is a lieutenant's duty.*
liberae esse civitatis, *to belong to a free state* (V. 7).
res erat multae operae ae laboris, *the operation cost great effort and toil* (V. 11).
erat magni periculi res, *it was a very dangerous thing.*

ii. <u>With dative of possession.</u> B. 190; AG. 231.
Est mihi, est tibi, *I have, you have.*
est Caesari, *Caesar has,*
Caesari nulla mecum amicitia est, *I have no friendship with Caesar, there is no friendship between Caesar and me* (CF. IV. 8).

iii. <u>With two datives.</u> B. 191, 2, *a*; AG. 233.

Erit mihi curae, *I will attend to it.*

dixit, sibi curae futurum esse, *he said that he would attend* **to it,**

mihi est cordi, it is agreeable to me, suits me.

ea Caesari usui erant, *those things were of use to Caesar.*

praesidio impedimentis erant, *they served as a guard for the baggage.*

his difficultatibus duae res erant subsidio, *two things served to offset these disadvantages* (II. 20).

haec magno Germanis dolori sunt, *these things are a cause of great vexation to the Germans* (V. 29).

iv. <u>With ablative of quality.</u> B. 224, 2; AG. 251.

Hi sunt specie tauri, *they have the appearance of a bull* (VI. 28).

capillo sunt promisso, *they have flowing hair* (V. 14).

ingenti magnitudine corporum sunt, *they are of gigantic stature* (I. 39).

NOTES ON VOCABULARY

In the preparation of this Vocabulary Meusel's *Lexicon Caesarianum* has been of greatest service; Lodge's *Vocabulary of High School Latin* has also been helpful. For the less obvious Latin etymologies Walde's *Lateinisches Etymolagisches Worterbuch* (second edition) has generally been followed; for the English derivatives, *The Century Dictionary* and *The New English Dictionary.*

For the Key to the English Pronunciation of Proper Names, and in other matters of English pronunciation, the Editor was indebted to Professor George Hempl.

ABBREVIATIONS

A list of Abbreviations is given on the following page.

ENGLISH PRONUNCIATION OF PROPER NAMES

After each Proper Name in the Vocabulary a Key to the English Pronunciation is given, thus:

Matrona, -ae, f., (Mat'ro-na)

The English long vowels (so called) have above them a macron or some mark indicative of quality; the short stressed vowels have no mark at all; the obscure unstressed vowels have a dot under them, thus:

	as in		*as in*		*as in*
a	'fate'	e	'hated'*	o	'democrat'*
a	'fat'	e	'her'	u	'use'
a	'idea'*	i	'pine'	u	'up'
a	'arm'	i	'pin'	u	'singular'*
a	'all'	i	'unity'*	u	'circus'*
e	'me'	o	'no'	U	'rude'
e	'met'	o	'not'	U	'full'

The chief stress, or accent, is indicated by ', the secondary by "; but the secondary stress is not marked when separated from another stress by a single intervening unstressed syllabic, for in that case one naturally puts it in the proper place.

* The obscure unstressed vowels are in effect very much alike, but they differ slightly according to the character of the adjoining consonants. They are most correctly sounded when one glides over them rapidly and naturally.

ABBREVIATIONS

References to the Gallic War are printed thus: I. 7 (Book I, chapter 7); to the Civil War, C. I. 7.
English Derivatives of Latin words are inserted at the end of the definitions, set off by a half-bracket, thus: [accuse.
* Implies that the form before which it stands is hypothetical.

abl.	*ablative*	inf.	*infinitive*
abs.	*absolute*	intes	*intensive*
acc.	*accusative*	inter.	*interrogative*
adj.	*adjective*	inter.	*interjection*
adv.	*adverb, adverbial*	intr.	*intransitive*
AG	*Allen & Greenough's Grammar*	irr.	*irregular*
B	*Bennett's Grammar*	l., ll.,	*line, lines*
C.	*Bellum Civile, Caesar's Civil War*	lit.	*literally*
causat.	*causative*	m.	*masculine*
cf.	*confer = compare*	n., neut.	*neuter*
chap	*chapter*	N.	*note*
comp.	*comparative.*	nom.	*nominative*
conj.	*conjunction.*	num.	*numeral*
dat.	*datative*	ord.	*ordinal*
decl.	*declension*	p.,p.	*page, pages*
def.	*defective*	part.	*participle*
dem.	*demonstrative*	pass.	*passive*
dep.	*deponent*	patr.	*patronymic*
dim.	*diminuative*	pers.	*person, personal*
distrib.	*distributative*	pf.	*perfect*
e.g.	*exempli gratia = for example*	pl.	*plural*
et al.	*et alibi = and elsewhere*	pos.	*positive*
et seq.	*et sequentia = and what follows*	pred.	*predicate*
etc.	*et cetera = and so forth*	prep.	*preposition*
excl.	*exclamation*	pres.	*present*
f.	*feminine*	pron.	*pronoun*
freq.	*frequentative*	eflex.	*reflexive*
fut.	*future.*	rel.	*relative*
gen.	*genitive*	sc. or scil.	*scilicet, scire licet = that is, namely*
i.e.	*id est = that is*	semi-dep	*semi-deponent*
imp.	*imperative*	sing.	*singular*
impers.	*impersonal.*	subj.	*subjunctive*
impf.	*imperfect*	sup.	*superlative*
inch.	*inchoative*	trans.	*translate, or translation*
indecl.	*indeclinable*	v.	*verb*
indef.	*indefinite*	voc.	*vocative*
indic.	*indicative*	1 2, 3, 4	*1st., 2nd., 3rd. 4th.verb conjugation*

VOCABULARY

A.

A., with proper names, = *Aulus.*

a. d. = ante diem.

ā, ab, abs, prep., with abl., *from, away from, out of; at, on; of agency, with the passive voice, by, on the part of; of time, from, since, after.* ā dextrō cornū, *on the right wing.* ā fronte, *in front.* ā tergō, *on the rear.* ab īnfimō, *at the bottom.* ab utrōque latere, *on both sides.* ā parvīs, *from childhood* (VI. 21, 3). **ab milibus passum octo,** *eight miles off.*

abdītus, -a, -um, [part, of ābdo], adj., *concealed, secluded.* (VI. 34, 3).

abdō, -dere, -didī, -ditus, [ab + dō], 3, *put away, remove; conceal.* sē abdere, *to hide one's self.*

abdūcō, -dūcere, -dūxī, -ductus, [ab + dūcō], 3, *withdraw; lead away, take off* (I. 11, 3). [abduct.

abeō, -īre, -iī, -itūrus, [ab + eō], irr., *go away, depart.* (VI. 43; VII. 50).

abesse, see absum.

abiciō, -icere, -iēcī, -iectus, [ab + iaciō], 3, *throw away, throw down; hurl* (V. 48). [abject.

abiēs, -ietis, f., *fir tree, spruce.* (V. 12).

abiungō, -iungere,-iūnxī, -iūnctus, [ab + iūngo], 3, *unyoke; separate, part* (III. 56).

abscīdō, -cīdere, -cīdī,-cīsus, [abs + caedō], 3, *cut off* (III. 14); *lop off, cutaway* (VII. 73).

absēns, [part, of absum], adj., *absent.* sē absente, *in his absence.* [absent

absimilis, -e, [ab + similis], adj., *unlike.*

absistō, -sistere, -stistī, [ab + sistō], 3, *withdraw, go away.*

abstineō, -tinēre, -tinuī, -tentus, [abs + teneō], 2, *hold back; refrain from* (I. 22); *spare, give quarter* (VII. 47). [abstain.

abstrahō, -trahere, -trāxī, -trāctus, [abs + trahō], 3, *drag away, drag off, take away by force,* [abstract.

absum, -esse, āfuī, āfutūrus, [ab + sum], irr., *be distant, be absent* or *away from; be wanting, be lacking.* longē abesse, *to be far away.* ā bellō abesse, *to be exempt from military service* (VI. 14). tōtō bellō abessent, *they took no part in the entire war* (VII. 63).

abundō, -āre, -āvī, [ab + undo, from unda, wave], 1, *overflow; abound in; be well provided with* (VII. 14, 64). [abundant.

abūtor, -ūtī, -ūsus, [ab + ūtor], 3, dep., *use up, misuse; waste* (C. III. 90). [abuse.

ac, see atque.

accēdō, -cēdere, -cessī, -cessūrus, [ad + cēdō], 3, *come to, draw near, approach; be added.* propius accēdere, *to come nearer* [accede.

accelerō, -āre, -āvī, -ātus, [ad + celerō, from celer], 1, *make haste, hasten.* (VII. 87). [accelerate.

acceptus, -a, -um, comp. -ior, sup. -issimus, [part, of accipiō], adj., *acceptable, welcome, dear.* (I. 3).

accidō, -cidere, -cidī, [ad + cadō], 3, *fall* (III. 14, 25); *happen, occur, turn out; befall, fall to the lot of.* Impers., accidit, *it happens,* [accident.

accīdō, -cīdere, -cīdī, -cīsus, [ad + caedō], 3, *cut into.* (VI. 27).

accipiō, -cipere, -cēpī, -ceptus, [ad + capiō], 3, *take to one's self, receive, accept; hear of, learn; incur,* ignōminiam accipere, *to incur disgrace* (VII. 17). [accept.

acclīvis, -e, [ad, cf. clīvus], adj., *sloping; up-hill, rising.*

acclīvitās, -tātis, [acclīvis], f., *upward slope, ascent,* (II. 18). [acclivity.

Accō, -ōnis, m., (ak' ō), a leader among the Senones. (VI. 4, 44; VII. 1).

accommodātus, -a, -um, comp. -ior, sup. -issimus, [part. of accommodō], adj., *suited, adapted.* (III. 13). [accommodate.

accommodō, -āre, -āvī, -ātus, [ad + commodō, from commodus], 1, *adjust, put on.* (II. 21).

accūratē, comp. -ius, sup. -issime, [accūratus], adv., *carefully.* Comp., accūrātius, *with greater pains* (VI. 22).

accurrō, -currere, -cucurrī, or -currī, -cursum est, [ad +currō], 3, *run to* (III. 5), *hasten to* (I. 22).

accūsō, -āre, -āvī, -ātus, [ad + causa], 1, *call to account, find fault with; reproach, accuse* [accuse.

ācer, ācris, ācre, comp. acrior, sup. acerrimus, adj., *sharp; of fighting, fierce* (C. III. 72). [acrid.

acerbē, comp. acerbius, sup. acerbissimē, [acerbus], adv., *bitterly.* sī acerbius inopiam ferrent, *if they found the scarcity too severe* (VII. 17).

acerbitās, -tātis, [acerbus], f., *bitterness, sourness;* pl., *sufferings* (VII. 17). [acerbity.

acerbus, -a, -um, comp. -ior, sup. -issimus, [ācer], adj., *bitter, harsh.*

ācerrimē, see ācriter.

acervus, -ī, m., *heap, pile.* (II. 32).

Achillās, -ae, ['Α χ ι λ λ ᾱ Σ, 'Α χ ι λ λ ᾱ Ε Ν Σ], m., *Achillas* (a-kil' as), an official under the young King Ptolemy of Egypt in 49 B.C., one of the slayers of Pompey. (C. III. 104).

aciēs, -eī, f., *edge;* of the eye, *keen look* (I. 39); of an army, *line of battle-line, army in battle array, battle.*

acquīrō, -quīrere, -quīsīvī, -quīsītus, [ad + quaerō], 3, *get in addition; gain further.* aliquid acquīrere, *to gain anything further* (VII. 59). [acquire.

ācriter, comp. ācrius, sup. ācerrimē, [ācer], adv., *sharply, fiercely, with vigor, courageously.* cum ācriter resisterētur, *when a vigorous resistance was offered* (V. 3).

āctuārius, -a, -um, [agō], adj., *easily driven, swift.* nāvis āctuāria, *swift vessel,* driven by oars as well as sails, (V. 1). [actuary.

āctus, see agō.

Acūtius, -ī, m., *Acutius Rufus* (a-kū' sh(y)us rū' fus), a partizan of Pompey. (C. III. 83).

acūtus, -a, -um, comp. -ior, sup. -issimus, [part. of acuō, *sharpen*], adj., *sharpened, sharp,* [acute.

ad, prep, with acc., *to, towards, up to;* of place, *in the vicinity of at, near to, by, in the presence of, among, on;* of time, *till, to, up to, until;* of purpose, especially with the gerundive constr., *for, in order to, for the purpose of, in;* of other relations, *with regard to, according to, in respect to, in consequence of, as to, in;* with words of number, with adverbial force, *about.* ad Genavam, *in the vicinity of Geneva.* ad multam noctem, *till late at night.* ad extrēmum, *at last, finally.* ad nunc modum, *after this manner.* ad vesperum, *towards evening.* ad ūnum, *to a man.* ad exercitum manēre, *to remain with the army* (V. 53). ad duodecim, *about twelve.* ad virtūtem, *in respect to valor.* (C. II. 6).

adāctus, see adigō.

adaequō, -āre, -āvī, -ātus, [ad + aequō], 1, *make equal to, bring up to a level with* (III. 12); *be equal to,* adaequāre cursum, *keep up with* (I. 48), *keep abreast of* (V. 8). [adequate.

adamō, -āre, -āvī, -ātus, [ad + amō], 1, *conceive a love for, covet.* (I. 31).

Adbucillus, -ī, m., (ad-bū-sil' us), an Allobrogian, father of Roucillus and Egus. (C. III. 59).

addō, -dere, -didī, -ditus, [ad + dō], 3, *add, join to; lay on* (VII. 23). addunt etiam dē Sabīnī morte, *they tell (him), further, about the death of Sabinus* (V. 41) [add.

addūcō, -ducere, -dūxī, -ductus, [ad + dūcō], 3, *lead to, bring, bring up to a place; lead, draw; induce,* prevail upon, *influence.* in eam sē consuētūdinem addūxērunt, *they have so trained themselves* (IV. 1). [adduce.

adēmptus, see adimō.

adeō, -īre, -iī, -itum est, [ad + eō], irr., *go to, come near, draw near, approach; reach, visit.*

adeo, [ad + eo, from is], adv., *so far, to such a degree; so, so much.*

adeptus, see adipīscor.

adequitō, -āre, -āvī, [ad + equitō, from eques], 1, *ride towards; ride up to* (I. 46).

adhaerēscō, -haerēscere, -haesī, [ad + haerēscō], 3, *stick, adhere; remain clinging* (V. 48).

adhibeō, -hibēre, -hibuī, -hibitus, [ad + habeō], 2, *hold toward; bring forward, bring in, call in, summon, admit; use, employ.*

adhortor, -ārī, -ātus, [ad + hortor], 1, dep., *encourage, rally, exhort, rouse, urge.*sē ipsī adhortantur, *they urge one another* (VI. 37).

adhūc, [ad + hūc], adv., *hitherto, until now, as yet.* (III. 22).

adiaceō, -iacēre, -iacuī, [ad + iaceō], 2, *lie near, border upon, be adjacent.* (VI. 33). [adjacent.

Adiatunnus, -ī, m., (ā" di-a-tun'us), a leader of the Sotiates. (III. 22).

adiciō, -icere, -iēcī, -iectus, [ad + iaciō], 3, *throw to, hurl; throw up; join to, add.*adiectā plānitiē, *with a plain adjacent* (III. 1). aggere ad mūnītiōnēs adiectō, *throwing up a mound before the fortifications* (V. 9).

adigō, -igere, -ēgī, -āctus, [ad + agō], 3, *drive (to), drive in; of missiles, cast, hurl (to);* of piles, *drive home* (IV. 17); of a tower, *move up* (V. 43); of an oath, *bind* (VII. 67, C. I. 76).

adimō, -imere, -ēmī, -ēmptus, [ad + emō], 3, *take away* (V. 6, C. I. 7); *cut off* (VII. 81).

adipīscor, -ipīscī, -eptus, [ad + apīscor, reach], 3, dep., *gain, obtain, secure.* (V. 39). [adept-

aditus, -ūs, [adeō], m., *approach, access; way of approach, means of access.* facilem aditum habēre, *to be easy of access* (III. 25); pl. *landing-places* (IV. 20).

adiūdicō, -āre, -āvī, -ātus, [ad + iūdicō], 1, *award* by judicial decision, *adjudge.* (VII. 37). [adjudicate.

adiungō, -iungere, -iūnxī, -iūnctus, [ad + iungō], 3, *join to, attach; add, unite with; annex.* [adjunct.

adiūtor, -ōris, [adiuvō], m., *helper, confederate* (V. 38); *mediator* (V. 41).

adiuvō, -iuvāre, -iūvī, adiūtus, [ad + iuvō], 1, *help, assist, support; render assistance, be of assistance.* [adjuvant.

Admagetobriga, -ae, f., (ad" ma-je-tob' ri-ga), a place in Gaul. (I. 31).

administer, -trī, [ad + minister], m., *assistant, helper; officiating priest* (VI. 16).

administrō, -āre, -āvī, -ātus, [ad + ministrō], 1, *render assistance; manage, carry on, administer; arrange for, get ready;* of orders, *execute, carry out.* [administer.

admīror, -ārī, -ātus, [ad + mīror], 1, dep., *wonder at, be surprised at; admire.* māximē admīrandum vidēbātur, *it seemed most surprising.* [admire.

admisceō, -ēre, admiscuī, admixtus, [a + misceō], 2, *mingle with, mix with.* (C. III. 48). [admix.

admittō, -mittere, -mīsī, -missus, [ad + mittō], 3, *let go; admit, receive; become guilty of, commit; incur* (IV. 25, C. III. 64). **facinus admittere,** *to commit a crime,***dēdecus admittere,** *to incur disgrace,* **admissīs equīs,** *with their horses at top speed,* lit. *let go* (C. II. 34). [admit.

admodum, [ad + acc. of **modus**], adv., lit. *up to the measure; quite, very;* with numbers, *fully, at least.*

admoneō, -ēre, -uī, -itus, [ad + moneō], 2, *warn,* [admonish.

admonitus, -ūs, [**admoneō**], m., *suggestion, advice.* (C. III. 92).

adnō, -nāre, [ad + nō, *swim*], 1, *swim to.* (C. II. 44).

adolēscō, -olēscere, -olēvī, -ultus, [ad + olēscō, *grow*], 3, *grow up, reach maturity.* (VI. 18). [adolescent.

adorior, -orīrī, -ortus, [ad + orior], 4, dep., *fall upon, attack, assail.*

adortus, pf. part. of **adorior,** *having attacked, attacking.*

adsum, -esse, affuī, [ad + sum], irr., *be at hand, be present; assist, help* (VII. 62).

adulēscēns, -entis, [**adolēscō**], adj., *young.* As noun, m., *young man, youth.*

adulēscentia, -ae, [**adulēscēns**], f., *youth.* (I. 20; C. II. 38). [adolescence.

adulēscentulus, -ī, [dim. of **adulēscēns**], m., *very young man, stripling.* (III. 21).

adventus, -ūs, [**adveniō**], m., *coming, approach, arrival,* [advent.

adversārius, -a, -um, [**adversor**], adj., *opposed.* As noun, **adversārīus, -ī,** m., *opponent, enemy,* [adversary.

adversus, -a, -um, sup. **-issimus,.** [part. of **advertō**], adj., *turned towards, fronting, in front, facing, opposite; unfavourable, adverse, unsuccessful.* **adversō colle,** *up the hill* (II. 19). **adversō flūmine,** *up the stream* (VII. 60). **adversīs hostibus occurrunt,** *they meet the enemy face to face* (II. 24). **in adversum ōs,** *full in the face* (V. 35). **rēs adversae,** *misfortune, disasters* (VII. 30). [adverse.

adversus, [**advertō**], prep. with acc. only, *opposite to; against* (IV. 14).

advertō, -tere, -tī, -sus, [ad + vertō], 3, *turn to, direct.* **animum advertō,** *notice, observe.* [advert.

advocō, -āre, -āvī, -ātus, [ad + vocō], 1, *call.* (VII. 52). [advocate.

advolō, -āre, -āvī, [ad + volō, *fly*], 1, *fly to; hasten to, rush upon.*

aedificium, -ī, [**aedificō**], n., *building.* [edifice.

aedificō, -āre, -āvī, -ātus, [**aedēs,** *building,* + FAC, in **faciō**], 1, *build, construct.*

Aeduus, -a, -um, adj., *Aeduan.* As noun, **Aeduus, -ī,** m., *an Aeduan;* pl., *Aeduans, the*

Aedui, (ed'ū-ī *or* ej' u-ī), a Gallic people, between the upper waters of the Sequana *(Seine)* and the Liger *(Loire)*, in alliance with the Romans before Caesar's arrival in Gaul and prominent throughout the Gallic War.

aeger, -gra, -grum, adj., *sick.* As noun, **aegrī, -ōrum,** m., pl., *the sick* (V. 40, C. III. 75).

aegerrimē, see **aegrē.**

aegrē, comp. **aegrius,** sup. **aegerrimē,** [**aeger**], adv., *with difficulty, scarcely, hardly,* **aegerrimē,** *with the greatest difficulty* (I. 13).

Aegyptus, -ī, [Α Ι Υ Η Π Τ Ο Σ], f., *Egypt.* (C. III. 104).

Aemilius, -ī, m., *Lucius Aemilius* (e-mil' i-us), a decurion in charge of a squad of Gallic cavalry. (I. 23).

aequāliter, [**aequālis,** *equal*], adv., *evenly, uniformly.* (II. 18).

aequinoctium, -ī, [**aequus + nox**], n., *equinox.* (IV. 36; V. 23). [equinox.

aequitās, -tātis, [**aequus**], f., *evenness; justness, fairness.* **animī aequitās,** *contentment* (VI. 22). [equity.

aequō, -āre, -āvī, -ātus, [**aequus**], 1, *equalize, make equal.* [equate.

aequus, -a, -um, comp. **aequior,** sup. **aequissimus,** adj., *level, even, flat; fair, just, equitable; like, equal; favourable, advantageous.* **aequō animō,** *with tranquil mind, without anxiety.***aequō Mārte,** *in a contest on equal footing* (VII. 19).

aerāria, -ae, [**aerārius,** *of copper*], 1., *copper mine.* (III. 21).

aerārium, -ī, [**aerārius,** *of copper*], n., *the public treasury* in Rome, *the treasury.* (C. I. 6).

aerātus, -a, -um, [**aes,** through *aerō, -āre*], adj., *sheathed with copper* or *bronze.* (C. II. 3).

aes, aeris, n., *copper; bronze,* an alloy of copper and tin; *money.* **aes aliēnum,** (lit., *another's money*), *debt* (VI. 13).

aestās, -tātis, f., *warm season, summer.*

aestimātiō, -ōnis, [**aestimō**], f., *valuation, appraisement.* [estimation.

aestimō, -āre, -āvī, -ātus, [**aes**], 1, *value, appraise, estimate; regard, consider.* [estimate.

aestīvus, -a, -um, [**aestās**], adj., *of summer.*

aestuārium, -ī, [**aestus**], n., *place overflowed at high tide,* (salt) *marsh.* (II. 28; III. 9). [estuary.

aestus, -ūs, m., *heat; tide.***ad aestūs vītandōs,** *to ward off the heat* (VI. 22). **minuente aestū,** *at ebb tide* (III. 12).

aetās, -tātis, f., *age, time of life; old age.* **aetāte cōnfectus,** *advanced in years.* **puerīlis aetās,** *age of childhood.* **per aetātem,** *by reason of age.*

aeternus, -a, -um, [for *aeviternus,* from **aevum**], adj., *everlasting, perpetual.* (VII. 77). [eternal.

Aetōlia, -ae, [Α Ι Τ Ω Λ Ι Α], f., (ē-tō'li-a), a

province of Greece, south of Epirus. (C. III. 61).

afferō, -ferre, attulī, allātus, [ad + ferō], irr., *bring, convey, deliver; bring forward, allege; produce, cause, occasion.* [afferent.

afficiō, -ficere, -fēcī, -fectus, [ad + faciō], 3, *do something to, treat, use; visit with, afflict, trouble, weaken, impair.* **beneficiō afficere,** *to treat with kindness* (I. 35; VII. 37). **laetitiā afficit,** *fills with joy* (V. 48). **māgnā difficultāte afficī,** *to be involved in great embarrassment* (VII. 6). **māgnō dolōre afficī,** *to be greatly annoyed* (I. 2). **māgnā affectus sollicitūdine,** *filled with deep anxiety* (VII. 40). **suppliciō afficere,** *to punish, visit* with punishment (I. 27); [affect.

affīgō, -fīgere, -fīxī, -fixus, [ad + fīgō], 3, *fasten to.* [affix.

affingō, -fingere, -fīnxī, -fictus, [ad + fingō], 3, *fashion; of a report, embellish* (VII. 1).

affīnitās, -tātis, [affīnis, from ad + fīnis], f., *relationship* by marriage, *kinship, connection.* [affinity.

affīrmātiō, -ōnis, [affirmō], f., *assurance.* (VII. 30). [affirmation.

affīxus, see **affīgō.**

afflīctō, -āre, -āvī, -ātus, [freq. of afflīgō], 1, *shatter, damage* (IV. 29); *strand, wreck* (III. 12).

afflīgō, -flīgere, -flīxī, -flīctus, [ad + flīgō, *strike*], 3, *dash against; throw down, knock down; shatter, damage.* [afflict.

affore (= **affutūrus esse**), future infinitive of **adsum.**

Āfrānius, -ī, m., *Lucius Afranius,* (a-frā′ ni-us), a lieutenant of Pompey defeated by Caesar in Spain in 49 B.C. (C. III. 83, 88).

Āfrica, -ae, f., (af′ri-ka), the Roman province of Africa. (C. II. 37).

Āfricus, -a, -um, [Āfrica], adj., *of Africa.* As noun, **Āfricus, -ī,** m. (originally sc. **ventus**), *southwest wind* (V. 8).

āfuisse, āfutūrus, see **absum.**

Agedincum, -ī, n., (aj-e-ding′ kum), chief city of the Senones, now *Sens.*

ager, agrī, m., *land* under cultivation, *field, territory, domain;* pl. *lands, territory, country, the country.***agrī cultūra,** *farming, agriculture.* **nihil agrī,** *no land* (IV. 1).

agger, -geris, [aggerō, ad + gerō], m., *that which is brought to a place, material for an embankment, filling* of earth and timber; *earth; embankment, mound, dike; rampart.* **aggerem petere,** *to get materials for the rampart* (II. 20). **aggerem exstruere,** *to build a rampart* (VII. 72). **multō aggere,** *with much earth* (VII. 23).

aggredior, -gredī, -gressus, [ad + gradior, *walk, go*], 3, dep., *approach; go against, attack, fall upon.* [aggressive.

aggregō, -āre, -āvī, -ātus, [ad + gregō, from grex, *flock*], 1, *bring together, join.* **sē aggregāre,**

to place one's self with (IV. 26), *to join one's self to* (VI. 12). [aggregate.

agitō, -āre, -āvī, -ātus, [freq. of agō], 1, *drive onward, impel; stir up, discuss* (VII. 2). [agitate.

agmen, -minis, [agō], n., *army on the march, marching column; line of march,* **agmen claudere,** *to bring up the rear* (I. 25, II. 19). **novissimum agmen,** *the rear.* **prīmum agmen,** *the van.* **in agmine,** *on the march* (III. 24, VII. 66).

agnōscō, -ere, agnōvī, [ad + gnōscō], 3, *recognize.* (C. II. 6).

agō, agere, ēgī, āctus, 3, *set in motion, drive, move forward; direct, conduct, guide; incite, urge; press forward, chase, pursue; drive off* as plunder, *rob; do, act, transact, perform; manage, carry on, accomplish; treat, discuss, confer, plead with;* of time, *spend, pass, live;* of court, *hold;* of sheds and towers, *bring up.* **conventūs agere,** *to hold court.***grātiās agere,** *to thank.* **vīneās agere,** *to bring up the vineae.* **cunīculōs agere,** *to extend the mines.* [act.

alacer, -cris, -cre, comp. **alacrior,** adj., *lively; eager, in high spirits.*

alacritās, -tātis, [alacer], f., *liveliness; enthusiasm.* [alacrity.

ālārius, -a, -um, [āla, *wing*], adj., *of the wing.* As noun, **ālāriī, -ōrum,** m., pl., *auxiliary troops posted on the wings, wing-men.*

Albicī, -ōrum, m., pl, (al′bi-sī), a small warlike people living north of Massilia. (C. II. 6).

albus, -a, -um, adj., *white.* **plumbum album,** *tin* (V. 12). [album.

alcēs, -is, f., *moose,* European *elk.* (VI. 27).

Alesia, -ae, f., (a-lē′sh[y]a *or* a-lē′zh [y]a), chief city of the Mandubians, now *Alise-Sainte-Reine.* (VII. 68-90).

Alexandrīa, -ae, [ΑΛΕΞΑΝΔΡΕΙΑ], f., (al-eg-zan′ dri-a), capital of Egypt. (C. III. 103, 104).

ali-, the form of **alius** in composition.

aliās, [alius], adv., *at another time.* **aliās. . .aliās,** *at one time. . .at another, sometimes . . . sometimes, now . . . now.* [alias.

aliēnō, -āre, -āvī, -ātus, [aliēnus], 1, *alienate, estrange.* **aliēnātā mente,** *deprived of reason* (VI. 41) [alienate.

aliēnus, -a, -um, [alius], adj., *belonging to another, another's; strange, foreign; unsuitable, unfavorable, disadvantageous.* As noun, **aliēnissimī, -ōrum,** sup., m., pl., *entire strangers* (VI. 31). [alien.

aliō, [alius], adv., *to another place, elsewhere.* (VI. 22).

aliquamdiū, [aliquī, diū], adv., *for some time, for a while.*

aliquandō, [alī- + quandō], adv., *at some time or other, sometime; at length* (VII. 27, 77).

aliquantus, -a, -um, [ali- + quantus], adj., *some, considerable.* Neut., **aliquantum,** as noun, *a little, somewhat.* **aliquantum itineris,** *some distance* (V. 10).

aliquī, aliqua, aliquod, [ali + qui], indefinite pronominal adj., *some, any, some other.*

aliquis (rarely **aliquī**), **aliqua, aliquid,** nom. and acc. pl., n., **aliqua,** [ali- + quis], indefinite pron., *some one, any one, anybody;* pl., *some, any* Neut., **aliquid,** *something, somewhat, anything.* **aliquid novī cōnsilī,** *some new scheme or other* (IV. 32). **aliquid calamitātis,** *some disaster* (V. 29). **aliquid sublevāre,** *to help somewhat* (I. 40).

aliquot [ali- + quot], num. adj., indecl., *some, several.*

aliter, [alis, alius], adv., *otherwise, differently.* **aliter ac,** *otherwise than, different from what.*

alius, -a, -ud, dat. **aliī,** adj., *another, some other, other, different, else,* **alius . . . alius,** *one . . . another, the one. . . the other;* pl., **aliī. . . aliī,** *some . . . other;* often as noun, **alius,** *another,* **aliī,** *others.* **aliā rē,** *with anything else* (I. 26). **alius aliā causā illātā,** *one alleging one reason, another, another* (I. 39). **longē alius atque,** *very different from.*

allātus, see **afferō.**

allicíō, -licere, -lexī, [ad + laciō *entice*], 3, *attract, allure.*

Allobrogēs, -um, (acc. **Allobrogas,** (I. 14, VII. 64), m., pl., (a-lob' ro-jēz), a Gallic people in the northeastern part of the Province. Acc. sing., **Allobrogem,** *an Allobrogian* (C. III. 84). Fig. 192.

alō, alere, aluī, altus, 3, *nourish, increase; maintain, keep; rear, foster, raise.*

Alpēs, -ium, 3, f., pl., *Alps,* general term for the mountains separating Cisalpine Gaul from Transalpine Gaul and Germany.

alter, -era, -erum, gen. **alterīus** or **alterius,** adj., often with the force of a noun, *one of two, the other, another; second.* **alter . . . alter,** *the one . . . the other.* **alterī . . . alterī,** *the one division, the one party . . . the other.* **ē quibus alter,** *one of whom* (V. 3). [alter.

alternus, -a, -um, [alter], adj., *in turn, alternate.* (VII. 23). [alternate.

alteruter, -tra, -trum, pronominal adj., *either of two.* (C. III. 90).

altitūdō, -inis, [altus], f., *height, depth;* of a beam, *thickness* (III. 13). [altitude.

altus, -a, -um, comp. **-ior,** sup. **-issimus,** [part. of **alō**], adj., *high, deep.* As noun, **altum, -ī,** n., *the deep, the open sea.*

alūta, -ae, f., *soft leather.* (III. 13).

am-, see **ambi-.**

ambactus, -ī, m., *vassal, dependant.* (VI. 15).

Ambarrī, -ōrum, m., pl., (am-bar' rī), a people east of the Arar *(Saône),* near its junction with the Rhone. (I. 11, 14).

ambi-, amb-, am-, an-, prep. found only in composition, *round about, around.*

Ambiānī, -ōrum, m., pl., (am-bi-ā'nī), a small state in Belgic Gaul. Fig. 193.

Ambibariī, -ōrum, m., pl. (am-bi-bā'ri-ī), a small state on the northwest coast of Gaul. (VII. 75).

Ambiliatī, -ōrum, m., pi., (am"bi-li'a-tī), a small state in Central Gaul. (III. 9).

Ambiorīx, -īgis, m., (am-bī'o-riks), a leader of the Eburones, who destroyed the Roman force under Sabinus and Cotta, and inspired the attack on Cicero's camp.

Ambivaretī, -ōrum, m., pi., (am-bi-var' e-tī), a people in Central Gaul, clients of the Aeduans.

Ambivaritī, -ōrum, m., pl. (am-bi-var'i-tī), a small state in Belgic Gaul. (IV. 9).

ambō, -ae, -ō, [cf. ambi-], adj., often used as noun, *both.* (V. 44, C. II. 6.)

āmentia, -ae, [āmēns, from ā + mēns], f., *madness, folly.*

āmmentum, -ī, n., *thong, strap,* for hurling a dart. (V. 48).

amīcitia, -ae, [amīcus], f., *friendship;* of a state, *friendship, alliance.*

amīcus, -a, -um, comp. **-ior,** sup. **-issimus,** [amō], adj., *friendly, faithful, well-disposed.* [amicable.

amīcus, -ī, [amō], m., *friend, ally.*

āmittō, -mittere, -mīsī, -missus, [ā + mittō], 3, *send away; let go, let slip, lose.*

amor, -ōris, [amō], m., *affection, love.*

amplificō, -āre, -āvī, -ātus, [amplus + faciō], 1, *make large, increase; extend.* [amplify.

amplitūdō, -inis, [amplus], f., *breadth, size; greatness, dignity.* [amplitude.

amplius, [comp. of **amplē,** from **amplus**], sup. **amplissimē,** adv., *more, further.*

amplus, -a, -um, comp. **-ior,** sup. **-issimus,** adj., *large* in extent, *great, extensive; distinguished, splendid, noble, prominent.* As noun, **amplius,** comp., n., *more,* **amplius obsidum,** *more hostages* (VI. 9). [ample.

an, inter. conj., *or, or rather, or indeed,* **-ne .. . an,** or **utrum . . . an,** *whether . . . or.*

an-, see **ambi-.**

Anartēs, -ium, m., pl., (an-är' tēz), a tribe on the Tibiscus *(Theiss),* in Dacia *(Hungary).*

Ancalitēs, -um, m., pl., (an-cal' i-tēz), a British tribe. (V. 21).

anceps, -cipitis, [an- + CAP in **caput**], adj., *two-headed, twofold, double.* **anceps proelium,** *battle on two fronts.*

ancora, -ae, [ΑΓΚΥΡΑ], f., *anchor.* **in ancorīs,**

at anchor. **tollere ancoram,** *to weigh anchor* (IV. 23). [anchor.

Andecumborius, -ī, m., (an" de-com-bō' ri-us), a leader among the Remi.

Andēs, -ium, or **Andī, -ōrum,** m., pl., (an' dēz, or an' dī), a Gallic people north of the Liger (*Loire*).

ānfrāctus, -ūs, [an-, cf. **frangō**] m., *curve* in a path or road, *bend, turn.* (VII. 46).

angulus, -ī, m., *corner.* (V. 13). [angle.

angustē, comp, **-ius,** sup. **-issimē,** [angustus], adv., *closely, in close quarters; scantily, sparingly.*

angustiae, -ārum, [angustus], f., pl., *narrow place, narrow part, defile, narrowness; straits, difficulties, perplexity; scarcity.*

angustus, -a, -um, comp. **-ior,** sup. **-issimus,** [cf. **angō,** *squeeze*], adj., *contracted, narrow, close.* Neut. as noun, **angustum, -ī,** *crisis* (II. 25); **rēs erat in angustō,** *matters had reached a crisis* (II. 25).

anima, -ae, f., *breath; soul, life* (VI. 14). [animate.

animadversiō, -ōnis, [animadvertō], f., *consideration; punishment* (C. III. 60). [animadversion.

animadvertō, -tere, -tī, -sus, [animus + advertō], 3, *turn the mind to, attend to; notice, observe, perceive.* **in eum animadvertō,** *inflict punishment upon him,* as we say "attend to him." (I. 19). [animadvert.

animal, -ālis, [anima], n., *living being, animal.* (VI. 17, 19). [animal.

animus, -ī, m., *soul, mind, consciousness; disposition, feelings; courage, spirit, temper, resolution.* **esse in animō,** *to intend.* [animus.

annōtinus, -a, -um, [annus], adj., *of the year before, last year's.* (V. 8).

annus, -ī, m., *year,* [annual.

annuus, -a, -um, [annus], adj., *of a year, yearly, annual.* (I. 16). [annuity.

ānser, -eris, m., *goose.* (V. 12).

ante, adv. and prep.:
(1) As adv., *in front; before, previously.* **ante quam,** *before.* **paulō ante,** *a little while before, a short time previously.* **paucīs ante diēbus,** *a few days before.*
(2) As prep., with acc., *before, in front of in advance of*

anteā, [ante + eā], adv., *previously, before, formerly.*

antecēdō, -cēdere, -cessī, [ante + cēdō], 3, go in advance, outstrip; *anticipate* (C. III. 6); *surpass, excel.* [antecedent.

antecursor, -ōris, [antecurrō], m., lit., fore-runner; pl., advance *guard, vanguard* (V. 47).

anteferō, -ferre, -tulī, -lātus, [ante + ferō], irr., *carry in front; place before, prefer* (V. 44).

antemna, -ae, f., *sail-yard.* [antennae.

antepōnō, -pōnere, -posuī, -positus, [ante + pōnō], 3, *place before; prefer, value above* (IV. 22).

antesignānus, -ī, [ante signum], m., *one in front of a standard;* pl., **antesignānī, -ōrum,** *soldiers before the standards* (C. III. 84).

antevertō, -tere, -tī, [ante + vertō], 3, *place before, take precedence.*

antīquitus [antīquus], adv., *in former times, long ago, anciently.*

antīquus, -a, -um, comp. **-ior,** sup. **-issimus,** [ante], adj., *old, former, old-time, ancient.* [antique.

Antistius, -ī, m., *Gaius Antistius Reginus* (an-tis' ti-us re-jī' nus), a lieutenant of Caesar.

Antōnius, -ī, m., *Marcus Antonius,* (mär' kus an-tō' ni-us), *Mark Antony* (born 83, died 30 B.C.), a lieutenant of Caesar in Gaul in 52 and 51 B.C., and afterwards in the Civil War; member of the Second Triumvirate, and rival of Octavianus. (VII. 81; C. III. 89).

aperiō, -perīre, -peruī, -pertus, 4, *open, uncover.* (VII. 22). [aperient.

apertē, -ius, -issimē, [apertus], adv., *openly, clearly, manifestly.*

apertus, -a, -um, comp. **-ior,** sup. **-issimus,** [part. of **aperiō**], adj., *open, uncovered; exposed, unprotected.* **loca aperta,** *open country.* **latus apertum,** *open flank, exposed flank.*

Apollō, -inis, m., (a-pol' ō), a divinity worshiped by the Greeks and Romans, identified by Caesar with a Gallic deity, (VI. 17).

Apollōnia, -ae, [' Α Π Ο Λ Λ Ω Ν Ι Α], f., (ap-o-lō'ni-a), a city in the Roman province of Macedonia, near the Adriatic Sea, about fifty miles south of Dyrrachium. (C. III. 75).

apparō, -āre, -āvī, -ātus, [ad + parō], 1, *prepare, make ready, get ready.* [apparatus.

appellō, -pellere, -pulī, -pulsus [ad + pellō], 3, *drive to, bring in;* of ships, *make for, put in, land.*

appellō, -āre, -āvī, -ātus, 1, *address, accost, call to, appeal to; call by name, name.* [appellate.

appetō, -petere, -petīvī, or **-iī, -petītus,** [ad + petō], 3, *strive after, seek; approach, draw near.* [appetite.

Appius, -ī, m., (ap' i-us), a Roman first name.

applicō, -plicāre, -plicāvī or **-plicuī, -plicātus,** [ad + plicō], fold, join. **sē applicāre ad,** *to lean against* (VI. 27). [applicant.

apportō, -āre, -āvī, -ātus, [ad + portō], 1, *carry to, bring.* (V. 1).

approbō, -āre, -āvī, -ātus, [ad + probō], 1, *approve, favour,* [approve.

appropinquō, -āre, -āvī, -ātum est, [ad + propinquō], 1, *approach, come near, draw near.*

appulsus, see **appellō.**

Apr., = **Aprilis.** (I. 6).

Aprilis, -e, adj., *of April.*

aptus, -a, -um, comp. **-ior,** sup. **-issimus,** adj., *fitted, adapted, suited; suitable, appropriate, ready.* [apt.

apud, prep., with acc. only, *at, with, near, close to, by; among, in the presence of.*

aqua, -ae, f., *water.* **mēnsūrae ex aquā,** *water-clocks* (V. 13). [aqueous.

aquātiō, -ōnis, [aquor], f., *obtaining water.* (IV. 11).

aquila, -ae, f., *eagle;* as an eagle of silver or gold on the end of a pole formed the chief ensign of the legion, *eagle, standard.* [aquiline.

Aquileia, -ae, f., (ak-wi-lē'ya), a city at the head of the Adriatic Sea. (I. 10).

aquilifer, -erī, [aquila + ferō], m., *bearer of the eagle, eagle-bearer.*

Aquītānia, -ae, f., (ak-wi-tā'ni-a), one of the three main divisions of Gaul.

Aquītānus, -a, -um, adj., *of Aquitania.* As noun, **Aquītānus, -ī,** m., *Aquitanian* (IV. 12); pl., *Aquitanians, Aquitani,* (ak-wi-tā' nī), inhabitants of Aquitania. (I. 1; III. 21).

aquor, -ārī, -atus, [aqua], 1, dep., *obtain water, get water.* (C. III. 97).

Arar, -aris, acc. **-im,** m., *Arar* (ā' rar) River, now *Saône* (sōn). It rises in the Vosges (vōzh) Mts., and flows southward into the Rhone.

arbiter, -trī, m., *witness; referee, commissioner* (V. 1). [arbiter.

arbitrium, -ī, [arbiter], n., *decision, arbitrament; authority.*

arbitror, -ārī, -ātus, [arbiter], 1, dep., *think, consider, believe.* [arbitrate.

arbor, -oris, f., *tree,* [arbor-vitae.

accessō, -sere, -sīvī, -sītus, 3, *cause to come, fetch; send for, summon, call in, invite.*

ārdeō, -ēre, ārsī, arsūrus, 2, *be on fire; be ablaze, be aroused; be eager, desire ardently.* [ardent.

Arduenna, -ae, f., (är-dū-en' na), *the Ardennes,* a forest-covered range of hills in the northeastern part of France, extending also into Belgium.

arduus, -a, -um, adj., *steep, high; hard, difficult.* [arduous.

Arecomicī, -ōrum, m., pi., (ar-e-kom' i-sī), a division of the Volcae, in the Province.

Arelās, -ātis, f., (är' e-las), a town in Southern Gaul, on the Rhone, north of Massilia; now *Arles.* (C. II. 5).

Aremoricus, -a, -um, [Celtic, **arē** = ad, + **mori,** = mare, 'by the sea'], adj., *Aremorican,* name applied to a group of small states along the northwest coast of Gaul (**Aremoricae cīvitātēs).**

argentum, -ī, n., *silver* (VI. 28); *silver-ware* (VII. 47; C. IN. 96). [argent.

argilla, -ae, f., *clay.* (V. 43). [argillaceous.

āridus, -a, -um, sup. **-issimus,** [āreō, *be dry*], adj., *dry.* As noun, **āridum, -ī,** n., *dry land, shore.* [arid.

ariēs, -ietis, m., *ram; battering-ram; prop, buttress* (IV. 17). [Aries.

Arīminum, -ī, n., (a-rim' i-num), a town in Italy on the Adriatic, the northernmost city in Italy proper; now *Rimini.* (C. I. 8).

Ariovistus, -ī, m., (a" ri-o-vis' tus), a German king, defeated by Caesar, 58 B.C.

Aristius, -ī, m., *Marcus Aristius,* (a-ris' ti-us), a military tribune. (VII. 42, 43).

arma, -ōrum, n., pl., *implements; implements of war, arms, armour, weapons;* of a ship, *equipment, tackle* (III. 14). **ad arma concurrere,** *to rush to arms.* **ab armīs discēdere,** *to lay down arms* (V. 41). **in armīs excubāre,** *to sleep under arms* (VII. 11). [arms.

armāmenta, -ōrum, [armō], n., pl., *implements; equipment;* of a ship, *rigging.* [armament.

armātūra, -ae, [armō], f., *armor, equipment.* **levis armātūrae peditēs,** *light infantry.* **levis armātūrae Numidae,** *light-armed Numidians* (II. 10). [armature.

armātus, -a, -um, sup. **armātissimus,** [part. of armō], adj., *armed, in arms, equipped.* As noun, **armātī, -ōrum,** m., pl., *armed men, warriors, soldiers.*

armō, -āre, -āvī, -ātus, [arma], 1, *provide with weapons, arm;* of a ship, *equip, fit out.* [arm.

Arpineius, -ī, m., *Gaius Arpineius,* (är-pi- nē' yus), a Roman knight, envoy of Caesar to Ambiorix. (V. 27, 28).

arripiō, -ripere, -ripuī, -reptus, [ad + rapiō], 3, *lay hold of, snatch.* (V. 33).

arroganter, comp. **-ius,** sup. [arrogāns], adv., *presumptuously, arrogantly.*

arrogantia, -ae, [arrogāns], f., *presumption, insolence,* [arrogance.

ars, artis, f., *skill; art, science* (VI. 17). [art.

artē, comp. **artius,** sup. **artissimē,** [artus], adv., *closely, tightly.*

articulus, -ī, [dim. of artus, *joint*], m., *joint, knuckle.* (VI. 27). [article.

artificium, -ī, [artifex, *artist*], n., *an art, trade; skill; craft, cunning.* [artifice.

artus, -a, um, comp. **-ior,** sup. **artissimus,** adj., *close;* of woods, *dense* (VII. 18).

Arvernus, -a, -um, adj., *of the Arverni, Arvernian.* As noun, **Arvernī, -ōrum,** m., pl., *Arvernians, the Arverni,* (är -ver nī), a powerful people about the upper part of the Elaver *(Allier);* their chief city, Gergovia, was unsuccessfully besieged by Caesar. Fig. 194.

arx, arcis, f., *citadel, stronghold.*

ascendō, -scendere, -scendī, -scēnsus, [ad + scandō, *climb*], 3, *ascend, climb up; mount.* [ascend.

ascēnsus, -ūs, [ascendō], m., *ascent, climbing; approach.*

ascīscō, ascīscere, ascīvī, ascītus, [ad + scīscō, *approve*], 3, *admit* to association with one's self, *accept.*

Asia, -ae, [Α ΣΙΑ], f., the Roman province *Asia,* (ā'sh[y]a, *or* ā' zh[y]a), including Phrygia, Lydia, Caria, and Mysia in Asia Minor. (C. III. 53).

aspectus, -ūs, [aspiciō, *look at*], m., *appearance, sight, look.* [aspect.

asper, -era, -erum, comp. -ior, sup. -rimus, adj., *rough, uneven; fierce, violent* (V. 45).

assiduus, -a, -um, [ad + SED, SID, in sedeō, *sit*], adj., *continuous, constant, incessant.* [assiduous.

assistō, -ere, astitī, [ad + sistō], 3, *stand near, stand by; appear* (VI. 18). [assist.

assuēfaciō, -facere, -fēcī, -factus, [assuētus + factō], 3, *accustom, habituate, familiarize, train.*

assuēscō, -suēscere, -suēvī, -suētus, [ad + suēscō, *become accustomed*], 3, *become accustomed to.* assuēscere ad hominēs, *to become domesticated* (VI. 28).

at, conj., *but, yet, but yet, at least.*

atque, ac, [ad + -que], conj.:
(1) Copulative, *and, and also, and even, and in particular.*
(2) Comparative, after words of likeness or unlikeness, *as, than.* idem atque, par atque, *the same as.* alius atque, *other than.* simul atque, *as soon as.*

Atrebās, -ātis, [Kel., = 'Possessor'], m., *an Atrebatian;* pl., *Atrebatians, the Atrebates,* (at-re-bā' tēz), a Belgic people.

Ātrius, -ī, m., *Quintus Atrius* (ā'trius), an officer in Caesar's army. (V. 9, 10).

attenuō, -āre, -āvī, -ātus, [ad + tenuō from tenuis], 1, *make thin; weaken, reduce in strength* (C. III. 89). [attenuate.

attexō, -ere, -texuī, attextus, [ad + texō], 3, *weave to, join on.* (V. 40).

Attiānus, -a, -um, [Attius], adj., *of Attius,* referring to P. Attius Varus. (C. II, 34).

attingō, -tingere, -tigī, -tāctus, [ad+ tangō], 3, *touch upon, touch; reach;* of territorial divisions, *border* on, extend to, adjoin.

Attius, -ī, m., *P. Attius Varus* (at' i-us vā'rus), *a lieutenant of Pompey in Africa.* (C. II. 34).

attribuō, -uere, -uī, -ūtus, [ad +tribuō], 3, *assign, allot.* [attribute.

attulī, see afferō.

Atuatuca, -ae, f., (at-ū-at' ū-ka), a stronghold in the territory of the Eburones,

Atuatucī, -ōrum, m., pl., (at-ū-at ū-sī), a warlike people on the left bank of the Meuse, descended from the Cimbrians and Teutons.

auctor, -ōris, [augeō], m., *originator, instigator; adviser, promoter, favorer.* auctōre hoste, *at the suggestion of the enemy* (V. 28). [author.

auctōritās, -tātis, [auctor], f., *influence, weight; prestige, authority, power.* [authority.

auctus, -a, -um, comp. auctior, [augeō], adj., *increased; rich.* (I. 43).

audācia, -ae, [audax], f., *boldness, daring, recklessness.* [audacity.

audācter, comp. audācius, sup. audācissimē, [audāx], adv., *boldly, courageously, fearlessly.*

audeō, audēre, ausus sum, 2, semi-dep., *venture, dare, risk; attempt.*

audiō, -īre, -īvī or -iī, -ītus, 4, *hear, listen to; hear of.* Present participle as Adj. in dictō audiens esse, *to be obedient to the word of command, to obey.* [audience.

audītiō, -ōnis, [audiō], f., *report, rumor, hearsay.* [audition.

augeō, augēre, auxī, auctus, 2, semi-dep., *increase, enlarge, augment, add to.* animus augētur, *courage is strengthened* (VII. 70).

Aulercus, -ī, m., *an Aulercan* (VII. 57); pl., *the Aulerci* (a-ler'si), a people of Central Gaul, of which Caesar mentions three branches, Brannovices (VII. 75), Cenomani (VII. 75), and Eburovices (III. 17, VII. 75).

Aulus, -ī, m., (â' lus), a Roman first name.

aureus, -a, -um, [aurum], adj., *of gold, golden.* (V. 12). [oriole.

aurīga, -ae, [aurea, *bridle,* + agō], m., *charioteer, driver.* (IV. 33).

auris, -is, f., *ear.* [aural

Aurunculeius, -i, m., *Lucius Aurunculeius Cotta,* (â" rung-kū-lē' yus kot' a), a lieutenant of Caesar, killed by the Eburones.

Auscī, -ōrum, m., pl., (â' sī), a people in the eastern part of Aquitania. (III. 27).

ausus, see audeo.

aut, conj., *or.* aut. . .aut, *either . . . or.* aut. . . aut. . . aut, *either . . . or. . . or.*

autem, conj., *but, however, on the contrary; and now, moreover.*

autumnus, -ī, m., *autumn.* [autumn.

auxiliāris, -e, [auxilium], adj., *auxiliary.* As noun, auxiliārēs, -ium, m., pl., *auxiliary troops, auxiliaries* (III. 25). [auxiliar.

auxilior, -ārī, -ātus, [auxilium], 1, dep., *render aid, assist, help.*

auxilium, -ī, [cf. augeō], n., *help, aid, assistance; relief, remedy, resource.* Pl., auxilia, *auxiliary troops, auxiliaries, allied forces.*

Avaricēnsis, -e, adj., *of Avaricum, at Avaricum.* (VII. 47).

Avaricum, -ī, n., (a-var'i-kum), largest and most strongly fortified city of the Bituriges, now *Bourges;* besieged and taken by Caesar, the inhabitants put to the sword.

avāritia, -ae, [**avārus,** *greedy*], f., *greed, covetousness.* [avarice.

āvehō, -vehere, -vexī, -vectus, [**ā + vehō**], 3, *carry off, carry away.*

āversus, -a, -um, sup. **āversissimus,** [part. of **āvertō**], adj., *turned away; behind, in the rear.* **āversum hostem,** *a retreating enemy, an enemy in flight.* **āversī ab hoste circumvenīrī,** *to be surrounded in the rear by the enemy* i.e. with their backs to the enemy (II. 26). [averse.

āvertō, -tere, -tī, -sus, [**ā + vertō**], 3, *turn away, turn aside, avert; divert, alienate, estrange.* [avert.

avis, -is, f., *bird.* (IV. 10). [aviation.

avus, -ī, m., *grandfather.*

Axona, -ae, f., (aks' o-na), a river in the southern part of Belgic Gaul, now *Aisne.*

B.

Bacēnis, -is, (sc. **silva**), f., (base' nis), a forest in Germany. (VI. 10).

Baculus, -ī, m., *Publius Sextius Baculus,* (bac' ū-lus), one of the bravest of Caesar's centurions. He distinguished himself in the battle with the Nervians (II. 25); his advice saved the day when Galba was attacked in the Alps (III. 5); and his heroic resistance checked a surprise attack on Cicero's camp (VI. 38).

Bagradās, or **Bagrada, -ae,** m., (bag' ra-das), an important river of Roman Africa, now *Medjerda.* (C. II. 38).

Baleārēs, -ium, [= ΒΑΛΙΑΡΕΙΣ, *slingers*], m., pl., (bal-e-ā'rēz), natives of the Balearic Islands, off the east coast of Spain; famous as slingers. (II. 7).

balteus, -ī, m., *belt, sword-belt.*

Balventius, -ī, m., *Titus Balventius,* (bal-ven' sh[y]-us), a brave centurion. (V. 35).

barbarus, -a, -um, [= ΒΑΡΒΑΡΟΣ], adj., *foreign, strange; rude, savage, uncivilized.* As noun, **barbarī, -ōrum,** m., pl., *strangers, foreigners; natives, barbarians.* [barbarous.

Basilus, -ī, m., *Lucius Minucius Basilus,* (mi-nū'sh[y]us bas' i-lus), an officer of Caesar, afterwards one of the conspirators against him; murdered in 43 B.C. on account of cruelty to his slaves.

Batāvī, -ōrum, m., pl., *the Batavians, Batavi,* (ba-tā' vī), a people dwelling near the mouth of the Rhine. (IV. 10).

Belgae, -ārum, m., pl., *the Belgians, Belgae,* (bel'jē), inhabitants of one of the three main divisions of Gaul, divided into many small states.

Belgium, -ī, n., (bel' j[y]um), *the land of the Belgians, Belgic Gaul, Belgium.* (V. 12, 25). [Belgium.

bellicōsus, -a, -urn, comp. **-ior,** sup. **-issimus,** [**bellicus**], adj., *warlike, fond of war.* (I. 10). [bellicose.

bellicus, -a, -um, [**bellum**], adj., *of war, martial, military.* (VI. 24).

bellō, -āre, -āvī, -ātus, [**bellum**], 1, *wage war, carry on war, fight.*

Bellovacī, -ōrum, m., pl., (be-lov'-a-sī), a powerful Belgic people.

bellum, -ī, n., *war, warfare,* **bellum gerere,** *to wage war.* **bellum īnferre,** *to make war.* **bellum parāre,** *to prepare for war.*

bene, comp. **melius,** sup. **optimē,** [**bonus**], adv., *well, ably, successfully.*

beneficiārius, -ī, [**beneficiārius, -a, -um,** from **beneficium**], m., *privileged soldier, who, by order of the commander, was exempt from ordinary tasks and detailed for special duties* (C. III. 88). [beneficiary.

beneficium, -ī, [**bene + faciō**], n., *kindness, favor, service.* [benefice.

benevolentia, -ae, [**benevolus**], f., *good will, friendly disposition, kindly feeling, friendship.* [benevolence.

Bibracte, -is, n., [bi-brak' tē], capital of the Aeduans, situated on a mountain now called *Mont Beuvray* (height, 2,690ft.).

Bibrax, -actis, f., (bī'braks), a town of the Remi, north of the Axona *(Aisne).* (II. 6).

Bibrocī, -ōrum, m., pl., (bib' ro-sī), a people in the southern part of Britain. (V. 21).

bīduum, -ī, [**bi-,** = **bis,** cf. **diēs**], n., *space of two days, two days.*

biennium, -ī, [**bi-,** = **bis,** cf. **annus**], n., *period of two years, two years' time.* (I. 3). [biennial.

Bigerriōnēs, -ōnum, m., pl., (bī" jer-ri-ō' nēz], a people in Aquitania. (III. 27).

bīnī, -ae, -a, [**bis**], distributive adj., *two by two, two each, by twos, two.*

bipedālis, -e, [**bi-,** = **bis,** + **pedalis,** from **pes**], .adj., *two feet in width, length, or height; two feet thick* (IV. 17).

bipertītō, [bipartītus, bi-, = **bis,** + **partītus**], adv., *in two divisions.* (I. 25; V. 32). [cf. bipertite.

bis, [for **duis,** cf. **duo**], num. adv., *twice.*

Biturīgēs, -um, m., pl., (bit-ū-rī' jēz), a people in Central Gaul (Fig. 195).

Boduognātus, -ī, m., (bod" ū-og-nā' tus), a leader of the Nervians. (II. 23).

Boiī, -ōrum, m., pl., *Boians, Boii* (bō' i-ī), a Celtic people once widely diffused over Central Europe (Fig. 196).

bonitās, -tātis, [**bonus**], f., *goodness, excellence;* of land, *fertility* (I. 28).

bonus, -a, -um, comp. **melior,** sup. **optimus,**

adj., *good, advantageous; pleasant, well-disposed, friendly,* **bonō animō esse,** *to be favorably disposed* (i. 6). As noun, **bonum,** n., *profit, advantage;* pl., **bona, -ōrum,** *goods, property, possessions,* [bonus; optimist.

bōs, bovis, gen. pl. **boum,** m. and f., *ox, bull, cow.* [bovine.

bracchium, -ī, [= B P A X I Q N], n., *arm, forearm.*

Brannovīcēs, -um, (bran-o-vī' sēz), m., pl., see **Aulercī.**

Brātuspantium, -ī, [Kel., = 'Valley of Judgment'], n., (brat-us-pan' sh[y]um), a stronghold of the Bellovaci. (II. 13).

brevis, -e, comp. **-ior,** sup. **-issimus,** adj., *short, brief,* [brief.

brevitās, -tātis, [**brevis**], f., *shortness* (II. 20); *smallness, small stature* (II. 30). [brevity.

breviter, comp. **-ius,** sup. **-īssimē,** [**brevis**], adv., *briefly, with few words, concisely.* (VII. 54).

Britannī, -ōrum, m., pl., *natives of Britain, Britons.*

Britannia, -ae, f., (bri-tan' i-a), *Britain.*

Britannicus, -a, -um, adj., *of Britain, British.* (V. 4).

brūma, -ae, [for *brevuma, sup. of **brevis,** sc. **diēs**], f., *winter solstice, shortest day; winter* (V. 13).

Brundisium, -ī, [B P E N T A Σ I O N], n., (brun-dizh' i-um), a city of Italy on the Adriatic, the principal port of embarcation for Greece; now *Brindisi.* (C. III. 87).

Brūtus, -ī, m., *Decimus Junius Brutus Albinus,* (jūn' yus brū'tus al-bī' nus), an officer of Caesar, both in the Gallic and in the Civil War; afterwards a conspirator against him.

būcinātor, -ōris, [**būcina,** *trumpet*], m., *trumpeter.* (C. II. 35).

C.

C, in expressions of number, = 100.

C, see **Gāius.**

Cabillōnum, -ī, n., an important city of the Aedui on the Arar, now *Châlon-sur-Saône.* (VII. 42, 90).

Cabūrus, -ī, m., *Gaius Valerius Caburus,* (va-lē'rj-us ka-bū'rus), a Gaul who received the Roman citizenship.

cacūmen, -inis, n., *end, point* (VII. 73); *peak, summit.* [cacuminous.

cadāver, -eris, [cf. **cadō**], n., *corpse, dead body.* [cadaver.

cadō, cadere, cecidī, cāsūrus, 3, *fall; be slain, die.* [chance.

Cadūrcī, -ōrum, m., pl., (ka-der' sī), a people in Aquitania. Sing. **Cadūrcus, -ī,** m., *a cadurcan* (VII. 5).

caedēs, -is, [**caedō**], f., *killing; slaughter, murder, massacre.*

caedō, caedere, cecīdī, caesus, 3, *cut, cut down; cut to pieces, slay.*

caelestis, -e, [**caelum**], adj., *heavenly.* As noun, **caelestēs, -ium,** m., pl., *the gods* (VI. 17). [celestial.

caelum, -ī, n., *heaven, the heavens, the sky.* (C. II. 5).

caerimōnia, -ae, f., *religious ceremony, sacred rite.* (VII. 2). [ceremony.

Caerōsī, -ōrum, m., pl., (se-rō'sī) a people in Belgic Gaul. (II. 4).

caeruleus, -a, -um, adj., *deep blue, dark blue.* (V. 14). [cerulean.

Caesar, -aris, m.:
(1) *Gaius Julius Caesar* (gā'yus jūl' yus sē' zar).
(2) *Lucius Julius Caesar,* consul in 64 B.C., a distant relative of the great Caesar, under whom he served as lieutenant, in 52 B.C. (VII. 65).

caespes, -itis, m., *sod, turf.*

calamitās, -tātis, f., *loss, damage; disaster, defeat.* [calamity.

Caletī, -ōrum, also **Caletēs, -um,** m., pl., (kal' e-tī, kal' e-tēz), a people near the mouth of the Sequana (*Seine*).

callidus, -a, -um, comp. **-ior,** sup. **-issimus,** [**calleō,** *be skillful*], adj., *skillful; tactful, crafty* (iii. 18).

cālō, -ōnis, m., *soldier's servant, camp servant.*

campester, -tris, -tre, [**campus**], adj., *of level ground, flat, level.*

campus, -ī, m.. *plain,* [campus.

Camulogenus, -ī, [Kel., = 'Son of Camulos,' i.e. 'Son of Mars'], m., (kam-ū-loj' e-nus), an Aulercan, commander of the Parisii against Labienus.

Canīnius, -ī, m., *Gaius Caninius Rebilus,* (ka-nin' i-us reb' i-lus), a lieutenant of Caesar's in the latter part of the Gallic War, and in the Civil War; made consul by Caesar for a few hours to fill a vacancy on the last day of December, B.C. 45. (VII. 83, 90; C. II. 34).

canō, canere, cecinō, 3, *sing; of a musical instrument, sound, play.*

Cantabrī, -ōrum, m., pl., *Cantabrians, Cantabri* (kan' ta-brī) a warlike people in northern Spain.

Cantium, -ī, n., *Kent, Cantium,* (kan-sh[y] um), a district in the southeast part of England.

capillus, -ī, [cf. **caput**], m., *hair of the head, hair.* [capillary.

capiō, capere, cēpī, captus, 3, *take, get; seize, capture; occupy, take possession of; select, win over, charm, captivate; receive; of vessels, reach, make; deceive* (I. 40). **initium capere,** *to begin.* **cōnsilium capere,** *to form a plan.* **dolōrem capere,** *to be grieved.* [capture.

Capitōlium, -ī, n., *the Capitol,* the temple of Jupiter, Juno, and Minerva on the Capitoline hill in Rome; sometimes referring to the hill as a whole, *the Capitoline hill.* (C. I.6). [Capitol.

capra, -ae, [**caper**], f., *she-goat.*

captīvus, -a, -um, [cf. **capiō**], adj., *taken prisoner, captured* (C. II. 5). As noun, **captīvus, -ī,** m., *captive, prisoner* (VI. 43). [captive.

captus, -a, -um, see **capiō.**

captus, -ūs, [**capiō**], m., *capacity; understanding, notion* (IV. 3).

Capua, -ae, f., (kap' ū-a), a city in Italy, in Campania. (C. III. 71).

caput, -itis, n., *head;* by metonymy, *person, man, life, safety;* of a river, *mouth* (IV. 10). **capite dēmissō,** *with the head bowed down* (I. 32). **capitis poena,** *capital punishment* (VII. 71). **duo milia capitum,** *two thousand souls.* [capital.

Carcasō, -ōnis, f., (kär' ka-sō), a town in southern Gaul, now *Carcassonne* (III. 20).

careō, -ēre, -uī, -itūrus, 2, *be without, lack, want.* (VI. 38; VII. 17).

carīna, -ae, f., *keel of a ship.*

Carnutēs, -um, m., pl., (kär' nū- tēz), a people in Central Gaul, north of the Liger (*Loire*); chief city, Cena-bum (Fig. 197).

carō, carnis, f., *flesh, meat,* [carnage.

carpō, -ere, -sī, -tus, 3, *pluck; censure, criticise* (iii. 17). [carp.

carrus, -ī, m., *cart, wagon.* [car.

cārus, -a, -um, comp. **-ior,** sup. **carissimus,** adj., *dear, precious.*

Carvilius, -ī, m., (kar-vil' i-us), one of four British rulers in Kent. (V. 22).

casa, -ae, f., *hut, cottage, barrack.*

cāseus, -ī, m., *cheese.* (VI. 22).

Cassī, -ōrum, m., pl., (kas' ī), a tribe in Britain. (V. 21).

Cassiānus, -a, -um, [**Cassius**], adj., *of Cassius.* (I. 13).

cassis, -idis, f., *helmet* of metal.

Cassius, -ī, m., *Lucius Cassius Longinus,* (kash' [y]us lon-jī' nus), praetor 111 B.C.; when consul, 107 B.C., he engaged in battle with the Tigurians in the territory of the Allobroges, and was defeated and slain. (I. 7, 12).

Cassivellaunus, -ī, [Kel., = 'the wonderfully Good'], m., *Cassivellaunus* (kas'' i-ve-lâ' nus), *Caswallon,* leader of the British army against Caesar in 54 B.C.

castellum, -ī, [dim. of **castrum**], n., *redoubt, fortress, stronghold.* [castle.

Casticus, -i, m., (kas' ti-kus), a prominent Sequanian. (I. 3).

castīgō, -āre, -āvī, -ātus, 1, *reprove.* (C. III. 60). [castigate.

castra, -ōrum, n., [pl. of **castrum,** *fortress*], *camp, encampment; military service* (I. 39); *day's march* (VII. 36). **castra movēre,** *to break camp.* **castra pōnere,** *to encamp, camp.* **in castrīs**

ūsum habēre, *to have experience in military service* (I. 39). **quīntīs castrīs,** *in five day's marches* (VII. 36). [-chester *in* Ro-chester, etc.

cāsus, -ūs, [**cadō**], m., *fall; chance, occurrence, happening, fortune; opportunity, event; accident, mishap, evil plight, death.* **cāsū,** *by chance.* **ad extrēmum cāsum,** *for the last extremity* (III. 5). [case.

Catamantāloedis, -is, [Kel., = 'Man of Even Temper'], m., (kat-a-man-ta-lē' dis), a leader among the Sequanians before Caesar's time. (I. 3).

catēnae, -ārum, f., pl., *chains; fetters.*

Caturīgēs, -um, [Kel., = 'Battle Kings'], m., pl., (kat-ū-ri' jēz), a Gallic people in the eastern part of the Province. (I. 10).

Catuvolcus, -ī, m., (kat-ū-vol' kus), a ruler of the Eburones; despairing of success in the war against Caesar, he took poison. (V. 24, 26; VI. 31).

causa, -ae, f., *cause, ground, reason; pretext, excuse; condition, state, case, suit.* **causā,** with gen., *for the sake of, on account of.* [cause.

cautē, comp. **-ius,** sup. **-issimē,** [**cautus,** from **caveō**], adv., *cautiously, carefully.* (V. 49).

cautēs, -is, f., *jagged rock, cliff.* (III. 13).

Cavarillus, -ī, [Kel., = from word meaning 'giant'], m., (kav-a-ril' us), an Aeduan of high rank. (VII. 67).

Cavarīnus, -ī, [Kel., = from word meaning 'giant'], m., (kav-a-rī' nus), a ruler among the Senones. (V. 54; VI. 5).

caveō, cavēre, cāvī, cautūrus, 2, *be on one's guard, beware of, take precaution; give security.* [cautious.

Cavillōnum, -ī, n., (kav-i-lō' num), an Aeduan city on the Arar, now *Châlon-sur-Saône.* (VII. 42, 90).

Cebenna, -ae, f., [Kel., = 'Back'], *Cebenna* (se-ben'a), *the Cévennes,* a mountain range in southern Gaul, about 250 miles long.

cēdō, cēdere, cessī, cessūrus, 3, *go away, depart, withdraw, retreat; yield, give up to; abandon.* **cēdentēs īnsequī,** *to follow up the retreating enemy* (II. 19). [cede.

celer, -eris, -ere, comp. **-ior,** sup. **celerrimus,** adj., *quick, speedy.*

celeritās, -tātis, [**celer**], f., *speed, quickness, swiftness, rapidity, dispatch.* [celerity.

celeriter, comp. **celerius,** sup. **celerrimē,** [**celer**], adv., *quickly, speedily, at once, immediately.*

cēlō, -āre, -āvī, -ātus, 1, *conceal, hide, keep secret.* (II. 32; VII. 80).

Celtae, -ārum, m., pl., *Celts, Celtae* (sel'tē) inhabitants of central Gaul, divided into many states.

Celtillus, -ī, m., (sel-til' us), an Arvernian

ruler, father of Vercingetorix. (VII. 4).

Cēnabēnsēs, -ium, [**Cēnabum**], m., pl., *the inhabitants of Cenabum.*

Cēnabum, -ī, n., (sen' a-bum), chief city of the Carnutes, later called *Aurelianensis Urbs,* whence comes *Orleans,* name of the city on the site of Cenabum.

Cēnimagnī, -ōrum, m., pl., (sen-i-mag' ni), a British people. (V. 21).

Cēnomanī, -ōrum, (se-nom'a-nī), see **Aulercī.**

cēnseō, -ēre, -uī, -us, 2, *estimate; think, hold, judge; decree, resolve upon, determine; vote for, favor.*

cēnsus, -ūs, [**cēnseō**], m., *count, enumeration.* (I. 29). [census.

centum, or **C,** indeclinable num. adj., *hundred.* [cent, *in* per cent.

centuriō, -ōnis, [**centuria**], m., *centurion.* [centurion.

cernō, cernere, crēvī, 3, *separate; distinguish, discern, see, perceive.*

certāmen, -inis, [**certō**], n., *contest, rivalry* (V. 44); *struggle, battle, engagement* (III. 14).

certē, comp. **certius,** [**certus**], adv., affirmative, *certainly, surely* (VI. 31); restrictive, *at least, at any rate* (IV. 25, V. 29, VII. 50).

certus, -a, -um, comp. **-ior,** sup. **-issimus,** [part. of **cernō**], adj., *certain, fixed, definite; positive, undoubted, trustworthy, true,* **certiōrem facere,** *to inform, certior fierī, to be informed.* Neut. as noun, **certī quid esset,** *what was really going on* (VII. 45); **prō certō,** *as a certainty, ascertain* (VII. 5). [certain.

cervus, -ī, m., *stag* (VI. 26); in military language, *stag's horns,* a device for hindering the approach of an enemy (VII. 72). [cervine.

cēterus, -a, -um, nom. sing. m. not in use, adj., *other, the other, the rest, remainder;* pl., *the rest, all the others, the other.* As noun, **cēterī, -ōrum,** m., pl., *the others, all the rest, everyone else;* **cētera, -ōrum,** n., pl., *the rest, all else, everything else.*

Ceutronēs, -um, m., pl. (sū' tro-nēz):
(1) A Belgic people, subject to the Nervians. (V. 39).
(2) A people in the eastern part of the Province. (I. 10).

chara, -ae, f., *chara,* a plant the tuberous roots of which were used by Caesar's soldiers for food. (C. III. 48).

Cheruscī, -ōrum, m., pl., (ke-rus' ī) a German people north of the Suebi. (VI. 10).

cibāria, -ōrum, [**cibārius,** from **cibus**], n., pl., *provisions, rations.*

cibus, -ī, m., *food, nourishment.*

Cicerō, -ōnis, m., *Quintus Tullius Cicero* (tul' i-us sis' e-rō), brother of Marcus Tullius Cicero, the orator, born about 102 B.C. He became a

lieutenant of Caesar in Gaul in 55, and made a heroic defence of his camp in 54; he held aloof from Caesar in the Civil War, but was reconciled with him in 47; he was put to death by order of the triumvirs in 43 B.C.

Ciliciēnsis, -e, [**Cilicia**], adj., *Cilician, of Cilicia,* a province in the southern part of Asia Minor.

Cimberius, -ī, m., (sim-bē' ri-us), a leader of the Suebi. (I. 37).

Cimbrī, -ōrum, m., pl., *Cimbrians, Cimbri* (sim' brī), a Germanic people that joined with the Teutones in the invasion of Gaul.

Cingetorīx, -īgis, [Kel., = 'King of Warriors'], m., (sin-jet' o-riks):
(1) Rival of Indutiomarus for the headship of the Treverans, and loyal to Caesar. (V. 3, 4, 56, 57; VI. 8).
(2) A British ruler. (V. 22).

cingō, cingere, cīnxī, cīnctus, 3, *surround, encircle; invest.* [cincture.

cippus. -ī, m., *stake, post.* (VII. 73).

circinus, -i, [= κιρκινος], m., *pair of compasses.* (I. 38).

circiter, [**circus,** circle], adv. and prep.:
(1) As adv., *about, not far from, near.*
(2) As prep., with acc. only, *about* (I. 50).

circuitus, -ūs, [**circumeō**], m., *a going around; detour, circuit, winding path, way around,* [circuit.

circum, [acc. of **circus,** circle], adv. and prep.:
(1) As adv., *about, around.*
(2) As prep. with acc., *around, about; in the neighborhood of, near, near by.*

circumcīdō, -cīdere, -cīdī, -cīsus, [**circum** + **caedō**], 3, *cut around, cut.* (V. 42).

circumcīsus, -a, -um, [part. of **circumcīdō**], adj., *cut off; steep, precipitous.* (VII. 36).

circumclūdō, -dere, -sī, -sus, [**circum** + **claudō**], 3, *encircle.* (VI. 28).

circumdō, -dare, -dedī, -datus, [**circum** + **dō,** place], 1, *place around, encompass, surround, encircle.*

circumdūcō, -dūcere, -dūxī, -ductus, [**circum** + **dūcō**], 3, *lead around; trace* (I. 38). [circumduct.

circumeō, -īre, -iī, -itus, [**circum** + **eō**], m., *go around, pass around; surround, encircle; go about, visit* for inspection (V. 2).

circumfundō, -fundere, -fūdī, -fūsus, [**circum** + **fundō**], 3, *pour around; surround, hem in;* pass. often used reflexively, *spread (themselves) around, crowd around.*

circumiciō, -icere, -iēcī, -iectus, [**circum** + **iaciō**], 3, *throw around, place around.* (II. 6).

circummittō, -mittere, -mīsī, -missus, [**circum** + **mittō**], 3, *send around.* (V. 51; VII. 63).

circummūniō, -īre, -īvī, -ītus, [**circum** +

mūniō], 4, *surround with walls, fortify; hem in* (II. 30).

circumplector, -plectī, 3, dep., *embrace, encompass, surround.* (VII. 83).

circumsistō, -sistere, -stetī or **-stitī**, [circum + sistō], 3, *stand around, surround, take a position around.*

circumspiciō, -icere, -exī, -ectus, [circum + speciō, *look*], 3, *look about, survey; ponder, consider; look about for, look over* (V. 31). [circumspect.

circumvāllō, -āre, -āvī, -ātus, [circum + vāllō], 1, *surround with a rampart, blockade.*

circumvehor, -vehī, -vectus, [circum + vehō], 3, pass. as dep., *ride around* (VII. 45); *sail around.*

circumveniō, -venīre, -vēnī, -ventus, [circum + veniō], 4, *come around, go around; surround, encompass; ensnare, overreach, deceive.* **per īnsidiās circumvenīrī**, *to be betrayed into ambush* (I. 42). [circumvent.

cis, prep. with acc., *on this side of.*

Cisalpīnus, -a, -um, [cis + Alpīnus], adj., *Cisalpine, on this* (the Italian) *side of the Alps.* [Cisalpine.

Cisrhēnānus, -a, -um, [cis + Rhēnānus], adj., *on this side* (the west side) *of the Rhine.* (VI. 2).

Cita, (sī' ta), see **Fūfius.**

citātus, -a, -um, comp. **-ior**, sup. **-issimus**, [citō], adj., *rapid.* (IV. 10).

citerior, -us, [citer, from cis], comp. adj., *on this side, hither, nearer.* **Gallia citerior**, *Cisalpine Gaul.* **Hispānia citerior**, *Hither Spain*, meaning the eastern part, afterwards called Tarraconensis (III. 23).

citō, -āre, -āvī, -ātus, [freq. of ciëō, *set in motion*], 1, *urge on.* (C. III. 96). [cite.

cito, comp. **citius**, sup. **citissimē**, [citus], adv., *speedily,* **citissimē**, *with the utmost rapidity* (IV. 33).

citrā, [citer, from cis], prep. with acc. only, *on this side of.*

citrō, [citer, from cis], adv., *hither.* **ultrō citrōque**, *to and fro, back and forth* (I. 42).

cīvis, -is, m. and f., *citizen, fellow-citizen.* [civil.

cīvitās, -tātis, [cīvis], f., *body of citizens, state, nation; citizenship* (I. 47). **multī ex cīvitāte**, *many of the citizens* (V. 25). [city

clam, [cf. cēlō], adv., *secretly.*

clāmitō, -āre, -āvī, -ātus, [freq. of clāmō], 1, *cry out loudly, shout.*

clāmor, -ōris, [cf. clāmō, *cry out*], m., *outcry, shout, din.* [clamor.

clandestīnus, -a, -um, [clam], adj., *secret, hidden.* vii. (I. 64). [clandestine.

clarē, [clārus], adv., *loudly, distinctly.* (C. III. 94).

clārus, -a, -um, comp. **-ior**, sup. **-issimus**, adj., *clear, distinct;* of the voice, *loud* (v. 30); *famous.* [clear.

classicum, -ī, [classicus, -a, -um, from classis], n., *trumpet signal.* (C. III. 82).

classis, -is, f., *a class; a fleet.* [class.

Claudius, -ī, m., *Appius Claudius Pulcher*, (klâ' di-us pul' ker), brother of Clodius (see below); praetor in 57 B.C., and consul in 54. (V. 1).

claudō, claudere, clausī, clausus, 3, *shut, close,* **agmen claudere**, *to bring up the rear.* [close.

clāvus, -ī, m., *nail, spike.* (III. 13).

clēmentia, -ae, [clēmēns], f., *forbearance, mercifulness.* [clemency.

Cleopātra, -ae, f., (klē-o-pā' tra), sister of the young Egyptian king, Ptolemy, and afterwards queen of Egypt. (C. III. 103).

cliēns, -entis, m., *retainer, dependent, client, adherent.* [client.

clientēla, -ae, [cliēns], f., *relation of client to patron, clientship, vassalage;* pl., *following of clients* (VII. 32), *dependencies* (VI. 12). [clientele.

clīvus, -ī, m., *slope.* (VII. 46).

Clōdius, -ī, m., (klō' di-us):

(1) *Publius Clodius Pulcher*, the enemy of Cicero, who as tribune in 58 B.C. drove the orator into exile; he was killed in 52 B.C. (VII. 1).

(2) *Aulus Clodius*, a mutual friend of Caesar and of Scipio. (C. III. 90).

Cn., = **Gnaeus** (nē' us), a Roman first name.

co-, see **com-.**

coacervō, -āre, -āvī, -ātus, [co- + acervō], 1, *heap up, pile up.* (II. 27).

coāctus, pf. pass. part. of **cōgō.**

coāctus, -ūs, [cōgō], m., only abl. sing. in use, *compulsion,* **coāctū cīvitātis**, *under compulsion from his state* (V. 27).

coagmentō, -āre, -āvī, -ātus, [coagmentum, cf. cōgō], 1, *fasten together.* (VII. 23). [coagment.

coartō, -āre, -āvī, -ātus, [co- + artō, *make close*], 1, *press together, crowd together.* (VII. 70).

Cocosātēs, -um, m., pl., (kok-o-sā' tēz), a people in Aquitania. (III. 27).

coëmō, -emere, -ēmī, -ēmptus, [co- + emō], 3, *buy up, purchase.*

coeō, -īre, -īvī or **-iī, -itum est**, [co- + eō], irr., *come together, join together.* (VI. 22).

coepī, -isse, coeptus, def., (present supplied by **incipiō**), *have begun, began.* With a pass. infinitive the pass. form, **coeptus est, coeptus erat**, is used (I. 47; II. 6; IV. 18).

coërceō, -ercēre, -ercuī, -ercitus, [co- + arceō, *shut up*], 2, *confine; restrain, check* (I. 17; V. 7). [coerce.

cōgitō, -āre, -āvī, -ātus, [co- + agitō], 1, *think about, think; intend, purpose, plan.* [cogitate.

cognātiō, -ōnis, [cognātus], f., *blood-relationship; blood-relations, kindred.* **mágnae cognātiōnis**, *having extended family* *connections* (VII. 32). [cognation.

cognōscō, -gnōscere, -gnōvī, cognitus, [co- + (g)nōscō], 3, *become acquainted with, learn, learn of, ascertain; be familiar with, know, recognize; spy out, examine; take cognizance of.* [cognisance.

cōgō, cōgere, coēgī, coāctus, [co- + agō], 3, *drive together, bring together, collect, gather, assemble; compel, force, oblige.* [cogent.

cohors, -hortis, f., *cohort, battalion,* the tenth part of a legion. [cohort.

cohortātiō, -ōnis, [cohortor], f., *encouraging, exhortation.* (II. 25).

cohortor, -ārī, -ātus, [co- + hortor], 1, dep., *encourage; urge, exhort; address* with encouraging words, **cohortātī inter sē,** *urging one another on.* [cohortative.

collabefīō, -fierī, -factus, [com- + labefīō, *be shaken loose*], pass., *be shattered.* (C. II. 6).

collātus, see **cōnferō.**

collaudō, -āre, -āvī, -ātus, [com- + laudō], 1, *praise warmly, commend.*

colligō, -āre, -āvī, -ātus, [com- + ligō, *bind*], 1, *bind together, fasten together.* (I. 25).

colligō, -ligere, -lēgī, -lēctus, [com- + legō, *gather*], 3, *gather together, collect, assemble; obtain, get.* **sē colligere,** *to gather themselves together; to form* in battle order (III. 19); *to recover themselves, rally,* [collect.

collis, -is, m., *hill, height, elevation.*

collocō, -āre, -āvī, -ātus, [com- + locō, *place*], 1, *place, set, post, station; set in order, arrange;* with or without **nūptum,** *give in marriage* (I. 18). [collocate.

colloquium, -ī, [colloquor], n., *conference, interview.* [colloquy.

colloquor, -loquī, -locūtus, [com- + loquor], 3, dep., *talk with, hold a conference, hold a parley.* **inter sē collocūtī,** *having conferred together* (IV. 30).

colō, colere, coluī, cultus, 3, *cultivate, till* (IV. 1; V. 12); *honor, worship* (VI. 17).

colōnia, -ae, [colōnus], f., *colony, settlement.* (VI. 24). [colony.

color, -ōris, m., *color.* [color.

com-, co-, prep., old form of **cum,** *with,* found only in composition; see **cum.**

combūrō, -ūrere, -ussī, -ūstus, [com- + *būrō, = ūrō, *burn*], 3, *burn up, consume* by fire. (I. 5). [combustion.

comes, -itis, [co- + eō], m. and f., *companion, comrade.* [count (title).

comitātus, -ūs, [comes], m., *retinue, company.* (C. III. 61, 96). [county.

comitia, -ōrum, [sing. **comitium,** *meeting-place* for elections], n., pl., *elections* (VII. 67; C. III. 82).

comitor, -ārī, -ātus, [comes], 1, dep.,

accompany, attend. (VI. 8).

commeātus, -ūs, [commeō], m., *passing to and fro, trip, voyage* (V. 23); *supplies, provisions,* often including grain, **frumentum.**

commemorō, -āre, -āvī, -ātus, [com- + memorō], 1, *call to mind, recount, relate.* [commemorate.]

commendō, -āre, -āvī, -ātus, [com- + mandō], 1, *commit* to one *for protection, entrust; ask favor for, commend.* [commend.

commentārius, -ī, [commentor], m., *note-book, source-book.* [commentary.

commeō, -āre, -āvī, -ātus, [com- + meō, *go*], 1, *go to and fro, visit, resort to.* (I. 1; VII. 36).

commīlitō, -ōnis, [com- + mīlitō, from mīles], m., *fellow-soldier, comrade.*

comminus, [com- + manus], adv., *hand to hand, at close quarters.*

commissūra, -ae, [committō], f., *joint, seam, juncture.* (VII. 72).

committō, -mittere, -mīsī, -missus, [com- + mittō], 3, *join, bring together, connect; entrust, commit; cause, do, perpetrate.* **committere proelium,** *to join battle, begin the engagement.* [commit.

Commius, -i, m., *Comm, Commius,* (kom' i-us), an Atrebatian, loyal and useful to Caesar (especially in the British campaigns) till the uprising in 52, when he became a commander in the Gallic army raised for the relief of Alesia.

commodē, comp. **-ius,** sup. **-issimē,** [commodus], adv., *conveniently, opportunely, to advantage; readily, easily; fitly, suitably, properly.* **nōn minus commodē — quam,** *just as readily as* (II. 20). **nōn satis commodē,** *not very conveniently* (III. 13).

commodus, -a, -um, comp. **-ior,** sup. **-issimus,** [com- + modus, i.e. *having full measure*], adj., *convenient, advantageous, easy; good, favourable; suitable, fit.* As noun, **commodum, -ī,** n., *convenience, advantage, profit.* [commodious.

commonefaciō, -facere, -fēcī, -factus, [commoneō + faciō], 3, *remind; impress upon* one (I. 19).

commoror, -ārī, -ātus, [com- + moror], 1, dep., *delay, linger.*

commoveō, -movēre, -mōvī, commōtus, [com- + moveō], 2, *disturb, disquiet, alarm; move, stir.* [commotion.

communicō, -āre, -āvī, -ātus, [commūnis], 1, *share together, share with, divide with; communicate, impart; consult with* (V. 36). [communicate.

commūniō, -īre, -īvī or **-iī, -ītus,** [com- + mūniō], 4, *fortify on all sides, strongly fortify, intrench.*

commūnis, -e, [com- + mūnus], adj., *common, in common, general, public; indiscriminate* (VI. 9).

commūnī cōnsiliō, *in accordance with the general plan, by common consent.* in commūnī conciliō, *at a general council* (II. 4; VII. 15). [common.

commūtātiō, -ōnis, [commūtō], f., *complete change, alteration.*

commūtō, -āre, -āvī, -ātus, [com- + mūtō], 1, *change, wholly change, alter; exchange* (VI. 22). [commute.

comparō, -āre, -āvī, -ātus, [com- + parō], 1, *prepare, make ready, get together; acquire, secure; amass,* (I. 18).

comparō, -āre, -āvī, -ātus, [com-par, *like*], 1, *match, compare.* [compare.

compellō, -pellere, -pulī, -pulsus, [com- + pellō], 3, *drive together, collect; drive, force.* [compel.

compendium, -ī, [com- + pendō], n., *profit, gain.* (VII. 43). [compend.

comperiō, -perīre, -perī, -pertus, [com- + PER in experior], 4, *ascertain, learn, discover, find out.* rēs comperta, *a settled fact, ascertained fact.* (VII. 42).

complector, -plectī, -plexus, [com- + plectō, *braid*], 3, dep., *embrace,* (I. 20); *surround, include, encompass* (VII. 72, 74). [complex.

compleō, -plēre, -plēvī, -plētus, [com- + pleō, *fill*], 2, *fill up, fill; complete, cover;* of troops, *fully occupy, fill full.* [complete.

complexus, see complector.

complūrēs, -a, [com- + plūrēs, from plūs], adj., pl., *several, a number of; many.* As noun, complūrēs, -ium, m., pl., *a great many, quite a number, many.*

comportō, -āre, -āvī, -ātus, [com-+ portō], 1, *bring in, carry, convey, bring over.* [comport.

comprehendō, -hendere, -hendī, -hēnsus, [com- + prehendō], 3, *grasp; seize; arrest, capture;* of fire, *catch* (V. 43). [comprehend.

comprobō, -āre, -āvī, -ātus, [com- + probō], 1, *approve fully, justify.*

cōnātum, -ī, [n. of cōnātus, part. of cōnor], n., *attempt, undertaking.*

cōnātus, -ūs, [cōnor], m., *attempt.*

cōnātus, pf. part. of cōnor.

concēdō, -cēdere, -cessī, -cessūrus, [com- + cēdō], 3, *withdraw, depart; give up, yield, cede; submit; allow, grant; grant permission, permit.* [concede.

concelebrō, -āre, -āvī, -ātus, [com- + celebrō], 1, *frequent; publish abroad, make known.* (C. III. 72).

concessus, -ūs, [concēdō], m., used only in abl. sing., *permission, leave.*

concīdō, -cīdere, -cīdī, [com- + cadō], 3, *fall down, fall; perish, be slain.*

concīdō, -cīdere, -cīdī, -cīsus, [com- + caedō], 3, *cut up, cut off; cut to pieces, kill, slay, destroy.*

conciliō, -āre, -āvī, -ātus, [concilium], 1, *win over, reconcile; win, gain, procure.* [conciliate.

concilium, -ī, n., *meeting, assembly.* [council.

concinō, -ere, -uī, [com- + canō], 3, *sound together.* (C. III. 92).

concitō, -āre, -āvī, -ātus, [com- + citō], 1, *rouse, stir up.*

conclāmō, -āre, -āvī, -ātus, [com-+ clāmō, *shout*], 1, *cry aloud together, shout, cry out.*

conclūsus, -a, -um, [conclūdō], adj., *confined, shut in.* (III. 9).

Conconnetodumnus, -ī, [Kel., = 'Great Helper in Slaughter'], m., (kon-kon" e -to-dum' nus), a chief of the Carnutes. (VII. 3).

concrepō, -āre, -uī, -itus, [com- + crepō, *rattle*], 1, *rattle, clash.* (VII. 21).

concurrō, -currere, -cucurrī or -currī, -cursum est, [com- + currō], 3, *run together, run up, rush; charge; gather; resort* (VI. 13). eō concursum est, *a rush was made to that point.* (II. 33). [concur.

concursō, -āre, [freq. of concurrō], 1, *rush to and fro, run about.*

concursus, -ūs, [concurrō], m., *running together; dashing together, collision* (V. 10; C. II. 6); *onset, charge* (VI. 8; VII. 62). [concourse.

condemnō, -āre, -āvī, -ātus, [com- + damnō], 1, *condemn, find guilty (of).* (VII. 19). [condemn.

condiciō, -ōnis, [com- + DIC, *declare*], f., *condition, situation, state; terms, stipulation.* [condition.

condōnō, -āre, -āvī, -ātus, [com- + dōnō], 1, *give up, overlook, disregard, pardon.* (I. 20). [condone.

Condrūsī, -ōrum, m., pl. (kon-drū' sī), a Belgic people on the right bank of the Mosa (Meuse).

condūcō, -dūcere, -dūxī, -ductus, [com- + dūcō], 3, *bring together, collect; hire.* manus conducta, *hired band, mercenary force* (V. 27). [conduce.

cōnfectus, see cōnficiō.

cōnferō, -ferre, -tulī, collātus, [com- + ferō], irr., *bring together, gather, collect, convey; compare* (I. 31); *ascribe, refer* (I. 40); *put off, postpone* (I. 40). sē cōnferre, *to betake one's self turn, proceed.* culpam cōnferre, *to cast the blame on.* [confer.

cōnfertus, -a, -um, comp. -ior, sup. -issimus, [part. of cōnferciō], adj., *crowded together, close, dense.*

cōnfestim, adv., *immediately, at once, speedily.*

cōnficiō, -ficere, -fēcī, -fectus, [com- + faciō], 3, *do thoroughly, complete, finish, accomplish, do; bring to an end, wear out, exhaust, enfeeble;* of troops, *bring together, furnish* (II. 4). **bellō Helvētiōrum cōnfectō,** *when the war with the Helvetii was over* (I. 30). **ante prīmam cōnfectam vigiliam,** *before the end of the first watch* (VII. 3). **māgnō itinere cōnfectō,** *having made a forced march* (II. 12). **cōnfectus vulneribus,** *exhausted with wounds.* [confectionery.

cōnfīdō, -fīdere, -fīsus sum, [com- + fīdō, *trust*], 3, semi-dep., *trust firmly, rely upon, have confidence in; believe, be confident.* [confide.

cōnfīgō, -fīgere, -fīxī, -fīxus, [com- + fīgō, *fasten*], 3, *fasten together, join.* (III. 13).

cōnfīnis, -e, [com- + fīnis], adj., *bordering on, adjoining.* (VI. 3).

cōnfīnium, -ī, [cōnfīnis], n., *boundary, frontier.* (V. 24). [confine.

cōnfīō, -fierī, [com- + fīō], irr., sometimes used instead of **cōnficior,** pass. of **cōnficiō,** *be accomplished, be done.* (VII. 58).

cōnfirmātiō, -ōnis, [cōnfīrmō], f., *assurance.* (III. 18). [confirmation.

cōnfirmātus, -a, -um, [cōnfīrmō], adj., comp. **cōnfirmātior,** *encouraged, confident.* (C. III. 84).

cōnfirmō, -āre, -āvī, -ātus, [com- + fīrmus], 1, *strengthen, confirm; arrange for, establish; reassure, encourage; assert, declare; assure.* **iūre iūrandō cōnfirmāre,** *to bind by an oath* (V. 27). [confirm.

cōnfīsus, -a, -um, see **cōnfīdō.**

cōnfiteor, -fitērī, -fessus, [com- + fateor, *confess*], 2, dep., *confess, acknowledge.* (V. 27). [confess.

cōnfīxus, -a, -um, see **cōnfīgō.**

cōnflagrō, -āre, -āvī, -ātus, [com- + flagrō, *blaze*], 1, *be in flames, be on fire.* (V. 43). [conflagration.

cōnflīctō, -āre, -āvī, -ātus, [freq. of cōnflīgō], 1, dep., *harass, assail.* (V. 35). [conflict.

cōnflīgō, -flīgere, -flīxī, -flīctus, [com- + flīgō, *strike*], 3, *dash together; contend, fight.*

cōnfluēns, -entis, [cōnfluō], m., *flowing together* of two streams, *confluence.* (IV. 15).

cōnfluō, -fluere, -flūxī, [com- + fluō], 3, *flow together; flock* (VII. 44). [confluent.

cōnfugiō, -fugere, -fūgī, [com- + fugiō], 3, *flee for refuge.* (VI. 5).

cōnfundō. -fundere, -fūdī, -fūsus, [com- + fundō], 3, *pour together; mass together* (VII. 75). [confound.

congerō, -gerere, -gessī, -gestus, [com- + gerō], 3, *bring together, collect.* (C. II. 37).

congredior, -gredī, -gressus, [com- + gradior, *step*], 3, dep., *come together, meet, unite with; join battle, engage, contend.*

congressus, -a, -um, see **congredior.**

congressus, -ūs, [congredior], m., *meeting; encounter, engagement* (III. 13). [congress.

coniciō, -icere, -iēcī, -iectus, [com- + iaciō], 3, *throw together, hurl, cast; throw up, throw; place, put.* **in fugam conicere,** *to put to flight.*

coniectūra, -ae, [coniciō], f., *inference.* [conjecture.

coniūnctim, [coniungō], adv., *jointly, in common.*

coniūnctus, -a, -um, comp. -ior, sup. -issimus, [part. of coniungō], adj., *connected; closely allied* (vii. 33). [conjunct.

coniungō, -iungere, -iūnxī, -iūnctus, [com- + iungō], 3, *join together, unite, join.* [conjoin.

coniūnx, coniugis, [coniungō], m. and f., *husband; wife, spouse* (vii. 14). [conjugal.

coniūrātiō, -ōnis, [coniūrō], f., *union bound by oath, league; conspiracy, plot.*

coniūrō, -āre, -āvī, -ātus, [com- + iūrō], 1, *take oath together* (vii. I); *form a league, conspire, plot.* [conjure.

cōnor, -ārī, -ātus, 1, dep., *endeavor, attempt, undertake, try.* **idem cōnārī,** *to make the same attempt* (i. 3).[conative.

conquiēscō, -ere, -quiēvī, -quiētūrus, [com- + quiēscō, *rest*], 3, *take complete rest, repose.* vii. 46.

conquīrō, -quīrere, -quīsīvī, -quīsītus, [com- + quaerō], 3, *seek out, hunt up; bring together, collect.*

conquīsītus, see **conquīrō.**

cōnsanguineus, -a, -um, [com- + sanguineus, from sanguis], adj., *of the same blood.* As noun, m., and f., *relative, kinsman;* pl., *kinsfolk, blood-relations.* [consanguineous.

cōnscendō, -scendere, -scendī, -scēnsus, [com- + scandō, *climb*], 3, *mount, ascend.* **nāvēs cōnscendere,** *to embark.*

cōnscientia, -ae, [cōnsciō], f., *knowledge* (v. 56); with **animī,** *moral sense, conscience* (C. III. 60), [conscience.

cōnscīscō, -scīscere, -scīvī, -scītus, [com- + scīscō, *approve*], 3, *decree, appoint; inflict, bring upon.* **sibi mortem cōnscīscere,** *to commit suicide* (i. 4; iii. 22).

cōnscius, -a, -um, [com-, cf. sciō], adj., *conscious, aware (of).* [conscious.

cōnscrībō, -scrībere, -scrīpsī, -scrīptus, [com- + scrībō], 3, *write* (v. 48); *enrol, levy, enlist.* [conscript.

cōnscrīptus, see **cōnscrībō.**

cōnsecrātus, -a, -um, [part. of cōnsecrō], adj., *holy, sacred.* [consecrate.

cōnsector, -ārī, -ātus, [cōnsequor], 1, dep., *follow up, pursue.*

cōnsecūtus, see **cōnsequor.**

cōnsēnsiō, -ōnis, [cōnsentiō], f., *common feeling, agreement.* vii. 76.

cōnsēnsus, -ūs, [cōnsentiō], m., *common feeling, agreement, understanding.* **omnium**

vestrum cōnsēnsū, *as you all agree* (VII. 77). [consensus.

cōnsentiō, -sentīre, -sēnsī, -sēnsus, [com- + sentiō], 4, *agree; plot together, conspire.* [consent.

cōnsequor, -sequī, -secūtus, [com- + sequor], 3, dep., *follow after, follow; pursue, overtake; obtain, secure, gain.* [consequence.

cōnservō, -āre, -āvī, -ātus, [com- + servō], 1, *save, spare;* of laws or rights, *observe, maintain.* [conserve. **cōnsīderātē,** [cōnsīderātus, from cōnsīderō], adv., *circumspectly.* Comp. **cōnsīderātius,** *with unusual caution* (C. III. 82).

Cōnsidius, -ī, in., *Publius Considius,* (kon-sid' j-us), an officer in Caesar's army.

cōnsīdō, -sīdere, -sēdī, -sessum, [com- + sīdō, *sit*], 3, *sit down, seat one's self; halt, encamp; take up an abode, establish one's self, settle.*

cōnsilium, -ī, [cf. cōnsulō], n., *consultation, deliberation, counsel; gathering for deliberation, council; advice; decision, plan, design, scheme; project, proposal; good judgment, prudence, discretion.* **cōnsilium inīre** or **habēre,** *to form a plan.* [counsel.

cōnsimilis, -e, [com- + similis], adj., *very like, quite like.*

cōnsistō, -sistere, -stitī, [com- + sistō, *set, place*], 3, *stand, stop, halt; take a position, be posted, make a stand; stay, remain; sojourn, settle; consist (in), depend (on).* **in orbem cōnsistere,** *to form a circle* (V. 33). **spēs in vēlīs cōnsistit,** *their hope depends on the sails* (III. 14). [consist.

cōnsobrīnus, -ī, [com-, cf. soror], m., *cousin.* (VII. 76). [cousin.

cōnsōlor, -ārī, -ātus, [com- + sōlor, *comfort*], 1, dep., *comfort, cheer, encourage.* [console.

cōnspectus, -ūs, [cōnspiciō], m., *sight, view, presence.* [conspectus.

cōnspiciō, -spicere, -spexī, -spectus, [com- + speciō, *look*], 3, *observe, behold, see, perceive.*

cōnspicor, -ārī, -ātus, 1, dep., *catch sight of, see, observe.*

cōnspīrō, -āre, -āvī, -ātus, [com- + spīrō, *breathe*], 1, *agree; combine, form a league, conspire* (III. 10). [conspire.

cōnstanter, comp. **-ius,** sup. **-issimē,** [cōnstāns], adv., *resolutely* (III. 25); *uniformly, unanimously* (II. 2).

cōnstantia, -ae, [cōnstāns], f., *firmness, resolution.* [constancy.

cōnsternō, -āre, -āvī, -ātus, 1, *alarm, terrify.* (VII. 30). [consternation.

cōnsternō, -sternere, -strāvī, -strātus, [com- + sternō], 3, *strew over, cover* (IV. 17); *strew, carpet* (C. III. 96). **cōnstīpō, -āre, -āvī, -ātus,** [com- + stīpō, *press*], 1, *crowd together, crowd closely.* (V. 43).

cōnstituō, -stituere, -stituī, -stitūtus, [com- + statuō], 3, *station, place, draw up; bring to a halt, stop* (VII. 47); of ships, *moor; appoint, establish; resolve upon, determine, decide, fix, settle.* [constitute.

cōnstō, -stāre, -stitī, -stātūrus, [com- + stō], 1, *stand firm; remain the same* (VII. 35); *remain, lie* (VII. 21); *depend on* (VII. 84); *cost* (VII. 19); *be made up of* (C. II. 36). **cōnstat,** impers., *it is certain, well-known, evident, it is clear.*

cōnsuēscō, -suēscere, -suēvī, -suētus, [com- + suēscō, *become used*], 3, *form a habit, become accustomed, be accustomed, be wont.*

cōnsuētūdō, -inis, [cōnsuēscō], f., *habit, practice, custom, usage; mode of life* (V. 14, VI. 21); *practice* in speaking a language (I. 47). **cōnsuētūdō vīctūs,** *standard of living* (I. 31). **praeter cōnsuētūdinem,** *contrary to custom* (VII. 61). [custom.

cōnsuētus, see **cōnsuēscō.**

cōnsul, -ulis, m., *consul,* one of the two chief magistrates at Rome, chosen annually. [consul.

cōnsulāris, -e, [cōnsul], adj., *consular.* (C. I, 6). [consular.

cōnsulātus, -ūs, [cōnsul], m., *consulship.* (I. 35). [consulate.

cōnsulō, -sulere, -suluī, -sultus, 3, *consult, deliberate, take counsel of;* with dat., *have regard for, look out for.*

cōnsultō, [cōnsulō], adv., *on purpose, designedly, purposely.*

cōnsultō, -āre, -āvī, -ātus, [freq. of cōnsulō], 1, *deliberate, take counsel.* (V. 53; VII. 77). [consult.

cōnsultum, -ī, [cōnsultus, from cōnsulō], n., *deliberation; resolution, decree, decision.*

cōnsūmō. -sūmere, -sūmpsī, -sūmptus, [com- + sūmō], 3, *use up, devour, eat up; waste, exhaust, destroy;* of time, *spend, pass.* [consume.

cōnsūmptus, see **cōnsūmō.**

cōnsurgō, -surgere, -surrēxī, consurrēctum est, [com- + surgō, *rise*], 3, *rise together, arise, stand up.*

contabulō, -āre, -āvī, -ātus, [com-, cf. tabula, *board*], 1, *construct of boards; build up in stories.* **mūrum turribus contabulāre,** *to cover the wall with towers* (VII. 22).

contāgiō, -ōnis, [cf. contingō], f., *contact.* (VI. 13). [contagion.

contāminō, -āre, -āvī, -ātus, [contāmen, = contāgiō], 1, *taint, pollute.* (VII. 43). [contaminate.

contegō, -tegere, -tēxī, -tēctus, [com- + tegō], 3, *cover, cover up* (VII. 85).

contemnō, -temnere, -tempsī, -temptus, [com- + temnō, *despise*], 1, *despise, hold in* *contempt.* [contemn.

contemptiō, -ōnis, [cf. **contemnō**], f., *a despising, contempt, scorn.*

contemptus, -ūs, [**contemnō**], m., *scorn.* [contempt.

contendō, -tendere, -tendī, -tentus, [com- + **tendō**], 3, *put forth effort, strive for, make effort, strive; demand* (VII. 63, C. III. 97); *hasten, make haste, push forward; struggle, contend, vie; maintain, insist, protest* (VI. 37, 41, 43). [contend.

contentiō, -ōnis, [**contendō**], f., *effort; struggle, fight, contest; dispute, controversy.* [contention.

contentus, -a, -um, [part. of **contineō**], adj., *satisfied.* [content.

contexō, -texere, -texuī, -textus, [com- + **texō,** weave], 3, *weave together, weave; bind together, join, construct.* [context.

continēns, -entis, [part. of **contineō**], adj., *adjoining; continuous, unbroken, consecutive.* **continentī impetū,** *without pausing* (VII. 28). As noun, (originally sc. **terra**), f., *mainland.* [continent.

continenter, [**continēns**], adv., *constantly, incessantly, without interruption, continually.*

continentia, -ae, [**continēns**], f., *self-restraint, moderation.* (VII. 52).

contineō, -tinēre, -tinuī, -tentus, [com- + **teneō**], 2, *hold together; hold; hold back, keep in hand; keep, retain, detain, shut in; of places and regions, hem in, bound, border; of space, fill* (I. 38); *of a rite, pass., consist of* (VII. 2). **sē continēre,** *to hold one's self, keep one's self, remain.* [contain.

contingō, -tingere, -tigī, -tāctus, [com- + **tangō**], 3, *touch, extend to, border on, reach; happen, fall to the lot of* (I. 43). [contact.

continuātiō, -ōnis, [verb **continuō**], f., *succession.* (III. 29). [continuation.

continuō, [**continuus**], adv., *forthwith, immediately, at once.*

continuus, -a, -um, [com-, cf. **teneō**], adj., *successive, uninterrupted.* [continuous.

cōntiō, -ōnis, [for *coventiō, co-, cf. **veniō**], f., *assembly, meeting* (V. 52, VII. 52); *address, harangue.* **hāc habitā cōntiōne,** *having delivered this address* (VII. 53).

cōntiōnor, -ārī, -ātus, [**cōntiō**], 1, dep., *address an assembly, make an address.* (C. I. 7).

contrā, [related to **com-**], adv. and prep.:
(1) As adv., *opposite, in opposition, on the other side; on the other hand, on the contrary* (V. 31).
contrā atque, *otherwise than, contrary to what* (IV. 13).
(2) As prep., with acc. only, *opposite to, facing, over against, contrary to; against, in hostility to, to the disadvantage of, in spite of; in reply to* (V. 29).

contrahō, -trahere, -trāxī, -trāctus, [com- + **trahō**], 3, *bring together, collect; draw in, contract, make smaller* (V. 49; VII. 40). [contract.

contrārius, -a, -um, [**contrā**], adj., *opposite, contrary.* **ex contrāriō,** *on the contrary* (VII. 30). [contrary.

contrōversia, -ae, [**contrōversus**], f., *dispute, debate, controversy, quarrel.* **minuere contrōversiās,** *to settle the questions at issue* (V. 26; VI. 23). [controversy.

contumēlia, -ae, f., *insult, indignity; of waves, buffeting* (III. 13). [contumely.

convalēscō, -valēscere, -valuī, [com- + **valēscō,** inch. from **valeō**], 3, *grow strong, get well, recover.* (VI. 36). [convalesce.

convallis, -is, [com- + **vallis**], f., *valley, ravine, defile.*

convehō, -vehere, -vexī, -vectus, [com- + **vehō**], 3, *bring together, collect, store.* (VII. 74).

conveniō, -venīre, -vēnī, -ventum est, [com- + **veniō**], 4, *come together, gather, assemble, meet, come in a body; come to an assembly* (V. 56); *be agreed upon* (I. 36, II. 19); impers., *be fitting* (VII. 85); *fall in with, meet* (I. 27). [convene.

conventus, -ūs, [cf. **conveniō**], m., *assembly, meeting; court.* [convent.

conversus, see **convertō.**

convertō, -vertere, -vertī, -versus, [com- + **vertō**], 3, *turn, direct, turn about, wheel around; change* (I. 41). **conversa signa īnferre,** *to face about and advance* (I. 25; II. 26). [convert.

Convictolitāvis, -is, acc. **-im,** (VII. 55), m., (kon" vik-to-li-tā' vis), an Aeduan whose claims to the office of Vergobret were sustained by Caesar.

convictus, see **convincō.**

convincō, -vincere, -vicī, -victus, [com- + **vincō**], 3, *prove clearly, establish, prove* (I. 40). [convict.

convocō, -āre, -āvī, -ātus, [com- + **vocō**], 1, *call together, summon, assemble.* [convoke.

coörior, -orīrī, -ortus, [co- + **orior**], 4, dep., *arise; of storm and wind, arise, rise, spring up; of war, break out* (III. 7).

coörtus, see **coörior.**

cōpia, -ae, [= co-opia, from co- + **ops**], f., *quantity, abundance, supply, plenty.* Pl., **cōpiae, -ārum,** *means, resources, wealth; forces, troops.*

cōpiōsus, -a, -um, comp. **-ior,** sup. **-issimus,** [**cōpia**], adj., *well-supplied, wealthy, rich.* (I. 23). [copious.

cōpula, -ae, [co- + AP in **aptus**], f., *band;* pl., *grappling-hooks* (III. 13). [copula.

cor, cordis, n., *heart.* **cordī esse,** *to be dear* (VI. 19). [cordial.

cōram, [co-, cf. **ōs,** face], adv., *face to face, in person.* **cōram adesse,** *to be present* (I. 32). **cōram perspicit** (V. 11) or **cernit** (VI. 8), *he sees with his* *own eyes.* As prep., with the ablative, *in the presence of.*

Coriosolitēs, -um, m., pl., (kō" ri-o-sol' i-tēz), a people along the northwestern coast of Gaul.

corium, -ī, n., *hide.* (VII. 22).

Cornēlius, -a, -um, adj., *of Cornelius, Cornelian.* **castra Cornēlia,** *Cornelian camp,* near Utica (C. II. 37). **cornū, -ūs,** n., *horn;* of a deer, *antler* (VI. 26); of an army, *wing.*

corōna, -ae, [= κ ο ρ ω ν η], f., *crown, wreath* (III. 16); of soldiers, *continuous cordon, cordon* (VII. 72). **sub corōnā vēndere,** *to sell into slavery* (III. 16). [crown.

corpus, -oris, n., *body.* [corporal.

corripiō, -ripere, -ripuī, -reptus, [com- + rapiō], 3, *snatch up; seize, carry away* (C. III. 64).

corrumpō, -rumpere, -rūpī, -ruptus, [com- + rumpō, *break*], 3, *spoil, destroy.* (VII. 55, 64). [corrupt.

cortex, corticis, m. and f., *bark* of a tree. (II. 33; C. III. 49).

Cōrus, -ī, m., *northwest wind.* (V. 7).

coss., = **cōnsulibus,** from **cōnsul.**

cotīdiānus, -a, -um, [cotīdiē], adj., *daily; ordinary, usual.*

cotīdiē, [quot + diēs], adv., *daily, every day.*

Cotta, -ae, m.:

(1) *L. Aurunculeius Cotta,* see **Aurunculeius.**

(2) *L. Aurelius Cotta* (â-rē' li-us kot' a), consul in 65 B.C. (C. I. 6).

Cotuātus, -i, m., (kot-ū-ā'tus), a leader of the Carnutes. (VII. 3).

Cotus, -ī, m., (kō' tus), an Aeduan, rival of Convictolitavis for the office of Vergobret. (VII. 32, 33, 39, 67).

crassitūdō, -inis, [crassus, *thick*], f., *thickness.* (III. 13; VII. 73).

Crassus, -ī, m., (kras' us):

(1) *Marcus Licinius Crassus,* member of the triumvirate with Caesar and Pompey, consul in 55 B.C.; perished in the disastrous Parthian expedition, 53 B.C. (I. 21; IV. 1).

(2) *Publius Licinius Crassus,* younger son of the triumvir, lieutenant of Caesar in Gaul, B.C. 58-56; returning to Rome in 55, he followed his father to the East and fell in the same battle, 53 B.C. (I. 52; II. 34; III. 7, 8, 9, 11, 20-27).

(3) *Marcus Licinius Crassus,* elder son of the triumvir, quaestor in Caesar's army after his brother Publius left Gaul. (V. 24, 46, 47; VI. 6).

Crāstinus, -ī, [crās], m., (kras' ti-nus), a brave soldier in Caesar's army. (C. III. 91, 99).

crātēs, -is, f., *wicker-work, wattle; hurdle, fascine.* [crate, grate.

crēber, -bra, -brum, comp. **crēbrior,** sup.

crēberrimus, adj., *thick, numerous, frequent, a great many.*

crēbrō, comp. **crēbrius,** sup. **crēberrimē,** [crēber], adv. *frequently, in quick succession.* (VII. 41).

crēdō, crēdere, crēdidī, crēditus, 3, *trust, believe, think, suppose; intrust, consign* (VI. 31). [creed, credit.

cremō, -āre, -āvī, -ātus, 1, *burn; burn to death* (I. 4.) [cremate.

creō, -āre, -āvī, -ātus, 1, *create, make; choose, elect, appoint.* [create.

crēscō, crēscere, crēvī, crētus, 3, inch., *grow; become great, become powerful* (I. 20); of a river, *become swollen* (VII. 55). [crescent.

Crētēs, -um, accusative **Crētas,** [Κ Ρ Η Τ Ε Σ], m., pl., *Cretans,* inhabitants of Crete.

Critognātus, -ī, m., (krit-og-nā' tus), a prominent Arvernian. (VII. 77, 78).

cruciātus,-ūs, [cruciō, *torture*], m., *torture, cruelty, torment, suffering.*

crūdēlitās, -tātis, [crūdēlis], f., *cruelty, barbarity.* [cruelty.

crūdēliter, comp. **crūdēlius,** sup. **crūdēlissimē,** [crūdēlis], adv., *cruelly, with cruelty.* (I. 31; VII. 38).

crūs, crūris, n., *leg.* (VI. 27).

cubīle, -is, [cf. cubō, *lie down*], n., *bed, resting-place.* (VI. 27).

culmen, -inis, n., *height, summit, top.* (III. 2). [culminate.

culpa, -ae, f., *blame, fault, error.* (IV. 27; V. 52). [culpable.

cultūra, -ae, [cf. colō], f., *tilling, cultivation,* [culture.

cultus, -ūs, [colō], m., *cultivation, care; mode of life, civilization.* [cult.

cum, prep, with ablative only, *with, along with, together with.* In composition the earlier form **com-** is used, which remains unchanged before **b, p, m,** but is changed to **col-** or **con-** before **l, cor-** or **con-** before **r, con-** before other consonants, and **co-** before vowels and **h;** implies doing anything *in concert with* others, or *thoroughly* and *completely.*With the personal pronouns and **quī, cum** is enclitic; as, **mēcum, nōbiscum, quibuscum.**

cum, conj., temporal, *when;* of definite time, *at the time when, when, while, as long as;* of indefinite time or repeated action, *whenever, as often as, at times when;* of relative time, descriptive or circumstantial, *when, while, after, on the occasion that, under the circumstances that, at the moment when;* of cause and concession, with subj., *since, inasmuch as, although, notwithstanding.*

cum . . . tum, *both . . . and, not only . . . but also.*

cum prīmum, *as soon as.*

cunctātiō, -ōnis, [cunctor], f., *delay, hesitation.* (III. 18, 24).

cunctor, -ārī, -ātus, 1, dep., *delay, hesitate.* (III. 23; IV. 25).

cūnctus, -a, -um, adj., *all together, all.* As noun, **cūnctī, -ōrum,** m., pl., *all in a body* (VII. II).

cuneātim, [**cuneātus, cuneus**], adv., *in the form of a wedge; in wedge-shaped masses* (VII. 28).

cuneus, -ī, m., *wedge;* of troops, *wedge-shaped mass* (VI. 40).

cunīculus, -ī, m., *rabbit;* in military language, *underground passage, mine.* (III. 21; VII. 22, 24).

cupidē, comp. **-ius,** sup. **-issimē,** [**cupidus**], adv., *eagerly, ardently.*

cupiditās, -tātis, [**cupidus**], f., *ardent desire, eagerness.* [cupidity.

cupidus, -a, -um, comp. **-ior,** sup. **-issimus,** [cf. **cupiō**], adj., *desirous, eager for, fond of.*

cupiō, cupere, cupīvī, cupītus, 3, *desire; wish well to* (I. 18).

cūr, adv., *why? wherefore?*

cūra, -ae, f., *care, attention, anxiety, trouble.* [cure (noun).

Cūriō, -ōnis, m., *Gaius Scribonius Curio,* (scri-bō' ni-us kū' ri-ō), a lieutenant of Caesar's army. (C. II. 3, 34 ET SEQ.).

cūrō, -āre, -āvī, -ātus, [**cūra**], 1, *take care, provide for, superintend, arrange.* **nāvēs aedificandās cūrāre,** *to have ships built* (V. 1). [cure (verb).

currus, -ūs, [cf. **currō**], m., *chariot.*

cursus, -ūs, [cf. **currō**], m., *running; speed; course.* **māgnō cursō,** *at full speed.* [course.

cūstōdia, -ae, [**cūstōs**], f., *a watching; guard; watch;* pl., *watch stations* (C. II. 5). [custody.

cūstōdiō, -īre, -īvī, -ītus, [**cūstōs**], 4, *guard, keep.* (VI. 4).

cūstōs, -tōdis, m. and f., *guard, keeper, watch.*

D.

D., with proper names, = **Decimus.**

D = quīngentī, 500.

d., see **a. d.**

Dācī, -ōrum, m., pl., *the Dacians, Daci* (dā' sī), a people living north of the lower course of the Danube River, in the countries now called *Hungary* and *Rumania.* (VI. 25).

Damasippus, -ī, see **Licinius.**

damnō, -āre, -āvī, -ātus, [**damnum**], 1, *condemn, sentence.* **capitis damnāre,** *to condemn to death* (C. III. 83). Part. as noun, **damnātī, -ōrum,** m., pl., *those condemned, criminals* (V. 55).

damnum, -ī, n., *loss.* (VI. 44).

Dānuvius, -ī, m., *the Danube.* (VI. 25).

dē, prep. with abl., denoting separation, *from;* of place and motion, *from, away from, out of;* of source, *of, from, out of, proceeding from, sprung from;* of the whole, partitively, *of, out of, from among;* of material, *made of, out of, from;* of

cause, *on account of, for, through, by;* of relation, *concerning, about, in respect to, of, in the matter of;* of time, *away from, after, during, in the course of, in.* **dē imprōvīsō,** *unexpectedly.*

dēbeō, dēbēre, dēbuī, dēbitus, [**dē + habeō**], 2, *owe;* pass., *be due;* followed by infin., *ought, must, should.* [debit.

dēcēdō, -cēdere, -cessī, -cessūrus, [**dē + cēdō**], 3, *go away, retire, withdraw; avoid, shun; die* (VI. 19).

decem, or **X,** indeclinable num., *ten.*

dēceptus, see **dēcipiō.**

dēcernō, -cernere, -crēvī, -crētus, [**dē + cernō**], 3, *pass judgment, decide; resolve upon, resolve, determine; assign* by vote (C. I. 6).

dēcertō, -āre, -āvī, -ātus, [**dē + certō,** *contend*], 1, *fight to a finish.* **proeliō dēcertāre,** *fight a decisive battle.*

dēcessus, -ūs, [**dēcēdō**], m., *departure, withdrawal.* [decease.

Decetia, -ae, f., (de-sē' sh[y]a), a town of the Aeduans, on the Liger (*Loire*). (VII. 33).

dēcidō, -cidere, -cidī, [**dē + cadō**], 3, *fall down, fall off.* [deciduous.

decimus, -a, -um, or **x,** [**decem**], num. adj., *tenth.* [decimal.

Decimus, -ī, m., (des' i-mus), a Roman first name.

dēcipiō, -cipere, -cēpī, -ceptus, [**dē + capiō**], 3, *catch; deceive* (I. 14). [deceive.

dēclārō, -āre, -āvī, -ātus, [**dē + clārō,** from **clārus**], 1, *make clear, announce.* (I. 50). [declare.

dēclīvis, -e, [**dē + clīvus**], adj., *sloping, descending.* As noun, **dēclīvia,** n., pl., *slopes, declivities* (VII. 88).

dēclīvitās, -tātis, [**dēclīvis**], f., *descent.* [declivity.

dēcrētum, -ī, [**dēcernō**], n., *decree, decision.* **dēcrētō stāre,** *to abide by the decision* (VI. 13). [decree.

decumānus, -a, -um, [**decimus**], adj., *of a tenth part, decuman.* **decumāna porta,** *rear gate* of the Roman camp, opposite the **porta praetōria.** (II. 24).

decuriō, -ōnis, [**decuria**], m., *decurion,* a cavalry officer in charge of a *decuria,* consisting of 10 horsemen.

dēcurrō, -currere, -cucurrī or **-currī, -cursūrus,** [**dē + currō**], 3, *run down, rush down, hasten.*

dēdecus, -oris, [**dē + decus,** *honor*], n., *disgrace, dishonor.* (IV. 25).

dēditīcius, -ī, [**dēditus,** from **dēdō**], adj., *that has surrendered, subject.* As noun, **dēditīciī, -ōrum,** m., pl., *prisoners of war, captives.*

dēditiō, -ōnis, [**dēdō**], f., *surrender.* **accipere** or **recipere in dēditiōnem,** *to receive by capitulation.* **in dēditiōnem venīre,** *to* surrender (VI. 3, 9).

dēditus, -a, -um, [part. of **dēdō**], adj., *devoted* (VI. 16).

dēdō, -dere, -didī, -ditus, [**dē** + **dō**], 3, *give up, surrender; devote* (III. 22).

dēdūcō, -dūcere, -dūxī, -ductus, [**dē** + **dūcō**], 3, *lead down; lead away, lead off, withdraw; lead, induce; conduct, bring;* of ships, *draw down, launch* (V. 2, 23); *bring home* as a bride, *marry* (V. 14). [deduce.

dēfatīgātiō, -ōnis, [**dēfatīgō**], f., *weariness, exhaustion.* (III. 19).

dēfatīgō, -āre, -āvī, -ātus, [**dē** + **fatīgō**, *weary*], 1, *tire out, exhaust.*

dēfectiō, -ōnis, [**dēficiō**], f., *a failing; desertion, revolt.* [defection.

dēfendō, -fendere, -fendī, -fēnsus, 3, *ward off, repel; defend, guard, protect.* [defend.

dēfēnsiō, -ōnis, [**dēfendō**], f., *defense.* (II. 7; VII. 23).

dēfēnsor, -ōris, [**dēfendō**], m., *defender, protector;* of piles protecting a bridge, *guards* (IV. 17).

dēfēnsus, see **dēfendō.**

dēferō, -ferre, -tulī, -lātus, [**dē** + **ferō**], irr., *bring down; carry away, bear away; bring (to), carry (to); refer (to), confer upon, lay before; report, announce.* [defer.

dēfessus, -a, -um, [part. of **dēfetīscor**], adj., *worn out, exhausted.* As noun, **dēfessus, -ī,** m., *one exhausted* (III. 4), pl., *the exhausted* (VII. 25, 41, C. III. 94).

dēfetīscor, -ī, dēfessus, [**dē** + **fatīscor**], 3, dep., *become exhausted* (VII. 88).

dēficiō, -ficere, -fēcī, -fectus, [**dē** + **faciō**], 3, *fail, be lacking; fall away, revolt, rebel.* **dēficere animō,** *to lose heart* (VII. 30). [deficit.

dēfīgō, -fīgere, -fīxī, fīxus, [**dē** + **fīgō**, *fasten*], 3, *make fast, fix, fasten; slick fast* (V. 44).

dēfīniō, -īre, -īvī, -ītus, [**dē** + **fīniō**] , 4, *set bounds to; define, fix, set* (VII. 83); *apportion* (C. III. 82). [define.

dēfore, see **dēsum.**

dēfōrmis, -e, comp. **-ior,** [**dē** + **fōrma**], adj., *ill-shaped* (IV. 2); *unsightly* (VII. 23). [deform.

dēfugiō, -fugere, -fūgī, [**dē** + **fugiō**], 3, *flee from, shun, avoid.*

dēiciō, -icere, -iēcī, -iectus, [**dē** + **iaciō**], 3, *throw down, cast down, throw; dislodge, drive from, rout;* of a ship, pass., *be carried* (IV. 28); of lots, *cast* (C. III. 6); *kill, destroy; disappoint.* **eā spē dēiectī,** *disappointed in this expectation* (i. 8). [dejection.

dēiectus, see **dēiciō.**

dēiectus, -ūs, [**dēiciō**], m., *descent, slope, declivity.* (II. 8, 22, 29).

deinceps, [dein, = deinde, + CAP in capiō], adv., *one after the other, in succession, in turn;*

without interruption (III. 29).

deinde, [dē + inde], adv., *thereafter, afterwards, then, next.*

dēlātus, see **dēferō.**

dēlectō, -āre, -āvī, -ātus, [freq. of **dēliciō**], 1, *please;* in pass., *have pleasure in* (IV. 2). [delectation.

dēlēctus, see **dēligō.**

dēleō, -ēre, -ēvī, -ētus, 2, *destroy, annihilate;* of disgrace, *wipe out* (II. 27). [delete.

dēlīberō, -āre, -āvī, -ātus, [**dē**, cf. **lībra**, *balance*], 1, *deliberate, ponder.* Impersonal, **dēlīberātur,** *the question is discussed* (VII. 15). [deliberate.

dēlibrō, -āre, —, -ātus, [**dē** cf. **liber**, *bark*], 1, *strip off the bark, peel.* (VII. 73).

dēlīctum, -ī, [**dēlinquō,** *do wrong*], n., *offence, crime.* (VII. 4). [delict.

dēligō, -āre, -āvī, -ātus, [**dē** + **ligō,** *bind*], 1, *bind fast, make fast, tie, fasten.*

dēligō, -ligere, -lēgī, -lēctus, [**dē** + **legō**], 3, *choose, select, pick out.*

dēlitēscō, -litēscere, -lituī, [**dē** + **latēscō,** from **lateō**], 3, *conceal one's self.* (IV. 32).

dēmentia, -ae, [**dēmēns**], f., *madness, folly.* (IV. 13). [dementia.

dēmessus, see **dēmetō.**

dēmetō, -metere, -messuī, -messus, [**dē** + **metō**], 3, *reap.* (IV. 32).

dēmigrō, -āre, -āvī, -ātus, [**dē** + **migrō**, *depart*], 1, *move from, withdraw; depart, migrate.*

dēminuō, -minuere, -minuī, -minūtus, [**dē** + **minuō**], 3, *lessen, make smaller; impair.* [diminish.

dēmissus, -a, -um, comp. **-ior** [part. of **dēmittō**], adj., *low.* (VII. 72).

dēmittō, -mittere, -mīsī, -missus, [**dē** + **mittō**], 3, *send down, let down.;* of the head, *bow* (I. 32). **dēmissae,** *letting themselves down* (VII. 47). **sē dēmittere,** *to go down, come down, descend* (V. 32; VI. 40; VII. 28). **sē animō dēmittere,** *to be discouraged* (VII. 29). [demit.

dēmō, dēmere, dēmpsī, dēmptus, [**dē** + **emō**], 3, *take down.* (V. 48).

dēmōnstrō, -āre, -āvī, -ātus, [**dē** + **mōnstrō**, *show*], 1, *point out, state, mention; show, explain.* [demonstrate.

dēmoror, -ārī, -ātus, [**dē** + **moror**], 1, dep., *delay, retard, hinder.*

dēmptus, see **dēmō.**

dēmum, adv., *at length, finally.*

dēnegō, -āre, -āvī, -ātus, [**dē** + **negō**], 1, *refuse, deny.* (I. 42). [deny.

dēnī, -ae, -a, [**decem**], distributive num. adj., *ten each, ten apiece.*

dēnique, adv., *at last, finally; in a word, in short: at any rate* (II. 33).

dēnsus, -a, -um, comp. **-ior,** sup. **-issimus,**

adj., *thick, closely packed, dense, crowded.* [dense.

dēnūntiō, -āre, -āvī, -ātus, [dē + nūntiō], 1, *announce, declare; threaten* (I. 36); *order* (VI. 10); *admonish* (C. III. 86). [denounce.

dēpellō, -pellere, -pulī, -pulsus, [dē + pellō], 3, *drive away, dislodge; of disease, ward off* (VI. 17).

dēperdō, -dere, -didī, -ditus, [dē + perdō, *destroy*], 3, *lose.*

dēpereō, -īre, -iī, -itūrus, [dē + pereō], irr., *be destroyed* (V. 23); *be lost, perish* (VII. 31, C. III. 87).

dēpōnō, -pōnere, -posuī, -positus, [dē + pōnō], 3, *lay aside, lay down, place; give up, resign* (VII. 33). [deposit.

dēpopulor, -ārī, -ātus, [dē + populor], 1, dep., *lay waste, plunder;* part. **dēpopulātus,** pass., *laid waste, devastated* (I. 11; VII. 77). [depopulate.

dēportō, -āre, -āvī, -ātus, [dē + portō], 1, *remove.* (III. 12). [deport.

dēposcō, -poscere, -poposcī, [dē + poscō], 3, *demand, earnestly desire.*

dēpositus, see **dēpōnō.**

dēprāvō, -āre, -āvī, -ātus, [dē, prāvus], 1, *distort, corrupt,* [deprave.

dēprecātor, -ōris, [dēprecor], m., *intercessor, mediator.* **eō dēprecātōre,** *by his intercession* (I. 9). [deprecator.

dēprecor, -ārī, -ātus, [dē + precor, *pray*], 1, dep., *pray to be delivered from, beg to escape; ask for quarter, beg for mercy* (IV. 7, VI. 4). [deprecate.

dēprehendō, -hendere, -hendī, -hēnsus, [dē + prehendō], 3, *catch, seize; surprise.*

dēprehēnsus, see **dēprehendō.**

dēprimō, -primere, -pressī, -pressus, [dē + premō], 3, *press down; sink* (C. II. 6, 7, 43). [depress.

dēpulsus, see **dēpellō.**

dērēctē, comp. **-ius,** [dērēctus], adv., *directly, straight up and down* (IV. 17).

dērēctus, -a, -um, [part. of dērigō], adj., *laid straight, straight; straight up and down, perpendicular.* [direct.

dērigō, -rigere, -rēxī, -rēctus, [dē + regō], 3, *lay straight; of a line of battle, draw up, form* (VI. 8). [dress.

dērīvō, -āre, -āvī, -ātus, [dē + rīvus, *brook*], 1, *draw off, turn aside.* (VII. 72). [derive.

dērogō, -āre, -āvī, -ātus, [dē + rogō], 1, *withdraw.* (VI. 23). [derogate.

dēscendō, -scendere, -scendi, dēscēnsum est, [dē + scandō, *climb*], 3, *come down, descend; with* ad *and the acc., resort to, stoop to.* [descend.

dēsecō, -cāre, -cuī, -ctus, [dē + secō], 1, *cut off.* (VII. 4).

dēserō, -serere, -seruī, -sertus, [dē + serō, *join*], 3, *leave, abandon, desert.* [desert.

dēsertor, -ōris, [dēserō], m., *deserter, runaway.* (VI. 23).

dēsertus, see **dēserō.**

dēsertus, -a, -um, comp. **-ior,** sup. **-issimus,** [part. of dēserō], adj., *deserted, solitary.* (V. 53).

dēsīderō, -āre, -āvī, -ātus, 1, *wish for, want, long for, miss; tack, lose;* pass. *often, especially of soldiers, be missing, be lost.* [desideratum.

dēsidia, -ae, [dēses, *idle,* cf. dēsideō], f., *indolence, idleness.* (VI. 23).

dēsignō, -āre, -āvī, -ātus, [dē + signō, *mark*], 1, *point out; indicate, evidence* (C. III. 96); *designate* (I. 18). [designate.

dēsiliō, -silīre, -siluī, -sultus, [dē + saliō, *leap*], 4, *leap down, jump down; from horses, dismount.*

dēsistō, -sistere, -stitī, -stitūrus, [dē + sistō], 3, *leave off, cease; desist from, stop, give up.* **dēsistere sententiā,** *to give up the notion* (VI. 4). [desist.

dēspectus, see **dēspiciō.**

dēspectus, -ūs, [dēspiciō], m., *a looking down; from an elevation, view.* **dēspectus in mare,** *view of the sea* (III. 14).

dēspērātiō, -ōnis, [dēspērō], f., *despair, hopelessness.* [desperation.

dēspērātus, -a, -um, comp. **-ior,** sup. **-issimus,** [part. of dēspērō], adj., *without hope, beyond hope, desperate.* (VII. 3). [desperate.

dēspērō, -āre, -āvī, -ātus, [dē + spērō], 1, *give up hope of, despair of, have no hope of.* [despair.

dēspiciō, -spicere, -spexī, -spectus, [dē + speciō, *look*], 3, *look down upon; despise, disdain.* [despise.

dēspoliō, -āre, -āvī, -ātus, [dē + spoliō], 1, *despoil, rob.* (II. 31). [despoil.

dēstinō, -āre, -āvī, -ātus, 1, *make fast, bind, stay.* **operī dēstinātī,** *detailed for the work* (VII. 72). [destine. **dēstituō, -stituere, -stituī, -stitūtus,** [dē + statuō], 3, *desert, abandon, leave.* (I. 16). [destitute.

dēstrictus, see **dēstringō.**

dēstringō, -stringere, -strīnxī, -strictus, [dē + stringō, *pluck off*], 3, *unsheathe, draw.* (I. 25; VII. 12).

dēsum, deesse, defuī, [dē + sum], irr., *be wanting, fail, lie lacking.* **hōc ūnum dēfuit,** *this was the only drawback* (IV. 26). **omnia deerant,** *there was a lack of everything* (IV. 29).

dēsuper, [dē + super], adv., *from above.* (I. 52).

dētendō, -ere, —, dētēnsus, [dē + tendō], 3, *relax; of tents, strike* (C. III. 85).

dēterior, comp. **-ius,** sup. **dēterrimus,** [dē], adj., *worse, poorer; of less value* (I. 36).

[deteriorate.

dēterreō, -terrēre, -terruī, -territus, [dē + terreō], 2, *frighten off, prevent, deter; repress* (V. 7). **dēterrēre nē, quō minus,** or **quīn,** *to prevent from.* [deter.

dētestor, -ārī, -ātus, [dē + testor], 1, dep., *curse, execrate.* [detest.

dētineō, -tinēre, -tinuī, -tentus, [dē + teneō], 2, *hold back.* (III. 12). [detain.

dētrāctus, see **dētrahō.**

dētrahō, -trahere, -trāxī, trāctus, [dē + trahō], 3, *draw off, take off; take away, remove.* [detract.

dētrectō, -āre, -āvī, -ātus, [dē + tractō], 1, *avoid.* (VII. 14).

dētrīmentōsus, -a, -um, [dētrīmentum], adj., *hurtful, detrimental.* (VII. 33).

dētrīmentum, -ī, [dē, cf. terō, *wear away*], n., *loss, damage, injury; loss in war, repulse, reverse, defeat.* **quid dētrīmentī,** *any harm* (C. I. 7). [detriment.

dēturbō, -āre, -āvī, -ātus, [dē + turbō, *disturb*], 1, *force back in disorder, dislodge.* (V. 43; VII. 86).

deūrō, -ūrere, -ussī, -ūstus, [dē + ūrō], 3, *burn up.* (VII. 25).

deus, -ī, m., *god.* [deity.

dēvehō, -vehere, -vexī, -vectus, [dē + vehō], 3, *carry away, remove, convey.* **equīs dēvexerat,** *he had brought on horseback* (I. 43).

dēveniō, -venīre, -vēnī, -ventūrus, [dē + veniō], 4, *come.* (II. 21).

dēvexus, -a, -um, [dēvehō], adj., *sloping.* As noun, **dēvexa, n., pl.,** *sloping places, slopes* (VII. 88).

dēvincō, -vincere, -vīcī, -victus, [dē + vincō], 3, *conquer completely, subdue.* (VII. 34, C. III. 87).

dēvocō, -āre, -āvī, -ātus, [dē + vocō], 1, *call away.* **in dubium dēvocāre,** *to risk, endanger* (VI. 7).

dēvōtus, [part. of dēvoveō], adj., *bound by a vow.* As noun, **dēvōtī, -ōrum, m., pl.,** *faithful followers* (III. 22). **dēvoveō, -vovēre, -vōvī, -vōtus,** [dē + voveō], 2, *vow, devote* (III. 22); *offer to the gods, consecrate* (VI. 17). [devote.

dexter, -tra, -trum, adj., *right.* [dexterous.

dextra, -ae, [dexter, sc. **manus**], f., *right hand.* (I. 20).

Diablintēs, -um, [Kel., = 'the Tireless'], m., pl., (dī-a-blin'tēz), a small people in northwestern Gaul, probably a division of the Aulerci. (III. 9).

diciō, -ōnis, pl. and nom. sing, not in use, f., *sway, sovereignty, authority, lordship.* (I. 31, 33; II. 34).

dicō, -āre, -āvī, -ātus, 1, *dedicate; devote, offer.* **sē dicāre in clientēlam, in servitūtem,** *to offer themselves as clients* (VI. 12), *as slaves* (VI. 13).

dīcō, dīcere, dīxī, dīctus, 3, *say, converse,*

speak; mention, tell, utter; appoint. **causam dicere,** *to plead a case.* of a day, *set.*

dictiō, -ōnis, [dīcō], f., *speaking; pleading.* (I. 4). [diction.

dictum, -ī, [dīcō], n., *saying, -word; command, order.* **dictō audiēns, audientēs,** *obedient to (his) order.* [dictum

dīdūcō, -dūcere, -dūxī, -ductus, [dis- + dūcō], 3, *lead in different directions* (VI. 34); *divide, separate* (III. 23); *distribute.* [diduce.

diēs, diēī, m. and f., *day; time* (I. 7). **multō diē,** *late in the day* (I. 22). **in diēs,** *day by day, every day.* **diem dīcere,** *to set a day.*

differō, differre, distulī, dīlātus, [dis- + ferō], irr., *spread, scatter* (V. 43); *put off, delay* (VII. II, C. III. 85); *differ, be different.* [differ.

difficilis, -e, comp. **difficilior,** sup. **difficillimus,** [dis- + facilis], adj., *difficult, hard.* [difficile.

difficultās, -tātis, [difficilis], f., *difficulty, trouble.* [difficulty.

difficulter, comp. **difficilius,** sup. **difficilimē,** [difficilis], adv., *with difficulty;* comp., *with too great difficulty.* (VII. 58).

diffīdō, -fīdere, -fīsus sum, [dis- + fīdō], 3, semi-dep., *distrust, lose confidence in, despair of.* [diffident.

diffīsus, -a, -um, part. of **diffīdō.**

diffluō, -ere, difflūxī, [dis- + fluō], 3, *flow in different directions, divide.* (IV. 10). [diffluent.

diffundō, -fundere, -fūdī, -fūsus, [dis- + fundō], 3, *pour forth; spread out, extend* (VI. 26). [diffuse.

digitus, -ī, m., *finger; as a measure, finger's breadth* (VII. 73), the 16th part of a Roman foot, . 728 of an inch. **digitus pollex,** *thumb as a measure* (III. 13). [digit.

dignitās, -tātis, [dignus], f., *worth, merit; self-respect* (VI. 8); *greatness, rank, reputation.* [dignity.

dignus, -a, -um, comp. **-ior,** sup. **-issimus,** adj., *worthy, worth, deserving.* (VII. 25).

dīiūdicō, -āre, -āvī, -ātus, [dis- + iūdicō], 1, *decide.* (V. 44). [dijudicate.

dīlēctus, see **dīligō.**

dīlēctus, -ūs, [dīligō], m., *levy, draft, enlistment.*

dīligenter, comp. **dīligentius,** sup. **dīligentissimē,** [dīligēns], adv., *carefully, punctually, with painstaking.* **parum dīligenter,** *with too little care* (III. 18).

dīligentia, -ae, [dīligēns], f., *care, painstaking, activity.* [diligence.

dīligō, -ligere, -lēxī, -lēctus, [dis- + legō, *choose*], 3, *love, prize.* (VI. 19).

dīmēnsus, see **dīmētior.**

dīmētior, -mētīri, -mēnsus [dis- + mētior], 4, dep., passive in Caesar, *measure, measure off*

(IV. 17); of work, *lay out* (II. 19). [dimension.

dīmicātiō, -ōnis, [dīmicō], f., *combat, engagement, encounter.* (VII. 86).

dīmicō, -āre, -āvī, -ātum est, [dis- + micō], 1, *fight, contend, struggle.*

dīmidius, -a,-um, [dis- + medius], adj., *half* (VI. 31). As noun, **dīmidium, -ī**, n., *half.*

dīmidiō minor, *a half smaller* (V. 13).

dīmittō, -mittere, -mīsī, -missus, [dis- + mittō], 3, *send in different directions, send about; dismiss, send off; let go, let slip, lose; abandon, leave; give up* (VII. 17); *disband* (II. 14). [dismiss.

dirimō, -imere, -ēmī, -ēmptus, [dis- + emō, take], 3, *take apart; break off, put an end to* (I. 46).

dīripiō, -ripere, -ripuī, -reptus, [dis- + rapiō, seize], 3, *tear asunder; ravage, plunder, pillage.*

dis- (dī-), inseparable prep., used only as a prefix with other words, adding the force of *apart, asunder, in different directions, utterly, entirely; not, un-.* In Composition **dis-** becomes **dif-** before **f**, **dir-** before vowels, **dī-** before **d, g, l, m, n, r**, and **v**.

Dīs, Dītis, m., with **pater**, *Dis pater* (dis pa' ter), *Father Dis, god of the Underworld.* (VI. 18).

discēdō, -cēdere, -cessī, -cessūrus, pf. pass. impers., **discessum est, [dis- + cēdō]**, 3, *go apart, disperse, scatter; depart, withdraw, leave, go away, go off.* **ab armīs discēdere**, *to lay down one's arms.*

disceptātor, -ōris, [disceptō, decide], m., *arbitrator, umpire, judge.* (VII. 37).

discernō, -cernere, -crēvī, -crētus, [dis- + cernō], 3, *distinguish between, know apart, keep separate* (VII. 75). [discern.

discessus, -ūs, [discēdō], m., *departure, going azuay.*

disciplīna, -ae, [discipulus], f., *instruction, training; system.* [discipline.

disclūdō, -clūdere, -clūsī, -clūsus, [dis- + claudō], 3, *keep apart, hold apart* (IV. 17); *separate* (VII. 8).

discō, discere, didicī, 3, *learn.*

discrīmen, -inis, [cf. discernō], n., *interval; crisis, peril* (VI. 38).

discutiō, -cutere, -cussī, -cussus, [dis- + quatiō, shake], 3, *shatter; remove, clear away* (VII. 8). [discuss. **disiciō, -icere, -iēcī, -iectus, [dis- + iaciō]**, 3, *drive asunder; disperse, scatter, rout* (I. 25; III. 20).

disiectus, see **disiciō.**

dispār, -paris, [dis- + pār], adj., *unequal, unlike.* (V. 16; VII. 39).

disparō, -āre, -āvī, -ātus, [dis- + parō], 1, *divide, separate.* [disparate.

dispergō, -spergere, -spersī, -spersus, [dis- + spargō, scatter], 3, *scatter, scatter about, disperse.* [disperse. **dispersus**, see **dispergō.**

dispōnō, -pōnere, -posuī, -positus, [dis- + ponō], 3, *set in various places, distribute; station, post.* [dispose.

disputātiō, -ōnis, [disputō], f., *discussion, debate, dispute.* [disputation.

disputō, -āre, -āvī, -ātus, [dis- + putō], 1, *treat, investigate, discuss.* (VI. 14). [dispute.

dissēnsiō, -ōnis, [dissentiō], f., *disagreement, dissension.* [dissension.

dissentiō, -sentīre, -sēnsī, -sēnsus, [dis- + sentiō], 4, *differ in opinion, disagree.* (V. 29; VII. 29). [dissent.

disserō, -serere, [dis- + serō, sow], 3, *plant here and there, place at intervals.* (VII. 73).

dissimulō, -āre, -āvī, -ātus, [dis- + simulō], 1, *make unlike; conceal, keep secret* (IV. 6). [dissimulate.

dissipō, -āre, -āvī, -ātus, 1, *scatter, disperse.* [dissipate.

dissuādeō, -suādēre, -suāsī, -suāsūrus, [dis- + suādeō], 2, *advise against, object, oppose.* (VII. 15). [dissuade.

distendō, -tendere, -tendī, -tentus, [dis- + tendō], 3, *stretch out.* (C. III. 92). [distend.

distineō, -tinēre, -tinuī, -tentus, [dis- + teneō], 2, *keep apart, hold apart, separate; hinder, delay* (VII. 37).

distō, -āre, [dis- + stō], 1, *stand apart, be separated, be distant.* **distantēs inter sē bīnōs pedēs**, *two feet apart* (VII. 23). [distant.

distrahō, -trahere, -trāxī, -trāctus, [dis- + trahō, draw], 3, *wrench asunder* (VII. 23); *draw apart* (C. III. 92). [distract.

distribuō, -tribuere, -tribuī, -tribūtus, [dis- + tribuō], 3, *distribute, divide, assign, apportion.* [distribute.

dītissimus, see **dīves.**

diū, comp. **diūtius**, sup. **diūtissimē**, adv., *long, for a long time.* **quam diū**, *as long as* (I. 17).

diurnus, -a, -um, [cf. diēs], adj., *of the day, by day.* [diurnal.

diūtinus, -a, -um, [diū], adj., *long continued, lasting.* (V. 52).

diūtissimē, see **diū.**

diūtius, see **diū.**

diūturnitās, -tātis, [diūturnus], f., *long continuance, length (of time), long duration.* (I. 40; III. 4).

diūturnus, -a, -um, comp. **-ior, [diū]**, adj., *long, prolonged.* (I. 14).

dīversus, -a, -um, [part. of dīvertō], adj., *opposite; separate, apart; different; remote* (VI. 25). [diverse.

dīvertō, -ere, -ī, -sus, [dis- + vertō], 3, *separate.* (II. 24). [divert.

dīves, -itis, comp. **dītior**, sup. **dītissimus**, adj., *rich, wealthy.* (I. 2).

Dīviciācus, -ī, m., (div" i-shi-ā' kus):
(1) An Aeduan of influence, loyal to Caesar, who at his intercession pardoned Dumnorix (I. 18-20), and the Bellovaci (II. 14, 15).
(2) A ruler of the Suessiones. (II. 4).

Dīvicō, -ōnis, m., (div'i-kō), leader of the Helvetians in their war with Cassius, 107 B.C., and head of an embassy to Caesar, 58 B.C. (I. 13, 14).

dīvidō, -videre, -vīsī, -vīsus, 3, *separate, divide.* [divide.

dīvīnus, -a, -um, comp. **-ior,** sup. **-issimus,** [**dīvus**], adj., *divine, sacred.* [divine.

dīvīsus, see **dīvidō.**

dō, dare, dedī, datus, irr., *give, give up, give over, grant; offer, furnish, allow.* **negōtium dare,** *to commission, direct* (II. 2). **sē ventō dare,** *to run before the wind* (III. 13). **in fugam dare,** *to put to flight.* **operam dare,** *to take pains* (V. 7). [date.

doceō, docēre, docuī, doctus, 2, *teach; inform; point out, state; show* (VI. 1). [doctor.

documentum, -ī, [**doceō**], n., *proof, warning.* (VII. 4). [document.

doleō, dolēre, doluī, dolitūrus, 2, *suffer; be grieved, be annoyed.*

dolor, -ōris, [**doleō**], m., *pain, suffering; grief, distress.* [dolors.

dolus, -ī, m., *cunning, fraud, deceit* (I. 13; IV. 13). [dole.

domesticus, a. -um, [**domus**], adj., *home, native, internal; their own* (II. 10); *of their own household* (C. III.60). **domesticum bellum,** *civil war* (V. 9). [domestic.

domicilium, -ī, [**domus**], n., *dwelling, abode, habitation.* [domicile.

dominor, -ārī, -ātus, [**dominus**], 1, dep., *be master, have dominion.* (II. 31). [dominate.

dominus, -ī, [**domō,** *subdue*], m., *master, lord.* (VI. 13). [dominie.

Domitius, -ī, m., (do-mish' [y]us):
(1) *Lucius Domitius Ahenobarbus,* consul with Appius Claudius Pulcher, 54 B.C. (V. 1), in the Civil War a general on the side of Pompey.
(2) *Gnaeus Domitius,* a cavalry officer in Curio's army in Africa. (C. II. 42).
(3) *Gnaeus Domitius Calvinus,* a general in Caesar's army. (C. III. 89).

domus, -ūs, f., *house, home.* [dome.

Donnotaurus, -ī, m., *Gaius Valerius Donnotaurus* (don-o-tâ' rus), a leader among the Helvii. (VII. 65).

dōnō, -āre, -āvī, -ātus, [**dōnum**], 1, *give, grant, confer.* (I. 47; VII. 11). [donate.

dōnum, -ī, [**dō**], n., *gift, present.*

dorsum, -ī, n., *back; of a mountain, long summit,* like the back of an animal (VII. 44). [dorsal.

dōs, dōtis, [cf. **dō**], f., *dowry, marriage portion.*

(VI. 19). [dot (dowry).

Druidēs, -um, [Kel. **druides,** 'the very wise'], m., pl., *Druids.*

Dubis, -is, [Kel. = 'the Black'], m., (dū'bis), a river in Gaul, tributary of the Arar *(Saône);* now the *Doubs.* (I. 38).

dubitātiō, -ōnis, [**dubitō**], f., *doubt, hesitation.* [dubitation.

dubitō, -āre, -āvī, -ātus, [**dubius**], 1, *be uncertain, doubt; hesitate, delay.*

dubius, -a, -um, adj., *doubtful, uncertain.* **nōn est dubium quīn,** *there is no doubt that* (I. 3). [dubious.

ducentī, -ae, -a, or **CC,** [**duo + centum**], adj., *two hundred.*

dūcō, dūcere, dūxī, ductus, 3, *lead, guide, conduct, bring, take; of a trench, make; protract, prolong, put off; think, consider, reckon.* **in mātrimōnium dūcere,** *to marry* (I. 9, 53). [ductile.

ductus, -ūs, [**dūcō**], m., *generalship, command.* (VII. 62; C. I. 7). [duct.

dum, conj., *while; until.*

Dumnorīx, -īgis, m., (dum' no-riks), an Aeduan, brother of Diviciacus, and son-in-law of Orgetorix; a bitter enemy of Caesar, and leader of an Aeduan anti-Roman party; slain by Caesar's orders while trying to escape from him, 54 B.C. (fig. 42.)

dumtaxat, [**dum + taxat**], adv., *merely, only.* (C. II. 41).

duo, -ae, -o, or **II,** adj., *two.* [duet.

duodecim, or **XII,** [**duo + decem**], indecl. num. adjective, *twelve.* [duodecimal.

duodecimus, -a, -um, [**duodecim**], num. adj., *twelfth.*

duodēnī, -ae, -a, gen. pl. **duodēnum** (VII. 36), [**duodecim**], distributive num. adj., *twelve at a time, by twelves.*

duodēseptuāgintā, or **LXVIII,** [**duo + dē + septuāgintā**], indeclinable num. adj., *sixty-eight.* (I. 29). **duodētrīgintā,** or **XXVIII,** [**duo + dē + trīgintā**], indeclinable num. adj., *twenty-eight.* (V. 2).

duodēvīgintī, -ae, -a, or **XVIII,** [**duo + dē + vīgintī**], num. adj., *eighteen.*

duplex, -icis, [**duo,** cf. **plicō,** *fold*], adj., *twofold, double.* [duplex.

duplicō, -āre, -āvī, -ātus, [**duplex**], 1, *make double, double.* [duplicate.

dūritia, -ae, [**dūrus**], f., *hardness; severe mode of life* (VI. 21). [duress.

dūrō, -āre, -āvī, -ātus, [**dūrus**], 1, *harden, make hardy.* (VI. 28).

Dūrocortorum, -ī, [Kel. = 'Fortified Enclosure'], n., (dū-ro-cor' torum), capital of the Remi, now *Reims.* (VI. 44).

dūrus, -a, -um, comp. **-ior,** sup. **-issimus,** adj., *hard, severe, difficult;* of a season, *inclement* (VII. 8).

Dūrus, -ī, m., *Quintus Laberius Durus,* (labē'ri-us dū'rus), a military tribune. (V. 15).

dux, ducis, [dūcō, *lead*], m., *leader, guide; general, commander.* [duke.

Dyrrachīnus, -a, -um, [Dyrrachium], adj., *at Dyrrachium, of Dyrrachium.* (C. III. 84, 87, 89).

Dyrrachium, -ī, [Δ Υ Ρ Ρ Α Χ Ι Ο Ν], n., (dir-rā' ki-um), a city on the east coast of the Adriatic, formerly called *Epidamnus;* now *Durazzo,* in Albania. (C. III. 53).

E.

ē, see **ex.**

eā, [properly abl. of **is,** sc. **parte**], adv., *there, on that side.* (V. 51).

Eburōnēs, -um, m., pl., (eb-ū-rō' nēz), a Belgic people north of the Treverans. In 54 B.C. they destroyed a detachment of Caesar's army under Sabinus and Cotta, and were afterwards almost exterminated by him.

Eburovīcēs, -um, m., pl., (eb" ū-ro-vi'sēz.), a division of the Aulerci.

ēdiscō, -discere, -didicī, [ex + discō], 3, *learn by heart.* (VI. 14).

ēditus, -a, -um, comp. **-ior,** [part. of ēdō], adj., *elevated; rising* (II. 8).

ēdō, -dere, -didī, -ditus, [ex + dō], 3, *put forth; inflict* (I. 31). [edit.

ēdoceō, -docēre, -docuī, -doctus, [ex + doceō], 2, *teach carefully, instruct, inform, tell.*

ēdūcō, -dūcere, -dūxī, -ductus, [ex + dūcō], 3, *lead out, lead forth;* of a sword, *draw* (V. 44). [educe.

effēminō, -āre, -āvī, -ātus, [ex + fēmina], 1, *make womanish, weaken, enervate.* (I. 1; IV. 2). [effeminate.

efferciō, -īre, effertus, [ex + farciō, *stuff*], 4, *fill in.* (VII. 23).

efferō, -ferre, extulī, ēlātus, [ex + ferō], irr., *bring out, carry forth, carry away* (I. 5; V. 45); *spread abroad, publish* (I. 46; VI. 14; VII. 1, 2); *lift up, pull up; extol* (C. III. 87); *elate* (V. 47, VII. 47). [elate.

efficiō, -ficere, -fēcī, -fectus, [ex + faciō], 3, *make out, bring about; accomplish, effect, produce; make, render; build, construct.* [effect.

effodiō, -fodere, -fōdī, -fossus, [ex + fodiō], 3, *dig out;* of the eyes, *gouge out* (VII. 4).

effossus, see **effodiō.**

effugiō, -fugere,-fūgī, [ex + fugiō], 3, *escape.*

effundō, -fundere, -fūdī, -fūsus, [ex + fundō], 3, *pour out.* **sē effundere,** of a crowd, *pour out, rush forth* (C. II. 7); of cavalry, *dash forth* (V. 19). [effusive.

egēns, egentis, comp. **egentior,** sup. **-issimus,** [part. of egeō], adj., *needy.* As noun, **egentēs, -ium,** m., pl., *the needy, destitute men* (VII. 4, C. III. 59).

egeō, egēre, eguī, 2, *lack, be in want (of).* (VI. 11).

egestās, -tātis, [egēns], f., *privation, destitution, want.* (VI. 24).

ego, meī, personal pron., *I;* pl. **nōs, nostrum,** *we.* [egotism.

egomet, pl. **nōsmet** [ego + -met, enclitic suffix = 'self'], personal pronoun, *I myself, ourselves.* (VII. 38).

ēgredior, -gredī, -gressus, [ex + gradior, *step*], 3, dep., *go out, go forth, come forth, leave;* from a ship, *land, disembark.*

ēgregiē, [ēgregius], adv., *remarkably well, admirably, splendidly.*

ēgregius, -a, -um, [ex + grex, *herd, crowd*], adj., *eminent, marked, distinguished, excellent.* [egregious.

ēgressus, see **ēgredior.**

ēgressus, -ūs, [ēgredior], m., *departure; disembarking, landing* (V. 8). [egress.

Egus, -ī, m., (ē' gus), an Allobrogian, son of Roucillus. (C. III. 59).

ēiciō, -icere, -iēcī, -iectus, [ex + iaciō], 3, *throw out, cast out, thrust out, expel; cast up* (V. 10). **sē ēicere,** *to rush, sally forth.* [eject.

eius modī, see **modus.**

ēlābor, -lābī, -lāpsus, [ex + lābor], 3, dep., *slip away; escape* (V. 37). [elapse.

ēlātus, see **efferō.**

Elaver, Elaveris, n., (el' a-ver), a tributary of the Liger (*Loire*), into which it flows from the south after a course of about 200 miles; now *Allier.*

ēlēctus, -a, -um, comp. **-ior,** sup. **-issimus,** [part. of ēligō], adj., *chosen, picked.* (II. 4; C. III. 91). [elect.

elephantus, -ī, [Ε Λ Ε Φ Α Σ], m., *elephant,* (VI. 28). [elephant.

Eleutetī, -ōrum, m., pl., (e-lū' te-tī) a people of Central Gaul. (VII. 75).

ēliciō, -licere, -licuī, [ex + laciō, *entice*], 3, *entice forth, lure forth; bring out, draw out.* [elicit.

ēloquor, -ī, ēlocūtus, [ex + loquor], 3, dep., *speak out, utter, declare.* (C. II. 34). [eloquent.

Elusātēs, -ium, m., pl., (el-ū-sā' tez), a people in Central Aquitania. (III. 27).

ēmigrō, -āre, -āvī, [ex + migrō, *depart*], I, *go forth, move, emigrate.* (I. 31). [emigrate.

ēmineō, -minēre, -minuī, 2, *project, stand out.* (VII. 72, 73). [eminent.

ēminus [ex + manus, *hand*], adv., *at a distance, from afar.* (VII. 24).

ēmissus, see **ēmittō.**

ēmittō, -mittere, -mīsī, -missus, [ex + mittō], 3, *send out; hurl, cast, shoot, discharge* (II. 23); *throw away, let go* (I. 25). [emit.

emō, emere, ēmī, ēmptus, 3, *buy, purchase.* (I. 16; II. 33).

ēnāscor, -nāscī, -nātus, [ex + nāscor], 3, dep., *grow out*; of branches, *shoot out* (II. 17).

enim [nam], conj., postpositive, *for, for in fact.* neque enim, *and (with good reason) for . . . not, for in fact . . . not.*

ēnītor, -ī, ēnīsus, [ex + nītor], 3, dep., *make effort* (C. II. 6); *force one's way out* (C. II. 34).

ēnūntiō, -āre, -āvī, -ātus [ex + nūntiō], 1, *report, reveal, disclose.* [enounce.

eō, abl. of is (44).

eō, [cf. is], adv., *thither, to that place, there.*

eō, īre, iī, itūrus, ītum est, irr., *go, pass, march, advance.*

eōdem [idem], adv., *to the same place; to the same thing* (I. 14), *to the same end* (IV. 11).

ephippiātus, -a, -um, adj., *riding with saddle-cloths.* (IV. 2).

ephippium, -ī, [Ε Φ Ι Π Π Ι Ο Ν, from Ε Π Ι + Ι Π Π Ο Σ], n., *saddle-cloth.* (IV. 2).

Ēpīrus, -ī, [" Η Π Ε Ι Ρ Ο Σ], f., (e-pī' rus), a province in the northern part of Greece, east of the Adriatic. (C. III. 47, 61).

epistula, -ae, [Ε Π Ι Σ Τ Ο Λ Η], f., *letter, despatch.* (V. 48). [epistle.

Eporēdorīx, -īgis, [Kel., = 'King of the running of horses' or 'King of men who ride after horses'], m., (ep-o-red' o-riks):
(1) A leader of the Aeduans, captured by Caesar. (VII. 67).
(2) A young Aeduan of rank, for a time friendly to Caesar, afterwards one of the commanders of the Gallic army raised for the relief of Alesia. (VII. 38, 39, 40, 54, 55, 63, 64, 76.)

epulae, -ārum, f., pl., *feast.* (VI. 28).

eques, -itis, [equus], m., *horseman, cavalryman, trooper*; as a member of a social order, *knight.*

equester, -tris, -tre, [eques], adj., *of cavalry, cavalry-.* [equestrian.

equitātus, -ūs, [equitō, *ride*], m., *cavalry; knighthood,* collectively *knights* (I. 31).

equus, -ī, m., *horse.* [equine.

Eratosthenēs, -is, [Ε Π Α Τ Ο Σ Θ Ε Ν Η Σ], m., (er-a-tos' the-nēz), a Greek, born at Cyrene, in Africa, B.C. 276; died about B.C. 196; librarian of the great library at Alexandria in Egypt, and famous as a geographer, mathematician, historian, and grammarian. (VI. 24).

ērēctus, -a, -um, comp. -ior, [part. of ērigō], adj., *high, elevated.* (III. 13). [erect (adj.).

ēreptus, see ēripiō.

ergā, prep. with acc., *towards.* (V. 54).

ergō, adv., *therefore, then.* (VII. 77).

ērigō, -rigere, -rēxī, -rēctus, [ex + regō], 3, *raise to a standing position* (VI. 27); *erect,* [erect (verb).

ēripiō, -ripere, -ripuī, -reptus, [ex + rapiō, *seize*], 3, *take away, snatch away; rescue, save* (I.

53). sē ēripere, *to rescue one's self, make one's escape.*

errō, -āre, -āvī, -ātus, 1, *wander; be mistaken, delude one's self* [err.

error, -ōris, [errō], m., *wandering; mistake* (C. III. 73). [error,

ērumpō, -rumpere, -rūpī, -ruptus, [ex + rumpō, *break*], 3, *burst forth, sally forth.* (III. 5). [erupt.

ēruptiō, -ōnis, [ērumpō], f., *a bursting forth; sally, sortie.* [eruption.

essedārius, -ī, [essedum], m., *fighter from a chariot, chariot-fighter.*

essedum, -ī, n., *two-wheeled war-chariot.* (IV. 32, 33; V. 9, 16, 17).

Esuviī, -ōrum, m., pl., (e-sū'vi-ī), a people in northwestern Gaul.

et, conj., *and.* et . . . et, *both . . . and.*

etiam [et + iam], conj., *also; even.* non solum . . . sed etiam, *not only . . . but also.*

etsī [et + sī], conj., *although, though, even if.*

ēvādō, -vādere, -vāsī, -vāsūrus, [ex + vādō], 3, *escape.* (III. 19). [evade.

ēvellō, -vellere, -vellī, -vulsus, [ex + vellō, *pluck*], 3, *pull out.* (I. 25).

ēveniō, -venīre, -vēnī, -ventūrus, [ex + veniō], 4, *turn out, happen.* (IV. 25).

eventus, -ūs, [cf. ēveniō], m., *outcome, result; chance, fortune* (VI. 42); *fate, accident* (IV. 31). [event.

ēvocātus, -ī, [part. of ēvocō], m., *veteran volunteer,* a soldier serving voluntarily after the completion of his time of service. (VII. 65).

ēvocō, -āre, -āvī, -ātus, [ex + vocō], 1, *call out, call forth, call, summon; invite* (V. 58). [evoke.

ēvolō, -āre, -āvī, [ex + volō, *fly*], 1, *fly forth, rush out, dash out.*

ex, often before consonants ē, prep. with abl., *out of, out from*; of place, *from, out of, down from*; of time, *from, since, after*; of source and material, *from, of*; of partition, *of, out of, from among*; of transition, *from, out of*; of cause, *from, by reason of, in consequence of*; of measure and correspondence, *according to, with, in, by, on.* ex unā parte, *on one side.* In composition ex becomes ef before f, ē before b, d, g, i consonant, l, m, n, and v.

exāctus, see exigō.

exagitō, -āre, -āvī, -ātus, [ex + agitō, freq. of agō], 1, *disturb, harass.* (II. 29; IV. 1).

exāminō, -āre, -āvī, -ātus, [exāmen, *tongue of a balance*], 1, *weigh.* (V. 12). [examine.

exanimō, -āre, -āvī, -ātus, [exanimus], 1, *deprive of life, kill*; pass., *be out of breath, weakened, exhausted* (II. 23, III. 19; C. III. 92).

exārdēscō, -ārdēscere, -ārsī, -ārsūrus, [ex + ārdēscō], 3, *take fire; be incensed* (V. 4).

exaudiō, -dīre, -dīvī, -dītus, [ex + audiō], 4,

hear distinctly, hear plainly.

excēdō, -cēdere, -cessī, -cessūrus, [ex + cēdō], 3, *go out, leave, withdraw, depart.* [exceed.

excellēns, -entis, comp. **-ior,** sup. **-issimus,** [excellō], adj., *surpassing, excellent.* (C. III. 99). [excellent.

excellō, -cellere, participial adj. **excelsus,** 3, *be eminent, surpass.* (VI. 13). [excel.

excelsus, -a, -um, comp. **-ior,** sup. **-issimus,** [part. of **excellō**], adj., *high* (VI. 26). [excelsior.

exceptō, -āre, -āvī, -ātus, [freq. of **excipiō**], 1, *catch up* with the hands, *take hold of* (VII. 47).

exceptus, see **excipiō.**

excīdō, -cīdere, -cīdī, -cisus, [ex + caedō], 3, *cut out; cut down* (VII. 50). [excise.

excipiō, -cipere, -cēpī, -ceptus, [ex + capiō], 3, *take out; take up* (VII. 3); *take in* (VII. 28); *cut off, catch* (VI. 28, 35; VII. 20); *receive, withstand* (I. 52, III. 5, IV. 17; C. III. 92); *cope with, encounter* (III. 13); *take the place of, relieve, succeed, follow* (V. 16; VII. 51, 88; C. II. 7, III. 87). [except.

excitō, -āre, -āvī, -ātus, [ex + citō, *move*], 1, *erect, raise rapidly* (III. 14; V. 40); *stir up, rouse, spur on; kindle* (VII. 24). [excite.

exclūdō, -clūdere, -clūsī, -clūsus, [ex + claudō], 3, *shut out, shut off, cut off; hinder, prevent.* [exclude.

excōgitō, -āre, -āvī, -ātus, [ex + cōgitō], 1, *think out, think of.* (V. 31). [excogitate.

excruciō, -āre, -āvī, -ātus, [ex + cruciō, from crux, *cross*], 1, *torment, torture.* [excruciate.

excubitor, -ōris, [excubō], m., *soldier in bivouac; watchman, sentinel.* (VII. 69).

excubō, -cubāre, -cubuī, [ex + cubō, *lie down*], 1, *lie out* of doors, *bivouac; keep watch, keep guard.*

exculcō, -āre, [ex + calcō, from calx, *heel*], 1, *tread down, pack down* by stamping. (VII. 73).

excursiō, -ōnis, [ex, cf. **currō**], f., *a running out; sally, sortie* (II. 30). [excursion.

excursus, -ūs, [excurrō], m., *a running forth; onset, attack* (C. III. 92). [excursus.

excūsātiō, -ōnis, [excūsō], f., *excuse, apology, defense.* (VI. 4).

excūsō, -āre, -āvī, -ātus, [ex, cf. causa], 1, *excuse, make excuse for.* (IV. 22). [excuse.

exemplum, -ī, [cf. eximō], n., *example, precedent;* as an example to warn others, *kind of punishment* (I. 31). [example.

exeō, -īre, -iī, -itum est, [ex + eō], irr., *go forth, go out; withdraw, leave.*

exerceō, -ercēre, -ercuī, -ercitus, [ex + arceō], 2, *exercise, practice; train, discipline.* [exercise.

exercitātiō, -ōnis, [exercitō, freq. of exerceō], f., *practice, exercise, training.*

exercitātus, -a, -um, comp. **-ior,** sup. **-issimus,** [exercitō, freq. of exerceō], adj.,

practiced, experienced, trained.

exercitus, -ūs, [exerceō], m., *army,* as a trained and disciplined body.

exhauriō, -haurīre, -hausī, -haustus, [ex + hauriō, *draw up*], 4, *take out.* (V. 42). [exhaust.

exigō, -igere, -ēgī, -āctus, [ex + agō], 3, *drive out;* of time, *spend, complete, end* (III. 28; VI. 1); of money, *demand, require* (C. I. 6). [exact.

exiguē [exiguus], adv., *barely, hardly.* (VII. 71).

exiguitās, -ātis, [exiguus], f., *smallness* (IV. 30); *scantness* (IV. 1); *small number, fewness* (III. 23); *shortness* (II. 21, 33).

exiguus, -a, -um, sup. **-issimus,** [exigō], adj., *small, scanty, little.*

eximius, -a, -um, [cf. eximō], adj., *distinguished, excellent.* (II. 8).

exīstimātiō, -ōnis, [exīstimō], f., *opinion, judgment* (I. 20; V. 44); *good name, reputation* (C.I. 7).

exīstimō, -āre, -āvī, -ātus, [ex + aestimō, *compute*], 1, *reckon; think, consider, judge, suppose, believe.*

exitus, -ūs, [exeō], m., *a going out, egress* (VII. 44); *passage* (VII. 28); *conclusion, end; issue, event, outcome.* [exit.

expediō, -pedīre, -pedīvī, -pedītus, [ex, cf. pēs], 4, *disengage, set free; get ready, make ready.* [expedite.

expedītiō, -ōnis, [expediō], f., *rapid march.* (V. 10). [expedition.

expedītus, -a, -um, comp. **-ior,** sup. **-issimus,** [part. of expediō], adj., *with light equipment, unencumbered, light-armed; convenient, easy.* **legiōnēs expedītae,** *legions in light marching order,* without baggage. As noun, **expedītus, -ī,** m., *soldier with light equipment, light-armed soldier.*

expellō, -pellere, -pulī, -pulsus, [ex + pellō], 3, *drive out, drive away, remove.* [expel.

experior, -perīrī, -pertus, 4, dep., *put to the test, try.* [expert.

expiō, -āre, -āvī, -ātus, [ex + piō, *appease*], 1, *atone for, make amends for.* (V. 52). [expiate.

expleō, -plēre, -plēvī, -plētus, [ex + pleō, *fill*], 2, *fill up, fill full; fill out, complete.*

explicō, -āre, -āvī and **-uī, explicitus, explicātūrus,** [ex + plicō, *fold*], 1, *unfold;* of troops, with **sē,** *deploy* (C. III. 93). [explicate.

explōrātor, -ōris, [explōrō], m., *scout, patrol.*

explōrātus, -a, -um, comp. **-ior,** sup. **-issimus,** [part. of explōrō], adj., *established, certain, settled, sure,* Neut. as noun in **prō explōrātō,** lit. *for a certainty, as certain* (VI. 5).

explōrō, -āre, -āvī, -ātus, 1, *search out, investigate, explore; spy out, reconnoitre; gain, secure.* [explore.

expōnō, -pōnere, -posuī, -positus, [ex +

pōnō], 3, *set out, put out; place in full view, array* (IV. 23); from ships, *set on shore, land; set forth, state, explain.* [expose.

exportō, -āre, -āvī, -ātus, [ex + portō], 1, *carry away.* (IV. 18). [export.

exposcō, -poscere, -poposcī, [ex + poscō], 3, *earnestly request, clamor for.* (VII. 19; C. III. 90).

exprimō, -primere, -pressī, -pressus, [ex + premō], 3, *press out; force out* (I. 32); *raise, increase* (VII. 22). [express.

expugnātiō, -ōnis, [expugnō], f., *storming, assault.* (VI. 41).

expugnō, -āre, -āvī, -ātus, [ex + pugno], 1, *take by storm, take by assault, capture.*

expulsus, see **expellō**.

exquīrō, -quīrere, -quīsīvī, -quīsītus, [ex + quaerō], 3, *seek out, search out* (I. 41); *ask for, inquire into* (III. 3). [exquisite.

exquīsītus, see **exquīrō**.

exsequor, -sequī, -secūtus, [ex + sequor], 3, dep., *follow up; maintain, enforce* (I. 4). [execute.

exserō, -serere, -seruī, -sertus, [ex + serō], 3, *thrust out; thrust out* from one's garments, *bare* (VII. 50).

exsertus, see **exserō**.

exsistō, -sistere, -stitī, [ex + sistō], 3, *appear; spring up, arise, ensue;* of a horn, *project* (VI. 26). [exist.

exspectō, -āre, -āvī, -ātus, [ex + spectō], 1, *look out for, wait for, await; look to see, expect.* [expect.

exspoliō, -āre, -āvī, -ātus, [ex + spoliō], 1, *deprive, rob.* (VII. 77).

exstinguō, -stinguere, -stīnxī, -stīnctus, [ex + stinguō], 3, *quench completely.* (V. 29). [extinguish.

exstō, -stāre, [ex + stō], 1, *stand out, project.* (V. 18). [extant.

exstruō, -struere, -strūxī, -strūctus, [ex + struō, *pile*], 3, *pile up, heap up; rear, build, construct, make* (VII. 72).

exsul, -ulis, m. and f., *outlaw, exile.* (V. 55).

exter or exterus, -a, -um, comp. exterior, sup. extrēmus, [ex] adj., *outward, outer.* Sup. extrēmus, *last, extreme, at the end.* As noun, extrēmī, -ōrum, m., pl., *the rear* (V. 10); neut. sing. in ad extrēmum, *at the end, finally* (IV. 4). [extreme.

externus, -a, -um, [exter], adj., *outward; foreign* (C. II. 5). [external.

exterreō, -ēre, -uī, -itus, [ex + terreō, *scare*], 2, *greatly frighten, terrify.*

extimēscō, -timēscere, -timuī, [ex + timēscō, *fear*], 3, *fear greatly, dread.* (III. 13).

extorqueō, -torquēre, -torsī, -tortus, [ex + torqueō, *twist*], 2, *force from; wrest from* (VII. 54). [extort.

extrā [exter], prep. with acc., *outside of beyond, without.* [extra.

extrahō, -trahere, -trāxī, -trāctus, [ex + trahō, *draw*], 3, *draw out; draw out to no purpose, waste* (V. 22). [extract.

extrūdō, -trūdere, -trūsī, -trūsus, [ex + trūdō], 3, *thrust out; shut out* (III. 12). [extrude.

exuō, -uere, -uī, -ūtus, 3, *strip, strip off, despoil, deprive.*

exūrō, -ūrere, -ussī, -ūstus, [ex + ūrō, *burn*], 3, *burn up.* (I. 5).

F.

faber, fabrī, m., *skilled workman, mechanic, artisan.* (V. 11). [fabric.

Fabius, -ī, m., (fā'bi-us):

(1) *Quintus Fabius Maximus* (mak' si-mus), called *Allobrogicus* (al-o-broj' i-kus), in honor of his victory over the Allobroges, Arvernians, and Ruteni in the year of his consulship, B.C. 121. (I. 45).

(2) *Gaius Fabius*, a lieutenant of Caesar in the Gallic War, and in the first year of the Civil War.

(3) *Lucius Fabius*, a centurion, killed at Gergovia. (VII. 47, 50).

(4) *Fabius, the Paelignian*, a soldier in Curio's army. (C. II. 35).

facile, comp. facilius, sup. facillimē, [facilis], adv., *easily, readily.*

facilis, -e, comp. facilior, sup. facillimus, [cf. faciō], adj., *easy, not difficult, not hard.* [facile.

facinus, -oris, [faciō], n., *action; wicked action, misdeed, crime.* facinus admittere or in sē admittere, *to become guilty of (a) crime.*

faciō, facere, fēcī, factus, 3, *do, make; act, perform, accomplish, form; bring about, cause; furnish, give.* For pass., fiō, fierī, factus sum, see fiō. certiōrem facere, *to inform,* imperāta facere, *to obey commands.* iter facere, *to march.* vim facere, *to use violence* (I. 8, V. 7). fidem facere, *to give assurances* (IV. 11). [factor.

factiō, -ōnis, [faciō], f., *party, political party; league.* [faction.

factū, pass. supine of faciō.

factum, -ī, [faciō], n., *deed, action, achievement.* [fact.

facultās, -ātis, [facilis], f., *ability, capability; opportunity, chance; abundance; supply* (III. 9). Pl., *resources, wealth.* [faculty.

fāgus, -ī, f., *beech-tree.* (V. 12).

fallō, fallere, fefellī, falsus, 3, *deceive, cheat; disappoint.*

falsus, -a, -um, [part. of fallō], adj., *false, ungrounded.* [false.

falx, falcis, f., *sickle; sickle-shaped hook.*

fāma, -ae, [cf. fārī, *to speak*], f., *report, rumor, common talk; reputation, fame* (VII. 77). [fame.

famēs, -is, f., *hunger, starvation.* [famine.

familia, -ae, [famulus, *servant*], f., *body of*

slaves in one household, *household; family* (VII. 33); including the whole body of serfs and retainers under the authority of a nobleman, *retinue* (I. 4). **pater familiae,** *head of a family, house-holder* (VI. 19); **patrēs familiae,** *heads of families* (C. II.44). **mātrēs familiae,** *matrons* (I. 50; VII. 26, 47, 48). **antīquissimā familiā,** *of a very old family* (VII. 32). **amplissimā familiā,** *of a very distinguished family* (VII. 37). [family.

familiāris, -e, comp. **-ior,** sup. **-issimus,** [**familia**], adj., *belonging to a family, private.* **rēs familiāris,** *private property, estate, private fortune* (I. 18; VII. 14, 64). As noun, **familiāris, -is,** m., *intimate friend, companion.* [familiar.

familiāritās, -ātis, [**familiāris**], f., *intimacy, close friendship.* [familiarity.

fānum, -ī, n., *shrine.* (C. I. 6). [fane.

fās, only nom. and acc. sing. in use, [cf. **fārī,** *to speak*], indecl., n., *right* according to the laws of God and nature. **fās est,** *it is right, allowable, lawful;* of an event, *it is predestined* (I. 50).

fascis, -is, m., *bundle* of reeds or twigs; especially pl., **fascēs, -ium,** *the fasces,* a bundle of rods with an axe, carried before the highest magistrates as an emblem of authority (C. III. 71).

fastīgātē [**fastīgātus**], adv., *sloping; slanting* (IV. 17).

fastīgātus, -a, -um, [cf. **fastīgium**], adj., *sloping, sloping down.* (II. 8).

fastīgium, -ī, n., of a roof, *top;* of a hill, *summit, peak* (VII. 69); *sloping side, slope, descent, declivity.*

fatīgō, -āre, -āvī, -ātus, 1, *weary.* (C. III. 95). [fatigue.

fātum, -ī, [cf. **fārī,** *to speak*], n., *fate, destiny.* (I. 39). [fate.

Faustus, -ī, see **Sulla.**

faveō, favēre, fāvī, fautūrus, 2, *be favorable, be inclined toward, favor, countenance.* [favour.

fax, facis, f., *torch, firebrand.* (VII. 24).

fēlīcitās, -ātis, [**felix,** *happy*], f., *good fortune* (I. 40; C. III. 73); *success* (VI. 43). [felicity.

fēlīciter, comp. **fēlīcius,** sup. **fēlīcissimē,** [**felix**], adv., *with good fortune, luckily, happily* (IV. 25; C. I. 7).

fēmina, -ae, f., *woman; female.* (VI. 21, 26). [feminine.

femur, -oris and **-inis,** n., *thigh.* (V. 35; VII. 73). [femoral.

fera, -ae, [**ferus,** *wild*], f., *wild beast, wild animal.* (VI. 25, 28).

ferāx, -ācis, comp. **ferācior,** sup. **ferācissimus,** [**ferō**], adj., *fertile, productive.* (II. 4). [feracious.

ferē, adv., *almost, nearly;* with words denoting time, *about; for the most part, as a rule, usually,* generally.

ferō, ferre, tulī, latus, irr., *bear, carry, bring; endure, support, suffer, hold out against; bear away; obtain, receive; assert, report, say* (VI. 17). **signa ferre,** *to advance.*

ferrāmentum, -ī, [**ferrum**], n., *iron tool.* (V. 42).

ferrāria, -ae, [**ferrum**], f., *iron mine.* (VII. 22).

ferreus, -a, -um, [**ferrum**], adj., *of iron, iron,* **ferreae manūs,** *grappling-hooks* (C. II. 6). [ferreous.

ferrum, -ī, n., *iron* (V. 12); figuratively, *the iron,* with a barbed point, at the end of a pike (I. 25), *sword* (V. 30).

fertilis, -e, comp. **-ior,** sup. **-issimus,** [**ferō**], adj., *fertile, fruitful, productive.* (VI. 24; VII. 13). [fertile.

fertilitās, -ātis, [**fertilis**], f., *productiveness.* (II. 4). [fertility.

ferus, -a, -um, adj., *wild; rude, savage, fierce.* [fierce.

fervefaciō, -facere, -fēcī, -factus, [**ferveō + faciō**], 3, *make hot, heat, heat red-hot.* (V. 43; VII. 22).

ferveō, -ēre, 2, *be boiling hot, be heated, glow.* Present Participle as Adj., **fervēns, -tis,** *red-hot* (V. 43). [fervent.

fībula, -ae, [cf. **fīgō,** *fasten*], f., *clasp; brace, bolt* (IV. 17).

fidēlis, -e, comp. **-ior,** sup. **-issimus,** [**fidēs**], adj., *faithful, trustworthy* (VII. 76); *true, loyal* (IV. 21).

fidēs, -eī, f., *good faith, fidelity, loyalty; pledge of good faith, promise; confidence, trust; protection, alliance.* [faith.

fīdūcia, -ae, [**fīdus**], f., *reliance, confidence, assurance.* [fiduciary.

figūra, -ae, [cf. **fingō**], f., *form, shape.* [figure.

fīlia, -ae, f., *daughter.*

fīlius, -ī, m., *son.* [filial.

fingō, fingere, fīnxī, fictus, 3, *form, shape; conceive, imagine, think of* (VI. 37); *invent, devise* (IV. 5); of the features, *change, control* (I. 39). [feign.

fīniō, fīnīre, fīnīvī, fīnītus, [**fīnis**], 4, *bound, define* (VI. 16); *measure, limit* (VI. 18, 25). [finite.

fīnis, -is, m., *limit, border, boundary, end.* Pl. *borders,* hence *territory, country, land.* [finis.

fīnitimus, -a, -um, [**fīnis**], adj., *bordering on, neighboring, adjoining.* As noun, **fīnitimī, -ōrum,** m., pl., *neighbours, neighbouring peoples.*

fiō, fierī, factus, irr., used as pass. of **faciō,** *be made, be done; be performed,* (II. 5); *become, take place, happen; come about, come to pass.* **certior fierī,** *to be informed.*

fīrmiter, [**fīrmus**], adv., *steadily, firmly.* (IV. 26).

fīrmitūdō, -inis, [**fīrmus**], f., *strength, solidity; rigidity.* (III. 13; IV. 17).

fīrmō, -āre, -āvī, -ātus, [fīrmus], 1, *make firm, strengthen, fortify*. (VI. 29).

fīrmus, -a, -um, comp. **-ior,** sup. **-issimus,** adj., *strong, firm; steadfast, powerful,* [firm.

fistūca, -ae, f., *rammer, pile-driver.* (IV. 17).

Flaccus, -ī, (flak'us), see **Valerius** (2) and (7).

flāgitō, -āre, -āvī, -ātus, 1, *ask earnestly, importune, demand.* (I. 16).

flamma, -ae, f., *blazing fire, flame, fire.* (V. 43; VI. 16). [flame.

flectō, flectere, flexī, flexus, 3, *bend, turn, curve.* (IV. 33; VI. 25). [flex.

Flegīnās, -ātis, m., *Gaius Fleginas* (fle-jī'nas), a Roman knight killed in action near Dyrrachium. (C. III. 71).

fleō, flēre, flēvī, flētus, 2, *weep, shed tears, cry.*

flētus, -ūs, [fleō], m., *weeping.*

flō, -āre, -āvī, -ātus, 1, *blow.* (V. 7).

flōrēns, -entis, comp. **-entior,** sup. **-entissimus, [flōreō,** *bloom*], adj., *flourishing, prosperous* (I. 30, IV. 3); *influential* (VII. 32).

flōs, flōris, m., *flower.* (VII. 73). [flower.

fluctus, -ūs, [cf. **fluō**], m., *wave.*

flūmen, -inis, [cf. **fluō**], n., *flowing water, current; stream, river.* **adversō flūmine,** *up the stream.*

fluō, fluere, flūxī, sup. **flūxum,** 3, *flow.* [flux.

fodiō, fodere, fōdī, fossus, 3, *dig, dig out.* (VII. 73).

foedus, foederis, n., *treaty, compact, league.* (VI. 2).

forāmen, -inis, [forō, *bore*], n., *hole.* (C. III. 53).

fore = **futūrum esse;** see **sum.**

forem = **essem;** see **sum.**

forīs, [foris, *door*], adv., *out of doors; outside of a city, without* (VII. 76).

fōrma, -ae, f., *shape, form.* [form.

fors, fortis, [cf. **ferō**], f., *chance, luck, accident.* (II. 21; VII. 87).

fortasse, [forte], adv., *perhaps, possibly.* (C. III. 60).

forte [abl. of **fors**], adv., *by chance, by accident; perchance, perhaps.*

fortis, -e, comp. **-ior,** sup. **-issimus,** adj., *strong; brave, courageous.* [fort.

fortiter, comp. **fortius,** sup. **fortissimē, [fortis],** adv., *bravely, boldly, courageously.*

fortitūdō, -inis, [fortis], f., *courage, bravery.* (I. 2). [fortitude.

fortuītō, [abl. of fortuītus, from forte], adv., *by chance.* [fortuitous.

fortūna, -ae, [fors], f., *luck, lot. fate, chance, fortune; good fortune; the goddess Fortune* (Fig. 198); Pl., *fortunes* (III. 12; V. 3; VI. 7; VII. 77); *possessions, property* (I. 11; V. 43; VI. 35; VII. 8). [fortune.

fortūnātus, -a, -um, comp. **-ior,** sup. **-issimus,** [part. of **fortūnō,** from **fortūna**], adj., *prosperous, fortunate.* (VI. 35). [fortunate.

forum, -ī, n., *market-place.* (VII. 28). [forum.

fossa, -ae, [cf. **fodiō**], f., *trench, intrenchment.* [fosse.

fovea, -ae, f., *pit, pitfall.* (VI. 28).

frangō, frangere, frēgī, frāctus, 3, *break; dash to pieces, wreck* (IV. 29); *crush, dishearten* (I. 31). [fracture.

frāter, -tris, m., *brother;* pl. as a name of honour applied to allies, *brethren* (I. 33, 44; II. 3).

frāternus, -a, -um, [frāter], adj., *of a brother, brotherly,* [fraternal.

fraudō, -āre, -āvī, -ātus, [fraus], 1, *cheat; embezzle* (C. III. 59, 60).

fraus, fraudis, f., *deception, imposition.* (VII. 40). [fraud.

fremitus, -ūs, [cf. **fremō,** *roar*], m., *uproar, noise, din.*

frequēns, -entis, comp. **frequentior,** sup. **-issimus,** adj., *in large numbers, crowded.* [frequent.

fretum, -ī, n., *strait.* **fretum Siciliae,** *Sicilian strait, strait of Messina* (C. II. 3).

frētus, -a, -um, adj., *relying on, depending on;* followed by abl.

frīgidus, -a, -um, comp. **-ior,** sup. **-issimus, [frīgeō,** *be cold*], adj., *cold.* (IV. 1). [frigid.

frīgus, frīgoris, n., *cold, cold weather.* Pl., *cold seasons, cold climate.*

frōns, frontis, f., *forehead; front.* **ā mediā fronte,** *in the middle of the forehead* (VI. 26). [front.

frūctuōsus, -a, -um, sup. **-issimus, [frūctus],** adj., *fruitful, fertile.* (I. 30).

frūctus, -ūs, m., *fruit, product; profit, interest, income* (vi. 19); *advantage, gain, reward* (VII. 27, 86). [fruit.

frūgēs, -um, f., pl., *produce, crops, fruits.* (I. 28). [frugal.

frūmentārius, -a, -um, [frūmentum], adj., *relating to grain* or *supplies of grain; productive of grain* (I. 10). **rēs frūmentāria,** *supply of grain, supplies.*

frūmentātiō, -ōnis, [frūmentor], f., *obtaining of grain, expedition in quest of grain.*

frūmentor, -ārī, -ātus, [frūmentum], 1, dep., *get grain, forage.*

frūmentum, -ī, n., *gram;* pl. often *crops of grain, grain-crops.*

fruor, fruī, frūctus, 3, dep., *enjoy;* followed by abl. (III. 22).

frūstrā, adv., *in vain, without effect; for nothing, without reason.* [frustrate.

Fūfius, -ī, m., *Gaius Fufius Cita* (fū' fi-us sī' ta), a Roman knight. (VII. 3).

fuga, -ae, f., *flight.* **in fugam dare,** *to put to flight, rout.*

fugiō, fugere, fūgī, 3, *flee, run away, make off;*

avoid, shun (VII. 30); *escape* (VII. 38).

fugitīvus, -a, -um, [**fugiō**], adj., *fleeing, runaway.* As noun, **fugitīvus, -ī,** m., *runaway slave* (I. 23). [fugitive.

fugō, -āre, -āvī, -ātus, [**fuga**], 1, *put to flight, rout.* (VII. 68).

fūmō, -āre, [**fūmus**], 1, *smoke.* (VII. 24). [fume.

fūmus, -ī, m., *smoke.* (II. 7; V. 48).

funda, -ae, f., *sling.*

funditor, -ōris, [**funda**], m., *slinger.*

fundō, fundere, fūdī, fūsus, 3, *pour* (VII. 24); *scatter, rout* (III. 6). [foundry.

fūnebris, -e [**fūnus**], adj., *funeral.* As noun, **fūnebria, -ium,** neuter plural, *funeral rites* (VI. 19).

fungor, fungī, fūnctus, 3, dep., *discharge, perform.* (VII. 25). [function.

fūnis, -is, m., *rope;* rope *cable* (III. 13, IV. 29, V. 10); *halyards* (III. 14).

fūnus, -eris, n., *funeral.* (VI. 19). [funeral.

furor, -ōris, [**furō,** *rage*], m., *rage, madness, fury.* [furor.

fūrtum, -ī, [**fūr,** *thief*], n., *theft.*

fūsilis, -e, [cf. **fundō**], adj., *molten.;* of clay, *kneaded, molded.* (V. 43). [fusile.

futūrus, -a, -um, see **sum.**

G.

Gabalī, -ōrum, m., pl., (gab'a-lī), a people in Southern Gaul, subject to the Arvernians. (VII. 7, 64, 75).

Gabīnius, -ī, m., *Aulus Gabinius* (ga-bin'i-us), consul with Lucius Calpurnius Piso, 58 B.C. (I. 6; C. III. 103).

gaesum, -ī, n., *heavy javelin* used by the Gauls. (III. 4).

Gaius, -ī, abbreviation **C.,** m., *Gaius* (gā' yus), sometimes in English written *Caius,* a Roman first name.

Galba, -ae, m., (gal'ba):

(1) *Servius Sulpicius Galba,* a lieutenant of Caesar in the earlier part of the Gallic War, Praetor at Rome in 54 B.C.; afterwards named among the conspirators who took Caesar's life. (III. 1-6).

(2) *Galba,* a ruler of the Suessiones. (II. 4, 13).

galea, -ae, f., *helmet.* (II. 21).

Gallia, -ae, [**Gallus**], f., *Gallia* (gal' i-a), *Gaul,* used of Transalpine Gaul, and of the middle one of its three parts, Celtic Gaul (I. 1); also of Cisalpine Gaul, and of the Province; once in the plural, Galliae, as referring to the several divisions (IV. 20). After Caesar's conquest the plural was used of three provinces in Transalpine Gaul (Fig. 199) [Gaul.

Gallicus, -a, -um, [**Gallus**], adj., *of Gaul, Gallic.*

gallīna, -ae, [**gallus,** *cock*], f., *hen.*

Gallus, -a, -um, adj., *Gallic.* As noun, m., *a*

Gaul; pl., **Gallī, -ōrum,** *Celts, Galli* (gal' ī), used by Caesar as referring to the inhabitants of *Gallia Celtica,* the middle of the three main divisions of Gaul.

Gallus, -ī, m., see **Trebius.**

Garumna, -ae, f., (ga-rum'na), the great river of southwestern France, which rises in the Pyrenees Mountains and flows in a northwesterly direction to the Atlantic Ocean, after a course of about 350 miles; now *Garonne.* (I. 1).

Garumnī, -ōrum, m., pl.,(ga-rum'nī), a people in Aquitania, probably near the sources of the Garonne. (III. 27).

Gatēs, -ium, m., pl., (gā' tēz), a people in Aquitania. (III. 27).

gaudeō, gaudēre, gāvīsus sum, 2, semi-dep., *rejoice, be glad.* (IV. 13).

gāvīsus, see **gaudeō.**

Geidumnī, -ōrum, [Kel., = 'the Impetuous'], m., pl., (je-dum' nī), a people of Belgic Gaul, clients of the Nervians. (V. 39).

Genava, -ae, f., (jen'a-va), a city of the Allobroges, on the lacus Lemannus; now *Geneva.* (I. 7).

gener, generī, m., *son-in-law.* (V. 56).

generātim [**genus**], adv., *by kind; by peoples, by tribes, nation by nation* (I. 51; VII. 19).

gēns, gentis, f., *clan, family* (VI. 22); *nation, people.* [gentile.

genus, generis, n., *birth, descent, family; race* (IV. 3; VII. 22, 42); *kind, species; class, rank; method, nature.* [genus.

Gergovia, -ae, f., (jer-gō' vi a), chief city of the Arvernians, situated on a narrow plateau (elevation. 2,440 ft.) about six miles south of Clermont-Ferrand.

Germānia, -ae, [**Germānus**], f., *Germany.* [Germany.

Germānicus, -a, -um, [**Germānī**], adj., *German.*

Germānus, -a, -um, adj., *of* or *from Germany, German.* As noun, **Germānī, -ōrum,** m., pl., *Germans, the Germans.* [German.

gerō, gerere, gessī, gestus, 3, *bear, carry; manage, transact, do, carry on; carry out, perform, accomplish;* of an office, *fill;* of war, *wage.* **comminus rem gerere,** *to engage in close contest* (V. 44). **rēs gerēbātur,** *the action was going on* (III. 14, VII. 80). **rem gestam perscrībit,** *he wrote a full account of what had been done* (V. 47). [jest, **gestus,** see **gerō.**

gladius, -ī, m., *sword.* [gladiolus.

glāns, glandis, f., *acorn; slingshot, bullet* hurled by a sling (V. 43; VII. 81). [gland.

glēba, -ae, f., *lump of earth, clod; lump, mass* (VII. 25). [glebe.

glōria, -ae, f., *fame, renown.* [glory.

glōrior, -ari, -atus, [gloria], 1, dep., *boast, brag* (I. 14).

Gnaeus, -ī, abbreviation Cn., m., (nē' us), a Roman first name.

Gobannitiō, -ōnis, m., (gob-a-nish' [y]ō), an uncle of Vercingetorix, hostile to him. (VII. 4).

Gorgobina, -ae, f., (gor-gob' i-na), a city in the country of the Aeduans, inhabited by Boians (VII. 9). Gracchī, -ōrum, m., pl., *the Gracchi*, (grak' ī), Tiberius and Gaius Sempronius Gracchus, leaders in reforms which led to violence; Tiberius Gracchus was killed in 133 B.C., Gaius in 121 B.C. (C. I. 7).

Graecus, -a, -um, [Γ Ρ Α Ι Κ Ο Σ], adj., *Greek, Grecian*. As noun, Graecus, -ī, m., *a Greek* (VI. 24).

Graiocelī, -ōrum, m., pl., (gra-yō'-se-lī), a Gallic people in the Alps. (I. 10).

grandis, -e, comp. -ior, sup. -issimus, adj., *large, great*, [grand.

Grānius, -ī, m., *Aulus Granius*, (grā'-ni-us), a Roman knight killed in action near Dyrrachium. (C. III. 71).

grātia, -ae, [grātus], f., *favor,gratitude; esteem, regard; recompense, requital* (I. 35, V. 27); *popularity; influence* (I. 9, 18, 20, 43, ETC.). Pl, grātiae, -ārum, *thanks*. grātiās agere, *to thank.* grātiā, *for the sake of* (VII. 43). [grace.

grātulātiō, -ōnis, [grātulor], f., *rejoicing, congratulation.* fit grātulātiō, *congratulations are offered.* [gratulation.

grātulor, -ārī, -ātus, [grātus], 1, dep., *offer congratulations, congratulate.* (I. 30). [gratulate.

grātus, -a, -um, comp. -ior, sup. -issimus, adj., *acceptable, pleasing* (VI. 16). Neut. as noun, grātum, -ī, *a kindness, a favor* (I. 44). [grateful.

gravis, -e, comp. -ior, sup. -issimus, adj., *heavy* (IV. 24); *heavily laden* (V. 8); *severe, hard, serious, troublesome;* of age, *advanced* (III. 16). [grave (adjective).

gravitās, -ātis, [gravis], f., *weight* (V. 16); *importance* (IV. 3). [gravity.

graviter, comp. gravius, sup. gravissimē, [gravis], adv., *heavily* (III. 14); *severely, warmly, bitterly; seriously, with great displeasure.*

graviter ferre, *to be annoyed, be disturbed.*

gravō, -āre, -āvī, -ātus, [gravis], 1, *weigh down.* Pass. as dep., *hesitate, be unwilling* (I. 35).

Grudiī, -ōrum, m., pl., (grū'di-ī), a Belgic people near the Nervians. (V. 39).

gubernātor, -ōris, [gubernō, *steer*], m., *helmsman, pilot.* [governor.

gustō, -āre, -āvī, -ātus, [gustus, *tasting*], 1, *taste, taste of.* [gustatory.

Gutruātus, ī, m., a leader of the Carnutes. (VII. 3).

H.

habeō, habēre, habuī, habitus, 2, *have, hold,* *possess, keep; regard, think, consider; account, repute, reckon;* of a count, *make* (I. 29). cēnsum habēre, *to take a census, make an enumeration* (I. 29). ōrātiōnem habēre, *to make a speech, deliver an address.* questiōnem habēre, *to conduct an investigation.* habēre sē aliter ac, *to be different from what.* [habit.

haesitō, -āre, -āvī, -ātus, [freq. of haereō], 1, *stick fast, remain fixed.* (VII. 19). [hesitate.

hāmus, -ī, m., *hook; barbed hook* (VII. 73). [hamate.

harpagō, -ōnis, [= Α Ρ Π Α Γ Η], m., *grappling-iron, grappling-hook,* a pole with an iron hook at the end. (VII. 81).

Harūdēs, -um, m., pl., (ha-rū'dēz), a German tribe between the Danube and the upper part of the Rhine.

haud, adv., *not at all, not.* (V. 54).

hedera, -ae, f., *ivy.* (C. III. 96).

Helvēticus, -a, -um, adj., *Helvetian.*

Helvēticum proelium, *the battle with the Helvetians* (VII. 9).

Helvētius, -a, -um, adj., *of the Helvetians, Helvetian,* cīvitās Helvētia, *the State of the Helvetians, Helvetian State,* divided into four cantons, the names of two of which, pāgus Tigurīnus, pāgus Verbigenus, are known (I. 12). As noun, Helvētiī, -ōrum, m., pl., *the Helvetians, Helvetii* (hel-vē'sh[y]ī).

Helviī, -ōrum, m., pl., (hel'vi-ī),a Gallic people in the Province.

Hercynius, -a, -um, adj., *Hercynian.* Silva Hercynia [in Greek Α Ρ Κ Υ Ν Ι Α Ο Ρ Η Ε Ρ Κ Υ Ν Ι Ο Ι Δ Ρ Υ Μ Ο Ι], a forest in southern Germany and Austria, which followed the course of the Danube from its source eastward beyond modern Vienna to the Carpathian Mountains. [hercynite.

hērēditās, -ātis, [hērēs, *heir*], f., *inheritance.* (VI. 13). [heredity.

Hibernia, -ae, f., *Hibernia* (hī-ber'ni-a), *Ireland.* (V. 13). [Hibernian.

hībernus, -a, -um, [hiems], adj., *of winter.* As noun, hīberna, -ōrum (sc. castra), n., pl., *winter-quarters.* [hibernal.

hīc, haec, hōc, gen. huius, dem. pron., *this, the following, he, she, it.*

hīc, [pron. hīc], adv., *here, at this place;* of time, *at this point.*

hiemō, -āre, -āvī, -ātūrus, [hiems]. 1, *pass the winter, winter.*

hiems, hiemis, f., *winter; wintry storm, stormy weather* (IV. 36).

hinc [hīc], adv., *hence, from this place, from this point.*

Hirrus, -ī, m., see Lūcīlius.

Hispānia, -ae, f., *Spain.* Pl., Hispāniae, -ārum, *Spanish provinces,* referring to the division into the two parts, **Hispānia citerior**, *Hither Spain*, and **ulterior**, *Further Spain* (C. III. 73). [Spain.

Hispānus, -a, -um, adj., *Spanish*. (V. 26). [spaniel, *i.e.* 'Spanish dog.'

homō, hominis, m. and f., *human being, man.*

honestus, -a, -um, comp. **-ior**, sup. **-issimus**, [**honōs**], adj., *honourable, noble; of good family.* (VII. 3; C. II. 5). **locō nātus honestō**, *of excellent family* (V. 45, C. III. 61). [honest.

honōrificus, -a, -um, comp. **honōrificentior**, sup. **-centissimus**, [**honōs**, cf. **faciō**], adj., *conferring honour, complimentary.* (I. 43). [honorific.

honōs, or **honor, -ōris**, m., *honour, esteem, respect, dignity; public office, office, post.* [honour.

hōra, -ae, [= ΩP Λ], f., *hour*, a twelfth part of the day, from sunrise to sunset, the Roman hours varying in length with the season of the year.

hordeum, -ī, n., *barley.* (C. III. 47).

horreō, horrēre, horruī, 2, *tremble at, shudder at, dread.* (I. 32).

horribilis, -e, comp. **-ior**, [**horreō**], adj., *dread-inspiring.* [horrible.

horridus, -a, -um, comp. **-ior**, [**horreō**], adj., *wild, frightful* (V. 14). [horrid.

hortātus, -ūs, [**hortor**], m., *encouragement, urging.* (C. III. 86).

hortor, -ārī, -ātus, 1, dep., *urge, encourage; exhort, incite, press.*

hospes, hospitis, m., *host; guest* (VI. 23); *friend bound by hospitality, guest-friend* (I. 53, V. 6). [host.

hospitium, -ī, [**hospes**], n., *relation of guest and host, tie of hospitality, hospitality.* [hospice.

hostis, -is, m., public *enemy, foe*; in this book both the sing., and the pl., **hostēs, -ium**, in most cases = *the enemy.* Cf. **inimīcus.** [host (army).

hūc, [**hīc**], adv., *hither, here, to this place.*

huius modī, see **modus.**

hūmānitās, -ātis, [**hūmānus**], f., *humanity; refinement, culture* (I. 1, 47). [humanity.

hūmānus, -a, -um, comp. **-ior**, sup. **-issimus**, [**homō**], adj., *of man, human* (C. I. 6); *refined, civilized* (IV. 3; V. 14). [human.

humilis, -e, comp. **-ior**, sup. **humillimus**, [**humus**, *ground*], adj., *low; shallow* (V. 1); *mean, humble, insignificant, weak.* [humble.

humilitās, -ātis, [**humilis**], f., *lowness* (V. 1); *humble position, insignificance* (V. 27). [humility.

I.

iaceō, iacēre, iacuī, iacitūrus, 2, *lie, lie prostrate; lie dead* (VII. 25). Pres. part. as noun, **iacentēs, -ium**, m., pl., *the fallen* (II. 27).

iaciō, iacere, iēcī, iactus, 3, *throw, cast, hurl; throw up, construct* (II. 12); of an anchor, *drop* (IV. 28).

iactō, -āre, -āvī, -ātus, [freq. of **iaciō**], 1, *throw, cast* (VII. 47); *throw about, jerk back and forth* (I. 25); *discuss, agitate* (I. 18); *boast of, vaunt* (C. III. 83).

iactūra, -ae, [**iaciō**], f., *a throwing; loss, sacrifice, cost.*

iactus, see **iaciō.**

iaculum, -ī, [cf. **iaciō**], n., *javelin.* (V. 43, 45).

iam, adv., *already, now; at once, immediately* (VI. 35, VII. 38); *at length* (I. 42); *actually* (III. 17); *in fact, indeed* (III. 9).

ibi or **ibī**, adv., *in that place, there.*

Iccius, -ī, m., (ik' sh[y]us), a leader of the Remi.

ictus, -ūs, [**īcō**, *strike*], m., *blow, stroke.* (I. 25; VII. 25).

Id., abbreviation for **Īdūs.**

idcircō, [**id** + abl. of **circus**], adv., *on that account, therefore.* (V. 3).

īdem, eadem, idem, eiusdem, dem. pron., *the same.* [identity.

identidem, [**idem et idem**], adv., *repeatedly, again and again.* (II. 19).

idōneus, -a, -um, adj., *suitable, convenient, fit, capable.*

Īdūs, -uum, f., pl., abbreviation **Īd.**, *the Ides*, the fifteenth day of March, May, July, and October; the thirteenth day of other months. (I. 7).

īgnis, -is, m., *fire.* Pl. **īgnēs**, *fire-signals, watch-fires* (II. 33). [igneous.

ignōbilis, -e, [**in-** + (g)**nōbilis**], adj., *unknown; obscure* (V. 28). [ignoble.

ignōminia, -ae, [**in-** + (g)**nōmen**], f., *disgrace, dishonor.* [ignominy.

ignōrō, -āre, -āvī, -ātus, [cf. **ignōscō**], 1, *be ignorant of, not to know, be unaware; overlook* (I. 27). **nōn ignōrāns**, *being not unfamiliar with* (VI. 42), *not unaware* (VII. 33). [ignore.

ignōscō, -gnōscere, -gnōvī, -gnōtus, [**in-** + (g)**nōscō**, *know*], 3, *pardon, overlook; forgive, excuse.*

ignōtus, -a, -um, comp. **-ior**, sup. **-issimus**, [**in-** + (g)**nōtus**], adj., *unknown; unfamiliar* (IV. 24).

illātus, see **īnferō.**

ille, illa, illud, illīus, dem. pron., used with or without a noun, *that; he, she, it.*

illīc [loc. of **ille**], adv., *there, in that place, in that region.* (I. 18; VII. 20).

illigō, -āre, -āvī, -ātus, [**in** + **ligō**, *bind*], 1, *tie on; bind* (IV. 17); *fasten* (V. 45).

illō [**ille**], adv., *thither, to that place; to that end* (IV. 11).

illūstris, -e, comp. **-ior**, sup. **-issimus**, [**in**, cf. **lūx**], adj., *prominent, distinguished; remarkable,* *noteworthy* (VII. 3). **illūstriōre locō nātus,** *of higher social position* (VI. 19). [illustrious.

Illyricum, -ī, n., (i-lir' i-kum), a region along the east coast of the Adriatic Sea, now *Istria* and *Dalmatia.* (II. 35; III. 7; V. 1).

imbēcillitās, -ātis, [imbēcillus, *weak*], f.. *weakness.* [imbecility.

imber, imbris, m., *rain, rainstorm.* **magnus imber,** *a violent rainstorm* (VII. 27).

imitor, -ārī, -ātus, 1, dep., *copy, imitate.* (VI. 40; VII. 22). [imitate.

immānis, -e, comp. **-ior,** sup. **-issimus,** adj., *huge, enormous, immense.*

immineō, -minēre, [in + mineō, *overhang*], 2, *overhang; be near at hand, threaten* (VI. 38). [imminent.

immittō, -mittere, -mīsī, -missus, [in + mittō], 3, *send into; send against* (VII. 40); of pikes, *hurl, cast* against (V. 44, VI. 8, C. III. 92); of timbers, *let down* into (IV. 17), *let in between* (IV. 17).

immolō, -āre, -āvī, -ātus, [in, cf. **mola,** *meal*], 1, lit. *sprinkle meal on* a victim for sacrifice; *sacrifice, offer up* (VI. 16, 17). [immolate.

immortālis, -e, [in- + mortālis, from **mors],** adj., *immortal.* [immortal.

immūnis, -e, [in- + mūnus], adj., *free from taxes.* (VII. 76). [immune.

immūnitās, -ātis, [immūnis], f., *freedom from public burdens, exemption* (VI. 14). [immunity.

imparātus, -a, -um, sup. **-issimus, [in- + parātus],** adj., *not ready, unprepared.* (VI. 30).

impedīmentum, -i, [impediō], n., *hindrance, interference* (I. 25; II. 25). Pl. **impedīmenta, -ōrum,** *heavy baggage, baggage; pack-animals* (VII. 45). [impediment.

impediō, -pedīre, -pedīvī, -peditus, [in, cf. **pēs],** 4, *hinder, obstruct, interfere with; prevent, disorder;* of the mind, *occupy, engage* (V. 7); *make unpassable* (VII. 57). [impede.

impedītus, -a, -um, comp. **-ior,** sup. **-issimus,** [part. of **impediō**], adj., *encumbered* with baggage, *hindered, hampered, obstructed, embarrassed; difficult, hard* (II. 28, III. 9); of places, *hard, inaccessible.*

impellō, -pellere, -puli, -pulsus, [in + pellō), 3, *strike against; urge, urge on, drive on, impel.* [impel.

impendeō, -pendēre, [in + pendeō, *hang*], 2, *hang over, overhang.* (I. 6; III. 2). [impend.

impēnsus, -a, -um, comp. **-ior,** [part, of **impendō,** *expend*], adj., *ample, great;* of price, *dear, high* (IV. 2). **imperātor, -ōris, [imperō],** m., *commander-in-chief, commander, general.* [emperor.

imperātōrius, -a, -um, [imperātor], adj., *of a commander, generals.* (C. III. 96).

imperātum, -ī, [imperō], n., *command, order.*

ad imperātum, *in accordance with his command* (VI. 2). **imperītus, -a, -um,** comp. **-ior,** sup. **-issimus, [in- + perītus],** adj., *inexperienced, unskilled, unacquainted with.* **tam** (I. 44), or **adeō** (V. 27) **imperītus rērum,** *of so little experience.*

imperium, -ī, [cf. **imperō],** n., *command, order; control, government, dominion; military authority.* **nova imperia,** *a revolution* (II. 1). [empire.

imperō, -āre, -āvī, -ātus, 1, *command, order; exercise authority over, rule* (I. 31, 36); *requisition, order to furnish, levy, draft, demand.* After **imperō, ut** is ordinarily to be translated by *to,* and **nē** by *not to,* with the infin. [imperative.

impetrō, -āre, -āvī, -ātus, [in + patrō, *execute*], 1, *obtain* by request, *procure, get; accomplish, bring to pass; gain one's request.* **rē impetrātā,** *the request having been granted, after the request had been granted.*

impetus, -ūs, [in, cf. **petō],** m., *attack, assault, charge; raid* (I. 44); *fury, impetuosity, force.* [impetus.

impius, -a, -um, [in + pius], adj., *wicked, impious.* As noun, **impiī, -ōrum,** m., pl., *the wicked* (VI. 13). [impious.

implicō, -āre, -āvī or **-uī, -ātus** or **-itus, [in + plicō,** *fold*], 1, *infold; interweave* (VII. 73). [implicate.

implōrō, -āre, -āvī, -ātus, [in + plōrō, *cry out*], 1, *beseech, implore* (I. 51); *invoke, appeal to* (V. 7, C, III. 82). **auxilium implōrāre,** *to solicit aid* (I. 31, 32). [implore.

impōnō, -ponere, -posuī, -positus, [in + pōnō], 3, *put on, place on, put; impose (upon); levy upon* (I. 44); of horses, *mount* (I. 42). [impose.

importō, -āre, -āvī, -ātus, [in + portō], 1, *bring in, import.* (I. 1; IV. 2; V. 12). [import.

improbus, -a, -um, comp. **-ior,** sup. **-issimus, [in- + probus,** *good*], adj., *bad, shameless.* (I. 17).

imprōvīsō [imprōvīsus], adv., *unexpectedly, suddenly.* (I. 13).

imprōvīsus, -a, -um, comp. **-ior, [in- + part. of prōvideō],** adj., *unforeseen, unexpected.* Neut. as noun in **dē imprōvīsō,** *unexpectedly, suddenly.*

imprūdēns, -entis, [contr. from **imprōvidēns, in- + part. of prōvideō],** adj., *unawares, off one's guard.* (III. 29; V. 15). [imprudent.

imprūdentia, -ae, [imprūdēns], f., *lack of foresight, indiscretion, ignorance.* [imprudence.

impūbēs, -eris, [in- + pūbēs], adj., *under age; unmarried* (VI. 21).

impugnō, -āre, -āvī, -ātus, [in + pugnō], 1, *attack, make an attack on* (I. 44); *fight* (III. 26). [impugn.

impulsus, -ūs, [impellō], m., *push; instigation* (V. 25). [impulse.

impulsus, see **impellō.**

impūne [impūnis, from in- + poena], adv., *without punishment, with impunity.* (I. 14).

impūnitās, -ātis, [impūnis, from in- + poena], f., *exemption from punishment, impunity.* (I. 14). [impunity.

īmus, see **īnferus.**

in, prep. with acc. and abl.:
(1) With the acc: of place, after verbs implying motion, *into, to, up to, towards, against;* of time, *until, till; for, with a view to;* of other relations, *to, in, respecting, concerning, according to, after, over.*
(2) With the abl.: of place, *in, within, on, upon, among, over;* of time, *in, in the course of, within, during, while;* of other relations, *involved in, under the influence of, in case of, in relation to, respecting.*In composition **in** retains its form before the vowels and most of the consonants; is often changed to **il-** before **l, ir-** before **r;** usually becomes **im-** before **m, b, p.**

in-, inseparable prefix, = *un-, not,* as in **incertus,** *uncertain.*

inānis, -e, comp. **-ior,** sup. **-issimus,** adj., *empty* (V. 23); *vain, useless* (VII. 19). [inane.

incautē, comp. **incautius,** [incautus], adv., *carelessly.* (VII. 27).

incautus, -a, -um, comp. **-ior,** [in- + cautus, cf. **caveō**], adj., *off one's guard.* (VI. 30). [incautious.

incēdō, -cēdere, -cessī, [in + cēdō, *go*], 3, *go forward, move (forward); come upon, enter* (C. III. 74).

incendium, -ī, [cf. incendō], n., *fire, conflagration.* [incendiary.

incendō, -cendere, -cendī, -cēnsus, [in, cf. **candeō,** *shine*], 3, *set on fire, burn; rouse, excite* (VII. 4). [incense.

incēnsus, see **incendō.**

inceptus, see **incipiō.**

incertus, -a, -um, comp. **-ior,** sup. **-issimus,** [in- + certus], adj., *uncertain, doubtful; undecided* (VII. 62); *indefinite* (VII. 16); of reports, *unreliable, unauthenticated* (IV. 5); of a military formation, *in disorder* (IV. 32).

incidō, -cidere, -cidī, [in + cadō], 3, with **in** and the acc., *fall in with, come upon, fall in the way of* (I. 53; VI. 30); *occur, happen* (VII. 3); of war, *break out* (II. 14, VI. 15). [incident.

incīdō, -cīdere, -cīdī, -cīsus, [in + caedō], 3, *cut into.* (II. 17). [incise.

incipiō, -cipere, -cēpī, -ceptus, [in + capiō], 3, *begin, commence, undertake.* [incipient.

incīsus, see **incīdō.**

incitātiō, -ōnis, [incitō], f., *a rousing, spurring on.* (C. III. 92).

incitō, -āre, -āvī, -ātus, [in + citō, *move rapidly*], 1, *urge, urge on, hurry;* of vessels,

drive forward with oars, *drive* (III. 14; IV. 25; VII. 60; C. II. 6); of horses, *urge on, spur;* of water, with **sē,** *rush against* (IV. 17), *run in* (III. 12); of men, *rouse, stir up, excite; spur on* (III. 10); *exasperate* (VII. 28). [incite.

incognitus, -a, -um, [in- + part. of cognōscō], adj., *unknown, not known.* (IV. 20, 29). [incognito.

incolō, -colere, -coluī, [in + colō], 3, intrans., *live, dwell;* trans., *inhabit, dwell in, live in.*

incolumis, -e, adj., *safe, unharmed, uninjured, unhurt.*

incommodē, comp. **-ius,** sup. **-issimē,** [incommodus], adv., *inconveniently; unfortunately* (V. 33).

incommodum, -ī, [incommodus], n., *inconvenience, disadvantage; misfortune, disaster, injury, defeat.* **quid incommodī,** *any harm* (VI. 13), *what disadvantage* (VII. 45).

incrēdibilis, -e, [in- + crēdibilis], adj., *beyond belief, extraordinary, incredible.* [incredible.

increpitō, -āre, [freq. of increpō, *chide*], 1, *reproach, rebuke* (II. 15); *taunt* (II. 30).

incumbō, -ere, incubuī, incubitus, [in + cumbō for cubō, *lie*], 3, *press upon; devote one's self to* (VII. 76). [incumbent.

incursiō, -ōnis, [incurrō], f., *invasion, raid, inroad.* [incursion.

incursus, -ūs, [incurrō], m., *onrush* (II. 20); *assault, attack* (VII. 36).

incūsō, -āre, -āvī, -ātus, [in- + causa], 1, *find fault with, accuse; chide, rebuke* (I. 40; II. 15).

inde, adv., of place, *from that place, thence;* of time, *after that, then* (VII. 48).

indicium, -ī, [cf. indicō, *reveal*], n., *information, disclosure.*

indīcō, -dīcere, -dīxī, -dictus, [in + dīcō], 3, *proclaim, declare;* of a council, *call, appoint.* [indict.

indictus, see **indīcō.**

indictus, -a, -um, [in- + dictus], adj., *unsaid;* of a case, *untried, without a hearing* (VII. 38).

indigeō, -ēre, indiguī, [indu, for in, + egeō], 2, *be in want of, lack.* (C. II. 35). [indigent.

indignē, comp. **-ius,** sup. **indignissimē,** [indignus], adv., *unworthily, shamefully.* (VII. 38).

indignitās, -ātis, [indignus], f., *shamefulness* (VII. 56); *indignity, ill-treatment* (II. 14). [indignity.

indignor, -ārī, -ātus, [indignus], 1, dep., *consider unworthy; be indignant* (VII. 19). [indignant.

indignus, -a, -um, comp. **-ior,** sup. **-issimus,** [in- + dignus], adj., *unworthy.* (V. 35; VII. 17).

indīligēns, -entis, comp. **-ior,** [in- + dīligēns], adj., *negligent, remiss.* (VII. 71).

indīligenter, comp. **-ius,** [indīligens], adv., *negligently, carelessly.* (II. 33).

indīligentia, -ae, [indīligens], f., *negligence,*

carelessness. (VII. 17).

indūcō, -dūcere, -dūxī, -ductus, [in + dūcō], 3, *lead in; lead on, induce, influence* (I. 2, 27); *cover* (II. 33). [induce.

inductus, see indūcō.

indulgentia, -ae, [indulgēns], f., *favor, kindness,* (VII. 63). [indulgence.

indulgeō, -dulgēre, -dulsī, 2, *be kind to, favor.* [indulge.

induō, -duere, -duī, -dūtus, 3, *put on* (II. 21); with sē, *pierce, stab themselves* (VII. 73, 82).

industria, -ae, [industrius], f., *activity, energy.* (C. II. 4, III. 73). [industry.

industriē, [industrius], adv., *actively, energetically.* (VII. 60, C. III. 95).

indūtiae, -ārum, f., pl., *truce, armistice.* (IV. 12, 13).

Indutiomārus, -ī, m., (in-dū″ sh(y)o-mā′ rus), a Treveran, rival of Cingetorix and hostile to Caesar.

ineō, -īre, -iī, -itus, [in + eō], irr., *enter, enter upon, begin;* of favour, *win* (VI. 43); of a plan, *form;* of an account or enumeration, *cast tip, make.*

inermis, -e, and (I. 40) inermus, -a, -um, [in- + arma], adj., *unarmed, without arms.*

iners, -ertis, comp. inertior, sup.

inertissimus, [in- + ars], adj., *indolent; unmanly* (IV. 2). [inert.

īnfāmia, -ae, [īnfāmis, from in- + fāma], f., *disgrace, dishonor.* [infamy.

īnfāns, -antis, comp. īnfantior, sup. -issimus, [in- + part. of for, *speak*], adj., *without speech.* As noun, m. and f., (lit. *one not speaking), child, infant* (VII. 28, 47). [infant.

īnfectus, -a, -um, [in- + factus], adj., *not done, unaccomplished.* īnfectā rē, *without accomplishing his (their) purpose* (VI. 12; VII. 17, 82).

īnferō, -ferre, intulī, illātus, [in + ferō], irr., *bring in, import* (II. 15); *throw upon* (VII. 22), *throw into* (VI. 19); of injuries, *inflict;* of hope and fear, *inspire, infuse;* of an excuse, *offer, allege* (I. 39); of wounds, *make, give.* bellum īnferre, *to make war.* signa īnferre, *to advance,* in equum īnferre, *to put on a horse* (VI. 30). [infer.

īnferus, -a, -um, comp. īnferior, sup. īnfimus or īmus, adj., *below, underneath;* comp., *lower, inferior;* sup., *lowest, at the bottom.* sub īnfimō colle, *at the foot of the hill* (VII. 49). Neut. as noun, ab īnfimō, *from the foot* (VII. 19), *at the bottom* (VII. 73); ad īnfimum, *toward the bottom* (VII. 73); ab īmō, *from the bottom* (III. 19), *at the lower end* (IV. 17). [inferior.

īnfestus, -a, -um, comp. -ior, sup. -issimus, adj., *hostile, threatening.*

īnficiō, -ficere, -fēcī, -fectus, [in + faciō], 3, *stain.* (V. 14). [infect.

īnfidēlis, -e, sup. -issimus, [in- + fidēlis],

adj., *unfaithful, untrustworthy.* (VII. 59). [infidel.

īnfīgō, -fīgere, -fīxī, -fīxus, [in + fīgō], 3, *fasten in.* (VII. 73). [infix.

īnfimus, see īnferus.

īnfīnītus, -a, -um, comp. -ior, [in- + fīnītus, from finiō], adj., *unlimited, boundless; vast, immense; numberless* (V. 12). [infinite.

īnfirmitās, -ātis, [īnfīrmus], f., *weakness, feebleness* (VII. 26); *fickleness* (IV. 5, 13). [infirmity.

īnfīrmus, -a, -um, comp. -ior, sup. -issimus, [in- + fīrmus], adj., *not strong, weak; depressed, timid* (III. 24); comp., *less strong* (IV. 3). [infirm.

īnflātē, comp. īnflātius, [īnflātus], adv., *boastfully.* (C. II. 39).

īnflectō, flectere, -flexī, -flexus, [in + flectō], 3, *bend.* (I. 25; II. 17). [inflect.

īnflexus, see īnflectō.

īnfluō, -fluere, -flūxī, [in + fluō], 3, *flow into, flow; drain into* (VII. 57). [influx.

īnfodiō, -fodere, -fōdī, -fossus, [in + fodiō], 3, *bury.* (VII. 73).

īnfrā, [for īnferā, sc. parte], adv. and prep.: (1) As adv., *below,* (IV. 36; VII. 61). (2) As prep., with acc., *below.* (VI. 28, 35).

īnfringō, -fringere, -frēgī, -frāctus, [in + frangō], 3, *break off; break, lessen* (C. III. 92). [infraction.

ingēns, -entis, comp. ingentior, adj., *large, vast, great;* of size of body, *huge* (I. 39).

ingrātus, -a, -um, comp. -ior, sup. -issimus, [in- + grātus], adj., *unacceptable, unwelcome.* [ingrate.

ingredior, -gredī, -gressus, [in + gradior, *step*], 3, dep., *advance; enter, go into* (II. 4; V. 9). [ingress.

iniciō, -icere, -iēcī, -iectus, [in + iaciō], 3, *throw in; lay on* (IV. 17); *place on, put on* (VII. 58); *inspire, infuse* (I. 46); of fear, *strike into* (IV. 19; VII. 55). [inject.

iniectus, see iniciō.

inimīcitia, -ae, [inimīcus], f., *enmity.* (VI. 12).

inimīcus, -a. -um, comp. -ior, sup. -issimus, [in- + amīcus], adj., *unfriendly, hostile.* As noun, inimīcus, -ī. m., *enemy, personal enemy,* as distinguished from hostis, *a public enemy; adversary.* [inimical.

inīquitās, -ātis, [inīquus], f., *unevenness; unfairness, unreasonableness; disadvantage.* inīquitās locī, *unfavourableness of (the) position, disadvantageous position.* [iniquity.

inīquus, -a, -um, comp. -ior, sup. -issimus, [in- + aequus]. adj., *uneven, sloping; unfavorable, disadvantageous; unfair, unjust* (I. 44).

initium, -ī, [cf. ineō], n., *beginning, commencement;* pl., *elements, first principles* (VI. 17). [initial.

initūrus, see ineō.

initus, -a, -um, see **ineō.**

**iniungō, -iungere, -iūnxī, -iūnctus, [in +
iungō],** 3, *fasten upon, impose.* (VII. 77). [enjoin.

iniūria, -ae, [iniūrius, in- + iūs], f., *wrong,
outrage, injustice, injury.* [injury.

iniussus, -ūs, [in- + iussus], m., only abl. in
use, *without command, without orders.* (I. 19; V.
28).

innāscor, -nāscī, -nātus, [in + nāscor], 3,
dep., *be born in, be latent in* (VII. 42, C. III. 92);
spring up in, arise in (I. 41). [innate.

innātus, -a, -um, see **innāscor.**

innītor, -nītī, -nīxus or **-nīsus, [in + nītor],** 3,
dep., *support one's self with, lean upon.* (II. 27).

innīxus, see **innītor.**

innocēns, -entis, comp. **innocentior,** sup.
-issimus, [in- + nocēns, from **noceō],** adj.,
blameless, innocent. As noun, **innocentēs,
-ium,** m., pl., *the innocent* (VI. 9), *innocent men*
(VI. 16). [innocent.

innocentia, -ae, [innocēns], f., *blamelessness,
integrity.* (I. 40). [innocence.

inopia, -ae. [inops, needy], f., *want, lack, need,
shortage, scarcity.*

inopīnāns, -antis, [in- + opīnāns, from
opīnor], adj., *not expecting, unawares, off one's
guard.*

inquam, inquis, inquit, present indicative,
def., *say, says.*

īnsciēns, -entis, [in- + sciēns, from **sciō],** adj.,
not knowing, unaware.

īnscientia, -ae, [īnsciēns], f., *ignorance, lack of
knowledge.*

īnscius, -a, -um, [in-, cf. **sciō].** adj., *not
knowing, unaware, ignorant.*

insecūtus, see **īnsequor.**

īnsequor, -sequī, -secūtus, [in + sequor], 3,
dep., *follow up, pursue, follow in pursuit*

īnserō, -serere, -seruī, -sertus, [in + serō], 3,
fasten in. (III. 14). [insert.

īnsidiae, -ārum, [cf. īnsideō], f., pl., *ambush,
ambuscade; artifice, device, trap, pitfall.* **per
īnsidiās,** *by stratagem* (I. 42; IV. 13). [insidious.

īnsidior, -ārī, -ātus, [īnsidiae], 1, dep., *lurk in
ambush, lie in wait.*

insigne, -is, [īnsignis], n., *sign, mark, signal;
decoration.* [ensign.

īnsignis, -e, comp. **-ior, [in + signum],** adj.,
noteworthy. (I. 12).

īnsiliō, -silīre, -siluī, [in + saliō, leap], 4, *leap
upon.* (I. 52).

īnsimulō, -āre, -āvī, -ātus, [in + simulō], 1,
charge with, accuse of; with gen. (VII. 20, 38).

īnsinuō, -āre, -āvī, -ātus, [in + sinuō, curve],
1, *push in;* with **sē,** *make one's way* (IV. 33).
[insinuate.

īnsistō, -sistere, -stitī, [in + sistō], 3, *stand,
stand upon, keep one's footing; press on; follow,*

pursue (III. 14). **tōtus īnsistit in,** *he devotes
himself wholly to* (VI. 5). [insist.

īnsolēns, -entis, [in-, soleō], adj., *unusual.*
īnsolēns bellī, *unaccustomed to war* (C. II. 36).
[insolent.

īnsolenter [īnsolēns], adv., *arrogantly,
haughtily.* (I. 14).

īnsolitus, -a, -um, [in- + solitus], adj.,
unaccustomed. (C. III. 85).

īnspectō, -āre, only pres. part. in use, [freq. of
īnspiciō], 1, *look at, look.* **īnspectantibus
nōbīs,** *under our own eyes* (VII. 25). [inspect.

īnstabilis, -e, [in- + stabilis, from **stō],** adj.,
unsteady. (IV. 23).

īnstāns, -antis, comp. **īnstantior,** [part. of
īnstō], adj., *impending, pressing.* (VI. 4). [instant.

īnstar, n., indecl., *likeness;* followed by gen.,
like (II. 17).

īnstīgō, -āre, -āvī, -ātus, 1, *urge on, incite.* (V.
56). [instigate.

**īnstituō, -stituere, -stituī, -stitūtus, [in +
statuō],** 3, of troops, *draw up, arrange; devise,
build, construct; make; make ready, furnish;
obtain* (III. 9); *establish, institute* (VI. 16); *undertake,
commence, begin; resolve upon, determine; train,
teach.* [institute (verb).

īnstitūtum, -ī, [īnstituō], n., *plan, practice* (I. 50;
VII. 24); *custom, usage* (IV. 20; VI. 18); *institution* (I.
1); *arrangement, disposition* (C. III. 84). [institute
(noun).

īnstitūtus, see **īnstituō.**

īnstō, -stāre, -stitī, -stātūrus, [in + stō], 1, *be
near at hand, approach; press on, press forward.*

īnstrūmentum, -ī, [īnstruō], n., *tool;* singular
with collective force, *stock, outfit.* **mīlitāre
īnstrūmentum,** *stock of weapons* (VI. 30).
[instrument.

**īnstruō, -struere, -strūxī, -strūctus, [in +
struō,** build], 3, *build, construct;* of troops,
draw up, form; fit out, equip, supply (V. 5; VII. 59; C.
III. 61). [instruct.

īnsuēfactus, -a, -um, [īnsuēscō + faciō], adj.,
accustomed, trained. (IV. 24).

īnsuētus, -a, -um, [part. of īnsuēscō], adj.,
unaccustomed.

īnsula, -ae, f., *island,* [insular.

īnsuper [in + super], adv., *above, on top.* (IV. 17;
VII. 23).

integer, -gra, -grum, comp. **integrior,** sup.
integerrimus, [in- + TAG in tangō], adj.,
*untouched, whole, unhurt, undamaged; fresh,
vigorous.* **rē integrā,** *at the outset* (VII. 30). As
noun, **integrī, -ōrum,** m., pl., *fresh troops,*
[integer.

integō, -tegere, -tēxī, -tēctus, [in + tegō], 3,
cover, cover over.

**intellegō, -legere, -lēxī, -lēctus, [inter +
legō],** 3, *understand, see clearly, realize,*

[intelligent.

intentus, -a, -um, comp. **-ior,** sup. **-issimus,** [part. of **intendō**], adj., *attentive, eager, intent.* [intent.

inter, prep. with acc., *between, among;* of time, *during, for* (I. 36). **inter sē,** *with each other, among themselves, with one another.*

intercēdō, -cēdere, -cessī, -cessūrus, [inter + cēdō], 3, *go between, be placed between* (II. 17); *lie between* (I. 39; V. 52; VII. 26, 46, 47); of time, *intervene, pass* (I. 7; V. 53); *take place, occur* (V. 11). [intercede.

intercessiō, -ōnis, [intercēdō], f., *interposition, protest.* (C. I. 7). [intercession.

intercipiō, -cipere, -cēpī, -ceptus, [inter + capiō], 3, *cut off, intercept.* [intercept.

interclūdō, -clūdere, -clūsī, -clūsus, [inter + claudō], 3, *shut off, cutoff; block up, blockade, hinder.*

interdīcō, -dīcere, dīxī, -dictus, [inter + dīcō], 3, *forbid, prohibit, exclude, interdict;* followed by a prohibition, *enjoin* (V. 58; VII. 40). [interdict.

interdiū, [inter, cf. **diēs**], adv., *in the daytime, by day.*

interdum, [inter + dum], adv., *for a time, for a season* (I. 14); *sometimes* (I. 39).

intereā, [inter + eā], adv., *in the mean time, meanwhile.*

intereō, -īre, -iī, -itūrus, [inter + eō], 4, *perish, be destroyed, die.*

interficiō, -ficere, -fēcī, -fectus, [inter + faciō], 3, *slay, kill.*

intericiō, -icere, iēcī, iectus, (inter + iaciō), 3, *throw between, place between, put between;* pass. part., **interiectus,** *lying between, intervening.* [interject.

interiectus, see **intericiō.**

interim, [inter + -im], adv., *in the mean time, meanwhile.*

interior, -ius, gen. **-ōris,** sup. **intimus,** [inter], adj. in comp. degree, *inner, interior.* As noun, **interiōrēs, -um,** m., pl., *those living in the interior* (V. 14), *those within* the city (VII. 82, 86). [interior.

interitus, -ūs, [intereō], m., *destruction, death.* (V. 47).

intermittō, -mittere, -mīsī, -missus, [inter + mittō], 3, *leave an interval, leave vacant; leave off, leave; stop, break, cease, discontinue; interrupt, suspend;* pass., of fire, *abate* (V. 43), of wind, *fail* (V. 8). **quā flūmen intermittit,** *where the river does not flow* (I. 38). **nocte intermissā,** *a night intervening* (I. 27). **intermissō spatiō,** *after an interval* (V. 15). [intermittent.

interneciō, -ōnis, [cf. **internecō,** *destroy*], f., *slaughter* (I. 13); *utter destruction* (II. 28). [internecine.

interpellō, -āre, -āvī, -ātus, 1, *interrupt; disturb, hinder* (I. 44). [interpellate.

interpōnō, -pōnere, -posuī, -positus, [inter + pōnō], 3, *place between, put between, interpose; put forward* (I. 42); *present, manifest* (IV. 32); of time, *suffer to elapse.* **fidem interpōnere,** *to pledge one's honor* (V. 6, 36). [interpose.

interpres, -pretis, m., *interpreter.* (I. 19; V. 36). [interpreter.

interpretor, -ārī, -ātus, [interpres], 1, dep., *explain, expound.* (VI. 13). [interpret.

interrogō, -āre, -āvī, -ātus, [inter + rogō], 1, *ask, question.* (VII. 20). [interrogate.

interrumpō, -rumpere, -rūpī, -ruptus, [inter + rumpō], 3, *break down, destroy.* (VII. 19, 34). [interrupt.

interscindō, -scindere, -scidī, -scissus, [inter + scindō], 3, *cut down* (II. 9); *cut through* (VII. 24).

intersum, -esse, -fuī, irr., *be between, lie between; be present at, take part in.* Impers., **interest,** *it concerns, is important.* **magnī interest,** *it is of great importance* (V. 4, VI. 1). **neque interest,** *and it makes no difference* (VII. 14). [interest.

intervāllum, -ī, [inter + vāllum], n., *room between two palisades, interval, space, distance.* [interval.

interveniō, -venīre, vēnī, -ventum est, [inter + veniō], 4, *arrive* (VI. 37); *appear, present one's self* (VII. 20). [intervene.

interventus, -ūs, [interveniō], m., *intervention.* (III. 15).

intexō, -texere, -texuī, -textus, [in + texō], *weave,* 3, *weave in, interweave.* (II. 33).

intoleranter, comp. **-ius,** sup. **-issimē,** [intolerāns], adv., *unendurably; violently* (VII. 51).

intrā, [for **interā** sc. **parte**], prep. with acc., *inside of, within.*

intrītus, [in- + part. of **terō,** *rub*], adj., *unworn; unwearied, fresh* (III. 26).

intrō, adv., *within, inside.*

intrō, -āre, -āvī, -ātus, [in + *trō,* cf. **trāns**], 1, *enter, go in.* [enter.

intrōdūcō, -dūcere, -dūxī, -ductus, [intrō + dūcō], 3, *lead into, bring into.* [introduce.

introeō, -īre, -īvī, [intrō + eō], irr., *go in; come in, enter* (V. 43).

introitus, -ūs, [introeō], m., *an entering; entrance* (V. 9). [introit.

intrōmissus, see **intrōmittō.**

intrōmittō, -mittere, -mīsī, -missus, [intrō + mittō], 3, *send into, send in; let in; bring in* (V. 58).

intrōrsus, [intrō + versus], adv., *within, inside.*

intrōrumpō, -rumpere, -rūpī, -ruptus, [intrō + rumpō, *break*], 3, *burst into; break in* (V. 51).

intueor, -tuērī, -tuitus, [in + tueor], 2, dep., *look upon.* (I. 32). [intuition.

intuleram, see īnferō.

intulī, see īnferō.

intus, adv., *within, on the inside.*

inūsitātus, -a, -um, comp. -ior, [in- + part. of ūsitor, freq. of ūtor], adj., *unfamiliar, unwonted, unprecedented.*

inūtilis, -e, comp. -ior, [in- + utilis], adj., *useless, unserviceable, of no use; disadvantageous* (VII. 27). [inutile.

inveniō, -venīre, -vēnī, -ventus, [in + veniō], 4, *come upon, find, discover; find out, learn* (II. 16). [invent.

inventor, -ōris, [inveniō], m., *originator, inventor.* (VI. 17). [inventor.

inveterāscō, -ere, inveterāvī, [in + veterāscō, from vetus], 3,*grow old; become established, become fixed* (V. 41); *establish one's self* (II. 1). [cf. inveterate.

invictus, -a, -um, [in- + part. of vincō], adj., *unconquerable, invincible.* (I. 36).

invideō, -vidēre, -vīdī, -vīsus, [in + videō], 2, *look askance at; envy.* (II. 31).

invidia, -ae, [invidus], f., *envy, jealousy,* [envy.

inviolātus, -a, -um, [in- + part. of violō], adj., *inviolable.* (III. 9). [inviolate.

invīsitātus, -a, -um, [in- + vīsitātus], adj., *unseen.* (C. II. 4).

invītō, -āre, -āvī, -ātus, 1, *invite, request* (I. 35; IV. 6); *entice, attract* (V. 51; VI. 35). [invite.

invītus, -a, -um, sup. -issimus, adj., *unwilling, reluctant.* sē invītō (I. 8; IV. 16), eō invītō (I. 14), *against his will.*

ipse, -a, -um, gen. ipsīus, dem. pron., *self; himself, herself, itself, themselves; he, they* (emphatic); *very.* ipsīus castra, *his own camp* (I. 21). hōc ipsō tempore, *just at this moment* (VI. 37). ipsum esse Dumnorīgem, *that Dumnorix was the very man* (I. 18).

īrācundia, -ae, [īrācundus], f., *anger, passion.* (VI. 5; VII. 42).

īrācundus, -a,-um, comp. -ior, [īra], adj., *passionate, quick-tempered.* (I. 31). [iracund.

irrīdeō, -rīdere, -rīsī, -rīsus, [in + rīdeō, laugh], 2, *laugh at, make fun of, ridicule.* (II. 30).

irridiculē, [in- + rīdiculē], adv., *without wit.* (I. 42).

irrumpō, -rumpere, -rūpī, -ruptus, [in + rumpō, break], 3, *break into, burst into, rush in.*

irruptiō, -ōnis, [irrumpō], f., *raid* (VII. 7); *attack* (VII. 70). [irruption.

is, ea, id, gen. eius, dem. pron., *he, she, it; that, this, the, the one; before* ut, is = tālis, *such; after* et, *and that too; after* neque, *and that not* (III. 2); *with comparatives, abl.* eō = *the, all the, as* eō magis, *all the more.*

iste, -a, -ud, gen. istīus, dem. pron., *that, that*

of yours. (VII. 77).

ita, [cf. is], adv., *in this way, so, thus; in the following manner, in such a way, accordingly.* nōn ita, *not so very, not very* (IV. 37; V. 47).

Italia, -ae, f., *Italy.* [Italy.

itaque, = et ita, *and so* (I. 52).

itaque, [ita + -que], adv., *and thus, accordingly, therefore, consequently.*

item, adv., *also, further; just so, in like manner.* [item.

iter, itineris, [cf. eō, īre], n., *journey, line of march; road, route.* magnum iter, *forced march,* from 20 to 25 miles a day. ex itinere, *directly after marching, from the line of march;* used of a force which turns from marching at once, without encamping, to attack an enemy in the field (I. 25), to storm a town (II. 6, 12; III. 21), or to retreat (II. 29). [itinerary.

iterum, adv., *again, a second time.*

Itius, -ī, m., *portus Itius*(ish' [y]us), harbor from which Caesar sailed to Britain, probably *Boulogne.*

itūrus, see eō.

iuba, -ae, f., *mane.* (I. 48.)

Iuba, -ae, m., *Juba* (jū' ba), a king of Numidia, who joined the side of Pompey in the Civil War.

iubeō, iubēre, iussī, iussus, 2, *order, give orders, hid, command.* [jussive.

iūdicium, -ī, [iūdex, *judge*], n., *legal judgment, decision, decree; place of judgment, trial* (I. 4); *opinion, judgment.* optimum iūdicium facere, *to pass a very favorable opinion* (I. 41). [judicial.

iūdicō, -āre, -āvī, -ātus, [iūdex], 1, *judge, decide; think, be of, the opinion; pronounce, declare* (V. 56). [judge (verb).

iugum, -ī, [IUG, cf. iungō], n., *yoke* (I. 7, 12; IV. 33); *of hills and mountains, ridge, summit, height.*

iūmentum, -ī, [for *iugumentum, root IUG in iungō], n., *yoke-animal, beast of burden, draught-animal,* used of horses, mules, and asses.

iūnctūra, -ae, [iungō], f., *juncture, joint.* (IV. 17). [juncture.

iūnctus, see iungō.

iungō, -ere, iūnxī, iūnctus, 3, *join together, join, connect, unite.* [join.

iūnior, see iuvenis.

Iūnius, -ī, m., *Quintus Junius* (jūn'-yus), a Roman of Spanish birth in Caesar's army. (V. 27, 28).

Iuppiter, Iovis, m., *Jupiter* (jū'piter). (VI. 17). Fig. 200. [jovial.

Iūra, -ae, m., *Jura* (jū'ra), a range of mountains extending from the Rhine to the Rhone (about 170 miles), and forming the boundary between the Helvetians and the

Sequanians. (I. 2, 6, 8).

iūrō, -āre, -āvī, -ātus, [iūs], 1, *take an oath, swear.* [jury.

iūs, iūris, n., *right, justice, authority.* **iūre bellī,** *by the laws of war* (I. 44; VII. 41). **in suō iūre,** *in the exercise of his own rights* (I. 36, 44). **iūs reddere,** *to render justice* (VI. 13). **iūs dīcere,** *to administer justice* (VI. 23). **iūra in hōs,** *rights over these* (VI. 13).

iūs iūrandum, iūris iūrandī, [iūs + gerundive of **iūrō], n., *oath.*

iussus, -ūs, [iubeō], m., used only in abl. sing., *order, bidding, command.* (VII. 3).

iūstitia, -ae, [iūstus], f., *justice, fair-dealing.* [justice.

iūstus, -a, -um, comp. **-ior,** sup. **-issimus, [iūs],** adj., *just, rightful, fair; proper, suitable, due.* [just.

iuvenis, -e, comp. **iūnior,** adj., *young.* As noun, **iūniōrēs, -um,** m., pl., *younger men,* of military age, under forty-six years (VII. 1). [junior.

iuventūs, -ūtis, [iuvenis] , f., *youth; young men.*

iuvō, -āre, iūvī, iūtus, 1, *help, aid, assist.*

iūxtā, adv., *near by, near.* [jostle.

K.

Kal. = **Kalendae.**

Kalendae, -ārum, f., pl., *Calends,* the first day of the month. [Calendar.

L.

L., with proper names = **Lūcius.**

Laberius, -ī, m., see **Dūrus.**

Labiēnus, -ī, m., *Titus Labienus* (lā-bi-ē' nus), the most prominent of Caesar's lieutenants in the Gallic War; in the Civil War he went over to the side of Pompey, but displayed small abilities as a commander, and fell at the battle of Munda, 45 B.C.

lābor, lābī, lapsus, 3, dep., *slip; go astray* (V. 3); *fail, be deceived, be disappointed* (V. 55). [lapse.

labor, -ōris, m., *toil, work, exertion, labor; endurance* (IV. 2). [labor.

labōrō, -āre, -āvī, -ātus, [labor], 1, *make effort, labor, strive* (I 31; VII. 31); *be hard pressed, be in distress, be in danger.* [labor (verb).

**labrum, -ī, [LAB, cf. lambō, lick], n., *lip* (V. 14); *edge* (VII. 72); *rim, brim* (VI. 28).

lac, lactis, n., *milk.* [lacteal.

lacessō, -ere, -īvī, -ītus, [obsolete **laciō,** *entice*], 3, *arouse, provoke; harass, assail, attack.*

lacrima, -ae, f., *tear.* [lacrimal.

lacrimō, -āre, -āvī, -ātus, [lacrima], 1, *shed tears, weep.* (VII. 38).

lacus, -ūs, m., *lake.* [lake.

laedō, laedere, laesī, laesus, 3, *injure; break, violate* (VI. 9).

laetitia, -ae, [laetus], f., *rejoicing, joy, delight.*

(V. 48, 52; VII. 79).

laetus, -a, -um, comp. **-ior,** sup. **-issimus,** adj., *joyful, glad.* (III. 18).

languidē, comp. **languidius, [languidus],** adv., *feebly, lazily.* (VII. 27).

languidus, -a, -um, comp. **-ior,** [cf. **languor],** adj., *weak, faint, exhausted.* (III. 5). [languid.

languor, -ōris, [langueō, *be faint*], m., *faintness; exhaustion, weariness* (V. 31). [languor.

lapis, -idis, m., *stone.* [lapidary.

lāpsus, see **lābor.**

laqueus, -ī, m., *noose.* (VII. 22).

largior, largīrī, largītus, [largus, *abundant*], 4, dep., *give freely, supply, bestow* (VI. 24); *bribe* (I. 18).

largiter, [largus, *abundant*], adv. *abundantly, much.* **largiter posse,** *to have great influence* (I. 18).

largītiō, -ōnis, [largior], 1., *lavish giving, bribery.* (I. 9). [largition.

**Lārīsa, -ae, [Λ A P I Σ Σ A], f. (la-ris' a), a city in Thessaly, now *Larissa.* (C. III. 96, 97, 98).

lassitūdō, -inis, [lassus, *weak*], f., *faintness, weariness.* [lassitude.

lātē, comp. **lātius,** sup. **lātissimē, [lātus],** adv., *widely, broadly, extensively.* **longē lātēque,** *far and wide* (IV. 35). **quam lātissimē,** *as far as possible.*

**latebra, -ae, [cf. lateō], f., *hiding-place.* (VI. 43). [latebricole.

lateō, latēre, latuī, 2, *lie hid* (II. 19); *be unnoticed* (III. 14). [latent.

lātissimē, see **lātē.**

lātitūdō, -inis, [lātus], f., *width, breadth, extent.* [latitude.

lātius, see **lātē.**

Latobrīgī, -ōrum, m., pl., (lat-o-bri'jī) a people near the Helvetians.

latrō, -ōnis, m., *freebooter, robber.*

latrōcinium, -ī, [latrōcinor, *plunder*], n., *freebooting, brigandage, robbery.* (VI. 16, 23, 35).

lātūrus, see **ferō.**

lātus, -a, -um, comp. **-ior,** sup. **-issimus,** adj., *broad, wide;* of territory, *extensive* (II. 4; VI. 22).

latus, -eris, n., *side;* of an army, *flank.* **latus apertum,** *exposed flank.* **ab latere,** *on the flank.* [lateral.

laudō, -āre, -āvī, -ātus, [laus], 1, *praise, commend, compliment.* [laud (verb).

laurea, -ae, [laurus, *laurel*], f., *laurel tree; laurel* (C. III. 71), [laureate.

laus, laudis, f., *praise, glory, commendation, distinction.* [laud.

lavō, -āre, lāvī, lautus and **lōtus, 1,** *wash;* pass. **lavārī,** used reflexively, *bathe* (IV. 1). [lave.

laxō, -āre, -āvī, -ātus, 1, *make wide, spread out, extend,* [laxative.

lēgātiō, -ōnis, [**lēgō,** *despatch*], f., *envoyship, mission* (I. 3); referring to persons (= **lēgātī**), *deputation, embassy, envoys,* [legation.

lēgātus, -ī [**lēgō,** *despatch*], m., *envoy;* of the army, *lieutenant, lieutenant-general.* [legate.

legiō, -ōnis, [cf. **legō,** *collect*], f., *legion.* [legion.

legiōnārius, -a, -um, [**legiō**], adj., *of a legion, legionary.* [legionary.

legō, -ere, lēgī, lēctus, 3, *bring together; single out, select* (C. III. 59); *read.* [legible.

legūmen, -inis, [**legō,** *gather*], n., *pulse.* (C. III. 47). [legume.

Lemannus, -ī, m., with **lacus,** *Lake Geneva.*

Lemovīcēs, -um, m., pl., (lem-o-vī'sēz), a Gallic people west of the Arvernians.

lēnis, -e, comp. **-ior,** sup. **-issimus,** adj., *smooth, gentle.* [lenient.

lēnitās, -ātis, [**lēnis**], f., *smoothness* (I. 12); *gentleness* (C. III. 98). [lenity.

lēniter, comp. **lēnius,** sup. **-issimus,** [**lēnis**], adv., *mildly, gently, slightly.*

lentē, [**lentus**], adv., comp. **lentius,** *slowly.* (C. II. 40).

Lentulus, -ī, m., (len' chūlus):
(1) *Lucius Lentulus,* consul in 49 B.C., a partisan of Pompey, who was with him at the time of the battle of Pharsalus (C. III. 96).
(2) See **Spinther.**

lēnunculus, -ī, m., *boat, skiff.* (C. II. 43).

Lepontiī, -ōrum, m., pl., (le-pon'-sh[y]ī), a people in the Alps.

Leptitānī, -ōrum, [**Leptis**], m., pl., (lep-ti-tā' nī), the inhabitants of Leptis Minor, a city on the coast of Africa southeast of Thapsus.

lepus, -oris, m., *hare.* (V. 12).

Leucī, -ōrum, m., pl., (lū' sī), a Gallic state south of the Mediomatrici. (I. 40).

Levācī, -ōrum, m., pl., (le-vā'sī), a Belgic people, dependents of the Nervians. (V. 39).

levis, -e, comp. **-ior,** sup. **-issimus,** adj., *light, slight;* of a report, *baseless, unfounded* (VII. 42); of an engagement, *unimportant* (VII. 36, 53). Comp., *more capricious* (V. 28); *less serious* (VII. 4).

levitās, -ātis, [**levis**], f., *lightness* (V. 34); *fickleness, instability* (II. 1; VII. 43). [levity.

leviter, [**levis**], adv., comp. **levius,** sup. **levissimē,** *lightly.* (C. III. 92).

levō, -āre, -āvī, -ātus, [**levis**], 1, *lighten; relieve, free from* (V. 27).

lēx, lēgis, f., *law, enactment.* [legal.

Lexoviī, -ōrum, m., pl., (leks-ō' vi-ī), a Gallic state on the coast west of the Sequana (*Seine*). Fig. 201.

libenter, comp. **libentius,** sup. **libentissimē,** [**libēns,** *glad*], adv., *willingly, gladly, cheerfully.*

līber, -era, -erum, comp. **-ior,** sup.

līberrimus, adj., *free, independent; unimpeded,*

unrestricted. [liberal.

līberālitās, -ātis, [**līberālis**], f., *generosity* (I. 18); *generous help* (I. 43). [liberality.

līberāliter, comp. **līberālius,** sup. **-issimē,** [**līberālis**], adv., *graciously, courteously, kindly.*

līberē, comp. **-ius,** [**līber**], adv., *freely, without hindrance* (VII. 49); *boldly* (V. 19); *openly* (I. 18; VII. 1).

līberī, -ōrum, m., pl., *children.*

līberō, -āre, -āvī, -ātus, [**līber**], 1, *set free, free; release, relieve.* [liberate.

lībertās, -ātis, [**līber**], f., *freedom, liberty, independence.* [liberty.

Libō, -ōnis, m., *Lucius Scribonius Libo* (skri-bō' ni-us lī' bō), a partisan of Pompey in the Civil War. (C. III. 90).

lībrīlis, -e, [**lībra,** *pound*], adj., *weighing a pound.* (VII. 81).

licentia, -ae, [**licēns, licet**], f, *lawlessness; presumption* (VII. 52). [license.

liceor, licērī, licitus, 2, dep., *bid, make a bid,* at an auction. (I. 18).

licet, licēre, licuit and **licitum est,** 2, impers., *it is allowed, lawful, permitted.* **licet mihi,** 1 *am allowed, I may.* **petere ut liceat,** *to ask permission.* [licit.

Licinius, -ī, m., *Licinius* (lī-sin' i-us), a Roman name:
(1) *Licinius Crassus,* see **Crassus.**
(2) *Licinius Damasippus* (dam-a-sip' us), a Roman senator on the side of Pompey in the Civil War. (C. II. 44).

līctor, -ōris, m., *lictor,* an attendant upon a Roman magistrate. (C. I. 6).

Liger, -eris, m., (lī'jer), *Loire,* which rises in the Cevennes (*Cebenna*) mountains, hows northwest, receives as a tributary the Allier (*Elaver*), flows west, and empties into the Atlantic, after a course of more than 500 miles, (III. 9; VII. 5, 11, 55, 59).

lignātiō, -ōnis, [**lignor,** from **lignum**], f., *getting wood.* (V. 39).

lignātor, -ōris, [**lignor,** from **lignum**], m., *wood-cutter.* Pl., *men sent to get wood, wood foragers* (V. 26).

līlium, -ī, n., *lily.* (VII. 73). [lily.

līnea, -ae, [**līneus,** from **līnum**], f., *line.* (VII. 23). [line.

Lingonēs, -um, m., pl., (ling'go-nēz), a Gallic people west of the Sequanians.

lingua, -ae, f., *tongue; language* (I. 1, 47). [language.

lingula, -ae, [dim. of **lingua**], f., *tongue of land.* (III. 12).

linter, -tris, f., *boat, skiff.*

līnum, -ī, n., *flax.* (III. 13).

līs, lītis, f., *strife; lawsuit; damages,* adjudged by legal process (V. 1).

Liscus, -ī, m., (lis' kus), chief magistrate

(vergobret) of the Aeduans in 58 B.C.
Litaviccus, -ī, m., (lit-a-vik' us), a prominent
Aeduan.

littera, -ae, f., *letter, character,* of the alphabet.
Pl. **litterae, -ārum,** *writing* (VI. 14); *letter,
despatch.* **litterae pūblicae,** *public records* (V. 47).
[letter.

lītus, -oris, n., *shore* of the sea, *strand, beach.*
[littoral.

locuplēs, -ētis, [locus, cf. **plēnus**], adj.,
wealthy, opulent. (C. III. 59).

locus, -ī, m., pl. **loca, -ōrum,** n., *place, ground;
position, situation; room; social position, rank,
standing; opportunity;* pl. **loca** often *region,
country.* [local.

locūtus, see **loquor.**

longē, comp. **longius,** sup. **longissimē,**
[longus], adv., *at a distance, far, by far.* Comp.,
of space, *further;* of time, *further, longer.* **quam
longissimē,** *as far as possible.*

longinquus, -a, -um, comp. **-ior,** [longus],
adj., *far removed, remote, distant; long-
continued, prolonged, lasting.* [longinquity.

longitūdō, -inis, [longus], f., *length.*
[longitude.

longurius, -ī, [longus], m., *long pole.*

longus, -a, -um, comp. **-ior,** sup. **-issimus,**
adj., *long, extended, distant;* used of either
space or time. **nāvis longa,** *battleship, galley.*

loquor, loquī, locūtus, 3, dep., *speak, say.*
[loquacious.

lōrīca, -ae, [cf. **lōrum,** *leather straps,* f., *cuirass*
of leather; *breastwork* (V. 40; VII. 72, 86). [loricate.

Lūcānius, -ī, m., *Quintus Lucanius* (lū-kā' ni-
us), a brave centurion. (V. 35).

Lūcīlius, -ī, m., a Roman name. **Lūcīlius
Hirrus** (lū-sil' i-us hir' us), a leader on the
side of Pompey in the Civil War. (C. III. 82).

Lūcius, -ī, m., (lū' sh[y]us), a Roman first
name; abbreviation, **L.**

Lucterius, -ī, m., (luk-tē' ri-us), a Cadurcan, a
helper of Vercingetorix in the great uprising
of 52 B.C.

lūctus, -ūs, [lūgeō], m., *mourning,
lamentation.* (C. II. 7).

Lugotorīx, -igis, m., (lū-got' o-riks), a British
chief. (V. 22).

lūna, -ae, f., *moon.* [lunar.

Lūna, -ae, f., *moon* as a divinity, *moon-goddess.*
(VI. 21).

Lutecia, -ae, f., (lū-tē'sh[y]a), a city of the
Parisii on an island in the Seine, *Paris.* (VI. 3;
VII. 57, 58).

lūx, lūcis, f., *light, daylight.* **prīmā luce,** at
daybreak.

lūxuria, -ae, [lūxus, *excess*], f., *high living,
luxury.* (II. 15). [luxury.

M.

M., with proper names = **Mārcus.**

M as a designation of number = 1000.

māceria, -ae, [cf. **mācerō,** *soften*], f., originally
wall of soft clay; wall of loose stone (VII. 69, 70.)

māchinātiō, -ōnis, [**māchinor,** *contrive*], f.,
mechanical appliance, machine. [machination.

maestus, -a, -um, sup. **-issimus,** [cf. **maereō,**
be sad], adj., *sad, dejected.*

magis, sup. **maximē,** [cf. **magnus**], adv. in
comp. degree, *more, rather.* **eō magis,** *all the
more.* Sup. **maximē,** *very greatly, exceedingly,
chiefly, especially.* **quam maximē,** *as much as
possible.*

magister, -trī, m., *master* of a ship, *captain* (C.
III. 43). [master.

magistrātus, -ūs, [**magister**], m., *magistracy,
civil office; one holding a magistracy, magistrate.*
[magistrate.

magnificus, -a, -um, comp. **magnificentior,**
sup. **-issimus,** [**magnus,** cf. **faciō**], adj.,
splendid, magnificent. (VI. 19). [magnificent.

magnitūdō, -inis, [**magnus**], f., *greatness,
extent; size, bulk;* of winds and waves, *violence.*
[magnitude.

magnopere, [for **magnō opere,** abl. of
magnum + opus], adv., *very much, greatly,
specially, deeply; earnestly, urgently.*

magnus, -a, -um, comp. **maior,** sup.
maximus, adj., *great, large, powerful;* of wind,
violent; of voices, *loud* (IV. 25). Sup., *greatest,
very great, largest, very large.* As noun,
maiōrēs, -um, m., pl., *forefathers, ancestors,*
maiōrēs natū, lit. *those older by birth, the old
men, elders* (II. 13, 28; IV. 13). [maximum.

maiestās, -ātis, [**maior**], f., *greatness, dignity.*
(VII. 17). [majesty.

maiōrēs, -um, see **magnus.**

malacia, -ae, [ΜΑΛΑΚΙΑ], f., *calm, dead cairn.*
(III. 15).

male, comp. **peius,** sup. **pessimē,** [**malus,**
bad], adv., *badly, ill, unsuccessfully.*

maleficium, -ī, [**maleficus**], n., *mischief,
wrong-doing, outrage, harm.*

mālō, mālle, māluī, [**magis + volō**], irr.,
prefer, choose rather, had rather.

mālus, -ī, m., *upright pole, upright;* of a ship,
mast. (III. 14; VII. 22).

mandātum, -ī, [part. of **mandō**], n.,
*commission, order; command; injunction,
instruction.* [mandate.

mandō, -āre, -āvī, -ātus, [**manus + dō**], 1,
commit, entrust, commission; order, direct.
[mandatory.

Mandubiī, -ōrum, m., pl., *Mandubians,
Mandubii* (man-dū' bi-ī), a Gallic people north
of the Aeduans; chief city Alesia, now *Alise-
Ste-Reine.*

Mandubracius, -ī, [Kel., = 'Son of the brewer

of barley-beer'], m., (man-du-brā'-sh[y]us), a British chieftain, loyal to Caesar. (V. 20, 22).

māne, adv., *in the morning.*

maneō, manēre, mānsī, mānsūrus, 2, *stay, remain; continue.* [manse.

manipulāris, -e, [manipulus], adj., *of a maniple.* As noun, manipulāris, -is, m., *soldier of a maniple, fellow-manipular.* (VII. 47, 50).

manipulus, -ī, [manus + PLE in pleō, the first standard of a maniple being a *handful* of hay raised on a pole], m., *company* of soldiers, *maniple,* one-third of a cohort. [maniple.

Mānlius, -ī, m., *Lucius Manlius* (man' li-us), a proconsul in Gaul. (III. 20).

mānsuēfaciō, -facere, -fēcī, -factus, pass.

mānsuēfīō, -fierī, [mānsuētus, *tame,* + faciō], 3, *make tame, tame.* (VI. 28).

mānsuētūdō, -inis, [mānsuētus, *tame*], f., *gentleness, compassion.*

manus, -ūs, f., *hand;* of troops, *band, force.* [manicure.

Mārcellīnus, -ī, m., *P. Cornelius Lentulus Marcellinus* (len' chū-lus mar-se-li' nus), a quaestor in Caesar's army in the Civil War. (C. III. 64).

Mārcellus, -ī, m., (*Gaius Claudius Marcellus* (klā' di-us mar-sel' lis), one of the consuls in 49 B.C. (C. I. 6).

Mārcius, -ī, m., *Marcius Rufius* (mär'si-us rū'fus), a quaestor in Curio's army (C. II. 43).

Marcomanī, -ōrum, m., pl., (mar-kom'a-nī) a Germanic people.

Mārcus, -ī, m., (mär' kus), a Roman first name, our *Mark.*

mare, -is, n., *the sea.* [marine.

maritimus, -a, -um, [mare], adj., *of the sea, by the sea, near the sea; maritime, sea-.* maritimae rēs, *naval operations* (IV. 23). [maritime.

Marius, -ī, m., *Gaius Marius* (mā'-ri-us), a great Roman general; born 157 B.C., near Arpinum, died 86 B.C.; famous for his victories over Jugurtha, and the Cimbrians and Teutons; seven times consul, remaining to the end the bitter foe of the aristocratic party. (I. 40).

Marrūcīnī, -ōrum, m., pl., (mär-ū-sī'nī), a people of Central Italy, on the Adriatic coast. (C. III. 34).

Mārs, Mārtis, m., *Mars* (märz), god of war (VI. 17). aequō Mārte, see aequus. [March.

mās, maris, m., *male.* (VI. 26). [male.

Massilia, -ae, [ΜΑΣΣΑΛΙΑ], f., (ma-sil'i-a), a city in southern Gaul, founded by Greeks from Phocaea; now *Marseilles.* (C. II. 3, 7).

Massiliēnsēs, -ium, [Massilia], m., pl., *inhabitants of Massilia, Massilians.*

matara, -ae, f., *javelin, spear.* (I. 26).

māter, -tris, f., *mother.* mātrēs familiae, *matrons.* [maternal.

māteria, -ae, and māteriēs, acc. (VII. 24)

māteriem, [māter], f., *material, stuff; timber, wood; woodwork* (VII. 23). [material.

māterior, -ārī, [māteria], 1, dep., *procure timber, get wood.* (VII. 73).

Matiscō, -ōnis, f., (ma-tis'kō), an Aeduan city on the Arar (*Saône*), now *Mâcon.* (VII. 90).

mātrimōnium, -ī, [māter], n., *marriage.* [matrimony.

Matrona, -ae, f., *Matrona* (mat'ro-na), *Marne,* a tributary of the Sequana (*Seine*), into which it flows four miles above Paris, after a course of more than two hundred miles. (I. 1).

mātūrē, comp. mātūrius, sup. mātūrrimē, [mātūrus], adv., *early.* quam mātūrrimē, *as early as possible* (I. 33).

mātūrēscō, [mātūrus],-ere, mātūruī, 3, *become ripe, ripen.* (VI. 29).

mātūrō, -āre, -āvī, -ātus, [mātūrus], 1, *make haste, hasten.* [maturate.

mātūrrimē, see mātūrē.

mātūrrimus, adj., *ripe; early* (IV. 20). [mature.

mātūrus, -a, -um, comp. -ior, sup.

Maurētānia, -ae, (mâ-re-tā' ni-a), a country of northern Africa reaching from Numidia west to the Atlantic Ocean. (C. I. 6).

maximē, [maximus], see magis.

maximus, see magnus.

Maximus, see Fabius (I).

medeor, -ērī, 2, dep., *heal; remedy, provide for* (V. 24). [medicine.

mediocris, -cre, [medius],adj., *common, ordinary;* of distance, *moderate, short.* [mediocre.

mediocriter, comp. mediocrius [mediocris], adv., *moderately, in a slight degree.*

Mediomatricī, -ōrum, m., pl., (mē"-di-o-mat' ri-sī), a Gallic people near the Rhine.

mediterrāneus, -a, -um, [medius + terra], adj., *inland.* (V. 12). [Mediterranean.

medius, -a, -um, adj., *middle, in the midst, mid-.* medius utrīusque, *halfway between both* (I. 34). media nox, *midnight.* dē mediā nocte, *just after midnight.* [medium.

Meldī, -ōrum, m., pl., (mel' dī), I Gallic people on the Matrona (*Marne*), east of the Parisii. (V. 5).

melior, adj., see bonus.

melius, adv., see bene.

membrum, -ī, n., *limb.* [member.

meminī, -isse, def., *remember, bear in mind.* (III. 6; VII. 37).

memor, -oris, adj., *mindful, remembering.* (C. II. 6.)

memoria, -ae, [memor], f., *memory, recollection, remembrance.* memoriā tenēre, *to recollect.* nostrā memoriā, *in our own day* (II. 4).

memoriā prōditum, *reported, handed down, by tradition* (V. 12). [memory.

Menapiī, -ōrum, m., pl., (me-nā'-pi-ī), a people in the northeast part of Belgic Gaul.

mendācium, -ī, [**mendāx,** *false*], n., *lie, falsehood.* [mendacious.

mēns, mentis, f., *mind; temper* (III. 19); *attitude of mind, feeling* (I. 41; VII. 64). **et mente et animō,** *heart and soul* (VI. 5). [mental.

mēnsis, -is, m., *month.*

mēnsūra, -ae, [**mētior**], f., *measuring* (VI. 25); *measure.* **ex aquā mēnsūra,** *water-clock* (V. 13). [measure.

mentiō, -ōnis, [MEN in **meminī**], f., *mention.* (vi. 38). [mention.

mercātor, -ōris, [**mercor,** *trade*], m., *trader, merchant.*

mercātūra,-ae, [**mercor,** *trade*], f, *traffic, trade;* pl., *commercial transactions* (VI. 17).

mercēs, -ēdis, f., *pay, hire.* (I. 31).

Mercurius, -ī, [cf. **merx,** *merchandise*], m., *Mercury,* messenger of the gods, patron of traders and thieves, promoter of eloquence, and conductor of souls to the lower world; also, patron divinity of athletes and athletics. (VI. 17).

mereō, -ēre, -uī, -itus, and **mereor, -ērī, -itus,** 2, dep., *deserve, merit; serve* (VII. 17). [merit.

merīdiānus, -a, -um, [**merīdiēs**], adj., *of mid-day.* **merīdiānō ferē tempore,** *about noon* (V. 8). [meridian.

merīdiēs, -eī, [**medī-diē,** loc.], m., *mid-day; south* (V. 13).

meritum, -ī, [part. of **mereō**], n., *merit, service.* [merit.

meritus, see **mereor.**

Messāla, -ae, m., *Marcus Valerius Messala* (va-lē' ri-us me-sā' la), consul, 61 B.C. (I. 2, 35).

Messāna, -ae, [ΜΕΣΣΗΝΗ], f., (mesā' na), a city of northeastern Sicily, now *Messina.* (C. II. 3).

-met, enclitic, *self;* see **egō.**

mētior, mētīrī, mēnsus, 4, dep., *measure, measure out, distribute.*

Metius, -ī, m., *Marcus Melius* (mē'-sh[y]us), an envoy of Caesar to Ariovistus.

Metlosēdum, -ī, n., (met-lo-sē'dum), a town of the Senones, on an island in the Sequana *(Seine),* 28 miles above Paris; later called Melodūnum, now *Melun.*

metō, metere, messuī, messus, 3, *reap.* (IV. 32).

metus, -ūs, m., *fear, apprehension.*

meus, -a, -um, [**mē**], adj., *my, mine.*

mīles, -itis, m., *soldier, foot soldier.*

mīlitāris, -e, [**mīles**], adj., *of a soldier, military.* **rēs mīlitāris,** *art of war.* [military.

mīlitia, -ae, [**mīles**], f., *military service,* (VI. 14, 18; VII. 14). [militia.

mīlle or **M,** indecl. adj., *a thousand.* As noun, **mīlia, -um,** n., pl., *thousand, thousands.* [mile.

Minerva, -ae, f., (mi-ner' va), goddess of wisdom and the arts; identified with a Gallic divinity (VI. 17).

minimē, see **parum.**

minimus, -a, -um, see **parvus.**

minor, -us, see **parvus.**

Minucius, see **Basilus.**

minuō, -uere, -uī, -ūtus, 3, *lessen, diminish, reduce;* of the tide, *ebb* (III. 12); of controversies, *settle, put an end to* (V. 26; VI. 23). [minute.

minus, see **parum.**

mīror, -ārī, -ātus, [**mīrus**], 1, dep., *wonder, wonder at.* (i. 32; v. 54).

mīrus, -a, -um, [**mīror**], adj., *wonderful, remarkable, marvellous.* **mīrum in modum,** *in a surprising manner* (I. 41).

miser, -era, -erum, comp. **-ior,** sup. **miserrimus,** adj., *wretched, unfortunate, pitiable; poor* (VI. 35). As noun, **miserī, -ōrum,** m., pl., *the wretched* (II. 28). [miser.

misericordia, -ae, [**misericors**], f., *pity, compassion, mercy.*

miseror, -ārī, -ātus, [**miser**], 1 , dep., *lament, deplore.* (I. 39; VII. 1).

missus, -ūs, [**mittō**], m., used only in abl. sing., *a sending, despatching.* **missū Caesaris,** *being sent by Caesar* (V. 27; VI. 7).

missus, -a -um, see **mittō.**

mītissimē, [**mītis,** *mild*], adv., sup., *very gently, very kindly.* **quam mītissimē potest,** *in as kind a manner as possible* (VII. 43).

mittō, mittere, mīsī, missus, 3, *send, dispatch; release, let go;* of weapons, *throw, hurl, shoot.* [missile.

mōbilis, -e, comp. **-ior,** sup. **-issimus,** [cf. **moveō**], adj., *fickle, changeable.* (IV. 5). [mobile.

mōbilitās, -tātis, [**mōbilis**], f., *quickness of movement, speed* (IV. 33, C. II. 6); *instability, changeableness* (II. 1). [mobility.

mōbiliter, [**mōbilis**], adv., *easily* (III. 10).

moderor, -ārī, -ātus, [**modus**], 1, dep., *keep under control* (IV. 33); *manage, control* (VII. 75). [moderate.

modestia, -ae, [**modestus**], f., *self-control; subordination* (VII. 52). [modesty.

modo, [**modus**], adv., *only, merely, even;* of time, *lately, just now* (VI. 39, 43). **nōn modo . . . sed etiam,** *not only . . . but also.*

modus, -ī, m., *measure, amount* (VI. 22); *plan* (V. 1); *manner, fashion, style.* **ad hunc modum,** *after this manner, in this way.* **eius modī,** *of such a character, of that kind.* **quem ad modum,** *in what way, how; in whatever way, just as* (I. 36). **modō,** abl., with a dependent genitive, *after the manner of, as* (IV. 17, 27). **nūllō modō,** *by no means* (VI. 12). **omnibus modīs,** *by all means, in* *every way* (VII. 14). [mode.

moenia, -ium, n., pl., *walls* of a city, *fortifications* as a whole.

mōlēs, -is, f., *mass, massive structure; dam, dike* (III. 12). [mole.

molestē, comp. **-ius**, sup. **-issimē**, [**molestus**, *troublesome*], adv., *with annoyance.*

mōlīmentum, -ī, [cf. **mōlior**, from **mōlēs**], n., *great effort.* (I. 34).

molitus, see **molō**.

molliō, -īre, -īvī, -ītus, [**mollis**], 4, *soften; make easy* (VII. 46).

mollis, -e, comp. **-ior**, sup. **-issimus**, adj., *pliant, gentle; smooth* (V. 9); *weak, yielding* (III. 19); *effeminate.*

mollitia, -ae (VII. 77), and (VII. 20) **mollitiēs, -ēī**, [**mollis**], f., *weakness, irresolution.*

molō, -ere, -uī, -itus, 3, *grind.*

mōmentum, -ī, [for * **movimentum**, cf. **moveō**], n., *movement; thrust, forward movement* (C. II. 6); *influence* (VII. 85); *importance, account* (VII. 39). [moment.

Mona, -ae, f., (mō′ na), the *Isle of Man,* in the Irish Sea. (V. 13).

moneō, -ēre, -uī, -itus, 2, *advise, warn, remind, admonish.*

mōns, montis, m., *mountain, mountain-range, elevation, height.* **summus mōns,** *top of the height* (I. 22). **rādīcēs montis,** *foot of the mountain* or *height* (I. 38; VII. 36). **sub monte,** *at the foot of the height* (I. 21, 48). [mount.

mora, -ae, f., *delay.*

morātus, -a, -um, see **moror**.

morbus, -ī, [cf. **morior, mors**], m., *disease, sickness.* (VI. 16, 17). [morbid.

Morinī, -ōrum, m., pl., (mot′ i-nī) a Belgic people, on the seacoast opposite Kent.

morior, morī, mortuus, 3, dep., *die.* (I. 4; VI. 13). [mortuary.

Moritasgus, -ī, m., (mor-i-tas′gus), a chief of the Senones. (V. 54).

moror, -ārī, -ātus, [**mora**], 1, dep., *delay, wait, stay; hinder, delay, check, impede.* [moratorium.

mors, mortis, f., *death.* [mortal.

mortuus, -a, -um, see **morior**.

mōs, mōris, m., *usage, custom, way, wont, practice.* Pl., *customs, manners.* [moral.

Mosa, -ae, f., *Mosa* (mō′ sa), *Meuse,* or *Maas,* which rises in the western spurs of the Vosges, pursues a northerly course till joined by the Waal, then flows westward into the North Sea.

mōtus, -ūs, [**moveō**], m., *movement, motion; disturbance, revolt, uprising.*

moveō, movēre, mōvī, mōtus, 2, *move, set in motion, remove;* of feelings, *disturb; stir, touch* (VII. 76). **castra movēre,** *to break camp.* [move.

mulier, -eris, f., *woman.*

mūliō, -ōnis, [**mūlus**], m., *muleteer, mule-driver.* (VII. 45).

multitūdō, -inis, [**multus**], f., *great number, host, large body; crowd.* [multitude.

multō, -āre, -āvī, -ātus, [**multa,** *a fine*], 1, *punish; deprive of,* byway of punishment (VII. 54; C. III. 83). [mulct.

multō, multum, comp. **plūs,** sup. **plūrimum,** [**multus**], adv., *much, by far, greatly.* **multum posse** or **valēre,** *to have great power, influence.*

multum, adv., see **multō**.

multus, -a, -um, adj., comp. **plūs,** sup. **plūrimus,** *much;* pl., *many.* As noun, m., pl., **multī, -ōrum,** *many* (people); **plūrēs, -ium,** *more, quite a number, several;* neut., sing., **multum,** *much;* **plūs,** *more;* **plūrimum,** *very much;* neut., pl., **multa,** *many things, many considerations.* **multō diē,** *late in the day, when the day was far spent* (I. 22). [plural.

mūlus, -ī, m., *mule.* (VII. 45). [mule.

Mūnātius, see **Plancus**.

mundus, -ī, m., *world, universe.* (VI. 14). [mundane.

mūnicipium, -ī, [**mūniceps**], n., *free town, municipality,* [municipal.

mūnīmentum, -ī, [**mūniō**], n., *fortification, defence, barrier.* (II. 17). [muniment.

mūniō, -īre, -īvī, -ītus, [**moenia**], 4, *fortify; protect, make secure.* **mūnīre iter,** *to construct a road* (VII. 58).

mūnītiō, -ōnis, [**mūniō**], f., *a fortifying, building of fortifications; works of fortification, fortification, intrenchment, defenses.* **mūnītiōnī castrōrum,** *for the fortifying of the camp* (V. 9). [munition.

mūnītus, -a, -um, comp. **-ior,** sup., **-issimus,** [part. of **mūniō**], adj., *fortified, protected, secure.* **mūnītissima castra,** *a camp very strongly fortified* (V. 57).

mūnus, -eris, n., *duty, service, function; present, gift* (I. 43). **mūnus mīlitiae,** *military service* (VI. 18).

mūrālis, -e, [**mūrus**], adj., *of a wall.* **mūrālis falx,** *wall-hook* (III. 14). **mūrāle pīlum,** *wall-pike* (V. 40; VII. 82). [mural.

mūrus, -ī, m., *wall; rampart, line of works* (I. 8). [mure, immure.

mūsculus, -ī, [dimin. of **mūs**], m., *little mouse;* in military language, *long shed, mousie.* (VII. 84). [muscle.

mutilus, -a, -um, adj., *maimed, broken.* **mutilae cornibus,** *without horns* (VI. 27).

mūtuor, -ārī, -ātus, [**mūtuus**], 1, dep., *obtain a loan of, borrow.* (C. III. 60).

N.

nactus, -a, -um, see **nancīscor**.

nam, conj., introducing an explanation or reason, *for;* as an enclitic without interrogative words, hardly translatable as a separate word, **quibusnam** (II. 30).

-nam; enclitic, *possible*; see **quisnam**.

Nammēius, -ī, m., (na-mē'yus), a Helvetian sent as envoy to Caesar. (I. 7).

Namnetēs, -um, m., pl., (nam' ne-tēz), a Gallic state north of the mouth of the Liger (*Loire*); the name survives in *Nantes*. (III. 9).

namque [**nam + -que**], conj., *for indeed, for truly, and (with good reason) for.*

nancīscor, -cīscī, nactus, and **nanctus**, 3, dep., *come upon, find, obtain; get, secure, get hold of.*

Nantuātēs, -um, [Kel., = 'Dwellers in the Valley'], m., pl., (nan-tu-ā'-tēz), a Gallic people southeast of Lake Geneva.

Narbō, -ōnis, m., (när' bō), capital of the Province, which was later named from it, *Gallia Narbonensis*; originally a city of the Volcae Arecomici, but made a Roman colony in 118 B.C.; now *Narbonne*. (III. 20; VII. 7).

nāscor, nāscī, nātus, 3, dep., *be born, produced; is found* (V. 12); *rise* (II. 18); *arise* (VI. 22; VII. 43). [nascent.

Nāsidiānus, -a, -um, adj., *of Nasidius*. (C. II. 7).

Nāsīdius, -ī, m., *Lucius Nasidius* (na-sid'i-us), a naval commander on the side of Pompey in the Civil War. (C. II. 3, 4).

Nasua, -ae, m., (nash' ū-a), a chieftain of the Suebi. (I. 37).

nātālis, -e, [**nātus**], adj., *of birth*. **diēs nātālis**, *birth-day* (VI. 18). [natal.

nātiō, -ōnis, [**nāscor**], f., *birth; people, tribe.* [nation.

nātīvus, -a, -um, [cf. **nātus**], adj., *natural, native.* (VI. 10). [native.

nātūrāliter, [**nātūrālis**], adv., *by nature, naturally.* (C. III. 92).

nātūra, -ae, [**nātus**, from **nāscor**], f., *nature, character; natural features, situation; nature of things, Nature.* **nātūrā et opere**, *naturally and artificially.* (V. 9, 21). [nature.

nātus, -ūs, [cf. **nāscor**], m., used only in abl. sing., *birth.* **maiōrēs nātū**, see **magnus**.

nauta, -ae, [for *nāvita from **nāvis**], m., *sailor, seaman.* (III. 9; V. 10).

nauticus, -a, -um, [= Ν Α Υ Τ Ι Κ Ο Σ], adj., *naval, nautical.* [nautical.

nāvālis, -e, [**nāvis**], adj., *naval*. As noun, **nāvālia, -ium**, n., pl., *shipyards.* (C. II. 3). [naval.

nāvicula, -ae, [dim. of **nāvis**], f., *boat, skiff* (I. 53); *small ship* (C. II. 3).

nāvigātiō, -ōnis, [**nāvigō**], f., *navigation, sailing; voyage.* [navigation.

nāvigium, -ī, [**nāvigō**], n., *vessel, boat.* See **speculātōrius**.

nāvigo, -āre, -āvī, -ātus, [**nāvis**, cf. **agō**], 1, *sail, go by water.* [navigate.

nāvis, -is, f., *ship, vessel;* for river navigation, *barge.* **nāvis longa**, *battleship, galley.* **nāvis onerāria**, *a transport* (Fig. 202). [nave.

nāvō, -āre, -āvī, -ātus, [(g)nāvus, *busy*], 1, *do with zeal.*

nē, adv., *not.* **nē . . . quidem**, *not . . . even.*

nē, conj., *that . . . not, lest, not to*, after words of fearing, *that*; after words of beseeching, ordering, commanding, *not to*. **nē quis**, *that no one.* **nē qua spēs . . .** *that no hope.* **dēterrēre nē . . .** *to frighten from.*

-ne, enclitic interrog. particle, *whether*. **-ne . . . an**, or **-ne . . . -ne** (VII. 14), *whether . . . or.*

nec, conj., see **neque**.

necessāriō, [**necessārius**], adv., *of necessity, unavoidably.*

necessārius, -a, -um, [**necesse**], adj., *needful, necessary; urgent, pressing.* As noun, **necessārius, -ī**, m., *relative, kinsman* (I. 11; C, III. 82). [necessary.

necesse, indeci. adj., *necessary, unavoidable, inevitable.*

necessitās, -tātis, [**necesse**], f., *necessity, need, urgency.* [necessity.

necessitūdō, -inis, [**necesse**], f., *close relationship, friendship.* (I. 43).

necne, [**nec + -ne**], conj., *or not.* **utrum . . . necne**, *whether or not* (I. 50).

necō, -āre, -āvī, -ātus, 1 , *put to death, kill, destroy.* [noyade.

nēcubi, [ne + *cubi for ubi], conj., *that nowhere, lest anywhere.* (VII. 35).

nefārius, -a, -um, [**nefās**], adj., *execrable, atrocious.* [nefarious.

nefās [ne, = **nē**, + **fās**], n., indecl., *a crime against divine law, impious deed.* **nefās est**, *it is wrong, it is not permitted* (VII. 40).

neglegō, -legere, -lēxī, -lēctus, [nec + legō], 3, *disregard, leave out of consideration, be indifferent to; neglect* (III. 27; IV. 38); *overlook, leave unnoticed* (I. 35, 36; III. 10). [neglect.

negō, -āre, -āvī, -ātus, 1, *deny, say not, say no*, often = **dīcit nōn**; *refuse* (V. 6, 27). [negative.

negōtiātor, -ōris, [**negōtior**], m., *wholesale dealer, wholesaler.* (C. III. 103). [negotiator.

negōtior, -ārī, -ātus, [**negōtium**], 1, dep., *transact business.* **negōtiandī causā**, *in order to carry on business*(VII. 3, 42, 55). [negotiate.

negōtium, -ī, [neg-, = **nē**, + **ōtium**], n., *business, enterprise, task; effort, trouble, difficulty.* **nihil negōtī**, *no trouble* (V. 38). **neque — quicquam negōtī**, *and not any — trouble* (II. 17). **negōtium dare**, *to direct, command* (II. 2).

Nemetēs, -um, m., pl., (nem' e-tēz), a Germanic people, settled west of the Rhine.

nēmō, dat. **nēminī**, [nē + * hemō = homō], m., *no one, nobody.*

nēquāquam [nē + quāquam, *anywhere*], adv.,

not at all, by no means.

neque or **nec** [ne, = nē, + -que], adv., *nor, and . . . not.* **neque . . . neque** or **nec,** *neither . . . nor.*

nē . . . quidem, see **nē.**

nēquīquam [nē + quīquam], adv., *in vain, to no purpose.* (II. 27).

Nervicus,-a,-um, adj., *of the Servians.* **Nervicum proelium,** *battle with the Nervians* (III. 5).

Nervius, -ī, m., *a Nervian* (V. 45). Pl., **Nerviī, -ōrum,** *the Nervians, Nervii* (ner' vi-ī), a warlike people of Belgic Gaul.

nervus, -ī, m., *sinew, muscle* (VI. 21); pl., *power, force* (I. 20). [nerve.

neu, see **nēve.**

neuter, -tra, -trum, gen. **neutrīus,** [nē + uter], pron. adj., *neither.* As noun, **neutrī, -ōrum,** m., pl., *neither side* (VII. 63), *neither force* (II. 9). [neuter.

nēve or **neu,** [nē + -ve, *or*], conj., *or not, and not, and that not, nor.* **neu . . . -que,** *and not . . . but* (II. 21). **neu . . . et,** *and not . . . but* (V. 34).

nex, necis, f., *death* by violence. **vītae necisque potestās,** *power over life and death, absolute power* (I. 16; VI. 19, 23).

nihil [ne, = nē, + hīlum, *trifle*], n., indecl., *nothing;* as adverbial acc., = emphatic **nōn,** *not at all.* [nihilism.

nihilō sētius, see **sētius.**

nihilum, -ī [ne, = nē + hīlum], n., *nothing.* **nihilō,** abl. of degree of difference, lit. *by nothing;* **nihilō minus,** *none the less.*

nimius, -a, -um, [nimis], adj., *excessive, too great.* (VII. 29; C. III. 96).

nisi [ne, = nē, + sī], conj., *if not, unless, except.* **Nitiobrogēs, -um,** m., pl., (nish-i-ob'ro-jēz), a people in Northern Aquitania.

nītor, nītī, nīxus and **nīsus,** 3, dep., *strive, endeavor; rely upon, depend on* (I. 13).

nix, nivis, f., *snow.* (VII. 8, 55).

nōbilis, -e, comp. **-ior,** sup. **-issimus,** [cf. **nōscō**], adj., *noted, renowned* (VII. 77); *of high rank, noble* (I. 2, 18; V. 22; VII. 67). As noun, **nōbilēs, -ium,** m., pl., *nobles, men of rank* (I. 44; VI. 13); **nōbilissimus, -ī,** m., *man of highest rank;* pl., *men of highest rank* (I. 7, 31). [noble.

nōbilitās, -tātis, [nōbilis], f., *nobility, rank* (II. 6); collective (for **nōbilēs**), *nobility, nobles, men of rank.* [nobility.

nocēns, -entis, comp. **nocentior,** sup. **-issimus,** [part. of **noceō**], adj., *guilty.* As noun, **nocentēs, -um,** m., pl., *the guilty* (VI. 9).

noceō, -ēre, -uī, -itūrus, 2, *hurt, do harm, injure.* **neque eīs nocērī posse,** *and that no harm could be done to them* (III. 14).

noctū, [cf. **nox**], adv., *by night, at night, in the night.*

nocturnus, -a, -um, [cf. **nox**], adj., *by night, of night.* **nocturnus labor,** *the toil of the night* (VII. 83). **nocturnum tempus,** *night-time* (V. 11, 40). [nocturnal.

nōdus, -ī, m., *knot; node,* on the joint of an animal (VI. 27). [node.

nōlō, nōlle, nōluī, [nē + volō], irr., *be unwilling, not wish, not want.* **nōlī, nōlīte,** with infin., *do not.*

nōmen, -inis, n., *name, appellation, title; reputation, renown; account.* **suō nōmine,** *on his own account* (I. 18), *on their own account* (VII. 75). [noun.

nōminātim [nōminō], adv., *by name.*

nōminō, -āre, -āvī, -ātus, [nōmen], 1, *name, call* by a name (VII. 73); *mention* (II. 18). [nominate.

nōn, adv., *not, no.* **nōn nihil,** *to some extent, somewhat* (III. 17). **nōn nūllus,** *some, several.* **nōn numquam,** *sometimes.*

nōnāgintā, or **XC,** indeclinable num. adj., *ninety.*

nōndum [nōn + dum], adv., *not yet.*

nōn nihil, see **nōn.**

nōn nūllus, -a, -um, see **nōn.**

nōn numquam, see **nōn.**

nōnus, -a, -um, [novem], numeral ord. adj., *ninth.* [noon.

Nōreia, -ae, f., (no-rē'ya), chief city of the Norici (nor'i-sī), now *Neumarkt.* (I. 5).

Nōricus, -a, -um, adj., *of the Norici, Norican* (I. 5). As noun, **Nōrica, -ae,** f., *Norican woman* (I. 53).

nōs, see **ego.**

nōscō, nōscere, nōvī, nōtus, 3, *obtain a knowledge of, learn;* in tenses from the pf. stem, *know, be familiar with, be acquainted with.*

nōsmet, see **egomet.**

noster, -tra, -trum, [nōs], pron. adj., *our, our own.* As noun, **nostrī, -ōrum,** m., pl., *our men, our side.* [nostrum.

nōtitia, -ae, [nōtus], f., *knowledge, acquaintance.* [notice.

notō, -āre, -āvī, -ātus, [nota, *mark*], 1, *brand* (C. III. 74); *reprimand, check* (C. I. 7). [note.

nōtus, -a, -um, comp. **-ior,** sup. **-issimus,** [part. of **nōscō**], adj., *known, well-known, familiar.*

novem, or **viiii,** indeclinable num. adj., *nine.*

Noviodūnum, -ī, [Celtic word, = 'Newtown'], n., (nō" vi-o-dū' num), name of three towns: (1) Of the Aeduans, on the right bank of the Liger (*Loire*); now *Nevers.* (VII. 55). (2) Of the Bituriges, south of Cenabum. (VII. 12, 14). (3) Of the Suessiones, on the Axona (*Aisne*). (II. 12).

novitās, -tātis, [novus], f., *novelty, newness,*

strangeness.

novus, -a, -um, adj., *new, fresh, strange.* Sup.
novissimus, *last, at the rear.* As noun,
novissimī, -ōrum, m., pl., *those at the rear, the rear.* **novissimum agmen,** *rear of the line of march, the rear.* [novice.

nox, noctis, f., *night.* **prīmā nocte,** *at nightfall* (I. 27). **multā nocte,** *late at night, when the night was far spent.* [nocti- in noctivagant, etc.

noxia, -ae, [**noxius, -a, -um,** *hurtful*], f., *hurt, offense, crime* (VI. 16).

nūbō, nūbere, nūpsī, supine **nūptum,** 3, *veil one's self* for marriage, *marry, wed.* (I. 18). [nuptial.

nūdō, -āre, -āvī, -ātus [**nūdus**], 1, *strip, make bare; clear* (II. 6); *expose, leave unprotected.*

nūdus, -a, -um, adj., *naked, bare; unprotected* (I. 25). [nude.

nūllus, -a, -um, gen. **nūllīus,** dat. **nūllī,** [**ne,** = **nē,** + **ūllus**], adj., *none, no.* As noun, especially in the dat., m., *no one.*

num, interrogative particle, expecting the answer No.

nūmen, -inis, [cf. **nuō,** *nod*], n., *divine will; divine majesty* (VI. 16).

numerō, -āre, -āvī, -ātus, [**numerus**], 1, *count, reckon.* (C. III. 53). [numerate.

numerus, -ī, m., *number, amount; estimation, account* (VI. 13). **obsidum numerō,** *as hostages* (V. 27). [number.

Numidae, -ārum, [Ν Ο Μ Α Σ, *wanderer,* pl. Ν Ο Μ Α Δ Ε Σ], m., pl., *Numidians,* a people in Northern Africa, in the country now called Algeria, famous as archers, and employed by Caesar as light-armed troops (II. 7, 10, 24). Numidians under Juba destroyed the army of Curio in 49 B.C. (C. II. 39, 41).

nummus, -ī, m., *piece of money, money, coin.* (v. 12).

numquam [**ne,** = **nē,** + **umquam**], adv., *never, not at any time.*

nunc, adv., *now, at present.*

nūncupō, -āre, -āvī, -ātus, [**nōmen,** cf. **capiō**], 1, *name publicly;* of vows, *offer publicly* (C. I. 6).

nūntiō, -āre, -āvī, -ātus, [**nūntius**], 1, *announce, report; give orders* (IV. 11). Impers. **nūntiātur,** *word is* brought, it is reported.

nūntius, -ī, m., *messenger, agent* (I. 44); *message, tidings.* [nuncio.

nūper, sup. **nūperrimē,** adv., *lately, recently.*

nūtus, -ūs, [**nuō,** *nod*], m., *nod, nodding* (V. 43); *bidding, command* (I. 31; IV. 23).

O.

ob, prep. with acc., *on account of, for.* **ob eam causam,** *for that reason.* **ob eam rem,** *on that account, therefore,* **quam ob rem,** *wherefore* (I. 34); *for what reason* (I. 50).

obaerātus, -a, -um, comp. **-ior,** [**ob,** cf. **aes**], adj., *in debt.* As noun, **obaerātus, -ī,** m., *debtor, serf* (I. 4).

obdūcō, -dūcere, -dūxī, -ductus, [**ob + dūcō**], 3, *lead forward;* of a trench, *prolong, extend* (II. 8).

obeō, -īre, -iī, -ītus, [**ob + eō**], irr., *go to meet; attend to.* **omnia per se obīre,** *to see to everything in person* (V. 33).

obiciō, -icere, -iēcī, -iectus, [**ob + iaciō**], 3, *throw before; place in front, place; put in the way, expose;* of taunts, *cast up at, twit of* (C. III. 96); of difficulties, *present* (VII. 59). [object.

obiectātiō, -ōnis, [**obiectō**], f., *reproach.* (C. III. 60).

obiectō, -āre, -āvī, -ātus, [freq. of **obiciō**], 1, *accuse of; twit of* (C. III. 48).

obiectus, -a, -um, see **obiciō.**

obitus, -ūs, [cf. **obeō**], m., *destruction.* (II. 29). [obituary.

oblātus, see **offerō.**

oblīquē, [**obliquus**], adv., *obliquely, with a slant.* (IV. 17).

oblīquus, -a, -um, adj., *slanting, crosswise.* (VII. 73). [oblique.

oblīvīscor, -līvīscī, -lītus, 3, dep., *forget.* [oblivion.

obsecrō, -āre, -āvī, -atus, [**ob + sacrō,** from **sacer**], 1, *beseech in the name of that which is sacred, implore, beg.* [obsecrate

obsequentia, -ae, [**obsequēns**], f., *compliance, complaisance.* (VII. 29).

observō, -āre, -āvī, -ātus, [**ob + servō**], *watch, observe* (VII. 16); *keep track of* (VI. 18); *heed, comply with* (I. 45; V. 35). [observe.

obses, -idis, [cf. **obsideō**], m. and f., *hostage.*

obsessiō, -ōnis, [cf. obsideo], f., *siege* (VII. 36); *blockade* (VI. 36).[obsession

obsessus, see **obsideō.**

obsideō, -sidēre, -sēdī, -sessus, [**ob + sedeō**], 2, *besiege, blockade;* of roads, *seize upon, block* (III. 23, 24; V. 40). [obsess.

obsidiō, -ōnis, [cf. **obsideō**], f., *siege, blockade; oppression* (IV. 19).

obsignō, -āre, -āvī, -ātus, [**ob + signō**], 1, *seal up, seal* (Fig. 203).

obsistō, -sistere, -stitī, [**ob + sistō**], 3, *withstand.* (VII. 29).

obstinātē [**obstinātus,** part. of **obstinō,** *persist*], adv., *firmly, steadfastly, persistently.* (V. 6).

obstrictus, -a, -um, see **obstringō.**

obstringō, -stringere, -strīnxī, -strictus, [**ob + stringō,** *tie*], 3, *bind, place under obligation.* (I. 9, 31).

obstruō, -struere, -strūxī, -strūctus, [**ob + struō,** *pile*], 3, *block up, stop up.* (V. 50, 51; VII. 41). [obstruct.

obtemperō, -āre, -āvī, -ātus, [ob + temperō], 1, *submit to, obey.*

obtentūrus, fut. act. part. of **obtineō.**

obtestor, -ārī, -ātus, [ob + testor], 1, dep., *call as witness, appeal to; implore, adjure.*

obtineō, -tinēre, -tinuī, -tentus, [ob + teneō], 2, *hold fast, maintain, keep, retain, hold* (I. 3); *get possession of, obtain* (I. 18; VI. 12); *possess, occupy, inhabit* (I. 1). [obtain.

obtrectātiō, -ōnis, [obtrectō], f., *disparagement.* (C. I. 7).

obveniō, -venīre, -vēnī, -ventūrus, [ob + veniō], 4, *fall in with, encounter* (II. 23); *fall to the lot of, fall to* (VII. 28, 81; C. I. 6).

obviam, [ob + acc. of **via**], adv., *in the way, against.* **obviam Caesarī proficīscitur,** *goes to meet Caesar* (VII. 12). **sī obviam venīrētur,** *if an advance should be made* (VII. 28).

occāsiō, -ōnis, [cf. **occidō**], f., *opportunity, favorable moment; surprise* (VII. 45). [occasion.

occāsus, -ūs, [cf. **occidō**], m., *going down, setting.* **sōlis occāsus,** *sunset, the west* (I. 1; IV. 28).

occidēns, -entis, [part. of **occidō**], adj., *of the sun, setting.* **occidēns sōl,** *the west* (V. 13). [Occident.

occidō,-cidere, -cidī, [ob + cadō], 3, *fall* (VI. 37).

occīdō, -cīdere, -cīdī, -cīsus, [ob + caedō], 3, *kill, slay.*

occīsus, -a, -um, see **occīdō.**

occultātiō, -ōnis, [occultō], f., *concealment.* (VI. 21).

occultē, comp. **-ius,** sup. **-issimē,** [occultus], adv., *secretly, in secret.*

occultō, -āre, -āvī, -ātus, [freq. of **occulō,** *cover*], 1, *hide, conceal; keep secret.*

occultus, -a, -um, comp. **-ior,** sup. **-issimus,** [part. of **occulō,** *cover*], adj., *hidden, secret, concealed.* As noun, **ex occultō,** *from ambush, in ambush* (VI. 34); **sē in occultum abdere,** *to go into hiding* (VII. 30); **in occultō,** *in hiding, in concealment* (II. 18; VI. 35; VII. 27, 35), *in a secret place* (I. 31, 32). [occult.

occupātiō, -ōnis, [occupō], f., *employment, engagement.* **occupātiōnēs reī pūblicae,** *business of state* (IV. 16). [occupation.

occupō, -āre, -āvī, -ātus, [ob, cf. **capiō**], 1, *seize upon, seize, take possession of; fill, occupy* (II. 8); *of the attention, engage, occupy.* **occupātus, -a, -um,** as adj., *engaged; busied* (II. 19). **occupārī in,** with abl., *to be engaged in, busy with.* [occupy.

occurrō, -currere, -currī, rarely **-cucurrī, -cursūrus,** [ob + currō], 3, *run to meet, come to meet, meet; meet with, fall in with, encounter; match, offset* (VII. 22); *come into mind, occur* (VII. 85). [occur.

Ōceanus, -ī, [Ωκεανος], m., *Ocean,* considered by Caesar as one body of water, including the Atlantic Ocean, the English Channel, and the North Sea; *the sea.* [ocean.

Ocelum, -ī, n., (ōs' e-lum), a town of the Graioceli in the Alps, west of modern Turin. (I. 10).

octāvus, -a, -um, [octō], numeral ord. adj., *eighth.* [octave.

octingentī, -ae, -a, or **DCCC,** [octō + centum], num. adj., *eight hundred.*

octō, or **VIII,** indeclinable num. adj., *eight.* [October.

octōdecim, or **XVIII,** [octō + decem], indeclinable num. adj., *eighteen.*

Octodūrus, -ī, [Kel., = 'Castle of Octos,' or 'Castle in a Defile'], m., (ok-to-dū' rus), chief town of the Veragri, in the Rhone valley southeast of Geneva. (III. 1).

octōgēnī, -ae, -a, or **LXXX,** [octō], distrib. num. adj., *eighty in each case.*

octōgintā, or **LXXX,** [octō], indeclinable num. adj., *eighty.*

octōnī, -ae, -a, [octō], distrib. num. adj., *eight each, eight at a time.*

oculus, -ī, m., *eye.* [oculist.

ōdī, ōdisse, ōsūrus, def., *hate.*

odium, -ī, [ōdī], n., *hatred.* [odium.

offendō, -fendere, -fendī, -fēnsus, 3, *hit against; hurt, wound* (I. 19). Impersonal, **offendī posset,** *injury could be inflicted, a disaster might occur* (VI. 36); **esset offēnsum,** *a reverse had been experienced* (C. III. 72). [offend.

offēnsiō, -ōnis, [offendō], f., *hurting, wounding; reverse.*

offerō, -ferre, obtulī, oblātus, [ob + ferō], irr., *bring before; offer, present; put in one's way, afford.* **sē offerre,** *to offer one's self* (VII. 89), *expose one's self* (VII. 77), *rush against* (IV. 12). [offer.

officium, -ī, [for *opificium,* **ops** + FAC in **faciō**], n., *service, duty; allegiance; sense of duty* (I. 40). **officium praestāre,** *to do one's duty* (IV. 25). [office.

Ollovicō, -ōnis,-m., (o-lov'i-kō) a king of the Nitiobroges. (VII. 31).

omittō, -mittere, -mīsī, -missus, [ob + mittō], 3, *lay aside, throw away* (VII. 88); *neglect, disregard* (II. 17). **omnibus omissīs rēbus,** *laying aside everything else* (VII. 34). [omit.

omnīnō, [omnis], adv., *altogether;* after negatives, *at all;* with numerals, *in all, altogether, only.* **nihil omnīnō,** *nothing at all.*

omnis, -e, adj., *every, all; as a whole.* As noun, pl., **omnēs, -ium,** m., *all men, all;* **omnia, -ium,** n., *all things, everything.* [omnibus.

onerārius, -a, -um, [onus], adj., *of burden;* see **nāvis.** [onerary.

onerō, -āre, -āvī, -ātus, [onus], 1, *load.* (V. 1). [onerate.

onus, -eris, n., *load, burden, weight; cargo* (V. 1). [onus.

opera, -ae, [opus], f., *effort, work, pains; service, aid, assistance.* dare operam, *to lake pains.* [opera.

opīniō, -ōnis, [opīnor, *think*], f., *idea, notion; good opinion, reputation; expectation.* opīniō timōris, *impression of fear.* iūstitiae opīniō, *reputation for fair dealing* (VI. 24). praeter opīniōnem, *contrary to expectation* (III. 3). [opinion.

oportet, oportēre, oportuit, 2, impers., *it is necessary, it is needful; it behooves; ought; is proper* (VII. 33).

oppidānus, -a, -um, [oppidum], adj., *of the town.* As noun, oppidānī, -ōrum, m., pl., *townspeople, inhabitants of the town.*

oppidum, -ī, n., *fortified town, city; fortified enclosure, stronghold* (V. 21).

oppleō, -ēre, -ēvī, -ētus, [ob + pleō], 2, *fill completely.* (C. III. 73).

oppōnō, -pōnere, -posuī, -positus, [ob + pōnō], 3, *place over against, set against, oppose.* [oppose.

opportūnē, sup. -issimē, [opportūnus], adv., *conveniently, seasonably, opportunely.*

opportūnitās, -ātis, [opportūnus], f., *fitness, favorableness, seasonableness; favorable situation, advantage,* [opportunity.

opportūnus, -a, -um, comp. -ior, sup. -issimus, adj., *fit, suitable, favorable, advantageous.* tempore opportūnissimō, *in the nick of time* (IV. 34). [opportune.

oppositus, -a, -um, [part. of oppōnō], adj., *placed opposite; lying in the way* (VII. 56). [opposite.

opprimō, -primere, -pressī, -pressus, [ob + premō], 3, *weigh down; overwhelm, crush; take by surprise, surprise, fall upon.* [oppress.

oppugnātiō, -ōnis, [oppugnō], f., *storming of a city or camp, assault, attack, besieging.*

oppugnō, -āre, -āvī, -ātus, [ob + pugnō], 1, *attack, assault; storm, besiege; take by storming.*

ops, opis, nom. and dat. sing. not in use, f., *help, power, might.* Pl., opēs, -um, *help* (VI. 21); *resources, means, wealth; influence; strength* (VII. 76). [opulent.

optātus, -a, -um, comp. -ior, sup. -issimus, [part. of optō], adj., *desired; welcome* (VI. 42).

optimē, see bene.

optimus, see bonus.

opus, n., used only in nom. and acc., *necessity, need.* opus est, *there is need, it is necessary.*

opus, operis, n., *work, labor; that produced by labor, structure, works; line of works, fortification.* Cf. quantus. [opus.

ōra, -ae, f., *coast, shore.* ōra maritima, *sea-coast* (IV. 20); *place put for people, inhabitants of the coast, people along the sea* (III. 8, 16).

ōrātiō, -ōnis, [ōrō], f., *speech, words, remarks, plea.* [oration.

ōrātor, -ōris, [ōrō], m., *speaker; envoy* (IV. 27). [orator.

orbis, -is, m., *circle.* in orbem cōnsistere, *to form a circle* (V. 33). orbis terrārum, *the world* (VII. 29). [orb.

Orcynia, -ae, f., (or-sin' i-a), with silva, *the Hercynian forest.* (VI. 24).

ōrdō, -inis, m., *row, series; layer* (VII. 23); *rank, order; century* (half a maniple), *company* (I. 40, V. 35); *officer commanding a century, centurion.* [order.

Orgetorīx, -īgis, [Kel., = 'the King who slays,' 'All-slaughtering King'], m., (or-jet' o-riks), a Helvetian nobleman who formed a plot to seize the supreme power.

Ōricum, -ī, [Ωρ ι κ ο ν], n., (or'i-cum), a seaport on the east coast of the Adriatic, now Palaeocastro, on the bay of Valona. (C. III. 90).

oriēns, -entis, [part. of orior], adj., *rising.* oriēns sōl, *rising sun; the east* (I. 1; V. 13; VII. 69). [orient.

orior, orīrī, ortus, 4, dep., *rise, arise; begin, spring from; start from* (I. 39). oriente sōle, *at sunrise* (VII. 3). ortā lūce, *at daybreak* (V. 8).

ōrnāmentum, -ī, [ōrnō], n., *decoration; distinction, honour* (I. 44; VII. 15). [ornament.

ōrnātus, -a, -um, comp. -ior, sup. -issimus, [part. of ōrnō], adj., *equipped.* [ornate.

ōrnō, -āre, -āvī, -ātus, 1, *furnish, equip; provide* (VII. 33).

ōrō, -āre, -āvī, -ātus, [ōs, *mouth*], 1, *plead, beg, entreat.* [orate.

ortus, -ūs, [orior], m., *rising.* ortus sōlis, *sunrise* (VII. 41).

ortus, see orior.

ōs, ōris, n., *mouth; face* (V. 35; VI. 39; C. III. 99). [oral.

Osismī, -ōrum, m., pl., (o-sis'mī), a small state in the northwest corner of Gaul.

ostendō, -tendere, -tendī, -tentus, [obs, for ob, + tendō], 3, *show, display; point out, set forth, declare.* ostentātiō, -ōnis, [ostentō], f., *display, show; ostentation* (VII. 53). ostentātiōnis causā, *in order to attract attention* (VII. 45). [ostentation.

ostentō, -āre, -āvī, -ātus, [freq. of ostendō], 1, *display, show;* with sē, *show off* (VII. 19).

ōtium, -ī, n., *rest, quiet, peace.*

ōvum, -ī, n., *egg.* (IV. 10). [oval.

P.

P. with proper names = Pūblius.

pābulātiō, -ōnis, [pābulor], f., *foraging, getting fodder.* [pabulation.

pābulātor, -ōris, [pābulor], m., *forager.* (V. 17).

pābulor, -ārī, -ātus, [pābulum], 1, dep., *forage, obtain fodder.*

pābulum, -ī, n., *fodder, forage.* [pabulum.

pācātus, -a, -um, comp. -ior, sup. -issimus, [part. of paco], adj., *peaceful, quiet.* [pacate.

pācō, -āre, -āvī, -ātus, [pāx], 1, *pacify, tranquilize.* [pacable.

pactum, -ī, [pacīscor], n., *agreement; manner, way* (VII. 83). [pact.

Padus, -ī, m., (pā' dus), *Po,* the great river of Northern Italy. (V. 24).

Paelignus, -a, -um, *Paelignian, of the Paeligni* (pe-lig' nī), a people of Central Italy, whose chief city was Corfinium. (C. II. 35).

Paemānī, -ōrum, m., pl., (pē-mā' nī), a people in Belgic Gaul. (II. 4).

paene, adv., *almost, nearly.*

paenitet, -ēre, -uit, 2, impers., *it makes sorry, it causes regret.* **eōs paenitet,** *they are sorry, regret* (IV. 5).[penitent.

pāgus, -ī, m., *district, canton,* generally referring to the inhabitants rather than to the country; *clan.* [pagan.

palam, adv., *openly, publicly.*

palma, -ae, f., *palm of the hand; hand* (VI. 26; C. III. 98). [palm.

palūdātus, -a, -um, *wearing a general's cloak* (palūdāmentum); as we say, *in uniform.* (C. I. 6).

palūs, -ūdis, f., *marsh, swamp, bog.*

palūster, -tris, -tre, [palūs], adj., *marshy, swampy* (VII. 20).

pandō, pandere, pandī, passus, 3, *spread out;* of hair, *dishevel* (VII. 48). **passīs manibus,** *with hands outstretched.*

pānis, -is, m., *bread;* pl., *loaves of bread* (C. III. 48). [pantry.

pār, paris, adj., *like, similar, same; equal; corresponding* (VII. 74). **pār atque,** *same as.* [par.

parātus, -a, -um, comp. -ior, sup. -issimus, [part. of parō], adj., *ready, prepared; provided.*

parcē, comp. -ius, [parcus], adv., *sparingly.* (VII. 71).

parcō, parcere, pepercī and parsī, parsūrus, 3, *use sparingly* (VII. 71); with dat., *spare, give quarter to.*

parēns, -entis, [pariō], m. and f., *parent.* [parent.

parentō, -āre, -ātus, [parēns], 1, *offer a sacrifice in honor of deceased parents or relatives; take vengeance for the death of any one, avenge* (VII. 17).

pāreō, pārēre, pāruī, 2, *obey; submit to, be subject to.*

pariō, parere, peperī, partus, 3, *bring forth; obtain, get, acquire.*

Parīsiī, -ōrum, m., pl., (pa-rish'[y]ī), a Gallic people on the Sequana *(Seine);* the name survives in *Paris.*

parō, -āre, -āvī, -ātus, 1, *prepare, make ready, make ready for; obtain, secure.* [pare.

pars, partis, f., *part, portion, share, number; region, district, division; side, direction; party, faction* (VI. 11, I. 15). **pars maior,** *the majority.* **ūnā ex parte,** *on one side.* **in omnēs partēs,** *in every direction.* [part.

Parthī, -ōrum, m., pl., *the Parthians,* a Scythian people in the region of the Caspian Sea. (C. III. 82).

particeps, -cipis, [pars, cf. capiō], adj., *sharing in.* (C. III. 60). [participle.

partim, [acc. of pars], adv., *partly, in part.*

partior, partīrī, partītus, [pars], 4, dep., *divide, divide up, share.* Part. **partītus** in a passive sense, *divided, shared.* [partite.

partus, see pariō.

parum, comp. minus, sup. minimē. adv., *too little, not enough.* Comp., *less.* Sup., *least, very little; not at all, by no means.* [minus.

parvulus, -a, -um, [dim. of parvus], adj., *very small; very young; slight, trifling.*

parvus, -a, -um, comp. minor, sup. minimus, adj., *small, trifling, insignificant.* Comp., *smaller, less.* As noun, minus, n., *less;* minimum, n., *the least.* **quam minimum spatī,** *as little time as possible* (III. 19). [minimum.

passim, [passus, from pandō], adv., *in all directions* (IV. 14); *here and there* (C. II. 38).

passus, -ūs, m., *step, pace;* as a measure of length, *pace* (reckoned as a double step, from the place where either foot is raised to the place where the same foot rests on ground again), = 5 Roman feet, or 4 feet, 10.25 inches by English measurement. **mīlle passūs,** *mile;* pl., **mīlia passuum,** *miles.* [pace.

passus, see pandō.

passus, see patior.

patefaciō, -facere, -fēcī, -factus, pass., patefīō, -fierī, -factus, [pateō + faciō], 3, *lay open, open.*

patēns, -entis, comp. patentior, [part. of pateō] adj., *open.* [patent.

pateō, patēre, patuī, 2, *be open, lie open, stand open; extend.*

pater, -tris. m., *father.* Pl, patrēs, -um, *fathers, forefathers.* [paternal.

patiēns,-entis, [patior], adj., comp. patientior, sup. patientissimus, *long-suffering, patient.* (C. III. 96). [patient.

patienter, comp. patientius, [patiēns], adv., *patiently.* (VII. 77).

patientia, -ae, [patiēns], f., *endurance* (VI. 24); *forbearance* (VI. 36). [patience.

patior, patī, passus, 3, dep., *suffer, bear,*

endure; permit, allow. [passive.

patrius, -a,-um, [**pater**], adj., *of a father; ancestral, of (their) forefathers* (II. 15).

patrōnus, -ī, [**pater**], m., *protector, patron.* (VII. 40). [patron.

patria, -ae, [**patrius,** sc. *terra*], f., *native land, fatherland* (C. II. 7).

patruus, -ī, [**pater**], m., *father's brother, uncle* on the father's side.

paucitās, -ātis, [**paucus**], f., *fewness, small number.* [paucity.

paucus, -a, -um, comp. **-ior,** sup. **-issimus,** adj., *little;* pl., *few.* As noun, **paucī, -ōrum,** m., pl., *few, only a few;* n., pl., **pauca, -ōrum,** *a few words* (I. 44).

paulātim, [**paulum**], adv., *little by little, by degrees; gradually; one by one* (IV. 30).

paulisper, [**paulum, per**], adv., *for a short time, a little while.*

paulō, [abl. of **paulus**], adv., *by a little, just a little.*

paululum [**paulus**], adv., *a very little, only a little.* (II. 8).

paulum, [neut. acc. of **paulus**], adv., *a little, somewhat.*

pāx, pācis, f., *peace.* [peace.

peccō, -āre, -āvī, -ātus, 1, *do wrong.*

pectus, -oris, n., *breast.* [pectoral.

pecūnia, -ae, [cf. **pecus,** *cattle*], f., *property; money.* Pl., **pecūniae,** *contributions of money* (C. I. 6).

pecūniārius, -a, -um, [**pecūnia**], adj., *of money, pecuniary.* [pecurfiary.

pecus, -oris, n., *cattle,* general term for domestic animals; *flesh* of cattle, *meat* (IV. 1).

pedālis, -e, [**pēs**], adj., *measuring a foot, a foot thick.* (III. 13). [pedal.

pedes, -itis, [**pēs**], m., *foot-soldier.* Pl, **peditēs, -um,** *infantry.*

pedester, -tris, -tre, [**pēs**], adj., *on foot.* **pedestrēs cōpiae,** *infantry.* **pedestre proelium,** *battle on land* (IV. 24). [pedestrian.

peditātus, -ūs, [**pedēs**], m., *infantry.*

Pedius, -ī, m., *Quintus Pedius* (pē'-di-us), nephew of Julius Caesar, under whom he served as lieutenant in the Gallic and Civil Wars. He was consul in 43 B.C. (II. 2, 11).

peior, see **malus.**

pellis, -is, f., *skin, hide.* [pelisse.

pellō, pellere, pepulī, pulsus, 3, *drive out, drive off; rout, defeat.*

Pelusium, -ī, [ΠΗΛΟΥΣΙΟΝ], n., (pe-lū'-shi-um), a city and fortress in Egypt, at the easternmost mouth of the Nile. (C. III. 103).

pendō, pendere, pependī, pēnsus, 3, *weigh out; pay.* [pendent.

penes, prep. with acc., *in the power of, in the possession of.*

penitus, adv., *far within.* (VI. 10).

per, prep. with acc., *through; across, along, over, among; during, in the course of; by, by the hands of, by means of, under pretense of; by reason of.* In oaths, *in the name of, by.* **per agrōs,** *over the country* (VI. 31; VII. 3). In composition, **per** adds the force of *through, thoroughly, very much, very.*

peragō, -agere. -ēgī, -āctus, [**per + agō**], 3, *finish, complete, bring to an end.*

perangustus, -a, -um, [**per + angustus**]; adj., *very narrow.* (VII. 15).

percellō, -ere, perculī, perculsus, 3, *beat down; cast down, demoralize* (C. III. 47).

perceptus, see **percipiō.**

percipiō, -cipere, -cēpī, -ceptus [**per + capiō**], 3, *get, secure, gain; hear* (V. 1); *learn* (VI. 8). [perceive.

percontātiō, -ōnis, [**percontor,** *inquire*], f., *questioning, inquiry.*

percurrō, -currere, -cucurrī or **-currī, -cursūrus,** [**per + currō**], 3, *run through; run along* (IV. 33).

percussus, see **percutiō.**

percutiō, -cutere, -cussī, -cussus, [**per + quatiō,** *shake*], 3, *thrust through.* (V. 44). [percuss.

perdiscō, -discere, -didicī, [**per + discō**], 3, *learn thoroughly, learn by heart.* (VI. 14).

perditus, -a, -um, comp. **-ior,** sup. **-issimus,** [part. of **perdō,** *ruin*], adj., *abandoned, desperate* (III. 17). As noun, **perditī, -ōrum,** m., pl., *desperate men, the desperate* (VII. 4).

perdūcō, -dūcere, -dūxī, -ductus, [**per + dūcō**], 3. *lead through, bring, conduct, convey; bring over, win over* (VI. 12); *draw out, prolong* (V. 31; C. III. 95); *extend, construct, make.*

perendinus, -a, -um, [**perendiē,** *day after tomorrow*], adj., *after tomorrow.* **perendinō diē,** *day after tomorrow* (V. 30).

pereō, -īre, -iī, -itūrus, [**per + eō**], lit., *perish, be lost.* [perish.

perequitō, -āre, -āvī, [**per + equitō,** *ride*], 1, *ride through* (VII. 66); *ride about* (IV. 33).

perexiguus, -a, -um, [**per + exiguus**], adj., *very small.*

perfacilis, -e, [**per + facilis**], adj., *very easy.*

perfectus, see **perficiō.**

perferō, -ferre, -tulī, -lātus, [**per + ferō**], irr., lit. *carry through; carry, convey, bring, report; endure, suffer; bear, submit to.*

perficiō, -ficere, -fēcī, -fectus, [**per + faciō**], 3, *finish, complete; perform, accomplish, carry out; cause, effect; bring about, arrange.* [perfect.

perfidia, -ae, [**perfidus**], f., *faithlessness, bad faith, treachery.* [perfidy.

perfringō, -fringere, -frēgī, -frāctus, [**per + frangō**], 3, *break through.*

perfuga, -ae, [perfugiō], m., *deserter.*

perfugiō, -fugere, -fūgī, [per + fugiō], 3, *flee for refuge, flee.*

perfugium, -ī, [cf. perfugiō], n., *place of refuge, refuge.* (IV. 38).

pergō, pergere, perrēxī, perrēctus, [per + regō], 3, *proceed, advance.*

perīclitor, -ārī, -ātus, [perīculum], 1, dep., *try, prove, make trial of, test; be in danger, incur danger* (VI. 34; VII. 56).

perīculōsus, -a, -um, comp. -ior, sup. -issimus, [perīculum], adj., *full of danger, dangerous.* (I. 33, VII. 8). [perilous.

perīculum, -ī, n., *trial, test* (I. 40); *attempt* (IV. 21); *risk, danger, hazard.* [peril.

perītus, -a, -um, comp. -ior, sup. -issimus, adj., *skilled, practiced; familiar with.*

perlātus, see perferō.

perlēctus, see perlegō.

perlegō, -legere, -lēgī -lēctus, [per + legō], 3, *read through, peruse.* (V. 48). [perlection.

perluō, -luere, -luī, -lūtus, [per + -luō, *wash*], 3, *wash.* Pass. used reflexively, *bathe* (VI. 21).

permagnus, -a, -um, [per + magnus], adj., *very large, very great.*

permaneō, -manēre, -mānsī, mānsūrus, [per + maneō], 2, *continue, slay, remain.* [permanent.

permisceō, -miscēre, -miscuī, -mixtus, [per + misceō, *mix*], 2, *mix, mingle.* (VII. 62).

permittō, -mittere, -mīsī, -missus, [per + mittō], 3, *give over, entrust, commit; grant, allow.* [permit.

permixtus, see permisceō.

permōtus, see permoveō.

permoveō, -movēre. -mōvī, -mōtus, [per + moveō], 2, *deeply move, disturb, alarm; arouse, stir; influence, induce.*

permulceō, -ēre, -sī, -sus, [per + mulceō, *soothe*], 2, *calm, soothe.* (IV. 6).

permulsus, see permulceō.

perniciēs, -eī, [per, cf. nex], f., *ruin, destruction.* (I. 20, 36).

perniciōsus, -a, -um, [perniciēs], adj., *ruinous.* (C. I. 7). [pernicious.

pernīcitās, -tātis, [pernīx, *nimble*], f., *quickness of movement, nimbleness.* (C. III. 84).

perpaucī, -ae, -a, [per + paucus], adj., *very few.* As noun, perpaucī, -ōrum, m., pl., *a very few.*

perpendiculum, -ī, [cf. perpendō], n., *plumb-line.* ad perpendiculum, *perpendicularly* (IV. 17). [perpendicular.

perpetior, -petī, -pessus, [per + patior], 3, dep., *bear patiently, endure.* (VII. 10; C. III. 47).

perpetuō [perpetuus], adv., *continually, constantly* (VII. 41); *always, forever* (I. 31).

perpetuus, -a, -um, [per, cf. petō], adj., *continuous, unbroken, unceasing, entire, perpetual.* As noun, in perpetuum, *for ever, ever after.* [perpetual.

perquīrō, -quīrere, -quīsīvī, -quīsītus, [per + quaerō], 3, *make careful inquiry about, inquire about.* (VI. 9).

perrumpō, -rumpere, -rūpī, -ruptus, [per + rumpō, *break*], 3, *break through, burst through, force a passage.*

perruptus, see perrumpō.

perscrībō, -scrībere, -scrīpsī , -scrīptus, [per + scrībō], 3, *write fully, report* in writing.

persequor, -sequī, -secūtus,[per + sequor], 3, dep., *follow up, pursue; assail, attack* (I. 13; V. 1); *avenge* (VII. 38). [persecute.

persevērō, -āre, -āvī, -ātus, [persevērus, *very strict*], 1, *continue steadfastly, persist.* [persevere.

persolvō, -solvere, -solvī, -solūtus, [per + solvō], 3, *pay in full, pay.* poenās persolvere, *to pay the penalty* (I. 12).

perspectus, see perspiciō.

perspiciō, -spicere, -spexī, -spectus, [per + speciō, *look*], 3, *see, look; inspect, survey; perceive, observe, ascertain.* [perspective.

perstō, -stāre, -stitī, -stātūrus, [per + stō], 1, *stand firmly, persist.*

persuādeō, -suādēre, -suāsī, -suāsum est, [per + suādeō, *persuade*], 2, *convince, persuade, prevail upon, induce,* mihi persuādētur, *I am convinced.* [persuade.

perterreō, -terrēre, -terruī, -territus, [per + terreō], 2, *greatly alarm, frighten, terrify, dismay.* Part., perterritus, -a, -um, often *panic-stricken.*

pertinācia, -ae, [pertināx, per + tenāx, from teneō], I., *obstinacy, stubbornness.* [pertinacity.

pertineō, -tinēre, -tinuī, [per + teneō], 2, *reach out, extend; pertain to, concern, belong to.* [pertain.

perturbātiō, -ōnis, [perturbō], f., *disturbance, confusion.* [perturbation.

perturbō, -āre, -āvī, -ātus, [per + turbō, *disturb*], 1, *disturb greatly, disorder, confuse.* [perturb.

pervagor, -ārī, -ātus, [per + vagor], 1, dep., *roam about.*

pervehō, -ere, pervexī, [per + vehō], 3, *carry through;* pass. with middle sense, *sail along* (C. III. 3).

perveniō, -venīre, -vēnī, -ventum est, [per + veniō], 4, *come (to), arrive (at), reach;* of an inheritance, *fall to* (VI. 19).

pēs, pedis, m., *foot;* as a measure of length, = . 9,708 English feet, or 296 millimetres. pedem referre, *to retreat.* [pedestrian.

pestilentia, -ae, [pestilēns], f., *plague, pestilence.* (C. III. 87). [pestilence.

petītus, see petō.

petō, petere, petīvī and petiī, petītus, 3, *make for, try to reach, seek; get, secure; beg, ask, request.* petere ut liceat, *to ask permission.*

Petrocoriī, -ōrum, m., pl., (pet-ro-ko'ri-ī), a Gallic people north of the Garumna *(Garonne)* river. (VII. 75).

Petrōnius, -ī, m., *Marcus Petronius* (pe-trō' ni-us), a centurion of the eighth legion (VII. 50).

Petrosidius, -ī, m., *Lucius Petrosidius* (pet-ro-sid' i-us), a brave standard-bearer. (V. 37).

phalanx, -angis, Greek acc. sing., (I. 52) phalanga, [φ ά λ α γ ξ], f. *compact host, mass, phalanx.* [phalanx.

Philippus, -ī, m., *Lucius Marcus Philippus* (fi-lip' us), consul in 56 B.C. (C. I. 6).

Pictonēs, -um, m., pl., (pik' to-nēz), a Gallic people bordering on the Atlantic south of the Liger *(Loire).* Fig. 205.

pietās, -ātis, [pius, *dutiful*], f., *dutiful conduct, devotion,* to the gods, one's country, or one's kindred; *loyalty* (V. 27). [piety.

pīlum, -ī, n., *javelin, pike.* [pile.

pīlus, -ī, [pīlum], m., with prīmus, *maniple of the triarii,* a division in the army containing the most experienced soldiers. prīmī pīlī centuriō, *first centurion of the first maniple of the triarii, first centurion* of the legion in rank (III. 5). prīmum pīlum dūcere, *to lead the first maniple of the triarii, to hold the rank of first centurion* (V. 35; VI. 38; C. III. 91).

pinna, -ae, f., *feather;* in military language, *battlement.* [pen.

Pīrustae, -ārum, m., pl., (pī-rus'tē) a people in Illyricum. (V. I).

piscātōrius, -a, -um, [piscātor, *fisherman*], adj., *of a fisherman.* nāvēs piscātōriae, *fishing-smacks* (C. II. 4). [piscatory.

piscis, -is, *m., fish.* (IV. 10). [Pisces.

Pīsō, -ōnis, m., (pī' sō):

(1) *Lucius Calpurnius Piso Caesoninus,* consul 112 B.C. (I. 12).

(2) *Lucius Calpurnius Piso Caesoninus,* consul with *Aulus Gabinius,* 58 B.C.; father-in-law of Caesar. (I. 6, 12).

(3) *Marcus Pupius Piso Calpurnianus,* consul with *M. Valerius Messala,* 61 B.C. (I. 2, 35).

(4) *Piso,* a brave Aquitanian. (IV. 12).

pix, picis, f., *pitch,* [pitch.

Placentia, -ae, f., (pla-sen'sh[y]a), a city in northern Italy, on the Po River; now *Piacenza.* (C. III. 71).

placeō, placēre, placuī, placitum est, 2, *please, be agreeable, be welcome to.* Used impersonally, placet, *it pleases, it seems good; it is agreed, it is settled; it is resolved, it is decided.* eī placuit, *he resolved* (I. 34). [please.

placidē, comp. -ius, [placidus], adv., *quietly, calmly.* (VI. 8).

plācō, -āre, -āvī, -ātus, 1, *appease, conciliate.* (VI. 16). [placate.

Plancus, -ī, m., *Lucius Munatius Plancus* (mū-nā'sh[y]us plang'-kus), a lieutenant in Caesar's army. (V. 24, 25).

plānē, comp. -ius, -issimē, [plānus], adv., *clearly, distinctly* (III. 26); *entirely, quite* (VI. 43).

plānitiēs, -ēī, [plānus], f., *level ground, plain.*

plānus, -a, -um, comp. -ior, sup. -issimus, adj., *level, even* (IV. 23); *flat* (III. 13). [plain.

plēbs, plēbis, or plēbēs, -eī, f., *the common folk, the common people, the masses.* apud plēbem, *among the masses.* [plebeian.

plēnē, comp. -ius, [plēnus], adv., *fully, completely.* (III. 3).

plēnus, -a, -um, comp. -ior, sup. -issimus, adj., *full.*

plērumque, [n. acc. of plērusque], adv., *commonly, generally, usually, for the most part.*

plērusque, -aque, -umque, [plērus, *very many*], adj., *very many, most.* As noun, plērīque, -ōrumque, m., pl., *the most, the greater part, the majority, most.*

Pleumoxiī, -ōrum, m., pl., (plū-mok'-si-ī), a Belgic people, subject to the Nervians. (V. 39).

plumbum, -ī, n., *lead.* plumbum album, *tin* (V. 12.) [plumber.

plūrēs, plūrīmus, see multus.

plūs, plūrimum, see multum.

pluteus, -ī, m., *breastwork* of planks or wickerwork, placed on ramparts (VII. 41), or on the stories of a tower (VII. 25); *wood construction* (VII. 72); movable *mantelet,* to protect besiegers.

pōculum, -ī, n., *cup, beaker.* (VI. 28).

poena, -ae, f., *compensation, fine* (V. 1); *punishment, penalty.* poenās pendere (VI. 9) or persolvere (I. 12), *to pay the penalty.* [penal.

pollex, pollicis, m., *thumb, great toe.*

polliceor, -licērī, -licitus, [por- + liceor], 2, dep., *promise, offer.* liberāliter pollicitus, *with generous promises* (IV. 21).

pollicitātiō, -ōnis, [pollicitor, freq. of polliceor], f., *promise, offer.*

pollicitus, see polliceor.

Pompeiānus, -a, -um, [Pompeius], adj., *of Pompey.* As noun, Pompeiānī, -ōrum, m., pl., *soldiers of Pompey, Pompey's men.* (C. III. 48, 72).

Pompeius, -ī, *m.,* (pom-pē' yus):

(1) *Gnaeus Pompeius Magnus, Pompey,* Caesar's father-in-law and rival, born B.C. 106; conquered by Caesar at the battle of Pharsalus, and afterwards murdered in Egypt.

(2) *Gnaeus Pompeius,* an interpreter serving under Titurius Sabinus. (V. 36).

pondus, ponderis, [cf. pendō], n., *heaviness,*

weight (ii. 29; vi. 27; vii. 22); *a weight* as a standard of value (v. 12); *quantity* (C. III. 96). [ponderous.

pōnō, pōnere, posuī, positus, 3, *place, put; lay down* (iv. 37); *set aside* (vi. 17); *station; pitch.* Pass. often *be situated, be dependent, depend on.* **castra pōnere,** *to pitch camp, encamp.* [positive.

pōns, pontis, m., *bridge.* [pontoon.

populātiō, -ōnis, [populor], f., *a laying waste, ravaging.* (i. 15).

populor, -ārī, -ātus, 1, dep., *lay waste, devastate.* i. II.

populus, -ī, m., *people* as a political *whole, nation.* [people.

por-, in composition, *forth, forward.*

porrigō, -rigere, -rēxī, -rēctus, [por- + regō], 3, *reach out, extend.* **porrēcta loca aperta pertinēbant,** *the open places lay extended,* i.e. *reached* (ii. 19).

porrō, adv., *moreover, furthermore.* (v. 27).

porta, -ae, f., *gate of a city, gateway; of a camp, gate, entrance, passage.* [porter (door-keeper).

portō, -āre, -āvī, -ātus, 1, *carry, bring, convey, take.* [portage.

portōrium, -ī, n., *toll, tax, customs duties.* i. 18; iii. I.

portus, -ūs, m., *harbor, haven.* [port.

poscō, poscere, poposcī, 3, *demand, ask for urgently; of things, require, make necessary* (vii. I).

positus, -a, -um, see **pōnō.**

possessiō, -ōnis, [cf. possīdō], f., *possession.* [possession.

possideō, -sidēre, -sēdī, [por- + sedeō], 2, *hold, occupy, possess.* i. 34; ii. 4; vi. 12. [possess.

possīdō, -sīdere, -sēdī, -sessus, [por- + sīdō], 3, *gain possession of, possess one's self of.* iv. 7.

possum, posse, potuī, [potis, *able,* + sum], irr., *be able, can; have power, have influence.* **multum posse,** *to have great influence;* **plūrimum posse,** *to have very great power, influence.* [posse.

post, adv., *afterwards, later, after;* with abl. of degree of difference. **annō post,** *a year later, the following year.* **paucīs post diēbus,** *a few days later.*

post, prep. with acc. only:
(1) Of place, *behind.* **post tergum,** *in the rear.*
(2) Of time, *after.* **post mediam noctem,** *after midnight.*

posteā [post eā], adv., *afterwards.* **posteā quam,** with the force of a conjunction, *after that, after.*

posterus, -a, -um, nom. sing. m. not in use, comp. **posterior,** sup. **postrēmus,** [post], adj., *the following, next.* As noun, **posterī, -ōrum,** m., pl., *posterity* (vii. 77). [postern.

postpōnō, -pōnere, -posuī, -positus, [post + pōnō], 3, *put after, lay aside.* **omnia postpōnere,** *to disregard everything else* (VI. 3). **omnibus rēbus postpositīs,** *laying everything else aside* (V. 7). [postpone.

postpositus, see **postpōnō.**

postquam [post + quam], conj., *after that, after, when;* **post** and **quam** are often separated by intervening words.

postrēmō [abl. of postrēmus, sc. tempore], adv., *at last, finally.*

postrīdiē, [locative from posterus diēs], adv., *the next day.* **postrīdiē eius diēī,** *the next day, the following day.*

postulātum, -ī, [part. of postulō], n., *demand, claim, request.*

postulō, -āre, -āvī, -ātus, 1, *claim, demand, ask, request; of things, require, make necessary, demand; accuse of* (C. III. 83). [postulate.

potēns, -entis, comp. **potentior,** sup. **-issimus,** [part. of possum], adj., *powerful.* As noun, **potentior, -ōris,** m., *one more powerful* (VI. 11); pl., *the more powerful* (II. 1; VI. 13, 22).

potentissimī, -ōrum, m., pl., *the most powerful* (VI. 22). [potent.

potentātus, -ūs, [potēns], m., *power, headship, supremacy.* (I. 31). [potentate.

potentia, -ae, [potēns], f., *might, power, influence.* [potency.

potestās, -ātis, [potis], f., *might, power, authority, lordship; possibility, opportunity.* **potestātem facere,** *to give opportunity; to grant permission* (IV. 15; V. 41).

potior, potīrī, potītus, [potis, *able,*] 4, dep., *obtain possession of become master of, acquire, obtain.*

potius, adv. in comp. degree, sup. **potissimum,** [potis], adv., *rather, more, preferably.* **potius quam,** *rather than.*

prae, prep. with abl., *in comparison with* (II. 30); *on account of* (VII. 44).

praeacuō, -cuere, -cuī, -cūtus, 3, *sharpen at the end.*

praeacūtus, -a, -um, [part. of praeacuō], adj., *sharpened at the end, sharpened, pointed; very sharp.*

praebeō, -ēre, praebuī, praebitus, [prae + habeō], 2, *hold forth; exhibit, manifest; furnish, provide* (II. 17); *produce* (III. 17). **opīniōnem praebēre,** *to create an impression* (III. 17, 25). [prebendary.

praecaveō, -cavēre, -cāvī, -cautus, [prae + caveō], 2, *take precautions.* (I. 38). [precaution.

praecēdō, -cēdere, -cessī, -cessūrus, [prae + cēdō], 3, *go before; surpass, excel* (i. I). [precede.

praeceps, -cipitis, [prae + CAP in caput], adj., *headlong, with great speed, head over heels* (II. 24; V. 17); *steep, precipitous* (IV. 33). [precipitous.

praeceptum, -ī, [part. of **praecipiō**], n., *order, command, instruction, injunction; precept.* (V. 35; VI. 36). [precept.

praecipiō, -cipere, -cēpī, -ceptus, [prae + capiō], 3, *anticipate* (VII. 9; C. III. 87); *order, direct, instruct.*

praecipitō, -āre, -āvī, -ātus, [praeceps], 1, *hurl headlong, fling down.* [precipitate.

praecipuē, [praecipuus], adv., *especially, specially, particularly.*

praecipuus, -a, -um, [prae + CAP in capiō], adj., *especial, particular.*

praeclūdō, -clūdere , -clūsī, -clūsus, [prae + claudō], 3, *close up, block.* (V. 9). [preclude.

praecō, -ōnis, m., *herald, crier.*

Praecōnīnus (pre-co-nī' nus), see **Valerius** (I).

praecurrō, -currere, -cucurrī or **-currī**, [prae + currō], 3, *run forward, hasten forward* (VI. 39; C. III. 34); *hasten in advance* (VII. 37); *anticipate* (VII. 9). [precursor.

praeda, -ae, [cf. **praehendō**], f., *booty, spoil, plunder.* [prey.

praedicō, -āre, -āvī, -ātus, [prae + dicō], 1, *make known, declare, announce; boast* (I. 44, C. II. 39). [preach.

praedīcō, -dīcere, -dīxī, -dictus, [prae + dicō], 3, *say beforehand; order, give orders, in advance* (C. III. 92). [predict.

praedō, -ōnis, [praeda], m., *robber, pirate.* (C. III. 104).

praedor, -ārī, -ātus, [praeda], 1, dep., *obtain booty, pillage, plunder.*

praedūcō, -dūcere, -dūxī, -ductus, [prae + dūcō], 3, *extend, make in front.* (VII. 46, 69).

praefectus, see **praeficiō**.

praefectus, -ī, [praeficiō], m., *commander, prefect; subsidiary official* (I. 39). [prefect.

praeferō, -ferre, -tulī, -lātus, [prae + ferō], irr., *carry before; put before, prefer to* (V. 54). **sē praeferre**, *to show one's self superior to* (II. 27). [prefer.

praeficiō, -ficere, -fēcī, -fectus, [prae + faciō], 3, *place in command of, appoint to command.*

praefīgō, -fīgere, -fīxī, -fīxus, [prae + fīgō, fasten], 3, *fix in front.* **sudibus praefīxīs**, *by driving stakes in front* (V. 18). [prefix.

praefringō, -fringere, -frēgī, -frāctus, [prae + frangō], 3, *break off, shatter.* (C. II. 6).

praemetuō, -ere, [prae + metuō, *fear*], 3, *be anxious.* (VII. 49).

praemittō, -mittere, -mīsī, -missus, [prae + mittō], 3, *send forward, send ahead, send in advance.* [premise.

praemium, -ī, [prae, cf. emō], n., *reward, distinction.* [premium.

praeoccupō, -āre, -āvī, -ātus, [prae + occupō], 1, *take possession of beforehand, seize first* (VII. 26). [preoccupy.

praeoptō, -āre, -āvī, -ātus, [prae + optō], 1, *choose rather, prefer.* (I. 25).

praeparō, -āre, -āvī, -ātus, [prae + parō], 1, *make ready beforehand, make ready, prepare.* [prepare.

praepōnō, -pōnere, -posuī, -positus, [prae + pōnō], 3, *set over, place in command of.*

praerumpō, -rumpere, -rūpī, -ruptus, [prae + rumpō, *break*], 3, *break off in front, break off.* (III. 14).

praeruptus, -a, -um, [part. of **praerumpō**], adj., *steep, precipitous.*

praesaepiō, -saepīre, -saepsī, -saeptus, [prae + saepiō], 4, *fence in; block, bar* (VII. 77).

praesaeptus, see **praesaepiō**.

praescrībō, -scrībere, -scrīpsī, -scrīptus, [prae + scrībō], 3, *give directions, direct* (I. 36, 40); *determine* (II. 20). [prescribe.

praescrīptum, -ī, [part. of **praescrībō**], n., *direction, order, instructions.* (I. 36). [prescript.

praesēns, -entis, comp. **-ior**, [part. of **praesum**], adj., *at hand, present.* [present.

praesentia, -ae, [praesēns], f., *presence* (V. 43); *present time.* **in praesentiā**, *for the present.* [presence.

praesentiō, -sentīre, -sēnsī, -sēnsus, [prae + sentiō], 4, *perceive beforehand.* (V. 54; VII. 30).

praesertim [prae, cf. serō, *join*], adv., *especially, particularly.*

praesidium, -ī, [praeses, *guard*], n., *guard, detachment, garrison, protection; post, redoubt; safety* (II. 11).

praestō, -stāre, -stitī, -stitus, [prae + stō], 1, *surpass, excel; exhibit, display, manifest; discharge, perform, do.* Impers. **praestat**, *it is preferable, it is better.*

praestō, adv., *at hand.* **praestō esse**, *to meet* (V. 26).

praesum, -esse, -fuī, [prae + sum], irr., *preside over; be at the head of have command of, have charge of.*

praeter, prep. with acc. only, *beyond* (I. 48); *except, besides; contrary to.*

praetereā [praeter + eā], adv., *besides, further.*

praetereō, -īre, -īvī or **-iī, -itus**, [praeter + eō], irr., *pass over* (VII. 25, 77); *pass, go by* (VII. 77). [preterit.

praeteritus, see **praetereō**.

praetermittō, -mittere, -mīsī, -missus, [praeter + mittō], 3, *pass over, let pass, allow to go by.*

praeterquam [praeter + quam], adv. with comparative force, *other than, besides.* (VII 77).

praetor, -ōris, [*praeitor from praeëō], m., *general, commander* (I. 21); *praetor*, a Roman magistrate, next in rank to the consul.

praetōrium, -ī, [praetōrius], n., *general's tent.* (C. III. 82).

praetōrius, -a, -um, [praetor], adj., *of the commander, general's* (I. 40, 42); *pretorian.* As noun, **praetōrius, -ī,** m., *ex-praetor, man of praetorian rank* (C. III. 82). [pretorian.

praetūra, -ae, [praetor], f., *the office of praetor, praetor ship* (C. III. 82).

praeūstus, -a, -um, [part. of **praeūrō**], adj., *burnt at the end, hardened at the end by burning.*

praevertō, -vertere, -vertī, [prae + vertō], 3, *outstrip; attend to first* (VII. 33).

prāvus, -a, -um, comp. **-ior,** sup. **-issimus,** adj., *bad, wicked.* (VII. 39).

precēs, see **prex.**

premō, -ere, -pressī, -pressus, 3, *press, harass, oppress;* pass., *be hard pressed, be beset, be burdened, be in need.* [press.

prēndō (for **prehendō**), **prēndere, prēndī, prēnsus,** 3, *take, grasp.* (I. 20).

pretium, -ī, n., *price, value.* [price.

prex, precis, f., generally pl., nom. and gen. sing. not in use, *prayer, entreaty, supplication; curse, imprecation* (VI. 31).

prīdiē, adv., *the day before, the previous day.* **prīdiē eius diēī,** *the day before that day, on the previous day* (I. 47).

prīmipīlus, -ī, [prīmus + pīlus], m., = **prīmus pīlus,** *first centurion;* see **pīlus.** (II. 25; C. III. 53).

prīmō [abl. of **prīmus**], adv., *at first, in the first place.*

prīmum [acc. of **prīmus**], adv., *first, before everything else, in the first place.* **quam prīmum,** *as soon as possible.* **cum prīmum,** *as soon as.*

prīmus, see **prior.**

prīnceps, -ipis, [primus + CAP in **capiō**], adj., *first, chief, at the front.* As noun, m., *leading man, leader,* pl. often *leading men.* [prince.

prīncipātus, -ūs, [prīnceps], m., *chief authority, headship.* [principate.

prior, -us, gen. **priōris,** adj. in comp. degree, sup. **prīmus,** [cf. **prō**], *former, previous, first.* As noun, **priōrēs, -um,** m., pl., *those in advance* (II. 11). Sup. **prīmus,** *first, the first.* As noun, **prīmī, -ōrum,** m., pl., *the foremost men, the first.* **prīma, -ōrum,** n., pl., in the phrase **in prīmīs,** *especially.* [prior, prime.

prīstinus, -a, -um, [*prīs, = prius, + -tinus], adj., *former, previous, earlier, old-time.* [pristine.

prius [prior], adv., *before, sooner, earlier.*

priusquam, prius quam, conj., *before, sooner than;* **prius** and **quam** are often separated by intervening words.

prīvātim [prīvātus], adv., *privately, as individuals,* opposed in meaning to **pūblicē.** (I. 17; V. 55).

prīvātus, -a, -um, [part. of **prīvō**], adj.,

private, personal. As noun, **prīvātus, -ī,** m., *private individual* (VI. 13). [private.

prīvō, -āre, -āvī, -ātus, 1, *rob, deprive.* (C. III. 90).

prō, prep. with abl. only, *in front of, before; for, in behalf of; instead of, as; on account of, in return for; in accordance with* (II. 31); *in proportion to, considering* (I. 2, 51; VI. 19; VII. 56, 74).

probō, -āre, -āvī, -ātus, [probus], 1, *approve; sliow to be worthy, display* (V. 44); *prove* (V. 27); *show, demonstrate* (I. 3). [probe.

prōcēdō, -cēdere, -cessī, [pro + cēdō], 3, *advance, go forward.* [proceed.

Procillus, (pro-sil'us), see **Valerius** (4).

prōclīnō, -āre, -āvī, -ātus, [prō + clīnō, *bend*], 1, *bend forward, lean forward;* pass., *become desperate* (VII. 42).

prōcōnsul, -ulis, [prō + cōnsul], m., *proconsul,* an ex-consul appointed as governor of a province.

procul, adv., *at a distance, from afar, far off.*

prōcumbō, -cumbere, -cubuī, [prō + cumbō, for **cubō,** *lie down*], 3, *fall prostrate* (VII. 15); *sink down* (II. 27); *be beaten down* (VI. 43); *lit down* (VI. 27); *lean forward* (IV. 17).

prōcūrātiō, -ōnis, [procūrō], f., *charge, management.* (C. III. 104).

prōcūrō, -āre, -āvī, -ātus, [prō + cūrō], 1, *look after, have charge of, regulate.* (VI. 13). [procure.

prōcurrō, -currere, -cucurrī or **-currī,** [prō + currō], 3, *run forward, hasten forward, rush forward.*

prōdeō, -īre, -iī, -itum est, [prōd-, for prō, + eō], irr., *come out, come forth, advance.*

prōdesse, see **prōsum.**

prōditiō, -ōnis, [prōdō], f., *treachery.*

prōditor, -ōris, [prodō], m., *traitor.*

prōditus, see **prōdō.**

prōdō, -dere, -didī, -ditus, [prō + dō], 3, *give forth, make known; transmit, hand down; surrender, betray; give up, abandon* (IV. 25).

prōdūcō, -dūcere, -dūxī, -ductus, [prō + dūcō], 3, *bring out, lead forth; prolong* (IV. 30). [product.

prōductus, see **prōdūcō.**

proelior, -ārī, -ātus, [proelium], 1, dep., *fight.*

proelium, -ī, n., *battle, combat, engagement.*

profectiō, -ōnis, [proficīscor], f., *departure, setting out.*

prōfectus, see **prōficiō.**

profectus, see **proficīscor.**

prōferō, -ferre, -tulī, -lātus, [prō + ferō], irr., *bring out, bring forth.*

prōficiō, -ficere, -fēcī, -fectus, [prō + faciō], 3, *effect, gain, accomplish.* [profit.

proficīscor, -ficīscī, -fectus, [prōficiō], 3, dep., *set out, depart; set out (for), proceed.*

profiteor, -fitērī, -fessus, [pro, = prō, + fateor, *confess*], 2, dep., *declare openly, avow* (VII. 2, 37);

VOCABULARY

477

offer, promise, [profess.

prōflīgō, -āre, -āvī, -ātus, [prō + **flīgō,** *strike*], 1, *put to flight, rout.* (II. 23; VII. 13). [profligate.

prōfluō, -fluere, -flūxī, [prō + **fluō**], 3, *flow forth.* (IV. 10).

prōfugiō, -fugere, -fūgī, [pro, = prō, + **fugiō**], 3, *flee, escape.*

prōfuī, see **prōsum.**

prōfundō, -fundere, -fūdī, -fūsus, [prō + **fundō**], 3, *pour forth.* **sē prōfūdit,** *rushed forward* (C. III. 93).

prōgnātus, -a, -um, [prō + (g)**nātus,** from (g)**nāscor**], adj., *sprung, descended.* (II. 29; VI. 18).

prōgredior, -gredī, -gressus, [prō + **gradior,** *step*], 3, dep., *advance, go forward, proceed.* [progress.

prōgressus, see **prōgredior.**

prohibeō, -hibēre, -hibuī, -hibitus, [prō + **habeō**], 2, *hold, restrain; keep off, prevent, hinder; cut off, shut off; protect, defend.* [prohibit.

prōiciō, -icere, -iēcī, -iectus, [prō + **iaciō**], 3, *throw forward, throw, fling, cast;* of arms, *throw down; abandon, lose* (II. 15). **sē prōicere,** *to leap down* (IV. 25), *to prostrate one's self* (I. 27, 31).

prōiectae, pass. as middle, *casting themselves* (VII. 26). [project.

proinde [prō + **inde**], adv., *hence, therefore, and so.* **prōinde ac sī.** *just as if* (C. III. 60).

prōmineō, -minēre, -minuī, 2, *bend forward, lean forward.* [prominent.

prōmiscuē [**prōmiscuus**], adv., *in common, promiscuously.* (VI. 21).

prōmissus, -a, -um, [part. of **prōmittō**], adj., of hair, *hanging down, flowing.* (V. 14).

prōmōtus, see **prōmoveō.**

prōmoveō, -movēre, -mōvī, -mōtus, [prō + **moveō**], 2, *move forward, push forward.* [promote.

prōmptus, -a, -um, comp. **-ior,** sup. **-issimus,** [part. of **prōmō,** *bring forward*], adj., *ready, quick.* [prompt.

prōmunturium, -ī, [cf. **prōmineō**], n., *headland.* (III. 12). [promontory.

prōnē [**prōnus**], adv., *bending forward, leaning forward.* (IV. 17).

prōnūntiō, -āre, -āvī, -ātus, [prō + **nūntiō**], 1, *tell openly, declare; announce, give notice.* Impers., **prōnūntiātur** *notice is given.* [pronounce.

prope, comp. **propius,** sup. **proximē,** adv., *near, nearly, almost;* followed by the acc., *near.*

proximē, *nearest, next, very near; last, most recently.*

prōpellō, -pellere, -pulī, -pulsus, [prō + **pellō**], 3, *drive away, put to flight, rout; force back* (V. 44). [propel.

properō, -āre, -āvī, -ātus, [**properus,** *quick*], 1, *hurry, make haste, hasten.*

propinquitās, -ātis, [**propinquus**], f., *nearness, vicinity; relationship* (II. 4). [propinquity.

propinquus, -a, -um, comp. **-ior,** [**prope**], adj., *near, neighboring.* As noun, **propinquus, -ī,** m., *relative;* pl., **propinquī, -ōrum,** m., *relatives, kinsfolk;* **propinquae, -ārum,** f., *female relatives* (I. 18).

propior, -us, gen. **propiōris,** adj. in comp. degree, sup. **proximus,** [cf. **prope**], positive wanting, *nearer.* **proximus, -a, -um,** *nearest, next, last,* of space or time. **proximā nocte,** *on the following night.* [proximate. **propius,** see **prope.**

prōpōnō, -pōnere, -posuī, -positus, [prō + **pōnō**], 3, *set forth, put forward, present; declare, explain; propose, intend; raise, display* (II. 20). [propose.

prōpositum, -ī, [**prōpositus**], n., *intention, purpose.* (C. III. 84).

prōpositus, see **prōpōnō.**

proprius, -a, -um, adj., *one's own, particular, peculiar, characteristic.* (VI. 22, 23). [proper.

propter, prep. with acc. only, *on account of, in consequence of.*

proptereā [**propter** + **eā**], adv., *for this reason, therefore.* **proptereā quod,** *because.*

prōpugnātor, -ōris, [**prōpugnō**], m., *defender.* (VII. 25).

prōpugnō, -āre, -āvī, -ātus, [prō + **pugnō**], 1, *come forth to fight* (V. 9); *fight on the defensive* (II. 7; VII. 86). **prōpulsō, -āre, -āvī, -ātus,** [freq. of **prōpellō**], 1, *drive off, drive back* (I. 49); *ward off, repel* (VI. 15).

prōra, -ae, [ΠΡΩΡΑ], f., *prow.* [prow.

prōruō, -ere, -uī, -utus, 3, *throw down; tear down* (III. 26).

prōsequor, -sequī, -secūtus, [prō + **sequor**], 3, dep., *follow after; follow up, pursue; address* (II. 5). [prosecute.

prōspectus, -ūs, [cf. **prōspiciō**], m., *view, sight.* **in prōspectū,** *in sight, visible* (V. 10). [prospect.

prōspiciō, -spicere, spexī, -spectus, [prō + **speciō,** *look*], 3, *look out, see to it* (V. 7); *provide for, look out for* (I. 23; VII. 50).

prōsternō, -sternere, -strāvī, -strātus, [prō + **sternō,** *scatter*], 3, *overthrow, utterly cast down, destroy.* (VII. 77). [prostrate.

prōsum, prōdesse, prōfuī, [prō, **prōd-,** + **sum**], irr., *be of advantage to.* (VI. 40).

prōtegō, -tegere, -tēxī, -tēctus, [prō + **tegō**], 3, *cover, protect.* [protect.

prōterō, -terere, -trīvī, -trītus, [prō + **terō**], 3, *wear away, destroy.* (C. II. 41).

prōterreō, -ēre, -uī, -itus, [prō + **terreō**], 2, *frighten away, drive off* by means of fright. (V.

58; VII. 81).

prŏtinus [prŏ + tenus], adv., *forthwith, at once, immediately.*

prŏturbō, -āre, -āvī, -ātus, [prŏ + turbō, *disturb*], 1, *drive away, repulse.* (II. 19; VII. 81).

prŏvectus, see **prŏvehō.**

prŏvehō, -vehere, -vexī, -vectus, [prŏ + vehō], 3, *carry forward* (V. 8); pass., in a middle sense, in **altum prŏvectae,** *putting out into the deep, putting out to sea* (28).

prŏveniō, -venīre, -vēnī, -ventum est, [prŏ + veniō], 4, *come forth; grow* (V. 24).

prŏventus, -ūs, [cf. **prŏveniō**], m., *issue, result, outcome.* (VII. 29, 80).

prŏvideō, -vidēre, -vīdī, -vīsus, [prŏ + videō], 2, *foresee, perceive in advance; provide for, look out for.* [provide.

prŏvincia, -ae, f., *province;* often *the Province,* the part of Transalpine Gaul subdued by the Romans before 58 B.C. [province.

prŏvinciālis, -e, [**prŏvincia**], adj., *of the province.* (VII. 7). [provincial.

prŏvīsus, see **prŏvideō.**

prŏvolō, -āre, -āvī, [prŏ + volō, *fly*], 1, *fly forward, dash forth.* (II. 19).

proximē, see **prope.**

proximus, -a, -um, see **propior.**

prūdentia, -ae, [**prūdēns,** for **prŏvidēns,** *far-seeing*], f., *foresight, good judgment.* (II. 4). [prudence.

Ptiāniī, -ōrum, m., pl., (tī-ā'ni-ī), a small state in Aquitania. (III. 27).

Ptolomaeus, -ī, [ΠΤΟΛΕΜΑΙΟΣ], m., *Ptolemy,* king of Egypt in 49 B.C., brother of Cleopatra. (C. III. 103).

pūberēs, -um, [adj. **pūbēs** used as a noun], m., pl, *adults.* (V. 56).

pūblicē [**pūblicus**], adv., *in the name of the state, as a state, publicly.*

pūblicō, -āre, -āvī, -ātus, [**pūblicus**], 1, *make public; confiscate* (V. 56; VII. 43). [publish.

pūblicus, -a, -um, adj., *of the state, public, common.* **litterae pūblicae.** *state documents* (V. 47). **rēs pūblica,** *the state, public business, public interest.* As noun, **pūblicum, -ī,** n., *a public place* (VI. 28; VII. 26). **in pūblicō,** *in a public place* (VI. 18).

Pūblius, -ī, m., (pub'li-us), a Roman first name.

pudet, pudēre, puduit or **puditum est,** 2, impers. form of **pudeō,** *it shames; it makes ashamed* (VII. 42).

pudor, -ōris, [cf. **pudeō**], m., *shame, sense of shame.*

puer, puerī, m., *child, boy.*

puerīlis, -e, comp. **-ior,** [**puer**], adj., *of a child.* [puerile.

pugna, -ae, f., *fight, combat, battle.*

pugnō, -āre, -āvī, -ātus, [**pugna**], 1, *fight, engage in battle.* **pugnātum est,** *the battle raged.*

pulcher, -chra, -chrum, comp. **-ior,** sup.

pulcherrimus, adj., *beautiful* (VII. 15); *noble* (VII. 77).

Pullō, -ōnis, m., (pul'ō), a brave centurion. (V. 44).

pulsus, see **pellō.**

pulsus, -ūs, [**pellō**], m., *stroke;* of oars, *movement* (III. 13). [pulse.

pulvis, pulveris, m., *dust.* [pulverize.

puppis, -is, i., *stern* of a ship. [poop.

purgō, -āre, -āvī, -ātus, [for *pūrigō; pūrus + agō], 1, *make clean; free from blame, excuse, clear.* **suī pūrgandī causā,** *in order to excuse themselves.* [purge.

Puteolī, -ōrum, m., pl., (pū-tē'o-lī), a city on the coast of Campania, now *Pozzuoli.* (C. III. 71).

putō, -āre, -āvī, -ātus, 1, *think, consider, believe, judge.* [putative.

Pȳrēnaeus, -a, -um, [ΠΥΡΗΝΑΙΟΣ], adj., *of Pyrene.* **Pȳrēnaeī montēs,** *the Pyrenees Mountains,* (I. 1).

Q.

Q. = **Quīntus.**

quā [abl. fem. of **quī,** originally sc. **viā** or **parte**], adv., *where.*

qua, nom. sing. fem., and neut. pl., of the indefinite pron. **quis,** or **quī.**

quadrāgēnī, -ae, -a, [**quadrāgintā**], num. distributive adj., *forty each, forty in each case.* (IV. 17; VII. 23).

quadrāgintā, or **XL,** [**quattuor**], indeclinable num. adj., *forty.*

quadringentī, -ae, -a, or **CCCC,** [**quattuor** + **centum**], numeral adj., *four hundred.*

quaerō, -ere, quaesīvī, quaesītus, 3, *look for, seek* (II. 21; VII. 37); *ask, inquire, make inquiry.* [query.

quaestiō, -ōnis, [cf. **quaerō**], f., *inquiry; examination, investigation.* [question.

quaestor, -ōris, [cf. **quaerō**], m.:
(1) *quaestor, state treasurer,* the lowest in rank of the great officers of state.
(2) *quarter-master, quaestor,* an officer accompanying the army on campaigns, having charge of money and supplies, sometimes detailed for military service in charge of troops.

quaestus, -ūs, [cf. **quaerō**], m., *getting* of money, *gain.* (VI. 17; C. III. 60).

quālis, -e, [cf. **quis**], inter. adj., *of what sort? what sort of?* (I. 21).

quam [**quī**], adv. and conj., *how much, how;* with superlatives (with or without **possum**), *as possible;* after comparatives and comparative expressions, *than, as;* with expressions of time, *after.* **quam vetus,** *how* *old.* **quam diū,** *as long as.* **nāvēs quam plūrimās,** *as many ships as possible.* **quam celerrimē,** *as quickly as possible.* **post diem quārtum quam,** *the fourth day after.*

quamvīs [quam + vīs, from volō], adv., *however much; however* (IV. 2).

quandō, adv., *ever, at any time.*

quantō opere, see **quantus.**

quantus, -a, -um, adj., *how great, how much, how large;* after **tantus,** *as;* **tantum . . . quantum,** *so much, so far . . . as.* As noun, with gen. of the whole, **quantum bonī,** *how much advantage, how great advantage* (I. 40); **quantum agrī,** *as much land as* (VI. 22). **quantō opere,** *how much, how deeply* (II. 5). **quantō opere . . . tantō opere,** *as much as ... so much* (VII. 52).

quantusvīs, quantavīs, quantumvīs, [quantus + vīs, from volō], adj., *however great, no matter how great.*

quārē [quā + rē], adv., *wherefore, and for this reason.*

quārtus, -a, -um, [quattuor], adj., *fourth.*

quartus decimus, or **XIIII,** *fourteenth.* [quart.

quasi [quam + sī], conj., *as if.*

quattuor, or **IIII,** indeclinable num. adj., *four.*

quattuordecim, or **XIIII,** [quattuor + decem], indeclinable num. adj., *fourteen.*

-que, enclitic conj., *and,* appended to a word which in construction belongs after it.

quem ad modum, see **modus.**

queror, querī, questus, 3, dep., *complain, lament; complain of make complaint of.* [querulous.

questus, see **queror.**

quī, quae, quod, gen. **cuius,** rel. and inter. pron.:
(1) As rel. pron., *who, which;* at the beginning of a clause often best rendered by a personal or demonstrative pron., with or without *and.* **īdem quī,** *the same as.*
(2) As inter. adj. pron., *what? what kind of?*

quī, quae or **qua, quod,** indef. pron., *any, any one,* or *anything,* used both as subst. and as adj. **sī quī,** if *any one.*

quicquam, see **quisquam.**

quīcumque, quaecumque, quodcumque, indef. pron., *whoever, whatever, whichever.*

quid, see **quis.**

quīdam, quaedam, quiddam, indef. pron., *a certain one, a certain thing.* As adj., **quīdam, quaedam, quod-dam,** *a certain, some, certain.*

quidem, adv., *indeed, at least.* **nē . . . quidem,** *not even.*

quidnam, see **quisnam.**

quiēs, -ētis, f., *rest, repose.* [quiet (noun).

quiētus, -a, -um, [part. of quiēscō, from quiēs], adj., *at rest, calm, quiet; peaceful, at peace.* [quiet (adj.).

quīn, [old abl. quī + ne], conj., *that not, but that, without;* after words expressing doubt or suspicion, *that;* after **dēterreō, retineō,** etc., trans. by *from* with a participle, **quīn etiam,** *moreover.*

quīncūnx, -ūncis, [quīnque + ūncia], f., *quīncūnx,* an arrangement of trees or other objects like the five spots on the dice (*quīncūnx*). (VII. 73).

quīndecim, or **XV,** [quīnque + decem], indeclinable num. adj., *fifteen.*

quīngentī, -ae, -a, or **D,** [quīnque + centum], num. adj., *five hundred.*

quīnī, -ae, -a, [quīnque], distrib. num. adj., *five each, five at a time.*

quīnquāgintā, or **L,** [quīnque], indeclinable num. adj., *fifty.*

quīnque, or **V,** indeclinable num. adj., *five.*

quīntus, -a, -um, [quīnque], adj., *fifth.* [quint. **Quīntus, -ī,** m., (kwin' tus), a Roman first name.

quis, — , quid, inter. pron., *who? what?* Neut. **quid,** with gen. of the whole, **quid cōnsiliī,** *what plan?* neut. **quid,** as adverbial acc., *why?* **quid vōs sectāminī,** *why do ye pursue?* (VI. 35).

quis, — , quid, indef. pron., *any one, anything.* As adj., **quī, quae** or **qua, quod,** *any.* **sī quis,** *if any one.* **nē quis,** *that not any one, that no one.* Neut. **quid,** with partitive gen., *any;* as, **sī quid cōnsilī,** *if any plan.*

quisnam, — , quidnam, inter. pron., *who, pray? what, pray?* As adj., **quīnam, quaenam, quodnam,** *of what kind, pray* (II. 30).

quispiam, — , quidpiam, indef. pron., *any one, anything* (VI. 17). As adj., **quispiam, quaepiam, quodpiam,** *any* (V. 35).

quisquam, — , quicquam, indef. pron., *any one, anything.* As adj., *any* (acc. **quemquam,** VI. 36).

quisque, — , quidque, indef. pron., *each one, each thing.* As adj., **quisque, quaeque, quodque,** *each.*

quisquis, — , quicquid, indef. rel. pron., *whoever, whatever.*

quīvīs, quaevīs, quidvīs, [quī + vīs, from volō], indef. pron., *any one, anything you please.* As adj., **quīvīs, quaevīs, quodvīs,** *any whatever.*

quō, see **quī.**

quō, adv. and conj.:
(1) **quō** [dat. or abl. of quī] I, adv., relative and interrogative. *whither, where;* indefinite, after **sī** and **nē,** *to any place, at any point, anywhere.*
(2) **quō** [abl. of quī], conj., used especially with comparatives, followed by subj., *in order that, that, that thereby.* **quō minus,** *that not,* often best translated by *from* with a

participle.

quoad [quō + ad], conj., *as long as* (iv. 12); *until, till* (iv. 11; v. 17, 24)

quod [acc. of **quī**], conj., *because, inasmuch as, since; as to the fact that, so far as.*

quō minus, see **quō** (2).

quoniam [**quom**, old form of **cum**, + **iam**], conj., *since, seeing that, because, inasmuch as.*

quoque, conj., following the emphatic word of a clause, *also, too.*

quōque, abl. of **quisque,** which see.

quōque = **et quō.**

quōque versus, see **versus.**

quot, indeclinable adj., *how many, as many as.* (iv. 22, vii. 19).

quotannīs [**quot** + abl. pl. of **annus**], adv., *yearly, every year.*

quotiēns [**quot**], adv., *as often as* (V. 34); *how often* (I. 43, C. III. 72). [quotient.

quotiēnscumque, [**quotiēns** + **cumque**], adv., *just as often as.* (C. I. 7).

R.

rādīx, -īcis, f., *root* (VI. 27); of an elevation, *foot, base.* **rādīcēs collis,** *the foot of the hill* (VII. 51, 69). **rādīcēs montis,** *the base of the height, the foot of the mountain.* [radish.

rādō, -ere, -rāsī, -rāsus, 3, *shave.* [razor.

raeda, -ae, f., *wagon* with four wheels. (I. 51; VI. 30).

rāmus, -ī, m., *branch, bough, limb.*

rapiditās, -ātis, [**rapidus,** *swift*], f., *swiftness.* (IV. 17). [rapidity.

rapīna, -ae, [cf. **rapiō,** *seize*], f., *pillaging, plundering.* (I. 15). [rapine.

rārus, -a, -um, comp. **-ior,** sup. **rārissimus,** adj., *not thick;* pl., *few, scattered, in small parties.* [rare.

rāsus, see **rādō.**

ratiō, -ōnis, [**reor, reckon**], f., *reckoning, enumeration; account; method, means, way; plan, theory, system, science; reason, ground; condition, situation.* **ratiōnem habere,** *to keep an account* (VI. 19), *take account of* (V. 27, VII. 71; C. III. 82). **ratiōne initā,** *having made calculation* (VII. 71). **abs tē ratiōnem reposcent,** *they will call you to account, will hold you responsible* (V. 30). [ratio, ration, reason.

ratis, -is, f., *raft.*

Rauracī, -ōrum, m., pl., (râ' ra-sī) a people along the upper Rhine, north of the Helvetians.

re-, red-, used only in composition, *again, back.*

rebelliō, -ōnis, [**rebellis,** from **re-** + **bellum**], f., *renewal of fighting, uprising.* **rebelliōnem facere,** *to enter into rebellion, rebel, revolt.* [rebellion.

Rebilus, (reb' i-lus), see **Canīnius.**

recēdō, -cēdere, -cessī, -cessūrus, [**re-** + **cēdō**], 3, *withdraw.* [recede.

recēns, -entis, adj., *fresh; recent, late.* As noun, **recentēs, -ium,** m., pl., *those who were fresh, the unwearied* (V. 16; VII. 48; C. III. 94). [recent.

recēnseō, -ēre, recēnsuī, [**re-** + **cēnseō**], 2, *review, mobilize.* (VII. 76).

receptāculum, -ī, [**receptō**], n., *place of shelter, retreat.* [receptacle.

receptus, see **recipiō.**

receptus, -ūs, [**recipiō**] m., *retreat; avenue of retreat* (VI. 9); *recall,* a signal given with a musical instrument to call soldiers back (VII. 47).

recessus, -ūs, [**recēdō**], m., *a receding; opportunity to draw back* (V. 43). [recess.

recidō, -cidere, -cidī, -cāsūrus, [**re-** + **cadō**], 3, *fall back; come upon, fall to the lot of* (VII. 1).

recipiō, -cipere, -cēpī, -ceptus, [**re-** + **capiō**], 3, *take back, get back, recover, win; receive, admit; take upon one's self* (C. III. 82). **sē recipere,** *to retreat, withdraw; to recover one's self* (II. 12; IV. 27, 34). **recipere in dēditiōnem,** *receive into submission.* [receive.

recitō, -āre, -āvī, -ātus, [**re-** + **citō,** *quote*], 1, *read aloud, recite.* (V. 48). [recite.

reclīnō, -āre, -āvī, -ātus, [**re-** + **clīnō,** *bend*], 1, *bend back.* **sē reclīnāre,** *to lean back* (VI. 27); part. **reclīnātus,** *leaning back* (VI. 27). [recline.

recordor, -ārī, -ātus, [**re-, cor**], 1, dep., *remember, call to mind.* (C. III. 47, 72, 73) [record.

recreō, -āre, -āvī, -ātus, [**re-** + **creō**], 1, *restore, renew.* (C. III. 74). [recreate.

rēctē, comp. **-ius,** sup. **-issimē,** [**rēctus**], adv., *rightly, properly; nobly* (VII. 80); *safely* (VII. 6).

rēctus, -a, -um, comp. **-ior,** sup. **rēctissimus,** [part. of **regō**], adj., *straight, direct.*

recuperō, -āre, -āvī, -ātus, [**re-,** cf. **capiō**], 3, *get back, recover.* [recuperate.

recūsātiō, -ōnis, [**recūsō**], f., *refusal, objection, protest.* (C. III. 98).

recūsō, -āre, -āvī, -ātus, [**re-,** cf. **causa**], 1, *refuse, make refusal, decline; raise objections* (V. 6).

redāctus, see **redigō.**

redditus, see **reddō.**

reddō, -dere, -didī, -ditus, [**red-** + **dō**], 3, *give back, restore, return; render, make* (II. 5). **iūs reddere,** *to dispense justice* (VI. 13). **supplicātiōnem reddere,** *to proclaim a thanksgiving* (VII. 90). **vītam prō vitā reddere,** *to give life for life* (VI. 16). [rendition.

redēmptus, see **redimō.**

redeō, -īre, -iī, -itum est, [**red-** + **eō**], irr., *go back, come back, return; slope down* (II. 8); *be reduced* (V. 48); *be referred* (VI. II). **ad gladiōs redīre,** *to resort to swords, draw swords* (C. III. 93).

redigō, -igere, -ēgī, -āctus, [**red-** + **agō**], 3,

force back; reduce; render, make (II. 27; IV. 3). [redact.

redimō, -imere, -ēmī, -ēmptus, [red- + emō], 3, *buy back, purchase;* of revenues, *buy up, farm* (I. 18). [redeem.

redintegrō, -āre, -āvī, -ātus, [red-+ integrō, *make whole]*, 1, *commence again, renew; revive.* [redintegrate.

reditiō, -ōnis, [cf. redeō] f., *a going back, retaining. (I. 5).*

reditus, -ūs, [cf. redeō] m., *returning, return.* (IV. 30; VI. 29, 36).

Redonēs, -um, m., pl., (red'o-nēz), a people in northwestern Gaul (Fig. 206).

redūcō, -dūcere, -dūxī, -ductus, [re- + dūcō], 3, *lead back, bring* or *conduct back; draw back* (VII. 22, 24); *carry back, put back* (VII. 72). [reduce.

refectus, see **reficiō.**

referō, -ferre, rettulī, -lātus, [re- + ferō], 3, *bring back, carry back* (IV. 28); *bring, carry, convey* to a place or person; *report, announce.* **pedem referre,** *to retreat.* **grātiam referre,** *to make return, requite.* [refer.

reficiō, -ficere, -fēcī, -fectus, [re- + faciō], 3, *repair, refit, restore;* of troops, *refresh* (III. 5; VII. 32, 83); *recruit* (C. III. 87). [refectory.

refrāctus, see **refringō.**

refringō, -fringere, -frēgī, -frāctus, [re- + frangō], 3, *break* (VII. 56); *burst in, break down* (II. 33). [refract.

refugiō, -fugere, -fūgī,[re- + fugiō], 3, *flee back* (V. 35); *flee away, escape.* [refuge.

Rēgīnus, (re-jī'nus), see **Antistius.**

regiō, -ōnis, [cf. regō, *keep straight]*, f., *direction, line; boundary; region, tract, territory.* **rēctā regiōne,** *in a direct line* (VII. 46); *along the line* (VI. 25). **ē regiōne,** *directly opposite.* [region.

rēgius, -a, -um, [rēx], adj., *kingly, royal.* (VII. 32; C. III. 104).

rēgnō, -āre, -āvī, -ātus, [rēgnum], 1, *be king, reign.* (V. 25). [reign.

rēgnum, -ī, [cf. regō], n., *kingship, sovereignty, royal power; absolute authority; territory* subject to a king or ruler, *kingdom,* [reign (noun.)

regō, -ere, rēxī, rēctus, 3, *keep straight; regulate; control, manage* (III. 13); *conduct, carry on* (VI. 17).

reiciō, -icere, -iēcī, -iectus, [re- + iaciō], 3, *throw back, hurl back* (I. 46); of ships, *cast back, carry back* (V. 5, 23); *drive back, repulse* (I. 24; II. 33); *cast away* (V. 30); *throw away* (I. 52). [reject.

reiectus, see **reiciō.**

relanguēscō, -ere, -uī, [re- + languēscō], 3, *become enfeebled, become enervated.* (II. 15).

relātus, see **referō.**

relēgō, -āre, -āvī, -ātus, [re- + lēgō, *depute]*, 1, *banish, remove, treat as an outlaw.* [relegate.

relīctus, see **relinquō.**

religiō, -ōnis, f., *religious scruple, religious obligation, religious observance, superstition.* [religion.

religō, -āre, -āvī, -ātus, [re- + ligō, *bind]*, 1, *bind back; bind fast* (C. II. 6).

relinquō, -linquere, -līquī, -līctus, [re- + linquō, *quit]*, 3, *leave, leave behind; desert, abandon;* of a siege or attack, *leave off, give up.* [relinquish.

reliquus, -a, -um, [cf. relinquō], adj., *remaining, left, the rest.* As noun, **reliquī, -ōrum,** m., pl., *the rest;* **reliquī,** gen. sing. neut., in **nihil reliquī,** *nothing left* (I. 11).

remaneō, -manēre, -mānsī, [re- + maneō], 2, *remain, stay behind.* [remain.

rēmex, -igis, [rēmus, cf. agō], m., *rower.* (III. 9).

Rēmī, -ōrum, m., pl., (rē' mī) a Belgic people, about the headwaters of the Axona (*Aisne*); chief city, Du-rocortorum, now *Reims.*

rēmigō, -āre, [rēmex], 1, *row.* (V. 8).

remigro, -āre, -āvī, [re- + migrō, *remove]*, 1, *move back, return.* (IV. 4, 27). [remigrate.

reminīscor, -minīscī, [re- + MEN in mēns], 3, dep., *remember, recollect.* (I. 13). [reminiscent.

remissus, -a, -um, comp. **-ior,** [part. of **remittō],** adj., *relaxed; mild.* **remissior,** *less severe* (V. 12). [remiss.

remittō, -mittere, -mīsī, -missus, [re- + mittō], 3, *send back; give back, restore* (VII. 20); *relax, diminish* (II. 15; V. 49); *impair, lose* (VI. 14); of a tax, *remit* (I. 44). [remit.

remollēscō, -lēscere, [re- + mollēscō, *grow soft]*, 3, *become weak.* (IV. 2).

remōtus, -a, -um, comp. **-ior,** sup. **-issimus,** [**removeō**], adj., *far off, remote.* (I. 31; VII. 1). [remote.

removeō, -movēre, -mōvī, -mōtus, [re- + moveō], 2, *move back, remove; dismiss* (I. 19). [remove.

remūneror, -ārī, -ātus, [re-, cf. **mūnus]**, 1, dep., *recompense, repay.* (I. 44). [remunerate.

rēmus, -ī, m., *oar.*

Rēmus, -ī, m., *one of the Remi, a Reman.*

rēnō, -ōnis, m., *reindeer skin, deerskin.* (VI. 21).

renovō, -āre, -āvī, -ātus, [re- + novō, from **novus]**, 1, *renew, again commence.* [renovate.

renūntiō, -āre, -āvī, -ātus, [re- + nūntiō], 1, *bring back word, announce; declare elected* (VII. 33). [renounce.

repellō, -pellere, reppulī, repulsus, [re- + pellō], 3, *drive back, force back, repulse.* [repel.

repente, [abl. of repēns, *sudden]*, adv., *suddenly.*

repentīnus, -a, -um, [repēns, *sudden]*, adj., *sudden, unexpected.*

reperiō, -perīre, repperī, repertus, 4, *find, find out; discover, ascertain, learn.*

repetō, -petere, -petīvī or **-petiī, -petītus, [re- + petō]**, 3, *seek again, again try to obtain* (V. 49);

demand (I. 31); *exact* (I. 30). [repeat.
repleō, -plēre, -plēvī, -plētus, [re- + pleō, *fill*], 2, *fill up; supply amply* (VII. 56). [replete.
repōnō, -pōnere, -posuī, -positus, [re- + pōnō], 3, *replace; place, rest* (C. II. 41). [repository.
reportō, -āre, -āvī, -ātus, [re- + portō], 1, *carry back, convey back.* [report.
reposcō, -poscere, [re- + poscō], 3, *demand, require.* (V. 30).
repraesentō, -āre, -āvī, -ātus, [re- + praesentō, from praesēns], 1, *do at once, do forthwith.* (I. 40). [represent.
reprehendō, -hendere, -hendī, -hēnsus, [re- + prehendō], 3, *hold back; criticize, blame.* [reprehend.
repressus, see **reprimō.**
reprimō, -primere, -pressī, -pressus, [re- + premō], 3, *restrain, check; repress.* [repress.
repudiō, -āre, -āvī, -ātus, 1, *reject, scorn.* (I. 40). [repudiate.
repugnō, -āre, -āvī, -ātus, [re- + pugnō], 1, *fight back, resist.* [repugnant.
repulsus, see **repellō.** [repulse.
requiēscō, -ere, requiēvī, requiētus, [re-+ quiēscō], 3, *take rest, rest.* (C. III. 98).
requīrō, -quīrere, -quīsīvī, -quīsītus, [re- + quaerō], 3, *require, demand* (VI. 34); *wish back again, miss* (VII. 63); *seek* (C. III. 35). [require.
rēs, reī, f., *matter, affair; circumstance, fact, transaction; object, project, business.* **rēs mīlitāris,** *warfare, military science.* **rēs novae,** *a revolution.* **praemia reī pecūniāriae,** *rewards in money* (C. III. 59). **quā rē,** *wherefore, and for this reason.* [real.
rescindō, -scindere, -scidī, -scissus, [re- + scindō], 3, *cut down, break up, destroy.* [rescind.
rescīscō, -scīscere, -scīvī, or -sciī, -scītus, [re- + scīscō, *inquire*], 3, *discover, find out.* (I. 28).
rescrībō, -scrībere, -scrīpsī, -scrīptus, [re- + scrībō], 3, *write again; enroll anew, transfer* from one branch of the service to another (I. 42). [rescribe.
reservō, -āre, -āvī, -ātus, [re- + servō], 1, *keep back, keep.* [reserve.
resideō, -sidēre, -sēdī, [re-+ sedeō, *sit*], *linger, remain.* [reside.
resīdō, -sīdere, -sēdī, [re- + sīdō, *sit down*], 3, *settle down, subside.* (VII. 64).
resistō, -sistere, -stitī, [re- + sistō, *set*], 3, *remain, stay; stand still* (C. II. 35); *oppose, withstand, offer resistance.* [resist.
respiciō, -spicere, -spexī, -spectus, [re- + speciō, *look*], 3, *look back* (II. 24; V. 43, C. 11. 35); *look at; consider* (VII. 77). [respect.
respondeō, -spondēre, -spondī, -spōnsus, [re- + spondeō, *promise*], 2, *answer, reply.* [respond.

respōnsum, -ī, [part. of respondeō], n., *answer, reply.* [response.
res pūblica, see **pūblicus.**
respuō, -spuere, -spuī, [re- + spuō], 3, *spit out; reject* (i. 42).
restinguō, -stinguere, -stīnxī, -stīnctus, [re- + stinguō, *quench*], 3, *put out, extinguish.* (vii. 24, 25).
restituō, -uere, -uī, -ūtus, [re- + statuō], 3, *replace, restore; renew, revive; rebuild*(i. 28). [restitution.
retentus, see **retineō.**
retineō, -tinēre, -tinuī, -tentus, [re- + teneō], 2, *restrain, detain, keep back; hold* (vii. 21). [retain.
retrahō, -trahere, -trāxī, -trāctus, [re- + trahō], 3, *bring back* by force. (v. 7). [retract.
revellō, -vellere, -vellī, -vulsus, [re- + vellō, *pull*], 3, *pull back* (i. 52); *tear away* (vii. 73).
reversus, see **revertor.**
revertō, revertī, [re- + vertō], 3, only in tenses from pf. stem, and **revertor, -vertī, -versūrus,** 3, dep., *return, go back.* [revert.
revinciō, -vincīre, -vinxī, -vinctus, [re- + vinciō], 4, *bind back, bind securely, fasten.*
revocō, -āre, -āvī, -ātus, [re- + vocō], 1, *call back, recall.* [revoke.
rēx, rēgis, [cf. regō, *rule*], m., *king, ruler, chieftain.*
Rhēnus, -ī, m., *the Rhine.*
Rhodanus, -ī, m., *the Rhone,* which rises in the Alps near the sources of the Rhine, and passing through Lake Geneva, follows at first a southwesterly direction, then flows south, reaching the Mediterranean after a course of about 500 miles.
rīpa, -ae, f., *bank* of a stream. [river.
rīvus, -ī, m., *stream, brook.* [rival.
rōbur, -oris, n., *oak* (ii. 13); *strength* (C. III. 87). [robust.
rogō, -āre, -āvī, -ātus, 1, *ask, request.* [rogation.
Rōma, -ae, f, *Rome.*
Rōmānus, -a, -um, [Rōma], adj., *Roman.* As noun, **Rōmānus, -ī,** m., *a Roman;* usually pl., *the Romans, Romans.* [Roman.
Rōscius, -ī, m., *Lucius Roscius* (rosh'-[y] us), a lieutenant in Caesar's army.
rōstrum, -ī, [cf. rōdō, *gnaw*], n., *beak;* of a ship, *beak.* [rostrum.
rota, -ae, f., *wheel.* [rotary.
Roucillus, -ī, m., (ru-sil' us), *an Allobrogian,* brother of Egus. (C. III. 59).
rubus, -ī, m., *briar, bramble.* (ii. 17).
Rūfus, -ī, [rūfus, *reddish*], m., (ru'-fus), a Roman cognomen.
rūmor, -ōris, m., *rumor, report, gossip.* [rumor.
rūpēs, -is, [cf. rumpō], f., *cliff.* (ii. 29).
rūrsus, [for revorsus, from revertō], adv.,

again, anew; in turn, on the contrary.

Rutēnī, -ōrum, m., pl., (ru-tē'ni), a Gallic people, west of the Cebenna *(Cévennes)* Mountains; part of them were in the Province, and were called **Rutēnī prōvinciālēs.**

Rutilus (ru' ti-lus), see **Semprōnius.**

S.

Sabīnus, see **Titūrius.**

Sabis, -is, m., *Sabis* (sā'bis), *the Sambre,* a river in the central part of Belgic Gaul flowing northeast into the Mosa *(Meuse).* (II. 16, 18).

Saburra, -ae, m., (sa-bū' ra), a general in Juba's army. (C. II. 38-42).

sacerdōs, -dōtis, [**sacer**, cf. **dō**], m. and f., *priest.* (VII. 33). [sacerdotal.

sacerdōtium, -ī, [**sacerdōs**], n., *priesthood. (C.* III. 82, 83).

sacrāmentum, -ī, [**sacrō**, *set apart as sacred*], n., *oath.* [sacrament.

Sacrātivir, -ī, m., *Marcus Sacrativir,* (sa-krat' i-vir), a Roman knight. (C. III. 71).

sacrificium, -ī, [**sacrificus**, from **sacrum** + FAC in **faciō**], n., *sacrifice.* (VI. 13, 16, 21). [sacrifice.

saepe, comp. **-ius**, sup. **-issimē**, adv. *often, frequently.* Comp., *too often* (III. 6). **saepe numerō**, *oftentimes, repeatedly.*

saepēs, -is, f., *hedge.* (II. 17, 22).

saeviō, -īre, -iī, -ītus, [**saevus**, *fierce*], 4, *rage; be violent* (III. 13).

sagitta, -ae, f., *arrow.*

sagittārius, -ī, [**sagitta**], m., *archer, bowman.* [Sagittarius.

sagulum, -ī, [dim. of **sagum**, *mantle*], n., *small cloak, cloak.* (V. 42).

sāl, salis, m., *salt.* (C. III. 37). [salad.

salīnae, -ārum, f., pl., [**sāl**], *saltworks.* (C. II. 37).

saltem, adv., *at any rate.* (C. I.6).

saltus, -ūs, m., *wooded valley, defile, glen, thicket.* (VI. 43; VII. 19).

salūs, -ūtis, [cf. **salvus**, *well*], f., *health, welfare; safety.* [salutary.

salūtō, -āre, -āvī, -ātus, [**salūs**], 1, *greet, address.* (C. III. 71). [salute.

Samarobrīva, -ae, f., (sam" a-ro-brī' va), a city of the Ambiani on the Samara *(Somme);* now *Amiens.*

sanciō, sancīre, sānxī, sānctus, 4, *make sacred; make binding, ratify.* [sanction.

sānctus, -a, -um, comp. **-ior**, sup. **-issimus**, [**sanciō**], adj., *hallowed, sacred.* [saint.

sanguis, -inis, m., *blood.* [sanguine.

sānitās, -tātis, [**sānus**], f., *soundness of mind, good sense.* [sanity.

sānō, -āre, -āvī, -ātus [cf. **sānus**], 1, *make sound; make good, remedy* (VII. 29).

Santonēs, -um, or **Santonī, -ōrum**, m., pl.,

(san' to-nēz, san' to-nī), a Gallic people on the seacoast north of the Garuinna *(Garonne).* Fig. 207.

sānus, -a, -um, comp. **-ior**, sup. **sānissimus**, adj., *sound, healthy, rational.* As noun, **prō sanō**, *as a prudent man* (V. 7). [sane.

sapiō, -ere, -īvī, 3, *taste; be sensible, understand* (V. 30). [sapient.

sarcinae, -ārum, [**sarciō**], f., pl., *packs,* carried by the soldiers on their backs.

sarciō, -īre, sarsī, sartus, 4, *mend; make good* (VI. I; C. III. 73); *wipe out* (C. III. 74). [sartorial.

sarmentum, -ī, [**sarpō**, *prune*], n., *a branch;* pl., *brushwood* (III. 18).

satis, adv., *enough, sufficiently, tolerably, rather;* often used as a noun, especially with a gen. of the whole as **satis causae**, *sufficient reason.*

satisfaciō [**satis** + **faciō**], **-facere, -fēcī, -factus**, irr., *satisfy, give satisfaction; make restitution* (I. 14, V. 1); *appease, placate* (VII. 89); *make apology, apologise* (I. 41, V. 54). [satisfy.

satisfactiō, -ōnis, [**satisfaciō**], f., *apology, excuse.* [satisfaction.

Sāturnīnus, -ī, m., *L. Appuleius Saturninus* (sat-ur-nī' nus), a tribune in 100 B.C. (C. I. 7).

satus, see **serō.**

saucius, -a, -um, adj., *wounded* (V. 36). As noun, **saucius, -ī**, m., *a wounded man* (III. 4).

saxum, -ī, n., *stone, rock.*

Scaeva, -ae, m., *Cassius Scaeva* (se'va), a brave centurion in Caesar's army. (C. III. 53).

scālae, -ārum, [cf. **scandō**, *climb*], f., pl., *ladder, scaling-ladder.* [scale.

Scaldis, -is, m., *the Schelde,* which rises in France near the headwaters of the *Somme* (Samara), and flows northeast to the sea. (VI. 33).

scapha, -ae, [ΣΚΑΦΗ], f., *skiff, small boat.*

scelerātus, -a, -um, comp. **-ior**, sup. **-issimus**, [part. of **scelerō**, from **scelus**], adj., *wicked, infamous* (VI. 34). As noun, **scelerātus, -ī**, m., *a crime-polluted man* (VI. 13).

scelus, sceleris, n., *crime, wickedness.* (I. 14).

scienter, comp. **scientius**, sup. **scientissimē**, [**sciēns**], adv., *cleverly, skilfully.* (VII. 22).

scientia, -ae, [**sciēns**], f., *knowledge, skill.* [science.

scindō, -ere, scidī, scissus, 3, *tear, cut, split; tear down, break down* (III. 5; V. 51).

sciō, scīre, scīvī, scītus, 4, *know, understand.*

Scīpiō, -ōnis, m., *Q. Caecilius Metellus Scipio* (sip' i-ō), a prominent partisan of Pompey, who married his daughter Cornelia as fifth wife. (C. III. 82, 83, 88, 90).

scorpiō, -ōnis, [ΣΚΟΡΠΙΩΝ],m., *a scorpion; scorpion,* a military engine (VII. 25). [scorpion.

scrībō, scrībere, scrīpsī, scrīptus, 3, *write, write down.* [scribe.

scrobis, -is, m. and f., *hole, pit; wolf-hole, wolf-pit.* [scrobicule.

scūtum, -ī, n., oblong *shield.*

sē, sēsē, see **suī.**

sē-, sēd-, in composition, *apart from, without.*

sēbum, -ī, n., *fat, tallow.* [sebaceous.

sēcessiō, -ōnis, [**sēcēdō**], f., *withdrawal.* (C. I. 7). [secession.

sēclūdō, -ere, -sī, -sus, [**sē- + claudō**], 3, *shut off.* (C. II. 97). [seclude.

secō, -āre, -uī, -tus, 1, *cut.* [sector.

sēcrētō [**sēcrētus**], adv., *secretly, privately.* (I. 18, 31).

sectiō, -ōnis, [**secō**], f., *booty,* [section.

sector, -ārī, -ātus, [freq. of **sequor**], 1, dep., *pursue, chase.* (VI. 35).

sectūra, -ae, [**secō**], f., *a cutting* through earth, *digging, excavation.* (III. 21).

secundum, [**sequor**], prep, with acc. only, *along, next to, by the side of* (II. 18; VII. 34); *according to* (IV. 17); *besides* (I. 33).

secundus, -a, -um, comp. **-ior**, sup. **-issimus**, [**sequor**], adj., *second, next; propitious, fortunate, favourable.* [second.

secūris, -is, [cf. **secō**], f., *axe;* pl. referring to the axes of the lictors, *the lictor's axe* (VII. 77).

sed, conj., *but; yet, but yet.*

sēd-, see **sē-.**

sēdecim, or **XVI**, [**sex + decem**], indeclinable num. adj., *sixteen.*

sēdēs, -is, [cf. **sedeō**, *sit*], f., *seat; habitation, abode, settlement, home.*

sēditiō, -ōnis, [**sēd- + itiō**, from **īre**], f., *mutiny, revolt.* (VII. 28). [sedition.

sēditiōsus, -a, -um, sup. **-issimus**, [**sēditiō**], adj., *mutinous.* [seditious.

Sedulius, -ī, m., (se-dū' li-us), a leader of the Lemovices. (VII. 88).

Sedūnī, -ōrum, m., pl., (se-dū' nī), a people in the Alps southeast of Lacus Lemannus (*Lake Geneva*).

Sedusiī, -ōrum, m., pl., (se-dū'- sh[y]-ī), a German tribe. (I. 51).

seges, -etis, f., *grain-field.* (VI. 36).

Segnī, -ōrum, m., pl., (seg' nī) a German tribe settled in Belgic Gaul. (VI. 32).

Segontiācī, -ōrum, m., pl., (seg"-on-shi-ā' sī), a people in the southern part of Britain. (V. 21).

Segovax, -actis, m., (seg' o-vaks), a British chieftain. (V. 22).

Segusiāvī, -ōrum, m., pl., (seg"ū- shi-ā' vī), a Gallic people, subject to the Aeduans. Fig. 208.

semel, adv., *once.* **semel atque iterum**, *time and again* (I. 31).

sēmentis, -is, [**sēmen**, *seed*], 1, *sowing, seeding* (I. 3).

sēmita, -ae, f., *path, by-way.*

semper, adv., *always, ever, constantly.*

Semprōnius, -ī, m., *Marcus Sempronius Rutilus* (sem-prō' ni-us ru' ti-lus), a Roman cavalry officer. (VII. 90).

senātor, -ōris, [cf. **senex**], m., member of the Roman Senate, *senator;* member of a Gallic state-council, *councillor, senator* (II. 28). [senator.

senātōrius, -a, -um, [**senator**], adj., *senatorial,* **ōrdō senātōrius**, *senatorial rank* (C. III. 83, 97). [senatorial.

senātus, -ūs, [cf. **senex**], m., *council of elders, senate,* [senate.

senex, -is, comp. **senior**, adj., *old, aged.* As noun, m., *old man* (I. 29); **seniōrēs, -um**, m., pl., *older men* (C. II. 4). [senile.

sēnī, -ae, -a, [**sex**], distrib. num. adj., *six each, six.* (I. 15).

Senonēs, -um, m., pl., (sen'o-nēz), a Gallic people south of the Matrona (*Marne*); chief city Agedincum, now *Sens.*

sententia, -ae, [cf. **sentiō**], f., *opinion, view, notion, conviction; decision, judgment.* **sententiam dīcere**, *to express an opinion.* **sententiās ferre**, *to vote* (C. III. 83). [sentence.

sentiō, sentīre, sēnsī, sēnsus, 4, *perceive* through the senses, *become aware, learn; feel, think; know.* [sense.

sentis, -is, m, *thorn-bush.* (II. 17).

sēparātim [**sēparātus**], adv., *separately, apart.*

sēparātus, -a, -um, [part. of **sēparō**], adj., *separate, marked off.* [separate.

sēparō, -āre, -āvī, -ātus, [**sē- + parō**], 1, *part, separate.* (VII. 63). [separate (verb).

septem, or **VII**, indeclinable num. adj., *seven.* [September.

septentriō, -ōnis, [**septem + triō**, *plough-ox*], m., generally pl., **septentriōnēs, -um**, *the seven plough-oxen*, the seven stars forming the constellation of the Great Bear; *the North.* [septentrional.

Septimius, -ī, m., *Lucius Septimius* (sep-tim' i-us), a military tribune. (C. III. 104).

septimus, -a, -um, [**septem**], num. adj., *the seventh.* [septimal.

septingentī, -ae, -a, or **DCC**, [**septem + centum**], num. adj., *seven hundred.* (V. 13; VII. 51).

septuāgintā, or **LXX**, indeclinable num. adj., *seventy.* [Septuagint.

sepultūra, -ae, [cf. **sepeliō**, *bury*], f., *burial.* (I. 26). [sepulture.

Sēquana, -ae, f., *Sequana* (sek'-wa-na), *the Seine*, the principal river of Northern France.

Sēquanī, -ōrum, m., pl., *the Sequanians, Sequani* (sek' wa-nī), a Gallic people west of the Jura; chief city Vesontio, now *Besançon.*

Sēquanus, -a, -um, adj., *Sequanian, of the Sequanians* (I. 31) As noun, **Sēquanus, -ī**, m., *a Sequanian* (I. 3).

sequor, -quī, -cūtus, 3, dep., *follow, follow after; pursue; take advantage of* (V. 8); *hold to, maintain* (VII. 63). **Caesaris fidem sequī,** *to attach one's self to Caesar* (V. 20, 56). [sequence.

Ser., = Servius.

sermō, -ōnis, m., *talk, conversation.* [sermon.

sērō, comp. **sērius,** sup. **-issimē, [sērus,** *late*], adv., *late; too late* (V. 29).

serō, serere, sēvī, satus, 3, *sow, plant.*

Sertōrius, -ī, m., *Quintus Sertorius* (ser-tō' ri-us), a Roman general. (III. 23).

servīlis, -e, [servus], adj., *servile, of slaves.* (I. 40; VI. 19). [servile.

serviō, -īre, -iī, -ītus, [servus], 4, *be the slave of, follow* (IV. 5); *devote one's self to* (VII. 34). [serve.

servitus, -tutis, [servus], f., *slavery, bondage, subjection.* [servitude.

Servius, -ī, m., (ser'vi-us), a Roman first name.

servō, -āre, -āvī, -ātus, 1, *save; keep, maintain, retain; save up* (VI. 19); *keep watch of, watch* (V. 19); *keep up the watch* (II. 33).

servus, -ī, m., *slave.* [serf.

sescentī, -ae, -a, or **DC, [sex + centum],** num. adj., *six hundred.*

sēsē, see **suī.**

sēsquipedālis, -e, [sēsqui-, *one half more,* + **pedālis; sēsqui- = sēmis,** *one half,* + **-que**], adj., *a foot and a half* in thickness. (IV. 17).

sēstertius, -a, -um, [for sēmis tertius, *three less one half*], num. adj., *two and a half* As subst., **sēstertius, -ī,** (originally sc. **nummus**), gen. pl. **sēstertium,** m., *sesterce,* a small silver coin, originally 2.5 *asses,* = about 4.10 cents.

sētius, adv., comp., *less.* **nihilō sētius,** *none the less, nevertheless.*

seu, see **sīve.**

sevēritās, -tātis, [sevērus, *severe*], f., *sternness, rigor, strictness.* (VII. 4). [severity.

sēvocō, -āre, -āvī, -ātus, [sē- + vocō], 1, *call apart, call aside.*

sex, or **VI,** indeclinable num. adj., *six.* [sextet.

sexāgintā, or **LX,** indeclinable num. adj., *sixty.*

Sextius, -ī, m., (seks' ti-us):
(1) *Publius Sextius Baculus,* see **Baculus.**
(2) *Titus Sextius,* a lieutenant.

sī, conj., *if whether.* **quod sī,** *but if, now if.* **sī quidem,** *if indeed, in so far as* (VI. 36).

Sibusātēs, -um, m., pl., (sib-ū-sā'-tēz), a people in Aquitania. (III. 27).

sīc, adv., *so, in this way, thus; as follows* (11. 4). **ut . . . sīc,** *as . . . so.* **sīc . . . ut,** *so . . . that.*

siccitās, -tātis, [siccus, *dry*], f., *dryness, drouth.*

Sicilia, -ae, f., the island of *Sicily.*

sīcut or **sīcutī, [sīc + utī],** adv., *just as, as.*

sīdus, -eris, n., *constellation;* pl., **sīdera,** *heavenly bodies,* sun, moon, and stars (VI. 14). [sidereal.

signifer, -ferī, [signum, cf. **ferō],** m., *standard-bearer, ensign.* (II. 25).

significātiō, -ōnis, [significō], f., *sign, signal, intimation; demeanor* (VII. 12). **significātiōnem facere,** *to give notice, convey information* (II. 33, V. 53, VI. 29). [signification.

significō, -āre, -āvī, -ātus, [signum, + FAC in faciō], 1, *show by signs, show, intimate, indicate; transmit the news* (VII. 3). [significant.

signum, -ī, n., *signal; standard, ensign.* **signum dare,** *to give the signal.* [sign.

Sīlānus, -ī, m., *Marcus Silanus* (si-lā' nus), a lieutenant of Caesar. (VI. 1).

silentium, -ī, [silēns, *silent*], n., *silence, stillness.* [silence.

Sīlius, -ī, m., *Titus Silius* (sil'i-us), a military tribune. (III. 7, 8).

silva, -ae, f., *wood, forest.* [sylvan.

silvestris, -e, [silva], adj., *covered with woods, wooded.* [sylvestral.

similis, -e, comp. **similior,** sup. **simillimus,** adj., *like, similar.* [similar.

similitūdō, -inis, [similis], f., *likeness, similarity.* [similitude.

simul, adv., *at the same time, at once; as soon as* (IV. 26). **simul . . . simul,** *both . . . and, partly . . . partly.* **simul atque,** *as soon as.*

simulācrum, -ī, [cf. simulō], n., *image.* (VI. 16, 17).

simulātiō, -ōnis, [cf. simulō], f., *pretense, deceit.* [simulation.

simul atque, see **simul.**

simulō, -āre, -āvī, -ātus, [similis], 1, *make like; pretend, feign* (I. 44; IV, 4). [simulate.

simultās, -tātis, [simul], f., *rivalry, jealousy, bitterness* toward a rival (V. 44).

sīn [sī + ne], conj., *if however, but if.*

sincērē [sincērus, *pure*], adv., *frankly, sincerely.* (VII. 20).

sine, prep. with abl. only, *without.*

singillātim, [singulī], adv., *one by one, singly.* (III. 2; V. 4, 52).

singulāris, -e, [singulī], adj., *one by one, one at a time* (IV. 26; VII. 8); *singular, extraordinary.* [singular.

singulī, -ae, -a, distrib. num. adj., *one to each, one by one, one apiece; separate, single.* [single.

sinister, -tra, -trum, adj., *left.* [sinister.

sinistra, -ae, [sc. manus], f., *left hand* (I. 25). **sub sinistrā,** *on the left* (V. 8).

sinistrōrsus [sinister + vorsus, cf. **vertō],** adv., *to the left.* (VI. 25).

sī quidem, see **sī.**

situs, -ūs, [cf. sinō], m., *situation, location, site.* [site.

sīve or **seu [sī + ve],** conj., *or if.* **sīve (seu) . . .**

sīve (seu), *if . . . or if, whether . . . or, either . . . or, it might be . . . or.*

socer, -erī, m., *father-in-law.* (I. 12).

societās, -tātis, [**socius**], f., *fellowship; alliance, confederacy* (VI. 2); *corporation, association* for business purposes (C. III. 103). [society.

socius, -ī, m., *comrade, ally;* in Caesar generally pl., **sociī**, *allies.* [social.

sōl, sōlis, m., *the sun.* **oriente sōle**, *at sunrise* (VII. 3). [solar.

Sōl, -is, m., *god of the sun, sun-god.* (VI. 21).

sōlācium, -ī, [cf. **sōlor**, *console*], n., *consolation, comfort.* (VII. 15). [solace.

soldurius, -ī, m., *retainer, follower, vow-beholden.* (III. 22).

soleō, -ēre, -itus sum, semi-dep., 2, *be wont, be accustomed.*

sōlitūdō, -inis, [**sōlus**], f., *wilderness, waste* (IV. 18; VI. 23). [solitude.

sollertia, -ae, [**sollers**, *skilful*], f., *skill, cleverness, ingenuity.*

sollicitō, -āre, -āvī, -ātus, [**sollicitus**, *agitated*], 1, *instigate, urge, incite; tamper with, tempt.* [solicit.

sollicitūdō, -inis, [**sollicitus**], f., *anxiety, apprehension.* [solicitude.

solum, -ī, n., *lowest part, ground;* of a trench, *bottom* (VII. 72). **agrī solum**, *the bare ground* (I. 11).

sōlum [acc. of **sōlus**], adv., *only.* **nōn sōlum . . . sed etiam**, *not only . . . but also.*

sōlus, -a, -um, gen. **sōlius**, adj., *only, alone.* [sole.

solvō, -ere, solvī, solūtus, [**se-**, = **sē-**, + **luō**, *loose*], 3, *loose; set sail* (IV. 23, 28; V. 23). [solve.

somnus, -ī, m., *sleep.* (C. II. 38).

sonitus, -ūs, [cf. **sonō**, *sound*], m., *noise, sound.* (VII. 60, 61).

sonus, -ī, m., *sound.* (VII. 47). [sound.

soror, -ōris, f., *sister.* **soror ex mātre**, *half sister on the mother's side* (I. 18). [sorority.

sors, sortis, f., *lot, chance.* [sort.

Sōtiātēs, -ium, m., pl., (sō-shi-ā'-tēz), a people in northern Aquitania. (III. 20, 21).

spatium, -ī, n., *space, distance; interval, time, period, duration.* **ā tantō spatiō**, *at so great a distance, so far off* (II. 30). **nactus spatium**, *having gained time* (V. 58). [space.

speciēs, -iēī, [cf. **speciō**, *look*], f., *sight, show, appearance; pretense.* **ad speciem**, *for show* (I. 51). [species.

spectō, -āre, -āvī, -ātus, [freq. of **speciō**, *look*], 1, *look at, regard* (I. 45; V. 29); *have in view* (C. III. 85); *face, lie* (I. 1; V. 13; VII. 69). [spectacle.

speculātor, -tōris, [**speculor**], m., *spy, scout.* [speculator.

speculātōrius, -a, -um, [**speculātor**], adj., *scouting, spying.* **speculātōrium nāvigium**,

spy-boat (IV. 26). [speculatory.

speculor, -ārī, -ātus, [cf. **specula**, *watch-tower*], 1, dep., *spy out, spy.* (I. 47). [speculate.

spērō, -āre, -āvī, -ātus, [cf. **spēs**], 1, *hope, expect.*

spēs, speī, f., *hope, expectation.*

Spinther, -ēris, m., (spin' ther), *P. Cornelius Lentulus Spinther*, a prominent adherent of Pompey in the Civil War. (C. III. 83).

spīritus, -ūs, [cf. **spīrō**, *breathe*], m., *breath, air;* pl., *haughtiness, pride* (I. 33; II. 4). [spirit.

spoliō, -āre, -āvī, -ātus, [**spolium**, *booty*], 1, *strip, despoil.* [spoil (verb).

spolium, -ī, n., usually in pl., *booty, spoils.* (C. II. 39). [spoil (noun).

sponte, abl., and **spontis**, gen., only forms in use of an obsolete nom. **spōns**, f., *of one's own accord, willingly.* **suā sponte**, *of their own accord, of their own initiative* (I. 44, VI. 14, C. III. 93); *on their own account, unaided* (V. 28; VII. 65); *by their own influence* (I. 9). [spontaneous.

stabiliō, -īre, -īvī, -ītus, [**stabilis**], 4, *make steady; make fast* (VII. 73).

stabilitās, -tātis, [**stabilis**], f., *steadiness.* (IV. 33). [stability.

statim [**stō**], adv., *on the spot; immediately, at once, straightaway.*

statiō, -ōnis, [cf. **stō**], f., *outpost, picket, guard; reserves* (V. 16). **in statiōne**, *on guard.* [station.

statuō, -uere, -uī, -ūtus, [**status**], 3, *set, place; determine, resolve; judge, think.* [statute.

statūra, -ae, [cf. **stō**], f., *height, stature.* (II. 30; VI. 21). [stature.

status, -ūs, [**stō**], m., *condition, position, situation.* [status.

stimulus, -ī, m., *goad; pricker* like a goad (VII. 73, 82). [stimulus.

stīpendiārius, -a, -um, [**stīpendium**], adj., *tributary, subject to payment of tribute* (I. 30, 36). As noun, **stīpendiāriī, -ōrum**, m., pl., *tributaries, dependents* (VII. 10). [stipendiary.

stīpendium, -ī, [**stips**, *coin*, cf. **pendō**, *weigh*], n., *tribute;* of soldiers, *pay.* [stipend.

stīpes, -itis, m., *stock of a tree, log.* (VII. 73).

stirps, -is, f., *stem; stock, race* (VI. 34).

stō, stāre, stetī, statūrus, 1, *stand, stand upright* (VI. 27); *be posted, be placed* (V. 35, 43); *abide by* (VI. 13).

strāmentum, -ī, [cf. **sternō**, *strew*], n., *thatch* of houses (V. 43); *pack-saddle* (VII. 45).

strepitus, -ūs, [**strepō**], m., *noise, uproar.*

stringō, -ere, strīnxī, strictus, 3, *bind tight;* of a sword, *draw* (C. III. 93). [stringent

struō, -ere, strūxī, strūctus, 3, *build, construct.* (C. III. 96).

studeō, -ēre, -uī, 2, *be eager for, strive for; be devoted to, pay heed to; eagerly desire, strive.* **novīs rēbus** or **imperiīs studēre**, *to desire a*

revolution.[student.
studiōsē, comp. **-ius,** sup. **-issimē,**
[**studiōsus,** *eager*], adv., *eagerly, diligently.*
studium, -ī, [cf. **studeō**], n., *eagerness, energy,
enthusiasm; goodwill* (I. 19); *pursuit.* **studia reī
mīlitāris,** *pursuits of war, military pursuits* (VI.
21). [study.
stultitia, -ae, [**stultus**], f., *folly, lack of foresight.*
(VII. 77).
stultus, -a, -um, adj., *foolish.* (C. III. 59). [stultify.
sub, prep.:
(1) With acc., after verbs of motion, *under,
towards, near to, just before.*
(2) With abl., *under, at the foot of, close by;* of
time, *on, in, during.*
subāctus, see **subigō.**
subdolus, -a, -um, [**sub + dolus**], adj., *crafty,
cunning.* (VII. 31).
subdūcō, -dūcere, -dūxī, -ductus, [**sub +
dūcō**], 3, *lead up* from a lower to a higher
position (I. 22, 24); of ships, *draw up, haul on
shore, beach* (IV. 29; V. II. 24).
subductiō, -ōnis, [**subdūcō**], 1., *hauling on
shore, beaching.* (V. 1).
subeō, -īre, -iī, -itūrus, [**sub + eō**], irr., *go
under* (I. 36); *come up, approach, go up (to),* from
a lower position (II. 25, 27; VII. 85); *undergo, suffer.*
subfodiō, -fodere, -fōdī, -fossus, [**sub +
fodiō**], 3, *stab underneath.* (IV. 12).
subfossus, see **subfodiō.**
subiciō, -icere, -iēcī, -iectus, [**sub + iaciō**], 3,
throw under, place near; throw from beneath (I. 26);
expose (IV. 36, C. III. 85); *make subject* (VII. 1, 77).
subiectus, -a, -um, comp. **-ior,** [**subiciō**], adj.,
lying near, adjacent. (V. 13). [subject.
subigō, -igere, -ēgī, -āctus, [**sub + agō**], 3,
subdue; constrain, reduce to straits (VII. 77).
subitō, [abl. of **subitus**], adv., *suddenly, on a
sudden.*
subitus, -a, -um, [**subeō**], adj., *sudden,
unexpected.*
sublātus, see **tollō.**
sublevō, -āre, -āvī, -ātus, [**sub + levō**], 1, *lift
up, support, hold up* (I. 48; VI. 27; VII. 47); *relieve,
assist, aid, support* (I. 16, 40; VII. 14, 65); of labor,
lighten (VI. 32); *retrieve* (C. III. 73).
sublica, -ae, f., *stake, pile.*
subluō, -luere, — , -lūtus, [**sub + luō**], 3, *wash*
(VII. 69); *flow at the foot of* (C. III. 97).
subruō, -ruere, -ruī, -rutus, [**sub + ruō**, *fall*],
3, *undermine.*
subsequor, -sequī, -secūtus, [**sub + sequor**],
3, dep., *follow close upon, follow after, follow up.*
[subsequent.
subsidium, -ī, [cf. **subsīdō**], n., *reserve, reserve
force, auxiliaries; support, relief, help, aid;
relieving force; resource, remedy.* **mittere
subsidiō,** *to send help.* [subsidy.

subsīdō, -sīdere, -sēdī, [**sub + sīdō,** *sit*], 3,
stay behind, remain behind. (VI. 36). [subside.
subsistō, -sistere, -stitī, [**sub + sistō,** *set*], 3,
halt, make a stand (I. 15); *hold out* (V. 10). [subsist.
subsum, -esse, [**sub + sum**], irr., *be near* (I. 25;
V. 29); of time, *be close at hand, not far off* (III. 27; V.
23, C. II. 97).
subtrahō, -trahere, -trāxī, -trāctus, [**sub +
trahō**], 3, *carry off, draw off underneath* (VII. 22);
withdraw, take away (I. 44). [subtract.
subvectiō, -ōnis, [**subvehō**], f., *transportation.*
(VII. 10).
subvehō, -vehere, -vexī, -vectus, [**sub +
vehō**], 3, *bring up.* (I. 16).
subveniō, -venīre, -vēnī, subventum est,
[**sub + veniō**], 4, *come to the help of, come to the
rescue of; assist, succor, render assistance.*
[subvention.
succēdō, -cēdere, -cessī, -cessūrus, [**sub +
cēdō**], 3, *come up, approach, advance; succeed* to
another's place, *take the place of, relieve, follow;
become the successor* (VI. 13); *prosper, succeed* (VII.
26). [succeed.
succendō, -cendere, -cendī, -cēnsus, [**sub,** cf.
candeō], 3, *set on fire, set fire to.*
succīdō, -cīdere, -cīdī, -cīsus, [**sub + caedō**],
3, *cut down.*
succumbō, -cumbere, -cubuī, [**sub + cumbō,**
for **cubō**], 3, *yield, succumb.* (VII. 86). [succumb.
succurrō, -currere, -currī, -cursum est, [**sub +
currō**], 3, *run to help, succor.* (V. 44; VII. 80).
[succor.
sudis, -is, f., *stake, pile.*
sūdor, -ōris, [cf. **sūdō,** *sweat*], m., *sweat; toil,
effort* (VII. 8). [sudary.
Suāba, -ae, [**Suēbus,** cf. **Suēbī**], f., *a Swabian
woman.* (I. 53).
Suēbī, -ōrum, [Ger., = 'Nomads'], m., pl., *the
Swabians, Suebi* (swē' bī), a powerful German
people.
Suessiōnēs, -um, m., pl., (swes-i-ō'-nēz), a
Belgic people north of the Matrona (*Marne*);
the name survives in *Soissons.*
sufficiō, -ficere, -fēcī, -fectus, [**sub + faciō**], 3,
hold out. (VII. 20). [suffice.
suffrāgium, -ī, n., *vote.* [suffrage.
Sugambrī, -ōrum, m., pl., (sū-gam'-brī), a
German people.
suggestus, -ūs, [**suggerō,** *raise up*], m.,
platform (VI. 3).
suī, sibi, sē or **sēsē,** nom. wanting, reflex.
pron., *himself, herself, itself, themselves, him,
her, it.*
Sulla, -ae, m., (sul' a):
(1) *Lucius Cornelius Sulla,* born 138 B.C.; consul
88, dictator 81-79 B.C.; leader of the
aristocratic party in the first Civil War, enemy
of Marius; died 78 B.C. (I. 21; C. I. 7).

(2) *Faustus Cornelius Sulla,* son of the dictator. (C. I. 6).

(3) *Publius Cornelius Sulla,* nephew of the dictator, who fought under Caesar. (C. III. 89, 99).

Sulpicius, -ī, m., (sulpish' [y]us):

(1) *Publius Sulpicius Rufus,* a lieutenant of Caesar in Gaul and afterwards in the Civil War. (IV. 22, VII. 90).

(2) *Servius Sulpicius,* Roman senator. (C. II. 44).

sum, esse, fuī, futūrus, irr., *be, exist.* [future.

summa, -ae, [summus; sc. **rēs],** f., *sum total, aggregate, whole* (I. 29; VI. II, 34; C. III. 89); *general management, control, administration; determination, deciding* (VI. 11). **summa imperī,** *the supreme command.* [sum.

sumministrō, -āre, -āvī, -ātus, [sub + ministrō, *serve],* 1, *supply, provide, furnish.*

summittō, -mittere, -mīsī, -missus, [sub + mittō], 3, *send secretly; send as reinforcement, send as help.* [submit.

summoveō, -movēre, -mōvī, -mōtus, [sub + moveō], 2, *force back.*

summus, see **superus.**

sūmō, sūmere, sūmpsī, sūmptus, 3, *take* (I. 7, 16; VII. 65); *take to one's self, take on, assume* (I. 33; II. 4); *put forth, expend, spend* (III. 14). **dē aliquō supplicium sūmere,** *to inflict punishment on any one* (I. 31; VI. 44).

sūmptuōsus, -a, -um, comp. **-ior, [sūmptus],** adj., *costly.* (VI. 19). [sumptuous.

sūmptus, -tūs, [sūmō], m., *expense.* (I. 18). [sumptuary.

superbē, comp. **-ius,** sup. **-issimē, [superbus,** *proud],* adv., *haughtily.*

superior, see **superus.**

superō, -āre, -āvī, -ātus, [superus], 1, *conquer, overcome, vanquish, defeat; surpass* (VI. 24); *surmount* (VII. 24); *rise above* (III. 14); *prove superior* (III. 14); *carry the day* (V. 31); *survive* (VI. 19). [superable.

supersedeō, -sedēre, -sēdī, [super + sedeō, *sit],* 2, *refrain from.* (II. 8). [supersede.

supersum, -esse, -fuī, [super + sum], irr., *remain, be left* (I. 23; III. 28; V. 22; C. III. 91); *survive* (I. 26; II. 27, 28).

superus, -a, -um, comp. **superior,** sup. **summus** or **suprēmus, [super],** adj., *above, on high.* Comp., **superior, -ius,** *higher, upper, superior;* of time, *former, earlier,* as **superiōre nocte,** *the previous night* (V. 10). Sup., **summus, a,-um,** *highest; greatest, very great; most important, chief; all together, all* (V. 17; VII. 41); often denoting a part, as **summus mōns,** *the top of the height* (I. 22). As noun, **summum, -ī,** n., *top, end.* **ab summō,** *from the top* (II. 18); *at the end* (VII. 73); *from the end* (VI. 26). [superior, supreme.

suppetō, -petere, -petīvī or **-iī, -petītus, [sub + petō],** 3, *be at hand, be available; hold out* (VII. 77, 85).

supplēmentum, -ī, [suppleō, *fill up],* n., *raw contingent,* a body of recruits under training, not yet assigned to the legions in which they will serve. [supplement.

supplex, -icis, m. and f., *suppliant.* (II. 28).

supplicātiō, -ōnis, [supplicō], f., *solemn thanksgiving, thanksgiving.* [supplication.

suppliciter [supplex], adv., *after the manner of a suppliant, humbly.*

supplicium, -ī, [cf. supplex], n., *punishment; death-penalty, execution.*

supportō, -āre, -āvī, [sub + portō], 1, *bring up, transport, convey.* [support.

suprā, adv. and prep.:

(1) As adv., *above; before, previously.*

(2) As prep., with acc., *above;* of time, *beyond, before* (VI. 19).

suscipiō, -cipere, -cēpī, -ceptus, [subs, for sub, + capiō], 3, *undertake, take up; take upon one's self, assume* (I. 3). **bellum suscipere,** *to commence war.* [susceptible.

suspectus, -a, -um, comp. **-ior,** adj., *under suspicion.* [suspect.

suspīciō, -ōnis, f., *suspicion; reason to suspect* (I. 4). [suspicion.

suspicor, -ārī, -ātus, [cf. suspiciō], 1, dep., *suspect, mistrust, surmise.*

sustentō, -āre, -āvī, -ātus, [freq. of sustineō], 1, *sustain, endure, bear, hold out.*

sustineō, -tinēre, -tinuī, -tentus, [subs, for sub, + teneō], 2, *hold up* (VII. 56); *check, pull up* (IV. 33); *hold out, bear, endure; hold out against, withstand.* [sustain.

sustulī, see **tollō.**

suus, -a, -um, [cf. suī], possessive pronominal adj., *his, her, its, their; his own, her own, their own,* etc.; with **locō, locīs,** *favorable to himself, to themselves.* As noun, **suī,** m., pl., *his, their friends, people, party, side;* **suum, -ī,** n., *their own* (I. 43); **sua,** n., pl., *his, her, their property, possessions.* **sē suaque,** *themselves and their possessions* (I. 11, II. 31).

Syria, -ae, [ΣΥΡΙΑ], f., (sir'i-a), a country lying east of the Mediterranean Sea, between Cilicia and Palestine; organized into a Roman province in 64 B.C. (C. I. 6, III. 103).

Syriacus, -a, -um, [Syria], adj., *Syrian.* (C. III. 88).

T.

T. = Titus (tī'tus), a Roman first name.

tabella, -ae, [dim. of **tabula**], f., *tablet; voting-tablet, ballot* (C. III. 83).

tabernāculum, -i, [taberna, *hut],* n., *tent, hut.* [tabernacle.

tabula, -ae, f., *board; writing-tablet; list* written

on a tablet (I. 29). [table.

tabulātum, -ī, [cf. **tabula**], n., *floor, storey.* (VI. 29). [tabulate.

taceō, -ēre, -uī, -ītus, 2, *be silent, remain silent* (i. 17); *say nothing of, pass over in silence* (I. 17).

tacitus, -a, -um, [part. of **taceō**], adj., *silent.* (i. 32). [tacit.

tālea, -ae, f., *stick, block* (VII. 73); *bar* (V. 12). [tally.

tālis, -e, adj., *such.*

tam, adv., *so, so very.*

tamen, adv., *yet, still, for all that, nevertheless, however.*

Tamesis, -is, m., *the Thames.*

tametsī [**tam**, = **tamen**, + **etsī**], conj., *although, though.*

tandem [**tam**], adv., *at length, finally; in* questions, *pray* (i. 40).

tangō, tangere, tetigī, tāctus, 3, *touch, border on.* (v. 3). [tact.

tantopere [**tantō opere**], adv., *so earnestly, with so great effort.* (i. 31).

tantulus, -a, -um, [dim. of **tantus**], adj., *so small, so slight, so trifling.*

tantum [acc. of **tantus**], adv., *only so much, so far, merely.* **tantum modo,** *only* (iii. 5).

tantundem [acc. neut. of **tantusdem**], adv., *just so much.* (vii. 72).

tantus, -a, -um, adj., *so great, so large, so much, so extensive, so important.* **tantus . . . quantus,** *so great, so much, only so much . . . as.*

Tarbellī, -ōrum, m., pl., (tar-bel' ī), a people in Aquitania, near the Ocean. (iii. 27).

tardē, comp. **-ius,** sup. **-issimē,** [**tardus**], adv., *slowly;* comp., *rather slowly* (iv. 23, C. III. 82).

tardō, -āre, -āvī, -ātus, [**tardus**], 1, *check, delay, impede, hinder.*

tardus, -a, -um, comp. **-ior,** sup. **-issimus,** adj., *slow.* Comp., *less active* (ii. 25). [tardy.

Tarusātēs, -ium, m., pl., (tär-ū-sā'-tēz), a people in Aquitania. (iii. 23, 27).

Tasgetius, -ī, m., (tas-jē'sh[y]us), a ruler of the Carnutes. (v. 25, 29).

Tauroīs, -entis, acc. **Tauroenta,** [Τ Α Υ Ρ Ο Ε Ι Σ], (tâ' ro-is), a fortified place on the seacoast near Massilia.

taurus, -ī, m., *bull.* (vi. 28). [Taurus.

Taximagulus, -ī, [Kel., = 'Slave of the god Taxis'], m., (tak-si-mag' ū-lus), a British chieftain. (v. 22).

taxus, -ī, I., *yew.* (vi. 31).

Tectosagēs, -um, m., pl., (tek-tos'-a-jēz), a division of the Volcae, in the Province; represented also by a branch settled near the Hercynian forest (vi. 24).

tēctum, -ī, [**tegō**], n., *roof* (i. 36); *house* (vii. 66).

tegimentum, -ī, [**tegō**], n., *covering.* (ii. 21; vi. 21). [tegument.

tegō, tegere, tēxī, tēctus, 3, *cover* (V. 43); *hide,*

conceal, protect.

tēlum, -ī, n., general word for *missile; dart, spear.*

temerārius, -a, -um, [**temere**], adj., *rash, headstrong.* (I. 31; VI. 20).

temere, adv., *blindly, recklessly, rashly* (I. 40, V. 28; VII. 37, C. III. 87); *without good reason* (IV. 20).

temeritās, -tātis, [cf. **temere**] I., *rashness, recklessness.* [temerity.

tēmō, -ōnis, m., *pole, tongue,* of a wagon or chariot. (IV. 33).

Tempē [Τ έμ π η], n., indeclinable pl., *Tempe,* a narrow valley, famed for its beauty, in the northern part of Thessaly, through which the river Xerias (ancient *Peneius*) flows eastward to the sea; it lies between Mt. Olympus and Mt. Ossa (Map 19, and Fig. 209).

temperantia, -ae, [**temperāns**, *temperate*], f., *moderation, sound judgment.* (I. 19). [temperance.

temperātus, -a, -um, comp. **-ior,** [**temperō**], adj., *moderate, temperate, mild* (V. 12). [temperate.

temperō, -āre, -āvī, -ātus, [cf. **tempus**], 1, *control one's self, refrain* (I. 7, 33) [temper.

tempestās, -tātis, [**tempus**], f., *weather; stormy weather, bad weather, storm.* [tempest.

templum, -ī, n., *temple.* (C. I. 7, II. 5). [temple.

temptō, -āre, -āvī, -ātus, [freq. of **tendō**], 1, *try, attempt; make an attack on, attack, assail* (VII. 73, 86); *try to win over* (VI. 2). [tempt.

tempus, -oris, n., *period of time; time, period; season; occasion, circumstances.* **prō tempore,** *according to the emergency* (V. 8). **in reliquum tempus,** *for the future, for all time to come.* **omnī tempore,** *always.* [temporal.

Tencterī, -ōrum, m., pl., (tengk'-te-rī), a German people, driven from their territories by the Suebi.

tendō, tendere, tetendī, tentus, 3, *stretch, extend; put up* (C. III. 82); *have one's tent* (VI. 37). [tend.

tenebrae, -ārum, f., pl., *darkness.*

teneō, tenēre, tenuī, 2, *hold, keep, occupy; hold in, keep in, hold back, restrain, hem in; bind* (I. 31). **sē tenēre,** *to keep one's self, to remain.* **memoriā tenēre,** *to remember* (I. 7, 14). [tenet.

tener, -era, -erum, comp. **-ior,** sup. **tenerrimus,** adj., *tender, young.* (II. 17). [tender (adj.).

tenuis, -e, comp. **tenuior,** sup. **tenuissimus,** adj., *thin; poor, trifling* (VI. 35); *feeble, delicate* (V. 40).

tenuitās, -ātis, [**tenuis**], f., *thinness; weakness; poverty, destitution* (VII. 17). [tenuity.

tenuiter, comp. **tenuius,** sup. **-issimē,** [**tenuis**], adv., *thinly.* (III. 13).

ter, num. adv., *three times, thrice.*

teres, -etis, [cf. terō, *rub*], adj., *smooth* (VII. 73).

tergum, -ī, n., *back.* ā tergō, post tergum, *in the rear, on the rear.* terga vertere, *to flee.* [tergant.

ternī, -ae, -a, [ter], distrib. num. adj., *by threes, three each.* [ternary.

terra, -ae, f., *earth; land, ground; territory, country, region.* [terrace.

Terrasidius, -ī, m., (ter-a-sid' i-us), an officer under Publius Crassus. (III. 7, 8).

terrēnus, -a, -um, [terra], adj., *of earth, earthy.* (I. 43). [terrain.

terreō, -ēre, -uī, -itus, 2, *frighten, terrify, alarm;* followed by quō minus, *deter, frighten* from an action (VII. 49).

territō, -āre, [freq. of terreō], 1, *frighten greatly, terrify.* metū territāre, *to fill with apprehension* (V. 6).

terror, -ōris, [cf. terreō], m., *fear, fright, alarm.* īnferre terrōrem, *to strike terror* (VII. 8). [terror.

tertius, -a, -um, [ter], num. ord. adj., *third.* tertius decimus, or XIII, *thirteenth.* [tertiary.

testāmentum, -ī, [cf. testor], n., *will.* (I. 39). [testament.

testimōnium, -ī, [cf. testis], n., *proof, evidence.* [testimony.

testis, -is, m. and f., *witness.*

testūdō, -inis, [cf. testa, *potsherd*], f., *turtle; turtle-shell roof, testudo,* a covering formed by the soldiers' shields held above their heads and overlapping (II. 6; V. 9; VII. 85); *turtle-shell shed,* a movable shed to protect soldiers near the enemy's wall (V. 12, 43, 52). [testudinate.

Teutomatus, -ī, m., (tū-tom'a-tus), a king of the Nitiobroges. (VII. 31, 46).

Teutonī, gen. -um, m., pl., *Teutons, Teutoni* (tū' to-nī); see Cimbrī.

Thessalia, -ae, [Θ Ε Σ Σ Α Λ Ι Α], f., *Thessaly,* the northeastern part of Greece. (C. III. 82).

Thrācēs, -um, m., pl., *Thracians,* natives of Thrace, east of Macedonia. (C. III. 95).

tignum, -ī, n., *log, pile.* (IV. 17).

Tigurīnus, -a, -um, adj., *Tigurian.* As noun, Tigurīnī, -ōrum, m., pl., *the Tigurians,* one of the four divisions of the Helvetians. (I. 12).

timeō, -ēre, -uī, 2, *fear, be afraid of; be afraid, be apprehensive* (I. 14, 41) Pres. part., as noun, timentēs, m., pl., *the fearful* (VII. 7).

timidē, comp. -ius, [timidus], adv., *timidly.* (III. 25; V. 33).

timidus, -a, -um, comp. -ior, sup. -issimus, [cf. timeō], adj., *timid, cowardly.* (I. 39; VI. 40). [timid.

timor, -ōris, [cf. timeō], m., *fear, apprehension, alarm.* [timorous.

Titūrius, -ī, m., *Quintus Titurius Sabinus* (tī-tū' ri-us sa-bī' nus), a lieutenant of Caesar.

Titus, -ī. m., (tī'tus), a Roman first name;

abbreviation, T.

tolerō, -āre, -āvī, -ātus, 1, *bear, support, endure; sustain* (VII. 77); *hold out* (VII. 71). [tolerate.

tollō, tollere, sustulī, sublātus, 3, *lift, raise;* of an anchor, *weigh* (IV. 23); *take on board* (IV. 28); *puff up, elate* (I. 15; V. 38, C. II. 37); *take away, remove* (VI. 17; VII. 14); *do away with* (I. 42).

Tolōsa, -ae, f., (to-lō' sa) a city in the Province, now *Toulouse.* (III. 20).

Tolōsātēs, -ium, [Tolōsa], m., pl., (tol-o-sā' tēz), a people in the territory of the Volcae Tectosages, in the Province, about Tolosa.

tormentum, -ī, [cf. torqueō, *twist*], n., *windlass* (VII. 22); as a military term, pl., *torsioners, engines, artillery* (VII. 41, 81); *missile,* thrown by the torsioners (IV. 25); *means of torture, rack, torture* (VI. 19; VII. 4). [torment.

torreō, torrēre, torruī, tostus, 2. *roast; burn, scorch* (V. 43). [torrid.

tot, indeclinable num. adj., *so many.*

totidem [tot], indeclinable num. adj., *just as many, just so many.*

tōtus, -a, -um, gen. tōtīus, adj., *the whole, all, all the, entire.* [total.

trabs, trabis, f., *beam, timber.*

trāctus, see trahō.

trādō, -dere, -didī, -ditus, [trāns + dō], 3, *hand over, give up, deliver, surrender; intrust, commit, confide; commend, recommend* (VII. 39); *hand down* (IV. 7); *teach, impart* (VI. 14, 17; VII. 22).

trādūcō, -dūcere, -dūxī, -ductus, [trāns + dūcō], 3, *lead across, bring over; lead, transport, transfer; win over* (VI. 12, VII. 37). [traduce.

trāgula, -ae, f., *dart, javelin,* perhaps having a barbed point, and hurled by means of a leather thong.

trahō, trahere, trāxī, trāctus, 3, *drag along* (I. 53); *draw along, drag* (VI. 38). [tract.

trāiciō, -icere, -iēcī, -iectus, [trāns + iaciō], 3, *throw across; strike through, pierce, transfix* (V. 35, 44; VII. 25, 82). [trajectory.

trāiectus, see trāiciō.

trāiectus, -ūs, [cf. trāiciō], m., *passage.* (IV. 21; V. 2).

trānō, -āre, -āvī, [trāns + nō, *swim*], 1, *swim across.* (I. 53).

tranquillitās, -ātis, [tranquillus, *still*], f., *stillness, calm* (III. 15). summa tranquillitās, *a profound calm* (V. 23). [tranquility.

trāns, prep. with acc. only, *across, over; on the further side of, beyond.*

Trānsalpīnus, -a, -um, [trāns + Alpīnus, from Alpēs], adj., *beyond the Alps, Transalpine.* (VII. 1, 6).

trānscendō, -scendere, -scendī, [trāns + scandō, *climb*], 3, *climb over* (VII. 70); of ships, *board* (III. 15). [transcend.

trānseō, -īre, -iī or -īvī, -itum est, [trāns +

eō], irr., *go over, go across, pass over, cross over; pass by, march through;* of time, *pass* (III. 2). [transit (verb).

trānsferō, -ferre, -tulī, -lātus, [**trāns + ferō**], irr., *carry across; transfer.* [transfer.

trānsfīgō, -fīgere, -fīxī, -fīxus, [**trāns + fīgō,** *fix*], 3, *pierce through, transfix.* [transfix.

trānsfīxus, see **trānsfīgō.**

trānsfodiō, -fodere, -fōdī, -fossus, [**trāns + fodiō**], 3, *pierce through, impale* (VII. 82).

trānsgredior, -gredī, gressus, [**trāns + gradior,** *walk, go*], 3, dep., *pass over, go across, cross.* (II. 19; VII. 25, 46). [transgress.

trānsitus, -ūs, [cf. **trānseō**], m., *going over, crossing* (V. 55; VI. 7; VII. 57). [transit (noun).

trānslātus, see **trānsferō.**

trānsmarīnus, -a, -um, [**trāns + mare**], adj., *beyond the sea.* (VI. 24). [transmarine.

trānsmissus, -ūs, [cf. **trānsmittō**], m., *passage.* (V. 13).

trānsmittō, -mittere, -mīsī, -missus, [**trāns + mittō**], 3, *send across, convey across.* (VII. 61). [transmit.

Trānspadānus, -a, -um, [**trāns + Padus**], adj., *beyond the Po.* (C. III. 87). [Transpadane.

trānsportō, -āre, -āvī, -ātus, [**trāns + portō**], 1, *carry over, convey across, transport.* [transport.

Trānsrhēnānus, -a, -um, [**trāns + Rhēnus**], adj., *beyond the Rhine, on the other side of the Rhine* (V. 2). As noun, **Trānsrhēnānī, -ōrum,** m., pl., *the people beyond the Rhine* (IV. 16; VI. 5). [Transrhenane.

trānstrum, -ī, [**trāns**], n., *thwart, cross-beam.* (III. 13).

trānsversus [part. of **trānsvertō**], adj., *crosswise.* (II. 8). [transverse.

Trebius, -ī, m., *Marcus Trebius Gallus* (trē' bi-us gal' us), an officer under Publius Crassus. (III. 7, 8).

Trebōnius, -ī, m., (tre-bō' ni-us): (1) *Gaius Trebonius,* quaestor 60 B.C., tribune of the people 55 B.C., a lieutenant of Caesar in the Gallic and Civil wars; afterwards one of the conspirators against Caesar's life. (2) *Gaius Trebonius,* a Roman knight. (VI. 40).

trecentī, -ae, -a, or **CCC,** [**trēs + centum**], num. adj., *three hundred.*

trepidō, -āre, -āvī, -ātus, [cf. **trepidus**], 1, *hurry about anxiously.* (V. 33; VI. 37) [trepidation.

trēs, tria, gen. **trium,** or **III,** num. adj., *three.*

Trēverī, -ōrum, m., pl., *Treverans, Treveri* (trev' e-rī), a Belgic people near the Rhine.

Trēverus, -a, -um, adj., *Treveran, of the Treveri* (II. 24).

Triārius, -ī, m., *Gaius Triarius* (tri-ā' ri-us), a commander under Pompey. (C. III. 92).

Tribocēs, -um, or **Tribocī, -ōrum,** [Kel., = 'the very Sweet'], m., pl., (trib' o-sēz, trib' o-sī), a

German people near the Rhine.

tribūnīcius, -a, -um, [**tribūnus**], adj., *of a tribune, tribunicial.* (C. 1. 7).

tribūnus, -ī, [**tribus,** *tribe*], m., *tribune.*

tribūnus mīlitum, *military tribune.* **tribūnus plebis,** *tribune of the people.* [tribune.

tribuō, -ere, -uī, -ūtus, [cf. **tribus**], 3, *assign, ascribe; allot, give, concede; grant, pay, render.***suae māgnopere virtūtī tribuere,** *to presume upon his valor* (I. 13).

tribūtum, -ī, [part. of **tribuō**], n., *tax, tribute.* (VI. 13, 14). [tribute.

trichila, -ae, f., *arbor, bower.* (C. III. 96).

trīduum, -ī, [**tri,** = **trēs,** cf. **dies**], n., *space of three days, three days.*

triennium, -ī, [**tri-,** = **trēs, + annus**], n., *period of three years, three years.* (IV. 4). [triennial.

trīgintā, or **XXX,** indeclinable num. adj., *thirty.*

trīnī, -ae, -a, [**trēs**], distrib. num. adj., *three each; three; threefold, triple* (I. 53). [trinal.

Trinovantēs, -um, m., pl., (trin-o-van' tēz), a tribe in Britain.

tripertītō, [**tripertītus, tri- + partītus**], adv., *in three divisions, in three columns.* [tripertite.

triplex, -icis, [**tri,** = **trēs,** cf. **plicō,** *fold*], adj., *threefold, triple.* [triple.

triquetrus, -a, -um, adj., *three-cornered, triangular.* (V. 13).

trirēmis, -e, [**tri,** = **trēs, + rēmus**], adj., *having three banks of oars.* (C. II. 6). [trireme.

trīstis, -e, comp. **-ior,** sup. **-issimus,** adj., *sad, dejected, disconsolate.* (I. 32).

trīstitia, -ae, [**trīstis**], f., *sadness, dejection.* (I. 32).

Troucillus, -ī, m., *Gaius Valerius Troucillus* (tru-sil' us), a Gaul who acted as interpreter for Caesar. (I. 19).

truncus, -ī, m., *trunk of a tree.* [trunk.

tū, tuī, pl. **vōs, vestrum,** personal pron., *thou, you.*

tuba, -ae, f., *trumpet.* [tuba.

tueor, tuērī, 2, dep., *gaze at, behold, watch; guard, protect, defend.*

tulī, see **ferō.**

Tulingī, -ōrum, m., pl., (tū-lin'jī) a people near the Helvetians.

Tullius, see **Cicero.**

Tullus, see **Volcacius.**

tum, adv., *then, at that time; there upon; besides, moreover.* **cum . . . tum,** *both . . . and, not only . . . but also.*

tumultuor, -ārī, -ātus, [**tumultus**], 1, dep., *make a disturbance; be in confusion* (VII. 61).

tumultuōsē, comp. **-ius,** sup **-issimē,** [**tumultuōsus**], adv., *with confusion.* Comp., *with more confusion* than usual (VII. 45).

tumultus, -ūs, m., *disturbance, confusion,*

disorder, uproar; uprising, rebellion (I. 40; V. 26). [tumult.

tumulus, -ī, [**tumeō,** *swell*], m., *mound, hillock.* [tumulus.

tunc, adv., *then, at that time, at this juncture.* (V. 41).

turba, -ae, f., *disorder, confusion.* (C. II. 35).

turma, -ae, f., *troop, squadron* of cavalry.

turmātim, [**turma**], adv., *by squadrons.* (C. III. 93).

Turonī, -ōrum, m., pl., (tū'ro-nī), a Gallic people, on the Liger *(Loire).*

turpis, -e, comp. **-ior,** sup. **-issimus,** adj., *ugly; disgraceful, shameful.*

turpiter, comp. **-ius,** sup. **-issimē,** [**turpis**], adv., *basely, disgracefully.*

turpitūdō, -inis, [**turpis**], f., *baseness, disgrace.* (II. 27). [turpitude.

turris, -is, f., *tower.* **turris ambulātoria,** *movable tower,* built on wheels so that it could be moved up to the wall of a besieged city. [tower.

Tūticānus, -ī, m., (tū-ti-kā'nus), a Gaul in Caesar's army. (C. III. 71).

tūtō, comp. **tūtius,** [abl. of **tūtus**], adv., *in safety, safely, securely.*

tūtus, comp. **-ior,** sup. **-issimus,** [part. of **tueor**], adj., *safe, secure.*

tuus, -a, -um, [**tū**], possessive pronominal adj., *thy, your.* (V. 44).

U.

ubi or **ubī,** adv., of place, *where;* of time, *when.* **ubi prīmum,** *as soon as.*

Ubiī, -ōrum, m., pl., *Ubians, Ubii* (ū' bi-ī), a German people.

ubīque [**ubī** + **-que**], adv., *anywhere, everywhere.* (III. 16). [ubiquity.

Ubius, -a, -um, adj., *Ubian, of the Ubians* (VI. 29).

ulcīscor, ulcīscī, ultus, 3, dep., *take vengeance on* (I. 14; IV. 19; V. 38); *avenge* (I. 12); *to take vengeance* (VI. 34).

ūllus, -a, -um, gen. **ūllīus,** adj., *any.* As noun, *anyone, anybody* (I. 8).

ulterior, -ius, [**ultrā**], adj. in comp. degree, *farther, beyond, more remote, more distant.* Sup. **ultimus,** *farthest, most distant, most remote; last.* As noun, **ulteriōrēs, -um,** m., pl., *those who were further off* (VI. 2); **ultimī, -ōrum,** m., pl., *the last* (V. 43). [ulterior, ultimate.

ultrā, prep. with acc. only, *on the farther, side of; beyond* (I. 48, 49).

ultrō, adv., *to the farther side; besides, moreover, also* (V. 28, VI. 35); *actually* (V. 40); *of one's own accord, voluntarily.*

ultus, see **ulcīscor.**

ululātus, -ūs, [**ululō,** *yell*], m., only in acc.

and abl., *shouting, yell.*

umerus, -ī, m., *shoulder.* (VII. 50, 56).

umquam, adv., *at any time, ever.*

ūnā [**ūnus**], adv., *into one place* (VII. 87); *in the same place* (II. 29; VII. 38); *at the same time; together, in company.* **ūnā cum.** *along with, together with.*

unde, adv., *whence, from which.*

ūndecim, or **XI,** [**ūnus** + **decem**], indeclinable num. adj., *eleven.*

ūndecimus, -a, -um, [**ūndecim**], num. ord. adj., *eleventh.*

ūndēquadrāgintā, or **XXXIX,** [**ūnus** + **dē** + **quadrāgintā**], indeclinable num. adj., *thirty-nine.*

ūndēvīgintī, or **XVIIII,** [**ūnus** + **dē** + **vīgintī**], indeclinable num. adj., *nineteen.* (I. 8).

undique [**unde** + **-que**], adv., *from all sides, on all sides, everywhere.*

ūniversus, -a, -um, [**ūnus** + **versus,** from **vertō**], adj., *all together, all, in a body; the whole of, entire.* As noun, **ūniversī, -ōrum,** m., pl., *all the men together, the whole body, all together.* [universe.

ūnus, -a, -um, gen. **ūnīus,** num. adj., *one; one alone, only one, only, sole; one and the same.* Pl., **ūnī,** *alone, only.* **ūnō tempore,** *at one and the same time.* **ad ūnum omnēs,** *all to a man* (V. 37). **Sēquanī ūnī,** *the Sequani only.* [unite.

urbānus, -a, -um, [**urbs**], adj., *of the city,* referring to Rome. [urban.

urbs, urbis, f., *city;* often *the city,* referring to Rome.

urgeō, urgēre, ursī, 2, *press;* pass., *be hard pressed* (II. 25, 26). [urge.

ūrus, -ī, m., *wild ox.* (VI. 28).

Usipetēs, -um, m., pl., (ū-sip' e-tēz), a German people.

ūsitātus, -a, -um, comp. **-ior,** sup. **-issimus,** [part. of **ūsitor**], adj., *usual; common, familiar* (VII. 22).

ūsque, adv., *as far as, even.* **ūsque ad,** *as far as;* of time, *up to, until* (I. 50; III. 15). **ūsque eō,** *even so far as this, even to this degree* (VI. 37; VII. 17).

ūsus, see **ūtor.**

ūsus, -ūs, [cf. **ūtor**], m., *use, practice, exercise, employment; experience, familiarity (with), skill; control; advantage, benefit; need, necessity.* **ex ūsū,** *of advantage.* [use (noun).

ut, utī, adv. and conj.:
(1) As adv., interrogative, *how* (I. 43, 46); relative, *as, just as.* **ut prīmum,** *as soon as.* **ut — ita,** *as — so, while — still.*
(2) As conj., with indic., *as* (I. 4); *when, as soon as* (I. 31); with subj., *that, so that; in order that; though, although* (III. 9).

uter, utra, utrum, gen. **utrīus,** pronominal adj., often used as subst., *which of two,* *whichever, which.*

uterque, -traque, -trumque, gen. **utrīusque,** [**uter** + **-que**], adj., *each, both.* As subst., **uterque, utrīusque,** m., *both, each.* Pl., **utrīque,** *both sides, both forces* (IV. 26; V. 50; VII. 70, 80, 85); *both peoples* (II. 16; VII. 7).

utī, see **ut.**

Utica, -ae, f, (ū'ti-ca), a city in northern Africa, on the sea-coast.

Uticēnsēs, -ium, m., pl., *Uticans, the inhabitants of Utica.* (C. II. 36).

ūtilis, -e, comp. **-ior,** sup. **-issimus,** [**ūtor**], adj., *useful, serviceable* (IV. 7; VII. 20); *helpful* (VII. 76).

ūtilitās, -ātis, [**ūtilis**], f., *usefulness, advantage, benefit.* [utility.

ūtor, ūtī, ūsus, 3, dep., *use, employ, adopt; avail one's self of, have, enjoy, find; observe, maintain; exercise, display, show.* [use (verb).

utrimque [**uterque**], adv., *on both sides.*

utrum, [**uter**], conj., *whether.* **utrum — an,** *whether — or.* **utrum — necne,** *whether — or not* (I. 50).

uxor, -ōris, f., *wife.* [uxorious.

V.

Vacalus, -ī, m., *Waal, Vacalus* (vak'a-lus), an arm of the Rhine, which flows west into the Meuse. (iv. 10).

vacātiō, -ōnis, [cf. **vacō**], f., *exemption.* (VI. 14). [vacation.

vacō, -āre, -āvī, -ātus, 1, *be unoccupied, lie waste.* [vacate.

vacuus, -a, -um, sup. **vacuissimus,** [**vacō**], adj., *empty, clear, vacant, unoccupied; destitute,* in **vacuus ab,** *destitute of* (II. 12). [vacuum.

vadum, -ī, n., *shoal, shallow* (III. 9, 12, 13; IV. 26); *ford, shallow place.*

vāgīna, -ae, f., *scabbard, sheath.* (V. 44).

vagor, -ārī, -ātus, 1, dep., *wander, wander about, roam about.*

valeō, -ēre, -uī, -itūrus, 2, *be powerful, be strong; have power, have influence; prevail.* [value.

Valerius, -ī, m., (va-lē' ri-us):

(1) *Lucius Valerius Praeconinus,* a lieutenant defeated and killed in Aquitania a few years before 56 B.C. (III. 20).

(2) *Gaius Valerius Flaccus,* a Roman governor in Gaul. (I. 47).

(3) *Gaius Valerius Caburus,* a Gaul who received the Roman franchise, B.C. 83. (I. 47; VII. 65).

(4) *Gaius Valerius Procillus,* son of (3); sent by Caesar as envoy to Ariovistus. (I. 47, 53).

(5) *Gaius Valerius Donnotaurus,* a Gaul, son of (3). (VII. 65).

(6) *Gaius Valerius Troucillus,* see **Troucillus.** (I. 19).

(7) *Valerius Flaccus,* an officer in Pompey's army. (C. III. 53).

Valetiācus, -ī, m., (val' e-shi-ā' kus), vergobret of the Aeduans in 53 B.C. (VII. 32).

valētūdō, -inis, [cf. **valeō**], f., *health.* (V. 40; VII. 78). [valetudinarian.

vallēs or **vallis, -is,** f., *valley.* [valley.

vāllum, -ī, [**vāllus**], n., *rampart set* with palisades, *wall, intrenchment.* [wall.

vāllus, -ī, m., *stake, pole; rampart stake, palisade;* rampart stakes in position, *stockade, palisade;* sharpened *point* (VII. 73).

Vangionēs, -um, m., pl., (van-jī'o-nēz), a German tribe. (I. 51).

varietās, -ātis, [**varius**], f., *variety, diversity* (VII. 23); *mottled appearance* (VI. 27). [variety.

varius, -a, -um, adj., *different, diverse.* [various.

Vārus, -ī, a Roman name: see **Attius.**

vāstō, -āre, -āvī, -ātus, [**vāstus**], 1, *lay waste, devastate.*

vastus, -a, -um, comp. **-ior,** sup. **-issimus,** adj., *vast, immense.* [vast.

vāticinātiō, -ōnis, [**vāticinor,** *predict*], f., *prophecy.* (I. 50). [vaticination.

Vatīnius, -ī, m., *Publius Vatinius* (va-tin' i-us), a partisan of Caesar. (C. III. 90).

-ve, enclitic conj., *or.*

vectīgal, -ālis, [cf. **vehō**], n., *tax, tribute* (V. 22); *revenue* (I. 18, 36).

vectīgālis, -e, [**vectīgal**], adj., *paying tribute, tributary.* (III. 8; IV. 3).

vectōrius, -a, -um, [**vector,** cf. **vehō**], adj., *for carrying.* **vectōrium nāvigium,** *transport ship* (V. 8). [vectorial.

vehementer, comp. **vehementius,** sup. **-issimē,** [**vehemēns,** *eager, violent*], adv., *vigorously, violently; exceedingly, greatly.*

vehō, -ere, vexī, vectus, 3, *carry.* **equō vectus,** *riding on horseback* (C. II. 44). [vehicle.

vel, [**volō**], conj., *or.* **vel . . . vel,** *either . . . or.* As adv., *even* (VII. 37).

Velānius, -ī, m., *Quintus Velanius* (ve-lā' ni-us), an officer under Crassus. (III. 7, 8).

Veliocassēs, -ium, and **Veliocassī, -ōrum,** m., pl., (vel" i-o-kas' ēz, vel" i-o-kas' ī), a small state north of the Sequana *(Seine).*

Vellaunodūnum, -ī, n., (vel" â-no-dū' num), a town of the Senones. (VII. 11, 14).

Vellaviī, -ōrum, m., pl., (ve-lā' vi-ī), a small state in the Cebenna *(Cévennes)* Mountains. (VII. 75).

vēlōcitās, -ātis, [**vēlōx**], f., *swiftness, speed.* (VI. 28). [velocity.

vēlōciter, comp. **vēlōcius,** sup. **vēlōcissimē,** [**vēlōx**], adv., *swiftly, quickly.* (V. 35).

vēlōx, -ōcis, comp. **-ior,** sup. **-issimus,** adj., *swift, fast.* (I. 48). [velox.

vēlum, -ī, n., *sail.* (III. 13, 14).

velut [vel + ut], adv., *just as.* velut sī, *just as if* (I. 32).

vēnātiō, -ōnis, [cf. vēnor, hunt], f., *hunting, hunting expedition.*

vēnātor, -ōris, [vēnor, hunt], m., *hunter.* (VI. 27).

vēndō, -dere, -didī, -ditus, [vēnum, sale, + dō], 3, *sell.* [vend.

Venellī, -ōrum, m., pl., (ve-nel' ī) a Gallic people, on the northwest coast (Fig. 210).

Venetī, -ōrum, m., pl., *Venetans, Veneti* (ven' e-tī), a sea-faring Gallic people, on the west coast.

Venetia, -ae, f., (ve-nē' sh[y]a), *the country of the Venetans.* (III. 9).

Veneticus, -a, -um, [Venetia], adj., *of the Venetans, Venetan.* Veneticum bellum, *the war with the Venetans* (III. 18; IV. 21).

venia, -ae, f., *pardon, forgiveness* (VI. 4); *permission* (VII. 15). [venial.

veniō, venīre, vēnī, ventum est, 4, *come.*

ventitō, -āre, -āvī, [freq. of veniō], 1, *come often, go often, keep coming.*

ventus, -ī, m., *wind.* [ventilate.

vēr, vēris, n., *spring,* prīmō vēre, *at the commencement of spring* (VI. 3). [vernal.

Veragrī, -ōrum, m., pl., (ver' a-grī), an Alpine tribe.

Verbigenus, -ī, m., *Verbigen, Verbigenus* (ver-bij' e-nus), a canton of the Helvetians. (I. 27).

verbum, -ī, n., *word.* verba facere, *to speak* (II. 14). [verb.

Vercassivellaunus, -ī, [Kel., = 'Supremely Good'], m., (ver-kas''-i-ve-lâ' nus), one of the four generals in command of the Gallic army raised for the relief of Alesia.

Vercingetorīx, -īgis, [Kel., = 'Great King of Warriors'], m., (ver-sin-jet'o-riks), an Arvernian, commander-in-chief of the Gallic forces in 52 B.C.

vereor, -ērī, -itus, 2, dep., *fear, be afraid; be afraid of, dread.*

vergō, -ere, 3, *lie, slope; be situated.* [verge.

vergobretus, -ī, m., [Celtic word, 'He that renders judgment'; as a title, 'Dispenser of Justice'], *vergobret,* title of the chief magistrate of the Aeduans. (I. 16).

veritus, see vereor.

vērō [abl. neuter of vērus], adv., *in truth, in fact, truly, certainly; but, but in fact, however.*

versō, -āre, -āvī, -ātus, [freq. of vertō], 1, *turn often; shift, change the position of* (V. 44). Pass.

versor, -ārī, -ātus, as dep., lit., *turn one's self about, move about in any place; dwell, live, be; be occupied, be engaged, be busy.* in bellō versārī, *to engage in war* (VI. 15). [versatile.

versus, -ūs, [vertō], m., *line, verse* (VI. 14). [verse.

versus, [part. of vertō], prep. and adv.:
(1) As prep., with acc. only, sometimes following a word governed by ad or in, *towards, in the direction of.* ad . . . versus, in . . . versus, *towards.*
(2) As adv., *turned, facing.* quōque versus, *in all directions* (III. 23; VII. 4, 14).

Verticō, -ōnis, m., (ver'ti-kō), a Nervian of rank. (V. 45, 49).

vertō, vertere, vertī, versus, 3, *turn, turn about; change.* terga vertere, *to turn and flee, to flee.*

Verucloetius, -ī, m., (ver-ū-klē'-sh[y]us), a Helvetian who went as envoy to Caesar. (I. 7).

vērus, -a, -um, comp. -ior, sup. vērissimus, adj., *true* (I. 18, 20); *right, proper, fitting* (IV. 8). As noun, vērum, -ī, n., *the truth.* vērī similis, *probable* (III. 13).

verūtum, -ī, [verū, spit for roasting meat], n., *dart.* (V. 44).

Vesontiō, -ōnis, m., (ve-son' sh[y]ō), chief city of the Sequanians, on the Dubis *(Doubs)* river; now *Besançon.* (I. 38, 39).

vesper, -erī, m., *evening,* [vespers.

vester, -tra, -trum, [vōs], possessive pronominal adj., *your, yours.*

vēstīgium, -ī, n., *footprint, track* (VI. 27); *spot, place* (IV. 2); of time, *moment, instant.* [vestige.

vestiō, -īre, -īvī, -ītus, [vestis], 4, *clothe* (V. 14; VII. 31); *cover* (VII. 23). [vestment.

vestis, -is, f., *clothing.* (VII. 47). [vest.

vestītus, -ūs, [cf. vestiō], m., *clothing, garb.* (IV. 1; VII. 88).

veterānus, -a, -um, [vetus], adj., *old, veteran.* (I. 24). [veteran.

vetō, -āre, -uī, -itus, 1, *forbid* (II. 20); *not allow* (VII. 33). [veto.

vetus, -eris, sup. veterrimus, adj., *old, former; ancient, long-standing.*

vetustās, -ātis, [vetustus, vetus], f., *antiquity, ancient times.* (C. I. 6).

vēxillum, -ī, [cf. vēlum], n., *banner, flag.*

vexō, -āre, -āvī, -ātus, [freq. of vehō], 1, *harass, assail* (I. 14; VI. 43); *lay waste, overrun* (II. 4; IV. 15). [vex.

via, -ae, f., *way, road; journey, march.* bīduī via, *a two days' march* (VI. 7). [via.

viātor, -ōris, [cf. via], m., *traveler, wayfarer.* (IV. 5).

vīcēnī, -ae, -a, [vīgintī], distrib. num. adj., *twenty each, twenty.*

vīcēsimus, -a, -um, [vīgintī], num. adj., *twentieth.* (VI. 21).

vīciēs [vīgintī], num. adv., *twenty times.* vīciēs centum milia passuum, *two thousand miles* (V. 13).

vīcīnitās, -ātis, [vīcīnus, near], f., *neighborhood; neighbors* (VI. 34). [vicinity.

vicis, -is, f., nom., dat. and voc. sing. and gen. and voc. pl. not in use, *change, succession.* in vicem, *in turn* (IV. 1, C. III. 98). [vicar.

victima, -ae, f., *victim.* (VI. 16). [victim.

victor, -ōris, [vincō], m., *conqueror, victor.* As adj., *victorious* (I. 31; VII. 20, 62). [victor.

victōria, -ae, [victor], f., *victory.* [victory.

victus, see vincō.

vīctus, -ūs, [vīvō], m., *living* (I. 31); *mode of life* (VI. 24); *food, provisions* (VI. 22, 23). [victuals.

vīcus, -ī, m., *village, hamlet.*

videō, vidēre, vīdī, vīsus, 2, *see, perceive, observe; understand.* Pass., generally as dep., videor, vidērī,

vīsus sum, *be seen, seem, appear; seem proper, seem good, seem best.* [vision.

Vienna, -ae, f., (vi-en' a), a city of the Allobroges; now *Vienne.* (VII. 9).

vigilia, -ae [vigil, *watchman*], f., *watching, sleeplessness* (V. 31, 32); *watch,* a division of the night; *sentry duty* (C. III. 49). [vigil.

vīgintī, or XX, indeclinable num. adj., *twenty.*

vīmen, -inis, n., *pliant shoot, twig, withe.* (II. 33; VII. 73). [Viminal.

vinciō, vincīre, vinxī, vinctus, 4, *bind.* (I. 53).

vincō, vincere, vīcī, victus, 3, *conquer, overcome, defeat, subdue; exceed, surpass* (VI. 43); *carry one's point, have one's own way* (V. 30).

victī, -ōrum, part., used as noun, m., pl., *the conquered.* [vincible.

vinculum, -ī, [vinciō], n., *chain, bond, fetters.* [vinculum.

vindicō, -āre, -āvī, -ātus, [cf. vindex], 1, *claim, demand* (VII. 76); *restore* to liberty (VII. 1); *inflict punishment* (III. 16). [vindicate.

vīnea, -ae, f., *arbor-shed, sappers' hut.*

vīnum, -ī, n., *wine.* [wine.

violō, -āre, -āvī, -ātus, [vīs], 1, *do violence to, maltreat* (VI. 23); *invade, lay waste* (VI. 32). [violate.

vir, virī, m., *man; husband* (VI. 19). [virile.

vīrēs, see vīs.

virgō, -inis, f., *maiden.* [virgin.

virgultum, -ī, [virga, *a shoot*], n., *small brush; fascine.* (III. 18; VII. 73).

Viridomārus, -ī, m., (vir'' i-do-mā'-rus), a prominent Aeduan.

Viridovīx, -īcis, m., (vi-rid'-o-viks), a leader of the Venelli. (III. 17-18).

virītim, [vir], adv., *man by man, to each individually.* (VII. 71).

Viromanduī, -ōrum, m., pl., (vir-o-man' du-ī), a Belgic people about the headwaters of the Samara (*Somme*) and the Scaldis (*Schelde*). Fig. 211.

virtūs, -tūtis, [vir], f., *manliness; courage, bravery, prowess; vigor, energy, initiative* (VII. 6, 59); *efficiency, effort* (V. 8; VII. 22); *worth* (I. 47). Pl.,

remarkable qualities, virtues (I. 44). [virtue.

vīs, acc. vim, abl. vī, pl. vīrēs, -ium, f., *strength* (VI. 28); *force, violence; influence, control* (VI. 14, 17); *number* (VI. 36). Pl., *physical powers, strength.* [vim.

vīsus, see videō.

vīta, -ae, [cf. vīvō], f., *life.* [vital.

vitium, -ī, n., *defect, failing, fault.* (C. II. 4, III. 72). [vice.

vītō, -āre, -āvī, -ātus, 1, *shun, avoid, try to escape.*

vitrum, -ī, n., *woad,* a plant used for dyeing blue. (V. 14).

vīvō, vīvere, vīxī, vīctūrus, 3, *live;* with abl., *sustain life, live on* (IV. 1, 10; V. 14). [vivacious.

vīvus, -a, -um, [cf. vīvō], adj., *living, alive.* As noun, vīvī, -ōrum, m., pl., *the living* (VI. 19). [vivisection.

vix, adv., *scarcely, barely; with difficulty, hardly* (I. 6; VI. 37; VII. 46).

Vocātēs, -ium, m., pl., (vo-kā' tēz), a people in Aquitania. (III. 23, 27).

Vocciō, -ōnis, m., (vok'sh[y]ō), a king of the Norici. (I. 53).

vocō, -āre, -āvī, -ātus, [cf. vōx], 1, *call, summon; call for, demand; name, call* (V. 21). [vocative.

Vocontiī, -ōrum, m., pl., (vo-kon'-sh[y]ī), a Gallic people in the Province. (I. 10).

Volcācius, -ī, m., *Gaius Volcacius Tullus* (vol-kā' sh[y]us tul' us), an officer in Caesar's army.

Volcae, -ārum, m., pl., (vol'sē), a Gallic people in the Province having two branches, Arecomicī and Tectosagēs.

volō, velle, voluī, irr., *be willing, wish, desire; mean, intend, purpose.*

voluntārius, -a, -um, [volō], adj., *willing; serving as a volunteer* (C. III. 91). As noun, voluntārius, -ī, m., *volunteer* (V. 56). [voluntary.

voluntās, -ātis, [volō], f., *will, wish, inclination, desire; good-will, loyalty* (I. 19; V. 4; VII. 10); *consent, approval* (I. 7, 20, 30, 39).

voluptās, -ātis, [volō], f., *pleasure, indulgence, enjoyment; amusement* (V. 12). [voluptuous.

Volusēnus, -ī, m., *Gaius Volusenus Quadratus* (vol-ū-sē' nus kwa-drā'-tus), a military tribune.

Vorēnus, -ī, m., *Lucius Vorenus* (vo-rē' nus), a centurion. (V. 44).

Vosegus, -ī, m., (vos' e-gus), a range of mountains in eastern Gaul, now *Vosges* (vozh).

vōtum, -ī, [voveō], n., *vow.* (C. I. 6). [vote.

voveō, vovēre, vōvī, vōtus, 2, *vow.* (VI. 16). [vow.

vōx, vōcis, f., *voice* (II. 13; V. 30; IV. 25); *utterance* (VII. 17); *word, reply* (I. 32). Pl. vōcēs, *words,*

sayings, language, speeches, statements. [voice.
Vulcānus, -ī, m., *Vulcan,* son of Jupiter and
Juno, god of fire and of work in metals. (VI.
21). [volcano.
vulgō [vulgus], adv., *generally, commonly,*
everywhere. (I. 39; II. 1; V. 33).
vulgus, -ī, n., *common people; multitude, crowd;*

of soldiers, *rank and file* (I. 46). [vulgar.
vulnerō, -āre, -āvī, -ātus, [vulnus], 1, *wound,*
hurt. [vulnerable.
vulnus, -eris, n., *wound.*
vultus, -ūs, m., *countenance, features,*
expression of face. (I. 39).

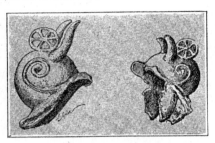

Figure 46. — Gallic helmets.

ENGLISH-LATIN VOCABULARY

Reproduced, with the consent of the authors, from *Latin Composition*, by Bernard M. Allen and John L. Phillips.

Regular verbs of the first conjugation are indicated by the figure I.

abandon, relinquō, -ere, -līquī, -līctus.
ability, virtūs, -tūtis, f. **natural ability,** ingenium, -iī, n. **have ability,** possum, posse, potuī.
able, be able, possum, posse, potuī.
about, concerning, dē, prep, with abl. **about, around,** circum, prep, with acc. **about** (with numerals), circiter.
accept, accipiō, -ere, -cēpī, -ceptus.
accident, cāsus, -ūs, m.
accomplish, perficiō, -ere, -fēcī, -fectus; cōnsequor, -ī, -secūtus.
account, on account of, propter, prep. with acc.
accuse, accūsō, I.
accustomed, be accustomed, soleō, -ēre, solitus.
across, trāns, prep, with acc.
act (noun), factum, -ī, n.
act (verb), faciō, -ere, fēcī, factus.
actively, ācriter.
admit, cōnfiteor, -ērī, -fessus.
adopt, of a plan, ūtor.
advance, prōgredior, -gredī, -gressus.
advantage, bonum, -ī, n.; commodum, -ī, n.
advise, moneō, -ēre, -uī, -itus.
affair, rēs, reī, f. **public affairs,** rēs pūblica.
afraid, be afraid, timeō, -ēre, -uī.
after, post, prep, with acc; postquam, conj.
afterward, post, posteā.
again, iterum.
against, in, ad, contrā, prepositions with acc.
ago, ante.
agriculture, agrī cultūra, -ae, f.
aid (noun), auxilium, -iī, n.
aid (verb), adiuvō, -āre, -iūvī, -iūtus, with acc.
alarm, permoveō, -ēre, -mōvī, -mōtus.
all, omnis, -e; tōtus, -a, -um.
allow, patior, patī, passus.
ally, socius, -iī, m.
almost, ferē, paene.
alone, sōlus, -a, -um.
already, iam.
also, quoque (postpositive). **not only . . . but also,** nōn modo . . . sed etiam.
although, cum, quamquam.
always, semper.
ambassador, lēgātus, -ī, m.
ambuscade, īnsidiae, -ārum, f., pl.
among, apud, prep, with acc.
ancestors, maiorēs, -um, m.

anchor, ancora, -ae, f. **at anchor,** ad ancoram.
and, et, atque, -que.
and . . . not, neque. **and so,** itaque.
announce, nūntiō, I.
another, alius, -a, -ud.
answer, respondeō, -ēre, -dī, respōnsus.
any, any one, anything, aliquis, aliqua, aliquid (quod); after sī, nisi or nē, quis, qua, quid (quod); with negatives, quisquam quidquam (pron.); ūllus, -a, -um (adj.).
appeal to, implōrō, I.
approach, appropinquō, I.
approve, probō, I.
arise, coörior, -īrī, -ortus.
arm, armō, I.
arms, arma, -ōrum, n.
army, exercitus, -ūs, m.
arouse, incitō, I.
arrival, adventus, -ūs, m.
arrive, perveniō, -īre, -vēnī, -ventum est.
as, just as, ut, sīcut, with indic. **as if,** quasi, velut sī. **as soon as,** simul atque.
ask, request, rogō, I. **ask, seek,** petō, -ere, -īvī or -iī, -ītus. **ask, inquire,** quaerō, -ere, -sīvī or -siī, -sītus.
assistance, auxilium, -iī, n.
at, in with abl.; ad with acc; sign of locative case.
Atrebatian, Atrebās, -ātis, m.
attack (noun), impetus, -ūs, m.
attack (verb), oppugnō, I; adgredior, -ī, -gressus; lacessō, -ere, -īvī or -iī, -ītus. **make an attack on,** impetum faciō in with acc.
attempt (noun), cōnātus, -ūs, m.
attempt (verb), cōnor, I.
authority, auctōritās, -tātis, f.
avenge, ulcīscor, -ī, ultus.
avoid, vītō, I.
await, exspectō, I.
away, be away, absum, abesse, āfuī, āfutūrus.

baggage, impedīmenta, -ōrum, n., pl.
band (of men), manus, -ūs, f.
barbarian, barbarus, -ī, m.
battle, pugna, -ae, f.; proelium, -iī, n.
be, sum, esse, fuī, futūrus. **be at hand,** adsum, adesse, affuī.
bear, ferō, ferre, tulī, lātus.
because, quod. **because of,** propter, prep, with acc.
befall, accidit, -ere, accidit.
before (adv.), ante, anteā.

before (conj.), prius quam, ante quam. before (prep.), ante, with acc.
before (adj.), prior, superior. **on the day before,** prīdiē.
beg, ōrō, I; petō, -ere, -īvī or -iī, -ītus.
began, coepī, coepisse, coeptus. Use the pass, when the inf. is pass.
begin, incipiō, (see **began**),
behalf, in behalf of, prō, prep, with abl.
behind, post, prep, with acc. **behind him, them,** etc., post tergum.
Belgians, Belgae, -ārum, m., pl.
believe, crēdō, -ere, crēdidī, crēditus; putō, I.
belittle, minuō, -ere, -uī, -ūtus.
betray, prōdō, -ere, -didī, -ditus.
between, inter, prep, with acc.
bitterly, ācriter.
board, go on board, nāvem (nāvēs) ascendō, -ere, -scendī, -scēnsus.
body, corpus, -oris, n.
both, each, uterque, utraque, utrum-que.
both . . . and, et . . . et.
boundaries, fīnēs, -ium, m.
brave, fortis, -e.
bravely, fortiter.
break down, perfringō, -ere, -frēgī, -frāctus.
bridge, pōns, pontis, m.
bring, ferō, ferre, tulī, lātus; dūcō, -ere, dūxī, -ductus, **bring about,** cōnficiō, -ere, -fēcī, -fectus.
bring on, upon, īnferō.
bring to, afferō, afferre, attulī, allātus; addūcō, -ere, -dūxī, -ductus. **bring together,** comportō, I.
Britain, Britannia, -ae, f.
Britons, Britannī, -ōrum, m., pl.
brother, frāter, -tris, m.
build, (of a bridge), faciō, -ere, fēcī, -factus. (of a road), muniō, -īre, -īvī, or -iī, -ītus. (of a rampart), perdūcō, -dūcere, -dūxī, -ductus.
building, aedificium, -iī, n.
burn, set fire to, incendō, -ere, -cendī, -cēnsus,
burning, incendium, -iī, n.
but, sed.
buy, emō, -ere, ēmī, emptus.
by, abl. case; ab, with abl. of agent.

call (by name), appellō, I.
camp, castra, -ōrum, n., pl.
can, possum, posse, potuī.
capture, capiō, -ere, cēpī, captus. (by storming), expugnō, I.
care, cūra, -ae, f.
carefully, dīligenter.
carriage with four wheels, wagon, raeda, f.
carry, ferō, ferre, tulī, lātus. **carry back,** referō, referre, rettulī, relātus. **carry on,** gerō,
-ere, gessī, gestus. **carry out, accomplish,** perficiō, -ere, -fēcī, -fectus.
case, causa, -ae, f. **in the case of,** in, prep, with abl.
cast off, cast out, abiciō, -ere, -iēcī, -iectus; ēiciō.
cause (noun), causa, -ae, f.
cause (verb), efficiō, -ere, -fēcī, -fectus; faciō, -ere, fēcī, factus.
cavalry (adj.), equester, -tris, -tre.
cavalry (noun), equitātus, -ūs, m.; equitēs, -um, m., pl.
Celts, Celtae, -ārum, m., pl.
centurion, centuriō, -ōnis, m.
certain (indef. pron.), quīdam, quaedam, quiddam.
certainly, certē.
chain, vinculum, -ī, n.
chance, occāsiō, -ōnis, f. **by chance,** forte,
charge, be in charge, praesum, -esse, -fuī. **put in charge,** praeficiō, -ere, -fēcī, -fectus.
chariot, currus, -ūs, m.
chief, chief man, prīnceps, -cipis, m.
children, puerī, -ōrum, m., pl. (free born), līberī, -ōrum, m., pl.
choose, legō, -ere, lēgī, lēctus; dēligō, -ere, -lēgī, -lēctus.
citizen, cīvis, -is, m.
city, urbs, urbis, f.
clear, make clear, dēclārō, I. **it is clear,** cōnstat.
client, cliēns, -entis, m.
close, be close at hand, subsum, -esse.
cohort, cohors, cohortis, f.
come, veniō, -īre, vēnī, ventum est. **come back,** redeō, -īre, -iī, -itum est. **come together,** conveniō, -īre, -vēnī, -ventum est. **come to pass, fio,** fierī, factum est. **come up, arise,** coörior, īrī, ortus
comfort, cōnsōlor, I.
command, iubeō, -ēre, iussī, iussus; imperō, I.
be in command, praesum, -esse, -fuī, with dat.
commander, imperātor, -ōris, m.
commence battle, proelium committō, -ere, -mīsī, -missus.
commit, do, faciō, -ere, fēcī, factus.
common, commūnis, -e. **common people,** plēbs, plēbis, f.
companion, socius, -iī, m.
compare, comparō, I.
compel, cōgō, -ere, coēgī, coāctus.
complain, queror, -ī, questus.
concern, it concerns, interest, -esse, -fuit.
concerning, dē, prep, with abl.
confer, colloquor, -ī, -locūtus.
conference, colloquium, -iī, n.

confess, cōnfiteor, -ērī, -fessus.
confidence, fidēs, -eī, f. **have confidence in,** cōnfīdō, -ere, -fīsus.
conquer, vincō, -ere, vīcī, victus; superō, I.
consider, believe, putō, I; exīstimō, I.
consider, regard, habeō, -ēre, habuī, habitus.
conspiracy, coniūrātiō, -ōnis, f.
conspire, coniūrō, I.
consul, cōnsul, -is, m.
consulship, cōnsulātus, -ūs, m. **in the consulship of,** abl. absol. with cōnsul.
consult, cōnsulō, -ere, -uī, -sultus.
contention, contentiō, -ōnis, f.
continent, continēns, -entis, f.
contrary to, contrā, prep, with acc.
convict, damnō, I.
council, cōncilium, -iī, n.
council of war, cōncilium, -iī, n.
counsel, advice, cōnsilium, -iī, n.
take counsel, cōnsulō, -ere, -uī, -sultus.
courage, virtūs, -ūtis, f. **have courage,** audeō, -ēre, ausus.
courageously, fortiter.
course, cursus, -ūs, m.
court of law, iūdicium, -iī, n.
covet, adamō, I.
crime, facinus, -oris, n.; scelus, -eris, n.
cross, trānseō, -īre, -iī, -itum est.
crowd, multitūdō, -inis, f.
crush, frangō, -ere, frēgī, frāctus.
custom, mōs, mōris, m.; cōnsuētūdō, -dinis, f.
cut down (of grain), succīdō, -ere, -cīdī, -cisus; (of abridge), rescindō, -ere, -scidī, -scissus.**cut off,** interclūdō, -ere, -clūsī, -clūsus.

daily, cotidiānus, -a, -um.
damage, afflīgō, -ere, -flīxī, -flīctus.
danger, perīculum, -ī, n.
dangerous, perīculōsus, -a, -um.
dare, audeō, -ēre, ausus.
daughter, fīlia, -ae, f.
day (noun), diēs, -eī, m. **on the next day,** postrīdiē. **on the day before,** prīdiē.
day (adj.), diurnus, -a, -um.
death, mors, mortis, f.
decide, cōnstituō, -ere, -uī, -ūtus.
decision, iūdicium, -iī, n.
declare, dēclārō, I; cōnfirmō, I.
decree, dēcernō, -ere, -crēvī, -crētus.
deed, factum, -ī, n.
deep, altus, -a, -um.
defeat, superō, I.
defend, dēfendō, -ere, -fendī, -fēnsus.
delay, wait, moror, I.
deliver (of a speech), habeō, -ēre, -uī, -itus.
demand (noun), postulātum, -ī, n.
demand (verb), imperō, I, with dat. of person

from whom; postulō, I, with ab and abl.
deny, negō, I.
depart, discēdō, -ere, -cessī, -cessum est.
descendants, posterī, -ōrum, m.
deserve, mereor, -ērī, meritus.
design (noun), cōnsilium, -iī, n.
desire, cupiō, -ere, -īvī or -iī, -ītus.
desirous, cupidus, -a, -um.
despoil, spoliō, I.
destroy, dēleō, -ēre, -ēvī, -ētus.
detain, teneō, -ēre, -uī; dētineō, -ēre, -uī, -tentus.
determine, cōnstituō, -ere, -uī, -ūtus.
devise, cōgitō, I.
devote, dō, dare, dedī, datus; dēdō, -ere, dēdidī, dēditus.
devoted, dēditus, -a, -um.
devotion, studium, -iī, n.
die, morior, morī, mortuus. **die, be put to death,** pass, of interficiō, -ere, -fēcī, -fectus.
die, perish, pereō, īre, -iī, -itūrus.
differ, differō, -ferre, distulī, dīlātus.
difference, there is a difference, interest, -esse, -fuit.
difficult, difficilis, -e.
difficulty, difficultās, -tātis, f.
diminish, dēminuō, -ere, -uī, -ūtus.
direction, pars, partis, f. **in that direction,** in eam partem,
disaster, calamitās, -tātis, f.
discover, reperiō, -īre, repperī, repertus.
disembark (trans.), ex nāvī (nāvibus) expōnō, -ere, -posuī, -positus; (intrans.), ex nāvī (nāvibus) ēgredior, ī, -gressus.
disgraceful, turpis, -e.
dislodge, summoveō, -ēre, -mōvī, -mōtus.
dismiss, dīmittō, -ere, -mīsī, -missus.
dismount, ex equō (equīs) dēsiliō, -īre, -uī, -sultus.
disorder, tumultus, -ūs, m.
disregard, neglegō, -ere, -lēxī, -lēctus.
distance, at a distance, procul, in locīs longinquīs.
disturb, commoveō, -ēre, -mōvī, -mōtus; perturbō, I.
divide, dīvidō, -ere, -vīsī, -vīsus.
do, faciō, -ere, fēcī, factus. **be done, happen,** fīō, fierī, factum est. **be done, go on,** pass, of gerō, -ere, gessī, gestus. **do not** (in prohibitions), nōlī, nōlīte, with inf.
doubt, dubitō, I. **there is no doubt,** nōn est dubium.
doubtful, dubius, -a, -um.
draw up (of soldiers), īnstruō, -ere, -strūxī, -strūctus; (of ships), subdūcō, -ere, -dūxī, -ductus.
drive, pellō, -ere, pepulī, pulsus. **drive back,** repellō, -ere, repulī, repulsus.

dry, āridus, -a, -um. **dry land,** āridum, -ī, n.
Dumnorix, Dumnorīx, -rīgis, m.
dust, pulvis, -veris, m.
duty, officium, -iī, n. **do one's duty,** officium praestō, -āre, -stitī, -stitus.

each (of any number), quisque, quaeque, quidque and quodque.
eager, cupidus, -a, -um.
eagle, aquila, -ae, f. eagle-bearer, aquilifer, -erī, m.
easily, facile.
easy, facilis, -e.
effort, labor, -ōris, m.
eight, octō.
either . . . or, aut . . . aut.
elect, faciō, -ere, fēcī, factus; creō, I.
else (adj.), reliquus, -a, -um. **nothing else,** nihil aliud.
eminent, clārus, -a, -um.
empty (of a river), īnfluō, īnfluere, -flūxī.
encounter, occurrō, -ere, -currī, -cursūrus, with dat.; subeō, -īre, -iī, -itus, with acc.
encourage, hortor, I.
end, fīnis, -is, m. **each end,** utraque pars, utrīusque partis, f.
endure, ferō, ferre, tulī, lātus.
enemy (in war), hostis, -is, m., hostēs, -ium, pl.; (personal), inimīcus, -ī, m.
enjoy, fruor, -ī, frūctus.
enlist, enroll, cōnscrībō, -ere, -scrīpsī, -scrīptus.
enough (adv. and indecl. noun), satis.
entreat, ōrō, I.
envoy, lēgātus, -ī, m.
equal, pār, paris; īdem, eadem, idem.
equinox, aequinoctiī diēs.
escape, effugiō, -ere, -fūgī.
establish, cōnstituō, -ere, -uī, -ūtus. **become established,** inveterāscō, -ere, -rāvī.
even, etiam. **not even,** nē . . . quidem. **even if,** etsī, etiam sī.
ever, umquam.
every, all, omnis, -e. **every, each,** quisque, quaeque, quidque and quodque. **everybody,** omnēs, -ium, m., pl. **everything,** omnia, omnēs rēs. **every part of,** tōtus, -a, -um; omnis, -e. **every sort of,** omnis, -e. **in every way,** omnī modō.
evidence, indicium, -iī, n.
evident, it is evident, cōnstat.
except, praeter, prep, with acc; nisi (conj.).
exchange, inter sē dō, dare, dedī, datus.
excuse, pūrgō, I.
exercise, exercitātiō, -ōnis, f.
exist, sum, esse, fuī, futūrus. **exposed,** apertus, -a, -um.
extend, pertineō, -ēre, -uī.

face to face, adversus, -a, -um.
fact, rēs, reī, f.
fall, cadō, -ere, cecidī, cāsūrus. **fall on, fall in with,** incidō, -ere, -cidī, -cāsūrus. **fall upon, overwhelm,** opprimō, -ere, -pressī, -pressus.
far, longē. **far and near,** longē lātēque.
farther, ulterior, -ius.
father, pater, -tris, m.
favorable, secundus, -a, -um.
fear (noun), timor, -ōris, m.; metus, -ūs, m.
fear (verb), timeō, -ēre, timuī.
feel, sentiō, -īre, sēnsī, sēnsus.
feeling, sēnsus, -ūs, m. **feelings,** animus, -ī, m.
fellow soldier, commīlitō, -ōnis, m.
few, paucī, -ae, -a. **not a few,** complūrēs, -ia or -a.
fickleness, levitās, -ātis, f.
field, ager, agrī, m.
fiercely, ācriter.
fifteen, quīndecim, XV.
fight (noun), pugna, -ae, f.; proelium, -iī, n.
fight (verb), pugnō, I; contendō, -ere, -tendī, -tentus; congredior, -ī, -gressus.
fill, compleō, -ēre, -ēvī, -ētus.
finally, dēnique, postrēmō.
find, inveniō, -īre, -vēnī, -ventus; nancīscor, -ī, nactus or nanctus. **find out,** reperiō, -īre, repperī, repertus.
finish, end, cōnficiō, -ere, -fēcī, -fectus.
finish, make perfect, perficiō, -ere, -fēcī, -fectus.
fire, set fire to, incendō, -ere, -cendī, -cēnsus.
first, prīmus, -a, -um. **at first,** prīmō. **in the first place,** prīmum.
fit, idōneus, -a, -um.
five, quīnque, V.
flank, latus, -eris, n.
flee, fugiō, -ere, -fūgī.
flight, fuga, -ae, f. **put to flight,** in fugam dō, dare, dedī, datus.
foe, see **enemy.**
follow, sequor, -ī, secūtus; īnsequor.
foot, pēs, pedis, m. **on foot,** pedibus.
for (conj.), nam, enim (postpositive).
for, in behalf of, prō, prep, with abl.
for, toward, in, prep, with acc; often expressed by dat. case.
force, vīs, f.
forces, cōpiae, -ārum, f., pl.
forest, silva, -ae, f.
forget, oblīvīscor, -ī, oblītus.
form, make, faciō, -ere, fēcī, factus; (of plans), capiō, -ere, cēpī, captus.
former, early, prīstinus, -a, -um.
fortify, mūniō, -īre, -īvī or -iī, -ītus.
fortune, good fortune, fortūna, -ae, f.

four, quattuor, IIII.
free, līber, -era, -erum. **free, unencumbered,** expedītus, -a, -um.
free, set free, līberō, I.
freedom, lībertās, -ātis, f.
friend, amīcus, -ī, m.
friendship, amīcitia, -ae, f.
frighten, terreō, -ēre, -uī, -itus.
from, sign of abl. case; ā or ab, ē or ex, dē, prepositions with abl.
front, frōns, frontis, f. **in front of,** prō, prep, with abl.; ante, prep, with acc.
full, plēnus, -a, -um.

gain, cōnsequor, -ī, -secūtus. **gain possession of,** potior, -īrī, -ītus, with abl.
gather, bring together, cōgō, -ere, coēgī, coāctus.
Gaul, Gallia, -ae, f.
Gauls, Gallī, -ōrum, m., pl.
general, dux, ducis, m.; imperātor, -ōris, m.
Germans, Gcrmānī, -ōrum, m., pl.
get to, arrive, perveniō, -īre, -vēnī, -ventum est. **get possession of,** potior, -īrī, -ītus, with abl.
give, dō, dare, dedī, datus.**give up,** see surrender, **give opportunity,** potestātem faciō, -ere, fēcī, factus.
glad, be glad, gaudeō, -ēre, gavīsus.
glory, glōria, -ae, f.
go, eo, ire, ivi, or il, itum est. **go back,** redeō, -īre, -iī, -itum est. **go out,** exeō, -īre, -iī, -itum est. **go on, be done,** pass, of gerō, -ere, gessī, gestus.
god, deus, deī, m.
good, bonus, -a, -um.
grain (threshed), frūmentum, -ī, n.; (growing or unthreshed), frūmenta, -ōrum, n., pl.
grain supply, rēs frūmentāria, reī frūmentāriae, f.
gratitude, grātia, -ae, f.
great, magnus, -a, -um.
greatly, magnopere.
grief, dolor, -ōris, m.
guard (noun), praesidium, -iī, n. **off one's guard,** inopināns, -antis. **on guard,** in statiōne (statiōnibus).

habit, cōnsuētūdō, -inis, f.
hand, manus, -ūs, f. **on the other hand,** contrā. **be at hand,** adsum, -esse, affuī.
happen, accidit, -ere, accidit; fit, fierī, factum est.
harbor, portus, -ūs, m.
harm, dētrīmentum, -ī, n.
hasten, contendō, -ere, -tendī, -tentus.
hastily, repente.
hate, ōdī, ōdisse, ōsūrus.

have, habeō, -ēre, -uī, -itus.
have in mind, propōnō, -ere, -posuī, -positus, with reflex.
he, is, hīc, ille. Usually not expressed.
hear, hear of, audiō, -īre, -īvī or -iī, -ītus.
height, altitūdō, -inis, f.
held, cf. hold.
help (noun), auxilium, -iī, n.
help (verb), adiuvō, -āre, -iūvī, -iūtus.
helpful, ūsuī, dat. of ūsus.
Helvetians, Helvētiī, -ōrum, m., pl.
here, hīc (adv.).
hesitate, dubitō, I, with inf.
hide, abdō, -ere, -didī, -ditus.
high (of position), superus, -a, -um. (of extent), altus, -a, -um. (of wind or tide), magnus, -a, -um.
himself, ipse (intensive); suī (reflexive) .
hinder, impediō, -īre, -īvī or -iī, -ītus.
hire, condūcō, -ere, -dūxī, -ductus.
his, eius; suus, -a, -um (reflex.).
hold, teneō, -ēre, -uī. (of an office), gerō, -ere, gessī, gestus. (of a council), habeō, -ēre, -uī, -itus.
home, house, domus, -ūs, f. **at home,** domī. **from home,** domō. (to one's) **home,** domum.
honor, honor, -ōris, m.
honorable, honestus, -a, -um.
hope (noun), spēs, -eī, f.
hope (verb), spērō, I.
horse, equus, -ī, m.
horseman, eques, -itis, m.
hostage, obses, -idis, m.
hostile, īnfēstus, -a, -um.
hour, hōra, -ae, f.
house, domus, -ūs, f.
how, in what degree, quam; **in what way,** quō modō, quem ad modum. **how many,** quot, quam multī, -ae, -a. **how much,** quantus, -a, -um; as subst., quantum, -i, n.
how often, quotiēns.
however (adv.), quamvīs.
however (conj.), autem (postpositive).
human, humānus, -a, -um.
hundred, centum, C.
hurl, coniciō, -ere, -iēcī, -iectus.
hurry (intrans.), contendō, ere, tendī, -tentus.
hurry off (trans.), rapiō, ere, -uī, raptus.

I, ego, meī. Usually not expressed.
if, sī. if not, nisi. if only, dum modo. **if** (in indirect questions), num, -ne. but if, quod sī; after another condition, sīn.
immortal, immortālis, -e.
import, importō, I.
importance, it is of importance, rēfert.
impunity, impūnitās, -ātis, f. **with impunity,** impūne.

in, in, prep, with abl.
increase (trans.), augeō, -ēre, auxī, auctus. (intrans.), crēscō, -ere, crēvī, crētus.
incredible, incrēdibilis, -e.
incur, subeō, -īre, -iī.
induce, addūcō, -ere, -dūxī, -ductus.
infantry, peditēs, -um, m., pl.; peditātus, -ūs, m.
inflict, īnferō, -ferre, intulī, illātus.
influence, auctōritās, -ātis, f.
influence (verb), addūcō, -ere, -dūxī, -ductus.
inform, certiōrem (certiōrēs) faciō, -ere, fēcī, factus.
inhabit, incolō, -ere, -uī.
injury, injūria, -ae, f.
inquire, quaerō, -ere, -sīvī or -iī, -sītus.
inspire, iniciō, -ere, -iēcī, -iectus, with dat. of person and acc. of thing.
intention, concilium, -iī, n.
interests of state, res publica, reī pūblicae, f. **highest interests of state,** summa rēs pūblica. **it is to the interest,** interest, interesse, interfuit.
intimate friend, familiāris, -is, m.
into, in, prep, with acc.
investigate, search into, quaerō, -ere, -sivī or -siī, -sītus. **investigate, inspect,** perspiciō, -ere, -spexī, -spectus.
invincible, invictus, -a, -um.
island, īnsula, -ae, f.
it, hīc, haec, hoc; is, ea, id.
Italy, Italia, -ae, f.
its, eius; suus, -a, -um (reflex.).
itself, ipse, ipsa, ipsum.

javelin, pīlum, -ī, n.
journey, iter, itineris, n.
judge, pass judgment, iūdicō, I.
jump down, dēsiliō, -īre, -uī, -sultus.
Jupiter, Juppiter, Jovis, m.
just as, sīcut.
justly, iūre.

keep, teneō, -ēre, -uī.
keep, hold, contineō, -ēre, -uī, -tentus.
keep, prevent, prohibeō, -ēre, -uī, -itus.
kill, interficiō, -ere, -fēcī, -fectus; occīdo, -ere, -cīdī, -cīsus.
knight, eques, -itis, m.
know, sciō, scīre, scīvī, scītus. **know, have learned,** cognōvī. **not know,** ignōrō, I; nesciō, -īre, -īvī.
known, nōtus, -a, -um.

lack, be lacking, be wanting, dēsum, -esse, -fuī.
lake, lacus. **Lake Geneva,** lacus Lemannus.
land, ager, agrī, m.

large, magnus, -a, -um. **large number,** multitūdō, -inis, f.
last (adv.), proximē. **at last,** tandem.
later (adv.), posteā.
latter, the latter, hīc, haec, hoc.
law, lēx, lēgis, f.
lay aside, dēpōnō, -ere, -posuī, -positus.
lay down (of arms), pōnō, -ere, posuī, positus.
lead, dūcō, -ere, dūxī, ductus. **lead across,** trādūcō, -ere, -dūxī, -ductus. **lead back,** redūcō, -ere, -dūxī, -ductus, **lead out,** ēdūcō, -ere, -dūxī, -ductus.
leader, dux, ducis, m.
leading man, prīnceps, -cipis, m.
leadership, prīncipātus, -ūs, m.
learn, cognōscō, -ere, -ōvī, -itus; reperiō, -īre, repperī, repertus.
leave, relinquō, -ere, -līquī, -līctus; discēdō, -ere, -cessī, -cessūrus, followed by ab with abl.
legion, legiō, -ōnis, f.
less, minor, minus, gen. minōris.
liberty, lībertās, -ātis, f.
lieutenant, lēgātus, -ī, m.
life, vīta, -ae, f.
line of battle, aciēs, -ēī, f.
listen to, audiō, -īre, -īvī or -iī, -ītus.
little, parvus, -a, -um.
a little while, breve tempus, -oris, n.
live, vīvō, -ere, vīxī, victus. **live in, inhabit,** incolō, -ere, -uī (with accusative).
long, longus, -a, -um. **for a long time,** diū.
look at, spectō, I.
lose, āmittō, -ere, -mīsī, -missus.
loud, magnus, -a, -um.
low, īnferus, -a, -um.

madness, furor, -ōris, m.; āmentia, -ae, f.
make, faciō, -ere, fēcī, factus.
make (of a plan), capiō, -ere, cēpī, captus; ineō, inīre, iniī, initus. **make war,** bellum faciō, or bellum īnferō, īnferre, intulī, illātus, both with dat. **make use of,** ūtor, -ī, ūsus.
man, homō, hominis, m.; vir, virī, m.**men, soldiers,** mīlitēs, -um, m.**a man who,** is quī.
many, multī, -ae, -a; complūrēs, -a or -ia.
march, iter, itineris, n.
march, make a march, iter faciō, -ere, fēcī, factus.
Mark, Mārcus, -ī, m.
marriage, mātrimōnium, -iī, n.
material, māteria, -ae, f.
matter, rēs, reī, f.
meet (trans.), conveniō, -īre, -vēnī, -ventum est, with acc.; occurrō, -ere, -currī, -cursūrus, with dat.
mercy, misericordia, -ae, f.

mere, ipse, -a, -um.
message, nūntius, -iī, m.
messenger, nūntius, -iī, m.
miles, mīlia passuum.
military matters, rēs mīlitāris, reī mīlitaris, f.
mind, mēns, mentis, f.; animus, -ī, m.
misdeed, facinus, -oris, n.
misfortune, calamitās, -ātis, f.
month, mēnsis, -is, f.
moon, lūna, -ae, f.
more (adj.), plūs, plūris; (adv.), magis.
moreover, autem (postpositive).
motive, causa, -ae, f.
move, moveō, -ēre, mōvī, mōtus.
moved, disturbed, commōtus, -a, -um.
much (adj.), multus, -a, -um; (adv.), multum; in comparisons, multō.
multitude, multitūdō, -inis, f.

name, nōmen, -inis, n.
narrow, angustus, -a, -um.
nation, nātiō, -ōnis, f.
nature, nātūra, -ae, f.
near at hand, be near at hand, adsum, -esse, affuī.
nearer (adj), propior, -ius; (adv.), propius.
nearly, ferē,
necessary, necessārius, -a, -um. it is necessary, opus est; necesse est.
neglect, neglegō, -ere, -lēxī, -lēctus.
neighbor, fīnitimus, -ī, m.
neither . . . nor, neque . . . neque; nec . . . nec.
never, numquam.
nevertheless, tamen.
new, novus, -a, -um.
news, nūntius, -iī, m.
next, proximus, -a, -um. on the next day, posterō diē.
night, nox, noctis, f. by night, noctū.
no, nūllus, -a, -um.
no one, nobody, nēmō, m. and f., gen. nūllīus, dat. nēminī, acc. nēminem, abl. nūllō.
noise, strepitus, -ūs, m.
not, nōn; in negative purpose, wish, or command, nē. and not, neque.
not only . . . but also, nōn sōlum . . . sed etiam.
not yet, nōndum.
notable, īnsignis, -e.
nothing, nihil (indecl.).
notice, animadvertō, -ere, -vertī, -versus.
now, at the present time, nunc; by this time, iam.
number, numerus, -ī, m.

obtain a request, impetrō, I.
occur, occurrō, -ere, -currī, -cursūrus.
of, concerning, dē, prep, -with abl.

offer, offerō, -ferre, obtulī, oblātus; of terms, ferō.
office, magistrātus, -ūs, m.; honor, -ōris, m.
often, saepe.
on, in, prep, with abl.
once, at once, statim.
one, ūnus, -a, -um. one . . . another, alius . . . alius. one who, is quī. only (adv.), modo.
only one, sōlus, -a, -um.
opinion, opīniō, -ōnis, f.
opportunity, facultās, -ātis, f.
oppose, resistō, -ere, -stitī.
oppress, premō, -ere, pressī, pressus.
or, aut; in questions, an.
order, iubeō, -ēre, iussī, iussus, with acc. and inf.; imperō, I, with dat., ut and subj. in order that, ut, with subj.
other, another, alius, -a, -ud. on the other hand, autem (postpositive).others, the remaining, cēterī, -ae, -a.
ought, dēbeō, -ēre, -uī, -itus; oportet, -ēre, oportuit.
our, noster, -tra, -trum.
our men, nostrī, -ōrum, m., pl.
outcry, clāmor, -ōris, m.
overwhelm, opprimō, -ere, -pressī, -pressus.
own, reflex, poss. adj., or gen. of ipse.

pack-animal, iūmentum, -ī, n.
pain, dolor, -ōris, m.
pardon, ignōscō, -ere, -nōvī, -nōtus.
part, pars, partis, f.
party, pars, partis, f.
pass judgment, iūdicō, I.
peace, pāx, pācis, f.
people, populus, -ī, m. their people (reflex.), suī, suōrum, m., pl.
perceive, perspiciō, -ere, -spexī, -spectus.
peril, perīculum, -ī, n.
perish, pereō, -īre, -iī, -itūrus.
permission, it is permitted, licet, licēre, licuit, with dat. and inf.
permit, patior, patī, passus, with acc. and inf.; permittō, -ere, -mīsī, -missus, with dat., ut, and subj.
personal enemy, inimīcus, -ī, m.
persuade, persuādeō, -ēre, -suāsī, -suāsum est, with dat., ut, and subj.
picked, dēlēctus, -a, -um.
pick out, dēligō, -ere, -lēgī, -lēctus.
pitch camp, castra pōnō, -ere, posuī, positus.
place (noun), locus, -ī, m.; pl. loca,-ōrum, n.
place (verb), collocō, I; pōnō, -ere, posuī, positus. place (in different positions), dīspōnō.
plan (noun), cōnsilium, -iī, n.
plan, arrange, cōnstituō, -ere, -uī, -ūtus.
plan, think (of), cōgitō, I.

pleasure, voluptās, -ātis, f.
plot, ambuscade, īnsidiae, -ārum, f., pl.
plot against, īnsidior, I, with dat.
point, at this point, hīc.
possession, gain possession of, potior, -īrī, -ītus.
power, ability, facultas, -ātis, f.; power, might, potentia, -ae, f.; military power, imperium, -iī, n.
powerful, to be very, plūrimum posse.
practice, exercitātiō, -ōnis, f.
praetor, praetor, -ōris, m.
praise, laus, laudis, f.
pray (verb), vōtum faciō, -ere, fēcī, factum, pray (in commands and questions),tandem.
prefer, mālō, mālle, māluī.
prepare, comparō, I; parō, I.
prepared, parātus, -a, -um.
preserve, cōnservō, I.
press hard, premō, -ere, pressī, pressus.
pretend, simulō, I.
prevail, valeō, -ēre, -uī, -itūrus.
prevent, prohibeō, -ēre, -uī, -itus, with inf.
not prevent, nōn dēterreō, -ēre, -uī, -itus, with quīn and subj.
previous, superior, -ius; prior, -us.
private, prīvātus, -a, -um.
privilege, give the privilege, potestātem faciō.
prolong, prōdūcō, -ere, -dūxī, -ductus.
proof, indicium, -iī, n.
property, rēs, reī, f.
proportion, in proportion to, pro.
prosperous, flōrēns, -entis.
protect, dēfendō, -ere, -dī, -fēnsus.
protection, praesidium, -iī, n.
prove, probō, I.
provided, provided that, dum.
province, prōvincia, -ae, f.
provision, make provision, prōvideō, -ēre, -vīdī, -vīsus.
public, pūblicus, -a, -um.
public welfare, rēs pūblica, reī pūblicae, f.
punish, ulcīscor, -ī, ultus.
punishment, supplicium, -iī, n.; poena, -ae, f.
purpose, mēns, mentis, f.
put down, conquer, superō, I.
put in charge, praeficiō, -ere, -fēcī, -fectus.
put to death, interficiō, -ere, -fēcī, -fectus.
put to flight, fugō, I.
put under the power, permittō, -ere, -mīsī, -missus.

quickly, celeriter.

rampart, vāllum, -ī, n.
rank, ōrdō, -inis, f.
rather, potius.

reach, perveniō, -īre, -vēnī, -ventum est, with ad and acc.
reach (of land), attingō, -ere, -tigī, -tāctus.
ready, parātus, -a, -um. get ready, comparō, I.
realize, intellegō, -ere, -lēxi, -lēctus.
reason, causa, -ae, f. for this reason, quā dē causā.
reasonable, iūstus, -a, -um.
reasonableness, ratiō, -ōnis, f.
recall, revocō, I.
receive, accipiō, -ere, -cēpī, -ceptus. receive under protection, in fidem recipiō.
recently, nūper.
recklessness, audācia, -ae, f.
regard, in regard to, dē with abl.
region, regiō, -ōnis, f.
reject, repudiō, I.
rejoice, gaudeō, -ēre, gāvīsus sum.
relief, subsidium, -iī, n.
remain, maneō, -ēre, mānsī, mānsūrus.
remove, tollō, -ere, sustulī, sublātus; removeō, -ēre, -mōvī, -mōtus.
renown, glōria, -ae, f.
repair, reficiō, -ere, -fēcī, -fectus.
repeatedly, saepe.
repent, paenitet, -ēre, -uit.
reply, respondeō, -ēre, -spondī, -spōnsus.
report, nūntiō, I.
report back, renūntiō, I.
republic, rēs pūblica, reī pūblicae, f.
reputation, opīniō, -ōnis, f.
request, obtain a request, impetrō, I.
reserve, reservō, I.
resist, resistō, -ere, -stitī, with dat.
rest of, remaining, reliquus, -a, -um.
restore, restituō, -ere, -uī, -ūtus; reddō, -ere, -didī, -ditus.
restrain, retineō, -ēre, -uī, -tentus; prohibeō, -ēre, -uī, -itus; reprimō, -ere, -pressī, -pressus.
retreat (noun), receptus, -ūs, m.
retreat (verb), recipiō, -ere, -cēpī, -ceptus, with reflexive.
return (noun), reditus, -ūs, m.
return, give back, reddō, -ere, -didī, -ditus.
return, go back, redeō, -īre, iī, -tum est; revertor, -ī. in return for, prō with abl.
revolt, tumultus, -ūs, m.
reward, praemium, -iī, n.
Rhine, Rhēnus, -ī, m.
Rhone, Rhodanus, -ī, m.
right, fair (adj.), aequus, a, um. right (in the sight of the gods), fās, n., indecl. noun.
rightly, iūre.
risk, perīculum, -ī, n.
river, flūmen, -inis, n.
road, via, -ae, f.; iter, itineris, n.
Roman, Rōmānus, -a, -um.
Rome, Rōma -ae, f.

royal power, regnum.
rule, regō, -ere, rēxī, rēctus.
rumor, rūmor, -ōris, m.
safe, incolumis, -e; tūtus, -a, -um.
safety, tūtō; translate when possible by adj., safe.
safety, salūs, -ūtis, f.
sail (verb), nāvigō, I.
sake, for the sake of, causā, following its gen.
same, īdem, eadem, idem.
savage, ferus, -a, -um.
save, cōnservō, I.
say, dīcō, -ere, dīxī, dictus.
sea, mare, -is, n.
secure, (adj.), tūtus, -a, -um.
secure (verb), cōnsequor, -I, -secūtus; conciliō, I; nancīscor, -ī, nactus.
see, see to it, videō, -ēre, vīdī, vīsus.
seek, petō, -ere, -ivī or -iī, -itus.
seem, videor, -ērī, vīsus.
seize, occupō, I; comprehendō, -ere, -hendī, -hēnsus.
self, myself, etc. If emphatic, ipse, -a, -um; if reflexive, meī, tuī, suī, etc.
senate, senātus, -ūs, m.
senator, senātor, -ōris, m.
send, mittō, -ere, mīsī, missus.
send ahead, praemittō, -ere, -mīsī, -missus.
send back, remittō, -ere, -mīsī, -missus.
send out or away (in different directions), dīmittō, -ere, -mīsī, -missus.
separate, dīvidō, -ere, -vīsī, -vīsus.
serious, gravis, -e.
servant, servus, -ī, m.
service, officium, -iī, n.; meritum, -ī, n.
service, be of service, prōsum, prōdesse, prōfuī.
set fire to, incendō, -ere, -cendī, -cēnsus,
set out, proficīscor, -ī, -fectus,
set sail, solvō, -ere, solvī, solūtus, with or without navem or nāvēs,
settle (down), cōnsīdō, -ere, -sēdī, -sessūrus.
seventh, septimus, -a, -um.
several, complūrēs, -a or -ia.
shield, scūtum, -ī, n.
ship, navis, -is, f.
war ship, nāvis longa.
short, brevis, -e.
shout, shouting, clāmor, -ōris, m.
show, ostendō, -ere, -dī, -tus; indicō, I; doceō, -ēre, -uī, doctus.
shrewdness, cōnsilium, -iī, n.
sight, cōnspectus, -ūs, m.
since, cum, with subj.; quoniam, with indic.
sister, soror, -oris, f.
situation, locus, -ī, m.; pl. loca, -ōrum, n.
skilful, skilled, perītus, -a, -um, with gen.

slave, servus, -ī, m.
slay, occīdō, -ere, -cīdī, -cīsus.
slight, parvus, -a, -um.
so (with adjectives and adverbs), tam; (with verbs), ita, sīc. **and so,** itaque. **so great,** tantus, -a, -um. **so long,** tam diū. **so long as,** dum, with indic. **so much** (as noun), tantum, -ī, n. **so often,** totiēns.
soldier, mīles, -litis, m.
some (adj.), aliquī, -qua, -quod; nōn nūllus, -a, -um; pl. as subst. **some one, something** (subst.), aliquis, aliquid. **some . . . others,** aliī . . . aliī. **some in one direction, others in another,** aliī aliam in partem. **there are some who,** sunt quī.
sometimes, nōn numquam.
soon, brevī tempore.
as soon as, simul atque.
sort, genus, -eris, n. **of this sort,** eius modī.
spare, parcō, -ere, pepercī or parsi, parsūrus.
speak, dīcō, -ere, dīxī, dictus.
speech, ōrātiō, -ōnis, f.
speed, celeritās, -ātis, f. **at full speed** (of horses), incitātus, -a, -um.
spot, locus, -ī, m; pl. loca, -ōrum, n.
spy, spy out, speculor, I.
stab, percutiō, -ere, -cussī, -cussus.
stand, stō, stāre, stetī, stātus. **stand, get a footing,** consistō, -ere, -stitī. **stand in the way of,** obsistō, -ere, stitī, with dat.
standard, signum, -ī, n.
start, proficīscor, -ī, profectus.
state, cīvitās, -ātis, f.
stay, maneō, -ēre, mānsī, mānsūrus.
still, now, nunc; **still, nevertheless,** tamen.
stir up, concitō, I.
storm, tempestās, -ātis, f.
strange, novus, -a, -um.
strangeness, novitās, -tātis, f.
strong, fīrmus, -a. -um.
such, of such a sort, talis, -e; **so great,** tantus, -a, -um.
suddenly, subitō.
sufficient, satis (indecl.), n.
sufficiently, satis.
suitable, idōneus, -a, -um, with dat. or ad with acc.
summon, vocō, I.
sun, sōl, sōlis, m.
supplies, commeātus, -ūs, m.
support, alō, -ere, -uī, altus or alitus.
suppose, crēdō, -ere, -didī, -ditus; exīstimō, I.
sure, certus, -a, -um.
surpass, superō, I, with acc.; praestō, -stāre, -stitī, -stitus, with dat.
surrender (oneself), dēdō, -ere, dēdidī, dēditus, with reflex.
surround, get around, circumveniō, -īre,

-vēnī, -ventus.
suspect, suspicor, I.
suspicion, suspīciō, -ōnis, f.
Swabians, Suēbī, -ōrum, m., pl.
sword, gladius, -iī, m.

take, bear, ferō, ferre, tulī, lātus. **take, lead,**
dūcō, -ere, dūxī, ductus. **take, take up,**
capture, capiō, -ere, cēpī, captus. **take away,**
ēripiō, -ere, -uī, -reptus. **take by storm,**
expugnō, I. **take place,** fīō, fierī, factum est.
take possession of, potior, -īrī, -ītus.
tear, lacrima, -ae,f.
tear up, ēripiō, -ere, -uī, -reptus.
tell, dīcō, -ere, dīxī, dictus; prōnūntiō, I. **tell,**
show, doceō, -ēre, -uī, doctus.
tempest, tempestās, -ātis, f.
ten, decem.
tenth, decimus, -a, -um.
terms, condiciō, -ōnis, f., sing, or pl.
terrify, perterreō, -ēre, -uī, -itus.
territory, territories, ager, agrī, m.; fīnēs,
-ium, m.
than, quam, or abl. after a comparative.
that (dem. pron.), ille, illa, illud; is, ea, id.
that, so that, in order that, ut; after verbs of
fearing, ne; after negative expressions of
doubt, quīn. **that . . . not,** introducing a
negative clause of purpose, nē. **would that,**
utinam.
their, suus, -a, -um (reflex.); eōrum.
them, cf. **he.**
then, at that time, tum. **then, therefore,**
igitur (usually postpositive).
there, in that place, ibi.
therefore, itaque.
these, cf. **This.**
thing, rēs, reī, f.
think, putō, I; exīstimō, I; arbitror, I. **think,**
feel, sentiō, -īre, sēnsī, sēnsus.
this, hīc, haec, hoc.
though, cum.
thousand, mīlle (indecl. adj.). **thousands,**
mīlia, -ium, n., pl. (followed by partitive
gen.).
threaten, impendeō, -ere.
three, trēs, tria. **a period of three days,**
trīduum, -ī, n. **three hundred,** trecentī, -ae, -a.
through, per, prep, with acc.
throw, iaciō, -ere, iēcī, iactus; coniciō, -ere,
-iēcī, -iectus.
throw back, rēiciō, -ere, -iēcī, -iectus.
throw down, away, abiciō, -ere, -iēcī, -iectus.
tide, aestus, -ūs, m..
tilling the land, agrī cultūra, -ae, f.
time, tempus, -oris, n. on time, ad tempus.
time and again, semel atque iterum.
timid, timidus, -a, -um.

to, ad, prep, with acc; often translated by dat.
to-day, hodiē.
together with, ūnā cum, with abl.
toward (in space), ad with acc.
town, oppidum, -ī, n.
trader, mercātor, -ōris, m.
transport, adj., onerārius, -a, -um.
travel, eō, īre, iī or ivī, itum est.
treachery, īnsidiae, -ārum, f., pl.
trial, iūdicium, -iī, n.
tribe, gēns, gentis, f.
tribune, tribūnus, -ī, m.
tribune of the people, tribūnus plēbis.
tributary, vectīgālis, -e.
troops, cōpiae, -ārum, f., pl.
true, vērus, -a, -um.
truth, vērum, -ī, n.
try, cōnor, I.
turn and flee, tergum vertō, -ere, vertī,
versum.
twelve, duodecim; XII.
two, duo, -ae, -o.

unacquainted, imperītus, -a, -um, with gen.
unbelievable, incrēdibilis, -e.
uncertain, incertus, -a, -um.
uncovered, nūdus, -a, -um.
understand, intellegō, -ere, -lēxī, -lēctus.
undertake, suscipiō, -ere, -cēpī, -ceptus.
ungrateful, ingrātus, -a, -um.
unharmed, incolumis, -e.
unjust, inīquus, -a, -um.
unjustly, iniūriā. unless, nisi.
unprepared, imparātus, -a, -um.
unskilful, imperītus, -a, -um.
until, ad, prep, with acc.
until, dum; quoad, conj.; when equivalent lo
before, prius quam.
urge, hortor, I; cohortor, I.
use (noun), ūsus, -ūs, m. of use, usuī (dative).
use, make use of, ūtor, -ī, ūsus.

vacant, lie vacant, vacō, I.
valor, virtūs, -ūtis, f.
vengeance, take vengeance on, ulcīscor, -ī,
ultus.
verdict, iūdicium, -iī, n.
very (adj.), ipse, -a, -um.
victory, victōria, -ae, f.
village, vīcus, -ī, m.
violence, vīs, f.
virtue, virtūs, -ūtis, f.
voice, vōx, vōcis, f.

wait, delay, moror, i.
wait for, exspectō, i.
wander about, vagor, i.
war, bellum, -ī, n.

warn, admoneō, -ēre, -uī, -itus.
way, manner, modus, -ī, m.
way, road, via, -ae, f.
we, nōs, gen., nostrum or nostrī.
weapon, tēlum, -ī, n.
weather, tempestās, -ātis, f.
weigh (of anchor), tollō, -ere, sustulī, sublātus.
welfare, salūs, -ūtis, f.
public welfare, rēs pūblica, reī pūblicae.
what (inter. pron.), quid; (inter. adj.), quī, quae, quod.
what (rel. pron.), (id) quod, (ea) quae.
what great, how great, quantus, -a, -um.
whatever, quidquid.
what sort of, quālis, -e.
when, cum; ubi.
where (place in which), ubi; (place to which), quō.
wherever, whithersoever, quocumque.
whether, num, -ne, sī, utrum.
which, see **who.**
which (of two), uter, utra, utrum.
while, dum.
who, what (inter, pron.), quis, quid.
who, which, what (rel. pron.), quī, quae, quod,
whoever, whatever, quīcumque, quaecumque, quodcumque.
whole, tōtus, -a, -um.
wholly, omnīnō.
why, cūr.
wicked, improbus, -a, -um.

wide, lātus, -a, -um.
width, lātitūdō, -inis, f.
wife, uxor, -ōris, f.
willing, be willing, volō, velle, voluī.
winter, hiems, hiemis, f.
pass the winter, hiemō, i.
winter quarters, hīberna, -ōrum, n., pl.
wisdom, cōnsilium, -iī, n.
wish, volō, velle, voluī.
not wish, nōlō, nōlle, nōluī.
with, cum, prep, with abl.
with, near, apud, prep, with acc.
withdraw, go away, discēdō, -ere, -cessī, -cessūrus.
without, sine, prep, with abl.
withstand, sustineō, -ēre, -uī, -tentus.
woman, mulier, -eris, f.
word, verbum, -ī, n.
work (noun), opus, operis, n.
work (verb), labōrō, i.
worth, virtūs, -ūtis,f.
would that, utinam.
wound, volnus, -eris, n.
wrong, do wrong, peccō, i.
year, annus, -ī, m.
every year, quotannīs.
yet, tamen.
yield, cēdō, -ere, cessī, cessūrus.
you, tū, tuī.
young man, adulēscēns, adulēscentis, m.
your (sing.), tuus, -a, -um; (plu.) vester, -tra, -trum.
zeal, studium, -iī, n.

Figure 26. — Bronze ball supposed to contain the ashes of Julius Caesar.

After the murder of Julius Caesar his body was taken to the Forum, and there burned.

In the Middle Ages his ashes were supposed to be preserved in the large round ball on the top of the obelisk which, till 1586, stood at the side of St. Peter's church in Rome, and now stands in the Piazza in front of St. Peter's. (Illustration from an engraving made in 1569.)

SOPHRON CATALOGUE
2013

Caesar's Commentaries: The Complete Gallic War. Revised. 8vo., xxiv,507 pp.; Introduction, Latin text of all eight Books, Notes, Companion, Grammar, Exercises, Vocabularies, 17 Maps, illus. all based on Francis W. Kelsey. ISBN 978-0-9850811 1 9 . . . . $19.95

Virgil's Aeneid Complete, Books I-XII. With Introduction, Latin text and Notes by W. D. Williams. 8vo., xxviii, 739 pp., 2 maps, Glossary, Index. ISBN 978-0-9850811 6 4 . . . . $27.95

Praxis Grammatica. **A New Edition.** John Harmer. 12 mo., xviii,116 pp.; Introduction by Mark Riley. **ISBN 978-0-9850811 2 6**. $3.95

The *Other* Trojan War. Dictys & Dares. 12 mo., xxii,397 pp.; Latin/English Parallel Texts; Frazer's Introduction & Notes, Index.

ISBN 978-0-9850811 5 7. . . . . $14.95

The Stoic's Bible: *a Florilegium for the Good Life.* Giles Laurén. 8vo., xxvi,610 pp., 2 illus., Introduction, Bibliography. ISBN 978-1-4538162 2 6. . . . . $24.95

Why Don't We Learn from History? B. H. Liddell Hart. 12 mo., 126 pp.

ISBN 978-0-9850811 3 3. . . . . $4.95

Quintilian. Institutionis Oratoriae. Liber Decimus. Text, Notes & Introductory Essays by W. Peterson. Foreword by James J. Murphy. 8vo., cvi,291 pp., Harleian MS facsimile, Indexes. ISBN 978-0-9850811-8-8 . . . . $19.95

Schools of Hellas. Kenneth Freeman. 12 mo., xxi,279 pp., illus., Indexes.

ISBN 978-0-9850811-9-5 . . . . . . $14.95

Cornelius Nepos Vitae. 12 mo., xviii,314 pp., 3 maps, notes, exercises, & vocabulary by John Rolf ISBN 978-0-9850811-7-1 . . . . $14.95

Available from SOPHRON (CreateSpace and Amazon worldwide)
73 Dean Road #3
Sacramento, CA 95815
liberdux@omsoft.com

Check or PayPal. Media mail: $3.75 first book $1.00 thereafter. Allow 4 weeks.

In Preparation:
The Stoic's Bible. Second, expanded edition.
Wilamowitz-Mollendorff / Marchant: Greek Reader.

CPSIA information can be obtained at www.ICGtesting.com
Printed in the USA
LVOW04s1228080115

421917LV00004B/65/P